United States Naval Aviation 1910–1995

Roy A. Grossnick

with contributions from

William J. Armstrong
W. Todd Baker
John M. Elliott
Gwendolyn J. Rich
Judith A. Walters

Naval Historical Center
Department of the Navy
Washington, D.C.

Library of Congress Cataloging-in-Publication Data

Grossnick, Roy A.
    United States naval aviation, 1910–1995 / Roy A. Grossnick ; with
contributions from William J. Armstrong ... [et al.]. — [4th ed.]
        p.   cm.
    Includes index.
    ISBN 0–945274–34–3 (case bound : alk. paper)
    1. United States. Navy—Aviation—Chronology.   I. Armstrong,
William J.   II. Title.
VG93.G7627   1997
359.94'0973—dc21   96–37481
                                                           CIP

For sale by the U.S. Government Printing Office
Superintendent of Documents, Mail Stop: SSOP, Washington, DC 20402-9328
ISBN 0-16-049124-X

Secretary of the Navy's
Advisory Committee on Naval History

Contents

Information on Photographs

The illustrations in this volume are official U.S. Navy, Marine Corps, Coast Guard or NASA (National Aeronautics and Space Administration) photographs. Negatives for most of these photographs are held by the National Archives and Records Administration's Still Pictures Branch. Photographs with an NH or NAH preceding the number are held by the Naval Historical Center's Photographic Section. U.S. Coast Guard photos, with USCG preceding the number, are held by either the Coast Guard Headquarters (History Office) or the National Archives (Still Picture Branch). The NASA photographs are held by NASA Headquarters, Public Affairs Office (News and Imaging Branch).

Photograph numbers for illustrations in the book appear at the end of the caption. Illustrations without a photo number were reproduced from non-numbered photographs in the Naval Historical Center's Aviation History Branch collection. An illustration with a number but not a letter prefix is a U.S. Navy photograph. Please be sure to add USN in front of these numbers when ordering them from the National Archives. The prefix K or KN means the original is in color, but it is still a USN photograph.

Foreword

The fourth edition of *United States Naval Aviation 1910–1995* is a testimony to Naval Aviation's achievements as it prepares to enter the 21st century and its first one hundred years of service. The Naval Historical Center's Aviation History Office has expanded on previous editions to make this chronology the quintessential reference work on Naval Aviation history.

This work is designed to provide naval personnel, historians and aviation enthusiasts with a general background on Naval Aviation history. It highlights the significant events and developments that shaped Naval Aviation from 1910 to 1995, rather than providing a detailed treatise of particular subjects or actions. It covers all aspects of Naval Aviation, including operational activities, technical developments and administrative changes.

To help make this book a more useful reference tool, Mr. Roy Grossnick and his expert staff have more than doubled the number of appendices, which include the most commonly requested subjects or data on Naval Aviation. The aim is to make this the first-source document that people use when they are looking for basic information on Naval Aviation. The book provides the opportunity to gain an insight and learn about the origins, achievements and traditions of Naval Aviation as it relates to the rich naval heritage of the United States.

Naval Aviation has undergone immense change since 1910. It now plays a defining role in the nation's defense structure and is on call to respond to military crises around the world. The past developments, as chronicled in this book, serve as a prologue to future developments in Naval Aviation.

William S. Dudley
Director of Naval History

Preface

The history of this book goes back to 1956 when the Deputy Chief of Naval Operations (Air) and Chief, Bureau of Aeronautics supported the preparation of a chronology for Naval Aviation. Their intent was to record events of special interest and lasting significance pertaining to the growth of U.S. naval air as an element of sea power, its employment and accomplishments in war and peace.

The writing project was undertaken by two history offices, the Naval Aviation History Office assigned to Deputy Chief of Naval Operations (Air) and the Historian's Office in the Bureau of Aeronautics. Under the initial directive, the two offices were permitted considerable leeway in defining the elements to be included in the chronology. Adherence to professional standards was paramount. Accuracy and comprehensive coverage of events and developments were key words for the project; its scope included the air elements of the Navy, Marine Corps, and the Coast Guard in time of war.

At the outset of the project, the historians in the two offices realized that "one of the drawbacks of chronologies as a form of exposition stems from the fact that they record, or chronicle, events with no attempt at explanation." Their chronology departed from that form, particularly for extended periods such as war campaigns and for developments in various technical areas. Some types of information, important to the history of Naval Aviation, became repetitious when included in a chronology. When such information was amenable to statistical or tabular treatment, it was incorporated in appendixes. Thus, the chronology project evolved into two parts: an actual chronology and various appendices providing invaluable facts and figures on subjects not suitable for the chronology but pertinent to the history of Naval Aviation.

The authors of the initial publication, *United States Naval Aviation 1910–1960*, did an admirable job in adhering to their professional objectives. Mr. Adrian O. Van Wyen, historian DCNO (Air), and Mr. Lee M. Pearson, historian, Bureau of Aeronautic/Bureau of Weapons, set the standards for future aviation historians to chronicle the history of Naval Aviation.

The first update, *United States Naval Aviation 1910–1970*, followed the basic scope and concept put forth in the earlier edition. Authors for this update were: Mr. Clarke Van Vleet, historian, DCNO (Air); Mr. Adrian O. Van Wyen, historian (Ret), DCNO (Air); and Mr. Lee M. Pearson, historian, Naval Air Systems Command. The second update, *United States Naval Aviation 1910–1980*, represented a more substantial upgrade to the publication. It retained the basic format but included more detailed appendices. The primary authors were Dr. William J. Armstrong, historian, Naval Air Systems Command, and Mr. Clarke Van Vleet, historian, DCNO (Air Warfare).

Many transformations in Naval Aviation have taken place since the first publication in the early 1960s. The world structure has undergone major realignments and old adversaries are now allies, or at least friends. People and machines are still the key ingredients for Naval Aviation. However, technology has come to play a very dominate role in how Naval Aviation projects its power in support of national defense objectives and our nation's heritage. The third update, *United States Naval Aviation 1910–1995*, attempts to bring into focus the myriad aspects of Naval Aviation and how they play a role in defense as well as the humanitarian side of their mission.

This edition, besides attempting to maintain the professional standards set by the early authors, has attempted to correct any errors in previous editions and make it the primary reference source on Naval Aviation for the Navy Department and researchers. It is not designed as a comprehensive source on Naval Aviation but as a basic guide to educate readers on Naval Aviation history. In order to accomplish this goal, the number of appendices covering commonly requested data on Naval Aviation has been more than doubled. The chronology provides a narrative flow of information, while the appendices provide an insight into the multiple functions of Naval Aviation. All aspects of Naval Aviation, including operational activities, administrative and personnel changes and technical developments, have been incorporated.

When drafting a reference work with such an extensive range of data, it is almost impossible to prevent errors. An exhaustive effort was made to check the accuracy of information in this book. When different sets of records or sources provided conflicting data, I selected the most accurate information based on reviewing all the possible sources. As the primary compiler for this edition, I accept full responsibility for any mistakes or errors of fact or misinterpretations that may have occurred in the book, and I welcome any corrections.

Roy A. Grossnick

Acknowledgments

I began working in the Naval Aviation History Office in 1980 and this book, in its editions as *United States Naval Aviation 1910–1970* and *1910–1980*, has been my primary reference source. It was the first source I used when a quick answer was needed on a particular Naval Aviation subject. Credit for making the book an indispensable reference tool must go to its past authors: Mr. Adrian O. Van Wyen, Mr. Lee M. Pearson, Mr. Clarke Van Vleet and Dr. William J. Armstrong.

Compiling a reference work of this magnitude was beyond the scope of just one person. The staff of the Naval Aviation History Office, both past and present, must be complimented on the work they have done over the years that contributed to updating the book. Special recognition goes to the contributors who are listed on the title page. Without the work done by Dr. William J. Armstrong, historian, Naval Air Systems Command, and Naval Aviation History Office staffers Mr. John M. Elliott, historian, retired; Ms. Judith A. Walters, historian; Ms. Gwendolyn J. Rich, archivist; and Mr. W. Todd Baker, historian, this edition would not have been possible. I extend to them my sincere thanks for all the extra time and diligent work they put into the project.

The *Naval Aviation News* magazine staff contributed their expertise in editing the manuscript. Their knowledge of Naval Aviation terminology and subject matter helped smooth out any writing discrepancies that may have crept into the text. Commander Diana T. Cangelosi's staff includes: Ms. Sandra K. Russell, Ms. Wendy E. Karppi, Journalists Second Class Gerald E. Knaak and E. Blake Towler, Mr. Morgan I. Wilbur, Art Director, and Mr. Charles C. Cooney, former Art Director.

Several people outside the Naval Historical Center also played a role in reviewing, making comments and providing information on special topics. Mr. Hal Andrews' vast knowledge of Naval Aviation, particularly its technical aspects, helped make this book a primary reference source for years to come. Lieutenant Commander Richard R. Burgess, USN (Ret.); Mr. Robert Lawson; Captain James E. Lesher, USNR (Ret.); and Mr. Leroy Doig III contributed to special sections in the appendices. A special thank-you goes to four people who spent considerable time reviewing the entire manuscript and making some excellent recommendations: Captain Rosario "Zip" Rausa, USNR (Ret.); Captain Richard C. Knott, USN (Ret.); Dr. William J. Armstrong and Dr. Jeffrey G. Barlow.

I would also like to recognize the professional staff in the Naval Historical Center who provided a wide range of support for the book. Mr. Bernard Cavalcante's Operational Archives Branch was always ready to assist in locating specific records, particularly Mrs. Kathy M. Lloyd, head of the Reference Section. The Ship's History Branch, headed by Mr. John C. Reilly, Jr., was instrumental in reviewing and documenting specific information on aviation ships. Ms. Jean L. Hort and her staff in the Navy Department Library provided the minute details that were easy to overlook. A special thank-you to Ms. Sandra J. Doyle for her strong support and liaison work. Perhaps the most important thanks go to Senior Historian Dr. Edward Marolda and Director Dr. William S. Dudley, who recognized the importance of continuing to update this reference source, supported the project and allocated the resources for publication.

The details surrounding the research and writing of a book are well recognized, but the administrative support necessary is usually forgotten in the flourish of getting the book to the printer. The center's Administrative Branch needs to be recognized for all the work it does in supporting the operations of the Naval Aviation History Branch. Branch head Lieutenant Carol Dula, USN, and her staff consistently responded to our administrative needs. Special recognition goes to Mr. Randy Potter for his technical computer support and to Ms. Donna Smilardo, the center's Budget Analyst, for keeping us out of the red ink.

Finally, I would like to thank my wife, Mary, and daughter, Maki, for being patient during the period of extended working hours necessary to get this book to publication. A special debt of gratitude is extended to Mr. John Grier, design and typesetting specialist of the Government Printing Office, for his layout efforts. For those I have not mentioned by name, let me say that your contributions are appreciated and are not forgotten.

Roy A. Grossnick

Glossary

1st MAW	First Marine Aircraft Wing
6thFLT	Sixth Fleet
7thFLT	Seventh Fleet
A&R	Assembly & Repair
A.P.	Armor Piercing
AAF	Army Air Forces
AAM	Air-to-air Missile
AAS	Army Air Service
ABATU	Advanced Base Aviation Training Unit
ACC	Air Combat Command
ACLS	Automatic Carrier Landing System
ACMR	Air Combat Maneuvering Range
ACNO (Air Warfare)	Assistant Chief of Naval Operations (Air Warfare)
ADM	Admiral
ADVCAP	Advanced Capability
AED	Aeronautical Engineering Duty
AEDO	Aeronautical Engineering Duty Officer
AEW	Airborne Early Warning
AEWWINGPAC	Airborne Early Warning Wing, Pacific
AFB	Air Force Base
AFEM	Armed Forces Expeditionary Medal
AIM	Air Launched Aerial Intercept Guided Missile
AIM	Aircraft Intermediate Maintenance
AIMD	Aircraft Intermediate Maintenance Department
AirDet/AIR DET	Air Detachment
AirLant/AIRLANT	Air Force, Atlantic Fleet or Commander, Air Force, U.S. Atlantic Fleet
AirPac/AIRPAC	Commander, Air Force, U.S. Pacific Fleet or Air Force, U.S. Pacific Fleet
ALARS	Air Launched Acoustical Reconnaissance
ALNAV	All Navy
ALVRJ	Advance Low Volume Ramjet
AMD	Aeronautical Maintenance Duty
AMO	Aviation Medical Officer
AMRAAM	Advanced Medium Range Air-to-air Missile
ANA	Association of Naval Aviation
ANG	Air National Guard
AOCP	Aviation Officer Continuation Pay
AOCS	Aviation Officer Candidate School
ARAPAHO	Name for a portable modular aviation facility for merchant ships
ARG	Amphibious Ready Group
ARM	Antiradiation Missile
ARPA	Advanced Research Projects Agency
ARPS	Automatic Radar Processing System

ASM	Air-to-surface Missile
ASMD	Anti-ship Missile Defense
ASO	Aviation Supply Office
ASROC	Antisubmarine Rocket Missile
ASTOVL	Advanced Short Takeoff/Vertical Landing
ASW	Antisubmarine Warfare
ATARPS	Advanced Tactical Aerial Reconnaissance Pod System
ATG	Air Task Group
ATU	Advanced Training Unit
BRAC	Base Closure and Realignment Commission
BTG	Basic Training Group
BuAer	Bureau of Aeronautics
BuC&R	Bureau of Construction and Repair
BuMed	Bureau of Medicine and Surgery
BuNav	Bureau of Navigation
BuOrd	Bureau of Ordnance
BuPers	Bureau of Naval Personnel
BuShips	Bureau of Ships
BuS&A	Bureau of Supplies and Accounts
BuWeps	Bureau of Naval Weapons
CO/co	Commanding Officer
CAA	Civil Aeronautics Authority
CAEWWS	Carrier Airborne Early Warning Weapons School
CAF	Confederate Air Force
CAINS	Carrier Aircraft Inertial Navigation System
CalTech	California Institute of Technology
CAP	Civil Air Patrol
CAP	Combat Air Patrol
CAPT	Captain
CARDIV	Carrier Division
CASU	Carrier Air Service Unit
CASU(F)	Combat Aircraft Service Units (Forward)
CC	Construction Corps
CCR	Circulation Control Rotor
CDR	Commander
CG	Commanding General
CIC	Combat Information Center
CincPac/CINCPAC	Commander in Chief, Pacific
CincPacFlt/CINCPACFLT	Commander in Chief, U.S. Pacific Fleet
CINCUS	Commander in Chief, U.S. Fleet
CIWS	Close in Weapons System (Phalanx)
CNATRA	Chief of Naval Air Training
CNR/CHNAVRSCH	Chief of Naval Reserarch
CNO	Chief of Naval Operations
COD	Carrier On-board Delivery
COIN	Counter Insurgency
ComAirLant	Commander, Naval Air Force, U.S. Atlantic Fleet
ComAirPac	Commander, Naval Air Force, U.S. Pacific Fleet
ComFAIR/COMFAIR	Commander, Fleet Air
COMHATWING	Commander, Heavy Attack Wing
COMHSLWINGPAC	Commander, Helicopter Antisubmarine Light Wing, U.S. Pacific Fleet
COMINCH	Commander in Chief, U.S. Fleet
COMINCUS	Commander in Chief, U.S. Fleet
COMLATWING	Commander, Light Attack Wing

COMMATWING	Commander, Medium Attack Wing
COMNAVAIRESFOR	Commander, Naval Air Reserve Force
COMNAVAIRLANT	Commander, Naval Air Force, U.S. Atlantic Fleet
COMNAVAIRPAC	Commander, Naval Air Force, U.S. Pacific Fleet
COMNAVFOR Somalia	Commander, Naval Forces Somalia
COMNAVSUPFOR	Commander, Naval Support Force
COMOPDEVFOR	Commander, Operational Development Force, U.S. Fleet
COMPATWING	Commander, Patrol Wing
COMSTRKFIGHTWING	Commander, Strike Fighter Wing
CONUS	Continental United States
DASH	Drone Antisubmarine Helicopter
DCNO	Deputy Chief of Naval Operations
DFC	Distinguished Flying Cross
DICASS	Directional Command Active Sonobuoy System
DMZ	Demilitarized Zone
DoD	Department of Defense
ECM	Electronic Countermeasures
ECMO	Electronic Countermeasures Operator/Officer
ECP	Enlisted Commissioning Program
EDO	Engineering Duty Officer
EFM	Enhanced Fighter Maneuverability
ELEX/COMNAVELEX	Naval Electronic Systems Command
ENS	Ensign
EW	Electronic Warfare
FAA	Federal Aviation Administration
FAETU	Fleet Airborne Electronics Training Units
FASOTRAGRULANT	Fleet Aviation Specialized Operational Training Group Atlantic
FAW	Fleet Air Wing
FAWTUPAC	Fleet All Weather Training Unit, Pacific
FBM	Fleet Ballistic Missile
FEWSG	Fleet Electronic Warfare Support Group
FLIR	Forward Looking Infrared Radar
FMS	Foreign Military Sales
FORSCOM	Forces Command
Ft	Feet
FTEG	Flight Test and Engineering Group
FY	Fiscal Year
G.P.	General Purpose
GCA	Ground Controlled Approach
Glomb	Guided Glider Bomb
GMGRU	Guided Missile Group
GMU	Guided Missile Unit
Halon	Fire Suppression Agent
HARM	High Speed Antiradiation Missile
HATWING	Heavy Attack Wing
HIPEG	High Performance External Gun
hp	Horsepower
HTA	Heavier-than-air
HUD/Hud	Heads up Display
Hvar	High Velocity Aircraft Rocket
IBM	International Business Machine Company
IFF	Identification Friend or Foe
IGY	International Geophysical Year
IO	Indian Ocean

IOC	Initial Operational Capability
IR	Imaging Infrared
JATO	Jet Assisted Takeoff
JCS	Joint Chiefs of Staff
JPATS	Joint Primary Aircraft Training System
KIA	Killed in Action
KIAS	Knots indicated air speed
KLM	Kuwait Liberation Medal
KPUC	Korean Presidential Unit Citation
KSM	Korean Service Medal
LAMPS	Light Airborne Multipurpose System
Lant/LANT	Atlantic
lbs	Pounds
LCAC	Air Cushion Landing Craft
LCDR	Lieutenant Commander
LCOL	Lieutenant Colonel
LDO	Limited Duty Officer
LGB	Laser Guided Bomb
LIC	Low Intensity Conflict
Loran/LORAN	Long Range Navigation Equipment
LRAACA	Long-range, Air Antisubmarine Warfare-capable Aircraft
LSO	Landing Signal Officer
LT	Lieutenant
LT (jg)	Lieutenant Junior Grade
LTA	Lighter-than-Air
LTV	Ling Temco Vought Corp.
MAC	Military Airlift Command
MACV	Military Assistance Command, Vietnam
MAD	Magnetic Airborne (or Anomaly) Detection
MAG	Marine Air Group
MAGTF	Marine Air Group Task Force
MATS	Military Air Transport Service
MAU	Master Augmentation Unit
MAW	Marine Air Wing
MAWSPAC	Medium Attack Weapons School, Pacific
MCAAS	Marine Corps Auxiliary Air Station
MCAF	Marine Corps Air Facility
MCAS	Marine Corps Air Station
Med	Mediterranean Sea
MEF	Marine Expeditionary Force
MEU	Marine Expeditionary Unit
MIA	Missing in Action
MiG	Russian aircraft designed by Artem I. Mikoyan and Mikhail I. Gurevich
MIRALC/SLBD	Mid Infrared Advanced Chemical Laser/Sea Lite Beam Director
MIT	Massachusetts Institute of Technology
MLS	Microwave Landing System
MRC	Major Regional Conflicts
MUC	Meritorious Unit Commendation
NAAF	Naval Air Auxiliary Facility
NAAS	Naval Air Auxiliary Station
NAB	Naval Air Base
NACA	National Advisory Committee on Aeronautics
NAD	Naval Aviation Depot
NADC	Naval Air Development Center

NADEP	Naval Aviation Depot
NAEC	Naval Air Engineering Center
NAESU	Naval Aviation Electronic Service Unit
NAF	Naval Air Facility
NAF	Naval Aircraft Factory
NAFC	Naval Air Ferry Command
NAILS	Naval Aviation Integrated Logistic Support Task Force
NALCOLANTUNIT	Naval Air Logistics Control Office, Atlantic Unit
NAMC	Naval Air Material Center
NAMO	Naval Aviation Maintenance Office
NAMTC	Naval Air Missile Test Center
NAO	Naval Aviation Observer
NAP	Naval Aviation Pilot/Naval Air Pilot
NAR	Naval Air Reserve
NARF	Naval Air Rework Facility
NARTU	Naval Air Reserve Training Unit
NARU	Naval Air Reserve Units
NAS	Naval Aeronautic Station
NAS	Naval Air Station
NASA	National Aeronautics and Space Administration
NASM	National Air Space Museum
NATC	Naval Air Test Center
NATMSACT	Naval Air Training Maintenance Support Activity
NATO	North Atlantic Treaty Organization
Natops/NATOPS	Naval Air Training and Operating Procedures Standardization Program
NATB	Naval Air Training Base
NATC	Naval Air Training Center
NATS	Naval Air Transport Service
NATEC	Naval Airship Training and Experimental Command
NATT	Naval Air Technical Training
NATTC	Naval Air Technical Training Center
NAVAIR	Naval Air Systems Command
NAVAIRSYSCOM	Naval Air Systems Command
NAVCAD	Naval Aviation Cadet
NavE	Navy Battle "E" Ribbon
NAVICP	Naval Inventory Control Point
NAVMAT/NMC	Naval Material Command
NavPro/NAVPRO	Naval Plant Representative Office
NAVRES/NR	Naval Reserve
Navstar	Navigation Satellite
NAWC	Naval Air Warfare Center
NAWC (WD)	Naval Air Warfare Center (Weapons Division)
NAWC (AD)	Naval Air Warfare Center (Aircraft Division)
NDSM	National Defense Service Medal
NEM	Navy Expeditionary Medal
NERV	Nuclear Emulsion Recovery Vehicle
NFO	Naval Flight Officer
NFRC	Naval Reserve Flying Corps
nm	Nautical Mile
NNV	National Naval Volunteers
NOB	Naval Operating Base
NORAD	North American Air Defense Command
NorLant	Northern Atlantic Ocean
NorPac	Northern Pacific Ocean

NOTS	Naval Ordnance Test Station
NRAB	Naval Reserve Aviation Bases
NRFC	Naval Reserve Flying Corps
NRL	Naval Research Lab/Naval Research Laboratory
NROTC	Naval Reserve Officer Training Corps
NS	Naval Station
NSF	National Science Foundation
NTPS	Naval Test Pilot School
NUC	Navy Unit Commendation
NVG	Night Vision Goggle
NVN	North Vietnam
NWC	Naval Weapons Center
O&R	Overhaul and Repair
OASU	Oceanographic Air Survey
OCS	Officer Candidate School
ODM	Operational Development Model
ONR	Office of Naval Research
OPNAV	Naval Operations
Ops	Operations
ORI	Operational Readiness Inspection
OSD	Office of Secretary of Defense
P/A	Pilotless Aircraft
Pac/PAC	Pacific
PASU	Patrol Aircraft Service Unit
PatSU/Patsu	Patrol Aircraft Service Unit
PatWing/PATWING	Patrol Wing
PLAT	Pilot Landing Aid Television
PMTC	Pacific Missile Test Center
Pol	Petroleum, Oil, Lubricants
POW	Prisoner of War
PPI	Plan Position Indicator
PUC	Presidential Unit Citation
Radar	Radio Detection and Ranging Equipment
RADM	Rear Admiral
RAF	Royal Air Force
RAM	Rolling Airframe Missile
RAST	Recovery Assist, Securing and Traversing System
RCA	Radio Corporation of America
RDT&E	Research, Development, Training and Evaluation
Ret	Retired
REWSON	Reconnaissance, Electronic Warfare and Special Operations
RFC	Canadian Royal Flying Corps
RimPac	Pacific Rim Exercise (Joint)
RIO	Radar Intercept Officer
RN	Royal Navy
RNAS	Royal Naval Air Station
ROK	Republic of Korea
RPV	Remotely Piloted Vehicle
RPV Star	Ship-deployable, Tactical Airborne Remotely Piloted Vehicle
RVN	Republic of Vietnam
RVNGC	Republic of Vietnam Meritorious Unit Citation (Gallantry Cross)
SAM	Surface-to-air Missile
SAR	Search and Rescue
SASM	Southwest Asia Service Medal

SCS	Sea Control Ship Concept
Seals	Sea-air-land Team
SEAPAC	Sea Activated Parachute Automatic Crew Release
SecDef/SECDEF	Secretary of Defense
SECNAV/SecNav	Secretary of the Navy
SEVENTHFLT	Seventh Fleet
SIXTHFLT	Sixth Fleet
SLAM	Standoff Land Attack Missile
SLCM	Sea/Surface Launched Cruise Missile
SLEP	Service Life Extension Program
Sol Rad	Solar Radiation
SoLant/SOLANT	Southern Atlantic Ocean
SOOS	Stacked Oscars on Scout System
SoPac/SOPAC	South Pacific
SPASUR	Navy Space Surveillance System
Sq	Square
SSM	Surface-to-surface Missile
STM	Supersonic Tactical Missile
STRATCOM	Strategic Command
SVN	South Vietnam
SWIP	System Weapons Integration Program
SWOD	Special Weapons Ordnance Device
TACAMO	Take Charge and Move out
Tacan/TACAN	Tactical Air Navigation System
TACELWING	Tactical Electronic Warfare Wing
TACGRU	Tactical Group
T&E	Test and Evaluation
TARPS	Tactical Aerial Reconnaissance Pod System
TERCOM	Terrain Contour Matching
TF	Task Force
TG	Task Group
TINS	Thermal Imaging Navigation Set
TRAM	Target Recognition Attack Multisensor
TraWing/TRAWING	Training Air Wing
TRIM	Trail Road Interdiction Mission
TWA	Trans World Airlines
UAV	Unmanned Aerial Vehicle
UDT	Underwater Demolition Team
U.K.	United Kingdom
U.S.	United States
UN	United Nations
UNSM	United Nations Service Medal
USA	U.S. Army
USACOM	U.S. Atlantic Command
USAF	U.S. Air Force
USCG	U.S. Coast Guard
USMC	U.S. Marine Corps
USN	U.S. Navy
USNR	U.S. Navy Reserve
USNRF	U.S. Navy Reserve Force
USNS	United States Naval Ship
USSR	Union of Soviet Socialist Republics
VADM	Vice Admiral
VAST	Versatile Avionics Shop Test

VCNO	Vice Chief of Naval Operations
VFAX	Advanced Experimental Fighter Aircraft
VLAD	Vertical Line Array DIFAR
VOD	Vertical on board Delivery
Vstol	Vertical/short Take-off and Landing
Vtol	Vertical Take-off and Landing
Vtol/stol	Vertical Take-off and Landing; Short Take-off and Landing
Vtxts	Navy Undergraduate Jet Flight Training System
VWS	Ventilated Wet Suit
WestPac/WESTPAC	Western Pacific Ocean
WNY	Washington Navy Yard
WTS	War Training Service
WW-I	World War I
WW-II	World War II

Note: Acronyms or abbreviations for squadron designations, air groups or air wings, aviation ship designations and aviation ratings may be found in appendices 16, 15, 3, and 14, respectively. Other appendices in the book also provide a limited number of more specialized acronym meanings.

PART 1

A Few Pioneers

1898–1916

The United States Navy's official interest in airplanes emerged as early as 1898. That year the Navy assigned officers to sit on an interservice board investigating the military possibilities of Samuel P. Langley's flying machine. In subsequent years there were naval observers at air meets here and abroad and at the public demonstrations staged by Orville and Wilbur Wright in 1908 and 1909. All were enthusiastic about the potential of the airplane as a fleet scout. By 1909, naval officers, including a bureau chief, were urging the purchase of aircraft.

It was in 1910 that a place was made for aviation in the organizational structure of the Navy. That was the year Captain Washington I. Chambers was designated as the officer to whom all aviation matters were to be referred. Although holding no special title, he pulled together existing threads of aviation interest within the Navy and gave official recognition to the proposals of inventors and builders. Before the Navy had either planes or pilots he arranged a series of tests in which Glenn Curtiss and Eugene Ely dramatized the airplane's capability for shipboard operations and showed the world and a skeptical Navy that aviation could go to sea.

Early in 1911 the first naval officer reported for flight training. By mid-year, the first money had been appropriated, the first aircraft had been purchased, the first pilot had qualified, and the site of the first aviation camp had been selected. The idea of a seagoing aviation force was beginning to take form as plans and enthusiasms were transformed into realities. By the end of the year a humble beginning had been made.

The need for more science and less rule of thumb was apparent to Captain Chambers. He collected the writings and scientific papers of leaders in the new field, pushed for a national aerodynamics laboratory, and encouraged naval constructors to work on aerodynamic and hydrodynamic problems. The Navy built a wind tunnel, and the National Advisory Committee for Aeronautics was established. The first real study of what was needed in aviation was conducted by a board under Chambers' leadership and included in its recommendations the establishment of a ground and flight training center at Pensacola, Fla., the expansion of research, and the assignment of an airplane to every major combatant ship of the Navy.

Progress in these early years was marked by an endurance record of six hours in the air; the first successful catapult launch of an airplane from a ship; exercises with the Fleet during winter maneuvers at Guantanamo Bay, Cuba; and combat sorties at Veracruz, Mexico. These were but some of the accomplishments by pioneer pilots. Their activity furthered the importance of aviation to the Navy. In 1914, Secretary of the Navy Josephus Daniels announced that the point had been reached "where aircraft must form a large part of our naval forces for offensive and defensive operations."

1898

25 March   Theodore Roosevelt, Assistant Secretary of the Navy, recommended to the Secretary that he appoint two officers "of scientific attainments and practical ability" who, with representatives from the War Department, would examine Professor Samuel P. Langley's flying machine and report upon its practability and its potentiality for use in war.

29 April   The first joint Army-Navy board on aeronautics submitted the report of its investigation of the Langley flying machine. Since the machine was a model of 12-foot wing span, its value for military purposes was largely theoretical, but the report expressed a general sentiment in favor of supporting Professor Langley in further experimentation.

1908

17 September   Lieutenant George C. Sweet and Naval Constructor William McEntee were official Navy observers at the first Army demonstration trials of the Wright flying machine at Fort Myer, Va.

2 December   Rear Admiral Willliam S. Cowles, Chief of the Bureau of Equipment, submitted a report on aviation prepared by Lieutenant George C. Sweet to the Secretary of the Navy. The report outlined the

1908—Continued

specifications of an airplane capable of operating from naval vessels on scouting and observation missions, discussed the tactical advantages of such capability for naval forces and recommended that a number of aircraft be purchased and "placed in the hands of the personnel of the Navy to further develop special features adapted to naval uses."

1909

16 August   A Bureau of Equipment request for authority to advertise for the construction of "two heavier than air flying machines" was disapproved by the Acting Secretary of the Navy with the comment: "The Department does not consider that the development of an aeroplane has progressed sufficiently at this time for use in the Navy."

1 September   Commander Frederick L. Chapin, U.S. Naval Attache at Paris, reported his observations at the Rheims Aviation Meet, expressing the opinion that "the airplane would have a present usefulness in naval warfare, and that the limits of the field will be extended in the near future," and in elaborating upon that theme prophetically noted two means by which aircraft could be operated from naval vessels. The first was the use of the Wright launching device (a catapult) to launch planes from the cleared quarterdeck of battleships, and the second was the construction of a floor (a flight deck) over the deck houses of auxiliary ships to provide the clear space required for take-off runs and landing aboard.

3 November   Lieutenant George C. Sweet was taken up as a passenger in the first Army Wright by Lieutenant Frank P. Lahm, USA, at College Park, Md. As a result, Sweet is credited with having been the first Navy officer to fly in an airplane.

1910

26 September   The Secretary of the Navy informed the U.S. Aeronautical Reserve (a new organization of private citizens formed to advance aeronautical science as a means of supplementing the national defense) that Captain Washington I. Chambers, Assistant to the Aid for Material, had been designated as the officer to whom all correspondence on aviation should be referred. This is the first recorded reference to a provision for aviation in Navy Department organization.

Eugene Ely Leaving Birmingham at Hampton Roads in the first takeoff from any ship, November 14, 1910 42878

1910—Continued

11 October The General Board, of which Admiral George Dewey was president, recommended to the Secretary of the Navy that, in recognition of "the great advances which have been made in the science of aviation and the advantages which may accrue from its use in this class of vessel," the problem of providing space for airplanes or dirigibles be considered in all new designs for scouting vessels.

7 October In a letter to the Secretary, the Chief of the Bureau of Steam Engineering, Captain Hutch I. Cone, pointed to "the rapid improvement in the design and manipulation of airplanes and the important role they would probably play" and requested authority to requisition an airplane for *Chester* (CL 1) and the services of an instructor to teach one or more officers to fly the machine.

13 October The Secretary of the Navy approved the recommendation of the Chief Constructor that an officer from the Bureau of Construction and Repair and another from the Bureau of Steam Engineering be appointed to investigate the subject of aviation and gain technical knowledge of airplanes, and directed that these officers keep Captain Washington I. Chambers, previously designated to serve in a similar capacity in the Secretary's office, fully informed of work contemplated and the results of all experiments.

22 October The International Aviation Tournament opened at Belmont Park, N.Y. Attending in an official capacity as Navy observers were the three officers recently named to investigate aviation: Captain Washington I. Chambers, Naval Constructor William McEntee, and Lieutenant N. H. Wright.

31 October The Chief of the Bureau of Construction and Repair suggested to the Secretary of the Navy that steps be taken to obtain one or more aeroplanes to develop their use for naval purposes and recommended that in the absence of specific funds for their purchase, specifications for the battleship *Texas* (Battleship No. 35) be modified so as to require its contractors to supply one or more aircraft as a part of their obligation.

14 November First take-off from a ship—Eugene Ely, a civilian pilot, took off in a 50-hp Curtiss plane from a wooden platform built on the bow of *Birmingham* (CL 2). The ship was at anchor in Hampton Roads, Va., and Ely landed safely on Willoughby Spit.

29 November Glenn H. Curtiss wrote to the Secretary of the Navy offering flight instruction without charge for one naval officer as one means of assisting "in developing the adaptability of the aeroplane to military purposes."

23 December The first naval officer to undergo flight training, Lieutenant Theodore G. Ellyson, was ordered to report to the Glenn H. Curtiss Aviation Camp at North Island, San Diego, Calif.

1911

18 January At 11:01 a.m., Eugene Ely, flying the same Curtiss pusher used to take off from *Birmingham* (CL 2), landed on a specially built platform aboard the armored cruiser *Pennsylvania* (Armored Cruiser No. 4) at anchor in San Francisco Bay, Calif. At 11:58 he took off and returned to Selfridge Field, San Francisco, completing the earliest demonstration of the adaptability of aircraft to shipboard operations.

26 January The first successful hydroaeroplane flight was made by Glenn H. Curtiss at North Island, San Diego, Calif. This important step in adapting aircraft to naval needs was witnessed by Lieutenant Theodore G. Ellyson, who assisted in preparing for the test.

1 February Glenn H. Curtiss made two successful flights from the water at San Diego, Calif., in his standard biplane using a single main float in place of the tandem triple float used in earlier tests. These take-offs demonstrated the superior efficiency of the sled profile float which was used on Navy hydroaeroplanes up to World War I.

10 February Acting Secretary of the Navy Beekman Winthrop directed the Point Loma, Calif., Wireless Station to cooperate with Captain Harry S. Harkness, U.S. Aeronautical Reserve, in experiments in connection with use of wireless from aeroplanes.

17 February In another of the early demonstrations of the adaptability of aircraft to naval uses, Glenn H. Curtiss taxied his hydroaeroplane alongside *Pennsylvania* (Armored Cruiser No. 4) at anchor in San Diego Harbor, was hoisted aboard and off again by ship's crane and then returned to base.

4 March The first funds for Naval Aviation were appropriated, providing $25,000 to the Bureau of Navigation for "experimental work in the development of aviation for naval purposes."

1911—Continued

Ely in Curtiss biplane comes aboard Pennsylvania in the first shipboard landing, January 18, 1911 428455

9 March The Wright Company made a formal offer to train one pilot for the Navy contingent upon the purchase of one airplane for the sum of $5,000. This offer was later made unconditional.

17 March Lieutenant John Rodgers, who became Naval Aviator No. 2, reported to the Wright Company at Dayton, Ohio, for instruction in flying.

1 April Captain Washington I. Chambers, the officer in charge of aviation, reported for duty with the General Board, a move suggested by Admiral George Dewey, when space for aviation was not available in the office of the Aid for Operations.

14 April The embryo office of Naval Aviation was transferred from the General Board and established in the Bureau of Navigation.

8 May Captain Washington I. Chambers prepared requisitions for two Curtiss biplanes. One, the Triad, was to be equipped for arising from or alighting on land or water; with a metal tipped propeller designed for a speed of at least 45 miles per hour; with provisions for carrying a passenger alongside the pilot; and with con-

Captain Washington Chambers 424786

1911—Continued

Sandbags, first arresting gear, halt Ely's plane 450108

trols that could be operated by either the pilot or the passenger. The machine thus described later became the Navy's first airplane, the A-1. Although these requisitions lacked the signature of the Chief of the Bureau of Navigation, necessary to direct the General Storekeeper to enter into a contract with the Curtiss Company, they did indicate Captain Chambers' decision as to which airplanes the Navy should purchase. From this, 8 May has come to be considered the date upon which the Navy ordered its first airplane and has been officially proclaimed to be the birthday of Naval Aviation.

27 June Lieutenant (jg) John H. Towers, who became Naval Aviator No. 3, reported for duty and instruction in flying at the Curtiss School, Hammondsport, N.Y.

1 July First flight of the A-1—At 6:50 p.m., Glenn H. Curtiss demonstrated the A-1, the first aircraft built for the Navy, taking off from and alighting on Lake Keuka at Hammondsport, N.Y. This flight was of 5 minutes' duration, and to an altitude of 25 feet. Three other flights were made the same evening, one by Curtiss with Lieutenant Theodore G. Ellyson as a passenger, and two by Ellyson alone.

Hoisting plane aboard Pennsylvania, February 1911 1051558

1911—Continued

Preparing A-1, first Navy plane, for wire launch 428450

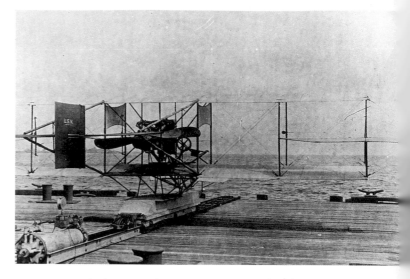

A-1 on the first catapult, Annapolis, July 1912 650864

3 July Lieutenant Theodore G. Ellyson flew the A-1 from Lake Keuka to Hammondsport, N.Y., on the first night flight by a naval aviator, landing successfully on the water on the second attempt without the aid of lights.

6 July Captain Washington I. Chambers was ordered to temporary duty at the Naval Academy in connection with the establishment of an aviation experimental station, the site for which had been previously selected on Greenbury Point, Annapolis, Md. Although not occupied by the aviators until September, this was the first base for Naval Aviation.

10 July Amphibious features of the Navy's first aircraft were demonstrated by Glenn H. Curtiss in the 24th flight of the Triad—the machine in which he took off from land, lifted the wheels while in the air, and landed in water.

13 July The Navy's second aircraft, the A-2, was set up and flown at Hammondsport, N.Y. The first flight was made by Glenn H. Curtiss, and the second by Lieutenant Theodore G. Ellyson.

23 August The officers on flight duty at Hammondsport, N.Y., and Dayton, Ohio, were ordered to report for duty at the Engineering Experiment Station, Naval Academy, "in connection with the test of gasoline motors and other experimental work in the development of aviation, including instruction at the aviation school" being set up on Greenbury Point, Annapolis, Md.

First Navy aircraft, the A-1 Triad Hydroaeroplane, taxing on Lake Keuka, Hammondsport, New York 1061484(NHF)

Lieutenant Ellyson gives Captain Chambers a flight in the A-1 424469

1911—Continued

7 September A memorable experiment in the Navy's search for a shipboard launching device was completed at Hammondsport, N.Y., when Lieutenant Theodore G. Ellyson made a successful takeoff from an inclined wire rigged from the beach down to the water. Ellyson's report contained the following description of the run: "The engine was started and run at full speed and then I gave the signal to release the machine. . . . I held the machine on the wire as long as possible as I wanted to be sure that I had enough headway to rise and not run the risk of the machine partly rising and then falling. . . . Everything happened so quickly and went off so smoothly that I hardly knew what happened except that I did have to use the ailerons, and that the machine was sensitive to their action."

16 September Plans to purchase flight clothing were described in a letter from Lieutenant Theodore G. Ellyson, who hoped to get the Navy Department to pay for them later. Requirements were previously outlined as a light helmet with detachable goggles, or a visor, with covering for the ears and yet holes so that the engine could be heard; a leather coat lined with fur or wool; leather trousers; high rubber galoshes and gauntlets; and a life preserver of some description.

20 September The attempt to equip aircraft with navigational instruments was reflected in a request of the Bureau of Navigation to the Naval Observatory for temporary use of a boat compass in experimental work connected with the development of aviation.

John Towers and Theodore Ellyson 427990

10 October Lieutenant Holden C. Richardson, CC, USN, reported to aviation at the Washington Navy Yard. Richardson became the Navy's first engineering and maintenance officer for aviation.

16 October Plans for a scientific test of hydroaeroplane floats at the Washington Navy Yard Model Basin were described in a letter from Captain Washington I. Chambers in which he stated that a model of the pontoons with Forlanini planes (hydrovanes) was nearly ready for test.

Holden C. Richardson (CC) 650871

17 October Searching for improved powerplants, Captain Washington I. Chambers, in a letter to Glenn H. Curtiss, discussed heavy oil (or diesel) engines and turbine engines similar in principle to those that, some 30 years later, would make jet propulsion practical. Chambers wrote, "In my opinion, this turbine is the surest step of all, and the aeroplane manufacturer who gets in with it first is going to do wonders."

25 October Lieutenants Theodore G. Ellyson and John H. Towers, on a flight in the A-1 from Annapolis, Md., to Fort Monroe, Va., to test the durability of the aircraft on cross-country flight, were forced down by a leaking radiator near Milford Haven, Va., having covered 112 miles in 122 minutes.

8 November Ensign Victor D. Herbster, later designated Naval Aviator No. 4, reported for flight instruction at the Aviation Camp at Greenbury Point, Annapolis, Md.

14 November The Navy's first major aircraft modification, conversion of the Wright B-1 landplane into a hydroaeroplane, was initiated with a telegraphic order to the Burgess Company and Curtiss, Marblehead, Mass., for a suitable float.

20 December Experiments with airborne wireless transmission were conducted at Annapolis, Md., by Ensign Charles H. Maddox in the A-1 airplane piloted by Lieutenant John H. Towers. The trailing wire anten-

1911—Continued

Herbster, Rodgers and Wiegand with B-1 1053801 (NHF)

na, reeled out after take-off, was found to be too weak, and no definite results were obtained.

26 December Search for a shipboard launching device continued as Captain Washington I. Chambers reported that the Bureau of Ordnance was interested in experimenting with a catapult for launching aeroplanes somewhat after the manner of launching torpedoes.

29 December The aviators at Annapolis, Md., were ordered to transfer with their equipment to North

Navy Wright, B-1 after installation of pontoon 428225

Island, San Diego, Calif. to set up an Aviation Camp on land offered for the purpose by Glenn H. Curtiss.

1912

9 March Interest in steel and aluminum as aircraft structural materials was evident in a letter from Assistant Naval Constructor Holden C. Richardson, who wrote to Captain Washington I. Chambers, "From all I can gather, there is little doubt that much greater confidence would be felt if pontoons were constructed with a metal skin. . . . It would be unwise to make any requisition for such a construction until a practically standard design has been developed."

11 March An early, if limited, interest in the helicopter was shown as the Secretary of the Navy authorized expenditure of not more than $50 for developing models of a helicopter design proposed by Chief Machinist's Mate F.E. Nelson of *West Virginia* (Armored Cruiser No. 5). The Secretary's accompanying policy implication was followed with a few exceptions for the next 30 years: "The Department recognizes the value of the helicopter principle in the design of naval aircraft and is following closely the efforts of others in this direction."

23 March Chief Electrician Howard E. Morin conducted experiments with wireless at Mare Island Navy Yard, San Francisco, Calif., in which he made transmissions from a dummy airplane fuselage hoisted to a height of 85 feet, which were received by a station at Point Richmond, Calif., 20 miles distant.

22 May 1st Lieutenant Alfred A. Cunningham, USMC, the first Marine Corps officer assigned to flight instruction and later designated Naval Aviator No. 5, reported to the Superintendent of the Naval Academy for "duty in connection with aviation" and subsequently was ordered to the Burgess Company at Marblehead, Mass., for flight instruction. This date is recognized as the birthday of Marine Corps aviation.

21 June Lieutenant Theodore G. Ellyson ascended 900 feet over Annapolis, Md. in 3 minutes and 30 seconds in the A-1.

20 July Comparative tests of Wright steel wire and Monel wire were conducted at Engineering Experiment Station Annapolis, Md., by the Aviation Camp. These, the earliest recorded Navy tests of aircraft structural materials, showed the Monel wire to be both free of corrosion and 50 percent stronger than the steel wire.

1912—Continued

25 July   Aircraft specifications—On the basis of the Navy's experience with its first airplanes, the Secretary of the Navy published "Requirements for Hydroaeroplanes," the first general specifications for naval aircraft. The purpose expressed by the Secretary was "to assist manufacturers in maintaining the highest degree of efficiency, while improving the factors which govern safety in aviation, without demanding anything that may not be accomplished under the limitations of the present state of the art and without confining purchases to the products of a single factory."

26 July   Tests of airborne wireless were continued at Annapolis, Md., using the Wright B-1 piloted by Lieutenant John Rodgers. On one flight, Ensign Charles H. Maddox, who was giving technical assistance to the aviators, sent messages to *Stringham* (Torpedo Boat No. 19) at a distance of about one and a half miles.

31 July   The Navy's first attempt to launch an airplane by catapult was made at Annapolis, Md., by Lieutenant Theodore G. Ellyson in the A-1. The aircraft, not being secured to the catapult, reared at about mid-stroke, was caught in a cross wind and thrown into the water. The pilot was not injured. This catapult, which was powered by compressed air, was constructed at the Naval Gun Factory, Washington Navy Yard, from a plan proposed by Captain Washington I. Chambers.

18 September   Lieutenant Bernard L. Smith, USMC, the second Marine officer assigned to flight training and later designated Naval Aviator No. 6, reported for instruction at the Aviation Camp at the Naval Academy in Annapolis, Md.

3 October   The Davis recoilless gun was given initial tests at Naval Proving Ground, Indian Head, Md. This gun was designed by Commander Cleland Davis to fire from an aircraft a caliber shell large enough to damage submarines but with a recoil slight enough to be absorbed by the aircraft.

6 October   Lieutenant John H. Towers, flying the Curtiss A-2, took off from the water at Annapolis, Md., at 6:50 a.m. and remained in the air 6 hours, 10 minutes and 35 seconds, setting a new American endurance record for planes of any type.

8 October   Tests of a Gyro 50-horsepower rotary motor were completed at the Engineering Experiment Station, Annapolis, Md. This, the Navy's first recorded attempt to utilize laboratory equipment and methods

Single-seat Curtiss trainer, similar to the A-2 428449

1912—Continued

in evaluating an aircraft engine, consisted of three brief dynamometer tests, followed by ground runs and flight tests.

8 October   Physical requirements for prospective naval aviators were first defined in Bureau of Medicine and Surgery Circular Letter 125221.

25 October   Ensign Godfrey deC. Chevalier, later designated Naval Aviator No. 7, reported for flight training at the Aviation Camp at Annapolis, Md.

12 November   The Navy's first successful launching of an airplane by catapult was made at the Washington Navy Yard by Lieutenant Theodore G. Ellyson in the A-3. The following month a flying boat was successfully launched from this catapult.

26 November   Lieutenant (jg) Patrick N. L. Bellinger, later Naval Aviator No. 8, reported for flight instruction at the Aviation Camp, Annapolis, Md.

30 November   The C-1, the Navy's first flying boat, was tested at Hammondsport, N.Y., by Lieutenant Theodore G. Ellyson. Its performance, as informally reported by Ellyson, was: "Circular climb, only one complete circle, 1,575 feet in 14 minutes 30 seconds fully loaded. On glide approximately 5.3 to 1. Speed, eight runs over measured mile, 59.4 miles per hour fully loaded. The endurance test was not made, owing to the fact that the weather has not been favorable, and I did not like to delay any longer."

Godfrey deC. Chevalier 466256

2 December   Ensign William D. Billingsley, later to become Naval Aviator No. 9, reported for duty at the Aviation Camp, Annapolis, Md., and was assigned to the Navy-Wright B-2 for instruction.

18 December   Lieutenant John H. Towers reported completion of a series of tests begun on 26 October to determine the ability to spot submarines from the air. He gave general conclusions that the best altitude for observation was about 800 feet; that submarines could be detected when running a few feet below the surface, but that the waters of Chesapeake Bay were too muddy for a fair test; and suggested that additional trials be held at Guantanamo Bay, Cuba.

19 December   President William H. Taft, acting on a recommendation made by the Secretary of the Navy, created a "Commission on Aerodynamical Laboratory" to determine the need for and a method of establishing such a laboratory. Navy members of the commission were Naval Constructor David W. Taylor and Captain Washington I. Chambers.

1913

6 January   The entire aviation element of the Navy arrived at Guantanamo Bay, Cuba, and set up the Aviation Camp on Fisherman's Point for its first operations with the fleet. The assignment, which included scouting missions and exercises in spotting mines and submerged submarines as part of the fleet maneuvers, served both to demonstrate operational capabilities of the aircraft and to stimulate interest in aviation among fleet personnel, more than a hundred of whom were taken up for flights during the eight-week stay.

Catapult launch of flying boat, Washington, D.C. 428462

1913—Continued

Base for first aviation operations with fleet at Fisherman's Point, Guantanamo Bay, Cuba, January 1913 652044

8 February   Lieutenant John H. Towers reported on experimental work underway at Guantanamo Bay, Cuba, including bombing, aerial photography, and wireless transmission, and stated: "We have become fairly accurate at dropping missiles, using a fairly simple device gotten up by one of the men. Have obtained some good photographs from the boats at heights up to 1,000 feet. I believe we will get some results with wireless this winter."

26 February   Action to provide the Navy with a wind tunnel, a basic tool in aeronautical research and development, was approved formally by the Chief Constructor of the Navy. The resulting tunnel, which was built at the Washington Navy Yard, remained in operation until after the end of World War II.

4 March   The Navy Appropriations Act for fiscal year 1914 provided an increase of 35 percent in pay and allowances for officers detailed to duty as flyers of heavier-than-air craft, limited to 30 the number of officers that could be so assigned, and further provided that no naval officer above the rank of lieutenant commander, or major in the Marine Corps, could be detailed to duty involving flying.

5 March   As a result of tests held at Guantanamo Bay, Cuba, 3-5 March, Lieutenant John H. Towers reported that submarines were visible from the air at depths of from 30 to 40 feet.

13 March   Captain Washington I. Chambers was awarded the medal of the Aeronautical Society for the year 1912 and cited for "his unusual achievements in

being the first to demonstrate the usefulness of the aeroplane in navies, in developing a practical catapult for the launching of aeroplanes from ships, in assisting in the practical solution of the hydroaeroplane by the production in association with others of the flying boat, in having been instrumental in the introduction into our halls of Congress of bills for a National Aerodynamic Laboratory, and a Competitive Test, and through his perseverance and able efforts in advancing the progress of Aeronautics in many other channels."

31 March   Aircraft instruments and allied equipment for installation in a new flying boat, the Burgess

Guantanamo 1913 — B. L. Smith, P. N. L. Bellinger, A. A. Cunningham, W. D. Billingsley (standing) V. D. Herbster, G. deC. Chevalier (seated) 426948

1913—Continued

Company and Curtiss D-1, were listed as: compass, altimeter, inclinometer, speed indicator, chart board, radio, and generator. Although the radio and generator were not installed, the remaining equipment was representative instrumentation on naval aircraft of the period.

10 April Performance standards for qualification as a Navy Air Pilot, and issuance of a certificate to all officers meeting the requirements, were approved by the Secretary of the Navy. They were described by Chambers as being different from those of the "land pilot" and more exacting than the requirements of the international accrediting agency, the Federation Aeronautique Internationale.

28 April Chief of the Bureau of Navigation Rear Admiral Victor Blue approved a proposal that the Navy Department, Glenn Curtiss, and the Sperry Company cooperate in testing the gyroscopic stabilizer on a new Navy airplane.

9 May President Woodrow Wilson approved the designation of representatives of governmental departments to serve on an advisory committee for the Langley Aerodynamical Laboratory which had been reopened by the Smithsonian Institution on 1 May. Navy members of the advisory committee were Captain Washington I. Chambers and Lieutenant Holden C. Richardson, CC, USN.

12 June Secretary of the Navy approved detailing Lieutenant Jerome C. Hunsaker, CC, USN, to the Massachusetts Institute of Technology to develop "a course of lectures and experiments on the design of aeroplanes and dirigibles, and to undertake research in that field." After making a tour of aeronautical research facilities in Europe, Hunsaker participated in establishing a course of aeronautical engineering at M.I.T. in the Department of Naval Architecture.

13 June Lieutenant (jg) Patrick N. L. Bellinger, flying the Curtiss A-3 at Annapolis, Md., set an American altitude record for seaplanes, reaching 6,200 feet.

20 June Ensign William D. Billingsley, piloting the B-2 at 1,600 feet over the water near Annapolis, Md., was thrown from the plane and fell to his death, the first fatality of Naval Aviation. Lieutenant John H. Towers, riding as passenger, was also unseated but clung to the plane and fell with it into the water, receiving serious injuries.

23 June A General Order fixed the cognizance of various bureaus in aviation in a manner paralleling the division of responsibility for naval vessels.

30 August A Sperry gyroscopic stabilizer (automatic pilot) was flight tested in the C-2 Curtiss flying boat by Lieutenant (jg) Patrick N. L. Bellinger at Hammondsport, N.Y.

30 August In a report to the Secretary of the Navy, the General Board expressed its opinion that "the organization of an efficient naval air service should be immediately taken in hand and pushed to fulfillment."

5 October Initial trials of the Navy's first amphibian flying boat—the OWL, or Over-Water-Land type—were completed at Hammondsport, N.Y., under the supervision of Lieutenant Holden C. Richardson, CC, USN. The aircraft, subsequently redesignated E-1, was the A-2 hydroaeroplane in which the pontoon was replaced with a flying boat hull containing a three-wheel landing gear.

7 October The Secretary of the Navy appointed a board of officers, with Captain Washington I. Chambers as senior member, to draw up "a comprehensive plan for the organization of a Naval Aeronautic Service." Its report, submitted after 12 days of deliberation, emphasized the need for expansion and for the integration of aviation with the fleet, and was in all respects the first comprehensive program for an orderly development of Naval Aviation. Its recommendations included the establishment of an Aeronautic Center at Pensacola, Fla., for flight and ground training and for the study of advanced aeronautic engineering; establishment of a central aviation office under the Secretary to coordinate the aviation work of the Bureaus; the assignment of a ship for training in operations at sea and to make practical tests of equipment necessary for such operations; the assignment of one aircraft to every major combatant ship; and the expenditure of $1,297,700 to implement the program.

17 December Captain Mark L. Bristol reported to the Navy Department for special duty as officer in charge of aviation, thereby relieving Captain Washington I. Chambers of that duty.

1914

6 January The Marine Corps element of the Aviation Camp at Annapolis, Md., under Lieutenant Bernard L. Smith, USMC, and equipped with a flying boat, an amphibian, spare parts, and hangar tents, was ordered to Culebra Island, P.R., for exercises with the Advance Base Unit.

1914—Continued

Pensacola 1914 with flying boats, hydroaeroplanes and tent hangars at the first permanent station 72-CN-6422

Henry C. Mustin 1061482

7 January   The Office of Aeronautics, with Captain Mark L. Bristol in charge, was transferred from the Bureau of Navigation to the Division of Operations in the Office of the Secretary of the Navy.

10 January   Secretary of the Navy Josephus Daniels announced that "the science of aerial navigation has reached that point where aircraft must form a large part of our naval force for offensive and defensive operations."

20 January   The aviation unit from Annapolis, Md., consisting of 9 officers, 23 men, 7 aircraft, portable hangars, and other gear, under Lieutenant John H. Towers as officer in charge, arrived at Pensacola, Fla., on board *Mississippi* (BB 23) and *Orion* (AC 11) to set up a flying school. Lieutenant Commander Henry C. Mustin, in command of the station ship *Mississippi* (BB 23) was also in command of the aeronautic station.

1914—Continued

16 February   Lieutenant (jg) James M. Murray, Naval Aviator No. 10, on a flight at Pensacola, Fla., in the Burgess D-1 flying boat, crashed to the water from 200 feet and was drowned.

20 February   The beginnings of Aviation Medicine were apparent in a letter to the Commanding Officer at Pensacola, Fla., on the subject of physical requirements for aviator candidates which expressed the opinion that useful information could be obtained by observing pilots during flight and by physical examination before and after flight. The letter further directed that this be considered and a program developed that would permit incorporation of such practice in the work of the flight training school.

9 March   The wind tunnel at the Washington Navy Yard was tested. Calibration required about three months, and its first use in July was a test of ship's ventilator cowling.

27 March   The original designations of aircraft were changed to two letters and a number of which the first letter denoted class, the second type within a class, and the number the order in which aircraft within class were acquired. Four classes were set up; A for all heavier-than-air craft, D for airships or dirigibles, B for balloons and K for Kites. Within the A Class, the letters L, H, B, X and C represented land machines, hydroaeroplanes, flying boats, combination land and water machines, and convertibles, respectively. Thus the third hydroaeroplane, formerly A-3, became AH-3, and the first flying boat, formerly C-1, became AB-1.

20 April   First call to action—In less than 24 hours after receiving orders, an aviation detachment of 3 pilots, 12 enlisted men, and 3 aircraft, under command of Lieutenant John H. Towers, sailed from Pensacola, Fla., on board *Birmingham* (CL 2) to join Atlantic Fleet forces operating off Tampico in the Mexican crisis.

20 April   Mr. A. B. Lambert of St. Louis, Mo., informed the Secretary of the Navy that the services of the Aviation Reserve, which he had organized the year before, were available for use in the Mexican crisis and listed the names of 44 members, 20 of whom could furnish their own aircraft.

21 April   A second aviation detachment from Pensacola, Fla., of one pilot, three student pilots, and two aircraft, commanded by Lieutenant (jg) Patrick N. L. Bellinger, embarked on *Mississippi* (BB 23) and

Aviation detachment at Veracruz 1914, Bellinger (right) in front of first plane to be hit by hostile gunfire 391984

1914—Continued

sailed for Mexican waters to assist in military operations at Veracruz, Mexico.

22 April The Bureau of Navigation approved formal courses of instruction for student aviators and student mechanics at the Flying School at Pensacola, Fla.

25 April On the first flight by the *Mississippi* (BB 23) aviation unit at Veracruz, Mexico, Lieutenant (jg) Patrick N. L. Bellinger piloted the AB-3 flying boat to observe the city and make a preliminary search for mines in the harbor.

28 April Lieutenant (jg) Patrick N. L. Bellinger and Ensign Walter D. LaMont made a flight in the AB-3 flying boat to photograph the harbor at Veracruz, Mexico.

2 May The AH-3 hydroaeroplane, piloted by Lieutenant (jg) Patrick N. L. Bellinger with Ensign W. D. LaMont as observer, flew the first mission in direct support of ground troops as Marines encamped near Tejar, Mexico, reported being under attack and requested the aviation unit at Veracruz, Mexico, to locate the attackers.

6 May The Curtiss AH-3 hydroaeroplane, piloted by Lieutenant (jg) Patrick N. L. Bellinger with Lieutenant (jg) Richard C. Saufley as observer, was hit by rifle fire while on a reconnaissance flight over enemy positions

The AH-7, Burgess-Dunne, flying over Pensacola 1061479

in the vicinity of Veracruz, Mexico—the first marks of combat on a Navy plane.

19 May As the need for scouting services diminished at Veracruz, Mexico, the aviation detachment resumed routine flight instruction while awaiting orders to return to Pensacola, Fla.

24 May The aeronautic detachment on board *Birmingham* (CL 2) arrived at Veracruz, Mexico, from Tampico to join the *Mississippi* (BB 23) detachment in the school routine of flight instruction.

26 May On the basis of flight tests, Lieutenant Holden C. Richardson, CC, USN, recommended that the Navy buy two swept-wing Burgess-Dunne hydroaeroplanes "so that the advantages and limitations can be thoroughly determined . . . as it appears to be only the beginning of an important development in aeronautical design." The aircraft which were subsequently obtained were designated AH-7 and AH-10.

1 July Aviation was formally recognized with the establishment of an Office of Naval Aeronautics in the Division of Operations under the Secretary of the Navy.

28 July Lieutenant (jg) Victor D. Herbster reported on bombing tests which he and Lieutenant Bernard L. Smith, USMC, carried out at Indian Head Proving Grounds, Stumpneck, Md. Both dummy and live bombs were dropped over the side of the machine from about 1,000 feet against land and water targets. Herbster reported his bombing would have been more accurate "if I had been able to disengage my fingers from the wind-wheel sooner."

21 August Lieutenant Commander Henry C. Mustin, Lieutenant Patrick N. L. Bellinger and 1st Lieutenant Bernard L. Smith, USMC, arrived in Paris, France, from *North Carolina* (ACR 12) for a two-day tour of aircraft factories and aerodromes in the immediate area. This temporary assignment, the first use of Naval Aviators as observers in foreign lands, was a precedent for the assignment of aviation assistants to naval attaches, which began the same month when Lieutenant John H. Towers was sent to London. In September Lieutenant (jg) Victor D. Herbster and 1st Lieutenant Bernard L. Smith reported to Berlin, Germany, and Paris, respectively.

16 November An administrative reorganization at Pensacola, Fla., shifted overall command from the station ship to headquarters ashore and the station was officially designated Naval Aeronautic Station, Pensacola.

1914—Continued

23 November The title "Director of Naval Aeronautics" was established to designate the officer in charge of Naval Aviation. Captain Mark L. Bristol, already serving in that capacity, was ordered to report to the Secretary of the Navy under the new title.

25 November To measure and record velocity and direction of winds, gusts, and squalls at the ends of the speed course at Pensacola, Fla., Director of Naval Aeronautics Captain Mark L. Bristol established requirements for special meteorological equipment to be installed there.

1915

1 February The Division of Naval Militia Affairs in the Bureau of Navigation directed that an aeronautic corps could be organized in each of the state Naval Militia.

3 March A rider to the Naval Appropriations Act created the National Advisory Committee for Aeronautics. Navy members in the original organization were Captain Mark L. Bristol and Lieutenant Holden C. Richardson, CC, USN.

3 March The Naval Appropriations Act of 1916 added enlisted men and student aviators to those eligible for increased pay and allowances while on duty involving flying; increased the amount previously provided for qualified aviators; and provided for the payment of one year's pay to the next of kin of officers and men killed in aircraft accidents. The same act also raised the limits on personnel assigned to aviation to a yearly average of not more than 48 officers and 96 men of the Navy and 12 officers and 24 men of the Marine Corps.

22 March The title "Naval Aviator" replaced the former "Navy Air Pilot" designation for naval officers qualified as aviators.

16 April The AB-2 flying boat was successfully catapulted from a barge by Lieutenant Patrick N. L. Bellinger at Pensacola, Fla. The catapult used had been designed in 1913 by Lieutenant Holden C. Richardson, CC, USN, and fabricated at the Washington Navy Yard. The success of this and subsequent launchings led to installation of the catapult aboard ship.

23 April Lieutenant Patrick N. L. Bellinger, in the Burgess-Dunne AH-10, established an American altitude record for seaplanes by ascending to 10,000 feet over Pensacola, Fla.

8 May Lieutenant (jg) Melvin L. Stolz, student aviator, was killed in a crash of the AH-9 hydroaeroplane at Pensacola, Fla.

First catapult launch from ship, Mustin in AB-2 439969

1915—Continued

28 May   The Naval Militia was informed that refresher flight training at Pensacola, Fla., was available for a limited number of its aviators.

1 June   The Navy let its first contract for a lighter-than-air craft to the Connecticut Aircraft Company, New Haven. It ordered one non-rigid airship which was later designated the DN-1.

7 July   In the initial step towards mobilizing science, Secretary of the Navy Josephus Daniels stated in a letter to Thomas A. Edison: "One of the imperative needs of the Navy, in my judgment, is machinery and facilities for utilizing the natural inventive genius of Americans to meet the new conditions of warfare." This letter led to the establishment of the Naval Consulting Board, a group of civilian advisors which functioned during the World War I period and included in its organization a "Committee on Aeronautics, including Aero Motors."

10 July   The Aeronautical Engine Laboratory had its beginnings at the Washington Navy Yard, Washington, D.C., with an authorization by the Secretary to outfit a building for testing aeronautic machinery.

10 July   After test of a sextant equipped with a pendulum-type artificial horizon, NAS Pensacola's commanding officer, Henry C. Mustin, reported that while the pendulum principle was basically unsatisfactory for aircraft use, a sextant incorporating a gyroscopically stabilized artificial horizon might be acceptable.

10 July   A standard organization prescribed by General Order was the first to provide for an aeronautic force within the Naval Militia. Its composition, paralleling that of other forces established at the same time, was in sections of not more than 6 officers and 28 enlisted men; two sections forming a division. Officers were in the "aeronautics duty only" category, the highest rank provided being that of lieutenant commander at the division level. Its enlisted structure provided that men taken in under regular ratings of machinist mates and electricians would perform duties as aeronautic machinists; carpenter mates would perform duties as aeronautic mechanics; and landsmen, the equivalent of today's strikers, would perform special duties.

22 July   Based on recommendations received from the Naval Aeronautic Station, Pensacola, Fla., the Director of Naval Aeronautics established requirements for 13 instruments to be installed in service aeroplanes: air speed meter, incidence indicator, tachometer, skidding and sideslip indicator, altitude barometer, oil gauge, fuel gauge, compass, course and distance indicator, magazine camera, binoculars, clock, and sextant. All except the navigational instruments, camera, binoculars, and clock were also required for school aeroplanes.

5 August   Lieutenant Patrick N. L. Bellinger, flying the Burgess-Dunne AH-10, spotted mortar fire for Army shore batteries at Fort Monroe, Va., signaling his spots with Very pistol flares.

11 August   The Naval Observatory requested the Eastman Kodak Company to develop an aerial camera with high-speed lens, suitable for photography at 1,000 to 2,000 yards altitude, and so constructed that the pressure of the air during flight would not distort the focus.

12 October   A directive was issued establishing an Officer in Charge of Naval Aeronautics under the newly created Chief of Naval Operations and giving authority for aviation programs in the Navy Department to the Chief of Naval Operations and to the Bureaus. Although this had the effect of abolishing the Office of the Director of Naval Aeronautics, that office continued to exist until the detachment of the incumbent director.

15 October   The Secretary of the Navy referred a proposal, made by Captain Mark L. Bristol, to convert a merchant ship to operate aircraft, to the General Board with the comment that there was a more immediate need to determine what could be done with *North Carolina* (ACR 12), already fitted to carry aeroplanes.

5 November   Lieutenant Commander Henry C. Mustin, in the AB-2 flying boat, made the first catapult launching from a ship, flying off the stern of *North Carolina* (ACR 12) in Pensacola Bay, Fla.

3 December   Lieutenant Richard C. Saufley, flying the Curtiss AH-14, set an American altitude record for hydroaeroplanes, reaching 11,975 feet over Pensacola, Fla., and surpassing his own record of 11,056 feet which he had set only three days before.

1916

6 January   Instruction commenced for the first group of enlisted men to receive flight training at Pensacola, Fla.

1916—Continued

11 January The Naval Observatory forwarded two magnetic compasses to Pensacola, Fla., for tests under all conditions. These compasses, modified from the British Creigh-Osborne design on the basis of recommendations by Naval Aviators, provided a model for the compasses widely used in naval aircraft during World War I.

21 January In a step that led to the establishment of an aviation radio laboratory at Pensacola, Fla., the Officer in Charge of Naval Aeronautics requested the Superintendent, Radio Service, to authorize the radio operators at the Pensacola Radio Station to experiment with aircraft radio. Simultaneously, four sets of radio apparatus for aeroplanes were received at Pensacola. Although initiation of developmental work did not begin immediately, by late July an officer and a civilian radio expert had been detailed to aircraft radio experimentation at Pensacola and the Bureau of Steam Engineering had ordered approximately 50 aircraft radio sets.

10 February The Bureau of Construction and Repair implemented a Navy Department decision by directing that designating numbers be assigned to all aircraft under construction and that these numbers be used for identification purposes until the aircraft were tested or placed in service at which time standard designations provided by the order of 27 March 1914 would be used. Numbers, beginning with 51-A, were simultaneously assigned to 33 aircraft. This was the introduction of serial numbers hereafter assigned to all aircraft.

4 March Captain Mark L. Bristol was detached as Director of Naval Aeronautics and both the title and the office ceased to exist. Captain Bristol was assigned to command *North Carolina* (ACR 12) and, under a new title of Commander of the Air Service, assumed operational supervision over all aircraft, air stations, and the further development of aviation in the Navy. Such aviation duties as remained in the Office of the Chief of Naval Operations were assumed by Lieutenant Clarence K. Bronson.

25 March Qualifications for officers and enlisted men in the Aeronautic Force of the Naval Militia were defined by General Order which, in each instance, were over and above those prescribed for the same ranks and ratings of the Militia. These extras, cumulative for ranks in ascending order, required ensigns to have knowledge of navigation (except nautical astronomy) and scouting problems, practical and theoretical

knowledge of aeroplanes and motors, and ability to fly at least one type of aircraft. Lieutenants (jg) were in addition to have some knowledge of nautical astronomy, principles of aeroplane design, and to qualify for a Navy pilot certificate. Additional requirements for lieutenants called for a greater knowledge of nautical astronomy and ability to fly at least two types of naval aircraft, while lieutenant commanders, the highest rank provided for the force, were also to have knowledge of Navy business methods used in aeronautics. Aviation mechanics were to have knowledge of aircraft maintenance and aviation machinists were to have similar knowledge of motors.

29 March Lieutenant Richard C. Saufley, flying a Curtiss hydroaeroplane at Pensacola, Fla., bettered his own American altitude record with a flight to 16,010 feet and on 2 April extended it again with a mark of 16,072 feet.

C. K. Bronson 416339

30 March The Secretary of the Treasury informed the Secretary of the Navy that Coast Guard officers Second Lieutenant Charles E. Sugden and Third Lieutenant Elmer F. Stone had been assigned to flight instruction at Pensacola, Fla., in accordance with an agreement between the two departments.

15 April An anchor and a two digit numeral, both in dark blue on a white background, were prescribed as "Distinguishing Marks for Naval Aeroplanes" in a Bureau of Construction and Repair drawing. The anchor and numeral were painted outboard on the upper and lower wing surfaces, the anchor was generally placed on the vertical tail surfaces and the numeral fore and aft on both sides of the fuselage.

1916—Continued

13 May The Chief of Naval Operations requested appropriate bureaus to undertake development of gyroscopic attachments for instruments and equipment, including compasses, bombsights, and base lines, the latter being a forerunner of the turn and bank indicator.

20 May Development of a gyroscopically operated bomb-dropping sight was initiated with the allocation of $750 to the Bureau of Ordnance to be used in placing an order with the Sperry Gyroscope Company.

22 May The Naval Observatory sent a color camera, made by the Hess-Ives Corporation, to the Naval Aeronautic Station at Pensacola, Fla., to determine whether color photography would be of value in aeronautic work.

3 June Formal instruction in free and captive balloons was instituted at Pensacola, Fla., when the Secretary of the Navy approved a course proposed by Lieutenant Commander Frank R. McCrary, and directed that it be added to the Bureau of Navigation Circular "Courses of Instruction and Required Qualifications of Personnel for the Air Service of the Navy."

9 June Lieutenant Richard C. Saufley, on an endurance flight in the AH-9 over Santa Rosa Island off Pensacola, Fla., crashed to his death after being in the air 8 hours and 51 minutes.

20 June A General Order, superseding that of 23 June 1913, was issued defining cognizance for aeronautics in the Navy Department. In addition to extending the subject from "Naval Aeroplanes" to "Aeronautics," this order embraced lighter-than-air and

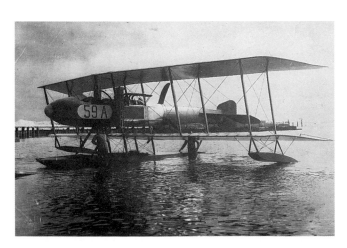

Experimental Gallaudet, propeller in the fuselage 1061646

certain heavier-than-air components that were not provided for in the earlier order.

12 July The AB-3 flying boat, piloted by Lieutenant Godfrey deC. Chevalier, was catapulted from *North Carolina* (ACR 12) while underway in Pensacola Bay, Fla. The launch completed calibration of the first catapult designed for shipboard use; *North Carolina* became the first ship of the U.S. Navy equipped to carry and operate aircraft.

17 July The first flight of the Gallaudet 59-A, a novel airplane with the propeller mounted in the fuselage aft of the wings, was made at Norwich, Conn., by David H. McCulloch and witnessed by Navy Inspector Lieutenant (jg) George D. Murray.

18 July Flight clothing allowances were established by the Secretary. Aviators were to be furnished helmets, goggles, and safety jackets. Enlisted men whose duties involved flying were to receive, in addition, wool head cover, suit, gauntlets, and boots.

22 July Serious interest in the development of light metal alloys for aeronautical use led Chief Constructor Rear Admiral David W. Taylor to request that the Aluminum Company of America apply its resources to the development of a suitable alloy, and for use in fabrication of Zeppelin-type girders.

8 August The Secretary clarified the place of aviation in the departmental organization by redefining the responsibilities of bureaus and offices for specific elements of the aviation program. While the new directive followed the division of cognizance over material established by the General Order of 20 June 1916, it went further in that it assigned the General Board responsibility for advising as to the numbers and general characteristics of aircraft, and in effect made the Bureau of Construction and Repair a lead bureau for aircraft development and procurement.

10 August Negotiation for the first aircraft production contract began with a telegram to Glenn H. Curtiss requesting him to "call at the Bureau [Construction and Repair] Monday with a proposition to supply at the earliest date practicable thirty school hydro aeroplanes." Specified characteristics included: two seats, loading of about four pounds per square foot, and power loading of about twenty pounds per horsepower. The telegram concluded, "Speed, climb and details of construction to be proposed by you. Rate of delivery is important and must be guaranteed." This telegram resulted in a contract for thirty N-9s which were delivered between November 1916 and

1916—Continued

K Model of 82-A, first aircraft designed and built by the Navy, under wind tunnel test 72-CN-6423

Ensign Wadleigh Capehart holds early semple bomb while straddling cockpit of a Burgess-Dunne 416327

1916—Continued

February 1917. The aircraft became the Navy's most popular training aircraft during World War I.

12 August The Secretary of the Navy agreed with the Secretary of War that the straight Deperdussin system of controlling aircraft in flight be adopted as the standard system for use in all aircraft of both services.

17 August The Secretary of the Navy approved a reorganization of the Naval Aeronautic Station, Pensacola, Fla. which reassigned the training of commissioned and enlisted personnel for aeronautic services with the fleet as a primary mission, and ordered the establishment of an Aeronautics School and departments for Manufacturing, Experimental Test and Inspection, Public Works, Supply and Medical.

29 August The Naval Appropriation Act for fiscal year 1917 provided for the establishment of a Naval Flying Corps to be composed of 150 officers and 350 enlisted men in addition to those provided by law for other branches of the Navy. It also provided for the establishment of a Naval Reserve Force of six classes including a Naval Reserve Flying Corps to be composed of officers and enlisted men transferring from the Naval Flying Corps; of surplus graduates of aeronautics schools; and of members of the Naval Reserve Force with experience in aviation.

9 September The initiation of formal flight testing as a basis for accepting new aircraft and the establishment of procedures for determining whether operational aircraft were safe to fly were provided for in an order issued by the Secretary.

12 September A demonstration of guided missile equipment—a piloted hydroaeroplane equipped with automatic stabilization and direction gear developed by the Sperry Company and P. C. Hewitt—was witnessed by Lieutenant Theodore S. Wilkinson of the Bureau of Ordnance at Amityville, Long Island, N.Y. Wilkinson reported: "The automatic control of the aeroplane is adequate and excellent. The machine left the water without difficulty, climbed to its desired height, maintained this altitude until the end of the run, when it dived sharply; and, unless controlled by the aviator, would have dived to the earth."

20 September The earliest extant instruction regarding color of naval aircraft was issued. This instruction canceled use of slate color and provided that wings, body and pontoon of the N-9 be finished with opaque yellow (or greenish-yellow) varnish.

Pilot E. F. Johnson and pioneer Naval photographer W. L. Richardson 452495

1916—Continued

11 October The Acting Secretary of War recommended to the Secretary of the Navy that a joint Army-Navy board be appointed to consider the requirements for developing a lighter-than-air service in the Army or Navy or both. With the Secretary's concurrence, there came into being an agency for interservice cooperation in aeronautics which under its later title, Aeronautical Board, functioned for over 30 years before being dissolved in 1948.

24 October The Bureau of Steam Engineering requested the Navy Yard, Philadelphia, Pa., to undertake development of a radio direction finder for use on aeroplanes, and specified that the apparatus be as light as possible and use wave lengths of 600 to 4,000 meters.

27 October The Chief of Naval Operations directed that all aircraft loaned or donated to the Naval Militia by private individuals or organizations be designated NMAH and be given numbers in sequence beginning with one.

8 November Lieutenant Clarence K. Bronson, Naval Aviator No. 15, and Lieutenant Luther Welsh, on an experimental bomb test flight at Naval Proving Ground, Indian Head, Md., were instantly killed by the premature explosion of a bomb in their plane.

17 November Efforts to develop high speed seaplanes for catapulting from ships led Chief Constructor David W. Taylor to solicit suitable designs from various manufacturers. Among the requirements were a speed range of 50 to 95 mph, two and a half hours endurance, and provisions for radio.

7 December Lieutenant Commander Henry C. Mustin reported that an Eastman Aero camera, tested at NAS Pensacola, Fla., at altitudes of 600 to 5,100 feet, was by far the best camera tested up to that time, and produced photographs very satisfactory for military purposes.

12 December Captain Mark L. Bristol was detached as Commander of the Air Service, and the functions of the command but not the title were transferred to Rear Admiral Albert Gleaves, Commander Destroyer Force, Atlantic Fleet.

30 December The Commission on Navy Yards and Naval Stations, authorized by the Act of 29 August 1916 for the purpose of selecting new sites for the expansion of Navy Yards and for submarine and air bases along the coast, submitted its preliminary report. For aviation the commission could only report that "the present development of aeronautical machines . . . and the practical experience so far obtained in the utilization of such machines to meet the tactical and strategical requirements of the fleet and the defense of the coast, is such as to preclude the determination at this time of any extensive system of aviation bases." The commission recommended that a joint Army-Navy board decide upon locations that might be used by both services.

Ken Whiting 1061480

W. McIlvain, USMC 1061483

PART 2

Test of Strength

1917–1919

A small group of pioneer Navy and Marine Corps aviators had nurtured the early growth of Naval Aviation, but it was too small and poorly equipped to wage war. When the call came in April 1917, one air station was operating, 48 aviators and students were available; 54 aircraft were on hand, but none of them had been designed for the work that would be required.

In the 19 months between declaration of war and the armistice, expansion was remarkable (see Appendix 4). Air stations sprang up on both sides of the Atlantic. Training programs were established at new air stations, on university campuses, and even with private industry. The Naval Reserve Flying Corps produced thousands of aviators, ground officers, mechanics and technical specialists. Aircraft of many types were produced, and one aircraft engine advanced from concept to mass production and operation.

The speed and breadth of the expansion produced expected chaos, but Naval Aviation nonetheless achieved a good wartime record. One of its units was the first from the United States to reach France. Naval aircraft flew more than 3 million nautical miles and attacked and damaged a dozen U-boats. By war's end, Navy and Marine Corps squadrons had organized the Northern Bombing Group which was preparing a round-the-clock air campaign which would have been the first strictly American air offensive of the war. When hostilities ceased, Navy and Marine Corps aviators were using 27 bases in Europe, two in Canada, one in the Canal Zone, one in the Azores, and 12 in the United States.

Naval Aviation's outstanding technical product of the war was the long-distance flying boat. Numerous types appeared but they all bore the look of a single family. The design progressed through the HS-1 and H-16 to the British original known as the F-5L, but all could trace their ancestry to the earlier work of Glenn H. Curtiss. The culmination of work with flying boats in the war was the Curtiss NC type. A product of naval constructors, a Yankee builder of aircraft, and New England yacht manufacturers, the NC type secured a place in aviation history in 1919 as the first aircraft to fly the Atlantic.

The flying boat was so impressive that many Naval Aviators urged its adoption as the major means of taking air power to sea. Others remained of the opinion that aircraft should fly from combatant ships of the fleet, and enthusiasts of lighter-than-air pointed to airship success in the war and urged development of their specialty. The logic of these claims, and the usefulness of these aeronautic types, were not ignored. The 1920s saw development in each area. But even as the war ended, sentiment in favor of the aircraft carrier was gaining currency. In 1919 the Navy decided to convert a collier to a carrier. This decision represented a modest beginning for a program which would occupy the attention of a host of ship builders, aircraft designers and naval tacticians for years to come.

1917

6 January A board of Army and Navy officers recommended to the Secretaries of the War and Navy Departments that an airship of the Zeppelin type be designed and constructed under the direction of the Chief Constructor of the Navy with funds provided equally by the Army and the Navy, and that a board of three Army and three Navy officers be created to insure effective interservice cooperation in prosecution of the work.

8 January A Benet-Mercie machine gun, installed in a flexible mount in the Burgess-Dunne AH-10, was fired at altitudes of 100 and 200 feet above Pensacola, Fla. Both the gun and the aircraft operated satisfactorily during the test.

10 January The first production order for aerial photographic equipment was initiated when the Naval Observatory issued requisitions for 20 aero cameras and accessories to be manufactured by the Eastman Kodak Company.

1917—Continued

15 January *Seattle* (Armored cruiser No. 11) arrived at Culebra, P.R., with an aviation detachment and aircraft on board, for fleet exercises in the Southern Drill Grounds. From this date until 23 March her air detachment operated from ship and temporary shore bases performing scouting and other missions in conjunction with fleet operations.

4 February The Secretary of the Navy directed that 16 nonrigid airships of Class B be procured. Contracts were issued subsequently to the Connecticut Aircraft Corporation, the Goodyear Tire & Rubber Company and the B. F. Goodrich Company.

5 February The Chief of Naval Operations recommended that, in view of the urgent military necessity, eight aeronautic coastal patrol stations be established.

10 February The National Advisory Committee for Aeronautics (NACA) established a patent subcommittee with Lieutenant John H. Towers as a member. The necessity for this subcommittee arose from the fact that the threat of infringement suits being brought by the holders of basic aeronautic patents was causing prohibitive prices for aircraft and general demoralization of the entire industry.

13 February At Pensacola, Fla., Captain Francis T. Evans, USMC, performed the first loop with a seaplane, an N-9 floatplane at 3,000 feet, and then forced it into a spin and successfully recovered. For this contribution to the science of aviation, he was later awarded the Distinguished Flying Cross.

12 March The first interservice agreement regarding the development of aeronautic resources and the operations of aircraft was submitted by a board of Army and Navy officers and approved by the Secretaries of the War and Navy Departments. The agreement recognized a general division of aeronautical functions along lines traditional to the services, but stressed the importance of joint development, organization, and operation, and enunciated basic principles whereby joint effort could be achieved in these areas.

13 March The Bureau of Construction and Repair directed that all seaplanes be finished in an opaque yellow color over all.

24 March The First Yale Unit of 29 men, among which were four destined to hold such high positions in the military departments as Assistant Secretary for War held by F. Trubee Davison, Assistant Secretary of the Navy for Air held by David S. Ingalls, Under Secretary of the Navy and Assistant Secretary of the Navy for Air held by Artemus L. Gates, and Secretary of Defense held by Robert A. Lovett; enlisted in the Naval Reserve Flying Force and four days later left college to begin war training at West Palm Beach. This was the first of several college groups to join up as a unit for war service.

6 April The United States declared that a state of war existed with Germany. The strength of Naval Aviation, Navy and Marine Corps combined, was: 48 officers and 239 enlisted men, 54 airplanes, 1 airship, 3 balloons, and 1 air station.

6 April The Secretary of the Navy, by approval of the recommendation of the Board on Flying Equipment, established standard flight clothing for the Naval Flying Service, and authorized its issuance as Title B equipage. Clothing consisted of a tan sheepskin long coat, short coat and trousers, moleskin hood, goggles, black leather gloves, soft leather boots, waders, brogans and life belts.

7 April By Executive Order, the president directed that the Coast Guard be transferred from the Treasury Department to operate as a part of the Navy until further orders.

14 April The Navy's first guided missile effort began when the Naval Consulting Board recommended to the Secretary of the Navy that $50,000 be apportioned to carry on experimental work on aerial torpedoes in the form of automatically controlled aeroplanes or aerial machines carrying high explosives.

20 April The Navy's first airship, DN-1, made its first flight at Pensacola, Fla. Its performance was unsatisfactory on several counts and, after only two more flights in this month, it was grounded and never flown again.

26 April The catapult installed on *Huntington* (ACR 5) was given its first dead load tests at Mare Island Navy Yard, San Francisco Bay, Calif.

27 April The Marine Aeronautic Company, Advance Base Force, was organized at Marine Barracks, Philadelphia Navy Yard, Pa., by the transfer of personnel from the Marine Aviation Section at Pensacola, Fla., from other Marine Corps units and from the Marine Corps Reserve Flying Corps. Captain Alfred A. Cunningham was in command.

1 May An expansion of the training program was approved which called for assignment of new classes every 3 months and the establishment of a course of

1917—Continued

Navy's first airship approaches floating hangar 19370

18 months duration to qualify officers as pilots of either seaplanes or dirigibles. The program also provided for training enlisted men as aviation mechanics and for selection of a few for pilot training and qualification as quartermaster.

4 May   The Commandant of the First Naval District was directed to assume control of the Naval Militia station at Squantum, Mass., for use in air training. On the same date, arrangements were completed to take over the Naval Militia station at Bay Shore, N.Y. These were two of several actions taken immediately after declaration of war to expand the flight training program while stations of a more permanent nature were being built.

5 May   The Secretary of War agreed to a proposal of the Secretary of the Navy that a joint board be established for the purpose of standardizing the design and specifications of aircraft. The board, subsequently established, was originally titled "Joint Technical Board on Aircraft, except Zeppelins."

5 May   Pensacola, Fla., reported on a test in which a Berthier machine gun, synchronized to fire through the propeller, was fired from a Curtiss R-3 taxiing on water and standing on the beach.

15 May   The Secretary of the Navy established an order of precedence for work involved in the preparation for war which placed "aircraft and their equipment" ninth on a list of twenty major fields of material procurement.

16 May   The Aircraft Production Board was established by resolution of the Council of National Defense as a subsidiary agency to act in an advisory capacity on questions of aircraft production and procurement. Membership included a representative from each service, the Navy's being Rear Admiral David W. Taylor. Reconstitution of the Board by Act of Congress on 1 October 1917, transferred its control to the War and Navy Departments, enlarged its membership for greater service representation, and changed its title to Aircraft Board.

17 May   Aircraft machine gun procurement— The Chief of Naval Operations requested purchase of 50 aircraft machine guns synchronized to fire through propellers and 50 for all-around fire.

17 May   Captain Noble E. Irwin was ordered to the Material Branch to relieve Lieutenant John H. Towers as Officer-in-Charge of the aviation desk in the Office of the Chief of Naval Operations. Lieutenant Towers, who remained as an assistant to Irwin, was given additional duty orders to the Bureau of Navigation as Supervisor, Naval Reserve Flying Corps.

17 May   The Navy awarded a contract to the Curtiss Exhibition Company to train 20 men of the Naval Reserve Flying Force as aviators at the company field at Newport News, Va.

18 May   Experimental self-sealing fuel tanks, consisting of double walled galvanized iron containing layers of felt, gum rubber and an Ivory soap-whiting paste, were demonstrated to representatives of the Army and Navy by the Bureau of Standards.

19 May   A distinguishing insignia for all United States Government aircraft was described in a general order which directed that it be placed on all naval aircraft. The insignia called for a red disc within a white star on a blue circular field to be displayed on the wings and for red, white and blue vertical bands on the rudder, with the blue forward.

19 May   The Secretary of the Navy directed that the building (bureau) number of each aircraft be placed in figures three inches high at the top of the white vertical band on each side of the rudder. As a result of this order, the practice of assigning numbers to aircraft, as AH, was discontinued and the building (bureau) or serial number became the sole means of identifying a particular aircraft.

1917—Continued

19 May The Chief of Naval Operations requested that two small seaplanes and one pilot be detailed for duty in connection with radio experimentation at Pensacola, Fla.

23 May The initial production program to equip the Navy with the aircraft necessary for war was recommended by the Joint Technical Board on Aircraft, to consist of 300 school machines, 200 service seaplanes, 100 speed scouts and 100 large seaplanes. The N-9 and R-6 were listed as the most satisfactory for school and service seaplanes, but the remaining two types were not sufficiently developed to permit a selection.

28 May *Huntington* (ACR 5) arrived at Pensacola, Fla., from Mare Island, Calif. While there, and until 1 August 1917, she was used in various aeronautic experiments involving the operation of seaplanes and kite balloons from her deck.

29 May The Navy awarded a contract to the Goodyear Tire & Rubber Company of Akron, Ohio, to train 20 men as LTA pilots.

30 May The Navy's first successful dirigible, the B-1, landed in a meadow 10 miles from Akron, Ohio, completing an overnight test flight from Chicago, Ill. The B-1 was manufactured at Akron by Goodyear, assembled in Chicago, and piloted on this flight by Goodyear pilot, Ralph H. Upson.

4 June The construction of five prototype models of 8- and 12-cylinder Liberty motors was authorized by the Aircraft Production Board and the Joint Technical Board on Aircraft. The design of these engines, based on conservative engineering practices especially adapted to mass production techniques, had been worked out in a room in a Washington, D.C., hotel by J. G. Vincent of the Packard Motor Car Company and E. J. Hall of the Hall-Scott Motor Car Company.

5 June The first U.S. military unit sent to France in World War I, the First Aeronautic Detachment, arrived in Pauillac, France, aboard *Jupiter* (AC 3). The Detachment, consisting of seven officers and 122 enlisted men, including the element aboard *Neptune* (AC 8) which arrived at St. Nazaire on 8 June, was commanded by Lieutenant Kenneth Whiting. Offloading was completed by 10 June.

11 June All aviation personnel and aircraft were transferred from *Seattle* (Armored cruiser No. 11) as she made ready for convoy duty at the Brooklyn Navy Yard, N.Y. Her raised catapult, while left on board, was lowered and secured to the deck where it would not interfere with normal operations at sea.

14 June The establishment of patrol stations along the Atlantic coast was implemented as the first contract for base construction was let. The contract covered sites on Long Island, N.Y., located at Montauk, Rockaway and Bay Shore.

Hispano-Suiza engine version of the N-9 trainer 1312

1917—Continued

17 June A joint Army-Navy Mission (called the Bolling Mission after its senior member, Major R. C. Bolling), of which the Navy members were Commander George C. Westervelt and Lieutenant Warren G. Child, sailed for Europe to study air developments among the Allies and recommend a policy and program for the American air services.

22 June Enlisted men of the First Aeronautic Detachment began preliminary flight training in Caudron landplanes under French instructors at the Military Aviation School, Tours, France. At about the same time, 50 men of the Detachment were sent to St. Raphael, France, for training as mechanics.

22 June Change No. 11 in uniform regulations was the first to make special provision for aviators. It provided for a summer service flying uniform of Marine Corps khaki in the same pattern and design as service whites, to be worn when on immediate active duty with aircraft. The order also provided for a working dress uniform made as a coverall from canvas, khaki or moleskin of the same color as the flying uniform.

4 July The first 8-cylinder Liberty motor arrived in Washington, D.C., for testing by the Bureau of Standards, having been assembled at the Packard Motor Car Company from parts made by manufacturers in plants scattered from Philadelphia, Pa., to Berkeley, Calif. Design, manufacture, and assembly of this motor had required less than six weeks.

7 July Lieutenant Kenneth Whiting, commanding the First Aeronautic Detachment, cabled the Secretary of the Navy reporting the results of his negotiations with the French in regard to training and establishment of air stations and requested departmental approval. Under the terms of the agreement, the first of several concerned with the expansion of Naval Aviation overseas, the French agreed to train personnel of the Detachment at existing French Army Aviation Schools (pilots at Tours, France, and mechanics at St. Raphael, France), and to start construction of three patrol stations for American use, located at Dunkirk, France, the mouth of the Loire River (Le Croisic, France), and the mouth of the Gironde (St. Trojan, France), and a training station at Lake Lancanau (Moutchic, France).

9 July A group of 24 potential Naval Aviators under Ensign Frederick S. Allen as Officer-in-Charge, reported at the University of Toronto for the start of flight training under the Canadian Royal Flying Corps (RFC). This training was arranged by an agreement with the Army and the RFC that 25 men from the Navy would be included in the contingent of 100 Americans for which the Government of Canada had agreed to provide flight training.

10 July A plan for training student officers of the Naval Reserve Flying Corps was circulated for comment. It proposed a program in three parts: (1) A Ground School for indoctrination into the Navy and study of subjects related to aircraft and flight, (2) a Preliminary Flight School for flight training through 5 to 10 hours of solo, and (3) a Completing Flight

American built HS flying boats moored at NAS Moutchic, one of the main training bases in France 1053802

1917—Continued

School for advanced flight training and qualification as a Naval Aviator and a commission as Ensign, USNRF. This plan was implemented without the benefit of a formal directive by the establishment of the Ground School in the same month and the later division of flight training into elementary and advanced courses.

23 July Ground instruction for prospective pilots and for aviation ground officers began at the Massachusetts Institute of Technology (MIT) with a class of 43 students comprising the Naval Air Detachment under command of Lieutenant Edward H. McKitterick. In this, and in similar programs later established at the University of Washington, Seattle, Wash., and the Dunwoody Institute, Minneapolis, Minn., large numbers of officers were indoctrinated and introduced to the fundamentals of aviation.

24 July A large obstacle to the effective expansion of aircraft production was removed by formation of the Manufacturers Aircraft Association to handle the business of a Cross Licensing Agreement by which member companies had full access to all patents held by other members at fixed low rates.

26 July The Army Navy Airship Board endorsed a proposal by the Bureau of Mines for the experimental production of helium and recommended the allotment of $100,000 to construct a small plant for the purpose. This action, subsequently approved by both Departments, initiated helium production in the United States.

27 July An act of Congress authorized the president to take possession of North Island, San Diego, Calif., for use by the Army and Navy in establishing perma-

nent aviation stations and aviation schools. The arrival of Lieutenant Earl W. Spencer on 8 November 1917, under orders to establish and command a station for the purpose of training pilots and mechanics and conducting coastal patrols, marked the beginning of the present NAS North Island.

27 July Construction of the Naval Aircraft Factory at the Navy Yard, Philadelphia, Pa., was authorized for the purposes of constructing aircraft, undertaking aeronautical developments and providing aircraft construction cost data.

8 August The approval by the Secretary of the Navy for plans to establish one training and three coastal patrol stations in France was the first of several dealing with an overseas base construction program that was expanded successively and ultimately provided 27

Woman at work in Naval Aircraft Factory, World War I (NH)2493

Naval Air Station at Treguier, France, showing HS-1 flying boats used in patrol over the English Channel 72979

1917—Continued

locations in France, England, Ireland and Italy, from which naval air units were operating at the close of the war.

10 August   Ground was broken for the Naval Aircraft Factory at the Philadelphia Navy Yard, Pa.

14 August   In an experiment initiated through the impetus of Rear Admiral Bradley A. Fiske, and conducted by Lieutenant Edward O. McDonnell at Huntington Bay, Long Island, N.Y., a dummy torpedo was launched from a seaplane, but struck the water at an unfavorable angle and ricocheted, nearly striking the plane. This event marked the beginning of serious Navy interest in launching torpedoes from aircraft.

15 August   The Bureau of Construction and Repair authorized the Curtiss Company to paint the wings of naval aircraft with "English-Khaki-Gray-Enamel" and all aircraft manufacturers to use either opaque yellow or clear varnish on floats and hulls. These, the initial variations to the color scheme that had been established the preceding March, were followed by so many other exceptions that no standard existed for the next six months. The trend, however, was to use an opaque yellow finish for school machines and to use a khaki finish, similar to that used on British aircraft, for service machines.

25 August   The NC flying boat development was initiated by Chief Constructor David W. Taylor in a memo which outlined certain general requirements of an airplane needed in war and directed his staff to investigate the subject further. In part, Taylor stated: "The 'United States [Liberty] Motor' gives good promise of being a success, and if we can push ahead on the airplane end, it seems to me the submarine menace could be abated, even if not destroyed, from the air. The ideal solution would be big flying boats or the equivalent, that would be able to fly across the Atlantic to avoid difficulties of delivery, etc."

25 August   The 12-cylinder Liberty motor passed a 50-hour test with a power output of 301 to 320 horsepower, preliminary to being ordered into mass production.

4 September   The technical members of the Bolling Mission, having just returned from studying air developments in Europe, submitted a report to the Secretaries of War and Navy. Among other things they recommended that air measures against submarines take precedence over all other air measures, that the

United States establish and operate as many coastal patrol stations in Europe as possible, and that European aircraft be obtained for use at those stations until the more satisfactory types manufactured in the United States became available.

7 September   In tests which led to additional orders for 300 Simon radio transmitters, radio signals, sent from an R-6 seaplane flying from NAS Pensacola, Fla., were received by Naval Radio Station New Orleans, La., 140 miles distant.

7 September   A forestry green winter service flying uniform, of the same design as the summer uniform, was authorized for all officers assigned to aviation duty.

7 September   A winged foul anchor was adopted as an official device to be worn on the left breast by all qualified Naval Aviators. Before the wings were issued, use of the letters "U.S.", which had been incorporated in the first design, was abandoned by order of 12 October 1917 and the design adopted was essentially that of the wings worn today.

8 September   A site at Naval Operating Base, Hampton Roads, Va., was established as an air training station and patrol base to conduct experimental work in seaplane operation. Detachments under training at the Curtiss School at Newport News, Va., and at Squantum, Mass., transferred to this location in October, and on 27 August of the next year, the Naval Air Station was formally established.

17 September   A kite balloon from *Huntington* (ACR 5) was hit by a squall and while being hauled down struck the water so hard that the observer, Lieutenant (jg) Henry W. Hoyt, was knocked out of the basket and caught underwater in the balloon rigging. As the balloon was pulled toward the ship, Patrick McGunigal, Ships Fitter First Class, jumped overboard, cleared the tangle and put a line around Lieutenant Hoyt so that he could be hauled up on deck. For this act of heroism, McGunigal was later awarded the Medal of Honor.

18 September   A production program of 1,700 operational type aircraft was established on the basis of a report issued this date by the Joint Technical Board on Aircraft.

26 September   Lieutenant Louis H. Maxfield, commanding the Naval Air Detachment at Akron, Ohio, reported the qualification of 11 students, including himself, as lighter-than-air pilots and requested their

1917—Continued

designation as Naval Aviator (Dirigible). These men, the first trained specifically as dirigible pilots, were subsequently assigned Naval Aviator numbers ranging from 94 to 104.

6 October   The Secretary of War authorized the Navy to use a part of the Army landing field at Anacostia, D.C., for the erection and maintenance of a seaplane hangar. Terms of use were within those of a revocable license and with the understanding that the Army might have joint use of the Navy area at any time. In the following January, NAS Anacostia, D.C., was established to provide a base for short test flights, to provide housing and repair services for seaplanes on test flights from NAS Hampton Roads, Va., and the Army station at Langley Field, Va., and to set up new seaplane types for study by those responsible for their construction and improvement.

11 October   The catapult, aircraft and all aeronautics gear were removed from *North Carolina* (ACR 12) at the Brooklyn Navy Yard, N.Y.

13 October   After serving on convoy duty without using her aeronautic gear except for one attempt with a kite balloon, *Huntington* (ACR 5) transferred her equipment ashore at New York. This transfer, and the subsequent departure of aviation personnel, marked the end of the operational test with aircraft on board combatant ships that had started with the *North Carolina* (ACR 12) in 1916.

14 October   The Marine Aeronautic Company at Philadelphia, Pa., was divided into the First Aviation Squadron, composed of 24 officers and 237 men, and the First Marine Aeronautic Company, composed of 10 officers and 93 men. On the same day, the First Marine Aeronautic Company transferred to the Naval Air Station at Cape May, N.J., for training in seaplanes and flying boats and on 17 October the First Aviation Squadron transferred to the Army field at Mineola, Long Island, N.Y., for training in landplanes.

16 October   The first power driven machine was started at the Naval Aircraft Factory, just 67 days after ground was broken.

21 October   First flight test of Liberty engine—The 12-cylinder Liberty engine was flown successfully for the first time in a Curtiss HS-1 flying boat at Buffalo, N.Y. This flight and other successful demonstrations led to the adoption of both the engine and the airplane as standard service types.

22 October   Special courses to train men as inspectors were added to the Ground School program at MIT with 14 men enrolled. Eventually established as an Inspector School, this program met the expanding need for qualified inspectors of aeronautical material by producing 58 motor and 114 airplane inspectors before the end of the war.

24 October   The first organization of U.S. Naval Aviation Forces, Foreign Service, which had evolved from the First Aeronautic Detachment, was put into operation as Captain Hutch I. Cone relieved Lieutenant Commander Kenneth Whiting of command over all Naval Aviation forces abroad.

24 October   Routine instruction in flight and ground courses began at NAS Moutchic, France, established as a training station serving naval air units in Europe.

2 November   Twelve men who had organized as the Second Yale Unit and had taken flight training at their own expense at Buffalo, N.Y., were commissioned as Ensigns, USNRF, and soon after received their designations as Naval Aviators.

5 November   To coordinate the aviation program, Captain Noble E. Irwin, Officer-in-Charge of Aviation, requested that representatives of bureaus having cognizance over some phase of the program meet regularly each week in his office for the purpose of discussing and expediting all matters pertaining to aviation.

9 November   Permission was received from the Argentine Government to use three Argentine Naval Officers, recently qualified as U.S. Naval Aviators, as instructors in the ground school at Pensacola, Fla.

10 November   A Navy "flying bomb," manufactured by the Curtiss Company, was delivered to the Sperry Flying Field at Copiague, Long Island, N.Y., for test. Also called an aerial torpedo, the flying bomb was designed for automatic operation carrying 1,000 pounds of explosive with a range of 50 miles and a top speed of 90 miles per hour. In addition to this specially designed aircraft, N-9s were also converted for automatic operations as flying bombs that were closely related to the guided missile of today.

14 November   A major step in assuring the success of the Navy's World War I aircraft production program was taken when the Secretary of War, Newton D. Baker, approved a recommendation "that priority be given by the War Department to naval needs for aviation material necessary to equip and arm seaplane bases."

1917—Continued

Ancestor of guided missile, World War I flying bomb 651988

15 November A Committee on Light Alloys, with Naval Constructor Jerome C. Hunsaker a member, was established within the NACA to intensify efforts to develop light metal alloys for aeronautical use.

18 November U.S. aerial coastal patrols in European waters began with Tellier seaplanes from LeCroisic, France, at the mouth of the Loire River. This seaplane patrol station, the first of eight established in France, was established 27 November under command of Lieutenant William M. Corry.

21 November A demonstration of the Navy N-9 flying bomb at Amityville, Long Island, N.Y., was witnessed by Major General George O. Squier, USA, Chief Signal Officer. Subsequently the Army established a parallel aerial torpedo project.

22 November A Tellier seaplane piloted by Ensign Kenneth R. Smith, with Electrician's Mate Wilkinson and Machinist's Mate Brady on board, was forced down at sea on a flight out of NAS LeCroisic, France, to investigate the reported presence of German submarines south of Belle Isle. Two days later, and only minutes before their damaged plane sank, they were rescued by a French destroyer. It was the first armed patrol by a U.S. Naval Aviator in European waters.

24 November In discussing the development of aircraft torpedoes and torpedo planes, the Chief of Naval Operations pointed out that available aircraft could carry no more than a 600-pound ordnance load and thus were incapable of delivering a torpedo with an explosive charge large enough to seriously damage a modern warship. This problem, the size of an effective torpedo versus the capabilities of aircraft, retarded torpedo plane development in World War I and continued as an important factor in the post war years.

1 December NAS Pauillac, France, was established as an active assembly and repair station supporting all naval air stations in France.

5 December The policy regarding helicopter development was established by the Secretaries of the War and Navy Departments on the basis of recommendations made by the Joint Technical Board on Aircraft. Basically, need for improvements in powerplants and propellers was recognized as necessary if a successful helicopter was to be obtained, but actual support of development efforts was to be limited to moral encouragement until a vendor had demonstrated a helicopter of military value.

7 December Fighter-type aircraft development was initiated with the Secretary's authorization for the Curtiss HA, or "Dunkirk Fighter." This single-pontoon seaplane was equipped with dual synchronized machine guns forward and dual flexible machine guns in the rear cockpit.

7 December The Naval Aeronautic Station Pensacola, Fla., was redesignated a Naval Air Station.

22 December The addition of an Aerography School in the training program at MIT was marked by the start of classes with one student enrolled. A major portion of the school's new instruction program was carried out at the Blue Hill Observatory, Harvard University, but some classes were also held at the Aerographic Laboratory on the MIT campus. Of 55 men enrolled in the school, 54 qualified as aerologists by the end of the war.

31 December The First Aviation Squadron of the Marine Corps, commanded by Captain William M. McIlvain, USMC, transferred from Mineola, N.Y., to Gerstner Field, Lake Charles, La., for advanced training in landplanes.

1918

1 January The Experimental and Test Department at Pensacola, Fla., was transferred to NAS Hampton Roads, Va., to overcome difficulties arising from the remoteness of the former location from the principal manufacturing and industrial areas.

1918—Continued

Naval aircraft on beach at Pensacola, World War I 426915

21 January The First Marine Aeronautic Company, Captain Francis T. Evans, USMC, commanding, arrived at Naval Base 13, Ponta Delgada, Azores, to fly antisubmarine patrols over convoy lanes in the Azores area.

25 January The Supervisor, Naval Reserve Flying Corps requested that Dr. Alexander McAdie, Director of Blue Hill Observatory, Harvard University, be enrolled as a Lieutenant Commander in the Naval Reserve and be assigned to the Aviation Office in CNO to organize a Naval Aerological Organization.

3 February Aerial gunnery training for prospective Naval Aviators and enlisted men began under Canadian Royal Flying Corps instructors at the Army field at Camp Taliaferro, Fort Worth, Tex.

8 February A change in national aircraft insignia was promulgated by the Navy which replaced the white star with concentric circles of red and blue around white, and reversed the order of the red, white and blue vertical bands on the rudder, placing the red nearest the rudder post.

21 February NAS Bolsena, Italy, was established, Ensign William B. Atwater commanding. The first of two air stations established in Italy during World War I, Bolsena was used primarily as a flying school.

22 February The Director of Naval Communications was requested to provide wireless transmitting and receiving equipment at five naval air stations on the Atlantic coast and at San Diego, Calif., and Coco Solo, Panama, to permit pilots on patrol to communicate with their bases. The following May, this request was expanded to cover all naval air stations.

22 February NAS Queenstown, Ireland, an assembly and repair station for all naval air stations in Ireland, was established, Lieutenant Commander Paul J. Peyton commanding.

26 February In recognition of the importance to flight operations of data on weather phenomena in the upper atmosphere, and acting largely on the recommendations of Lieutenant Commander Alexander McAdie, formerly of Harvard University's Blue Hill Observatory, the Chief of Naval Operations established an allowance list of aerographic equipment for air stations abroad.

28 February The president issued a proclamation, effective in 30 days, that prohibited private flying over the United States, its territorial waters and its possessions without a special license issued by the Joint Army and Navy Board on Aeronautic Cognizance.

1 March The dirigible station at Paimboeuf, France, where several aviation personnel had been on duty with the French since November 1917, was taken over by American forces and established as a Naval Air

1918—Continued

Station, Lieutenant Commander Louis H. Maxfield in command.

3 March Dirigibles in France—The AT-1 (Astra-Torres), having been obtained from the French on 1 March, made its first flight under American control at Paimboeuf, France. Prior to the armistice, the Navy obtained 12 dirigibles from the French.

6 March The Bureau of Navigation established instrument allowances for naval aircraft allotting a compass, two altimeters and a clock for service seaplanes and flying boats; a compass, altimeter, clock and statoscope for dirigibles and free balloons; and an altimeter and clock for kite balloons and training planes.

6 March An unmanned flying-bomb type plane was launched successfully and flown for 1,000 yards at the Sperry Flying Field, Copiague, Long Island, N.Y. The launching device was a falling weight type catapult.

7 March The Office of the Director of Naval Aviation was established in the Office of the Chief of Naval Operations and the Aviation Section became a Division.

9 March A revised training program for Naval Aviators, Seaplanes, was initiated which provided that, after a period of general training, all student aviators specialize in one of three general types of seaplanes; that they follow a syllabus which divided the program into elementary, advanced, and advanced specialization courses; and designated the stations at which the respective courses would be given.

15 March The Bureau of Construction and Repair directed that all new naval aircraft be painted in low visibility naval gray enamel.

19 March As combat operations underlined the need for Aviation Intelligence Officers, Commander, Naval Aviation Forces, Foreign Service, distributed a circular letter defining the duties and functions performed by such officers at Royal Navy Air Stations with the suggestion that provisions for similar services be made at naval air stations "as may seem expedient." Supplementary letters clarified the duties and functions and on 31 October it was specifically stated that Aviation Intelligence Officers be specially trained for this work.

19 March A formation of flying boats, on long range reconnaissance off the German coast, was attacked by German seaplanes. Ensign Stephan Potter shot down one of the attackers and was credited officially as being the first American Naval Aviator to shoot down an enemy seaplane.

21 March The HA seaplane, or "Dunkirk Fighter," made its first flight at Port Washington, Long Island, N.Y., with Curtiss test pilot Roland Rohlfs at the controls and Captain Bernard L. Smith, USMC, occupying the second seat.

25 March Ensign John F. McNamara, flying out of RNAS Portland, England, made the first attack on an enemy submarine by a U.S. Naval Aviator. For his attack, reported by Admiral Sims as "apparently successful," Ensign McNamara was commended by the Secretary of the Navy for his "valiant and earnest efforts on this particular occasion."

27 March The first aircraft built at the Naval Aircraft Factory, the H-16, Serial No. A-1049, was flown for the first time. The H-16 was used in antisubmarine patrol from U.S. and European stations, and for this purpose was equipped with two 230-pound bombs and five Lewis machine guns; one forward, two aft, and two amidships.

30 March The Curtiss 18-T or "Kirkham" triplane fighter was ordered from Curtiss Engineering Corporation. This single-engine, two-seater landplane was fitted with two synchronized and two flexible guns.

First NAF-built H-16 leaving assembly building NAF 2121

1918—Continued

15 April The First Marine Aviation Force, commanded by Captain Alfred A. Cunningham, USMC, was formed at NAS Miami, Fla., from personnel of the First Aviation Squadron and the Aeronautic Detachment, USMC, both of which had disbanded the day before. A Headquarters Company and four squadrons designated A, B, C and D, were organized within this Force on 16 June and it was later transferred overseas to operate as the Day Wing of the Northern Bombing Group.

16 April The first detachment of trained aerologists, consisting of nine officers and 15 enlisted men, departed for duty at naval air stations in Europe.

17 April Lieutenant William F. Reed, Jr., reported at NAS Pensacola, Fla., for what was then called "aerographical" duty, the first such assignment ever made to a naval air station.

23 April The first shipment of Liberty engines to Naval Aviation units in France was received at the assembly and repair station, NAS Pauillac, France.

27 April The airship AT-1, commanded by Lieutenant Frederick P. Culbert and a crew made up of Ensigns Merrill P. Delano, Arthur D. Brewer and Thomas E. McCracken, completed a 25-hour 43-minute flight out of Paimboeuf, France, during the course of which three convoys were escorted through a mined zone. For their flight, the longest on record for an airship of the type, the commanding officer

and crew were officially commended by the French Minister of Marine.

30 April Northern Bombing Group—The Secretary of the Navy approved a plan, recommended by the General Board and developed by U.S. Naval Forces in Europe, for air operations to be undertaken in the Dunkirk-Zeebrugge region against German submarine support facilities by a specially organized unit later designated the Northern Bombing Group, and directed that bureaus and offices expedite assembly of the necessary personnel and equipment.

6 May NAS Coco Solo, Panama, was established, Lieutenant Ralph G. Pennoyer commanding, to maintain patrols over the seaward approaches to the Panama Canal.

15 May The Bureau of Steam Engineering reported that the Marconi SE 1100 radio transmitter, designed for use on the H-16 flying boat, had demonstrated dependability in voice communications at distances up to 50 nautical miles and in code communications at up to 120 nautical miles. This was one of the first radio sets used in, and the first tube set developed for, naval aircraft.

18 May The Chief of Naval Operations set training goals to provide pilots for foreign service, and to meet them, directed that eight elementary training squadrons be operated, two at Key West, Fla., four at Miami, Fla., and two at Bay Shore, N.Y.; that elementary training at Pensacola, Fla., be discontinued as

Curtiss (Krikham) 18-T experimental fighter 1061648

1918—Continued

soon as students on board were graduated; and that six advanced training squadrons be organized there to begin training patrol plane and night bomber pilots as soon as practicable.

24 May The first consignment of American-built flying boats, six HS-1s aboard *Houston* (AK 1) and two aboard *Lake Placid* (a Navy cargo ship), arrived at Pauillac, France.

13 June The first American-built aircraft to be assembled in France, an HS-1, made its first flight at Pauillac, France, piloted by Lieutenant Charles P. Mason, USN, with Commander James B. Patton, USN, and Lieutenant William B. Jameson, USNRF, as passengers.

19 June NAS Pensacola, Fla., began taking upper atmospheric weather soundings to provide information on wind velocity and direction, needed for navigational training flights. Recording instruments were carried aloft by a kite balloon, a technique developed by the station meteorological officer, Lieutenant W. F. Reed.

30 June The first Navy pilots of the Night Wing, Northern Bombing Group, to take special training with British units, marked the completion of their course by participating as observers in a night bombing raid by Royal Air Force (RAF) Squadron 214.

1 July An act of Congress repealed all laws relating to the National Naval Volunteers (NNV) and authorized the president to transfer as a class all its members, in their confirmed ranks and ratings, to the Naval Reserve, the Naval Reserve Flying Corps or the Marine Corps Reserve.

7 July The Naval Aircraft Factory completed its first order for 50 H-16 flying boats.

20 July The RAF Station, Killingholme, England, from which U.S. Navy pilots had been flying patrols since February 1918, was turned over to American forces and established as a Naval Air Station, Lieutenant Commander Kenneth Whiting in command.

21 July A surfaced German submarine, firing on a tugboat and three barges three miles off Nauset Beach on Cape Cod, Mass., was attacked by two seaplanes from NAS Chatham, Mass. After firing on both aircraft, the submarine submerged and escaped.

24 July NAS Porto Corsini, Italy, the only U.S. Navy seaplane patrol station established in Italy during World War I, was placed in operating status, Lieutenant Wallis B. Haviland commanding.

25 July The Secretary of War approved a recommendation by the Joint Army and Navy Airship Board, thus completing an inter-service agreement which assigned responsibility for the development of rigid airships to the Navy.

27 July The N-l, first experimental aircraft designed and built at the Naval Aircraft Factory, made its fourth successful flight and its first test of the Davis gun for which it was designed. Lieutenant Victor Vernon piloted and Lieutenant Sheppard operated the gun which gave what was reported as a very satisfactory performance against a target moored in the Delaware River near the factory.

30 July Headquarters Company and Squadrons A, B, and C of the First Marine Aviation Force arrived at Brest, France, on board *DeKalb* (a Navy troop transport). Upon disembarking, they proceeded to airdromes between Calais, France, and Dunkirk, France, for operations as the Day Wing, Northern Bombing Group. With the arrival, the squadrons were redesignated 7, 8, and 9 respectively.

HS flying boats at Naval Air Station Brest, one of two receiving and assembly plants established in France 1053803

1918—Continued

5 August A flying boat piloted by Ensign Ashton W. Hawkins with Lieutenant (jg) George F. Lawrence as second pilot, took off from NAS Killingholme, England, in rain and poor visibility at 10:30 p.m. to patrol a course intercepting a reported Zeppelin raid. The patrol was made in good weather above the clouds without sighting the enemy and came down through heavy weather at South Shields, England, at 5:30 a.m. almost out of fuel. It was the first American night combat patrol out of Killingholme and may have been the first of the war by a U.S. Naval Aviator.

11 August Ensign James B. Taylor made the initial flight in the Loening M-2 Kitten landplane at Mineola, Long Island, N.Y. This aircraft, which was intended for use aboard ship, was not successful; but is of special interest because it was the first monoplane developed under Navy contract; was one of the smallest aircraft ever built for the Navy with an empty weight of less than 300 pounds, and, although equipped with a British ABC motor for flight, was designed for use with a two-cylinder Lawrance 30-horsepower air-cooled engine which was the predecessor of the large American air-cooled radial engines.

15 August Independent offensive operations of the Northern Bombing Group began as Ensign Leslie R. Taber of Air Squadron 1, piloted a Caproni bomber in a night raid on the submarine repair docks at Ostend, Germany. Ensign Charles Fahy was second pilot and D. C. Hale rear gunner on the flight.

19 August NAS Halifax, Nova Scotia, the first of two air stations established in Canada, was placed in operating status to conduct patrols over the northern approaches to the Atlantic coast, Lieutenant Richard E. Byrd commanding.

19 August In trial runs observed by Naval Constructors Holden C. Richardson and Charles N. Liqued, the Kirkham 18-T experimental triplane fighter, built by the Curtiss Company, achieved speeds of 161, 162, and 158 miles per hour, over a measured course.

21 August A flight of bombers and fighters from NAS Porto Corsini, Italy, was intercepted by a superior force of Austro-Hungarian planes over the Austro-Hungarian naval base at Pola on the Adriatic Sea. During the ensuing fight, one American plane was forced down 3 miles from the harbor entrance. Ensign Charles H. Hammann, whose fighter plane was also damaged, evaded his pursuers and landed alongside the downed pilot; took him on board and flew back to base. For his extraordinary heroism in effecting the rescue under hazardous conditions, Ensign Hammann was later awarded the Medal of Honor.

1 September In a reorganization of aviation forces abroad, the Commander, U.S. Naval Aviation Forces, Foreign Service, was assigned to the Staff of the Commander, U.S. Naval Forces Operating in European Waters, as the Aide for Aviation, and unit commands were set up for France, England, Ireland, Italy, and the Northern Bombing Group to control and direct the operations of stations and units in their respective areas.

3 September The first naval air operations from bases in Ireland began from NAS Lough Foyle with patrols over the North Channel entrance to the Irish Sea.

23 September The flywheel catapult, a forerunner of those installed aboard the *Lexington* and *Saratoga,* was used successfully to launch a flying bomb at Copiague, Long Island, N.Y. Development of this catapult by the Sperry Company had been undertaken in connection with the Bureau of Ordnance flying bomb project.

23 September The Aircraft Radio School at Pensacola, Fla., began a course of instruction for Aircraft Radio Electricians which included code work, semaphore and blinker study, gunnery, and laboratory work. This school was transferred subsequently to Harvard University.

24 September Lieutenant (jg) David S. Ingalls, while on a test flight in a Sopwith Camel, sighted an enemy two-seat Rumpler over Nieuport. In company with another Camel he attacked and scored his fifth aerial victory in 6 weeks to become the Navy's first ace. For this and other meritorious acts while serving as a fighter pilot with Royal Air Force Squadron 213, he was awarded the Distinguished Flying Cross by the British Government and the Distinguished Service Medal by the president of the United States.

25 September Chief Machinist's Mate Francis E. Ormsbee went to the rescue of two men in a plane which had crashed in Pensacola Bay, Fla. He pulled out the gunner and held him above water until help arrived, then made repeated dives into the wreckage in an unsuccessful attempt to rescue the pilot. For his heroism, Chief Ormsbee was awarded the Medal of Honor.

1 October Some of the earliest recorded food-dropping missions were flown by Marine Corps pilots

1918—Continued

Captain Francis P. Mulcahy, Captain Robert S. Lytle, and Lieutenant Frank Nelms. On this day and the next, they made repeated low level runs in the face of enemy fire and delivered 2,600 pounds of food and badly needed supplies to a French regiment surrounded by German troops near Stadenburg.

4 October The first of the NC flying boats, the NC-1, made its initial flight at NAS Rockaway, N.Y., with Commander Holden C. Richardson, CC, and Lieutenant David H. McCulloch pilots.

14 October The first raid-in-force by the Northern Bombing Group in World War I was made by eight planes of Marine Day Squadron 9, which dropped 17 bombs totaling 2,218 pounds on the German held railroad junction at Thielt, Belgium. For extraordinary heroism on this and on an earlier raid in engaging enemy aircraft at great odds, 2nd Lieutenant Ralph Talbot, and his observer, Gunnery Sergeant Robert G. Robinson, were later awarded the Medal of Honor.

15 October The Bureau of Steam Engineering reported that five Hart and Eustiss reversible pitch propellers were under construction for use on twin-engine dirigibles. In addition, two Hart and Eustiss variable pitch propeller hubs for the F-5L were being ordered.

17 October A pilotless N-9 training plane, converted to an automatic flying machine, was launched successfully at Copiague, Long Island, N.Y., and flew a prescribed course, although the distance gear failed to land the airplane at a preset range of 14,500 yards. The plane was last seen over the Bay Shore Air Station at an altitude of 4,000 feet, flying eastward.

22 October The twin-engine dirigible C-1, commanded by Major Bernard L. Smith, USMC, and with crew consisting of Lieutenant Ralph A. D. Preston, USNRF, Lieutenant (jg) Donald T. Hood, USNRF, Ensign Warner L. Hamlen, USNRF, Ensign Marcus H. Estorly, USNRF, and two civilian mechanics, M. Roulette and James Royal, was delivered at NAS Rockaway, N.Y., having flown that day from Akron, Ohio, via Washington, D.C. The Aero Club of America later awarded Smith and Hamlen its Medal of Merit for this flight.

11 November An armistice was signed ending the hostilities of World War I. In the 19 months of the United States' participation, the strength of Naval Aviation had grown to a force of 6,716 officers and 30,693 men in Navy units, and 282 officers and 2,180 men in Marine Corps units, with 2,107 aircraft, 15 dirigibles, and 215 kite and free balloons on hand. Of these numbers 18,000 officers and men and 570 aircraft had been sent abroad.

17 November NAS Hampton Roads, Va., reported that an H-16 flying boat, equipped with a radio direction finder using the British six-stage amplifier, received signals from the Arlington, Va., radio station at a distance of 150 miles.

22 November Lieutenant Victor Vernon and Mr. S. T. Williams dropped a 400-pound dummy torpedo from an F-5L at the Naval Aircraft Factory in the initial test of a torpedo launching gear upon which development had begun the preceding July.

23 November Use of titles "Navigation Officer" and "Aerographic Officer" in naval air station organization was authorized by the Chief of Naval Operations to identify officers trained to perform the special duties involved.

27 November The NC-1 took off from Rockaway Beach, N.Y., with 51 persons aboard, establishing a new world record for persons carried in flight.

2 December Efforts to develop aircraft to operate from ships were renewed by the Office of the Chief of Naval Operations request that the Bureau of Construction and Repair provide aircraft of the simplest form, lightly loaded, and with the slowest flying speed possible.

12 December In a test to determine the feasibility of carrying fighter aircraft on dirigibles, the C-1 lifted an Army JN-4 in a wide spiral climb to 2,500 feet over Fort Tilden, N.Y., and at that height released it for a free flight back to base. The airship was piloted by Lieutenant George Crompton, Dirigible Officer at NAS Rockaway, N.Y., and the plane by Lieutenant A. W. Redfield, USA, commanding the 52d Aero Squadron based at Mineola, N.Y.

26 December Ensign Thomas E. Maytham, piloting a B-type airship, completed a flight from Key West, Fla., to Tampa, Fla., Cape Sable, Fla., Palm Beach, Fla., and return that covered approximately 690 miles. This bettered his earlier endurance mark of 32 hours with a continuous flight of 40 hours 26 minutes. Although recognized only as an American record, this time surpassed by more than 25 hours the existing world mark.

30 December Lieutenant Thomas C. Rodman, piloting an H-16 flying boat at Pensacola, Fla., scored the

1918—Continued

Navy's first win in the Curtiss Marine Trophy Race, an annual competition set up by Glenn H. Curtiss in 1915 to encourage seaplane development. The contest was on the basis of miles traveled in 10 hours of flight, with extra mileage credit for passenger load. In winning, Rodman carried 11 passengers 670 statute miles and received credit for 970 miles.

1919

23 January Ensign Fitzwilliam W. Dalrymple and Chief Machinist's Mate Frederick H. Harris took off at NAS Miami, Fla., in a single-engine pusher flying boat, HS-2L, and with benefit of special gas tanks, remained airborne for 9 hours 21 minutes.

3 February Captain George W. Steele, Jr., assumed command of Fleet Air Detachment, Atlantic Fleet, on board his flagship, *Shawmut* (CM 4), in the Boston Navy Yard, Mass. Established for the purpose of testing the capabilities of aviation to operate with fleet forces, the new command marked the beginning of a permanent provision for aviation in fleet organization. Although all elements of the detachment were not immediately assembled, its composition was: *Shawmut* (CM 4) flagship and tender, a seaplane squadron of six H-16 flying boats under Lieutenant Commander Bruce G. Leighton, an airplane division of three landplanes under Lieutenant Commander Edward O. McDonnell on *Texas* (BB 35) and a kite-balloon division of six balloons on various ships and the *Shawmut* (CM 4), under Lieutenant (jg) John G. Paul.

9 February The submission of aerological data, obtained at various naval air stations, to the U.S. Weather Bureau for use in coordinated study of weather conditions, commenced with the report submitted by NAS Pensacola, Fla.

17 February The Fleet Air Detachment which had completed assembly at Guantanamo Bay, Cuba, on the 15th, began operations with the fleet by participating in long range spotting practice. On this day and in subsequent exercises, the detachment gave a practical demonstration of the capabilities of aircraft and of the advantages to be derived from the coordinated employment of air and surface units.

7 March In a test at NAS Hampton Roads, Va., Lieutenant (jg) Frank M. Johnson launched an N-9 landplane from a sea sled making approximately 50 knots. The sea sled was a powerful motor boat designed to launch an aircraft at a point within range

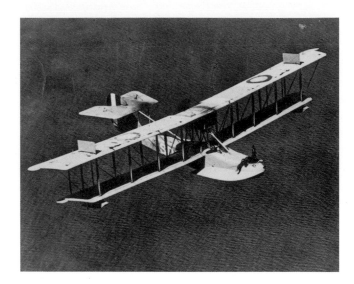

HS-2L flying boat powered by Liberty motor 1053768

of the target and had been developed experimentally at the recommendation of and under the guidance of Commander Henry C. Mustin as a means of attacking German submarine pens. The sea sled was manufactured by Murray and Tregurtha of South Boston, Mass.

9 March Lieutenant Commander Edward O. McDonnell, piloting a Sopwith Camel, made the first flight from a turret platform on a U.S. Navy battleship as he successfully took off from the No. 2 turret of *Texas* (BB 35), lying at anchor at Guantanamo Bay, Cuba.

12 March The feasibility of using voice radio and telephone relay for air to ground communications was demonstrated as Lieutenant Harry Sadenwater, in an airborne flying boat, carried on a conversation with the Secretary of the Navy who was seated at his desk in the Navy Department some 65 miles away.

13 March The Chief of Naval Operations issued a preliminary program for postwar naval airplane development. Specialized types desired were fighters, torpedo carriers and bombers for fleet use; single-engine, twin-engine and long distance patrol and bomber planes for station use; and a combination land and seaplane for Marine Corps use.

21 March A gyrocompass developed by the Sperry Gyroscope Company for the Navy was tested in an aircraft. Although this particular instrument was not found acceptable, this is the first recorded instance of tests of this device which was later to prove an invaluable navigational instrument for long-range flight.

7 April The Seaplane Squadron and *Shawmut* (CM 4) of Fleet Air Detachment left Guantanamo Bay,

1919—Continued

Cuba, for the United States after almost seven weeks of participation in fleet exercises, during which time the squadron had operated entirely afloat and had no support from shore bases.

8 April   Captain Thomas T. Craven was detached from the Bureau of Navigation for duty in the Office of the Chief of Naval Operations where, in the following month, he relieved Captain Noble E. Irwin as Director of Naval Aviation.

10 April   The roll-up of naval air stations in Europe, which had begun on 31 December 1918 with the disestablishment of Porto Corsini, Italy, was completed as the Assembly and Repair Base at Eastleigh, England, was demobilized.

26 April   An F-5L flying boat, equipped with two 400-hp Liberty engines and piloted by Lieutenant H. D. Grow out of Hampton Roads, Va., completed a flight of 20 hours and 19 minutes in which it covered 1,250 nautical miles. Although the flight was not made under FAI supervision and was prior to the date on which seaplanes were recognized as a separate class for record purposes, this time was better than any recognized seaplane duration record until May 1925.

28 April   Lieutenant Commander Richard E. Byrd, who developed and tested navigational equipment for the forthcoming transatlantic flight, requested the Naval Observatory to supply bubble levels which he adapted for attachment to navigational sextants, thereby providing an artificial horizon which made it possible to use these instruments for astronomical observations from aircraft.

8 May   Seaplane Division One, comprised of three NC flying boats, took off from NAS Rockaway, N.Y. at 10:00 a.m. for Halifax, Nova Scotia, on the first leg of a projected transatlantic flight. Commanding the Division, and the NC-3, was Commander John H. Towers. The NC-4 was commanded by Lieutenant Commander Albert C. Read. The NC-1 was commanded by Lieutenant Commander Patrick N. L. Bellinger.

14–15 May   The airship C-5, Lieutenant Commander Emory W. Coil commanding, made a record flight from Montauk Point, Long Island, N.Y., to St. Johns, Newfoundland, covering the 1,050 nautical miles in 25 hours and 50 minutes.

16 May   Around 6 p.m., three NC flying boats took off from Trepassey Bay, Newfoundland, for the long overwater flight to the Azores.

16 May   Ensign Herbert C. Rodd, radioman on the NC-4, intercepted a radio message from the steamship *George Washington* 1,325 miles distant. A radio message from one of the NCs was also intercepted by the radio station, Bar Harbor, Maine, when the plane was 1,400 miles away.

17 May   After more than 15 hours in the air, the NC flying boats neared the Azores. At 1323 GMT, the NC-4 landed at Horta, Azores. The other NC boats were not so fortunate; both had lost their bearings in thick fog and landed at sea to determine their positions. But in landing they sustained damage and were unable to resume flight. The NC-3 drifted backwards toward the Azores and arrived at Ponta Delgada, Azores, at 6:30 p.m. on 19 May. The NC-1 sustained additional damage in the heavy seas and was taken under tow by the Greek steamer *Ionia,* but the tow lines soon parted. *Gridley* (DD 92) then attempted to tow the NC-1 but the aircraft pulled adrift again and broke up and sank. Her entire crew was taken on board *Ionia* and arrived at Horta, Azores at 12:30 p.m. on 18 May.

27 May   `At 8:01 p.m. the NC-4 landed in the harbor at Lisbon, Portugal, completing the first crossing of the Atlantic Ocean by air. The only one of three NC boats to reach the Azores by air, the NC-4 arrived the afternoon of the 17th, and after a layover of 10 days, covered the last leg of the crossing to Lisbon. Lieutenant Commander Albert C. Read was in command and Lieutenant Elmer F. Stone, USCG, Lieutenant James L. Breese, Lieutenant (jg) Walter K. Hinton, Ensign Herbert C. Rodd and Chief Machinist's Mate Eugene S.

C-5 airship attempted transatlantic crossing 1061650

1919—Continued

Rhoads made up the crew. The NC-4 flight terminated at Plymouth, England, on 31 May.

12 June A contract was issued for the construction of a revolving platform at Hampton Roads, Va., for use in experimental development of techniques and equipment for landing aircraft aboard ship.

21 June The Bureau of Construction and Repair reported a modification to the aircraft color scheme whereby stretched fabric surfaces were to be finished with aluminum enamel. Thus, wing and tail surfaces and in some instances the fuselage surfaces were to be aluminum-colored while the specified color for other exterior surfaces continued to be naval gray enamel.

23 June The General Board submitted the last of a series of reports to the Secretary of the Navy on a policy for developing a naval air service. On the conclusion that aviation had become an essential arm of the fleet, the board urged adoption of a broad program for peacetime development that would establish a naval air service "capable of accompanying and operating with the fleet in all waters of the globe." Approved with some modification by the Secretary on 24 July, this program provided the direction for a number of actions taken in the following months.

25 June NAS Anacostia, D.C., reported experiments in which aircraft carried aloft instruments to measure temperature and humidity of the upper atmosphere.

1 July The Secretary of the Navy authorized installation of launching platforms on two main turrets in each of the eight battleships.

2 July The Officer-in-Charge of the Navy Detachment under instruction in landplanes at the Army Air Service School, Langley Field, Va., reported that the 27 Naval Aviators on board had completed the preliminary flight phase in JN-4s and were rapidly nearing the end of the formation flight syllabus in DH aircraft. This training was in preparation for the operation of landplanes from battleship turrets.

11 July The Naval Appropriations Act for fiscal year 1920 made several important provisions for the future of Naval Aviation. Among others it provided for conversion of *Jupiter* (AC 3) into an aircraft carrier, later named *Langley*; for conversion of two merchant ships into seaplane tenders, only one of which, later named *Wright* (AZ 1), was completed, and for construction of one rigid dirigible later designated ZR-1 and named *Shenandoah* and purchase of another from abroad later designated ZR-2 (R-38). In a more restrictive sense, the act limited to six the heavier-than-air stations that could be maintained along the coasts of continental United States.

NC-4, commanded by LCDR A. C. Read, completed first transatlantic flight, Lisbon, Portugal, May 27, 1919 650875

1919—Continued

Crew of the NC-4—1st LT E. F. Stone, USCG, CMM E. C. Rhoads, LT(jg) Walter Hinton, ENS H. C. Rodd, LT J. L. Breese, LCDR. A. C. Read—with CAPT R. H Jackson 1061649

SecNav with transatlantic flyers (1) Read, SecNav Daniels, Towers, Asst SecNav Roosevelt, Bellinger (2) Rodd, Sadenwater, Barin, Richardson, McCulloch, (3) Breese, Lavender (4) Rhoads, Christensen, Stone, Hinton 45354

1919—Continued

1 August To merge aviation with other naval activities, the Aviation Division of the Office of the Chief of Naval Operations was abolished and its functions reassigned to other divisions and to the Bureau of Navigation. The Director of Naval Aviation retained his title as head of the Aviation Section of the Planning Division. In the reorganization, the Aircraft Test Board was transferred to the Board of Inspection and Survey.

9 August Construction of the rigid airship ZR-1, the future *Shenandoah* and the Navy's first rigid airship, was authorized by the Secretary of the Navy. This airship was constructed at the Naval Aircraft Factory and assembled at Lakehurst, N.J.

19 August The Secretary of the Navy ordered use of the pre-war white star national insignia on all naval aircraft in place of the concentric circle design adopted for the war. By this order, the red, white and blue vertical bands on the rudder reverted to their prewar position, blue being forward.

23 August A general order directed that during dirigible flights parachutes be carried for each person on board. The following November, this directive was amplified to apply also to flights in kite balloons and added the further requirement that life preservers be carried in all lighter-than-air craft during flights over water.

22 October The Secretary of War approved the Navy's request that 18 Naval Aviators and 10 mechanics be given landplane training at the Air Service Training School at Carlstrom Field, Arcadia, Fla., and two days later approved a similar program at March Field, Riverside, Calif. This training, an extension of the program already conducted under the Army at Langley Field, Va., had been requested by the Secretary of the Navy as necessary to the successful operation of scouting aircraft from battleship turrets.

1 November The Aerological School at NAS Pensacola, Fla., opened with a class of one Marine Corps and four Navy officers.

18 November The Secretary of the Navy informed the Secretary of War that, in response to his request, arrangements had been made for six Army men to attend the enlisted men's course in meteorology at Pensacola, Fla., and suggested they report about 1 December when classes were scheduled to start.

21 November Engineering plans for the conversion of *Jupiter* (AC 3) to an aircraft carrier, originally completed 5 July were modified, and a summary specification was issued by the Bureau of Construction and Repair. In addition to an unobstructed "flying-on and flying-off deck," stowage space for aircraft and facilities for repair of aircraft, the new plans provided for catapults to be fitted on both forward and aft ends of the flying-off deck.

5 December The Secretary of the Navy approved the basic agreement covering procurement of the R-38 (ZR-2) rigid airship from the British Air Ministry.

F-5L American adaptation of British flying boat 644471

F-boat, a World War I trainer, at Pensacola 177954

The Curtiss H-12, a twin engine flying boat, represented an early World War I step in aircraft development NH 60768

Thomas-Morse S-5 powered with rotary engine 1053765

Sea sled, high speed boat for transport and launch of bombers, Caproni landplane on board, November 1918 229907

Turret platform helped adapt planes to ships 428436

Davis recoilless ASW gun, mounted on H-1 1053766

Launching torpedo from R-type aircraft, a means of increasing Naval aviation's offensive power 1061481

Gondola of C-class with bomb in rack 1053767

PART 3

The Twenties

1920–1929

The twenties stand out in the history of Naval Aviation as a decade of growth. The air arm steadily increased in size and strength while improving its administrative and operational position within the Navy. The period began under the leadership of a director without authority to direct. It ended with a flourishing Bureau of Aeronautics. In the early 1920s a small air detachment in each ocean fleet proved themselves effective under conditions at sea. At the end, three carriers were in full operation, patrol squadrons were performing scouting functions, and aircraft were regularly assigned to battleships and cruisers. Together these elements played important roles in the annual fleet war games.

Impressive technical progress also characterized the period. With slim funds, the radial air-cooled engine was developed into an efficient and reliable source of propulsion. Better instruments came into use, and an accurate bomb-sight was developed. Aircraft equipped with oleo struts and folding wings enhanced the operating capability of carriers. Each year, aircraft flew faster, higher and longer. Of the many world records placed on the books, U.S. Naval aircraft set their share.

Tactics were developed. Dive bombing was established almost before anyone knew enough about it to call it by name. Marine Corps expeditionary troops learned through experience the value of air support. The techniques of torpedo attack, scouting, spotting for gunfire and operating from advanced bases, were investigated and learned. The skills of naval pilots turned the airplane to new uses in polar exploration and photographic survey. It was evident everywhere that the Navy was solving its basic and unique problem of taking aviation to the sea.

But the period was also one of controversy that went beyond the Navy. Newspapers reported angry statements by the proponents of air power and virulent retorts from its opponents. There were charges of duplication, inefficiency, prejudice and jealousy. There was discussion over the role of air power and such issues as the role of the services in coastal defense. Even the further need for a Navy was questioned. Naval Aviators were unhappy with their career limita-

tions and lack of command responsibility. The aircraft industry was discontented with small peacetime orders and government procurement policies and government competition. Most of this controversy was typical of a new technology developing at a rapid pace, but not all of the questions would be answered before the decade's end.

1920

8 January The policy of the Army and Navy relating to aircraft was published for the information and guidance of the services. It defined the functions of Army, Navy and Marine aircraft as a guide to procurement, training and expansion of operating facilities; it set forth the conditions under which air operations would be coordinated in coast defense; it enunciated the means by which duplication of effort would be avoided; and it provided for the free exchange of technical information. An outgrowth of discussion in the previous year, this statement was one of many in a long line of interservice agreements on function and mission which spanned the years to and beyond the more familiar Key West and Newport agreements reached by the Joint Chiefs of Staff in 1948.

19 January Commandant, NAS Pensacola, Fla., reported that in the future no student would be designated a Naval Aviator or given a certificate of qualification as a Navy Air Pilot unless he could send and receive 20 words a minute on radio telegraph.

20 January The development and purchase of 200-hp radial air-cooled engines from the Lawrance Aero Engine Corporation was initiated with an allocation of $100,000 to the Bureau of Steam Engineering for this purpose.

17 March To overcome an acute shortage of pilots, a change in the flight training program was approved which separated the heavier-than-air (seaplane) and the lighter-than-air (dirigible) courses; and reduced the overall training period from nine to six months for the duration of the shortage.

1920—Continued

27 March A successful test of the Sperry gyrostabilized automatic pilot system in an F-5L was completed at Hampton Roads, Va.

2 April NAS Hampton Roads, Va., reported that successful night weather soundings had been made since January, using candlelighted free balloons to measure the force and direction of the wind.

1 May Developmental and experimental work in metal construction for aircraft was disclosed in a Bureau of Construction and Repair report. Twelve German Fokker D-VII planes, which used welded steel extensively, were to be obtained from the Army and two sets of metal wings for the HS-3 flying boat were being procured from Charles Ward Hall.

18 June A reversible pitch propeller designed by Seth Hart and manufactured by the Engineering Division, Army Air Service, was installed on the C-10 airship at Rockaway Beach. That same month a Hart reversible pitch propeller was ordered for the VE-7.

22 June The Bureau of Navigation announced plans to select four officers for a two-year postgraduate course in aeronautical engineering at the Naval Academy and M.I.T., and asked for volunteers for the fall semester. Part of the requirement was that appointees take flight instruction and qualify as Naval Aviatiors after completing their studies.

28 June Six F-5Ls of the Atlantic Fleet Airboat Squadron, commanded by Lieutenant Commander Bruce G. Leighton, returned to Philadelphia, Pa., completing a seven-month cruise through the West Indies on which the squadron logged 12,731 nautical miles, including 4,000 flown on maneuvers with the fleet.

6 July In a test of the radio compass as an aid to navigation, an F-5L left Hampton Roads, Va., and flew directly to *Ohio* (BB 12), 94 miles at sea in a position unknown to the pilot. Without landing, the plane made the return trip to Hampton Roads, Va., this time navigating by signals from Norfolk, Va.

12 July A general order provided for the organization of the naval forces afloat into the Atlantic, Pacific and Asiatic Fleets; and for the formation of type forces within each designated Battleship, Cruiser, Destroyer, Submarine, Mine, Air and Train. Under this order, the Air Detachments in each fleet became Air Forces.

17 July The Secretary prescribed standard nomenclature for types and classes of naval vessels, including aircraft, in which lighter-than-air craft were identified by the type "Z" and heavier-than-air craft by "V". Class letters assigned within the Z type were R, N and K for rigid dirigibles, non-rigid dirigibles and kite balloons respectively, while F, O, S, P, T and G were established for fighter, observation, scouting, patrol, torpedo and bombing and Fleet planes as classes within the V type.

17 September The site of the naval aviation activities on Ford Island was officially designated NAS Pearl Harbor, T.H.

4 November The third of a series of tests to determine the effectiveness of aerial bombs against ships was completed, using the old battleship *Indiana* (Battleship No. 1) as a target. The tests which began on 14 October were conducted at Tangier Sound in the Chesapeake Bay under carefully controlled conditions to determine both the accuracy with which bombs could be dropped on stationary targets and the damage caused by near-misses and direct hits.

1921

20 January The Secretary of the Navy approved a recommendation that development of radio-controlled aircraft be undertaken by the Bureau of Ordnance and the Bureau of Engineering.

20 January A Naval Aircraft Factory design of a turntable catapult, powered by compressed air, was approved by the Bureau of Construction and Repair for fabrication at the Philadelphia Navy Yard, Pa.

Aircraft were launched from capital ships by turntable catapult, shown on a pier at NAF with an N-9 428435

1921—Continued

7 March   Captain William A. Moffett relieved Captain Thomas T. Craven as Director of Naval Aviation.

15 March   The Metallurgical Laboratory at the Naval Aircraft Factory, Philadelphia, Pa., reported that a high-strength, chromium-vanadium steel alloy had proven satisfactory both in extensive laboratory tests and in the actual manufacture of aircraft fittings. These findings marked an important advance in the development of metal as a high-strength aircraft structural material.

16 June   Two CR-1 Curtiss racers were ordered, the first of the series with which Navy and Army fliers captured many world speed records.

1 July   The following basic ratings were established in the Aviation Branch: Aviation Machinist's Mate, Aviation Metalsmith, Aviation Carpenter's Mate, Aviation Rigger and Photographer. Although prior to this time certain general service ratings had been identified parenthetically as pertaining to aviation, qualifications for them required meeting the standards of the general rating in addition to those required for the aviation specialty. The ratings established on this date were the first concerned specifically with aviation and based solely on aviation requirements.

12 July   An Act of Congress created a Bureau of Aeronautics, charged with matters pertaining to naval aeronautics as prescribed by the Secretary of the Navy.

W. A. Moffett the first Chief of the Bureau of Aeronautics 466366

21 July   The bombing tests—The German battleship *Ostfriesland* was sunk by heavy bombs dropped by Army bombers in the last of a series of tests to determine the effectiveness of air weapons against combatant ships, and the means by which ship design and construction might counter their destructive capability. The tests, in which the Army participated at the invitation of the Navy, were carried out off the Virginia Capes beginning 21 June. On that day, the German submarine U-117 was sunk by 12 bombs dropped from Navy F-5Ls at 1,100 feet. On the 29th, Navy aircraft located the radio-controlled U.S. battleship ex-*Iowa* (Battleship No. 4) in 1 hour and 57 minutes after being alerted of her approach somewhere within a 25,000 square mile area and attacked with dummy bombs. On 13 July, Army bombers sank the German destroyer G-102, and on the 18th the German light

The Ostfriesland under attack in 1921 Army-Navy bombing test. Mining effects of hits like this sank her 161903

cruiser *Frankfurt* went down under the combined effect of 74 bombs delivered by Army and Navy aircraft. Tests against the *Ostfriesland* began on 20 July when Army, Navy and Marine Corps planes dropped 52 bombs, and they ended the next day when the Army delivered eleven 1,000- and 2,000-pounders. The Navy had originally planned the tests to provide detailed technical and tactical data on the effectiveness of aerial bombing against ships and the value of compartmentation in enabling ships to survive bomb damage; the Army participated for the purpose of portraying the superiority of air power over sea power. The divergence in purposes and resulting differences in operational plans were not reconciled and, in consequence, the Navy's purposes were not realized. The significance of the tests was hotly debated, and became a bone of contention between a generation of Army and Navy air officers. The one firm conclusion that could be drawn was that aircraft, in unopposed attack, could sink capital ships.

1921—Continued

1 August   A World War I high-altitude bombsight, mounted on a gyroscopically stabilized base, was tested by the Torpedo Squadron, Atlantic Fleet at Yorktown, Va., marking the successful completion of the first phase of Carl L. Norden's development of an effective high-altitude bombsight for the Bureau of Ordnance.

9 August   Rear Admiral Bradley A. Fiske, USN (Ret.), proposed as a landing surface for aircraft carriers, "a nice soft cushion" so mounted "that it would take up the forward motion of the airplane and not check its forward velocity at once."

10 August   A General Order established the Bureau of Aeronautics, and defined its duties under the Secretary of the Navy as comprising "all that relates to designing, building, fitting out, and repairing Naval and Marine Corps aircraft;" gave it authority to recommend to the Bureau of Navigation and the Commandant of the Marine Corps on all matters pertaining to aeronautic training and the assignment of officer and enlisted personnel to aviation; described the scope of its relationships with other bureaus having cognizance of aeronautical materials and equipment; and also directed that special provision be made in its organization to furnish information "covering all aeronautic planning, operations and administration that may be called for by the Chief of Naval Operations."

11 August   Practical development of carrier arresting gear was initiated at Hampton Roads as Lieutenant Alfred M. Pride taxied an Aeromarine onto the dummy deck, and engaged arresting wires. These tests resulted in the development of arresting gear for *Langley*, consisting essentially of both athwartship wires attached to weights, and fore and aft wires.

24 August   During its fourth trial flight, the R-38 (ZR-2) rigid airship purchased by the Navy from the Royal Air Force, broke into two parts and fell into the Humber River at Hull, England. It carried to their deaths 28 British nationals and 16 Americans, including Air Commodore E. M. Maitland and Commander Louis H. Maxfield, the latter the prospective American commanding officer.

1 September   The Bureau of Aeronautics began functioning as an organizational unit of the Navy Department, under its Chief, Rear Admiral William A. Moffett.

26 October   A compressed air, turntable catapult, in its first successful test, launched an N-9 seaplane piloted by Commander Holden C. Richardson from a pier at the Philadelphia Navy Yard, Pa.

3 November   A Curtiss-Navy racer, powered by a 400-hp Curtiss engine, on loan to the builder and piloted by Bert Acosta, won the Pulitzer Race at Omaha with a world record speed of 176.7 mph.

1 December   The first flight of an airship inflated with helium gas was made at Norfolk, Va. The airship, the C-7, was piloted by Lieutenant Commander Ralph F. Wood.

16 December   *Wright*, a seaplane tender and balloon carrier, was commissioned the AZ 1 at New York, N.Y., with Captain Alfred W. Johnson in command.

20 December   To meet requirements expressed by several Pacific Fleet commands, the commanding officer of NAS San Diego, Calif., was authorized to establish a school for training Naval Aviators in the use of landplanes.

Wright, AV1 with seaplane on board; the first U.S. Naval vessel especially fitted as an aircraft tender 1053778

1922

16 January   Parachutes issued for heavier-than-air use—The Bureau of Aeronautics directed that Army-type seat pack parachutes be shipped to Marine Corps aviation units in Haiti, the Dominican Republic, Guam and Quantico, Va.

6 February   The Washington Treaty, limiting naval armament, was signed in Washington, D.C., by representatives of the British Empire, France, Italy, Japan and the United States. The treaty established a tonnage ratio of 5-5-3 for capital ships of Great Britain, the United States and Japan respectively, and a lesser figure for France and Italy. The same ratio for aircraft carrier tonnage set overall limits at 135,000-135,000-81,000 tons. The treaty also limited any new carrier to 27,000 tons with a provision that, if total carrier tonnage were not exceeded thereby, nations could build two carriers of not more than 33,000 tons each or obtain them by converting existing or partially constructed ships which would otherwise be scrapped by this treaty.

7 February   The completion of a 50-hour test run of the Lawrance J-1, 200-hp, radial aircooled engine by the Aeronautical Engine Laboratory, Washington Navy Yard, D.C., foreshadowed the successful use of radial engines in naval aircraft.

2 March   Experimental investigation and development of catapults using gunpowder was initiated, eventually producing a new type catapult for use in launching aircraft from capital ships.

20 March   *Langley,* converted from the collier *Jupiter* (AC 3) as the first carrier of the U.S. Navy, was commissioned at Norfolk, Va., under command of her Executive Officer, Commander Kenneth Whiting.

25 March   Research Laboratory as had been provided for in a public law passed in August 1916. Following the construction of necessary buildings at Bellevue, D.C., the Aircraft Radio Laboratory from NAS Anacostia, D.C., the Naval Radio Research Laboratory from the Bureau of Standards and the Sound Research Section of the Engineering Experiment Station were consolidated at the new organization prior to its establishment in July 1923. In view of the research orientation of this facility, it was generally called the Naval Research Laboratory, and its name was officially changed to that by the Naval Appropriations Act of 1926.

27 March   To comply with a provision of the law establishing the Bureau of Aeronautics that its chief and at least 70 percent of its officers be either pilots or observers, the Bureau of Aeronautics defined the functions and qualifications of Naval Aviation Observers, and recommended a course of study for their training. Upon its approval by the Bureau of Navigation, Rear Admiral William A. Moffett reported for training, and on 17 June 1922 qualified as the first Naval Aviation Observer.

29 March   A change in the aircraft designation system was promulgated which added the identity of the manufacturer to the model designation. Symbols consisted of a combination of letters and numbers in which the first letter identified the manufacturer and the second, the class (or mission) of the aircraft. Thus MO was a Martin observation plane. Numbers appearing between letters indicated the series of designs within the class built by the same manufacturer (the 1 being omitted) and numbers following a dash after the class letter indicated modifications of the basic model. Thus, the second modification of the MO became MO-2, while the second-design observation plane built by Martin became M2O.

The first carrier, Langley, converted from the collier, Jupiter, with fighters and torpedo planes aboard 185915

1922—Continued

1 April   Descriptive specifications of arresting gear of the type later installed in *Lexington* and *Saratoga* were sent to various design engineers, including Carl L. Norden and Warren Noble. "The arresting gear will consist of two or more transverse wires stretched across the fore and aft wires . . . [and which] lead around sheaves placed outboard to hydraulic brakes. The plane after engaging the transverse wire is guided down the deck by the fore and aft wires and is brought to rest by the action of the transverse wire working with the hydraulic brakes."

22 April   The Secretary of the Navy approved a recommendation of the general board that one spotting plane be assigned to each fleet battleship and cruiser, and that the feasibility of operating more aircraft from these ships be tested.

24 April   In efforts to increase the service life of aircraft engines beyond the 50 hours then required, the Bureau of Aeronautics issued a contract to the Packard Motor Car Company for the 300-hour test of a Packard 1A-1551 dirigible engine. Such endurance testing, whereby the weaker components of an engine were identified in runs to destruction, and then redesigned for longer life, came to be an important step both in increasing the operating life of engines and in the development of new high performance engines.

25 April   The first all-metal airplane designed for the Navy made its first flight. The ST-1 twin-engine torpedo plane, built by Stout Engineering Laboratory, was test-flown by Eddie Stinson. Although this aircraft possessed inadequate longitudinal stability, its completion marked a step forward in the development of all-metal aircraft.

24 May   Routine operation of catapults aboard ship commenced with the successful launching of a VE-7 piloted by Lieutenant Andrew C. McFall, with Lieutenant DeWitt C. Ramsey as passenger, from *Maryland* (BB 46) off Yorktown, Va. A compressed air catapult was used. As catapults were installed on other battleships and then on cruisers, the Navy acquired the capability of operating aircraft from existing capital ships. Techniques were thus developed for supporting conventional surface forces, particularly in spotting for ships guns, and experimentation was conducted with aerial tactics that would later be further developed by carrier aviation. Perhaps more important, the capabilities and limitations of aircraft were demonstrated to officers and men throughout the Navy.

31 May   In the National Elimination Balloon Race at Milwaukee, Wisc., the Navy was represented by two balloons: one manned by Lieutenant Commander Joseph P. Norfleet and Chief Rigger James F. Shade, and the other by Lieutenant William F. Reed and Chief Rigger K. Mullenix. Norfleet's balloon was filled with helium, the first use of the gas in a free balloon. Reed finished third in the race with a distance of 441 miles and was the only Navy qualifier for the International Balloon Race to be held at Geneva, Switzerland, later in the year.

17 June   The practice of numbering aircraft squadrons to conform to the number of the ship squadron they served, was changed to a system of numbering all squadrons serially by class in the order in which they were initially authorized. The use of letter abbreviations to indicate mission was also adopted.

17 June   In anticipation of a reorganization that would merge the Atlantic and Pacific Fleets into a U.S. Fleet, the fleet aviation commands, whose titles had previously been changed from Air Forces to Air Squadrons, were retitled Aircraft Squadrons of the Scouting and Battle Fleets. These commands would replace the Atlantic and Pacific Fleets, respectively.

26 June   The rigid airship *Los Angeles* (ZR-3) was ordered from the Zeppelin Airship Company, Friedrichshafen, Germany. This zeppelin, part of World War I reparations, was obtained as a non-military aircraft under the terms approved by the Conference of Ambassadors on 16 December 1921.

1 July   Eight medical officers, the first to report for flight training, began their instruction at NAS Pensacola, Fla. Four had previously completed the flight surgeon's course at the Army Technical School of Aviation Medicine.

1 July   Congress authorized conversion of the unfinished battle cruisers *Lexington* and *Saratoga* to aircraft carriers, as permitted under the terms of the Washington Treaty.

1 July   Navy men began training in the care and packing of parachutes when 10 Chief Petty Officers reported for two months instruction at the Army School at Chanute Field, Rantoul, Ill.

3 July   Class XVI, the first class of student Naval Aviators to be trained in landplanes, began training at Pensacola, Fla.

1922—Continued

17 July   The Chief of Naval Operations forwarded a list of Bureau and Division representatives to the Bureau of Navigation with the request that they be ordered to meet as a board for the purpose of drawing up tactical doctrine governing the employment of spotting aircraft in fleet fire control.

27 September   The first mass torpedo practice against a live target was conducted off the Virginia Capes by 18 PT aircraft of Torpedo and Bombing Plane Squadron One. The squadron attacked the designated target, *Arkansas* (BB 33), which was one of a formation of three battleships that were maneuvering while running at full speed. The attack lasted over a 25 minute period during which the aircraft approached the ships from port and starboard and released 17 Mk VII Model 1 "A" torpedoes at distances of 500 to 1,000 yards and obtained eight hits on the designated target. Subsequent analysis emphasized artificialities which prevented the practice from demonstrating combat capability of either the surface or air units but the outstanding fact demonstrated was that torpedoes could be successfully launched from aircraft, and be made to run straight.

27 September   Commanding officer, NAS Anacostia, D.C., proposed that radio could be used to detect the passage of a ship at night or during heavy fog. The means proposed, the "Beat method of detection," resulted from the unexpected nature of a radio signal observed by Commander A. Hoyt Taylor and Mr. L. C. Young of the Aircraft Radio Laboratory, NAS Anacostia, when a passing river steamer interrupted experimental high frequency radio transmissions between Anacostia and a receiver across the river at Hains Point, D.C. The observation and analysis of the phenomenon was a basic step in the chain of events that led to the U.S. Navy's invention of radar.

8 October   The Curtiss Marine Trophy Race for seaplanes, held at Detroit, Mich., as an event of the National Air Races, was won by Lieutenant Aldophus W. Gorton, flying a TR-1 powered by a Lawrance, J-1 engine. He averaged 112.6 mph over the 160 mile course. Second place went to Lieutenant Harold A. Elliott in a Vought VE-7H.

14 October   Lieutenants Harold J. Brow and Alford J. Williams, flying CR-2 and CR-1 Curtiss Racers with Curtiss D-12 engines, finished third and fourth in the Pulitzer Trophy Race at Detroit, Mich., making speeds of 193 and 187 mph, respectively.

H. J. Brow with 1922 Curtiss CR Pulitzer Racer 1053781

1922—Continued

17 October The first carrier takeoff in the U.S. Navy was made by Lieutenant Virgil C. Griffin in a Vought VE-7SF from *Langley,* at anchor in the York River.

VE-7, type to make the first Langley take-off 651598

26 October Lieutenant Commander Godfrey deC. Chevalier, flying an Aeromarine, made the first landing aboard the carrier *Langley* while underway off Cape Henry.

14 November Lieutenant Commander Godfrey deC. Chevalier, Naval Aviator No. 7, died in the Naval Hospital, Portsmouth, of injuries received in a plane crash two days before at Lochaven, near Norfolk, Va.

18 November Commander Kenneth Whiting, piloting a PT seaplane, made the first catapult launching from the carrier *Langley,* while she was at anchor in the York River.

29 November Lieutenants Ben H. Wyatt and George T. Owen, piloting DH-4Bs, arrived at San Diego, Calif., and completed a round trip transcontinental flight that began from the same place on 14 October. The planes made the trip in short hops, flying a southern route through Tucson, Ariz., New Orleans, La., and Pensacola, Fla., on the outward leg; and from Washington, D.C., through Dayton, Ohio, Omaha, Nebr., Salt Lake City, Utah, and San Francisco, Calif., on the homeward leg; completing the 7,000-mile trip in about 90 hours of flight. Layovers caused by mechanical difficulties, bad gasoline, weather and lack of navigating equipment accounted for most of the elapsed time.

An aeromarine practices landings aboard Langley; LCDR G. deC. Chevalier made first landing on October 26, 1922 215821

An aerial camera on the gun mount of a DH-4 1053779

1923

6 February Transfer of the Aeronautical Engine Laboratory from the Washington Navy Yard, D.C., to the Naval Aircraft Factory was authorized by the Secretary of the Navy, thereby clearly establishing the Naval Aircraft Factory as the center of the Navy's aeronautical development and experimental work.

12 February The Bureau of Navigation informed the Commandant at Pensacola, Fla., that two year's service in an operating unit subsequent to graduation from flight training was no longer a requirement for designation as a Naval Aviator.

18–22 February Aviation was employed in a U.S. Fleet Problem for the first time as Problem I was worked out to test the defenses of the Panama Canal against air attack. Blue Fleet and Army coastal and air units defending the Canal, were assisted by the operations of 18 patrol planes of Scouting Plane Squadron 1 based on the tenders *Wright* (AZ 1), *Sandpiper* (AM 51) and *Teal* (AM 23). The lack of carriers and planes for the attacking Black Fleet was made up by designating two battleships as simulated carriers. On the approach one of these, *Oklahoma* (BB 37), launched a seaplane by catapult to scout ahead of the force (21 Feb.), and early the next morning a single plane representing an air group took off from Naranyas Cays, flew in undetected and, without either air opposition or antiaircraft fire, theoretically destroyed Gatun Spillway with 10 miniature bombs.

21 February Tests of aircraft handling were made aboard *Langley* with Aeromarines operating in groups of three. Results showed that it required two minutes to prepare the deck after each landing; and in the best time for the day three planes were landed in seven minutes.

21 February In recognition of the fact that the newer aircraft engines offered advantages of longer life and lower cost, the Bureau of Aeronautics issued guidelines that severely restricted the repair and reuse of engines over two years old. Through this means, the Navy was able to expend promptly its residual stocks of World War I engines and equip most new aircraft with newer engines. More importantly, freed of the millstone of stocks of obsolescent engines, the Navy could aggressively sponsor the development of improved aircraft engines to meet its various requirements.

7 March Navy participation in aviation fuel research and development was indicated in the Aeronautical Engine Laboratory report on systematic tests, conducted by the Bureau of Standards, on mixtures of alcohol-gasoline and benzol-gasoline. Industrial and governmental research with fuels, of which this was a part, eventually resulted in the development of tetraethyl-lead as an additive for aviation fuels and of iso-octane as a standard for antiknock characteristics.

10 March The aircraft model designation system was modified by reversing the order of letters in the

1923—Continued

combination, placing the class letter first and manufacturer's letter last. Thus, the designation FB indicated a fighter built by Boeing. Although this modification applied only to new aircraft and did not change designations already assigned, the system so established remained in use until 1962.

15 March The training of nucleus crews for the rigid airships *Shenandoah* (ZR-1) and *Los Angeles* (ZR-3), which had been underway since 1 July 1922 at NAS Hampton Roads, Va., opened at a new location when ground school work started at NAS Lakehurst, N.J., under Captain Anton Heinan, lighter-than-air expert, formerly of the German Navy.

15 April The Naval Research Laboratory reported that equipment for radio control of aircraft had been demonstrated in an F-5L, and was found satisfactory up to a range of 10 miles. It also stated that radio control of an airplane during landing and takeoff was feasible.

17 April Lieutenant Rutledge Irvine, flying a Douglas DT equipped with a Liberty engine, established a world altitude record for Class C airplanes with a useful load of 1,000 kilograms, reaching 11,609 feet over McCook Field, Dayton, Ohio.

26 May The Chief of the Bureau of Aeronautics agreed with the Chief of the Air Service that it would be advantageous to both the aviation industry and the military services to work under identical aeronautic specifications whenever possible and further stated that he considered it desirable for the Army and Navy to work together toward that end immediately. When Lieutenant Ralph S. Barnaby was ordered to McCook Field as the bureau's representative at an interservice conference on standardization in December, a series of annual meetings was initiated that continued until 1937, when the Aeronautical Board assigned a full-time staff to carry on the work.

6 June Planes and pilots of Aircraft Squadrons, Battle Fleet, established seven world records for Class C seaplanes at San Diego, Calif., as follows:

Lieutenant (jg) Mainrad A. Schur, in a DT-2 torpedo plane, set the speed record for 500 kilometers at 72 mph.

Lieutenant Henry T. Stanley, in an F-5L patrol plane, set distance and duration records with a payload of 250 kilograms at 574.75 miles and 10 hours, 23 minutes, 58 seconds.

Lieutenant Herman E. Halland, in an F-5L patrol plane, set distance and duration records with a 500-kilogram payload at 466 miles and 7 hours, 35 minutes, 54 seconds.

Two versions of the Douglas DT torpedo plane 426931

1923—Continued

Lieutenant Robert L. Fuller, in a DT-2 torpedo plane, set distance and duration marks with a 1,000-kilogram payload at 205.2 miles and 2 hours, 45 minutes, 9 seconds.

7 June   Pilots at San Diego, Calif., continued their assault on the record books with eight new world marks for Class C seaplanes as follows:

Lieutenant Earl B. Brix, in a DT-2, set an altitude record of 10,850 feet for planes carrying a 250-kilogram useful load.

Lieutenant Robert L. Fuller, in an F-5L, set an altitude record of 8,438 feet for planes carrying a 500-kilogram load.

Ensign Edward E. Dolecek, in an F-5L, set an altitude record of 7,979 feet for planes with a 1,000-kilogram load.

Lieutenant Cecil F. Harper, in a DT-2, set the altitude record of 13,898 feet for planes with no useful load.

Lieutenant Henry T. Stanley, in an F-5L, with a 1,500-kilogram load, set the duration mark at 2 hours, 18 minutes, and an altitude record of 5,682 feet.

Lieutenant Herman E. Halland, in an F-5L with a 2,000-kilogram load, set a duration record of 51 minutes and an altitude record of 4,885 feet.

12 June   Lieutenant (jg) Mainrad A. Schur, flying a DT-2 Douglas torpedo plane powered with a Liberty engine, set three world records at San Diego, Calif., for Class C seaplanes with a duration mark of 11 hours, 16 minutes, 59 seconds, a distance mark of 792.25 miles, and a speed of 70.49 mph for 1,000 kilometers.

13 June   At San Diego, Calif., Lieutenant Ralph A. Ofstie, in a TS seaplane equipped with a Lawrance J-1 engine, set world speed records for Class C seaplanes for 100 and 200 kilometers with speeds of 121.95 and 121.14 mph, respectively.

21 July   The Bureau of Aeronautics established a policy of assigning experimental airplanes to fleet squadrons for operational evaluation before adopting them as service types.

13 August   Constructive action towards building an effective aviation branch of the Naval Reserve Force was marked by the establishment of Naval Aviation Reserve Units at Fort Hamilton, N.Y., and Squantum, Mass.

4 September   *Shenandoah* (ZR-1) made its first flight at NAS Lakehurst, N.J., Captain Frank R. McCrary commanding.

28 September   U.S. Navy aircraft won first and second place in the international seaplane race for the Schneider Cup at Cowes, England, and in winning established a new world record for seaplanes with a speed of 169.89 miles per hour for 200 kilometers. Lieutenant David Rittenhouse, the new record holder, marked up 177.38 miles per hour for the race and Lieutenant Rutledge Irvine placed second with 173.46 mph. Both were flying CR-3s equipped with Curtiss D-12 engines.

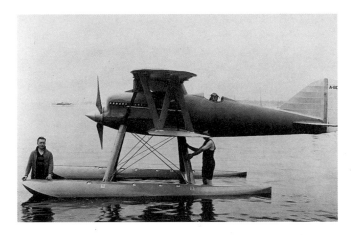

CR-3, winner of 1923 Schneider Trophy Race 175426

6 October   Navy planes swept the Pulitzer Trophy Race at St. Louis, Mo., taking the first four places all at faster speeds than the winning time of the previous year. Both first and second place bettered the world's speed mark, with the winner Lieutenant Alford J. Williams in an R2C, setting the new records for 100 and 200 kilometers at 243.812 and 243.673 mph, respectively.

2 November   Lieutenant Harold J. Brow, flying an R2C-1 equipped with a Curtiss D-12 engine, established a world speed record at Mitchel Field, Long Island, N.Y., averaging 259.47 mph in four flights over the 3-kilometer course.

Al Williams' R2C won the 1923 Pulitzer Race 458279

1923—Continued

4 November   Lieutenant Alford J. Williams, flying an R2C-1 equipped with a Curtiss D-12 engine, raised the world speed record to 266.59 mph at Mitchel Field, Long Island, N.Y., bettering the record set by Lieutenant Harold J. Brow only two days before.

5 November   A series of tests, designed to show the feasibility of stowing a seaplane aboard the submarine S-l and launching it, were completed at the Hampton Roads Naval Base, Va. A crew from *Langley,* supervised by Lieutenant Commander Virgil C. Griffin, had cooperated with the S-l's Commanding Officer, Lieutenant Powel M. Rhea, in carrying out the tests which involved removing a disassembled Martin MS-1 from a tank on the submarine, assembling it, and launching it by submerging the submarine.

6 November   Lieutenant Alford J. Williams, in an R2C-1, climbed to 5,000 feet in 1 minute, bettering the best previously reported climb of 2,000 feet in the same time.

16 November   The Bureau of Aeronautics directed that all aircraft attached to vessels of the fleet be overhauled once every six months.

3 December   The establishment of a special service squadron, for the purpose of developing long-distance scouting planes, was approved by the Chief of Naval Operations. The squadron, designated VS Squadron 3, was initially based at NAS Anacostia, D.C., and commanded by Lieutenant Commander Charles P. Mason.

7 December   The Bureau of Aeronautics established a new designation system for catapults whereby a type letter, "A" for compressed air, "P" for powder, and "F" for flywheel, indicated the energy source while major design modifications were indicated by Mark numbers. Under this system, the compressed air, turntable catapult demonstrated at the Naval Aircraft Factory and installed aboard *Maryland* (BB 46) was designated type "A" Mark I, and *Langley's* catapult was designated type "A", Mark III. This designation system was subsequently extended, with some modification, to include other energy sources, notably the type letter "H" for hydraulic catapults.

1924

3 January   VT Squadron 20, commanded by Lieutenant Commander George D. Murray, sailed from San Diego, Calif., on board *Vega* (AK 17) for transfer to the Philippine Islands to operate from *Ajax* (AG 15) as the first air unit of the Asiatic Fleet.

4 February   The Bureau of Aeronautics directed that the practice of striping or camouflaging aircraft be discontinued and that by 1 July all aircraft should be painted in accordance with the prescribed naval gray except stretched fabric on wing and tail and some fuselage surfaces which were to be aluminum. The one exception permitted was that all squadrons of a station, force, or fleet could uniformly paint the upper wing chrome yellow or other color to increase visibility in case of forced landing.

26 February   VS Squadron 3 was authorized to fly one division of CS seaplanes from Anacostia, D.C., to

Al Williams, speed record holder with R3C-1 459589

1924—Continued

Miami, Fla, and Key West, Fla., and return, for the purpose of conducting service tests under actual operating conditions.

8 March The race for the Curtiss Marine Trophy at Miami was won by Lieutenant L. V. Grant in a Vought VE-7, at an average speed of 116.1 mph.

21 March The Bureau of Aeronautics directed that service parachutes be used by all personnel on all flights.

21 April The Bureau of Aeronautics requested the Bureau of Steam Engineering to investigate development of a single-wave radio sending and receiving set, suitable for installation in fighting planes, with a 20-mile sending radius, and powered by a small battery or engine driven generator.

2 May A DT plane, carrying a dummy torpedo, was launched by catapult from *Langley,* at anchor in Pensacola Bay, Fla. The plane was piloted by Lieutenant W. M. Dillion and also carried Lieutenant Stanton H. Wooster as gunnery officer.

19 June The Bureau of Ordnance issued a contract to the Ford Instrument Company for development of an antiaircraft director for shipboard fire control.

22–23 June Lieutenants Frank W. Wead and John D. Price, in a Curtiss CS-2 equipped with one Wright T-3 Tornado engine, set five world records for Class C sea-planes at Anacostia, D.C.; one for distance with 963.123 miles; one for duration for 13 hours, 23 minutes, 15 seconds; and three for speeds of 73.41 mph for 500 kilometers, 74.27 mph for 1,000 kilometers, and 74.17 mph for 1,500 kilometers.

24 June A technical order was issued which prescribed the external color of naval aircraft. Overall color was to be aluminum enamel with clear varnish on wooden spars and struts. Naval yellow enamel was to be used on the top surfaces of upper wings of training planes and yellow or other high visibility color could similarly be applied to all aircraft of any station, force or fleet.

11–12 July Lieutenants Frank W. Wead and John D. Price, flying a CS-2 equipped with a Wright Tornado engine, broke world records for Class C seaplanes at Ana-costia, D.C., with new marks for distance of 994.19 miles and for duration of 14 hours, 53 minutes, 44 seconds.

23 July The Bureau of Aeronautics announced that it was assuming cognizance of pigeon boxes for use in aircraft.

8 August *Shenandoah* (ZR-1) secured to the mooring mast on *Patoka* (AO 9) while underway in Narragansett Bay, remained moored to the ship during her passage to anchor off Jamestown, R.I., and cast off next day, almost 24 hours later. This was the first use of the mooring mast erected aboard ship to facilitate airship operations with the fleet.

In first use of mooring mast aboard ship, the airship, Shenandoah, moored to Patoka, August 8, 1924 19-N-9670

1924—Continued

11 August Observation planes from the light cruiser *Raleigh* (CL 7) took off from the water near the Arctic Circle on the first of several reconnaissance flights over the Greenland coast from Angmagsalik to Cape Farewell to locate suitable emergency landing areas for the Army flyers, then crossing the Atlantic, via Iceland, on the last leg of their round-the-world flight.

15 August In the first use of rigid airships with the fleet, *Shenandoah* (ZR-1) departed Lakehurst, N.J., to take part in a Scouting Fleet problem 300 miles at sea. She discovered the "enemy" fleet but heavy rains forced her early retirement to base where she arrived 17 August after 40 hours in the air.

1 September A parachute school opened at NAS Lakehurst, N.J., to train enlisted men in the care, operation, maintenance and testing of parachutes—the first school of its kind in the Navy.

15 September An N-9 seaplane, equipped with radio control and without a human pilot aboard, was flown on a 40-minute flight at the Naval Proving Grounds, Dahlgren, Va. Although the aircraft sank from damage sustained while landing, this test demonstrated the practicability of radio control of aircraft.

18 September The repair ship *Medusa* (AR 1) was commissioned and a section of VO-2, consisting of two officers and 20 men, was organized and assigned as a ship-plane repair detail to support the operations of VO-1.

10 October A CS-2 seaplane, piloted by Lieutenants Andrew Crinkley and Rossmore D. Lyon, landed at Quantico, Va., after a continuous flight from NAS Anacostia, D.C., of 20 hours, 28 minutes, and 1,460 miles logged. Although the flight exceeded world records for endurance and distance, it was not officially timed and therefore not an official record.

15 October The rigid airship ZR-3 was delivered at NAS Lakehurst, N.J., completing a 5,000-mile flight from Friedrichshafen, Germany, in 81 hours under the command of Dr. Hugo Eckener, and with prospective commanding officer, Captain George W. Steele aboard.

16 October Emergency use of parachute—Following a mid-air collision over Coronado, Calif., Gunner William M. Coles, USN, of VF Squadron 1, made a successful emergency parachute jump from his JN.

25 October When all foreign entrants withdrew from the Schneider Cup Race to be held at Bayshore Park, Md., the United States agreed to cancel the race rather than win by a flyaway. Instead, the Navy staged a series of record attempts in which the scheduled contestants and other naval aircraft put 17 world records in the book for Class C seaplanes as follows: Lieutenant George T. Cuddihy, in a CR-3 powered with a Curtiss D-12 engine, broke a maximum world speed record of almost two years standing with 188.078 mph.

Lieutenant Ralph A. Ofstie, in a CR-3 with a Curtiss D-12 engine, broke world speed records for 100, 200 and 500 kilometers with marks of 178.25 mph for the 100 and 200 and 161.14 for the 500.

Lieutenant George R. Henderson, in a PN-7 flying boat equipped with two Wright T-2 engines, set four records for speed over 100 and 200 kilometers with loads of 250 and 500 kilograms, all at 78.507 mph; and four records with a useful load of 1,000 kilograms with a speed of 78.507 mph for 100 and 200 kilometers, a distance record of 248.55 miles and a duration record of 5 hours, 28 minutes, 43 seconds.

Lieutenant Osborne B. Hardison, also in a PN-7, set world records for speed over 100 kilometers, and for distance with a useful load of 1,500 kilograms at 68.4 mph and 62.137 miles, and three more with a useful load of 2,000 kilograms in speed for 100 kilometers at 68.4 mph, distance 62.137 miles, and duration 1 hour, 49 minutes, 11.9 seconds.

25 October The rigid airship *Shenandoah* (ZR-1), commanded by Lieutenant Commander Zachary Lansdowne, landed at NAS Lakehurst, N.J., completing a round-trip transcontinental cruise that began on 7 October and covered 9,317 miles in 258 hours of flight. The trip included stops at Fort Worth, Tex., San Diego, Calif., and a stay of 11 days on the west coast, including a flight to Camp Lewis at Tacoma, Wash.

11 November Lieutenant Dixie Kiefer piloted a plane in a successful night catapult launch from *California* (BB 44) at anchor in San Diego, Calif., harbor. The launch at 9:46 p.m. was aided only by searchlights trained about 1,000 yards ahead.

14 November Qualifications for Flight Surgeons were agreed upon by the Chiefs of the Bureau of Aeronautics and the Bureau of Medicine and Surgery, which required medical officers to complete the three-month course at the U.S. Army School of Aviation Medicine and three months of satisfactory service with a Naval Aviation unit before designation. The requirement that a medical officer so qualified also make flights in aircraft was limited to emergencies and the desire of the officer.

1924—Continued

17 November   *Langley* reported for duty with the Battle Fleet, thereby ending over two years in experimental status and becoming the first operational aircraft carrier in the U.S. Navy. On 1 December she also became the flagship of Aircraft Squadrons, Battle Fleet.

25 November   Mrs. Calvin Coolidge christened the ZR-3 as *Los Angeles* (ZR-3) at NAS Anacostia, D.C. As a part of the ceremony it was commissioned a ship of the Fleet, with Captain George W. Steele commanding.

13 December   The NM-1, an all-metal airplane, was flown at the Naval Aircraft Factory. This aircraft was designed and built for the purpose of developing metal construction for naval airplanes and was intended for Marine Corps expeditionary use.

14 December   A powder catapult was successfully demonstrated in the launching of a Martin MO-1 observation plane from the forward turret of the battleship *Mississippi* (BB 41) at Bremerton, Wash. The aircraft was piloted by Lieutenant L. C. Hayden with Lieutenant William M. Fellers as passenger. Following this demonstration, the powder catapult was widely used on battleships and cruisers.

1925

17 January   A special board, headed by the Chief of Naval Operations, Admiral Edward W. Eberle, submitted its report to the Secretary of the Navy. Appointed on 23 September 1924 to consider recent developments in aviation and to recommend a policy for the development of the Navy in its various branches, the board devoted most of its discussion to the importance of the battleship, but in its recommendations gave prominence to aviation. For this branch, it recommended that carriers be built up to treaty limits, that *Lexington* and *Saratoga* be completed expeditiously, that a new 23,000-ton carrier be laid down, and that a progressive aircraft building program be established to insure a complete complement of modern planes for the fleet. In regard to personnel, the board recommended expansion of aviation offerings at the Naval Academy, assignment of all qualified academy graduates to aviator or observer training after two years of sea duty, and the establishment of a definite policy governing assignment of officers to aviation.

22 January   VF Squadron 2, the first trained to operate as a squadron from a carrier, began landing practice on *Langley* off San Diego, Calif. This was also the beginning of the *Langley* operations as a unit of Aircraft Squadrons, Battle Fleet.

4 February   Commanding officers were made responsible for determining when aircraft attached to vessels of the fleet required overhaul, and an earlier order of 1923 was canceled which had required complete overhaul of such aircraft every six months.

2–11 March   Fleet Problem V, the first to incorporate aircraft carrier operations, was conducted off the coast of Lower California. Although the air activity of *Langley* was limited to scouting in advance of the Black Fleet movement to Guadalupe Island, the performance was convincing enough for the Commander in Chief, Admiral Robert E. Coontz, to recommend that completion of *Lexington* and *Saratoga* be speeded up as much as possible. The Admiral also recommended that steps be taken to insure development of planes of greater durability, dependability and radius, and that catapult and recovery gear be further improved. He also reported that experience now permitted catapulting of planes from battleships and cruisers as routine.

11 March   Routine aerological sounding flights— NAS Anacostia, D.C., reported arrangements were being made for daily weather flights to an altitude of 10,000 feet to obtain weather data and to test upper-air sounding equipment. These flights commenced in mid-April, and the following February the schedule was extended to include Saturday, Sunday and holiday flights, with the altitude being increased to 15,000 feet.

13 March   Rear Admiral William A. Moffett was appointed for a second tour of duty as Chief of the Bureau of Aeronautics.

2 April   The feasibility of using flush-deck catapults to launch landplanes was demonstrated by catapulting a DT-2 landplane, piloted by Lieutenant Commander Charles P. Mason, with Lieutenant Braxton Rhodes as passenger, from the *Langley,* moored to its dock in San Diego, Calif.

8 April   Lieutenant John D. Price, piloting a VF-1 plane, made a night landing on *Langley,* at sea off San Diego, Calif., and was followed on board by Lieutenants Delbert L. Conley, Aldolphus W. Gorton and Rossmore D. Lyon. Except for an accidental landing on the night of 5 February when Lieutenant Harold J. Brow stalled while practicing night approaches, these were the first night landings made on board a U.S. carrier.

1925—Continued

8 April Almost two years after the special aviation uniform had been abolished, new uniforms of forestry green for winter and khaki for summer were authorized for Naval Aviators, Observers, and other officers on duty involving flying. Although there were minor modifications to the original design in later years, this uniform, in khaki, was adopted for the entire Navy in 1941.

1–2 May Lieutenants Clarence H. Schildhauer and James R. Kyle, on a test flight over Philadelphia, Pa., of the PN-9 manufactured at the Naval Aircraft Factory, broke the world endurance record for Class C seaplanes, remaining in the air for 28 hours, 35 minutes, 27 seconds. The plane, a metalhulled flying boat equipped with two Packard engines, was used by Commander John Rodgers later in the year on his record flight toward Hawaii.

Rodger's PN-9 on mainland to Hawaii flight, forced down after record distance, sailed 450 miles to Kaui 426936

5 May The Secretary of the Navy approved reorganization of certain departments at the Naval Academy as required to make aviation an integral part of the curriculum; the establishment of a program, beginning with the Class of 1926, to give three months of special ground and flight instruction to all midshipmen; and additional instruction as necessary to qualify each graduate as an aviator or observer during the first two years after graduation.

29 May The standard color of naval aircraft was modified: hulls and floats of seaplanes were to be painted navy gray; wings, fuselages, landing gear, etc., aluminum color; and the top surface of upper wings, stabilizers and elevators, orange-yellow.

17 June The Naval Air Detail, under Lieutenant Commander Richard E. Byrd of the MacMillan Expedition, sailed from Boston with three Loening amphibians aboard *Peary* (DD 340). *Bowdoin* (a civilian research ship) joined *Peary* (DD 340) off Wiscasset, Maine, and after a 3,000-mile voyage, the expedition reached Etah in North Greenland on 1 August to begin an aerial exploration of the area that covered 30,000 square miles before the end of the month.

1 July When a law, enacted 28 February, became effective, the Naval Aviation Reserve began to organize into 10 squadrons of four divisions each. Authorized squadron complements for each of three scouting and three bombing squadrons were established at 40 officers and 130 men, and for each of four fighting squadrons at 18 officers and 20 men.

1 September Commander John Rodgers, Lieutenant Byron J. Connell and a crew of three in a PN-9,

A traditional Hawaiian greeting to Rodgers and crew at Kaui 184669

1925—Continued

attempting a flight from San Francisco, Calif., to Honolulu, T.H. (Territory of Hawaii) were forced down by lack of fuel shortly after 4:00 in the afternoon. Lost at sea for 10 days in spite of extensive air and sea search, Commander Rodgers and his crew rigged sail from the wing fabric and set course for Kaui Island. After covering about 450 miles by sail, they were sighted on 10 September by the submarine R-4, 10 miles from their goal. The 1,841.12 statute miles, flown from 31 August to their forced landing was accepted by the F.A.I. as a new world airline distance record for Class C seaplanes that remained unbeaten for almost five years.

3 September   The rigid dirigible *Shenandoah* (ZR-1) was torn apart in a severe line squall before daylight over Byesville, Ohio. The control car and after section of the hull fell directly to the ground, while the forward section with seven men aboard free-ballooned for an hour before they landed safely 12 miles from the scene of the crash. In all there were 29 survivors, but 14 were killed including Lieutenant Commander Zachary Lansdowne, the commanding officer.

29 September   The Chief of Naval Operations directed that all heavier-than-air Naval Aviators, not already qualified to pilot landplanes, be given training in landplane operation.

3 October   In view of the need for an accumulation of upper air data for improved weather forecasting, the Bureau of Aeronautics requested that aircraft squadron flagships take upper air soundings twice a day when at sea.

5 October   VJ-1B, first of the Utility Squadrons, was formed at San Diego, Calif., from personnel of VS-2B and assigned to Aircraft Squadrons, Battle Fleet. Lieutenant John F. Moloney was the first commanding officer.

26 October   The two Navy entries in the Schneider Cup Race at Bay Shore Park, Md., flown by Lieutenants George Cuddihy and Ralph A. Ofstie, were forced out of the race on the last lap with engine trouble.

27 October   Oleo shock-absorbing landing gear for aircraft was reported in use on NB-1, FB-1, UO-1, SC-2 and new bombing planes being constructed by the Naval Aircraft Factory, Douglas and Boeing.

30 November   The President's Aircraft Board, better known as the Morrow Board, after its senior member, submitted its report to President Calvin Coolidge. On the basis of views expressed in extended hearings by prominent civilian and military leaders, the board made recommendations in regard to the aviation industry and military aviation that were of far reaching importance and influenced a number of legislative actions taken in the following months. Its recommendations against a separate air force and in favor of representation for aviation on operational commands and high level administrative offices, and its recognition of the need for a policy of long-range procurement and standard replacement schedules were among those of special interest to the Navy.

14 December   The Lampert Committee, set up on 24 March 1924 by the House of Representatives as the Select Committee of Inquiry into the Operations of the United States Air Services, filed its report. It favored establishment of a Department of National Defense and an adequate representation of aviation in the high military councils. It showed particular concern over the state of the aircraft industry and recommended that the government cease competing with the industry in the production of aircraft, engines and accessories; that the requirement of competitive bidding be abolished in favor of other restrictions promoting the best interests of the Government; that the War and Navy Departments each spend $10 million annually for new flying equipment; and that a five-year construction and procurement program be carried out.

18 December   Competitive trials of Consolidated, Curtiss and Huff Daland aircraft, designed as land, sea gunnery and training planes were completed at NAS Anacostia, D.C. These trials led to the procurement of the Consolidated NY series of training planes which continued in use into the 1930s.

1926

21 April   The Secretary of the Navy directed that beginning with the Class of 1926, all graduates of the Naval Academy be given a course of 25 hours of flight instruction during their first year of sea duty and that, for the purpose of providing this instruction, flight schools be established at the naval air stations at Hampton Roads, Va., and San Diego, Calif.

9 May   Lieutenant Commander Richard E. Byrd and Aviation Pilot Floyd Bennett, flying a trimotor Fokker named the Josephine Ford, made the first flight over the North Pole, reaching it at 9:03 GCT. After circling the Pole, they returned to base at Kings Bay, Spitzbergen, Norway completing the round trip in 15 and one half hours.

1926—Continued

F6C-1 Curtiss fighter powered by D-12 engine 460634

14 May The Curtiss Marine Trophy Race, held off Hains Point, D.C., over the Potomac, was won by Lieutenant Thomas P. Jeter in a Curtiss F6C-1 Hawk with a speed of 130.94 mph.

6 June The last elements of the Alaskan Aerial Survey Expedition departed Seattle, Wash., for Alaska. The expedition, under command of Lieutenant Ben H. Wyatt, was composed of the tender *Gannet* (AM 41), the barge YF 88 housing a photo lab, and three Loening amphibians. The work of the expedition, which extended through the summer and into September, was performed in cooperation with the Department of the Interior for early aerial mapping of Alaska.

16 June The Bureau of Aeronautics reported that the emergency barricade on *Langley* had successfully prevented landing aircraft from crashing into planes parked on the flight deck.

24 June An Act of Congress, implementing the recommendations of the Morrow Board pertaining to the Navy, provided that command of aviation stations, schools and tactical flight units be assigned to Naval Aviators; that command of aircraft carriers and tenders be assigned to either Naval Aviators or Naval Aviation Observers; that the office of an Assistant Secretary of the Navy be created to foster naval aeronautics; and that a five year aircraft program be set up under which

the number on hand would be increased to reach 1,000 useful planes.

1 July Provisions of a law enacted 24 June became effective, establishing a requirement that the number of enlisted pilots be not less than 30 percent of the total number of pilots on active duty in the Navy.

2 July The Distinguished Flying Cross was authorized by Congress as an award for acts of heroism or extraordinary achievement in aerial flight by any member of the armed services including the National Guard and the Reserves. The award was retroactive to 6 April 1917.

10 July Edward P. Warner took the oath of office as the first Assistant Secretary of the Navy for Aeronautics.

First Assistant Secretary of the Navy for Air E. P. Warner

1926—Continued

28 July The submarine S-1, commanded by Lieutenant C. B. Momsen, surfaced and launched a Cox-Klemin XS-2 seaplane, flown by Lieutenant D. C. Allen. It also recovered the aircraft and submerged completing the first cycle of operations in a series of tests investigating the feasibility of basing aircraft on submarines.

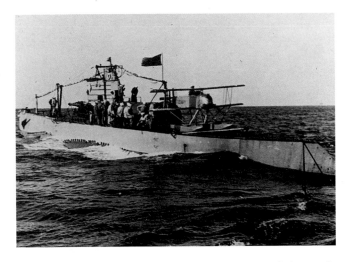

S-1 demonstrates the feasibility of operating aircraft from submarines in tests with XS-2 seaplane, 1926 1053777

9 August In a day of tests to determine the speed with which aircraft could be operated at sea, pilots of VF Squadron 1 completed 127 landings aboard *Langley*. As a result of the experience gained, the same squadron later landed 12 planes in 21 minutes under the emergency conditions created when the ship ran into a heavy mist.

18 August A contract was let to the Aircraft Development Corporation, Detroit, Mich., for a metal-clad airship designated ZMC-2. The descriptive term "metal-clad" resulted from the fact that the ZMC-2's lightly framed hull was covered with gas-tight stressed-aluminum skin. It was also to be pressure-rigid in that the shape of the hull was to be maintained by positive internal gas pressure.

27 August Commander John Rodgers, Naval Aviator No. 2, on a flight from NAS Anacostia, D.C., crashed in the Delaware River near the Naval Aircraft Factory dock and received injuries from which he died on the same day.

22 October In a display of tactics developed by VF Squadron 2, Lieutenant Commander Frank D. Wagner led the F6C-2 Curtiss fighters in a simulated attack on the heavy ships of the Pacific Fleet as they sortied from San Pedro. Coming down in almost vertical dives from 12,000 feet at the exact time of which the fleet had been forewarned, the squadron achieved complete surprise and so impressed fleet and ship commanders with the effectiveness of their spectacular approach that there was unanimous agreement that such an attack would succeed over any defense. This was the first fleet demonstration of dive-bombing and although the tactic had been worked out by the demonstrating squadron in an independently initiated project, the obvious nature of the solution to the problem of effective bomb delivery was evident in that the same tactic was similarly and simultaneously being developed by VF Squadron 5 on the east coast.

13 November Lieutenant Christian F. Schilt, USMC, flying an R3C-2, took second in the Schneider Cup Race at Hampton Roads, Va., with an average speed of 231.363 mph. This was the last Navy participation in international racing competition.

19 November *Maryland* (BB 46) conducted experimental firing with the Mark XIX antiaircraft fire control system which had been developed by the Ford Instrument Company and which incorporated a stabilized line of sight to aid in tracking approaching aircraft.

13 December Rear Admiral Joseph M. Reeves, commanding Aircraft Squadrons, Battle Fleet, reported on the results of the first dive bombing exercise ("light bombing," as it was then called) to be conducted in the formal fleet gunnery competition. One Marine and two Navy fighter squadrons and three Navy observation squadrons participated. The Marine and Navy fighters made 45 degree dives from 2,500 feet and at

FB-5 fitted for longitudinal arresting wires 458533

1926—Continued

an altitude of 400 feet, dropped 25 pound fragmentation bombs; observation squadrons similarly attacked from 1,000 feet. Pilots of VF-2, commanded by Lieutenant Commander Frank D. Wagner and flying F6Cs and FB-5s, scored 19 hits with 45 bombs on a target 100 feet by 45 feet. The uses visualized for this tactic included disabling or demolishing flight decks, destroying enemy aircraft in flight, attacking exposed personnel on ship or shore and attacking light surface craft and submarines.

1927

1 January A flight test section was established as a separate department at NAS Anacostia, D.C., with Lieutenant George R. Henderson in charge.

1 January To test the feasibility of using enlisted pilots in fleet squadrons, VF Squadron 2, manned with four Naval Aviators and 10 Aviation Pilots, was established at San Diego, Calif., Lieutenant Commander James M. Shoemaker commanding.

18 January Lieutenant Commander John R. Poppen, MC, reported for duty in charge of the Aviation Section of the Naval Medical School, Washington, D.C., marking the beginning of a three month period during which the entire resources of the school were devoted to intensive instruction in aviation medicine. The institution of this program also marked the beginning of

Flight Surgeon training in the Navy and the discontinuance of an interservice agreement in effect since 1922, by which Navy Medical Officers were trained in this specialty at the Army School for Flight Surgeons.

9 March The first passenger transport, the JR-1 trimotor, was purchased from the Ford Motor Company following a demonstration at NAS Anacostia, D.C.

14 April Lieutenant George R. Henderson, flying a Vought O2U Corsair equipped with a Pratt & Whitney Wasp engine, broke the world altitude record for Class C seaplanes with a useful load of 500 kilograms, reaching 22,178 feet over Washington, D.C.

23 April Lieutenant Steven W. Callaway, flying a Vought O2U Corsair at Hampton Roads, Va., set a new 100-kilometer world speed record for Class C seaplanes with a 500 kilogram useful load, at 147.263 mph.

30 April Lieutenant James D. Barner, flying a Vought O2U Corsair at Hampton Roads, Va., broke the 500-kilometer world speed record for Class C seaplanes carrying a useful load of 500 kilograms with a speed of 136.023 mph.

5 May Lieutenant Carleton C. Champion took off from Hampton Roads, Va., in a Wright Apache, equipped with a Pratt & Whitney Wasp engine and NACA supercharger, and climbed to an altitude of 33,455 feet, breaking the existing world record for Class C seaplanes by better than 3,000 feet.

Battleship-based O2Us (Vought Corsairs) of 1920s 426930

1927—Continued

21 May   Lieutenant Rutledge Irvine, in a Vought O2U Corsair equipped with a Pratt & Whitney Wasp engine, established a world record for Class C Seaplanes for 1,000 kilometers at Hampton Roads, Va., with a speed of 130.932 mph.

23 May   A major advance in the transition from wooden to metal aircraft structures resulted from the Naval Aircraft Factory's report that the corrosion of aluminum by salt water—hitherto a serious obstacle to the use of aluminum alloys on naval aircraft—could be decreased by the application of anodic coatings.

27 May   Dive bombing came under official study as the Chief of Naval Operations ordered the Commander in Chief, Battle Fleet, to conduct tests to evaluate its effectiveness against moving targets. Carried out by VF Squadron 5S in late summer and early fall, the results of these tests generated wide discussion of the need for special aircraft and units, which led directly to the development of equipment and adoption of the tactic as a standard method of attack.

1 July   A new system of squadron designation became effective providing, in addition to the standard class designation letters and identification number, a suffix letter to indicate the fleet, force, or unit to which the squadron was assigned. Under this system VF-1B was Fighting Squadron 1 of Battle Force.

1 July   The practice of sending Naval Reserve aviation officers to one year of training duty with the fleet after graduation from Pensacola, Fla., began with the assignment of the first group of 50 newly commissioned ensigns.

4 July   Lieutenant Carleton C. Champion, flying a Wright Apache powered with a Pratt & Whitney engine, reached 37,995 feet over Anacostia, D.C., thereby breaking his own world altitude record for Class C seaplanes, established 2 months earlier. This height exceeded any previously reached by heavier-than-air aircraft.

8 July   Lieutenant Byron J. Connell and Naval Aviaton Pilot S. R. Pope, flying a PN-10 equipped with two Packard engines, set new world duration and distance records for Class C seaplanes with a useful load of 2,000 kilograms, and a new world duration record with a 1,000 kilogram load, on the same flight out of San Diego, logging 11 hours 7 minutes 18 seconds in the air and a distance of 947.705 miles.

17 July   Major Ross E. Rowell, USMC, led a flight of five DHs in a strafing and dive bombing attack against bandit forces surrounding a garrison of U.S. Marines at Ocotal, Nicaragua. Although instances of diving attacks had occurred during World War I and Marine Corps pilots had used the same technique in Haiti in 1919, this attack was made according to doctrine developed in training and is generally considered as the first organized dive bombing attack in combat.

25 July   Three weeks after breaking the seaplane altitude record, Lieutenant Carleton C. Champion took off from Anacostia, D.C., in a Wright Apache rigged as a landplane and reached 38,419 feet, establishing a new world record that stood for 2 years.

15–16 August   Lieutenants Byron J. Connell and Herbert C. Rodd, flying out of San Diego in a PN-10 patrol plane equipped with two Packard engines, broke three world records for Class C seaplanes; distance with a 500-kilogram load, and duration with a 500-kilogram load, with marks of 1,569.0 miles and 20 hours 45 minutes 40 seconds in the air.

18 August   Lieutenants Byron J. Connell and Herbert C. Rodd took off from San Diego, Calif., in a PN-10 flying boat with a useful load of 7,726 pounds, and climbed to 2,000 meters to break the world record for the greatest payload carried to that altitude by a Class C seaplane.

16 November   *Saratoga,* first carrier and fifth ship of the Navy to bear the name, was placed in commission at Camden, N.J., Captain Harry E. Yarnell commanding.

14 December   *Lexington,* first carrier and fourth ship of the Navy to carry the name, was commissioned at Quincy, Mass., Captain Albert W. Marshall commanding.

1928

5 January   The first takeoff and landing on *Lexington* was made by Lieutenant Alfred M. Pride in a UO-1 as the ship moved from the Fore River Plant to the Boston Navy Yard in Massachussetts.

6 January   Lieutenant Christian F. Schilt, USMC, flying an O2U-1, made the first of 10 flights in which he landed in a street of the village of Quilahi, Nicaragua, and evacuated 18 wounded officers and men while under hostile fire. For this feat, which he accomplished in three successive days, Schilt was awarded the Medal of Honor.

1928—Continued

Saratoga with a deck-load of aircraft USN 1027066

1928—Continued

Schilt gets medal of honor USMC 521201

11 January   The first takeoff and landing on *Saratoga* was made by her Air Officer, Commander Marc A. Mitscher in a UO-1.

27 January   *Los Angeles* (ZR-3) made a successful landing on *Saratoga* at sea off Newport, R.I., and remained on board long enough to transfer passengers and take on fuel, water and supplies.

1 February   Joint Army-Navy nomenclature for aircraft engines became effective whereby standard type names were assigned to engines based upon the cubic inches of piston displacement—to the nearest ten. Under this scheme, the Vee type Curtiss D-12 engine received the standard type name Curtiss V-1150 and the air-cooled radial J-5 Whirlwind became the first Wright R-790.

27 February   Commander Theodore C. Ellyson, the first Naval Aviator, and Lieutenant Commander Hugo Schmidt and Lieutenant Rogers Ransehounsen, crashed to their deaths in a Loening amphibian in Chesapeake Bay while on a night flight from Norfolk, Va., to Annapolis, Md.

28 February   An order was issued limiting the application of standard type names for aircraft engines to air-cooled engines of recent design. For example, the standard type name, Curtiss V-1150, was abolished and this engine was reassigned its earlier D-12 designation. On the other hand, the designation Wright R-790 was retained with provisions for use of R-790-A to indicate a major modification while earlier models of this engine kept the old designations, J-2, J-3 and J-4.

28 February   The contract for the XPY-1 flying boat was issued to the Consolidated Aircraft Corporation. This aircraft, which was designed for alternate installation of two or three engines, was the first large monoplane flying boat procured by the Navy, and was the initial configuration which evolved into the PBY Catalina.

UO-1 makes landing on Saratoga, CV 3 424479

1928—Continued

3–5 May   Lieutenants Arthur Gavin and Zeus Soucek, in a PN-12 equipped with two Wright Cyclone engines, set the world duration record for Class C seaplanes in a flight of 36 hours 1 minute over Philadelphia, Pa.

11 May   An Act of Congress provided that duty performed by officers assigned to airships which required them to make regular and frequent aerial flights, could be certified by the Secretary as service equivalent to sea duty.

19 May   Major Charles A. Lutz, USMC, won the Curtiss Marine Trophy Race at Anacostia, D.C., in an F6C-3, making a speed of 157.6 mph over the 100-mile course.

25–26 May   Lieutenants Zeus Soucek and Lisle Maxson, in a PN-12 powered by two Wright engines, set world marks for Class C seaplanes with a 1,000-kilogram useful load: speed over 2,000 kilometers at 80.288 mph; distance at 1,243.20 miles; and duration at 17 hours 55 minutes 13.6 seconds.

12 June   *Lexington* anchored in Lahaina Roads, Hawaii, at the end of a speed run from San Pedro, Calif., to Honolulu, Hawaii, that broke all existing records for the distance with an elapsed time of 72 hours and 34 minutes.

26 June   Lieutenant Arthur Gavin, piloting a PN-12 powered with two Pratt & Whitney Hornet engines, set a world altitude record of 15,426 feet at Philadelphia, Pa., for Class C seaplanes with a payload of 2,000 kilograms.

27 June   Lieutenant Arthur Gavin, in a PN-12 equipped with two 525-hp Pratt & Whitney engines, made a world record altitude flight of 19,593 feet at Philadelphia for Class C seaplanes with a useful load of 1,000 kilograms.

30 June   A contract was issued to the Martin Company for development of the XT5M-1 "diving bomber," which, in a later production version, became the BM-1. This aircraft and the Naval Aircraft Factory's similar XT2N-1 were the first dive bombers designed to deliver a 1,000-pound bomb.

11–12 July   A PN-12, powered with two Pratt & Whitney engines and piloted by Lieutenant Aldolphus W. Gorton and Chief Boatswain Earl E. Reber, in a flight out of Philadelphia, Pa., set five world records for Class C seaplanes as follows: distance and speed for 2,000 kilometers with both 1,000- and 2,000-kilogram loads at 1,336 miles and 81.043 mph; and a duration mark of 16 hours, 39 minutes with a 2,000-kilogram load.

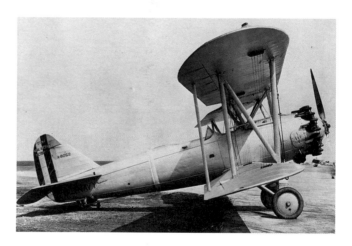

The XT2N-1 heavy dive bomber built by NAF 462160

Air races were featured in the 1920s. LT A. W. Gorton in TR-1 won the 1922 Curtiss Marine Trophy Race 65098

Lexington off Diamond Head, Lexington and Saratoga were constructed on battle cruiser hulls 416531

1928—Continued

25 July   The removal of bow and stern catapults on *Langley* was authorized since neither had been operated in three years.

6 October   Contracts for the 6,500,000 cubic foot rigid airships ZRS-4 and ZRS-5, subsequently christened *Akron* (ZRS-4) and *Macon* (ZRS-5), were let to the Goodyear Zeppelin Corporation, Akron, Ohio.

14 December   Fourteen fighting-plane radio telephone sets, operating on a frequency of 3,000 to 4,000 kilocycles and featuring an engine-driven generator, were shipped to VB-2B Squadron aboard the *Saratoga* for service tests. This equipment had been designed at NAS Anacostia, D.C., and manufactured at the Washington Navy Yard, D.C., in order to provide early evaluation of radio equipment in single-seat aircraft.

1929

16 January   Experience in night flying became a requirement for all heavier-than-air Naval Aviators and Naval Aviation Pilots of the Navy and Marine Corps. The Chief of Naval Operations ordered that prior to 1 July 1930, each qualified aviator pilot an aircraft on 10 hours of night flying involving at least 20 landings, and that student aviators meet the same requirement during the first year of their first duty assignment.

21 January   The Naval Proving Ground recommended that three prototypes of the production version of the Mark XI Norden bombsight be accepted and reported that on the first trial two of the three sights had placed a bomb within 25 feet of the target.

23–27 January   The carriers *Lexington* and *Saratoga* appeared in fleet exercises for the first time, attached to opposing forces in Fleet Problem IX. The most notable event of the Problem was the employment of *Saratoga* by the attacking Black Fleet to achieve its primary objective, the theoretical destruction of the Panama Canal. This carrier was detached from the main force and with an escorting cruiser, sent on a wide southward sweep before turning north to approach within striking distance of the canal. On the morning of the 26th, while it was still dark, she launched a strike group of 69 aircraft which arrived over the target undetected shortly after dawn and completed the theoretical destruction of the Miraflores and Pedro Miguel Locks without opposition. This demonstration made a profound impression on naval tacticians and in the 1930 maneuvers, a tactical unit, built around the aircraft carrier, appeared in force organization for the first time.

1 March   The Secretary directed that 33 officers of the Construction Corps and one officer of the line designated for Engineering Duty Only (EDO), with such additional Naval Constructors and EDO officers as the exigencies of the Navy permitted and the needs of the Bureau of Aeronautics required, be assigned to duty in the Aeronautical Organization.

1 March   In an effort to increase the proportion of officers completing the flight training course at Pensacola, Fla., and thereby reducing per capita training expense, the indoctrination courses at Hampton Roads, Va., and San Diego, Calif., were changed to elimination courses that would emphasize flight familiarization to determine aptitude and be open only to those meeting the physical requirements for aviators.

13 March   Rear Admiral William A. Moffett was appointed for a third consecutive tour as Chief of the Bureau of Aeronautics.

9 April   The feasibility of abandoning fore-and-aft wire arresting gear was confirmed in operations aboard *Langley*. These, and similar operations aboard *Saratoga* later that month, culminated a year of experimental development on the landing platform at Hampton Roads, Va., and led to the Secretary's authorizing, in September, the physical removal from the carriers of the fore-and-aft wires and associated equipment.

4–6 May   In winning the National Elimination Balloon Race with a flight from Pitt Stadium, Pittsburgh, Pa., to Savage Harbor, Prince Edward Island, Canada, Lieutenant Thomas G. W. Settle and Ensign Wilfred Bushnell won the Litchfield Trophy, qualified for the International Race to be held later in the year, and established world distance records for balloons in three categories from 1,601 to 4,000 cubic meters capacity with a flight of 952 miles.

8 May   The Bureau of Aeronautics announced the policy of providing all carrier airplanes with brakes and wheel type tail skids, following successful operations of a T4M so equipped in tests carried out aboard *Langley* in conjunction with the elimination of the fore-and-aft wire arresting gear.

8 May   Lieutenant Apollo Soucek, flying a Wright Apache equipped with a 425-hp Pratt & Whitney Wasp engine, set a new world record for Class C landplanes, reaching 39,140 feet over NAS Anacostia, D.C.

10 May   The Distinguished Flying Cross was awarded to Lieutenant Alford J. Williams by the Secretary of the

1929—Continued

Soucek in his Apache during the altitude record flight #80-G-416204

Navy for extraordinary achievement in aerial flight during March 1928 in which he studied the action of aircraft in violent maneuvers and inverted flight, and developed and applied principles of operation which contributed directly to safety in flight and the development of more accurate methods of testing the performance capabilities of aircraft.

25 May   The race for the Curtiss Marine Trophy, held at NAS Anacostia, D.C., was won by Lieutenant William G. Tomlinson in an XF7C-1 with a speed of 162.52 mph.

4 June   Lieutenant Apollo Soucek, in a Wright Apache equipped with a Pratt & Whitney Wasp engine, set the new world altitude mark for Class C seaplanes at 38,560 feet.

11 June   General standards for shielding aircraft engine ignition, essential to long range radio reception, were established at a conference held at the Bureau of Standards. Navy representatives included Lieutenant Commander Allen I. Price from the Bureau of Aeronautics and C. B. Mirick and L. A. Hyland from the Naval Research Laboratory. Basic techniques for shielding airborne radio from ignition interference had been developed by a naval radio group at the Bureau of Standards at the close of World War I and had per-

mitted some rather remarkable radio reception. Although some use of ignition shielding had been made throughout the 1920s, the results generally indifferent in that adequate shielding had brought with it undue cost in terms of aircraft maintenance or degradation of aircraft performance. At the June 1929 conference, spokesmen for aircraft, engine and radio fields and for magneto, sparkplug and cable specialties considered each other's problems sympathetically in order to develop practical shielding standards. Within the next year or so ignition shielding was generally applied to naval aircraft and a requirement for ignition shielding was included in the 1932 edition of the "General Specification for the Design and Construction of Airplanes for the United States Navy."

9 August   The ZMC-2, a metal clad 200,000-cubic foot airship built by Aircraft Development Corporation, made its first flight at Grosse Ile (Detroit) Airport, Mich. This airship, subsequently delivered to NAS Lakehurst, N.J., was utilized several years for training purposes.

20 August   Lieutenant Aldolphus W. Gorton, flying a specially equipped UO-1, made several successful hook-ons to the trapeze of *Los Angeles* (ZR-3) over NAS Lakehurst, N.J. Earlier attempts by the same pilot on 3 July were foiled when the hook failed to operate after making contact with the trapeze.

1929—Continued

29 November The first flight over the South Pole was made in a Ford trimotor named the Floyd Bennett. The flight was commanded by Commander Richard E. Byrd who also did the navigating. Bernt Balchen was pilot, Harold June was co-pilot and radio operator and Captain Ashley McKinley, USA, photographer. Takeoff from Little America on McMurdo Sound was at 10:29 p.m. on the 28th, New York time, and the Pole was reached at 8:55 a.m. on the 29th. The round trip, including a fuel stop on the return flight, required almost 19 hours.

27 December Based upon scores obtained with the new Norden gyrostabilized MARK XI bombsight during fleet exercises, the Bureau of Ordnance reported that the sight gave about 40 percent more hits than earlier bombsights.

The ZMC-2 metal-clad airship completed in 1929 21724

Lieutenant A. W. Gorton flying a Vought UO-1 makes hook-on landing on Los Angeles, a German-build rigid airship. 461642

F4Bs of Fighter Squadron VF-1B in formation 426947

Martin bomber drops torpedo 184698

The SC-1 scout bomber and torpedo plane 1053780

Ford trimotor, early pas-
senger transport, RR-5
5370

PD-1 patrol planes conducting high altitude horizontal bombing 184590

Airships J-4 and L-1 flying over Barnegat Bay 463784

Mine layer Aroostook, first ship assigned to aviation in the Pacific served as a seaplane tender 1919–1931 1053770

F-5L and DT aboard Teal, a Bird-class tender 1053769

T4M-1 is released from Langley arresting gear, fiddle bridges, in background, supported fore and aft wires 426932

PART 4

The Thirties

1930–1939

The Thirties began quietly with an international treaty extending previous agreements to reduce naval armament, but as the years passed they quietly dissipated as the nations of the world moved inexorably toward war.

In the United States, the period began with disturbing indications of a dark economic depression that soon became harsh reality. Forced by this circumstance to effect rigid economies, the expansion of Naval Aviation was slowed, the aircraft inventory was barely sufficient to equip operating units, research and development programs suffered, and operations were curtailed drastically. But as the nation began its program to recover prosperity through the initiation of public works, money was made available for more naval aircraft, for new ships and for modernizing naval air stations. The upward swing began.

In spite of the hardships, there were surprising gains in aviation technology. Engineers and aircraft manufacturers produced more dependable products, aircraft equipment and components were refined and improved, and aircraft performance rose sharply. Better radios of reduced size, more accurate bombsights, supercharged power plants, controllable-pitch propellers, efficient retractable landing gear and folding wings; all contributed to the improvement of aircraft performance and made airplanes better instruments of war. Hydraulic arresting gear and catapults were installed aboard aircraft carriers. Better methods of recovering battleship and cruiser observation planes were developed. The feasibility of instrument flight was demonstrated ashore and at sea. Radio controlled planes of dependable performance were put to practical use as targets for AA gunners. Engineers and designers learned more about the value of streamlining and clean design.

In operations, there was a change as whole squadrons began to turn in the record performances previously accomplished by individual pilots. Tactical innovations of the 1920s became fleet doctrine. Three new aircraft carriers joined the fleet, raising the operational total high enough to equip peacetime forces with a respectable seagoing air arm. Naval Aviation acquired broader respect and, as it achieved prominence in both fleet organization and operations, became a truly integrated arm of naval power.

Only in the field of lighter-than-air were there serious setbacks. Crashes of the *Akron* (ZRS-4) and the *Macon* (ZRS-5) sounded the death knell of the Navy's rigid airship program; and in spite of favorable reports from investigating committees, continued successes in Germany, and repeated recommendations as to its value in specialized operations; the rigid airship was finished. By association, the non-rigid airship almost followed it into oblivion.

As the decade drew to its close, the ominous rumblings of limited wars, that had echoed across both oceans throughout the period, grew louder. Naval expansion was authorized; the pilot training program was stepped up. Ships that would make history in World War II were designed and laid down. Aircraft that would operate from their decks, in the bold advance across the Pacific, were on the drawing boards; and some were getting their feel of the air. As the rumblings burst forth into the full force of a European war and the United States declared its neutrality; the Navy, strongly bolstered by aviation, patrolled the Atlantic seaboard in operations that were strangely similar to those which the same units would later perform under conditions of war.

1930

16 January *Lexington* completed a 30-day period in which she furnished electricity to the city of Tacoma, Wash., during an emergency arising from a failure of the city's power supply. The electricity supplied by the carrier totaled 4,251,160 kilowatt-hours.

29 January Hydraulic arresting gear, a type which eventually proved capable of great refinement to absorb the energy of heavy aircraft landing at high speeds, was reported to be under development at NAS Hampton Roads, Va.

1930—Continued

31 January Lieutenant Ralph S. Barnaby made a successful air-to-ground glider flight, dropping from the rigid dirigible *Los Angeles* (ZR-3) at an altitude of 3,000 feet over Lakehurst, N.J.

7 February Action to develop a means of recovering seaplanes by ships underway was initiated by a request from the Bureau of Aeronautics that the Naval Aircraft Factory study the problem and work up designs for a system adaptable in recovering seaplanes of the O2U-3 type.

14 February The first monoplane designed for carrier operations, a Boeing Model 205 fighter later purchased by the Navy and designated XF5B-1, was delivered to NAS Anacostia, D.C., for test. The Board of Inspection and Survey in its report commented adversely on the XF5B-1's landing, takeoff and high altitude characteristics, but recommended further development to obtain a rational comparison of monoplane and biplane types.

15 February The design of retractable landing gear, particularly attractive for use in fighting planes because of its promise to improve performance and thereby enhance military value, had progressed to the point that the Naval Aircraft Factory was authorized to construct working models as a means of establishing the practicability of various retracting mechanisms.

21 March The Martin XT5M-1, first dive bomber designed to deliver a 1,000-pound bomb, met strength and performance requirements in diving tests.

21 April The Bureau of Navigation issued a circular letter directing that no more enlisted applicants be recommended for pilot training. When men already in the system or under instruction completed their course in early 1932, this order caused a temporary lull in enlisted pilot training.

22 April A naval treaty was signed at London, England, by the signatories of the Washington Naval Treaty which carried forward the general limitations of that earlier agreement and provided for further reductions of naval armament. Under the terms applicable to Naval Aviation, the definition of an aircraft carrier was broadened to include ships of any tonnage designed primarily for aircraft operations; and it was agreed that installation of a landing-on or flying-off platform on a warship designed and used primarily for other purposes would not make that ship an aircraft carrier; and further, that no capital ship in existence on 1 April 1930 would be fitted with such a platform or deck.

31 May The last Curtiss Marine Trophy Race, an annual event for service seaplanes, was won by Captain Arthur H. Page, USMC, in an F6C-3 Curtiss fighter with a speed of 164.08 mph. The race was staged over the Potomac off NAS Anacostia, D.C.

First experimental monoplane fighter, XF5B-1 460387

1930—Continued

4 June   On the first anniversary of his seaplane altitude record, Lieutenant Apollo Soucek took off from Anacostia in a Wright Apache landplane equipped with a Pratt & Whitney 450-hp engine; and, flying to a new height of 43,166 feet, regained the world altitude record he had held briefly in 1929.

21 July   Captain Arthur H. Page, USMC, piloted an O2U from a sealed hooded cockpit on an instrument flight of about 1,000 miles from Omaha, Nebr., to NAS Anacostia, D.C., via Chicago, Ill., and Cleveland, Ohio; the longest blind flight to date. Lieutenant Vernon M. Guymon, USMC, acted as safety pilot and took over the controls only for the landings after Captain Page had brought the plane over the fields at 200 feet.

Page and Guymon made long blind flight 1930 460434

1 September   In the race for the Thompson Trophy in Chicago, Ill., Captain Arthur H. Page, USMC, flying an XF6C-6, was the only military entry. Page gained and increased an early lead but on the 17th of 20 laps crashed to his death, a victim of carbon monoxide poisoning.

5 November   The Director of Naval Research Laboratory reported that Mr. Leo C. Young and Mr. L. A. Hyland, while conducting experiments in the directional effects of radio, had detected an airplane flying overhead. This led to the formal establishment of a project at the Naval Research Laboratory for "Detection of Enemy Vessels and Aircraft by Radio."

28 November   The Chief of Naval Operations, Admiral William V. Pratt issued a new naval air policy, effective 1 April 1931, which essentially reorganized aviation and established it as an integral part of the fleet to operate with it under the direct command of the Commander-in-Chief U.S. Fleet (CINCUS). The policy stressed the importance of fleet mobility and the need for offensive action in protecting against invasion from overseas, assigned the development of the offensive power of the fleet and advanced base forces as the primary task of Naval Aviation, and relegated participation in coast defense to the status of a secondary task. To complete the change, the policy also directed that air stations in strategic naval operating areas henceforth be assigned to, and operate under the Fleet; and only such other stations as necessary for training, test, aircraft repairs and similar support functions would be maintained under shore command.

2 December   The seaplane tender *Aroostook* (CM 3), one utility and two patrol squadrons of the Battle Fleet reported for duty to Commander Base Force, thereby providing that command with its first aviation organization.

1931

8 January   Further development of dive-bombing equipment and tactics was insured as tests completed at the Naval Proving Grounds, Dahlgren, Va., showed that displacing gear eliminated the recently encountered danger of a bomb colliding with its releasing airplane.

9 January   An agreement was announced between the Chief of Naval Operations, Admiral William V. Pratt and the Army Chief of Staff, General Douglas MacArthur, governing the operations of their respective air forces, which climaxed a long standing interservice controversy over the division of responsibilities for coast defense. Under the terms, the functions of the two air forces were closely associated with those of their parent services; the naval air force was defined as an element of the fleet to move with it and to carry out its primary mission; and the Army Air Corps as a land-based air arm to be employed as an essential arm of the Army in performing its general mission, including defense of the coast at home and at possessions overseas.

22 January   The Navy ordered its first rotary winged aircraft, the XOP-1 autogiro, from Pitcairn Aircraft, Incorporated.

25 February   A new pilot training syllabus was issued which added a course in Advanced Seaplane

1931—Continued

XOP-1, first Navy Autogiro arrives at Anacostia 215856

Training and returned the courses in Bombing and Torpedo, and Observation and Gunnery, dropped in November 1929, thereby expanding the regular flight course to 258.75 hours and, for those also taking Advanced Combat, to 282.75 hours. The ground school course was also expanded in some areas and with the inclusion of a short course in photography, totaled 386.5 hours.

2 March A propeller development program, which led to the adoption of variable pitch propellers, was initiated with the award of a contract to Hamilton Standard Propeller Company for two such propellers suitable for use on fighting planes.

3 March A recommendation that two officers from the postgraduate aeronautical engineering group be selected for study at the California Institute of Technology (CalTech) was approved. As a result, the policy of assigning postgraduate students to civilian institutions was broadened to permit greater specialization, and for the next three school years students were assigned in two groups: one to MIT where emphasis was on aircraft engines, the other to CalTech for study of aircraft structures.

31 March When a disastrous earthquake shook Nicaragua and destroyed most of the city of Managua, *Lexington* was ordered from Guantanamo Bay, Cuba, to assist other Navy and Marine units in relief operations. Early the next afternoon, she inaugurated carrier aircraft relief operations in the U.S. Navy, by launching five planes carrying medical personnel, supplies and provisions to the stricken city.

1 April A reorganization of the U.S. Fleet into Battle, Scouting, Submarine and Base Forces provided for the appointment of type commanders for each type of ship and for aircraft, and designated the aviation type commands in the Battle, Scouting and Base Forces as Commander Aircraft (name of Force).

2 April A contract for the XFF-1 two-seat fighter, the first naval aircraft to incorporate retractable landing gear for the purpose of improving aerodynamic cleanness and thereby increasing performance, was issued to Grumman.

9 April A contract was issued to the Glenn L. Martin Company for 12 BM-1 dive bombers. This aircraft, which was a further development of the XT5M-1, was the first dive bomber capable of attacking with a heavy (1,000 pound) bomb to be procured in sufficient quantity to equip a squadron.

FF-1, first fighter with retractable landing gear 1061485

BM-1, dive bomber carrying 1000-pound bomb 1053772

1931—Continued

1 June   New specifications for aircraft markings were issued which directed use of 20-inch-wide colored bands around the fuselage of section leader planes, assigning royal red, white, true blue, black, willow green and lemon yellow for sections 1 through 6 respectively. The same order permitted use of distinguishing colors on the empennage whenever two or more squadrons of the same class operated together.

1 July   The Naval Air Stations at Coco Solo, C.Z. and Pearl Harbor, T.H., were redesignated Fleet Air Bases to conform with their transfer to the U.S. Fleet and their function of providing mobile air units for fleet operations.

19–20 July   A Navy balloon, piloted by Lieutenant Thomas G. W. Settle and Lieutenant (jg) Wilfred Bushnell, won the Litchfield Trophy and the National Elimination Balloon Race at Akron, Ohio, with a distance of 195 miles to Marilla, N.Y., thereby qualifying for the International Race.

10 September   Rear Admiral William A. Moffett directed that the bureau's program for test and evaluation of variable-pitch propellers be expedited and noted that in recent tests at NAS Anacostia, D.C, a variable-pitch propeller on a Curtiss F6C-4 had provided a 20 percent reduction in takeoff run and a slight increase in high speed.

23 September   Lieutenant Alfred M. Pride piloted the Navy's first rotary wing aircraft, an XOP-1 autogiro, in landings and takeoffs aboard *Langley* while underway.

26 September   The keel for *Ranger*, first ship of the U.S. Navy to be designed and constructed as a carrier, was laid at the Newport News Shipbuilding and Drydock Company, Newport News, Va.

30 September   The Bureau of Aeronautics reported that studies were being conducted on catapulting landplanes on wheels. This, the preliminary step in the development of flush deck catapults for launching landplanes from carriers, visualized the installation of

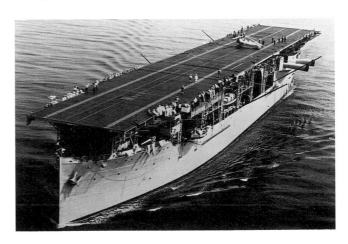

XOP-1 Autogiro landing aboard Langley 215836

The 14,500-ton Ranger, CV-4, was the first American ship designated as an aircraft carrier from the keel up 428440

1931—Continued

powder catapults on hangar decks. The development was expanded to include the use of compressed air, and by the end of 1932 the Naval Aircraft Factory had successfully launched an O2U-3 landplane with this latter gear.

7 October In a bombing demonstration conducted from an altitude of 5,000 feet against the anchored target ship *Pittsburgh* (Armored Cruiser No. 4), 50 percent hits were obtained with the newly developed Norden Mark XV bombsight as compared to slightly over 20 percent hits with the earlier Mark XI model.

7 October Evaluation of the experimental K Class airship, the K-1, was begun at NAS Lakehurst, N.J. It featured an enclosed all-metal car and a 320,000 cubic-foot envelope, which made it the largest non-rigid airship designed especially for the Navy until that time.

27 October The rigid airship *Akron* (ZRS-4), having made its first trial flight on 23 September 1931 at Akron, Ohio, was commissioned at NAS Lakehurst, N.J., with Lieutenant Commander Charles E. Rosendahl as Commanding Officer.

2 November Marine Scouting Squadrons VS-14M and -15M embarked on *Saratoga* and *Lexington*, respectively, to operate as an integral part of Aircraft, Battle Force. These squadrons, first of the Marine air units assigned to carriers, were carrier-based until late 1934; and from then until 1941, other Marine squadrons maintained some carrier proficiency through periodic operations afloat.

3 November The rigid dirigible *Akron* (ZRS-4) made a 10-hour flight out of Lakehurst, N.J., carrying aloft 207 persons, a new record for the largest number of individuals carried into the air by a single craft.

9 December *Langley* completed nine days of operations off the New England coast in which the cold weather operating capabilities of carrier deck gear and carrier aircraft, and the effectiveness of protective flight clothing were given a practical test.

1932

9 January The Secretary of the Navy informed the Secretary of War of work being conducted at the Naval Research Laboratory in detecting ships and aircraft by radio and suggested that since one obvious application of the method was in air warning systems for large areas, the Army might be interested in undertaking further work.

24 March The Army Air Corps, in response to enthusiastic reports from its observers who had witnessed the performance of the Mk XV Norden bombsight in trials against *Pittsburgh* (Armored Cruiser No. 4) the previous October, requested the Navy to provide it with 25 Mk XV sights. This was the Army's first commitment for the Navy-developed sight that was to become essential to high altitude precision bombing in World War II.

2 April Torpedo Squadron 5A (ex-VT-20) sailed from the Philippines aboard *Jason* (AC 12). When VS-8A, the only squadron remaining in the area, was disestablished

Langley was converted from a carrier to a seaplane tender by removal of forward flight deck 465883

1932—Continued

the following June, aviation in the Asiatic Fleet was reduced to the observation aircraft on board cruisers.

2 May   The Bureau of Aeronautics directed that hydraulic cylinder type arresting gear be installed on *Langley* to replace weight type gear used earlier. This decision resulted from operational experience of *Langley* with two sets of hydraulic gear installed in June and September 1931.

18 May   With enough qualified students on hand to fill several classes at Pensacola, Fla., the practice instituted in 1930 of waiving the requirement of two years of sea duty before assignment to elimination flight training was discontinued. In effect, this marked the beginning of almost a year in which no new prospective aviators were enrolled.

1 June   The resignation of the Assistant Secretary of the Navy for Aeronautics David S. Ingalls was accepted by the president and it was announced that, as an economy measure, the appointment of a successor was not contemplated. The office remained vacant until 1941.

30 June   *Los Angeles* (ZR-3) was decommissioned for economy reasons at NAS Lakehurst, N.J., after eight years of service and over 5,000 hours in the air.

1 July   The requirement of an earlier law that 30 percent of the Navy's pilots be enlisted men, was reduced to 20 percent as an amending act became effective. The restrictive nature of the requirement was modified by an additional provision that it was applicable except when, in the opinion of the Secretary of the Navy, it was impracticable to obtain the required number of enlisted pilots.

28 July   Research into the physiological effects of high acceleration and deceleration, encountered in dive bombing and other violent maneuvers, was initiated through a Bureau of Aeronautics allocation of funds to the Bureau of Medicine and Surgery for this purpose. The pioneer research, pointing to the need for anti-G or anti-blackout equipment, was performed at Harvard University School of Public Health by Lieutenant Commander John R. Poppen, MC, under the direction of Dr. C. K. Drinker.

25–27 September   The International Balloon Race, held at Basel, Switzerland, was won by Lieutenant Thomas G. W. Settle and Lieutenant Wilfred Bushnell in a flight which ended on the Polish-Latvian border near Vilna and established a new world distance record of 963.123 miles for balloons in three categories of volume.

10 November   A contract for 125 sets of GF radios was issued to the Aviation Radio Corporation. This was the first production order for radio equipment suitable for installation in single-seat fighters.

22 November   Following tests of the OP-1 autogiro in Nicaragua, Major Francis P. Mulcahy, USMC, reported that the autogiro's chief value in expeditionary duty was in inspecting small fields recommended by ground troops as landing areas, evacuating medical "sitting" cases, and ferrying important personnel.

1933

4 January   A new plan for postgraduate work was approved which combined the existing programs for specialists and for the General Line, and extended the aeronautical engineering program to three years. Under the new plan, all officers selected for postgraduate work began with one year in the School of the Line. Those demonstrating ability and interest in advanced technical specialties were given a second year in that area of study and, in the third year, were sent to a civilian institution for work, in most instances leading to a Master of Science degree.

25 January   The Bureau of Navigation announced that the assignment of naval officers to flight training at Pensacola, Fla., would be resumed in May or June, or almost a year since the last group had been assigned.

16 February   The president presented to Colonel Nathan D. Ely, USA (Ret), the Distinguished Flying Cross, awarded posthumously to Colonel Ely's son, Eugene B. Ely, for extraordinary achievement as a pioneer aviator and for significant contribution as a civilian to the development of aviation in the Navy when in 1910 and 1911 he demonstrated the feasibility of operating aircraft from ships.

1 April   Fleet Aviation was reorganized and assigned to two principal commands each exercising type functions within his Force, and one of whom, Commander Aircraft, Battle Force, served as type commander for all fleet aircraft. Carriers, with their aircraft, were assigned to Battle Force and all tender-based air and Fleet Air Bases at Pearl Harbor, T.H., and Coco Solo, C.Z., were assigned to Base Force. The command Aircraft Scouting Force was abolished.

1933—Continued

4 April The rigid airship *Akron* (ZRS-4) crashed in a severe storm off Barnegat Light, N.J. Among the 73 fatalities were Rear Admiral William A. Moffett, Chief, Bureau of Aeronautics, and Commander Frank C. McCord, Commanding Officer of *Akron* (ZRS-4).

18 April Lieutenant George A. Ott piloting an O2U seaplane, with Lieutenant (jg) Bruce A. Van Voorhis as passenger, made the first operational test of a device, later called the Plane Trap, installed on the stern of *Maryland* (BB 46). Proposed by Lieutenant Lisle J. Maxson, the device was a V-shaped float attached to the stern of the ship by a system of struts which permitted it to ride at an even depth in the water. In operation, the seaplane taxied toward the float pushing a knobbed probe on the nose of its pontoon into the V-float which engaged the probe and held the seaplane in position for hoisting aboard. The device was an immediate success and proposals were made to install the same gear on five additional battleships.

29 April The Bureau of Aeronautics recommended resumption of postgraduate instruction in aerology which had been suspended in 1929. By the end of the year, arrangements were completed for a two-year course at the Postgraduate School and a third year at a civilian university.

6 June Two Franklin gliders were received at NAS Pensacola, Fla., for use in a test to determine whether inclusion of glider training in the student flight syllabus would replace or simplify elimination flight training and thereby reduce dual instruction time. Instructor training in the new craft began immediately under the direction of Lieutenant Ralph S. Barnaby, and glider training, as an experimental feature of the training program, continued into 1936.

13 June A contract for the development of special radio equipment for making blind landings aboard carriers was issued to the Washington Institute of Technology.

16 June Under the terms of the National Industrial Recovery Act, the president allotted $238 million to the Navy for the construction of new ships, including two aircraft carriers. In less than two months, contracts were awarded for carriers Nos. 5 and 6, eventually commissioned as *Yorktown* and *Enterprise*.

22 June A new underway recovery device, proposed by Lieutenant George A. Ott, senior aviator on *Maryland* (BB 46), was tested at sea off Point Firmin,

Calif. The device resembled a cargo net fitted with a wood spreader at its forward edge and canvas underneath which, when towed by the ship, rode the surface forward and was slightly submerged aft so that the seaplane could taxi on it and catch the net with a hook on the bottom of its pontoon. Recovery over the stern was successful on the first attempt. An alongside recovery, necessary for ships with cranes amidships, was tried next. With the net trailing from a boom, the seaplane again caught the net but then swung into the ship and crumpled its wing. In spite of the partial failure, the possibilities of the plane net were apparent and later adjustments corrected the initial deficiencies.

23 June *Macon* (ZRS-5), having made its first flight on 21 April, was commissioned at Akron, Ohio, with Commander Alger H. Dressel as commanding officer.

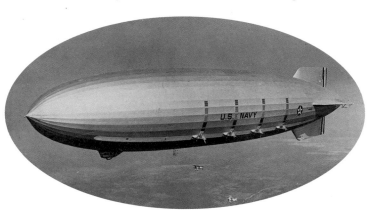

Macon ZRS-5 prepares to take protective fighters on board. There was space for five planes in the hangar 4284422

8 August Commander, Aircraft Battle Force, requested authority to use variable-pitch propellers during forthcoming exercises on six Boeing F4B-4s of VF-3, based aboard *Langley*, and on one F4B-4 of VF-1, based aboard *Saratoga*. This request, which stemmed from successful trials conducted by VF-3 aboard the *Langley*, marked the initial service acceptance of the variable-pitch propeller.

9 August Commander Battle Force, commenting on tests of the plane net made by *Maryland* (BB 46), pointed out that construction of the net and pontoon hook were well within the capacity of ships company and directed that all battleships under his command experiment with, and attempt to develop, techniques for underway recovery.

2–4 September The Navy balloon of Lieutenant Commander Thomas G. W. Settle and Lieutenant Charles H. Kendall took second place in the Gordon Bennett International Balloon Race at Chicago with a

The Boeing F4B-4 carrier fighter of the 1930s 462618

distance of 776 miles, and their 51 hours in the air set new world records for duration in three categories of volume.

7–8 September   Six Consolidated P2Y-1 flying boats of Patrol Squadron 5F, under the command of Lieutenant Commander Herman E. Halland, flew nonstop from Norfolk, Va., to Coco Solo, C.Z., making a record distance formation flight of 2,059 miles in 25 hours 19 minutes.

12 October   The rigid airship *Macon* (ZRS-5) departed NAS Lakehurst, N.J., bound for her new home on the west coast at NAS Sunnyvale, Calif. Following the Atlantic coast down to Macon, Ga., and then westward over the southern route to the west coast, the airship arrived at Sunnyvale in the afternoon of the 15th, completing the 2,500 mile nonstop flight in approximately 70 hours.

17 October   In an effort to prevent a shortage of pilots as a result of the curtailment in training, additional instruction was authorized for specially recommended student Naval Aviators, who had failed to qualify on their first attempt or whose training had been interrupted. In the next month, authorization of a

requalification course for Naval Aviators and Naval Aviation Pilots, who had been on nonflying duty, was directed toward the same end.

24 October   Development of anti-blackout equipment was initiated with an authorization to the Naval Aircraft Factory to develop and manufacture a special abdominal belt in accord with specifications prepared by Lieutenant Commander John R. Poppen, MC, for use by pilots in dive bombing and other violent maneuvers.

28 October   A contract was issued to Consolidated for the XP3Y-1 flying boat, marking the initiation of Navy sponsored development of the PBY Catalina series of flying boats.

17 November   The sum of $7,500,000 was allotted to the Navy from funds provided under the National Industrial Recovery Act of 16 June 1933, for the procurement of new aircraft and equipment, thereby permitting the Bureau of Aeronautics to maintain its 1,000-plane program, to equip operating aircraft with modern navigation instruments and radios, and to make other improvements in naval aircraft and their accessories which were not possible under the annual appropriation.

1933—Continued

20 November Lieutenant Commander Thomas G. W. Settle and Major Chester L. Fordney, USMC, flying a 600,000 cubic foot free balloon, set a world's altitude record of 61,237 feet in a flight into the stratosphere with departure from Akron, Ohio, and landing near Bridgeton, N.J.

20 December To effect the organization of the aviation element of the newly formed Fleet Marine Force, Aircraft Squadrons East Coast Expeditionary Forces was redesignated Aircraft One, Fleet Marine Force, and Aircraft Squadrons West Coast Expeditionary Forces became Aircraft Two, Fleet Marine Force.

1934

10–11 January Six Consolidated P2Y-1s of Patrol Squadron 10F, Lieutenant Commander Knefler McGinnis commanding, made a nonstop formation flight from San Francisco, Calif., to Pearl Harbor, T.H., in 24 hours 35 minutes, thereby bettering the best previous time for the crossing, exceeding the best distance of previous mass flights, and breaking a nine-day-old world record for distance in a straight line for Class C seaplanes with a new mark of 2,399 miles.

P2Y-1s of Patrol Squadron 10-F made first non-stop formation flight from San Francisco to Pearl Harbor 426937

14 March Dr. A. Hoyt Taylor, head of the Radio Division of the Naval Research Laboratory, authorized a project for development of pulse radar (as it was later called) to detect ships and aircraft. The basic concept, which had been proposed by Leo C. Young, involved special sending, receiving and display equipment all mounted in close proximity. This equipment would send out pulses of radio energy of a few microseconds in duration separated by time intervals that were tens to thousands of times longer than the duration of a pulse. Reception of an echo would indicate a target; time of travel to the target and back, the distance; and directional sending or receiving antenna, the bearing. As compared to the beat in a continuous radio wave, a technique which had been under development at the Naval Research Laboratory for nearly four years, the pulse technique promised to be of much greater utility because it would provide range and bearing as well as detection and because the entire apparatus could be installed aboard a single ship. The feasibility of the pulse technique was based upon new developments of the radio industry including the cathode ray tube, high power transmitting tubes and special receiving tubes.

27 March An act of Congress, approved by the president and popularly known as the Vinson-Trammell Act, established the composition of the Navy at the limit prescribed by the Washington and London Naval Treaties. The act authorized construction of a number of ships, including one aircraft carrier of about 15,000 tons, and in other matters relating to aviation authorized the president to procure naval aircraft for ships and naval purposes in numbers commensurate with a treaty Navy. It also provided that not less than 10 percent of the authorized aircraft and engines be manufactured in government plants. Under the authorization, *Wasp* was laid down in 1936.

28 April The equipment and techniques of alongside recovery by plane net had developed to the point that Commander, Cruisers Battle Force, issued a directive describing the method that would be used by all ships of his command. The success of the method was such that the only plane trap in use, that on *Maryland* (BB 46) was removed in June and underway recovery of seaplanes by battleships and cruisers soon became routine.

1 May Lieutenant Frank Akers made a hooded landing in an OJ-2 at College Park, Md., in the first demonstration of the blind landing system intended for carrier use and under development by the Washington Institute of Technology. In subsequent flights, Lieutenant Akers took off from Anacostia, D.C., under a hood and landed at College Park, Md., without assistance.

22 May The NS-1, a single-engine biplane trainer, was ordered from Stearman Aircraft Company, Wichita, Kans.

4 June *Ranger* was commissioned at Norfolk, Va., Captain Arthur L. Bristol commanding.

21 June First landings and takeoffs were made aboard *Ranger* by the ship's aviators led by Lieutenant Commander Arthur C. Davis. After completing normal

1934—Continued

operations, the ship went full speed astern and aircraft landed using the bow arresting gear.

30 June A contract was issued to Douglas for the XTBD-1 torpedo bomber. This aircraft was the prototype for the TBD Devastator which remained in operational use through June 1942.

Curtiss F9C-2s with airship hoop-on gear 441982

Devastator torpedo plane 1061904

F9C-1 being hoisted into hangar of Akron 441980

18 July Fourteen Naval Academy graduates, Class 1933, reported at Pensacola, Fla., for special training toward qualification as Naval Aviators. Their designation in January 1935 climaxed a series of events over the somewhat devious route of an honorable discharge upon graduation in 1933; because of lack of vacancies in the Navy, enrollment and training as Flying Cadets in the Army Air Corps; acceptance of the Navy offer of a commission in either the Navy or Marine Corps; and finally, completion of the special course at Pensacola.

19 July Lieutenant Harold B. Miller and Lieutenant (jg) Frederick N. Kivette, flying F9C-2s without their wheel landing gear, dropped from the trapeze of *Macon* (ZRS-5) to scout for *Houston* (CA 30) returning from a cruise in the Pacific with President Franklin D. Roosevelt on board. Because of the improved performance of the air-

craft on this first flight without landing gear, it became standard operating procedure to fly *Macon* (ZRS 5) planes from the trapeze in this configuration.

1 August Lieutenant (jg) Charles H. Kendall and Lieutenant (jg) Howard T. Orville, in a 206.4-mile flight from Birmingham, Ala., to Commerce, Ga., won the National Elimination Balloon Race and qualified for the international race.

1 November The Naval Aircraft Factory was authorized to manufacture and test a flush-deck hydraulic catapult, Type H Mark I. This catapult was designed to launch landplanes from aircraft carriers and was the Navy's initial development of a hydraulic catapult, a type which was to prove capable of extensive refinement and which eventually was to be accepted as a primary means of launching landplanes from carriers.

1934—Continued

15 November Plans to install hydraulic flush deck catapults aboard carriers were formalized in a Bureau of Aeronautics request that space be reserved on *Yorktown* and *Enterprise* for two bow catapults on the flight deck and one athwartships on the hangar deck.

18 November A contract was issued to the Northrop Corporation for the XBT-1, a two-seat Scout and 1,000-pound dive bomber. This aircraft was the initial prototype in the sequence that led to the SBD Dauntless series of dive bombers introduced to the fleet in 1938 and used throughout World War II.

XBT-1, heavy dive bomber, forerunner of SBD 1053784

14 December Reinflation of the rigid airship *Los Angeles* (ZR-3) was completed, and she became airborne in the hangar at NAS Lakehurst, N.J., after nearly three years of decommissioned status. Although not flown again, she continued in use as a test and experimental ship for another five years and, after having served that purpose, was stricken from the inventory on 29 October 1939. Dismantling was completed in 7 weeks.

15 December The Secretary of the Navy approved acceptance of the XO3C-1, a single-engine biplane observation seaplane; subsequently converted to the XSOC-1. Aircraft of this type were operated from battleships and cruisers from late 1935 through World War II.

21 December Flight test of the NS-1, Stearman biplane trainer, was completed at NAS Anacostia, D.C.

1935

5 January The Bureau of Navigation stated that Lieutenant Commander John R. Poppen, MC, would be ordered to the Naval Dispensary, Philadelphia Navy Yard, with additional duty at the Naval Aircraft Factory, to observe pilots, conduct their annual physi-

Curtiss SOC-1 catapulted from heavy cruiser 41061

1935—Continued

cal examinations and work on hygienic and physiological aspects of research and development projects. This was the first assignment of a Flight Surgeon to the Naval Aircraft Factory other than as part of a specific project.

14 January Squadrons assigned to *Ranger* made the first of a series of cross-country flights from Norfolk, Va., to Hartford, Conn., and Buffalo, N.Y., to test the functioning of carrier aircraft, special equipment, and flight clothing under the exacting conditions to be encountered in cold weather. When the tests were completed on 2 February, the lessons learned were used in preparing for tests aboard *Ranger* the next winter.

22 January The Federal Aviation Commission, appointed by the president as provided in the Air Mail Act of 12 June 1934, submitted its report which in essence set forth a broad policy covering all phases of aviation and the relation of the government thereto. A major share of its recommendations referred to commercial and civil aviation and in general stressed the needs for a strong air transport, for expanding airport facilities, for improving provisions for aviation in government organization, and for supporting the welfare of the aviation industry, particularly through the establishment of more realistic procurement practices and policy. For military aviation, the commission recommended: continued study of air organization toward more effective employment of aviation and closer interservice relationships, expansion of experimental and development work and its close coordination through the NACA, expansion of the Reserve organizations and larger appropriations to support them, and a modification of personnel policies to permit assignment of officers with special engineering ability and industrial experience to continuous duty related to their specialty.

9 February The XN3N-1, prototype of the Yellow Peril primary trainer, was ordered from the Naval Aircraft Factory.

12 February After encountering a severe gust of wind which caused a structural failure, the rigid airship *Macon* (ZRS-5) crashed off Point Sur, Calif., with two fatalities.

12 March The Navy issued a contract to Pitcairn Autogiro Company to remove the fixed wings from the XOP-1, thereby converting it to the XOP-2 which thus became the Navy's first heavier-than-air aircraft without fixed wings.

15 April Passage of the Aviation Cadet Act created the grade of Aviation Cadet in the Naval and Marine Corps Reserves. The act set up a new program for pilot training in which otherwise qualified college graduates between the ages of 18 and 28 would be eligible for one year of flight instruction, benefits of pay, uniform gratuities and insurance; and would, after serving three additional years on active duty, be commissioned as Ensigns or Second Lieutenants, be paid a bonus of $1,500, and be returned to inactive duty as members of the Reserves.

1 May A new pilot training syllabus was issued requiring completion of about 300 hours of flight instruction and 465 hours of ground school in a total time of one year. The new course made no differentiation between student Naval Aviators and Student Aviation Pilots, but specified an additional 90 hours of indoctrination courses for members of the Reserve.

5 June The designation of specially qualified officers for the performance of aeronautical engineering duty only (AEDO) was authorized by an act of Congress. The appointment of a board in September to select the first officers for this AEDO designation and the subsequent approval of its report by the Secretary brought about the assignment of 11 officers of the line and 33 from the Construction Corps to this new specialist category.

20 July The first class of Aviation Cadets to report for flight training convened at NAS Pensacola, Fla. First of the group to become a Naval Aviator was Elliott M. West who was designated on 12 June 1936 and assigned number 4,854.

XN3N, Yellow Peril, training plane built at NAF 1061654

1935—Continued

30 July The first blind landing aboard a carrier was made by Lieutenant Frank Akers, who took off from NAS San Diego, Calif., in an OJ-2 with hooded cockpit, located *Langley* underway in an unknown position, and landed aboard catching the number four arresting wire. Lieutenant Akers subsequently received a Distinguished Flying Cross for this flight.

26 September The president approved a joint Army-Navy proposal for the transfer of air station properties, climaxing several years of study and discussion of the joint use of aviation facilities in certain areas. By this approval and a subsequent Executive Order, the Army agreed to turn over to the Navy: Rockwell Field on North Island, Calif., Luke Field on Ford Island, T.H., and Bolling Field at Anacostia, D.C., while the Navy agreed to turn over to the Army the Naval Air Station at Sunnyvale, Calif. In this exchange, it was understood that the Army would construct new fields at Bolling adjoining its previous location, and Hickam Field on Oahu, T.H.

Naval Air Station Anacostia (foreground), old Bolling Field (background) prior to acquisition by Navy 1061655

First production monoplane fighter, Brewster F2A 16054

5 October The first G Class airship, the G-1, was delivered to NAS Lakehurst. This airship, formerly the Defender of Goodyear's commercial fleet, was used by the Navy for training purposes.

14–15 October Lieutenant Commander Knefler McGinnis, Lieutenant (jg) James K. Averill, NAP Thomas P. Wilkinson, and crew of three flew an XP3Y-1 Consolidated patrol plane, powered with two 825-hp Pratt & Whitney engines, from Cristobal Harbor, Canal Zone, to Alameda, Calif., in 34 hours 45 minutes and established new world records for Class C seaplanes of 3,281.383 miles airline distance and 3,443.255 miles brokenline distance.

XP3Y-1 commanded by K. McGinnis set 3443-mile record on flight from Panama to Alameda, October 1935 1053771

15 November The Chief, Bureau of Aeronautics, approved recommendations from a fighter design competition and thereby initiated development of the Grumman XF4F-1 biplane and the Brewster XF2A-1 monoplane. The developmental sequence thus set in motion, although it included many subsequent changes and modifications, provided prototypes of the Navy's first-line fighters in use when the United States entered World War II.

1936

20 January The Bureau of Engineering, acting in response to a request from the Bureau of Aeronautics, initiated naval support to the Bureau of Standards for the development of radio meteorographs. These instruments, later renamed radiosondes, were to be attached to small free bal-

1936—Continued

loons and sent aloft to measure pressure, temperature and humidity of the upper atmosphere, and to transmit this information to ground stations for use in weather forecasting and flight planning.

22 January   *Ranger,* with 23 aircraft on board, arrived in Cook Inlet, Alaska, and began three weeks of operational tests to study the effects of cold weather on operating efficiency and to determine material and other improvements necessary for increasing carrier capabilities under extreme weather conditions.

18 March   The flight test of the XN3N-1, prototype of the Yellow Peril, a primary trainer biplane, was completed at NAS Pensacola, Fla.

1 April   The Marine Corps Aviation Section, which had been set up independently under the Commandant in the previous year, was established as a Division. With the change, the Officer-in-Charge was given the title Director of Aviation and as such continued to serve in the dual capacity of advisor to the Commandant on aviation and head of the Marine Corps organization in the Bureau of Aeronautics, under an arrangement which had been in effect since the establishment of that Bureau.

28 April   R. C. Guthrie and Robert M. Page, at the Naval Research Laboratory, began testing a laboratory model of a pulsed radio wave detection device (pulse radar). As tests proceeded, aircraft were detected at distances up to 25 miles.

6 May   Construction of the facility, which was later named the David W. Taylor Model Basin, was authorized by legislation, providing buildings and appliances for use by the Bureau of Construction and Repair in investigating and determining shapes and forms to be adopted for U.S. vessels, including aircraft.

11 June   In an effort to adapt commercial airplane maintenance techniques to naval use, the Bureau of Aeronautics authorized Commander, Aircraft Base Force, to provide patrol squadrons with an extra aircraft for use as a rotating spare to replace squadron planes that were undergoing maintenance inspection.

10 July   The Chief, Bureau of Aeronautics, approved a program of improvements to the F4F and F2A fighters being developed by Grumman and Brewster. Most important were the conversion of the Grumman design from a biplane to the monoplane XF4F-2 prototype for the F4F Wildcat of World War II, and the

installation of larger engines in both, which promised a top speed of 300 mph.

21 July   Lieutenant Commander Delmer S. Fahrney received orders to report to the Chief of the Bureau of Aeronautics and the Director of the Naval Research Laboratory for duty in connection with an experimental project. This marked the initial step in implementation of a recommendation made by the Chief of Naval Operations the preceding May that radio controlled aircraft be obtained for use as aerial targets. Fahrney, in his subsequent report, not only proposed a procedure for developing radio controlled target planes but also recognized the feasibility of using such aircraft as guided missiles.

23 July   A contract was awarded to Consolidated for the XPB2Y-1 four-engined flying boat. This aircraft had been selected for development as a result of a design competition held late the previous year, and in later configurations, it became the Navy's only four-engined flying boat to be used as a patrol plane during World War II.

7 August   A change in the flight syllabus was approved which placed more emphasis on instrument flying. The new course, which was inserted between the service seaplane and fighter courses, was given by a new instrument flying unit formed at Pensacola, Fla., for the purpose, and included six hours in Link trainers, nine hours of modified acrobatics in NS aircraft, and two hours radio range flying under the hood.

19 August   Lieutenant Boynton L. Braun, pilot and ACOM W. B. Marvelle completed test bombing against the submarine R-8 off the Virginia Capes. Flying a T4M-1 at an altitude of 2,500 feet, they dropped twelve 100-pound bombs in a 2-day period and obtained four near-misses with a cumulative effect which caused the submarine to sink.

15 September   *Langley,* first aircraft carrier of the U.S. Navy, was detached from Battle Force and assigned to Commander, Aircraft Base Force, for duty as a seaplane tender. After a brief period of operation, she went into the yard for conversion, from which she emerged early in 1937 with the forward part of her flight deck removed.

1937

27 February   Expansion of the Working Committee of the Aeronautical Board and the extension of its functions to include work in aeronautical standardization, were approved by the Secretaries of the War and Navy Departments. By this decision, interservice

1937—Continued

efforts in standardization changed from a part-time program of annual conferences to one employing a joint staff of officers and civilians on a full-time basis.

15 March   The Bureau of Aeronautics assigned distinguishing colors to each aircraft carrier for use as tail markings by all squadrons on board, thereby changing the existing practice of assigning colors to squadrons and eliminating the confusion resulting when squadrons transferred from one carrier to another.

21–22 June   Patrol Squadron 3, with 12 PBY-1 Catalinas under the command of Lieutenant Robert W. Morse, flew nonstop from San Diego, Calif., to Coco Solo in the Canal Zone, completing the 3,292-mile flight in 27 hours and 58 minutes.

30 May   A contract was issued to the Martin Company for the XPBM-1 two-engined flying boat patrol plane. The aircraft was the initial prototype in the PBM Mariner series of flying boats used during and after World War II.

1 July   The system of designating squadrons was revised to provide for numbering each carrier squadron according to the hull number of its carrier, each battleship and cruiser squadron the same as the number of its ship division, each Marine Corps squadron according to its Aircraft Group, and patrol squadrons serially without regard to assignment. The change also abolished the use of suffix letters to indicate organizational assignment, except for Naval District and Reserve squadrons, and interposed the M for Marine Corps squadrons between the V prefix and mission letters.

2 July   The Navy agreed to accept transfer of Army airships and lighter-than-air equipment. Included in the transfer were the airships TC-13 and TC-14, used for antisubmarine patrol in the early stages of World War II.

15 July   The Ship Experimental Unit was placed in operating status at the Naval Aircraft Factory and made responsible for development and testing of equipment and techniques for carrier landings. This unit consisted of officers and men which were transferred from NAS Norfolk, Va., where this function had been performed since 1921.

6 August   A contract was issued to Goodyear for two new non-rigid airships, the L-1 for training purposes, and the K-2 for coastal patrol.

9 August   The contractor's demonstration flights of the XOZ-1 rotary-winged aircraft, which included a water takeoff, were completed at the Naval Aircraft Factory. Pennsylvania Aircraft Corporation had modified this aircraft from an N2Y-1 trainer into an experimental gyroplane by installing a new engine and a rotary wing with cyclic control.

9 September   The XPBS-1, a four-engined monoplane flying boat built by Sikorsky Aircraft, made its first flight. This aircraft, constructed as a long-range patrol plane, was later used as a transport.

30 September   *Yorktown* was commissioned at Norfolk, Va., with Captain Earnest D. McWhorter in command.

1 October   Patrol aviation with its tenders was transferred from Base Force and assigned to the reestablished type command, Aircraft Scouting Force. With the change, five Patrol Wings, numbered 1 through 5, were established as separate administrative commands over their assigned squadrons.

17 December   The XPTBH-2, a twin-float seaplane designed by Hall Aluminum Aircraft Company, Inc. for patrol and torpedo attack, was accepted by the Navy. This was the last twinfloat torpedo plane developed for the Navy.

23 December   A successful unmanned radio-controlled flight was made with a JH-1 drone, at the Coast Guard Air Station, Cape May, N.J. Takeoff and landing were made using a landbased radio set; for flight maneuvers, control was shifted to an airborne TG-2.

1938

21 April   The delivery of the XF2A-1 to the Langley Memorial Aeronautical Laboratory of the National Advisory Committee for Aeronautics marked the initiation of full-scale wind tunnel tests to determine means of decreasing aerodynamic drag and thereby increasing high speed. These tests, conducted at the recommendation of Commander Walter S. Diehl, indicated that the speed of the XF2A-1 could be increased 31 mph over the 277 mph already achieved, and led to the utilization of this technique in other high-performance aircraft, by both the Army and the Navy. The data thus obtained was also directly applicable to the design of new aircraft.

12 May   *Enterprise* was commissioned at Newport News, Va., Captain Newton H. White commanding.

1938—Continued

Enterprise, CV-6 preparing to get underway with all planes of her air group on the flight deck 13554

17 May   The Naval Expansion Act, among its provisions for Naval Aviation, authorized an increase in total tonnage of underage naval vessels amounting to 40,000 tons for aircraft carriers, and also authorized the president to increase the number of naval aircraft to "not less than" 3,000. Carriers built as a result of this authorization were *Hornet* and *Essex*, laid down in 1939 and 1941, respectively.

1 June   The routine use of radiosondes (or radio meteorographs, as they were then called) to obtain data on weather conditions in the upper atmosphere was initiated at NAS Anacostia, D.C. By the close of the year, *California* (BB 44) and *Lexington* were also outfitted to use radiosondes.

8 June   After over two years of evaluation by fleet squadrons and various shore-based naval air activities, the antiblackout or abdominal belt, intended for use by pilots in dive bombing and other violent maneuvers, was returned to a developmental status with a finding by the Commander, Aircraft Battle Force, that the advantages of this belt were not sufficient to offset its disadvantages.

8 June   By policy established by the Secretary of the Navy, the provisions for maintenance of aircraft aboard carriers and aircraft tenders were limited to those required for upkeep and minor repairs.

1 July   New command billets titled Commander, Carrier Air Group, were authorized, and carrier squadrons were organized into groups each designated by the name of the carrier to which it was assigned.

23 August   A contract was issued to Martin for the XPB2M-1 four-engine flying boat. Initially intended as a patrol plane, this craft was later converted to the PB2M-1R Mars transport and served as a prototype for the JRM series of flying boats.

24 August   In the first American use of a drone target aircraft in anti-aircraft exercises, *Ranger* fired upon a radio-controlled JH-1 making a simulated horizontal bombing attack on the fleet. This not only heralded a new departure in anti-aircraft practice, but also indicated that radio-controlled aircraft could be used as a training device in the fleet.

14 September   A radio-controlled N2C-2 target drone engaged in a simulated dive-bombing attack against the battleship *Utah* (BB 31) in test firing of antiaircraft battery. The proponents of guided missile development view this as the first demonstration of the air to surface missile.

15 October   A new specification prescribing color for naval aircraft was issued. Trainers were to be finished in orange-yellow overall with aluminum colored floats or landing gear. The color of service aircraft remained essentially as prescribed in 1925, aluminum overall with orange-yellow on wing and tail surfaces that were visible from above.

2 November   A revision of the pilot training syllabus was approved instituting minor adjustments in the flight program and changes of greater significance in the ground program. A special course was added for flight surgeons, celestial navigation was added for

1938—Continued

enlisted students, and gameboard problems were introduced as a practical approach to instruction in scouting and search.

1 December The Hepburn Board, appointed by the Secretary of the Navy in accordance with the act of 17 May, reported on its survey of the aviation shore establishment. Recognizing the demands that would have to be met if the approach of war should precipitate a great expansion, the Board recommended for aviation the enlargement of 11 existing stations and the erection of 16 new ones, including Oahu (Kaneohe), Midway, Wake, Guam, and five other Pacific Islands.

16 December The K-2 airship was delivered to NAS Lakehurst, N.J., for trials. This was the prototype for the World War II K Class patrol airships, of which 135 were procured.

The non-rigid airship K-2, prototype for World War II LTA fleet 1053773

1939

27 March Following the successful experimental refueling of patrol planes by the submarine *Nautilus* (SS 168), the Commander-in-Chief U.S. Fleet (CIN-CUS), directed that Submarine Division Four and Patrol Wing Two conduct refueling tests at frequent intervals and carry out an Advanced Base problem each quarter to develop to the utmost the possibilities for refueling patrol planes under various conditions.

7 April An amphibian version of the PBY flying boat was ordered from Consolidated. This aircraft, the first successful amphibian patrol plane procured by the

Navy, was the prototype for the PBY-5A which was widely used in World War II.

15 May A contract was issued to Curtiss-Wright for the XSB2C-1 dive bomber, thereby completing action on a 1938 design competition. The preceding month, Brewster had received a contract for the XSB2A-1. As part of the mobilization in ensuing years, large production orders were issued for both aircraft, but serious managerial and developmental problems were encountered which eventually contributed to discarding the SB2A and prolonged preoperational development of SB2C. Despite this, the SB2C Helldiver would become the principal operational carrier dive bomber.

27 May Lieutenant Colonel Alfred A. Cunningham, first U.S. Marine Corps aviator, died at his home in Sarasota, Fla. He reported for flight training at Annapolis, Md., on 22 May 1912, a day now celebrated as the birthday of Marine Corps aviation; and in a relatively short aviation career, served with distinction in many capacities. During World War I, he organized and commanded the first Marine aviation unit, was among those proposing operations later assigned to the Northern Bombing Group and was commanding officer of its Day Wing. In the postwar period, he served as the first administrative head of Marine Corps aviation and then commanded the First Air Squadron in Santo Domingo.

13 June *Saratoga* and the tanker *Kanawha* (AO 1) completed a 2-day underway refueling test off the coast of southern California, thereby demonstrating the feasibility of refueling carriers at sea, a technique which was to prove vitally important to operations in areas where bases were not available.

13 June The Aviation Cadet Act of 1935 was revised to provide for the immediate commissioning as ensigns or second lieutenants of all cadets on active service and the future commissioning of others upon completion of flight training. The law also extended the service limitation to seven years after completion of training of which the first four would be required, and provided for promotion to the next higher grade on the basis of examination after three years of service. A reduction in the bonus payment upon release to inactive duty was made with the provision that aviation cadets already serving in the fleet be given the option of remaining on the old pay scale with the $1,500 bonus or of accepting commissioned pay and the new $500 discharge payment.

1 July A standard system of numbering patrol squadrons in reference to wings was adopted by which

1939—Continued

the first digit of a squadron designation number became the same as the wing to which it was attached.

1 July By Executive Order, the Aeronautical Board, the Joint Board (later Joint Chiefs of Staff), the Joint Economy Board and the Munitions Board all previously functioning by an understanding between the Secretary of War and the Secretary of the Navy, began functioning under the direction and supervision of the president as Commander-in-Chief of the Army and Navy.

13 July A Fleet Air Tactical Unit was authorized by the Chief of Naval Operations to provide research and advisory activities relating to operational use of new aircraft.

4 August *Yorktown* and *Enterprise* made successful launchings of SBC-3 and O3U-3 aircraft from flight deck and hangar deck catapults in the first practical demonstration of launching aircraft from carriers by means of a hydraulic flush-deck catapult and in the first demonstrations of catapulting aircraft from the hangar deck.

24 August The Acting Secretary approved the detailing of a medical officer to the Bureau of Aeronautics for the purpose of establishing an Aviation Medical Research Unit.

30 August Lieutenant Commander Thurston B. Clark, flying a twin-engined XJO-3 equipped with tricycle landing gear, made 11 landings aboard and take-offs from *Lexington* off Coronado Roads, thereby demonstrating the basic adaptability of twin-engined aircraft and of tricycle landing gear to carrier operations.

5 September The president proclaimed the neutrality of the United States in the European War and directed that the Navy organize a Neutrality Patrol. In complying therewith, the Chief of Naval Operations ordered the Commander, Atlantic Squadron to establish combined air and ship reconnaissance of the sea approaches to the United States and West Indies for the purpose of reporting and tracking any belligerent air, surface, or underwater units in the area.

8 September The president proclaimed the existence of a limited national emergency and directed measures for strengthening national defenses within the limits of peacetime authorizations.

Scout-Observation O3U-1 amphibious version 1061651

1939—Continued

11 September In the first redeployment of patrol squadrons on the Neutrality Patrol, VP-33, equipped with Catalinas, transferred from the Canal Zone to Guantanamo Bay, Cuba, for operations over the Caribbean. Two days later, the Catalinas of VP-51 arrived at San Juan, P.R., from Norfolk, Va., to patrol the southern approaches to the Caribbean through the Lesser Antilles.

21 September VP-21, with 14 PBY aircraft, took off from Pearl Harbor, T.H., for the Philippines via Midway, Wake and Guam, and with its arrival became the first patrol unit in the Asiatic Fleet since 1932. This squadron and another which arrived later the next year, were the nucleus of Patrol Wing 10, formed in the Philippines in December 1940.

1 October To achieve an immediate expansion of pilot training, the syllabus was revised to set up a program of concentrated instruction which reduced the length of the training period from 12 to 6 months. The new program provided a primary course in landplanes and a basic phase in service landplanes and instrument flying for all students, and restricted each student in the advanced program to specialization in either patrol and utility aircraft, observation planes, or carrier aircraft. Ground school was similarly concentrated and shortened from 33 to 18 weeks.

14 October The Naval Aircraft Factory was authorized to develop radio control equipment for use in remote controlled flight-testing of aircraft so that dives, pullouts, and other maneuvers could be performed near the aircraft's designed strength without risking the life of a test pilot.

1 December Ensign A. L. Terwilliger was designated a Master Horizontal Bomber, the first Naval Aviator in a fleet squadron to so qualify.

8 December To effect a higher degree of coordination in research, the Secretary of the Navy directed that the Bureaus of Aeronautics and Ordnance acting separately, and the Bureaus of Engineering and Construction and Repair, acting as one unit, designate an officer to head a section in the respective Bureaus devoted to science and technology and also to act as a liaison officer with the Naval Research Laboratory and as a member of the Navy Department Council for Research. By the same order, the duties performed in the Office of the Chief of the Naval Operations concerned with research and invention were transferred to the Office of the Secretary and placed under the administration of the Director, Naval Research Laboratory.

20 December A contract was issued to Consolidated for 200 PBY type aircraft to support an increase in patrol plane squadrons growing out of Neutrality Patrol requirements. This was the largest single order for naval aircraft since the end of World War I.

OS2U Kingfisher used on shipboard and for inshore patrol 407887

The landing signal officer waves off an SB2U 1053782

SB2U-1 ready for take-off from Saratoga 105378

Lexington, Yorktown, Ranger and Enterprise 1061652

Camera man in SU-1 shoots oblique photograph 458706

Curtiss SBC-4 Marine Corps Scout dive bomber 16455

Vought SBU-1 Scout dive bomber 1061653

Curtiss XF11-C was later redesignated XBF2C-1 46266

The Douglas RD-2 amphibian in executive colors 5206

Marine Corps field, Quantico, 1931; the base for aircraft squadrons, east coast expeditionary force 1053789

PART 5

World War II

1940–1945

Thirty years after the Navy had acquired its first airplane, and only 19 years after it had acquired its first aircraft carrier, Naval Aviation faced the supreme test of war. When it was called upon to carry the fight to the enemy, it not only carried out its tasks, but forged ahead to become the very backbone of fleet striking power.

If it had not already been shown in combat before the United States entered the war, all doubts as to the potency of naval air power were removed by the infamous, yet skillfully executed attack on Pearl Harbor, when Japanese carrier aircraft in one swift stroke eliminated a major portion of the Navy's heavy surface power. That our own forces had the kernel of a similar potential was demonstrated on a much smaller scale as carrier forces struck the first retaliatory blows.

The geographic position of the United States put it squarely between two wars that had little in common. Air operations on the Atlantic side, except for participation in three amphibious operations, were essentially a blockade and a campaign to protect ships delivering raw materials to our factories and war munitions and reinforcements to our Allies. In the Pacific, it was a matter of stopping an enemy advance which, in a few short months, had spread over all the western and parts of the south and central Pacific, and then carrying out the bitterly contested task of driving him homeward across the broad expanse of an island-dotted sea.

The country was hardly ready for either campaign. The Navy and Marine Corps air arms could muster only 7 large and 1 small aircraft carriers, 5 patrol wings and 2 Marine aircraft wings, 5,900 pilots and 21,678 enlisted men, 5,233 aircraft of all types including trainers, and a few advanced air bases. But aided by its distance from the enemy and fortunate in its industrial power, the United States built the ships, planes and equipment. Its military forces trained the land, sea and air forces that ultimately beat down the enemy, drove them from strategically located bases, cut off their raw materials, and placed the allied forces in position to launch final air and amphibious offensives. These offensives were made unnecessary as the awesome destructive power of the atom was released upon Hiroshima and Nagasaki.

For the first time in history, naval engagements were fought entirely in the air without opposing surface forces sighting each other. New words and phrases entered the aviator's lexicon; words like air support, hunter-killer, JATO, CIC, CAP, bogie, scramble and splash. Radar pierced the night and gave new eyes to the fleet; advances in technology, particularly in electronics, improved the defense and added power to the offense. The scientist contributed directly to the war effort in both the development of specialized equipment and in the application of scientific principles to operational tactics. Logistics took on new importance. Refueling and replenishment at sea were developed to a high art and increased the mobility and staying power of fleet forces.

In the course of the war, Navy and Marine pilots destroyed over 15,000 enemy aircraft in the air and on

Exploding depth charge and line of splashes from machinegun bullets bring the end of German submarine 44360

101

the ground, sank 174 Japanese warships, including 13 submarines, totaling 746,000 tons, sank 447 Japanese merchant ships totaling 1,600,000 tons and, in the Atlantic, destroyed 63 German U-boats. (In combination with other agents, Navy and Marine air helped sink another 157,000 tons of war and 200,000 tons of merchant ships and another six Japanese and 20 German submarines.) It was a creditable record, but the Navy's air arm did not play an entirely independent role. It operated as it had developed, as an integral part of naval forces, contributing its full share to the power of the fleet and to the achievement of its mission in controlling the sea.

Many have said that World War II witnessed the full development of aviation, but generalities are often misleading. Many of the opinions expressed before the war on the effect of air power on naval operations were shown up as misconceived, if not false, theories. The bombing tests of the 1920s proved to some that navies were obsolete and that no ship could again operate within the range of land-based air, but carrier task force operations in the war gave little credence to such conclusions. Advocates of independent air power questioned both the possibility and the usefulness of close air support for troops, but such support was proven not only possible but indispensable. Those who questioned the importance of the airplane to navies were equally off the mark. The disappointment of naval officers who visualized decisive fleet engagements in the tradition of Trafalgar and Jutland was no doubt as great as that of the air power theorists who had seen their predictions go awry. By test of war it had become exceedingly clear that neither an Army nor a Navy could either survive or achieve an objective in war without first achieving air superiority. It had also become clear that neither could exert as much force by itself as it could with the aid of air striking power. Aviation had indeed come of age.

1940

4 January Project Baker was established in Patrol Wing 1 for the purpose of conducting experiments with blind landing equipment.

15 February Commander-in-Chief, U.S. Fleet (COM-INCH), noting that reports on air operations in the European War stressed the need of reducing aircraft vulnerability, recommended that naval aircraft be equipped with leak-proof or self-sealing fuel tanks and with armor for pilots and observers. Although the Bureaus of Aeronautics and Ordnance had been investigating these forms of protection for two years, this formal statement of need gave added impetus and accelerated procurement and installation of both armor and self-sealing fuel tanks.

24 February The Bureau of Aeronautics issued a contract for television equipment, including camera, transmitter, and receiver, that was capable of airborne operation. Such equipment promised to be useful both in transmitting instrument readings obtained from radio-controlled structural flight tests, and in providing target and guidance information necessary should radio-controlled aircraft be converted to offensive weapons.

27 February Development of the "Flying Flapjack," a fighter aircraft with an almost circular wing, was initiated with notice of a contract award to Vought-Sikorsky Aircraft for the design of the V-173—a full-scale flying model (as distinguished from a military prototype). This design, based upon the research of a former NACA engineer, Charles H. Zimmerman, was attractive because it promised to combine a high speed of near 500 mph with a very low takeoff speed.

29 February The Bureau of Aeronautics initiated action that led to a contract with Professor H. O. Croft at the University of Iowa, to investigate the possibilities of a turbojet propulsion unit for aircraft.

19 March To assist in the identification of U.S. aircraft on the Neutrality Patrol, Fleet activities were authorized to apply additional National Star Insignia on the sides of the fuselage or hull of aircraft so employed.

22 March Development of guided missiles was initiated at the Naval Aircraft Factory with the establishment of a project for adapting radio controls to a torpedo-carrying TG-2 airplane.

23 April Commander Donald Royce was designated to represent the Navy on an Army Air Corps Evaluation Board for rotary-wing aircraft. This board was established incidental to legislation directing the War Department to undertake governmental development of rotary-wing aircraft.

25 April *Wasp* was commissioned at Boston, Mass., Captain John W. Reeves, Jr., commanding.

20 May The Commanding Officer of the destroyer *Noa* (DD 343) reported on successful operations conducted off the Delaware Capes in which an XSOC-1, piloted by Lieutenant George L. Heap, was hoisted over the side for takeoff and was recovered by the ship while underway. As an epilogue to preliminary operations conducted at anchor on 15 May, Lieutenant

1940—Continued

Heap made an emergency flight transferring a stricken seaman from *Noa* in Harbor of Refuge, Del., to the Naval Hospital, Philadelphia, Pa.

27 May The Secretary of the Navy directed that six destroyers of the DD 445-class be equipped with catapult, plane, and plane handling equipment. DDs 476-481, *Pringle, Stanly, Hutchins, Stevens, Halford,* and *Leutze,* were selected subsequently. Shortcomings in the plane hoisting gear led to removal of the aviation equipment from the first three ships prior to their joining the fleet in early 1943. In October 1943, after limited aircraft operations by *Stevens* and *Halford,* aviation equipment was ordered removed from them and plans for its installation on *Leutze* were canceled.

14 June The Naval Expansion Act included authorization for an increase in aircraft carrier tonnage of 79,500 tons over the limits set 17 May 1938, and a revision of authorized aircraft strength to 4,500 useful airplanes.

15 June Congress revised its previous action and set the aircraft ceiling at 10,000 useful airplanes, including 850 for the Naval Reserve, and not more than 48 useful airships.

25 June The Aeronautical Engineering Duty Only (AEDO) designation was abolished and all men appointed to that special duty were designated for Engineering Duty Only (EDO).

25 June The Chief of Naval Operations promulgated plans for an expanded flight training program calling for the assignment of 150 students per month beginning 1 July, and a regular increase to an entry rate of 300 per month within a year.

27 June The president established a National Defense Research Committee to correlate and support scientific research on the mechanisms and devices of war. Among its members were officers of the War and Navy Departments appointed by the respective Secretaries. Although research on the problems of flight was specifically excluded from its functions, this organization made substantial contributions in various fields of importance to Naval Aviation, including airborne radar.

14 July The initial meeting of what became the National Defense Research Committee's Division 14, or Radar Division, was attended by Alfred L. Loomis, Ralph Bowen, E. L. Bowles and Hugh H. Willis. In this

and subsequent meetings with other scientists, this group defined its mission as "to obtain the most effective military application of microwaves in minimum time." In carrying out this mission, Division 14 developed airborne radar used in the Navy for aircraft interception, airborne early warning and other more specialized applications.

19 July Authorization for a further expansion of the Navy provided an increase of 200,000 tons in the aircraft carrier limits set the previous month, and a new aircraft ceiling of 15,000 useful planes. The act also allowed further increases in aircraft strength on presidential approval.

5 August The Chief Of Naval Operations established general ground rules for exchange of scientific and technical information with a British mission, generally known as the Tizard Mission after its senior member Sir Henry Tizard. In general, free exchange of information was expected on matters concerning aviation, including the field later called radar. The degree of exchange actually achieved surpassed expectations so that the coming of the Tizard Mission served as a benchmark in the interchange of scientific and technical information regarding World War II weaponry.

12 August The Bureau of Ordnance requested informally that the National Defense Research Committee sponsor development, on a priority basis, of proximity fuzes with particular emphasis on anti-aircraft use. Such fuzes had been under consideration for some time and the decision to undertake development followed receipt from the Tizard Mission of reports of British progress.

17 August Section T (so called for its Chairman, Dr. Merle A. Tuve) of Division A, National Defense Research Committee, was established to examine the feasibility of various approaches to developing a proximity fuze. Eight days later, a contract was issued to the Department of Terrestrial Magnetism, Carnegie Institution of Washington, for the research that culminated in the radio VT fuze for anti-aircraft guns and both radio and photoelectric VT fuzes for bombs and rockets.

29 August The exchange with the British Tizard Mission of scientific and technical information concerning radar began at a conference attended by Sir Henry Tizard, two of his associates, and representatives of the U.S. Army and Navy including Lieutenant John A. Moreno of the Bureau of Aeronautics. The initial conference dealt primarily with the British techniques for detecting German bombers but touched

1940—Continued

upon means of identifying friendly aircraft. In follow-on meetings, British developments of shipboard and airborne radar were also discussed. A British disclosure growing out of this exchange of particular importance for airborne radar application was the cavity magnetron, a tube capable of generating high power radio waves of a few centimeters in length.

2 September In exchange for 50 four-stack destroyers, Great Britain, by formal agreement ceded to the United States for a period of 99 years, sites for naval and air bases in the Bahamas, Jamaica, St. Lucia, Trinidad, Antigua, and British Guiana, and extended similar rights freely and without consideration for bases in Bermuda and Newfoundland. Acquisition of these sites advanced our sea frontiers several hundred miles and provided bases from which naval ships and aircraft could cover strategically important sea approaches to our coast and to the Panama Canal.

3 October The Chief of Naval Operations requested the Naval Attaché in London to obtain samples of a variety of British radio echo equipment (radar), including aircraft installations for interception (AI), surface vessel detection (ASV) and aircraft identification (IFF).

5 October The Secretary of the Navy placed all divisions and aviation squadrons of the Organized Reserve on short notice for call to active duty and granted authority to call Fleet Reservists as necessary. On the 24th, the Bureau of Navigation announced plans for mobilizing the aviation squadrons, which called for one third to be ordered to active duty by 7 November and all by 1 January 1941.

9 October The Secretary of the Navy approved a recommendation by the General Board, that 24 of the authorized submarines be equipped to carry aviation gasoline for delivery to seaplanes on the water. This was in addition to *Nautilus* (SS 168) which had demonstrated her ability to refuel patrol planes and had conducted a successful test dive to 300 feet with aviation gasoline aboard; and to *Narwhal* (SC 1) and *Argonaut* (SF 7) which were being altered to carry 19,000 gallons of aviation gasoline each.

11 October The Technical Aide to the Secretary of the Navy, Rear Admiral Harold G. Bowen, proposed a program for development of radio ranging equipment (radar) which formed the basis for the Navy's pre-war development program. In addition to identification equipment and ship-based radar, this program included an airborne radar for surface search.

23 October Within the Atlantic Squadron, an administrative command was set up for carrier aviation entitled, "Aircraft, Atlantic Squadron."

24 October An administrative command for patrol aviation in the Atlantic Squadron was set up under the title, "Patrol Wings, Atlantic Squadron."

28 October The Chief of Naval Operations reported that aircraft with some form of armor and fuel protection were just beginning to go into service use, and that within a year all fleet aircraft, except those assigned Patrol Wing 2, would have such protection.

1 November A reorganization of the fleet changed the administrative organization of aviation by dividing the forces between two oceans. This was the beginning of the independent development of forces according to strategic requirements. In the Atlantic, aviation was transferred from Scouting Force to Patrol Force, which was formed in place of the Atlantic Squadron as a fleet command parallel to Scouting Force, and set up under Commander, Aircraft Patrol Force and Commander, Patrol Wings Patrol Force. In the Pacific, Patrol Wings remained attached to Scouting Force under the combined command Commander, Patrol Wings U.S. Fleet and Commander, Aircraft Scouting Force.

11 November The first general meeting of the Radiation Laboratory was held at the Massachusetts Institute of Technology (MIT). The Radiation Laboratory, as principal scientific and developmental agency of Division 14 of NDRC, was to become instrumental in many aspects of airborne radar development.

15 November The seaplane tender *Curtiss*, first of two ships of her class, was commissioned at Philadelphia, Pa., Commander Samuel P. Ginder commanding.

15 November Naval air operations began from Bermuda. First to operate were the planes of Patrol Squadron 54 based on *George E. Badger* (DD 196).

16 November The Bureau of Aeronautics established a catapult procurement program for *Essex* class carriers. One flight deck catapult and one athwartships hangar deck catapult were to be installed on each of 11 carriers.

18 November The Chief of Naval Operations authorized use of the abbreviation, "RADAR," in unclassified correspondence and conversation and directed that the phrase, Radio Detection and Ranging Equipment, be used in lieu of terms such as Radio Ranging Equipment, Radio Detection Equipment, Radio Echo Equipment, or Pulse Radio Equipment.

30 December   The Bureau of Aeronautics directed that fleet aircraft be painted in non-specular colors. Ship-based aircraft were to be light gray all over; patrol planes were to be light gray except for surfaces seen from above which were to be blue gray.

1941

1 February   The Atlantic and Pacific Fleets were established, completing the division begun the previous November and changing the titles of aviation commands in the Atlantic Fleet to "Aircraft, Atlantic Fleet" and "Patrol Wings, Atlantic Fleet." No change was made in the Pacific Fleet aviation organization at this time.

10 February   As an initial step in training patrol plane pilots to make blind landings, using radio instrument landing equipment which was being procured for all patrol aircraft and their bases, a one-month course of instruction began under Project Baker. This was attended by one pilot from each of 13 squadrons; by one radioman from each of five patrol wings; and by two radiomen from each of five Naval Air Stations.

26 February   An extensive modification of aircraft markings added National Star Insignia to both sides of the fuselage or hull and eliminated those on the upper right and lower left wings; discontinued the use of colored tail markings, fuselage bands and cowl markings; made removal of vertical red, white and blue rudder stripes mandatory; and changed the color of all markings, except the National Insignia, to those of least contrast to the background.

1 March   Support Force, Atlantic Fleet, was established for operations on the convoy routes across the North Atlantic. Its component patrol squadrons were placed under a Patrol Wing established at the same time.

11 March   The president was empowered by an act of Congress to provide goods and services to those nations whose defense he deemed vital to the defense of the United States, thus initiating a Lend-Lease program under which large quantities of the munitions and implements of war were delivered to our allies. *Archer* (BAVG 1) was transferred on 17 November

1941, as the first of 38 escort carriers transferred to the United Kingdom during the war.

17 March   The Chief of the Bureau of Aeronautics approved a proposal for establishing a special NACA committee to review promptly the status of jet propulsion and recommend plans for its application to flight and assisted takeoff.

28 March   The Commanding Officer of *Yorktown* after five months operational experience with the CXAM radar, reported that aircraft had been tracked at a distance of 100 miles and recommended that friendly aircraft be equipped with electronic identification devices and carriers be equipped with separate and complete facilities for tracking and plotting all radar targets.

19 April   Development of a Guided Glider Bomb (Glomb) was initiated at the Naval Aircraft Factory. The Glomb was designed to be towed long distances by a powered aircraft, released in the vicinity of the target, and guided by radio control in its attack. It was equipped with a television camera to transmit a view of the target to the control plane.

20 April   The first successful test of electronic components of a radio-proximity fuze was made at a farm in Vienna, Va., as a radio oscillator, or sonde, which had been fired from a 37-mm pack howitzer, made radio transmissions during its flight. The demonstration, that radio tubes and batteries could be constructed sufficiently rugged to withstand firing from a gun, led Section T of the National Defense Research Committee to concentrate upon the radio-proximity fuze for anti-aircraft guns.

26 April   The Naval Aircraft Factory project officer reported that an unmanned O3U-6 airplane under radio control had been successfully flight-tested beyond the safe bounds of piloted flight and that the information thus obtained had been of great value in overcoming flutter encountered at various speeds and accelerations.

28 April   *Pocomoke*, first of two seaplane tenders of her class, was commissioned at Portsmouth, Va., Commander John D. Price commanding.

30 April   In an initial step towards establishing a glider development program, the Naval Aircraft Factory was requested to undertake preliminary design of a personnel and equipment transport glider. As work progressed and requirements were further clarified, development was initiated for 12- and 24-place

1941—Continued

amphibian gliders to be constructed of wood or plastic by firms not already engaged in building military aircraft.

30 April Commanding Officer, NAS Lakehurst, N.J., directed that the metal-clad airship, ZMC-2, be salvaged and the car complete with engines, instruments and appurtenances be assigned to the Lighter-Than-Air Ground School at Lakehurst. The ZMC-2, completed in August 1929, had been flown over 2,250 hours.

2 May Fleet Air Photographic Unit, Pacific, was established under Commander, Aircraft Battle Force, preceding by one day the establishment of a similar unit in the Atlantic Fleet under Commander, Patrol Wings Atlantic.

3 May Project Roger was established at the Naval Aircraft Factory to install and test airborne radar equipment. Its principal assignment involved support of the Radiation Laboratory at the Massachusetts Institute of Technology and the Naval Research Laboratory in various radar applications including search and blind bombing and in radio control of aircraft.

8 May The establishment of Aviation Repair Units 1 and 2 was directed to provide a nucleus of aircraft repair and maintenance personnel ready for overseas deployment as advanced bases were established.

10 May The Naval Aircraft Factory reported that it was negotiating with the Radio Corporation of America for the development of a radio altimeter suitable for use in radio-controlled assault drones.

15 May The seaplane tender *Albemarle* arrived at Argentia, Newfoundland, to establish a base for Patrol Wing, Support Force operations and to prepare for the imminent arrival of VP-52, the first squadron to fly patrols over the North Atlantic convoy routes.

21 May The Bureau of Aeronautics requested the Engineering Experiment Station, Annapolis, Md., to undertake development of a liquid-fueled assisted takeoff unit for use on patrol planes. This marked the Navy's entry into the field that later came to be called jet assisted takeoff (JATO), and was the Navy's first

Launching a PBM Mariner, a dramatic demonstration of the utility of newly developed jet-assisted takeoff (JATO) 415346

development program, other than jet exhaust from reciprocating engines, directed towards utilizing jet reaction for aircraft propulsion.

27 May The president proclaimed that an unlimited national emergency confronted the country, requiring that its military, naval, air, and civilian defenses be put on the basis of readiness to repel any and all acts or threats of aggression directed toward any part of the Western Hemisphere.

2 June *Long Island,* first escort carrier of the U.S. Navy, was commissioned at Newport News, Va., Commander Donald B. Duncan commanding. Originally designated AVG 1, *Long Island* was a flush-

Long Island, first escort carrier of the U.S. Navy, was converted from the cargo ship Mormacmail 26567

1941—Continued

deck carrier converted in 67 working days from the cargo ship *Mormacmail.*

4 June   The Naval Aircraft Factory reported that development of airborne television had progressed to the point that signals transmitted by this means could be used to alter the course of the transmitting plane.

11 June   An Aircraft Armament Unit was formed at NAS Norfolk, Va., with Lieutenant Commander William V. Davis as Officer-in-Charge, to test and evaluate armament installations of increasing complexity.

28 June   To strengthen the provisions for utilizing science in war, the president created the Office of Scientific Research and Development and included in its organization the National Defense Research Committee and a newly established Committee on Medical Research.

30 June   Turboprop engine development was initiated as a joint Army-Navy project, with a Navy contract to Northrop Aircraft for the design of an aircraft gas turbine developing 2,500-hp at a weight of less than 3,215 pounds.

1 July   The first landing, takeoff, and catapult launching from an escort carrier were made aboard *Long Island,* by Lieutenant Commander William D. Anderson, commanding officer of VS-201.

1 July   The Test, Acceptance and Indoctrination Units that had been established at San Diego, Calif., and Norfolk, Va., in May to fit out new patrol aircraft and to indoctrinate new crews in their use, were expanded and set up as separate commands. The San Diego Unit, which retained its original name, was placed under Commander, Aircraft Scouting Force, and the Norfolk unit became Operational Training Squadron under Commander, Patrol Wings Atlantic.

1 July   Patrol Wing, Support Force, was redesignated and established as Patrol Wing 7, Captain Henry M. Mullinix commanding.

3 July   The Seaplane tender *Barnegat*, first of 26 ships of her class, was commissioned at Bremerton, Wash., Commander Felix L. Baker commanding.

4 July   Planes of Patrol Squadron 72, based on *Goldsborough* (DD 188), flew protective patrols from Reykjavik, Iceland, until the 17th, to cover the arrival of Marine Corps garrison units from the United States.

7 July   The First Marine Aircraft Wing, composed of a Headquarters Squadron and Marine Air Group 1, was organized at Quantico, Va., under command of Lieutenant Colonel Louis E. Woods. It was the first of its type in the Marine Corps and the first of five wings organized during the war period.

8 July   Patrol Wing 8 was established at Norfolk, Va., Commander John D. Price commanding.

12 July   The Naval Research Laboratory was transferred from the Office of the Secretary of the Navy to the cognizance of the Bureau of Ships, and a Naval Research and Development Board was established in the Office of the Secretary of the Navy composed of representatives of the Chief of Naval Operations and the Bureaus of Aeronautics, Ordnance, Ships, and Yards and Docks, and led by a civilian scientist with the title Coordinator of Research and Development. Dr. Jerome C. Hunsaker served as coordinator until December when he was relieved by Rear Admiral Julius A. Furer.

17 July   The organization for development of proximity fuzes was realigned so that Section T could devote its entire effort to radio-proximity fuzes for anti-aircraft projectiles. Responsibility for photoelectric and radio fuzes for bombs and rockets was transferred to Section E of the National Defense Research Committee at the National Bureau of Standards.

18 July   Commander James V. Carney, Senior Support Force Staff Officer, reported that British type ASV radar has been installed in one PBY-5 each of VP-71, VP-72, and VP-73 and two PBM-1s of VP-74. Initial installation of identification equipment (IFF) was made about the same time. In mid-September radar was issued for five additional PBM-1s of VP-74 and one PBY-5 of VP-71, and shortly thereafter for other aircraft in Patrol Wing 7 squadrons. Thereby the Wing became the first operational unit of the U.S. Navy to be supplied with radar-equipped aircraft. Its squadrons operated from Norfolk, Va., Quonset Point, R.I., and advanced bases on Greenland, Newfoundland and Iceland during the last months of the neutrality patrol.

18 July   Aviation was given representation on the highest of the Army and Navy boards as membership of the Joint Board was revised to include the Deputy Chief of Staff for Air and the Chief of the Bureau of Aeronautics.

21 July   The requirement that all students assigned to the carrier-plane phase of flight training be given time in each of the three basic aircraft types was abolished,

1941—Continued

and the practice of assigning students to specialized training in either fighters, scout bombers or torpedo planes began.

25 July Thirty P-40s and three primary training planes of the 33rd Pursuit Squadron, Army Air Forces, were loaded aboard *Wasp* at Norfolk, Va., for transport to Reykjavik, Iceland.

28 July To establish a continuing organization for training flight crews, the Chief of Naval Operations directed that action be taken as expeditiously as practicable to provide additional gunnery and tactical training in the pilot training program; to establish within the Atlantic and Pacific Fleets at Norfolk, Va., and San Diego, Calif.; Advanced Carrier Training groups to indoctrinate newly designated Naval Aviators in the operation of current model carrier aircraft; and to assign a number of patrol squadrons in each fleet the primary task of providing familiarization, indoctrination, advanced gunnery and tactical training for new flight crews.

28 July The Operational Training Squadron of the Atlantic Fleet, and the Test, Acceptance and Indoctrination Unit of the Pacific Fleet were redesignated Transition Training Squadron, Atlantic and Pacific, respectively.

29 July The Secretary of the Navy approved the installation of a Radar Plot aboard carriers as "the brain of the organization" protecting the fleet from air attack. The first installation was planned for the island structure of *Hornet*.

1 August A Microwave (AI-10) radar developed by the Radiation Laboratory and featuring a Plan Position Indicator (PPI) was given its initial airborne test in the XJO-3 at Boston Airport. During the test flights, which continued through 16 October, Radiation Laboratory scientists operated the radar and devised modifications while naval personnel from Project Roger (usually Chief Aviation Pilot C. L. Kullberg) piloted the aircraft. During the tests, surface vessels were detected at ranges up to 40 miles; radar-guided approaches against simulated enemy aircraft were achieved at ranges up to 3.5 miles. Operational radars which were developed from this equipment were capable of searching a circular area and included the ASG for K-type airships and the AN/APS-2 for patrol planes.

1 August The Bureau of Aeronautics requested the Naval Research Laboratory to develop radar guidance equipment for assault drones, both to relay target information to a control operator and to serve as automatic homing equipment. This marked the initiation of radar applications to guided missiles.

6 August Patrol Squadrons 73 and 74 initiated routine air patrols from Reykjavik, Iceland, over North Atlantic convoy routes.

6 August In recognition of the radical change which radar was causing in the method of using fighters to protect the fleet, the Chief of Naval Operations issued a "Tentative Doctrine for Fighter Direction from Aircraft Carriers" and directed that carriers and other ships equipped with radar immediately organize fighter direction centers.

7 August The Chief, Bureau of Aeronautics issued a preliminary plan for installing radar in naval aircraft. Long range search radar (British ASV or American ASA) was to be installed in patrol planes. Short range search radar (British Mk II ASV modified for Fleet Air Arm or American ASB) was to be installed in one torpedo plane in each section commencing with the TBF while space needed for search radar was to be reserved in new scout-dive-bombers and scout-observation planes. Interception equipment, when available, would be installed in some F4Us and a British AI Mk IV radar was being installed in an SBD with a view to its use as an interim interceptor. The plan also included installation of appropriate radio altimeters in patrol and torpedo planes, and recognition equipment in all service airplanes.

5 September Artemus L. Gates, Naval Aviator No. 65 and member of the First Yale Unit of World War I, took the oath of office as Assistant Secretary of the Navy for Aeronautics; the first to hold the office since the resignation of David S. Ingalls in 1932.

9 September The Bureau of Aeronautics requested the National Defense Research Committee and the Naval Research Laboratory to develop an interceptor radar suitable for installation in single engine, single seat fighters such as the F4U.

1 October The Aviation Supply Office was established at Philadelphia, Pa., under the joint cognizance of the Bureau of Aeronautics and the Bureau of Supplies and Accounts, to provide centralized control over the procurement and distribution of all aeronautical materials regularly maintained in the general stock.

8 October Organizational provision for guided missiles was made in the fleet by the establishment o[

1941—Continued

"Special Project Dog" in Utility Squadron 5, to test and operate radio-controlled offensive weapons and to train personnel in their use. VJ-5 was also directed to develop a radio-controlled fighter plane—"aerial ram" or "aerial torpedo"—to be flown into enemy bomber formations and exploded.

13 October The Bureau of Aeronautics directed that all fleet aircraft be painted non-specular light gray except for surfaces seen above which were to be blue-gray. In late December, this color scheme was extended to shore-based airplanes except trainers.

20 October *Hornet* was commissioned at Norfolk, Va., Captain Marc A. Mitscher commanding.

21 October In tests with MAD gear (Magnetic Airborne Detector), a PBY from NAS Quonset Point, R.I., located the submarine S-48. The tests were carried out in cooperation with the National Defense Research Committee.

29 October Patrol Squadron 82 received the first of a planned full complement of PBO-1s at NAS Norfolk, Va. Assignment of these aircraft, actually destined for the British and painted with British markings, was the beginning of what became an extensive use of land

planes by patrol squadrons during the war and, although it was not yet apparent, was the first move toward the eventual elimination of the flying boat from patrol aviation.

1 November By Executive Order, the president directed that, until further orders the Coast Guard operate as a part of the Navy subject to the orders of the Secretary of the Navy.

18 November Doctor L. A. DuBridge of the Radiation Laboratory reported that the initial design of a 3-cm aircraft intercept radar was completed.

26 November *Kitty Hawk*, first of two aircraft ferries, was commissioned, Commander C. E. Rogers commanding.

1 December Patrol Wing 9 began forming at Quonset Point, R.I., with Lieutenant Commander Thomas U. Sisson as prospective commanding officer.

7 December Japanese carrier aircraft launched a devastating attack on ships at Pearl Harbor, Hawaii, and on the military and air installations in the area. The three aircraft carriers of the Pacific Fleet were not present. *Saratoga*, just out of overhaul, was moored at San Diego, Calif. *Lexington* was at sea about 425 miles southeast of Midway toward which she was

Pearl Harbor Sunday morning, December 7, 1941; aircraft burning from attack by Japanese Carrier-based air 19948

1920—Continued

Enterprise, known as "The Big E" was in almost continuous action during World War II 704377

headed to deliver a Marine Scout Bombing Squadron. *Enterprise* was also at sea about 200 miles west of Pearl Harbor, returning from Wake Island after delivering a Marine Fighter Squadron there. Her Scouting Squadron 6, launched early in the morning to land at Ewa Airfield, Hawaii, arrived during the attack and engaged enemy aircraft.

9 December The Secretary of the Navy authorized the Bureau of Ships to contract with the RCA Manufacturing Company for a service test quantity of 25 sets of ASB airborne search radar. This radar had been developed by the Naval Research Laboratory (under the designation XAT) for installation in dive bombers and torpedo planes.

10 December Aircraft from *Enterprise* attacked and sank the Japanese submarine I-70 in waters north of the Hawaiian Islands. This was one of the submarines

used to scout the Hawaiian area in connection with the Pearl Harbor attack and was the first Japanese combatant ship sunk by United States aircraft during World War II.

10 December Antisubmarine patrols over the South Atlantic were initiated by Patrol Squadron 52, equipped with Catalinas operating from Natal, Brazil.

12 December The Naval Air Transport Service (NATS) was established under the Chief of Naval Operations to provide rapid air delivery of critical equipment, spare parts, and specialist personnel to naval activities and fleet forces all over the world.

14 December Patrol Wing 10 departed Cavite and, with its two patrol squadrons and four seaplane tenders, began withdrawal from the Philippines. Before reaching Australia it operated from various bases along

1941—Continued

the way, including Balikpapan, Soerabaja, and Ambon in the Netherlands East Indies.

15 December Patrol Wing 8 transferred from Norfolk, Va., to Alameda, Calif., for duty on the west coast.

16 December The Secretary of the Navy approved an expansion of the pilot training program from the existing schedule of assigning 800 students per month to one calling for 2,500 per month thereby leading to a production of 20,000 pilots annually by mid-1943.

17 December The Naval Research Laboratory reported that flight tests in a PBY of radar utilizing a duplexing antenna switch had been conducted with satisfactory results. The duplexing switch made it possible to use a single antenna for both transmission of the radar pulse and reception of its echo; thereby, the necessity for cumbersome "yagi" antenna no longer existed, a factor which contributed substantially to the reliability, and hence the effectiveness, of World War II airborne radar.

17 December Seventeen SB2U-3 Vindicators of VMSB-231, led by a PBY of Patrol Wing 1, arrived at Midway Island from Oahu, Hawaii, completing the longest mass flight by single-engine aircraft then on record in 9 hours, 45 minutes. It was the same squadron that was en route to Midway on 7 December aboard *Lexington* when reports of the attack on Pearl Harbor forced the carrier to turn back short of her goal.

18 December Two-plane detachments from Patrol Wings 1 and 2, based in Hawaii, began scouting patrols from Johnston Island.

18 December Following an operational loss of an American Volunteer Group (Flying Tigers) aircraft and the ensuing confrontation between the pilot, Eriksen Shilling, and a group of Chinese, "blood chits" were developed. The Flying Tigers were a U.S. volunteer group formed by Major General Claire L. Chennault for operations in the China-Burma-India theater. The first blood chits were printed on silk by Chinese Intelligence and stitched on the back of the American's flight jackets. It showed the flag and promised a reward for assisting the bearer. The message was printed in several languages. Blood chits were later used by the fast carrier groups in the Pacific during World War II, in the Korean and Vietnam wars and in Desert Storm. Another item similar to blood

chits was the "Barter Kit." It was issued during the Cuban Missile Crisis and Vietnam and included gold coins, watches, etc. . . . to barter for assistance if downed.

25 December Two-plane detachments from squadrons at Pearl Harbor and Kaneohe, Hawaii, began patrols from Palmyra Island, a principal staging base to the South Pacific.

1942

2 January The first organized lighter-than-air units of World War II, Airship Patrol Group 1, Commander George H. Mills commanding, and Airship Squadron 12, Lieutenant Commander Raymond F. Tyler commanding, were established at NAS Lakehurst, N.J.

5 January A change in regulations, covering display of National Insignia on aircraft, returned the star to the upper right and lower left wing surfaces and revised rudder striping to 13 red and white horizontal stripes.

7 January Expansion of Naval Aviation to 27,500 useful planes was approved by the president.

11 January *Saratoga,* while operating at sea 500 miles southwest of Oahu, Hawaii, was hit by a submarine torpedo and forced to retire for repairs.

11 January Patrol Squadron 22, with PBY-5 Catalinas, joined Patrol Wing 10 at Ambon, the first aviation reinforcements from the Central Pacific to reach southwest Pacific Forces opposing the Japanese advance through the Netherlands East Indies.

14 January The formation of four Carrier Aircraft Service Units (CASU) from four small Service Units, previously established in the Hawaiian area, was approved.

16 January To protect the advance of Task Force 8 for its strike against the Marshall and Gilbert Islands, planes of Patrol Squadron 23 began daily searches of the waters between their temporary base at Canton Island and Suva in the Fijis. These were the first combat patrols by aircraft in the South Pacific.

23 January The first naval aircraft to operate in the Samoan Islands, OS2Us of VS-1-D14, arrived with Marine Corps reinforcements from San Diego, Calif.

29 January Five-inch projectiles containing radio-proximity fuzes were test fired at the Naval Proving Ground, Dahlgren, Va., and 52 percent of the fuzes

1942—Continued

functioned satisfactorily by proximity to water at the end of a 5-mile trajectory. This performance, obtained with samples selected to simulate a production lot, confirmed that the radio-proximity fuze would greatly increase the effectiveness of anti-aircraft batteries and led to immediate small scale production of the fuze.

30 January   The Secretary of the Navy authorized a glider program for the Marine Corps consisting of small and large types in sufficient numbers for the training and transportation of two battalions of 900 men each.

1 February   The Secretary of the Navy announced that all prospective Naval Aviators would begin their training with a three months' course emphasizing physical conditioning and conducted by Pre-Flight Schools to be established at universities in different parts of the country. The training began at the Universities of North Carolina and Iowa in May, the University of Georgia and St. Mary's College, Calif., in June, and at Del Monte, Calif., in January 1943.

1 February   First U.S. Carrier Offensive—Task Forces 8 (Vice Admiral William F. Halsey) and 17 (Rear Admiral Frank J. Fletcher), built around the carriers *Enterprise* and *Yorktown,* bombed and bombarded enemy installations on the islands of Wotje, Kwajalein,

Attacking Japanese torpedo plane is shot down by antiaircraft fire from carriers raiding Marshall Islands 201986

Jaluit, Makin, and Mili in the Marshall and Gilbert Islands.

12 February   The Chief of Naval Operations promulgated an advanced base program using the code names "Lion" and "Cub" to designate major and minor bases, and in July added "Oaks" and "Acorns" for aviation bases. This was the beginning of a concept of functional components which developed as the war progressed and which provided planners and commanders with a means of ordering standardized units of personnel, equipment, and material to meet any special need in any area, in much the same manner as ordering from a mail-order catalogue.

16 February   A Navy developed Air-Track blind landing system was in daily use in Iceland for landing flying boats. Other blind-landing systems were in various phases of development, and work on the Ground Controlled Approach system had progressed to the point that Navy personnel had made talk-down landings at the East Boston (Commonwealth) Airport, Mass.

17 February   Commander-in-Chief, U.S. Fleet authorized removal of athwartships hangar deck catapults from *Wasp, Yorktown, Enterprise* and *Hornet.*

21 February   The seaplane tender *Curtiss* and Patrol Squadron 14 arrived at Noumea, New Caledonia, to begin operations from what became a principal Navy base in the South Pacific during the first year of the war.

23 February   The Bureau of Aeronautics outlined a comprehensive program which became the basis for the wartime expansion of pilot training. In place of the existing 7-months course, the new program required eleven and one half months for pilots of single or twin-engine aircraft and twelve and one half months for four-engine pilots; and was divided into three months at Induction Centers, three months in Primary, three and one half months in Intermediate and two or three months in Operational Training, depending on type aircraft used.

24 February   First Wake Island Raid—A striking force, (Vice Admiral William F. Halsey) composed of the carrier *Enterprise* with cruiser and destroyer screen, attacked Wake Island.

26 February   The Navy's Coordinator of Research and Development requested the National Defense Research Committee to develop an expendable radio sonobuoy for use by lighter-than-air craft in antisubmarine warfare.

1942—Continued

27 February   The seaplane tender *Langley,* formerly first carrier of the U.S. Navy, was sunk by enemy air attack 74 miles from her destination while ferrying 32 AAF P-40s to Tjilatjap, Java.

1 March   Carrier Replacement Air Group 9 was established at NAS Norfolk, Va., under command of Commander William D. Anderson. It was the first numbered Air Group in the Navy and marked the end of the practice of naming air groups for the carriers to which they were assigned.

1 March   Ensign William Tepuni, USNR, piloting a Lockheed Hudson, PBO, of VP-82 based at Argentia, Newfoundland, attacked and sank the U-656 southwest of Newfoundland—the first German submarine sunk by U.S. forces in World War II.

2 March   Regularly scheduled operations by the Naval Air Transport Service were inaugurated with an R4D flight from Norfolk, Va., to Squantum, Mass.

4 March   First Raid on Marcus—*Enterprise,* as part of Task Force 16 (Vice Admiral William F. Halsey), moved to within 1,000 miles of Japan to launch air attacks on Marcus Island.

7 March   Patrol Wing 10 completed withdrawal from the Philippines and the Netherlands East Indies, and established headquarters in Perth, Australia, for patrol operations along the west coast of Australia.

7 March   The practicability of using a radio sono-buoy in aerial anti-submarine warfare was demonstrated in an exercise conducted off New London, Conn., by the K-5 blimp and the S-20 submarine. The buoy could detect the sound of the submerged submarine's propellers at distances up to three miles, and radio reception aboard the blimp was satisfactory up to five miles.

8 March   Inshore Patrol Squadron VS-2-D14, which had arrived at Bora Bora, on 17 February, inaugurated air operations from the Society Islands.

9 March   VR-1, the first of 13 VR squadrons established under the Naval Air Transport Service during World War II, was established at Norfolk, Va., Commander Cyril K. Wildman commanding.

10 March   A carrier air strike, launched from *Lexington* and *Yorktown* in the Gulf of Papua, flew over the 15,000-foot Owen Stanley Mountains on the tip of New Guinea to hit Japanese shipping engaged in landing troops and supplies at Lae and Salamaua. One converted light cruiser, a large minesweeper, and a cargo ship were sunk and other ships damaged.

10 March   A contract with the Office of Scientific Research and Development became effective whereby Johns Hopkins University agreed to operate a laboratory which became known as the Applied Physics Laboratory. This was one of several important steps in the transition of the radio-proximity fuze from development to large scale production. Other steps taken within the next 6 weeks included the organizational transfer of Section T from the National Defense Research Committee directly to the Office of Scientific Research and Development and the relocation of most of the Section T staff from the Carnegie Institution of Washington to the Applied Physics Laboratory at Silver Spring, Md.

26 March   Unity of command over Navy and Army air units operating over the sea to protect shipping and conduct antisubmarine warfare was vested in the Navy.

29 March   The forward echelon of Marine Fighter Squadron 212 arrived at Efate to construct an air strip from which the squadron initiated operations in the New Hebrides on 27 May.

6 April   The administrative command Aircraft, Atlantic Fleet, was redesignated Carriers, Atlantic Fleet.

7 April   To provide aviation maintenance men with special training required to support air operations at advanced bases, Aircraft Repair Units 1 and 2 were merged to form the Advanced Base Aviation Training Unit (ABATU) at Norfolk, Va.

9 April   A radio controlled TG-2 drone, directed by control pilot Lieutenant Moulton B. Taylor of Project Fox, made a torpedo attack on *Aaron Ward* (DD 483) steaming at 15 knots in Narragansett Bay. Taylor utilized a view of the target obtained by a television camera mounted in the drone, and directed the attack so that the torpedo was released about 300 feet directly astern of the target and passed under it.

10 April   A reorganization of the Pacific Fleet abolished the Battle and Scouting Forces and set up new type commands for ships and aviation. With the change, titles of the aviation type commands became Carriers, Pacific, and Patrol Wings, Pacific.

1942—Continued

Hornet with B-25 bombers on board enroute to launching point for the first Tokyo raid, 1942 1061486

18 April Raid on Tokyo—From a position at sea 668 miles from Tokyo, the carrier *Hornet* launched 16 B-25s of the 17th AAF Air Group led by Lieutenant Colonel Jimmy H. Doolittle, USA, for the first attack on the Japanese homeland. *Hornet* sortied from Alameda, Calif., 2 April, made rendezvous with *Enterprise* and other ships of Task Force 16 (Vice Admiral William F. Halsey) north of the Hawaiian Islands, and proceeded across the Pacific to the launching point without making port.

18 April A Night Fighter Development Unit was established to be located at NAS Quonset Point, R.I. This unit, originally named Project Argus was renamed Project Affirm to avoid confusion with the electronic element (Argus Unit) of an advanced base. Project Affirm's official purpose was development and test of night fighter equipment for Navy and Marine Corps aircraft; in addition it developed tactics and trained officers and men for early night fighter squadrons and as night fighter directors.

19 April Two tests of the feasibility of utilizing drone aircraft as guided missiles were conducted in Chesapeake Bay. In one, Utility Squadron VJ-5, utilizing visual direction, crash-dived a BG-1 drone into the water beyond its target, the wreck of *San Marcos* and a live bomb exploder in the drone failed to detonate. The second and more successful test was conducted by Project Fox from CAA intermediate field, Lively, Va., using a BG-2 drone equipped with a television camera to provide a view of the target. Flying in a control plane 11 miles distant, Lieutenant Moulton B. Taylor directed the drone's crash-dive into a raft being towed at a speed of eight knots.

20 April *Wasp* on special ferry duty out of Glasgow, Scotland, entered the Mediterranean and launched 47 RAF Spitfires to Malta. When the operation was duplicated on 9 May, it was the occasion for Winston Churchill's message, "Who says a Wasp cannot sting twice?"

24 April A new specification for color of naval aircraft went into effect. The color of service aircraft remained non-specular light gray with non-specular blue-gray on surfaces visible from above. Advanced trainers were to be finished in glossy aircraft gray with glossy orange yellow on wing and aileron surfaces visible from above while primary trainers were to be finished glossy orange-yellow with gray landing gear.

30 April The Air Operational Training Command was established with headquarters at Jacksonville, Fla. Four days later the Naval Air Stations at Jacksonville, Miami, Fla., Key West, Fla, and Banana River, Fla., and their satellite fields were assigned to the new command.

4–8 May Battle of Coral Sea—In the first naval engagement in history fought without opposing ships making contact, United States carrier forces stopped a Japanese attempt to land at Port Moresby, Papua, New Ginea, by turning back the covering carrier force. Task Force 17 (Rear Admiral Frank J. Fletcher) with the carrier *Yorktown*, bombed Japanese transports engaged in landing troops in Tulagi Harbor, damaging several and sinking one destroyer (4 May); joined other Allied naval units including Task Force 11 (Rear Admiral Aubrey W. Fitch) with the carrier *Lexington* south of the Louisiades (5 May); and after stationing an attack

1942—Continued

U. S. dive bombers attack the Japanese aircraft carrier Shokaku during the battle of the Coral Sea, May 1942 17422

group in the probable track of the enemy transports, moved northward in search of the enemy covering force. Carrier aircraft located and sank the light carrier *Shoho* covering a convoy (7 May), while Japanese aircraft hit the separately operating attack group and sank one destroyer and one fleet tanker. The next day the Japanese covering force was located and taken under air attack, which damaged the carrier *Shokaku*. Almost simultaneously enemy carrier aircraft attacked Task Force 17, scoring hits which damaged *Yorktown* and set off uncontrollable fires on *Lexington,* as a result of which she was abandoned and was sunk (8 May). Although the score favored the Japanese, they retired from action and their occupation of Port Moresby by sea was deferred and finally abandoned.

10 May   The possibility of increasing the range of small aircraft, by operating them as towed gliders, was demonstrated at the Naval Aircraft Factory when Lieutenant Commanders William H. McClure and Robert W. Denbo hooked their F4Fs to tow lines streamed behind a twin-engined BD (Army A-20), cut their engines and were towed for an hour at 180 knots at 7,000 feet.

10 May   *Ranger,* on a transatlantic ferry trip, reached a position off the African Gold Coast and launched 60 P-40 Warhawks of the Army Air Force to Accra, from which point they were flown in a series of hops to Karachi, India, for operations with the 10th AAF. This was the first of four ferry trips made by *Ranger* to deliver AAF fighters across the Atlantic, the subsequent launches being accomplished on 19 July 1942, 19 January 1943, and 24 February 1943.

10 May   VS-4-D14 (Inshore Patrol Squadron) arrived in the Tonga Islands with the base construction and garrison convoy and set up facilities to conduct antisubmarine patrols from Nukualofa Harbor on Tongatabu.

11 May   The president ordered that an Air Medal be established for award to any person who, while serving in any capacity in or with the Army, Navy, Marine Corps, or Coast Guard after 8 September 1939, distinguishes or has distinguished himself by meritorious achievement while participating in aerial flight.

15 May   The design of the National Star Insignia was revised by eliminating the red disc in the center of the star, and use of horizontal red and white rudder striping was discontinued.

15 May   The Chief of Naval Operations ordered that an Assistant Chief of Naval Operations (Air) be established to deal with aviation matters directly under the Vice Chief of Naval Operations and that the Chief of the Bureau of Aeronautics fill the new office as additional duty. In complying with a further provision of the order that such readjustment of functions be made as would serve the interest of the order, the Vice Chief of Naval Operations subsequently concentrated the aviation functions already being performed in his office into a new Division of Aviation. The office was abolished in mid-June 1942.

15 May   A VR-2 flight from Alameda, Calif., to Honolulu, Hawaii, the first transoceanic flight by NATS aircraft, initiated air transport service in the Pacific.

20 May   Rear Admiral John S. McCain reported for duty as Commander, Aircraft, South Pacific, a new command established to direct the operations of tender and shore-based aviation in the South Pacific area.

26 May   The feasibility of jet-assisted takeoff was demonstrated in a successful flight test of a Brewster F2A-3, piloted by Lieutenant (jg) C. Fink Fischer, at NAS Anacostia, D.C., using five British antiaircraft solid propellant rocket motors. The reduction in takeoff distance was 49 percent.

27 May   The transfer of Patrol Wing 4 from Seattle, Wash., to the North Pacific began with the arrival of Commander, Kodiak, Alaska.

3–4 June   In an attempt to divert forces from the Midway area, a Japanese carrier force launched small raids on Dutch Harbor, Aleutian Islands, hitting twice on the third and once on the fourth and doing consid-

1942—Continued

erable damage to installations ashore. PBYs located the carriers on the fourth but attacks by 11th AAF bombers were unsuccessful.

3–6 June The Battle of Midway—A strong Japanese thrust in the Central Pacific to occupy Midway Island, was led by a four-carrier Mobile Force, supported by heavy units of the Main Body (First Fleet) and covered by a diversionary carrier raid on Dutch Harbor in the Aleutians. This attack was met by a greatly outnumbered United States carrier force composed of Task Force 17 (Rear Admiral Frank J. Fletcher) with *Yorktown,* and Task Force 16 (Rear Admiral R. A. Spruance) with *Hornet* and *Enterprise,* and by Navy, Marine Corps, and Army air units based on Midway. Planes from Midway located and attacked ships of the Japanese Occupation Force 600 miles to the west (3 June), and of the Mobile Force (4 June) as it sent its aircraft against defensive installations on Midway. Concentrating on the destruction of Midway air forces and diverted by their torpedo, horizontal, and dive bombing attacks, the Japanese carriers were caught unprepared for

Formation of Grumman TBF Avengers 417667

the carrier air attack which began at 0930 with the heroic but unsuccessful effort of Torpedo Squadron 8, and were hit in full force at 1030 when dive bombers hit and sank the carriers *Akagi, Kaga,* and *Soryu.* A Japanese counter attack at noon and another 2 hours later, damaged *Yorktown* with bombs and torpedoes so severely that she was abandoned. In the late afternoon, U.S. carrier air hit the Mobile Force again, sinking *Hiryu,* the fourth and last of the Japanese carriers in action. With control of the air irretrievably lost, the Japanese retired under the attack of Midway-based aircraft (5 June) and of carrier air (6 June) in which the heavy cruiser *Mikuma* was sunk and the *Mogami*

severely damaged. Japanese losses totaled two heavy and two light carriers, one heavy cruiser, 258 aircraft, and a large percentage of their experienced carrier pilots. United States losses were 40 shore-based and 92 carrier aircraft, the destroyer *Hammann* (DD 412) and the carrier *Yorktown,* which sank 6 and 7 June respectively, the result of a single submarine attack. The decisive defeat administered to the Japanese put an end to their successful offensive and effectively turned the tide of the Pacific War.

1942—Continued

4 June The TBF Grumman Avenger flown by pilots of a shore-based element of Torpedo Squadron 8, began its combat career with attacks on the Japanese Fleet during the Battle of Midway.

10 June Patrol planes of Patrol Wing 4 discovered the presence of the enemy on Kiska and Attu, Aleutian Islands—the first news of Japanese landings that had taken place on the 7th.

10 June A formal organization, Project Sail, was established at NAS Quonset Point, R.I., for airborne testing and associated work on Magnetic Airborne Detectors (MAD gear). This device was being developed to detect submarines by the change that they induced in the earth's magnetic field. Principal developmental efforts were being carried out by the Naval Ordnance Laboratory and the National Defense Research Committee. In view of the promising results of early trials made with airships and an Army B-18, 200 sets of MAD gear were then being procured.

11–13 June PBY Catalinas, operating from the seaplane tender *Gillis* in Nazan Bay, Atka Island, hit ships and enemy positions on Kiska, Aleutian Islands, in an intense 48-hour attack which exhausted the gasoline and bomb supply aboard *Gillis*, but was not successful in driving the Japanese from the island.

13 June Long Range Navigation Equipment (LORAN), was given its first airborne test. The receiver was mounted in the K-2 airship and, in a flight from NAS Lakehurst, N.J., accurately determined position when the airship was over various identifiable objects. The test culminated with the first LORAN homing from a distance 50 to 75 miles offshore during which the LORAN operator, Dr. J. A. Pierce, gave instructions to the airship's commanding officer which brought them over the shoreline near Lakehurst on a course that caused the commanding officer to remark, "We weren't [just] headed for the hangar. We were headed for the middle of the hangar." The success of these tests led to immediate action to obtain operational LORAN equipment.

15 June *Copahee*, Captain John G. Farrell commanding, was commissioned at Puget Sound Navy Yard, first of 10 escort carriers of the Bogue Class converted from Maritime Commission hulls.

16 June Congress authorized an increase in the airship strength of the Navy to 200 lighter-than-air craft.

17 June The development of Pelican, an antisubmarine guided missile, was undertaken by the National Defense Research Committee with Bureau of Ordnance sponsorship. This device consisted of a glide bomb which could automatically home on a radar beam reflected from the target.

17 June Following the abolition of the newly created office of the Assistant Chief of Naval Operations (Air), the earlier order establishing an aviation organization in the Office of the Chief of Naval Operations was revised to the extent that the Director of the Aviation Division became responsible directly to the Vice Chief of Naval Operations.

17 June A contract was awarded to Goodyear for the design and construction of a prototype model M scouting and patrol airship with 50 percent greater range and volume (625,000 cu. ft.) than the K Class. Four model M airships were procured and placed in service during World War II.

25 June Preliminary investigation of early warning radar had proceeded to the point that the Coordinator for Research and Development requested development be initiated of airborne early warning radar including automatic airborne relay and associated shipboard processing and display equipment. Interest in early warning radar had arisen when Admiral Ernest J. King remarked to Dr. Vannevar Bush, head of the Office of Scientific Research and Development, that Navy ships need to see over the hill, i.e. beyond the line of sight.

26 June Scheduled Naval Air Transport Service operations between the west coast and Alaska were initiated by VR-2.

27 June The Naval Aircraft Factory (NAF) was directed to participate in the development of high altitude pressure suits with particular emphasis upon testing existing types and obtaining information so that they could be tailored and fitted for use in flight. The Navy thus joined the Army which had sponsored earlier work on pressure suits. The NAF expanded its endeavors in the field of high altitude equipment which then included design of a pressure cabin airplane and construction of an altitude test chamber.

29 June Following an inspection of Igor I. Sikorsky's VS-300 helicopter on 26 June, Lieutenant Commander Frank A. Erickson, USCG, recommended that helicopters be obtained for antisubmarine convoy duty and life-saving.

1942—Continued

3 July   In the first successful firing of an American rocket from a plane in flight, Lieutenant Commander James H. Hean, Gunnery Officer of Transition Training Squadron, Pacific Fleet, fired a retro-rocket from a PBY-5A in flight at Goldstone Lake, Calif. The rocket, designed to be fired aft with a velocity equal to the forward velocity of the airplane, and thus to fall verti-

PBY-5A, amphibious version of the Catalina flying boat, carries retro-rockets for antisubmarine warfare 700504

cally, was designed at the California Institute of Technology. Following successful tests, the retro-rocket became a weapon complementary to the magnetic airborne detector with Patrol Squadron 63 receiving the first service installation in February 1943.

7 July   An agreement was reached between the Army and Navy, which provided that the Army would deliver to the Navy a specified number of B-24 Liberators, B-25 Mitchells, and B-34 Venturas to meet the Navy's requirement for long range landplanes. Also, the Navy would relinquish its production cognizance of the Boeing Renton plant to the Army for expanded B-29 production and limit its orders for PBYs to avoid interference with B-24 production.

12 July   Patrol Wings were reorganized to increase the mobility and flexibility of patrol aviation. Headquarters Squadrons were authorized for each wing to furnish administrative and maintenance services to attached squadrons. Geographic areas of responsibility were assigned to each wing, and permanent assignment of squadrons was abolished in favor of assignment as the situation required.

19 July   The seaplane tender *Casco* established an advanced base in Nazan Bay, Atka, Aleutian Islands, to support seaplane operations against Kiska, which

included antishipping search, bombing of enemy positions, and cover for surface force bombardments.

24 July   The Bureau of Aeronautics issued a Planning Directive calling for procurement of four Sikorsky helicopters for study and development by Navy and Coast Guard aviation forces.

1 August   A J4F Widgeon, piloted by Ensign Henry C. White of Coast Guard Squadron 212, based at Houma, La., scored the first Coast Guard kill of an enemy submarine with the sinking of the German U-166 off the passes of the Mississippi.

7 August   Marine Aircraft Wings, Pacific was organized at San Diego, Calif., under command of Major General Ross E. Rowell for the administrative control and logistic support of Marine Corps aviation units assigned to the Pacific Fleet. In September 1944, this command was renamed Aircraft, Fleet Marine Force, Pacific.

7 August 1942–9 February 1943   Capture of Guadalcanal—Air support for the U.S. Marines' first amphibious landing of World War II was provided by three carriers of Air Support Force (Rear Admiral Leigh Noyes), and by Navy, Marine, and Army units of Aircraft, South Pacific (Rear Admiral John S. McCain) operating from bases on New Caledonia and in the New Hebrides. Carrier forces withdrew from direct support (9 Aug) but remained in the area to give overall support to the campaign during which they participated in several of the naval engagements fought over the island. *Saratoga* sank the Japanese light carrier *Ryujo* in the Battle of the Eastern Solomons (23–25 Aug); *Enterprise* was hit by carrier-based bombers (24 Aug) and forced to retire; *Saratoga* was damaged by a submarine torpedo (31 Aug) and forced to retire; and *Wasp* was sunk by a submarine (15 Sep) while escorting a troop convoy to Guadalcanal. *Hornet,* in Task Group 17 (Rear Admiral George D. Murray), hit targets in the Buin-Tonolei-Faisi area (5 Oct); attacked beached Japanese transports and supply dumps on Guadalcanal; destroyed a concentration of seaplanes at Rekata Bay (16 Oct); and, with *Enterprise,* fought in the Battle of Santa Cruz (26–27 Oct) in which she was sunk by air attack. In final carrier actions of the campaign, *Enterprise* took part in the last stages of the Naval Battle for Guadalcanal (12–15 Nov), assisting in sinking 89,000 tons of war and cargo ships, and in the Battle of Rennel Island (29–30 Jan) in which two escort carriers also participated. Ashore, air forces in great variety provided direct support. Navy patrol squadrons flew search, rescue, and offensive missions from sheltered coves and harbors. Marine Fighter

1942—Continued

Escort carriers taking station to provide amphibious troops with close air support during an invasion 1053753

An SBD over Enterprise, Saratoga in the background, 1942

1942—Continued

Squadron 223 and Scout Bombing Squadron 232, delivered by the escort carrier *Long Island,* initiated operations from Henderson Field on Guadalcanal (20 Aug) and were joined within a week by AAF fighter elements and dive bombers from *Enterprise,* and by other elements as the campaign progressed. Until the island was secure (9 Feb), these forces flew interceptor patrols, offensive missions against shipping, and close air support for the Marines and for Army troops relieving them (13 Oct). Marine air units carrying the major air support burden accounted for 427 enemy aircraft during the campaign.

10 August   The headquarters of Patrol Wing 3 shifted within the Canal Zone from NAS Coco Solo to Albrook Field for closer coordination with the Army Air Force Command in the defense of the Panama Canal.

12 August   *Cleveland* (CL 55), operating in the Chesapeake Bay, demonstrated effectiveness of the radio-proximity fuze against aircraft by destroying three radio-controlled drones with four proximity bursts fired from her five inch guns. This successful demonstration led to mass production of the fuze.

12 August   *Wolverine* (IX 64) was commissioned at Buffalo, N.Y, Commander George R. Fairlamb commanding. This ship and *Sable* (IX 81), commissioned the following May, were Great Lakes excursion ships converted for aviation training and as such they operated for the remainder of the war on the inland waters of Lake Michigan. They provided flight decks upon which hundreds of Student Naval Aviators qualified for carrier landings and many flight deck crews received their first practical experience in handling aircraft aboard ship.

13 August   Commander-in-Chief, U.S. Fleet directed that an Aircraft Experimental and Developmental Squadron be established about 30 September 1942 at NAS Anacostia, D.C. This squadron, which replaced the Fleet Air Tactical Unit, was to conduct experiments with new aircraft and equipment in order to determine their practical application and tactical employment.

15 August   Patrol Wing 11 was established at Norfolk, Va., Commander Stanley J. Michael commanding. Five days later the Wing moved to San Juan, P.R., for operations under the Caribbean Sea Frontier.

20 August   The designation of escort carriers was changed from AVG to ACV.

24 August   *Santee,* Captain William D. Sample commanding, was placed in commission at the Norfolk Navy Yard, Va.; the first of four escort carriers of the Sangamon Class converted from Cimarron Class fleet oilers.

30 August   The occupation of Adak, Alaska, by Army forces and the establishment of an advanced seaplane base there by the tender *Teal,* put North Pacific forces within 250 miles of occupied Kiska and in a position to maintain a close watch over enemy

A PBY Catalina flying over the Aleutians near Adak 405443

shipping lanes to that island and to Attu, Aleutian Islands. The tender *Casco,* conducting support operations from Nazan Bay, was damaged by a submarine torpedo and temporarily beached.

1 September   U.S. Naval Air Forces, Pacific, Rear Admiral Aubrey W. Fitch commanding, was established for the administrative control of all air and air service units under the Commander-in-Chief, Pacific (CINCPAC), replacing the offices of Commander, Carriers Pacific, and Commander, Patrol Wings Pacific. The subordinate commands Fleet Air West Coast, Fleet Air Seattle, and Fleet Air Alameda were established at the same time.

6 September   The first Naval Air Transport Service flight to Argentia, Newfoundland, marked the beginning of air transport expansion along the eastern seaboard that during the month extended briefly to Iceland and reached southward to the Canal Zone and Rio de Janeiro, Brazil.

7 September   Air Transport Squadron 2, based at Alameda, Calif., established a detachment at Pearl Harbor, Hawaii, and began a survey flight to the South Pacific as a preliminary to establishing routes between San Francisco, Calif., and Brisbane, Australia.

1942—Continued

16 September Patrol Wing 12 was established at Key West, Fla., Captain William G. Tomlinson commanding, for operations under the Gulf Sea Frontier.

19 September Commander, Patrol Wing 1 departed Kaneohe, Hawaii, for the South Pacific to direct the operations of patrol squadrons already in the area. Headquarters were first established at Noumea, New Caledonia, and subsequently at Espiritu Santo, Guadalcanal, and Munda.

1 October Airship Patrol Group 3, Captain Scott E. Peck commanding, was established at Moffett Field, Calif., to serve as the administrative command for airship squadrons operating on the west coast.

1 October Three functional training commands were established for Air Technical Training, Air Primary Training, and Air Intermediate Training, with headquarters initially at Chicago, Ill., Kansas City, Mo., and Pensacola, Fla., respectively.

12 October Naval Air Centers Hampton Roads, Va., San Diego, Calif., Seattle, Wash., and Hawaiian Islands, and Naval Air Training Centers Pensacola, Fla., and Corpus Christi, Tex., were established to consolidate under single commands the complex of Naval Aviation facilities that had become operational in the vicinity of certain large air stations.

15 October Patrol Wing 14, Captain William M. McDade commanding, was established at San Diego, Calif., for operations under the Western Sea Frontier and for duties concerned with equipping, forming, and establishing patrol squadrons.

17 October Inshore Patrol Squadrons (VS), engaged in coastal antisubmarine reconnaissance and convoy duty under the Sea Frontiers, were transferred to Patrol Wings for administrative control.

19 October The initial installation and deployment of the ASB-3 airborne search radar was reported. This radar, developed by the Naval Research Laboratory for carrier based aircraft, had been installed in five TBF-1s by NAS New York, N.Y., and five SBD-3s by NAS San Pedro, Calif. One aircraft of each type was assigned to Air Group Eleven *(Saratoga)* and the others shipped to Pearl Harbor, Hawaii. Remaining sets on the initial contract for 25 were to be used for spare parts and training.

22 October Westinghouse Electric and Manufacturing Company, by amendment to a design study contract, was authorized to construct two 19A axial flow turbojet powerplants. Thereby, fabrication was initiated of the first jet engine of wholly American design.

28 October Procurement of the expendable radio sonobuoy for use in antisubmarine warfare was initiated as the Commander-in-Chief, U.S. Fleet directed the Bureau of Ships to procure 1,000 sonobuoys and 100 associated receivers.

31 October Air Transport Squadrons Pacific was established over the NATS squadrons based in the Pacific and those on the west coast flying the mainland to Hawaii routes.

1 November Patrol Wings were redesignated Fleet Air Wings, and to permit the organization of patrol aviation on the task force principle, the practice of assigning a standard number of squadrons to each Wing was changed to provide for the assignment of any and all types of aircraft required by the Wing to perform its mission in its particular area.

1 November Airship Patrol Group 1 at NAS Lakehurst, N.J., was redesignated Fleet Airship Group 1.

2 November NAS Patuxent River, Md., was established to serve as a facility for testing experimental airplanes, equipment and material, and as a NATS base.

2 November Fleet Air Wing 6, Captain Douglas P. Johnson commanding was established at NAS Seattle, Wash.

8–11 November Invasion of North Africa—Carrier aircraft from *Ranger* and escort carriers *Sangamon*, *Suwannee,* and *Santee* of Task Group 34.2 (Rear Admiral Ernest D. McWhorter) of the Western Naval Task Force, covered the landings of Army troops near Casablanca, Morocco, (8 Nov) and supported their operation ashore until opposing French forces capitulated (11 Nov). The escort carrier *Chenango* accompanied assault forces to the area and launched her load of 78 AAF P-40s (10–11 Nov) for operations from the field at Port Lyautey, Morocco.

13 November Patrol Squadron 73 arrived at Port Lyautey, Morocco, from Iceland via Bally Kelly, Ireland, and Lyncham, England. Supported by the seaplane tender *Barnegat*, the squadron began antisubmarine operations from French Morocco over the western Mediterranean, the Strait of Gibraltar, and its approaches. Patrol Squadron 92 also arrived at Port Lyautey on the same day via Cuba, Brazil, Ascension Island, and West Africa.

1942—Continued

16 November   Naval Aviation's first night fighter squadron, VMF(N)-531, was established at MCAS Cherry Point, N.C., with Lieutenant Colonel Frank H. Schwable in command. After initial training with SNJs and SB2A-4s, the squadron was assigned twin-engined PV-1 aircraft equipped with British Mark IV type radar.

23 November   The VS-173, a full-scale model of a fighter aircraft with an almost circular wing, made its first flight at the Vought-Sikorsky plant, Stratford, Conn. A military version of this aircraft, the XF5U-1, was constructed later but never flown.

1 December   Fleet Air Wing 15, Captain George A. Seitz commanding, was established at Norfolk, Va., for operations under the Moroccan Sea Frontier.

1 December   Fleet Airship Wing 30, Captain George H. Mills commanding, was established at NAS Lakehurst, N.J., to administer Atlantic Fleet Airship Groups and their component squadrons.

1 December   Airship Patrol Group 3 at NAS Moffett Field, Calif., was redesignated Fleet Airship Wing 31.

26 December   The Chief of Naval Operations approved the merger of the Service Force Aviation Repair Unit and Advanced Cruiser Aircraft Training Unit, established in October 1941 and June 1942 respectively, to form a Scout Observation Service Unit (SOSU) with a mission to maintain battleship and cruiser aircraft and to indoctrinate pilots in their specialized operations. This SOSU, the first of three established during World War II was established 1 January 1943.

27 December   *Santee*, first of 11 escort carriers assigned to Hunter-Killer duty, sortied Norfolk with Air Group 29 on board for free-roving antisubmarine and anti-raider operations in the South Atlantic.

31 December   After pointing out that the need for airborne radar was so apparent and urgent that peacetime methods of procurement and fleet introduction could not be followed, the Chief of the Bureau of Aeronautics requested the Naval Research Laboratory to continue to provide personnel capable of assisting fleet units in the operation and maintenance of radar equipment until a special group of trained personnel could be assembled for that purpose. This special group developed within a few months into the Airborne Coordination Group which

provided trained civilian electronics specialists to fleet units throughout the war and into the postwar period.

31 December   *Essex*, Captain Donald B. Duncan commanding, was placed in operating status at Norfolk, Va.; the first of 17 ships of her class commissioned during World War II.

1943

1 January   Naval Reserve Aviation Bases (NRAB) engaged in Primary Flight Training in all parts of the country were redesignated Naval Air Stations (NAS) without change of mission. This was the end of the NRABs except for Anacostia, D.C., which was abolished on 7 July 1943, and Squantum, Mass., which became an NAS on 1 September 1943.

1 January   Air Force, Atlantic Fleet, was established, Rear Admiral Alva D. Bernhard commanding, to provide administrative, material, and logistic services for Atlantic Fleet aviation in place of the former separate commands Fleet Air Wings, Atlantic, and Carriers, Atlantic, which were abolished. By the same order Fleet Air, Quonset, was established as a subordinate command.

1 January   Ground Controlled Approach equipment (GCA) was called into emergency use for the first time when a snowstorm closed down the field at NAS Quonset Point, R.I., a half hour before a flight of PBYs was due to arrive. The GCA crew located the incoming aircraft on their search radar, and using the control tower as a relay station, "talked" one of them into position for a contact landing. This recovery was made only 9 days after the first successful experimental demonstration of GCA.

5 January   The first combat use of a proximity fuzed projectile occurred when *Helena* (CL 50) off the south coast of Guadalcanal, destroyed an attacking Japanese dive bomber with the second salvo from her 5-inch guns.

7 January   A change in the pilot training program was implemented by the opening of Flight Preparatory Schools in 20 colleges and universities in all parts of the country. Under the new program, students began their training at these schools with three months of academic work fundamental to ground school subjects, then proceeded to War Training Service courses conducted by the Civil Aeronautics Administration at universities for two months training in ground subjects and elementary flight under civilian instructors; then to

1943—Continued

the Pre-Flight Schools for three months of physical conditioning; and finally to Navy flight training beginning at one of the Primary Training Bases.

7 January   Development of the first naval aircraft to be equipped with a turbojet engine was initiated with the issuance of a Letter of Intent to McDonnell Aircraft Corporation for engineering, development, and tooling for two VF airplanes. Two Westinghouse 19-B turbojet engines were later specified and the aircraft was designated XFD-1. It became the prototype for the FH-1 Phantom jet fighter.

10 January   Fleet Air Wing 15 headquarters was transferred from Norfolk, Va., to Port Lyautey, French Morocco, to direct patrol plane operations in the Mediterranean and Gibraltar Strait area.

12 January   The Chief of Naval Air Operational Training directed that aircraft operating from stations under his command be marked for identification purposes with letters and numerals in three groups separated by a dash. The first group provided a letter identification of the station, the second a letter identifying the unit type and the third the number of the aircraft in the unit. The order also provided that when more than one unit was on board a station, a number be added to the station letter. Thus J2-F-22 identified the aircraft as from Jacksonville, Fla., OTU #2 Fighter Training Unit, plane number 22.

14 January   *Independence*, Captain George R. Fairlamb, Jr., commanding, was placed in commission at Philadelphia, Pa.; the first of nine light carriers of her class constructed on Cleveland Class cruiser hulls.

15 January   Captain Spencer "Seth" H. Warner, Head of the Flight Statistics Desk of the Bureau of Aeronautics, introduced Grampaw Pettibone, in the *BuAer News Letter*. Pettibone, a cartoon character drawn by Lieutenant Robert Osborn, was produced as a safety feature in the hope of cutting down on pilot-error accidents. Gramps went on to become famous through the postwar decades as Osborn, after leaving the Navy, continued to contribute his character to *Naval Aviation News* magazine.

17 January   Following tests conducted at NAS San Diego, Calif., by six experienced pilots flying F4U-1s, the commanding officer of VF-12, Commander Joseph C. Clifton, reported that anti-blackout suits raised their tolerance to accelerations encountered in gunnery run and other maneuvers by three to four Gs.

1 February   Bombing Squadron, VB-127, was established at NAS Deland, Fla., with Lieutenant Commander William K. Gentner in command. The squadron was equipped with PV-1 Venturas and, although not the first land plane patrol squadron in the Navy, was the first to have the VB designation.

1 February   A new specification prescribing color and marking of naval aircraft became effective. A basic camouflage color scheme was provided for use on fleet aircraft which consisted of semigloss sea blue on surfaces viewed from above and non-specular insignia white on surfaces viewed from below. The terminology "basic non-camouflage" and "maximum visibility" were introduced for the color schemes described in April 1942, and used on intermediate and primary trainers.

1 February   Regulations governing display of National Insignia on aircraft were again revised by the order to remove those on the upper right and lower left wing surfaces.

11 February   A contract was issued to the Ryan Aeronautical Corporation for the XFR-1 fighter. This aircraft incorporated a conventional reciprocating engine for use in normal operations and the turbojet for use as a booster during takeoffs and maximum performance flights. Development and production were handled on a crash basis to equip escort carrier squadrons at the earliest possible date. However, numerous bugs were encountered which prevented the FR-1's assignment to combat.

11 February   The Vought F4U Corsair was flown on a combat mission for the first time when 12 planes of VMF-124 based on Guadalcanal escorted a PB2Y Dumbo to Vella Lavella to pick up downed pilots. The flight was uneventful. Its first combat action came two days later when pilots from the same squadron ran into air opposition while escorting PB4Ys of VP-51 on a daylight strike against enemy shipping in the Kahili area of Bougainville.

13 February   The Naval Air Transport Service was reorganized and the establishment of Wings was directed for the Atlantic and west coast squadrons.

15 February   Commander-in-Chief, U.S. Fleet assigned responsibility for sea-going development of helicopters and their operation in convoys to the Coast Guard and directed that tests be carried out to determine if helicopters operating from merchant ships would be of value in combating submarines.

1943—Continued

The landing signal officer bringing in a F4U 41221

16 February Fleet Air Wing 16, Captain R. D. Lyon commanding, was established at Norfolk. Va.

17 February Lighter-than-air operations over the Caribbean were initiated from Edinburgh Field, Trinidad, by the K-17 of Airship Patrol Squadron 51.

19 February A Letter of Intent was issued to Vega Airplane Company for two XP2V-1 patrol planes, thereby initiating development of the P2V Neptune series of land-based patrol aircraft.

21 February–1 November Advance up the Solomons Chain—In a series of amphibious operations, directly and indirectly supported by Marine Corps, Navy and Army units of Aircraft, South Pacific, and Aircraft, Solomons, Central Pacific Forces moved from Guadalcanal up the Solomon Islands towards the Japanese naval base at Rabaul. Begin-

ning with the unopposed landing in the Russells (21 Feb), these forces leapfrogged through the islands establishing bases and airfields as they went. Moving into Segi of the New Georgia Group (21 Jun), through Rendova, Onaivisi, Wickham Anchorage, Kiriwini and Woodlark (30 Jun), Viru (2 Jul), Zanana (2 Jul), Rice Anchorage (5 Jul), Vella Lavella (15 Aug), Arundel (27 Aug), and Treasury Islands (27 Oct), they reached Bougainville where landings on Cape Torokina were additionally supported by carrier air strikes (1, 2 Nov) on the Buka-Bonis airfields.

24 February The Naval Photographic Science Laboratory was established at NAS Anacostia, D.C., under the direction of the Bureau of Aeronautics to provide photographic services to the Navy and to develop equipment and techniques suitable for fleet use.

1943—Continued

1 March   Air Transport Squadrons, West Coast, was established at NAAS Oakland, Calif., with control over all NATS squadrons west of the Mississippi except those on the mainland to Honolulu, Hawaii, run.

1 March   A revision of the squadron designation system changed Inshore Patrol Squadrons to Scouting Squadrons (VS), Escort Fighting Squadrons (VGF) to Fighting Squadrons (VF), Escort Scouting Squadrons (VGS) to Composite Squadrons (VC) and Patrol Squadrons (VP) operating land type aircraft to Bombing Squadrons (VB). This revision also redesignated carrier Scouting Squadrons (VS) as VB and VC and as a result the types of squadrons on *Essex* Class carriers was reduced to three. In spite of this change, the aircraft complement of their Air Groups remained at its previous level of 21 VF, 36 VSB and 18 VTB.

1 March   Fleet Airship Group 2, Captain Walter E. Zimmerman commanding, was established at NAS Richmond, Fla., and placed in charge of lighter-than-air operations in the Gulf Sea Frontier.

4 March   Changes to the characteristics of *Essex* Class carriers were authorized by the Secretary of the Navy, including installation of a Combat Information Center (CIC) and Fighter Director Station, additional anti-aircraft batteries, and a second flight deck catapult in lieu of one athwartships on the hangar deck.

5 March   *Bogue*, with VC-9 on board, joined Task Group 24.4 at Argentia, Newfoundland, and began the escort of convoys to mid-ocean and return. Although *Santee* had previously operated on hunter-killer duty, *Bogue* was the center of the first of the hunter-killer groups assigned to convoy escort.

15 March   Fleet Air Wing 4 headquarters moved westward on the Aleutian chain from Kodiak to Adak, Alaska.

20 March   Forty-two Navy and Marine Corps Avengers, on a night flight from Henderson Field, mined Kahili Harbor, Bougainville. A coordinated attack on Kahili airfield by AAF heavy bombers contributed to the success of this, the first aerial mining mission in the South Pacific.

23 March   The Training Task Force Command was established with headquarters at NAS Clinton, Okla., to form, outfit and train special units for the operational employment of assault drone aircraft.

Rocket weapons, being installed on a plane 468849

29 March   Tests of forward firing rockets projectiles from naval aircraft were completed at the Naval Proving Ground, Dahlgren, Va., using an SB2A-4 aircraft.

29 March   Air Transport Squadrons, Atlantic, was commissioned at Norfolk, Va., to supervise and direct operations of NATS squadrons based on the Atlantic seaboard.

1 April   Aircraft Antisubmarine Development Detachment, Commander Aurelius B. Vosseller in command, was established at NAS Quonset Point, R.I., under Air Force, Atlantic Fleet, to develop tactical training programs and techniques that would make full use of newly developed countermeasures equipment.

1 April   The first Navy night fighter squadron, VF(N)-75, was established at Quonset Point, R.I., Commander William J. Widhelm, commanding.

4 April   The Naval Aircraft Factory reported that, in tests of an automatic flying device for use on towed gliders, the LNT-1 had been towed automatically without assistance from the safety pilot.

14 April   Fleet Air Wing 16 transferred from Norfolk, Va., to Natal, Brazil, to direct patrol plane antisubmarine operations under the Fourth Fleet in the South Atlantic.

1943—Continued

21 April   Captain Frederick M. Trapnell made a flight in the Bell XP-59A jet Airacomet at Muroc, Calif.—the first jet flight by a U.S. Naval Aviator.

3 May   Air Transport Squadron 1 (VR-1), based at Norfolk, Va., extended the area of its operations with a flight to Prestwick, Scotland, via Reykjavik, Iceland. This was the first R5D operation in the Naval Air Transport Service.

4 May   The first regular patrols began from Amchitka, Aleutian Islands, extending the search coverage by Fleet Air Wing 4 beyond Attu toward the Kurile Islands.

4 May   To expedite the evaluation of the helicopter in antisubmarine operations, the Commander-in-Chief, U.S. Fleet directed that a "joint board" be formed with representatives of the Commander-in-Chief, U.S. Fleet; the Bureau of Aeronautics; the Coast Guard; the British Admiralty and the Royal Air Forces. The resulting Combined Board for the Evaluation of the Ship-Based Helicopter in Antisubmarine Warfare was later expanded to include representatives of the Army Air Forces, the War Shipping Administration and the National Advisory Committee for Aeronautics.

7 May   Navy representatives witnessed landing trials of the XR-4 helicopter aboard the merchant tanker *Bunker Hill* in a demonstration sponsored by the Maritime Commission and conducted in Long Island Sound. The pilot, Colonel R. F. Gregory, AAF, made about 15 flights, and in some of these flights he landed on the water before returning to the platform on the deck of the ship.

11–30 May   Occupation of Attu—Air support for the landing of Army troops (11 May) and for their operations ashore was provided by Navy and Marine units on the escort carrier *Nassau* (11–20 May), and by the Navy and Army units of North Pacific Force (11–20 May). This was the first use of CVE based aircraft in air support in the Pacific and the debut of a Support Air Commander afloat. His team consisted of three officers and a radioman and his post was a card table aboard *Pennsylvania* (BB 38). Colonel W. O. Eareckson, USA, an experienced Aleutian pilot, was in command of the unit.

15 May   The Naval Airship Training Command was established at Lakehurst, N.J., to administer and direct lighter-than-air training programs at the Naval Air Centers, Lakehurst and Moffett Field, Calif., and to direct the Experimental and Flight Test Department at Lakehurst.

18 May   The program for the use of gliders as transports for Marine Corps combat troops was canceled, thereby returning the Navy's glider development to an experimental basis.

22 May   Grumman Avengers of VC-9, based on *Bogue*, attacked and sank the German submarine U-569 in the middle north Atlantic scoring the first sinking of the war by escort carriers on hunter-killer patrol.

24 May   Special Project Unit Cast was organized at NAS Squantum, Mass., to provide, under Bureau of Aeronautics direction, the services required to flight test the electronics equipment being developed at the Radiation and Radio Research Laboratories.

7 June   The establishment of NAF Attu, within 1 week of its capture from the Japanese, brought Fleet Air Wing 4 bases to the tip of the Aleutian chain, nearly 1,000 miles from the Alaskan mainland and 750 miles from Japanese territory in the Kuriles.

7 June   Commander-in-Chief, U.S. Fleet established a project for airborne test, by Commander, Fleet Air, West Coast, of high velocity, "forward shooting" rockets. These rockets, which had nearly double the velocity of those tested earlier at Dahlgren, Va., had been developed by a rocket section, led by Dr. C. C. Lauritsen, at the California Institute of Technology under National Defense Research Committee auspices and with Navy support. This test project, which was established in part on the basis of reports of effectiveness in service of a similar British rocket, completed its first airborne firing from a TBF of a British rocket on 14 July and of the CalTech round on 20 August. The results of these tests were so favorable that operational squadrons in both the Atlantic and Pacific Fleets were equipped with forward firing rockets before the end of the year.

10 June   Lieutenant Commander Frank A. Erickson, USCG, proposed that helicopters be developed for antisubmarine warfare, "not as a killer craft but as the eyes and ears of the convoy escorts." To this end he recommended that helicopters be equipped with radar and dunking sonar.

15 June   President Franklin D. Roosevelt approved a ceiling of 31,447 useful planes for the Navy.

28 June   A change in the design of the National Star Insignia added white rectangles on the left and right sides of the blue circular field to form a horizontal bar, and a red border stripe around the entire design. The following September, Insignia Blue was substituted for the red.

1943—Continued

29 June NAS Patuxent River, Md., began functioning as an aircraft test organization with the arrival of the Flight Test unit from NAS Anacostia, D.C.

29 June Elements of VP-101 arrived at Brisbane from Perth, Austrailia, thereby extending the patrol coverage of Fleet Air Wing 10 to the east coast of Australia and marking the beginning of a northward advance of patrol operations toward the Papuan Peninsula of New Guinea.

5 July The first turbojet engine developed for the Navy, the Westinghouse l9A, completed its 100-hour endurance test.

8 July *Casablanca*, first of her class and first escort carrier designed and built as such, was placed in commission at Astoria, Oreg., Captain Steven W. Callaway commanding.

14 July The Secretary of the Navy issued a General Order forming the Naval Air Material Center, consisting of the separate commands of the Naval Aircraft Factory, the Naval Aircraft Modification Unit, the Naval Air Experimental Station and the Naval Auxiliary Air Station. This action, effective 20 July, consolidated in distinct activities the production, modification, experimental, and air station facilities of the former Naval Aircraft Factory organization.

15 July New designations for carriers were established which limited the previous broadly applied CV symbol to *Saratoga, Enterprise* and carriers of *Essex* Class, and added CVB (Aircraft Carriers, Large) for the 45,000 ton class being built and CVL (Aircraft Carriers, Small) for the 10,000 ton class built on light cruiser hulls. The same directive reclassified escort carriers as combatant ships and changed their symbol from ACV to CVE.

15 July The airship organization of the U.S. Fleet was modified. Fleet Airship Wings 30 and 31 were redesignated Fleet Airships, Atlantic, and Pacific respectively. Airship Patrol Groups became Airship Wings. Airship Patrol Squadrons became Blimp Squadrons, and the addition of two more wings and the establishment of Blimp Headquarters Squadrons in each wing was authorized.

18 July The airship K-74, while on night patrol off the Florida coast, attacked a surfaced U-boat and in the gun duel which followed was hit and brought down—the only airship lost to enemy action in World War II. The German submarine, U-134, was damaged enough to force her return to base, and after surviving two other attacks on the way, was finally sunk by British bombers in the Bay of Biscay.

19 July The Naval Aircraft Factory was authorized to develop the Gorgon, an aerial ram or air-to-air missile powered by a turbojet engine and equipped with radio controls and a homing device. The Gorgon was later expanded into a broad program embracing turbojet, ramjet, pulsejet, and rocket power; straight wing, swept wing, and canard (tail first) air frames; and visual, television, heat-homing, and three types of radar guidance for use as air-to-air, air-to-surface and surface-to-surface guided missiles and as target drones.

22 July Since there had been no operational need for arresting gear and related equipment for landing over the bow of aircraft carriers, the Vice Chief of Naval Operations approved its removal.

23 July Patrol Squadron 63, the first U.S. Navy squadron to operate from Great Britain in World War II, arrived at Pembroke Dock, England, to assist in the antisubmarine patrol over the Bay of Biscay.

2 August Fleet Airship Wings 4 and 5, Captain Walter E. Zimmerman and Commander John D. Reppy commanding, were established at Maceio, Brazil, and Edinburgh Field, Trinidad, for antisubmarine and convoy patrols in the South Atlantic and southern approaches to the Caribbean.

4 August The Chief of Naval Air Intermediate Training directed that Aviation Safety Boards be established at each training center under his command.

5 August COMINCH directed the use of Fleet Air Wing commanders in subordinate commands of Sea Frontiers and suggested their assignment as Deputy Chiefs of Staff for Air.

15 August The arrival of Aircraft Experimental and Development Squadron (later Tactical Test) from NAS Anacostia, D.C., to NAS Patuxent River, Md., completed the transfer of aircraft test activities.

15 August The landing of U.S. Army and Canadian troops on Kiska, Aleutian Islands, by a Naval Task Force made the first use in the Pacific of Air Liaison Parties (ALP) with forces ashore. Although the enemy had deserted the island, the landing provided opportunity to prove that the principle of the ALP was sound and that rapid and reliable voice communications between front line commanders and the Support Air Control Unit afloat were possible.

1943—Continued

K-class airship on escort duty in Atlantic protects a convoy of merchantmen against German submarines 428465

18 August   To give Naval Aviation authority commensurate with its World War II responsibility, the Secretary of the Navy established the Office of the Deputy Chief of Naval Operations (Air), charging it with responsibility for "the preparation, readiness and logistic support of the naval aeronautic operating forces." By other orders issued the same day, five divisions were transferred from the Bureau of Aeronautics to form the nucleus of the new office and Vice Admiral John S. McCain took command as the first DCNO (Air).

21 August   Headquarters, Fleet Air Wing 7 was established at Plymouth, England, to direct patrol plane operations against submarines in the Bay of Biscay, the English Channel and the southwest approaches to England.

29 August   The formation of combat units for the employment of assault drone aircraft began within the Training Task Force Command as the first of three Special Task Air Groups was established. The component squadrons, designated VK, began establishing on 23 October.

VAdm. John S. McCain, USN 236837

1943—Continued

Essex and Independence class carriers, the fast carrier task forces were built around ships of these types 301754

30 August   Second Strike on Marcus—Task Force 15 (Rear Admiral Charles A. Pownall), built around *Essex*, the new *Yorktown* and *Independence* launched nine strike groups in a day-long attack on Japanese installations on Marcus Island, the first strikes by *Essex* and *Independence* Class carriers, and the first combat use of the Grumman F6F Hellcat.

1 September   Two light carriers of Task Group 11.2 (Rear Admiral Arthur W. Radford) and Navy patrol bombers from Canton Island furnished day and night air cover for naval units landing occupation forces on Baker Island, east of the Gilberts.

15 September   Fleet Air Wing 17, Commodore Thomas S. Combs commanding, was established at

Grumman F6F Hellcat laden with rockets and droppable fuel tank taking off from Hancock 259064

1943—Continued

Brisbane, Australia, for operations in the Southwest Pacific area.

15 September   French Patrol Squadron 1 (VFP-1), manned by "Fighting French" naval personnel trained under U.S. Navy control, was established at NAS Norfolk, Va.

18 September   A three-carrier task force (Rear Admiral Charles A. Pownall), attacked Tarawa, Makin, and Abemama Atolls in the Gilbert Islands.

18 September   Training was assigned as a primary mission to Fleet Air Wing 5 at Norfolk, Va., and Fleet Air Wing 9 assumed responsibility for all patrol plane operations in the Eastern Sea Frontier.

27 September   The beginning of airship operations in the South Atlantic was marked by the arrival of the K-84, of Blimp Squadron 41, at Fortaleza, Brazil.

30 September   An advance detachment of Bombing Squadron 107, equipped with PB4Y Liberators, arrived at Ascension Island to join AAF units on antisubmarine barriers and sweeps across the narrows of the South Atlantic.

1 October   Air Force, Atlantic Fleet, was reorganized and Fleet Air, Norfolk, and Fleet Airships, Atlantic, were established as additional subordinate commands.

1 October   The authorized complement of fighters in *Essex* Class carrier air groups was raised, increasing the total aircraft normally on board to 36 VF, 36 VB and 18 VT. The authorized complement for CVL groups was established at the same time as 12 VF, 9 VB and 9 VT and revised in November 1943 to 24 VF and 9 VT and remained at that level through the war.

4 October   In conjunction with her duties in protecting North Atlantic convoy routes to Russia, *Ranger* launched two strikes against German shipping in Norway—one in and around Bodo Harbor; the other along the coast from Alter Fjord to Kunna Head.

5 October   Coast Guard Patrol Squadron 6 was established at Argentia, Newfoundland, Commander

PB4Y-1 Liberator, a long-range patrol plane 65159

1943—Continued

D. B. MacDiarmid, USCG, commanding, to take over the rescue duties being performed by naval aircraft in Greenland and Labrador.

5–6 October   Second Wake Raid—Task Force 14 (Rear Admiral Alfred E. Montgomery), composed of six new carriers, seven cruisers, and 24 destroyers, making it the largest carrier task force yet assembled, bombed and bombarded Japanese installations on Wake Island. In the course of the two-day strike, ship handling techniques for a multicarrier force, devised by Rear Admiral Frederick C. Sherman's staff on the basis of experience in the South Pacific, were tested under combat conditions. Lessons learned from operating the carriers as a single group of six, as two groups of three, and as three groups of two, provided the basis for many tactics which later characterized carrier task force operations.

6 October   The Naval Airship Training Command at Lakehurst, N.J., was redesignated the Naval Airship Training and Experimental Command.

12 October   The Bureau of Ordnance established a production program for 3,000 Pelican guided missiles at a delivery rate of 300 a month.

16 October   The Navy accepted its first helicopter, a Sikorsky YR-4B (HNS-1), at Bridgeport, Connecticut, following a 60 minute acceptance test flight by Lieutenant Commander Frank A. Erickson, USCG.

Coastguardsmen test capability of Navy's first helicopter, HNS-1, for air-sea rescue at NAS New York 1061902

31 October   Lieutenant Hugh D. O'Neil of VF(N)-75, operating from Munda, New Georgia, destroyed a Betty during a night attack off Vella Lavella, the first kill by a radar-equipped night fighter of the Pacific Fleet. Major Thomas E. Hicks and Technical Sergeant Gleason from VMF(N)-531 provided ground-based fighter direction.

1 November   A detachment of Bombing Squadron 145, equipped with Venturas, began operations from Fernando Noronha Island, extending the area of Fleet Air Wing 16 antisubmarine patrols over the South Atlantic toward Ascension Island.

1 November   First Rabaul Strike—A two-carrier task force (Rear Admiral Frederick C. Sherman) delivered an air attack on the naval base at Rabaul damaging several warships of the Japanese Second Fleet.

8 November   The Chief of Naval Operations directed that Aviation Safety Boards, similar to those in the Intermediate Training Command, be established in the Primary and Operational Training Commands.

8 November   The Naval Ordnance Test Station, Inyokern, California, was established for research, development and testing weapons and to provide primary training in their use. It initially supported the California Institute of Technology which, through the Office of Scientific Research and Development, was undertaking the development and testing of rockets, propellants and launchers.

11 November   Second Rabaul Strike—Three heavy and two light carriers organized in two carrier task forces (Rear Admirals Frederick C. Sherman and Alfred E. Montgomery), hit Japanese naval shipping at Rabaul sinking one destroyer and damaging ships, including two cruisers. In this attack SB2C Curtiss Helldivers were used in combat for the first time.

13–19 November   Army and Navy aircraft of Task Force 57 (Rear Admiral John H. Hoover), based on islands of the Ellice, Phoenix, and Samoan Groups and on Baker Island, conducted long-range night bombing attacks on Japanese bases in the Gilbert and Marshall Islands as a preliminary to the invasion of the Gilberts.

18–26 November   Occupation of the Gilbert Islands—Six heavy and five light carriers of Task Force 50 (Rear Admiral Charles A. Pownall) opened the campaign to capture the Gilberts with a two-day air attack on airfields and defensive installations in the islands (18–19 Nov), covered the landings of Marines and

1943—
Continued

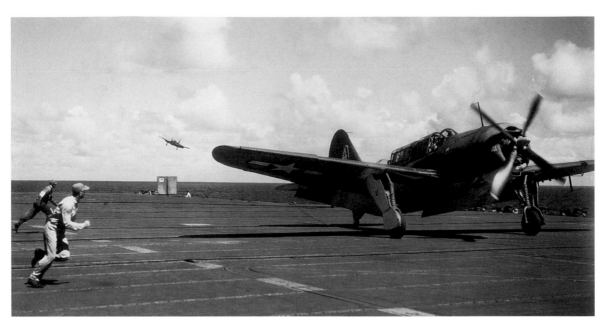

Flight deck crew preparing to release SB2C from arresting gear and clear the deck for approaching aircraft 469432

Army troops on Tarawa and Makin Atolls (20 Nov) and on Abemama (21 Nov), and supported their operations ashore (21–24 Nov). Eight escort carriers, operating with the Attack Forces, covered the approach of assault shipping (10–18 Nov), flew antisubmarine and combat air patrols in the area, and close support missions on call (19–24 Nov). After the islands were secure (24 Nov), one carrier group remained in the area for another week as a protective measure. The first unit of the garrison air force, VF-1, took off from escort carriers *Barnes* and *Nassau* (25 Nov) and landed on Tarawa airstrip. One escort carrier, *Liscome Bay* was lost (24 Nov) to submarine attack, and the light carrier *Independence* was damaged (20 Nov) by air attack. The first attempts at night interception from carriers were made during the campaign by a team of two Hellcats and one radar-equipped Avenger operating from *Enterprise* and led by the Air Group Commander, Lieutenant Commander Edward H. (Butch) O'Hare. In operation the fighters flew wing on the Avenger and after being vectored to the vicinity of the enemy aircraft by the ship's fighter director relied on the Avenger's radar to get within visual range. On the first occasion (24 Nov) no intercepts were made but on the second (26 Nov) the enemy was engaged in the first aerial battle of its type which so disrupted the attack that the flight was credited with saving the task group from damage.

O'Hare, Ace and night fighter 1061488

1943—Continued

27 November   The first of the Martin Mars flying boats was delivered to VR-8 at NAS Patuxent River, Md.

30 November   On her first operational assignment, the Martin Mars, in the hands of Lieutenant Commander W. E. Coney and crew of 16, took off from Patuxent River, Md., carrying 13,000 pounds of cargo that was delivered at Natal, Brazil, in a nonstop flight of 4,375 miles and of 28 hours 25 minutes duration.

30 November   A department of Aviation Medicine and Physiological Research was authorized at the Naval Air Material Center, to study physiological factors particularly as related to design of high speed and high altitude aircraft.

1 December   Aircraft, Central Pacific, Rear Admiral John H. Hoover commanding, was established under Commander, Central Pacific, for operational control of defense forces and shore-based air forces in the area.

1 December   The Naval Air Ferry Command was established as a Wing of the Naval Air Transport Service. It assumed the functions previously performed by Aircraft Delivery Units in ferrying new aircraft from contractor plants and modification centers to embarkation points for ultimate delivery to the fleet.

4 December   At the close of the Gilberts Campaign, two groups of Task Force 50 (Rear Admiral Charles A. Pownall), composed of four heavy and two light carriers and screening ships, bombed airfields and shipping at Wotje and Kwajalein Atolls in the Marshall Islands.

8 December   A striking force of two carriers, six battleships, and 12 destroyers bombed and bombarded enemy installations on Nauru, to the west of the Gilberts.

15 December   Observation Fighter Squadron 1 (VOF-1), first of three of its type brought into existence during World War II, was established at Atlantic City, N.J., with Lieutenant Commander William F. Bringle in command.

17 December   Commander, Aircraft, Solomons, joined in the air campaign to reduce the Japanese Naval Base at Rabaul with a fighter sweep of Navy, Marine Corps, and New Zealand planes led by Marine ace Major Gregory Boyington. Intensive follow-up attacks through February 1944 assisted in the establish-

Marine's top ace, Pappy Boyington, reads an order to pilots of his fighter squadron in the South Pacific 1061487

ment of encircling allied bases. Rabaul remained under air attack until the war's end, the last strike being delivered by Marine Corps PBJs on 9 August 1945.

18 December On the basis of his belief that tests indicated the practicability of ship-based helicopters, the Chief of Naval Operations separated the pilot training from test and development functions in the helicopter program. He directed that, effective 1 January 1944, a helicopter pilot training program be conducted by the U.S. Coast Guard at Floyd Bennett Field, N.Y., under the direction of the Deputy Chief of Naval Operations (Air).

20 December The Naval Air Training Command was established at Pensacola, Fla., to coordinate and direct, under the Chief of Naval Operations, all Naval Aviation training in the activities of the Primary, Intermediate, and Operational Training Commands.

20 December Two Catalinas of Patrol Squadron 43, at Attu, flew the first Navy photo reconnaissance and bombing mission over the Kuriles.

20 December Commander Frank A. Erickson, USCG, reported that Coast Guard Air Station, Floyd Bennett Field, N.Y., had experimented with a helicopter used as an airborne ambulance. An HNS-1 helicopter made flights carrying, in addition to its normal crew of a pilot and a mechanic, a weight of 200 pounds in a stretcher suspended approximately 4 feet beneath the float landing gear. In further demonstrations early the following year, the stretcher was attached to the side of the fuselage and landings were made at the steps of the dispensary.

25 December Aircraft from a two-carrier task group (Rear Admiral Frederick C. Sherman) attacked shipping at Kavieng, New Ireland, as a covering operation for landings by the Marines in the Borgen Bay area of New Britain on the following day.

31 December Fleet Air Wing 17 departed Australia and set up headquarters at Samarai on the tip of the Papuan Peninsula of New Guinea.

1944

3 January Helicopter Mercy Mission—Commander Frank A. Erickson, USCG, flying an HNS-1 helicopter, made an emergency delivery of 40 units of blood plasma from lower Manhattan Island, N.Y., to Sandy Hook,

N.J., where the plasma was administered to survivors of an explosion on the destroyer *Turner* (DD 648). In this, the first helicopter lifesaving operation, Commander Erickson took off from Floyd Bennett Field, N.Y., flew to Battery Park on Manhattan Island to pick up the plasma and then to Sandy Hook. The flight was made through snow squalls and sleet which grounded all other types of aircraft.

11 January The first U.S. attack with forward-firing rockets was made against a German U-boat by two TBF-1Cs of Composite Squadron 58 from the escort carrier *Block Island*.

16 January Lieutenant (jg) S. R. Graham, USCG, while en route from New York, N.Y., to Liverpool, England, in the British freighter *Daghestan* made a 30 minute flight in an R-4B (HNS-1) from the ship's 60 by 80-foot flight deck. Weather during the mid-winter crossing of the North Atlantic permitted only two additional flights and, as a result, the sponsoring Combined Board for Evaluation of the Ship-based Helicopter in antisubmarine warfare concluded that the helicopter's capability should be developed in coastal waters until models with improved performance became available.

18 January Catalinas of VP-63, based at Port Lyautey, Morocco, began barrier patrols of the Strait of Gibraltar and its approaches with Magnetic Airborne Detection (MAD) gear and effectively closed the strait to enemy U-boats during daylight hours until the end of the war.

29 January–22 February Occupation of the Marshall Islands—Six heavy and six light carriers, in four groups of Task Force 58 (Rear Admiral Marc A. Mitscher), opened the campaign to capture the Marshalls (29 Jan) with heavy air attacks on Maloelap, Kwajalein, and Wotje. On the first day the defending enemy air forces were eliminated and complete control of the air was maintained by carrier aircraft during the entire operation. Eight escort carriers, attached to the Attack Forces of the Joint Expeditionary Force, arrived in the area early the morning of D-day. Aircraft from the carriers flew cover and antisubmarine patrols for attack shipping and assisted two fast carrier groups, providing air support for landings on Kwajalein and Majuro Atolls (31 Jan), Roi and Namur (1 Feb), and for operations ashore. The AGC command ship, used for the first time during this campaign, provided greatly improved physical facilities for the Support Air Commander. Here, the Support Air Commander first assumed control of Target Combat Air Patrol, previously vested in carrier units, and a

1944—Continued

Force Fighter Director on his staff coordinated fighter direction. Two fast carrier groups to the west kept Eniwetok Atoll neutralized until the initial objectives were achieved. Their early achievement permitted the second phase of the campaign, Seizure of Eniwetok, earlier than the planned date of 10 May. The landings (17 Feb) and the ground action were supported by aircraft from one fast carrier group and one escort carrier group. Covering operations were provided by the First Strike on Truk (17–18 Feb), carried out by the Truk Striking Force (Vice Admiral R. A. Spruance), built around three fast carrier groups. In a two-day attack, the carriers launched 1,250 combat sorties against this key naval base and exploded the myth of its impregnability with 400 tons of bombs and torpedoes, sinking 37 war and merchant ships aggregating 200,000 tons and doing heavy damage to base installations. In this action the first night bombing attack in the history of U.S. carrier aviation was carried out by VT-10 from *Enterprise* with 12 radar equipped TBF-1Cs. The attack, delivered at low level, scored several direct hits on ships in the harbor. In a brief enemy air attack on the same night, *Intrepid* was hit by an aerial torpedo. For the campaign, night fighter detachments of VF(N)-76 and VF(N)-101 (assigned F6F-3s and F4U-2s equipped with AIA radar) were assigned to five carriers and, while not widely used, were on occasion vectored against enemy night raiders.

30 January To effect the neutralization of Wake Island during the Marshalls operation, two squadrons of Coronados from Midway Island made the first of four night bombing attacks. Repetitions of the 2,000-mile round trip mission were completed on 4, 8, and 9 February.

2 February The last of the World War II ceilings for Navy aircraft, calling for an increase to 37,735 useful planes, was approved by the president.

Adm. Marc Mitscher

Invasion of the Marshalls. Japanese airstrip at Engebi burning after attack by U.S. carrier based planes 221248

1944—Continued

Loading torpedoes on SB2C for strike on ships 1053796

3 February Flight Safety Bulletin No. 1 was issued jointly by the Deputy Chief of Naval Operations (Air) and the Chief of the Bureau of Aeronautics, announcing their intention to issue consecutively numbered bulletins concerning the safe operation of naval aircraft.

4 February In a test of refueling operations with *Altamaha* off San Diego, Calif., the K-29 of Blimp Squadron 31 made the first carrier landing by a nonrigid airship.

4 February The first photo reconnaissance of Truk was made by two PB4Ys of VMD-254 on a 12-hour night flight from the Solomon Islands. Cloud cover prevented complete coverage but the information acquired was useful in planning the carrier strike which hit later in the month.

15 February A new command, Forward Area, Central Pacific (Rear Admiral John H. Hoover), was established to control the operations of shorebased air forces and naval forces assigned to the Ellice, Gilbert, and Marshall Islands.

20 February On completion of the strike on Truk, a small unit composed of *Enterprise,* one cruiser, and six destroyers (Rear Admiral John W. Reeves) separated from the main force and launched two air strikes on Jaluit.

23 February Two carrier groups of Task Force 58 (Rear Admiral Marc A. Mitscher), after successfully fending off a series of determined enemy air attacks during the night, hit targets on Saipan, Tinian, Rota, and Guam for the dual purpose of reducing enemy air strength in the Marianas and to gather photo intelligence for the impending invasion. The combined efforts of pilots and antiaircraft gunners accounted for 67 enemy aircraft shot down and 101 destroyed on the ground.

24 February The first detection of a submerged enemy submarine by the use of MAD gear was made by Catalinas of VP-63, on a MAD barrier patrol of the approaches to the Strait of Gibraltar. They attacked the U-761 with retrorockets, and with the assistance of two ships and aircraft from two other squadrons, sank it.

4 March A reduction in flight training was visualized as the total outputs for 1944, 1945, and 1946 were fixed at 20,500, 15,000 and 10,000 pilots respectively.

1944—Continued

6 March   A new specification for color of naval aircraft went into effect. The basic camouflage scheme, used with fleet aircraft, was modified slightly to provide for use of non-specular sea blue on upper fuselage surfaces; airfoil surfaces visible from above remained semigloss sea blue and other surfaces visible from below, semigloss insignia white. A new basic non-camouflage color scheme, all aluminum, was specified for general use on aircraft not in the combat theater. The maximum visibility color scheme used on primary trainers became glossy orange yellow overall.

15 March   The twin-engined North American Mitchell, PBJ, was taken into combat for the first time in its naval career in an attack on Rabaul by pilots of Marine Bombing Squadron 413.

18 March   Task Group 50.10 (Rear Admiral Willis A. Lee), composed of *Lexington,* two battleships, and a destroyer screen, bombed and bombarded bypassed Mili in the Marshalls.

20 March   Two escort carriers provided cover and airspot for the battleship and destroyer bombardment of Kavieng and nearby airfields in a covering action for the occupation of Emirau.

22 March   A new specification for color of fighter aircraft went into effect. It directed that fighters be painted glossy sea blue on all exposed surfaces.

26 March   Corsairs of VMF-113 from Engebi flew the first fighter escort for AAF B-25s on the 360 mile bombing mission against Ponape, and were so effective in destroying enemy interceptors that later missions over the island were unmolested.

27 March   *Saratoga* (Captain John H. Cassady) and three destroyers, assigned to temporary duty with the Royal Navy, joined the British Eastern Fleet in the Indian Ocean approximately 1,000 miles south of Ceylon.

30 March–1 April   Strikes on the Western Carolines—In an operation designed to eliminate opposition to the landings at Hollandia and to gather photo intelligence for future campaigns, a strong Fifth Fleet force, built around Task Force 58 (Vice Admiral Marc A. Mitscher) with 11 carriers, launched a series of attacks on Palau, Yap, Ulithi, and Woleai, and shipping in the area. Aerial mining of Palau Harbor by Torpedo Squadrons 2, 8, and 16, was the first such mission by carrier aircraft and the first large scale daylight mining operation of the Pacific war. The attacks accounted for 157 enemy aircraft destroyed, 28 ships of 108,000 tons sunk, and denial of the harbor to the enemy for an estimated 6 weeks.

15 April   Air-Sea Rescue Squadrons (VH) were formed in the Pacific Fleet to provide rescue and emergency services as necessary in the forward areas. Prior to this time the rescue function was performed as an additional duty by regularly operating patrol squadrons.

16 April   Carrier Transport Squadron, Pacific, was established for administrative and operational control over escort carriers assigned to deliver aircraft, spare parts, and aviation personnel in direct support of Pacific Fleet Operations.

18 April   In preparation for the campaign to occupy the Marianas, photo-equipped Liberators of VD-3 obtained complete coverage of Saipan, Tinian, and Aguijan Islands. For the 13-hour flight from Eniwetok and return, B-24s of the AAF flew escort for the photo planes and bombed the islands in a diversionary action. This was the first mission by shore-based aircraft over the Marianas.

19 April   *Saratoga,* operating with the British Eastern Fleet, participated in the carrier strike on enemy installations at Sabang in the Netherlands East Indies.

21–24 April   Landings at Hollandia—Task Force 58 (Vice Admiral Marc A. Mitscher) supported the landings of Southwest Pacific Forces in the Hollandia-Aitape section of the north New Guinea coast. The force of five heavy and seven light carriers organized in three groups, launched preliminary strikes on airfields around Hollandia and at Wakde and Sawar (21 April), covered the landings (22 April) at Aitape, Tanahmerah Bay, and Humboldt Bay, and supported troop movements ashore (23–24 April). Eight escort carriers of Task Force 78 (Rear Admiral Ralph E. Davison) flew cover and antisubmarine patrols over ships of the Attack Group during the approach and provided support for the amphibious assault at Aitape. Carrier aircraft accounted for the destruction of 30 enemy aircraft in the air and 103 on the ground.

23 April   VR-3 operated the first regularly scheduled NATS transcontinental hospital flight between Washington, D.C., and March Field, Calif.

26 April   Headquarters of Fleet Air Wing 4 was established on Attu, western most island of the Aleutians.

1944—Continued

29 April–1 May   Second Carrier Strike on Truk— Task Force 58 (Vice Admiral Marc A. Mitscher), returning to Majuro from the Hollandia operation, launched a 2-day attack on enemy installations and supply dumps at Truk. In addition to damage ashore, three small ships were sunk and 145 enemy aircraft destroyed. Task Group 58.1 (Rear Admiral Joseph J. Clark), detached from the main force on the second day, flew protective cover for a cruiser bombardment of Satawan, and on 1 May supported bombardment of Ponape with air cover and bombing and strafing attacks.

1 May   The command Aircraft, Central Pacific, was dissolved and its functions assumed by Commander, Marshalls Sub-Area.

4 May   A board headed by Rear Admiral Arthur W. Radford and known by his name, submitted a report that had a direct effect on aviation planning during the latter part of the war and, with modifications to fit the needs of peacetime, extended its influence long after the war. The Integrated Aeronautic Program for Maintenance, Material and Supply, which evolved from its recommendations, was essentially a plan involving the assignment of new planes to combat units; return of aircraft to the United States for reconditioning and reassignment after specified combat tours; the retirement of second tour aircraft before maintenance became costly; and the support of the aeronautical organization through the use of factors and allowances for pools, pipelines, and reconditioning kept realistic by frequent appraisal.

8 May   The seaplane tender *Kenneth Whiting*, first of four ships of the class, was commissioned at Tacoma, Wash., Commander Raymond R. Lyons in command.

8 May   Commander, Naval Forces, Northwest African Waters, approved the assignment of nine Naval Aviators from Cruiser Scouting Squadron 8 (VCS-8) to the 111th Tactical Reconnaissance Squadron (TRS) of the 12th Army Air Force for flight training and combat operations in North American P-51C Mustangs. Previous combat experience with Curtiss SOC Seagulls and Vought OS2U Kingfishers being used in air spotting and reconnaissance missions proved both types were vulnerable to enemy fighters and antiaircraft fire. The higher performance of fighters such as the P-51 was expected to result in a reduction of casualties on these missions. A total of 11 Naval Aviators participated in combat operations from the cockpits of P-51s while assigned to the 111th TRS in support of the cam-

paign in Italy and the invasion of southern France. On 2 September 1944 all Naval Aviators assigned to the 111th returned to their ships, ending a four month long association between the 111th TRS and VCS-8.

13 May   To distinguish between fixed and rotary wing heavier-than-air craft, the helicopter class designation VH plus a mission letter (i.e. VHO for observation and VHN for training) was abolished and helicopters were established as a separate type designated H. The previous mission letters thus became classes designated O, N, and R for observation, training and transport respectively.

13 May   To meet the needs of the fleet for aviation personnel trained in the use of electronics countermeasures equipment, the Chief of Naval Operations directed that on 1 June, or as soon thereafter as practicable, the Chief of Naval Air Technical Training establish a school to be known as Special Projects School for Air, located initially at NAAS San Clemente Island, Calif.

15 May   The first of 16 special transatlantic flights was made by NATS aircraft to the United Kingdom to deliver 165,000 pounds of minesweeping gear essential to the safety of assault shipping during the Normandy invasion. The delivery was successfully completed 23 May.

17 May   The Bureau of Aeronautics authorized CGAS Floyd Bennett Field, N.Y., to collaborate with the Sperry Gyroscope Company in making an automatic pilot installation in a HNS-1 helicopter.

An OS2U Kingfisher is taxied onto the plane net for an underway recovery by a cruiser 299540

1944—Continued

17 May *Saratoga* participated in the carrier air strike of the British Eastern Fleet on the Japanese base at Soerabaja, Java.

19–20 May Third Raid on Marcus—Planes from a three-carrier task force (Rear Admiral Alfred E. Montgomery) hit Marcus with a predawn fighter sweep and strafed and bombed the island for two consecutive days.

23 May Third Wake Raid—Carrier Task Group 58.6 (Rear Admiral Alfred E. Montgomery) shifted from Marcus to hit Wake with five composite bombing, strafing and rocket strikes.

29 May The only U.S. carrier lost in the Atlantic, *Block Island*, was torpedoed and sunk by a German U-boat while engaged in hunter-killer operations in the Azores area.

31 May Commander, Training Task Force was directed to establish on 1 June, within his command at NAS Traverse City, Mich., a detachment to be known as Special Weapons Test and Tactical Evaluation Unit to conduct such tests of special weapons and other airborne equipment as were assigned.

1 June Airships of ZP-14, assigned to antisubmarine operations around Gibraltar, completed the first crossing of the Atlantic by non-rigid airships. The flight began 29 May from South Weymouth, Mass., and ended at Port Lyautey, French Morocco, covering a distance of 3,145 nautical miles in 58 hours. Including time for stop overs at Argentia, Newfoundland, and the Azores, the airships moved their area of operations across the Atlantic in 80 hours.

1 June Air Transport Squadron 9 (VR-9) was formed at Patuxent River, Md., and VR-12 at Honolulu, Hawaii, to function as headquarters and maintenance squadrons for their respective commands, NATS Atlantic and NATS Pacific.

Airships of ZP-14 from South Weymouth arrive Port Lyautey, Morocco, for ASW patrols over Gibraltar 232195

1944—Continued

4 June Off Cape Blanco, Africa, a hunter-killer group (Captain Daniel V. Gallery), composed of the escort carrier *Guadalcanal,* with VC-8 aboard, and five destroyer escorts, carried out a determined attack on the German submarine U-505, forcing it to surface. Boats from the destroyer escort *Pillsbury* (DD 133) and the carrier reached the submarine before scuttling charges could accomplish their purpose and the U.S. Navy found itself with a prize of war.

5 June The Deputy Chief of Naval Operations (Air) reported that Aviation Safety Boards, established in one large command, had in one-quarter of operation reduced the fatal accident rate by 47 percent. He directed the establishment of similar boards in other commands outside of advanced combat areas and the appointment of a flight safety officer in each squadron.

6 June Allied Invasion of Normandy—Seventeen Naval Aviators taken from aviation units on battleships and cruisers were assigned to bombardment duty as part of VCS-7. They operated with units of the British Fleet Air Arm and Royal Air Force, flying gunfire spotting missions in RAF Spitfires over the Normandy beaches from D-Day until 26 June.

11 June–10 August Occupation of the Marianas— Task Force 58 (Vice Admiral Marc A. Mitscher), built around seven heavy and eight light carriers, opened the campaign to occupy the Marianas Islands with a late afternoon fighter sweep (11 Jun) that destroyed one-third of the defending air force. In bombing and strafing attacks on shore installations and on shipping in the immediate area on succeeding days, this force prepared the way for the amphibious assault of Saipan (15 Jun), supported operations ashore with daily offensive missions, kept the area isolated with attacks on airfields and shipping in the Bonin and Volcano Islands to the north (15–16, 24 Jun, 3–4 Jul, 4–5 Aug), and successfully defended the operation against an attack by major fleet forces in the Battle of the Philippine Sea (19–20 Jun). On the first day (19 Jun) TF 58 repelled a day-long air attack from carriers and shore bases, destroying 402 enemy planes, and the next day (20 Jun) launched an air attack late in the afternoon on the retreating Japanese Fleet, sinking the carrier *Hiyo* and two fleet oilers.

Air cover for assault and close air support for operations ashore was provided by aircraft from an initial force of 11 escort carriers attached to Attack Forces. A Navy seaplane squadron VP-16, moved into the area (16 Jun) and began operations from the open sea. Garrison aircraft were ferried in by escort carriers to operate from captured airfields. First to arrive were Marine observation planes of VMO-4 (17 Jun), AAF P-47's (22 Jun), and Marine Corps Night Fighter Squadron 532 (12 Jul). After organized resistance ended on Saipan (9 Jul), troops landed on Guam (21 Jul) and on Tinian (24 Jul).

As the campaign neared successful completion, three groups of Task Force 58 left the area temporarily for strikes on the Western Carolines (25–28 Jul). Palau, Yap, Ulithi and other islands were taken under attack

A Japanese plane shot down during an attack on the escort carrier Kitkun Bay, Marianas Campaign 238363

1944—Continued

while photographic planes obtained intelligence of enemy defenses. This done, the groups steamed north for the fourth side of the campaign on the Bonins and Volcanoes. By the time Guam was secure (10 Aug), carrier aircraft had accounted for 110,000 tons of enemy shipping sunk and 1,223 aircraft destroyed. In this campaign, groups of the fast carrier force retired in turn to advanced fleet bases for brief periods of rest and replenishment, thus initiating a practice that became standard operating procedure during all future extended periods of action.

12 June In the first deployment of a guided missile unit into a combat theater, elements of Special Task Air Group 1 arrived in the Russell Islands in the South Pacific.

24 June The Chief of Naval Operations promulgated plans which provided for a drastic reduction in the pilot training program. This required the transfer of some students already in Pre-Flight, and prior stages of training and the retention of enough to maintain a course in Pre-Flight schools expanded to 25 weeks. The program of "deselection" and voluntary withdrawal of surplus students was instituted by the Chief of Naval Air Training early in the next month. The resulting reductions were directly responsible for the discontinuance of the War Training Service Program in August, closing the Flight Preparatory Schools in September and the release of training stations which began in September.

26 June Seaplane tender *Currituck*, first of four ships of her class, was commissioned at Philadelphia, Pa., Captain William A. Evans commanding.

29 June The Parachute Experimental Division was established at Lakehurst, N.J., for research, development, and testing of parachutes and survival gear.

29 June Carrier Air Groups were standardized for all commands under the following designations: CVBG, large carrier air group; CVG, medium carrier air group; CVLG, light carrier air group; CVEG, escort carrier air group (*Sangamon* class); and VC, escort carrier air group (*Long Island, Charger, Bogue,* and *Casablanca* class).

30 June The Naval Aircraft Modification Unit of the Naval Air Material Center, Philadelphia, Pa., was relocated at Johnsville, Pa., where facilities for intensified efforts in guided missile development and quantity modification of service airplanes were available.

6 July A Special Air Unit was formed under Commander, Air Force, Atlantic Fleet (COMAIRLANT), with Commander James A. Smith, Officer-in-Charge, for transfer without delay to Commander, Fleet Air Wing 7 in Europe. This unit was to attack German V-1 and V-2 launching sites with PB4Y-1s converted to assault drones.

6 July The Bureau of Aeronautics authorized Douglas to proceed with the design and manufacture of 15 XBT2D airplanes. The single-seat divebomber and torpedoplane thus initiated, was designed jointly by BuAer and Douglas engineers. Through subsequent development and model redesignation, these aircraft became the prototypes for the AD Skyraider series of attack planes.

14 July To achieve economy of effort and unity of purpose by coordinating all safety functions through a central organization, a Flight Safety Council was established by the joint action of the Deputy Chief of Naval Operations (Air) and the Chief of the Bureau of Aeronautics, to plan, coordinate, and execute flight safety programs.

14 July PB4Y Liberators of VB-109, based at Saipan, made the first strike on Iwo Jima by shore-based planes.

27 July Fleet Air Wing 17 headquarters moved to Manus in the Admiralty Islands.

29 July In the first successful test of the Pelican guided missile, conducted 44 miles offshore from NAS New York, N.Y., two of the four launched against the target ship *James Longstreet* were hits.

29 July A detachment of Liberators of Bombing Squadron 114 from Port Lyautey, Morocco, was established under British command at Lajes Airfield in the Azores Islands for antisubmarine operations.

31 July The Accelerated Field Service Test Unit at Patuxent River, Md., was redesignated Service Test and established as a separate department.

5 August The Fast Carrier Task Force was reorganized into First and Second Fast Carrier Task Forces, Pacific, commanded respectively by Vice Admiral Marc A. Mitscher and Vice Admiral John S. McCain.

7 August Carrier Division 11 was established at Pearl Harbor, Hawaii, Rear Admiral Matthias B. Gardner commanding. This division, composed of carriers *Saratoga* and *Ranger,* was the first in the U.S. Navy specifically established for night operations.

1944—Continued

10 August Naval Air Bases commands were established within each Naval District, the Training Command, and for Marine Corps Bases, and were charged with the military direction and administrative coordination of matters affecting the development and operational readiness of aviation facilities in their respective areas.

10 August The operating aircraft complement of Carrier Air Groups was revised to 54 VF, 24 VB and 18 VT with the provision that four night fighters and two photo planes be included among the 54 VF.

11 August An electric powered rescue hoist was installed on an HNS-1 helicopter at CGAS Floyd Bennett Field, N.Y. During the ensuing four day test period, in which flights were conducted over Jamaica Bay, the feasibility of rescuing personnel from the water and of transferring personnel and equipment to and from underway boats was demonstrated. Six weeks later, a hydraulic hoist, which overcame basic disadvantages of the electric hoist, was installed and successfully tested, leading to its adoption for service use.

11 August Dr. M. F. Bates of the Sperry Gyroscope Company submitted a brief report of the trial installation and flight test of a helicopter automatic pilot (cyclic pitch control) in an HNS-1 at CGAS Floyd Bennett Field, N.Y.

15–29 August Landings in Southern France—Two United States and seven British escort carriers of the Naval Attack Force (Rear Admiral T. H. Troubridge, RN) supplied defensive fighter cover over the shipping area, spotted for naval gunfire, flew close support missions, made destructive attacks on enemy concentrations and lines of communication and otherwise assisted Allied troops landing between Toulon and Cannes, France, and advancing up the Rhone Valley.

20–23 August The nonrigid airship K-111, under command of Lieutenant Commander Frederick N. Klein, operating in conjunction with the Escort Carrier *Makassar Strait* off San Diego, Calif., demonstrated the feasibility of refueling and replenishing airships from aircraft carriers. In this operation of 72.5 hours duration, the airship's crew was relieved every 12 hours and its engines were operated continuously. In one evolution, the airship remained on deck for 32 minutes.

24 August The first night carrier air group, CVLG(N)-43, was established at Charlestown, R.I. Its component squadrons VF(N)-43 and VT(N)-43, the lat-ter the first of the night torpedo squadrons, were established the same day.

24 August Fleet Air Wing 10 moved forward from Perth, Australia, to Los Negros in the Admiralty Islands, to support the advance of Southwest Pacific Forces on the Philippines.

31 August–30 September Occupation of Palau and Morotai—Simultaneous landings by Central and Southwest Pacific Forces were preceded by wide-flung operations of four carrier groups of Task Force 38 (Vice Admiral Marc A. Mitscher), which committed only part of its strength in direct support and operated principally in covering action. TG 38.4 (Rear Admiral Ralph E. Davison) opened the campaign with attacks on the Bonin and Volcano Islands (31 Aug-2 Sep). The entire Fast Carrier Force hit the Palau area (6–8 Sep), leaving TG 38.4 to maintain the neutralization of Palau, and moved against the Philippines with fighter sweeps over Mindanao airfields (9–10 Sep) and strikes in the Visayas (12–14 Sep). Here TG 38.1 (Vice Admiral John S. McCain) separated to hit Mindanao (14 Sep) and to support landing on Morotai by Southwest Pacific Forces (15 Sep). The landings were preceded by bombing and strafing attacks and were supported (15–16 Sep) by TG 38.1 aircraft and additionally by six escort carriers of TG 77.1 (Rear Admiral Thomas L. Sprague). Landings on Peleliu by Central Pacific Forces (15 Sep) were preceded by preliminary carrier air attacks (12–14 Sep) from TG 38.4 and from four CVEs of Carrier Unit One (Rear Admiral William D. Sample). Continued support was given by the same fast carrier group (15–18 Sep) and until the end of the month by a total of 10 escort carriers operating in TG 32.7 (Rear Admiral Ralph A. Ofstie). Carrier air support was also provided for landings on Agaur (17 Sep), Ulithi (23 Sep), and the shore-to-shore movement from Peleliu to Ngesebus (28 Sep) support for the latter including strikes by Marine Corps land-based units from Peleliu, the first of which, VMF(N)-541, had arrived 24 September. Following the action at Morotai, TG 38.1 rejoined the main body of Fast Carriers which then launched strikes on airfields and shipping around Manila (21–22 Sep) and hit airfields, military installations, and shipping in the central Philippines (24 Sep) before retiring. In this month of action, carrier planes destroyed 893 enemy aircraft and sank 67 war and merchant ships totalling 224,000 tons.

Enemy weakness in the central Philippines, uncovered by carrier air action, changed plans for reentry into the Philippines, shifting the assault point from southern Mindanao to Leyte and advancing the assault date from mid-November to 20 October.

1944—Continued

Fire spreads from napalm dropped by Marine fighter flying air support during Peleliu invasion USMC 97976

1 September Project Bumblebee (as it was later known) came into being as the Bureau of Ordnance reported that a group of scientists from Section T of the Office of Scientific Research and Development were investigating the practicability of developing a jet-propelled, guided, anti-aircraft weapon. Upon completion of the preliminary investigation, a developmental program was approved in December by the Chief of Naval Operations. In order to concentrate upon the guided missile phase of the anti-aircraft problem, the OSRD and Applied Physics Laboratory of Johns Hopkins University, completed withdrawal, also in December, from the proximity fuze program which thus came completely under the Bureau of Ordnance.

3 September Lieutenant Ralph Spaulding of Special Air Unit, Fleet Air Wing 7, flew a torpex-laden drone Liberator from an airfield at Feresfield, England, set radio control and parachuted to ground. Ensign James M. Simpson, controlling the Liberator's flight from a PV, sought to hit submarine pens on Helgoland Island; however, he lost view of the plane in a rain shower during the final alignment and relying only upon the drone's television picture of the terrain hit the barracks and industrial area of an airfield on nearby Dune Island.

3 September Fourth Wake Raid—A strike group of one carrier, with cruisers and destroyers, hit enemy positions on Wake.

6 September A contract was awarded to McDonnell Aircraft Corporation for development of the Gargoyle, or LBD-1, a radio controlled low-wing gliding bomb fitted with a rocket booster and designed for launching from carrier-based dive-bombers and torpedo planes against enemy ships.

6 September As the scope of the aviation safety program was enlarged, a Flight Safety Section was established in the Office of the Deputy Chief of Naval Operations (Air), and was assigned the direction and supervision of the aviation safety program.

9 September Fleet Air Wing 17 moved forward to the Schouten Islands to direct patrol plane operations supporting the occupation of Morotai by Southwest Pacific Forces.

11 September Commander, Fleet Air Wing 1, based on *Hamlin*, transferred from Espiritu Santo in the South Pacific to Guam to direct the operations of patrol squadrons in the Central Pacific.

18 September The Pelican guided missile production program was terminated and the project returned to a developmental status. Despite reasonable success during the preceding six weeks, this decision was made because of tactical, logistic and technical problems involved in its use.

1944—Continued

27 September Guided missiles were used in the Pacific, as Special Task Air Group 1, from its base on Stirling in the Treasury Islands, began a combat demonstration of the TDR assault drone. The drones had been delivered to the Russell Islands by surface shipping and flown 45 miles to bases in the Northern Solomons where they were stripped for pilotless flight and armed with bombs of up to 2,000 pounds. For combat against heavily defended targets, a control operator in an accompanying TBM guided the drone by radio and directed the final assault by means of a picture received from a television camera mounted in the drone. In the initial attack, against antiaircraft emplacements in a beached merchant ship defending Kahili airstrip on South Bougainville, two out of four TDRs struck the target ship.

1 October Patrol Squadrons (VP) and multi-engine bombing squadrons (VB) were renamed and redesignated patrol bombing squadrons (VPB).

7 October A new Bureau of Aeronautics color specification went into effect which provided seven different color schemes for aircraft depending upon design and use. The most basic change was the use of glossy sea blue all over on carrier based aircraft and on seaplane transports, trainers and utility aircraft. The basic non-specular camouflage color scheme, semigloss blue above and nonspecular white below, was to be applied to patrol and patrol bombing types and to helicopters. For antisubmarine warfare, two special camouflage schemes—gray on top and sides and white on bottom, or white all over—were prescribed with the selection dependent upon prevailing weather conditions (this had been used by COMNAVAIRLANT since 19 July 1943). All aluminum was to be used on landplane transports and trainers and landplane and amphibian utility aircraft. Orange-yellow was to be used upon target-towing aircraft and primary trainers. Another new scheme, glossy red, was specified for target drones.

7 October Provision was made for the optional use by tactical commanders of special identification markings on combat aircraft, such markings preferably to be applied with temporary paint.

10 October–30 November Occupation of Leyte— The opening blow of the campaign was struck (10 Oct) by Task Force 38 (Vice Admiral Marc A. Mitscher) against airfields on Okinawa and the Ryukyus. This force, built around 17 carriers hit airfields on northern Luzon (11 and 14 Oct), on Formosa (12–14 Oct), and

in the Manila area (15 Oct), destroying 438 enemy aircraft in the air and 366 on the ground in 5 strike days. These and other strikes concentrated on reinforcement staging areas and effectively cleared the air for the landing (20 Oct) of Southwest Pacific Army troops on Leyte. Fast carrier support of the ground campaign was supplemented (18–23 Oct) by the action of 18 CVEs organized in three elements under TG 77.4 (Rear Admiral Thomas L. Sprague).

A major disruptive effort by the Japanese Fleet was opposed by the Fast Carrier Force of the Third Fleet (Vice Admiral William F. Halsey) and by surface and air elements of the Seventh Fleet (Vice Admiral Thomas C. Kinkaid) in three related actions of The Battle for Leyte Gulf (23–26 Oct). As the Japanese Fleet, in three elements identified as Southern, Central, and Northern Forces, converged on Leyte Gulf from as many directions, Fast Carrier Force aircraft (24 Oct) hit the Southern Force in the Sulu Sea, attacked the Central Force in the Sibuyan Sea, sinking the 63,000 ton battleship *Musashi* and a destroyer, and was itself under air attack resulting in the loss of *Princeton*. Seventh Fleet surface elements turned back the Southern Force in a brief intensive action before daylight in the Battle of Surigao Strait (25 Oct), sinking two battleships and three destroyers. The Japanese Central Force made a night passage through San Bernardino Strait and at daylight took under fire six escort carriers and screen of TG 77.4, and was opposed by a combined air and ship action in the Battle Off Samar (25 Oct), in which *Gambier Bay*, two destroyers, and one destroyer escort were sunk by enemy gunfire and three Japanese heavy cruisers were sunk by carrier air. At the same time the Fast Carrier Force met the Northern Force in the Battle Off Cape Engano, sinking the heavy carrier *Zuikaku* and light

Attack on Japanese cruiser, Battle for Leyte Gulf 47012

1944—Continued

carriers *Chiyoda, Zuiho,* and *Chitose,* the latter with the assistance of cruiser gunfire. Off Leyte, Kamikaze pilots, in the first planned suicide attacks of the war, hit the escort carriers, sinking *St. Lo* and damaging *Sangamon, Suwannee* (AO 33), *Santee, White Plains, Kalinin Bay,* and *Kitkun Bay.* As remnants of the Japanese Fleet limped homeward through the Central Philippines, (26–27 Oct) carrier aircraft sank a light cruiser and four destroyers, to bring Japanese battle losses to 26 major combatant ships totaling over 300,000 tons.

Direct air support in the Leyte-Samar area was assumed by Allied Air based at Tacloban (27 Oct) and 2 days later the escort carriers retired. Later one group operated at sea to protect convoys from the Admiralties

Navy Ace, David McCampbell 258198

Kamikaze barely misses the carrier Sangamon 700580

against air and submarine attack (19–28 Nov) and another group performed the same services (14–23 Nov) for convoys from Ulithi. The Fast Carrier Force also continued support for 2 days attacking airfields on Luzon and in the Visayas (27–28 Oct), shipping near Cebu (28 Oct), and Luzon airfields and shipping in Manila Bay (29 Oct). In supporting operations during October, carrier aircraft destroyed 1,046 enemy aircraft.

Requirements for continued carrier air support for the campaign caused cancellation of a planned Fast

1944—Continued

Carrier Strike on Tokyo, and Task Force 38 (now under Vice Admiral John S. McCain) sortied from Ulithi to hit Luzon and Mindoro airfields and strike shipping in Manila Bay (5–6 Nov), sinking a heavy cruiser and other ships; hit a reinforcement convoy of four transports and five destroyers in Ormoc Bay (11 Nov) sinking all but one destroyer; shifted to Luzon and the Manila area (13–14 Nov) and sank a light cruiser, four destroyers, and 20 merchant and auxiliary ships; hit the same areas again (19 and 25 Nov), sinking another heavy cruiser and several auxiliaries; and wound up the month's operations with an aerial score of 770 enemy aircraft destroyed. During these actions, the force was under several Kamikaze attacks which damaged the carriers *Intrepid* (29 Oct), *Franklin* and *Belleau Wood* (30 Oct), *Lexington* (5 Nov), *Essex, Intrepid,* and *Cabot* (25 Nov)—two seriously enough to require Navy Yard repairs.

14 October The Amphibious Forces Training Command, Pacific, was directed to form mobile Air Support Training Units to train Carrier Air Groups and Marine Corps squadrons in the technique of close air support operations.

17 October Commander, Fleet Air Wing 10, on *Currituck,* arrived in Philippine waters and directed

patrol plane operations in support of the occupation of Leyte.

19 October Commander, Fleet Air Wing 17 moved to Morotai, N.E.I., to support Southwest Pacific operations against the Philippines.

21 October A new command, Marine Carrier Air Groups, was established under Aircraft, Fleet Marine Force, Pacific to direct the formation and training of Marine Corps squadrons destined to operate from air support escort carriers. Current plans called for the formation of six Marine Carrier Air Groups, each composed of a fighter and a torpedo squadron, four of them to be assigned to escort carriers and two to function as replacement and training groups.

25 October In recognition of the difference in functions performed, Carrier Aircraft Service Units and Patrol Aircraft Service Units, operating at advanced bases, were redesignated Combat Aircraft Service Units (Forward), short title CASU(F), while those in the continental United States and Hawaii retained the original title.

26 October The last attack in a month long demonstration of the TDR assault drone was made by Special Task Air Group, thereby concluding the first use of the guided missile in the Pacific. During the demonstration a total of 46 drones were expended, of which 29

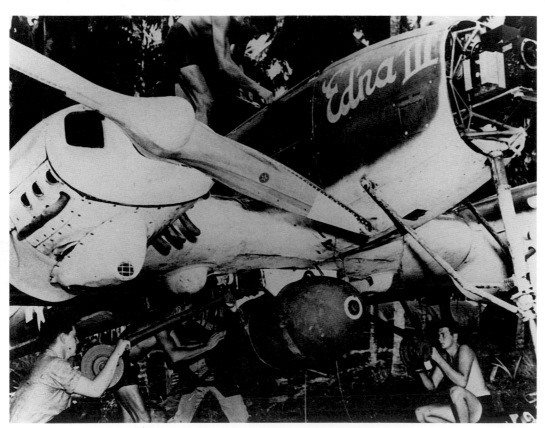

TDR-1, assault drone, being prepared for attack
1053775

1944—Continued

reached the target areas: two attacked a lighthouse on Cape St. George, New Ireland, making one hit which demolished the structure; nine attacked anti-aircraft emplacements on beached ships achieving six direct hits and two near misses; and 18 attacked other targets in the Shortlands and Rabaul areas making 11 hits.

6 November   Recognition of the future importance of turbojet and turboprop powerplants led the Bureau of Aeronautics to request the Naval Air Material Center to study requirements for a laboratory to develop and test gas-turbine powerplants. This initiated action which led to the establishment of the Naval Air Turbine Test Station, Trenton, N.J.

17 November   The Bureau of Aeronautics reported that technical studies were underway to determine the feasibility of launching an adaptation of the JB-2, a U.S. Army version of the German V-l Buzz Bomb, from escort carriers for attacks on enemy surface vessels and shore targets. Modifications visualized included installation of radio controls and a radar beacon. As subsequently developed, this became the Loon.

23 November   Training Task Force Command was dissolved and its facilities, personnel and equipment reallocated.

27 November   *Commencement Bay*, first of her class built from the last U.S. escort carrier design, was commissioned at Tacoma, Wash., Captain Roscoe L. Bowman commanding.

29 November   The changing character of the war was reflected in a revision of the aircraft complement of *Essex* Class Carrier Air Groups to 73 VF, 15 VB and 15 VT. The fighter complement was to be filled by two squadrons of 36 planes each plus one for the Air Group Commander and to include four VF(N), two VF(P) and two VF(E). The change to the new figures was gradual, beginning with the assignment of Marine fighter squadrons in December and continued with the establishment of VBF squadrons the following month.

30 November   Fleet Air Wing 10 headquarters became shore based on Jinamoc Island in the Philippines.

1 December   Electronics Tactical Training Unit was established at NAS Willow Grove, Pa., to train personnel of the Airborne Coordinating Group as instructors in the operation of all newer types of airborne electronics apparatus including search, navigation, identification, and ordnance radar.

7 December   *Chourre* was commissioned as the first aviation repair ship of the U.S. Navy, Captain Andrew H. Bergeson commanding.

11 December   The steady decline in U-boat activity in the Caribbean during the year permitted a reduction of blimp operations over the southern approaches, and Fleet Airship Wing 5 at Trinidad was disestablished.

12 December   Three Evacuation Squadrons (VE) were established in the Pacific from Air Sea Rescue Squadron elements already providing evacuation services.

13 December   Escort Carrier Force, Pacific (Rear Admiral Calvin T. Durgin), was established for administrative control over all escort carriers operating in the Pacific, excepting those assigned to training and transport duty.

14–16 December   Support of the Landings on Mindoro—Six escort carriers of Task Unit 77.12.1 (Rear Admiral Felix B. Stump) and Marine Corps shore-based air flew cover for the passage of transport and assault shipping through the Visayas (12–14 Dec). The escort carriers provided direct support for landings by Army troops (15 Dec) and in the assault area (16–17 Dec). On the night of D-day Navy seaplanes joined with operations from Mangarin Bay. The covering support of Task Force 38 (Vice Admiral John S. McCain), with seven heavy and six light carriers, began with fighter sweeps over Luzon airfields (14 Dec) and continued with successive combat air patrols relieved on station, which spread an aerial blanket over Luzon (14–16 Dec) and effectively pinned down all enemy aircraft on the island and accounted for a major share of the 341 enemy aircraft destroyed in the brief campaign.

18 December   Third Fleet units, refueling east of the Philippines, were overtaken by an unusually severe typhoon which formed nearby. Three destroyers capsized in the high seas and several ships were damaged, including four light carriers of Task Force 38 and four escort carriers of the replenishment group.

28 December   Marine Corps Fighter Squadrons 124 and 213, the first to operate from fast carriers in combat, reported for their first tour of carrier duty aboard *Essex* in Ulithi.

30 December   The specification on aircraft color was amended to provide that patrol and patrol bombing landplanes received a color scheme that was in general similar to that prescribed for carrier based airplanes. Specifically, the patrol and patrol bombers were to be painted semigloss sea blue on top and bottom surfaces of wings and on all horizontal tail surfaces; other tail surfaces and the fuselage were to be non-specular sea blue.

1945

1 January Carrier Training Squadron, Pacific, composed of two carrier divisions, was established in the Pacific Fleet to provide operational control over carriers employed in training Carrier Air Groups out of Pearl Harbor and San Diego.

2 January Eighteen Fighter Bomber Squadrons (VBF) were established within existing Carrier Air Groups to adjust their composition to the needs of changed combat requirements in the Pacific.

2 January Headquarters, Fleet Air Wing 17, based on *Tangier*, directed patrol plane support of the Lingayen Gulf operations from San Pedro Bay.

3–22 January Invasion of Luzon—Southwest Pacific Force operations against Luzon were directly supported by Seventh Fleet escort carriers in Task Group 77.4 (Rear Admiral Calvin T. Durgin) and indirectly by the fast carriers in Task Force 38 (Vice Admiral John S. McCain) of Third Fleet and Central Pacific Forces. Task Group 77.4, with 17 escort carriers, covered the approach of the Luzon Attack Force against serious enemy air opposition from Kamikaze pilots which sank *Ommaney Bay* (4 Jan), and damaged several ships including escort carriers *Manila Bay* and *Savo Island* (5 Jan). It conducted preliminary strikes in the assault area (7–9 Jan), covered the landings in Lingayen Gulf (9 Jan), and supported the inland advance of troops ashore (9–17 Jan). Among the ships damaged by Kamikaze pilots opposing the landings were the escort carriers *Kadashan Bay* and *Kitkun Bay* (8 Jan), and *Salamaua* (13 Jan). Task Force 38, with seven heavy and four light carriers in three groups and one heavy and one light carrier in a night group, and accompanied by a Replenishment Group with one hunter-killer and seven escort carriers, concentrated on the destruction of enemy air power and air installations in surrounding areas. In spite of almost continuous bad weather which hampered flight operations during the entire month, this force launched offensive strikes on Formosa and the Ryukyus (3–4 Jan), a two day attack on Luzon (6–7 Jan) and on

fields in the Formosa-Pescadores-Ryukyus area (9 Jan), destroying over 100 enemy aircraft and sinking 40,000 tons of merchant and small combatant ships in one week of preliminary action. During the night (9–10 Jan) Task Force 38 made a high-speed run through Luzon Strait followed by the Replenishment Group which passed through Balintang Channel, for Operations in the South China Sea (9–20 Jan). Strikes (12 Jan), over 420 miles of the Indo-China coast, reached south to Saigon and caught ships in the harbor and in coastal convoys with devastating results, sinking 12 tankers, 20 passenger and cargo vessels and numerous small combatant ships, totaling 149,000 tons. Moving northward to evade a typhoon, the force hit targets at Hong Kong, the China Coast, and Formosa (15 Jan) and next day concentrated on the Hong Kong area damaging enemy shore installations and sinking another 62,000 tons of shipping. As inclement weather persisted, the force left the South China Sea with an after dark run through Balintang Channel (20 Jan) and hit Formosa, the Pescadores, and Okinawa against enemy air opposition which damaged *Ticonderoga* and *Langley* (20 Jan) and repeated the attack in the Ryukyus the next day to finish off three weeks of action with an aerial score of over 600 enemy aircraft destroyed and 325,000 tons of enemy shipping sunk.

11 January The Bureau of Ordnance assigned the first task on Project Bumblebee to the Applied Physics Laboratory, thus formally establishing the program for development of a ram-jet powered, guided, antiaircraft weapon from which the Talos, Terrier, and Tartar missiles eventually emerged.

29–31 January Six escort carriers of Task Group 77.4 (Rear Admiral William D. Sample) provided air cover and support for landings by Army troops at San Antonio near Subic Bay (29 Jan), on Grande Island in the same area (30 Jan) and at Nasugbu, south of the entrance to Manila Bay (31 Jan).

6 February The Chief of Naval Operations directed that, following a period of training at NAS Kaneohe Bay, Hawaii, VPB Squadrons 109, 123, and 124 of Fleet Air Wing 2 be equipped to employ the SWOD Mark 9 (Bat) glide bomb in combat.

15 February The West Coast Wing of the Naval Air Transport Service was disestablished and its squadrons reassigned to the Pacific and Atlantic Wings.

16 February–16 March Capture of Iwo Jima—The Marine Corps assault of 19 February was preceded and supported by two separate carrier elements of the Central Pacific Force. The first of these was Task Force

1945—Continued

58 under Vice Admiral Marc A. Mitscher, the second was Task Group 52.2 under Rear Admiral Calvin T. Durgin. On 16–17 February Mitscher moved against Japan with nine heavy and five light carriers in four groups, and two heavy carriers in a night group. Carrier aircraft hit Japanese air bases in the Tokyo plains. From 19 to 23 February, his forces supported Marine Corps landings and operations on Iwo Jima and flew neutralization strikes against the Bonins. On 25 February, he returned for a second strike on Tokyo. On 1 March he struck at Okinawa and the Ryukyus and then retired to Ulithi, leaving in his wake 648 enemy aircraft destroyed and 30,000 tons of merchant shipping sunk.

Task Group 52.2 began the campaign with nine escort carriers; it was later augmented by two more escort carriers and one night CV. On 16–18 February, Admiral Durgin carried out air strikes on Iwo Jima's shore defenses to reduce their resistance to the impending Marine Corps landing. From 19 February to 11 March he flew missions in direct support of Marine Corps ground operations and neutralized airstrips in the Bonins.

In counter attacks, the Japanese were not entirely unsuccessful. On 21 February a Kamikaze raid upon Task Group 52 sank the escort carrier *Bismarck Sea,* seriously damaged *Saratoga,* and did minor damage to *Lunga Point*. But new air defense elements in the U.S. Fleet were functional and noteworthy; they included the altitude-determining radar on LSTs and a Night Fighter Director in the Air Support Commander's organization.

Other U.S. operations deserve mention. Task Group 50.5, under Commodore Dixwell Ketcham, was based in the Marianas. The Group's shore-based aircraft conducted shipping reconnaissance and air-sea rescue between Japan and Iwo Jima. They also flew offensive screens for carrier raids and expeditionary forces. Similar operations were carried out by patrol planes of Fleet Air Wing 1 from tenders anchored in the lee of Iwo Jima (28 Feb–8 Mar). Marine Corps Observation Squadrons 4 and 5, which arrived on CVEs and on LSTs equipped with Brodie gear, began operations from Iwo Jima airfields on 27 February. Army fighters were flown in from Saipan on 6 March, and Marine Corps Torpedo Squadron 242 arrived on 8 March; they flew day and night combat air patrols and provided all air support upon the departure of the last CVEs on 11 March. Iwo Jima was secured on 16 March.

19 February   Commander, Fleet Air Wing 1 went to sea aboard *Hamlin* to direct patrol squadrons in support of the Iwo Jima campaign and remained in the area until the island was secure.

26 February   Headquarters, Fleet Air Wing 17 was established ashore at Clark Field on Luzon.

3 March   The Naval Air Transport Service was reorganized and established as a Fleet Command with headquarters at NAAS Oakland, Calif., to operate under the immediate direction of COMINCH and CNO.

3 March   The Naval Air Technical Training Command was incorporated into the Naval Air Training Command.

7 March   Commanding Officer, CGAS Floyd Bennett Field, N.Y., reported that a dunking sonar suspended from an XHOS-1 helicopter had been tested successfully.

7 March   The tandem rotor XHRP-X transport helicopter, built under Navy contract by P-V Engineering Forum made its first flight at the contractor's plant at Sharon Hill, Pa., with Frank N. Piasecki as pilot and George N. Towson as copilot.

8 March   A rocket powered Gorgon air-to-air missile was launched from a PBY-5A and achieved an estimated speed of 550 mph in its first powered test flight, conducted off Cape May, N.J., under the direction of Lieutenant Commander Moulton B. Taylor.

17 March   Responsibility for evacuating wounded personnel was assigned to the Naval Air Transport Service.

18 March–21 June   The Okinawa Campaign—The last and, for naval forces, the most violent of the major amphibious campaigns of World War II was supported by three separately operating carrier forces, by tender-based patrol squadrons, by Marine and Army air units based in the immediate area and by Army and Navy air units based in other areas. On 28 May a change in overall command from the Fifth Fleet (Admiral R. A. Spruance) to the Third Fleet (Admiral William F. Halsey) took place, which changed all task number designations from the 50s to the 30s. (In this account, first designations are used throughout.)

The fast carriers of Task Force 58 (Vice Admiral Marc A. Mitscher) began the attack. With an original strength of 10 heavy and six light carriers, this force launched neutralization strikes on Kyushu, Japan (18–22 Mar), destroying 482 enemy aircraft by air attack and another 46 by ship's gunfire, and began pre-assault strikes on Okinawa (23 Mar). During these preliminaries, Kamikaze pilots, employing conventional aircraft, bombs, and Baka flying bombs (first observed on 21 Mar) retaliated with attacks which seri-

1945—Continued

Marine F4U in rocket attack on Okinawa USMC 129356

ously damaged the carrier *Franklin* and scored hits on four others. For the next three months the fast carrier force operated continuously in a 60-mile-square area northeast of Okinawa and within 350 miles of Japan, from which position it neutralized Amami Gunto airfields, furnished close air support for ground operations, intercepted enemy air raids, and on occasion moved northward to hit airfields on Kyushu.

Task Group 52.1 (Rear Admiral C. T. Durgin), originally 18 escort carriers strong, conducted pre-assault strikes and supported the occupation of Kerama Retto (25–26 Mar), joined in the pre-assault strikes on Okinawa (27–29 Mar) and, from a fairly restricted operating area southeast of the island, supported the landings and flew daily close support for operations ashore until the island was secure (21 Jun). The arrival

A Japanese bomber, hit by antiaircraft guns while attacking an Essex class carrier, leaves a trail of fire 313866

1945—Continued

in May of two CVEs with Marine Carrier Air Groups on board marked the combat debut in Marine Air Support carriers.

Task Force 57 (Vice Admiral H. B. Rawlings, RN), a British task force built around four carriers equipped with armored flight decks, operated south of Okinawa (26 Mar–20 Apr and 3–25 May), from which position it neutralized airfields on Sakishima Gunto and Formosa, and intercepted air raids headed for the assault area. Subject to frequent suicide attacks, all four carriers took hits in the course of their action, but all remained operational.

Patrol squadrons of Fleet Air Wing 1, based on seaplane tenders at Kerama Retto, conducted long-range antishipping search over the East China Sea to protect assault forces from enemy surface force interference, flew antisubmarine patrols in the immediate area, and provided air-sea rescue services for carrier operations from D minus 1 day to the end of the campaign.

Army and Marine Corps troops landed on the western shores (1 Apr) against light opposition, established a firm beachhead, and captured Yontan airfield the same day. Supporting shore-based air moved in behind the landings led by the OY-1 spotting planes (3 Apr). As ground opposition stiffened, Marine Corps elements of the Tactical Air Force began local air defense patrols (7 Apr) and shortly started their close air support mission. A Navy landplane patrol squadron joined forces ashore (22 Apr) and extended the range of seaplane search operations, and an Army fighter squadron began operations from Ie Shima (13 May).

Strong Japanese air opposition developed (6 Apr) in the first of a series of mass suicide attacks involving some 400 aircraft. In seven mass raids, interspersed with smaller scattered ones, during the critical period (6 Apr–28 May), the Japanese expended some 1,500 aircraft, principally against naval forces supporting the campaign. In the three month's struggle against the humanly guided missiles of the Kamikaze force, the U.S. Navy took the heaviest punishment in its history. Although Task Force 58 lost no carriers during the campaign, one light and eight heavy carriers were hit: *Enterprise, Intrepid, Yorktown* (18 Mar), *Franklin, Wasp* (19 Mar), *San Jacinto* (6 Apr), *Hancock* (7 Apr) *Enterprise, Essex,* (11 Apr) *Intrepid* (16 Apr) *Bunker Hill* (11 May), and *Enterprise* (14 May). Three escort carriers of Task Force 52, *Wake Island* (3 Apr), *Sangamon* (4 May), and *Natoma Bay* (6 Jun), were also damaged.

Opposition from Japanese naval surface forces was brief and ineffective. A task force made up of *Yamato,* the world's largest battleship, one light cruiser, and eight destroyers, took part in what was to be the last sortie by the Japanese Navy and was beaten decisively by carrier aircraft in the Battle of the East China Sea (7 Apr). Only four Japanese destroyers survived the encounter.

Carrier air support was on a larger and more extensive scale than any previous amphibious campaign. Fast and escort carrier planes flew over 40,000 action sorties, destroyed 2,516 enemy aircraft, and blasted enemy positions with 8,500 tons of bombs and 50,000 rockets. Marine Corps squadrons ashore destroyed another 506 Japanese aircraft and expended 1,800 tons of bombs and 15,865 rockets on close air support missions. Task Force 58's time on the line (18 Mar–10 Jun) was surpassed by the escort carriers (24 Mar–21 Jun), but of several records for continuous operations in an active combat area that were marked up by the carriers during the campaign, the most outstanding was logged by *Essex,* with 79 consecutive days.

21 March   The development of a rocket-powered surface-to-air guided missile, was initiated as the Bureau of Aeronautics awarded a contract for 100 experimental Larks to the Ranger Engine Division of Fairchild.

26 March   Commander, Fleet Air Wing 1, based on *Hamlin,* arrived at Kerama Retto to direct the operations of patrol squadrons assigned to support the assault and capture of Okinawa.

14 April   Commander, Fleet Air Wing 10, arrived at Puerto Princessa, Palawan, to direct patrol plane operations against the shipping in the South China Sea and along the Indo-China coast.

23 April   PB4Ys of Patrol Bombing Squadron 109 launched two Bat glide bombs against the enemy shipping in Balikpapan Harbor, Borneo, in the first

Bat, WWII automatic homing Navy missile 701606

1945—Continued

combat employment of the only automatic homing bomb to be used in World War II.

1 May CVBG-74, the first large Carrier Air Group in the U.S. Navy, was established at NAAF Otis Field, Mass., for duty on *Midway*.

2 May First Helicopter Rescue—Lieutenant August Kleisch, USCG, flying a HNS-1 helicopter rescued 11 Canadian airmen that were marooned in northern Labrador about 125 miles from Goose Bay.

4 May Fleet Air Wing 18, Rear Admiral Marshall R. Greer commanding, was established at Guam to take over the operational responsibilities in the Marianas area, previously held by Fleet Air Wing 1.

8 May V-E Day—The president proclaimed the end of the war in Europe.

9 May U-249, the first German submarine to surrender after the cessation of hostilities in Europe, raised the black surrender flag to a PB4Y of Fleet Air Wing 7 near the Scilly Islands off Lands End, England.

10 May In a crash program to counter the Japanese Baka (suicide) bomb, the Naval Aircraft Modification Unit was authorized to develop Little Joe, a ship-to-air guided missile powered with a standard JATO unit.

19 May The Office of Research and Inventions was established in the Office of the Secretary of the Navy to coordinate, and from time to time to disseminate to all bureaus full information with respect to all naval research, experimental, test and developmental activities and to supervise and administer all Navy Department action relating to patents, inventions, trademarks, copyrights, royalty payments, and similar matters. By this order, the Naval Research Laboratory and the Special Devices Division of the Bureau of Aeronautics were transferred to the newly established office.

5 June Cognizant commands and offices were informed of plans, permitted by the cessation of hostilities in Europe, for the future employment of Atlantic patrol aviation which called for the disestablishing of four Wings and 23 Patrol, five Inshore Patrol, and seven Composite Squadrons, and for the redeployment of seven Patrol Squadrons to the Pacific.

10 June After the close of hostilities in Europe, Fleet Air Wing 15 departed from Port Lyautey, Morocco, for Norfolk, Va.

13 June A ramjet engine produced power in supersonic flight in a test conducted by the Applied Physics Laboratory at Island Beach, N.J. The ramjet unit was launched by a booster of four 5-inch high velocity aircraft rockets and achieved a range of 11,000 yards, nearly double that of similarly launched, cold units.

15 June Fleet Airship Wing 2 at Richmond, Fla., was disestablished.

15 June Experimental Squadrons XVF-200 and XVJ-25 were established at Brunswick, Maine, to provide, under the direct operational control of COMINCH, flight facilities for evaluating and testing tactics, procedure, and equipment for use in special defense tasks particularly those concerned with defense against the Kamikaze.

16 June Naval Air Test Center, Patuxent River, Md., was established to be responsible for aviation test functions formerly assigned to NAS Patuxent River.

20 June Fifth Wake Raid—Three carriers of Task Group 12.4 (Rear Admiral Ralph E. Jennings) launched five strikes against enemy positions on Wake Island.

27 June Fleet Air Wing 16 was disestablished at Recife, Brazil.

30 June–3 July Landings at Balikpapan—Marine Corps and Navy squadrons, aboard three escort carriers of Task Group 78.4 (Rear Admiral William D. Sample), provided close air support, local combat air patrol, and strikes on military installations, in support of landings by Australian troops (1 Jul) at Balikpapan, Borneo.

10 July–15 August Carrier operations against Japan—Task Force 38 (Vice Admiral John S. McCain), initially composed of 14 carriers and augmented by one other later in the period, operated against the Japanese homeland in a series of air strikes on airfields, war and merchant shipping, naval bases and military installations from Kyushu in the south to Hokkaido in the north. The force was a part of Third Fleet under Admiral William F. Halsey, who was in overall command. Operations were supported by a replenishment group and an antisubmarine group, both with escort carriers in their complement, and were supplemented (after 16 Jul) by operations of British Carrier Task Force 37 (Vice Admiral H. B. Rawlings, RN) composed of four carriers and a screen. The attack began with heavy air strikes on airfields in the Tokyo plains area (10 Jul), shifted to airfields and shipping in the northern Honshu-Hokkaido area (14-

1945—Continued

15 Jul), and returned to Tokyo targets (17 Jul) and naval shipping at Yokosuka (18 Jul). The attack hit Inland Sea shipping in the Kure area and airfields on northern Kyushu (24 Jul), swept up the Sea to the Osaka area and to Nagoya (25 Jul), and then repeated the sweep (25, 28 and 30 Jul). After moving southward (1 Aug) to evade a typhoon, the force moved northward to clear the Hiroshima area for the atomic bomb drop and hit the Honshu-Hokkaido area (9–10 Aug), and Tokyo (13 Aug). On 15 August at 0635, when

Admiral Halsey sent a message to his forces announcing the end of hostilities and ordering the cessation of offensive air operations, the first carrier strike of the day had already hit Tokyo and the second was approaching the coastline as it was recalled.

In this final carrier action of World War II, carrier aircraft destroyed 1,223 enemy aircraft of which over 1,000 were on the ground, and sank 23 war and 48 merchant ships totaling 285,000 tons.

13 July Captain Ralph S. Barnaby, commanding the Johnsville Naval Aircraft Modification Unit, reported

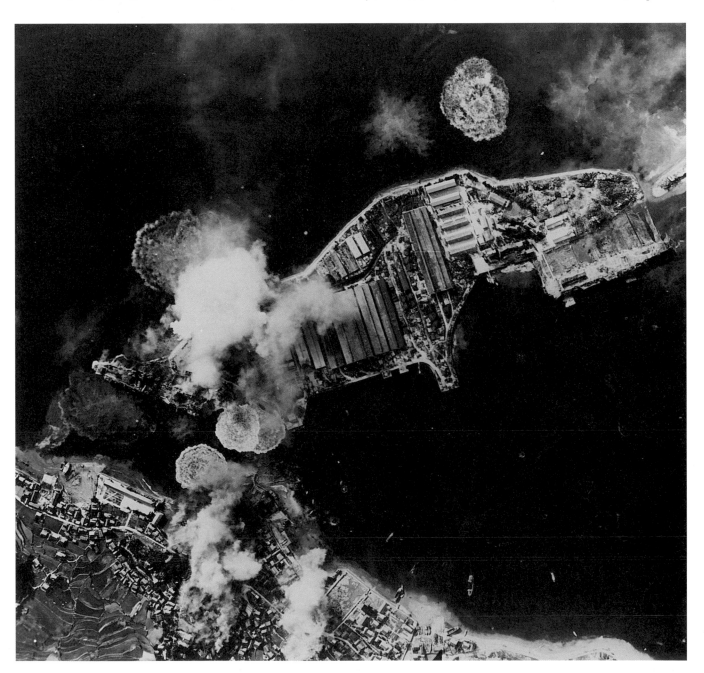

Planes of the Third Fleet attack camouflaged carriers in assault on Japanese naval base at Kure, July 1945 490162

1945—Continued

that the LBD-1, or Gargoyle, air-to-surface missile, in a series of 14 test flights including two at service weight, had made five satisfactory runs, thereby demonstrating that it was potentially capable of carrying out its mission.

14 July Fleet Air Wing 12 was disestablished at Key West, Fla.

14 July Commander, Fleet Air Wing 7, embarked on *Albemarle* at Avonmouth, England, for transfer of headquarters to the United States at Norfolk, Va.

14 July Commander, Fleet Air Wing 1, aboard *Norton Sound* set up his command base in Chimu Wan, Okinawa, and directed patrol plane operations over the East China Sea, the Yellow Sea, and the coastal waters of Japan from that location until the end of the war.

15 July Fleet Airship Wing 4 at Recife, Brazil, was disestablished.

18 July Sixth Wake Raid—*Wasp* returned to action after battle repairs and overhaul at Puget Sound, Wash., launched air strikes against targets on Wake.

19 July Fleet Air Wing 9 was disestablished at NAS New York, N.Y.

20 July Little Joe, a rocket-propelled surface-to-air missile, made two successful flights at Applied Physics Laboratory (Johns Hopkins University) test station at Island Beach, N.J.

20 July Fleet Airborne Electronics Training Units (FAETU) were established in the Atlantic and Pacific Fleets to train airborne early warning crews in the theory, operation and maintenance of their equipment.

24 July Marine Corps pilots, operating from the escort carrier *Vella Gulf,* attacked Japanese positions on Pagan Island in the Marianas, and two days later hit Rota in the same island group.

28 July Fleet Air Wing 15 was disestablished at Norfolk, Va.

1 August Seventh Wake Raid—Task Group 12.3, composed of one carrier, one battleship and destroyer screen, bombed and bombarded Wake.

4 August Fleet Air Wing 7 was disestablished at Norfolk, Va.

6 August Eighth Wake Raid—*Intrepid,* while en route from Pearl Harbor, Hawaii, to join forces off Japan, bombed buildings and gun positions on Wake Island.

6 August Escort carriers from TG 95.3 (Rear Admiral Calvin T. Durgin), covering a cruiser force operating in the East China Sea, launched strikes on shipping in the harbor at Tinghai, China.

9 August Naval Aviator Commander Frederick L. Ashworth, USN, participated in the delivery of the second atomic bomb. The weapon was released by a B-29 over Nagasaki, Japan. Ashworth had supervised and coordinated the field tests of the atomic bomb.

14 August Japan accepted the terms of unconditional surrender and on the same day, which was the 15th in the Western Pacific, hostilities ceased.

21 August The Asiatic Wing, Naval Air Transport Service, was established at NAS Oakland, Calif., Captain Carl F. Luethi in command, to operate and maintain air transport support of establishments and units in the Western Pacific and Asiatic theaters. Early in September, Wing headquarters was established on Samar in the Philippines, and on 15 November transferred to NAB Agana, Guam.

2 September The formal surrender of Japan, on board *Missouri* (BB 63) in Tokyo Bay, marked V-J Day and the end of World War II.

10 September *Midway,* first of the 45,000 ton class aircraft carriers, was placed in commission at Newport News, Va., with Captain Joseph F. Bolger in command.

3 October As the initial attempt to establish an earth satellite program, the Bureau of Aeronautics established a committee to evaluate the feasibility of space rocketry.

10 October The Office of Chief of Naval Operations was reorganized and four new Deputy Chiefs were set up for Personnel, Administration, Operations and Logistics on the same level as the existing Deputy Chief of Naval Operations (Air). The reorganization, which was by direction of the Secretary of the Navy and in accord with Executive Order, abolished Commander-in-Chief, U.S. Fleet, and transferred command of the operating forces to the Chief of Naval Operations.

17 October A type designation letter K for pilotless aircraft was added to the basic designation system,

1945—Continued

replacing the previous Class designation VK. Classes A, G and S within the type were assigned for pilotless aircraft intended for attack against aircraft, ground targets, and ships respectively.

29 October The Committee to Evaluate the Feasibility of Space Rocketry recommended that detailed studies be made to determine the feasibility of an Earth Satellite Vehicle. This led the Bureau of Aeronautics to issue contracts to one university and three companies for theoretical study, and preliminary design of a launch vehicle and for determining by actual test the specific impulse of high energy fuels including liquid hydrogen-oxygen.

1 November The Naval Air Training Command was reorganized with headquarters at NAS Pensacola, Fla., and the following subordinate commands: Naval Air Advanced Training, Naval Air Basic Training, Naval Air Technical Training, and a newly formed Naval Air Reserve Training. By this change the titles Naval Air Operational Training and Naval Air Intermediate Training ceased to exist and the facilities of the former Naval Air Primary Training Command were incorporated into Basic Training or absorbed by the Reserve Program.

5 November Ensign Jake C. West, with VF-41 embarked on *Wake Island* for carrier qualifications with the FR-1, lost power on the forward radial engine of his FR-1 shortly after take-off, forcing him to start his aft jet engine. He returned to the ship and made a successful landing, the first jet landing aboard a carrier.

29 November The Special Weapons Test and Tactical Evaluation Unit was redesignated Pilotless Aircraft Unit and in the next month was transferred to MCAS Mojave, Calif., and directed to operate detachments at NAF Point Mugu, Calif., as necessary.

1 December Fleet Air Wing 6 was disestablished at NAS Whidbey Island, Wash.

28 December The president directed that the Coast Guard be transferred from the Navy and returned to the jurisdiction of the Treasury Department.

Marine fighters on Henderson Field. This airbase was vitally important during the Guadalcanal Campaign 45345

PV-1, Medium range land-based patrol plane 41693

Hoisting PBM Mariner aboard tender. Normal servicing was performed from boats 428461

Bombs on plane frame carrier 1053797

Loading ammo in fighter 1061656

Navy night fighters, a flight of F6F Hellcats painted black 407243

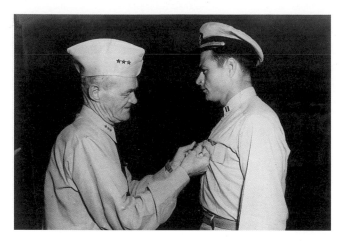

Navy Ace C. E. Harriss receives DFC from ADM Mitscher 297413

USMC Ace Joe Foss tells how one almost got away 35197

Fighter direction team for combat air patrol 428460

The fleet at Ulithi with fast carriers Wasp, Yorktown, Hornet, Hancock and Ticonderoga anchored in a row 294129

PART **6**

Postwar Years

1946–1949

The years following the greatest war in history were highlighted by the problems of demobilization, organizational readjustment and an uneasy international situation not in itself related to the outcome of the war.

Demobilization was rapid. Ships were retired to a mothball fleet; aircraft were placed in storage. Shore stations at home and abroad were deactivated. Within a year after the end of hostilities the on-board figures for the men of Naval Aviation fell to a mere one-quarter of the World War II peak. Only a skeleton of the wartime force remained to carry new operational demands that arose before the forces required for peace could be organized.

The unsettled international situation raised new, yet old, problems for the Navy. Within months fleet elements assigned to areas for the purpose of supporting occupation forces were given the additional and familiar task of supporting the nation's policy in areas on opposite sides of the world. A task force built around one or two carriers cruised the Mediterranean and as the years passed became a fixture in that sea. A similar force in the western Pacific provided the same tangible symbol of American might and determination to support the free peoples of the world.

Organizational readjustment took place at several levels. At the top there were problems of adjusting to a new departmental organization formed by what was really only compromise agreement. At the bureau and office level there were problems of reducing staffs and of realigning the functional elements of technical and administrative units to meet new requirements. In the fleet there were problems of transition, partly in size but particularly in weapons and tactics developed either as a result of combat experience or of technological advances. The introduction of jet aircraft posed special problems for carrier operations, proving once again that after the machine was developed navies had the additional problem of finding the means of taking it to sea. Superimposed were new concepts based upon guided missiles which had been introduced during World War II, but which were still in embryonic development and which required additional efforts in all

areas from design through operational deployment. In all of these, the degree of difficulty was increased by the need to complete the transition without even a temporary loss of combat effectiveness.

It was a period in which changes occurred at an ever accelerating rate and came to be accepted as normal. Technological and scientific advances built rapidly upon each other, and, almost before they could be turned to an advantage, new and greater advances had been made. It was a period of constant readjustment in plans, continual adaptation in force organization, and repeated revision of tactical doctrine. There was no time to sit back for deliberate study of the lessons of war and the careful examination of the various possibilities to determine the most favorable course of action. There existed an urgency that was not lessened by the realization of the truly destructive power that was now available to mankind.

In other respects, however, the period was a repetition of the twenties. There was the same clamor for a separate air force and for a merger of the services, but this time both were successfully accomplished in the unification of three services into a single department of defense. The study of aviation and national air policy by a president's commission and a congressional committee was reminiscent of the Morrow Board and Lampert Committee of 1925. There was new agreement among the services on their respective missions and functions. There was also dispute. As the services sought larger shares of a decreasing budget, old charges of duplication were raised; navies were again declared obsolete. This time the whipping boy was not the battleship, but the aircraft carrier. They were said to be too expensive and too vulnerable. Their capability to perform so-called strategic missions was supposedly a duplication of effort, and if they were not used in that fashion their use was too limited to warrant their existence. Carrier supporters retaliated with criticism of the newest long-range bomber—the B-36—which was equally vulnerable, expensive, and entirely unable to live up to its billing. The Secretary of Defense canceled the carrier already under construction, designed to carry Navy long-range attack planes, and the Secretary of the Navy resigned in protest. The argument raged and the whole affair seemed out of hand as it reached the fantastic situation in which one service was publicly deciding for another not only how its mission should be carried out but what was needed to do it. But the whole affair came to a halt after Congressional hearings gave the Navy a chance to be heard and when war in Korea provided more immediate problems and a greater national appreciation of the necessity for adequate military forces in an era when survival of the free world was at stake.

1946

2 January FAW-17 was disestablished in Japan.

26 January The Naval Aviation Ordnance Test Station was established at NAAS Chincoteague, Va., under the cognizance of the Bureau of Ordnance and under the air station for administration and logistic support. The establishing order also provided for the transfer from Johnsville of all Bureau of Ordnance guided missile test facilities and staff to operate at the new location with a mission to perform tests and modifications as necessary to develop aviation ordnance and guided missiles.

1 February A major reorganization of the Bureau of Aeronautics aligned the technical divisions into two groups according to function, one titled Research Development and Engineering, and the other Material and Services. An additional Assistant Chief was established over each group and the former Assistant Chief, whose staff divisions were also strengthened by the reorganization, was given the title of Deputy and Assistant Chief.

1 March Operation Frostbite—*Midway* with elements of Air Group 74 on board, and accompanied by three destroyers, left Norfolk, Va., under command of Rear Admiral John H. Cassady to conduct cold weather tests in Davis Strait. In the period 7–22 March, these units operated as a carrier task force off the coast of Labrador and above the Arctic Circle, conducting flight operations with World War II type aircraft and the newer F8F Bearcat, the combination prop and jet FR-1 Fireball, and the HNS-1 helicopter.

2 March The Chief of Naval Operations established an aircraft storage program whereby up to 6,000 aircraft of types in operation were to be stored against future needs and an additional 360 F6F-5s for future conversion to drones.

5 March The Secretary of the Navy approved the conversion of two submarine hulls into guided-missile launching vessels. *Cusk* (SS 348) and *Carbonero* (SS 337) were later selected for this conversion.

7 March The Chief of Naval Operations directed that Ground Controlled Approach equipment (GCA) be adopted as the standard blind landing system for the Navy.

11 March A modification of the class designation of naval aircraft eliminated the VB and VT used for bomber and torpedo aircraft and set up VA to identify aircraft with a primary mission of attacking surface targets. This change was responsible for the subsequent redesignation of most BT2D and BTM aircraft as AD and AM.

12 March In a reorientation and consolidation of Navy guided-missile developments, the Chief of Naval Operations directed that Glomb, Gorgon II-C, and Little Joe be discontinued; that Gargoyle, Gorgon II-A, Gorgon III-A, and Dove be limited to test and research vehicles; that the Loon be continued as a launching test vehicle and a possible interim weapon; that the Bat be completed; and that Kingfisher, Bumblebee, and Lark be continued as high priority missile developments.

15 March The Chief, Bureau of Aeronautics formally proposed to the Commanding General, Army Air Forces that a joint Army-Navy project be established for development of an earth satellite.

25 March The XHJD-1, the first twin engine helicopter, made a hovering flight. Designed for the Navy by the McDonnell Aircraft Corporation, this helicopter was intended for experimental use in a flight develop-

The F8F Bearcat, a popular post-war fighter 277123

1946—Continued

Midway, first of the 45,000-ton-class carriers, was placed in commission 10 September 1945 362123

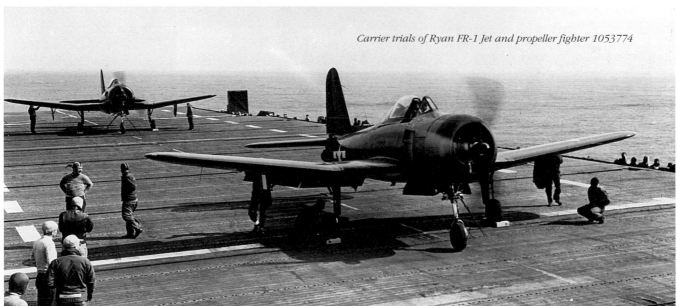

Carrier trials of Ryan FR-1 Jet and propeller fighter 1053774

Carbonero launches the Loon, an early step in the adaptation of the guided missile to the submarine 402800

1946—Continued

Twin rotor XHJD-1 designed for helicopter flight development 395920

ment program and for tactical use in utility and air-sea rescue operations.

3 April A contract was issued to Douglas for the design and construction of the XF3D-1 night fighter.

15 May The designation of patrol squadrons reverted to its prewar status with the change from VPB to VP.

21 May The Chief of Naval Operations outlined a program for the operational introduction of the Bat (SWOD Mk 9) which called for its assignment to VP-104 of the Atlantic Fleet and VP-115 of the Pacific Fleet and directed transfer to VP-104 of all PB4Y-2s already modified to operate the Bat missile.

22 May The initial operational tests of an XCF dunking sonar carried by in HO2S helicopter were completed off Key West, Fla. During a three-month period in which the tests were conducted, Lieutenant Stewart R. Graham, USCG, and Ensign William H. Coffee, USCG, piloted the helicopter and Lieutenant Commander Roy Rather, Dr. J. J. Coop, and Mr. C. V. Scott operated the sonar which provided good sonic and supersonic listening ranges and a high degree of bearing accuracy against both conventional and snorkel type submarines.

29 May The Aeronautical Board acted upon the Bureau of Aeronautics proposal for a joint Army-Navy earth satellite project by approving the establishment of an Earth Satellite Subcommittee to coordinate projects already underway.

6 June The Joint Research and Development Board was created by charter of the Secretaries of War and Navy for the purpose of coordinating all research and development activities of joint interest to the two departments. Its several committees embraced aeronautics, atomic energy, electronics, geographical exploration, geophysical sciences and guided missiles.

24 June A contract was issued to North American Aviation, Inc., for the design and construction of three

A twin-jet F3D Skynight on carrier approach 652827

1946—Continued

XAJ-1 aircraft, thereby beginning active development of a long-range carrier-based bomber capable of delivering nuclear weapons.

25 June   A contract was issued to Chance Vought for the development and construction of three XF7U-1 aircraft. This was a tailless, high performance fighter, equipped with tricycle landing gear, powered with twin turbojet engines, and designed for carrier operation.

26 June   The Aeronautical Board agreed unanimously that the knot and the nautical mile be adopted by the Army Air Forces and Navy as standard aeronautical units of speed and distance, and directed that use of the terms be specified in all future procurement of air speed indicators, charts, related equipment, and future issues of applicable handbooks and technical orders.

1 July   Operation Cross Roads—Tests to determine effects of atomic bombs on naval targets were conducted at Bikini Atoll in the Pacific. In the first test, a Nagasaki-type bomb, dropped from a B-29 at 30,000 feet on ships anchored in the lagoon, sank five of them outright and did heavy damage to nine others. A shallow underwater burst on the 25th raised the total number sunk directly or indirectly to 32 of the 83 ships of all types used in the tests. Among them were the aircraft carriers *Saratoga,* sunk in shallow water on

the 25th after 19 years of active service, and *Independence,* which was so heavily damaged and contaminated that she was no longer fit for use. Although these tests had broad national impact, to the Navy and to Naval Aviation they not only made clear the importance of nuclear weapons in control of the sea but they also provided much detailed data on the effects of nuclear blasts and a sound technical basis for intensification of efforts to develop tactics and equipment whereby the damage of such attacks against a naval task force could be held to a minimum.

1 July   The Naval Air Reserve Program was formally activated under the Naval Air Training Command, with 21 Reserve activities already in operation.

1 July   VX-3 was established at NAS New York, N.Y., to study and evaluate the adaptability of helicopters to naval purposes.

3 July   FAW-8 was disestablished at NAS Alameda.

11 July   To establish clear-cut relationships for aircraft maintenance, the Chief of Naval Operations directed the disestablishment of all CASUs and other maintenance units and their replacement by Fleet Aircraft Service Squadrons (FASRON) by 1 January. The new FASRONs were to be of three kinds according to aircraft types serviced, and were designed to promote higher standards and greater uniformity and efficiency in aircraft maintenance.

21 July   In the first U.S. test of the adaptability of jet aircraft to shipboard operation, an XFD-1 Phantom piloted by Lieutenant Commander James Davidson,

F7U-1 a tailless twin-net fighter by Vought 419488

Davidson landed FH on CVB 1053757

1946—Continued

Phantom on Franklin D. Roosevelt 1053790

made successful landings and takeoffs (deck-launched without catapults) on board *Franklin D. Roosevelt*.

1 August An act of Congress established the Office of Naval Research in the Navy Department to plan, foster and encourage scientific research. The new office came into being on 21 August 1946 by redesignation of the Office of Research and Inventions which had been established by Secretarial order in May 1945.

13 August Congress approved the Hale Plan, also known as the "Flying Midshipmen" or Aviation Midshipmen Program. It was part of the program issued by Vice Admiral James L. Holloway when he was Chief of Naval Personnel. The program was designed to provide the Navy with qualified pilots in the post-World War II period following the loss of a large segment of experienced Naval Aviators returning to civilian life. For those who joined the program, it

offered to pay for two years of college and training as a naval aviator in exchange for a service obligation. Personnel completing their flight training and designated a Naval Aviator were not automatically commissioned at the same time. They remained as aviation midshipman and were ordered to the fleet, serving as pilots but not as a commissioned officer. After a period of service in the fleet these "flying midshipmen" usually received their commission. The "Flying Midshipmen" program was replaced by the Naval Aviation Cadet program in early 1950. Of the 3,000 Aviation Midshipmen, approximately 1,800 were designated Naval Aviators. Many Aviation Midshipmen were recalled to active during the Korea War.

14 August The Chief of Naval Operations standardized missile terminology within the Navy to the extent that he directed the term "Guided Missiles" be used for all types developed by the Navy. Past practice was

1946—Continued

continued, however, in that authorization was given to continue as model designations, and in the description of missile classes, the Bureau of Ordnance term "Special Weapons Ordnance Device (SWOD)" and the Bureau of Aeronautics term "Pilotless Aircraft (P/A)."

15 August   An Instrument Flight Standardization Board was established at NAS Anacostia, D.C., under the operational control of the Deputy Chief of Naval Operations (Air), for the purpose of determining the means by which the instrument flight proficiency of pilots could be improved.

1 September   A reorganization of the Office of the Deputy Chief of Naval Operations (Air) placed its divisions into four groups titled Plans, Personnel, Readiness, and Air Logistics. An Air Planning Group was also set up on the DCNO (Air) staff to facilitate planning on the top policy level and to coordinate and direct the work of all divisions toward the same goals.

29 September–1 October   The Truculent Turtle, a Lockheed P2V Neptune (bureau number 89082), manned by Commanders Thomas D. Davies, Eugent P. Rankin, Walter S. Reid and Lieutenant Commander Roy H. Tabeling, flew from Perth, Australia to Columbus, Ohio, in 55 hours 17 minutes, and broke the world's record for distance without refueling with a flight of 11,235.6 miles.

Davies commanded the Turtle 703095

The Truculent Turtle flew nonstop Perth, Australia to Columbus 703094

1946—Continued

1 October Naval Air Missile Test Center, Point Mugu, Calif., was established to conduct tests and evaluation of guided missiles and components, Captain Albert N. Perkins, commanding.

2 October A recommendation was made by the Bureau of Aeronautics that the designation XF9F-2 be adopted in lieu of XF9F-1, thereby reflecting a decision to abandon development of the XF9F-1 four-engine night fighter in favor of a single engine day fighter. Involved in this decision was the substitution of a Rolls Royce Nene engine for Westinghouse 24Cs, an action that led to American production of the Nene.

30 October Under a project conducted by NAMC Philadelphia, Pa., Lieutenant (jg) Adolph J. Furtek made a successful ejection from a JD-1, flying at about 250 knots at 6,000 feet over Lakehurst, N.J. It was the Navy's first live test of an ejection seat.

3 November The airship XM-1 landed at Naval Air Facility, Glynco, Ga., completing a flight of 170.3 hours, a world record for duration in self-sufficient flight for any type aircraft. The flight, with Lieutenant Harold R. Walton in command, left Lakehurst, N.J., on 27 October, followed the Atlantic coast to Savannah, Ga., then seaward to the Bahamas, to Florida, to Cuba, over the Gulf of Mexico and back toward NAF Glynco.

7 November A letter identification system for marking all Navy and Marine aircraft, including those of the training command and the Naval Air Reserve, was adopted. Letters were assigned to all carriers and to wings, groups and squadrons not assigned to carrier operations. In addition, a wide orange stripe around the fuselage, forward of the empennage, was ordered placed on all aircraft of the Naval Reserve. By a change issued the following month (12 Dec), the assignment of letters to carriers was discontinued and the letters were assigned instead to Carrier Air Groups and to Marine squadrons operating on CVEs.

8 November The Office of the Deputy Chief of Naval Operations (Special Weapons) was disestablished and its functions relating to guided missiles were reassigned to a new Assistant Chief of Naval Operations (Guided Missiles) and a Guided Missiles Division, both established under DCNO (Air).

11 November Lieutenant Colonel Marion E. Carl, USMC, flying a jet propelled P-80A made two catapult launches, four free take-offs and five arrested landings aboard *Franklin D. Roosevelt*. His first catapult launches were on 1 November. These operations were part of an extensive investigation of the carrier suitability of jet aircraft which had begun on 29 June 1945 with the delivery of a P-80A to NAS Patuxent River, Md.

15 November To correct the results of demobilization which had left squadron numbers all out of sequence and a system of no apparent order, sweeping changes were made in air unit designation. Carrier Air Groups of four types were designated according to their assigned ship, as CVBG for Battle Carrier, CVG for Attack Carrier, CVLG for Light Carrier and CVEG for Escort Carrier. Carrier squadrons were limited to Fighter and Attack, thus abolishing the VBF, VB and VT designations, and were assigned suffix letters to indicate their carrier type assignment. Patrol squadrons were redesignated to show in addition to the VP, an abbreviation of their aircraft class, as VP-MS-1 for Patrol Squadron 1 operating medium seaplanes. Observation squadron numbers again followed the parent ship division but suffix letters B or C were added to differentiate between battleship and cruiser units. The VJ for utility became VU, VPP replaced the VD for photographic squadrons, and VPM replaced VPW for meteorological squadrons. Reserve units were changed to the same system but were assigned consecutive numbers of a higher series. Marine Corps units were not affected by the change.

20 November At Cleveland, Ohio, an F8F Grumman Bearcat with Lieutenant Commander Merl W. Davenport as pilot, took off in a distance of 115 feet from a standing start and climbed to 10,000 feet in 94 seconds.

25 November The report of a board, headed by Rear Admiral Thomas S. Combs and established to consider the steps required to adapt the Integrated Aeronautic Maintenance, Material and Supply Program to postwar conditions, was approved. Recommendations were largely concerned with measures to improve program administration such as providing for exact planning, rigid adherence to schedules and complements, the receipt of complete information from the field, and its proper evaluation. Many touched on areas so critical that action was taken before final approval.

6 December Captain Victor D. Herbster, Naval Aviator No. 4, died at the Naval Hospital, St. Albans, N.Y. He served continuously in aviation from 8 November 1911, when he reported for flight training at Annapolis, Md., to his retirement on 1 July 1936. Upon his return to active service in August 1940, he again served in aviation until his final retirement on 29 March 1946.

1946—Continued

31 December Special Unit Project Cast was disestablished and its personnel, material and functions transferred to the Air Support Division, National Research Laboratory (NRL), which had been established 1 September at NATC Patuxent River, Md., to provide the NRL with flight test services as necessary to its electronics equipment research and development program.

1947

2 January Unit identification letters, assigned in November, were ordered displayed on both sides of the vertical fin and rudder and on the upper right and lower left surfaces near the wing tips. This placement required relocation of several standard markings on aircraft.

2 January A new specification for aircraft color was issued providing for the use of glossy sea blue on all shipboard and water based aircraft and all helicopters; aluminum was retained for landplane transports, utility planes and advanced training planes; and glossy orange yellow was similarly retained for primary trainers. Special color schemes included land camouflage (olive drab above and light gray below) for Marine observation planes; glossy insignia red for target drones; target towing aircraft were to have glossy orange-yellow wings, and glossy sea blue fuselage with glossy insignia-red wing bands and rudder.

14 January A horizontal red stripe, centered on the white horizontal bar, was added to the National Star Insignia.

29 January From a position 660 miles off the Antarctic Continent, *Philippine Sea* launched to Little America the first of six R4D transport aircraft which she had ferried from Norfolk, Va., as a part of Operation Highjump. The first plane off, which was also the first carrier takeoff for an R4D, was piloted by Commander William M. Hawkes and carried Rear Admiral Richard E. Byrd as a passenger.

2 February Colonel Bernard L. Smith, second Marine and sixth naval aviator, died from injuries received when his car was hit by a train at Coral Gables, Fla. From 18 September 1912, when he reported for flight training at Annapolis, Md. until his resignation on 20 January 1920, he served with Marine and Navy aviation elements in a variety of duties including intelligence assignments overseas. For six years 1931–37, he was a member of the Naval Reserve, then transferred to the Marine Corps Reserve and returned to active duty in World War II, during which he again served with distinction until his retirement in December 1946.

12 February The Loon guided missile was launched from *Cusk* (SS 348) off Point Mugu in the first firing of a guided missile from a submarine.

1 March The development of titanium alloys for aeronautical applications was initiated by a Bureau of Aeronautics contract with P. R. Mallory & Co. for study of methods of producing titanium metal and alloys and of determining their essential properties.

4 March Operation Highjump—Air operations in the Antarctic ended. From 24 December 1946, six PBMs, based on seaplane tenders, operated in the open seas around the continent of Antarctica, and from 9 February, six R4Ds operated ashore from the airstrip at Little America. Together these aircraft logged 650 hours on photographic mapping flights covering 1,500,000 square miles of the interior, and 5,500 miles of coastline, or the equivalent of about half the area of the United States and its entire coastline—Atlantic, Pacific, and Gulf coasts combined.

30 April A standard system of designating guided missiles and assigning them popular names was adopted for use by the Army and Navy. The basic designation adopted was a two-letter combination of the three letters A (Air), S (Surface), U (Underwater), in which the first letter indicated the origin of the missile and the second letter its objective; followed by the letter M for missile. Thus a surface-to-air missile was designated SAM. This basic designation was followed by a model number; odd for Army and even for Navy. For popular names, it was agreed that ASMs would be named for birds of prey, AAMs for other winged creatures, SAMs for mythological terms, and SSMs for astronomical terms or bodies.

20 May The Secretary of the Navy directed that within the period 1 June–1 August 1947, the U.S. Navy Pre-Flight at NAS Ottumwa, Iowa, be relocated and redesigned U.S. Naval School, Pre-Flight, NAS Pensacola.

4 June The Chief of Naval Operations approved new aircraft carrier characteristics to be incorporated in an improvement program titled "Project 27A", by which *Essex* Class carriers were modified to meet the new operating requirements resulting from developments in aircraft and weapons. The principal changes involved in the program were directed toward a capability for operating aircraft of up to 40,000 pounds,

1947—Continued

and included installation of two H-8 catapults, strengthening the flight deck and clearing it of guns, increasing elevator capacity and adding special provisions for jet aircraft such as blast deflectors, increased fuel capacity and jet fuel mixers. *Oriskany,* first of nine carriers modernized under this project, began conversion at the New York Naval Shipyard on 1 October 1947.

7 June FAW-10 was disestablished at NAB Sangley Point, Philippines.

17 June The Navy awarded a contract to Douglas for design study and engineering data for a delta winged fighter. On the basis of the technical information thus obtained, the Navy subsequently initiated development of the XF4D-1.

26 June Development of low drag bombs was initiated as the Bureau of Aeronautics authorized Douglas Aircraft (El Segundo) to undertake design of a bomb release system with smooth flight characteristics at subsonic speeds. This development was undertaken to overcome the aircraft buffeting which was induced by conventional bombs when carried externally at three-quarters the speed of sound. The basic goal was development of an external store shape which could house conventional bombs, machine guns, rockets, etc. and be adapted to use as an external fuel tank.

30 June FAW-18 was disestablished at NAS Agana, Guam, in the Marianas.

9 July A Gorgon IV (PTV-2), powered by a subsonic ram-jet engine, was air-launched from a P-61C and made a 28-second free flight at the Naval Air Missile Test Center, Point Mugu, Calif.

24 July The adaptation of the helicopter to amphibious warfare was initiated when the Chief of Naval Operations established a requirement for a type capable of transporting assault troops from an escort carrier and setting them down ashore along with their necessary combat equipment and supplies.

26 July The National Security Act of 1947 became law providing the most basic reorganization of defense activities since the creation of the Navy Department in 1798. The law established the National Security Council, the Central Intelligence Agency, the National Security Resources Board, the National Military Establishment and the Office of Secretary of Defense. Within the National Military Establishment it estab-

lished a third service, the U.S. Air Force, the Joint Chiefs of Staff, the Research and Development Board and the Munitions Board. It also defined the United States Navy as "including such aviation as may be organic therein."

7 August An Act of Congress restored the Aeronautical Engineering Duty Only (AEDO) designation abolished in 1940, by authorizing the assignment of qualified officers of the line, including those designated EDO.

13 August Naval Air Development Station, Johnsville, Pa., was established replacing the Naval Aircraft Modification Unit. Its mission was development of aircraft electronics, guided missiles and aviation armament.

20 August Commander Turner F. Caldwell, piloting the Douglas Skystreak D-558-1, broke the world's speed record flying at 640.663 mph over the three-kilometer course at Muroc, Calif.

25 August Major Marion E. Carl, USMC, flying the Douglas Skystreak D-558-1, set a new world's speed record of 650.796 mph over the three-kilometer course at Muroc, Calif.

25 August Tests of the Douglas low drag bomb shape were begun at the Southern California Cooperative Wind Tunnel at Pasadena, Calif.

D-558-1 research airplane, set 1947 speed record 704422

1947—Continued

Col. Carl set speed record USMC 11986

6 September A V-2 rocket was successfully launched from the flight deck of *Midway* in the first firing of a large bombardment rocket from a ship at sea. While the missile behaved abnormally after take-off, the feasibility of the operation was demonstrated and considerable experience was gained.

17 September James V. Forrestal, Secretary of the Navy, took the oath of office as first Secretary of Defense. The following day the National Security Act of 1947 became effective and the Departments of the Army, Navy and Air Force were constituted as integral parts of the National Military Establishment.

30 September The Research and Development Board was formally set up in the National Military Establishment as Dr. Vannevar Bush took office as Chairman. This board, which superseded the Joint Research and Development Board, functioned in areas dealing with research and development coordination, planning and direction. At its first meeting, 19 December, the credentials of all members were accepted by the Board, one of two Navy members being the Deputy Chief of Naval Operations (Air).

1 November The U.S. Naval Parachute Unit moved from NAS Lakehurst, N.J., to NAS El Centro, Calif. Its mission was research, development and testing of parachutes, parachute recovery systems and ejectable seat capsules.

28 November *Norton Sound* was assigned to the Operational Development Force for use as an experimental rocket-firing ship. Necessary alterations were performed at the Philadelphia Naval Shipyard, Pa., beginning the following March.

The Viking research rocket, fired from Norton Sound, May 1950, reached an altitude of 106 miles 415261

1947—Continued

1 December HMX-1 was established at MCAS Quantico, Va., Colonel Edward C. Dyer commanding. Its mission was to develop techniques and tactics for the various uses of helicopters in amphibious operations.

19 December A New Development Board was established to review the programs of the various bureaus and offices and to recommend the priorities of development projects to the Chief of Naval Operations. This Board was replaced in May 1948 by a Research and Development Review Board consisting of the Chief of Naval Research and officers in the Office of the Chief of Naval Operations responsible for development.

19 December The Research and Development Board directed its Committee on Guided Missiles to coordinate the Earth Satellite Vehicle Project, thereby taking this function over from the Aeronautical Board.

30 December The President's Air Policy Commission, Thomas K. Finletter, Chairman, submitted its report based on extensive hearings covering a period of over three months. The report, "Survival in the Air Age," was a broad review of the international situation in terms of the proven effectiveness of air power and its added potential for destruction with the advent of the atomic bomb. The report stressed the need to maintain military forces large enough to make aggression dangerous and particularly emphasized the urgency of building up strong military aviation with its supporting industry and civil air transport, and of encouraging a progressive research and development program to maintain the existing margin of superiority held by the United States.

1948

1 January The headquarters of the Naval Air Basic Training Command was transferred from Corpus Christi, Tex., to NAS Pensacola, Fla., and Naval Air Training Bases, Corpus Christi was disestablished. At the same time, the Naval Air Advanced Training Subordinate Command was established at NAS Corpus Christi.

1 March The Congressional Committee on National Aviation Policy, headed by Senator Owen Brewster, submitted its report which, although differing in some respects with the earlier report submitted by the President's Air Policy Commission, was a general reiteration of its conclusions in regard to the effect of air power on the national security and the need for a national policy that would build a strong military air force supported by a healthy aircraft industry and civil aviation.

4 March A Test Pilot Training Division was established at the Naval Air Test Center, Patuxent River, Md., to instruct experienced fleet pilots in aeronautical engineering and techniques of flight testing. Ten years later this Division became the U.S. Naval Test Pilot School.

10 March The carrier suitability of the FJ-1 Fury jet fighter was tested on board *Boxer* off San Diego, with a number of landings and takeoffs by Commander Evan P. Aurand and Lieutenant Commander Robert M. Elder of VF-5A.

FJ-1 Fury, early design of an all-jet fighter 1053785

1948—Continued

29 March The Technical Evaluation Group of the Research and Development Board noted that an earth satellite was feasible but recommended that none be constructed until utility could be clearly established.

30 March The establishment of a Naval Air Reserve Advisory Council was approved by the Secretary of the Navy. The purpose of the Council, which was composed of 50 aviation Reserve officers appointed from civil life, was to make available to the Navy the experience and continuing advice of reservists who had held key positions while on active duty during the war.

1 April HU-1, the first of its type in the U.S. Navy, was established at NAS Lakehurst, N.J., Commander Maurice A. Peters commanding.

21 April The Secretary of Defense issued a memorandum for the Secretaries within his Department, attaching a paper defining the functions of the armed forces and the Joint Chiefs of Staff. Based on the policy embodied in the National Security Act, this was the first functions paper drawn up by the services after their reorganization and was commonly referred to as the Key West agreement.

27 April In the first carrier launchings of planes of this size and weight, two P2V-2 Neptunes, piloted by Commander Thomas D. Davies and Lieutenant Commander John P. Wheatley, made JATO takeoffs from *Coral Sea*, off Norfolk, Va.

1 May Changes in aircraft marking specifications made it mandatory for carrier squadrons to use distinguishing colors on propeller spinners and across the top of the vertical fin and rudder. The colors insignia red, insignia white, light blue, light yellow, light green, and black outlined in white, were assigned to squadrons one through six respectively of each carrier air group. The changes also required that arresting hooks be painted in alternate four-inch bands of black and white.

5 May The submarine *Cusk* (SS 348) launched a Loon missile off the Naval Air Missile Test Center, Point Mugu, Calif., guided it over a 46-mile course and splashed it within 100 yards of its target, Begg Rock.

5 May VF-17A, equipped with 16 FH-1 Phantoms, became the first carrier qualified jet squadron in the U.S. Navy. In three days of operations aboard *Saipan* (CVL 48), all squadron pilots plus Commander, Air Group 17 were qualified with a minimum of eight takeoffs and landings each.

8 May The Michelson Laboratory of the U.S. Naval Ordnance Test Station, China Lake was dedicated. The opening of this laboratory was a major step in the transition of the station from a rocket test range to a research and development activity specially equipped to study the various aspects of rocketry and guided missiles.

18 May A contract was issued to Goodyear Aircraft Corporation for design of an ASW airship with an envelope volume of 825,000 cubic feet, approximately double that of the K class airship of World War II. Through subsequent contractual action which was initiated in September, one ZPN airship was ordered.

25 May Two Support Wings were established and placed under Commander, Fleet Logistic Support Wings, to provide, subsequent to the merger of Navy and Air Force air transport commands, such air logistic support services over routes of sole Navy interest as would be required for internal administration and the fulfillment of the Navy's mission.

1 June The Naval Air Transport Service and the Air Transport Service of the Air Force Air Transport Command, were consolidated to form the Military Air Transport Service (MATS) as a unified element of the National Military Establishment under the command and direction of the U. S. Air Force.

4 June To establish and maintain close relationships between the operating forces and planning agencies, arrangements were made for an Air Board to meet quarterly, with DCNO (Air), the Chief of BuAer, ComAirLant and ComAirPac as principal members.

4 June The Airborne Coordinating Group was renamed U.S. Naval Aviation Electronics Service Unit (NAESU).

11 June The Chief of Naval Operations issued standards for training aviators as helicopter pilots and provided that helicopter pilots previously trained by the Coast Guard or VX-3 would retain their qualification.

18 June The Chief, Bureau of Aeronautics authorized the Naval Air Missile Test Center to train, on a noninterfering basis, the Air Force's First Experimental Guided Missile Group in the operation of the Lark guided missile.

22 June Flight training was opened to men between the ages of 18 and 25, with at least two years of college, under a plan that was in essence a reactivation of the Aviation Cadet program. Candidates were

1948—Continued

The P4M Mercator, a long-range patrol plane 1053755

required to serve on active duty for four years after which they would be returned to inactive duty as members of the Reserve, but a limited number were to be given the opportunity to remain on active duty with possibilities for transferring to the regular Navy. First of the new Aviation Cadets under this program reported for training in the latter part of August.

29 June Development of TACAN (tactical air navigation system) was initiated by a Bureau of Ships contract to the Federal Telecommunications Laboratory for development of a surface beacon and airborne receiver that were capable of determining the direction of the aircraft from the surface station. Stringent accuracy requirements were based upon needs growing out of World War II carrier operational experience. A year later, following tests of the initial model, contracts were issued to the same company for development of equipment that would also measure distance.

1 July The Naval Air Transport Service, which had remained in being after the establishment of MATS to assist in the transfer of Navy units to the new organi-

zation, was disestablished after 6½ years of distinguished service.

1 July The importance of rockets in the future of Naval Aviation was emphasized by the establishment of the U.S. Naval Aeronautical Rocket Laboratory, Lake Denmark, N.J. It provided a rocket testing facility on the east coast, similar in function to the Air Force Rocket Test Facility at Muroc, Calif.

3 July Ordnance aspects of the low drag bomb development were initiated as the Chief of Naval Operations requested the Bureau of Ordnance to develop a 250-pound bomb on the lines of the Douglas shape and a container to the same lines that could carry a number of conventional 250-pound bombs.

6 July VAW-1 and VAW-2, were established in the Pacific and Atlantic Fleets with responsibilities for organizing and training AEW teams for carrier operations. Although AEW aircraft had operated from carriers at an earlier date and a land based squadron,

1948—Continued

VPW-1, had been established on 1 April 1948 with a secondary mission of AEW, those squadrons were the first to be organized specifically for the AEW mission and the first to provide the fleet with AEW services from carriers.

20 July   The Chief of Naval Operations directed that the standard composition of Carrier Air Groups be changed to three fighters and two attack squadrons, thus adding one fighter squadron to each group. To compensate for this increase, squadron aircraft complements were slightly reduced.

22 July   Assembly and Repair Departments (A&R) at Navy and Marine Corps air stations were renamed Overhaul and Repair Departments (O&R.)

23 July   The Assistant Secretary of the Navy for Air approved a plan to develop the Jacksonville area as a Fleet Aviation Center. The plan included reactivation of Cecil Field, Fla., and Mayport, Fla., to help support the air groups assigned to the Center, and the relocation of the Naval Air Advanced Training Command based at NAS Jacksonville.

29 July   The president approved the construction, in a private shipyard, of a flush-deck 65,000-ton aircraft carrier, subsequently named *United States,* for which funds had been provided in the Naval Appropriation Act 1949.

1 August   Because the National Security Act of 1947 had assigned most of its functions to other boards and some duplication appeared to exist, the Aeronautical Board was dissolved after over 30 years as an interservice agency for cooperation in aviation.

17 August   The Chief of Naval Operations informed the Chief of the Bureau of Aeronautics of his intention to assign antisubmarine warfare as a primary mission to most of the patrol squadrons, and requested that the Bureau institute a vigorous program to outfit patrol planes in service with the necessary equipment.

28 August   The Caroline Mars, a JRM-2 flying boat, landed at Chicago with 42 persons on board and a 14,000-pound payload, after a record nonstop flight from Honolulu, Hawaii, of 4,748 miles in 24 hours, 12 minutes.

1 September   The system of group and squadron designations, in effect since November 1946, was sim-

The Philippine Mars, a JRM Naval transport, makes jet-assisted take-off at Alameda en route to Honolulu 1053758

1948—Continued

plified. Carrier Air Groups became CVG without regard to their carrier assignment; carrier squadrons VF and VA were assigned two or three digit numbers, the first of which was the same as the parent air group, and suffix letters were dropped. Patrol squadrons reverted to the simple VP designation. Special designations for transport squadrons, as VRF and VRU, became VR. Some VC squadrons became VAW to reflect their air warning mission, while others became VFN or VAN to reflect all-weather capability.

5 September The JRM-2 Caroline Mars of VR-2, on a 390-mile flight from Patuxent River, Md., to Cleveland, Ohio, carried a 68,282-pound cargo, the heaviest payload ever lifted in an aircraft.

1 October Modification of the seaplane tender *Norton Sound* was completed at the Philadelphia Naval Shipyard, and after a brief shakedown she was placed in operation as the Navy's first guided missile experimental and test ship.

27 October Operation Vittles—VR-6 and -8 of the Military Air Transport Service, were ordered to move from their Pacific bases to Germany to take part in the Berlin Airlift.

1 November The Naval Air Advanced Training Command was transferred from NAS Jacksonville, Fla., to NAS Corpus Christi, Tex., in accordance with plans to convert the Jacksonville area into a fleet aviation center.

5 November To meet the requirements of landing aircraft weighing up to 50,000 pounds at speeds as high as 105 knots, a project was initiated at the Naval Aircraft Factory for design of Mark 7 high energy absorption arresting gear.

9 November Navy transport squadrons, transferred from the Pacific to assist in Operation Vittles, began flying cargo into Berlin.

17 December To meet the mounting requirements for transatlantic airlift in support of Operation Vittles, VR-3 was switched from flying the domestic routes to the Westover, Mass., to Frankfurt, Germany, run.

1949

23 January *Palau* completed a 12-day test period off the New England coast developing the capability of carriers to conduct air operations under cold and severe weather conditions. This marked the Navy's continued interest in cold weather tests, first demonstrated on the *Langley* in the same area 18 years before.

26 January *Norton Sound*, the nation's first guided-missile experimental test ship, launched its first missile, the Loon, off the Naval Air Missile Test Center, Point Mugu, Calif.

Norton Sound, converted from a seaplane tender to the Navy's first guided missile ship, fires a Loon 415146

27 January The Chief of Naval Operations authorized conversion of all new-construction cruisers to accommodate helicopters.

3 February The Lockheed R6O Constitution, commissioned the day before at NAS Alameda, Calif., inaugurated her transcontinental service, from Moffett Field, Calif., to Washington, D.C., by establishing a new record for personnel carried on a transcontinental flight. With 78 passengers and 18 crewmen, the 92-ton plane crossed the continent in 9 hours and 35 minutes.

25 February The Caroline Mars, a JRM-2 flying boat, broke the world record for passenger lift by transporting 202 men from NAS Alameda to San Diego, Calif., and broke it again the same day on the return flight with a load of 218 men. These loads were in addition to a four-man crew.

4 March The Caroline Mars, a JRM-2 flying boat of Transport Squadron 2, set a new record for persons carried aloft by transporting 263 passengers and a crew of six on a Fleet Logistic Air Wings flight from San Diego, Calif. to Alameda, Calif. The flight was of 2 hours 41 minutes duration and the passengers were the officers and men of Air Group 15 on a routine transfer of station.

1949—Continued

7 March   A P2V-3C, piloted by Captain John T. Hayward of VC-5 was launched from *Coral Sea* off the Virginia Capes with a 10,000-pound load of dummy bombs, flew across the continent to drop its load on the west coast and returned nonstop to land at NAS Patuxent River, Md.

31 March   The best monthly total of the Berlin Airlift to date was made as U.S. aircraft delivered 154,475 tons of cargo to the city. In making its contribution to the total, VR-8 set an all-time airlift record of 155 percent efficiency for the month, and daily utilization of 12.2 hours per aircraft.

5 April   The disestablishing of the last of the observation squadrons, VO-2, marked the end of one era and the beginning of another as a plan to use helicopters in place of fixed-wing aircraft aboard battleships and cruisers was put into effect, with the changeover scheduled for completion by 30 June.

23 April   Construction on *United States* was halted by order of the Secretary of Defense Louis Johnson.

19 May   The JRM-1 Marshall Mars broke the record for number of people carried on a single flight when 301 passengers and a crew of seven were flown from Alameda, Calif. to San Diego, Calif.

15 July   Douglas pilots flying an XF3D-1 completed an initial flight evaluation of the low drag external store shape at Edwards AFB, Calif. Carrying two of these shapes, the aircraft had a top speed of 51 knots greater than when carrying two conventional 2,000-pound bombs and 22 knots greater than with two 150-gallon external fuel tanks.

31 July   The participation of VR-6 and -8 in the Berlin Airlift ended. During their eight months in Germany, these squadrons flew a total of 45,990 hours, carried 129,989 tons of cargo into Berlin, and established a record of payload efficiency and aircraft utilization at the unparalleled figure of better than 10 hours per day per plane for the entire period.

1 August   The Naval Air Development Center, Johnsville, Pa., was established and the Naval Air Development Station was disestablished. The mission of the Center was development of aircraft electronics, pilotless aircraft and aviation armament, and research and development in the field of aviation medicine pertaining to the human centrifuge. These functions were performed by four laboratories appropriately named.

9 August   The first use in the United States of a pilot-ejection seat for an emergency escape, was made by Lieutenant Jack L. Fruin of VF-171 from an F2H-1 Banshee while making over 500 knots in the vicinity of Walterboro, S.C.

F2H Banshee McDonnell Fighter 1053787

10 August   The National Security Act of 1947 was amended providing for a limited increase in the authority of the Secretary of Defense and replacing the National Military Establishment with the Department of Defense. It further provided that the three military departments would continue to be separately administered and that Naval Aviation would "be integrated with the naval service . . . within the Department of the Navy."

1 October   In accordance with an interservice agreement reached in July, an exchange program to indoctrinate selected Air Force and Navy pilots (including the Marines) in the operational and training activities of each other's service, began with the exchange of 18 pilots from each service for the period of 1 year. The agreement provided that all pilots be qualified in the type of aircraft operated by the unit to which they were assigned and that each would occupy a regular pilot's billet in his new assignment.

1949—Continued

5 October In a demonstration of naval air capabilities, a Neptune P2V-3, piloted by Commander Frederick L. Ashworth, took off from the carrier *Midway* at sea off Norfolk and flew to the Panama Canal, then northward over Corpus Christi, Tex., and on to NAS San Diego, Calif., completing a 4,800-mile nonstop, nonrefueling flight in 25 hours and 40 minutes.

30 October Lieutenant Guiseppe A. Rullo and M. D. Kembro, CAP, flew a Sikorsky helicopter, HO3S, from NAS Seattle, Wash., to NAS Alameda, Calif., in 10 hours and 50 minutes and unofficially bettered the existing distance record for helicopters with a flight of 755 miles.

1 December In a reorganization of air transport services, the Atlantic and Pacific Fleet Logistic Support Wings ceased to exist and all air transport units were consolidated under a single command — the Fleet Logistic Air Wing.

9 December A reorganization of the Naval Air Reserve was completed in which 128 Fighter, 41 Attack, 25 Composite, 29 Patrol, 26 Transport, 57 Service, and 5 Blimp Squadrons were placed under command of 27 Air Wings established at as many Reserve Air Stations spread throughout the country.

P2V Neptune JATO take-off from Midway 407668

Firing Lark surface to air missile, at Pt. Mugu 400916

The Aerobee, high altitude sounding rocket 408012

Skyraider displays its capacity and versatility 419472

P5M-1 Marlins show new shape of boat hulls 1053754

F6F fires Tiny Tim, rocket with a heavy punch 705452

*The XF5U-1, the first short
take-off fighter 1053786*

F7F Tigercat twin engine fighter by Grumman USMC 44731

The AM-1 Mauler carries 9000 lb. payload 706902

Flight test of an early jet fighter, F6U-1, Pirate 419467

Flight deck of Coral Sea portrays activity with jets, props, and helicopters as F2H Banshees fly over 626130

Vertical envelopment exercise, Marines aboard Palau, embark in HRP-1s for landing on beach 707741

HRP-1, Tandem rotor transports of Marine Experimental Helicopter Squadron 1, take-off from Quantico 1053788

HTLs taking off from carrier 424773

The landing signal officer directs an HO3S helicopter landing aboard Franklin D. Roosevelt 1053756

Three converted Essex-class carriers are moored at North Island in this 1955 view of a modern air station 1053798

Ships on a leash, Essex-class carriers and other element of the reserve Fleet mothballed at Puget Sound 428458

PART 7

Korean Operations

1950–1953

The outbreak of war in Korea caught U.S. military services in the midst of a transition. The establishment of the Department of Defense in 1947 and its reorganization in 1949 required readjustments within the services to which none had become completely acclimated. Successive decreases in the military budget and the prospect of more to come had reduced the size of all services, and a reorganization of operating forces to keep within prescribed limits was in process. New weapons and equipment had not been completely integrated, and tactical doctrine and new operating techniques for their most effective employment were still being developed. This was particularly apparent in Naval Aviation, where the introduction of jet aircraft had created a composite force in which like units were equipped with either jet or propeller-driven aircraft having wide differences in performance characteristics, maintenance and support requirements, and tactical application.

Combat requirements in Korea were quite different from those of the island-hopping campaign of World War II. Only the landings at Inchon, two and a half months after the shooting began, followed the familiar pattern. The UN's intention to confine the battle area to the peninsula resulted in a limitation of air operations in support of troops. This was a normal enough mission for carrier air, but the need to sustain it for extended periods over an extremely large landmass made quite a difference. Carrier forces also flew deep support missions; attacked enemy supply lines; roamed over enemy territory looking for targets of opportunity; bombed enemy bridges; interdicted highways and railroads; attacked refineries, railroad yards and hydroelectric plants; and escorted land-based bombers on special missions. All were carried out effectively, but were new experiences for units trained to interdict enemy sea-lines of communication and ward off attack by enemy naval forces.

The see-saw action on the ground as the battle line shifted and as action flared up and quieted again required great flexibility of force and demanded the ability to carry out a variety of missions, but after the first six months of the war, the overall air campaign developed into a monotonous, although serious, routine. It was a battle described by Commander Task Force 77 in January 1952 as "a day-to-day routine where stamina replaces glamour and persistence is pitted against oriental perseverance."

Compared to World War II, Korea was a small war. At no time were more than four large carriers in action at the same time. Yet in the three years of war, Navy and Marine aircraft flew 276,000 combat sorties, dropped 177,000 tons of bombs and expended 272,000 rockets. This was within 7,000 sorties of their World War II totals in all theaters and bettered the bomb tonnage by 74,000 tons, and the number of rockets by 60,000. In terms of national air effort, the action sorties flown by Navy and Marine Corps aircraft rose from less than 10 percent in World War II to better than 30 percent in Korea.

There was another and perhaps greater difference between the two wars. Support of forces in Korea required major attention from the planners and of units assigned to logistic supply, but action in Korea was only a part of the total activity of the period. Outside the combat area fleet forces continued their training operations on the same scale as before, and fleet units were continuously maintained on peaceful missions in the eastern Atlantic and in the Mediterranean. Research and development, although accelerated, did not shift to emphasize projects having direct application to the war effort but continued on longer range programs directed toward progressively modernizing fleet forces and their equipment with more effective weapons. New facilities for test and evaluation were opened. Advances in guided missiles reached new highs indicating their early operational status, and ships to employ them were being readied. Firings of research missiles like Loon, Lark and Viking from shore installations and from ships provided both useful data and experience. Terrier, Talos, Sparrow, Sidewinder, and Regulus passed successive stages of development. Research in high-speed flight, assisted by flights of specially designed aircraft, provided data leading to new advances in aircraft performance. The carrier modernization program continued and was revised to incorporate the steam catapult and the angled deck, together representing the most significant advance in aircraft carrier operating capability since World War II.

In a period when Naval Aviation was called upon to demonstrate its continuing usefulness in war and its particular versatility in adapting to new combat requirements, it also moved forward toward new horizons.

1950

10 January *Norton Sound* departed Port Hueneme on a 19-day cruise in Alaskan waters where it launched two Aerobees, one Lark, and one Loon, and tested an auxiliary propulsion system for the Lark under severe conditions. In addition to its crew, the ship carried 27 observers representing the Army, Navy, and Air Force, including 8 scientists connected with the Aerobee upper atmosphere research program.

13 January In the first successful automatic homing flight of a surface-to-air guided missile, a Lark, CTV-N-10, launched at the Naval Air Missile Test Center, NAMTC Point Mugu, Calif., passed within lethal range of its target, an F6F drone, making the simulated interception at a range of 17,300 yards and an altitude of 7,400 feet.

7 February In a demonstration of carrier long-range attack capabilities, a P2V-3C Neptune, with Commander Thomas Robinson in command, took off from *Franklin D. Roosevelt* off Jacksonville, Fla., and flew over Charleston, S.C., the Bahamas, the Panama Canal, up the coast of Central America and over Mexico to land next day at the Municipal Airport, San Francisco, Calif. The flight, which covered 5,060 miles in 25 hours, 59 minutes, was the longest ever made from a carrier deck.

8 March Operation Portrex, the largest peacetime maneuvers in history and the first to employ airborne troops in an amphibious operation, was brought to a climax with a combined amphibious and airborne assault on Vieques Island. The Joint Armed Service Exercise, which began 20 February and extended through 14 March, was staged to evaluate joint service doctrine for combined operations, to service test new equipment under simulated combat conditions, and to provide training for the defense forces of the Caribbean Command.

10 March The Secretary of Defense announced that the Bureau of Aeronautics, under a research program begun in 1946, had developed a new lightweight titanium alloy for use in jet aircraft engines. The alloy was described as being as strong as high-strength steel and only half as heavy, highly resistant to corrosion, and so composed as to retain its basic properties at high temperatures.

22 March The submarine *Cusk* (SS 348), from a position off the Naval Air Missile Test Center, NAMTC Point Mugu, Calif., launched a Loon guided missile and, at the midway point of a 50-mile flight, surrendered control to the guidance station on San Nicolas Island. This station completed the first successful operation involving transfer of guidance by splashing the missile 360 yards from the center of the target, Begg Rock.

1 April The Naval Air Rocket Test Station, Lake Denmark, N.J., was established, superseding the Naval Aeronautical Rocket Laboratory, for the purposes of testing and evaluating rocket engines, components and propellants, and training service personnel in handling, servicing and operating rocket engines.

8 April A PB4Y Privateer of VP-26, with 10 men on board, was lost over the Baltic Sea after being attacked by Soviet aircraft.

18 April The experimental model of the Consolidated Vultee P5Y, a 60-ton seaplane, passed its initial flight test at San Diego, Calif. The plane was equipped with four Alison T-40 turboprop engines, each rated at 5,500 hp and each turning 15-foot contra-rotating propellers.

21 April The first carrier takeoff with the AJ-l heavy attack plane was made from *Coral Sea* by Captain John T. Hayward, commanding VC-5.

The AJ-1, carrier-based heavy attack plane 197506

21 April   The heaviest aircraft ever launched from a carrier, a P2V-3C, piloted by Lieutenant Commander Robert C. Starkey of VC-6, took off from *Coral Sea* with a gross weight of 74,668 pounds.

3 May   The submarine *Cusk* (SS 348) launched a Loon guided missile, and after submerging, tracked and controlled the missile's flight to a range of 105 miles.

11 May   A Viking missile was successfully launched from *Norton Sound* near Christmas Island, south of Hawaii. It was the first Viking launched from a ship and set a new altitude record for American-built single-stage rockets of 106.4 statute miles.

15 May   The Navy announced the completion of a new test chamber at the Ordnance Aerophysics Laboratory, Daingerfield, Tex., making it possible for the first time to conduct tests of full-scale ramjet engines up to 48 inches in diameter at simulated altitudes up to 100,000 feet.

19 June   The Caroline Mars (JRM-2) completed the 2,609-mile flight from Honolulu, T.H., to San Diego, Calif., with 144 men aboard for the largest passenger lift over the Pacific on record.

25 June   The U.S. Government asked for an emergency meeting of the UN Security Council to consider the invasion of the Republic of South Korea launched by North Korean forces early in the morning of the 25th (Korean time). The council, meeting later the same day, adopted a resolution calling for the cessation of hostilities and the withdrawal of North Korean forces above the 38th parallel, and also calling on all members to assist the UN in the execution of the resolution.

27 June   The president announced that he had ordered sea and air forces in the Far East to give support and cover to Republic of Korea forces and had ordered the Seventh Fleet to take steps to prevent an invasion of Formosa.

27 June   In a night meeting the UN Security Council adopted a resolution calling upon all its members to assist the Republic of Korea in repelling the armed attack on its territory.

30 June   President Truman announced that, in keeping with the UN Security Council request for support to the Republic of Korea (ROK) in repelling the invaders and restoring peace, he had authorized the USAF to bomb military targets in North Korea, the use of Army ground troops in action to support ROK forces, and had directed a naval blockade of the entire Korean coast.

3 July   Carrier aircraft went into action in Korea for the first time. *Valley Forge* with Air Group 5, and HMS *Triumph* operating in the Yellow Sea, launched strikes on airfields, supply lines and transportation facilities in and around Pyongyang, northwest of Seoul. This was the first combat test for the Grumman F9F Panther and the Douglas AD Skyraider. It was also the occasion for the first Navy kills in aerial combat during the war and the first shoot-down by a Navy jet, as F9F pilots of VF-51 Lieutenant (jg) Leonard H. Plog and Ensign Elton W. Brown, Jr. shot down two Yak-9s on the first strike over Pyongyang.

8 July   To obtain maximum effectiveness in the employment of all air resources in the Far East Command and to ensure coordination of air efforts, Commander in Chief, Far East approved and adopted as policy the agreement of Commander, Naval Forces, Far East and Commanding General, Far East Air Forces. Under it, the Navy controlled the operations of its carrier aircraft whenever they were on missions assigned to Commander, Naval Forces, Far East and of its shore-based aircraft whenever they were on naval missions. On all other missions, the operations of naval aircraft, both carrier and shore-based, were under the Air Force. For shore-based Marine air this control was direct, but for naval aircraft the control was of a coordination type. The selection of targets and their priority by a General Headquarters Joint Service Target Analysis Group ensured that the air campaign was coordinated with the overall objectives.

12 July   The command Naval Air, Japan was set up in Tokyo to provide an interim staff to administer the expanding aviation forces in the Far East, and on 9 August was formally established as Fleet Air, Japan, with Rear Admiral George R. Henderson in command.

16 July   Fleet Air Wing 1 headquarters moved from Guam to Naha on Okinawa to direct patrol squadron operations in the Formosa Strait.

18 July   *Valley Forge* and HMS *Triumph* returned to action with strikes on airfields, railroads and factories at Hungham, Hamhung, Numpyong, and Wonsan, and did particularly heavy damage to the oil refinery at Wonsan, North Korea. For the remainder of the month, this force struck deep behind enemy lines and flew close support missions as required while shifting entirely around the peninsula from the Sea of Japan to

AD Skyraider prepares to take off on close support mission 428637

Wonsan refinery after carrier strike 707876

the Yellow Sea, in operations intended to relieve the pressure on UN forces which were fighting a delaying action while withdrawing toward Pusan.

20 July Fourteen squadrons of the Organized Reserve were activated for duty with Naval Aviation forces. Included were eight carrier-fighter and two carrier-attack squadrons, one antisubmarine squadron, two patrol squadrons, and one Fleet Aircraft Service squadron.

22 July *Badoeng Strait* arrived at Yokosuka, Japan, with elements MAW-1 on board. Four days later, *Sicily* arrived at the same port with a load of ammunition, and on 1 August, *Philippine Sea* reported to Commander, Seventh Fleet in Buckner Bay, Okinawa. These were the first carrier reinforcements to arrive in the Far East and the beginning of carrier deployment to the combat area that, by the war's end, totalled 11 attack, one light and five escort carriers sent into action—some for two or three tours.

23 July *Boxer* arrived in Yokosuka, Japan, with a load of 145 P-51 and 6 L-5 Air Force aircraft, 19 Navy aircraft, 1,012 passengers, and 2,000 tons of additional cargo, all urgently needed for operations in Korea. In

1950—Continued

making this delivery, *Boxer* broke all existing records for a Pacific crossing, steaming from Alameda, Calif. to Yokosuka in 8 days and 16 hours.

27 July   To meet the requirements of supporting combat forces in Korea, Fleet Logistic Air Wing, Pacific, was established as a unit of the Pacific Fleet and independent from the existing Fleet Logistic Air Wing.

3 August   Elements of VMO-6, equipped with HO3S helicopters and OY observation planes, began operations in Korea, supporting the First Provisional Marine Brigade in the vicinity of Changwon. Among the services rendered by the helicopters on their first day in a combat area were the delivery of rations and water to troops on a mountain and the evacuation of the more severe heat casualties.

3 August   VMF-214, operating from the escort carrier *Sicily* in Tsushima Strait, began the combat operations of the First Marine Aircraft Wing in Korea with a rocket and incendiary bomb attack on Chinju. *Badoeng Strait*, with VMF-323 on board, joined the action three days later and thus began a long service of close air support by Marine squadrons from light and escort carriers.

4 August   FAW-6 was established at Tokyo, Japan, under Acting Commander Captain John C. Alderman, and assigned operational control over all United States and British patrol squadrons in the Japan-Korea area.

5 August   *Valley Forge* and *Philippine Sea* began what was to become almost three years of continuous fast carrier operation, with attacks on enemy lines of communication in southwestern Korea and close support missions on the Pusan perimeter.

7 August   ZP2K-1 (subsequently redesignated ZSG-2), a K-class airship modernized and equipped with inflight refueling equipment and attachments for picking up sea water as ballast, was delivered to the Navy.

7 August   Flight of a helicopter under automatic control was made at Mustin Field, Philadelphia, Pa., using an HO3S-1 helicopter equipped with a single axis automatic pilot. Successful test of this instrument confirmed the feasibility of a helicopter automatic pilot which was being developed under the leadership of L. S. Guarino at the Aeronautical Instrument Laboratory, Naval Air Material Center.

24 August   In a test conducted at the Naval Ordnance Test Station, Inyokern, Calif., a Terrier surface-to-air guided missile intercepted an F6F drone at a range of more than 11 miles from the point of launch.

31 August   Pilots of VC-5 completed carrier qualifications on board *Coral Sea* in the AJ-1 Savage, marking the introduction of this long-range attack bomber to carrier operations.

15 September   Landings at Inchon—Under heavy support by naval gunfire and aircraft, elements of the

Heavily armed Corsair on pre-dawn launch 419929

1950—Continued

First Marine Division landed on Wolmi Island at 0630 and, after landing craft were regrouped and the tide was again favorable, followed up with a successful assault of the mainland at Inchon.

Beginning 12 September carrier support was provided by two carriers in preliminary strikes in the objective area and on highways leading into Seoul, and was augmented by two escort carriers the day before the landing and by the arrival of *Boxer* on D-day. The HMS *Triumph,* operating with the Blockade and Covering Force, provided air defense for the assault forces enroute. As the troops advanced inland, carrier support continued until 3 October with close air support missions and strikes against enemy lines of communications.

18 September Fleet Logistic Air Wing was replaced by Fleet Logistic Air Wing, Atlantic/Continental, and assigned status parallel to that of the previously established Fleet Logistic Air Wing, Pacific.

19 September Two days after the capture of Kimpo Airfield by troops working inland from Inchon, the first elements of MAW-1 arrived from Japan, and early the next morning began air operations from Kimpo with strikes supporting troops advancing on Seoul.

23 September An HO3S-1 helicopter, equipped with an automatic pilot developed by the Aeronautical Instruments Laboratory, was successfully flown with three axis automatic control at Mustin Field, Philadelphia, Pa.

2 October The Bureau of Aeronautics authorized the establishment of Project Arowa (Applied Research: Operational Weather Analysis) at Norfolk, Va., for the purpose of developing basic meteorological research data into practical weather forecasting techniques.

10 October The carrier force moved into action off the east coast of Korea with strikes and sweeps from Wonsan to Chongjin in preparation for amphibious landings at Wonsan. When a heavy concentration of mines in the harbor delayed the scheduled landings, the carrier attack shifted northward and inland to assist the advance of UN forces which, by the time the landings were made on the 26th, had swept past the intended objective area and were advancing toward the Yalu River.

28 October The Chief of Naval Operations directed that each station, air group, wing, and squadron establish a permanent Instrument Flight Board to check the instrument flying proficiency of Naval Aviators and Naval Aviation pilots and to supervise and coordinate the instrument training of all pilots attached. It was further directed that, with certain exceptions, all Group I Naval Aviators maintain a valid instrument rating after 18 months from date.

29 October The fast carrier force retired to Sasebo, Japan, as the advance of UN forces toward the Yalu River rapidly reduced the area which could be attacked and there was no further need for its services.

31 October The National Advisory Committee for Aeronautics (NACA) issued a report on tests at the Langley Aeronautical Laboratory in which a wind tunnel was used to determine the characteristics of a fully submerged, high-speed submarine. The interrelationships of basic naval sciences dealing with aeronautics and naval architecture were thus reemphasized.

6 November As enemy opposition stiffened, the fast carrier forces returned to action, attacking targets in their assigned area east of the 127th meridian. Two days later, the force was given a primary mission of cutting off Chinese Communist reinforcements from Manchuria by destroying the international bridges across the Yalu River.

9 November The initial strikes against bridges crossing the Yalu River at Sinuiju were opposed by enemy MiG-15s. In this, the first encounter of Navy jets with

Amen downed Navy's first MiG

1950—Continued

MiGs, the commanding officer of VF-111, Lieutenant Commander William T. Amen, in an F9F Panther, scored one kill and became the first Navy pilot in history to shoot down a jet aircraft.

10 November   The Naval Guided Missile Training Unit No. 21, under training to operate Terrier missiles, was relocated from the Naval Ordnance Test Station Inyokern, China Lake, Calif. to *Norton Sound*, and redesignated a fleet activity under Commander, Air Force, Pacific Fleet.

29 November   Emergency conditions on the front lines, created by the deep penetration of a communist offensive, required a shift of emphasis in fast carrier operations from bridge strikes to close air support. As the situation worsened, support operations of carrier forces were intensified through December to cover the withdrawal of troops toward east coast ports and their evacuation by ships, and continued into January as the Communist advance rolled past the 38th parallel and was slowly brought to a halt.

6 December   Five days after arriving from Korea, *Valley Forge* sailed from San Diego under emergency orders to return to action in Korea.

7 December   As the southward advance of communist forces required the evacuation of airfields in northern Korea, VMF-214 took off from Yonpo and

landed on board *Sicily* off Hungnam without a break in its close air support operations.

17 December   The light carrier *Bataan*, with VMF-212 embarked, joined forces in the Sea of Japan protecting the evacuation of troops from Hungnam and other ports. *Bataan* was pressed into service after delivering replacement aircraft to Japan and her squadron was one of those which evacuated from Yonpo early in the month.

18 December   VP-892, the first all-Reserve squadron to operate in the Korean war zone, began operations from Iwakuni, Japan.

19 December   President Truman proclaimed a national emergency.

1951

16 January   As a step in the implementation of a program providing for early service evaluation of the Terrier and Sparrow 1 air-defense missiles, together with the development of production engineering information and the establishment of production facilities, an advance order was placed with the Sperry Gyroscope Company for 1,000 Sparrow 1 air-to-air missiles.

29 January   Task Force 77 began a series of air attacks against rail and highway bridges along the east coast of northern Korea. With the additional assign-

A Corsair drops napalm bomb in close support of troops 1061489

1951—Continued

Sparrow I air-to-air missiles on wing of F3D 1023526

ment of bombing highways and lines of communication in northeast Korea, its responsibilities for interdiction would occupy a major share of its attention until the end of the war.

1 February   The first of two heavy attack wings, HATWING-1, was established at Norfolk, Va., Captain Robert Goldthwaite commanding. Its first squadron, VC-5, reported for duty the next day.

5 February   Six AJ-1 and three P2V-3C aircraft of VC-5 departed Norfolk for Port Lyautey, French Morocco, via Bermuda and the Azores. Completion of the flight on the 8th by all but one AJ, which was grounded at Lajes, Azores, by lack of spare parts, was the first transatlantic flight by carrier-type aircraft.

8 February   Marine fighter squadrons returned to Korea after a period in Japan, and began support operations from the airfield at Pusan, South Korea.

6 March   A Talos missile, powered by a ramjet engine, was launched by the Naval Ordnance Test Station, and operated two minutes in the longest full-scale ramjet flight yet achieved.

29 March   CVG-101, composed of Reserve squadrons called to active duty from Dallas, Tex.; Glenview, Ill.; Memphis, Tenn.; and Olathe, Kans., flew its first combat missions from *Boxer*—the first carrier strikes by Reserve units against North Korean forces.

29 March   A Regulus XSSM-N-8 test vehicle, operating under airborne command, took off from the lake bed at Edwards AFB, Muroc, Calif., circled the field, and landed successfully.

31 March   A program for development of a propeller-driven vertical takeoff fighter was initiated with issuance of a contract to Convair for the XFY-1. A somewhat similar aircraft, the XFO-1 (later redesignated XFV-1), was ordered from Lockheed three weeks later as an alternate solution to the design problems.

2 April   Two F9F-2B Panthers of VF-191, each loaded with four 250- and two 100-pound general-purpose bombs, were catapulted from *Princeton* for an attack on a railroad bridge near Songjin, North Korea. This was the first Navy use of a jet fighter as a bomber.

Test of Regulus I surface-to-surface missile, JATO launches Bird and main engine provide long range 1053792

A submarine fires a Regulus I guided missile 636833

1951—Continued

Deflector diverts jet exhaust on F9F takeoff 423763

ADs destroy Hwachon Dam in only aerial torpedo in use in Korea 428678

8–15 April When reports indicated the possibility of an amphibious attempt on Formosa from the China coast, Task Force 77 left the Korean area temporarily to make a show of strength in the Formosa Strait. From 11 to 14 April the force steamed off the China coast and flew aerial parades outside the international limit off the mainland.

1 May In the first and only use of aerial torpedoes in Korean combat, 8 Skyraiders and 12 Corsairs from *Princeton* made an attack on the Hwachon Dam. Destruction and damage to the flood gates released the waters of the reservoir into the Pukhan River and prevented Communist forces from making an easy crossing.

1 June MAW-1 inaugurated the policy of basing one squadron immediately in the rear of the First Marine Division to provide ground alert aircraft which were on call through the Joint Operations Center for close air support missions.

Preparing Skyraider for strike 428982

1951—Continued

Arming F9Fs 20mm guns 1030116

12 June Two PB4Y-2s of VP-772 were transferred from NAS Atsugi, Japan, to Pusan, South Korea, to fly flare dropping missions for Marine Corps night attack aircraft. The success of the operation, which was conducted as an experiment, was such that the practice of assigning specially equipped patrol aircraft for this purpose was continued.

17 June Postwar research on high-speed, jet-propelled seaplanes had progressed to the point that a contract was issued to Convair for development of a delta-winged, hydroski-equipped research seaplane with fighter characteristics. Through subsequent redesign, the aircraft became the XF2Y-1.

18 June The ZPN-1 airship made its first flight.

1 July The Naval Air Turbine Test Station was established at Trenton, N.J. Its mission was test and evaluation of turbojet, turboprop, ramjet, pulsejet engines and accessories and components.

10 July The UN military representatives, headed by Vice Admiral C. Turner Joy, arrived at Kaesong, Korea, for armistice discussions with Communist leaders. Thus began many trying months in which negotiations were alternately suspended and reopened while hostilities continued unabated.

7 August The McDonnell XF3H-1 Demon, an experimental model of a Navy shipboard jet fighter, completed its first flight at St. Louis, Mo.

7 August A Viking high-altitude sounding rocket, developed by the Naval Research Laboratory and launched at the White Sands Proving Grounds, N.M., achieved an altitude of 135.3 miles.

7 August The Navy's sonic research plane, the D-558-2 Skyrocket, piloted by Douglas test pilot William B. Bridgeman, set an unofficial world speed record of 1,238 mph over Muroc, Calif.

8 August The Secretary of the Navy established the classification AVM for Auxiliaries, Guided Missiles Ships, and changed the designation of *Norton Sound* from AV 11 to AVM 1.

15 August The Douglas Skyrocket D-558-2, the Navy's sonic research plane, piloted by William B. Bridgeman, reached 79,494 feet over Muroc, Calif., the highest altitude achieved by man to that date.

23 August *Essex*, veteran of World War II and first of the postwar converted carriers to go into action, joined Task Force 77 off the east coast of Korea and launched her planes in combat. On this strike, F2H-2 Banshees flown by pilots of VF-172 went into action for the first time.

25 August F2H Banshees and F9F Panthers from *Essex*, operating with Task Force 77 in the Sea of Japan, provided fighter escort for Air Force B-29s on a high altitude bombing mission against the marshalling yards at Rashin on the extreme northeast border of Korea.

2 September HMR-161, equipped with HRS-1s, arrived Pusan, South Korea, aboard *Sitkoh Bay* and flew ashore prepared to perform transport, assault,

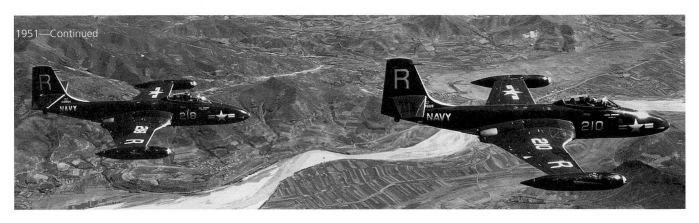

1951—Continued

F2H Banshees from Essex seek out North Korean targets 433959

and supply missions for the First Marine Division. On 13 September it began its support of the First Marine Division with Operation Windmill I. In this initial combat test of transport helicopter capabilities, the squadron lifted one day's supplies for the First Marine Battalion on a seven-mile carry from its base to the forward area.

7 September   In its first shipboard launching, a Terrier surface-to-air missile was fired from *Norton Sound* and simulated an interception of an F6F target drone.

15 September   The Department of Defense Joint Parachute Test Facility, consisting of Navy and Air Force parachute units, was established under the management control of the Bureau of Aeronautics at NAAS El Centro, Calif.

21 September   As activity on the front quieted down and the lines remained fairly stable, the Fast Carrier Task Force was relieved of its close air support duties and ordered to concentrate its attack on railroad tracks as a part of the interdiction program.

3 October   HS-1, first of its kind in the Navy, was established under the command of Commander Joseph T. Watson, Jr. at NAS Key West, Fla.

6 November   A Neptune patrol bomber of VP-6 failed to return from a weather reconnaissance mission over international waters off Siberia after Soviet planes fired upon it.

1 December   The U.S. Naval Aviation Safety Activity was established at Norfolk, Va., under the Chief of Naval Operations to promote the aviation safety program and to direct specific effort toward maintaining the highest practicable level of aviation safety throughout the Navy. In April 1955, this activity was redesignated the Naval Aviation Safety Center.

11 December   ATG-1, operating from *Valley Forge*, flew its first combat mission, attacking coastal rail lines and bridges in northeast Korea. This was the first of the ATGs formed after experience in Korea had demonstrated that five squadrons then in Carrier Air Groups could not be operated effectively in combat from *Essex* class carriers. Temporary withdrawal of one squadron from each group scheduled for deployment provided the units from which ATGs were formed. These temporary groups, which were not formally established and existed from 1951 to early 1959. As many as eight were in existence by 1955.

12 December   The Kaman K-225 helicopter, equipped with a Boeing YB-502 turbine engine, made its first flight at Windsor Locks, Conn. This Navy-sponsored development was the first demonstration of the adaptability of gas-turbine engines to helicopters.

19 December   A test of emergency assembly capabilities with nuclear weapons was conducted aboard *Philippine Sea* at San Diego, Calif., marking the initial and successful introduction of special weapons in the Pacific fleet.

1952

4 January   The new classifications CAG and CLG were established for heavy and light cruiser guided missile ships and *Boston* (CA 69) and *Canberra* (CA 70) were changed to (CAG 1) and (CAG 2), respectively.

1 February   The Chief of Naval Operations approved a modification of the Project 27A carrier conversion program which provided an increase in the capacity of deck operating equipment. Changes included use of more powerful arresting gear, higher performance catapults and a replacement of the number three centerline elevator with a deck-edge type of greater capacity. Conversion of three *Essex* class carri-

1952—Continued

ers incorporating these modifications was completed in 1954 under Project 27C (Axial Deck).

1 April Guided Missiles Service Unit No. 211 was formed at the Naval Mine Depot, Yorktown, Va. This, the first of six scheduled Terrier units, was made up of personnel who had been trained by Guided Missiles Training Unit No. 2 at the Consolidated Vultee Aircraft Corporation, San Diego, Calif.

28 April The Navy announced that the British-developed steam catapult would be adopted for use on U.S. aircraft carriers, with the first installation on *Hancock.* This decision followed tests conducted during the first three months of the year at the Naval Shipyard, Philadelphia, Pa.; the Naval Operating Base, Norfolk, Va.; and at sea, during which U.S. naval aircraft were launched by this device from HMS *Perseus.*

8 May The Fleet Air Gunnery Unit was established as an integral part of the operating forces of the Pacific Fleet under Commander Air Force, Pacific Fleet. Its mission was to provide air gunnery training on an individual and tactical unit basis for units of the Pacific Fleet.

16 May Two Terrier missiles were fired separately at F6F-5K target drones and each destroyed its target, thereby culminating the Terrier developmental program and permitting emphasis to be shifted to production of the first tactical model.

26 May The Navy's first, and for many years the world's largest, wind tunnel was disestablished at the Naval Gun Factory, Washington, D.C. Completed in 1914, the 8-by-8-foot wooden tunnel served the Navy for over 30 years as an aerodynamic laboratory for research in aircraft design.

26–29 May The feasibility of the angled-deck concept was demonstrated in tests conducted on a simulated angled deck aboard *Midway* by Naval Air Test Center pilots and Atlantic Fleet pilots, using both jet and prop aircraft.

17 June The Aviation Medical Acceleration Laboratory was dedicated at the Naval Air Development Center. This laboratory, which featured a human centrifuge with a 110-foot arm capable of producing accelerations of up to 40 Gs, was designed and constructed as a research tool for investigating pilot reactions to accelerations encountered in high-speed flight at various temperatures and altitudes and later also proved useful in the astronaut training program.

20 June A contract was issued for the construction of a 7-foot-by-10-foot slotted throat transonic wind tunnel at the David Taylor Model Basin.

23–24 June Combined elements of Air Force, Navy and Marine Corps virtually destroyed the electric power potential of North Korea with attacks on prime military targets which had been bypassed through almost two years of war. On the 23d, the main effort was directed against the hydroelectric plant at Suiho, 40 miles up the Yalu River from Antung, Manchuria. The attacks continued the next day with more attention being given to the plants at Chosen, Fusen and Kyosen. This two-day attack, which involved over 1,200 sorties, was the largest single air effort since the close of World War II and the first to employ planes from all the U.S. services fighting in Korea.

1 July To provide the fleet with officers and enlisted personnel trained in the operation, maintenance and control of surface, and submarine-launched guided missiles, the Naval Guided Missile School was established at the Fleet Air Defense Training Center, Dam Neck, Virginia Beach, Va. The Naval Air Guided Missile School (advanced) was also established at the Naval Air Technical Training Center, NAS Jacksonville, Fla., to provide aviation personnel trained in the maintenance of air-launched guided missiles.

11–12 July In one of the major coordinated air efforts of the war, Navy, Marine, Air Force, Australian, and British air elements launched a round-the-clock attack on the railroad yards and industrial facilities at Pyongyang.

14 July The keel of *Forrestal*, the first of the 59,900-ton aircraft carriers, was laid at the Newport News Shipbuilding and Drydock Company, Newport News, Va.

1 August The Naval Air Special Weapons Facility was established at Kirtland AFB, Albuquerque, N.Mex., thereby providing for naval participation in various programs involved in the application of nuclear weapons to aircraft.

28 August In the first of six attacks on North Korean targets, Guided Missile Unit 90, based aboard *Boxer,* launched an explosive-laden F6F-5K drone under control of two ADs against a railroad bridge at Hungnam.

29 August The new UN philosophy of mass air attack was again demonstrated in the record-breaking around-the-clock raid on Pyongyang. The entire car-

1952—Continued

rier air force of Task Force 77 teamed up with 5th AF, MAW-1, Republic of Korea Air Force and British air elements to spread destruction on the supply concentrations in and about the city.

1 September *Mississippi* (EAG 1), having been outfitted with Terrier surface-to-air missiles at the Norfolk Naval Shipyard, reported to Commander Operational Development Force to participate in the missile's evaluation.

3 September The Naval Ordnance Test Station, Inyokern, Calif., fired the first fully configured Sidewinder air-to-air missile, thereby initiating an extensive period of developmental testing.

8 September Deputy Chief of Naval Operations (Air) became responsible for all phases of basic and technical training of personnel for air launched missiles. However, the training program was to be administered through the Commander Naval Air Technical Training Command. The Bureau of Personnel had formerly been responsible for all individual training.

15 September VX-4 was established as a unit of Air Force, Pacific Fleet, at the Naval Air Missile Test Center (NAMTC) to conduct operational evaluation tests of air-launched missiles. The squadron's initial test assignment was to assist with tests of Sparrow I.

1 October Aircraft carriers designated CV and CVB were reclassified as Attack Carriers and assigned the designation CVA.

3 November A Regulus Assault Missile (RAM) was launched from *Norton Sound* off the Naval Air Missile Test Center (NAMTC) and landed on San Nicolas Island in the first shipboard demonstration of the RAM missile system.

12 November The final configuration of the ZP3K (later ZSG-3) nonrigid airship was flown and accepted at NAS Lakehurst. The airship was a modernized antisubmarine configuration of the K model and was designed especially for carrier-based operation. Thirty K-class airships were so configured.

18 November The feasibility of using a helicopter as an aerial minesweeper was demonstrated in the first of a series of tests conducted by VX-1 pilots flying an HRP-1 helicopter off Panama City, Fla.

16 December *Princeton*, operating in the Sea Test Range of the Naval Air Missile Test Center (NAMTC), catapulted F2H-2P control planes and then launched a Regulus assault missile. The pilots of the control planes guided the missile to a target point on San Nicolas Island, where they transferred control to other pilots who successfully landed the missile.

1953

12 January In the initiation of test operations aboard the Navy's first angled deck carrier, *Antietam,*

F9F Panther takes off from Antietam during the operational suitability tests of angled flight deck 477063

Captain Samuel G. Mitchell, the ship's commanding officer, landed aboard in an SNJ. During the next four days, six aircraft models made landings, touch-and-go landings, night landings, and takeoffs in winds of varying force and direction.

18 January A P2V of VP-22, conducting patrol of Formosa Strait, was shot down off Swatow, China, by Communist Chinese antiaircraft fire. Rescue operations were hampered by shore battery gunfire and high seas, the latter causing the Coast Guard rescue plane to crash on takeoff. Total losses from the incident were 11 men, 7 of them from the P2V crew.

9–10 February A maximum effort strike against supply concentrations and transport targets from Wonsan through Songjin to Chongjin was launched by the carriers of Task Force 77.

13 February The first full guidance flight of a Sparrow III missile was conducted at the Naval Air Missile Test Center.

1 March Aircraft from Task Force 77 heavily damaged the hydroelectric plant at Chosen and four days later repeated the attack, cutting the penstocks and destroying sections of the main power plant.

6 March *Tunny* (SSG 284), outfitted at the Mare Island Naval Shipyard, San Fransico Bay, Calif., to launch Regulus surface-to-air missiles, was commissioned.

19 March Task Force 77 launched a heavy strike against the city of Chongjin, North Korea, completely ravaging the industrial section of the city.

20 March The ZP2N-1 (later ZPG-2) airship made its first flight at Akron, Ohio. The airship was the production model of the nonrigid N class but with an envelope of 975,000 cubic feet. It was originally designed for mid-ocean antisubmarine warfare and convoy-escort operations and contained provisions for inflight refueling, reprovisioning and servicing. A total of 17 of these airships were procured in ASW and AEW configurations. The AEW configured airships were designated ZPG-2W.

9 April The XF2Y-1 Sea Dart, an experimental delta-wing jet seaplane equipped with hydroskis, made its first flight at San Diego, Calif.

3 May Commanding General, Far East Air Forces listed 30 major North Korean airfields to be maintained unserviceable in order to limit Communist air action and to prevent augmentation of their air arm preceding the date of a possible armistice. Responsibility for six of these fields was assigned to Task Force 77 and the naval air campaign featured periodic attacks upon them until the end of the war.

21 May An AD-4 Skyraider took off from NAS Dallas, Tex., with a bomb load of 10,500 pounds. Combined with the weight of its guns, ammunition, fuel and pilot, its total useful load of 14,491 pounds was 3,143 pounds more than the weight of the aircraft.

7–19 June The major effort of carrier air was directed on a round-the-clock basis against the Communist front line and supporting positions to counter an apparent effort by the enemy to gain ground prior to a possible armistice.

23 June Lieutenant Commander George H. Whisler, Jr., while attached to VR-31, completed the first transcontinental round-trip solo flight between sunrise and sunset. Lieutenant Commander Whisler departed NAS Norfolk, Va., at 0518 in an F9F-6 Cougar (BuNo 127432) and landed at NAS North Island, Calif., at 0905 local time, after stops at NAS Memphis, Tenn., and Webb AFB, Texas. After 50 minutes on the ground Lieutenant Commander Whisler departed NAS North Island, Calif., in an F3D-2 Skyknight (BuNo 127076) headed for NAS Norfolk, Va. He refueled at NAS Dallas and arrived at NAS Norfolk, Va., at 1921, local time.

25 June Task Force 77 deployed four F4U-5N Corsairs to Kimpo to operate under the 5th AF for an indefinite period. The purpose was to intercept night attacks being made on the field by aircraft flying too slowly to be intercepted by jets.

30 June The Research and Development Board and three other activities of the Department of Defense were abolished as the president's Reorganization Plan No. 6 became effective. The functions of these activities were assigned to the Secretary of Defense, six new Assistant Secretaries of Defense were created, and the chairman of the Joint Chiefs of Staff was given managerial control of the Joint Chiefs.

8 July The designation Antisubmarine Support Aircraft Carrier (CVS) was established for attack carriers assigned to antisubmarine warfare, and five CVAs assigned the new mission were redesignated effective one month from date.

10 July The Naval Air Development Unit was established at South Weymouth, Mass., to participate in development and testing of equipment designed for antisubmarine warfare and air defense.

1953—Continued

11 July   Major John F. Bolt, USMC, downed his fifth and sixth MiGs while operating with the Fifth Air Force in Korea, becoming the first Naval Aviator to attain five victories in jet aerial combat.

12 August   In the first successful shipboard launching of a fully guided Terrier, the missile was fired from *Mississippi* (EAG 1), and hit its target, an approaching F6F drone.

20 August   Lieutenant Colonel Marion E. Carl, USMC, piloted the D-558-2 Skyrocket to a new altitude record of 83,235 feet over Edwards AFB, Calif.

Marine Ace Major Bolt USMC 348324

15 July   *Tunny* (SSG 284) launched a Regulus missile off Naval Air Missile Test Center (NAMTC). This, the first submarine launching of a Regulus, was completed with a simulated attack after which the missile was successfully recovered on San Nicolas Island.

25 July   Pilots of Task Force 77 flew 538 offensive and 62 defensive sorties—their record for one day of operations in the Korean War.

27 July   On the final day of the Korean War, Task Force 77 expended its major effort on transportation facilities, with airfields a secondary target. The attacks destroyed or damaged 23 railroad cars, 11 railroad bridges, 1 railroad tunnel, 9 highway bridges, and numerous buildings.

27 July   United Nations and Communist representatives signed an armistice at Panmunjom, bringing hostilities to a halt in Korea.

D-558-2, high speed research aircraft in which LtCol. Marion E. Carl made flights at 1,143 mph and 83,235 feet 651837

1953—Continued

2 September Project 110, a conversion plan for *Midway*-class carriers, was promulgated. Basic changes were the same as those for the angled-deck version of Project 27C but with the addition of a modified C-11 steam catapult in the angled-deck area.

11 September In its first successful interception, a Sidewinder air-to-air missile, test fired at the Naval Ordnance Test Station, Inyokern, Calif., sent an F6F drone down in flames.

1 October *Hornet* completed conversion at the New York Naval Shipyard; the last of nine *Essex* class carriers modernized under Project 27A.

3 October A new official world speed record of 752.943 mph over a 3-kilometer course was set by the F4D Skyray at Muroc, Calif. Piloted by Lieutenant Commander James F. Verdin, this was the first carrier aircraft to establish this record in its normal combat configuration.

16 October A Douglas F4D-1 carrier fighter, flown by test pilot R. O. Rahn, broke the 100-kilometer closed course speed record at 728.114 mph.

19 November The Chief of Naval Operations endorsed the common utilization of the Fleet Air Gunnery Unit by the Pacific and Atlantic Fleets and the Marine Corps "as a step towards increased emphasis and standardization in the combat employment of aircraft armament."

3 December The Steam Catapult Facility, NAMC, Philadelphia, Pa., was established by Hon. James H. Smith, Assistant Secretary of the Navy for Air, with the launching of F9F and AD aircraft.

3 December The first successful test of super circulation (boundary layer control) on a high-speed airplane, an F9F-4 Panther, took place at the Grumman Aircraft Corporation field at Bethpage, Long Island, N.Y. John Attinello, a BuAer engineer, was credited with developing this practical application of the aerodynamic principle.

19 December The Navy and Bureau of Standards announced that under a joint project with the code name "Tinkertoy" methods had been developed for the automatic manufacture of electronics equipment and that a sonobuoy assembled by this method was in production. Tinkertoy was a technique for utilizing automatic machinery to attach basic electronic components to ceramic wafers and to build the wafers up into modules which could be readily assembled into complete units. Its importance at the time was viewed as breaking an electronics production bottleneck. In a broader view it was a step towards the development of microelectronics and solid state circuitry.

Speedster Verdin in Skyray 630092

Helicopter supplies outpost 433345

Wings for medics. Helicopters were used to fly battle casualties from the front to rear area hospitals 420530

Landing in a rice paddy USMC 131109

HTLs preparing to takeoff from Valley Forge in western Pacific 424772

Interdiction. Repeated attacks denied railroad to stubborn foe 1053759

Locomotive, but no railroad 1053760

An AD Skyraider test fires the Mighty Mouse, a high speed long-range air-to-air rocket, at NOTS Inyokern 707573

F9F Panther jets dump reserve fuel before landing on Princeton upon return from air strike over Korea 429191

Two Petrels, air-to-surface guided mis-siles, suspended beneath the wings of a P2V Neptune patrol plane 687387

The P5M-2 Martin Marlin fea-tures a "T" tail 1053791

XF7U-1 Cutlass, Vought's tailless twin-jet fighter, taking off from Midway during carrier evaluation 432148

*AJ-1 Savage landing aboard
Lake Champlain 630663*

F2Hs en route to target pass Lake Champlain 630627

*Early version of
Lockheed WV,
radar picket
plane for long-
range patrol, on
seaward exten-
sion of Dewline
1053793*

At the end of a patrol flight a P5M-2 Martin Marlin sets down at NAS Sangley Point in the Philippine Islands 676502

PART **8**

The New Navy

1954–1959

In spite of the truce in Korea, peace in the world remained on unsteady footing. Within months, the worsening situation in the Far East, a series of crises in the Middle East, and a general deterioration in international relations gave new importance to the traditional practice of deploying naval forces to trouble spots of the world. As tension grew, hostility became open; and as international maneuverings led to incidents and demands which threatened world peace, naval forces were called upon to represent the nation in critical areas. On different occasions these forces evacuated refugees, patrolled troubled waters, provided support to menaced nations, and presented a physical symbol of freedom as a bulwark between the aggressor and the oppressed.

The period was also marked by technological and scientific advances of such magnitude that the Navy and Naval Aviation passed through a change greater than any in their previous history. The effective exploitation of these advances enhanced the speed, firepower, versatility, and mobility of naval, sea and air forces. Guns were being replaced by guided missiles, capability to deliver nuclear weapons was increased, aircraft speeds jumped from sub- to supersonic, the adaptation of nuclear power to aircraft was under investigation, and an increased knowledge of space gave evidence of its future effect on surface operations.

Guided missiles of several types were perfected and placed into operation. Air-to-air missiles became standard equipment on interceptors; a ground-support type was deployed by fleet squadrons. Air defense missiles were on board operating ships. Air-to-surface missiles were assigned to the Naval Air Reserve, and an interceptor missile was introduced into flight training. The fleet ballistic missile, Polaris, was deployed on nuclear- powered submarines.

A new class of carriers was built and the basic carrier modernization program was completed. Carrier forces, strengthened by these additions and improvements, operated a whole new family of aircraft with high performance capabilities. The successful application of nuclear power to ships of several types reached a new height by the construction of a new

carrier utilizing the advantages of this newfound source of power.

Accompanying the intensive application of technological advances were extensive reorganizations within the Navy Department by which greater emphasis was placed on research. New provisions were made for utilizing developments in space, and closely related activities in technical fields were brought together by the merger of two bureaus. Similar adjustments in the fleet provided a more uniform organization for carrier aviation, set up special task groups for the progressive improvement of antisubmarine tactics, provided completely equipped mobile amphibious squadrons ready to operate in the new tactics of vertical assault, and revised the Reserve program to provide units trained and equipped to perform specific tasks immediately upon mobilization.

All these advances in technology and all the improvements in weapons and equipment created a new Navy which paradoxically continued to play its traditional role in controlling the sea. Defense of the nation and of its commerce, deterrence of aggression, and readiness in time of war to destroy any active enemy power remained the Navy's basic tasks.

Events of the latter part of the 1950s were largely dominated by the space program. As a new age loomed upon the horizon, questions were raised and investigations made regarding the state of the nation's scientific attainment, the quality of its educational program, and the relative position of its progress in missilery. Successful orbits by Explorer I and Vanguard provided the first of a number of convincing answers. Within months, the orbit of man-made satellites became almost commonplace and the fantasy of man in space began to take on realistic form as tests demonstrated the feasibility of retrieving objects from orbit and an astronaut training program was launched.

1954

1 January The Naval Air Weapons Systems School was established at Jacksonville, Fla., to train cadres in

1954—Continued

maintenance of air-launched guided missiles, aircraft armament control systems, missile external control equipment, and bomb directors.

1 April   The first transcontinental flights in less than four hours were made by three pilots of VF-21 in F9F Cougars in a 2,438-mile flight from San Diego, Calif., to Floyd Bennett Field, N.Y., with aerial refueling over Hutchinson, Kans. Lieutenant Commander Francis X. Brady made the crossing in 3 hours 45 minutes 30 seconds, Lieutenant (jg) John C. Barrow took 3 hours 46 minutes and 49 seconds, and Lieutenant W. Rich made it in 3 hours 48 minutes even. Official timers were not present.

19 April   Model designations for airships were modified to conform with designations for heavier-than-air aircraft. Basically, the envelope designation letters "K" and "N" were replaced by manufacturer's letters, standard suffix numbers and letters were uniformly applied and the patrol class of airships was divided into patrol and antisubmarine classes. Thus the ZPN became the ZPG-1 and the ZP2K became the ZSG-2.

25 May   A ZPG-2 airship, commanded by Commander Marion H. Eppes, landed at NAS Key West, Fla., after a record breaking flight of 200.1 hours or more than eight days in the air. The flight, which began at NAS Lakehurst, N.J., ranged over the Atlantic as far north as Nova Scotia, out to Bermuda and Nassau and southward over the Caribbean and Gulf of Mexico. For his achievement on this flight, Commander Eppes was awarded the Distinguished Flying Cross and later the 1955 Harmon International Trophy for Aeronauts.

27 May   The Chief of Naval Operations approved Project 125 of the carrier improvement program which in general provided for installing an angled deck, enclosing the bow to improve seaworthiness, and making other changes to further modernize the carriers that had completed the earlier Project 27A.

1 June   Commander Henry J. Jackson, in an S2F-1, was catapulted from *Hancock* in the initial operational test of the C-11 steam catapult. As tests continued throughout the month, a total of 254 launchings were made with the S2F, AD-5, F2H-3, F2H-4, FJ-2, F7U-3 and F3D-2.

15 June   To coordinate and guide the extensive aeronautical research, development, and material activities in the Fourth Naval District, including the Philadelphia, Pa., Johnsville, Pa., Trenton, N.J., and

First operation of steam catapult, Hancock launches an S2F-1 638785

Lakehurst, N.J., areas, the Naval Air Development and Material Center was established at Johnsville, Pa., Rear Admiral Selden B. Spangler, Commander.

22 July   The XZS2G-1 (formerly XZP5K-1) made its first flight at Goodyear Aircraft Corporation, Akron, Ohio. This airship, designed as a replacement for the K Class airship, was fitted with inverted "Y" control surfaces.

26 July   Two AD Skyraiders of Air Group 5 from *Philippine Sea* were attacked by two LA-7 type aircraft while searching for survivors of a Cathay Pacific airliner shot down three days before off Hainan Island. The AD pilots returned fire and splashed both attackers.

4 September   A P2V of VP-19, on routine reconnaissance over international waters, was attacked by two MiG aircraft and forced to ditch off the Siberian coast. Nine of the crew escaped and were later rescued, but one went down with the plane.

31 October   Ensign Duane L. Varner of VF-34 completed a 1,900-mile nonstop, nonrefueling, transcontinental flight from Los Alamitos, Calif., to Cecil Field, Fla., in 3 hours and 58 minutes in an F2H-2 Banshee.

1954—Continued

The S2F, Tracker anti-submarine search and attack plane, comes in for a landing on Valley Forge 1053776

2 November The XFY-1 delta wing experimental fighter, piloted by J. F. Coleman, made a successful flight at NAS Moffett Field, Calif., consisting of vertical takeoff, transition to horizontal flight and return to vertical position for landing. The first free vertical takeoff had been made on 1 August. For his contribution to the art of flying in testing the XFY-1, Coleman was later awarded the Harmon International Trophy for 1955.

1955

17 January VX-6 was established at NAS Patuxent River, Md., for operations with Task Force 43 in Operation Deep Freeze. This squadron provided services for parties based ashore on Antarctica and made courier flights between that continent and New Zealand.

21 January The Flying Platform, a one-man helicopter of radical design, made its first flight at the Hiller plant in Palo Alto, Calif. Although the flight occurred during ground tests and was therefore accidental, it was successful in all respects.

27 January A North American FJ-3 Fury, piloted by Lieutenant Commander William J. Manby, Jr., of VF-33, set a new unofficial climb mark by reaching 10,000 feet from a standing start in 73.2 seconds at NAS Oceana, Va.

XFY-1, experimental vertical take-off fighter 709126

1955—Continued

1 February   Task Force 43, Captain George J. Dufek commanding, was activated to plan Antarctic operations scheduled to begin in the fall under the code name Operation Deep Freeze. The mission of the force on its first expedition was to build facilities and airstrips and deliver supplies in support of U.S. participation in the International Geophysical Year 1957-58.

1 February   VP-23 left Tarragona, Spain, for NAS Port Lyautey, Morocco, after six days of intensive training at the Spanish Military Air Base at Reus. This was the first operation of U.S. forces from bases in Spain.

6 February   After steaming from the Atlantic to the Pacific around the Cape of Good Hope, *Midway* reported to Commander Task Force 77 for operations in the China Seas. This marked the first operation of ships of her class in the western Pacific.

12 February   The evacuation of 24,000 military and civilian personnel of the Republic of China from the Tachen Islands, off the China coast, was completed without incident under cover of surface ships and carrier air of the Seventh Fleet.

13 February   An F3H-1N Demon, piloted by McDonnell test pilot C. V. Braun, set the unofficial record for climb to 10,000 feet at 71 seconds.

16 February   The Bureau of Aeronautics issued instructions describing new color schemes that would be used on all new Navy and Marine Corps aircraft beginning 1 July 1955 and applied on all currently operating aircraft within the next two years. The familiar sea blue was changed to light gull gray on top and glossy white below for carrier aircraft, all-over seaplane gray for water based aircraft and all-over light gull gray for helicopters. Bare aluminum was retained for utility types and land plane transports, the latter having in addition a solar heat reflecting white top. Orange-yellow remained the color for primary trainers, but the advanced trainer scheme was changed to international orange and insignia white. Other changes were olive drab above and glossy white below for land observation types and a combination of orange-yellow, engine gray and insignia red for target drones and target tow aircraft.

23 February   An F4D Skyray, piloted by Douglas test pilot R. O. Rahn, reached 10,000 feet in 56 seconds, the fourth unofficial climb record set by Navy carrier fighters in less than a month.

24 February   The Chief of Naval Operations directed that the term "angled" be used in lieu of "canted," "slanted," and "flamed," which had been used variously in describing the deck of aircraft carriers in which the landing runway was offset from the line of the keel.

24 February   The first R3Y-1 Tradewind, a high-speed seaplane transport equipped with four Allison turboprop engines, was delivered to NATC Patuxent River, Md., for service suitability evaluation and trials. Intended for the long-range over-water transportation of military cargo, this plane was also suitable for use as a personnel or troop transport and for the air evacuation of wounded.

22 March   A Navy R6D of VR-3, assigned to MATS, crashed and exploded at 0203 on Pali Kea Peak, 15 miles northwest of Honolulu, Hawaii, killing all on board. The 57 passengers and 9 crew members lost in this tragedy made it the worst heavier-than-air crash in naval aviation history.

25 March   The Chance Vought XF8U-1, a jet carrier fighter, exceeded the speed of sound on its first flight, made at Edwards AFB.

4 April   The Jet Transitional Training Unit was established at NAS Olathe, Kans., to provide student training for aviators transferring from shore to sea duty in the rank of commander and below. In addition to providing refresher training for these "desk pilots," the unit was responsible for training pilots making the transition from prop to jet type aircraft.

30 April   Admiral John H. Towers, Naval Aviator No. 3, died. His long and distinguished career had begun on 26 June 1911, when he reported for flight instruction at the Curtiss Flying School, Hammondsport, N.Y., and extended through many important aviation and fleet commands including Chief of the Bureau of Aeronautics, Commander, Air Force Pacific, Commander, Second Carrier Task Force and Commander in Chief, Pacific Fleet. Upon his retirement from active duty on 1 December 1947, he was serving as Chairman of the General Board.

2 May   The Navy announced the Aviation Officer Candidate Program, open to college graduates between the ages of 19 and 26. The new program paralleled the Aviation Cadet Program insofar as flight training was concerned, but in recognition of the higher scholastic attainment of its candidates, offered a commission as Ensign, USNR, upon completion of the four month preflight course.

1955—Continued

Vought F8U-2N Crusader, all-weather fighter is equipped with heat-seeking air-to-air missile Sidewinder 1061492

F8U steam catapult launch from Hancock 1053762

1955—Continued

5 May VP-1, with 12 P2V-5 Neptunes, returning from duty in the Far East by way of Asia, Europe, and North Africa, arrived at NAS Whidbey Island, Wash. Although a tour of duty separated the Pacific Ocean leg from the rest of the flight, this was the first round-the-world flight by a Navy squadron.

12 May The classification of naval vessels was revised to provide the designation CVHE for Escort Helicopter Aircraft Carrier and CVU for Utility Aircraft Carrier. The carriers were redesignated one month later.

1 June VQ-1, the first squadron of its type in the U.S. Navy, was established at NAS Iwakuni, Japan, with Lieutenant Commander Eugene R. Hall in command. First aircraft assigned were P4M-1Q Mercators.

22 June A P2V-5 Neptune of VP-9, while on patrol in the Aleutian area, was attacked by two MiG-15s, which set fire to the starboard engine and forced the Neptune to crash on St. Lawrence Island, near Gambell. There were no fatalities.

1 July NAAS Mayport, Fla., was established, completing the program begun in 1948 of converting the Jacksonville, Fla., area into a Fleet Aviation Center. Mayport provided docking facilities for carriers alongside the airstrip, thus permitting the rapid loading or unloading of special equipment and personnel and the easy movement of carrier air units ashore or afloat.

1 July *Thetis Bay,* in the process of conversion to its new mission, was reclassified as an assault Helicopter Aircraft Carrier and redesignated CVHA 1.

14 July The Martin P6M Seamaster, a swept-wing seaplane powered with four J-71 jet engines and in-

The XP6M-1 Seamaster, new water-based aircraft 1053800

corporating a new hull design, made its first flight. Designed for minelaying and reconnaissance tasks, and adaptable to other missions, this plane initially demonstrated great promise for the offensive potential of the operating forces.

22 August As VX-3 began operational evaluation of the mirror landing system installed on *Bennington,* Commanding Officer Commander Robert G. Dose, flying an FJ-3 Fury, made the first landing with the device. Two days later Lieutenant Commander Harding C. MacKnight made the first night landing in an F9F-8 Cougar. The squadron's favorable report formed the basis for a decision to procure the mirror landing system for installation on aircraft carriers and at certain shore stations.

12 September The Navy announced that all fighters in production would be fitted with gear for inflight refueling, thus establishing the technique as a standard operational procedure.

16 September Guided Missile Group ONE (GMGRU-1) was established at San Diego, Calif., to provide trained detachments to operate the Regulus assault missile from aircraft carriers and to support the employment of the Regulus on cruisers and submarines of the Pacific Fleet. Ten days later, GMGRU-2 was established at Chincoteague, Va., to provide the same services in the Atlantic Fleet.

27 September Navy responsibilities in connection with plans to launch an earth satellite during the International Geophysical Year (1957–1958), which included technical management of the Department of Defense portion of the program, were assigned to the Chief of Naval Research.

1 October *Forrestal,* the first of four ships of her class, was placed in commission at the Norfolk Naval Shipyard, Portsmouth, Va., Captain Roy L. Johnson in command.

10 October *Saipan* with HTU-1 aboard, left Tampico, Mexico, after a week of disaster relief operations for the inhabitants of the area. During these operations, the helicopters rescued 5,439 persons marooned on rooftops, trees and other retreats, and delivered 183,017 pounds of food and medical supplies, thus earning the commendation of the Task Group Commander and the best wishes of a thankful people.

11 October The Navy announced achievement of the initial step toward an eventual goal of monitoring surface weather in uninhabited portions of the world

1955—Continued

First carrier of a new class, Forrestal, was designed especially for operation of jet aircraft 709972

1 November Boston (CAG 1), Terrier missile ship and the world's first guided-missile cruiser, was placed in commission at the Philadelphia, Pa., Naval Shipyard, Captain Charles B. Martell commanding.

8 November The Secretary of Defense established a National Ballistic Missile Program, involving joint Army-Navy development of an intermediate range ballistic missile, for both shipboard and land-based operations. This resulted in Navy support for the Army's liquid-propellant missile, Jupiter, being developed at the Redstone Arsenal, Ala., in order to adapt it for use as a fleet ballistic missile.

9 November The Chief of Naval Operations informed the Chief of the Bureau of Ships of his intention to equip each angled-deck carrier with mirror landing systems and requested that equipment for 12 installations be procured during the fiscal years 1956 and 1957.

and thereby providing improved weather forecasting for use in both flight and surface operations. Automatic meteorological stations, developed by the Office of Naval Research and the Bureau of Aeronautics, were set adrift in the hurricane lanes north of Puerto Rico and provided continuous weather data on tropical storm Janet. Subsequent progress included a moored automatic weather station, one of which in September 1960 provided the first alert on tropical storm Ethel; unit stations on Antarctica, initially in 1956 but more successfully in 1960; and nuclear energy power as a source for data collection and transmission beginning in 1964.

15 October Lieutenant Gordon Gray, piloting a Douglas A4D-1 Skyhawk, broke the Class C world speed record for 500 kilometers with a speed of 695.163 mph at Muroc, Calif.

14 November The flagship of Rear Admiral George J. Dufek, Commander, Task Force 43, sailed from Norfolk, Va., for New Zealand to rendezvous with the ships of the task force for the southward voyage to Antarctica. Operating under the code name Operation Deep Freeze, the mission of this force was to establish bases on Antarctica for geophysical studies during the coming year.

1 December An element of Fleet All Weather Training Unit, Pacific (FAWTUPAC), was assigned to the Continental Air Defense Command to operate as a fighter-interceptor group under U.S. Air Force control. When FAWTUPAC was disestablished on 2 May 1958, this element was given squadron status and designated VF(AW)-3.

4 December On one flight of a project set up to evaluate the all-weather capabilities of airships,

1955—Continued

Lieutenant Commander Charles A. Mills operated a ZPG airship in the vicinity of South Weymouth, Mass., in an ice-accreting experiment unparalleled in lighter-than-air history. In spite of heavy airship icing, propeller icing, severe vibration and flying ice particles, Mills piloted his airship, directed the collection of data, returned to the field under instrument conditions, and made a ground-controlled approach landing in a manner that retained a maximum amount of ice on the ship for analysis on the ground. For his achievement on this and other flights during the evaluation, Lieutenant Commander Mills was awarded the 1956 Harmon International Trophy for Aeronauts.

20 December   Two P2V Neptunes and two R5D Skymasters of VX-6 forged the first air link with the continent of Antarctica with a flight from Christchurch, New Zealand, to McMurdo Sound.

1956

3 January   ZW-1, Commander John L. Mack commanding, was established at NAS Lakehurst, N.J.—the first lighter-than-air unit of its type.

10 January   Airborne Early Warning Wing, Pacific, Captain Edward C. Renfro commanding, was established at NAS Barbers Point, Hawaii, to supervise and direct units flying defensive patrols protecting the continental United States and Hawaii against surprise attack.

7 March   Fleet assignment of the F3H-2N Demon, all-weather fighter, began with the delivery of six F3H-2Ns to VF-14 at NAS Cecil Field.

An F3H-2N firing air-to-air Sparrow III missiles 1061490

12 March   VA-83, equipped with F7U-3M Cutlass aircraft and Sparrow I missiles, departed Norfolk, Va., aboard *Intrepid* for duty in the Mediterranean in the first overseas deployment of a naval missile squadron.

12 March   The Assistant Secretary of Defense for Research and Development established a titanium alloy sheet rolling program and designated the Bureau of Aeronautics as coordinator. Thereby an organized effort of the armed services and the titanium industry was established to improve titanium alloys with particular emphasis upon strength, uniformity and fabricating characteristics for use in aircraft and missiles.

20 March   The Ballistic Missile Committee, Office of the Secretary of Defense, approved a Navy program for development of solid-propellant motors for use in ship-based ballistic missiles.

31 March   Five A3D-1 aircraft were ferried from NAS Patuxent River, Md., to VAH-1 at NAS Jacksonville, Fla., completing the first delivery of Skywarriors to a fleet unit.

3 April   The Navy announced that the Petrel, an air-to-surface guided missile designed for use by patrol aircraft against shipping, was in operational use from the P2V-6Ms of VP-24.

23 April   Cognizance of Project Vanguard (an earth satellite launching program) within OPNAV was assigned to the Guided Missiles Division of DCNO (Air). The division was responsible for advising the Chief of Naval Operations on general aspects of the program, and supporting and assisting the Office of Naval Research in the resolution of problems, other than fiscal, arising within the Navy Department and at missile test activities of other services.

25 April   The Chief of Naval Operations announced that mirror landing systems would be installed in the near future at all principal Naval Air Stations for improvement of air traffic control and reduction of landing accidents.

26 April   The Naval Aircraft Factory at Philadelphia, Pa., was renamed the Naval Air Engineering Facility (Ships Installations) and its mission revised to include research, engineering, design, development, and limited manufacturing of devices and equipment for launching and recovering aircraft and guided missiles. Redesignation ceremonies on 1 June marked the passing of a name prominent in Naval Aviation since World War I.

1956—Continued

An A3D-2 aerial tanker, refuels an F4H-1 1042033

Equipment development encompasses all phases of Naval Aviation, mirror landing system brings in A3D 698382

29 May   The ship designation system was modified to provide for use of the suffix "N" to identify vessels propelled by nuclear energy.

25 June   U.S. Naval Ordnance Plant, Indianapolis, Ind., a facility devoted to research, development, production, and repair of aviation fire control equipment was redesignated U.S. Naval Avionics Facility. This facility had been established early in World War II for development and production of aviation ordnance including the Norden bombsight. Its redesignation completed an internal Navy realignment whereby the Bureau of Ordnance had received complete responsibility for solid propellant rocket motors and the Bureau of Aeronautics had received complete responsibility for aviation fire control equipment.

27–28 June   The first annual Fleet Air Gunnery Meet was held at NAAS El Centro, Calif. Six teams, selected from Navy and Marine Corps shore-based fighter units and composed of the squadron commander and three pilots, competed with two firings each at 15,000 and 25,000 feet. Top team honors and the Earle Trophy went to VF-112 of AirPac, and individual honors to Lieutenant (jg) H. N. Wellman of VF-43 of AirLant.

7 July   VW-12 and Maintenance Squadron 2 were established at NAS Barbers Point, Hawaii, for patrol duty along the Pacific Distant Early Warning Line of the Continental Air Defense System.

12 July   The Chief, Bureau of Aeronautics, approved a reorganization of the Office of Assistant Chief for Research and Development, whereby various technical divisions with closely related functions were regrouped under appropriately titled officers. Thereby a

1956—Continued

reorganization of the entire bureau, which had been initiated a year earlier, was completed. This included the establishment of an Assistant Chief for Plans and Programs with a concomitant strengthening of planning functions and a division of the Material and Services group into two groups titled "Procurement" and "Maintenance and Support," each under an Assistant Chief.

14 July In the initial overseas deployment of a Sidewinder missile unit, VA-46, equipped with F9F-8s, departed from Norfolk, Va., on *Randolph* for operations with the Sixth Fleet in the Mediterranean. Deployment of the Sidewinder was extended to the western Pacific the following month as VF-211, equipped with FJ-3s, departed the west coast on *Bon Homme Richard* for operations with the Seventh Fleet.

20 July *Thetis Bay* (CVHA 1), the first helicopter assault carrier, was commissioned at San Francisco, Calif., Captain Thomas W. South II, commanding. Formerly CVE 90, *Thetis Bay* was converted to operate helicopters and to accommodate 1,000 Marine combat troops to be flown ashore in the vertical development tactics of amphibious assault.

31 July An A3D Skywarrior, flown by Lieutenant Commanders P. Harwood and Alton R. Henson, and Lieutenant Roy R. Miears, demonstrated the performance capabilities of new carrier jet attack aircraft with a 3,200-mile nonstop, nonrefueling flight from Honolulu, Hawaii to Albuquerque, N. Mex., in 5 hours and 40 minutes, with an average speed of 570 mph.

15 August The Avionics Division was established in the Research and Development Group of the Bureau of Aeronautics with Captain William E. Sweeney as Director. Formed by a merger of the Electronics and Armament Divisions and the Navigation Branch of the Airborne Equipment Division, its establishment was both the direct result of a rapid expansion of electronics techniques in aviation armament and air navigation, and a recognition of the need for closely coordinated effort for their most effective application.

21 August An F8U-1 Crusader, piloted by Commander Robert W. Windsor, Jr., captured the Thompson Trophy with a new national speed record of 1,015.428 mph over the 15-kilometer course at Naval Ordnance Test Station, China Lake, Calif. This production model carrier fighter, equipped during its record performance with full armament of 20mm cannon and dummy ammunition, was the first opera-

Marine helicopter squadron HMR-362 demonstrates rescue at sea while operating with Thetis Bay *1053795*

1956—Continued

tionally equipped jet plane in history to fly faster than 1,000 mph.

22 August Lieutenant Commander Virgil Solomon set down the Marianas Mars (JRM) on waters off NAS Alameda, Calif., after a flight from Honolulu, Hawaii, and completed the last scheduled passenger run for Mars aircraft.

22 August A P4M Mercator, while on night patrol out of Iwakuni, Japan, reported that it was under attack by aircraft over international waters, 32 miles off the China coast, and was not heard from again. Carrier

Cdr. R. W. Windsor in F8U-1 1061494

and land-based air and surface ships, searching for the plane, found wreckage, empty life rafts, and the bodies of two crew members.

30 August The Air Coordinating Committee approved a common military-civil short range air navigation system called VORTAC. This system consisted of a combination of the Navy developed TACAN (Tactical Air Navigation System) with the Civil Aeronautic Authority's VOR (Very High Frequency Omnirange direction finder). The Air Coordinating Committee action resulted in the installation of ground beacons on the civil airways that served both civilian and military aircraft, each using their own specialized equipment.

1 September In the race for the North American Trophy, an event of the National Air Show, four FJ-3

Furies of VF-24 took off from *Shangri-La* at sea off the Pacific coast of Mexico and flew nonstop, 1,198 miles to Oklahoma City, Okla., without refueling. The winner was Lieutenant (jg) D. K. Grosshuesch, with a time of 2 hours 13 minutes 38.6 seconds for an average speed of 537.848 mph.

2 September On the second day of the National Air Show, Lieutenant (jg) R. Carson flying an F3H-2N Demon of VF-124 captured the McDonnell Trophy with a nonstop, nonrefueling flight from *Shangri-La* off San Francisco, Calif., to Oklahoma City, Okla., covering the 1,436 miles in 2 hours 32 minutes 13.45 seconds for an average speed of 566.007 mph.

3 September Two A3D Skywarriors, piloted by Captain John T. Blackburn, commanding Heavy Attack Wing 1 (HATWING-1), and Commander Charles T. Frohne, were launched from *Shangri-La* off the Oregon coast, flew across a finish line at the National Air Show, Oklahoma City, Okla., and continued on to Jacksonville, Fla., without refueling. In completing the 1,543.3-mile leg from the *Shangri-La* to Oklahoma City in 2 hours 32 minutes 39.7 seconds for an average speed of 606.557 mph, Captain Blackburn was awarded the Douglas Trophy. With this flight a 3-day demonstration of carrier mobility was completed, in which *Shangri-La* had launched aircraft to the same destination from widely separated points while moving from Mexico to Oregon.

21 September An F11F-1 Tiger, piloted by Grumman test pilot Tom Attridge, shot itself down while conducting test firings off eastern Long Island, N.Y., by running into 20mm projectiles it had fired only seconds before.

Test model of Grumman F11F-1, supersonic fighter 1011277

1956—Continued

2 October *Enterprise* was ordered stricken from the Navy list and put up for sale as scrap. Launched just 20 years before and commissioned 12 May 1938, she was in more action during World War II than any other carrier, was a pioneer in night combat operations, and was recipient of both the Presidential Unit Citation and the Navy Unit Commendation. Decommissioned in the demobilization period following the war, she was laid up with the Reserve Fleet at Bayonne, N.J., and never returned to active service.

5 October Three Cougar jets, piloted by Commanders Gerald A. Robinson and Donald Mitchie, and Ensign Ronald K. Hess of VF-144, made a round trip transcontinental flight from Miramar, Calif., to Long Island, N.Y., with fueling stops each way at Olathe, Kans., in an elapsed time of 10 hours 49 minutes 11 seconds. Although better than the existing record of 11 hours 18 minutes 27 seconds, the flight was not officially observed and therefore not officially recognized.

11 October An R6D-1 of Air Transport Squadron 6 on a scheduled MATS flight from Lakenheath, England, to Lajes in the Azores, disappeared over the Atlantic with 50 passengers and 9 crewmembers on board. Extensive search by ships and aircraft for the next 14 days found debris from the plane, but no survivors.

16 October Five students received Naval Observer Wings; the first graduates of the Navigator-Bombardier School at NAS Corpus Christi, Tex., which began 26 May.

29 October The Suez crisis erupted into open warfare and all major fleet units were sent to sea under conditions of maximum readiness. The Sixth Fleet, in the Mediterranean, was ordered to evacuate U.S. citizens from the area. Aircraft provided cover and heavy combatant ships stood by while ships and destroyers of the amphibious group and units of Air Force transport squadrons went into Alexandria, Egypt, Haifa, Tel Aviv, Israel, Amman, Jordan, and Damascus, Syria, and evacuated some 2,200 persons by 3 November. Operations by Sixth Fleet, in the area for several weeks, included the logistic support of the first UN International Forces which arrived in the area in November.

31 October Seven Navy men landed in an R4D Skytrain on the ice at the South Pole—the first to stand at the spot since Captain Robert F. Scott of the Royal Navy reached it in January 1912. The seven men were:

Crew of the first plane to land at South Pole, 31 October 1956. AD2 John P. Strider, RAdm. George J. Dufek, Lcdr. Conrad S. Shinn, Lt. John Swadner, AT2 William Cumbie, Capt. William M. Hawkes, and Capt Douglas L. L. Cordiner 805653

Rear Admiral George J. Dufek, Commander, Task Force 43 and Commander, Naval Support Forces, Antarctica; Captain Douglas L. L. Cordiner, C.O., VX-6; Captain William. M. Hawkes, co-pilot; Lieutenant Commander Conrad S. Shinn, pilot; Lieutenant John Swadener, navigator; J. P. Strider, AD2, crew chief; and William Cumbie, AT2, radioman. The party remained at the pole for 49 minutes setting up navigational aids to assist the future delivery of materials and equipment for constructing a scientific observation station at the spot.

2 November The Navy announced award of a contract to Westinghouse Electric to design and furnish reactor components for a nuclear-powered aircraft carrier.

8 November A Navy Stratolab balloon, manned by Lieutenant Commanders Malcolm D. Ross and M. Lee Lewis, bettered the existing world altitude record by soaring to 76,000 feet over the Black Hills of South Dakota on a flight designed to gather meteorological, cosmic ray, and other scientific data necessary to improved safety at high altitudes. For this record ascent, the men were awarded the 1957 Harmon International Trophy for Aeronauts.

9 November A Sikorsky HR2S helicopter, piloted by Major Roy L. Anderson, USMC, at Windsor Locks, Conn., began a 3-day assault on world records, setting three new marks as follows: 9 November, carried a payload of 11,050 pounds to an altitude over 12,000 feet; 10 November, carried 13,250 pounds to over

1956—Continued

HR2S assault helicopter can lift three jeeps USMCA 150310

7,000 feet; and 11 November, set a speed record of 162.7 mph over a three-kilometer course.

29 November The ZSG-4, first airship fitted with a dacron envelope, made its first flight at NAS Lakehurst, N.J.

3 December *Compass Island* (EAG 153), the first ship converted to support the Fleet Ballistic Missile Program, was commissioned at the New York Naval Shipyard. On the same day the first Terrier missile destroyer, *Gyatt* (DD 712) was commissioned at Boston, Mass.

7 December The Secretary of Defense directed that air transport operations be placed under a Single Manager Service, and designated the Military Air Transport Service of the U.S. Air Force as its operating agency. This directive, which was implemented on 1 July 1957, required that the Navy transfer to this agency all of the transport aircraft it was operating under MATS and all four-engine land transports of the Fleet Logistic Air Wings except for 30 which could be retained for fleet service and administrative airlift.

8 December The Secretary of Defense authorized the Navy to proceed with the development of the solid-propellant Polaris Fleet Ballistic Missile as a sub-

marine-launched weapon system and to terminate its participation in the liquid-propellant Jupiter program.

8 December A Martin Viking rocket was successfully fired at Cape Canaveral, Fla., in a test of launching equipment, tracking, and telemetry instruments intended for the Vanguard earth satellite.

Firing a Polaris from George Washington 1053794

1956—Continued

17 December The WF-2 Tracer, a carrier early warning plane adapted from the TF-1 design, made its first flight at the Grumman plant, Peconic River, Long Island, N.Y.

1957

1 January The Naval Air Experimental Station, Philadelphia, Pa., one of the four subcommands grouped together to form the Naval Air Material Center (NAMC) in 1943, was disestablished and consolidated with the NAMC.

3 January The last operational Catalina, a PBY-6A of NARTU Atlanta, was ordered retired from service.

10 January The Naval Air Mine Defense Development Unit, established under an officer in charge on 31 August 1956, was established as a full command at Panama City, Fla., to develop and evaluate aviation systems, materials, and techniques for mine countermeasures.

14–24 January In an evaluation of their all-weather capability, ZPG airships of ZW-1, operating in relays from South Weymouth, Mass., maintained continuous radar patrol over the North Atlantic 200 miles off the New England coast through some of the worst storms experienced in the area in years.

18 January TF-1Qs, first naval aircraft equipped for electronics jamming, were first received by VA(AW)-35 at San Diego, Calif.

1 February Lieutenant Commander Frank H. Austin, Jr., MC, completed the Test Pilot Training Program at NATC Patuxent River, Md., and became the first Navy Flight Surgeon to qualify as a test pilot.

4 February The Chief of Naval Operations set forth a new policy for billet assignment which provided that aviators and nonaviators would be assigned alternately as either the senior or next senior officer of each important policy generating and administrative billet and that assignment to all billets of commander level and above would be filled by aviators and nonaviators in the ratio of their respective numbers on board.

9 February The Robertson Committee, chaired by the Deputy Secretary of Defense Reuben B. Robertson, Jr., and formed to study means of shortening the time required to develop aircraft, issued its final report. The committee concluded that through streamlining management and administrative processes and thereby eliminating wasted motion, the development of weapon systems could be accomplished in significantly less time than had been required since World War II. To this end, the services were taking specific action to correct a number of problems. Among the steps taken by the Navy were establishing program

The WF-2, a carrier-based early warning plane 1033433

1957—Continued

managers for each weapon program within the Bureau of Aeronautics and a Long Range Objectives Group in the Office of the Chief of Naval Operations.

21 February   In recognition of the increasing importance of weather information to naval operations, the Naval Aerology Branch, OP-533, was given status as the Naval Weather Service Division, OP-58.

7 March   A turbo-catapult, powered by the exhaust of six jet engines and designed primarily for use by Marine Corps expeditionary forces, launched its first aircraft at Georgetown, Del. The airplane, an AD-4NA, weighing 16,400 pounds and piloted by Joseph Barkley, all-American engineering test pilot, was launched at a speed of 90 knots in a run of 210 feet.

15 March   A ZPG-2 airship, commanded by Commander Jack R. Hunt, landed at NAS Key West, Fla., after a flight that began 4 March at South Weymouth, Mass., and circled over the Atlantic Ocean toward Portugal, the African coast and back for a new world record in distance and endurance, covering 9,448 statute

Cdr. Hunt briefing ZPG-2 crew 1009749

miles and remaining airborne 264 hours 12 minutes without refueling. For his accomplishment in commanding the airship on this flight, Commander Hunt was awarded the 1958 Harmon International Trophy for Aeronauts.

21 March   An A3D-1 Skywarrior, piloted by Commander Dale W. Cox, Jr., broke two transcontinental speed records; one for the round trip from Los Angeles, Calif., to New York, N.Y., in 9 hours 31 minutes 35.4 seconds; and the other for the east to west flight in 5 hours 12 minutes 39.24 seconds.

25 March   The first F8U-1 Crusader was delivered to a fleet unit, VF-32, in the record time of two years after the first flight of the experimental model.

5 April   In the Second Annual Naval Air Weapons Meet, VMF-314 won the Earle Trophy for first place in air gunnery, and VA-26 took the Kane Trophy for best in the air-to-ground competition. Best individual score of the meet was made by Commander Alexander Vraciu, Commanding Officer of VF-51 and Navy Ace in World War II.

12 April   Scheduled production of the Sparrow I air-to-air missile was completed by the Sperry Farragut Company, Bristol, Tenn., with delivery of the last missile on order.

13 April   Aviation officer distribution functions, performed by the Office of Deputy Chief of Naval

ZPG-2 departs South Weymouth on a nonstop 11-day flight 1009746

1957—Continued

Operations (Air) since its formation in 1943 and by the Bureau of Aeronautics prior to that time, were transferred to the Bureau of Naval Personnel.

21 April *Antietam* reported for duty to the Chief of Naval Air Training at Pensacola, Fla., providing that command with its first angled deck carrier for use in flight training.

25 April The Sixth Fleet sailed to the eastern Mediterranean, remaining for a week in a show of strength supporting the President's warning against the Communist threat to the independence of Jordan.

30 April The Naval Aviation Medical Center at Pensacola, Fla., was established, combining under a single command the clinical, training, and research functions of the Naval School of Aviation Medicine and the Pensacola Naval Hospital.

1 May A two-part rocket, made up from the first stage of a Viking and a prototype of a third stage, was launched from Cape Canaveral, Fla., in the second

Launching Vanguard, May 1957 709847

successful test of the Vanguard earth satellite launching vehicle.

6 May ZPG-2W, an early-warning airship with a large radar antenna mounted within the envelope, made its first flight at Akron, Ohio.

17 May *Badoeng Strait*, the last escort carrier in service with the fleet, was decommissioned at Bremerton, Wash.

23 May A drone HTK-1 helicopter, carrying a safety pilot, operated from the fantail of *Mitscher* (DL 2) in the vicinity of Narragansett Bay, Mass. These tests and others, conducted in February off Key West, Fla., in which a piloted HUL-1 carried Mk 43 torpedoes in flights to and from *Mitscher,* demonstrated the feasibility of assigning torpedo carrying drone helicopters to destroyers and led to the development of the Drone Anti-Submarine Helicopter (DASH) which was later embodied in the QH-50C.

27 May The first T2V-1 Sea Star jet trainer was delivered to the Naval Air Advanced Training Command at Corpus Christi, Tex.

28 May In a reorganization of the Naval Air Reserve program, the Chief of Naval Operations directed that the 73 Auxiliary Air Units located throughout the country be disestablished during the next six months.

6 June Two F8U Crusaders and two A3D Skywarriors flew nonstop from *Bon Homme Richard* off the California coast to *Saratoga* off the east coast of Florida. This, the first carrier-to-carrier transcontinental flight, was completed by the F8Us in 3 hours 28 minutes and by the A3Ds in 4 hours 1 minute.

27 June Lieutenant Commander Malcolm D. Ross, USN, and Charles B. Moore of the Arthur D. Little Co., successfully completed a Stratolab balloon flight to investigate the interior of a thunderstorm, ascending from the top of Mount Withington near Socorro, N. Mex., into the towering cumulus cloud above the mountain. The flight was the first of a series conducted during the summer under the sponsorship of the Office of Naval Research and the Bureau of Aeronautics.

30 June A program to gather daily weather data over the Pacific, North America, and the Atlantic by the use of transosonde balloons was inaugurated with the release of the first balloon from NAS Iwakuni, Japan. Set to float at 30,000 feet, the balloons carried instruments which reported pressure and temperature every two hours. The duration of each flight was

1957—Continued

planned for from five to eight days with the termination point somewhere in the Atlantic, short of the European coast.

15 July   After the establishment of the Single Manager for Airlift Service, the Fleet Logistic Air Wings were abolished and transport squadrons not assigned to the Single Manager Service were redesignated Fleet Tactical Support Squadrons (VR) and reassigned to operate directly under the control of Fleet commanders.

16 July   An F8U-1P Crusader (bureau number 144608), piloted by Major John H. Glenn, Jr., USMC, broke the transcontinental speed record with a crossing from Los Alamitos, Calif., to Floyd Bennett Field, N.Y. in 3 hours 22 minutes 50.05 seconds for an average speed of 723.517 mph. This was the first upper atmosphere supersonic flight from the West Coast to the East Coast.

Maj. J. H. Glenn crossed the continent at supersonic speed 1061493

16 July   Two A3D Skywarriors, on a routine flight to join VAH-2 at NAS Barbers Point, Hawaii, made the Pacific flight from NAS Moffett Field, Calif., to Honolulu, Hawaii, in the record time of 4 hours 45 minutes.

30 July   The first pilotless helicopter flight was made at Bloomfield, Conn. Built by Kaman Aircraft, under

joint Army-Navy contract, the new helicopter was designed on the basis of principles developed experimentally under Navy contract using a modified HTK.

30 July   Air Force, Pacific Fleet, and Air Force, Atlantic Fleet, were retitled to become Naval Air Force, Pacific Fleet, and Naval Air Force, Atlantic Fleet.

12 August   An F3D Skynight, with Lieutenant Commander Don Walker aboard, was landed on *Antietam,* at sea off Pensacola, Fla., by the Automatic Carrier Landing System. This landing began the first shipboard test of the system designed to bring planes aboard in all weather conditions without help from the pilot. In the period 12–20 August more than 50 fully automatic landings were completed.

27 August   The Navy announced that all Naval Aviator candidates, except Aviation Cadets, entering flight training after 1 January 1958 would be obligated to serve 3½ years on active duty after completing the course instead of the 2 years previously required.

28 August   The ground level ejection seat, designed and developed by the Martin-Baker Aircraft Co., Ltd., of England, and under evaluation by Grumman Aircraft for the Navy, was demonstrated at NAS Patuxent River, Md. A successful ejection was made by Lieutenant Sydney Hughes, RAF, from an F9F-8T flying just above the ground at 120 mph.

3 September   The XKDT-1, a solid-propellant rocket-powered target drone, made its first flight in a launch from an F3H Demon over NAMTC Point Mugu, Calif.

28 September   *Alameda County,* converted from LST 32, was redesignated an Advance Aviation Base ship, AVB 1. The first of her class, the new ship was designed to provide fuel, spare parts, technicians and facilities necessary to establish and operate an airstrip for patrol and carrier aircraft in locations where there were no base facilities.

30 September   *Saipan,* last of the light carriers, was decommissioned.

1 October   The Naval Air Test Facility (Ship Installations) was established at NAS Lakehurst, N.J., with Commander Richard M. Tunnell, commanding, to evaluate aircraft launching and recovery systems and to support their development.

11 October   An A3D Skywarrior of VAH-4 bettered the mainland to Hawaii time with a control-tower to

1957—Continued

Test of Talos, supersonic surface-to-air missile 710376

control-tower flight from San Francisco, Calif., to Honolulu, Hawaii, in 4 hours 29 minutes 55 seconds.

15 October   The Talos Defense Unit, a land-based version of the Talos shipboard missile system and designed to launch Talos missiles automatically, was accepted from the Radio Corporation of America by Rear Admiral Frederick S. Withington, Chief of the Bureau of Ordnance. It was turned over to Lieutenant General E. L. Cummings, Chief of Army Ordnance, for evaluation at the White Sands Proving Ground and possible use at Army anti-aircraft installations.

16 October   *Lake Champlain,* with HMR-262 embarked, arrived at Valencia, Spain, to give aid to thousands made homeless by a flood.

13 November   The 1,000-mile Regulus II bombardment missile was fired at Edwards AFB, Calif., in its first launch with rocket boosters. After a 48-minute flight, the 11-ton missile was returned to the field by control aircraft.

21 November   Project Arowa was terminated and its personnel and records were transferred to the Navy Weather Research Facility, Norfolk, Va., which had been established the preceding month.

22 November   The first Reserve Squadron to fire guided missiles as a part of its regular training, VP-834 from NAS Floyd Bennett Field, N.Y., completed two weeks training at NAS Chincoteague, Va., in which it fired Petrel air-to-surface missiles under the supervision of Guided Missile Unit 11.

9 December   Cognizance of research and development programs for space vehicles was transferred from DCNO (Air) to ACNO (Research and Development) and responsibilities for what was formerly Project Vanguard were broadened to include all space vehicle programs prosecuted by the Office of Naval Research in the extension of, or following, Vanguard.

1958

9 January   Pacific Fleet air units began delivery of emergency supplies to inhabitants of several islands in the Marshalls, severely damaged by typhoon Ophelia.

9 January   *Princeton,* with Navy and Marine Corps aircraft embarked, and two destroyers from the Seventh Fleet and *Duxbury Bay* from the Middle East Force, ended seven days of relief operations for flood victims in Ceylon.

3 February   The Chief, Bureau of Aeronautics, appointed a Weapons System Team to accelerate development and fleet introduction of the A2F (A-6) aircraft. This team was under the chairmanship of the program manager and staffed with representatives from Production, Maintenance and Contracts Divisions and the Research and Development Group. The latter representative, the R&D Project Officer (or class desk officer), was also chairman of an R&D Project Team which included representatives of Avionics, Airborne Equipment and Power Plant Divisions. This action and the assignment of systems management responsibilities to the airframe contractor marked important steps in the implementation of the management concepts recommended by the Robertson Committee.

4 February   The keel of the world's first nuclear powered aircraft carrier, *Enterprise,* was laid at Newport News, Va.

13 February   A selected Reserve was set up within the overall Reserve Organization to provide fully trained and equipped forces and units for direct and immediate deployment to specific active duty assignment upon the commencement of hostilities. The entire Naval Air Reserve was incorporated into the new organization.

14 February   Operational evaluation of the air-to-air Sparrow III began as VX-4 fired the first missile.

1 March   An early warning WV-2E prototype, with a rotodome radar antenna mounted on the fuselage, was accepted from Lockheed and assigned to the Naval Air

1958—Continued

Development Unit at NAS South Weymouth, Mass., for preliminary evaluation.

7 March   *Grayback* (SSG 574), the first submarine built from keel up with guided-missile capability, was commissioned at Mare Island, Calif.

10 March   The Chief of Naval Operations approved a reorganization of carrier aviation that would create uniform air groups, provide a more permanent group assignment to ships, and permit a reduction of assigned units and aircraft without also reducing combat readiness. The new organization also provided for a permanent replacement Air Group to be established on each coast and made responsible for the indoctrination of key maintenance personnel, the tactical training of aviators, and conducting special programs required for the introduction of new models of combat aircraft.

17 March   A 3¼ pound earth satellite was placed in orbit by a Vanguard rocket fired from Cape Canaveral, Fla., in a test of the system designed for launching earth satellites for the International Geophysical Year. The highly successful scientific satellite, designed and developed under supervision of the Office of Naval Research, proved that the earth is slightly pear-shaped. Its solar-powered batteries continued to transmit for over 6 years and at last reports the satellite was expected to remain in orbit for as long as 2,000 years.

19 March   VX-4 launched the first Bullpup missile, beginning its operational evaluation.

23 March   In the first practical test of the Fleet Ballistic Missile underwater launching apparatus, a dummy Polaris missile was sent into the air off San Clemente Island, Calif.

2 April   An important step in the development of the Drone Anti-Submarine Helicopter for operation from destroyers was taken as an existing Bureau of Aeronautics contract with Gyrodyne for the RON-1 rotocycle (one man helicopter) was amended to provide for the development, installation and flight test of remote control equipment.

8 April   Airborne firing tests of HIPEG (High Performance External Gun) in F3H-2N aircraft commenced at Naval Aviation Ordnance Test Station, Chincoteague, Va. This twin-barreled, high-speed 20mm aircraft machine gun was developed for a pod installation on aircraft, thereby making it interchangeable with other aviation ordnance.

11 April   Rear Admiral John S. Thach issued the first Operation Order to Task Group Alfa, formed in the Atlantic Fleet to accelerate the development of antisubmarine tactics and to improve fleet readiness in antisubmarine warfare. Admiral Thach is also remembered for the "Thach Weave," an aircraft tactic which he pioneered in World War II.

18 April   In the Third Annual Naval Air Weapons Meet at El Centro, Calif., in which 15 specially selected squadrons participated, top honors in their class went to: VF-111 in air-to-air (day), VF-213 in air-to-air (all-weather), VA-126 in air-to-ground, and VAH-5 in heavy attack.

18 April   Lieutenant Commander George C. Watkins, piloting an F11F-1F Tiger at Edwards AFB, Calif., broke the world altitude record for the second time in three days, this time setting the mark at 76,939 feet.

21 April   To clarify command relationships and to permit the closer integration of Navy units into the

Task group alpha on parade portrays diversity and complexity of antisubmarine warfare equipment 1048502

1958—Continued

Single Manager Airlift Service, the Chief of Naval Operations directed that Navy squadrons be organized in Naval Air Transport Wings, one for the Pacific and another for the Atlantic.

4 May Practical test of an all-jet program in basic training began as 14 students reported to ATU-206 at Forrest Sherman Field, Pensacola, Fla., for instruction in the T2V Sea Star.

10 May Naval Missile Facility Point Arguello, Calif., was established as an activity of the National Pacific Missile Range.

11 May Lieutenant Commander Jack Neiman completed a 44-hour simulated high altitude flight in the pressure chamber at NAS Norfolk under conditions existing between 80,000 and 100,000 feet.

17 May Four F3H Demons and four F8U Crusaders completed nonstop trans-Atlantic crossings in Operation Pipeline, a practical test of the speed with which carrier aircraft could be delivered from the East Coast to the Sixth Fleet, in the Mediterranean.

22–23 May Major Edward N. LeFaivre, USMC, piloted an F4D-1 at NAMTC Point Mugu, Calif., to five world records in speed of climb to 3,000, 6,000, 9,000, 12,000, and 15,000 meters with marks of 44.392, 66.095, 90.025, 111.224, and 156.233 seconds.

26 May The HSS-1N helicopter, capable of day and night antisubmarine warfare under instrument flight conditions, was publicly flown at NAS Corpus Christi, Tex., by Sikorsky test pilot Jack Stultz.

27 May The twin jet F4H all-weather interceptor made its first flight at St. Louis, Mo., with R. C. Little, Chief Test Pilot for McDonnell Aircraft at the controls.

28 May *Galveston* (CLG 3), the first Talos missile cruiser, was placed in commission.

16 June The Pacific Missile Range, Point Mugu, Calif., was established under Navy management to provide range support to the Department of Defense and other government agencies in guided missiles, satellite and space vehicle research, development, evaluation, and training. This was the third National Missile Range to be established and the first from which a satellite could be safely fired into polar orbit.

20 June The Advanced Research Projects Agency (ARPA) requested the Naval Research Laboratory to modify its "Minitrack" system, which had been developed under Project Vanguard to produce a capability for detecting, identifying and predicting the orbits of nonradiating objects in space. Out of this request a Navy Space Surveillance System (SPASUR) was developed which began producing useful data in June 1959 and on 2 February 1960 established the existence of an unknown object in orbit and later identified it as the re-entry vehicle of *Discoverer V* which had been assumed lost.

26 June A TF-1 of VR-21 at San Diego, Calif., delivered a J-34 engine to *Yorktown* 300 miles at sea, in the first delivery of an aircraft engine by carrier-on-board delivery (COD).

1 July The Pacific extension of the Continental Air Defense Dewline went into full operation.

1 July Submarine Squadron 14, the first Fleet Ballistic Missile Submarine Squadron, was established under the Atlantic Fleet Submarine Force with Captain Norvell G. Ward, commanding.

1 July The first joint CAA-Navy Radar Air Traffic Control Center (RATCC) went into operation at NAS Miramar, Calif.

The F4H-1, McDonnell Phantom II, in which Cdr. L.E. Flint established a world altitude record of 98,560 ft. 710526

1958—Continued

15 July   While aircraft from *Essex* and *Saratoga* flew cover from long range, and ships of the Sixth Fleet stood by, amphibious units landed 1,800 Marines on the beach near Beirut to support the Lebanese government and to protect American lives. In the days following, land, sea, and air reinforcements were sent to the area and order was maintained without untoward incident.

23–31 July   The feasibility of creating or destroying cloud formations by release of carbon black into the atmosphere was established in tests conducted off the Florida coast by VW-4, commanded by Commander Nicholas Brango, under the overall direction of Dr. Florence W. van Straten of the Naval Weather Service Division, Op-58.

29 July   Commander Malcolm D. Ross and Lieutenant Commander M. Lee Lewis made a balloon ascension to 82,000 feet, carrying a record load of 5,500 pounds and remaining in the air 34½ hours. The primary purpose of the flight was to test and evaluate the sealed cabin system designed to carry an externally mounted telescope for the observation of the atmosphere of Mars and was thus an operational and logistic rehearsal for coming events.

6 August   The Department of Defense Reorgani-zation Act of 1958 was approved. Effective six months from this date, the new law provided a more direct civilian control over military operations through the offices of the Secretary of Defense, the Joint Chiefs of Staff and the respective service secretaries; provided for the establishment of unified or specified combatant commands, to direct the operations of units assigned from the respective services, responsible for the accomplishment of their military mission directly to the President and the Secretary of Defense; and revised the secretarial structure of the Department by reducing the number of Assistant Secretaries of Defense from nine to seven, limiting the number within each service department to three, specifying that one of them be an Assistant Secretary for Financial Management, and revoked the statutory provision for an Assistant Secretary of the Navy for Air. The law also maintained the separate organization of each service under its own Secretary and defined the Navy Department as including Naval Aviation and the U.S. Marine Corps.

19 August   In its first successful flight a Tartar surface-to-air missile, fired at the Naval Ordnance Test Station, China Lake, intercepted an F6F drone.

23 August   An act of Congress created the Federal Aviation Agency and assigned it broad responsibilities involving operation of airways; the regulation of air traffic including military; and the establishment of airports and missile and rocket sites. The Act also provided for military participation in performance of the Agency's functions, for military deviations from air traffic regulations in an emergency, and for appeal to the President of disagreements concerning the location of military airports.

Norton Sound launches surface-to-air Tartar 710498

24 August   After Chinese Communists began heavy shelling of the Kinmen Islands and there were renewed indications of naval activity in Taiwan Straits, units of the Seventh Fleet moved to the Taiwan area to support the Republic of China in a firm stand against aggression. As tension remained high and warlike action continued, ship reinforcements, including aircraft carriers, were sent to the area. By October the tension lessened and the situation became somewhat stabilized.

25 August   Commander Forrest S. Petersen made his first flight in the X-15. Peterson was the Navy's research pilot in the NASA X-15 program. Between this date and 30 January 1962, he made five X-15 flights and logged about forty minutes. The X-15 program was a NASA effort to research the problems associated with controlled, manned aircraft flown at extreme altitude (as much as 250,000 feet) at Mach + speed (as much as 4,093 mph). Petersen's notable area of specialty in the program was exploration of the angle of attack envelope to obtain information on aerodynamic heating and stability and control.

1958—Continued

28 August As the situation in Lebanon was somewhat eased, *Essex* and four destroyers left the Sixth Fleet and transited the Suez Canal en route to join the Seventh Fleet forces off Taiwan, where tension was still high.

29 August The Lockheed Electra, selected in April as the plane most closely meeting requirements for long range antisubmarine warfare, made its first flight in the external configuration of the P3V-1.

1 September An Antisubmarine Warfare Laboratory was established at the Naval Air Development Center, Johnsville, Pa.

5 September A Coordinator, Missile Ranges, was established on the staff of the Deputy Chief of Naval Operations (Air) to serve as his principal advisor on missile range matters, to determine operating requirements, and to coordinate the establishment of policies relating to missile range use.

6 September *Norton Sound,* operating midway between the southern extremities of South America and Africa, fired its third and final atomic tipped rocket to an altitude of about 300 miles. This series of test firings, called Project Argus, had included shots on 27 and 30 August; it was conducted for the Advanced Research Projects Agency. The nuclear explosions produced a visible aurora and a radiation belt around the earth which extended 4,000 miles into space and lasted for several weeks, and provided highly significant scientific and military data.

8 September Lieutenant Richard H. Tabor, MC, wearing a Goodrich lightweight full-pressure suit, completed a 72-hour simulated flight in the pressure chamber at NAS Norfolk, in which he was subjected to altitude conditions as high as 139,000 feet.

15 September Lieutenant William P. Lawrence became the first Naval Aviator to fly at twice the speed of sound in a fleet-type aircraft, F8U-3 Crusader. Lawrence, the project officer, was on an evaluation flight at Edwards Air Force Base, Calif.

16 September In its first launch at sea, the Regulus II was fired from the submarine *Grayback* (SSG 574), off the California coast, and, under radio command, flown inland in a simulated bombardment to Edwards AFB, Calif.

28 September In a preliminary test of equipment to be used in IGY solar eclipse studies, an ASP rocket,

accelerated by a Nike missile booster, was fired from *Point Defiance* (LSD 31) near Puka Puka Island to 800,000 feet, the highest altitude ever reached by a ship-launched rocket.

30 September The final annual report of the National Advisory Committee for Aeronautics was issued by its Chairman, General James H. Doolittle. The forwarding letters pointed out that at the close of business that day, the NACA would cease to exist and that all facilities and employees would be absorbed by the National Aeronautics and Space Administration to be established the following day. Final Navy members were Vice Admiral William V. Davis, Jr., and Rear Admiral Wellington T. Hines.

30 September Operation Deep Freeze IV began as Rear Admiral George J. Dufek, Commander Naval Support Force, Antarctica, and four of his staff arrived at McMurdo Sound aboard an R5D of VX-6.

1 October Project Vanguard was transferred from the Navy to the National Aeronautics and Space Admin-istration. The following 17 February, NASA successfully launched the first full scale Vanguard earth satellite.

8 October FJ-4Bs of VMA-212 and -214 landed at NAS Atsugi, Japan, after a trans-Pacific flight from MCAS Kaneohe, Hawaii, with layovers at Midway and Guam. Designated Operation Cannonball, the flight in two sections of 12 aircraft, refueled from Air Force KB-50 tankers in the vicinity of Wake Island and from Navy AJs near Iwo Jima.

10 October The terms "aerology" and "aerological officer" became obsolete as use of "meteorology" and "meteorological officer" in their place was directed by the Secretary of the Navy.

2 October To provide a highly mobile unit capable of employing Marine Corps helicopter squadrons and combat troops in the fast-landing concept of vertical envelopment, the Commander in Chief, Atlantic Fleet announced the formation of a new amphibious squadron composed of *Boxer,* and four LSDs equipped with helicopter platforms.

10 November The first permanent Marine Aviation Detachment afloat was activated on board *Boxer* to provide supply, maintenance, and flight deck control functions necessary to support the operations of Marine helicopter squadrons and combat troops assigned.

5 December *Observation Island* (EAG 154) equipped with launching, fire control, navigational,

1958—Continued

and other devices called for in the Fleet Ballistic Missile testing program, was commissioned at the Norfolk Naval Shipyard, Va.

5 December A sounding rocket, Hugo, fired from a Navy Terrier-type missile launcher at NASA's pilotless Aircraft Research Station at Wallops Island, Va. to a height of 86 miles, obtained the first extremely high altitude photographs of a frontal cloud formation. Project Hugo was conducted by the Office of Naval Research with assistance from Bureau of Aeronautics, NASA and the U.S. Weather Bureau and utilized a rocket camera package designed and constructed by New Mexico State University.

8 December The first firing of a Sparrow III air-to-air missile by a squadron deployed outside of the continental limits was conducted by VF-64, based aboard *Midway* and equipped with F3Hs. Eleven days later, VF-193, aboard *Bon Homme Richard,* conducted a similar exercise. Both squadrons were deployed with the Seventh Fleet in the western Pacific.

12 December The Secretary of the Navy directed termination of the Regulus II bombardment missile program as a measure necessary to achieve an overall balance in missile weapons systems within available resources.

16 December The Intermediate Range Ballistic Missile (IRBM) portion of the Pacific Missile Range, at Point Mugu, Calif., was inaugurated with the successful firing of a Thor from Vandenburg AFB, Calif.

19 December The Naval Air Missile Test Center, Point Mugu, Calif., was redesignated U.S. Naval Missile Center, Point Mugu, and placed under the military command of Commander, Pacific Missile Range.

28 December Nine ships of an antisubmarine group, including *Yorktown,* were diverted from operations at sea to aid the people of Koniya, Japan, made homeless by a fire which swept through the town and destroyed most of its dwellings. Within 24 hours of the disaster, the group delivered food, medicines, clothing, blankets, and tents to the needy. Men from the group assisted on the scene until Japanese relief agencies could cope with the situation.

1959

21 January Tests at Indianhead, Md., of a new type movable nozzle for the Polaris, demonstrated a successful major advance in the directional control of ballistic missiles.

24 January Major John P. Flynn and Captain Clifford D. Warfield of MAW-2, made a nonstop, nonrefueling flight in A4D Skyhawks from El Toro, Calif., to Cherry Point, N.C., covering 2,082 miles in 4 hours 25 minutes.

27 January The Naval Air Development and Material Command, Johnsville, Pa., was redesignated Naval Air Research and Development Activities Command, and its scope was expanded to include aeronautical research and development activities in the Third Naval District.

5 February In accordance with the provisions of the Defense Reorganization Act of 1958, the Office of Assistant Secretary of the Navy for Air was abolished. Functions of the office were assumed by the Secretary of the Navy pending an appointment to fill the newly created Office of Assistant Secretary for Research and Development.

16–19 February Units of the Naval Air Reserve participated for the first time in a full-scale fleet exercise. Fifty-five crews from selected Naval Air Reserve units and 36 P2V and S2F aircraft took part in an antisubmarine defense exercise on the West Coast with elements of the Pacific Fleet and the Canadian Navy.

24 February The operational deployment of the Talos missile was marked by its first firing at sea by *Galveston* (CL 93) in the vicinity of Roosevelt Roads, P.R.

10 March The Chief of Naval Operations approved transfer of LTA training from the Naval Air Training Command to Commander Naval Air Force, Atlantic and the cessation of the requirement that all LTA students also have HTA training.

11 March The HSS-2 amphibian all-weather antisubmarine warfare helicopter made its first flight piloted by Sikorsky test pilot R. S. Decker.

13 March Aviation Cadet E. R. Clark soloed in a TT-1 Pinto, the first student in Naval Aviation history to solo a jet without previous experience in propeller aircraft.

9 April Four Naval Aviators, Lieutenant Colonel John H. Glenn, USMC, Lieutenant Commander Walter M. Schirra, Lieutenant Commander Alan B. Shepard, Jr., and Lieutenant Malcolm Scott Carpenter, USN, were among the seven men selected as prospective astronauts under Project Mercury—a basic program in the development of space exploration and manned orbital flight.

15–22 April Elements of the Naval Air Reserve took part in Exercise Slamex, conducted by Commander,

1959—Continued

The HSS-2 Sikorsky all-weather ASW helicopter 710394

Antisubmarine Defense Force, Atlantic—their second participation in a fullscale fleet exercise since the organization of the Selected Reserve. Operating from Naval Air Stations at Brunswick, Maine; Quonset Point, and Lakehurst, N.J., with P2V and S2F aircraft, 78 crews from 12 Reserve stations conducted round-the-clock flight operations for seven days, logged 2,800 accident-free flight hours, maintained an aircraft availability of better than 85 percent and reported 75 submarine contacts.

25 April   Bullpup was first deployed overseas when VA-212, equipped with FJ-4B Furies, sailed from Alameda, Calif. on board *Lexington* to join the Seventh Fleet in the western Pacific. The following August, VA-34, equipped with A4Ds sailed from the East Coast aboard *Saratoga* to join the Sixth Fleet, thus extending Bullpup deployment to the Mediterranean.

26 April   HU-2 pilots of the ice breaker *Edisto* (AG 89) homeward bound from the Antarctic, completed

Bullpup air-to-surface missiles are carried by FJ-4B 710127

1959—Continued

10 days of rescue operations in the Montevideo area of Uruguay during which they carried 277 flood victims to safety.

28 April   The office of the Assistant Chief of Naval Operations (Research and Development) was disestablished and replaced by a new Deputy Chief of Naval Operations (Development), with authority and responsibility to execute the research, development, test, and evaluation responsibilities of the Chief of Naval Operations. Vice Admiral John T. Hayward, who was head of the disestablished office, became the new Deputy for Development.

5 May   The Guided Missiles Division was transferred in its entirety from DCNO (Air) to the newly established office of DCNO (Development), and its Director was designated Assistant Chief of Naval Operations (Development).

7 May   The classification of 36 escort carriers, designated CVE, CVU, and CVHE, was changed to AKV, Cargo Ship and Aircraft Ferry. The change was accompanied by a change of hull numbers and marked the end of the escort carrier as a combatant ship of the U.S. Navy.

15 May   The classification of four support carriers (CVS) and seven light carriers (CVL) was changed to Auxiliary Aircraft Transport (AVT). This change removed the CVL designation from the Navy Vessels Register.

15 May   To centralize and strengthen the research and development program, more direct channels for technical control and program guidance over the Operational Development Force were established in the Office of the Chief of Naval Operations. The mission of the force was revised and broadened to include test and evaluation and, reflected the changes, its title was changed to "Operational Test and Evaluation Force."

26 May   A concept of aircraft maintenance, which provided for the assignment of responsibility directly to the unit having custody of the aircraft and for a gradual elimination of FASRONS, was approved for implementation.

27 May   As a reflection of the ever-broadening scope of a unit which owed its beginning to the needs of Naval Aviation, the Naval Weather Service Division, with its functions and personnel, was transferred from DCNO (Air) to DCNO (Fleet Operations and Readiness.)

8 June   The bombardment missile Regulus I, fired by the submarine *Barbero* (SS 317) 100 miles off the Florida coast, delivered a package of Post Office mail ashore at Mayport, Fla., after a 22-minute flight.

16 June   A P4M Mercator, on a routine flight over international waters off Korea, was fired upon by two MiGs. The attack wounded one crewman and so damaged the plane that it made an emergency landing at Miho, Japan, with both starboard engines and some of the flight controls inoperative.

19 June   A ZPG-3W, first of four airships designed for use in air warning patrol and largest nonrigid ever built, was delivered to NAS Lakehurst, N.J.

11 July   The Marine Aviation Cadet program was reinstituted after a lapse of 18 years as a class of 12 MarCads began their preflight training course at NAS Pensacola, Fla.

13 July   The Chief of Naval Operations approved the policy recommendations of the Connolly Board that enunciated organizational responsibilities in the Office of the Chief of Naval Operations. Essentials of the policy were that the Navy would use space to accomplish naval objectives, that it would participate fully in space technology and that astronautics would have high priority in overall research and development.

14 July   A two-stage Nike-Asp solid-propellant rocket fired from Naval Missile Facility, Point Arguello, Calif., was the first of 12 designed to record radiation 150 miles up and also the first ballistic missile fired from the new facility.

15 July   The Aviation Safety Division of DCNO (Air) was changed to a staff office, headed by a coordinator, to act as principal advisor to DCNO (Air) in all matters of air safety and to coordinate the planning and implementation of aviation safety programs throughout the Navy.

22 July   Within DCNO (Air), the Office of the Coordinator, Missile Ranges was disestablished and its functions assigned to a simultaneously established Astronautics Division, charged with assisting DCNO (Air) in performing his overall responsibility for directing the Navy astronautic program, including the formulation of plans, policies, and the determination of requirements.

28 July   The Naval Research Laboratory issued its initial report indicating the feasibility of adapting Omega navigation to aircraft use. This report, prepared by A.

1959—Continued

F. Thornhill of the Radio Division, was a theoretical analysis of the problems involved in designing an airborne receiver. It also described Omega navigation as a phase comparison radio navigation technique utilizing very low frequency radio waves of such range that six appropriately located shore based transmitters would provide world wide coverage.

30 July　The Navy announced that Advanced Training Command units and Reserve squadrons would receive Sidewinder air-to-air missiles. The following week the program was implemented when the Advanced Training Unit 203, at NAAS Kingsville, Tex., began training operations carrying Sidewinders on their F11F jets.

flood-stricken Taiwan during which it airlifted 1,600,540 pounds of cargo and 833 passengers on 898 missions.

25 August　During suitability trials on board *Independence* an A3D piloted by Lieutenant Commander Ed Decker took off at a gross weight of 84,000 pounds—the heaviest aircraft ever to take off from a carrier.

27 August　The ballistic missile Polaris was fired for the first time from a ship at sea by *Observation Island,* off Cape Canaveral, Fla.

1 September　The Bureau of Naval Weapons was formed. The first Chief of the new bureau, Rear Admiral Paul D. Stroop, took the oath of office on 10 September.

Sidewinder air-to-air missiles on F9F-8 Cougar 699330

3 August　The first flight test of the antisubmarine missile Subroc was successfully completed by a launch from a shore installation at NOTS China Lake, Calif.

18 August　An act of Congress established the Bureau of Naval Weapons and provided that the Bureaus of Aeronautics and Ordnance would be abolished upon transfer of all their functions.

20 August　Marine Helicopter Squadron 261, operating from *Thetis Bay,* completed a week of relief operations in

9 September　Navy air and surface units located and recovered an Atlas boosted Mercury capsule in an area 700 miles short of the predicted point of impact in the Atlantic Ocean.

18 September　The Air Warfare Division of DCNO (Air) was disestablished and its functions pertaining to aviation combat readiness were transferred to DCNO (Fleet Operations and Readiness). A new branch was established in the Aviation Plans Division to perform planning requirement functions previously assigned to the disestablished division.

1959—Continued

25 September The last class of LTA students also qualified in HTA, completed training at NAS Glynco, Ga. The last man to receive the dual designation was Ensign John B. Hall.

30 September Airship flights by the Reserves of Naval Air Reserve Training Unit, Lakehurst, N.J., marked the end of the airship training program conducted for 12 years under the Chief of Naval Air Reserve Training.

1 October An R5D Skymaster, piloted by Lieutenant Commander John A. Henning of VX-6, arrived at NAF McMurdo Sound, Antartica, after a flight from Christchurch, New Zealand. The arrival of Rear Admiral David M. Tyree, Commander, Naval Support Force Antartica, on this first flight of the season marked the operational implementation of Operation Deep Freeze 60.

1 October Fleet Air San Diego was established with Rear Admiral Dale Harris in command.

6 October *Kearsarge* left Nagoya, Japan, after relief operations in the wake of a typhoon. Some 6,000 persons were evacuated, 200,000 pounds of supplies and medicines were delivered and over 17,000 typhoid and antibiotic shots were administered to prevent the spread of disease.

2 November A student training flight at NAS Pensacola, Fla., by 2nd Lieutenant David K. Mosher, USMC, and his instructor Lieutenant Commander Rieman A. MacDonell, inaugurated use of the T2J Buckeye in basic training.

30 November The Airship Training Group at NAS Glynco, Ga., was disestablished ending lighter-than-air training in the U.S. Navy.

1 December The Bureaus of Aeronautics and Ordnance were abolished as the Chief of the Bureau of Naval Weapons Rear Admiral Paul D. Stroop relieved their Chiefs, Rear Admirals Robert E. Dixon and Miles H. Hubbard, and the Bureau of Naval Weapons absorbed their functions.

WEPS Chief, Stroop relieves Chiefs BuAer-BuOrd, Dixon and Hubbard 710604

The T2J-1, advanced trainer by North American 1061491

1959—Continued

The XF2Y-1, hydro ski fighter, during taxi trials 708780

An XF4D-1 lands aboard Coral Sea during trials 63014

A3D is launched by Forrestal's steam catapult 1053799

Carrier light attack plane, the Douglas A4D-1 1006922

1959—Continued

The A3J-1, Vigilante, all-weather attack plane, designed to deliver weapons from high or low altitude 1039888

HUP demonstrates air-sea rescue 680099

jet light attack; VA-85 the prop light attack; and VAH-4 the heavy attack. Top individual scorer was 1st Lieutenant G. A. Davis, USMC, of VMF-232 competing in the Day Fighter shoot.

6 December   Commander Lawrence E. Flint, Jr., USN, piloting a McDonnell F4H-1 Phantom II powered by two GE J-79 engines bettered the existing world altitude record by reaching 98,560 feet over Edwards AFB, Calif.

7 December   *Dewey* (DLG 14), the first of a new class of guided missile destroyer leaders designed to employ the air defense missile Terrier III, was commissioned at the Boston Naval Shipyard, Mass.

30 December   The first Fleet Ballistic Missile submarine *George Washington* (SSBN 598) was placed in commission at Groton, Conn., Commander George B. Osborn commanding. The first of nine nuclear powered ballistic missile submarines authorized by Congress, she was launched on 9 June 1959.

4 December   Crack teams from selected fleet squadrons completed four days of competitive gunnery, bombing, and missile firing at MCAAS Yuma, Ariz., in the championship round of the annual weapons meet. VF(AW)-3 took the all weather fighter title in the F4D Class and VF-41 won it in F3H Class. VMF-232 won the day fighter competition; VA-56 the

*Guided missile ship Mississippi fires
Terrier surface-to-air missile 659363*

HSL anitsubmarine helicopter 1053761

Saratoga on duty with the Sixth Fleet in the Mediterranean, departs from August Bay, Sicily 1038502

Coral Sea, Midway and Hancock at NAS Alameda, a huge industrial complex linking shore to sea 1053763

Sinews of the Sixth Fleet, Intrepid and Independence prepare at Norfolk for duty in Mediterranean 1053764

PART 9

The Sixth Decade

1960–1969

The year 1961 marked the golden anniversary of Naval Aviation. It was a year filled with many nostalgic memories of past glories and also a year in which Naval Aviation attained new stature as an effective fighting force. One nuclear-powered and two conventionally powered attack carriers joined the operating forces, perhaps the greatest array of carrier-air might added during peacetime to any fleet in a single year. Before the decade was out, two more attack carriers had been commissioned and another was taking form on the ways. Four new amphibious assault ships, and others built to exploit the unique capabilities of helicopters in vertical assault and replenishment, joined the fleet. New high-performance aircraft went into operation. Vertical and short-takeoff-and-landing aircraft were developed; one went into service. New types of missiles appeared and such old standbys as Sparrows and Sidewinders were given new capabilities. On the other side of the ledger, the blimp and the flying boat, long-familiar figures in Naval Aviation, became victims of the relentless march of technology.

Efforts to conquer space began in earnest as manned orbital flight became a reality and a series of successes culminated in the first manned lunar landing. More than half the nation's astronauts had Navy backgrounds—Naval Aviators made the first American suborbital and orbital flights. Navy flight surgeons joined in the study of physiological effects of space flight. A Navy space surveillance system helped forge the necessary links for a continuous watch on space. Satellites developed by Navy scientists expanded our knowledge of space, and a Navy satellite navigation system gave to all nations an accurate means of traveling the earth's oceans. Carriers or amphibious assault ships, were at sea in both oceans during all orbiting periods to cover an emergency landing, and were always on station to recover the astronauts and their spacecraft upon their return to earth.

Support of the space program was responsible for a number of organizational adjustments within the Navy Department as well as for formation of a Recovery Force command in the fleet. Broader and more basic changes in departmental structure resulted from a series of high-level studies directed toward clarifying lines of authority and responsibility. The bureau system was abolished, and material support was centralized under a strengthened Material Command placed under direct control of the Chief of Naval Operations. New impetus was given to the project manager concept and other changes radiated outward to the operating forces and the shore establishment.

In other respects, the Navy's traditional role in controlling the sea remained unchanged. Revival of the old technique of naval blockade during the Cuban missile crisis found a modern Navy fully capable of performing it. Operating forces were near at hand to give aid to the stricken when hurricanes, typhoons, and earthquakes struck in widely distant points. The round-the-world cruise of a nuclear-powered task force and operations in the Indian Ocean carried the flag into many foreign ports. Crises in Africa, the Middle East, over Berlin and the threat of war in Caribbean nations, found naval forces ready to evacuate American nationals and by their presence to reaffirm the Navy's role in keeping the peace. In Southeast Asia, the nation responded to aggressive actions with retaliatory air strikes. As retaliation developed into war and the nation's commitment increased, the burden of the Navy's air war was carried by aircraft of the Seventh Fleet. The requirement for sustained naval action and support of operations ashore posed major problems for logistic planners and force commanders alike, as the action became progressively heavier despite repeated attempts to halt the fighting and to settle differences at the conference table.

1960

1 January Electronics Countermeasures Squadrons were redesignated Fleet Air Reconnaissance Squadrons, without change of their VQ letter designation.

15 January The Naval Weather Service Division was transferred from the Office of DCNO (Operations & Readiness) to the staff of the Vice Chief of Naval Operations, and an Office of the U.S. Naval Weather

1960—Continued

Service was set up as a field activity under the management control of the Chief of Naval Operations. The responsibilities of the new office included management control of the integrated Fleet Weather Central system and technical direction of meteorological matters within the shore establishment and the operating forces.

26 January The first of two giant unmanned balloons was launched from *Valley Forge,* at sea south of the Virgin Islands. Almost as high as a 50-story building and with a cubic capacity greater than that of the rigid airship *Akron,* the balloons carried 2,500 pounds, including 800 pounds of emulsion sheets to record cosmic-ray activity. The first balloon achieved an altitude of 116,000 feet and remained aloft 8 hours, while the second reached 113,000 feet and made a flight of

Valley Forge prepares to launch Skyhook balloon 1046721

26½ hours. The balloons were tracked by early warning aircraft from the carrier and shore bases, and the instruments were recovered by a destroyer. The project was under the joint sponsorship of the National Science Foundation (NSF) and the Office of Naval Research (NRL).

25 February A Navy R6D transport, carrying members of the Navy Band and a team of antisubmarine specialists, collided with a Brazilian airliner over Sugar Loaf Mountain, Rio de Janeiro. The accident took the lives of all 26 persons on board the airliner and all but 3 of the 38 Navy men on board the R6D.

29 February The Department of Defense announced that two new developments in airborne mine countermeasures had been successfully demonstrated to Navy and Defense officials by the Navy Mine Defense Laboratory and the Navy Air Mine Defense Development Unit at Panama City, Fla. The first was air-portable minesweeping gear that enabled a helicopter to become a self-sufficient aerial minesweeper; the second was equipment for transferring the minesweeping-gear towline from a surface minesweeper to a helicopter, from one helicopter to another, or from a helicopter to a surface minesweeper.

29 February Navy and Marine Corps personnel from Port Lyautey were flown to the Agadir area of Morocco to aid inhabitants of the city razed by a severe earthquake. Before rescue and relief operations were over, a Navy-wide effort brought food and clothing to the stricken people from Reserve and other units as far away as Seattle, Wash.

1 March A ZPG-3W airship of ZW-1 returned to NAS Lakehurst, N.J., from an Air Defense Command barrier patrol over the North Atlantic after having been on station for 49.3 hours and 58 hours in the air. This new record for continuous patrol more than doubled the best time logged by its predecessor, the smaller ZPG-2W.

18 March On the first firing test of Project Hydra, conducted at Naval Missile Center, Point Mugu, a 150-pound rocket was successfully ignited underwater and launched into the air. The test demonstrated the feasibility of launching rockets while floating upright in the water and gave promise of eliminating the cost of launching pad construction and allowing greater freedom in the choice of launching sites.

25 March In the first launch of a guided missile from a nuclear powered submarine, *Halibut* (SSGN 587), fired a Regulus I during training exercises off Oahu, Hawaii.

1960—Continued

26 March Elements of MAW-1 participating in Exercise Blue Star established an operational jet airstrip on the south shore of Taiwan within 72 hours of the amphibious landing. The 3,400-foot strip was surfaced with expeditionary airfield matting, equipped with MOREST arresting gear, portable TACAN equipment, portable mirror landing system, lower control system, and supported by a portable fuel tank farm. A4D aircraft operated from the strip with the assistance of JATO, and F4Ds and F8Us used afterburners for takeoff.

1 April CVSG-53 and -59, each composed of one HS and two VS squadrons, were established at NAS North Island, Calif. This marked the beginning of a reorganization of antisubmarine aviation which called for the formation of nine CVSGs and for the assignment of an additional replacement CVSG and a patrol squadron in each fleet to perform functions paralleling those being carried out by the previously established replacement carrier air groups.

13 April The navigation satellite Transit 1B was placed into orbit by a Thor-Able-Star rocket launched from Cape Canaveral, Fla. Designed by the Applied Physics Laboratory, the satellite emitted a radio signal at a precise frequency. Surface receiving stations used a measurement of the signal's doppler shift to determine their position with high accuracy. Among other experiments performed in connection with this launch,

Ground antenna for the navigation satellite 1105433

an uninstrumented satellite, mounted pickaback, was successfully separated and placed in its own orbit. Thereby, the feasibility of launching multiple satellites with a single vehicle was demonstrated.

19 April The Secretary of the Navy established the Naval Space Surveillance Facility, Dahlgren, Va.

1 May Seventeen Basic Training Groups of the Naval Air Training Command were redesignated training squadrons (VT) and established as separate units, each under a commanding officer.

3 June Test launchings of Bullpup air-to-surface missiles from a Marine Corps HUS-1 helicopter were successfully completed at Naval Air Test Center, Patuxent River, Md.

10 June Seven helicopters of HS-4 from *Yorktown* rescued 53 merchant seamen from the British freighter *Shun Lee* which was breaking up on Pratas Reef, 500 miles northwest of Manila, Philippines. Under storm conditions in the wake of Typhoon Mary, the helicopter took 25 men from the wreck and 28 more from Pratas Island inside the reef.

21 June *Norfolk* (DL 1), from a position off Key West, Fla., fired an antisubmarine rocket missile (ASROC) in a public demonstration, marking the completion of a two-month technical evaluation. This missile featured a rocket-powered airframe carrying a homing torpedo, or alternatively, a depth charge.

22 June The navigation satellite Transit 2A was placed into orbit by a Thor-Able-Star rocket launched from Cape Canaveral, Fla. A Naval Research Laboratory Sol Rad I (Solar radiation) satellite, mounted pickaback, was also placed in orbit. In addition to further developing the Doppler navigation techniques, Transit 2A confirmed the practicability of using satellites for precise geodetic survey, provided critical measurements of the effect of the ionosphere on electromagnetic waves, and provided measurements of high frequency cosmic noise requested by the Canadian Government. The 2A had an operating life of 2½ years.

1 July The first Carrier On-board Delivery squadron, VRC-40 was established at NAS Norfolk, Commander John H. Crawford commanding.

1 July In a successful demonstration of the operating capabilities of a drone helicopter designed for use in antisubmarine warfare from destroyers, an experimental DSN-1 made an at-sea landing aboard *Mitscher* (DL 2), off the coast of Long Island, N.Y. Although the

1960—Continued

drone was manned by a safety pilot, the helicopter was flown by remote control from shore and maneuvered around the ship and into position for a landing before the pilot took command and made the final let down.

1 July To support the operations of the Pacific Missile Range, Calif., a Pacific Missile Range Facility was established at Eniwetok, Marshall Islands.

9 July *Wasp* sailed from Guantanamo Bay for the coast of Africa to support UN attempts to quiet disorders in the newly independent states of the Congo. By the time of her departure in early August, the carrier had supplied a quarter of a million gallons of gasoline in support of the UN airlift.

18 July The Navy terminated the Corvus air-to-surface missile program in order to permit increased emphasis upon other weapons systems offering a wider scope of employment.

20 July A Polaris ballistic missile was launched for the first time from *George Washington* (SSBN 598) while submerged at sea off Cape Canaveral, Fla. The missile broke clear of the water, ignited in the air and streaked more than 1,000 miles toward its target down the Atlantic Missile Range.

21 July The Navy announced that a contract for the development of the Missileer aircraft for launching the Eagle long-range air-to-air guided missile was being issued to the Douglas Aircraft Corporation.

1 August The Naval Air Rocket Test Station, Lake Denmark, N.J., was disestablished and the land was turned over to the Army for incorporation in Picattinny Arsenal. Navy liquid rocket development projects were transferred to other activities, primarily the Naval Ordnance Test Station, China Lake, Calif.; the Naval Propellant Plant, Indian Head, Md.; and the Naval Weapons Laboratory, Dahlgren, Va.

2 August A Naval Research Laboratory Aerobee rocket, instrumented to study the ultraviolet spectrum of the sun, was launched at the White Sands Missile Range, N. Mex., and soared over 90 miles into the atmosphere. As the rocket returned to earth, its nose cone separated from the main section and was parachuted to the ground.

11 August In the first recovery of an object after it had been in orbit, a Navy HRS-3 helicopter operating from *Haiti Victory* (T-AK-238) off the Pacific Missile

Range, Calif., recovered the instrumented capsule discharged by *Discoverer XIII* on its 17th pass around the earth. The capsule was located about 330 miles northwest of Honolulu, Hawaii, by Air Force planes which directed the ship toward the spot. Recovery was made less than three hours after the capsule hit the water.

2 September Captain Holden C. Richardson, Naval Aviator No. 13, died at Bethesda, Md. A man of many attainments, Captain Richardson was the Navy's first engineering test pilot, helped develop the Navy's first catapults, was one of the designers of the NC boats supervised their construction and piloted one of them on the transatlantic attempt, was a pioneer designer of flying boat hulls, and one of the original members of NACA.

5 September An F4H-1 Phantom II, piloted by Lieutenant Colonel Thomas H. Miller, USMC, set a new world record of 500 kilometers over the triangular course at Edwards AFB, Calif., with a speed of 1,216.78 mph.

19 September The NASA Nuclear Emulsion Recovery Vehicle (NERV) was launched from the Naval Missile Facility, Point Arguello, Calif., by an Argo D-8 rocket. The instrumented capsule reached an altitude of 1,260 miles and landed 1,300 miles down range where it was recovered by Navy ships.

25 September An F4H-1 Phantom II, piloted by Commander John F. Davis, averaged 1,390.21 mph for 100 kilometers over a closed circuit course, bettering the existing world record for the distance by more than 200 mph.

20 October The Department of Defense announced establishment, under Navy management, of an Army-Navy-Air Force program to develop the prototype of an operational vertical takeoff and landing aircraft for the purpose of testing its suitability for air transport service.

10 November The Secretary of Defense directed that the Navy Space Surveillance System and the Air Force Space Track System, each performing similar services over different sections of the surveillance network, be placed under the control of the North American Air Defense Command (NORAD) for military functions.

15 November The Polaris Fleet Ballistic Missile Weapon System became operational as *George Washington* (SSBN 598) departed Charleston, S.C., with a load of 16 A-1 tactical missiles.

1960—Continued

17 November At the request of the threatened countries, President Eisenhower ordered a naval patrol of Central American waters to intercept and prevent any Communist-led invasion of Guatemala and Nicaragua from the sea. The patrol was carried out by a carrier and destroyer force which remained in the area until recalled on 7 December.

13 December An A3J Vigilante piloted by Commander Leroy A. Heath, with Lieutenant Henry L. Monroe as bombardier-navigator, climbed to 91,450.8 feet over Edwards AFB, Calif., while carrying a payload of 1,000 kilograms. This performance established a new world altitude record with payload and surpassed the existing record by over four miles.

Cdr. L. A. Heath and Lt. H. L. Monroe flew A3J to above 91,000 feet
NH 69962

19 December Fire broke out on the hangar deck of *Constellation* in the last stages of construction at the New York Naval Shipyard. Fifty civilian workers died in the blaze.

22 December Helicopters of HS-3 and HU-2 from *Valley Forge* rescued 27 men from the oiler SS *Pine Ridge* as she was breaking up in heavy seas 100 miles off Cape Hatteras, N.C.

1961

31 January A Marine Corps helicopter of HMR(L)-262 made an at sea recovery of a Mercury capsule, bearing the chimpanzee Ham, after it had completed a 15-minute flight reaching 155 miles high and 420 miles down range. The capsule was launched by a Redstone rocket from Cape Canaveral, Fla., in a preliminary test for manned space flight.

1 February The Space Surveillance System, with headquarters at the Naval Weapons Laboratory, Dahlgren, Va., was established, Captain David G. Woosley commanding. By this action, the system which had been functioning as an experimental research project since 1959, became an operational command.

21 February The navigation satellite Transit 3B, carrying Lofti (low frequency transionospheric satellite) pickaback, was put into orbit by a Thor-Able-Star rocket, fired from Cape Canaveral, Fla. Improper burning of the second stage and its failure to separate from the payload prevented achievement of the planned orbital path. Despite this, during the Transit's 39 days in orbit, prototype navigational messages containing ephemerides and time signals were inputted into its memory and reported back thereby providing the first complete demonstration of all features of the navigation satellite system.

6 March The Secretary of Defense established Defense policies and responsibilities for development of satellites, antisatellites, space probes and supporting systems. Each Military Department was authorized "to conduct preliminary research to develop new ways of using space technology to perform its assigned function." Although research, development, test and engineering of Department of Defense space development programs and projects were to be the responsibility of the Air Force, provisions were made for granting exceptions thereby leaving the door ajar to the possibility of the Navy developing a unique space capability.

10 April C-130BL Hercules of VX-6, piloted by Commander Loyd E. Newcomer and carrying a double crew of 16 and a special crew of five, landed at Christchurch, New Zealand, completing the emergency evacuation from Byrd Station, Antarctica, of Leonid Kuperov, a Soviet exchange scientist who was suffering from an acute abdominal condition. The round trip flight out of Christchurch was the first to pierce the winter isolation of the Antarctic Continent.

21 April The Office of the Pacific Missile Range Representative, Kaneohe, Hawaii, was redesignated

1961—Continued

and established as the Pacific Missile Range Facility, Hawaiian Area, to serve as the mid-Pacific headquarters for missile and satellite tracking stations located in the Hawaiian and Central Pacific areas.

29 April *Kitty Hawk*, the first of a new class of attack carriers equipped with Terrier anti-air missiles, was commissioned at Philadelphia, Pa., Naval Shipyard, Captain William F. Bringle commanding.

4 May A world record balloon altitude of 113,739.9 feet was reached in a two-place open gondola Stratolab flight by Commander Malcolm D. Ross and Lieutenant Commander Victor A. Prather (MC). Launched from *Antietam* off the mouth of the Mississippi, the balloon, which was the largest ever employed on manned flight, reached its maximum altitude 2 hours and 36 minutes after takeoff 136 miles south of Mobile, Ala. This achievement was marred by the death of Lieutenant Commander Prather, who fell from the sling of the recovery helicopter and died on board the carrier about an hour after being pulled from the water.

5 May Commander Alan B. Shepard, Jr., USN, became the first American to go into space as he completed a flight reaching 116 miles high and 302 miles down range from Cape Canaveral, Fla. His space capsule, *Freedom 7*, was launched by a Redstone rocket and recovered at sea by an HUS-1 helicopter of HMR(L)-262 which transported it and Commander Shepard to *Lake Champlain*.

Kitty Hawk, first carriers of new class 1069225

1961—Continued

Shepard's recovery completes first U.S. manned space flight NH69954

17 May An HSS-2 helicopter flown by Commander Patrick L. Sullivan and Lieutenant Beverly W. Witherspoon, set a new world class speed record of 192.9 mph for 3 kilometers at Bradley Field, Windsor Locks, Conn.

24 May Three F4H Phantom II fighters competing for the Bendix Trophy bettered the existing record for transcontinental flight from Los Angeles to New York. The winning team of Lieutenant Richard F. Gordon, pilot, and Lieutenant (jg) Bobbie R. Young, RIO, averaged 870 mph on the 2,421.4 mile flight and set a new record of 2 hours, 47 minutes.

24 May Commander Patrick L. Sullivan and Lieutenant Beverly W. Witherspoon, flying an HSS-2 helicopter set another new world class speed record with a mark of 174.9 mph over a 100-kilometer course between Milford and Westbrook, Conn.

1 June Ships of the Second Fleet, including *Intrepid, Shangri-La,* and *Randolph,* were ordered to stand by off southern Hispaniola when a general uprising seemed about to follow the assassination of President Trujillo of the Dominican Republic.

21 June The Secretary of the Navy approved plans for terminating the lighter-than-air program that would disestablish all operational units by November, put eight of the 10 remaining airships in storage and deactivate the Overhaul and Repair shop at Lakehurst, N.J.

29 June The navigation satellite Transit 4A was put into a nearly circular orbit at about 500 miles by a Thor-Able-Star rocket fired from Cape Canaveral. Although Greb and Injun satellites riding pickaback did not separate from each other, both operated satisfactorily. Transit 4A was the first space vehicle to be equipped with a nuclear powered generator.

10 July The first NATOPS (Naval Air Training and Operating Procedures Standardization) Manual was promulgated with the distribution of the HSS-1 manual. This manual prescribed standard operating proce-

Sullivan and Witherspoon NH 69959

dures and flight instructions which were peculiar to the HSS-1 and complemented the more technical information contained in the HSS-1 Flight Manual (or handbook). As the NATOPS system developed, NATOPS Flight Manuals were issued which consolidated flight and operating instructions with the handbook information, the first being that for the F9F-8T dated 15 December 1963. Further publications included the NATOPS Manual, which contained generalized instructions covering air operations, and other manuals dealing with such subjects as carrier operations, air refueling, instrument flight, and landing signal officer procedures.

18 July   The first of a series of 10 unguided rocket launches was made at Naval Missile Center, Point Mugu, Calif., to develop an economical research rocket using a standard booster. Called Sparro-air, the rocket was designed and built at Point Mugu by combining two Sparrow air-to-air missile rocket motors. It was launched from an F4D Skyray to an altitude of 64 miles.

21 July   Captain Virgil I. Grissom, USAF, the second American man-in-space, completed a 15 minute, 118 mile high flight 303 miles down the Atlantic Missile Range. Premature blowoff of the hatch cover caused flooding of the capsule and made its recovery impossible, but Grissom was picked up from the water by a second helicopter and delivered safely to *Randolph.*

3 August   The Director of Defense Research and Engineering approved revisions to the tri-Service Vertical Take-Off and Landing (VTOL) program whereby administrative responsibility for a tilting wing aircraft (later developed as the XC-142) was transferred from the Navy to the Air Force but with the three services continuing to share the cost equally.

26 August   *Iwo Jima* was commissioned at Bremerton, Wash., Captain T. D. Harris commanding. First of the amphibious assault ships to be designed and built as such, the new ship was 602 feet overall, of 17,000 tons standard displacement, and equipped to operate a helicopter squadron and an embarked detachment of Marine combat troops in the "vertical envelopment" concept of amphibious assault.

28 August   The Naval Ordnance Test Station, China Lake, Calif., reported on tests of Snakeye I mechanical retardation devices which were being developed to permit low altitude bombing with the MK 80 family of low drag bombs. Four designs of retarders (two made

by Douglas and two by NOTS) had been tested in flight, on the station's rocket powered test sled, or in the wind tunnel. One of Douglas' designs had shown sufficient promise that a contract had been issued for a number of experimental and prototype units.

28 August   Lieutenant Hunt Hardisty, pilot, and Lieutenant Earl H. DeEsch, RIO, flew an F4H Phantom II over the 3-kilometer course at Holloman AFB, N. Mex., and averaged 902.769 mph for a new low altitude world speed record.

11 September   Task Force 135, commanded by Rear Admiral F. J. Brush, composed of *Shangri-La* and *Antietam,* two destroyers, an attack transport and two fleet tugs, was ordered to the Galveston-Freeport area of Texas for disaster relief operations in the wake of Hurricane Carla.

1 October   In response to the call of the president as a result of renewed tension over the divided city of Berlin, units of the Naval Reserve, including five patrol and 13 carrier antisubmarine squadrons of the Naval Air Reserve, reported for active duty.

16 October   The Astronautics Operations Division, Op-54, with mission, functions and personnel, was transferred from the Office of DCNO (Air) to Op-76 of the Office of DCNO (Development).

23 October   The Polaris A-2 was fired from underwater for the first time as *Ethan Allen* (SSBN 608) fired it 1,500 miles down the Atlantic Missile Range.

31 October   Fleet Airship Wing One and ZP-1 and ZP-3, the last operating units of the LTA branch of Naval Aviation, were disestablished at NAS Lakehurst, N.J.

6 November   *Antietam* left British Honduras for Pensacola after 4 days of relief operations following hurricane Hattie. Helicopters, from VT-8 and HMR(L)-264, carried over 57 tons of food, water and medical supplies and transported medical and other relief personnel to the people in Belize, Stann Creek and other points hit by the hurricane.

22 November   Lieutenant Colonel Robert B. Robinson, USMC, flying an F4H-1 Phantom II, set a world speed record, averaging 1606.3 mph in two runs over the 15 to 25-kilometer course at Edwards AFB, Calif.

25 November   The nuclear-powered *Enterprise* was commissioned at Newport News, Va., Captain Vincent P. DePoix commanding.

1961—Continued

*Iwo Jima built
as amphibious
assault ship
NH 69957*

*Hancock ord-
nanceman with
Snakeye bombs
114345*

*Skyburner pilot R. B. Robinson stands alongside F4H
with which he set 1606.3 mph record NH69958*

Enterprise, first nuclear-powered aircraft carrier, with planes spotted on flight deck 1063056

1 December An HSS-2 helicopter, flown by Captain Bruce K. Lloyd and Commander Don J. Roulstone, laid claim to three new world speed records over a course along Long Island Sound between Milford and Westbrook, Conn., with performances of 182.8 mph, 179.5 mph, and 175.3 mph for 100, 500, and 1,000 kilometers, respectively.

5 December Commander George W. Ellis piloted an F4H Phantom II on another world record, surpassing the existing record for altitude sustained in horizontal flight with a height of 66,443.8 feet over Edwards AFB, Calif.

6 December In a joint Navy-Air Force ceremony, new wings were pinned on America's first astronauts, Commander Alan B. Shepard, Jr., USN, and Captain Virgil I. Grissom, USAF. The new designs displayed a

B. Lloyd and E. Roulstone NH 69961

1961—Continued

shooting star superimposed on the traditional aviator wings of the respective services.

8 December The landing field at NAS Anacostia, Washington, D.C., was closed at 0500 hours, all approach procedures were terminated and air traffic facilities ceased operation. Thus, ended the career of a station unique for the variety of its operations and services, and in terms of continuous operations, the fourth oldest in the U.S. Navy.

14 December Installation of the Pilot Landing Aid Television system (PLAT) was completed on *Coral Sea*, the first carrier to have the system installed for operational use. Designed to provide a video tape of every landing, the system was useful for instructional purposes and in the analysis of landing accidents making it a valuable tool in the promotion of safety. By early 1963, all attack carriers had been equipped with PLAT and plans were underway for its installation in antisubmarine carriers and at shore stations.

30 December An HSS-2 helicopter flown by Commander Patrick L. Sullivan and Captain David A. Spurlock, USMC, at Windsor Locks, Conn., bettered its old three-kilometer world record at 199.01 mph.

1962

1 January Three new Fleet Air Commands were established under Commander, Naval Air Force Atlantic, one with headquarters at Keflavik, Iceland, one at Bermuda and the other in the Azores.

17 January First air operations were conducted by *Enterprise* as Commander George Talley made an arrested landing and catapult launch in an F8U Crusader. Although three TF Traders of VR-40 had taken off from her deck on 30 October 1961 to transport VIPs to the mainland after observing sea trials, Commander Talley's flights marked the start of *Enterprise* fleet operations.

23 January The last of 18 F8U-2N Crusaders VMF(AW)-451, arrived at Atsugi, Japan, from MCAS El Toro, Calif., completing the first transpacific flight by a Marine Corps jet fighter squadron. Stops were made at Kaneohe, Hawaii, Wake Island, and Guam and air refueling was provided by GV-1 tankers. The flight was led by Lieutenant Colonel Charles E. Crew, commanding officer of the squadron.

24 January Two Navy F4H Phantom II fighters, designated F-110A by the Air Force, arrived at Langley AFB, Va., for use in orientation courses preliminary to the assignment of Phantom's to units of the Air Force Tactical Air Command.

26 January To overcome deficiencies disclosed during operation of ships equipped with surface-to-air missiles, the Chief of the Bureau of Naval Weapons designated an Assistant Chief for Surface Missile Systems who was to head a special task force and direct all aspects of surface missiles within the Bureau and to act with the Chief of Naval Personnel and the Bureau of Ships on matters involving these Bureaus.

5 February An HSS-2 Sea King became the first helicopter to exceed 200 mph in an officially sanctioned trial. Piloted by Lieutenant R. W. Crafton, USN, and Captain Louis K. Keck, USMC, over a course along the Connecticut shore from Milford to New Haven, the antisubmarine helicopter broke the world record for 15 to 25 kilometers with a speed of 210.65 mph.

L. K. Keck and R.W. Crafton NH69960

1962—Continued

8 February A detachment of VP-11 at NAS Argentia, New Foundland, began ice reconnaissance flights over the Gulf of St. Lawrence to aid in evaluating satellite readings of ice formations transmitted by Tiros 4 which was put into orbit the same day.

20 February Lieutenant Colonel John H. Glenn, USMC, in Mercury spacecraft *Friendship 7,* was launched from Cape Canaveral, Fla., by an Atlas rocket. His three turns about the earth were the first U.S. manned orbital flights. He was recovered some 166 miles east of Grand Turk Island in the Bahamas by *Noa* (DD 841) and then delivered by helicopter to *Randolph.*

Navy men on first astronaut team:

Shepard (NH69953)

Glenn (NH69952)

Carpenter (NH69951)

Schirra made six orbits NASA62MA7-24

Glenn begins orbital flight NASA62MA6-112

1962—Continued

21 February   The F4H-1 Phantom II established new world records for climb to 3,000 and 6,000 meters with times of 34.52 and 48.78 seconds. Lieutenant Commander John W. Young and Commander David M. Longton piloted the plane on its respective record flights at NAS Brunswick, Maine.

1 March   New world climb records to 9,000 and 12,000 meters were established at NAS Brunswick, Maine, when an F4H-1 piloted by Lieutenant Colonel William C. McGraw, USMC, reached those altitudes from a standing start in 61.62 and 77.15 seconds, respectively.

3 March   The F4H-1 continued its assault on time-to-climb records at NAS Brunswick, Maine, as Lieutenant Commander Del W. Nordberg piloted the Phantom II to an altitude of 15,000 meters in 114.54 seconds.

31 March   Lieutenant Commander F. Taylor Brown piloted the F4H-1 Phantom II at NAS Point Mugu, Calif., to a new world time-to-climb record for 20,000 meters with a time of 178.5 seconds.

3 April   Lieutenant Commander John W. Young piloted the F4H-1 to its seventh world time-to-climb record by reaching 25,000 meters in 230.44 seconds at NAS Point Mugu, Calif.

McGraw, Longton, Nordberg and Young set five F4H time-to-climb records at NAS Brunswick 711031

F4H-1 completed time-to-climb record sweep in project high jump 1143454

1962—Continued

12 April The F4H-1 made a clean sweep of world time-to-climb records as Lieutenant Commander Del W. Nordberg piloted a Phantom II at Point Mugu, Calif., on a climb to 30,000 meters in 371.43 seconds. Speed attained was better than 3 miles per minute, straight up.

30 April The Naval Air Research and Development Activities Command was disestablished and responsibility for overall management and coordination of the aeronautical research and development activities in the Third and Fourth Naval Districts was returned to the Bureau of Naval Weapons.

10 May A Sparrow III fired from an F4H-1 scored a direct hit in a head-on attack on a Regulus II missile while both were at supersonic speed. The interception, made in the test range of the Naval Air Missile Center at Point Mugu, Calif., was the first successful head-on attack made by an air-launched weapon on a surface launched guided missile.

22 May The Navy's first space satellite command, the Navy Astronautics Group, was established at the Pacific Missile Range Headquarters, Point Mugu, Calif., under command of Commander James C. Quillen, Jr. In addition to its other duties, the new command was given responsibility for operating the Transit Navigational System being developed by the Navy for the Department of Defense.

24 May Lieutenant Commander M. Scott Carpenter in *Aurora 7* was launched into orbit from Cape Canaveral, Fla., on the second U.S. manned orbital flight. Upon completing three orbits he returned to earth, landing in the Atlantic 200 miles beyond the planned impact area. He was located by a Navy P2V, assisted by para-rescue men, dropped from an Air Force RC-54 and, after almost three hours in the water, picked up by an HSS helicopter from *Intrepid* and returned safely to the carrier. His capsule was retrieved by *John R. Pierce* (DD 753).

29 May Vice Admiral Patrick N. L. Bellinger, USN (Ret.), died in Clifton Forge, Va. His long and distinguished career as Naval Aviator No. 8 began on 26 November 1912 when he reported for flight training at Annapolis, Md., and ended with his retirement 1 October 1947 while serving on the General Board. As one of the pioneers in Naval Aviation, he conducted many experiments, scored a number of "firsts" and made several record flights.

1 June The final report on the titanium alloy sheet rolling program was issued by the Materials Advisory Board of the National Research Council, thereby terminating this program as a formally organized effort. Achievements of the program during the six years included acquiring metallurgical and engineering data for a number of titanium alloys and familiarizing the aerospace industry with their properties and methods of fabrication. High strength, heat-treated sheet alloys developed under this program were soon utilized in a number of aircraft including the A-7, later models of the F-4, the Air Force SR-71 and in deep submergence vehicles used in oceanographic research. The success of this effort also led to the establishment of a similar refractory metal sheet rolling program to develop metals for use at extremely high temperatures.

A-7 attack plane carries bombs and missiles NH69970

26 June The 1,500-mile-range Polaris A-2 missile became operational as *Ethan Allan* (SSBN 608) departed Charleston, S.C. carrying 16 of the A-2 missiles.

29 June A Polaris missile was fired 1,400 miles down range from Cape Canaveral, Fla., carrying the new bullet-nose shape to be used in the A-3 advanced Polaris. The first flight model of the A-3 was successfully fired from the same base on 7 August 1962.

1 July The commands Fleet Air Patuxent and Naval Air Bases, Potomac River Naval Command were established and assigned as additional duty to Commander Naval Air Test Center, Patuxent River, Md.

1 August Squadrons of the Naval Air Reserve that had been called up in October 1961, were released to inactive duty, reducing the strength of the naval air operating forces by 18 squadrons and 3,995 officers and men.

1962—Continued

31 August The passing of an era was marked at NAS Lakehurst, N.J., by the last flight of a Navy airship. The flight also marked the end of a year's service by the two airships kept in operation after the discontinuance of the lighter-than-air program for use as airborne aerodynamics and research laboratories in the development of VTOL/STOL aircraft and ASW search systems. Pilots on the last flight were Commanders Walter D. Ashe and Robert Shannon and the passengers included lighter-than-air stalwarts Vice Admiral Charles E. Rosendahl, USN (Ret.), and Captain Fred N. Klein, USN (Ret.). Many lighter-than-air men from many parts of the country were on hand to observe and to lend a hand in docking the airship after its last flight. This ended a 45-year LTA saga that began with the DN-1, the Navy's first airship.

12 September A Grumman Albatross, UF-2G, piloted by Lieutenant Commander Donald E. Moore, climbed to 29,460 feet over Floyd Bennett Field, N.Y., and set a new world altitude record for amphibians carrying a 1,000 kilogram load. On the same day, Lieutenant Commander Fred A. W. Franke, Jr., piloted the Albatross to a new record for amphibians with a 2,000 kilogram load with a climb to 27,380 feet.

15 September Lieutenant Commander Richard A. Hoffman, piloting a Grumman Albatross, UF-2G, set a new world 5,000 kilometer speed record for amphibians carrying a 1,000 kilogram load with a speed of 151.4 mph on a course from Floyd Bennett Field to Plattsburgh, N.Y., to Dupree, S. Dak., and return to Floyd Bennett Field, N.Y.

17 September Nine pilots selected to join the nation's astronauts were introduced to the public at Houston, Tex. The three Navy men on the new team were: Lieutenant Commander James A. Lovell, Jr., Lieutenant Commander John W. Young, and Lieutenant Charles Conrad, Jr.

18 September A joint Army-Navy-Air Force regulation was issued establishing a uniform system of designating military aircraft similar to that previously in use by the Air Force. By it, all existing aircraft were redesignated using a letter, dash, number, and letter to indicate in that order, the basic mission or type of aircraft, its place in the series of that type, and its place in the series of changes in its basic design. Under the system, the Crusader, formerly designated F8U-2, became the F-8C indicating the third change (C) in the eighth (8) of the fighter (F) series. Provision was also made for indicating status of the aircraft and modifica-

tions of its basic mission by prefix letters. Thus the YF8U-1P became the YRF-8A symbolizing a prototype (Y) of the photoreconnaissance (R) modification of the F-8A aircraft.

3 October *Sigma 7*, piloted by Commander Walter M. Schirra, USN, was launched into orbit by a Mercury-Atlas rocket from Cape Canaveral, Fla., and after nearly six orbits and a flight of over 160,000 miles, landed in the Pacific, 275 miles northeast of Midway Island. Helicopters dropped UDT men near the capsule and it and Commander Schirra were hoisted aboard *Kearsarge*.

Schirra emerges from Mercury 8 on recovery ship Kearsarge NH69950

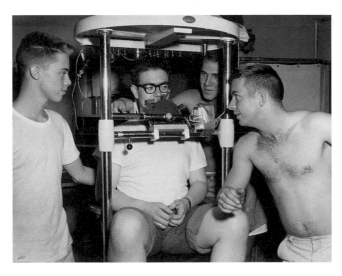

Response to space stimuli is studied 110522

1962—Continued

8 October   To strengthen the air defense of the southeastern United States, VF-41, equipped with F-4B Phantoms, was transferred from NAS Oceana, Va., to NAS Key West, Fla., for duty with the U.S. Air Force in the North American Air Defense Command (NORAD).

16 October   The Chief of Naval Operations directed that a few helicopters be converted to aerial minesweepers for use in a mine countermeasures development and training program and eventual assignment to fleet squadrons. The RH-46A (HRB-1) was initially designated for this conversion but the RH-3A (HSS-2) was later substituted.

17 October   VMA-225 completed a two-way crossing of the Atlantic between MCAS Cherry Point, N.C., and NS Rota, Spain. Lieutenant Colonel Edwin A. Harper, USMC, led the flight of 16 A-4C Skyhawks (A4D) which left Cherry Point on the 8th, flew to Bermuda and directly to Rota. After a brief layover, the flight returned to Cherry Point by way of Lajes in the Azores and Bermuda. Refueling on both east and west flights was provided by 10 Marine KC-130F Hercules tankers of VMGR-252.

19 October   As operational units began moving to patrol stations in Florida to counter the threat posed by missiles and bombers in Cuba, all aircraft and squadrons not required for air defense, reconnaissance and antisubmarine patrol were relocated to prevent overcrowding.

23 October   VFP-62, which had been flying photo reconnaissance over the missile sites in Cuba since the 15th, flew the first low-level photo mission over Cuban territory. For its outstanding accomplishment during this crisis, in the period 15 October–26 November 1962, this squadron was awarded the Navy Unit Commendation which was presented personally by the president on 26 November 1962.

24 October   As the president imposed a blockade of Cuba which he had announced in his TV broadcast two days earlier, ships of the blockading force were in position at sea, *Enterprise, Independence, Essex* and *Randolph,* and shore-based aircraft were in the air, patrolling their assigned sectors. On the same day the service tours of all officers and enlisted men were extended indefinitely.

31 October   The geodetic satellite Anna, developed for the Department of Defense under Bureau of Naval Weapons management, was placed into orbit from Cape Canaveral, Fla. The Anna satellite contained three independent sets of instrumentation to validate geodetic measurements taken by several organizations participating in the Anna worldwide geodetic research and mapping program.

5 November   Two Marine Corps helicopter squadrons began, as additional duty, a transition training program in which some 500 Marine aviators qualified in fixed-wing aircraft would be trained to operate helicopters. The need for the special program arose from the increased proportion of helicopters in the Marine Corps, coupled with an overall shortage of pilots and the inability of the Naval Air Training Command to absorb the additional training load within the time schedule allotted.

20 November   As agreement was reached over the removal of missiles and bombers from Cuba, the naval blockade was discontinued and the ships at sea resumed their normal operations. Next day, the extensions of service ordered in October were cancelled.

30 November   The Bureau of Naval Weapons issued a contract to the Bell Aerosystems Co., for construction and flight test of two VTOL research aircraft with dual tandem-ducted propellers. Thereby the tri-service VTOL program was expanded to include a tilting duct craft to be developed under Navy administration in addition to the tilting wing XC-142 and the tilting engine X-19A both of which were administered by the Air Force.

1 December   Two new commands, Fleet Air Caribbean and Naval Air Bases, Tenth Naval District, were established and assigned as additional duty to Commander, Caribbean Sea Frontier.

14 December   The Naval Air Material Center at NAS Lakehurst, N.J., was renamed Naval Air Engineering Center.

18 December   Transit 5A, a prototype of the Navy's operational navigation satellite, was launched into a polar orbit by a four-stage Blue Scout rocket fired at the Naval Missile Facility, Point Arguello, Calif. The satellite's radio failed after 20 hours in orbit and prevented its utilization for navigation purposes. However, certain secondary experiments were successful.

19 December   An E-2A piloted by Lieutenant Commander Lee M. Ramsey was catapulted off *Enterprise* in the first shipboard test of nose-tow gear designed to replace the catapult bridle and reduce launching intervals. Minutes later the second nose-tow launch was made by an A-6A.

E-2A is used for early warning and to control tactical aircraft 1143451

1963

7–13 January Helicopters from NAS Port Lyautey, Morocco, NS Rota, Spain and *Springfield* (CLG 7) flew rescue and relief missions in the flooded areas of Beth and Sebou Rivers in Morocco. Over 45,000 pounds of food, medicines and emergency supplies were flown in and some 320 marooned persons were lifted to safety.

29 January A Walleye television glide bomb, released from a YA-4B, made a direct impact on its target at the Naval Ordnance Test Station, China Lake, Calif., in the first demonstration of its automatic homing feature.

9 February The Secretary of the Navy approved with minor modification the recommendations of his Advisory Committee on the Review of the Management of the Department of the Navy, commonly known as the Dillon Board for its chairman John H. Dillon. With this approval, he set into motion a series of changes in lines of authority and responsibility that would be implemented during the year, most of which were outlined in a General Order issued on 1 July 1963.

22 February An LC-130F Hercules of VX-6 made the longest flight in Antarctic history covering territory

Walleye, a missile that sees 1112651

1963—Continued

never before seen by man. The plane which was piloted by Commander William H. Everett and carried Rear Admiral James R. Reedy among its passengers, made the 3,470 mile flight from McMurdo Station, south beyond the South Pole to the Shackleton Mountain Range and then southeastward to the pole of inaccessibility and returned to McMurdo in 10 hours and 40 minutes.

25 February The transmitter in the Navy-developed Solar Radiation I satellite was restarted after 22 months of silence. Launched 22 June 1960 with Transit 2A in the first of the pickaback firings, the 42-pound satellite provided detailed data on solar storms for eight months and was turned off on signal from earth on 18 April 1961 when magnetic drag reduced the satellite's spin to a level too low for useful scanning of the sun.

8 March The Department of Defense and National Aeronautics and Space Administration (NASA) announced an agreement establishing working arrangements concerning the nonmilitary applications of the Transit navigation satellite system. Under it NASA assumed responsibility for determining the suitability of Transit equipment for nonmilitary purposes, while the Navy retained its responsibility for overall technical direction and for research and development as necessary to meet and support military requirements.

1 April To bring their title in line with their functions, Replacement Air Groups (RAG) were redesignated Combat Readiness Air Groups (CRAG).

8 May The Air Force announced that two squadrons of A-1E Skyraiders would be added to the 1st Air Commando Group at Hurlburt AFB, Fla. This decision followed field tests of two Skyraiders loaned by the Navy in mid-1962 and led to a further decision, announced by the Secretary of the Air Force in May 1964, that 75 Skyraiders would be sent to Vietnam as replacements for B-26 and T-28 aircraft employed there by the 1st Air Commando Wing.

16 May *Kearsage* recovered Major L. Gordon Cooper, USAF, and his *Faith 7* capsule, 80 miles southeast of Midway, after his 22-orbit flight.

13 June Lieutenant Commanders Randall K. Billings and Robert S. Chew, Jr., of NATC Patuxent River, Md., piloting an F-4A Phantom II and an F-8D Crusader aircraft, made the first fully automatic carrier landings with production equipment on board *Midway* off the California coast. The landings, made "hands off" with

both flight controls and throttles operated automatically by signals from the ship, highlighted almost 10 years of research and development and followed by almost 6 years the first such carrier landing made with test equipment.

20 June The last student training flight in the P-5 Marlin by VT-31 at NAS Corpus Christi, Tex., marked the end of the seaplane in the flight training program. The pilot and instructor was Lieutenant Phillip H. Flood; the student was Ensign Arnold J. Hupp.

29 June FAW-10 was established at NAS Moffett Field, Calif., Captain John B. Honan commanding.

1 July General Order No. 5 set forth new policies and principles governing the organization and administration of the Navy and directed their progressive implementation. It redefined the principal parts of the Navy, adding a Naval Military Support Establishment as a fourth part under a Chief of Naval Material, responsible directly to the Secretary of the Navy and with command responsibilities over the four material bureaus and major project managers and an overall task of providing material support to the operating forces of the Fleet and the Marine Corps.

1 August VMF (AW) squadrons equipped with F-4B aircraft were redesignated VMFA squadrons.

2 August Shortly after midnight, an F-3B Demon piloted by Lieutenant Roger Bellnap, launched the first of a series of five planned space probes designed to measure the ultraviolet radiation of the stars. The probe, a two-stage solid-propellant Sparroair, was launched from a nearly vertical altitude at 30,000 feet over the Pacific Missile Range and reached a peak altitude of 66 miles.

23–24 August In a joint Weather Bureau-Navy project titled Stormfury, a Navy A-3B Skywarrior piloted by Commander John F. Barlow of VAH-11 seeded Hurricane Beulah with silver iodide particles in an experiment to determine whether the energy patterns of large storms could be changed. Although the second day seedings appeared to have some effect, results were considered too indefinite to draw firm conclusions.

6 September Five SH-3A helicopters of HS-9 based at NAS Quonset Point, R.I., rescued 28 workmen from two Texas Towers oilwell platforms shaken by gales and heavy seas off Cape Cod, Mass.

18 September To provide the continuing action necessary for effective management of the inactive air-

1963—Continued

craft inventory, an informal Review Board was established with representation from CNO, the Bureau of Naval Weapons, the Aviation Supply Office, and the storage facility at Litchfield Park, Arizona, to review the inventory at least every six months for the purpose of recommending the retention or disposal of specific models.

18 October The selection of 14 men for a new astronautic team was announced by NASA. Among those chosen were five naval aviators: Lieutenant Commander Richard F. Gordon, Jr., Lieutenant Commander Roger B. Chaffee, Lieutenant Alan L. Bean, Lieutenant Eugene A. Cernan, and Captain Clifton C. Williams, USMC.

25 October Navy ships and aircraft began departing from Port-au-Prince after nearly two weeks of relief operations in Haiti, laid waste by Hurricane Flora. Four Navy ships, including the carrier *Lake Champlain* and the amphibious assault ship *Thetis Bay,* aided by Navy and Marine Corps cargo aircraft from east coast stations, delivered nearly 375 tons of food, clothing and medical supplies donated by relief agencies, and provided other assistance to the stricken populace.

26 October The long range A-3 Polaris missile was launched for the first time from *Andrew Jackson* (SSBN 619), a submerged submarine, cruising about 30 miles off Cape Canaveral, Fla.

8 November During 8, 21 and 22 November, Lieutenant James H. Flatley III, and his crew members, Lieutenant Commander Smokey Stovall and ADJ1 Ed Brennan, made 21 full-stop landings and takeoffs in a C-130F Hercules on board *Forrestal.* From this test the Navy concluded that the C-130 could carry 25,000 pounds of cargo and personnel 2,500 miles and land on a carrier. However, the C-130 was considered too risky for use in routine COD operations.

30 November The Secretary of Defense approved use of funds effective 1 July 1964, for the purpose of placing Naval Aviation Observers in the same pay status as pilots.

2 December The Chief of Naval Material reported to the Secretary of the Navy for duty as his assistant for Naval Material Support and assumed supervision and command of the four material bureaus—Naval Weapons, Ships, Supplies and Accounts, and Yards and Docks.

6 December Transit 5BN-2 was launched into polar orbit by a Thor-Able-Star rocket from Vandenberg AFB, Calif. This, the first navigation satellite to become operational, provided data for use by surface and submarine forces.

20 December Carrier Air Groups (CVG), were redesignated Carrier Air Wings (CVW).

21 December *Saratoga* began receiving weather pictures from the Tiros 8 weather satellite while moored at Mayport, Fla. This was the start of an operational investigation of shipborne readout equipment in which *Saratoga* continued to receive test readings from Tiros, in port and at sea, through May 1964 and from the experimental weather satellite Nimbus in September 1964.

1964

1 January Fleet Air Wings, Pacific was established with Rear Admiral David J. Welsh in command.

1 January The last three seaplane tenders under Commander, Naval Air, Atlantic (COMNAVAIRLANT), *Duxbury Bay, Greenwich Bay* and *Valcour,* were transferred to Cruiser-Destroyer Force Atlantic. Although the employment of these ships as seaplane tenders had been secondary to their use as flagships for Commander, Middle East Force, for several years, this transfer was the final step in the phaseout of patrol seaplanes in the Atlantic Fleet.

15 January The commands Fleet Air Southwest Pacific and Fleet Air Japan were disestablished.

15 January Carrier Divisions 15, 17, and 19 were designated Antisubmarine Warfare Groups 1, 3, and 5 respectively and transferred from Commander, Naval Air, Pacific (COMNAVAIRPAC) to Commander, Antisubmarine Warfare Force, Pacific (COMASWFOR-PAC) for administrative control. Mission of the new groups was to develop antisubmarine carrier group tactics, doctrine and operating procedures including coordination with patrol aircraft operations.

17 February An Office of Antisubmarine Warfare Programs was established under the Chief of Naval Operations to exercise centralized supervision and coordination of all antisubmarine warfare planning, programming and appraising.

28 February A helicopter piloted by Commander Dale W. Fisher of HU-1 made the first landing on the deck of the combat store ship *Mars* (AFS 1) during her

1964—Continued

shakedown cruise off San Diego. Although the concept of vertical replenishment at sea had been discussed and tested as early as 1959 and helicopter platforms had been installed on certain logistics ships since then, commissioning of *Mars* provided the first real opportunity to incorporate the helicopter into the fleet logistic support system.

9 March   A ceremony was held at the David Taylor Model Basin Aerodynamics Laboratory commemorating the 50th anniversary of its establishment. Originally set up at the Washington Navy Yard, the Laboratory was moved to its present location at Carderock, Md., in 1944. Captain Walter S. Diehl, USN (Ret.), an aerodynamics authority of world repute, attended the ceremony and received a citation for his outstanding contributions to the work of the Laboratory.

13 March   Instructions were issued to redesignate all Heavy Attack Squadrons, VAH, upon assignment of RA-5C aircraft, as Reconnaissance Attack Squadrons, RVAH.

23 March   Two Marine helicopter crews of VMO-1 rescued 11 sick, injured and wounded members of a road engineering party that had survived attacks by hostile Indians in the dense jungle of the Amazon basin near Iquitos, Peru. Their helicopters were transferred ashore in the Canal Zone from *Guadalcanal* and were airlifted to Iquitos by a U.S. Air Force C-130.

28 March   Within five hours after a devastating earthquake struck in Alaska, the seaplane tender *Salisbury Sound* was underway from NAS Whidbey Island, Wash., to render assistance and P-3A Orions and C-54 Skymasters, moving up from Moffett Field, Calif., were en route with emergency supplies. For 14 days the ship provided power and heat to the severely damaged Naval Station at Kodiak while its crew served in many capacities to help people on shore.

1 April   The last of 15 astronauts completed a helicopter flight familiarization program at Ellyson Field, as a phase of their training for lunar landings. The training was designed to simulate the operation of the Lunar Excursion Module of Project Apollo. Instituted by the Navy at the request of NASA, the program was scheduled in a series of two-week courses for two students and had been in progress since 12 November 1963.

4 April   Commanded by Rear Admiral Robert B. Moore, the Concord Squadron composed of *Bon Homme Richard, Shelton* (DD 790), *Blue* (DD 744), *Frank Knox* (DD 742), and fleet oiler *Hassayampa* (AO 145) of Seventh Fleet, entered the Indian Ocean from the Pacific and began a six-week cruise which carried it near Iran, the Arabian peninsula, down the African Coast and into many ports along the way for goodwill visits.

23 April   The Chief of Naval Operations broadened the opportunities for Naval Aviators to qualify as helicopter pilots by extending responsibilities for transition training to commands outside the Flight Training Command.

1 May   A P-3A Orion, commanded by Captain Paul L. Ruehrmund of VX-1, returned to NAS Key West,

P-3, newest antisubmarine patrol aircraft NH 69967

1964—Continued

Fla., completing an 18-day, 26,550 nautical mile flight which, in several stages, carried it around the world. On the over-water leg of the flight, the plane dropped explosive sound signals to assist Naval Ordnance Laboratory scientists studying the acoustical properties of the sea as a medium for sound transmission over long distances.

7 May   The Chief of Naval Operations informed the Chief of Naval Personnel of an agreement by which the U.S. Air Force and U.S. Coast Guard would train Navy pilots in the techniques of operating HU-16 seaplanes in Search and Rescue and requested its implementation.

24 June   PHC Clara B. Johnson of VU-7 was designated an aerial photographer and became the first WAVE with the right to wear the wings of an aircrewman.

26 June   An LC-130F Hercules, commanded by Lieutenant Robert V. Mayer of VX-6, completed a round-trip flight from Christchurch, New Zealand, to Antarctica in an emergency evacuation of Petty Officer B. L. McMullen, critically injured in a fall. Two planes, with teams of medical specialists on board, flew from NAS Quonset Point, R.I., to Christchurch where one plane stood by while the other undertook the hazardous flight.

29 June   A new specification for the color of naval aircraft was issued which changed the color scheme for patrol aircraft assigned to antisubmarine work to gull gray with white upper fuselage.

1 July   The Pacific Missile Range facilities at Point Arguello, Calif., and on Kwajalein Atoll were transferred from Navy to Air Force and Army command, respectively.

2 August   North Vietnam motor torpedo boats that attacked *Maddox* (DD 731) patrolling international waters in the Gulf of Tonkin, were damaged and driven off by ships gunfire and rocket and strafing attacks by aircraft from *Ticonderoga*.

5 August   On orders from the president to take offensive action toward preserving our right to operate in international waters, aircraft from Seventh Fleet carriers *Constellation* and *Ticonderoga* attacked motor torpedo boats and their supporting facilities at five locations along the North Vietnam coast. In 64 attack sorties against the concentrations, these aircraft sank or seriously damaged 25 boats and destroyed a major part of their petroleum stores and storage facilities.

15 August   The president announced existence of a program to develop a counterinsurgency (COIN) airplane designed to perform a variety of missions in peace and war. The Navy Department, as the designated Department of Defense development agency, selected North American Aviation Co., as the contractor for construction of the prototype, later assigned for designation OV-1OA and the name Bronco.

29 August   *Boxer* and two LSDs arrived off the coast of Hispaniola to give medical aid and helicopter evacuation services to people in areas of Haiti and the Dominican Republic badly damaged by Hurricane Cleo.

28 September   The Polaris A-3, Fleet Ballistic Missile, became operational as *Daniel Webster* (SSBN 626) departed Charleston, S.C., with a full load of the new missiles.

30 September   Three ski-equipped LC-130 Hercules aircraft of VX-6 took off from Melbourne, Australia; Christchurch, New Zealand and Puntan Arenas, Chile, respectively, and made flights to Antarctica, landing on Williams Field at McMurdo Sound. The flight from Melbourne, the first in history from Australia to Antarctica, passed over the South Pole to drop a 50-pound sack of mail to the wintering-over party, then landed at Byrd Station before proceeding to McMurdo Sound. The arrival of Rear Admiral James R. Reedy, Commander Naval Support Forces, Antarctica, on this flight, on 1 October, marked the official opening of Operation Deep Freeze '65.

1 October   *Franklin* (AVT 8), formerly CVS, CVA and CV 13, was stricken from the Navy Register—first of the World War II Essex Class carriers to be labeled unfit for further service.

3 October   Operation Sea Orbit ended as *Enterprise* and *Long Beach* (CGN 9) arrived at Norfolk and *Bainbridge* (CGN 7) reached Charleston, S.C. This task force, the world's first composed entirely of nuclear powered ships, left Gibraltar on 31 July, sailed down the Atlantic and around Africa, across the Indian and Pacific Oceans, and around Cape Horn, completing a 65 day and 30,216 nautical mile round-the-world cruise without taking on either fuel or provisions.

17 November   Helicopters of HMM-162 from *Princeton,* began delivery of 1,300 tons of food and clothing to people in the inland areas of South Vietnam flooded by heavy rains following a typhoon.

1964—Continued

26 November Nine helicopters of HU-2 and four from NAS Lakehurst, N.J., assisted the Coast Guard in the rescue of 17 men from the Norwegian tanker *Stolt Dagali* cut in two by collision with the Israeli liner *Shalom* off the New Jersey coast.

17 December Commander Theodore G. Ellyson, Naval Aviator No. 1, was enshrined in the National Aviation Hall of Fame at Dayton, Ohio—first naval officer to be so honored.

1965

1 January In accordance with the provision of General Orders prescribing the organization and administration of the Navy, all Naval Air Bases Commands were disestablished.

12 January The Department of Defense announced that the Transit all-weather navigation satellite system had been in operational use since July 1964. This system, when completely developed, would consist of four satellites in polar orbit and would provide a ship at the equator with a navigational fix once an hour.

19 January *Lake Champlain* recovered an unmanned Project Gemini space capsule launched from Cape Kennedy, Fla., in a suborbital flight 1,879 miles down the Atlantic Missile Range and within 23 miles of the carrier.

7 February In retaliation for a damaging Viet Cong attack on installations around Pleiku, a fighter-bomber strike, launched from the carriers *Ranger, Coral Sea,* and *Hancock,* blasted the military barracks and staging areas near Dong Hoi in the southern sector of North Vietnam.

8 February The title and designation of Naval Aviation Observers, 135X, were changed to Naval Flight Officers, 132X, to be effective 1 May.

6 March A Sikorsky SH-3A helicopter, piloted by Commander James R. Williford, took off from *Hornet* berthed at North Island, Calif., and 15 hours and 51 minutes later landed on *Franklin D. Roosevelt* at sea off Mayport, Fla. The flight surpassed the existing distance record for helicopters by more than 700 miles.

8 March With surface and air units of Seventh Fleet standing by, 3,500 Marines, including a helicopter squadron and supporting units, landed without opposition at Da Nang, an air base near the northern border of South Vietnam.

12 March Four enlisted men completed 24 days of living in a rotating room in a test conducted at Pensacola, Fla., by the Naval School of Aviation Medicine to determine the spinning rate men can endure without discomfort and to check out procedures for conditioning men for space flight.

23 March Astronauts Virgil Grissom and John Young landed their *Gemini 3* spacecraft east of Bermuda roughly 50 miles from the intended splash point. The craft was spotted by Coast Guard helicopter about 20 minutes after the landing and within an hour the two astronauts were picked up by helicopter and delivered to *Intrepid*.

26 March Seventh Fleet air units began their participation in Operation Rolling Thunder, a systematic bombing of military targets throughout North Vietnam waged by land and ship based air, as pilots from the carriers *Coral Sea* and *Hancock* launched strikes on island and coastal radar stations in the vicinity of Vinh Son.

15 April Carrier pilots of Seventh Fleet joined the battle in South Vietnam with a strike against Viet Cong positions near Black Virgin Mountain. Their attack was so successful that future in-country missions were assigned to Seventh Fleet, and to carry them out, one carrier was normally operated at what was called Dixie Station off the coast of South Vietnam. Dixie operations continued from 20 May 1965 to 4 August 1966 when land-based air was well enough established to handle most of the required air attacks in that area.

19 April Six Navy and two Marine Corps aviators emerged from two sealed chambers at the Aerospace Crew Equipment Laboratory, Philadelphia, Pa., after a 34-day test to learn the physical effect of prolonged stays in confined quarters and a low-pressure pure oxygen atmosphere.

27 April As revolt in the Dominican Republic threatened the safety of American nationals, *Boxer* sent her Marines ashore while embarked helicopter pilots of HMM-264 began an airlift in which over 1,000 men, women and children were evacuated to ships of the naval task force standing by.

10 May Seaspar, a surface-to-air version of the Sparrow III air-to-air missile, was fired in the Pacific Missile Range test area from *Tioga County* (LST 1158) on its first shipboard test.

12 May Some 1,400 men of the 3rd Battalion, 3rd Marines landed at Chu Lai, South Vietnam, from *Iwo Jima* and an APA and LSD.

1965—Continued

18 May Members of the Naval Air Reserve began a volunteer airlift supporting operations in Vietnam. On weekend and other training flights from their home stations to the west coast, Hawaii, and Southeast Asia, these pilots and crews, flying C-54 and C-118 aircraft of the Air Reserve, carried key personnel and urgently needed cargo to the combat zone, logging over 19,000 flight hours in the first 18 months of the operation.

1 June The new Marine Corps expeditionary airfield at Chu Lai, South Vietnam, 52 miles south of the major base at DaNang, became operational as the first aircraft arrived and the first combat missions took off from the strip.

7 June The *Gemini 4* spacecraft of J. A. McDivitt and E. H. White splashed down in the Atlantic about 40 miles off target after a four-day flight. Minutes later Navy frogmen dropped from a helicopter to attach the flotation collar and in less than an hour after landing the astronauts were aboard *Wasp* which had kept position for possible landings in each orbit since blastoff on 4 June.

17 June While escorting a strike on the barracks at Gen Phu, North Vietnam, Commander Louis C. Page and Lieutenant Jack E. D. Batson, flying F-4B Phantoms of VF-21 and *Midway,* intercepted four MiG-17s and each shot down one, scoring the first U.S. victories over MiGs in Vietnam.

17 June *Independence* with CVW-7 on board, arrived at Subic Bay for duty with Seventh Fleet. Her arrival, from the Atlantic Fleet around the tip of Africa, added a fifth attack carrier to naval forces operating off Vietnam.

Independence with fighters on forward deck 1047141

1965—Continued

23 June   In an unusual mission for ships of her type, the seaplane tender *Currituck* carried out a shore bombardment of Viet Cong positions in the Mekong Delta area of South Vietnam.

30 June   Seven years after its establishment, the Pacific extension of Dewline ceased to operate and Barrier Force, Pacific and Airborne Early Warning Barrier Squadron, Pacific went out of existence.

1 July   FAW-8 was established at NAS Moffett Field, Calif., Captain David C. Kendrick commanding.

1 July   The Navy's first Oceanographic Air Survey Unit (OASU) was established at NAS Patuxent River, Md., Commander Harold R. Hutchinson commanding. Tasks assigned included aerial ice reconnaissance in the North Atlantic and Polar areas and aerial operations concerned with worldwide magnetic collection and observation, known as Project Magnet.

1 July   Helicopter Utility Squadrons (HU) were redesignated Helicopter Combat Support Squadrons (HC) and Utility Squadrons (VU) were redesignated Fleet Composite Squadrons (VC) as more representative of their functions and composition.

14 July   *Yorktown* left San Diego for Subic Bay on a turnaround trip to deliver urgently needed materials to forces operating in and around South Vietnam.

13 August   To achieve the increase in personnel necessary to carry out missions created by the requirements of a deteriorating international situation, a temporary policy was established which deferred the separation of officers and enlisted men from active service.

26 August   The barrier air patrol over the North Atlantic ended as an EC-121J Warning Star of VW-11 landed at Keflavik, Iceland. The landing also signaled a change in which a new and advanced radar system took over from the aircraft and men of Naval Aviation who for the past 10 years had maintained constant vigil over the northern approaches to the American continent.

29 August   *Gemini 5* splashed down into the Atlantic 90 miles off target after a record breaking eight-day space flight, and 45 minutes later Navy frogmen helped astronauts Gordon Cooper and Charles Conrad out of their space capsule and aboard a helicopter for flight to the prime recovery ship *Lake Champlain*.

31 August   President Johnson approved a policy on the promotion and decoration of astronauts by which each military astronaut would receive, upon the completion of his first space flight, a one grade promotion up to and including colonel in the Air Force and Marine Corps and captain in the Navy, and Gemini astronauts completing a successful space flight would receive the NASA Medal for Exceptional Service (or cluster).

1 September   In accord with the provision of an act of Congress, the Secretary of the Navy authorized additional pay to flight deck personnel for duty performed in the hazardous environment of flight operations on the decks of attack and antisubmarine carriers.

11 September   Lead elements of the First Cavalry Division, U.S. Army, with their helicopter and light observation aircraft, went ashore at Qui Nhon, South Vietnam, from *Boxer* in which they had been transported from Mayport, Fla., by way of the Suez Canal.

24 September   As the accelerated frequency of manned space flights placed increasing demands upon Navy recovery capabilities, a flag officer was designated CNO Representative and Navy Deputy to the DOD Manager for Manned Space Flight Support Operations and given additional duty as Commander, Manned Space Recovery Force, Atlantic. His assigned mission was to coordinate and consolidate operational requirements with all commands providing Navy resources in support of manned space flights.

14 October   The A-1, 1,200 nautical mile range, Polaris missile was retired from duty with the return of *Abraham Lincoln* (SSBN 602) to the United States for overhaul and refitting with the 2,500 nautical mile range Polaris A-3.

15 October   To expand Pacific airlift capabilities, VR-22 was moved from its base at NAS Norfolk to the west coast at NAS Moffett Field, Calif.

2 December   The nuclear powered *Enterprise,* carrying the largest air wing (CVW-9) deployed to the western Pacific to that time, joined the action off Vietnam with strikes on Viet Cong installations near Bien Hoa.

16 December   *Wasp* recovered Captain Walter M. Schirra and Major Thomas P. Stafford, USAF, in their *Gemini 6A* spacecraft one hour after their landing in the western Atlantic about 300 miles north of Puerto Rico. The astronauts had completed a one-day flight

1965—Continued

during which they made rendezvous with *Gemini 7* and kept station with it for three and one-half orbits.

18 December   Helicopters of HS-11 recovered Lieutenant Colonel Frank Borman, USAF, and Commander James A. Lovell, in the western Atlantic about 250 miles north of Grand Turk Island and delivered them to *Wasp*. During their 14-day flight in *Gemini 7,* the astronauts carried out many experiments in space, including station keeping with *Gemini 6A,* and established a new duration record for manned space flight.

20 December   The Secretary of the Navy established a Director of Naval Laboratories on the staff of the Assistant Secretary for Research and Development and directed that he also serve as Director of Laboratory Programs in the Office of Naval Material. Subsequently, administrative responsibility for laboratories was transferred to this dual office while test and evaluation facilities, such as Naval Air Test Center, Naval Missile Center, and Naval Air Engineering Center were placed under the command of the Naval Air Systems Command.

1966

20 January   A contract for production of the Walleye television homing glide bomb was issued to the Martin Marietta Corporation.

26 February   The first unmanned spacecraft of the Apollo series, fired into suborbital flight by a Saturn 1B rocket from Cape Kennedy, Fla., was recovered in the southeast Atlantic 200 miles east of Ascension Island by a helicopter from *Boxer*.

1 March   The Naval Air Transport Wing, Atlantic was disestablished.

2 March   *Constellation* began receiving weather data from the operational weather satellite Essa 2. Her equipment was the second experimental shipboard installation of receivers capable of presenting a picture of major weather patterns taken from space and its evaluation was a continuation of that begun on board *Saratoga* with the satellites Tiros 8 and Nimbus in late 1963 and 1964.

16 March   *Leonard F. Mason* (DD 852) recovered astronauts Neil A. Armstrong and David R. Scott in *Gemini 8,* who after completing the first space docking with another satellite, experienced control difficul-

ties which necessitated an emergency landing in the Pacific 500 miles east of Okinawa.

17 March   The X-22A VTOL research aircraft made its first flight at Buffalo, N.Y.

X-22A, for vertical takeoff and landing 1111306

31 March   Flight test of a Helicopter Capsule Escape System, involving recovery of personnel by separation of the inhabited section of the fuselage from the helicopter proper, demonstrated the feasibility of its use during inflight emergencies. The test was conducted at NAF El Centro, Calif., with an H-25 helicopter.

4 April   NASA announced selection of 19 men for the Astronaut Team, among whom were 11 who had qualified as Naval Aviators including John S. Bull, Ronald E. Evans, Thomas K. Mattingly, Bruce McCandless II, Edgar D. Mitchell and Paul J. Weitz on active duty in the Navy and Gerald P. Carr and Jack R. Lousma on active duty in the Marine Corps. Don L. Lind (USNR), and Vance D. Brand and Fred W. Haise, Jr. (former Marine pilots), were selected as civilians.

5 April   The Secretary of Defense approved a joint request from the Secretaries of the Navy and Air Force that Navy air transport units be withdrawn from the Military Airlift Command. The withdrawal was accomplished by disestablishing Navy units during the first half of 1967.

10 April   Two Navy enlisted men, and a Medical Officer and a civilian electronics technician acting as observers, began spinning at 4 rpm in the Coriolis Acceleration Platform of the Naval Aerospace Medical Institute at NAS Pensacola, Fla. It was the beginning of a 4-day test to determine the ability of humans to adapt to a new form of rotation such as may be used in space stations to produce artificial gravity.

1966—Continued

18 April In a reorganization of Naval Air Basic Training Command schools at NAS Pensacola, Fla., the Naval Pre-Flight School was redesignated Naval Aviation Schools Command and six existing schools became departments of the new command. The six schools were: Aviation Officer Candidate, Flight Preparation, Survival Training, Instructor Training, Indoctrination for Naval Academy and NROTC Midshipman, and Aviation Officer Indoctrination.

1 May A reorganization of the Navy Department became effective which placed material, medical, and personnel supporting organizations under command of the Chief of Naval Operations, abolished the Naval Material Support Establishment and its component bureaus and in their place set up the Naval Material Command, composed of six functional, or systems, commands titled: Air, Ships, Electronics, Ordnance, Supply, and Facilities Engineering.

11 May The Commanding Officer of MAG-12 piloted an A-4 Skyhawk on a catapult launch from the Marine Expeditionary Airfield at Chu Lai, Vietnam. It was the first combat use of the new land based catapult capable of launching fully loaded tactical aircraft from runways less than 3,000 feet long.

15 May *Intrepid,* operating as an attack carrier although still classified as an antisubmarine carrier (CVS), joined Seventh Fleet carriers in action off Vietnam. On the first day, her air wing (CVW-10), composed entirely of attack squadrons, flew 97 combat sorties against Viet Cong troop concentrations and supply storage areas around Saigon.

18 May The XC-142A tri-service V/STOL transport made its first carrier takeoffs and landings during tests conducted aboard *Bennington* at sea off San Diego. The tests, including 44 short and six vertical takeoffs, were made with wind over the deck varying from zero to 32 knots. Lieutenant Roger L. Rich, Jr., along with other Navy, Marine, and Army pilots took turns at the controls.

6 June *Wasp* recovered *Gemini 9* astronauts Thomas P. Stafford and Eugene A. Cernan 345 miles east of Cape Kennedy after their 72-hour space flight on which they made successful rendezvous with another satellite and Cernan spent well over an hour outside the spacecraft. The astronauts elected to remain in their space craft during the recovery and were hoisted aboard the carrier.

7 June A C-130 Hercules, piloted by Commander Marion Morris of VX-6, returned to Christchurch, New Zealand, after a flight to McMurdo Station, Antarctica, to evacuate Robert L. Mayfield, UT-2, who had been critically injured in a fall. It was the third emergency air evacuation from Antarctica during the winter night.

16 June An attack by A-4 Skyhawks and F-8 Crusaders from *Hancock* in an area 24 miles west of Thanh Hoa, was the first carrier strike on petroleum facilities since 1964 and the beginning of what became a systematic effort to destroy the petroleum storage system of North Vietnam.

1 July Three North Vietnam torpedo boats came out to attack *Coontz* (DLG 9) and *Rogers* (DD 876) operating about 40 miles off shore on search and rescue missions. Aircraft from *Constellation* and *Hancock* made short work of the attackers, sinking all three with bombs, rockets, and 20mm cannon fire. After the attack, *Coontz* pulled 19 survivors from the water.

19 July The Chief of Naval Operations established the LHA program to bring into being a new concept of an amphibious assault ship. Plans developed through preliminary study envisioned a large multipurpose ship with a flight deck for helicopters, a wet boat well for landing craft, a troop carrying capacity of an LPH and a cargo capacity nearly that of an AKA.

21 July A helicopter assigned to HS-3 from *Guadalcanal* recovered astronauts John W. Young and Michael Collins after their landing in the Atlantic 460 miles east of Cape Kennedy, Fla. The astronauts had

The XC-142A vertical takeoff and landing aircraft during trials aboard Bennington NH 69968

1966—Continued

Helicopters from Wasp approach astronauts E.A. Cernan and T. P. Stafford at end of Gemini 9A flight NASA66H725

Guadalcanal, amphibious assault ship, crew formation recalls its Gemini recovery role NH 69955

1966—Continued

*Recovery of Collins
and Young
NASA66H1030*

spent over 70 hours in space, had docked with an Agena satellite and Collins had made a space stand and a space walk.

25 August *Hornet* recovered the second unmanned space craft of the Apollo series after its suborbital flight about 500 miles southeast of Wake Island.

3 September Naval Air Test Center pilots completed a 2 day shipboard suitability trial of the RH-3A helicopter minesweeper aboard *Ozark* (MCS 2) on the open sea. This trial completed the Center's evaluation of the helicopter for the minesweeper role. The following year the ship and a helicopter detachment from newly established HC-6 were utilized in a mine countermeasures development and training program in the Atlantic Fleet and a detachment from HC-7 was prepared for training and operation on *Catskill* (MCS 1) in the Pacific.

8 September An A-3A Skywarrior, equipped with a Phoenix missile and its control system, located, locked on at long range and launched the missile scoring an intercept on a jet target drone. The event occurred over the Navy Pacific Missile Range near San Nicolas Island. Although the Phoenix had been launched successfully before, this was the first full scale test employing all functions of the missile control system.

15 September A helicopter assigned to HS-3 from *Guam* recovered *Gemini 11* astronauts Charles Conrad and Richard Gordon at sea 700 miles off Cape Kennedy, Fla. The recovery marked the end of a three-day mission in space in which the astronauts completed several dockings with an Agena satellite, established a new altitude record of over 850 miles and Gordon made a walk in space.

16 September Helicopters from *Oriskany* rescued the entire crew of 44 men from the British merchant ship *August Moon* as she was breaking up in heavy seas on Pratas Reef 175 miles southeast of Hong Kong.

26 October Fire broke out on the hangar deck of *Oriskany* while operating in the South China Sea off Vietnam, resulting in the loss of 44 officers and men. Heroic efforts by the crew against great odds prevented greater loss of life and damage to the ship.

8 November The Chief of Naval Operations approved a reorganization of the Naval Air Reserve involving the disestablishment of all Air Wing Staffs and establishing in place of each an administrative unit titled Naval Air Reserve Staff and a training unit titled Naval Air Reserve Division (Fleet Air).

15 November *Wasp* made the last recovery of the Gemini program, picking up astronauts James A.

1966—Continued

Lovell, Jr., and Edwin A. Aldrin, Jr., and their spacecraft 600 miles southeast of Cape Kennedy. The astronauts were lifted from their spacecraft to the ship by an SH-3A helicopter of HS-11.

1967

26 February The first application of aerial mining in Vietnam occurred when seven A-6As, led by Commander Arthur H. Barie of VA-35's Black Panthers, planted minefields in the mouths of the Song Ca and Song Giang rivers. This operation was aimed at stopping coastal barges from moving supplies into immediate areas.

1 April The status of Overhaul and Repair Departments at six Navy and one Marine Corps air station was changed to that of separate commands, each titled Naval Air Rework Facility.

12 April A wing insignia for Aviation Experimental Psychologists and Aviation Physiologists was approved. The new design was similar to Flight Surgeons Wings except for use of the gold oak leaf of the Medical Service Corps in place of the leaf with acorn of the Medical Corps.

24 April Seventh Fleet carrier aircraft launched their first strikes on MiG bases in North Vietnam with an attack on Kep Airfield, 37 miles northeast of Hanoi. The attack was delivered by A-6 Intruders and A-4 Skyhawks from *Kitty Hawk* and was followed-up by another A-6 attack the same night. While providing cover for the bombers during the first attack, Lieutenant Commander Charles E. Southwick and Lieutenant Hugh Wisely, flying F-4B Phantom IIs of VF-114, each were credited with a probable MiG-17 kill in aerial combat.

15 May The Chief of Naval Operations directed that a new department titled Aircraft Intermediate Maintenance (AIMD) be established in all operating carriers except the one operating with the Naval Air Training Command. The function of the new department was to assume responsibility for maintenance afloat formerly held by Air Wing and Air Group commanders.

19 May Two A-7A Corsair II aircraft, piloted by Commander Charles Fritz and Captain Alex Gillespie, USMC, made a trans-Atlantic crossing from NAS Patuxent River, Md., to Evreux, France, establishing an unofficial record for long distance, nonrefueled flight by light attack jet aircraft. Distance flown was 3,327 nautical miles; time of flight was seven hours and one minute.

24 May The seaplane tender *Currituck* returned to North Island, Calif., after completing a 10-month tour in the western Pacific and the last combat tour for ships of her type.

Electronics enables A-6 to bomb accurately through clouds 1143448

1967—Continued

8 June Aircraft launched from *America* to aid *Liberty* (AGTR 5) as she was under attack by Israeli aircraft and motor torpedo boats, were called back before reaching their destination when a message of regret and apology was received from Tel Aviv. Commander, Sixth Fleet, then sent medical teams on board destroyers to the scene to aid in caring for the wounded.

18 June The first scheduled winter flight to Antarctica was successfully completed when a Navy LC-130F of VX-6 flying from Christchurch, New Zealand, landed at Williams Field, seven miles from McMurdo Station. Although earlier winter flights had been made to Antarctica as a result of medical emergencies, this was the first planned flight.

30 June Naval Air Transport Wing, Pacific, was disestablished at NAS Moffett Field, Calif.

1 July DODGE satellite was placed into orbit by a Titan III-C fired from Cape Kennedy, Fla. DODGE (an acronym for Department of Defense Gravity Experiment) was developed by the Applied Physics Laboratory under management of the Naval Air Systems Command to provide a three-axis passive stabilization system that could be used on satellites orbiting the earth at synchronous altitudes. In addition to demonstrating the basic feasibility of this form of stabilization, Dodge carried color television cameras and on 25 July made the first full-disc color photograph of the earth.

1 July The title of the Office of the Naval Weather Service was changed to Naval Weather Service Command and its mission modified to ensure fulfillment of Navy meteorological requirements and the Department of Defense requirements for oceanographic analyses; and to provide technical guidance in meteorological matters. On the same date, the Naval Weather Service Division, Op-09B7, was disestablished and its functions assigned to the new command.

1 July Naval Air Propulsion Test Center, with headquarters at Trenton, N.J., was established by merger of the Naval Air Turbine Test Station, Trenton, N.J., and the Aeronautical Engine Laboratory of NAEC Philadelphia, Pa.

19 July Air Transport Squadron Three, last Navy component of the Military Airlift Command, was disestablished at McGuire AFB, N.J., ending an interservice partnership that began in 1948 when Navy and Air Force transport squadrons combined to form the Military Air Transport Service.

29 July Fire broke out on the flight deck of *Forrestal* as aircraft were being readied for launch over Vietnam. Flames engulfed the fantail and spread below decks touching off bombs and ammunition. Heroic effort brought the fires under control, but damage to aircraft and the ship was severe and the final casualty count was 132 dead, two missing and presumed dead, and 62 injured.

29 July The vice president announced that the Navy Navigation Satellite System, Transit, would be released for use by merchant ships and for commercial manufacture of shipboard receivers.

15 August The Aircraft Carrier Safety Review Panel held its first meeting. Headed by Admiral James S. Russell, USN (Ret.), the panel was appointed to examine actual and potential sources of fire and explosions in aircraft carriers with the object of minimizing their occurrence and damage and to propose further improvement in the equipment and techniques used to fight fires and control damage by explosion.

10 October Rear Admiral Albert Cushing Read, USN (Ret.), Naval Aviator No. 24, died in Miami, Fla. Well known commander of the NC-4 on the first flight across the Atlantic in 1919, Admiral Read made many contributions during his Naval Aviation career which began in July 1915 and carried through to his retirement in September 1946.

31 October *Currituck*, last seaplane tender in service, was decommissioned at Mare Island, Calif., and transferred to the Reserve Fleet.

6 November An SP-5B Marlin of VP-40 at NAS North Island, Calif., made the last operational flight by seaplanes of the U.S. Navy. With Commanders Joseph P. Smolinski and George A. Surovik as pilot and copilot and 15 passengers including Rear Admiral Constant A. Karaberis on board, the flight ended seaplane patrol operations in the Navy. For more than fifty years, seaplanes had been a mainstay in the Navy's enduring effort to adequately integrate aeronautics with the fleet.

9 November *Bennington* recovered the unmanned *Apollo 4* spacecraft about 600 miles northwest of Hawaii and after its 8½-hour orbital flight.

1968

19 January A C-130 Hercules of VR-24 and helicopters from NAF Sigonella, Italy, delivered food, clothing and medicine to the west coast of Sicily to aid

1968—Continued

Bennington prepares to recover Apollo 4 capsule NASA 67H1536

some 40,000 persons made homeless by an earthquake in the region of Montevago.

23 January When word was received of the capture of *Pueblo* (AGER 2) by a North Korean patrol boat, a Task Group, composed of *Enterprise* and screen, was ordered to reverse course in the East China Sea and to run northward to the Sea of Japan where it operated in the vicinity of South Korea for almost a month.

27 January At the call of the president in the emergency created by the seizure of *Pueblo* (AGER 2), six carrier squadrons of the Naval Air Reserve reported for active duty.

28 March The Secretary of the Navy approved establishment of a new restricted line officer category (152x) called the Aeronautical Maintenance Duty Officer (AMDO).

31 March President Johnson announced that as an indication of American willingness to make concessions opening the way to peace talks with the North Vietnamese, the bombing of targets north of the 20th parallel would stop on the following day.

4 April The *Apollo 6* unmanned spacecraft was recovered after its orbital flight by *Okinawa* about 380 miles north of Hawaii.

3 May The Aviation and Submarine Safety Centers were combined to form the Naval Safety Center. At the same time the Office of the Assistant Chief of Naval Operations (Safety) was established.

22 June The keel for *Nimitz* was laid at Newport News, Va.

1 July To insure a more rapid and efficient transition to combat status in the event of mobilization, the Naval Air Reserve was reorganized into wings and squadrons known collectively as the Naval Air Reserve Force, and effective 1 August, Commander Naval Air Reserve Training assumed additional duty as Commander, Naval Air Reserve Force.

6 July VMO-2 stationed at Da Nang, South Vietnam, received the first OV-10A Broncos to arrive in South Vietnam. The aircraft, specifically developed for counterinsurgency warfare, was immediately employed for forward air control, visual reconnaissance and helicopter escort.

24 August A change in uniform regulations provided a new breast insignia for Navy and Marine Corps

1968—Continued

personnel qualified as Flight Officers. The new wings replaced the old Naval Aviation Observers wings effective 31 December.

16 September The Department of Defense announced that six naval air reserve squadrons called to active duty immediately after the seizure of *Pueblo* (AGER 2) would be returned to inactive status within the next six weeks.

22 October Helicopters of HS-5 from *Essex* located and recovered astronauts Walter M. Schirra, Donn F. Eisele, and R. Walter Cunningham about 285 miles south of Bermuda and delivered them safely to the ship. It was the end of an 11-day mission in space and the first manned flight of the Apollo program.

1 November In response to orders from the president, all bombing of North Vietnam was halted at 2100 Saigon time. The last Navy mission over the restricted area was flown earlier in the day by Commander Kenneth E. Enney in an A-7 Corsair II from *Constellation*.

6 November The lighter-than-air hangar at NAS Lakehurst, N.J., was designated a National Historic Landmark by the National Park Service of the Department of the Interior.

27 December Helicopters of HS-4 hovered over *Apollo 8* after it ended its historic flight around the moon with a predawn splashdown in the Pacific within three miles of *Yorktown*. At first light, astronauts Frank Borman, James A. Lovell, and William A. Anders were picked up by helicopters and carried to the ship.

Schirra, Eisele, and Cunningham aboard recovery ship Essex after orbiting earth for 11 days in Apollo 7 NASA68H986

*New way,
A-7 launch
with nose
tow gear
119077*

Old way, launching with catapult bridle 1110446

27 January Commander, Naval Air Systems Command directed that the Naval Aviation Integrated Logistic Support Task Force be phased out. This Task Force, generally known as NAILS, had made an in depth study of aviation logistics with particular emphasis on spares and repair parts support management. Among other things, it recommended that a NAILS Center be established.

1969

3 January VAL-4, the first Navy squadron of its type, was established at NAS North Island, Calif., to operate the OV-10A Bronco. When VAL-4 deployed to Vietnam in March, it became an important part of the brown-water Navy, operating from two airfields in the Mekong Delta to provide direct support for U.S. and Vietnamese Navy Riverine operations.

14 January A fire aboard *Enterprise* resulting from detonation of a MK-32 Zuni rocket warhead overheated by exhaust from an aircraft starting unit, took 27 lives, injured 344 and destroyed 15 aircraft. Repairs to the ship were completed at Pearl Harbor, Hawaii, in early March.

An F-4B from VF-143 fires Zuni rockets during Seventh Fleet operation in South China Sea 110794

1969—Continued

3 February The Naval Air Systems Command issued a contract to Grumman for development of the F-14A fighter and manufacture of six experimental aircraft. The F-14, intended as a high performance replacement for the F-4 and abortive F-111B, will feature a variable-sweep wing and carry the Phoenix missile.

13 February *Randolph* was decommissioned, and placed in the Reserve Fleet. This was followed on 30 June by the decommissioning of *Essex*, which was placed in reserve, and on 1 December by the decommissioning of *Boxer* which was sold for scrap.

13 March Apollo 9 Astronauts James A. McDivitt, USAF, David R. Scott, USAF, and Russell L. Schweickart were recovered by a helicopter from HS-3 off *Guadalcanal* after completing a 10-day orbit of the earth.

14 April North Korean aircraft shot down an unarmed EC-121 propeller-driven Constellation which was on a routine reconnaissance patrol over the Sea of Japan from its base at Atsugi, Japan. The entire 31-man crew was killed. U.S. response was to activate Task Force 71 to protect such flights over those international waters in the future. Initially, the TF consisted of the carriers *Enterprise, Ticonderoga, Ranger,* and *Hornet* with cruiser and destroyer screens.

26 May Apollo 10 Astronauts Thomas P. Stafford, USAF, John W. Young, USN, and Eugene A. Cernan, USN, were recovered by HS-4 off *Princeton* after making an 8-day orbit of the earth.

26 May A new, major development in carrier fire prevention occurred when *Franklin D. Roosevelt* put to sea from Norfolk Naval Shipyard, Va., after an ll-month overhaul which included installation of a deck edge, spray system using the new seawater compatible, fire-fighting chemical, Light Water.

1 June On a flight from Stephenville, Newfoundland, to Mildenhall, England, Lieutenant Colonel R. Lewis, USMC, and Major C. L. Phillips, USMC, piloted an OV-10 Bronco to a world record of 2,539.78 miles for point to point distance for light turbo-prop aircraft.

24 June The first operational "hands off" arrested landing using the AN/SPN-42, Automatic Carrier Landing System, on a carrier was performed by Lieutenant Dean Smith and Lieutenant (jg) James Sherlock of VF-103 when their Phantom II landed aboard *Saratoga*. AN/SPN-42 was an outgrowth of SPN-10 which was first tested in 1957 but was found not to meet all fleet requirements.

30 June Personnel on duty in the naval aeronautical organization at the end of the fiscal year, in round

OV-10A, light armed reconnaissance aircraft 1143446

1969—Continued

numbers, included a grand total of 177,000 with 28,500 officers of whom 15,200 were HTA pilots. Enlisted men numbered 147,700 of whom 27 were pilots. Respective figures for Marine Aviation were: 72,500; 9,600; 5,600; 62,800, and 5.

14 July The first A-7E Corsair II assigned to an operational squadron was delivered to VA-122, the A-7 West Coast training squadron at NAS Lemoore, Calif. The A-7E version of the Vought Corsair II incorporates heads-up-display (HUD) and Project Map Display (PMDS) whereby vital information from flight and navigation instruments are projected into the pilots normal field of vision, thereby permitting him to concentrate on his mission without looking down at instruments. Service use of this equipment culminated a development effort of more than 15 years duration.

24 July Apollo 11 Astronauts Neil A. Armstrong, ex-USN, Edwin E. Aldrin, Jr., USAF, and Michael Collins, USAF, were recovered by HS-4 off *Hornet* after the first moon landing during which Armstrong and Aldrin walked on the moon, 20–21 July. The first person to set foot on the moon was a naval aviator, Neil Armstrong.

1 August The Naval Air Systems Command issued a contract to Lockheed Aircraft Corporation for development of the S-3A, a carrier based antisubmarine warfare plane designed for all weather operation and equipped with modern detection and data processing equipment. It was scheduled to replace the S-2 Tracker in the seventies.

17 August Hurricane Camille swept into the Gulf Coast near Gulfport, Miss., leaving many people homeless and causing heavy property damage. Naval Aviation performed emergency assistance and HT-8 received a letter from the president praising it for services rendered during the disaster.

31 August Two LC-130s of VXE-6 arrived at McMurdo Sound, Antarctica, six weeks in advance of the opening of Operation Deep Freeze 70. Among the passengers were Rear Admiral David F. Welch, Commander Naval Support Force, Antarctica, and seven scientists.

1 September The Naval Aviation Integrated Logistic Support Center, Patuxent River, Md., was established to provide intensified logistics management for Naval Aviation.

8 September As part of Project Birdseye, the Arctic ice-survey mission initiated in March 1962 to gather ice-flow information for the Naval Oceanographic Office, VXN-8 provided ice surveillance for SS *Manhattan* during the ship's historic voyage from the East Coast of the United States to Alaska through the ice-packed Northwest Passage.

30 September CVSG-57 was disestablished followed by the disestablishment of CVW-10 on 28 November and CVSG-52 on 15 December.

22 October The Naval Air Systems Command and the United Kingdom executed a Memorandum of Agreement whereby the Hawker-Siddely Harrier, a vertical take-off and landing aircraft, could be purchased. A subsequent Letter of Offer covered procurement of 12 aircraft with initial delivery in January 1971. The Harrier, U.S. designation AV-8A, was being procured for operational use by the Marine Corps as a result of interest generated in September 1968 when Marine Aviators Colonel

Pilots converting to the AV-8A learn new vocabulary

1969—Continued

Marine Harrier demonstrates its hover capabilities

Thomas H. Miller, Jr. and Lieutenant Colonel Clarence M. Baker flew the aircraft in England. The Harrier was a further development of the Kestrel, which in early phases received developmental support from the United States and West Germany as well as the United Kingdom.

24 November The Apollo 12 Astronauts, an all-Naval Aviator crew of Richard F. Gordon, Jr., Charles Conrad, Jr., and Alan L. Bean, were recovered by HS-4 off *Hornet* after circling the moon, and in a lunar module, landing there with Conrad and Bean on 19 November for 31½ hours.

Three of the first four men on the moon have flown for the Navy NASA-AS12497278

UH-1B on Mekong Delta patrol 1143447

A C-2 Greyhound makes carrier on board delivery to Kitty Hawk during operation off Vietnam 1143450

QH-50D drone helicopter on ASW mission 1143449

CH-46A during vertical replenishment NH 69969

CH-46A for vertical assault HN69966

SP-2H, on patrol inspects a Vietnamese junk 1115829

H-2 stands plane guard during flight operations K31638

Marine CH-53A, Sea Stallion, lifts large Truck NH 69965

Shrike antiradar missiles HN69964

Mounting Gun-pod on A-4 4710124

Light water in washdown system, used for fighting fire

Assembling A-7 turbofan TF-30 engine NH69963

Reloading M-60 machine gun on UH-1B helicopter K58290

Echo II test at Lakehurst 1143455

Task Force 77 units in the Tonkin Gulf, Oriskany (center), as seen from signal bridge of Constellation 1143453

Human centrifuge used in study of space flight 1036457

Nuclear-powered Enterprise, Long Beach, and Bainbridge preparing for 1964 round the world cruise 1103800

Naval air interdicts Vietcong supply route by destroying highway bridge with bombing NH 69956

Helos deliver guns and ammo to troops USMC 184967

Advanced aviation base ship, Tallahatchie County, decommissioned in 1970

Iroquois come in for refueling from LC-130 Hercules during deepfreeze K87381

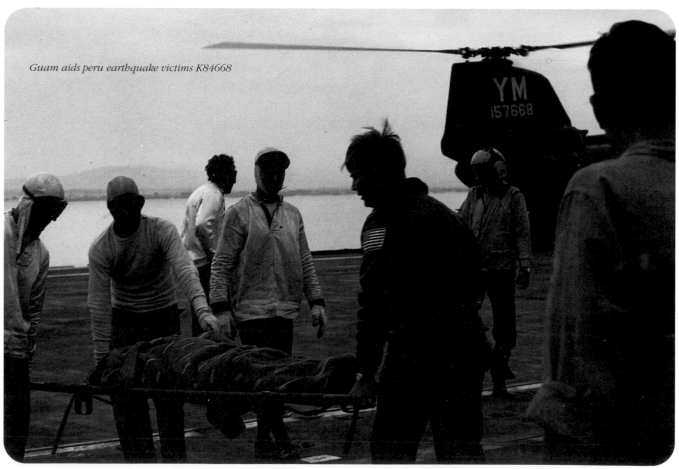

Guam aids peru earthquake victims K84668

PART 10

The Seventies

1970–1980

Naval Aviation began its seventh decade with the United States heavily embroiled in the Vietnam War and 1980 ended with carriers *Dwight D. Eisenhower* and *Ranger* deployed in the Indian Ocean. The country had no sooner ended its long military involvement in Vietnam than it faced a growing crisis in the Middle East, a crisis that reached hostile proportions late in 1979 when Iranian hoodlums captured the United States Embassy in their capital city, Tehran.

Throughout the 1970s, the American public became increasingly aware of the country's critical dependence upon oil from foreign sources. During this time, an acute consciousness of the United States' position as a two-ocean nation reemphasized the reliance upon the U.S. Navy to keep sea lanes open and commerce moving unhampered.

For nearly ten years, the burden of the Navy's air action fell upon the carriers and aircraft of the Seventh Fleet. To meet this responsibility, naval air relied on established weapons and material and introduced new ones. The Walleye, a television-guided glide bomb designed to home automatically on target, was tested successfully in combat. Helicopters flexed their muscle in a combat role and served also as aerial tanks and flying freight trains. Land-based patrol aircraft, in Operation Market Time, scoured the coastline of South Vietnam to search out enemy infiltrating vessels and locate surface forces for interception. In 1972, Operations Linebacker I and II waged heavy interdiction and bombing campaigns against North Vietnam. Aircraft of the Seventh Fleet performed the most extensive aerial mining operation in history, blockading the enemy's main avenues of supply. An uneasy truce finally resulted in the United States disengaging itself from Vietnam in 1973. Two years later, Naval Aviation was called upon to assist in the evacuation of refugees fleeing the North Vietnamese takeover of South Vietnam. In 1979, naval air power helped rescue thousands of Indochinese who took to the high seas in poor vessels to escape mounting tyranny in their homelands.

Against the unrelenting need for vigilance was pitted a declining material inventory and difficulty in retaining experienced personnel. Much of the 1970s can hardly be called bountiful for Naval Aviation. As the surplus of equipment left over from Vietnam eroded through constant use, money for replenishment was not abundant. The high inflation rate that beset the world's industrial nations plagued defense budgets and drove downward the purchasing power of military salaries. Nevertheless, Naval Aviation continued to make headway in the areas of research and development.

Early in the 1970s, the Navy introduced the F-14 Tomcat, and the Marine Corps accepted the AV-8 V/STOL Harrier. At the end of the decade, a new fighter/attack aircraft, the F/A-18 Hornet, was undergoing flight trials. The submarine threat was confronted by the addition to the fleet of the light airborne multipurpose system (LAMPS) which combined shipboard electronics with the SH-2D helicopter. As 1980 drew to a close, the latest LAMPS version was under test in a new Navy airframe, the SH-60B Seahawk. Also at decade's end, the Navy's latest heavy-lift helicopter, the CH-53E, was ready for acceptance by a Marine Corps squadron. Airframes were not the only items which saw advance. The fields of electronics, missiles, and crew systems also benefited from improvements. Finally it should be mentioned that during the 1970s two nuclear supercarriers, *Nimitz* and *Dwight D. Eisenhower* were commissioned; a third, *Carl Vinson*, was launched.

As Naval Aviation began its eighth decade, there was no serious reason to doubt that its superior record of achievement would endure. Aircraft, integrated with the fleet, would continue to provide the United States with the strongest naval power on earth.

1970

15 January *Bennington*, *Valley Forge* and *Tallahatchie County* were decommissioned. As a part of the continuing ship reduction program, this was followed by the decommissioning of *Princeton* on 13 February, *Hornet* on 26 June and *Yorktown* on 27 June. Earmarked in 1970 for decommissioning in 1971 were *Bon Homme Richard* and *Shangri-La*.

1970—Continued

31 January *Midway* was recommissioned following a four-year conversion-modernization at the San Francisco Bay Naval Shipyard, Calif. Other ship developments that followed were the commissioning of *Inchon* on 20 June, completing *Ticonderoga's* conversion from CVA to CVS in May, and laying the keel of *Dwight D. Eisenhower* on 15 August.

10 February As part of the U.S. withdrawal from Vietnam, two Marine squadrons, VMFA-542 and VMA-223, returned to Marine Corps Air Station El Toro, Calif. The same month, VMA-211 and MAG-12 were reassigned to Japan. In September, VMFA-122, VMFA-314 and VMA(AW)-242, as well as two aviation support units, H&MS-13 and MABS-13, returned to the U.S. On 13 October, the last Marines left Chu Lai, a base from which they had been operating since 1965.

16 March The crash of an EC-121 reconnaissance plane took the lives of 23 Navy passengers at Da Nang Air Base, South Vietnam.

28 March The first North Vietnamese MiG kill since the 1 November 1968 bombing halt occurred when Lieutenant Jerome E. Beaulier and Lieutenant (jg) Stephen J. Barkley in an F-4 Phantom II of VF-142 off *Constellation* shot down a MiG-21 while escorting an unarmed Navy reconnaissance plane on a mission near Thanh Hoa, North Vietnam.

1 April CVWR-20 and CVWR-30 were established followed by CVSGR-70 and CVSGR-80 on 1 May. This was a continuation of a program initiated in July 1968 to give Naval Air Reserve an improved combat readiness. The reorganization placed all carrier-type squadrons in two reserve carrier air wings and two carrier ASW groups. Twelve VP and three VR squadrons joined the carrier squadrons under the control of Commander Naval Air Reserve Force.

10 April The A-4M Skyhawk made its first flight at the McDonnell Douglas plant at Palmdale, Calif. This aircraft was equipped with a high power engine (nearly 50 percent more thrust than that of the Skyhawk from 1954) and brake parachute; these features made it particularly adaptable for operations from short airfields in forward areas.

17 April Apollo 13 astronauts James A. Lovell, Jr., USN; John L. Swigert, Jr., ex-USAF; and Fred W. Haise, Jr., ex-USMCR, were recovered by HS-4 off *Iwo Jima* after their abortive moon flight.

2 May A VC-8 helicopter rescued twenty-six persons from a Dutch Antillean Airlines DC-9 ditched in the Caribbean. The helicopter was piloted by Lieutenant Commander James E. Rylee and Lieutenant (jg) Donald Hartman; crewmen were ADC William Brazzell and AD Calvin Lindley.

9 May Approximately 30 U.S. Navy craft, helicopters and OV-10 Bronco aircraft participated with the combined South Vietnamese/U.S. Riverine Force in operations into the Mekong River Corridor to neutralize sanctuary bases in that area. This followed the initial series of strikes by combined U.S.-RVN ground forces against enemy sanctuaries in Cambodia during the first week of May.

31 May Following Peru's earthquake which took 50,000 lives, injured 100,000 and made 800,000 homeless, *Guam* and HMM-365 provided victims with over 200 tons of relief supplies and transported over 1,000 evacuees and medical patients on 800 mercy flights. Before *Guam* left the Peruvian coast on 21 June, her crewmen spent two days in Lima at the invitation of a grateful Peruvian government.

1 June CVW-4 and -12 were disestablished, followed by the disestablishment of CVSG-51 on 30 June.

9 June Sikorsky pilot James R. Wright and copilot Colonel Henry Hart, USMC, flying a Marine Corps CH-53D, established a New York, N.Y., to Washington, D.C., record for helicopters of 156.43 mph with an elapsed time of 1 hour, 18 minutes and 41.4 seconds from downtown to downtown. The following day they established a New York, N.Y., to Boston, Mass., record for helicopters of 162.72 mph with a city to city time of 1 hour, 9 minutes, 23.9 seconds.

30 June As a result of reductions in force levels, personnel on duty in the naval aeronautical organization at the end of the fiscal year, in round numbers, included a grand total of 162,600 with 25,900 officers of whom 14,500 were pilots. Enlisted men numbered 135,900 of whom 22 were pilots. Respective figures for Marine Aviation were: 72,000 total; 9,900 officers of whom 5,700 were pilots; 62,000 enlisted men and 4 enlisted pilots.

1 July Naval Air Systems Command Liaison Office, Dayton, Ohio, was disestablished. This marked the end of an office that had its beginning in October 1920, when the Navy detailed an aviation officer to McCook Field to observe and report on experimental work.

1970—Continued

17 July The P-3C began deployed operations as VP-49 took over patrol responsibilities at Keflavik, Iceland. This ASW aircraft, which was described in an unveiling ceremony 14 months earlier as "two or three times as effective as anything we now have," featured the latest antisubmarine warfare equipment including directional sonobuoys, a high capacity computer and related displays.

8 September The Department of Defense modified its basic space policy (established in March 1961) by providing that functional responsibilities of the services would be considered in assigning programs for development and acquisition of space systems. In addition, the Director of Defense, Research and Engineering would assure that specific space programs administered by one service would be broad enough to meet the related needs of other services.

25 September A Condor television-guided air-to-surface missile was launched by an A-6A at a standoff distance from its target. The aircraft was 56 miles from the target when the missile made a direct impact. The test was conducted at the Naval Weapons Center, China Lake, Calif.

25 September As a result of the Jordanian crisis caused by Palestinian commando attempts to unseat the monarchy in Amman, *John F. Kennedy* joined *Saratoga* and *Independence* in the Mediterranean, followed by seven other U.S. Navy ships, including *Guam* on 27 September. This strengthened the Sixth Fleet to some 55 ships which served as a standby force in case U.S. military protection was needed for the evacuation of Americans and as a counterbalance to the Soviet Union's Mediterranean fleet.

25 October Sailors and Marines completed four days of assistance and relief to thousands of Filipinos left homeless, hungry and injured by Typhoon Joan which had struck southern Luzon and Catanduanes Island in the Republic of the Philippines, leaving 600 dead and 80,000 without shelter. Over 300 tons of rice, flour, blankets and fuel were air-lifted by HMM-164, while galleymen aboard *Okinawa* worked round-the-clock baking over 5,000 loaves of bread, and inland, medics groped by flashlight to aid the injured.

29 October Following the ravages of Typhoon Kate and flood waters that inundated some 140 square miles of Vietnam south of Da Nang, the helicopter forces of 1st Marine Aircraft Wing performed rescue and relief operations for over 9,000 South Vietnamese.

Initial rescue operations began when MAG-16 evacuated some 900 people the first day during floods termed the worst since 1964.

21 November Navy planes dropped flares along the coast of North Vietnam to divert attention from an Army-Air Force search and rescue team that searched a vacated prisoner-of-war compound at Son Tay, 20 miles west of Hanoi.

21–22 November In response to attacks on unarmed U.S. reconnaissance aircraft, 200 U.S. aircraft conducted protective reaction air strikes against North Vietnamese missile and antiaircraft sites south of the 19th parallel. The strike forces included Marine Corps and Navy aircraft from *Hancock, Ranger,* and *Oriskany.*

24 November The Senate Preparedness Investigating Subcommittee completed a three-day "Investigation into Electronic Battlefield Program," which dealt with the development and use of sensor surveillance to locate hostile forces in South Vietnam and thus take the night away from the enemy. As representatives of the Services and OSD explained to the committee, the program had its beginnings in 1966 when the Navy sought to adapt the air-dropped radio sonobuoy to ground use by replacing the hydrophone with a microphone. In the initial phase, the project was called ALARS (for Air Launched Acoustical Reconnaissance) which was a part of the TRIM (Trail Road Interdiction Mission) Project. In August 1966 a scientific study group proposed a broader air-supported barrier system, and in September, the Secretary of Defense established the Defense Communications Planning Group to implement the concept and later expanded the mission to cover a variety of tactical applications with a variety of sensors. Although the air-supported sensor responsibility was eventually assigned to the Air Force (under the code name Igloo White), the initial combat mission was carried out from November 1967 to June 1968 by a newly established Navy squadron, VO-67, equipped with 12 OP-2E aircraft.

24 November A T-2C modified by North American Rockwell to a super-critical wing configuration was test flown by North American test pilot Edward A. Gillespie at Columbus, Ohio. The supercritical wing, based upon theoretical development by Dr. Richard Whitcomb of NASA, promised to delay the onset of transonic shock separation, buffeting, and other undesirable aerodynamic phenomena and thus give greater flexibility to aircraft intended for operation in the sonic speed regimen.

1970—Continued

25 November   The Chief of Naval Material established a Navy Space Project Office with responsibility for the integration and coordination of space activities within the purview of the Naval Material Command and with responsibility for management of designated space projects.

21 December   The F-14A aircraft, piloted by Grumman test pilots Robert Smyth and William Miller, made its first flight at Grumman's Calverton, Long Island, N.Y., plant.

1971

1 January   Task Force 77, the Attack Carrier Striking Force Seventh Fleet, continued operations off Vietnam on Yankee Station, the "on line" area in the Gulf of Tonkin, with missions consisting of interdiction of the Ho Chi Minh Trail in Laos, air support for allied ground forces in South Vietnam (SVN), photographic reconnaissance, combat air patrols and electronic warfare. On station at the beginning of the year were *Hancock* and *Ranger*.

6 January   The Marine Corps/Navy's first AV-8 Harrier was accepted by Major General Homer S. Hill, USMC, at Dunsfold, England. The Harrier was the first vertical take-off and landing (V/STOL) fixed-wing aircraft ever accepted for use as a combat aircraft by U.S. armed forces.

19 January   *Enterprise* completed sea trials with her newly designed nuclear reactor cores which contained enough energy to power her for the next ten years.

22 January   The Navy's most advanced antisubmarine warfare aircraft, the land-based P-3C Orion, established a world record in the heavyweight turboprop class for long distance flight. The production model aircraft, piloted by Commander Donald H. Lilienthal with a crew of eight, set the record with a flight of 6,857 statute miles over the official great circle route from NAS Atsugi, Japan, to NAS Patuxent River, Md. The flight, which topped the Soviet Union's IL-18 turboprop record of 4,761 miles set in 1967, lasted 15 hours, 21 minutes. In order to avoid Russia's Kamchatka Peninsula, the Lilienthal flight actually covered 7,010 miles.

26 January   The AV-8A Harrier arrived at the Naval Air Test Center, Patuxent River, Md. for commencement of Board of Inspection and Survey trials.

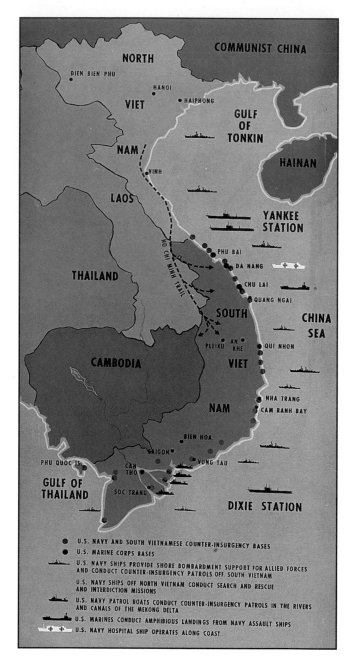

Southeast Asia.

27 January   A P-3C at the Naval Air Test Center, Patuxent River, Md. with Commander Donald H. Lilienthal as Plane Commander established a world speed record for its class of 501.44 mph over the 15 to 25 km course.

27 January   NAVAIR expedited procurement of the TCW-33P VWS (Ventilated Wet Suit) to permit its issuance to VS and VP squadrons during the winter of 1971–1972. The evaluation of 3,100 ventilated wet suits had begun in 1969 and enthusiastic acceptance by flight crews led to the decision that the suits should

1971—Continued

AV-8A Harrier (VTOL) comes in for a recovery on board Guadalcanal K-89288

be procured for early issue rather than phased in as stocks of the Mk 5 anti-exposure suit were depleted.

29 January The Navy's newest carrier-based electronic warfare aircraft, the sophisticated EA-6B Prowler, entered service with VAQ-129 at NAS Whidbey Island, Wash. The Prowler, a derivative of the two-place A-6 Intruder, was lengthened to accommodate a four-place cockpit and replaced the A-3 Skywarrior. VAQ-129 (redesignated from VAH-10 in 1970) became the replacement training squadron when it commenced instructing aircrew and ground support replacement personnel for all the Navy's Prowler squadrons.

31 January Alternating on Yankee Station, *Hancock, Ranger* and *Kitty Hawk* flew a total of 3,214 sorties during the month, of which 3,128 delivered ordnance in Laos. A-6 and A-7

A-6 Intruder releasing ordnance during bombing mission over Vietnam NAH-003854

1971—Continued

aircraft were particularly effective in attacking truck traffic, the enemy having put a seasonally high number of trucks on the road, averaging close to 1,000 per day.

4 February   A P-3C, at the Naval Air Test Center, Patuxent River, Md., with Commander Donald H. Lilienthal as Plane Commander, set a world record for its class of 45,018.2 feet altitude in horizontal flight.

5 February   The Navy announced the first successful test-firing of a Condor air-to-surface missile armed with a live warhead. The missile, which was fired from an A-6 Intruder jet aircraft and guided by television, scored a direct hit on a target ship, which was out of sight from the launching aircraft.

8 February   Commander Donald H. Lilienthal and crew in their P-3C completed the assault on world records for unlimited weight turboprop planes, establishing an altitude record of 46,214.5 feet, and time-to-climb records of 3,000 meters in 2 minutes 51.7 seconds; 6,000 meters in 5 minutes 46.3 seconds; 9,000 meters in 10 minutes 26.1 seconds; and 12,000 meters in 19 minutes 42.2 seconds.

17 February   The Weapons Systems Explosive Safety Review Board approved service use of the pyrotechnic seeding device, WMU-1/B. This unit, consisting of a silver iodide (catalyst) generator, became the first weather modification unit released for production and general use by the Navy. Later that year this device was used over the island of Okinawa to enhance rainfall and thus replenish the island's water reserves.

24 February   The Navy disclosed that an electronic eavesdropper, developed at the Naval Air Development Center, Warminster, Pa., had been used in Southeast Asia since June 1967. Called the Acoubuoy, it was dropped along trails and broadcasted passing sounds to aircraft up to 20 miles away.

28 February   In Vietnam during the month, two carriers remained on station throughout the period as strike sorties rose to an average of 122 per day because of a 40 percent increase in enemy truck movements from the previous month, averaging more than 1,400 a day. A program was extended to A-7 aircraft night all-weather seeding missions heretofore flown exclusively by the A-6. The computer release of flares over targeted road segments was followed by visual delivery of seeds which allowed the enemy minimal chances of spotting the emplaced mine fields.

9 March   Construction began on the joint U.S./U.K. naval air and radio communications station located on the Indian Ocean atoll of Diego Garcia. Later in the month, Naval Mobile Construction Battalion 40, supported by U.S. surface vessels, commenced the major construction effort.

10 March   On Yankee Station, *Ranger* and *Kitty Hawk* set a record of 233 strike sorties for one day and went on during the ensuing six-day period to mark up a strike effectiveness record that exceeded record performances by TF-77 during the previous three-year period.

16 March   The first SH-2D LAMPS (Light Airborne Multi-Purpose System) helicopter test flight took place at Kaman's Bloomfield, Conn., facility. This flight followed testing aboard *Sims* (DE 1059) to determine deck strength for helicopter operations. It was announced later in the month that 115 H-2 helicopters would be committed to the LAMPS program. The LAMPS system was configured to extend the range of ASW and ASMD on destroyers, frigates, and destroyer escorts as an airborne extension of the ships' own detection systems.

29 March   The first active AIM-9G missile was launched from an NUH-2H helicopter by the Weapons System Test Division of NATC.

31 March   In Vietnam, strike sorties launched by the carriers serving on Yankee Station during the month totaled 4,535 of which 4,479 were sorties delivering ordnance. These figures were up by 1,074 and 1,065, respectively, from the previous month. Over 680 Acoubuoy seed and interdiction package missions were flown during the month with unknown results. Approximately 75 percent of the interdiction packages, however, obtained one or more road cuts while implanting Acoubuoy seeds.

1 April   HM-12, the Navy's first helicopter squadron devoted exclusively to mine countermeasures, was established at NAS Norfolk, Va. The mission of HM-12 was to remove or eliminate enemy mines from sealanes and amphibious operating areas. To accomplish this task HM-12 helicopters towed specially designed mechanical magnetic and acoustic minesweeping equipment which would activate the enemy mines, thereby eliminating them as a threat to future operations in the area. HM-12 employed CH-53A Sea Stallions until they received the Sikorsky RH-53D built specifically for mine countermeasures.

1971—Continued

5 April   Modernization of the Naval Air Reserve continued when the first A-7 Corsair IIs were received by VA-303 at NAS Alameda, Calif. The first reserve squadron to operate the modern jet, VA-303 received its full complement of 12 aircraft by the end of June. Less than four months later, VA-303 made the initial reserve A-7 squadron deployment, marking the first extended deployment of a reserve squadron on other than annual active duty training.

16 April   The A-4M Skyhawk entered squadron service with VMA-324 and VMA-331 at MCAS Beaufort, S.C. The most advanced in the A-4 series, the aircraft featured a new self-contained starter, carried twice as much 20mm ammunition, and had 20 percent more thrust (11,200 pounds). The new model Skyhawk, the seventh major version, was developed specifically for the Marine Corps and was capable of delivering all air-to-ground weapons in the naval inventory.

16 April   VMA-513 at MCAS Beaufort, S.C., took delivery of three AV-8A Harrier aircraft, thereby becoming the first operational high performance V/STOL squadron in the United States.

30 April   In Vietnam during the month, three carriers assigned to TF-77—*Ranger, Kitty Hawk*, and *Hancock*—provided a constant two carrier posture on Yankee Station. Hours of employment remained unchanged with one carrier on daylight hours and one on the noon to midnight schedule. Strike emphasis was placed on the interdiction of major Laotian entry corridors to South Vietnam (SVN). Strike sorties delivering ordnance totalled 3,648. Fifteen strike sorties were flown into North Vietnam (NVN) during the month.

1 May   A board to study and make recommendations on Aeronautical Engineering Duty personnel policies, which had been appointed the preceding 14 December with Rear Admiral Daniel K. Weitzenfeld as senior member, submitted its report. The board reported that the AED community was at full strength and had an excellent base of aspirants from which to select new applicants. A number of recommendations were made to further the careers of Aeronautical Engineering Duty Officers (AEDO) and their use by the Navy. The more significant recommendations included achieving "a limited joining with the AMD (152) group in recognition of a common purpose in support of Naval Aviation," and identifying billets which could be filled by either Aeronautical Engineering Duty or Aeronautical Maintenance Duty Officers.

18 May   In Vietnam, *Midway,* after relieving *Hancock* on 10 May, commenced single carrier operations on Yankee Station until the end of the month. This had not been in effect since January, when *Kitty Hawk* served a two-week "on station" tour alone. During the one-carrier operations, *Ranger* and *Kitty Hawk* were away for upkeep periods in Japan.

21 May   Technical evaluation of a new fire control system with a helmet-mounted sight was begun at the Naval Air Test Center, Patuxent River, Md.

28 May   The Secretary of Defense announced measures to strengthen the Sixth Fleet. He said that fleet readiness was to be improved by the almost continuous presence of a helicopter carrier, and by a substantial increase in the hours flown by maritime air patrols and the ship-operating days of sea patrols. This followed an earlier announcement by the Pentagon on 24 May that the Sixth Fleet would be strengthened in response to the growing Soviet naval power.

31 May   As in previous months in Vietnam, strike emphasis was placed on the interdiction of Laotian entry and throughout corridors to SVN. Southern Laotian routes leading to Cambodia also received increased emphasis during the month. Although weather cancellations remained at a comparatively low level, conservation of strike sorties was still accomplished by limiting carrier sorties to 60–70 per day, resulting in a total of 2,645 sorties that delivered ordnance. Two protective reaction strikes were carried out in NVN during the month. NVN surface-to-air missile (SAM) coverage south of 20° N continued at a high level. The increased SAM threat required additional aircraft in support of strike and reconnaissance flights.

28 June   A proposal by the Naval Training Command Board to consolidate all naval training was approved. The board had convened under the direction of the CNO on 8 February. Training had been under review since World War II by official study groups and boards, the first being the Hopwood Board in 1955 which recommended that training be divorced from the Bureau of Naval Personnel. Major recommendations of the Naval Training Command Board established a single training command, Chief of Naval Training, with headquarters at Pensacola, Fla. Chief of Naval Technical Training was established at Memphis, Tenn. Education and programs which had been under the Chief of Naval Personnel were placed under the new command of Director of Naval Education and Training. Three former air training staffs were consolidated into a single staff with eight training wings to be

1971—Continued

located at major pilot training bases. Public announcement of the new single training command was made on 21 July and became effective on 1 August.

29 June Light gull gray, Federal Standard Color No. 36440, applied to carrier aircraft was replaced with glossy light gull gray Federal Standard Color No. 16440. This change was directed by MIL-C-18263F (AS) of this date.

30 June During June in Vietnam, the realignment of carriers continued as *Midway* departed Yankee Station on 5 June, relieved by *Kitty Hawk,* and *Oriskany* commenced strike operations on 16 June. A total of 14 two-carrier days and 16 single-carrier days during the month resulted in a monthly strike sortie count of 2,431. The Navy's strike sortie count for Fiscal Year 1971 thus came to 32,230 sorties, 172 under the annual ceiling. June strike operations were under the influence of the southwest monsoons with attendant clouds and rain.

7 July The last active duty A-1 Skyraider, an NA-1E, was retired. The aircraft, which had been assigned to the Naval Air Test Center, Patuxent River, Md., and was used in many test programs there, including slow speed and ordnance release, was turned over to the Confederate Air Force, Harlingen, Texas for museum display.

13 July Deputy Secretary of Defense David Packard issued a new directive defining policy for acquisition of major defense systems. Basically, Mr. Packard sought to return authority to the military departments, subject to approval by the Secretary of Defense, at key points in the development acquisition process. Among the various points of the policy were increased emphasis upon the project manager (called program manager in the DOD directive), reiteration of the importance of maintaining a strong technology base, and the definition of the entire development-acquisition process as three distinct phases: (1) program initiation, (2) full-scale development, and (3) production/deployment. The new directive emphasized the importance of making accurate cost predictions and realistic schedule forecasts and of relating the military benefits anticipated from a new technology to the cost of the technology. To reduce the magnitude of risk, prototyping was to be part of the advanced development effort; operational suitability of a system was to be tested and evaluated before it was committed to large scale production—thus the popular description of the policy as "fly before buy."

24 July CVSGR-80 began ASW operations from *Ticonderoga*. It was the first time in naval history that the Naval Air Reserve had demonstrated the capability for immediate employment of fleet-size wings and groups, fully manned, properly equipped, and operationally ready to perform all phases of carrier operations.

26 July The Apollo 15 spacecraft was launched from the Kennedy Space Center for a lunar mission. On 30 July the lunar module Falcon commanded by Colonel David R. Scott, USAF, with Lieutenant Colonel James B. Irwin, USAF, a Naval Academy graduate, class of 1951, separated from the command ship, *Endeavor,* with Major Alfred M. Worden, USAF, and landed on the moon in the Hadley-Apennine area. The crew accumulated 66 hours, 55 minutes on the moon's surface before they departed on 2 August. Five days later, *Okinawa,* primary recovery ship for Task Force 130, accomplished the recovery of the Apollo 15 crew after splashdown in the Pacific. The mission was the first of three moon flights geared directly to scientific investigation and achieved far more than all the previous lunar missions combined.

28 July HC-7 was awarded the Presidential Unit Citation, the second Navy helicopter squadron to receive the citation for duty in Vietnam. The other helo squadron to win the award was HA(L)-3. Operating from ships at sea on Yankee Station, HC-7 SAR detachments were credited with rescuing 76 U.S. aviators from Vietnam waters. During the early stages of the conflict, the squadron had made several overland rescues in NVN under intense enemy fire.

30 July In Vietnam, with *Oriskany, Midway* and *Enterprise* serving intermittently on station, a total of 22 two-carrier days and nine single-carrier days resulted in a strike sortie count of 2,001. Strike operations during the month of July were disrupted when the carriers on station evaded three different typhoons—Harriet, Kim and Jean. A slight increase in SVN strike sorties occurred during the month. These were mainly visual strikes against enemy troop positions and in support of U.S. helicopter operations.

30 July The Navy accepted the first operational BQM-34E Firebee II aerial jet target. The Firebee II had been developed by Ryan Aeronautical Company under contract to the Naval Air Systems Command and was designed to maneuver at greater speeds and altitudes than the standard Firebee target previously in use. Jet-powered, the remote-controlled target system was rated at Mach 1.5, offering subsonic and supersonic mission capabilities.

1971—Continued

3 August Pilots of VMA-142, -131 and -133 began qualification landings in A-4Ls aboard *Independence*. During a three-day period, four active duty and 20 reserve pilots operated aboard the carrier. This was the first time that Marine Air Reserve squadrons qualified in carrier duty.

26 August VAW-124 flew the carrier-based early warning E-2B nonstop across the Atlantic. The Hawkeye left NAS Norfolk, Va., flew over Newfoundland, Canada, and Lajes, Azores, to reach *America* which was deployed to the Sixth Fleet in the Mediterranean.

31 August During the month, dual carrier operations were conducted only during the first week; and, as of the 16th, *Enterprise* filled in the remainder of the month alone on station. Thus, a total of 8 two-carrier days and 23 single-carrier days represented a near reversal of July's carrier mix, producing a strike sortie count for the month of 1,915.

30 September Single carrier operations on Yankee Station were conducted throughout the month, except for one two-carrier day. The schedule had *Enterprise* flying the first four days, *Oriskany* the middle of the month and *Midway* completing the last four days. The single carrier posture, combined with the low intended sortie rate, produced 1,243 strike sorties during the month. *Oriskany* flyers participated in a joint USAF/USN protective reaction strike in southern NVN on 21 September.

5 October HC-4 at NAS Lakehurst, N.J., accepted its first SH-2D LAMPS helicopter, making it the first fleet operating unit to use the new LAMPS configured Seasprite. One week later at NAS Imperial Beach, Calif. HC-5 became the first West Coast-based helicopter squadron to receive the new Seasprite.

8 October About one hundred officers and men of the Mobile Mine Countermeasure Command and four CH-53 Sea Stallion helicopters were airlifted from Norfolk, Va., and Charleston, S.C., to the Sixth Fleet at Souda Bay, Crete, by C-5s of the 437th Military Airlift Wing in a demonstration of the world-wide quick reaction mine countermeasures capability. A detachment of four CH-53As from HM-12 recorded the first overseas deployment of the new helicopter. The detachment began sweeping operations upon arrival at Souda Bay. From 2 to 7 November the squadron participated in the first integration of airborne minesweeping operations into an amphibious assault exercise, conducted from *Coronado* (LPD 11).

29 October HS-15, the first sea control ship squadron, was established at NAS Lakehurst, N.J. The squadron was devised tactically to protect convoys and vessels not operating with or within the protective range of carriers. Tests along these lines were conducted subsequently aboard *Guam* utilizing the SH-3H Sea King helicopters of HS-15 and Marine Corps AV-8A Harriers of VMA-513. Tests included V/STOL and helo compatibility, antisnooper and antisurface tactics, bow and cross axial landings, night operations and shipboard control of airborne intercepts.

31 October On Yankee Station during the month, single carrier operations were conducted except for the last day. *Midway* completed her final line period 10 October, with *Enterprise* taking over the next day for the remainder of the month. *Oriskany* joined the last day, and together the three carriers recorded a total of 1,024 ordnance-delivering strike sorties, 30 of them in SVN, the remainder in Laos. The air warfare posture in NVN was altered 20 October through the deployment of six MiG aircraft south of 20° N—two each at Vinh, Quan Lang and Bai Thuong.

8 November The jet-powered S-3A, the Navy's newest antisubmarine warfare aircraft, made its official roll-out at Lockheed's Burbank California facility. Christened the Viking, the aircraft was designed to replace the aging S-2 Tracker.

17 November The Office of the Assistant Secretary of Defense reported that the Navy had been designated the lead service in making aircraft ready for use in Project Grass Catcher—the interception of drug smugglers. During January and February 1972, four OV-10s were loaned to the Bureau of Customs.

30 November Preliminary evaluation of the F-14A was conducted at Grumman's Calverton, N.Y., facility by a team from NATC Patuxent River, Md. The Tomcat was designed for all fighter missions, including air-to-air combat and fleet defense.

30 November Alternating on Yankee Station, *Oriskany*, *Constellation* and *Enterprise* provided 22 two-carrier days on the line, delivering 1,766 ordnance-bearing strike sorties, twelve and nine of them into NVN and SVN, respectively. Two reconnaissance missions were flown during the month, with the airfield at Vinh the mission assignment. Escort aircraft on both missions expended ordnance in a protective reaction role against firing antiaircraft artillery sites near the field. Other protective reaction strikes were executed.

1971—Continued

2 December   NAF Cam Ranh Bay, South Vietnam, was disestablished and patrol squadron detachments which had routinely rotated at NAF Cam Ranh Bay were deployed to NAS Cubi Point, R.P. At Cam Ranh Bay the patrol squadrons were part of the Vietnam Air Patrol Unit under the operational control of Commander, Fleet Air Wing 8 or 10. Operational tasking could also come from Commander, Task Force 77, on Yankee Station or Commander, Seventh Fleet. The patrol squadrons worked closely with Commander, Vietnam Coastal Surveillance Force. Their missions were to provide air patrol coverage for SVN along her coast line to detect any infiltration of NVN trawlers taking men and supplies into SVN. These missions were known as Market Time patrols. Patrol squadrons also provided aerial reconnaissance and ASW patrols for naval forces operating from Yankee Station and other areas of the Gulf of Tonkin and the South China Sea.

2 December   Commander George W. White, at the Naval Air Test Center, Patuxent River, Md., became the first Navy test pilot to fly the F-14A Tomcat. By the end of 1971, nine of the aircraft were assigned to various flight test programs. Purchase plans had called for an eventual total of 313 aircraft—301 for operations and 12 for research and development.

8 December   Amphibious Group Alpha, formed around *Tripoli*, was directed to move from Okinawa to the vicinity of Singapore in anticipation of a possible Indian Ocean deployment. This followed indications by the head of the UN relief mission in Dacca, East Pakistan/Bangladesh that as a result of the Indo-Pakistani war, which began on 3 December, evacuation of foreign civilians by means of carrier-based helicopters might be required.

8 December   Commander-in-Chief, U.S. Pacific Fleet (CINCPACFLT) confirmed a requirement previously enunciated by Commander, Naval Air Force Pacific Fleet, for a system of video coverage of the entire launch and recovery sequence of carrier operations.

10 December   *Enterprise* and other units from Yankee Station formed Task Force 74 and departed Vietnamese waters for the Indian Ocean. On 12 December the Royal Air Force evacuated Western nationals from East Pakistan/Bangladesh, thereby eliminating the requirement for an American evacuation operation. Task Force 74 entered the Indian Ocean on 15 December, as a show of force in connection with the Indo-Pakistani war.

12 December   VX-4 reported on an extensive series of evaluations of the helmet mounted sight, the Visual Target Acquisition System, in the F-4 that had commenced in 1969. While the report cited a number of shortcomings, it concluded that the helmet sight was superior to operational equipment used by fighter pilots in air-to-air combat.

15 December   VMA(AW)-224, part of CVW-15 on board *Coral Sea*, arrived on Yankee Station. VMA(AW)-224 was the first Marine Corps squadron to fly combat missions into NVN from a carrier operating on Yankee Station.

31 December   During 1971 HAL-3, the Seawolves, the only light attack helicopter squadron in the Navy, flew 34,746 hours in squadron aircraft in support of their mission to provide quick reaction armed helicopter close air support for all naval forces and South Vietnamese forces operating in the southern part of SVN. During their flights in 1971, HAL-3 expended 16,939,268 rounds of 7.62mm ammunition; 96,696 2.75-inch rockets; 32,313 40mm grenade rounds; and 2,414,096 rounds of .50 cal. machine gun ammunition in carrying out their assigned missions. HAL-3 lost six aircraft during 1971.

31 December   *Constellation* and *Enterprise* operated on Yankee Station together during the month until 10 December, when the latter was unexpectedly directed to transit to the Indian Ocean where she operated as

UH-1B helicopter from HAL-3 flies low over the Mekong Delta, South Vietnam NAH-002810

1971—Continued

flagship for the newly formed TF-74 for the possible evacuation of U.S. citizens from East Pakistan in connection with the Indo-Pakistani war. *Constellation's* tour was extended to the end of the month due to the new contingency operations. *Coral Sea* came on the line 15 December. A total of 2,462 ordnance delivery strike sorties were flown during the month. The number of surface-to-air missile firing incidents increased and the bold excursions by MiG aircraft into Laos prompted both the USAF and USN to develop new tactics, combining efforts, to suppress the MiG threat. A major protective reaction strike effort by both USAF and USN commenced 26 December and terminated 30 December. In this period, TF-77 flew 423 strike sorties employing all-weather A-6A systems backed up by A-7Es as pathfinders, with Dong Hoi, Quang Khe and Vinh the major targets assigned to the Navy. During the month, the Laser Guided Bomb (LGB) was introduced by squadrons aboard *Constellation*. Initially, 16 trial LGB drops were road cuts, with subsequent targets antiaircraft artillery sites. In the coming year, LGBs were to be used effectively against heretofore seemingly indestructible targets in NVN, such as heavy steel bridge structures built into solid rock.

1972

1 January The area of responsibility assigned to Commander-in-Chief, Pacific (CINCPAC), was shifted westward to include the Indian Ocean and the Persian Gulf. U.S. naval communications, refueling and logistical airstrip facilities continued under construction on the island of Diego Garcia to assist in covering the new area of responsibility for the U.S. Navy.

6 January Training Air Wing Five was established at Whiting Field, Fla. The new wing was composed of Naval Air Stations Whiting and Ellyson Fields; VT-2, VT-3 and VT-6; and HT-8. This was the first training wing established under the reorganization of the Naval Air Training Command. The wing was established to coordinate and supervise training activities that previously had been the responsibility of each station and squadron.

18 January *Enterprise* joined *Constellation* on Yankee Station following her tour in the Indian Ocean in December 1971, where she had shown force and the flag in connection with the Indo-Pakistani war and the buildup of Soviet naval forces off the Indian subcontinent.

18 January *Guam* began the first in a series of tests to analyze the sea control ship concept (SCS). SCS was a concept in which a shipboard platform would have a smaller complement of aircraft than the large carriers (CVA) and would maintain control of sea lines/lanes in low threat areas of the world. A SCS ship would be designed to carry the V/STOL aircraft as well as helicopters, in order to provide protection of underway replenishment groups, mercantile convoys, amphibious assault forces and task groups with no aircraft carrier in company.

19 January Lieutenants Randall H. Cunningham and William P. Driscoll in an F-4 of VF-96 off *Constellation* shot down a MiG-21, the first enemy aircraft downed since 28 March 1970, when Lieutenants Jerome E. Beaulier and Steven J. Barkley in an F-4 of VF-142 off *Constellation* downed a MiG-21. The 19 January action occurred during a protective reaction strike in response to earlier antiaircraft artillery and surface-to-air missile firings from the area which had menaced an RA-5C reconnaissance plane and its escorts. This accounted for the Navy's 33rd MiG shot down in the Vietnam war since the first shoot down on 17 June 1965, downed by Commanders Louis C. Page and John J. Smith in an F-4 of VF-21 off *Midway*.

21 January The S-3A Viking, the Navy's newest ASW aircraft, conducted its maiden test flight from Lockheed's Palmdale, Calif., facility. The S-3A met the Navy's requirements for a 400 knot plus aircraft with a 2,000 mile sub hunting range to replace the aging S-2 Tracker. The S-3A, while about the same size as the S-2, had twice the speed and range of the Tracker. It had been equipped with the latest sensor and weapon systems and could cover nearly three times the area of the S-2 Tracker.

31 January With only light ground action, limited troop contacts and the withdrawal of U.S. ground troops continuing during the month, the level of air operations also remained low, a situation which continued generally throughout the first three months of the year. During January, a total of only eight Navy tactical air attack sorties were flown in South Vietnam (SVN). In North Vietnam (NVN), there was very little attack effort except for some protective reaction strikes. *Coral Sea*, *Constellation* and *Enterprise* served intermittently on Yankee Station during the month.

11 February As a result of the shift from conventional to jet aircraft, the Navy announced that the Aviation Machinist's Mate Class B school on reciprocating engines, located at the Naval Air Technical Training Command, NAS Memphis, Tenn., was closing.

LT Cunningham shows how he and LT(jg) Driscoll bagged MiGs 1151717

Pre-flight pilot briefing for combat mission over Vietnam.

1972—Continued

11 February   The Navy announced that the development and installation of mufflers on engine test cells at the Naval Air Rework Facility, Alameda, Calif., had eliminated 85 percent of the audible noise in testing jet engines for the A-3.

29 February   During the month, naval air attack sorties in SVN had risen to 733 compared to 8 during January. The increase was due to the preemptive operations by allied forces in preparation for an expected large-scale enemy offensive during Tet which did not materialize. *Constellation*, *Coral Sea* and *Hancock* served overlapping tours on Yankee Station, assuring two to three carriers on station at a time during most of the month.

10 March   There were limited attack strikes into NVN; however, protective reaction strikes increased significantly. During the period 5 January through 10 March there were 90 protective reaction strikes by USN and USAF aircraft against surface-to-air missile and antiaircraft artillery installations, compared to 108 such raids during the entire year of 1971.

16 March   HAL-3, the only armed UH-1 Navy helicopter squadron to serve in Vietnam, was disestablished. HAL-3 and VAL-4 were the only Navy air units to be homeported in-country. HAL-3 provided valuable gunship support for Navy and Army riverine operations in the Mekong Delta from 1967 to their disestablishment. During this time HAL-3 pioneered various tactics in support of patrol boats and shore installations. They operated from various bases in the Mekong Delta and from specially-equipped Patrol Craft Tenders (AGP) (former LSTs).

23 March   VMA-513 completed the Harrier DOD sortie rate validation and demonstrated the capability of the AV-8A to respond rapidly and repeatedly to requests for close air support while operating from austere forward bases. During the ten-day test, the squadron flew 376 sorties with a complement of six aircraft.

24 March   A QF-4B target aircraft that the Naval Air Development Center, Warminster, Pa., had converted from a combat configuration into a maneuvering target, was delivered to the Naval Missile Center for testing. The QF-4B would fulfill the requirement for a full-size, high-altitude, supersonic, maneuvering aerial target capable of flying at altitudes in excess of 50,000 feet and at airspeeds exceeding twice the speed of sound.

29 March   The BQM-34E, supersonic Firebee II, was utilized by the Atlantic Fleet Weapons Range for the first time in missile defense exercises with *Wainwright* (DLG 28). The target was launched from a DP-2E at an altitude of 20,000 feet and accelerated to Mach 1.52 while testing the ship's ability to withstand penetration of high altitude, high speed enemy craft.

29 March   Due to the fleet requirements for qualified aircrew personnel, the Naval Air Technical Training Unit's Photographer's Mate Class "A" School initiated flight training again as part of the course. The flight training requirements for the Photographer's Mate Class "A" School had been dropped 16 years earlier.

30 March   Naval Air attack sorties in SVN had dropped from 733 in February to 113 during March. On 23 March the U.S. canceled further peace negotiations in Paris, France, because of a lack of progress in the talks. This was followed by the North Vietnamese invasion of SVN. This "Easter or Spring Offensive" was the result of the long buildup and infiltration of NVN forces during previous months and presaged some of the most intense fighting of the entire war. The NVN invasion prompted increased air operations by the carriers in support of South Vietnamese and U.S. forces. The carriers on Yankee Station when NVN invaded on 30 March were *Hancock* and *Coral Sea*. During the month four carriers had rotated on Yankee Station; they were *Constellation*, *Kitty Hawk*, *Coral Sea* and *Hancock*.

1 April   VAL-4, the last Navy combat force in Vietnam, was withdrawn. VAL-4 flew the OV-10 Bronco and its mission had been to provide quick reaction and close support for river patrol boats and the mobile riverine forces in South Vietnam.

5 April   Operation Freedom Train involved Navy tactical air sorties against military and logistic targets in the southern part of NVN that were involved in the invasion of SVN. The operating area in NVN was limited initially to between 17° and 19°N. However, special strikes were authorized against targets above the 19th parallel on various occasions. The magnitude of the North Vietnamese offensive indicated that an extended logistics network and increased resupply routes would be required to sustain ground operations by NVN in their invasion of SVN. Most target and geographical restrictions that were placed in effect since October 1968 concerning the bombing in NVN were lifted gradually and the list of authorized targets expanded. Strikes in NVN were against vehicles, lines of communication (roads, waterways, bridges, railroad bridges and railroad tracks), supply targets, air defense targets

1972—Continued

and industrial/power targets. Aircraft involved in Freedom Train operations were from *Hancock, Coral Sea, Kitty Hawk* and *Constellation*. By the end of April, operations were permitted in NVN throughout the region below 20° 25′N and many special strikes above the 20th parallel had also been authorized.

6 April Heavy air raids were conducted against NVN, the first since October 1968 when a halt was called on heavy raids. Since the bombing halt in October 1968, the U.S. air effort had been concentrated on interdicting men and supplies moving along the routes into SVN. Except for protective reaction strikes and a five-day operation at the end of 1971, called Proud Deep, very few heavy attack missions had been flown into NVN. The U.S. heavy reactionary raids were prompted by a massive invasion of SVN by six North Vietnamese divisions, that by 6 April involved 12 of North Vietnam's 13 divisions. The objectives of these heavy raids were: (1) destruction of all NVN aggression-supporting resources, (2) harassment and disruption of enemy military operations, and (3) reduction and impediment of movements of men and materials through southern NVN.

6 April Elements of two Phantom II Marine squadrons, VMFA-115 and VMFA-232, flew into Da Nang from Iwakuni, Japan, as part of the reinforcing effort in support of SVN troops, particularly around Quangtri. VMFA-212 arrived from Kaneohe, Hawaii, on 14 April. Targets for Marine sorties were enemy tanks, trucks and troops, giving SVN forces a chance to regroup and reestablish a line of defense north and west of Hue.

6 April The Navy's new air superiority fighter, the F-14 Tomcat, arrived at Naval Air Test Center, Patuxent River, Md. The swing-wing, twin-engine Grumman aircraft arrived for a series of catapult launches, automatic carrier landing system checks, airspeed system calibrations and weight and balance checks to determine its suitability for naval operations.

7 April During the week ending 7 April, the Navy flew 680 sorties in SVN to counter the NVN troop concentrations and their equipment flow, and to support the SVN forces with close air support, direct air support and interdiction missions. This was more than five times the number of sorties the Navy flew for the entire month of March.

11 April The Harpoon anti-ship missile underwent its first drop test at the Naval Missile Center, Point Mugu, Calif. The missile, developed by McDonnell Douglas Corporation, was dropped from 20,000 feet by a P-3 Orion operated by the Missile Center. The Harpoon was designed to be launched from aircraft or ships from a stand-off range against enemy ship targets.

12 April The new P-3C Acoustic Sensor Operator Trainer (Device 14B44) was made available for training aircrew personnel at Fleet Aviation Specialized Operational Training Group, Pacific Detachment. It was designed to train aircrewmen in the operation of sensor stations on the P-3C Orion aircraft. The simulator could duplicate the real world conditions of underwater acoustical data and also simulate the detection, classification and localization procedures of the AQA-7 Jezebel system on board the P-3C Orion.

14 April The Navy averaged 191 sorties per day in SVN, a 97 percent increase over the previous week. Sorties concentrated west and north of Quangtri City with interdiction and direct air support flown in the area. Carriers on Yankee Station were *Constellation, Hancock, Coral Sea,* and *Kitty Hawk.*

16 April Apollo 16 was launched successfully from Kennedy Space Center, Fla., for a lunar highlands investigation. The astronaut team was composed of Captain John W. Young, Lieutenant Colonel Charles M. Duke, USAF, and Lieutenant Commander Thomas K. Mattingly. Astronauts Young and Mattingly, the Navy members of the Apollo 16 crew, landed on the moon four days later to conduct scientific research.

16 April Aircraft from *Coral Sea, Kitty Hawk* and *Constellation* flew 57 sorties in the Haiphong area in support of U.S. Air Force B-52 strikes on the Haiphong petroleum products storage area. This operation was known as Freedom Porch.

25–30 April An example of Naval Air action against enemy positions inside central and south SVN during NVN's spring offensive occurred the last six days of April as *Hancock's* VA-55, -164 and -211 struck enemy held territory around Kontum and Pleiku and *Constellation's* VA-146, -147 and -165, hit areas around the besieged city of Anloc in support of SVN troops, some only 40 miles outside the capital of Saigon. Targets attacked included artillery fire bases, enemy tanks, bunkers, troop positions, ammunition caches and gun emplacements.

27 April HC-1, aboard *Ticonderoga,* recovered Apollo 16 after it splashed down in the south Pacific.

1972—Continued

28 April The AIM-54A Phoenix missile was launched from an F-14 for the first time. The aircraft was flying from Point Mugu, Calif.

30 April Operations by Navy and Marine Corps aircraft in Vietnam had expanded significantly throughout April, with a total of 4,833 Navy sorties in SVN and 1,250 sorties in NVN. The Marine Corps flew 537 sorties in SVN. The dramatic increase in Navy sorties was supported by directing all four carriers operating in the western Pacific to the support of operations in Vietnam. *Coral Sea* and *Hancock* were on Yankee Station when the North Vietnamese spring offensive began. *Kitty Hawk* was ordered to Yankee Station on 1 April and arrived on 3 April. *Constellation* was ordered to Yankee Station on 2 April and arrived on the line 7 April. Between 8 and 30 April the Navy effort grew gradually from 240 sorties a day to a peak of over 300, resulting in a monthly average of 270 sorties per day.

1 May While flying weather was good for the first seven days of May, the Navy averaged 97 attack sorties daily into NVN while flying an average of 168 a day into SVN. The Navy's efforts at this time were still concentrated in support of SVN forces attempting to stem the NVN offensive, then a month old. SVN troops were retreating toward Hue. Quangtri City had fallen 1 May and an attack against Hue appeared imminent. The city of Anloc remained surrounded by the NVN. The first week of May also witnessed NVN's newly deployed combat support surface-to-air missiles, the SA-7 Grail infrared-seeker missile.

4 May The Navy's first night carrier landing trainer was unveiled at NAS Lemoore, Calif. This trainer permitted pilots to simulate night landings of the A-7E on carrier decks.

5 May VP-9 aircraft departed NAS Moffett Field, Calif., for NAS Cubi Point, R.P., to augment the VP units tasked with ocean surveillance air patrols in relationship to the mining of NVN harbors and the corresponding movement of Communist bloc ships.

6 May In the second most active dog-fight day of the war, Navy flyers shot down two MiG-17s and two MiG-21s. Scoring the kills were flyers from VF-111 and VF-51 aboard *Coral Sea* and two planes from VF-114 off *Kitty Hawk*.

8 May For the first time in more than three weeks, U.S. forces attacked targets in the vicinity of Hanoi, with Navy pilots flying 50 attack sorties. Another 96 sorties were flown in southern NVN between the capital and the DMZ, while 99 were directed against the enemy in SVN.

9 May Operation Pocket Money, the mining campaign against principal NVN ports, was launched. Early that morning, an EC-121 aircraft took off from Da Nang airfield to provide support for the mining operation. A short time later, *Kitty Hawk* launched 17 ordnance-delivering sorties against the Nam Dinh railroad siding as a diversionary air tactic. Poor weather, however, forced the planes to divert to secondary targets at Thanh and Phu Qui which were struck at 090840H and 090845H, Vietnam time, respectively. *Coral Sea* launched three A-6A and six A-7E aircraft loaded with mines and one EKA-3B in support of the mining operation directed against the outer approaches to Haiphong Harbor. The mining aircraft departed the vicinity of *Coral Sea* at 090840H in order to execute the mining at precisely 090900H to coincide with the President's public announcement in Washington that mines had been seeded. The A-6 flight led by the CAG, Commander Roger E. Sheets, was composed of Marine Corps aircraft from VMA-224 and headed for the inner channel. The A-7Es, led by Commander Leonard E. Giuliani and made up of aircraft from VA-94 and VA-22, were designated to mine the outer segment of the channel. Each aircraft carried four MK 52-2 mines. Captain William R. Carr, USMC, the bombardier/navigator in the lead plane, established the critical attack azimuth and timed the mine releases. The first mine was dropped at 090859H and the last of the field of 36 mines at 090901H. Twelve mines were placed in the inner segment and the remaining 24 in the outer segment. All MK 52-2 mines were set with 72-hour arming delays, thus permitting merchant ships time for departure or a change in destination consistent with the President's public warning. It was the beginning of a mining campaign that planted over 11,000 MK 36 type destructor and 108 special MK 52-2 mines over the next eight months. It is considered to have played a significant role in bringing about an eventual peace arrangement, particularly since it so hampered the enemy's ability to continue receiving war supplies.

10 May Operation Linebacker I, the heavy strike of targets in most of NVN, evolved and lasted until restrictions on operations above 20°N were imposed 22 October. The operation was an outgrowth of Freedom Train and the President's mining declaration which also stated that the U.S. would make a maximum effort to interdict the flow of supplies in NVN. On this first day of Linebacker I, the Navy shifted its attacks from targets in southern NVN to the coastal

1972—Continued

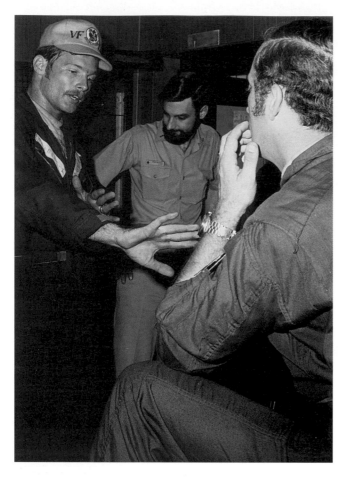

LT Dose of VF-92 explains MiG manuever 1151760

region embracing Haiphong north to the Chinese border. In all, 173 attack sorties were flown in this region this day, although another 62 were directed into SVN in continuing support of allied forces there.

It was the most intensified air-to-air combat day of the entire war. Navy flyers shot down eight MiGs. An F-4 Phantom II, from VF-96 on board *Constellation,* while engaged in aerial combat over Haiphong shot down three MiGs for the first triple downing of enemy MiGs by one plane during the war. Lieutenant Randall H. Cunningham was the pilot and Lieutenant (jg) William P. Driscoll was the RIO of the F-4. These three MiG downings, coupled with their 19 January and 8 May downing of two MiGs, made them the first MiG aces of the Vietnam War. Three other kills were scored by planes of VF-96 and one by VF-92 off *Constellation* and one by VF-51 off *Coral Sea.*

During the five and one-half month period of Linebacker I, the Navy contributed more than 60 percent of the total sorties in NVN, with 60 percent of this effort in the "panhandle", the area between Hanoi and the DMZ. Tactical air operations were most intense

during the July-September quarter with 12,865 naval sorties flown. Most attack sorties in NVN fell into two classes—armed reconnaissance and strike. The former was directed usually against targets of opportunity within three main areas—near Hanoi, Haiphong and the Chinese border. Strike operations were preplanned and usually directed at fixed targets. Most types of fixed targets, not associated with armed reconnaissance, required approval by the Commander-in-Chief, Pacific, or by the Joint Chiefs of Staff, prior to attack. Principal Navy aircraft were the A-7 and A-6, which accounted for roughly 60 and 15 percent of the Navy's attack sorties, respectively. About 25 percent of the Navy's effort was at night. Carriers participating in the initial May-June operations from Yankee Station were *Constellation, Coral Sea, Hancock, Kitty Hawk, Midway* and *Saratoga.*

10 May   Commander, Naval Air Systems Command, promulgated a plan for management of advanced prototype development and demonstration of a thrust-augmented wing Attack Plane-Fighter Vertical/Short Takeoff and Landing aircraft. A prototype development manager was to be established under the Deputy Commander for Plans and Programs and was to be assisted by a small cadre of management and technical personnel located in the Assistant Commander for Research and Technology's organization and at the contractor's facility.

11 May   Naval aircraft flying from *Coral Sea, Midway, Kitty Hawk* and *Constellation* laid additional mine fields in the remaining ports of significance in NVN—Thanh Hoa, Dong Hoi, Vinh, Hon Gai, Quang Khe and Cam Pha as well as the Haiphong approaches. This early mining was not confined solely to the seven principal ports. Other locations were also seeded early in the campaign, including the Cua Sot, Cap Mui Ron, and the river mouths, Cua Day and Cua Lac Giang, south of Don Son and the Haiphong port complex.

12 May   The 72-hour delay arming time on the initial mines laid at Haiphong was up at 120900H Vietnam time. Nine ships at Haiphong had taken advantage of the grace period to depart the port. Twenty-seven ships remained. Both Soviet and Soviet-bloc ships headed for Haiphong at the time had diverted to different destinations, thus avoiding a direct confrontation with the mine fields.

13 May   CH-53 and CH-46 helicopters of HMM-164 aboard *Okinawa* airlifted 1,000 South Vietnamese Marines from SVN's 369th Marine Corps Brigade from a landing zone near Hue to an area 24 miles northwest of the city behind NVN lines.

1972—Continued

CH-53A Sea Stallion supplying Marines S-54231-A

14 May   During the first two weeks of May, and the fourth day of Linebacker I, 992 military targets in NVN had been attacked by Navy pilots. Storage areas accounted for 17 percent, roads and trucks 15 percent, railroads 13 percent and bridges other than rail for 11 percent of the targets hit. The number of targets attacked would be increased by nearly 50 percent by the end of the month as Linebacker gained momentum.

17 May   Two A-4 Marine squadrons, VMA-311 and -211, arrived from Japan at the recently reactivated base at Bien Hoa, SVN. These units concentrated air strikes against enemy troops surrounding An Loc and

responded to calls from counterattacking SVN forces attempting to gain ground in adjacent areas.

18 May   The scope of the air war in Vietnam changed when the Uong Bi electric power plant near Haiphong was struck. This marked the beginning of strikes on a class of targets formerly avoided, including power plants, shipyards and the Haiphong cement plant. Over 60 of the Navy's more than 200 sorties into NVN that day were in the Haiphong region, the first since 10 May.

25 May   The Secretary of the Navy signed the Incidents at Sea Agreement between the U.S. and

1972—Continued

USSR. Since 1945 Naval Aviation history recorded 15 serious incidents of firing on U.S. Navy planes by Communist bloc aircraft. The agreement was designed to help prevent unintentional accidents between the two navies and help reduce tension on or over the high seas.

31 May During the month, the Navy had flown 3,949 attack sorties against NVN as compared to 1,250 during April; continuing attack sorties into SVN numbered 3,290 for May compared to 4,833 in April. While naval sorties in SVN had dropped by over 500 from the previous month of April, USMC air attack sorties in support of allied forces in SVN increased from 543 in April to 1,502 during May. Targets in NVN hit by naval planes increased to 2,416 in May from 719 during April, with railroads accounting for 16 percent, roads and trucks 14, storage areas 13 and bridges 10 percent of the targets hit. Enemy MiGs shot down over NVN by naval flyers during May totaled 16, including 11 MiG-17s, two MiG-19s and three MiG-21s, while the Navy lost six planes, including two F-4s and two A-7s to SA-2 surface-to-air missiles, and one F-8 and one RA-5 to unknown causes, probably surface-to-air missiles. With *Saratoga* joining the other five carriers on Yankee Station during the month, carrier strength totaled six, the greatest number since the war began. Meanwhile, by the end of the month, the term "quasi-stalemate" best described the war situation in SVN. The SVN army was still regrouping and holding on, and the forward thrust of the NVN seemed to be halted.

20 June VMA(AW)-533 with A-6A Intruders arrived at the remote jungle base of Nam Phong, known as the "Rose Garden," in the east central plains of Thailand in juxtaposition to the NVN attacks in the SVN highlands. Roads, aircraft parking and storage areas had been hacked out of the jungle by a joint USN/USMC engineering team in preparing this advance base. Between 23 May and 18 June the following Marine Corps units had arrived in preparation for operations against the invading NVN forces: Task Force Delta; VMGR-152, Det D with KC-130 Hercules; H&MS-36, Det D with CH-46 Sea Knights; VMFA-115 with F-4B Phantom IIs and VMFA-232 with F-4J Phantom IIs.

21 June VF-31 aircraft from *Saratoga* shot down a MiG-21. This was the third MiG downing by Navy pilots during June. On 11 June VF-51 aircraft from *Coral Sea* shot down two MiG-17s in the Nam Dinh area of NVN.

21 June The Chief of Naval Material directed that the Commander, Naval Electronic Systems Command (ELEX) take on the responsibility and authority for final decisions involving development, acquisition and support for equipment and capabilities providing platform-to-platform command, control and communications (C3) involving satellites, air, surface and sub-surface elements. The directive involved a proposal to rename the ELEX to reflect this assignment and prohibited large scale lateral movements between the systems commands. Despite these qualifications, a dispute arose as to whether ELEX should undertake detailed management of most electronic material program or apply control through broad gauged decisions. The decision has resulted in the transfer of Project Management Offices for Space (PM-16) and Reconnaissances, Electronic Warfare and Special Operations (or REWSON—PM-7) from the Chief of Naval Material to the Commander, ELEX (as PME-107) and in the redesignation of the Naval Air Systems Command's Electronic Warfare Project Management Office as REWSON followed by the physical merging of the two REWSON project management offices with a double hatting of the incumbents.

23 June HS-2, -15, -74 and -75 came to the aid of flood stricken residents in the Wilkes-Barre, Scranton and Pottstown areas of Pennsylvania. Besides the extensive rescue and evacuation work conducted by these squadrons they were also involved in transporting medical supplies and personnel, equipment, food and clothing to the flood victims.

29 June NAVAIR announced the formation of a "Buddy-Up" Program whereby reserve officers attached to Naval Air Systems Command Reserve Units would establish a working relationship with various Naval Air Systems Command activities. This was envisioned as developing into a means whereby the reserve officers would identify and undertake to perform meaningful project work for the activities.

30 June Navy tactical air attack sorties in SVN during June were 2,021. This was a considerable decrease in comparison to the April and May figures. The decrease reflected the stalemate on the ground in SVN. Navy attack sorties against Linebacker I targets in NVN involved 3,844 sorties in June. Linebacker I attack sorties against the road transport system, water transport craft and storage targets increased from the pre-June levels. The greatest number of Navy concentrated strikes, which involved 10 or more attack aircraft striking a compact cluster of tactical targets, was flown from April through June and comprised 40 percent of the total Navy attack effort.

1972—Continued

30 June The Naval Air Rework Facility and the Naval Air Station at North Island, Calif., submitted to the Naval Civil Engineering Laboratory an interim report on pollution studies. A follow-on final report was published in August with the title "Environmental Collection Data Base." It contained methodological information on effective means of measuring the extent of various types of environmental pollution, related some pollutants to particular industrial or operational activity, and contained quantitative data on the extent of pollution found to be present. Thus, it provided an important first step in devising plans to lessen the environmental impact of pollution produced by naval operational and industrial air activities.

1 July A reorganization of the Naval Air Training system occurred when the Naval Air Advanced Training Command was disestablished and the Chief of Naval Air Training was relocated to Corpus Christi, Tex. This action was part of the Navy's effort to consolidate training under a concept called "single base training." When pilots completed their primary training they were assigned to a specific program involving training in either jets, props or helos. This training would be completed at one specific training base where the pilots would finish their instruction before receiving their wings. The new structure/organization came under the control of the Chief, Naval Air Training Command.

1 July Tactical Electronic Warfare Wing 13 (TACEL-WING-13) was disestablished at NAS Whidbey Island, Wash. It had been established to introduce the complex electronic warfare EA-6B Prowler into fleet service.

15 July A three-day test demonstration of the ability of the UH-2C Seasprite to fire Sparrow III missiles against surface targets was completed at the Pacific Missile Range, Sea Test Range, Calif. The helicopter, modified to carry a single missile mounted on a rail launcher, fired four missiles during the course of the demonstration.

22 July *Tripoli* arrived in Subic Bay, R.P., with HMM-165 on board to provide relief support after record rains caused disastrous flooding in the central Luzon valley between Manila and Lingayen Gulf. Tens of thousands of people were affected and additional ships were tasked for Philippine flood relief operations.

31 July The Navy began night operations regularly on 24 May and during June and July night sorties constituted 30 percent of the total Navy attack effort in NVN, relying primarily on the A-7 and A-6. About 45 percent of the Navy armed reconnaissance effort was at night during June and July. The A-7 flew about as many night sorties as it did day sorties. The A-6 flew more night than day armed reconnaissance sorties during the summer months. The total number of Navy night sorties during June and July were 1,243 and 1,332 respectively. Three to four carriers were maintained on Yankee Station during the summer months. The carriers involved were *Constellation*, *Coral Sea*, *Hancock*, *Kitty Hawk*, *Midway*, *Saratoga*, *Oriskany* and *America*.

31 July There was a dramatic change in NVN's air defense effort during the summer months. During the earlier periods of April and May, the Navy air effort in NVN involved intensive air-to-air combat and a large number of surface-to-air missile (SAM) firings. In contrast, during June and July there was an increase in Linebacker I Navy attack sorties, but there was a decrease in the number of air-to-air combat incidents and SAM firings. MiG kills decreased to three in June by Navy aircraft and zero in July compared to 16 MiG kills by Navy aircraft in May. After mid-June, almost all North Vietnamese aircraft sighted or engaged were MiG-21s. Navy/MiG encounters were primarily against MiG-21s, representing a considerable change from May, when 11 of 16 Navy kills were MiG-17s.

5 August *New Orleans* relieved *Tripoli* in Philippine flood relief operations. HMM-165 transferred to *New Orleans* to continue support due to their knowledge of terrain and problems inherent in the flood relief operations.

5 August A Naval Air Test Center pilot made the first fully automated landing aboard *Ranger* in an F-4J Phantom II. The test landing device linked the plane's controls with a computer aboard ship and enabled the aircraft to land with the pilot's hands off the controls. The system was developed to make safer landings at night and in low visibility conditions.

7 August An HC-7 Det 110 helicopter, aided by planes from *Saratoga* and *Midway*, conducted a search and rescue mission for a downed aviator in NVN. The pilot of an A-7 aircraft from *Saratoga* had been downed by a surface-to-air missile about 20 miles inland, northwest of Vinh, on 6 August. The HC-7 helicopter flew inland over mountainous terrain to rescue the pilot. The rescue helicopter used its search light to assist in locating the downed pilot and, despite receiving heavy ground fire, was successful in retrieving the pilot and returning to an LPD off the coast of NVN. This was the deepest penetration of a rescue heli-

1972—Continued

copter into NVN since 1968. HC-7 Det 110 continued its rescue efforts and by the end of 1972 it had successfully conducted 48 rescues during the year, 35 of those under combat conditions.

17 August The Naval Material Command and the Air Force Systems Command reached an agreement relating to Navy and Air Force responsibilities for aircraft engine production at the Pratt & Whitney Aircraft Divisions, East Hartford, Conn., and West Palm Beach, Fla. The Memorandum of Agreement provided that an Air Force Deputy Plant Representative and staff be assigned to the Naval Plant Representative Office (NAVPRO) to represent the F-15 Program Director on F-15 matters and to advise the NAVPRO on the in-plant management of Air Force engine programs.

29 August John Konrad, Vought Aeronautics test pilot, made the first flight in a two-place version of the A-7E that the company had developed to demonstrate to the Air Force and the Navy the advantages of such a configuration for use as an advanced trainer or for such tactical duties as electronics countermeasures.

31 August Although Marine Corps air efforts were concentrated in SVN, the Marines contributed significantly to U.S. efforts in NVN to prevent offloading and transportation of supplies from Chinese merchant ships at Hon La and Hon Nieu. HMA-369, with seven AH-1J helicopters, using the Cobra weapons system, operated from *Denver* (LPD 9) against water transport traffic in late June, and from *Cleveland* (LPD 7) in early August. HMA-369's operations during August were extended to include night surveillance and attack. In addition HMA-369 helicopters served as airspotters for naval gunfire and as airborne tactical controllers for fixed-wing aircraft attacking lucrative targets.

The Navy flew 4,819 sorties in August against NVN. The downward trend of Navy attack sorties in SVN continued during July and August. The stepped-up campaign in the Mekong Delta accounted for a sharp rise in Marine Corps air activity in SVN. The Marine Corps air effort rose from 8 percent of the total air effort in SVN during May to 43 percent during August.

11 September VMFA-333 flying off *America* downed a MiG-21 near Phuc Yen airfield in North Vietnam. This was the only MiG kill for the Navy/Marine Corps during September and brought the grand total of MiGs downed by Navy/Marine Corps pilots to 55 since the war began.

30 September During September the number of Navy tactical air attack sorties decreased from the level flown in August. There were 3,934 Navy tactical air attack sorties flown into NVN, down by about 800 from the August total. During July and August, more than 45 percent of the Navy armed reconnaissance sorties were at night. However, in September, only 31 percent of the armed reconnaissance sorties were flown at night. In SVN the Navy flew 1,708 tactical air attack sorties, a decrease from the level flown in August. About half of the Navy's tactical air sorties were close and direct air support sorties in SVN. Marine Corps activity stayed relatively high during September because of stepped-up ground activity in the Mekong Delta. Marine Corps tactical air sorties for September were 1,296. Carriers operating on Yankee Station during the month of September were *Hancock, Kitty Hawk, Midway, Saratoga, Oriskany* and *America*.

1 October The first two F-14 Tomcat squadrons were formed at NAS Miramar San Diego, Calif. The new squadrons carried the designations VF-1 and VF-2. These squadrons were established to receive the Navy's first new fighter plane in 14 years, the McDonnell Douglas F-4 Phantom II was introduced in 1958.

8 October The first F-14 Tomcat, the Navy's new sophisticated fighter, was delivered to VF-124. VF-124 was designated the F-14 training squadron for all F-14 fighter squadrons of the Pacific and Atlantic Fleet.

23 October The U.S. ended all tactical air sorties into NVN above the 20th parallel and brought to a close Linebacker I operations. This goodwill gesture of terminating the bombing in NVN above the 20th parallel was designed to help promote the peace negotiations being held in Paris, France. During May through October, the Navy flew a total of 23,652 tactical air attack sorties into NVN. U.S. tactical air sorties during Linebacker I operations helped stem the flow of supplies into NVN, thereby limiting the operating capabilities of North Vietnam's invading army. Carriers involved in Linebacker I operations were *Enterprise, Constellation, Coral Sea, Hancock, Kitty Hawk, Midway, Saratoga, Oriskany* and *America*.

31 October During October the total number of Navy tactical air sorties into NVN was 2,661. Tactical air sorties into SVN during October were 2,097 and 1,599 for the Navy and Marine Corps, respectively. Air operations in SVN followed the general pattern of the ground war. NVN increased their small-scale attacks throughout SVN in an apparent effort to gain territory before a possible cease-fire. Thus, the main objective

1972—Continued

of Navy and Marine Corps tactical air sorties were close and direct air sorties in support of allied ground troops, with a view toward frustrating the enemy's desire to acquire territory before a cease-fire agreement was signed.

22 November Groundbreaking ceremonies for the new Naval Aviation Museum building were officiated by Admiral Arthur W. Radford, USN (Ret). Admiral Radford, former Chairman of the Joint Chiefs of Staff, was the Chairman of the Naval Aviation Museum Association, Inc., a non-profit organization of Naval Aviation enthusiasts who labored since 1965 to finance and create the first part of the new museum building. All funds for the building of the first phase of the museum were contributed by private individuals and organizations. The museum was designed to be built in three phases. The first phase consisted of 65,000 sq. ft. of floor space with future expansion of 140,000 sq. ft. The Naval Aviation Museum was established at NAS Pensacola, Fla., in December 1962 by the authority of the Secretary of the Navy. It had been housed in a temporary building until enough money had been accumulated to build the first phase of the new museum building.

30 November The majority of the Navy's tactical air sorties in SVN during October and November can best be described as close and direct air support attacks. Targets attacked during these sorties accounted for more than 75 percent of all known targets during October and November. The percentage of Navy sorties flown for interdiction purposes in SVN decreased markedly during October and November compared to the previous levels in the spring and summer months.

13 December An HC-1 Detachment Five SH-3G Sea King helicopter, stationed aboard *Oriskany,* rescued a VFP-63 pilot involved in operations in the Tonkin Gulf while on Yankee Station. This was the fifteenth pilot rescued by HC-1 detachments while they were operating aboard a carrier on Yankee Station during 1972. During 1972 HC-1 rescued a total of 36 people, including the 15 pilots.

17 December During the period 23 October through 17 December there was a U.S. bombing halt above the 20th parallel in NVN. No MiG kills or U.S. losses were recorded during this period. Three to four carriers were maintained on Yankee Station during the bombing halt. Carriers alternating on Yankee Station were: *Enterprise, Kitty Hawk, Midway, Saratoga, Oriskany, America* and *Ranger.*

18 December Linebacker II operations were initiated on 18 December when negotiations in the Paris peace talks stalemated. The Linebacker II operations ended on 29 December when the North Vietnamese returned to the peace table. These operations involved the resumed bombing of NVN above the 20th parallel and was an intensified version of Linebacker I. The reseeding of the mine fields was resumed and concentrated strikes were carried out against surface-to-air missile and antiaircraft artillery sites, enemy army barracks, petroleum storage areas, Haiphong naval and shipyard areas, and railroad and truck stations. Navy tactical air attack sorties under Linebacker II were centered in the coastal areas around Hanoi and Haiphong. There were 505 Navy sorties in this area during Linebacker II. Between 18 and 22 December the Navy conducted 119 Linebacker II strikes in North Vietnam. Bad weather was the main limiting factor on the number of tactical air strikes flown during Linebacker II. The following carriers participated in Linebacker II operations: *Enterprise, Saratoga, Oriskany, America* and *Ranger.*

19 December HC-1 helicopters, aboard *Ticonderoga,* recovered the crew of Apollo 17 after splashdown. The Apollo 17 crew consisted of Naval

Helicopter from HS-6 recovering astronauts from Apollo 14 lunar mission.

Apollo 14 capsule after splashdown in the Pacific Ocean awaiting recovery.

Aviators Captain Eugene A. Cernan and Commander Ronald E. Evans and geologist Harrison H. Schmidt. This recovery marked the end of NASA's Apollo lunar program. Naval Aviation squadrons and naval surface units performed all the recovery operations for the 11 Apollo missions. There were 33 astronauts involved in the Apollo program, 22 of whom had Navy backgrounds.

23 December An example of attack squadron action during the year is portrayed by the following partial roundup of operations by VA-56 which ended its seventh line period this date. Flying combat with CVW-5 off *Midway* during portions of every month since April, the squadron recorded a total of 180 days on the line, engaged in 5,582.9 combat hours, flew over 3,000 sorties, performed 2,090 and 781 day and night carrier landings, respectively, and amassed a total of 6,301 flight hours during its line periods. It conducted strikes against such targets as the Haiphong, Ninh Binh, Ha Tinh, Kien An, Tam Da and Than Hoa bridge complexes, the Haiphong, Vinh, Doung Nham and Nam Dinh petroleum areas, and the Gia Lam railroad yards across the Red River from Hanoi. Other actions included mining operations and protective flights for four search and rescue (SAR) missions, including one at night inside NVN, and one

for two Air Force officers downed off the coast. During the line periods, four of the unit's A-7Bs were lost to antiaircraft artillery and surface-to-air missile fire, with two pilots taken prisoner-of-war, one listed as missing in action, and one retrieved.

25 December A Christmas day bombing/tactical air attack recess went into effect during which none of the U.S. air services flew sorties. Since the beginning of the heavy raids against the Hanoi/Haiphong complex on 18 December to persuade NVN to return to the conference table and release the American POWs, 420 raids by B-52s had been conducted, with 18 December accounting for 122, the highest number. Carrier strikes from TF-77 and tactical aircraft from Thailand supplemented the raids, mainly to suppress missile sites and confuse the NVN air defense systems. Heavy attacks were resumed on 26 December, with 113 B-52 raids, the next highest sortie count. Targets, as before, were powerhouses, railroads, missile assembly points, command and control stations, fuel reserves, airfields and railroad marshaling yards. By the end of the 27th, intercepted enemy messages indicated NVN was losing its missile potential as new missiles could not be moved from assembly points to the launchers.

1972—Continued

28 December   An F-4J Phantom II, from VF-142 on board *Enterprise*, downed a MiG-21. This was the 24th MiG downed by Navy/Marine Corps pilots during 1972. The total MiG downings by Navy/Marine Corps pilots during the Vietnam war from the first in June 1965 through December 1972 were 56. Statistics for Navy/Marine Corps downings of MiGs during 1972:

Constellation:	VF-96, 8 MiGs
	VF-92, 1 MiG
Coral Sea:	VF-51, 4 MiGs
	VF-111, 1 MiG
Midway:	VF-161, 4 MiGs
Kitty Hawk:	VF-114, 2 MiGs
Saratoga:	VF-103, 1 MiG
	VF-31, 1 MiG
America:	VMFA-333, 1 MiG
Enterprise:	VF-142, 1 MiG

29 December   Heavy raids around Hanoi, which had been resumed the day after the Christmas bombing halt, were eased as NVN showed indications of returning to the conference table. The over 700 sorties by B-52s during the 11 heavy-bombing days were believed accountable for the eventual resumption of negotiations which led to the peace agreement and the release of American POWs. On 28 and 29 December, during a total of 160 raids, no B-52s were lost to NVN air defenses, indicating the virtual paralysis of the system. Only two percent—15 B-52s were lost from over 700 raids during the whole 11-day heavy bombing period.

30 December   The U.S. called another bombing halt in North Vietnam and the Navy ended all tactical air sorties above the 20th parallel. The bombing halt was called when North Vietnam returned to the negotiating table to continue the Paris peace talks.

31 December   During 1972 the Navy conducted 33.9 percent of all tactical air attack sorties flown in SVN. There were 23,802 tactical air attack sorties flown and 160,763 general purpose bombs delivered by Navy fixed-wing aircraft, with Marine Corps fixed-wing aircraft delivering 111,859 general purpose bombs in SVN during 1972. The Navy and Marine Corps each lost five fixed-wing aircraft in SVN during 1972. In NVN the Navy conducted more than 60 percent of the tactical air attack sorties flown, for a total of 28,093. The Navy and Marine Corps lost 49 aircraft in NVN during this period. In 1972 the carriers spent a total of 1,403 on-line days at Yankee Station, with an average on-line period of slightly more than 25 days for each carrier. Carrier and Carrier Air Wings on Yankee Station during 1972 were:

Hancock with CVW-21	
Kitty Hawk with CVW-11	
Oriskany with CVW-19	
America with CVW-8	
Enterprise with CVW-14	
Midway with CVW-5	
Saratoga with CVW-3	
Constellation with CVW-9	
Coral Sea with CVW-15	
Ranger with CVW-2	

Marine Corps squadrons operating off carriers on Yankee Station during 1972 were VMA(AW)-224, VMCJ-2 and VMFA-333. Marine Corps land-based fixed-wing squadrons in Southeast Asia during 1972 were VMFA-115, VMFA-212, VMFA-232, VMA(AW)-533, VMCJ-1, VMA-211, VMA-311, VMGR-151, H&MS-15, and H&MS-12.

1973

1 January   A major reorganization in naval reserve affairs got under way as a result of the announcement two days earlier by the Secretary of the Navy that the Naval Surface and Air Reserve Commands would be consolidated into Commander Naval Reserve Force located in New Orleans, La.

8 January   Representatives of the U.S. and Greek navies signed an accord in Athens formally granting the U.S. Sixth Fleet home port facilities in the Athens vicinity. Under the arrangement, one of the Sixth Fleet's two carrier task forces in the Mediterranean Sea would be stationed in the Athens area.

12 January   VF-161, flying off *Midway*, shot down a North Vietnamese MiG-17, the last enemy "kill" of the war, making a total of 57 MiGs shot down by Navy and Marine Corps pilots during the Vietnam conflict.

27 January   The Vietnam cease-fire, announced four days earlier, came into effect and *Oriskany*, *America*, *Enterprise* and *Ranger*, on Yankee Station, cancelled all combat sorties into North and South Vietnam. During the U.S. involvement in the Vietnam conflict (starting in 1961 and ending on 27 January 1973) the Navy lost 526 fixed-wing aircraft and 13 helicopters to hostile action. The Marine Corps lost 193 fixed-wing aircraft and 270 helicopters to enemy action during the same period. Operation Homecoming, the repatriation of U.S. POWs between 27 January and 1 April, began and NVN and the Viet Cong released 591 POWs. Of the 591 POWs released during Operation Homecoming, 145 were Navy personnel, all but one of whom were Naval Aviation personnel.

1973—Continued

Former POW CDR William R. Stark is greeted by his family upon his arrival at NAS Miramar, Calif.

27 January   Task Force 78 was formed to conduct minesweeping operations in North Vietnamese waters under the code name Operation Endsweep. It consisted of surface minesweeping elements and an Air Mobile Mine Countermeasures Command. The latter was made up of HM-12, HMH-463 and HMM-165, organized into units Alpha through Delta, an airborne mine countermeasures planning element, command and control element, an aircraft element and a material element.

28 January   Aircraft from *Enterprise* and *Ranger* flew 81 combat sorties on the first day of the Vietnam cease-fire against lines-of-communication targets in Laos. The corridor for overflights was between Hue and Da Nang in SVN. These combat support sorties were flown in support of the Laotian government which had requested this assistance and it had no relationship with the cease-fire in Vietnam.

1 February   The U.S. Third Fleet was reactivated at Pearl Harbor, Hawaii, with the merger of the First Fleet and Antisubmarine Warfare Forces, Pacific Fleet. The change was made to reduce fleet staffs and achieve economies while retaining control of operational units, including some 100 ships and 60,000 men serving a 50-million-square mile area from the West Coast to beyond Midway Island.

3 February   Task Force 78 flagship *New Orleans,* with escort ships, began a six-day mine countermeasures exercise in Subic Bay, R.P., in preparation for scheduled Endsweep operations in NVN.

5 February   Commander, Task Force 78, and other Navy mine demolition experts met with North Vietnamese leaders in Haiphong to discuss Operation Endsweep, the clearing of mines in NVN.

6 February   Surface minesweepers of Task Force 78 began preliminary sweeping to prepare an anchorage in deep water off the approaches to Haiphong Harbor. Ships of the force included *New Orleans* and *Inchon.* The ocean anchorage would be used by command and supply ships of the U.S. Navy in on-scene support of minesweeping of NVN harbors, coastal and inland waterways. During the operation Task Force 78 ships were joined by *Tripoli.*

Minesweeping TF-78 on Operation Endsweep off Haiphong Harbor.

6 February   NAVAIR established a policy that new avionics equipment generally be designed for automatic troubleshooting with the general purpose Versatile Avionics Shop Test (VAST) computerized equipment. This policy significantly improved the maintenance of avionics equipment through use of the VAST system which was designed with the capability to test the majority of avionics within the Naval Aviation inventory.

11 February   Aircraft from *Constellation* and *Oriskany* operating on Yankee Station, the location of which was changed to a position off the coast of the northern part of South Vietnam, flew strikes against

1973—Continued

targets in southern Laos. Combat sorties from carriers on Yankee Station against targets in Laos had continued since the cease-fire in Vietnam.

14 February   The Pentagon announced a step-up of U.S. air strikes in Laos to 380 daily, an increase of 100. Aircraft from *Oriskany* and *Enterprise* flew about 160 of these sorties into Laos on this date.

25 February   Planes from *Ranger* and *Oriskany* flew combat support missions over Cambodia. The combat support sorties were flown in support of the government of Cambodia at its request.

27 February   Airborne mine countermeasures began off Haiphong during Operation Endsweep. This was a "first" in mine warfare as airborne minesweeping had never been done with "live" mines. A CH-53 Sea Stallion from HM-12 made two sweeps in the Haiphong shipping channel. All operations were abruptly halted and minesweeping task force moved to sea as the President called for "clarification . . . on a most urgent basis" of Hanoi's delay in releasing American POWs.

4 March   The withdrawal of U.S. troops from Vietnam resumed and the naval minesweeping force returned to its position off Haiphong. Minesweeping operations continued in and around Haiphong and the harbor was reopened after being closed for ten months because of the U.S. naval mining which began in May 1972. In addition, *America* was ordered to depart the Far East for the U.S. This was the initial move in reducing the number of carriers serving in Southeast Asia from six to three by mid-June 1973.

21 March   VXN-8 returned to NAS Patuxent River, Md., from Project Magnet deployment to the Southern Hemisphere under the direction of the U.S. Naval Oceanographic Office. During the deployment, two flights were made around the world within the Southern Hemisphere, and an over-the-South-Pole flight by an RP-3D on 4 March was a first for that type of aircraft.

29 March   The remaining U.S. combat forces left South Vietnam; and the United States Military Assistance Command, Vietnam (MACV), was disbanded, officially ending U.S. military involvement in South Vietnam. The last phase of Operation Homecoming was concluded when the final group of 148 American POWs was released by Hanoi. This brought the total to 591 POWs released, 566 of whom were U.S. military personnel with 144 being naval pilots and aircrewmen.

29–31 March   *Forrestal* led two other Sixth Fleet ships into Tunisian waters where Sea King helicopters from the carrier evacuated some 200 persons and airlifted four tons of relief supplies to flood victims in Tunisia.

1 April   Two new air wings were established as the final phase of the reorganization of the AirLant community, completing the functional wing concept: Air Antisubmarine Wing One with VS-22, -24, -27, -30, -31 and -32 and Helicopter Antisubmarine Wing One with HS-1, -3, -5, -7 and -11.

13 April   The Secretary of the Navy announced that an agreement with the United Kingdom had been signed providing for an eight-month joint study of an advanced V/STOL Harrier involving participation by Rolls-Royce, Hawker-Siddeley, Pratt & Whitney Aircraft and McDonnell Douglas. The overall aim was to determine the feasibility of joint development of an advanced concept V/STOL incorporating a Pegasus 15 engine and an advanced wing.

16 April   The Cruise Missile Project Office was established in the Naval Air Systems Command with responsibility to develop both tactical and strategic versions of the cruise missile.

30 April   The last Marine NAP (enlisted Naval Aviation Pilot) retired. He was Master Gunnery Sergeant Patrick J. O'Neil, who enlisted during World War II and completed over 30 years of active duty.

3–9 May   Fighting broke out between Lebanese army units and Palestinian guerrillas in Lebanon. Martial law was declared. Among U.S. forces in the Mediterranean, *John F. Kennedy* and *Forrestal* were alerted for possible contingencies. A cease-fire agreement between Lebanese and Palestinian negotiators stabilized the situation.

8 May   In a ceremony at the Douglas Aircraft Division, Long Beach, Calif., the first McDonnell Douglas C-9B Skytrain jet transports were accepted by the Navy and delivered to Fleet Tactical Support Squadrons One and Thirty. A commercial version of the DC-9, the C-9B had a maximum 32,444 pound payload range of 1,150 statute miles with a ferry range of about 3,400 miles. It accommodated 107 passengers five-abreast.

18 May   A four-day trial of a prototype glide slope indicator was completed aboard *Truxtun* (CGN 35). The indicator, developed by the Naval Air Engineering Center, consisted of a hydraulically stabilized Fresnel lens. It was one of several steps taken to achieve an all weather capability with LAMPS helicopters.

1973—Continued

25 May The first production RH-53D Sea Stallion, specially configured for the airborne mine counter-measures mission, arrived at the Naval Air Test Center, Patuxent River, Md., for weapons systems trials. Navy preliminary evaluation and the initial phase of the Board of Inspection and Survey trials had begun at Sikorsky Aircraft Division on 15 May.

25 May Skylab II, carrying a three-man, all-Navy crew of Captain Charles Conrad, Jr., Commander Joseph P. Kerwin, MC, and Commander Paul J. Weitz, rendezvoused with the earth-orbiting Skylab I workshop. Among the crew's first tasks was repairing the Skylab I meteoroid shield and solar array system which had been damaged during launch. The crew boarded the workshop, made repairs, conducted medical experiments and studied solar astronomy and earth resources for 28 days before returning to earth on 22 June.

7 June The Deputy Secretary of Defense directed the Navy to produce preliminary plans for a $250-million prototype development plan for a jet fighter aircraft costing less than the F-14 Tomcat missile-armed fighter.

13 June The National Aeronautics Association presented the Robert J. Collier Trophy for 1972 jointly to the Navy's Task Force 77 and to the Seventh and Eighth Air Forces for their "demonstrated expert and precisely integrated use of advance aerospace technology" in Operation Linebacker II, the 11-day air campaign in December 1972 against North Vietnam that "led to the return of the U.S. prisoners of war."

22 June The all-Navy crew of Skylab II astronauts was recovered after their 28-day mission in space by HC-1 and flown aboard *Ticonderoga*.

30 June FAW-1 and -2 were redesignated Patrol Wings 1 and 2. This was the end of the use of the FAW (Fleet Air Wing) designation and beginning of the Patrol Wing designation which had been used prior to World War II.

27 July Operation Endsweep was closed officially and Task Force 78 was disbanded. During the six months of its existence, the airborne element had made 3,554 sweeping runs totaling 1,134.7 sweeping hours in 623 sorties. The surface elements had made 208 sweeping runs of 308.8 hours. The aviation material casualties were three helicopters lost in operational accidents. Mine logistics carrier station operations in the Gulf of Tonkin were conducted by *Enterprise, Oriskany, Ranger,* and *Coral Sea* at various periods and their respective aircraft flew support sorties for Operation Endsweep.

28 July Skylab III commanded by Captain Alan L. Bean, USN, in company with civilian doctor Owen K. Garriott and Major John R. Lousma, USMC, was launched into space.

31 July HSL-33, the Navy's first squadron dedicated solely to providing LAMPS detachments for LAMPS-configured ships of the Pacific Fleet, was established at NAS Imperial Beach, California.

15 August After intensive bombing for more than six months, the U.S. ended its combat involvement in Cambodia, as voted by Congress on 30 June. Aircraft from carriers *Ranger* and *Oriskany* had conducted combat sorties in Cambodia during February. After March 1973, carriers on Yankee Station conducted carrier air patrols; electronic intelligence patrols; surface, subsurface, and surveillance coordinator patrols; and training, tanker, communications relay and reconnaissance sorties.

16 August The F-14's quick-reaction dogfight capability was demonstrated at the Pacific Missile Range, Point Mugu, Calif. when, from a distance of less than a mile, the aircraft shot down a maneuvering QT-33 target drone with a Sparrow III missile.

29 August HM-12 received the first RH-53D Sea Stallion helicopters. The RH-53Ds were configured especially for minesweeping operations.

6 September A BQM-34E Firebee II target drone, equipped with a graphite-epoxy composite wing, was test flown successfully at the Point Mugu Sea Test Range, Calif., reaching a speed of Mach 1.6 at 40,000 feet and a maximum acceleration of six Gs. The graphite-epoxy composite would save 40 percent of the weight of metal counterparts in various aeronautical applications. The test wing was designed and fabricated by the Naval Air Development Center, Warminster, Pa.

7 September The Navy announced that the Blue Angels flight demonstration team planned to switch to the slower, smaller and less expensive A-4F Skyhawks rather than continue to use the F-4J Phantoms they had been flying since 1969.

25 September The three astronauts of Skylab III made a successful splashdown in the Pacific, ending a record 59-day, 24-million-mile flight. They were recovered by HC-1 and flown aboard *New Orleans*. During Skylab III, Captain Alan L. Bean, USN, Commander of Skylab III, set a new record for the most time in space, eclipsing Navy Captain Charles Conrad's record of 49 days, three hours, and 37 minutes.

1973—Continued

The S-3A Viking making its first catapult launch from Forrestal as part of its initial carrier suitability tests C121073

1 October The formal Board of Inspection and Survey service acceptance trials of the S-3A began at the Naval Air Test Center, Patuxent River, Md. The tests were to utilize seven S-3A aircraft during a four-month period, including weapons system checkouts, carrier suitability, flying qualities and performance, and propulsion and airframe evaluation.

5 October *Midway*, with CVW-5 embarked, put into Yokosuka, Japan, marking the first home porting of a complete carrier task group in a Japanese port as a result of the accord arrived at on 31 August 1972 between the U.S. and Japan. In addition to the morale factor of dependents housed at a foreign port, the development had strategic significance because it facilitated continuous positioning of three carriers in the Far East at a time when the economic situation demanded the reduction of carriers in the fleet.

8–13 October Task Force 60.1 with *Independence*, Task Force 60.2 with *Franklin D. Roosevelt* and Task Force 61/62 with *Guadalcanal* were alerted for possible evacuation contingencies in the Middle East. *John F. Kennedy*, in the Atlantic, was directed to a holding area off Gibraltar.

9 October The Pentagon announced that *Guadalcanal*, an amphibious assault ship with U.S. Marines aboard, was operating in the eastern Mediterranean Sea as part of the Sixth Fleet. Other elements of the fleet were moving toward Crete, including *Independence* and *Franklin D. Roosevelt*, on alert as a result of the 1973 Yom Kippur war between Arab and Israeli forces.

19–24 October Some 50 A-4 aircraft were flown from the U.S. to supply Israel, staging through the Azores and *Franklin D. Roosevelt* which was located south of Sicily. When necessary, *John F. Kennedy*, off Gibraltar and *Independence*, off Crete, also provided assistance. On the 24th, *Iwo Jima* entered the Mediterranean with reinforcing Marines.

27 October Due to the situation in the Middle East, the U.S. government ordered a worldwide "precautionary alert" of its military forces. Possible unilateral intervention by the Soviet Union was feared. By 28 October, three U.S. aircraft carriers and two amphibious assault carriers were off Crete.

1973—Continued

29 October   The Defense Department announced that a naval task force centering around *Hancock* had been ordered to the Indian Ocean. This was prompted by the Middle East war and the consequent Arab oil embargo and was the first of four task groups deployed into the Indian Ocean in 1974 to focus on such areas as the entrance to the Persian Gulf and the entrance to the Red Sea.

16 November   Skylab IV, commanded by Lieutenant Colonel Gerald P. Carr, USMC, and with a crew consisting of Lieutenant Colonel William R. Pogue, USAF, and Edward G. Gibson, civilian, was launched at the Kennedy Space Center, Fla. The scheduled 56-day "open-ended" space flight had among its aims study of the Comet Kohoutek, earth resources and the sun.

21 November   In the first test of its full arsenal of Phoenix missiles, an F-14 operating over the Pacific Missile Sea Test Range, Calif., fired six Phoenix missiles and guided them simultaneously at six separate targets 50 miles away, obtaining four direct hits.

1 December   The Blue Angels became the Navy Flight Demonstration Squadron (Blue Angels) and was designated a shore activity located at NAS Pensacola, Fla.

Bow view of Tarawa, the first ship in the new class of Amphibious Assault Ships, underway

1973—Continued

7 December   *Tarawa*, the first of a new class of amphibious assault ships, was launched at Pascagoula, Miss.

17 December   *Iwo Jima* departed Tunisia after three days of flood relief assistance by her helicopters which conducted refugee rescue, equipment deliveries and other flood associated missions.

20 December   Two women physicians, Lieutenants Jane O. McWilliams and Victoria M. Voge, graduated from the Naval Flight Surgeon Training Program, to become the first women naval flight surgeons.

20 December   The Naval Air Engineering Center was relocated officially from Philadelphia, Pa., to NAS Lakehurst, N.J., and authority and responsibility for the air station was reassigned to the Chief of Naval Material to be exercised through NAVAIR. Subsequently, on 8 January 1974, the Air Station was placed under the Naval Air Engineering Center. Thereby, the basic organization arrangements involved in relocation of the Naval Air Engineering Center from League Island, Philadelphia to NAS Lakehurst were completed although the physical transfer would be phased over much of 1974. The relocation was part of the Shore Establishment Realignment announced by the Secretary of Defense in March of 1973. Thus, an affiliation between Naval Aviation and the League Island site at Philadelphia, which began with the establishment of the Naval Aircraft Factory in 1917, was terminated except for a few residual aviation oriented functions.

31 December   Ellyson Field, NAS Pensacola, Fla., officially became the Naval Education and Training Program Development Center to administer the Navy's enlisted advancement system, including the development of advancement and special examinations as well as administering and conducting various courses, studies and training programs.

1974

18 January   The Secretary officially named the Navy's fourth nuclear-powered carrier *Carl Vinson*. The name was chosen in honor of Carl Vinson's contributions to the national defense during his fifty years in the House of Representatives.

4 February   VT-4 students aboard *John F. Kennedy* conducted the final flights of the TF-9J Cougars.

5 February   The Naval Aerospace Institute at Pensacola, Fla., announced that the repatriated Navy and Marine Corps prisoners-of-war from Vietnam were scheduled to come to Pensacola for periodic checks of their physical and mental status.

8 February   Skylab IV astronauts Lieutenant Colonel Gerald P. Carr, USMC, mission commander, Dr. Edward Gibson, and Lieutenant Colonel William Pogue, USAF, landed in the Pacific after a record-setting 84 days in space. They were recovered by HC-1 which flew them aboard *New Orleans*. This event marked the 32nd astronaut retrieval by Naval Aviators since the space program began in 1961.

20 February   The S-3A Viking ASW aircraft was introduced officially in the Navy in ceremonies at NAS North Island, Calif. VS-41 accepted the first aircraft. The Viking, a highly advanced, carrier-qualified jet aircraft, was designed to replace the older, propeller-driven S-2 Tracker which had been the Navy's primary carrier-based submarine hunter for over twenty years.

ADM Thomas B. Hayward, CNO, delivering remarks at the launching ceremony for Carl Vinson in 1980 KN-29933

1974—Continued

22 February Lieutenant (jg) Barbara Ann Allen became the Navy's first designated female aviator when she received her Wings of Gold in a ceremony at NAS Corpus Christi, Tex.

1 March Sikorsky's triple-turbine helicopter, the YCH-53E, the largest and most powerful helicopter in the western world, made its first flight. The CH-53E was a growth version of the CH-53 which had been in Navy service since 1965.

1 March *John F. Kennedy* commenced a year-long overhaul at Norfolk Naval Shipyard to be converted to handle the new CV concept (an air wing capable of performing strike and ASW operations) and to operate the new F-14 Tomcat fighter as well as the S-3A Viking.

15 March *Intrepid* was decommissioned and placed in the reserve fleet after thirty years of service to the Navy. Since her commissioning on 16 August 1943, *Intrepid* had seen duty as a CV, CVA and CVS. During World War II her air groups shot down 266 enemy planes, destroyed 298 more on the ground and damaged 178 others.

18 March The first operational F-14 Tomcat fighter aircraft made its maiden landings and takeoffs from *Enterprise*. The operations were conducted by VF-1 and -2 of CVW-14.

22 March Rear Admiral Brian McCauley arrived in Cairo, Egypt, with a small military planning staff to help plan the clearing of the Suez Canal of unexploded ordnance. The United States, Egypt, France, and the United Kingdom were involved in the project known as Nimbus Star.

2 April The last C-54 Skymaster in the Navy's flying inventory was retired to storage. The twenty-nine-year-old C-54Q saw its last service with the Naval Test Pilot

An F-14A Tomcat from VF-1 comes in for a recovery aboard Enterprise 161723

1974—Continued

School, NAS Patuxent River, Md. The Skymaster, BuNo 56501, had flown almost 15,000 hours with more than 2,500,000 nautical miles since its acceptance on 24 March 1945.

11 April At the Naval Missile Center, Point Mugu, Calif., the P-3 Orion fired its first Harpoon missile. The aircraft involved was a P-3A; the missile scored a direct hit on a remote-controlled *Septar* target boat.

14 April The Navy donated the ASW carrier *Yorktown* to Charleston, S.C., for the city's National Naval Museum. The "Fighting Lady" had spent 25 years with the Pacific Fleet before being transferred to the Atlantic in 1969. She was decommissioned 27 June 1970.

22 April A twelve-plane detachment of RH-53D Sea Stallions from HM-12 began minesweeping the Suez Canal as part of Project Nimbus Star.

4 June NAVAIR established an Aircraft Survivability/Vulnerability branch. This office was created in response to the need for a thoroughly coordinated Navy technical program addressing the need for better aircraft survivability in combat.

5 July Two Marine Corps aviators, Major John H. Pierson and his co-pilot, Major David R. Shore, flew an OV-10A Bronco 4,480 kilometers from NAS Whidbey Island, Wash., to Homestead AFB, Fla. This flight set a new world record for distance in a straight line by a Class C-1-F, Group II aircraft. The National Aeronautics Association sanctioned the record.

22 July As a result of the conflict between Turkish and Greek Cypriot forces on Cyprus, the U.S. Ambassador to Cyprus, Roger Davies, requested the evacuation of U.S. citizens. In a joint Navy/Marine Corps effort, HMM-162 from the Sixth Fleet carrier *Inchon* evacuated 466 people, 384 of them U.S. citizens, in only five hours. *Forrestal* provided air cover for the operation.

5 August The world's largest unmanned balloon was launched successfully from Fort Churchill in Manitoba, Canada. The flight was sponsored by the Office of Naval Research and NASA's Office of Space Science. The facilities of the Navy's Skyhook program were used for the launch. The entire flight train—balloon, an 800-pound instrument package, and a parachute—lifted to an altitude of 155,000 feet. As the balloon rose to float altitude it assumed a fully inflated form of 512 feet in diameter with a volume of 50.3 million cubic feet. The balloon traveled 500 miles west and was tracked by Project Skyhook's DC-3.

9 August The Navy announced the first acceptance by VQ-4 of an EC-130 Hercules TACAMO aircraft.

10 August Sikorsky's YCH-53E, Number 1, flew in a hover at a gross weight of 71,700 pounds. It carried an external load of 17.8 tons and hovered at a wheel height of fifty feet. This was the heaviest gross weight ever flown—and the heaviest payload ever lifted—by a helicopter in the western world.

24 August Navy and Marine Corps helicopters completed six days of disaster flood relief work in central Luzon, R.P. Aircraft from NAS Cubi Point, R.P., *San Jose* (AFS 7), *Tripoli* and Clark AFB, R.P., provided airlift of emergency food supplies.

RH-53D Sea Stallion of HM-12 minesweeping the Suez Canal 1151672

1974—Continued

28 August   The Chief of Naval Operations released a formal VFAX operational requirement directing NAVAIR to perform industrial solicitation and full-scale development. The VFAX concept was by this time under management by NAVAIR's PMA-265. The aircraft that finally emerged from the VFAX concept was the McDonnell Douglas F/A-18 Hornet.

14 September   The SEU-3/A Lightweight Ejection Seat manufactured by the Stencel Aero Engineering Company primarily for the AV-8A Harrier was approved for service use.

17 September   *Enterprise* sailed from San Francisco, Calif., with VF-1 and -2 aboard. This event marked the initial deployment of the Grumman F-14 Tomcat, the Navy's newest fighter.

17 September   The prototype LAMPS MK-III H-2/SR helicopter was delivered to the Kaman Aerospace Corporation for flight certification tests. Prior to this delivery, Naval Air Development Center, Warminster, Pa., engineers completed extensive design modifications which were required to incorporate the LAMPS MK-III developmental avionics package.

2 October   The Joint Logistics Commanders signed an agreement making Dupont's HT-4 the standard fabric for all flight suits.

19 November   The Central Treaty Organization Exercise Midlink 74 got underway as the largest naval exercise ever held in the Arabian Sea. Participating were forces from the United States, United Kingdom, Iran, Pakistan, and Turkey. *Constellation* was part of the eight-ship force from the United States.

2 December   The Navy's Advanced Low Volume Ramjet (ALVRJ) successfully completed its first free flight at the Pacific Missile Range at Point Mugu, Calif. The ALVRJ was a unique propulsion system designed for high performance missiles. It was developed for NAVAIR by LTV.

1975

3 January   The Association of Naval Aviation was formally founded "to stimulate and extend appreciation of Naval Aviation . . . past, present and future." The non-profit organization became open to any officer, enlisted person or civilian who contributed to, or was interested in, U.S. Naval Aviation.

17 January   The first production model of Lockheed's updated P-3C Orion was delivered to VX-1, the Navy's antisubmarine warfare evaluation squadron at NAS Patuxent River, Md. New avionics and software included a versatile computer language, the Omega world-wide navigation system, increased sound-processing sensitivity, a tactical display scope, improved magnetic tape transport, and a seven-fold increase in computer memory capacity from 65,000 to 458,000 words.

21 January   *Saratoga*, along with three other surface vessels, was released from contingency response off Cyprus. *Saratoga* had been maintaining a response alert for possible assistance in the evacuation of American citizens from the strife-torn island.

28 January   The AIM-54 Phoenix missile was given approval for service use.

9 February   *Enterprise* responded to calls for disaster relief from the island nation of Mauritius which was struck on 6 February by Typhoon Cervaise. Arriving at Port Louis on the 12th, carrier personnel spent more than 10,000 man-hours rendering such assistance as restoring water, power and telephone systems, clearing roads and debris, and providing helicopter, medical, food and potable water support to the stricken area.

15 February   The Sikorsky YCH-53E transport helicopter completed Navy Preliminary Evaluation conducted by the Naval Air Test Center, Patuxent River, Md., and HMX-1.

2 March   The F-14A Tomcat and the Phoenix Missile system were given approval for service use.

17 March   The S-3A Viking was given approval for service use.

18 March   NAVAIR established an Assistant Commander for Test and Evaluation and assigned to him the functions involving management of T & E and its facilities. This important organizational development had its direct origins in a decision by the Secretary of Defense (SECDEF) made in mid-1960s which stressed the need for adequate Test and Evaluation (T & E) data to provide a basis for determining whether new equipment was developed sufficiently to warrant procurement for service use. In a much more historic sense, the establishment of the Assistant Commander, Test and Evaluation was part of Naval Aviation's long-standing commitment to a consolidation of T & E. This commitment resulted, as early as 1942, in the creation of NAS Patuxent River, Md., as a facility for testing experimental airplanes, equipment, and material.

1975—Continued

23 March   Hancock, en route from Subic Bay, R.P., as relief for Enterprise, on station in the South China Sea, loaded HMH-463 at Pearl Harbor, Hawaii, for transport to the southwest Pacific. The unit would support operations in case evacuations of American and other nationals from areas of the Indochinese peninsula became necessary. Meanwhile, North Vietnamese forces continued their advance southward and were poised to cut off the entire northern quarter of the Republic of Vietnam some 300 miles north of Saigon.

1 April   Eugene Taylor "Smokey" Rhoads, Chief Aviation Pilot, USN, died at the Veterans Hospital, San Diego, Calif. Rhoads was a member of the flight crew that made the first trans-Atlantic flight in May 1919 in the NC-4.

12 April   Operation Eagle Pull was activated for Cambodia. Twelve CH-53 Sea Stallions of HMH-462 evacuated 287 persons from Phnom Penh to Okinawa. Among those evacuated were U.S. Ambassador John Gunther Dean and Cambodian President Saukhm Khoy, as well as newspapermen and other foreign

nationals. Upon completion of the evacuation, helicopters of HMH-463 from Hancock, retrieved the elements of the 31st Marine Amphibious Unit which had established the perimeter from which the evacuees had been rescued.

13 April   The Naval Aviation Museum was dedicated at Pensacola, Fla. All funds for construction of the 68,000-square-foot structure had been donated privately. The building was presented to the Navy by the Naval Aviation Museum Foundation, Inc. It replaced the small temporary museum set up in 1962. Among the 72 vintage aircraft at the museum, a feature attraction was the original NC-4, the first airplane to fly the Atlantic Ocean. Plans, and an ongoing drive for privately donated funds, called for continued expansion of the new museum through three more stages to eventually reach 260,000 square feet of floor space.

19 April   Midway, Coral Sea, Hancock, Enterprise and Okinawa responded to possible evacuation contingencies by deploying to waters off Vietnam as North Vietnam overran two-thirds of South Vietnam and pronounced the carriers' presence a brazen challenge and a violation of the 1973 Paris Peace Accords.

Sailors from Durham (LKA 114) lending a hand K-107587

Sailor from Durham (LKA 114) cares for two Vietnamese children separated from their mother during the evacuation K-107619

1975—Continued

29 April In a period of three hours, Operation Frequent Wind was carried out by U.S. Navy and Marine Corps helicopters from the Seventh Fleet. Frequent Wind involved the evacuation of American citizens from the capital of South Vietnam under heavy attack from the invading forces of North Vietnam. The military situation around Saigon and its Tan Son Nhut airport made evacuation by helicopter the only way out. President Ford ordered the evacuation when Viet Cong shelling forced the suspension of normal transport aircraft use at Tan Son Nhut. With fighter cover provided by carrier aircraft, the helicopters landed on Saigon rooftops and at Tan Son Nhut to evacuate the Americans. The airport became the main helicopter landing zone; it was defended by Marines from the 9th Amphibious Brigade flown in for that purpose. All but a handful of the 900 Americans in Saigon were evacuated. The last helicopter lifted off the roof of the United States Embassy at 7:52 p.m. carrying Marine security guards.

Flight from Saigon as Communists take over in 1975.

Escaping South Vietnamese pilot and family land aboard Midway, plane is now at Naval Aviation Museum, Pensacola, Fla.

1975—Continued

30 April VW-4, the Hurricane Hunters, was disestablished. Established 15 November 1952 as VJ-2 and redesignated VW-4 in 1953, it was the Navy's last squadron specifically detailed for hurricane reconnaissance. During its more than 30 years of service, VW-4 made major contributions to meteorological science, oceanographic research, the National Weather Service, and the Naval Weather Service Command.

2 May *Midway* off-loaded at Utapao, Thailand, over 40 USAF helicopters used in South Vietnam evacuation operations. At the same time, carrier personnel assisted in the recovery and on-loading from the Utapao Airport of over 95 South Vietnamese Air Force craft, including F-5 fighters and A-37 light bombers, which had been flown into Utapao when South Vietnam fell to the Communists. The aircraft were transported to Guam.

2 May Development of a new carrier-based fighter by the McDonnell Douglas and the Northrop aircraft corporations was announced by NAVAIR. To be designed for speeds in excess of Mach 1.5, a combat ceiling in excess of 45,000 feet and a radius of action of more than 400 nautical miles, development was to emphasize improved maneuvering performance, reliability, and maintainability.

5 May The first training class for a new type of physician, the Aviation Medical Officer (AMO), began at the Naval Aerospace Medical Institute, Pensacola, Fla. The program was initiated because of the acute shortage of flight surgeons. The AMOs were not scheduled to undergo flight training nor be assigned duty involving flying; instead, they were to augment the efforts of flight surgeons where aeromedical workloads were heavy, performing flight physicals and providing routine medical care.

12–14 May *Coral Sea* participated with other Navy, Air Force and Marine forces in the recovery of the American merchantship SS *Mayaguez* and her 39 crewmen, illegally seized on 12 May in international waters by a Cambodian gunboat controlled by the Communist Khmer Rouge. Protective air strikes were flown from the carrier against the Cambodian mainland naval and air installations as USAF helicopters with 288 Marines from Battalion Landing Teams 2 and 9 were launched from Utapao, Thailand, to rescue the crew and secure the merchantman. Eighteen Marines, airmen and Navy corpsmen were lost in action. Alerted for response, but not utilized before the release of the commandeered ship and crew on the 14th, were *Hancock*, operating as an LPH platform, and *Okinawa*.

1 July All U.S. naval gunfire training activities at the Puerto Rican island of Culebra were terminated through a joint Washington-San Juan agreement, ending a controversy that had dragged on for years. The announcement indicated that air-to-ground weapons training at Culebra Cays would continue for a limited time only because of previously scheduled training activities.

1 July The aircraft carrier designation CVA was replaced with CV. This change was made to improve the accuracy of designations in modern warfare. By removing the letter A, which stood for attack, the new designation CV could serve a multipurpose air, surface, and ASW role, depending on the type of aircraft carried.

24 July HS-6 operating off *New Orleans* recovered the Apollo spacecraft and astronauts Vance D. Brand (former Navy pilot), Thomas P. Stafford (USAF) and Donald K. Slayton (USAF). This splashdown marked the end of the Apollo-Soyuz mission, the first joint U.S.-Soviet space effort, and the end of the Apollo Program. It was also the final planned at-sea recovery in the U.S. space program.

28 July The U.S. Senate cleared the way for construction at Diego Garcia by voting to expand the U.S. support facility on the Indian Ocean island. It ended a long dispute over construction at the installation, permitting the Navy to begin an $18.1 million expansion to include aircraft runway extension, petroleum-oillubricants storage areas, a pier and additional power plant facilities.

29 July The Navy created the lighter-than-air project office at the Naval Air Development Center, Warminster, Pa. The purpose of this office was to enhance expertise in lighter-than-air technology within the Navy.

1 August A KA-3B Skywarrior, attached to VAQ-208, completed the longest nonstop flight ever made by a carrier-based tactical jet aircraft. The flight originated at the Naval Station, Rota, Spain, and ended at NAS Alameda, Calif. It covered a distance of 6,100 miles and lasted 13 hours.

2 August The Commandant of the Marine Corps announced that the twelve Marine Corps fighter/attack squadrons would remain an all F-4 Phantom force until their replacement by F-18 aircraft beginning in the early 1980s. The Marine Corps was scheduled originally to be equipped with four squadrons of the F-14 Tomcats, but instead these four would be used to transition four Navy fighter squadrons from F-4s to F-14s, thus retaining the authorized 18- squadron Navy force for overall air defense.

1975—Continued

14 August The newly commissioned *Nimitz* completed refresher training at Guantanamo Bay, Cuba, before beginning her cruise with a nuclear task force to northern European waters. The world's largest ship at the time, *Nimitz* had an overall length of 1,092 feet, an extreme breadth of 292 feet, a flight deck area of four and a half acres, and displaced 95,000 tons with a combat load. The Navy's second nuclear carrier, *Nimitz* was named in honor of the World War II hero and former Chief of Naval Operations, Fleet Admiral Chester W. Nimitz.

Nimitz commissioned on 3 May 1975 1161470

26 Septmber The Chief of Naval Operations approved the popular name Tomahawk for the Navy's SLCM.

3 October VMGR-352 took delivery of the first KC-130R Hercules refueler/transport.

22 October The Chief of Naval Operations and Defense Systems Acquisition Review Council initiated new policies on development and operational test and evaluation functions along with weapon system acquisition.

24 October The Navy reported that a new method of conducting Shrike pilot training programs had been developed. This method consisted of captive flight firings linked to a communications pod and was performed at the Air Combat Maneuvering Range at Yuma, Ariz. The new method could be adopted to all versions of the A-4 Skyhawk, A-6 Intruder and A-7 Corsair aircraft.

27 October *Inchon* and five surface vessels served as a contingency evacuation force, with *John F. Kennedy* in support, as U.S. citizens were advised to evacuate their dependents from Lebanon due to prolonged government instability and increased armed skirmishing among political factions in the country.

1 November Effective this date, the Naval Aerospace Recovery Facility at NAF El Centro, Calif., was disestablished and the mission statement of the National Parachute Test Range, also at El Centro, was modified to absorb its function. The Naval Air Facility was assigned to the CNO for command and support.

25 November The first launch in the XJ521 Program took place at Point Mugu. The XJ521 was an air-to-air medium range missile resulting from modifications by the United Kingdom to the American Sparrow AIM-7E-2. The missiles were fired from an F-5 aircraft at QT-33 targets.

6 December H-46 Sea Knight helicopters from NAS Whidbey Island, Wash., began search and rescue operations in the northwestern Washington state areas flooded by heavy rains. Four days of this humanitarian work saw a total of 113 people evacuated after being stranded by the flood waters.

8 December The first production prototype of Sikorsky's three-engine, multimission CH-53E transport helicopter made its first flight at the company's Connecticut plant. The flight of about 30 minutes consisted of low-altitude hovering and limited maneuvering.

1976

28 January The Navy awarded a contract for an initial funding of $16 million to the McDonnell Douglas Corporation to begin full-scale development of the new F-18 Air Combat Fighter.

11 February The first Terrain Contour Matching (TERCOM) Guidance Test Vehicle was flown using a modified Navy Firebee drone. TERCOM was then used in the Tomahawk Cruise Missile.

1976—Continued

18 February   The night attack weapons system, a modified air-to-surface Maverick missile designed to enhance the performance of night tactical and strike aircraft, scored a direct hit on a moving M-48 tank during a test conducted at the Naval Weapons Center, China Lake, Calif.

2 March   Two VS-22 Lockheed S-3A Viking aircraft landed aboard *Saratoga* off the coast of Italy, completing the first Atlantic crossing by S-3A Vikings. The S-3A Vikings departed NAS Cecil Field, Fla., and made stops at NAS Bermuda, NAS Lajes, Azores, and NS Rota, Spain, before landing on *Saratoga*. Their flight across the Atlantic proved that rapid augmentation of S-3A Viking carrier antisubmarine assets was possible from long distances.

20 May   Bell Helicopter's AH-1T made its first flight. The following week the AH-1T flew to 120 knots and did mild sideslips, climbs and descents.

26 May   A contract for a new Navy multi-engine aircraft trainer to be designated T-44A was awarded to Beech Aircraft. The aircraft would replace the TS-2A.

28 May   Helicopter crews from HS-4 aboard *Ranger;* detachments from HC-3 on *Camden* (AOE 2), *Mars* (AFS 1) and *White Plains* (AFS 4); and helicopters from NAS Cubi Point, R.P., assisted in the Philippine disaster relief efforts in the flood ravaged areas of Central Luzon. Over 1,900 people were evacuated; more than 370,000 pounds of disaster relief supplies and 9,340 gallons of fuel were provided by Navy and Air Force helicopters.

29 May   *Tarawa* was commissioned at Ingalls Shipbuilding Division of Litton Industries in Pascagoula, Miss. *Tarawa* was the first of five in a class of amphibious assault ships to join the fleet.

5 June   The Navy launched the first fully guided Tomahawk cruise missile over the White Sands Missile Range in New Mexico. The missile was airborne for 61

CH-46 helicopters from HMM-163 operating from Tarawa K-114732

1976—Continued

minutes after it was released from the wing of a Pacific Missile Test Center, Patuxent River, Md., A-6 Intruder aircraft at an altitude of 11,500 feet. This was the first in a series of flights intended to test the functional operation of the test vehicle's capability to perform navigation, guidance updates, and low-terrain following maneuvers. It was also the first test flight using a turbofan engine, previous tests had utilized the turbojet engine.

6 June An A-6 Intruder successfully test fired the tactical version of the Tomahawk cruise missile using the TERCOM navigation system. The Tomahawk was designed as a long-range weapons system with strategic and tactical application which could be launched from tactical and strategic aircraft, surface ships, submarines and land platforms.

24 June The Navy accepted its first T-34C Mentor aircraft. The new aircraft would replace the aging T-34B and T-28B/C used in primary and basic flight training. It would be the first training command aircraft to have maintenance and supply support provided by civilian contractors.

24 June The Navy's Air-Launched Low Volume Ramjet (ALVRJ) set a new distance record traveling over 100 nautical miles at sustained speeds of over 1,700 miles per hour. This was the fifth flight for the ramjet at the Navy's Pacific Missile Test Center at Point Mugu, Calif.

30 June A new eight-inch laser-guided projectile, developed jointly by the Navy and Marine Corps, was fired successfully from the new major caliber light weight gun mounted in *Hull* (DD 945).

30 June A Naval Aviation tradition came to an end when brown shoes were stricken from the officers' and chiefs' uniforms. The tradition initially distinguished the Brown Shoe Navy of the aviators from the black shoes of the surface officers.

1 July The Navy's Sea-Air Operations Gallery, part of the new National Air and Space Museum of the Smithsonian Institution, was opened to the public. The Sea-Air Operations Gallery presented a "you are there" mock-up of an aircraft carrier's hangar deck, bridge and preflight operations room. Audio/visual presentations of take-offs and landings from a carrier were presented in the bridge areas. The hangar deck included Navy aircraft past and present. Famous events in Naval Aviation history were depicted throughout the gallery.

6 July *Coral Sea* was presented the Meritorious Unit Commendation for her actions during the *Mayaguez* crisis in May 1975. *Coral Sea* played a major role in the return of SS *Mayaguez* after Cambodian gunboats seized the merchant ship on the high seas off the coast of Cambodia. *Coral Sea* provided air support to the landing of Marines at Koh Tang Island as CVW-15 conducted strikes on specified military targets.

9 July The CH-46 Sea Knight helicopter's effectiveness and life were extended with the delivery of the first two CH-46E prototypes. The major modifications to the CH-46E helicopters were new T-58-GE-16 engines, an Omega-Doppler navigation system, new crashworthy pilot and copilot seats, a combat crashworthy fuel system, a new rescue hoist and an infrared suppressor for engine exhaust.

12 July *Ranger* and her escort ships of Task Force 77.7 entered the Indian Ocean and were assigned to operate off the coast of Kenya in response to a threat of military action in Kenya by Ugandan forces. A VP-17 P-3 aircraft visiting Nairobi and a U.S. Middle East Force ship visiting Mombassa further demonstrated U.S. friendly ties and support for Kenya during her crisis with Uganda.

12 July The Navy phased out the last C-117 (Douglas DC-3), perhaps the most famous transport plane of all time. The last C-117 was flown from Pensacola, Fla, to Davis Monthan Air Force Base, Ariz., the boneyard for obsolete military aircraft.

27 July *America* and other elements of Task Force 61, with *Nimitz* standing by, supported the evacuation of 160 Americans and 148 other nationals from Beirut, Lebanon. The amphibious transport ship *Coronado* (LPD 11) removed the evacuees from Lebanon and arrived in Athens on 29 July. During January through July 1976 the contingency evacuation force for the "Lebanon Civil War Crisis" involved, at different intervals, the support of *America*, *Nimitz*, *Iwo Jima*, *Independence*, *Guadalcanal* and *Saratoga*.

27 July The first phase of a program to develop the AV-8B Harrier, a version of the current AV-8A with improved payload and range, was approved by the Department of Defense.

13 August An HU-16 Albatross, the Navy's last operational seaplane made its final water landing in Pensacola Bay, Fla. After two-touch-and-go landings the aircraft was flown to Sherman Field where it was turned over to the Naval Aviation Museum in Pensacola.

1976—Continued

A P-3B Orion from VP-17 on patrol in the Pacific Ocean.

20 August   *Ainsworth* (FF 1090) became the first ship to have installed a production version of the Harpoon Command and Launch Missile System.

21 August   A Navy task force headed by *Midway* made a show of force off the coast of Korea in response to an unprovoked attack on two U.S. Army officers who were killed by North Korean guards on 18 August. *Midway's* response was in support of a U.S. demonstration of military concern vis-à-vis North Korea.

29 August   The Navy's last S-2 Tracker aircraft, operating with VS-37, was withdrawn from active service. Many of the pilots who flew the Tracker credit it with being the Navy's most versatile airplane of its era. The S-2 entered service with VS-26 in February 1954 and provided the Navy with 22 years of active service.

15 September   Test flights began on the east coast air combat maneuvering range (ACMR) under construction off the coast of Cape Hatteras, N.C. This follow-on system to the Navy ACMR at Yuma, Ariz., would provide air combat training for East Coast squadrons.

17 September   The new space shuttle program was unveiled by NASA. Of the 28 astronauts in the space program, 12 had either a Navy or Marine Corps aviation background.

29 September   The Navy's Ship-Deployable, Tactical, Airborne Remotely-Piloted Vehicle (RPV) (STAR) achieved the first automatically closed-loop recovery of an RPV into a net-encapsulated arresting assembly. The test occurred at the National Parachute Test Range, El Centro, Calif.

30 September   *Oriskany*, the last Essex-class attack carrier, was decommissioned at San Francisco, Calif., and placed in the mothball fleet. *Oriskany* saw extensive action in the Korean and Vietnam conflicts.

4 October   The first overseas operational commitment on a carrier for the AV-8A aircraft began when VMA-231, equipped with the AV-8A Harrier, embarked on *Franklin D. Roosevelt* and departed for the Mediterranean Sea for a Sixth Fleet deployment.

5 November   The latest model of the Sea Cobra helicopter, the AH-1T, was turned over to the Marine Corps from Bell Helicopter Textron for further testing. The new version offered an improved payload of 4,392 pounds over the previous payload of 2,739 pounds.

13 November   The first at-sea firing tests of the SM-2 (extended range) guided missile from *Wainwright* (CG 28) were completed, using a modified Terrier fire control system to control the missile flight. *Wainwright's* test capped a highly successful five-year program with observers reporting excellent accuracy.

1976—Continued

1 December Naval Air Facility, China Lake, Calif., was disestablished after more than 30 years as a separate command, and became part of the Naval Weapons Center.

1 December NAAS Saufley Field, Fla., was disestablished. The closing of the basic tactical and combat flying base brought to an end one of the early fields used in association with the training of Naval Aviators at NAS Pensacola, Fla. The primary training installation was opened for flight purposes in 1940 and named after Richard C. Saufley, Naval Aviator #14, who was killed while on a record endurance flight on 9 June 1916 after being in the air 8 hours and 51 minutes. Saufley Field was used initially by aviation students practicing landings and takeoffs away from the normal flight pattern at NAS Pensacola. Established as NAAS Saufley Field in 1943, aviation students in basic training received instructional courses in ground training, formation flying, and cross-country flying employing the SNJ Texan and T-28 aircraft.

1977

6 January The first F404 development engine was tested successfully at the General Electric plant in Lynn, Mass., approximately a month ahead of schedule.

13 January NAS Jacksonville, Fla., announced that two AV-8A Harrier aircraft had made a bow on approach and landing aboard *Franklin D. Roosevelt*. This may have been the first time in Naval Aviation history that a fixed-wing aircraft made a bow-on, downwind landing aboard a carrier at sea. This landing, with jets facing aft, demonstrated that V/STOL aircraft could be landed aboard a carrier without many of the conditions necessary for fixed-wing, non-V/STOL aircraft.

14 January For the first time, an all-nuclear-powered task group was operating in both deployed fleets. The Seventh Fleet task group was composed of *Enterprise* and her nuclear-powered escort ships, while the Sixth Fleet task group had *Nimitz* with her nuclearpowered escort ships.

31 January The TA-7C, a two-seat Corsair II converted from an earlier model and designated a combat crew and instrument trainer, was delivered to the Navy for use at NAS Cecil Field, Fla., and NAS Lemoore, Calif. Replacement pilots for the light attack squadrons flying A-7s would train in the TA-7Cs.

27 February *Enterprise* and her escort ships were directed to operate off the east African coast in response to public derogatory remarks against the U.S. by the President of Uganda and his order that all Americans in Uganda meet with him.

1 March The Naval Air Rework Facility and Naval Air Station at Lakehurst, N.J., were disestablished and the mission of the Naval Air Engineering Center was modified to absorb their functions.

1 March The Navy's new F/A-18 fighter/attack aircraft was assigned the name Hornet, a name often used for Navy ships-of-the-line. The plane, scheduled for fleet delivery in the early 1980s, would replace the F-4 Phantom II and the A-7 Corsair II.

24 March Initial service acceptance trials for the CH-53E Super Stallion were completed at NATC. The growth version of the CH-53E had three turbine engines instead of two. The Super Stallion carried mission loads of 16 tons compared to nine tons for the CH-53D. It had 7 rotor blades instead of 6 and could accommodate 56 troops.

25 March NAVAIR announced that its Advanced Concepts Division and the Naval Air Development Center, Warminster, Pa., were testing a lighter-than-air craft known as Aerocrane. This project represented the first government-sponsored study of lighter-than-air flight in several years.

5 April The Navy took delivery of the new T-44A trainer at NAS Corpus Christi, Tex. The Beech aircraft signaled a significant modernization trend in the Navy's flight program. The T-44A would eventually replace the TS-2A Tracker, flown by training squadrons since the early 1960s.

8 April The Navy's first E-2C ARPS aircraft joined the fleet at NAS Norfolk, Va., assigned to VAW-121. The ARPS aircraft was designed to improve the radar capability in its mission of airborne early warning. VAW-121 was scheduled to receive three additional ARPS aircraft that year, making it the first ARPS squadron.

12 April An operational requirement was established for night vision capability in U.S. Marine Corps transport helicopters.

21 April *Franklin D. Roosevelt*, the first carrier to launch a jet plane, 21 July 1946, returned to the U.S. from her last overseas deployment prior to her decommissioning on 1 October 1977.

1977—Continued

22 June The new OV-10D Bronco series, undergoing test and evaluation at NATC's Strike Aircraft Test Directorate, Patuxent River, Md., was equipped with a night vision sensor which allowed the two-man crew to pinpoint targets in the dark. Called FLIR, for Forward Looking Infrared Radar, the sensor could detect the thermal radiation from all objects in its field of view, including individual soldiers. While primarily designed to provide a "night eyes" capability, FLIR also offered various degrees of vision through camouflage, dust, smoke, haze and light fog. It was also to be used for navigation; terrain avoidance and surveillance; target detection, recognition and tracking; gun laying; and as a landing aid.

13 July An F-4J Phantom II landed for the first time using the microwave landing system (MLS) at the FAA Test Facility at Atlantic City, N.J. A pilot from the Naval Air Test Center, Patuxent River, Md., was at the controls. The MLS was designed to reach out electronically, catch the target aircraft, and fly it to a safe landing without the aircraft's pilot touching the controls.

23 July Rear Admiral Alan B. Shepard, Jr., USN, was inducted into the Aviation Hall of Fame. He was cited for outstanding contributions to aviation as a Naval Aviator, instructor and test pilot, and for his contributions to space technology. He was the first American launched into space and the fifth to walk on the moon.

11 August The first CH-46E Sea Knight with newly developed fiberglass rotor blades was flown by Marine Corps helicopter pilots. The helicopter was the first of 400 to be retrofitted with new rotor blades which were less susceptible to corrosion and fatigue damage.

26 August The Navy unveiled its new XFV-12A vertical/short takeoff and landing research aircraft at the Rockwell International facility in Columbus, Ohio. The XFV-12A, a single engine, single seat, thrust-augmented wing prototype high-performance fighter aircraft, was designed to operate from small ships.

29 August The first production model of the P-3C Orion update II arrived at NATC for technical evaluation. It incorporated the latest in avionics and weapons systems, including a turret-mounted infrared detection device to drop out of the nose to identify targets day or night. The aircraft also had the Harpoon air-to-surface missile system.

1 September The LAMPS MK III helicopter contractors were selected by the Navy. Sikorsky Aircraft Division was selected to build the helicopter and General Electric's aircraft engine group was selected to provide the engines. The LAMPS helicopter was intended to carry a crew of three, fly 170 miles an hour and operate at altitudes up to 10,000 feet.

30 September The Joint Cruise Missile Project Office was established in the Naval Material Command with the Navy and Air Force sharing responsibility for developing a cruise missile. The Cruise Missile Project Office had been a project of the Naval Air Systems Command.

1 October The Naval Aviation Logistics Center became fully operational at Patuxent River, Md. The new center was responsible for the implementation, coordination and management of Navy-wide depot-level aviation maintenance programs.

31 October The Department of Defense directed a significant relocation of the essential mission of the National Parachute Test Range at El Centro, Calif. The Range had been responsible for RDT&E for parachute systems and for providing common airfield support to aviation units. With this change, the RDT&E mission was moved to the Naval Weapons Center at China Lake, Calif. The airfield support mission remained at El Centro with the existing Naval Air Facility there.

14 November The Chief of Naval Air Training formally accepted the T-34C aircraft manufactured by Beech Aircraft Corporation. The T-34C, a turboprop, two-place trainer, was to replace the T-34B and T-28 training aircraft.

1978

2 February The Tomahawk cruise missile was launched successfully from the submarine *Barb* (SS 220) and flew a fully guided land attack test flight that terminated at Edwards AFB, Calif. This was the first launch of the Tomahawk from a submarine.

9 February The first satellite of the new Navy Fleet Satellite Communications System was launched. This system satisfied the need for worldwide tactical command, control and communications for the entire fleet.

16 February Eleven of the 35 astronaut candidates selected to participate in NASA's space shuttle program were Navy personnel. Eight of the Navy selectees were in the pilot training program and the other three were trained as mission specialists.

1978—Continued

27 February A contract for the CH-53E Super Stallion helicopter was awarded to Sikorsky Aircraft to begin full-scale production. The CH-53E provided the Navy and Marine Corps with a heavy-lift helicopter, able to lift twice as much as the earlier D model.

28 February The Department of Defense authorized full-scale development of Sikorsky Aircraft's SH-60B LAMPS MK III helicopter. The aircraft was designed primarily for antisubmarine and antiship missions and to be deployed aboard frigates, destroyers and cruisers.

17 March NASA selected four two-man crews for early orbital flights of the space shuttle. Captain John W. Young, USN, was selected as commander and Commander Robert L. Crippen, USN, as pilot for the first scheduled orbital test. Colonel Joe H. Engle, USAF, and Commander Richard H. Truly, USN, were selected as the backup crew. Also included in the first group of two-man crews was Lieutenant Colonel John R. Lousma, USMC.

10 April The first TA-7C attack trainer arrived at NATC Patuxent River, Md., for Board of Inspection and Survey trials. The TA-7C was designed to provide a position for both the instructor and the student in the aircraft, thus providing a more efficient method of instruction while reducing fuel consumption about one-half. The new two-seater would also reduce the number of aircraft required for transition training.

14 April The first of 12 C-2A Greyhounds rolled off the SLEP line at NARF North Island, Calif. SLEP would add between seven and ten years of service to the carrier-on-board-delivery aircraft. There was no other aircraft in the Navy's inventory which could carry as many supplies and personnel to a carrier at sea.

9 June Rear Admiral William L. Harris, NWC Commander, accepted the Daedalian Weapons Systems Award in San Antonio, Tex., on behalf of the Naval Weapons Center and the Naval Air Systems Command. The Order of Daedalians, a national fraternity of military pilots, selected NWC and NAVAIR as co-winners of the 1978 award in recognition of the success of these two Navy commands in working together as a team in the development and improvement of a family of heat-seeking guided missiles known as Sidewinder. The Daedalian Weapons System Award and accompanying perpetual trophy was presented annually by the Order of Daedalians to the individual, group or organization, military or civilian, judged to have developed the most outstanding weapon system. The recipient was selected from nominations submitted by the Departments of the Army, Navy, and Air Force on a rotating basis.

8 July The Naval Air Test and Evaluation Museum at NAS Patuxent River, Md., opened its doors to the public for the first time. Its premier exhibition depicted the full scope of test and evaluation in Naval Aviation. The displays were varied, showing the many different types of aircraft which have passed through the Patuxent River test facility over the years.

21 July The final flight of the service acceptance trials for the AH-1T Cobra helicopter gunship was made at Naval Air Test Center, Patuxent River, Md. The helo carried an increase of more than 200 percent in its armament payload and was designed to fly farther and fight longer and harder over a target than previous models of the Cobra.

22 July Captain Holden C. Richardson was inducted into the National Aviation Hall of Fame at Dayton, Ohio. Naval Aviator #13, Captain Richardson was the first Naval Aviation engineering officer to be so honored.

2–3 August The mock-up of the SH-60B ASW helicopter was put through shipboard compatibility trials aboard *Arthur W. Radford* (DD 968). Earlier trials were conducted July 25-26 aboard *Oliver Hazard Perry* (FFG 7). The SH-60B was being developed by Sikorsky Aircraft.

3 August NAVAIR reported a major advance in the technology of escape systems. During the summer, the Naval Weapons Center at China Lake, Calif., successfully tested a vertical-seeking ejection seat. While carrying a dummy crew member, the seat was fired downward from a suspended test module. It traveled downward less than 45 feet before reversing direction and traveling upward; it then parachuted safely to the ground. These tests demonstrated that the vertical-seeking seat would make it possible to safely eject upside down, within 50 feet of the surface, thus greatly increasing the safety envelope of ejection seats.

14 September A Navy technical evaluation was completed on the CH-53E Super Stallion helicopter to determine if performance had been altered by changes made since the initial trials conducted by the Board of Inspection and Survey. The Super Stallion successfully completed the 60-hour test program.

1978—Continued

15 September   The test-bed P-3C Orion was delivered to the Naval Air Development Center, Warminster, Pa., for the Update III program. The aircraft featured an advanced signal processor developed by IBM which provided a four-fold improvement in isolating sounds of submerged targets from ocean background noise. Lockheed California Company was the prime contractor of the P-3C and had been involved with its development over the past 17 years.

9 November   The U.S. Marine Corps' newest light attack aircraft, the AV-8B, flew for the first time at McDonnell Douglas Corporation in St. Louis, Mo. The AV-8B Harrier had more than double the payload and radius of its predecessor, the AV-8A.

18 November   The Navy's new strike fighter, the F/A-18 Hornet, made its first flight at McDonnell Douglas Corporation in St. Louis, Mo. The Hornet was designed for a combat radius of more than 550 miles and a ferry range of more than 2,000 miles.

18 December   Commander, NAVAIR formally established the undergraduate Jet Pilot Training System Project. This project was designed to provide Naval Aviation with an integrated training program consisting of aircraft, simulators, academics, and training management. VTXTS was aimed at the intermediate and advanced jet training levels.

27 December   *Constellation* and her escort ships were directed to the vicinity of Singapore in response to the internal crisis in Iran and because of vital U.S. interests in the Persian Gulf area. On 2 January 1979, the president directed *Constellation* and her escort ships to remain on station in the South China Sea and not enter the Indian Ocean.

1979

16 January   The first F/A-18 Hornet arrived at NATC Patuxent River, Md., for evaluation trials. Testing during the year included in-flight refueling, land-based catapult launchings and arrested landings, speed tests and at-sea carrier takeoffs and traps aboard *America*.

24 January   Vice President Walter P. Mondale presented Lieutenant Colonel Herbert Fix with the Harmon International Aviation Trophy. Colonel Fix received the award for his role as Commanding Officer of HMH-463 during the evacuations of Phnom Penh and Saigon in 1975. The citation praised Colonel Fix for carrying out his missions "without casualties

among the aircrews of 16 rotary wing aircraft in HMH-463, although the operations took place under combat conditions involving antiaircraft fire, machine gun and small arms fire, and in part at night with few navigational aids." Colonel Fix was the first U.S. Marine Corps pilot to receive the Harmon Trophy. At the time of the award, he was Project Manager for the H-1/H-3 Helicopters Project Office at the Naval Air Systems Command.

25 January   The Navy's YAV-8B, the Harrier prototype built by McDonnell Douglas, arrived at the Naval Air Test Center, Patuxent River, Md., to test its aerodynamic improvements not found in the AV-8A.

28 January   *Constellation* and her escort ships were released from contingency operations in the South China Sea. The contingency operations had been issued in response to the internal crisis in Iran. The crisis abated when the Shah of Iran departed for exile on 16 January. Due to the uneasy situation in Iran all U.S. government dependents and nonessential American citizens were ordered to evacuate the country on 30 January.

9 February   The Secretary of the Navy announced that the helicopter portion of the Navy's LAMPS MK III was to be known officially as the Seahawk. Designated SH-60B, the Sikorsky helicopter took its name from the Curtiss SC-1 Seahawk which was a catapult launched, noncarrier, float plane of late World War II.

The newest plane in the Navy inventory, the F/A-18 Hornet, is examined by naval officers.

1979—Continued

14 February The Tomahawk missile was launched from the nuclear powered attack submarine *Guitarro* (SSN 665) off the California coast. This successful test was part of a planned series of three submarine launches and flight tests of the Tomahawk conducted between February and June which demonstrated the missile's over-the-horizon capability to search for, locate, and conduct simulated attacks on a target ship at sea.

27 February The Navy took delivery of the last A-4 Skyhawk from the McDonnell Douglas Corporation, setting a record for the longest production run for any U.S. military aircraft. Built as an attack bomber and as a two-place trainer, the A-4 had been in continuous production for 26 years. The final Skyhawk off the production line was an A-4M attack bomber built for operation by the Marine Corps. It was the 2,960th Skyhawk manufactured by McDonnell Douglas and was delivered to VMA-331.

7 March *Constellation* and her escort ships were ordered to the Gulf of Aden in response to the conflict between North and South Yemen. The Gulf of Aden and the Persian Gulf were considered vital waterways for the passage of petroleum products to the U.S. and her allies.

11 March A P-3B Orion from NATC Patuxent River, Md., flew the first transoceanic flight guided by NavStar, the space-based radio navigation system. The six-hour flight was from NAS Barbers Point, Hawaii, to NAS Moffett Field, Calif. The NavStar system comprised 24 satellites in earth orbit providing radio navigational information.

20 March The last variant of the P-2 Neptune rolled off the production line at ceremonies in Japan. This was the longest production run of any aircraft type in history, 34 years from the first model which was built in 1945 in Burbank, California by the Lockheed Corporation. The P-2 was the mainstay of the U.S. Navy's ASW patrol fleet during the 1950s and early 1960s until it was replaced by the P-3 Orion.

26 March The AV-8A Harrier was used at NATC Patuxent River, Md., to test a new ski jump ramp developed by the British to cut down the takeoff distance for the Harrier. The new ski jump ramp was designed with a 12-degree angle of elevation and was 130 feet long. The total takeoff distance for a Harrier using the new ramp was 230 feet compared with the 930-foot runway necessary for a Harrier to make a no-catapult, flat-surface launch. NATC Patuxent River was evaluating the ramp for possible use in the fleet.

16 April *Midway* relieved *Constellation* as the Indian Ocean contingency carrier. *Midway* and her escort ships continued a significant American naval presence in the oil-producing region of the Arabian Sea and Persian Gulf.

21 April The Navy's Supersonic Tactical Missile test vehicle made its first flight at the Pacific Missile Test Center, Point Mugu, Calif. This advanced integral rocket/ramjet test vehicle was developed by Vought. It was described as a major step toward development of a new generation of high performance, air-to-surface tactical standoff missiles.

23 April In a ceremony at NAS Norfolk, Va., Vice Admiral Forrest S. Petersen transferred ownership of the last Kawanishi H8K2 flying boat to the Japanese Museum of Maritime Science. Code named Emily by the allies during World War II, the big craft was brought to the United States by the Navy late in 1945 to undergo tests at Patuxent River, Md. When the tests were completed, the Emily was stored at Norfolk and outlasted all its sister aircraft. In July 1979, the Museum of Maritime Science transported the Emily to Tokyo.

30 April A RH-53D Sea Stallion from HM-12 set a new nonstop, transcontinental flight record by flying from Norfolk, Va., to San Diego, Calif. The helicopter flew 2,077 nm in 18.5 hours, air refueling from an Air National Guard HC-130 Hercules. The flight demonstrated the long-range, quick-response capability of the RH-53D helicopter and was commanded by Lieutenant Rodney M. Davis.

22 May The first of two McDonnell Douglas AV-8C Harriers arrived at NATC Patuxent River, Md., for service acceptance trials. Improvements built into this aircraft over the AV-8A included a new UHF radio, a chaff and flare dispensing system, lift improvement devices, a radar warning system and secure voice equipment.

30 May *Midway* and her escort ships were released from contingency operations in the Arabian Sea and departed for the Pacific.

12 June The Deputy Secretary of Defense approved the mission element need statement for the VTXTS. This system represented a major step toward meeting the continuing requirement to provide undergraduate pilot training for student Naval Aviators and transition students of the U.S. Navy and Marine Corps.

1979—Continued

20 June   Lieutenant Donna L. Spruill became the first Navy woman pilot to carrier qualify in a fixed-wing aircraft. Lieutenant Spruill piloted a C-1A Trader to an arrested landing aboard *Independence*.

1 July   With the disestablishment of U.S. Army Executive Flight Detachment, HMX-1 became the single source of helicopter support for the White House.

17 July   *Saipan* was operating off the coast of Nicaragua for possible evacuation of American diplomats and others due to the turmoil surrounding the fall of that government.

18 July   VP-23, flying the P-3C Orion, fired the new Harpoon missile. VP-23 was the first operational fleet patrol squadron to receive, fire and make an operational deployment with the Harpoon missile. On August 17, a ceremony at NAS Brunswick, Maine, marked the introduction of the Harpoon antiship missile into operational service as an air-launched weapon.

19 July   The President announced he had instructed the U.S. Seventh Fleet to aid the Vietnamese "boat people" and assist them to safety. U.S. Naval Aviation and surface units of the Seventh Fleet stepped up patrolling, assistance and rescue efforts in support of these Vietnamese refugees.

Aerial view, taken by a P-3B Orion from VP-22, of boat people aboard their small craft displaying an "SOS" sign 1175289

21 July   Neil A. Armstrong, a Navy pilot during the Korean War, was inducted into the Aviation Hall of Fame in Dayton, Ohio. He served as an experimental test pilot for the National Advisory Committee for Aeronautics and flew a variety of high speed aircraft including the X-15. Later, after being selected as an Astronaut by NASA, he served as command pilot of the Gemini 8 mission, during which he participated in the first docking of a spacecraft. His most notable achievement came as commander of the Apollo 11 Lunar Landing Mission when he became the first man to step on the moon.

24 July   The Bell XV-15 successfully converted in flight from the helicopter mode to the fixed-wing mode. The XV-15 flight test program was founded as a joint U.S. Navy/NASA/Army research effort to evaluate the tilt rotor concept.

27 July   The Navy's newest turbo-jet-powered aerial target, the Northrop BQM-74C, successfully completed its first flight over the Pacific Missile Test Center, Point Mugu, Calif. The 33-minute flight also marked the first airborne launch of the BQM-74C when the target was launched from under the wing of an A-6 Intruder. Following completion of the flight, the BQM-74C was safely landed at sea, retrieved, and returned to Point Mugu for inspection, refurbishment, and eventual reuse. The BQM-74C was the only target in the world using a Digital Avionics Processor which allowed it to provide realistic low cost antiship cruise missile simulation in training.

30 August   The first prototype of the Navy's SH-60B Seahawk helicopter was unveiled at the Sikorsky

Vietnamese refugee boarding White Plains (AFS 4) after being rescued from their 35 foot boat in the South China Sea NAH-002785

1979—Continued

Aircraft Division at Stratford, Conn. The SH-60B was designed to operate from destroyers, frigates and cruisers in performing its role in the LAMPS mission— detecting, classifying, locating and destroying hostile submarines and surface vessels over extended ranges. Secondary missions for the helicopter included search and rescue, medical evacuation and general fleet support. The SH-60B was officially dubbed the Seahawk in February 1979.

30 August A U.S. Navy CH-53D Sea Stallion helicopter of VR-24 lifted a 12-foot bronze statue of the Madonna and Child to the top of Mt. Tiberius on Capri, Italy, to replace one which had been destroyed by lightning. The statue was too large to be transported overland.

15 September The first UC-12B for the Navy arrived at NATC Patuxent River, Md., for preliminary evaluation tests. The UC-12B is the military version of the Beechcraft Super King Air 200 which was purchased by the Navy to replace aging reciprocating engine aircraft and supplement the Navy's transport inventory. The UC-12B was designed to carry 8 to 12 passengers. It had a maximum cruise speed of 300 mph and a range up to 1,760 miles. The aircraft could operate from short, grass runways and fly at 31,000 feet. It had advanced solid state avionics which could automatically navigate the plane through bad weather conditions. The UC-12B had been designed for reliability, maintainability and low cost of operation, with a configuration which lent itself to a variety of transport, training and utility missions.

18 September The Circulation Control Rotor made its first flight using the airframe and propulsion system from an HH-2D helicopter. This CCR was initiated by the Navy as an advanced rotor system with improved performance, reduced maintenance requirements, and reduced vibration levels from extant rotor systems.

28 September RVAH-7 was disestablished, closing the history on the last RA-5C Vigilante squadron in the Navy. The Vigilante had provided 15 years of tactical support to the fleet as a photographic reconnaissance plane and had served valiantly in Vietnam with integrated intelligence sensors and photographic equipment. Some of the RA-5C Vigilantes were planned for use as drones.

1–8 October The AV-8C Harrier shipboard trials were conducted aboard *Saipan*. Testing consisted of 33 flights involving short take-offs, vertical take-offs and vertical landings by the AV-8C.

11 October *Nassau* and other amphibious ships headed for Guantanamo Bay, Cuba, in a show of force ordered by the President in response to maneuvers by a Russian combat brigade in Cuba. On 17 October, 1,800 Marines landed in Guantanamo Bay as a demonstration of naval power in the wake of the Soviet refusal to withdraw the Russian combat brigade from Cuba.

14 October The A-6E TRAM aircraft was introduced into the fleet, at NAS Oceana, Va. The A-6E TRAM provided the U.S. Navy with the finest all-weather attack system in the world.

28 October *Kitty Hawk* and her escort ships were directed to operate south of the Korean peninsula in response to the assassination of South Korean President Park Chung Hee on 26 October.

30 October The F/A-18 Hornet made its first landing at sea aboard *America* for five days of sea trials. A total of 32 catapult and arrested landings were completed.

4 November One Naval Aviator and 14 Marines were among the more than 60 Americans taken hostage when the United States Embassy in Tehran, Iran, was seized by a mob of Iranian revolutionaries. Spokesmen for the mob demanded that the United States return to Iran the deposed Shah who was in a New York hospital at the time.

18 November *Midway* and her escort ships, which had been operating in the Indian Ocean, arrived in the northern part of the Arabian Sea in connection with the continuing hostage crisis in Iran.

20 November The last RA-5C Vigilante in the Navy departed NAS Key West, Fla., on her final flight. The RA-5C was one of the Navy's finest and only all-weather carrier based reconnaissance aircraft. With this final flight, the entire reconnaissance inventory of 156 Vigilante aircraft was phased out.

21 November *Kitty Hawk* and her escort ships were directed to sail to the Indian Ocean to join *Midway* and her escort ships which were operating in the northern Arabian Sea. The two carrier forces provided the U.S. with A-6 and A-7 attack aircraft and F-4 and the modern F-14 fighter aircraft, which could respond to a variety of situations if called upon during the Iranian hostage crisis.

1979—Continued

3 December   *Kitty Hawk* and her escort ships arrived on station in the northern Arabian Sea for contingency operations during the Iranian hostage crisis. This was the first time since World War II that the U.S. Navy had two carrier task forces in the Indian Ocean in response to a crisis situation.

12 December   The development program for the LAMPS MK III SH-60B Seahawk helicopter reached a major milestone when the aircraft completed its first flight at the Sikorsky test facility in West Palm Beach, Fla.

17 December   The first two-seater F/A-18 Hornet arrived at NATC Patuxent River, Md., for armament and stores separation testing. During 1979 NATC had conducted 416 flights in the F/A-18 for a total of 555 hours testing the new fighter/attack plane. On 12 December NATC completed a successful live firing of a Sidewinder missile from the F/A-18.

21 December   The Defense Department announced a three-ship nuclear-powered carrier battle group from the Sixth Fleet would deploy to the Indian Ocean to relieve the Seventh Fleet carrier battle group led by *Kitty Hawk*. The Sixth Fleet carrier battle group consisted of the nuclear-powered *Nimitz* and her nuclear-powered escort ships.

24 December   A massive Soviet airlift of 5,000 Russian airborne troops and equipment into the Afghanistan capital of Kabul was conducted. The U.S. protested the large influx of Soviet troops which the Soviet Union claimed were there at the request of the Afghanistan government. On 27 December, a Soviet-backed coup installed a new president in Afghanistan. Two carrier task forces centering around *Midway* and *Kitty Hawk* continued contingency operations in the northern Arabian Sea.

31 December   During 1979, Navy carrier forces responded to five crisis situations around the world. The following carriers responded for contingency operations: *Constellation* responded to the crisis which involved North and South Yemen; *Saipan* responded during the Nicaraguan turmoil; *Nassau* was involved in the response to Russian combat troops in Cuba; *Kitty Hawk* responded to the alert in Korea; and *Midway* and *Kitty Hawk* conducted contingency operations during the Iranian hostage crisis.

31 December   U.S. Navy surface and aviation forces of the Seventh Fleet continued their patrols and rescue assistance efforts connected with the Vietnamese boat people following the President's order in July. During the last six months of 1979, Navy ships embarked over 800 Vietnamese refugees. Vietnamese refugees picked up by merchant vessels with the aid of P-3 patrol aircraft totaled over 1,000.

1980

1 January   *Midway* and *Kitty Hawk* continued on contingency operations in the Arabian Sea in response to 53 Americans held hostage at the American Embassy in Teheran, Iran, since 4 November 1979.

1 January   VP-23 deployed from Keflavik, Iceland, to Diego Garcia and made its first operational flight out of the Indian Ocean base within ten days after receiving orders, thereby demonstrating its rapid deployment capability.

2 January   A detachment of P-3B Orions of VP-10, deployed at Rota, Spain, flew photoreconnaissance missions to locate areas damaged in an earthquake which struck the Azores the day before, killing some 50 persons and injuring another 500.

4 January   *Nimitz* rendezvoused with her nuclear-powered escort ships in the Mediterranean and headed to the Indian Ocean via Africa's Cape of Good Hope to relieve *Kitty Hawk* which was on contingency duty. This left *Forrestal*, the only carrier with the Sixth Fleet, in the Med.

4 January   The first TA-7C Corsair II assigned to the Pacific Missile Test Center, Point Mugu, Calif., was test flown.

7 January   Reconnaissance Attack Wing One was disestablished. The wing had consisted of nine fleet squadrons, one training squadron and a support command which had provided tactical reconnaissance for Navy carrier deployments. The phaseout coincided with the final retirement from the fleet of all RA-5C Vigilantes on 20 November 1979 and the disestablishment of the last RVAH squadron on 28 September 1979.

22 January   *Nimitz* and her escort ships joined *Midway* and *Kitty Hawk* and their escort ships on station in the Arabian Sea. The following day *Kitty Hawk* departed for Subic Bay, R.P., having spent 64 days in operations connected with the Iranian crisis.

1980—Continued

5 February *Coral Sea* relieved *Midway* which had been on contingency operations in the Arabian Sea since the Iranian hostage crisis broke out in November 1979.

29 February VMO-1 began flying the new OV-10D Bronco observation plane at New River, N.C. The D version, manufactured by Rockwell International, had the FLIR and laser rangefinder designator systems. The new systems enabled the pilot to locate a target at night or in bad weather and then pinpoint the exact range and location with a laser beam. An automatic video tracker computer system locked on to a moving target with information provided by the infrared system. The TV-like video display gave the pilot and observer a computer-assisted sighting capability. Conventional improvements included the upgraded T-76 turboprop engine, larger fiberglass propellers and an increased fuel capacity.

1 March It was reported that the CNO had proposed to the Secretary of Defense a plan to reactivate the *Essex*-class carrier *Oriskany* and several other major moth-balled ships to help fulfill the Navy's missions in the Indian Ocean and other areas.

6 March *Nassau* began a month-long cruise to the Caribbean to demonstrate U.S. capability to defend the Panama Canal in accordance with the 1979 treaty with Panama. *Nassau* had a 400-man Marine detachment, CH-46 Sea Knight and CH-53 Sea Stallion helicopters and AV-8A Harriers on board.

16 April *Dwight D. Eisenhower* and her nuclear-powered escort ships departed East Coast ports en route to the Indian Ocean to relieve *Nimitz*. This was the second all nuclear-powered task force to head for the Indian Ocean since the beginning of the Iranian hostage crisis. Two days later, *Constellation* and her escort ships departed Subic Bay, R.P., steaming to the Indian Ocean to relieve *Coral Sea*.

24 April Eight RH-53D Sea Stallions operating from *Nimitz* in the Arabian Sea took part in a joint task force operation to rescue the American hostages in Tehran, Iran. The mission was later aborted at a desert refueling site. Subsequently, one of the helicopters collided with a C-130 Hercules aircraft resulting in the loss of eight lives. All other personnel were evacuated on the remaining C-130s.

30 April *Constellation* and her task group relieved *Coral Sea* and her escort ships. *Coral Sea* had been on station for 89 days in connection with the Iranian crisis.

5 May *Saipan* and other Navy ships provided humanitarian search and rescue support operations for the vast sealift of Cuban refugees heading for the U.S. through the Florida Straits. The Navy ships had been diverted from the annual combined training exercise Solid Shield to undertake the mission.

8 May Arriving in the Arabian Sea from the U.S. via the Cape of Good Hope, *Dwight D. Eisenhower* conducted turnover with *Nimitz*, which had been involved in Iranian contingency operations for 115 consecutive days.

26 May The President embarked on *Nimitz* off Norfolk, Va., and thanked the men of *Nimitz* and her escort ships for their sacrifice during an extended nine-month deployment to the Mediterranean and the Indian Ocean. *Nimitz* had spent 144 straight days at sea in connection with the Iranian hostage crisis.

27 May *Coral Sea* was diverted to standby duty south of the Cheju-Do Islands in the Sea of Japan in response to conditions of civil unrest in the Republic of Korea. She was relieved by *Midway* three days later.

31 May P-3 Orions from various patrol squadrons of Patrol and Reconnaissance Force, Seventh Fleet, continued their search, begun the previous year, for refugees in the South China Sea and Gulf of Thailand. These aircraft had investigated more than 15,000 radar contacts and dropped radio transmitters and/or refugee survival packs to people in distress. To this date, over 2,500 refugees had been rescued through efforts by all elements of the Navy.

3 June The first AGM-65E laser Maverick missile was fired at Eglin AFB, Fla., from a Marine Corps A-4M Skyhawk. The missile was the laser-guided version of the USAF's air-to-ground Maverick with a heavier warhead. It was being developed by Hughes Aircraft Company for use by the Marine Corps in close-air support of combat troops.

15 June A loading demonstration of the F/A-18 Hornet was held at NATC Patuxent River, Md. The aircraft showed off some of its weapons capabilities, among them the 20mm Vulcan cannon, AIM-7F advanced Sparrow, AIM-9L Sidewinder, flare dispensers, rocket launchers, advanced fuel-air explosives, and a Rockeye and other bombs. Hornet weaponry also included Walleye, Maverick, Harpoon and HARM missiles, and laser-guided bombs.

1980—Continued

23 June   The Navy granted approval for service use for two advanced sonobuoys. The AN/SSQ-2 Directional Command Active Sonobuoy System and the AN/SSQ-77 Vertical Line Array DIFAR represented the first major improvements in the sonobuoy field since the AN/SSQ-53 DIFAR was introduced in 1968. These sonobuoys reinforced their article's unique position as the vital link between the search aircraft and "enemy in liquid space." They provided a three-to-five fold improvement over existing active and passive airborne sensors.

8 July   The Navy terminated its support operations at Key West, Fla., for the Cuban refugees. Eleven Navy ships as well as P-3 Orion patrol aircraft assisted the unofficial freedom flotilla which involved civilian boats crossing the Florida Straits to transfer Cuban refugees to the U.S. Over 115,500 had arrived from Mariel, Cuba, since the freedom flotilla began.

18 July   Charles "Pete" Conrad, former Navy pilot and NASA astronaut, became the twelfth former Naval Aviator to be enshrined in the prestigious Aviation Hall of Fame, Dayton, Ohio.

30 July   An automatic parachute release system developed by Vought Corporation was designed to save the lives of pilots who ejected from their aircraft under adverse conditions. The new system, developed with U.S. Navy funding, was called SEAPAC. It had seawater activated switches which automatically released the parachute harness when a pilot entered the water.

31 July   A T-2C Buckeye was launched successfully from a fixed-angle, three-degree ski jump at Naval Air Test Center, Patuxent River, Md. This launch was the first part of feasibility demonstrations to evaluate the use of ramps for takeoffs by conventional, as opposed to V/STOL, aircraft.

31 July   A Limited Duty Officer aviator program for second class, first class and chief petty officers, pay grades E-5 through E-7, was established, with the first 35 enlisted personnel selected and scheduled to report to NAS Pensacola, Fla., in April 1981. After completing aviation officer indoctrination, primary flight and maritime (prop) training, the new officers were assigned to an initial three-year tour as primary flight instructors. Major objectives of the program were to improve utilization and retention of aviators, provide further upward mobility for enlisted personnel, improve the flight instructor program and provide for replacement of aviators in selected shipboard billets.

17 August   *Midway* relieved *Constellation* to begin another Indian Ocean deployment and complement the *Dwight D. Eisenhower* task group still on contingency duty in the Arabian Sea.

22 September   *Dwight D. Eisenhower* and *Midway* continued contingency operations in the northern Arabian Sea as war erupted between Iraq and Iran.

12 October   Ships of the Amphibious Force, Sixth Fleet, including *Guadalcanal,* began assisting the victims of a massive earthquake which devastated the Algerian city of Al Asnam. The ships took up positions 20–25 miles offshore to render helicopter support in the disaster relief efforts.

6 November   *Ranger* and accompanying ships of her task group relieved *Midway* in the northern Arabian Sea. *Midway* thus completed her second Indian Ocean deployment in connection with the Iranian crisis, for a total of 157 days on the line.

11 November   For the first time, the LAMPS SH-60B Seahawk worked with the RAST system aboard a ship underway. The guided-missile frigate *McInerney* (FFG 8) conducted the shipboard aspect of the exercise which included mainly electronic communications and not an actual landing. This test was conducted from the Bath Ironworks and Yard at Bath, Maine.

13 November   VFA-125, the Navy's first F/A-18 Hornet squadron, was established at NAS Lemoore, Calif. The new squadron would train Navy and Marine Corps personnel to fly and maintain the new fighter-attack aircraft.

22 November   Aircraft carrier suitability tests of the Tomahawk II medium range air-to-surface missile were completed.

25 November   RH-53D Sea Stallions from VR-24, together with units of the U.S. Army and Air Force, began disaster relief assistance to victims of the devastating earthquake at Avellino, Italy, on 23 November which killed over 3,000 persons and made many more homeless. Commander, Fleet Air Mediterranean, headquartered at Naples, was director of U.S. military support efforts.

8 December   *Independence* and her escort ships relieved *Dwight D. Eisenhower* and her task force which had been involved in Iranian contingency operations since 8 May. *Dwight D. Eisenhower* returned to Norfolk, Va., on 22 December after a 251-day deployment, the longest underway deployment for a Navy

1980—Continued

ship since World War II. She had been underway for 152 continuous days.

31 December   Carrier operations during 1980 in connection with the Iranian crisis consisted of 10 tours by eight attack carriers (two with two tours each) in the Indian Ocean/Arabian Sea. The carriers accumulated a grand total of 723 days on station. Those with over 100 contingency days on station during the year included *Dwight D. Eisenhower,* whose two tours totaled 199 days; *Midway,* with two tours representing 118 days; *Constellation,* with 110 days; and *Nimitz,* with 108 days. Other carriers involved in contingency operations in the Indian Ocean were *Coral Sea, Ranger, Independence* and *Kitty Hawk.*

An F-4 Phantom II in colorful 1976 bicentennial markings.

An E-2 Hawkeye in colorful 1976 bicentennial markings.

An H-3 in colorful 1976 bicentennial markings.

A TA-4J Skyhawk in colorful 1976 bicentennial markings.

Pilot ejecting from aircraft aboard Shangri-La NH-90350

F-4J Phantom of VF-21 making a successful barricade arrested landing aboard Ranger.

PART 11

The Diamond Anniversary Decade

1981–1990

The eighth decade of Naval Aviation was characterized by a buildup of its forces, the rise of world-wide acts of terrorism and Naval Aviation's involvement in response to the various crises throughout the world.

The decade began with American Embassy personnel being held as hostages in Iran. As had been the case since the Cold War began, carriers were on station in response to the crisis. The latter part of the 1970s had seen an increase in the number of carrier deployments to the Indian Ocean. In the 1980s that trend was increased and strengthened. Undoubtedly, this was the result of the ongoing and increasing problems in the Middle East, eastern Africa and the subcontinent of Asia.

During the 1980s, Naval Aviation saw a resurgence in its strength and capabilities. There was an increase in its building programs and new technology research. Many of Naval Aviation's aircraft for the 1990s and the 21st century were introduced in the 1980s. They included the F/A-18 Hornet, the SH-60B LAMPS MK III Seahawk and its derivatives, the MH-53E and the AV-8B Harrier II. A new aircraft concept was introduced with the rollout of the V-22 Osprey, a fixed-wing, tilt-rotor aircraft capable of vertical take-off and landing and horizontal flight (VTOL). Missile development kept pace with the aircraft. New introductions into the operating inventory included the HARM, Skipper, Hellfire and the cruise missile (Tomahawk). The platforms for these missiles also kept pace with developments. Additional nuclear-powered aircraft carriers were commissioned and more were authorized for construction. A new class of multipurpose amphibious assault ship (LHD) was commissioned with more scheduled for completion or under construction.

The decade of the 1980s was special for Naval Aviation. In 1986 it celebrated its 75th anniversary. Throughout the year, many of the advances in the development of Naval Aviation were lauded, as were the men and women who contributed to its growth. Naval Aviation's continued involvement in international events was emphasized and its need to maintain its readiness and capabilities was reaffirmed .

Naval Aviation's involvement in international events—major highlights of the 1980s—began with Iran and the continuing hostage crisis, 1979–1981. Libyan operations in 1981, 1986 and 1989 demonstrated Naval Aviation's air-to-air and strike capabilities. In 1983, a carrier and amphibious task force took part in Operation Urgent Fury and the re-establishment of democracy in the Caribbean island of Grenada. Operations in and around Lebanon kept Naval Aviation occupied during the mid-1980s. Responding to hijacking and terrorism in the Mediterranean basin was an ongoing requirement for most of the 1980s. The other hot spot for Naval Aviation was the Persian Gulf and the Iran-Iraq war. Naval Aviation was involved in numerous periods of short-lived combat operations in the Persian Gulf area. The escorting of reflagged oil tankers and the monitoring of the Iran-Iraq war kept Naval Aviation on the line from the mid-1980s. As the decade ended, a new crisis appeared when Iraq invaded Kuwait and the UN imposed an economic blockade on Iraq to force its withdrawal from Kuwait.

The activities of Naval Aviation were not limited to a combat role. In 1982, the U.S. Navy began working closely with U.S. Customs and the Coast Guard to curb the influx of drugs into the country. Navy E-2C Hawkeye aircraft became a permanent participant in helping to detect drug smugglers. Other activities included continued involvement in the manned space program and assistance during natural disasters, both at home and abroad.

The 1980s ended on a high note, featuring a continued détente between the U.S. and the Soviet Union. During this decade, Naval Aviation continued to show its diversity and multiple capabilities.

1981

1 January The names of the first group of selectees for the new Naval Aviation Hall of Honor at the Naval Aviation Museum in Pensacola, Fla., were made public. The 12 men approved for enshrinement by the Chief of Naval Operations on 10 July 1980 were:

1981—Continued

Admiral John H. Towers; Eugene B. Ely; Lieutenant Colonel Alfred A. Cunningham; Rear Admiral Richard E. Byrd, Jr.; Commander Theodore G. Ellyson; Glenn H. Curtiss; Vice Admiral Patrick N. L. Bellinger; Rear Admiral William A. Moffett; Rear Admiral Albert C. Read; Lieutenant Commander Godfrey deC. Chevalier; Captain Holden C. Richardson; and Warrant Officer Floyd Bennett.

6 January   The LAMPS MK III ASW system went to sea for the first time. Off the northeastern coast of Florida, the SH-60B Seahawk landed aboard *McInerney* (FFG 8) underway by using the new RAST gear. RAST was designed to recover a helicopter in seas with ship movements up to a 28 degree roll, 5 degrees of pitch and heaving of 15 feet per second. The primary mission of the SH-60B was antisubmarine warfare. It also provided surveillance and targeting information on surface vessels, performed search and rescue (SAR) operations and was used for vertical replenishment and gunfire support.

10 January   Aircraft from the naval stations at Guantanamo Bay, Cuba, and Roosevelt Roads, P.R., responded to a request by the Jamaican government for assistance in fighting a fuel oil storage tank fire in the Montego Bay area. The aircraft flew in fire fighters, equipment and light water.

15 January   A Tomahawk cruise missile was launched from the submerged submarine *Guitarro* (SSN 665) off the California coast and impacted the target at a range of more than 100 miles. The test was repeated six days later with the same results. In another test conducted on 20 March, the missile hit the target at a range of more than 200 miles. These tests successfully demonstrated the Tomahawk's capability to search for, locate and attack a target at sea.

20 January   Iran released 52 Americans who had been held hostage since 4 November 1979, when the American Embassy in Tehran was seized. Twelve members of the hostage group were active duty Navy and Marine Corps personnel. Commander Don A. Sharer was the only member of the group from the Naval Aviation community. A Naval Flight Officer, he was a naval advisor at the time of the embassy takeover and the senior member of the Navy and Marine Corps hostages.

31 January   The era of Enlisted Naval Aviators came to a close when the last enlisted pilot, Master Chief Robert K. Jones, retired after 38 years of naval service. Enlisted pilots had performed their duties for over 61 years as Naval Aviators on combat missions, as transport pilots and as instructors. The program for Enlisted Naval Aviators officially ended in 1947.

Master Chief Air Controlman Robert K. Jones (right foreground) conducts a pre-flight check of a US-2B Tracker.

1981—Continued

19 February VFA-125 became the first squadron to receive the new F/A-18 Hornet for fleet operations. The Hornet was the Navy's newest strike fighter and had been undergoing extensive operational test and evaluation at Patuxent River, Md., and by VX-4 at Point Mugu, Calif. VFA-125's mission was to train maintenance personnel and pilots for future Hornet squadrons.

16 March An A-6 Intruder from VA-115 on board *Midway* sighted a downed civilian helicopter in the South China Sea. *Midway* immediately dispatched HC-1 Det 2 helicopters to the scene. All 17 people aboard the downed helicopter were rescued and brought aboard the carrier. The chartered civilian helicopter was also plucked out of the water and lifted to *Midway's* flight deck.

23 March The F/A-18 Hornet began climatic testing by the Air Force's 3246th Test Wing at the McKinley Climatic Laboratory, Eglin Air Force Base, Fla. The tests were designed to evaluate the F/A-18 airframe's ability to withstand the wide range of temperatures and climatic conditions which the aircraft would experience in its everyday operations.

12 April Space Shuttle *Columbia* was launched at Cape Canaveral, Fla. The first reusable space vehicle was manned by an all-Navy crew consisting of Naval Aviators Captain John Young, USN (Ret), and Captain Robert Crippen. Two days later, after 36 orbits around the earth, the shuttle returned to earth and touched down safely at Edwards Air Force Base, Calif. The vehicle was then prepared for its next flight into space. The space orbiter was designed to carry satellite payloads into space and conduct manned experiments.

13 April AV-8A Harriers were deployed as a Marine Air Group aboard an LHA for the first time. Marine Air Group 32, composed of VMA-231 and -542, began its Sixth Fleet deployment aboard *Nassau*.

15 April Admiral John S. Thach, one of the Navy's early fighter tacticians, died. He was commanding officer of VF-3 when World War II began and was perhaps best known for developing a two-plane fighter tactic which proved to be effective against the highly maneuverable Japanese Zero. This innovation became known as the "Thach Weave" and was taught to Navy and Army Air Force pilots alike.

4 May *America* transited the Suez Canal, the largest warship ever to do so. She was the first U.S. carrier to travel through the canal since 1 June 1967, when *Intrepid* navigated the waterway.

19 May Astronauts Captain John W. Young, USN (Ret), and Captain Robert L. Crippen, USN, were presented medals by the President at White House ceremonies for their successful mission on the first orbital flight of the Space Shuttle *Columbia*. Astronaut Young received the congressional Space Medal of Honor, the seventh person so honored. Five of the seven have been Navy or Marine Corps Aviators.

20 May TACGRU One and subordinate commands, TACRONS 11 and 12, were established. Their mission was to perform all functions relating to tactical control of aircraft in support of amphibious operations.

The F/A-18 Hornet during climatic testing at Eglin AFB, Fla.

1981—Continued

Space Shuttle Columbia, with its all Navy crew, touches down at Edwards AFB, Calif., after its first flight.

26 May   During night air operations on *Nimitz*, an EA-6B Prowler from VMAQ-2 crash landed on the flight deck and careened into parked aircraft on the bow. Fourteen men lost their lives. The men of *Nimitz* and CVW-8 prevented further loss of life and damage to the carrier by prompt rescue, damage control and fire prevention operations. On 30 June, *Nimitz* returned to operations at sea after two days in port in Norfolk to repair the damage incurred as a result of the 26 May crash.

1 June   Patrol Wing 10 was established in ceremonies held at NAS Moffett Field, Calif. The operational patrol wing would act as the middle link between the patrol squadrons and Commander, Patrol Wings, Pacific. This was the third time that the Patrol Wing 10 designation had been used. It was originally established in December 1940, disestablished in June 1947, established in June 1963 and disestablished once more in 1973. In early 1942, PBY squadrons of the patrol wing fought courageous delaying actions against the Japanese as Allied forces were driven southward from the Philippines. Later in the war, the legendary Black Cats operated under Patrol Wing 10.

6 June   The Order of Daedalians presented their Weapon System Award for Outstanding System Achievement to NAVAIR. The specific system which occasioned the award was NAVAIR's A-6E TRAM project.

15 June   The Blue Angels, the Navy's Flight Demonstration Squadron, celebrated their 35th anniversary. Since its beginning, the squadron had flown the F8F Bearcat, F6F Hellcat, F9F Panther, F9F-5 Cougar, F11F-1 Tiger, F-4J Phantom II, and the A-4 Skyhawk.

16 June   The first fleet operational CH-53E Super Stallion helicopter, built by Sikorsky Aircraft Division, was delivered to Marine Air Group 26 for assignment to HMH-464. The newly improved CH-53E, the western world's largest helicopter, could transport cargo of over 16 tons or ferry 55 fully equipped Marines. It was also capable of delivering aircraft on board carriers.

29 June   The Secretary of Defense approved full production of the F/A-18 Hornet. The aircraft had met all requirements for use as a Navy and Marine Corps fighter and would replace the aging F-4 Phantom II.

1 July   VS-0294 was established at NAS North Island, Calif. The reserve unit's mission would be to train and qualify pilots, NFOs, aircrewmen and maintenance personnel to augment fleet carrier ASW squadrons. The reserve squadron, with the exception of maintenance personnel, would train on simulators or trainers, which were realistic mock-ups of S-3A aircraft, thereby reducing the high cost of utilizing actual aircraft.

1981—Continued

7 July   A strike by the Professional Air Traffic Controllers Organization led the President to assign 116 Navy and Marine Corps air traffic controllers to civilian airport towers.

8 July   A newly modified model 24 Lear jet arrived at NAS Patuxent River, Md., to be used as part of the Naval Test Pilot School's fleet of flying teaching aids. The Lear jet was equipped with a flight control system which allowed changes in the aircraft's flying qualities to meet instructional needs. Test pilot students could be exposed to handling characteristics ranging from a transport to the F/A-18 in this aircraft.

9 July   U.S. Naval Aviation officials and representatives from the Federal German Navy Air Arm marked the 25th anniversary of the program established in 1956 for the training of German naval pilots, flight officers and flight surgeons at U.S. Naval Aviation facilities. The ceremonies were conducted at NAS Pensacola, Fla., and included the Chief of Naval Air Training and the Deputy Commander-in-Chief German Fleet.

23 July   VMFA-312 received a camouflaged F-4S Phantom II sporting a new paint scheme which was being tested by NAVAIR. The new camouflage was a scientifically designed, counter-shaded gray, tactical paint scheme to help the plane to escape visual detection.

19 August   Two F-14 Tomcats of VF-41 shot down two Libyan Su-22 Sukhoi aircraft over international waters. Flying off *Nimitz*, the Tomcats were on a reconnaissance mission for a missile-firing exercise being conducted by U.S. ships from two carrier battle groups when they were fired on by the Libyan planes. The VF-41 Tomcats, part of CVW-8, were piloted by Commander Henry M. Kleeman and Lieutenant Lawrence M. Muczynski with the respective RIOs Lieutenants David J. Venlet and James Anderson.

28 September   The first night flight of a conventional land attack Tomahawk cruise missile was conducted over White Sands Missile Range, N.Mex. A Navy A-6 equipped with the Tomahawk cruise missile took off from the Pacific Missile Test Center, Point Mugu, Calif., and flew to White Sands. The aircraft used the Tomahawk's terrain contour matching updates to guide it to the range. Once inside the range, the missile was launched from the A-6 and flew a complex night land attack mission.

5 October   The AGM-88A HARM missile made its first live warhead launch. The missile was fired from

an A-7E against *Savage* (DER 368). The test was conducted from the Pacific Missile Test Center.

14 October   The Naval Aviation Hall of Honor was dedicated at the Naval Aviation Museum, Pensacola, Fla. The first 12 selectees were enshrined during the dedication.

28 October   Walter Hinton, the last surviving participant in the historic NC-4 flight, died. The flight, made in May 1919, was the world's first trans-Atlantic flight.

31 October   Newport News Shipbuilding, Newport News, Va., laid the keel for CVN 71, and the name for the new carrier was announced officially as *Theodore Roosevelt*. Secretary of Defense Caspar Weinberger delivered the address during a ceremony at Newport News, Va.

5 November   The McDonnell Douglas AV-8B Harrier flew for the first time. The AV-8B, developed by McDonnell Aircraft Company with British Aerospace participation, was an advanced version of the AV-8A already in service with the Marine Corps.

7 November   VMAQ-4 was established at NAS Whidbey Island, Wash. The squadron was the first Marine Corps reserve squadron to fly the EA-6A Intruder.

13 November   The Secretary of the Navy announced the forthcoming retirement of Admiral Hyman G. Rickover, Director of the Division of Naval Reactors. Admiral Rickover was known as the father of the nuclear-powered submarine and was also responsible for the development of nuclear-powered surface ships, including aircraft carriers. Admiral Rickover's contributions to Naval Aviation had been duly recognized on 21 July 1970, when he was awarded honorary Naval Aviator wings.

14 November   Astronauts Captain Richard H. Truly, USN, and Colonel Joe H. Engle, USAF, brought Space Shuttle *Columbia* back to earth after two days in space. They were the first men to fly into space and return in a previously used spacecraft. *Columbia* had its maiden voyage in April 1981.

17 November   The first firing of the Harpoon Block 1B missile occurred aboard *Fletcher* (DD 992). This successful launch was a milestone in missile development by NAVAIR. The air-launched version of the Harpoon made its initial carrier deployment in October 1981 with VA-65 aboard *Constellation*.

1981—Continued

2 December Captain Cecil E. Harris, USN (Ret), died. He was the Navy's second highest scoring ace during World War II and was credited with downing 24 enemy aircraft.

1982

8 January The F/A-18 Hornet made its first fully automatic landing on a simulated carrier deck field at Naval Air Test Center, Patuxent River, Md.

28 January The new Limited Duty Officer Aviator Program, in which enlisted personnel could receive flight training and be commissioned, was inaugurated by Antisubmarine Warfare Aircrewman First Class Michael A. Gray and Chief Yeoman Douglas L. McGowan, Jr., when they completed their flight training and received their wings and commission. This was the first time that noncommissioned officers completed flight training since the NAVCAD program ended in 1968.

3 February *John F. Kennedy* transited the Suez Canal from the Mediterranean Sea to the Red Sea, the largest warship ever to pass through the Canal. She was en route to the Indian Ocean for an extended deployment.

13 February VF-84, stationed aboard *Nimitz*, returned to Norfolk from the Mediterranean, completing the first operational deployment of the TARPS on the F-14 Tomcat. TARPS was designed to be carried by the F-14 for low to medium altitude photoreconnaissance missions.

5 March The Navy assumed command of the government plant representative office at McDonnell Douglas Corporation's St. Louis, Mo., facilities. The Navy replaced the Air Force plant representative office which had been responsible for contract administration at the McDonnell Douglas plant for the past 11 years.

16 March The Vice President announced the U.S. Navy would be actively working with U.S. Customs officials and the U.S. Coast Guard to curb the influx of drugs into the United States. The Navy's E-2C Hawkeye aircraft became a permanent participant in helping detect drug smugglers.

18 April 40th anniversary of the Doolittle raid on Tokyo. The event was celebrated on 14 April with a flyover of Washington, D.C., by four rebuilt B-25 aircraft. General Doolittle, USAF (Ret), was on hand to greet the pilots after the flyover. During the Tokyo raid in 1942, B-25s had been launched from the carrier *Hornet*.

22 May Marine Corps Aviation celebrated its 70th anniversary, marking the day when 1st Lieutenant Alfred A. Cunningham, USMC, reported to the Superintendent of the Naval Academy for "duty in connection with aviation."

2 June The AV-8B Harrier II made the first flight of its Navy Preliminary Evaluation. This advanced version of the AV-8 was designed to have twice the performance of its predecessor.

7 June The Navy received an advanced version of the Harpoon missile called the Block 1B Harpoon. The new missile had an improved radar-guidance system and was capable of flying at lower altitudes than the initial Harpoons, which were delivered to the fleet starting in 1977. The new capability reduced the risk of detection by defense radar. The Harpoon was programmed to be the Navy's basic antiship weapon for the rest of this century.

25 June The history of the Navy's C-121 (previous designations include PO, WV, R7O and R7V) ended after 33 years of service when the last Warning Star (other popular names were Constellation, Super Constellation and Super Connie) was retired from active service with VAQ-33. The Constellation began its naval career in August 1949 and served in a wide variety of roles and missions during its active duty with the Navy.

25 June The greatest concentration of U.S. Navy air power in the Mediterranean Sea was the result of the battle groups of *Forrestal* and *Independence* joining forces with *Dwight D. Eisenhower* and *John F. Kennedy* during the latter part of June. After steaming together in the eastern Mediterranean Sea for several days, *Forrestal* and *Independence* relieved *Dwight D. Eisenhower* and *John F. Kennedy*, the latter sailing home to Norfolk, Va., after a long deployment.

30 June The last active duty photographic squadron (VFP-63) was disestablished. VFP-63's disestablishment also brought to a close the era of the F-8 Crusader squadrons on active duty in the Navy. The only F-8 and photographic squadrons still left in existence were reserve squadrons VFP-206 and VFP-306, NAF Washington, D.C.

30 June Chief of Naval Operations Admiral Thomas B. Hayward, the Navy's number one aviator, retired. Admiral Hayward, the 21st CNO, assumed the position on 1 July 1978. He was a graduate of the Naval Academy, Class of 1944, and was designated a Naval Aviator on 26 July 1950.

1982—Continued

7 July In a change of command ceremony, Mr. Walter Wagner became the Naval Air Systems Command's first civilian project manager. Mr. Wagner relieved Captain John E. Hock, Jr., as project manager for the E-2/C-2 airborne tactical data system.

13 July Lieutenant Commander Barbara Allen Rainey, the first woman to be designated a Naval Aviator, was killed in an aircraft accident during a training flight. She was an instructor with VT-3 when the accident occurred.

Barbara Allen in the early days of her career.

30 July Ensign Jannine Weiss became the first enlisted woman to receive her wings and commission under the new Limited Duty Officer Aviator Program.

31 July The last Guided Missile Unit was disestablished after 29 years of service. GMU-41 was established on 11 May 1953, with a varied mission. It provided missile training and technical support to ships and squadrons, and supported units involved in test and evaluation of missiles and associated equipment in the fleet environment.

2 August The XV-15, Bell Helicopter's experimental vertical lift aircraft, piloted by Navy test pilot Lieutenant Commander John Ball and Bell's test pilot Dorman Cannon, conducted its first at-sea shipboard landings and takeoffs on *Tripoli*. A tilt-rotor aircraft, the XV-15 had a conventional fixed wing, with engines and rotors mounted on the wingtips, which were capable of swiveling to provide either vertical or horizontal flight.

5 August The Naval Air Test Center successfully completed tests on the first aircraft tire made entirely of guayule natural rubber. The Goodyear tire was mounted on the right main landing gear of an F-4J Phantom II and subjected to a series of maximum gross weight takeoffs and landings. Maximum weight for the test aircraft was 56,000 pounds.

8 August The Chief of Naval Operations established the first NAVPRO outside the U.S. in Melbourne, Australia. The new NAVPRO's duty would be to administer U.S. contracts with Australian companies that were involved in building the F/A-18 for the Royal Australian Air Force.

24 September Naval Air Systems Command awarded to McDonnell Douglas, teamed with British Aerospace and Sperry, a pre-full-scale development contract for the VTXTS. The VTXTS was designed around the British Aerospace Hawk with appropriate simulators, academics, a training management system, and support equipment.

30 September Acting as executive agent for a tri-service program, NAVAIR signed a $400,000 contract with the Gila River Indian Community of Sacaton, Ariz., to research, develop and establish a prototype domestic guayule rubber industry in the United States. If successful, this industry would reduce U.S. depen-

1982—Continued

dence on supplies of 100-percent imported natural rubber. Potential military applications for guayule rubber were aircraft tires, jet engine mounts, hydrophone arrays, truck tires, tank treads, submarine acoustic tiles and medical supplies.

1 October Master Chief Avionics Technician Billy C. Sanders assumed the duties of Master Chief Petty Officer of the Navy. He was the second person with an aviation background to hold the position since it was established on 1 March 1967. Master Chief Thomas S. Crow, who preceded Sanders, was the first.

1 October Helicopter Tactical Wing One was established at NAS Norfolk, Va. The new wing consisted of HC-6, HC-16, HM-12, HM-14 and HM-16. It was responsible for the administrative and operational activities of these helicopter squadrons with regard to training, material support and overall readiness. Captain John W. Osberg was its first commander.

7 October ARAPAHO at-sea testing was completed at the Norfolk International Terminal, Norfolk, Va., when the 18,000-ton container ship Export Leader—configured with a portable modular aviation facility—returned to port after having logged 178 day and 45 night helicopter landings. ARAPAHO was a research and development project to demonstrate the feasibility of equipping merchant ships with emergency aviation support in wartime and of operating ASW helicopters and other combatant aircraft from these vessels.

16 October *Saratoga* conducted her first sea trials since entering the shipyard as the first carrier to undergo SLEP. She was completing the final phase of the modernization and overhaul program.

28 October The 30th anniversary of the first flight of the A-3 Skywarrior, affectionately known as the Whale. The aircraft had been in the fleet since 1956 and had been used as a heavy bomber, radar trainer, electronics reconnaissance platform, tanker, tanker-electronics jammer, photoreconnaissance platform, dedicated electronics jammer, airborne weapons test bed and VIP transport.

11 November The first operational flight of the Space Shuttle *Columbia* was launched with astronauts Vance D. Brand, Robert F. Overmyer, William B. Lenoir and Joe P. Allen aboard. Astronauts Brand and Overmyer were former Navy and Marine Corps aviators, respectively. Lenoir and Allen were civilians. This was the first time four astronauts were aboard the shut-

tle for a flight. Previous test flights conducted by the Space Shuttle *Columbia* carried only two astronauts.

15 December *Naval Aviation News* celebrated its 65th year of publication. The Navy's oldest periodical in continuous print and one of the oldest aviation magazines in the country, the magazine originally began as a weekly bulletin published by the Chief of Naval Operations.

1983

7 January The first F/A-18 Hornets entered operational service (excluding operational training squadrons) with the Black Knights of VMFA-314, replacing the F-4 Phantom II. This transition marked the beginning of the replacement of F-4 and A-7 aircraft with the Hornet.

21 January HSL-41 was established with Commander Michael B. O'Connor Jr., as the Seahawks' first commanding officer. The squadron would be flying the new Sikorsky SH-60B Seahawk and, as the LAMPS MK III fleet readiness squadron, would train pilots, aircrew and maintenance personnel for SH-60B fleet squadrons.

11 March The first fleet CH-53E Super Stallion was delivered to the HM-12 Sea Dragons. The CH-53E could transport heavier loads over longer distances than previous helicopters used for logistics in the fleet.

The new heavy lift CH-53E Super Stallion in flight.

1983—Continued

Modifications included the addition of a third engine, a larger main rotor system and changes to the tail rotor. These changes would allow the CH-53E to carry three times the payload of its predecessor, the RH-53D.

21 March   Carrier aviation experienced another first when an all-female flight crew from VRC-30 Truckin' Traders conducted an operational mission in a C-1A Trader that terminated in a carrier arrested landing aboard *Ranger*. The aircraft was commanded by Lieutenant Elizabeth M. Toedt and the crew included Lieutenant (jg) Cheryl A. Martin, AD3 Gina Greterman and ADAN Robin Banks.

25 March   Fighter Attack Squadrons were redesignated Strike Fighter Squadrons. They would be flying the F/A-18 Hornet. The VFA designation used for the Fighter Attack Squadrons remained the same for the Strike Fighter Squadrons.

1 April   Naval Air Reserve Units (NARU) were redesignated Naval Air Reserve (NAR): NAR Alameda, Calif., NAR Jacksonville, Fla., NAR Memphis, Tenn., NAR Norfolk, Va., NAR Whidbey Island, Wash., NAR Point Mugu, Calif., and NAR North Island, Calif.

7 April   VF-201 and -202, Naval Reserve fighter squadrons, participated in National Week '83 exercises. This was the first time that tactical air reserve units conducted joint operations with the Sixth Fleet. The two squadrons with their F-4N Phantom IIs deployed from NAS Dallas, Tex., to NAS Sigonella, Sicily, via NAS Oceana, Va.; Gander, Newfoundland; Lajes, Azores; and Rota, Spain.

1 May   RVAW-110 and -120 were redesignated VAW-110 and -120. Responsible for training personnel in early warning services for future assignment to fleet units, the VAW-110 Greyhawks were based at Norfolk, Va., and the VAW-120 Firebirds at NAS Miramar, Calif.

2 May   Lieutenant Leslie E. Provow, a Naval Aviator assigned to VRC-40, the Codfish Airlines, became the first woman to be designated a Landing Signal Officer.

6 May   HC-4 was established, permanently based at NAS Sigonella, Sicily, and flying the CH-53E Super Stallion. Its mission was to provide vertical on-board delivery (VOD) for the Sixth Fleet.

23 May   The Navy's EX-50 Advanced Lightweight Torpedo made its first launch from a tactical aircraft, the S-3A Viking, at NATC Patuxent River, Md.

10 June   Lieutenant Colleen Nevius became the first woman Naval Aviator to graduate from the U.S. Naval Test Pilot School at Patuxent River, Md., and be designated a Navy Test Pilot.

Lieutenant Colleen Nevius.

23 June   The British-built airship, Skyship 500, arrived at NATC Patuxent River, Md., for test and evaluation. The Navy and Coast Guard were interested in the airship for possible maritime patrol, search and rescue and geo-survey missions.

1 July   A new alignment of NAVAIR headquarters was implemented. The position of Deputy Commander was established. It was headed by a civilian, Dr. Angelo J. DiMascio. The realignment was designed to provide a corporate management perspective enabling NAVAIR to operate more efficiently.

6 July   A Marine Corps CH-53E Super Stallion flew coast to coast in a 15-hour flight from Patuxent River, Md., to MCAS Tustin, Calif. It was refueled four times by a Marine Corps KC-130 Hercules.

23 July   The U.S. Navy's only World War I ace, David S. Ingalls, was enshrined in the National Aviation Hall of Fame in Dayton, Ohio. Mr. Ingalls was honored for his service in World War I, in World War II in the Naval Air Transport Service and in his postwar role in commercial aviation.

1983—Continued

1 August A Marine Corps OV-10A Bronco landed on *Nassau* flight deck. This was the first time a Bronco had ever landed on an LHA. The recovery opened up the possibility of a future role for the OV-10A in amphibious operations.

25 August The Navy Department accepted the production prototype of the P-3C Orion Update III. The aircraft was flown to NATC Patuxent River, Md., for test and evaluation by VX-1. It was expected to be twice as effective in submarine detection as the Update II because it would provide increased effectiveness in the acoustic processing system.

29 August The first flight of the AV-8B Harrier II production model was conducted at the McDonnell Douglas plant in St. Louis, Mo.

30 August Lieutenant Commander Dale A. Gardner was a crew member aboard the Space Shuttle *Challenger*, becoming the first Naval Flight Officer (NFO) in space.

1 September The MH-53E Super Stallion production prototype made its first flight. The MH version of the CH-53E heavy-lift helicopter was developed to meet the Navy's needs for airborne mine countermeasures missions. The MH versions would also augment the VOD requirements of the Navy.

20 September The first launch of the Navy's AGM-65F IR Maverick missile took place. It was launched from an A-7E Corsair II and made a direct hit on a destroyer target. The AGM-65F was the latest addition to the Maverick family of air-to-ground missiles and was designed to enhance the Navy's antiship capabilities.

26 September The first takeoffs of an F/A-18 Hornet from a ski-jump ramp were conducted at NAS Patuxent River, Md. The tests were part of an evaluation of conventional jet aircraft using an upward curved ramp to shorten takeoff roll.

28 September The Seahawks of HSL-41 received their first production SH-60B. HSL-41 was the Navy's first LAMPS MK III squadron.

1 October A reorganization of Commander, Naval Reserve Force (formerly Chief of Naval Reserve) included a change in which Commander, Naval Air Reserve Force reported to Commander, Naval Reserve Force instead of to the Chief of Naval Operations. The restructuring was designed to improve command and control of the Naval Reserve Force and enhance combat readiness.

1 October The new Naval Space Command was established, with former astronaut Captain Richard H. Truly as its first commander. The new command con-

An AV-8B Harrier II full-scale development model undergoing heavy load tests prior to the first flight of the production model.

1983—Continued

solidated the Navy's present space-related activities under one organization. Elements that were placed under the new command included the Naval Space Surveillance System, Naval Astronautics Group and activities supporting the Fleet Satellite Communications System.

3 October   Ensign Don E. Slone received his Wings of Gold as a Naval Flight Officer, becoming the first former enlisted man to complete the Enlisted Commissioning Program and the Aviation Officers Candidate School.

25 October   Combat amphibious assault operations on Grenada were supported by aircraft from CVW-6 aboard *Independence*. Surveillance operations were provided by patrol squadrons and support operations by several reserve VR units.

23 November   A modified CH-46 lifted off Boeing Vertol's flight ramp at Philadelphia, Pa., for its first flight. The modified CH-46 carried improvements that, when incorporated in all the H-46s, would extend the service life of the Navy/Marine Corps fleet of H-46 aircraft through the 1990s.

4 December   In a strike against Syrian positions in Lebanon by CVW-6 and CVW-3 aircraft, two aircraft (an A-7 Corsair II and an A-6 Intruder) were lost to antiaircraft fire. This was the first loss of Navy fixed-wing aircraft in combat since the end of the Vietnam conflict in January 1973.

27 December   The Secretary of the Navy announced the assignment of the name *Wasp* to LHD 1. The LHD 1 was the first of a new class of amphibious assault ships designed to accommodate new air-cushioned landing craft, as well as conventional landing craft, the AV-8 Harrier and all types of helicopters.

1984

4 January   Lieutenant Robert O. Goodman, an NFO from VA-85 deployed aboard *John F. Kennedy*, returned to the U.S. after being held as a POW for a month in Syria. His A-6E had been shot down on 4 December 1983, while participating in a retaliatory strike in Lebanon.

10 January   HC-1 received its first two CH-53E helicopters. Capable of lifting over 16 tons, the Super Stallion was the largest and most powerful helicopter in the western world. HC-1 was the only Navy West

Coast squadron to fly the CH-53E. The squadron would also continue to fly the SH-3G Sea Knight in its current role.

12 January   The first AV-8B Harrier was received at MCAS Cherry Point, N.C., by VMAT-203. With over 25 percent of the structural weight composed of carbon epoxy composite material, the AV-8B offered twice the payload and radius of the AV-8A.

3 February   Space Shuttle *Challenger* flew with a crew of Naval Aviators. The spacecraft commander, Vance D. Brand, was a Marine Corps aviator for five years. The two Navy members were Captain Bruce McCandless II and Commander Robert L. Gibson.

13 February   The last instructional flight of the T-28 Trojan was flown by Ensign Michael Lee Gierhart of VT-27, ending the aircraft's 31-year career of training Naval Aviators.

Lieutenant Robert O. Goodman at a press conference following his return from captivity in Syria.

1984—Continued

12 March   A Beech Aircraft AQM-37 variant target was flown to Mach 4.2 (2,775 mph) at 102,000 feet at the Navy's Pacific Missile Test Center, Point Mugu, Calif.

12 March   ComPatWingsPac, Commodore Daniel J. Wolkensdorfer presented the Air Force Commendation Medal to VP-40 for the squadron's participation in the search for survivors of Korean Air Lines flight 007, shot down by a Soviet SU-17 Flagon interceptor. VP-40, during the midst of its deployment to northern Japan, provided P-3 Orions which served as the primary search platform, while the USAF maintained operational control of the effort.

14 March   The last T-28 in the Training Command, BuNo 137796, departed for Naval District Washington to be displayed permanently at NS Anacostia, D.C.

20 March   Lieutenant Catherine H. Osman was the first female pilot to land a helicopter (HH-46A) aboard the battleship *Iowa* (BB 61).

26 April   The first EA-6B ICAP-2 Prowler, BuNo 161776, was delivered to the Navy. Fifteen EXCAP models already with the fleet would be upgraded.

28 April   The first MAU was established at NAS Brunswick, Maine. Similar in composition to a reserve VP squadron, the MAU's purpose was to train Naval Reserve personnel in the same type of aircraft being operated by active duty patrol squadrons so that the reserve flight crews could rapidly augment those squadrons in an emergency. Squadron augment units, predecessors of the MAUs, were scheduled to consolidate into the MAUs when they were established.

8 May   The first aviation supply wings were presented at the 73rd annual Aviation Ball by Vice Admiral Robert F. Schoultz, Deputy Chief of Naval Operations (Air Warfare), to: Vice Admiral Eugene A. Grinstead, Jr., SC, USN; Rear Admiral Andrew A. Giordano, SC, USN (Ret); and Commodore John H. Ruehlin, SC, USN, Commanding Officer, Aviation Supply Office, Philadelphia, Pa. Plans for the establishment of a Naval Aviation Supply Officer Program and the authorization of a breast insignia (wings) for qualifying Supply Corps officers had been in progress since 1982.

2 July   CVWR-20 concluded its first at-sea deployment since 1978 when it returned from a week aboard *Dwight D. Eisenhower*. This also marked the first time in four years that CVWR-20 operated as a complete air wing and the first deployment of the A-7E Corsair II with a reserve squadron, VA-203.

21 July   World War II Marine Corps ace Joseph J. Foss was among four individuals enshrined in the National Aviation Hall of Fame to recognize their outstanding contributions to aviation and their achievements in air and space technology.

This T-28B displayed at NS Anacostia marked the end of the era for the Trojan in the Training Command when it was transferred from VT-27.

1984—Continued

25 July Commodore Oakley E. Osborn, ComPatWingsPac, acccpted the first Navy P-3C Orion Update III from Lockheed during a ceremony held at NAS Moffett Field, Calif. VP-31 would train personnel in the operation of the updated P-3 beginning with VP-40, the first fleet operational squadron scheduled to receive the aircraft.

17 August HM-14, after receiving a Joint Chiefs of Staff notice of tasking for rapid deployment to the Gulf of Suez, commenced mine-hunting operations that continued for 22 consecutive days in the troubled area. Earlier, on 6 August, HM-14 had embarked aboard *Shreveport* (LPD 12) with four RH-53Ds which were later augmented by others from the squadron's detachment, as well as an RH-53D from HM-12.

13 September The newly configured S-3B Viking made its first flight at Lockheed facilities in Palmdale, Calif. The latest version of the Viking featured improved avionics and weapons systems, including the Harpoon missile.

22 September HM-14 conducted flight operations to support logistics, medevacs and embassy personnel evacuation after a terrorist bombing of the U.S. Embassy Annex in Beirut, Lebanon.

26 September The XV-15 tilt-rotor aircraft demonstrator completed two weeks of concept tests at NATC Patuxent River, Md.

2 October The U.S. Navy signed a contract to initiate full-scale development of the T-45TS Jet flight training system by McDonnell Douglas. The system's aircraft, the T-45, would replace the T-2Cs and TA-4Js used by the Chief of Naval Air Training in the intermediate and advanced phases of jet flight training.

12 October VF-301's acceptance of its first F-14 Tomcat marked the introduction of the F-14 into the Naval Air Reserve Force as part of the Navy's total force defense concept.

28 November Deliveries of the F/A-18 Hornet were resumed four months after the McDonnell Douglas Corporation announced it would bear costs of modifications to correct a fatigue-related problem in the tail area of the aircraft.

30 November *Nimitz*, with CVW-8 embarked, sortied in response to national tasking. After the Cuban government denied the U.S. Coast Guard permission to tow a U.S. vessel which had lost power and drifted into Cuban waters, a brief show of force by *Nimitz* difused the incident. The carrier later resumed a scheduled four-day port visit to St. Thomas, V.I.

8 December VA-105 Gunslingers returned from a six-month deployment to MCAS Iwakuni, Japan, in the Western Pacific. The squadron's assignment to MAG-12, 1st MAW marked the first time a Navy squadron participated in the Marine Corps Unit Deployment Program and the first time a Navy squadron came under the operational control of the Marine Corps since World War II.

28 December VXE-6 rescued the aircrew and passengers of a downed LC-130 Hercules near McMurdo Station in the Antarctic. The successful rescue was made by another LC-130 in unexplored terrain under extreme environmental conditions within 16 hours of the incident.

31 December The first T-47A for Naval Flight Officer navigation training was delivered to the Naval Air Training Command by Cessna Aircraft Corporation under a five-year agreement with the Navy, which encompassed a total training concept. Cessna would provide maintenance and support of the T-47A aircraft, which would replace T-39Ds used in flight officer training.

1985

7 January The Navy selected the F-16N for its aggressor aircraft program. The purchase of 14 of the new aircraft from General Dynamics included supporting material and services. These aircraft would simulate Soviet tactical aircraft during the Navy's air-to-air combat training for fighter pilots.

24 January VA-83 became the first fleet operational squadron to fire successfully an AGM-88 HARM. The missile was launched from an A-7E Corsair II piloted by Lieutenant Commander John Parker who was assigned to a HARM detachment deployed to Naval Weapons Center, China Lake, Calif.

30 January The AV-8B Harrier II became the U.S. Marine Corps' newest tactical aircraft when it began operational service with combat squadron VMA-331 at MCAS Cherry Point, N.C. The new AV-8B was designed to provide close air support for Marine ground troops.

17 February *Independence*, the third carrier to undergo SLEP, arrived at the Philadelphia Naval Shipyard, Pa., for a modernization and overhaul

The F-16N used by the Navy's adversary squadrons.

The new AV-8B Harrier II shows its versatility.

designed to extend her service life by 15 years. Indy's flight deck systems would be improved to allow the recovery of high-performance aircraft while the ship traveled at lower speeds. Major changes also included the overhaul of two NATO Seasparrow missile launchers with two others to be installed along with three Phalanx CIWS. Other improvements would result in significant savings in fuel consumption for *Independence.*

21 February   The F/A-18 Hornet strike fighter and the LAMPS, which used the SH-60B Seahawk ASW helicopter, deployed overseas for the first time. Both systems operated as part of Battle Group Delta headed by *Constellation* in a routine deployment with the Seventh Fleet to the Western Pacific and Indian Ocean. The Hornets replaced the A-7E Corsair IIs operated by two squadrons assigned to CVW-14, making *Constellation* the Navy's first carrier to have F/A-18s assigned to her air wing. The SH-60B Seahawk helicopter operated as the air subsystem of the LAMPS MK III weapon system, deployed aboard *Crommelin* (FFG 37).

1 March   The Undergraduate Naval Flight Officer Training System Upgrade was introduced at NAS Pensacola, Fla., when the first class of prospective NFOs began training on the Cessna T-47A Citation. As part of the new training system upgrade, T-47As replaced the T-39D Saberliners that had been used to train NFOs since 1965.

6 March   The Naval Air Systems Command and United Technologies' Sikorsky Aircraft signed a contract for full-scale development and production options for a carrier-borne version of the SH-60B Seahawk. Designated SH-60F, the variant would be used to protect the inner perimeter of carrier battle groups from enemy submarines.

29 March   The Navy awarded a contract to the McDonnell Douglas Corporation for development of night attack capabilities for the F/A-18 Hornet aircraft. About 750 F/A-18s would be outfitted with a navigational forward-looking infrared pod, a television-like heads up display, night vision goggles for the pilot, and other improvements.

1985—Continued

1 April   VP-68 completed its move from NAS Patuxent River, Md., to NAF Washington, D.C., located at Andrews AFB. Relocation of the reserve antisubmarine warfare squadron, which operated the P-3B Orion, was to make room for the JVX test program at NAS Patuxent River, but also helped balance base loading at NAF Washington. The V-22 Osprey, formerly the JVX, a multiservice, tilt-rotor V/STOL aircraft, was scheduled for testing at the Naval Air Test Center starting in 1988.

12 April   VAQ-133 returned the last fleet EA-6B EXCAP aircraft, BuNo 159585, to Grumman Aircraft Corporation for ICAP II modification at the company's facilities on Long Island, N.Y. VAQ-133 began its transition to the ICAP II EA-6B in January 1985.

26 April   David Sinton Ingalls, Naval Aviator No. 85 and the Navy's only World War I flying ace, died at his home in Chagrin Falls, Ohio, after a stroke. Ingalls was a member of the First Yale Unit before he was ordered to the Royal Flying Corps and later assigned to Royal Air Force Squadron Number 213, located in Berguess, France. He shot down four enemy planes and one aerial balloon during the war and later served as Assistant Secretary of the Navy for Aeronautics during the Hoover administration.

30 May   The keel was laid for *Wasp* during ceremonies at Ingalls Shipbuilding in Pascagoula, Miss. First of a new class of amphibious ships, the LHD was designed to accommodate helicopters such as the CH-53E Super Stallion and SH-60B Seahawk, as well as the MV-22 Osprey tilt-rotor aircraft and the AV-8B Harrier II.

14 June   *Nimitz* was called to the coast of Lebanon for contingency operations in support of United States efforts to release American hostages held in Beirut.

19 June   The Navy announced the selection of the Goshawk as the popular name for the T-45A trainer, which was a part of the T-45 training system (formerly VTXTS) scheduled to replace the T-2C and TA-4J aircraft operated by the Training Command. The name Goshawk was previously applied by Curtiss to the F11C-2 fighters which were manufactured for the Navy in 1933.

After a launch from an F/A-18 Hornet, the AMRAAM streaks toward its target during testing at Pacific Missile Test Center, Point Mugu, Calif.

1985—Continued

19 June The first new C-2A with more powerful engines was delivered to NATC Patuxent River, Md., for three months of flight testing. Engines with more horsepower than those of fleet C-2As were installed in the aircraft, and the tests evaluated the effect of the updated engines on aircraft performance and flying qualities.

8 July VAW-120, traditionally an E-2C training squadron, received its first upgraded C-2A Greyhounds for training replacement personnel. Initial operational capability of the aircraft was achieved on time following the delivery of five aircraft in October to VR-24, NAS Sigonella, Italy.

15–17 July The maintainability phase of the AMRAAM was demonstrated successfully at the Pacific Missile Test Center, Point Mugu, Calif. The missile was being tested and evaluated for both the Navy and Air Force by the Air Force Systems Command, Joint Systems Program Office, Eglin AFB, Fla. The demonstration, repeated several times a day for three days, proved it possible to load four AMRAAMs onto the wings of an F/A-18 Hornet in less than 15 minutes. Loading time was critical to the Navy in combat situations both ashore and on board aircraft carriers. Unloading procedures, which were not to exceed four minutes, were performed in an average of two minutes.

29 August The Secretary of the Navy announced the decision to home port *Nimitz*'s carrier battle group at Everett, Wash., in the Puget Sound region, scheduled as the home port for up to 15 ships.

2 September Reserve squadron HSL-84 completed its deployment of two detachments aboard reserve frigates which marked the first time in Naval Reserve history that a reserve LAMPS detachment was embarked aboard a ship for an extended period of time. While at sea for two weeks beginning 16 August, Det 1 assigned to *Grey* (FF 1054) and Det 2 assigned to *Lang* (FF 1060) operated as part of a five-ship all-Reserve squadron.

10 October Four of seven Navy F-14s of VF-74 and -103 launched from *Saratoga* intercepted an Egyptian 737 airliner in international waters and directed it to Sigonella, Sicily. The airliner was carrying four Arab terrorists who had earlier hijacked the Italian cruise ship *Achille Lauro* on 7 October and murdered a U.S. citizen. During the operation, the F-14s were refueled by Navy KA-6D tankers. Other aircraft which assisted in the intercept were Navy E-2C Hawkeyes of VAW-125, EA-6B Prowlers and an Air Force C-135.

13 October *Coral Sea* returned to the Mediterranean Sea for her first Sixth Fleet deployment since 1957. Commanded by Captain Robert H. Ferguson, with CVW-13 embarked, it was also the first deployment of the F/A-18 to the Mediterranean. The aircraft were assigned to VFA-131 and -132.

15 October A Tomahawk antiship missile was launched from *Norton Sound* at the Pacific Missile Test Center's Sea Test Range off the coast of California. The test successfully demonstrated the missile's vertical launch system as well as its ability to search for, find and strike a target at sea. The Tomahawk was capable of carrying either a nuclear or conventional warhead.

19 October VFA-303, the first Naval Reserve squadron to transition the F/A-18, received its first aircraft during ceremonies at NAS Lemoore, Calif. Delivery of the eight aircraft ended two years of preparation at NAS Alameda, Calif., where the squadron was home ported until its move to Lemoore in 1983 for training in the Hornets. Later, on 31 October, Lieutenant Bram B. Arnold of VFA-303 landed aboard *Ranger*, becoming the first Reserve pilot to land an F/A-18 aboard an aircraft carrier.

28 October The first prototype model of the S-3B Viking, an operational capability upgrade to the S-3A, arrived at NATC Patuxent River, Md., for developmental test and evaluation. The "B" configuration, extensively updated with state-of-the-art avionics and the Harpoon missile control and launch system, was developed to counter the threat of the new generation of sophisticated Soviet submarines and to enhance the aircraft's multimission capability.

The new S-3B Viking during tests at Naval Air Test Center, Patuxent River, Md.

1985—Continued

31 October   Cuts in deployment schedules were ordered by CNO to eliminate excessive at-sea periods for ships and aircraft squadrons. This was intended to enhance efficient use of the expanded Navy; and, at the same time, allow crews more time at home with their families. During an interview, the CNO announced major turnaround ratios of 2:1 or better, assuring sailors that battle groups would spend a maximum of six months at sea.

9–17 November   A detachment from VP-66 participated in Operation Hat Trick II operating out of NS Roosevelt Roads, P.R. It was a coordinated operation with the Coast Guard in the war against illegal drug traffic. The operation involved general area surveillance and location of suspect vessels.

13 December   VC-10 was tasked to fly cover for a U.S. warship exercising rights of navigation in international waters off the southern coast of Cuba. VC-10's regular mission was to provide air service for U.S. Atlantic Fleet ships and aircraft and air defense of Guantanamo Bay, Cuba.

1986

8 January   With its change of command, CVW-8 became the first air wing to incorporate the wing commander/deputy commander concept (Super CAG), which provided an improved focus on power projection and enhanced tactical development and strike planning. Under this system, the wing commander, O-6, was directly responsible to the assigned battle group commander, both ashore and afloat, and additionally to the carrier commanding officer when embarked. Captain Frederick L. Lewis relieved Captain Daniel L. Rainey, Jr., as Commander, CVW-8, in a ceremony at NAS Oceana, Va. As part of the restructuring, Carrier Air Wing 8 (CVW-8) was redesignated as a "major sea command," reporting to Commander, Carrier Group 8 and additionally to commanding officer, *Nimitz* when embarked.

13 January   The T-39 Sabreliner completed its final flight for the U.S. Navy as a training aircraft when VT-86, based at NAS Pensacola, Fla., retired its last T-39D. BuNo 150983 was included among six of the eight remaining Sabreliners which were sent to Davis Monthan AFB, Ariz. Two others were scheduled for use as VIP transports at other Navy and Marine Corps air stations. The T-39 aircraft had completed 20 years and 300,000 hours of service within the Naval Flight Officer program.

15 January   The Royal Maces of VA-27 officially became the first recipients of the Grampaw Pettibone Trophy during a ceremony at the Officer's Club on the Washington Navy Yard, D.C. Commander Joseph P. Sciabarra, CO of the NAS Lemoore, Calif.-based squadron, accepted the award from Secretary of the Navy John F. Lehman. The trophy was commissioned by Paul Warner, son of the originator of Grampaw Pettibone, and would be awarded annually to the individual or organization that contributed the most toward aviation safety awareness through written communications.

22 January   Vice President George H. W. Bush was the key participant at the official inaugural marking the year-long observance of the 75th Anniversary of Naval Aviation at the National Air and Space Museum, Washington, D.C. Secretary of Defense Caspar Weinberger and Secretary of the Navy John F. Lehman also attended.

28 January   Naval Aviator and astronaut Commander Michael John Smith and six other astronauts were killed in a massive explosion of the space shuttle *Challenger* shortly after its launch from Kennedy Space Center, Fla. The explosion was triggered by escaping propellant combustion products, which cut into the shuttle's liquid-fuel booster. Commander Smith was a graduate of the U.S. Naval Academy and the only Navy member of the space shuttle crew.

20 February   Rear Admiral Richard H. Truly was appointed the Associate Administrator of Space Flight within the National Aeronautics and Space Administration. Truly was designated a Naval Aviator in October 1960 and had served as Commander, Naval Space Command since its establishment in 1983.

18 March   The second F-21 Kfir squadron, and the first assigned to the Marine Corps, was established as VMFT-401 at MCAS Yuma, Ariz. Appropriately nicknamed Snipers, the squadron provided adversary training support to the Fleet Marine Force and other units. VF-43, at NAS Oceana, Va., was the first Navy squadron to receive the F-21s (Israeli-built fighter).

24–25 March   Libyan Operations—VP-56 provided ASW patrol assets for "Freedom of Navigation" exercises in the Gulf of Sidra for American carrier aircraft operating in international waters. On 24 March Libyan armed forces fired missiles at U.S. Navy forces operating in the Gulf of Sidra. Following the Libyan missile firings, VAQ-137 co-authored a plan to destroy the Libyan SA-5 missile radar site at Surt. The plan was executed using the electronic capabilities of the

1986—Continued

An Israel F-21A Kfir used by the Navy and Marine Corps for adversary training.

Rockeye cluster bombs used against Libyan corvettes are transported across Coral Sea's flight deck by aviation ordnancemen.

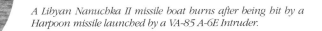

A Libyan Nanuchka II missile boat burns after being hit by a Harpoon missile launched by a VA-85 A-6E Intruder.

The end of an era arrives with the departure of VF-151's F-4S Phantom IIs from Midway and a transpacific flight to NAS North Island, Calif. VF-151 and VF-161 were the last fleet squadrons deployed with the F-4.

1986—Continued

deployed VAQ squadrons and the HARM missile capability of the VA squadrons. VA-81, with its A-7E Corsair IIs, participated in the retaliatory strike against the Surt SA-5 missile site by acting as the decoy group for VA-83s A-7Es, which fired their HARMs against the site, putting it out of action. On the same day, A-6A Intruders from VA-34 attacked and damaged a Libyan Combattante II G-class fast attack missile craft with a Harpoon missile. This was the first operational use of a Harpoon in combat. A follow-up attack by VA-85 aircraft using Rockeye bombs resulted in the sinking of the Combattante. More action followed—Intruders of VA-85 attacked a Libyan Nanuchka II-class missile corvette and dropped Rockeye cluster bombs on the corvette. The damaged Nanuchka II was forced to return to the port of Benghazi. On 25 March a second Nanuchka II-class missile corvette was attacked by a couple of VA-55 Intruders. However, their Rockeyes missed the corvette. This attack was followed up by Intruders from VA-85, firing a Harpoon which destroyed the vessel.

25 March   The final carrier launching of a Navy fleet F-4S Phantom II was completed by pilot Lieutenant Alan S. Colegrove and radar intercept officer Lieutenant Greg Blankenship of VF-151. The aircraft was launched from *Midway* during flight operations in the East China Sea. The F-4 was scheduled for replacement by the F/A-18 Hornet.

28 March   VFA-106, the Atlantic Fleet F/A-18 readiness squadron, graduated its first class of replacement pilots. Nine of the 10 graduates were aviators assigned to the VFA-137 Kestrals, which were established in 1985.

29 March   Lieutenant Commander Donnie L. Cochran, the first African American member of the U.S. Navy's precision flight demonstration squadron, the Blue Angels, completed his initial performance during the team's air show held at Luke AFB, Ariz. Lieutenant Commander Cochran was selected in September 1985 for the number three position on the flight team based at Pensacola, Fla.

14–15 April   Operation El Dorado Canyon—F/A-18 Hornets from CVW-13 aboard *Coral Sea* and A-7E Corsair IIs from *America* conducted air-to-surface Shrike and HARM missile strikes against Libyan surface-to-air missile sites at Benghazi and Tripoli, minutes before attacks by the Navy's A-6Es from the two carriers and the Air Force's F-111s. Intruders from VA-55 and -34 conducted a low-level bombing raid on ter-

A VA-55 A-6E Intruder lands on Coral Sea. Intruders from VAs 55 and 34 struck terrorist targets in Benghazi, Libya.

rorist targets in Benghazi, Libya. Aircraft from VA-55 hit the Benina airfield and VA-34 struck the Benghazi military compound. Navy E-2C Hawkeyes and EA-6B Prowlers, along with Marine Corps Prowlers, provided electronic countermeasures and command control capabilities for aircraft involved in the strikes against Libya. CVW-1's F-14A Tomcats and CVW-13's F/A-18 Hornets provided fighter support for the operations.

28 April   *Enterprise* transited the Suez Canal, becoming the first nuclear-powered carrier to do so, as it steamed toward the Mediterranean to relieve *Coral Sea*. The transit began at 0300 and took approximately 12 hours to complete.

2 May   The feasibility of blimps for active duty was determined by a Navy board and later recommended to the Secretary of the Navy for funding. Studies concerning the usefulness of Navy airships were completed earlier in 1985.

2 May   The Navy initiated a contract for the V-22 tiltrotor aircraft with the team of Bell Helicopter Textron, Fort Worth, Tex., and Boeing-Vertol Company, Philadelphia, Pa., as codevelopers of the joint-services aircraft.

5 May   The Secretary of the Navy designated 1986 as the Diamond Anniversary of Naval Aviation, during which significant historical Naval Aviation achievements would be recognized in events throughout the year.

1986—Continued

5 May A reenactment flight of the original NC-4's transatlantic crossing took place as one of the 75th Anniversary commemorative events. The flight was made with two privately owned PBY Catalina flying boats, one painted with the original NC-4 colors, as a reenactment of the original NC-4's trans-Atlantic crossing that began on 8 May 1919. The flight originated from NAS Pensacola, Fla., and commenced the original route from NAS Rockaway Beach, N.Y., and ended in Lisbon, Portugal. The flight was one of the events commemorating the 75th Anniversary of Naval Aviation.

One of the PBY Catalinas that participated in the NC-4 reenactment flight.

13 May The first Shrike launch by a Navy EA-6A was completed by VAQ-209 when Lieutenant Commanders E. L. Brandt and M. J. Corcoran conducted a live firing of an AGM-45 Shrike missile at Naval Weapons Center, China Lake, Calif. The launch occurred during the reserve squadron's annual two weeks of active duty for training.

27 May The helicopter landing trainer IX-514 was approved for use by student Naval Aviators after testing was conducted using UH-1N, SH-3H, SH-60B, and TH-57 aircraft. The training craft provided a platform to shipboard-qualify student helicopter pilots before they joined the fleet.

1 June MAWSPac, previously composed of personnel from VA-128, was officially designated as a separate shore command. During an establishment ceremony on 16 June at NAS Whidbey Island, Wash., Commander Richard P. Dodd was designated as the first commanding officer of the combat readiness training school, which was under the operational and administrative control of Commander, Medium Attack Tactical Electronic Warfare Wing, U.S. Pacific Fleet.

6 June The first Naval Aviation Cadet in 17 years began active duty when Captain Bobby C. Farrar, deputy commander of the Navy Recruiting Command, swore in his son, Sean. The program, which allows personnel to enter aviation officer candidate school and eventually flight training without a college degree, had been suspended in 1969.

28 June As a tribute to the 75th Anniversary of Naval Aviation and Glenn H. Curtiss, a week of festivities began at Hammondsport, N.Y. Events included a reenactment of the Navy's first flight of the A-1 and a permanently mounted scale model of the aircraft, which was unveiled at dedication ceremonies on the shore of Keuka Lake on 29 June.

1 July The Helistat, a flight demonstrator lighter-than-air craft under development by Piasecki Aircraft Company for use by the Forestry Service, crashed at NAEC Lakehurst, N.J., during flight tests. The Helistat was powered by the engines and rotor systems of four SH-34J Seabat helicopters attached to a ZPG-2 airship envelope.

1 July A formal airship development program was approved for the U.S. Navy by Secretary of the Navy

The IX 514, a new training deck for student helicopter pilots.

1986—Continued

John F. Lehman. The naval airship program was initiated in 1985 to provide an airborne early warning capability for a non-carrier battle group with secondary missions of air antisubmarine warfare and search and rescue.

5 August VAQ-131 performed the first fleet launch of a AGM-88A HARM missile from a fleet EA-6B at Naval Weapons Center, China Lake, Calif. The missile was fired from a Prowler flown by Lieutenant Robert Smith, pilot; Lieutenant Commander Kenneth P. Parks, ECMO 1; Lieutenant Michael J. Quinlan, ECMO 2; and commanding officer Commander William F. Headridge, ECMO 3.

18 August An AMRAAM launched at Pacific Missile Test Center, Point Mugu, Calif., from a modified F/A-18 Hornet intercepted its target flying at low altitude in a high clutter environment when it shot down a QF-86 drone. The F/A-18 was flying 890 feet above sea level over the Pacific at Mach .49 and the drone was flying at Mach .68 at 625 feet above the water.

19 August *Carl Vinson*, with CVW-15 aboard, performed fleet operations in the Bering Sea, making it the first carrier since World War II to perform such operations in that part of the world. The carrier returned to NAS Alameda, Calif., on 5 February 1987.

19 August Tests of the CAI Mod 2, an optical landing system for the AV-8B on LHA-class ships, were initiated aboard *Belleau Wood* (LHA 3) for day/night operations. The tests were conducted through 29 August and again from 6-23 October.

1 September The Coral Sea concept, approved by the Secretary of the Navy to provide *Coral Sea* and *Midway* with two squadrons of eight A-6Es each, was initiated with VA-65's assignment to CVW-13 aboard *Coral Sea*. VA-65 was previously assigned to CVW-7.

10 September When *America* returned from its Mediterranean deployment, it marked the first battle group to spend no more than six months overseas as part of the Navy's efforts to reduce deployments. Having deployed to the Sixth Fleet on 10 March 1986, the carrier was relieved by *John F. Kennedy* with Carrier Air Wing 3 (CVW-3).

29 September The Navy's F-14A Plus Super Tomcat completed its maiden flight as it hit Mach 1.1 at 25,000 feet and a maximum altitude of 35,000 feet during engine compatibility and flutter tests performed by

Grumman test pilot Joe Burke. The aircraft was powered by new F110-GE-400 turbofan engines with approximately 35 percent more thrust than current F-14A TF30s.

1 October VRF-31, the Navy's last aircraft ferry squadron, was disestablished at NAS Norfolk, Va. The squadron was established originally as VRF-1 and received its current designation in 1957. It became the Navy's only ferry squadron when VRF-32, on the West Coast, was disestablished in 1972.

17–18 September VFP-206, the Navy's last photoreconnaissance squadron, performed the last catapult and carrier landing of the F-8 aboard *America* when Lieutenant Commander Barry D. Gabler made the final landing.

20 September Naval Aviation personnel were authorized by ALNAV message 202001Z Oct to wear brown shoes and khaki socks with summer khaki uniforms to become effective on 1 April 1987. All officers with aviation designators, qualified flight surgeons, aviation physiologists and enlisted personnel in pay grades E-7 and above were included in the new regulation, which specified a low-quarter, brown leather dress shoe with plain toe. The brown shoes had been removed as part of the uniform on 1 July 1976 after being part of the Naval Aviator's uniform since 1913.

3 November VR-57 flew a C-9B aircraft into the port city of Quingdao in the Peoples Republic of China, becoming the first naval aircraft to do so since the port was closed to the U.S. in 1949. The flight preceded by two days the visit of three naval ships to the port. VR-57, a reserve squadron based at NAS North Island, Calif., was commanded by Commander A. W. Boyce.

31 December VC-8 launched three H-3 helicopters on short notice to support rescue efforts at the Dupont Plaza Hotel fire in San Juan, Puerto Rico. Called the worst hotel disaster in U.S. history, 75 persons stranded on the roof of the hotel were rescued in twilight and darkness by the Redtails.

1987

5 January The first extended deployment for the AV-8B Harrier II began when VMA-331 deployed aboard *Belleau Wood* for a six-month western Pacific cruise.

6 January Reserve CVW-77 and -78 loaned E-2C Hawkeyes to the U.S. Customs Service and the Coast Guard to bolster their federal drug enforcement efforts.

1987—Continued

12 January   The airfield at MCAS Camp Pendleton, Calif., was designated Munn Field in honor of Lieutenant General John C. Munn. The general had been Assistant Commandant of the Marine Corps and the first Marine Aviator ever to command Camp Pendleton.

19 February   The Navy's E-6A Hermes prototype flew for the first time. Flight testing of the new aircraft began on 1 June. The E-6A was a militarized version of Boeing's 707-320B and was scheduled to replace the EC-130 TACAMO aircraft. These aircraft provided an airborne communications link between the Navy's ballistic missile submarine force and national command authorities.

18 March   VF-301 took part in an AIM-54A Phoenix missile launch at the Pacific Missile Test Range, Point Mugu, Calif. This was the first use of a Phoenix by a Naval Air Reserve squadron.

19 March   The SH-60F CV-Helo conducted its first flight. It was ordered by the Navy in early 1985 as the replacement for the SH-3H Sea King ASW helicopter utilized for the inner-zone defense of carrier battle groups.

29 March   VFP-206, the Navy's last light photographic squadron, was disestablished at NAF Washington, D.C. This was also the end of the F-8 Crusader era in Naval Aviation. Some VFP-206 RF-8Gs were sent to the storage facility at Davis-Monthan AFB, Ariz., while one was transferred to the National Air and Space Museum. The last two Navy

The E-6A at Boeing Field in Seattle, Wash., during its flight test program.

1987—Continued

RF-8Gs were assigned to the Naval Air Systems Command for test support purposes. The F-14A TARPS aircraft would take on the reserve requirements for photoreconnaissance.

30 March   The Navy conducted the first flight of its new BQM-126A target drone at Pacific Missile Test Center, Point Mugu, Calif. It was designed as a lower cost, state-of-the-art replacement for targets currently used. It was capable of flying from sea level up to 40,000 feet.

31 March   As part of a reorganization approved by the Under Secretary of the Navy, NARFs were redesignated Naval Aviation Depots (NADEP); the Naval Aviation Logistics Center became the Naval Aviation Depot Operations Center; and the Aircraft Intermediate Maintenance Support Office assumed the new title Naval Aviation Maintenance Office. This reorganization centralized support for fleet aviation maintenance.

1 April   HM-12 was the first fleet squadron to receive the MH-53E Sea Stallion. This new airborne mine counter-measures helicopter provided a greater tow tension capability, longer on-station time and a new digital automatic flight control system.

6 April   The first of 26 F-16N Fighting Falcon supersonic aggressor aircraft was received by the Navy.

25 April   The Blue Angels, the Navy's Flight Demonstration Squadron, conducted its first air show using their newly assigned aircraft, F/A-18 Hornets.

18 May   Oscar 13, a Navy satellite designed to function as part of the Navy's Transit Satellite Navigation System, celebrated its 20th year of service. It was then the oldest active U.S. satellite.

22 May   Marine Corps Aviation celebrated its 75th anniversary. On 22 May 1912, 1st Lieutenant Alfred A.

Cunningham, USMC, reported to the Naval Aviation Camp at Annapolis, Md., for duty in connection with aviation. Marine Corps Aviation has been an active and important part of Naval Aviation ever since.

5 June   The Navy Department awarded a contract to Westinghouse-Airship Industries to build a prototype airship for fleet operations as an airborne early warning and communications platform. The Navy terminated its lighter-than-air program in 1961 and ceased operation of its last airship in 1962.

22 June   The Navy's newest transport aircraft, the C-20D Gulfstream IV, was received by Fleet Logistics Support Wing Detachment, NAF Washington, D.C.

The C-20D Gulfstream

26 June   The night-attack version of the AV-8B Harrier II conducted its maiden flight at McDonnell-Douglas' St. Louis, Mo., facility. This was followed by operational test and evaluation of the aircraft later in the summer. The upgrade to this aircraft would greatly expand the operational envelope by utilizing state-of-the-art navigation equipment and night-vision devices.

30 June   The Navy received its first SH-60F Seahawk (Carrier Inner Zone Helicopter). Operational test and evaluation of the aircraft began in December. The SH-60F would replace the SH-3H Sea King used by HS squadrons.

30 June   VX-5 conducted the first successful firing of a HARM from an A-6E Intruder. This was the first in a series of missile launches planned to test the SWIP

1987—Continued

configuration for the A-6E. The new configuration would also allow the Intruder to be armed with Harpoon and Maverick missiles. These weapons systems would provide increased availability of standoff weapons for Navy carrier air wings.

6 July SH-60B and SH-2F helicopters, modified for Special Middle East Force duties, were deployed. The modifications included special mission defensive equipment, such as the M-60 machine gun and special countermeasure and infrared electronic devices.

10 July The Navy awarded a contract to Boeing to upgrade a P-3 to the Update IV version, which would include an updated avionics suite to address the problem of the newer, quieter submarines.

14 July VAQ-131 began the first Pacific Fleet deployment of the EA-6B with HARM aboard *Ranger*.

15 July Commander Naval Air Force, U.S. Pacific Fleet initiated extensive modifications to LAMPS MK I and MK III aircraft to increase survivability and surface surveillance capability during Persian Gulf operations.

25 July Naval Aviator Admiral Thomas H. Moorer was enshrined in the National Aviation Hall of Fame in Dayton, Ohio.

27 July HM-14 was called upon for a rapid response deployment to the Persian Gulf and departed 72 hours later with its RH-53Ds to counter mines being laid by Iranian forces. HM-14 assets were flown by USAF C-5 and C-141 aircraft to Diego Garcia where its helicopters were reassembled and placed aboard *Guadalcanal*. The squadron conducted sweeping and hunting operations in the Persian Gulf until relieved by surface mine-sweeping units.

1 August Distribution began to Pacific Fleet aviation units for laser eye protection devices to counter the emerging laser threat.

1 August Commander, Naval Air Force, U.S. Atlantic Fleet began support of an average of five to seven LAMPS helicopter detachments operating on convoy duty in the Persian Gulf.

10 August The first of four new P-3 Weapons Systems Trainers (2F140) was received by the Navy at NAS Moffett Field, Calif. The trainers provided state-of-the-art capabilities for training personnel in ASW.

21 August COMNAVAIRPAC Vice Admiral James E. Service retired and relinquished his Gray Eagle title to Lieutenant General Frank E. Petersen, Commanding General, Marine Corps Development and Education Command, Quantico, Va. General Petersen was designated a Naval Aviator in October 1952, becoming the first African American aviator in the Marine Corps. He was the first African American to receive the Gray Eagle award.

10 September VC-6 Det 1 deployed aboard *Iowa* (BB 61) with the Pioneer RPV for a NATO and Indian Ocean cruise. This marked the beginning of battleship-operated RPVs providing independent reconnaissance and naval gunfire support capabilities.

The Navy's Pioneer RPV (Remotely Piloted Vehicle).

19 September *Wasp* was christened. She was the first of a new class of amphibious assault ships (LHD). Her primary mission was to deploy and land elements of a Marine air and ground task force during an assault by employing helicopters, landing craft and amphibious vehicles. The ship would operate the AV-8B Harrier II, as well as various types of helicopters, and the new air cushion landing craft (LCAC).

21 September The Navy received the first updated version of the F/A-18 Hornet, the F/A-18C. Upgrades included the advanced medium-range air-to-air missile, and the infrared imaging Maverick missile. This version provided for reliability, survivability and maintainability of the fuel system and additional growth capabilities in the areas of computer memory, speed and interface channels for the mission computer.

29 September *Coral Sea* departed for a Mediterranean cruise operating under a new concept called the "Coral Sea configuration." To help streamline aircraft maintenance, the two attack squadrons on board used a shared maintenance concept.

1987—Continued

30 September   The deployment of the first AV-8B Harrier II to the Mediterranean Sea began as *Nassau* left her home port of Norfolk Va., en route to the Mediterranean. The AV-8Bs on board were assigned to VMA-231.

8 October   HML(A)-169 became the first Marine Corps squadron to deploy operationally with the new AH-1W Super Cobra. The unit deployed to the Persian Gulf aboard *Okinawa* (LPH 3). The AH-1W was capable of simultaneously employing the Hellfire, TOW and Sidewinder missiles. It also had a new heads-up display and bigger engines to give the ground support gunship greatly increased mission capabilities.

30 October   The Navy established the designation C-28A, which would be assigned to a Cessna 404 (Titian Ambassador) 8- to 10-passenger, twin-engine plane. The aircraft would be used to transport personnel and cargo.

16 November   The Navy accepted the first production F-14A (Plus) Tomcat. The aircraft was part of a two-step program leading to the F-14D, an advanced air superiority aircraft. Improvements in the F-14A (Plus) included two new, more powerful engines and better reliability, operability, maintainability and fuel consumption.

5 December   VP-62 became the first Reserve patrol squadron to transition to the Navy's most current maritime patrol plane, the P-3C Orion Update III. The Update III featured state-of-the-art computer integration equipment, an improved infrared detection system, a Harpoon air-to-surface missile capability and the ability to carry a variety of other weapons.

7 December   The Naval Test Pilot School at NAS Patuxent River, Md., received the first of three HH-65 Dolphin helicopters on loan from the Coast Guard.

10 December   The X-31A designation was established and was applied to the enhanced fighter maneuverability (EFM) technology demonstrator aircraft which was never intended for production. The EFM was designed to provide dramatic improvements in maneuver agility for fighter aircraft during close-in aerial combat, as well as in transonic and supersonic engagements and in-ground attack applications.

15 December   The YEZ-2A designation was established and was assigned to the Navy's operational development model (ODM) airship. Potential use for the YEZ-2A airship was as an organic asset of surface action groups to serve as a fuel-efficient, long-endurance airborne platform for area surveillance and communications, command and control.

The F-14A (PLUS) at Grumman's Calverton, N.Y., flight test facility.

1987—Continued

17 December The first fleet S-3A Viking, retrofitted to an S-3B configuration, entered service with VS-27 at NAS Cecil Field, Fla. This update provided major weapon systems improvements, including a new acoustic processor, new electronic support measures system, target imaging radar, the Harpoon missile, and an electronic countermeasures system. The modifications greatly increased the Viking's multiple-mission capability.

21 December Changes to the Office of Chief of Naval Operations, required by the Goldwater-Nichols DoD Reorganization Act of 1986, resulted in the Deputy Chief of Naval Operations (Air Warfare) being redesignated Assistant Chief of Naval Operations (Air Warfare). This organization had been established originally on 18 August 1943 as Deputy Chief of Naval Operations (Air) and modified on 15 July 1971 to Deputy Chief of Naval Operations (Air Warfare).

21 December The Secretary of the Navy announced he had approved the opening of aircrew assignments to women for the Navy's two shore-based fleet air reconnaissance squadrons flying EP-3 Orions.

31 December For the first time in its history, the Naval Air Reserve Force completed a full calendar year without a major aircraft mishap. During 1987, the force consisted of 52 operational squadrons and over 400 aircraft.

1988

11 January Colonel Gregory "Pappy" Boyington, top World War II Marine Corps ace, died at age 75. He was CO of the VMF-214 Black Sheep during World War II and was credited with the destruction of 28 Japanese aircraft. On 3 January 1944, he was shot down over Rabaul, captured by the Japanese and was a POW for the next 20 months. Colonel Boyington received

A close-up of Gregory "Pappy" Boyington in World War II flight gear.

the Medal of Honor for his actions in combat while CO of VMF-214 from 12 September 1943 to 3 January 1944.

17 March Vanguard I, the world's longest orbiting man-made satellite, built by the Naval Research Laboratory, marked its 30th anniversary in space. It was the first satellite to use solar cells to power its instrumentation. Although the satellite's radio transmitter was no longer operative, it provided a wealth of information on air density, temperature ranges and micrometeorite impact during its six years of transmitting.

11 April The Navy's first F-14A (Plus) to be assigned to an operational squadron was accepted by VF-101 at NAS Oceana, Va. The F-14A (Plus) had two General Electric F-110 engines that each developed 7,000 pounds more thrust than the original Tomcat power plants. This additional power greatly extended the performance capabilities of the aircraft.

16 April The Navy's new trainer, the T-45A Goshawk, took its maiden flight at Douglas Aircraft Company, Long Beach, Calif. The T-45 was scheduled to become the Navy's primary aircraft for training Naval Aviators.

The T-45A Goshawk in flight.

18 April The Navy retaliated against Iran following the 14 April incident in which *Samuel B. Roberts* (FFG 58) struck an Iranian mine in international waters. The retaliation involved both surface and air units. CVW-11 squadrons from *Enterprise* were the major aviation participants. VAW-117's Nighthawks provided airborne early warning tracking and analysis of targets as well as air intercept control. The initial American strikes centered around a surface group action against two Iranian oil platforms that had been identified as support bases for Iranian attacks on merchant shipping. Elements of CVW-11 provided air support for the surface groups in the form of surface combat air patrols, flying A-6E Intruders and A-7E Corsair IIs, and combat air patrols with F-14 Tomcats.

1988—Continued

The Iranian oil platforms targeted for a retaliation strike following the damaging of Samuel B. Roberts (FFG 58) by an Iranian mine in international waters.

The initial action began with coordinated strikes by two separate surface groups. One group, consisting of two destroyers and one amphibious ship, attacked the Sassan platform while the other group, comprising a guided missile cruiser and two frigates, attacked the Sirri platform. Iranian response to the destruction of the two oil platforms involved the dispatching of numerous gunboats to prey on various targets in the Persian Gulf. Following an attack by Iranian Boghammar speedboats on an American-flagged supply ship and a Panamanian-flagged ship, A-6Es from VA-95 were vectored in on the speedboats by an American frigate. The aircraft dropped Rockeye cluster bombs on the speedboats, sinking one and damaging several others.

Action continued to escalate. *Joshan,* an Iranian Combattante II Kaman-class fast attack craft, challenged *Wainwright* (CG 28) and her surface group. The American ships responded to the challenge by sinking *Joshan.* Fighting continued when the Iranian frigate *Sahand* departed Bandar Abbas and challenged elements of an American surface group. She was observed by two VA-95 A-6Es while they were flying surface combat air patrol for *Joseph Strauss* (DDG 16).

Sahand launched missiles at the A-6Es, and the Intruders replied with launches of two Harpoons and four laser-guided Skipper bombs. This was followed by a Harpoon firing from *Joseph Strauss.* The weapons delivered against *Sahand* were successful.

Fires blazing on her decks eventually reached her magazines resulting in the final explosions that led to her sinking. The loss of *Sahand,* one of Iran's most modern ships, was not enough to stop the suicidal sorties of the Iranian Navy. A sister ship, *Sabalan,* departed her port for operations in the gulf. She fired on several A-6Es from VA-95 with a surface-to-air missile. One of the Intruders responded with a laser-guided bomb that hit *Sabalan* and stopped her dead in the water. The Iranian frigate was taken in tow by an Iranian tug with the stern partially submerged. VA-95's aircraft, as ordered, did not continue the attack. This action ended the retaliatory strikes against Iran that began as a result of Iranian mining in international waters.

6 May   A prototype F/A-18D Hornet equipped as an advanced night attack aircraft made its maiden flight at McDonnell Douglas in St. Louis, Mo. The night attack version was equipped with a new FLIR sensor called TINS designed to help pilots navigate and assist in locating, identifying and attacking ground targets at night. The F/A-18D was a two-seat model and would employ a pilot and Naval Flight Officer in tactical missions.

16 May   The production model of the Navy's new E-6A communications aircraft arrived at NATC Patuxent River, Md., for extensive electromagnetic testing.

1988—Continued

23 May   The revolutionary tilt-rotor aircraft, the V-22 Osprey, made its debut during rollout ceremonies at Bell Helicopter's facility in Arlington, Tex. The V-22 combined the attributes of a helicopter and a turbo-prop aircraft and was developed from the start to serve the needs of all four armed services.

14 June   The Sunday Punchers of VA-75 became the first fleet A-6 squadron to launch a HARM. CO Commander John T. Meister and operations officer Lieutenant Commander Richard D. Jaskot scored a direct hit on a target ship. The missile was fired from a new A-6E SWIP aircraft. The modified aircraft was upgraded to launch the latest air-to-surface missiles including HARM, Harpoon and Maverick, as well as its normal array of air-to-surface weapons.

14 June   Reserve VP-62 fired its first AGM-84 Harpoon missile and scored a direct hit, signaling a new chapter in Naval Aviation history. The missile was launched from the Broadarrows' new P-3C Orion Update III aircraft during coordinated fleet operations with other 2nd Fleet units. Based at NAS Jacksonville, Fla., the squadron had been selected earlier as the first Reserve patrol squadron to receive the P-3C as part of the Navy's horizontal integration program.

13 July   Carrier Airborne Early Warning Weapons School was established as a separate command on the same principles as Top Gun and Strike University. Emphasis would be on warfare training for E-2C Hawkeye aircrews.

22 July   Reserve VA-304 took delivery of a KA-6D, marking the introduction of the Intruder to the Naval Air Reserve. By September 1988 the squadron had three KA-6Ds and two A-6Es.

2 August   *Constellation* successfully fought a severe fire in the main engineering space using the installed HALON firefighting equipment; this was the first carrier use of the system in fighting a fire.

5 August   Dwaine L. Lyon received his Wings of Gold and was commissioned an ensign, becoming the first NAVCAD to complete the jet strike training pipeline since the NAVCAD program was reinstituted in 1986. The program, which began in 1935, was an important source of Naval Aviators until it was terminated in 1965. Under the revived NAVCAD program, aviation cadets with a minimum of two years of college or its equivalent would undergo flight training as noncommissioned officers.

17 August   The maiden flight of the Navy's new Helicopter Combat Support aircraft, HH-60H, was conducted at Sikorsky Aircraft, Stratford, Conn. The helicopter was a derivative of the SH-60F. The primary mission of the new HH-60H would be strike rescue with secondary tasks involving special warfare missions. The HH-60Hs were the first new aircraft purchased for and operated exclusively by the Naval Air Reserve.

30 September   The Navy's last operational reciprocating-engine aircraft, a C-1A Trader (BuNo 146048), retired from active service and was transferred to the Naval Aviation Museum, NAS Pensacola, Fla. The C-1A had been based at the air station, providing carrier onboard delivery support for the Navy's training carrier *Lexington*.

1 October   HCS-5 was established at NAS Point Mugu, Calif., the first squadron of its kind. HCS-5 was a Reserve squadron with a primary mission of combat search and rescue (strike rescue) and special warfare support. It would operate the HH-60H Seahawk.

3 October   The aircraft designation A-12A was established, designating a new carrier-based, attack aircraft with a two-man crew. The A-12 aircraft program was canceled in 1991.

14 October   The Navy selected Lockheed Aeronautical Systems Company to develop a replacement for the P-3C Orion maritime patrol aircraft. The new aircraft, designated LRAACA for long-range, air antisubmarine warfare-capable aircraft, would have new fuel-efficient, modern-technology turboprop engines to increase its range and efficiency, an increased payload capability and an improved avionics suite. The program was canceled in 1990.

3 November   The Navy's first SLAM, AGM-84E, rolled out at McDonnell Douglas' facility in St. Charles, a suburb of St. Louis, Mo. SLAM was a derivative of the Harpoon antiship missile system. It was designed for deployment from carrier-based aircraft and allowed an aircraft to attack land targets and ships in port or at sea from an extended range, in excess of 60 nautical miles.

10 November   Ensign Joy D. Warner became the first woman to earn her Wings of Gold through the newly reinstated NAVCAD program. She joined the program in June 1987 and completed basic flight training with HT-8.

1988—Continued

29 November The Navy Department transferred an F-4S Phantom II (BuNo 157307) to the Smithsonian's National Air and Space Museum, upon its arrival at Dulles International Airport, Va. This F-4 saw action in Vietnam and was a MiG killer. On 21 June 1972 the F-4, piloted by Commander Samuel C. Flynn, Jr., with Lieutenant William H. John as radar intercept officer, shot down a MiG-21. The F-4 was assigned to VF-31 operating off *Saratoga* at the time. The museum planned to display the F-4 in a future Vietnam war exhibit.

31 December The Aviation Officer Continuation Pay (AOCP) program was terminated and a new program was instituted on 1 January 1989. Called Aviation Continuation Pay (ACP), the new program applied only to pilots and Naval Flight Officers below pay-grade O-5. Determination of eligible communities and payment rates was based on analysis of current year group shortages, department head requirements and other pertinent management factors. ACP payment could reach up to $12,000 for each year of the contract if the officer agreed to remain on active duty to complete 14 years of continuous service.

31 December The year 1988 ended as the "safest in aviation history" for the Navy/Marine Corps team, according to Secretary of the Navy William L. Ball. 48 class "A" mishaps were recorded—down to 2.16 mishaps per 100,000 flight hours for 1988.

1989

4 January Two F-14A Tomcats flown by crews from VF-32 of NAS Oceana, Va., downed two hostile Libyan MiG-23 aircraft in the central Mediterranean north of the Libyan port of Tobruk over international waters. The squadron was deployed with CVW-3 aboard *John F. Kennedy*, which had been participating in routine training exercises off the northeastern tip of the Libyan coast when the group was approached by the two Flogger jets from the Al Bumbah air base. After repeated attempts for a peaceful intercept, the VF-32 Swordsmen fired their missiles, downing the MiGs.

20 January George H. W. Bush, former Naval Aviator, was inaugurated as the 41st president of the United States during an outdoor ceremony at the U.S. Capitol. As a member of VT-51 during World War II, Bush was shot down while operating a TBM Avenger in the Pacific.

23 February The Navy's Mid Infrared Advanced Chemical Laser/Sea Lite Beam Director (an experimental high-energy laser system) destroyed a Vandal supersonic missile in a test conducted at the White Sands Missile Range, N.Mex. This was the first time a high-energy laser system successfully engaged and destroyed a Vandal missile, flying low and fast in a cruise missile profile. The laser system was designed to show that a laser could acquire, track, and focus enough energy on a supersonic target to destroy it.

19 March The V-22 Osprey tilt-rotor aircraft made its first flight at Bell Helicopter Textron's Flight Research Center, Arlington, Tex. The aircraft reached a maximum speed of 20 knots and an altitude of 30 feet during a 15-minute flight in the helicopter mode, which initiated phase one of flight tests. The V-22 was the first modern weapons system designed from conception to meet the requirements of all four U.S. armed services.

31 March VP-62 completed transition to the P-3C Update III, the newest production Orion, marking the first time in Reserve patrol history that a Reserve squadron received the latest state-of-the-art aircraft.

3 April An A-6E modified with a new composite wing made its first flight at Wichita, Kans. Manufactured by Boeing from graphite/epoxy composite materials, the new wing was stronger than the original metal wing on the Intruder. Grumman Aircraft Systems Division would install the wings on its newly manufactured A-6s. The new wings would be installed by Navy depots on the older A-6s.

16 April The VS-30 Diamondcutters became the first fleet S-3 squadron to fire a Harpoon antiship missile. The launch resulted in a direct hit on the target by a detachment assigned to VS-30 as it participated in exercise North Star '89 aboard *America*.

19 April While operating in the Caribbean, *Coral Sea* responded to a call for assistance from *Iowa* (BB 61) due to an explosion in the battleship's number two gun turret in which 47 crew members were killed. The explosive ordnance disposal team from *Coral Sea* removed volatile powder charges from the ship's 16-inch guns and flooded powder magazines. *Coral Sea* also dispatched a surgical team and medical supplies. VC-8, using SH-3G helicopters, also performed medevac and logistical support to *Iowa*.

15 May H. Lawrence Garrett III was sworn in as the 68th Secretary of the Navy, succeeded William L. Ball III. Secretary Garrett was commissioned as a Naval Aviation Cadet in 1964 and served as a Naval Flight Officer with VP-50 in Vietnam.

1989—Continued

The new V-22 Osprey in flight.

22 June HS-10 accepted the Navy's first SH-60F CV-Helo inner zone antisubmarine warfare aircraft during a ceremony at NAS North Island, Calif. In October, HS-10 became the Navy's only SH-60F fleet readiness squadron when it transferred all SH-3 training to HC-1 and HS-1.

24 June The first development free-flight test of a SLAM resulted in a direct hit against a simulated surface-to-air missile communication site at San Nicholas Island, Pacific Missile Test Center Range, Calif. The carrier-based aircraft missile was launched from an A-6E (SWIP) Intruder. During its flight it was controlled from an F/A-18 Hornet using the Walleye data link for man-in-the-loop control. SLAM was a derivative of the Harpoon missile system, manufactured by McDonnell Douglas.

1 July Rear Admiral Richard H. Truly, serving as the Associate Administrator for Space Flight, Office of Space Flight, National Aeronautics and Space Administration, retired from the Navy and was confirmed by Congress as the administrator of NASA. A Naval Aviator, Rear Admiral Truly was selected as an astronaut in 1965 and was credited with bringing U.S. backing into an active space program after the Space Shuttle *Challenger* accident.

1 July The Naval Aviation Museum officially changed its name to the National Museum of Naval Aviation.

8 July HCS-5, NAS Point Mugu, Calif., accepted the first Sikorsky HH-60H strike rescue and special warfare operations helicopters. The HH-60H was the first aircraft to be produced specifically for the Naval Air Reserve.

22 July Admiral Marc A. Mitscher, Naval Aviator #33, was enshrined in the National Aviation Hall of Fame. In 1919, Mitscher commanded the NC-1, one of the three seaplanes that attempted the first airborne trans-Atlantic crossing. Only NC-4 was successful. In 1928, Mitscher made the first takeoff and landing on *Saratoga* in a Vought UO-1. His distinguished service during World War II included command of *Hornet*; Patrol Wing 2; Fleet Air, Noumea; and units of the U.S. Army Air Force, Navy and Marine Corps aviation groups, and contingents of the Royal New Zealand Air Force. Of particular significance was his command of Task Force 58. Mitscher received many citations for his wartime service.

1 August *Coral Sea* and *America* departed early from separate port visits when they were diverted to the eastern Mediterranean as a show of force in the wake of the suspected hanging of Marine Corps Lieutenant Colonel William R. Higgins by Middle East terrorists, and threats to other hostages. Lieutenant Colonel Higgins had been kidnapped in February 1988 while a member of the United Nations peacekeeping forces in Lebanon. *Midway*, operating with Battle Group Alfa, was originally scheduled to participate in Pacific Exercise-89 but instead was repositioned to fill the carrier commitment in the Indian Ocean. The carrier remained on station in the northern Arabian Sea until mid-October, extending its deployment by one month.

3 August *Ranger* rescued 39 Vietnamese refugees, adrift for 10 days on a barge in heavy seas and monsoon rains in the South China Sea, about 80 miles from NAS Cubi Point, R.P. SH-3s from HS-14 assisted. An A-6 from VA-145 spotted the barge, which had apparently broken loose from its mooring near a small island off the coast of Vietnam with 10 men on board. Twenty-nine other refugees from a sinking refugee boat climbed aboard the barge when it drifted out to sea. After examination by medical personnel, all were flown to NAS Cubi Point for further processing.

3 August VQ-3 took delivery of two Boeing E-6A Hermes at Seattle, Wash. The arrival of the new strategic communications aircraft marked the entry of the newest generation of TACAMO aircraft into the fleet. The E-6A would eventually replace the Lockheed EC-130Q Hercules in both VQ-3 and its Atlantic Fleet counterpart, VQ-4.

25 August A NASA-designed Scout rocket launched two Navy navigation satellites from Vandenberg AFB, Calif. This marked the culmination of the planned launch program for the TRANSIT system that began in 1962. The Navy relied on TRANSIT for precise position information anywhere on the earth and in all weather conditions. The two satellites were launched "piggy-back" style using the SOOS (Stacked Oscars on Scout) system.

7 September An NS-3A modified as the aerodynamic prototype of the ES-3A made its first flight. Sixteen ES-3As would eventually replace the EA-3B Skywarrior in fleet air reconnaissance squadrons.

12 September The Coast Guard retired its last Sikorsky HH-52A Sea Guard. The HH-52A served over 26 years as the Coast Guard's primary short-range, search and rescue helicopter. It was replaced by the Aerospatiale HH-65A Dolphin.

14 September The first Sikorsky HH-60J Jayhawk medium-range, search and rescue helicopter rolled out in Stratford, Conn. It would replace the Sikorsky HH-3F in Coast Guard service.

14 September The V-22 Osprey made its first flight in full airplane mode. The part helicopter, part air-plane tilt-rotor aircraft was airborne for about one hour at Bell Helicopter Textron's Arlington, Tex., facility.

14 September The Navy Aircrew Common Ejection Seat successfully completed a 600-knot dual ejection from an F-14D test sled at China Lake, Calif.

17–21 September Under the direction of Commander, Fleet Air, Caribbean, a number of Navy and Marine Corps squadrons—including HC-2 (Det VI), VP-93, and VC-8—responded to the destruction brought by Hurricane Hugo to the Caribbean by flying in needed supplies to Puerto Rico and evacuating the seriously injured to hospitals.

22 September VMFT-401 transferred its last F-21A Kfir, marking the retirement of this Israeli-built fighter from U.S. Naval Aviation. The F-21A served as an aggressor aircraft.

30 September VAK-208 was disestablished as the last Navy squadron dedicated solely to the mission of aerial refueling. Assigned to Reserve Carrier Air Wing 20, the squadron provided aerial refueling and pathfinder support since its establishment as VAQ-208 in July 1970. It was redesignated VAK-208 on 1 October 1979. Reserve carrier air wing aerial refueling was assumed by VA-304 and -205, transitioning to the A-6E and the KA-6D Intruders.

1 October HAL-4, a Naval Reserve squadron, was officially redesignated HCS-4 with an added mission of strike rescue. HAL-4 was the last Navy gunship squadron.

17 October An earthquake in northern California brought response from HM-15 Detachment 3 and HC-1. Both conducted lifts of food, water, and relief materials to the heavily damaged areas. HC-11 Det 3 also participated in the disaster relief. The amphibious assault ship *Peleliu* provided food and shelter to homeless earthquake victims.

29 October The developmental prototype of the Advanced Capability version of the Grumman EA-6B made its first flight.

1 November NAS Pensacola, Fla., became the last Chief of Naval Air Training command to fully convert to civilian contractors for maintenance on aircraft. In the past, the work had been done by Navy personnel in maintenance ratings. Having the work performed by a civilian company was considered more cost-effective.

1989—Continued

3 November   The designation VH-60N was approved for the version of the H-60 helicopter to be used as the worldwide executive transport. Personnel from HMX-1 were responsible for flying the President and his staff in this helicopter.

6–7 November   VX-1 set a Naval Aviation record for flying the longest nonstop, air-refueled flight in the E-6A TACAMO aircraft. Two refuelings were made in flight utilizing Air Force KC-10s from March AFB, Calif.

1–2 December   *Midway* and *Enterprise*, originally scheduled to conduct joint operations, were put on alert status for Operation Classic Resolve in response to a coup attempt in Manila, R.P. After the situation subsided, *Midway* returned to her home port at Yokosuka, Japan; and *Enterprise* continued her deployment in the Indian Ocean.

2 Decermber   VAQ-309 officially received the EA-6B Prowler during ceremonies at NAS Whidbey Island, Wash., becoming the first reserve squadron to operate the modern electronic warfare aircraft.

1990

25 January   A helicopter crew from *Guadalcanal* rescued three fishermen after their boat went under three miles off Cape Henry, Va.

25 January   HSL-45 Detachment 10; HSL-33 Detachment 3; and HSL-35 Detachment 1 responded to a distress call from the Chinese merchant vessel *Hauzhu*, reported to be sinking 40 miles off the northern coast of the Philippines. Nineteen crew members were recovered.

21 March   The SH-2G helicopter was introduced at a flyout ceremony at the Kaman Aerospace Corporation's production facility in Bloomfield, Connecticut. The SH-2G was an upgraded version of the SH-2F helicopter, which was part of the LAMPS MK I. Improvements included a sonobuoy data processing system, changes in the tactical navigation system, more powerful engines, composite rotor blades, an infrared target detection system and several countermeasures systems.

27 March   HS-2 became the first Navy squadron to receive the SH-60F inner-zone combat aircraft for operational deployment with the fleet at a ceremony at NAS North Island, Calif. The SH-60F, made by Sikorsky, was a derivative of the SH-60B Seahawk LAMPS MK III helicopter.

17 April   The Lockheed Aeronautical Systems Company formally delivered the last P-3 Orion (BuNo 163925) to the U.S. Navy in a ceremony at Palmdale, Calif. It was the 548th P-3 accepted by the Navy since deliveries began in August 1962.

18 May   NAVAIR established the model designation BQM-145A for the medium-range unmanned aerial vehicle. The BQM-145A was a programmable reconnaissance drone that could be launched from various tactical aircraft and also from the ground.

18 May   The night attack F/A-18D Hornet was introduced into service at the Marine Corps Air Station El Toro, Calif. The F/A-18D was the first two-seat Hornet designated to fly tactical as opposed to training missions. It would replace the A-6 Intruder as the Marine Corps' day/night attack aircraft.

3 June   Three days after President Bush ordered an amphibious task force off the coast of Liberia, *Saipan*, *Ponce* (LPD 15) and *Sumter* (LST 1181) began their watch over the events in Liberia ready to assist any additional evacuation of U.S. citizens, should they be threatened by the rebel uprising there.

24 June   The wreckage of the Navy's rigid airship, *Macon* (ZRS-5), was located by the Navy submersible *Sea Cliff* (DSV 4) off the coast of Point Sur, Calif., where it had crashed on 12 February 1935. At the time, *Macon* was carrying four Curtiss F9C-2 Sparrowhawk biplane fighters. They were spotted near the wreck of the *Macon*.

26 June   The first ship launch of the SLAM was conducted from a Harpoon canister aboard the guided missile cruiser *Lake Champlain* (CG 57). The launch was controlled from a LAMPS MK III helicopter, with video images downlinked to the ship's command information center via the helicopter's Walleye data link pod. The test was conducted at Pacific Missile Test Center's sea test range.

12 July   Commander Rosemary Bryant Mariner relieved Commander Charles Hughes Smith as commanding officer of VAQ-34. Commander Mariner was the first woman selected to command an operational aviation squadron.

Commander Rosemary Bryant Mariner.

1990—Continued

16 July The largest earthquake to strike the Philippines in 14 years rocked Manila and left many northern areas of Luzon destroyed. Marine helicopters assigned to Marine Corps Air Group Task Force 4-90 and HMM-164(C) hauled food, water and medical supplies. CH-46E, CH-53D, and CH-53E helicopters were used for transports, while searches for survivors were conducted by UH-1N and AH-1W helicopters and OV-10 observation planes. Navy SH-3G helicopters assigned to VC-5 at NAS Cubi Point also flew resupply and medical missions. VC-5 helicopters delivered cement-cutting saws and trained operators in rescue parties to help free victims trapped in the rubble.

20 July The Navy terminated a contract with Lockheed Aeronautical Systems for the P-7A for default. The P-7A, formerly known as LRAACA (long-range air anti-submarine warfare capable aircraft), was the planned replacement for the P-3 maritime patrol aircraft.

31 July HC-9, the Navy's only combat search and rescue helicopter unit, was disestablished. Its mission passed to two Navy Reserve special operations squadrons: HCS-5 at Point Mugu, Calif., and HCS-4 at NAS Norfolk, Va. HC-9 had been established in August 1975.

2 August The NAVSTAR navigation satellite was boosted into orbit by a Delta rocket. This was the latest in a series of spacecraft capable of pinpointing the location of U.S. military units.

2 August Iraq invaded Kuwait. At the time, eight U.S. Navy Middle East Force ships were in the Persian Gulf. The carrier battle group of *Independence* with CVW-14 aboard was in the Indian Ocean, and *Dwight D. Eisenhower* with CVW-7 was in the Mediterranean. *Independence*'s battle group was directed to proceed to the northern Arabian Sea in support of Operation Desert Shield, a UN sanctioned economic blockade of Iraq.

5 August *Independence*'s battle group arrived on station in the Gulf of Oman.

5 August 90–9 January 91 Operation Sharp Edge was authorized by the State Department on 5 August to evacuate noncombatants caught in the civil war in Liberia. *Saipan* and other ships were stationed off the Liberian coast. Marines from 22nd Marine Expeditionary Unit were flown into the American embassy compound in Monrovia, Liberia. The MEU's air combat element, HMM-261(C), was comprised of CH-46Es from HMM-261, CH-53Ds from HMH-362, UH-1Ns and AH-1Ts from HMLA-167, and AV-8Bs from VMA-223. On 28 November a cease-fire was accepted by the opposing Liberian factions and on 30 November the limited evacuation of noncombatants from Monrovia terminated, with a total of 2,609 evacuated, including 330 U.S. citizens. Operation Sharp Edge concluded on 9 January 1991.

7 August *Saratoga* left the U.S. for a previously scheduled deployment to the eastern Mediterranean, with CVW-17 aboard.

7 August *Dwight D. Eisenhower* and her battle group transited the Suez Canal and entered the Red Sea on 8 August.

7 August The EP-3E Aries II, an electronic version of the P-3C, arrived at NAS Patuxent River, Md., to begin four months of extensive performance testing.

15 August Leading a carrier battle group, *John F. Kennedy* deployed from her home port, Norfolk, Va., with CVW-3 aboard. The battle group would be available for potential relief of the *Dwight D. Eisenhower* battle group or additional tasking to be determined by the situation in the Middle East.

16 August Consistent with UN Security Council Resolution 661, a multinational maritime intercept operation involving Naval Aviation forces began intercepting ships going to or from Iraq and Kuwait.

22 August *Saratoga* transited the Suez Canal to take up her station in the Red Sea, where she would relieve *Dwight D. Eisenhower* who would then proceed home.

30 August *John F. Kennedy*'s battle group transited the Strait of Gibraltar en route to the Mediterranean Sea.

3 September *Dwight D. Eisenhower* transited the Strait of Gibraltar en route to home port.

6 September Amphibious assault ship *Nassau* transited the Suez Canal.

7 September Amphibious assault ships *Iwo Jima* and *Guam* transited the Suez Canal.

14 September *Nassau* arrived in the Gulf of Oman.

14 September *John F. Kennedy*'s battle group transited the Suez Canal into the Red Sea.

1990—Continued

Dwight D. Eisenhower transits the Suez Canal en route to operations in the Red Sea.

16 September   *Iwo Jima* and *Guam* arrived in the Gulf of Oman.

1 October   *Independence* transited the Strait of Hormuz en route to the Persian Gulf.

3 October   *Independence* conducted flight operations in the Persian Gulf. She was the first carrier to do so since 1974, when *Constellation* operated there.

4 October   *Independence* left the Gulf after spending three days in its relatively confined and shallow waters. A Pentagon spokesman said the aircraft carrier had successfully completed its mission which was "to demonstrate to our friends and allies in the region that it is possible to put a carrier in the Gulf and carry out operations."

8 October   The two U.S. Marine Corps UH-1N Huey helicopters based on the amphibious assault ship *Okinawa* in the Gulf of Oman disappeared with eight

men aboard during "routine night training operations." No survivors were found.

28 October   U.S. Marines from the amphibious transport ship *Ogden* (LPD 5) boarded the Iraqi vessel *Amuriyah*, bound for Iraq through the Gulf. The vessel refused to halt despite summons from U.S. and Australian ships. The allied ships fired shots across *Amuriyah*'s bow and warplanes from *Independence* buzzed low in warning passes. The Marine boarding party found no banned cargo and the Iraqi craft was allowed to proceed.

1 November   *Midway,* with CVW-5 aboard, replaced *Independence* in the northern Arabian Sea.

8 November   President Bush announced a decision to double the number of carrier battle groups deployed in support of Operation Desert Shield. *Ranger* with CVW-2, *America* with CVW-1, and *Theodore Roosevelt* with CVW-8 were scheduled to be

1990—Continued

on station by 15 January 1991. The three were to join *Saratoga*, *John F. Kennedy*, and *Midway*.

15 November U.S. and Saudi forces began Operation Imminent Thunder, an eight-day combined amphibious landing exercise in northeastern Saudi Arabia which involved about 1,000 U.S. Marines, 16 warships, and more than 1,100 aircraft. Close air support was provided by Marine aircraft as well as planes from *Midway*, which had entered the Gulf from the northern Arabian Sea for the exercise.

16 November The Navy's newest fighter, the Grumman F-14D Super Tomcat, was formally accepted for fleet service in a ceremony held at NAS Miramar, Calif.

29 November The UN Security Council approved a resolution authorizing the use of military force unless Iraq vacated Kuwait by 15 January 1991.

8 December *Ranger*, with CVW-2 aboard, departed San Diego, Calif., on an unscheduled deployment in support of Operation Desert Shield.

20 December *Independence* returned to her San Diego, Calif., home port from her Persian Gulf deployment.

21 December An Israeli-chartered liberty ferry shuttling 102 crew members from the Israeli port of Haifa back to *Saratoga* capsized and sank off the coast of Israel. Israeli military and police officers rushed out in boats and helicopters to pull sailors from the water. Helicopters flew injured men to two hospitals in Haifa. Twenty U.S. sailors died. In addition, a crew member was missing and presumed drowned.

28 December *America*, with CVW-1 aboard, and *Theodore Roosevelt*, with CVW-8, departed Norfolk, Va., on deployment in support of Operation Desert Shield.

On 3 February 1984, Navy astronaut Captain Bruce McCandless II became the first person to walk untethered in space.

A VFA-113 Hornet aboard Constellation.

A Marine Harrier operating off Tarawa.

A Marine AH-1W Sea Cobra.

A loaded F/A-18 Hornet.

PART 12

The First Half of the Nineties

1991–1995

The first half of the 1990s has been characterized by changes in the world order, containment of localized fighting and a revamped naval strategy. As 1991 began, the 15 January deadline for the UN-ordered withdrawal of Iraqi troops from Kuwait neared; and U.S. aircraft carriers advanced to locations near the Persian Gulf. On 16 January, (the night of 17 January in the Middle East), Tomahawk cruise missiles were launched at pre-programmed targets by nine U.S. Navy ships in the Mediterranean, Persian Gulf and Red Sea; just in time to be shown on the evening news. Later that same evening, President George H. W. Bush addressed the nation and announced that the liberation of Kuwait had begun and a massive armada of naval, air force and Allied aircraft struck targets in Iraq.

The Gulf War was the first war the public could see in real time. TV viewers around the world saw first hand the awesome military might of the United States as it liberated Kuwait. The Gulf War was short and on 27 February, President Bush declared that Kuwait had been liberated. However, UN economic sanctions against Iraq remained in effect. Naval Aviation was actively involved in patrolling Iraq during the remainder of the first half of the decade. It was involved in supporting UN-imposed sanctions against Iraq and limiting Iraq's threat to its minorities and neighbors.

In October 1994, after Iraqi troops again massed on the Kuwaiti border, President Clinton dispatched *George Washington* to the Red Sea, to protect Kuwait from possible invasion. Iraq withdrew from the Kuwaiti border and recognized the sovereignty of Kuwait, but UN economic sanctions on Iraq remained in place. In 1995, *Constellation, Theodore Roosevelt* and *Independence* patrolled Iraq's "no-fly zone" during Operation Southern Watch.

The Soviet Union had cooperated with the United States during the Gulf War. It was the first U.S.-Soviet coordinated effort since World War II. Soviet *glasnost* (openness) and *peristroika* (re-structuring) were bringing about changes and unrest in the Soviet Union. In August 1991, an attempted coup triggered the dissolution of the Soviet Union into its component republics. On 25 December 1991, Mikhail Gorbachev formally resigned as president of a Soviet Union that no longer existed.

The collapse of the Soviet Union left the United States as the world's only superpower. The new world order presented regional rather than global threats and challenges. In response, the Navy developed a new strategy promulgated in the white pater entitled "...From the Sea." The paper emphasized littoral warfare—along the coastlines—and maneuver from the sea.

The new global situation called for the downsizing of the Navy's personnel and material. With the Soviet Union no longer a threat, the Clinton administration supported a smaller defense budget. For Naval Aviation it was the largest draw-down since World War II. Many aviation squadrons and naval shore facilities were disestablished, reorganized or consolidated.

The break-up of the composite state of Yugoslavia into its constituent republics presented the first major challenge to the Navy's "...From the Sea" strategy. In a referendum in the spring of 1992, a majority of those in the Republic of Bosnia-Herzegovina voted for independence from the remains of Yugoslavia. The Bosnian Serbs reacted by proclaiming that the Republic of Bosnia-Herzegovina was a constituted part of Yugoslavia, now only consisting of Serbia and Montenegro. Fighting broke out between the Serbs, Croats, and Slavic Moslems in Bosnia-Herzegovina and the republic was divided along ethnic lines.

Along the coastline of Bosnia-Herzegovina, aircraft carriers kept watch over the situation from the Adriatic Sea and provided support for Operation Provide Promise—the United Nations relief effort—and Operation Deny Flight, which monitored the air space over Bosnia-Herzegovina to prevent the warring parties from using it in warfare.

On her last deployment (1994), *Saratoga* provided support for Operations Deny Flight and Provide Promise. *Saratoga* then returned to Mayport, Fla., where she was decommissioned in August 1994.

Dwight D. Eisenhower and *America* continued the support of Operation Deny Flight from the Adriatic

Sea. On 30 August 1995, aircraft from *Theodore Roosevelt* carried out the initial early morning strikes that began Operation Deliberate Force, action against Serb military targets in Bosnia.

The Dayton Accords, signed in Paris in December 1995, by the Bosnian Federation and the Bosnian Serbs, brought a hope for peace in Bosnia-Herzegovina. Operation Joint Endeavor enforced the military aspects of this peace by providing a stable environment in which the civil aspects could proceed. Operation Deny Flight, begun in 1993, then came to an end. President Bill Clinton called up reserves to participate in Operation Joint Endeavor.

The initial half of the 1990s marked a first for women in the Navy. In April 1993, Secretary of Defense Les Aspin dropped most of the restrictions that prohibited women from engaging in aerial and naval combat. Later in the year, Congress supported the secretary's decision to allow women in combat by repealing the Combat Exclusion Law. In October 1994, *Dwight D. Eisenhower* became the first aircraft carrier to deploy with women permanently assigned on board.

In the first half of the 1990s, Naval Aviation continued to adjust to changing world events, the development of new technology and new strategies in order to serve the Nation in peace and war.

1991

1 January HC-4 relocated its detachment from Jeddah, Saudi Arabia, to Hurghada, Egypt, constructed an airhead operating site within 48 hours, and began transporting passengers, cargo, and mail to the Red Sea battle groups during Operation Desert Shield.

2–5 January CH-53E helicopters from *Guam* helped insert Marines into the U.S. Embassy compound in Mogadishu, Somalia, during Operation Eastern Exit, which rescued U.S. Ambassador James K. Bishop, the Soviet ambassador, and other foreign nationals caught in the Somali civil war.

6 January *Saratoga* transited the Suez Canal en route to the Red Sea to participate in Operation Desert Shield.

7 January Secretary of Defense Richard Cheney canceled the A-12 Avenger carrier-based aircraft program. The action was based on the inability of the contractors—General Dynamics and McDonnell Douglas—to design, develop, fabricate, assemble, and test A-12 aircraft within the contract schedule and to deliver an aircraft that met contract requirements. This was the largest weapons contract cancellation ever by the Pentagon.

9 January *America* transited the Strait of Gibraltar and arrived in the Mediterranean Sea, and then prepared for participation in Operation Desert Shield.

12 January Congress voted 52 to 47 in the Senate and 250 to 183 in the House on a joint resolution that gave President George H. W. Bush the support he sought for military action against Iraq.

12 January *Ranger* battle group arrived on station in the northern Arabian Sea and participated in Operation Desert Shield.

12 January Amphibious Group Three (with the Fifth Marine Expeditionary Brigade embarked) arrived on station in the Arabian Sea. Eighteen ships, including *Okinawa, Tarawa, Tripoli* and *New Orleans* were to join the 13-ship Amphibious Group Three, to comprise the largest amphibious task force since the Korean War.

12 January *Midway* battle group reentered the Persian Gulf and participated in Operation Desert Shield.

14 January *Theodore Roosevelt* battle group passed through the Suez Canal and assumed battle station in the Red Sea.

15 January *America* battle group transited the Suez Canal and arrived on station in the Red Sea.

15 January *Ranger* with CVW-2 on board, and her battle group transited the Strait of Hormuz to station in the Persian Gulf.

16 January *Theodore Roosevelt* transited the Bab el-Mandeb Strait from the Red Sea to the Gulf of Aden.

16 January At 4:50 p.m. EST, a squadron of fighter-bombers took off from an air base in central Saudi Arabia. Targets in Iraq and Kuwait began being hit before 7:00 p.m. EST. (It was the night of 17 January in the Middle East.) At the time, six Navy battle groups, two battleships, and a 31-ship amphibious task force were operating in the Red Sea, Persian Gulf, and Arabian Sea areas. The Navy had more than 100 ships in the area and 75,000 Navy personnel afloat and ashore, while more than 67,000 Marines ashore comprised a Marine Expeditionary Force and nearly 18,000 Marines embarked aboard naval vessels brought the Marine Corps presence to nearly 85,000.

1991—Continued

16 January President George H. W. Bush addressed the nation at 9:00 p.m. EST and announced that the liberation of Kuwait from Iraq, Operation Desert Storm, had begun.

A P-3C over the Arabian desert during Operation Desert Storm.

17 January Over 100 Tomahawk cruise missiles were launched at preprogrammed targets by nine U.S. Navy ships in the Mediterranean, Persian Gulf, and Red Sea. This was the start of Operation Desert Storm and the first combat launch of the Tomahawk missile. The Navy launched 228 combat sorties from *John F. Kennedy*, *Saratoga*, and *America* in the Red Sea; *Midway* and *Ranger* in the Persian Gulf; and *Theordore Roosevelt* en route to the Persian Gulf.

17 January An F/A-18C from *Saratoga*'s VFA-81 was shot down by an Iraqi surface-to-air missile. Pilot Lieutenant Commander Michael Speicher became the first American casualty of the Persian Gulf War.

17 January At 7:15 p.m. EST (2: 15 a.m. local time), an estimated eight Iraqi Scud missiles attacked the Israeli cities of Haifa and Tel Aviv, causing property damage. The Pentagon announced that stationary Scud sites in Iraq had been destroyed and the mobile sites were being sought out. The U.S. was also preparing to send additional Patriot antimissile batteries to Israel.

17 January F/A-18Cs piloted by Lieutenant Commander Mark Fox and Lieutenant Nick Mongillo of VFA-81, assigned to *Saratoga*, each shot down a MiG-21. They were the first-ever aerial victories for the Hornet.

18 January Navy lost two additional aircraft, both A-6s. The crewmen, Lieutenants Jeffrey Zaun and Robert Wetzel of *Saratoga*'s VA-35 and Lieutenants Charles Turner and William Costen of *Ranger*'s VA-155 were first reported missing and later as announced as being prisoners of war.

18 January A Marine Corps OV-10A observation aircraft was shot down by Iraqi forces. Lieutenant Colonel William R. Acree and Chief Warrant Officer 4 Guy Hunter of VMO-2 were both captured.

18 January *Nicholas*' HSL-44 (Det 8) SH-60Bs provided air targeting while a Kuwaiti patrol boat, two Army helicopter gunships, and *Nicholas* (FFG 47) engaged and neutralized Iraqi forces on nine oil platforms in the Durrah oil field. The Iraqi forces were manning antiaircraft artillery sites on the platforms. This was the first combined helicopter, missile, and surface ship gun engagement of the war and resulted in the destruction of the positions and capture of the first Iraqi prisoners of wars.

19 January *Theodore Roosevelt* and her battle group transited the Strait of Hormuz and entered the Persian Gulf.

19 January The first combat use of SLAM occurred when launched from A-6 Intruders and A-7 Corsair IIs based aboard *John F. Kennedy* and *Saratoga*.

20 January Iraqi television broadcast ran what it claimed were interviews with three U.S. and four Allied military airmen shot down in the war in the Persian Gulf. The U.S. State Department called the Iraqi charge d'affaires in Washington to protest that the broadcast was contrary to the Third Geneva Convention governing treatment of prisoners of war and to demand that any prisoners be given immediate access to representatives of the International Committee of the Red Cross, the internationally recognized overseer of the convention. The tapes were shown on U.S. television the following day.

20 January Department of Defense announced that an Iraqi artillery battery was destroyed by a Navy A-6 and an Air Force A-10 aircraft.

21 January President George H. W. Bush signed an executive order designating the Arabian Peninsula areas, airspace, and adjacent waters as a combat zone.

21 January An F-14 was downed by a surface-to-air missile over Iraq. Pilot Lieutenant Devon Jones and Radar Intercept Officer Lieutenant Lawrence Slade of *Saratoga*'s VF-103 were reported missing. Lieutenant Jones was recovered the following day, but Slade was captured as a prisoner of war.

1991—Continued

21 January *Theodore Roosevelt* battle group arrived on station in the Persian Gulf.

23 January Navy A-6s disabled an al-Qaddisiya-class Iraqi tanker that had been collecting and reporting intelligence data. The A-6s also attacked and sank a Winchester-class hovercraft (being refueled by the tanker) and a Zhuk patrol boat.

24 January Navy A-6s attacked and destroyed an Iraqi Spasilac minelayer. An A-6 sank an Iraqi Zhuk-class patrol boat and another Iraqi minesweeper hit an Iraqi mine while attempting to evade the A-6 fire. A-6s and F/A-18s attacked the Umm Qasr Naval Base.

24 January The first Kuwaiti territory, the island of Jazirat Qurah, was reclaimed.

28 January Navy A-6s attacked Iraqi ships at Bubiyan Channel, at Umm Qasr Naval Base, and in Kuwait harbor.

28 January Captain Michael Berryman of VMA-311 was captured by Iraqi forces after his AV-8B Harrier was shot down.

30 January Navy A-6s attacked three Iraqi landing craft in the vicinity of Shatt al-Arab Channel.

30 January All 18 F/A-18s aboard *Saratoga* delivered 100,000 pounds of MK-83 1,000-pound bombs on Iraqi positions in Kuwait. This was the largest amount of bomb tonnage carried in a single mission.

1 February VAW-123 coordinated aircraft on the first of 11 Scud missile patrols flown from 1-7 February. On 3 February, *America* confirmed the destruction of two Scud-related vehicles.

2 February A Navy A-6 with crew members Lieutenant Commander Barry Cooke and Lieutenant Patrick Kelly Connor, from *Theodore Roosevelt's* VA-36, were shot down by antiaircraft fire. The crewmen were reported missing. This was *Theodore Roosevelt's* first combat loss of the war.

5 February A Navy F/A-18A crashed while returning from a combat mission. The pilot, Lieutenant Robert Dwyer of VFA-87 from *Theodore Roosevelt*, was killed.

6 February An F-14A from VF-1, off *Ranger*, piloted by Lieutenant Stuart Broce, with Commander Ron McElraft as Radar Intercept Officer, downed a MI-8 Hip helicopter with an AIM-9M Sidewinder missile.

7 February A-6s attacked and heavily damaged two Iraqi patrol boats in the northern Persian Gulf near al-Faw Peninsula.

8 February A-6s attacked and neutralized an Iraqi training frigate co-located with a TMC-45 class patrol boat (Exocet capable craft) at Cor al-Zubayr.

9 February Captain Russell Sanborn, USMC, was captured by Iraqi forces after his VMA-231 AV-8B was shot down.

14 February *America* battle group transited the Strait of Hormuz en route to operations in the Persian Gulf.

15 February *America* became the first and only carrier to conduct strikes from both sides of the Arabian Peninsula.

18 February An Iraqi mine blasted a 20-by-30 foot hole in the forward section of the 18,000-ton helicopter carrier *Tripoli* during mine clearance operations in the northern Persian Gulf. After continuing her duty for five days, *Tripoli*, the flagship of the minesweeping operation, returned to a shipyard drydock in Bahrain for a month of repairs.

20 February *America's* VS-32 became the first S-3 squadron to engage, bomb, and destroy a hostile vessel, an Iraqi gunboat.

20–24 February Using the AV-8B Harrier, the VMA-331 Bumblebees flew 243 sorties along the Iraqi border and throughout Kuwait.

23 February *America*, *Midway*, *Theodore Roosevelt*, and *Ranger* were in the Persian Gulf. *John F. Kennedy* and *Saratoga* were operating from the Red Sea.

23 February Aircraft from *America* destroyed a Silkworm (antiship) missile battery after Iraq unsuccessfully fired a missile at *Missouri* (BB 63).

23 February A VMA-542 AV-8B Harrier was shot down by Iraqi forces. Captain James Wilbourn, USMC was killed in action.

23 February The SAR team from NAS Lemoore, Calif., saved a 19-year-old male who had been missing for five days. He was found on a 6,000-foot elevation in very rocky terrain at the southern edge of Sequoia National Park. The SAR team was called in to assist the Tulare County Sheriff's Department.

1991—Continued

S-3 Vikings fly over burning Kuwaiti oil fields.

24 February   Operation Desert Sabre, the ground offensive against Iraq, began. General Norman Schwarzkopf's plan was based on the classic principles of war: deception, concentration of force, and speed.

25 February   Two Marine Corps aircraft were shot down by Iraqi forces. Captain Scott Walsh was rescued after his VMA-542 AV-8B was lost. Major Joseph Small was captured and Captain David Spellacy was killed when their OV-1OA was shot down.

26 February   A-6Es from *Ranger's* VA-155 bombed Iraqi troops fleeing Kuwait City to Basra in "bumper to bumper" convoys along two multi-lane highways. Numerous tanks, armored vehicles, jeeps, cars, and tractor-trailers were destroyed.

27 February   At 9:00 p.m. EST, President George H. W. Bush declared that Kuwait had been liberated and that the Persian Gulf War over. At midnight EST, all U.S. and coalition forces would suspend further offensive combat operations.

27 February   Forty Iraqi soldiers, thinking it was manned, surrendered to battleship *Wisconsin's* (BB 64) RPV when it flew over their position.

27 February   Captain Reginald Underwood, USMC was killed when his VMA-331 AV-8B was shot down by Iraqi forces.

3 March   CH-46 helicopters with loudspeakers rounded up surrendering Iraqi troops on Faylaka Island. The enemy prisoners of war were ferried by helicopter to *Ogden* (LPD 5) for further transport to Saudi prisoner of war facilities.

4 March   Iraq released POWs including the Navy's Lieutenants Jeffrey Zaun, Robert Wetzel, and Lawrence Slade. The prisoners of war were turned over to U.S. officials by the International Committee of the Red Cross near the Jordanian border station of Ruwayshid.

4 March   *America* departed the Persian Gulf and returned to the Red Sea after conducting 3,008 combat sorties during the war.

6 March   *New Orleans,* with a minecountermeasures squadron on board and four mine-countermeasures ships, led minesweeping activities.

6 March   President George H. W. Bush reported to a joint session of Congress, "Aggression is defeated. The war is over."

1991—Continued

8 March   Lieutenant Kathy Owens became the last pilot to land on the training carrier *Lexington* after the Navy made a quick decision late in the day to decommission the ship. She was the first woman pilot to get that distinction on a carrier, which was the first to have women crew members. Lieutenant Owens has flown with VRC-40—a C-2 squadron based in Norfolk, Va.—since January 1990. Lieutenant Paul Villagomez, AMH1 Donnie E. Kicklighter, and AD2 Mark F. Pemrick were also members of the flight crew.

11 March   *Saratoga* and *Midway* battle groups departed the Persian Gulf area for their respective homeports. *Saratoga* transited the Suez Canal en route to Mayport, Fla.; *Midway* departed the Persian Gulf en route to Yokosuka, Japan.

12 March   *John F. Kennedy* transited the Suez Canal en route to the Mediterranean.

13 March   President George H. W. Bush established the Southwest Asia Service Medal by executive order. It would be awarded to U.S. military personnel who served in the Persian Gulf area during the operations.

16–22 March   *America* conducted a port visit to Hurghada, Egypt, making the first port call of the deployment after 78 consecutive days at sea.

17 March   *Tripoli* was awarded the Combat Action Ribbon for being endangered by enemy mine attack on 18 February.

28 March   *John F. Kennedy* and *Saratoga*, leading their battle groups, arrived at their home ports of Norfolk, Va., and Mayport, Fla., respectively. They were the first battle groups involved in the Persian Gulf War to return to the U.S.

29 March   *Kitty Hawk*, her flight deck modified to accommodate F/A-18 Hornet aircraft, left the Philadelphia Naval Shipyard, Pa., to conduct sea trials. This was the first time the 80,000-ton carrier had moved under her own power since arriving in Philadelphia three and one-half years before undergoing a SLEP overhaul.

1 April   *Theodore Roosevelt* transited the Strait of Bab el-Mandeb and began three weeks of Red Sea operations.

3 April   *America* transited the Suez Canal and returned to the Mediterranean.

6 April   Iraq accepted United Nations terms for a formal cease-fire in the Persian Gulf War.

8 April   *America* transited the Strait of Gibraltar and returned to the Atlantic.

8 April   Having left from both NAS Sigonella, Sicily, and Hurghada, Egypt, for Diyarbakir, Turkey, on April 6, HC-4 detachments flew Secretary of State James A. Baker III and his party of 60 along the border between Turkey and civil war-torn Iraq to a remote Kurdish refugee camp. A popular uprising in Kurdistan had taken place in March against Saddam Hussein, but the Iraqi forces quickly recaptured the main towns and cities of Kurdistan. The Iranians had allowed the Kurds to flee into their country, but the Turks had not, and the Kurds were stranded in the mountains in the cold.

A flight of VA-72 A-7E Corsair IIs after departing John F. Kennedy en route home following their service in Desert Storm. VA-72 and VA-46 were the last two A-7 squadrons operational deployed.

1991—Continued

9 April   HC-4 returned to Incirlik, Turkey, to become the primary and first heavy lift helicopter combat logistics support asset for Operation Provide Comfort. The squadron delivered massive amounts of relief aid to Kurdish refugees and flew needy people to safe havens.

9 April   UN Security Council approved Resolution 689 establishing a United Nations-Iraq-Kuwait Observer Mission to monitor the permanent cease-fire.

11 April   The Persian Gulf War came to its official conclusion at 10:00 a.m. EDT as UN Security Council Resolution No. 687, establishing a permanent cease-fire in the Persian Gulf War, went into effect.

11 April   After 28 years in production and 548 deliveries, the final P-3 Orion was turned over to the Navy. The ceremonies were held at Lockheed Aeronautical Systems Company's Palmdale, Calif., production facility.

15 April   NAVAIR established the HH-1N designation for many of the H-1 Huey helicopters. The redesignation was to be completed by 30 September.

17 April   *Midway* returned from the Persian Gulf War to her home port of Yokosuka, Japan.

17 April   Secretary of Defense Richard Cheney signed an order directing military commanders to begin implementing the president's plan, announced the previous day at a press conference, which called for the establishment of several encampments in northern Iraq. U.S., British, French, and Turkish military personnel had been delivering relief supplies to the refugees. The U.S. Sixth Fleet's 24th Marine Expeditionary Unit commenced operations 17 hours after arrival at the Humanitarian Service Support Base at Silopi, Iraq. A forward humanitarian service support base was also established at Diyarbakir, Turkey.

18 April   *America* returned from the Persian Gulf War to Norfolk, Va.

20 April   *Theodore Roosevelt* transited the Suez Canal and began support of Operation Provide Comfort, the Allied nations' effort to aid Kurdish refugees who were in danger of extermination in the aftermath of the Persian Gulf War.

20 April   *Theodore Roosevelt* joined the U.S. naval forces, including *Guadalcanal*, positioned off Turkey to support an estimated 7,000 American ground troops participating in Operation Provide Comfort, the relief effort for Kurdish refugees.

1 May   The Navy redesignated all F-14A aircraft that had undergone the A+/A(Plus) conversion as F-14B aircraft.

7–8 May   Two A-6E Intruders on a reconnaissance mission over northern Iraq were attacked by Iraqi artillery units. These were the first confirmed incidents of hostile fire since Allied forces began occupying a designated security zone for Kurdish refugees. The planes were unscathed, continued their mission, and returned safely to *Theodore Roosevelt*, positioned off the coast of Turkey to support U.S. military operations in northern Iraq.

12 May   Eight ships of an amphibious assault group headed by *Tarawa* arrived to begin a large-scale relief effort in Bangladesh, which had been devastated by a cyclone on 30 April. During Operation Sea Angel, CH-53 Sea Stallions, CH-46 Sea Knights, UH-1N Iroquois and AH-1T Sea Cobras carried food, medical supplies, and rescued people who had been isolated by the floods.

15 May   The ES-3A Shadow made its first flight at the Lockheed plant in Palmdale, Calif.

22 May   The House Armed Services Committee voted to allow women to fly combat missions in Air Force, Navy, and Marine Corps aircraft. The measure was included in an amendment to the 1992 defense budget.

23 May   Commander, Naval Forces, Middle East declared the Kuwaiti port of Ash-Shuwaikh free of ordnance and Iraqi mines, making it the fifth and final in a series of port-clearing missions by Allied forces.

30 May   *Forrestal*, leading a battle group, departed from its home port of Mayport, Fla., for a scheduled deployment to the Mediterranean Sea to relieve the *Theodore Roosevelt* battle group on station in the eastern Mediterranean in support of Operation Provide Comfort.

3 June   An LC-130 Hercules based at NAS Point Mugu, Calif., landed at McMurdo Station, Antarctica, to complete the first mid-winter medical evacuation of critically ill personnel since 1966. Navy pilots and crew from VXE-6 evacuated a member of New Zealand's Division of Science and Industrial Research.

6 June   *America* was among the 10 U.S. Navy ships whom, returning from the Persian Gulf, sailed into New York Harbor as part of the city's fourth annual Fleet Week celebration.

1991—Continued

10 June A traditional New York ticker tape Parade of Heroes saluted all the men and women who served during Operations Desert Shield and Desert Storm culminated the city's Fleet Week.

12–27 June After rumbling for three days, Mount Pinatubo in the Philippines began erupting. Subic Bay Naval Complex suffered major damage. *Abraham Lincoln* with CVW-11 aboard; *Midway* and her battle group; plus three ships from the Amphibious Readiness Group Alpha, led by *Peleliu*, participated in Operation Fiery Vigil to evacuate the disaster victims. VFA-94, HSL-47, and VC-5 were among those who assisted with the effort.

A VC-5 TA-4J Skyhawk departing NAS Cubi Point, P.I., during eruptions from Mt. Pinatubo.

18 June *Tripoli* turned over her duties as flagship for Commander, U.S. Mine Countermeasures Group, to *Texas* (CGN 39). The group had located and destroyed nearly 1,200 mines in the Persian Gulf.

18–19 June VP-4, in combination with the Coast Guard, carried out a SAR mission and saved two men and one woman who had been forced to ditch from

their Grumman Albatross seaplane, approximately 600 miles east of Oahu.

23 June *Tripoli* transited the Strait of Hormuz en route to San Diego, Calif., her home port, completing a tour in the Persian Gulf which began on 1 December 1990.

28 June *Theodore Roosevelt* battle group returned to Norfolk, Va. She was the last carrier involved in the Persian Gulf War to return to its home port.

8 July An E-2C Hawkeye from Norfolk, Va., based VAW-122 aboard *Forrestal* was ordered to be shot down after suffering an engine fire that could not be extinguished. All five aircrewmen parachuted from the aircraft and were recovered within minutes by helicopters from *Forrestal* and *Yorktown* (CG 48). The incident occurred during a routine flight in support of Operation Provide Comfort.

10 July The President approved the list of military base closures proposed by the Defense Base Closure and Realignment Commission (BRAC). The list included two naval air stations and one Marine Corps air station: NAS Moffett Field, Calif.; NAS Chase Field, Tex.; and MCAS Tustin, Calif.

13 July *Nimitz* battle group turned over operations in the Persian Gulf to *Abraham Lincoln* battle group and transited the Strait of Hormuz.

29 July Grumman delivered the last scheduled production EA-6B Powler carrier-based electronic warfare aircraft to the Navy during ceremonies held at its Calverton, N.Y., plant.

30 July *Kitty Hawk* left her berth at the Philadelphia Naval Ship Yard, Pa., after 40 months of repairs and new equipment. She was the fourth carrier overhauled at the shipyard under SLEP.

31 July The Senate voted overwhelmingly to overturn a 43-year-old law that barred women from flying warplanes in combat. The new measure, an amendment to the military budget bill for the 1992 fiscal year, permitted, but did not require, the armed forces to allow women to fly combat missions.

19 August The Naval Air Reserve celebrated its 75th anniversary.

27 August A ceremony at NAS Jacksonville, Fla., marked the introduction of the SH-60F Seahawk into operational service with the Atlantic Fleet. HS-3 was the first East Coast squadron to trade its SH-3H Sea Kings for the new helicopter.

1991—Continued

27 August The last U.S. Navy participants of the Persian Gulf War arrived home, including *New Orleans*, with HMM-268 embarked.

6 September The U.S. Navy made its first flight in the X-31A aircraft at Patuxent River, Md. The X-31 was the first international experimental aircraft development program undertaken by the U.S. Rockwell International was the U.S contractor and Messerschmitt-Bolkow-Blohm was the German contractor. The X-31 was a project of the Advanced Research Projects Agency (ARPA).

7 September Following the banquet of the annual Tailhook Association convention held at the Las Vegas Nevada Hilton, a number of Navy and Marine Corps aviators gathered at parties held throughout the hotel. Accusations of sexual misconduct were alleged. The events surrounding the incidents during the Tailhook Association convention promulgated an intense campaign to increase awareness throughout the Navy—specifically new programs and policies that addressed sexual misconduct and sexual harrasment.

27 September The Douglas A-3 Skywarrior retired from active duty at ceremonies hosted by VAQ-33, NAS Key West, Fla. Ed Heinemann, the designer of the A-3, was on hand. The EA-3Bs of VQ-2 were the last operational "Whales" in the Navy and had served in the Persian Gulf War.

27 September In a televised address, President George H. W. Bush announced that the U.S. would unilaterally reduce nuclear arms, including the withdrawal of all tactical nuclear weapons from Navy ships. Among many provisions, the order directed that all Navy air-deliverable nuclear weapons be withdrawn from all aircraft carriers and stored or destroyed as would all such weapons associated with land-based naval aircraft, such as patrol planes.

1 October Naval Weapons Center, China Lake, Calif.; Naval Air Development Center, Warminster, Pa.; and Naval Ordnance Missile Test Station, White Sands, N.Mex.; were transferred into NAVAIR. The action was in preparation for the consolidation of all naval air activities under the Naval Air Warfare Center, which would be an activity of NAVAIR.

18 October An F/A-18 successfully launched an improved version of the SLAM at the White Sands Missile Range, N.Mex.

20–23 October Naval Aviation units based in the San Francisco Bay area at NAS Alameda, NAS Moffett Field, and NS Treasure Island provided assistance to the fire-fighting efforts during the fire in the Oakland-Berkeley, Calif., area. HS-85 provided airlift support with SH-3s. Reservists were put on alert.

8 November The decommissioning ceremony for *Lexington* was held at NAS Pensacola, Fla. CNO Admiral Frank B. Kelso II was the principle speaker. *Lexington* had been commissioned in 1943 and in World War II was famous as the "Blue Ghost" that the Japanese could not sink. In 1962, she assumed duty as the training carrier assigned to the Naval Air Training Command in Pensacola, Fla. During her career she had been assigned the following designations: CV 16, CVS 16, CVT 16 and AVT 16.

9 November Two HS-9 helicopter crews of CVW-17 assigned to *Saratoga* rescued three commercial fishermen from their sinking boat 50 miles off Mayport, Fla. A Coast Guard helicopter saved a fourth. The fishermen were taken aboard *Saratoga* for medical care.

12 November A ceremony at NAS Corpus Christi, Tex., marked the establishment in September of the Naval Air Training Maintenance Support Activity. Captain David Timmons was the first CO. The establishment of NATMSACT was the culmination of a trend over 15 years toward maintaining training aircraft with contract civilians in place of military personnel.

4 December U.S. Navy T-45A Goshawk made its first aircraft carrier landing aboard *John F. Kennedy*.

1992

1 January Naval Air Warfare Center (NAWC) was established under the Commander, Naval Air Systems Command. The new activity's first commander was Rear Admiral George Strohsahl. NAWC was to have two divisions: Aircraft (AD) and Weapons (WD).

2 January The Naval Air Warfare Center Aircraft Division (NAWC AD) was established at NAS Patuxent River, Md. Rear Admiral Strohsahl was its first commander (acting). Rear Admiral (sel.) Barton Strong was scheduled to arrive in February or March to assume command of the division. Under the realignment, NAS Patuxent River reported to Commander, NAWC AD. NAWC AD was responsible for aircraft, engines, avionics, and aircraft support. It absorbed activities of the Naval Air Development Center, Warminster, Pa.; the Naval Air Engineering Center, Lakehurst, N.J.; the Naval Air Propulsion Center, Trenton, N.J.; the Naval Avionics

1992—Continued

Center, Indianapolis, Ind.; and the Naval Air Test Center, Patuxent River, Md. The operating site at Warminster was eventually to be consolidated at Patuxent River, Md.

2 January Flight Test and Engineering Group (FTEG) was established under NAWC AD. The Naval Air Test Center (NATC) Patuxent River, Md., was disestablished the same day. The old NATC directorates became directorates under FTEG. Captain Robert Parkinson, former NATC deputy commander, became the director of FTEG.

9 January The Department of Defense announced its acceptance of an offer from the government of Saudi Arabia to award its Kuwait Liberation Medal to members of the U.S. armed forces who directly participated in Operation Desert Storm. The award had been estab-

lished by King Fahd bin Abdul Aziz of Saudi Arabia to honor the outstanding performance of coalition forces in their historic liberation of Kuwait last year.

13 January In a memorandum, Secretary of the Navy (SECNAV) directed the Navy and Marine Corps to integrate VMFA and VMAQ squadrons into Navy CVWs, in order to reduce the requirements for F-14s, F/A-18s, and EA-6Bs. Historically, Marine tactical squadrons had operated frequently as part of carrier air wings, but rarely had this concept been institutionalized in any permanent form.

18 January VMFA-112 at NAS Dallas, Tex., the last operational squadron to fly the F-4 Phantom II, held a retirement ceremony for its last F-4. The last operational flight was made by Colonel John Brennan of the VMFA-112 on 10 January. The first flight of the Navy's Phantom II, the F4H-1, had taken place on 27 May 1958.

An F-14 Tomcat flies over a liberated Kuwait.

1992—Continued

19 January   Naval Aviation History Office commemorated its fiftieth anniversary by preparing for its move to new quarters in the Washington Navy Yard.

21 January   The Naval Air Warfare Center Weapons Division (NAWC WD) was established during a ceremony at Point Mugu, Calif., Rear Admiral William E. Newman was its first commander. NAWC WD headquarters was located at Point Mugu and China Lake, with a facility at White Sands. NAWC WD was responsible for aircraft weapons and weapons systems, simulators and targets. It absorbed the activities of the Pacific Missile Test Center, Point Mugu, Calif; the Naval Weapons Center, China Lake, Calif.; the Naval Weapons Evaluation Facility, Albuquerque, N.Mex.; and the Naval Ordnance Missile Test Station, White Sands, N.Mex.

21 January   The Naval Air Station, Point Mugu, Calif. was disestablished, with Naval Air Weapons Station, Point Mugu, taking its place the same day. This action left NAVAIR with NAS Patuxent River, Md., as the command's only remaining air station. At one time, NAVAIR had NAS Lakehurst, N.J., and NAS Point Mugu.

22 January   Naval Air Weapons Station, China Lake, Calif., was established at the site of the former Naval Weapons Center.

23 January   The first production U.S. Navy T-45A Goshawk jet trainer rolled out at the McDonnell Aircraft facility in St. Louis, Mo. The T-45 Training System is the Navy's first totally integrated training system, combining computer-based academics, simulators, trainer aircraft, and a training integration system and contractor logistic support.

31 January   The Navy took delivery of the last production A-6 Intruder from Grumman, closing out over 31 years of Intruder production. The aircraft was to be delivered to VA-145 at NAS Whidbey Island, Wash.

4 February   Mr. Pete Williams, the Assistant Secretary of Defense (Public Affairs), stated that the Navy's goal of active carriers was twelve.

5 February   *Forrestal*, the Navy's first super carrier was redesignated a training carrier at her new home port, NAS Pensacola, Fla. This brought the Navy's total of active carriers down to 14 active and one training carrier. *Forrestal* was scheduled to replace *Lexington* as the Navy's training carrier.

6 February   A ceremony at NAS Barbers Point, Hawaii, marked the beginning of HSL-37's transition from the SH-2F Seasprite helicopter to the SH-60B.

11 February   VA-34 Blue Blasters became the first fleet A-6E squadron to fire a AGM-65E laser-guided Maverick missile during an exercise in the Arabian Gulf.

14 February   VMFA(AW)-225 formally accepted the first fleet two-seat F/A-18D Hornet at MCAS El Toro, Calif. This was the first aircraft capable of operating the new ATARPS.

24 February   McDonnell Douglas and British Aerospace reached an exclusive partnership agreement, pending U.S. government approval to work together to develop and produce advanced short takeoff/vertical landing (ASTOVL) strike fighter aircraft.

4 March   NAWC AD Patuxent River, Md., officially stood up in ceremonies held at NAS Patuxent River. Rear Admiral (Sel.) Barton Strong assumed command of the division.

4 March   VAW-113 at NAS North Island, Calif., became the first fleet squadron to accept delivery of the E-2C Group II aircraft, which was equipped with the new APS-145 radar.

10 March   The Department of Defense announced its plan for the withdrawal from the Philippine Naval Facility at Subic Bay. Major milestones in the plan included: closure of DoD dependents schools in June; transfer of the majority of dependents throughout the summer months; relocation of Fleet Logistics & Support Squadron 50 to Anderson AFB, Guam, in August; disestablishment of the ship Repair Facility in September; and formal final turnover of the facility to the Philippine government in December.

21 March   *Independence* with CVW-5 on board, departed Subic Bay, the last carrier scheduled to call at the base before its closure.

31 March   NASA announced that Lieutenant Commander Wendy B. Lawrence had been chosen to be among the space agencys' new astronauts. Lieutenant Commander Lawrence was the first Navy woman line officer Naval Aviator astronaut.

1 April   Fleet Electronic Warfare Support Group (FEWSG) merged with the Fleet Deception Group, Atlantic to form the Fleet Practical Readiness Group. The new command, based at Naval Amphibious Base, Little Creek, Va., assumed operational control of FEWSG's electronic aggressor squadrons VAQ-33, -34, and -35.

1992—Continued

1 April   By CNO direction, the remaining A-7 aircraft in the active inventory were to be retired by 1 April. The decision was partially reversed, however, in order to retain 11 TA-7C and 3 EA-7L aircraft on strength with NAWC as chase aircraft for various programs, including the Tomahawk missile program.

8 April   McDonnell Douglas delivered the 6,000th production missile of the Harpoon (AGM-84) program to the Navy during a ceremony at the Company's manufacturing facility in St. Charles, Mo. The Harpoon had been used successfully by Naval Aviation in combat against Libyan and Iranian forces and, in its SLAM version, against Iraqi forces.

13–25 March   In response to a request from Italian authorities to save the town of Zafferana from a lava flow advancing from Mount Etna, two Marine CH-53E Super Stallions from HMM(C)-226 aboard *Inchon* augmented by a CH-53E from Sigonella-based HC-4 placed 8000-pound concrete blocks in the path of the lava. As geologists had hoped, the concrete forced open another lava vent further down the mountain away from the town.

22 March   U.S. and Australia began Coral Sea '92, joint military exercises off the east coast of Australia, coinciding with the 50th anniversary of the Battle of the Coral Sea.

1 May   The first class of flight instructors from VT-21, assigned to train the next generation of Naval Aviators in the new T-45A Goshawk, began their own training in the T-45A.

1 May   Strategic Communications Wing ONE was established at Tinker AFB, Okla. Operationally, the wing reported to U.S. StratCom and coordinated all TACAMO Operations. The Navy's two TACAMO squadrons, VQ-3 and VQ-4, relocated to Tinker. Administratively the wing would report to CINC-PACFLT via COMNAVAIRPAC to organize, equip, maintain and train subordinate commands and liaison with host Tinker AFB.

7 May   The last TACAMO EC-130 began its final deployment from NAS Patuxent River, Md., with VQ-4. VQ-4 was undergoing a transition from the EC-130Q aircraft to the new E-6A Mercury.

The E-6A Mercury in flight.

1992—Continued

22 May VQ-5 at NAS Agana, Guam, took delivery of its first ES-3A electronic reconnaissance aircraft, marking the operational service entry of this new electronic reconnaissance version of the S-3 aircraft.

31 May Four aviators of the VS-21 Fighting Redtails attached to *Independence* assisted a sea rescue of 19 crewmen from a sinking Panamanian cargo ship, located 580 nautical miles off the coast of Diego Garcia in the Indian Ocean.

27 June VT-21 became operational as the Navy's first training squadron to give instructions on the T-45A Goshawk.

1 July Helicopter Sea Control Wing 3 was redesignated Helicopter Antisubmarine Light Wing 1 absorbing Helicopter Sea Control Wing 1 at the same time, placing all Atlantic Fleet Helicopter Antisubmarine Light squadrons (HSLs) under one wing.

10 July The last production Grumman F-14D Tomcat was delivered to the Navy. The F-14D was powered by two General Electric F-110-GE-400 augmented turbofans with afterburners of 27,000 pounds per engine. This model had improved avionics, ECCM, and enhanced radar. This marked the end of 22 years of production of the F-14 Tomcat fighter.

20 July The fourth prototype of the V-22A Osprey tilt-rotor aircraft crashed into the Potomac River on approach to MCAF Quantico, Va., killing three Marines and four Boeing employees. The remaining three prototypes were grounded pending the results of the mishap investigation. The mishap was blamed on mechanical failure.

22 July In a press conference at the Pentagon, Acting Secretary of the Navy Sean O'Keefe and CNO Admiral Frank B. Kelso II announced a sweeping reorganization of the OPNAV staff. The plan, developed by Admiral Kelso, aligns the OPNAV staff with the Joint Staff. The reorganization was scheduled to be in effect on 1 January 1993. The Assistant Chiefs of Naval Operations (ACNO) for Submarine Warfare (OP-02), Surface Warfare (OP-03), Air Warfare (OP-05), and Naval Warfare (OP-07) would merge into one staff under the DCNO for Resources, Warfare Requirements and Assessment (code N8), a three-star flag officer. The new designation assigned to ACNO (Air Warfare (OP-05)) was Director, Air Warfare (N88).

24 July *Saratoga* became the first U.S. aircraft carrier ever to conduct sustained flight operations in the Adriatic Sea. She was sent there in response to the strife in the former Yugoslavian republic of Bosnia-Herzegovina. Deployed with the *Saratoga* was the amphibious ship *Iwo Jima*.

5 August The Pentagon announced that it would ask contractors to develop a less expensive version of the V-22 Osprey tilt-rotor aircraft.

10 August The OPNAV Staff commenced the administrative conversion to N-codes. The reorganization would provide closer liaison with the Army and Air Force and optimize early cross-service technology and requirements discussions. The ACNO (Air Warfare) (OP-05) became N88, one echelon under N8 the DCNO (Resources, Warfare Requirements & Assessment.)

12 August Commander-in-Chief, U.S. Pacific Fleet, announced the formation of six permanent battle groups.

22–26 August Hurricane Andrew, the most expensive natural disaster ever to strike the U.S., ravaged the Bahamas, Florida and Louisiana, leveling Homestead AFB, Fla. Naval Aviation units were called into action to help relieve the suffering of hundreds of thousands of Americans. Navy ships with supplies and repair capabilities steamed from East Coast ports for Florida.

23 August *Independence* entered the Persian Gulf prepared to enforce an Allied ban on Iraqi flights over south Iraq below the 32nd parallel. On 26 August President George H. W. Bush announced that the United States and its allies had informed Iraq that in 24 hours Allied aircraft would fly surveillance missions in southern Iraq and were prepared to shoot down any Iraqi aircraft flying south of the 32nd parallel. The action was precipitated by Iraq's failure to comply with UN Resolution 688 which demanded that the Iraqi Government stop the repression of its Shiite population in southern Iraq.

27 August Operation Southern Watch—Persian Gulf allies began to enforce the ban on Iraqi planes from flying south of the 32nd parallel. Any Iraqi planes that violated the ban would be shot down. *Independence* and *Saratoga*, and the amphibious ship *Iwo Jima* participated. Twenty Navy aircraft from CVW-5 aboard *Independence* in the Persian Gulf were the first coalition aircraft on station over Iraq as Operation Southern Watch began. Southern Watch was the enforcement of a ban on Iraqi warplanes and helicopters from flying

1992—Continued

south of the 32nd parallel and attacking Shiite Moslem ethnic groups in the marshes of southern Iraq. Any Iraqi aircraft caught airborne would be shot down. Marine Corps AV-8B Harriers from *Tarawa* also supported the operation.

28 August Typhoon Omar devastated Guam. Joint Task Force Marianas coordinated the relief efforts of all the military services. Naval Aviation units involved in relief efforts included NAS Agana, Guam, HC-5, VRC-50, VQ-1, VR-59 and VQ-5.

4 September Two CH-53E and two AH-1W helicopters from *Iwo Jima*, stationed in the Adriatic in support of the UN relief efforts to the Bosnian capital of Sarajevo, rushed to the scene of an Italian Air Force G.222 transport downed by a SAM. The helicopters drew fire from the ground, but were undamaged.

4 September Commander Linda V. Hutton assumed command of VRC-40 becoming the first woman to command an Atlantic Fleet aircraft squadron.

11 September Hurricane Iniki, the strongest storm to hit the Hawaiian Islands in 90 years, devastated 75 to 80 percent of the island of Kauai. NAS Barbers Point and its tenant commands provided volunteers and assisted local residents. *Belleau Wood* sailed to Kauai with troops and relief supplies. Pacific Missile Range Facility, Barking Sands on Kauai was only slightly damaged and served as a hub of relief flight operations. Navy and Marine Corps aircraft flew in supplies and personnel. VP-1 and HSL-37 also participated in the relief effort.

14 September *Forrestal* arrived at Philadelphia Naval Shipyard, Pa., from NAS Pensacola, Fla., to commence a 14-month $157-million complex overhaul. *Forrestal* would then be used as a training carrier. The Navy, however, decided in early 1993 to mothball *Forrestal* in Philadelphia and leave the Navy without a dedicated training carrier.

16 September President George H. W. Bush dispatched the *Tarawa* Amphibious Ready Group to the coast of Somalia as part of Operation Provide Relief, a multinational effort to relieve the massive starvation in the country. The Marine Harrier (AV-8B) aircraft and helicopters from HMM-161(R) stood ready offshore to protect relief teams and transport aircraft bringing in a contingent of Pakistani peace-keeping troops to Mogadishu, the capital city.

16 September *Ranger* arrived on station in the Persian Gulf in support of Operation Southern Watch, enforcing the no-fly zone over Iraq south of the 32nd parallel.

28 September Secretary of the Navy Sean O'Keefe, CNO Admiral Frank B. Kelso II and Commandant of the Marine Corps General Carl E. Mundy, Jr. signed a new Navy/Marine Corps strategy, entitled ". . From the Sea." The new strategy was developed in response to the shift in the threat from global to regional. It emphasized littoral warfare and maneuver from the sea.

30 September The four functional wings (Helicopter Wings, Atlantic; Patrol Wings, Atlantic; Strike-Fighter Wings, Atlantic; and Tactical Wings, Atlantic) of COMNAVAIRLANT were disestablished in a sweeping change that eliminated an entire echelon of command in the administrative structure of Naval Aviation on the East Coast.

30 September The Naval Base at Subic Bay, the last military base in Southeast Asia, was turned over formally to the Philippine Government.

7 October *John F. Kennedy*, with CVW-3 on board, and her battle group left for a six-month deployment to the Mediterranean Sea to relieve *Saratoga*. The tensions in the area involved the civil war in the former Yugoslavia and conflicts with Iraq's president Saddam Hussein.

15 October HS-14 became the first U.S. squadron to land aircraft (the SH-3H Sea King) on the deck of a Russian warship, RNS *Admiral Vinogradov*, a Udaloy-class destroyer.

22 October The Department of Defense announced the awarding of a contract to the Bell-Boeing Joint Program Office for the modification and test of a V-22 derivative. The aircraft was in consonance with the Secretary of Defense letters of 2 July 1992 to Congressional leadership. It was a scaled-down version of the V-22 tilt-rotor aircraft.

24 October The Atlantic Fleet reorganized into six permanent battle groups. The forming of permanent battle groups was a major change in fleet composition. Previous Navy plans called for forming battle groups for specific workups and deployments.

30 October NAS Cubi Point, Republic of the Philippines, was disestablished ending almost a century of American military presence in the Philippines. The occasion was marked by a public ceremony.

1992—Continued

The complex wing and rotor folding arrangement of the MV-22A Osprey.

The MV-22A Osprey.

1992—Continued

3 November   The Presidential Commission on the Assignment of Women in the Armed Forces recommended against allowing military women to fly in combat, but for allowing women to serve in some combat ships.

7 November   In support of Operation Provide Promise, an ARG centered on *Guam* with HMM-261 (reinforced) embarked, relieved *Iwo Jima* ARG, with HMM-365 (reinforced) aboard, in the Adriatic.

14 November   The Rolling Airframe Missile (RAM) System was installed on *Peleliu*. RAM is a lightweight, quick reaction, high-firepower weapon system.

14 November   *Lexington*, the Navy's unsinkable "Blue Ghost" of World War II was officially turned over to the city of Corpus Christi, Tex., during a ceremony. *Lexington*, a memorial/museum ship, was opened for public tours.

7 December   The Navy and McDonnell Douglas Aerospace finalized the $3.715 billion development contract for the advanced F/A-18E/F. The cost-plus incentive contract covers 7.5 years of engineering and support activities, including the manufacturing and testing of seven flight test aircraft and three ground test airframes.

7 December   *Ranger* and her task force, diverted from the Persian Gulf, sailed off the coast of Somalia in support of Operation Restore Hope, the UN-authorized effort to relieve mass starvation amid factional fighting in Somalia.

9 December   Under the leadership of U.S. Armed Forces, Operation Restore Hope began in the early morning darkness. The preannounced landing of U.S. Marines was witnessed by millions of U.S. primetime television viewers. Initially HMM-164 (reinforced from *Tripoli*) provided all of the Marine helicopter support to ground forces in Somalia.

16 December   Five air traffic controllers from *Kitty Hawk* were sent aboard *Leahy* (CG 53) to establish approach control services in and out of Mogadishu in support of Operation Restore Hope. Approaching aircraft were picked up from a VAW-114 E-2C Hawkeye, which tracked flights and issued advisories from about 200 miles out. Once the flights were within 50 miles, the *Leahy* team took over and led them to within visual range of the airport, about 10 miles away.

19 December   Relieving *Ranger* off Somalia, aircraft off *Kitty Hawk* assumed the missions of photo-reconnaissance, armed reconnaissance, and show of force to discourage opposition to Operation Restore Hope.

27 December   Iraqi jets violated the "no-fly zone" below the 32nd Parallel resulting in the loss of a MiG-25 to an AIM-120 AAMRAM missile fired by a U.S. Air Force F-16D. *Kitty Hawk*, diverted from relief efforts off the coast of Somalia to the Persian Gulf, dispatched F-14A and F/A-18A fighters in support of Operation Southern Watch.

1993

1 January   In a reorganization of the OPNAV Staff, the position of ACNO (Air Warfare)/(OP-05), held by Rear Admiral Riley D. Mixon, became Director, Air Warfare (N88) reporting to the DCNO (Resources, Warfare Requirements and Assessment)/(N8). N88 was reduced from a three-star to a two-star billet.

13 January   Squadrons from CVW-15, embarked on *Kitty Hawk* in the Persian Gulf, launched 35 aircraft to lead a coalition strike on Iraqi missile sites. *Kitty Hawk* had been in the Indian Ocean in support of Operation Restore Hope, but was ordered into the Persian Gulf after an Iraqi MiG-25 violated the UN-imposed no-fly zone in southern Iraq on 27 December 1992.

17 January   Four U.S. Navy ships in the Persian Gulf and Red Sea launched Tomahawk cruise missiles at the Zaafaraniyah Nuclear Fabrication Facility located in the Baghdad area. The facility made nuclear weapons parts.

18 January   *John F. Kennedy* battle group moved on station in the eastern Mediterranean in response to Iraqi violation of the UN imposed "no-fly zone".

23 January   An A-6E of VA-52 launched a laser-guided bomb at an Iraqi anti-aircraft site after the crew thought it was being fired on.

4 February   Commander, Amphibious Squadron 43 embarked on *Tripoli* was relieved as Commander, Naval Forces Somalia (COMNAVFOR SOMALIA) by DESRON 17 embarked on *William H. Standley* (CG 32). COMNAVFOR SOMALIA was charged with providing direct support for Operation Restore Hope, the UN embargo directed by Security Council Resolution 733. *Tripoli* amphibious task unit was the first U.S. military presence on station near the Horn of Africa. It set the base of operations for Operation Restore Hope, the largest peacetime humanitarian mission ever undertaken.

1993—Continued

17 February The Aircraft Carrier Memorial, a 10-ft. black obelisk honoring those who served aboard U.S carriers, was dedicated at NAS North Island, San Diego, Calif.

25 February *John F. Kennedy* battle group entered the Adriatic in support of Operation Provide Promise—the UN effort to supply Bosnia-Herzegovina with food and supplies.

4 March *Constellation* departed Philadelphia Naval Shipyard, Pa., the fifth and last carrier to complete SLEP.

17 March *Saipan* ARG sailed from the East Coast to relieve *Guam* in the Adriatic in support of Operation Provide Promise—the UN effort to supply Bosnia-Herzegovina with food and supplies.

18 March *Kitty Hawk* battle group was relieved by *Nimitz* battle group and headed for home, after having operated in the Indian Ocean and Persian Gulf and participated in Operations Restore Hope and Southern Watch.

23 March The ARG centered around *Wasp* arrived off Somalia to support UN relief efforts in Operation Restore Hope. Marine helicopters and Harriers from HMM-263 embarked on *Wasp* flew sorties in support of Marines in Somalia.

31 March Two VQ-2 EP-3E aircraft were on station over the Adriatic providing crucial support to the delivery of humanitarian air drops over eastern Bosnia-Herzegovina in Operation Provide Promise.

1 April Sea Strike Wing One was redesignated Sea Control Wing LANT. The Air Antisubmarine Squadrons were redesignated Sea Control Squadron; the short designator "VS" was retained. The name change reflected the broader and all-encompassing VS mission, particularly in light of the increased multi-mission versatility of the S-3B aircraft.

8 April *Tripoli* amphibious task force arrived in Pearl Harbor, Hawaii, after a five-month deployment in support of Operation Restore Hope—the UN effort to relieve mass starvation in Somalia. During the support, task force units recovered 30,000 pieces of ordnance and disposed of more than 100,000 pounds of explosives collected from caches throughout the Somali countryside; launched more than 2000 aircraft sorties from *Tripoli* and *Juneau* (LPD 10); delivered more than 175,000 meals and 25,000 gallons of water.

Tripoli off the coast of Mogadishu, Somalia.

1993—Continued

An SH-60B flies past Rushmore (LSD 47) off the coast of Somalia en route to Tripoli.

Marines prepared to embark a waiting CH-46E helo on Tripoli during early hours of Operation Restore Hope.

12 April   NATO officials in conjunction with the UN began the enforcement of a "no-fly zone" over Bosnia-Herzegovina, known as Operation Deny Flight. NATO had proposed the "no-fly zone" to the UN Security Council, who passed Resolution 802. Twelve F/A-18 Hornet strike-fighter aircraft from CVW-8 embarked on *Theodore Roosevelt* were transferred to NATO in support of the operation. Other aircraft and ships from *Theodore Roosevelt*'s battle group provided support. The Mediterranean ARG emarked on *Saipan* provided SAR/TRAP duties.

22 April   A VAQ-209 Starwarriors' EA-6B fired the first successful over-the-horizon HARM Missile using targeting data from space delivered directly to the cockpit.

26 April   VC-6 carried out the first launch of a Pioneer UAV from an amphibious vessel, *Denver* (LPD 9). VC-6 Det 2, NAS Patuxent River, Md., made the launch.

28 April   Secretary of Defense Les Aspin lifted the ban on combat flights for women and opened up additional ships to women. Secretary Aspin further stated that he would forward a draft proposal to Congress, which would remove the last legislative barrier to the assignment of women to combat vessels. The CNO, Admiral Frank B. Kelso II, concurred.

29 April   Following the Secretary of Defence's decision to expand combat roles for women, CNO Admiral Frank B. Kelso II, opened six enlisted Naval Aviation ratings to women: Aviation Antisubmarine Warfare Operator (AW), Electronic Warfare Technician (EW), Fire Controlman (FC), Gas Turbine Technician (GS), Gas Turbine Technician-Electrical (GSE), and Gas Turbine Technical-Mechanical (GSM).

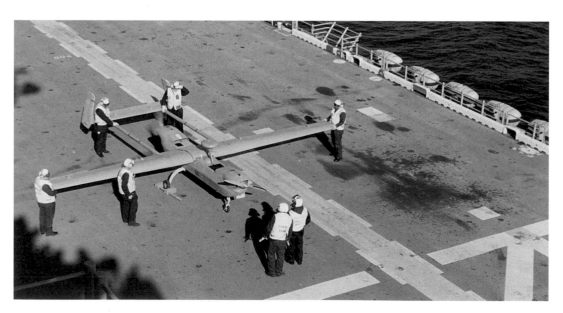

A Unmanned Aerial Vehicle aboard Essex for testing.

1993—Continued

5 May   Commander, Helicopter Antisubmarine Light Wing, U.S. Pacific Fleet (COMHSLWINGPAC) was established in a ceremony at NAS North Island, Calif.; Captain John R. Brown was the first commander of the new type wing.

6 May   Lieutenant Commander Kathryn P. Hire, a Naval Reservist, was selected to be assigned to VP-62. She was the Navy's first woman to become eligible to compete for assignments in aircraft engaged in combat missions.

7 May   Speaking to aviators at the seventh annual Naval Aviation Symposium in Pensacola, Fla., Vice Admiral Ronald J. Zlatoper, Chief of Naval Personnel, outlined the Navy's plan to open new opportunities for women. The first squadron expected to be assigned women was VAQ-130. CVW-3, embarked on *Dwight D. Eisenhower* and CVW-11 on *Abraham Lincoln* were also scheduled to be assigned women.

17 May   Chairman of the Joint Chiefs of Staff, General Colin Powell, approved the Armed Forces Expeditionary Medal for Operation Restore Hope veterans.

1 June   Commander, Strike Fighter Wing, Pacific, changed from a flag-level functional wing to a type wing, as part of the ongoing reorganization of the wings in the Pacific Fleet.

8 June   Commander, Patrol Wing 2 (COMPATWING), was disestablished after 56 years of service.

11 June   Ground breaking took place at NAS Patuxent River, Md., for the new Aircraft Technology Laboratory.

26 June   U.S. Navy surface vessels launched a successful strike on the Iraqi Intelligence Service headquarters building in Baghdad. The action was in response to Iraq's attempt on former President George H. W. Bush's life while on a visit to Kuwait in April. *Theodore Roosevelt* and *Arleigh Burke* (DDG 51) were dispatched to the Red Sea to reinforce the area.

14 July   Secretary of Defense Les Aspin approved an order directing U.S. aircraft to deploy and join NATO's planned air support to the UN protection force in Bosnia. In response to this order, *Theodore Roosevelt* returned to the Mediterranean in support of Operation Deny Flight—the enforcement of the "no-fly zone" over Bosnia-Herzegovina.

11 August   *America* deployed from Norfolk, Va., to relieve *Theodore Roosevelt* in Operation Deny Flight missions over Bosnia-Herzegovina.

17 August   A VAQ-209 Starwarriors' EA-6B and VP-60 Cobras' P-3 conducted the first successful over-the-horizon HARM and Harpoon War-at-Sea strike using targeting data from space delivered directly to the cockpit.

1 September   The Clinton Administration unveiled a new plan for cutting the armed forces based on the Bush Administration's doctrine that the United States should be prepared to fight two simultaneous major regional conflicts and one low intensity conflict. The plan called for 11 battle groups and one carrier to serve as both a reserve and training carrier. The Bush plan had called for 12 battle groups.

3 September   AMRAAM achieved initial operating capability for the Navy with CVW-11 aboard *Abraham Lincoln*.

9 September   NAS Jacksonville, Fla., VP-30 merged with VP-31 based at Moffett Field, Calif., to form the Navy's largest aviation squadron. The consolidation was the result of the military's downsizing. It enabled the Navy to train all P-3 aircraft crews in Jacksonville.

11 September   The Navy's first "supercarrier" *Forrestal* was decommissioned at Pier 6E at the Philadelphia Naval Shipyard, Pa. *Forrestal* was the first carrier designed and built to land jet powered aircraft.

1 October   The NAVCAD program was disestablished. The program was begun during World War II, and initially called the V-5 and then the V-12 program. It was disestablished in 1966, but later reinstated in 1986 to help train more pilots for the planned 600-ship fleet.

1 October   U.S. Atlantic Command (USACOM) became responsible for joint training and deploying of all continental U.S.-based forces. This merged the Army's Forces Command (FORSCOM), the Navy's Atlantic Fleet, the Air Force's Air Combat Command (ACC) and the Marine Forces Atlantic into a single combat command. The Atlantic Command would support all U.S. involvement in UN peacekeeping operations and respond to natural disasters within the United States. The command would also plan for the land defense of the United States.

1 October   The Naval Training Systems Center, Orlando, Fla., was redesignated the Naval Air Warfare Center, Training Systems Division, with no change of mission.

1993—Continued

1 October The first phase of a new Joint Primary Training Program began as five Air Force aviators reported to NAS Whiting Field, Pensacola, Fla., while flight instructors from the Navy, Marine Corps and Coast Guard reported to Randolph AFB, Tex., for training.

15 October Secretary of the Navy John H. Dalton announced the consolidation of Aviation Officer Candidate School (AOCS) and Officer Candidate School (OCS) in Pensacola, Fla. The consolidated school would be called Officer Candidate School and would be located at the Naval Aviation Schools Command in Pensacola. Both aviation and non-aviation officer candidates would attend. The consolidation would save about $1.9 million annually.

17 October *New Orleans* and *Guadalcanal* ARGs arrived off the coast of Mogadishu, Somalia. The ARGs joined the *Abraham Lincoln* which had arrived five days earlier. *Guadalcanal* ARG had been operating in the Adriatic Sea, off the coast of Bosnia-Herzegovina, in support of Operations Provide Promise and Deny Flight.

29 October *America* transited the Suez Canal heading south to relieve *Abraham Lincoln* operating off the coast of Somalia. *Abraham Lincoln* then could return to Alameda, Calif., ending a scheduled six-month deployment.

16 November Aviation Antisubmarine Warfare Operator rating (AW) was changed to Aviation Warfare Systems Operator. The change reflected the broadened scope of responsibilities. The existing rating badge and abbreviation "AW" did not change.

24 November The X-31 International Test Program announced its first two supersonic flights. Aircraft Number 1 flew nine flights achieving Mach 1.08 at an altitude of 37,500 feet. The enhanced fighter maneuverability demonstrator aircraft was being developed by the Navy, the Defense Advanced Research Projects Agency, and the German Ministry of Defense.

30 November President William Clinton signed legislation lifting the ban on women serving on combat ships.

1 December Secretary of the Navy John H. Dalton announced the first assignment of women to combat ships to begin by June 1994, pending notification of Congress as required by the fiscal year 1994 Defense Authorization Bill. *Dwight D. Eisenhower* and *Abraham Lincoln* were both scheduled to be the first carriers to embark women. *John C. Stennis* was scheduled to embark women at the end of 1994.

9 December The V-22 Osprey returned to Patuxent River, Md., from facilities in Wilmington, Del., to begin full engineering manufacturing development testing at the Naval Air Warfare Center Aircraft Division. The new program would usher in a new Integrated Test Team concept of test and evaluation for Naval Aviation.

16 December *Independence* returned to the Arabian Gulf in support of Operation Southern Watch, which ensured Iraqi compliance with the UN imposed "no-fly zone" south of the 32nd parallel.

1994

1 January The Navy began training aviators at NAS Kingsville, Tex., using the new T-45 Training System, which included the T-45 Goshawk jet trainer. The Goshawk was to replace the aging T-2 Buckeye and TA-4 Skyhawk.

18 January In a press briefing held at the Pentagon, Chief of Naval Operations Admiral Frank Kelso II emphasized that while the naval forces of the future will have a smaller number of ships, aircraft and Navy/Marine Corps personnel, the capability of these smaller forces would be significant due to the wise use of technologies and prudent cost-cutting measures.

1 February *Saratoga*, with CVW-17 embarked, took station in the Adriatic Sea. The carrier's Joint Task Group would participate in a variety of U.S., NATO and UN missions throughout the Mediterranean, Black and Red Seas. *Saratoga* and CVW-17 were to provide combat air patrol and command control and surveillance aircraft for Operations Deny Flight and Provide Promise off the coast of Bosnia-Herzegovina.

18 February Ensign Alta DeRoo became the first female Naval Aviator to receive her wings in the E-2 Hawkeye community during a ceremony held in Norfolk, Va.

21 February Lieutenant Shannon Workman became the first female combat pilot to pass successfully fleet carrier qualifications. She was embarked on board *Dwight D. Eisenhower* and assigned to VAQ-130 based at NAS Whidbey Island, Wash. Lieutenant Workman was slated to be one of four female aviators to deploy aboard *Dwight D. Eisenhower* in October.

1994—Continued

3 March *Peleliu* ARG joined the *Inchon* ARG off the coast of Somalia to support the withdrawal of U.S. troops from Somalia.

3 March The last A-6E *Intruder* to receive a composite wing at Naval Aviation Depot, Norfolk, Va., marked the end of the A-6 Composite Rewing Program. The Navy had begun the program in 1990 to replace the metal wings normally used on the aircraft as they reached the end of their fatigue life.

7 March Sixty-three women received orders to *Dwight D. Eisenhower*—the first combat ship to have women permanently assigned.

17 March The X-31 Enhanced Fighter Maneuver-ability aircraft flew at Mach 1.2 using thrust vectoring vanes instead of its tail surfaces for control. This flight was a significant "first" in aviation history.

19 March A T-45 Goshawk, the first U.S. Navy training jet equipped with a digital cockpit (Cockpit-21), was flown by an experimental test pilot in an inaugural flight from McDonnell Douglas facilities in St. Louis, Mo.

24 March The last American military transport ship to depart Somalia, Training Ship *Empire State*, left Modgadishu while *Peleliu* AGR remained off the coast in support of UN operations in Somalia.

31 March The popular name Peregrine was assigned to the BQM-145A medium-range unmanned aerial vehicle.

1 April The first operational flight of the Airborne Multisensor Pod System took place at Naval Air Warfare Center Weapons Division, Point Mugu, Calif.

28 April A *Saratoga*-based F/A-18 Hornet crashed in the Adriatic Sea during takeoff from the carrier, killing the pilot. The death was the first among the NATO allies conducting air operations in support of Bosnia.

29 April The U.S. Navy Penguin (AGM-119B) missile MK-2 Mod 7 reached initial operational capability (IOC) and was launched for the first time by a fleet unit on 25 June when an SH-60B from *Hewitt* (DD 966) fired an operational missile. Penguin is a short-range, inertially guided antiship missile system. HSL-51 Det 6 accomplished the firing at the Pacific Missile Range Facility off the coast of Hawaii as part of RIM-PAC 94 exercises.

2 May Two F-14B Tomcats from VF-103 aboard *Saratoga* delivered three GBU-16 (Paveway II) laser-guided bombs to direct hits at Capo Frasca Target Complex, Sardinia, Italy. This was the first time the F-14 had accomplished this feat.

5 May The House Armed Services Committee approved $3.65 billion for the then-unnamed aircraft carrier CVN 76 and advance procurement for the large-deck amphibious ship LHD 7 as part of its $263.3 billion defense budget for 1995. CVN 76 will become the Navy's twelfth aircraft carrier supported by the Department of Defense's Bottom-Up Review.

16–17 May Russian pilots tested nine F/A-18 Navy fighter jets at Patuxent River, Md., while U.S. Navy pilots sat in the back seat.

5–6 June *George Washington* hosted the nation's top leaders, including President William Clinton and First Lady Hilary Rodham Clinton, on the occasion of the 50th anniversary of D-Day. *George Washington* was first off the coast of Portsmouth, England, and then at sea off the invasion beaches of Omaha and Utah and nearby Pointe du Hoc, where Americans landed on D-Day.

28 June The Georgia-built P-3C Orion rolled out of the assembly hangar at Lockheed Aeronautical Systems Company in Marietta marking the "official" return to production of the maritime patrol aircraft. The aircraft were for the Republic of Korea.

1 July A ceremony marked the closing of NAS Moffett Field, Calif. The air station was commissioned originally as NAS Sunnyvale in 1933. It was the home port of the Navy's dirigible *Macon* (ZRS-5). After *Macon* went down in a storm off Point Sur in 1935, the Navy transferred NAS Sunnyvale to the U.S. Army. The station reverted to the Navy in 1942 and was redesignated NAS Moffett Field, in honor of Rear Admiral W. A. Moffett, who was killed in the crash of the dirigible *Akron* (ZRS-4) in 1933.

1 July The schedule for the Joint Primary Aircraft Training System (JPATS) flight evaluation at Wright-Patterson AFB, Ohio, was established. Aircraft from various manufacturers would be evaluated from 24 July through 8 October. JPATS would replace the T-34C and T-37B with a common training system, including aircraft academics and simulators.

6 July *Inchon* Amphibious Ready Group (ARG) departed Norfolk, Va., en route to the Caribbean waters off the coast of Haiti. The four-ship ARG would aug-

1994—Continued

Former president George Bush, also a Naval Aviator during World War II, visited George Washington in August 1995 to mark the 50th anniversary of V-J day.

ment combined forces already in that region assigned to enforce UN Security Council sanctions aimed at restoring democracy to Haiti.

7 July The popular name White Hawk was established for the VH-60N, whose primary mission was to provide worldwide executive transport in support of the president and his staff.

31 July Lieutenant Kara Hultgreen made her first qualifying landing in an F-14A on board *Constellation*, 110 miles southwest of San Diego, Calif. She thus became the first fully qualified female Tomcat pilot. Lieutenant Hultgreen was assigned to VF-213 at NAS Miramar, Calif. Lieutenant (jg) Carey Dunai, also in an F-14, became the second woman to reach the milestone with her qualifying trap moments later.

17 August *Inchon* ARG returned to its home port of Norfolk, Va. It was relieved by the *Wasp* ARG off the coast of Haiti in support of Operation Support Democracy.

31 August Five Navy MH-53 minesweeper helicopters arrived at MCAS Tustin, Calif., as the H-53 training of both Navy and Marine Corps personnel began to consolidate. With the disestablishment of HM-12, the Navy's H-53 fleet readiness squadron, the Marines assumed the training responsibility in HMT-302.

12–13 September A unique operation developed due to the situation in Haiti. *Dwight D. Eisenhower* and *America* deployed with a large contingent of Army helicopters on board, but no air wings. The carriers headed for the Caribbean in support of President William Clinton's policy to restore democracy to Haiti. *Dwight D. Eisenhower* also embarked Navy squadrons HS-7, HCS-4 and HC-2. This was the first time that carriers deployed operationally with a large contingent of Army helicopters and no air wing on board.

America with a large contingent of army units aboard for deployment to Haiti.

1994—Continued

Army helos leave the deck of Dwight D. Eisenhower.

27 September   After completing the most extensive over-haul in U.S. Navy history at Newport News Shipbuilding, Va., the world's first nuclear-powered aircraft carrier, *Enterprise*, returned to her home port at Norfolk, Va.

30 September   The aircraft model designation TC-18F was established for two Boeing 707-382B aircraft. The aircraft had been extensively modified to include cockpit avionics and a universal air refu-eling receptacle for dry contacts only. The Naval Training Support Unit at Tinker AFB, Okla., was using these aircraft to train pilots for the VQ-3 and -4 TACAMO (take charge and move out) mission aboard E-6A aircraft.

1 October   NAS Fort Worth, Tex., was established as a joint reserve force base. The air station would be home for the Navy and Marine Corps squadrons formerly based at NAS Dallas, Tex., which was closing, and NAS Memphis, Tenn., which would no longer be an air station.

1 October   Commander, Patrol Wings, U.S. Atlantic Fleet, was established in Norfolk, Va., with Rear Admiral Michael D. Haskins as its first commander.

5 October   The first aviator class to use the T-45 Training System (T45TS) received their wings and graduated from VT-21 in a ceremony at NAS Kingsville, Tex. The T-45 Goshawk, a modified version of the British Aerospace Hawk, is the aircraft element of the integrated T45TS, which includes simulators and academic training.

7 October   President William Clinton dispatched *George Washington*, with CVW-7 embarked, and its battle group to the Red Sea to protect Kuwait from the Iraqi troops massing on its border. *George Washington* arrived in the Red Sea 10 October. Additionally, the *Tripoli* Amphibious Ready Group, with 2,000 embarked Marines, moved to the northern Persian Gulf.

1994—Continued

20 October   *Dwight D. Eisenhower* completed a Mediterranean deployment. She initially had the most advanced technology available in the fleet and become the first aircraft carrier to have women permanently assigned.

25 October   Lieutenant Kara S. Hultgreen, the first woman to fully qualify as an F-14 Tomcat pilot, was killed in a training accident while attempting to land on board *Abraham Lincoln*. She was with VF-213.

28 October   Ground was broken for a hangar that would become the new home of VP-30 at NAS Jacksonville, Fla. The fleet readiness squadron trained Navy pilots, naval flight officers, airborne systems specialists and ground maintenance personnel in the operation of the P-3 Orion patrol aircraft. VP-30 became the sole Navy P-3 fleet readiness squadron in October 1993 upon the disestablishment of VP-31 on the West Coast.

15 November   Commander Donnie Cochran assumed command of the Blue Angels, becoming the first African-American skipper of the Navy's flight demonstration squadron. Commander Cochran had commanded VF-11, NAS Miramar, Calif., and had flown with the Blues from 1985 to 1988.

6 December   The "Spirit of Naval Aviation" a monument dedicated to the thousands of Navy, Marine Corps and Coast Guard aviation personnel who have earned Wings of Gold, was unveiled at the Smithsonian's Air and Space Museum, Washington, D.C. The monument would be displayed at the National Museum of Naval Aviation, Pensacola, Fla.

8 December   NASA announced the selection of five Naval Aviators to be among its 19 new astronaut candidates for the space shuttle pilot instruction program: Lieutenant Commander Scott Altman, VF-31; Commander Jeffery Ashby, VFA-94; Lieutenant Commander Joe Edwards, Jr., Joint Staff; Commander Dominic Gorie, VFA-106; and Lieutenant Susan Still, VF-101, the first female Naval Aviator to be chosen for this program. Naval reservist Lieutenant Commander Kathryn Hire was also selected for training as a mission specialist.

20 December   Robert C. Osborn died at his home in Salisbury, Conn., at the age of 90. He had drawn the cartoon "Grampaw Pettibone" in *Naval Aviation News* for over 51 years. During World War II he was the creator of the "Dilbert the Pilot" and the "Spoiler the Mechanic" posters, which were seen throughout the Navy, and the "Sense" pamphlets.

CO of the Blue Angels, Commander Donnie Cochran.

Robert C. Osborn in his later years.

1995

17 January   The T-45A Goshawk and its associated training system elements completed a successful Department of Defense Milestone III review. The approval meant that prime contractor McDonnell Douglas would continue to produce 12 T-45As per year for a total buy of 174 aircraft to be completed through 2003.

2 February   Secretary of the Navy John H. Dalton announced that President William Clinton had approved his recommendation to name the *Nimitz*-class aircraft carriers under construction: *Harry S. Truman* and *Ronald Reagan*.

14 February   A ceremony was held to break ground for the new Naval Air Technical Training Center to be built at historic Chevalier Field at NAS Pensacola, Fla. The field was named for Lieutenant Commander Godfrey de Courcelles Chevalier, an aviation pioneer who made the first underway carrier landing aboard *Langley* on 26 October 1922.

Harry S. Truman under construction.

The T-45A Goshawk training aircraft.

1995—Continued

17 February   Ground breaking began at NAS Patuxent River, Md., for a new facility to house the Naval Air Systems Command Headquarters to be relocated from Arlington, Va.

28 February–2 March   Naval and Marine forces from *Belleau Wood* conducted amphibious landings in Mogadishu, Somalia, to establish a rear guard security perimeter in support of Operation United Shield, which ensured a safe and orderly withdrawal of the UN forces in Somalia. *Essex* ARG also participated in this operation.

1 March   *Inchon* was redesignated MCS 12 and scheduled for a 13-month overhaul at Pascagoula, Miss., and conversion into a mine countermeasures support ship. *Inchon* had just completed a year operating off the coasts of Somalia, Bosnia and Haiti.

2 March   Lieutenant Commander Wendy Lawrence became the first female Naval Aviator in space when she launched as a crew member and mission specialist on the Space Shuttle *Endeavour*. The mission was commanded by Commander Stephen Oswald, USNR, a Naval Aviator. Lieutenant Commander Lawrence was also the first female Naval Academy graduate astronaut.

6 March   The first F-117A stealth fighter engine was inducted into depot-level repair at Naval Aviation Depot, Jacksonville, Fla.

14 March   Naval Aviator and astronaut Captain Michael A. Baker, USN, was assigned as the NASA manager of operational activities at the Gagarin Cosmonaut Training Center in Star City, Russia, near Moscow. The assignment coincided with the launching of Naval Aviator Captain Norman Thagard, USMC, and two cosmonauts aboard a Soyuz rocket for a three-month stay aboard Russia's space station Mir.

Lieutenant Commander Lawrence was the first Navy woman line officer Naval Aviator astronaut.

10 April   VA-196, NAS Whidbey Island, Wash., accepted the last rewinged A-6E Intruder (BuNo 159579). Naval Aviation Depot, Alameda, Calif., had rewinged 23 A-6s since June 1989.

3 May   AW3(NAC) Carly Renee Harris became the first aircrew-qualified woman Aviation Warfare Systems Operator in the S-3 Viking community. She was assigned to VS-22, NAS Jacksonville, Fla.

20 May   *Theodore Roosevelt* and CVW-8 transited the Suez Canal from U.S. Central Command to the Adriatic Sea to participate in Operation Deny Flight.

26 May   *Theodore Roosevelt*, with CVW-8's 36 F/A-18 and 14 F-14 aircraft embarked, arrived in the Adriatic Sea to maintain a presence in response to the increased ethnic tension in Bosnia-Herzegovina, cutting short her participation in Exercise Trident Express in the central Mediterranean Sea.

1 June   The Department of Defense unveiled the low-observable Tier III Minus unmanned aerial vehicle known as Dark Star in a ceremony held at Lockheed's Skunk Works in Palmdale, Calif.

8 June   CH-53 Sea Stallions, AH-1W Sea Cobras and AV-8B Harriers from the 24th Marine Expeditionary Unit aboard *Kearsarge* rescued Captain Scott O'Grady, USAF, after he was shot down while flying over Bosnia on 2 June in support of Operation Deny Flight.

27 June–7 July   Naval Aviator and astronaut Captain Robert Gibson, USN, commanded the Space Shuttle *Atlantis* on the first U.S. shuttle—Russian space station docking mission, STS-71. The mission was the first joint docking mission between the two countries since the Apollo-Soyuz test project flight in 1975.

1995—Continued

30 June The 36-year-old *Independence* became the oldest ship in the Navy's active fleet and the first carrier in history to hold that distinction. Captain David P. Polatty III was presented the "Don't Tread on Me" Navy Jack in a formal ceremony on 1 July. The flag was received from *Mauna Kea* (AE 22) following her decommissioning ceremony.

14 July An F-14D Tomcat from NAWCAD Patuxent River, Md., flew for the first time using a new Digital Flight Control System designed to protect aviators against unrecoverable "flat spins" and carrier landing mishaps.

19 August The winter fly-in to McMurdo Station, Antarctica, began with LC-130 Hercules aircraft of VXE-6 delivering supplies and support personnel. They would construct the ice runway in preparation for the 1995–1996 season's surge of scientists and support workers. This would be the 40th season for Operation Deep Freeze.

30 August F/A-18 Hornets, F-14 Tomcats, S-3 Vikings and ES-3A Shadows under the guidance of EA-6B Prowlers and E-2 Hawkeyes from *Theodore Roosevelt* led the initial attacks on Bosnian Serb military targets in Bosnia during Operation Deliberate Force. The air strikes, approved by both NATO and the UN, targeted air defense missile sites, radar sites and communication facilities.

1–3 September Traveling on board *Carl Vinson*, President William Clinton and the First Lady attended the 50th anniversary commemoration of the end of World War II in Hawaii.

9–30 September *America* and embarked CVW-1 conducted strike and flight operations in the Adriatic Sea in support of Operation Deliberate Force.

1 October VAW-77 "Night Wolf" was established at NAS Atlanta, Ga., and would work in tandem with the Coast Guard and other federal law enforcement agencies to combine and coordinate operations of the nation's counternarcotics forces.

1 October The Naval Aviation Supply Office, Philadelphia, Pa., was disestablished. The Naval Inventory Control Point (NAVICP), Philadelphia/Mechanicsburg, Pa., was established in its place. The new command took over both the functions of ASO and the Ships Parts Control Center at Mechanicsburg, which was also disestablished. NAVICP Philadelphia would be commanded by a Deputy for Aviation under Commander NAVICP, Philadelphia/Mechanicsburg who would report to Commander, Naval Supply Systems Command. The Aviation Supply Office was established on 1 October 1941 to provide centralized control of all aeronautical materials regularly maintained in general stock.

29 November The F/A-18E Super Hornet made its first flight from St. Louis' Lambert International Airport, Mo.

The F/A-18E on its maiden flight.

1995—Continued

11 December   *America* with embarked CVW-1 arrived on station in the Adriatic Sea to begin Operation Joint Endeavor. *Wasp* ARG joined *America* in the Adriatic and began supporting Operation Joint Endeavor on 18 December.

14 December   The final Dayton Accords concerning Bosnia-Herzegovina were signed in Paris, France, by the Bosnian Federation and the Bosnian Serbs. Operation Joint Endeavor under NATO leadership was to oversee the military aspects of peace implementation, and Operation Deny Flight ended.

21 December   The end of Operation Deny Flight was commemorated at Dal Molin Airport, Vincenza, Italy. Operation Deny Flight began in 1993 and provided air cover and close air support to UN Protection Forces' military operations, stopped the use of air power as an instrument of war in Bosnia-Herzegovina, and provided the firepower for air strikes in Operation Deliberate Force that contributed to the peace process.

John C. Stennis heads to sea.

An F-14 Tomcat from VF-143 flies over a destroyed Iraqi radar site.

Abraham Lincoln gets her island during construction.

An F-14 and A-6E conduct low level flight operations over Saudi Arabia.

The decommissioned Saratoga under tow en route to Philadelphia, Pa.

An old maneuver in Naval Aviation, spelling out words on the flight deck.

The eyes of the fleet, the E-2C Hawkeye.

The venerable A-6E Intruder firing a missile.

An EP-3E in flight.

The SH-60B Seahawk.

EA-6B Prowlers in flight.

The History of Naval Aviator and Naval Aviation Pilot Designations and Numbers, The Training of Naval Aviators and the Number Trained (Designated)

T he evolution of the programs and policies regarding the designation of Naval Aviators and Naval Aviation Pilots is one of confusion, ambiguities, inadequate centralized administration of record keeping and inconsistencies in the implementation of a new and young aviation organization into the Navy. During the early period, divergent views on aviation within the Navy and the onset of World War I brought a great influx of new people, programs, policies, aircraft and air stations into a fledgling Naval Aviation. When the U.S. entered World War I, Naval Aviation consisted of one operating air station, 48 aviators and student aviators, and 54 aircraft on hand. It was ill equipped to handle the huge growth precipitated by the U.S. entry into World War I.

Background on the Evolution of Naval Aviators

The Navy's aviation program had an aviator before it acquired its first aircraft. Lieutenant Theodore G. Ellyson was ordered to training in December 1910 at the Glenn Curtiss aviation camp in San Diego, Calif. The Navy received its first aircraft from the Curtiss Company in July 1911. Flight instruction at that time was informal and remained so for the next couple of years. Ellyson became a pilot when Curtiss agreed he

could fly an airplane. Subsequently Ellyson taught John Towers to fly. But flying the airplane was only part of the drill. The student also had to become totally familiar with the mechanics of his machine and be able to repair and rebuild it. Formality arrived when Captain Washington I. Chambers, the Navy's first Director of Naval Aeronautics, declared the requirements for becoming a Navy pilot to follow the same rules employed by the Aero Club of America (the American chapter of the Federation Aeronautique Internationale). Prior to the Navy establishing these standards, some Navy flyers held pilot certificates from the Aero Club of America.

Officers assigned to the "aviation element" of the Navy and who qualified as pilots were formally recognized for their duty as flyers on 4 March 1913 by the Navy Appropriations Act for fiscal year 1914. This act provided an increase of 35 percent in pay and allowances for officers detailed to duty as flyers of heavier-than-air craft. On 10 April 1913, the Secretary of the Navy approved performance standards for qualification and the issuance of a certificate as a "Navy Air Pilot" to qualified officers. Captain Chambers had requested the certificate in his letter of 4 April 1913 to the Chief of Bureau of Navigation. His letter of request states, "The requirements for a Navy Air Pilot are different from those of the land pilot and are purposely made more exacting than those of the 'license' issued by the International Aeronautical Federation." To receive a Navy Air Pilot certificate an officer had to pass the advanced training course and become highly skilled as a flyer or pass an examination by a board of qualified officers. The Bureau of Navigation was identified as the Navy organization responsible for issuing the Navy Air Pilot certificate to qualified officers. The issuance of the Navy Air Pilot certificate was subject to a delay of almost two years from the date the Secretary of the Navy had approved issuing a Navy Air Pilot certificate.

Even though performance standards for qualification as a Navy Air Pilot were established in April 1913, it was not until a year later, on 22 April 1914, that the Bureau of Navigation, which was responsible for all Navy training, approved a course of instruction for student flyers and aviation mechanics. It is obvious that there were delays in establishing aviation programs and policies by the Bureau of Navigation. On 9 January 1915, Admiral Bradley A. Fiske pointed out to the Bureau of Navigation that unless some officers were recognized as qualified and were given certificates, no board of experts could be appointed to examine the qualifications of new applicants. He recommended that certificates be issued to Ellyson, Towers, Mustin, Bellinger, Herbster, Smith and Chevalier, and that they be numbered 1 through 7 and dated sequentially from 1 January 1914 for Ellyson to 1 July 1914 for Chevalier. The Bureau of Navigation followed up on Admiral Fiske's recommendation and, in accordance with what the Secretary of the Navy had approved almost two years before, sent out letters dated 21 January 1915 forwarding Navy Air Pilot Certificates to the seven offices mentioned above, numbering and dating them as Admiral Fiske had recommended. However, the Bureau of Navigation and NAS Pensacola, Fla., continued to follow the procedure of identifying those students completing the elementary flight course at Pensacola as "Naval Aviators" to differentiate them from pilots who had completed the advance course of requirements and qualified as Navy Air Pilots.

Before the Bureau of Navigation could continue its follow up work and issue more Navy Air Pilot Certificates, Congress revised the law on flight pay, and, in a new bill approved 3 March 1915, used the term "Naval Aviator" in specifying those eligible for flight pay. This bill, the Naval Appropriations Act, fiscal year 1916, added enlisted men and student aviators to those eligible for increased pay and allowances while on duty involving flying. It also increased the amount previously provided for qualified aviators. The language of the act provided "flight pay" only for "Naval Aviators", those fliers completing the elemen-

tary flight course at Pensacola. It did not cover those who had qualified as the best pilots and received the Navy Air Pilots certificate. Hence, on 22 March 1915, in order to include those pilots designated Navy Air Pilots, a change was made to the Secretary of the Navy's performance standards certificate whereby the designation "Navy Air Pilot" was changed to "Naval Aviator". This was the beginning of the primary emphasis being placed on the designation Naval Aviator. However, the Navy continued to make references to Navy Air Pilots. In March and April 1915, qualified aviation boards, appointed to give exams at Pensacola, recommended designation of five men as follows: Saufley for a Naval Aviator Certificate dated 6 March, McIlvain for a Navy Air Pilot Certificate dated 10 March, Bronson for orders dated 6 April with the designation Navy Air Pilot, Whiting and Richardson for Naval Aviator Certificates dated 10 and 12 April. The reason for the different use of Naval Aviator and Navy Air Pilot terminology is not known, but the recommendations were approved with a modification as reported by the Bureau of Navigation on 25 May 1915, that all five men had been issued Navy Air Pilot Certificates, numbers 8 through 12. The use of the Navy Air Pilot Certificate and designation continued even after the Secretary of the Navy issued his order to change the designation to Naval Aviator.

Confusion over the issue of Naval Aviator or Navy Air Pilot designations continued within Navy organizations. On 5 May 1915, the Secretary of the Navy informed Whiting: "You are hereby designated as a Naval Aviator for duty involving flying in aircraft, including balloons, dirigibles and airplanes, in accordance with an Act of Congress approved March 3, 1915." The conflict or confusion seems to be in terminology. It was the opinion at that time that an official statement was legally necessary for an individual on flying duty (necessary only in the sense of receiving extra pay while assigned to a job involving actual flying in an aircraft) and that the "Certificates" were only evidence of qualification as an aviator. Thus, on 21 May 1915, the Secretary of the Navy signed a circular letter directing that commanding officers "issue orders detailing officers of the Navy and Marine Corps to Duty as Naval Aviators or Student Naval Aviators when they are required to actually fly or operate these machines." Therefore, regardless of the title on the "Certificates", these orders used the title associated with the law.

In January 1916, the Bureau of Navigation issued its "Course of Instructions and Required Qualifications of Personnel for the Air Service of the Navy." This syllabus mentions eleven classifications for personnel assigned to aeronautic duty. For officers they include: Student Naval Aviator, Naval Aviator, Navy Air Pilot, aeroplane, Navy Air Pilot, dirigible and Military Aviator. The remaining groups were for enlisted personnel classifications. One of the major reasons for the confusion regarding designations was the involvement of several different organizations within the Navy making policy decisions on Naval Aviation without adequate coordination of terminology or standardizing its applications. Terminology was used for different purposes, such as identifying an individual qualified to pilot an aircraft and, for pay purposes, identifying an individual involved in flight but not necessarily as the pilot.

On 1 May 1917 a new course of instruction was presented as a revision without specifying what it revised, although it must have taken the place of the course dated January 1916. The new course stated that officers detailed to aeronautic duty will be classed as: Student Naval Aviator, Naval Aviator, and Navy Air Pilot, either for seaplanes or dirigibles. Completion of the course of instruction for Student Naval Aviator (Seaplane) qualified the student for advancement to elementary and solo flying. Upon completion of that stage the student took the exam for Naval Aviator (seaplane) and was then eligible for what appears to be the advanced course. For this course the instruction stated: "Upon successful completion of the examination the Naval Aviator (seaplane) will be designated Navy Air Pilot (seaplane) and issued a certificate numbered according to his standing in the class with which he qualified as a Navy Air Pilot (seaplane)." A revision to the May 1917 course of instruction was issued 1 January 1918, and the term Navy Air Pilot was not mentioned. In this revision, officers and men detailed for pilot duty were classed as student Naval Aviators and Naval Aviators, seaplane or dirigible. By this time the U.S. was fully engaged in World War I, the Naval Aviation training program had expanded, and the question of title finally seemed to be settled. It took almost three years, from 22 March 1915, when the SecNav order was issued to change Navy Air Pilot to Naval Aviator, to January 1918, before the terminology Navy Air Pilot was dropped from instructions issued by the Navy.

Designation List of Naval Aviators

Confusion in the designation list of Naval Aviators seems to have been tied with the precedence for the designation date of a Naval Aviator and its connection with the adoption of the gold wings insignia (Naval Aviator Wings). A 13 November 1917 Bureau of Navigation letter states, "The Bureau is now compiling a list of all officers and men who are qualified as Naval Aviators, in order that new pins may be delivered as shortly after they are received from the manu-

facturers as possible." This is followed by a BuNav report to Pensacola, Fla., stating, "The new Naval Aviator's pins have been delivered to the Bureau of Navigation and they will be sent out as soon as they can be engraved to show the Aviator's number, his name and branch of service."

There is some question as to whether BuNav produced a list of Naval Aviators at this time. However, the CNO's Aviation Office had a listing of 282 numbers that was forwarded to BuNav under a letter dated 19 January 1918 with the following:

"1. Enclosure (a) is a list of qualified Naval Aviators given in numerical sequence.

2. This list was compiled after careful examination of all the records of this office and numbers assigned according to the date of qualification as Naval Aviator in all cases where such date is shown by the records; but due to the fact that those officers of the regular service who were the first to enter aviation were not required to take a Naval Aviator's test but were merely designated 'Naval Aviator' or 'Navy Air Pilot' because of their recognized qualification as such, the numbers assigned in such cases were determined by the date upon which they were ordered to aviation duty and the length of such duty, full consideration being given each and every individual case so affected.

3. Additions to the attached list will be forwarded to the Bureau from time to time and as rapidly as the students now under instruction pass the necessary test for qualification as Naval Aviators."

The following list, except for the omission of fractional numbers and the differences in two names, is accepted as the precedence list of early Naval Aviators.

Naval Aviator Number	Name	Service	Navy Air Pilot Number
1	Ellyson, Theodore G.	USN	1
2	Rodgers, John	USN	
3	Towers, John H.	USN	2
4	Herbster, Victor D.	USN	5
5	Cunningham, Alfred A.	USMC	14
6	Smith, Bernard L.	USMC	6
7	Chevalier, Godfrey deC	USN	7
8	Bellinger, Patrick N. L.	USN	4
9	Billingsley, William D.	USN	
10	Murray, James M.	USN	
11	Mustin, Henry C.	USN	3
12	McIlvain, William M.	USMC	9
13	Richardson, Holden C.	USN	12
14	Saufley, Richard C.	USN	8
15	Bronson, Clarence K.	USN	10
16	Whiting, Kenneth	USN	11
17	Maxfield, Louis H.	USN	13
18	McDonnell, Edward O.	USN	
19	Capehart, Wadleigh	USN	

Naval Aviator Number	Name	Service
20	Spencer, Earl W., Jr.	USN
21	Bartlett, Harold T.	USN
22	Murray, George D.	USN
23	Corry, William M.	USN
24	Read, Albert C.	USN
25	Johnson, Earle F.	USN
26	Evans, Francis T.	USMC
27	Paunack, Robert R.	USN
28	Scofield, Harold W.	USN
29	Child, Warren G.	USN
30	Dichman, Grattan C.	USN
31	Young, Robert T.	USN
32	Gillespie, George S.	USN
33	Mitscher, Marc A.	USN
34	Strickland, Glenn B.	USN
35	Monfort, James C.	USN
36	Cabaniss, Robert W.	USN
37	Chase, Nathan B.	USN
38	Stone, Elmer F.	USCG
39	McKitterick, Edward H.	USN
40	Leighton, Bruce G.	USN
41	Griffin, Virgil C.	USN
42	Cecil, Henry B.	USN
43	Sugden, Charles E.	USCG
44	Bressman, Augustus A.	USN
45	Ramsey, DeWitt C.	USN
46	Hull, Carl T.	USN
47	Peyton, Paul J.	USN
48	Kirkpatrick, Robert D.	USN
49	Geiger, Roy S.	USMC
50	Bonner, Walter D.	USN
51	Murphy, Thomas H.	USN
52	Mason, Charles P.	USN
52½	Salsman, James	USN
53	Simpson, Frank, Jr.	NNV
54	Donahue, Robert	USCG
55	Brewster, David L. S.	USMC
55½	Sunderman, John T.	USN
56	Barin, Louis T.	NNV
57	Parker, Stanley V.	USCG
58	Masek, William	USN
59	Coffin, Eugene A.	USCG
60	Eaton, Phillip B.	USCG
61	Enos, George	USN
62	Varini, Giochino	USN
63	Hawkins, Clarence A.	USN
64	Ruttan, Charles E.	USN
65	Gates, Artemus L.	USNRF
65½	Laud-Brown, Wellesley	USNRF
66	Lovett, Robert A.	USNRF
67	Ames, Allan W.	USNRF
68	Gould, Erl C. B.	USNRF

Naval Aviator Number	Name	Service
69	Walker, Guy A.	USN
70	Kilmer, Oliver P.	USN
71	Talbot, Peter	USN
72	Davison, Henry P.	USNRF
73	Vorys, John M.	USNRF
74	MacLeish, Kenneth A.	USNRF
75	Beach, Charles F.	USNRF
76	Farwell, John D.	USNRF
77	Sturtevant, Albert D.	USNRF
78	Read, Russell B.	USNRF
79	Brush, Graham M.	USNRF
80	James, Oliver B.	USNRF
81	Rockefeller, William	USNRF
82	McIlwaine, Archibald G.	USNRF
83	Read, Curtis S.	USNRF
83½	Gartz, Richard C.	USNRF
84	Ireland, Robert L.	USNRF
85	Ingalls, David S.	USNRF
86	Walker, Samuel S.	USNRF
87	Smith, Kenneth R.	USNRF
88	Lynch, Francis R. V.	USNRF
89	Lawrence, George F.	USNRF
89½	Merrill, Norman E.	NNV
90	McLaughlin, Guy	USN
91	McCrary, Frank R.	USN
92	Coombe, Reginald G.	USNRF
93	Landon, Henry H., Jr.	USNRF
94	Culbert, Frederic P.	USN
95	Feher, Anthony	USN
95a	Fitzsimon, Ricardo	Argentine Navy
95b	Pouchan, Ceferino M.	Argentine Navy
95c	Zar, Marcos A.	Argentine Navy
96	Coil, Emory W.	USN
96½	Chamberlain, Edmund G.	USMC
97	Strader, Ralph M.	USNRF
98	Talbot, Andrew B.	USNRF
99	Whitehouse, William P.	USNRF
100	Crompton, George	USNRF
100½	Pennoyer, Ralph G.	USN
100¾	Presley, Russell A.	USMC
101	Hamlen, Warner	USNRF
102	Little, Charles G.	USNRF
103	Brewer, Arthur D.	USNRF
104	Delano, Merrill P.	USNRF
104½	Kiely, Ralph	USN
105	Lansdowne, Zachary	USN
105½	Douglas, Gilbert W.	USNRF
106	Bell, Colley W.	USNRF
107	Chadwick, Noel	USNRF
108	Ditman, Albert J.	USNRF
109	Donnelly, Thorne	NNV
110	Carter, R. C.	USNRF

Naval Aviator Number	Name	Service
110½	Allen, Charles L.	USN
111	Stone, George W.	USN
111½	Bradford, Doyle	USNRF
112	Atwater, William B.	USNRF
112½	Webster, Clifford L.	USNRF
113	Fallon, Nugent	USNRF
114	Williams, Arthur S.	USNRF
115	Dietrich, Arthur F.	USN
116	Palmer, Carlton D.	USN
117	Murray, Cecil D.	USNRF
118	Taylor, Moseley	USNRF
119	Townsend, Richard S.	USNRF
120	Walton, Mark W.	USNRF
121	Depew, Ganson G.	USNRF
122	Goodyear, Frank	USNRF
123	McCormick, Alexander A.	USNRF
124	Schieffelin, John J.	USNRF
125	Rodman, Thomas C.	USNRF
126	Smith, Edward T.	USNRF
127	Otis, James S.	USNRF
128	Hawkins, Ashton W.	USNRF
129	Lufkin, Chauncey F.	USNRF
130	Potter, Stephen	USNRF
131	Fuller, Percival S.	USNRF
132	Decernea, Edward	USNRF
133	Ott, George A.	USN
134	Geary, John W.	USNRF
134½	Wetherald, Royal W.	USNRF
135	Hinton, Walter	USN
136	Willcox, Westmore	USNRF
137	Lee, Benjamin II	USNRF
138	Stone, Emory A.	USNRF
139	Fuller, Charles F.	USNRF
140	Hutchins, Hurd	USNRF
141	Stocker, Robert M.	USNRF
142	Foster, John C.	USNRF
143	Allen, Frederic S.	USNRF
144	Amory, Francis I.	USNRF
145	Read, Duncan H.	USNRF
146	Goldthwaite, Duval R.	USNRF
147	McCann, Richard H.	USNRF
148	Wright, Arthur H.	USNRF
149	Swift, Henry	USNRF
150	Butler, Stuart M.	USNRF
151	Gordon, Harry B.	USNRF
152	Zunino, Frank A.	USNRF
153	Shea, Edward L.	USNRF
154	Forrestal, James V.	USNRF
155	Brackenridge, Gavin	USNRF
156	Gibson, Harold F.	USNRF
157	Mudge, William F.	USNRF
158	Clarkson, William F.	USNRF
159	McCoid, Paul H.	USNRF
160	Halstead, Jacob S.	USNRF
161	Randolph, Robert D.	USNRF
162	Matter, Robert	USNRF
163	Warburton, William J.	USNRF
163½	Peterson, Herman A.	NNV
164	Rutherford, John	NNV
165	Laughlin, George M. III	NNV
166	Evans, George B.	NNV
167	Johnson, Albert R.	NNV
168	McCulloch, David H.	USNRF
169	Peirce, Thomas J. H.	NNV
170	Page, Phillips W.	USNRF
171	Shaw, George W.	USNRF
172	Peck, Lyman S.	USNRF
173	Humphreys, William Y., Jr.	NNV
174	Berger, Frederick G. B.	NNV
175	Boyd, Theodore P.	NNV
175½	Alexander, William H.	USN
176	White, Lawrence G.	NNV
177	Coddington, Dave H.	NNV
178	Kerr, Robert H.	USN
179	Whitted, James A.	USN
180	Haskell, Armory L.	USNRF
181	Hyde, Russell N.	USNRF
182	Keyes, Kenneth B.	USNRF
183	Warren, Alfred K.	USNRF
184	Eaton, Joseph A.	USNRF
185	Peterson, William L.	USNRF
186	Stanley, Henry T.	USNRF
187	Remey, John T.	USNRF
188	Palmedo, Roland	USNRF
189	Forbes, Duncan P.	USNRF
190	Allen, Francis G.	USNRF
191	Baker, Charles S.	USNRF
192	Greenough, Charles W.	USNRF
193	Ames, Charles B.	USNRF
194	Hofer, Myron A.	USNRF
195	Ives, Paul F.	USNRF
196	Clark, Robert F.	USNRF
197	Brewer, Edward S.	USNRF
198	Dumas, Gardner D.	USNRF
199	McNamara, John F.	USNRF
200	Rowen, Harold J.	USNRF
201	Compo, George L.	USNRF
202	Perrin, John	USNRF
203	Hutchinson, Lester B.	USNRF
204	MacCaulay, Donald M.	USNRF
205	Lochman, Dean E.	USNRF
206	Moore, Lloyd Ray	USN
207	Thomas, Reginald de Noyes	USNRF
208	Clements, James R.	USNRF

Naval Aviator Number	Name	Service
209	Schermerhorn, Horace	USNRF
210	Murphy, Dudley B.	USNRF
210½	Grosvenor, Theodore P.	USNRF
211	Roe, George T.	USNRF
212	Teulon, Arthur P.	USNRF
213	Marriner, Walter T.	USN
214	Pumpelly, Harold A.	USNRF
215	Biggers, Robert L.	USNRF
216	Farmer, Charles R.	USNRF
217	Rumill, George E.	USNRF
218	Greenfield, Edwin R.	USNRF
219	Weld, Lothrop M.	USNRF
220	Phelan, James	USNRF
220½	West, Winfield M.	USNRF
221	Lancto, Joseph W.	USNRF
222	Wilcox, Harold M.	USNRF
223	Hawkins, Rees	USNRF
224	Wenz, Edward A.	USNRF
225	Alvord, Donald B.	USNRF
226	Baum, James E., Jr.	USNRF
227	Smith, Frank S.	USNRF
228	Hawkins, Samuel S.	USNRF
229	Clapp, Kenneth H.	USNRF
230	Dowell, Benjamin B.	USNRF
231	Ostridge, Charles L.	USNRF
232	Bergin, Thomas M.	USNRF
233	Gadsden, Philip H.	USNRF
234	Graves, Justin D.	USNRF
235	Connolly, Leo W.	USNRF
236	McAdoo, William G., Jr.	USNRF
237	Wheeler, Oscar G.	USNRF
238	Benjamin, Henry R.	USNRF
239	Souther, Arthur F.	USNRF
240	Roberts, Charles H.	USNRF
241	Harris, Frederick M.	USNRF
242	Naylor, Henry R.	USNRF
243	Voorhees, Dudley A.	USNRF
244	Maxwell, Howard W., Jr.	USNRF
245	King, Frederick E.	USNRF
246	Lamar, Lamartine E.	USNRF
247	Bancroft, Frederick W., Jr	USNRF
248	Griswold, Rettig A.	USNRF
249	Chapman, Thomas H.	USNRF
250	Frothingham, Philip B.	USNRF

The confusion regarding precedence and the assignment of numbers resulted in some qualified individuals being left off the list of Naval Aviator numbers. During World War I qualified civilian aviators joined the naval service and served as Naval Aviators. They were qualified pilots who flew as a Navy pilot or Naval Aviator but did not receive a Naval Aviator number or were overlooked in the assignment of a number because of administrative problems during the huge war build-up.

The Bureau of Navigation (redesignated Bureau of Naval Personnel [BuPers] in 1942) continued to issue Naval Aviator numbers and was the sole source until 31 July 1942. In a SecNav letter, dated 31 July 1942, the old method of designating Naval Aviators (the assignment of numbers) was discontinued. The following system was put in place:

Commandant, Naval Air Station, Pensacola, Fla., is directed to commence a series of numbers for the foregoing designations as Naval Aviator (HTA) Number P1, P2, P3, etc.

Commandant, Naval Air Station, Jacksonville, Fla., is directed to commence a similar series as Naval Aviator (HTA) Number J1, J2, J3, etc.

Commandant, Naval Air Station Corpus Christi, Tex., is directed to commence a similar series as Naval Aviator (HTA) Number C1, C2, C3, etc.

Commanding Officer, Naval Air Station, Miami, Fla., is directed to commence a similar series, as Naval Aviator (HTA) Number M1, M2, M3, etc.

Commanding Officer, Naval Air Station, Norfolk, Va., is directed to commence a similar series, as Naval Aviator (HTA) Number N1, N2, N3, etc.

Commanding Officer, Naval Air Station, Alameda, Calif., is directed to commence a similar series as Naval Aviator (HTA) Number A1, A2, A3, etc.

Commanding Officer, Naval Air Station, Lakehurst, N.J., is directed to commence a similar series as Naval Aviator Number L1, L2, L3, etc.

Commanding Officer, Naval Air Station, Moffett Field, Calif., is directed to commence a similar series as Naval Aviator (LTA) Number S1, S2, S3, etc.

This letter also stated: "The original letter of designation will be delivered directly to the individual without prior reference to the Navy Department for approval." Copies of the letter of designation were to be forwarded to the Bureau of Personnel, Bureau of Aeronautics, Commandant, U.S. Marine Corps, and Bureau of Medicine and Surgery (in the case of Flight Surgeons). Because of the decentralization of this numbering system a complete listing of Naval Aviators and their designation numbers has not been found for the World War II period even though the Bureau of Personnel was to receive a copy of all the letters of designation.

On 28 November 1942, a Secretary of Navy letter issued a modification to the commands designating Naval Aviators. Changes in this letter were as follows:

The Commandant, Naval Air Training Center, Pensacola, Fla., assumed the duties of designating Naval Aviators vice the Commandant, Naval Air Station, Pensacola. There is no indication the use of the numbering series P1, P2, P3, etc. . . . was changed.

The Commandant, Naval Air Training Center, Corpus Christi, Tex., assumed the duties of designating Naval Aviators vice the Commandant, Naval Air Station, Corpus Christi. There is no indication the use of the numbering series C1, C2, C3, etc. . . . was changed.

The Commandant, Naval Air Center, Hampton Roads, Va., was directed to assume the duties of designating Naval Aviators vice the Commanding Officer, Naval Air Station, Norfolk, Va. There is no indication the use of the numbering series N1, N2, N3, etc. . . . was changed.

This system remained in effect until 1949. A Secretary of the Navy letter of 29 March 1949 canceled its previous letters regarding designation of Naval Aviators (letters of 31 July 1942, 28 November 1942 and 9 January 1943) and authorized the Commander, Naval Air Training; Commander, Naval Air Advanced Training; and the Chief of Naval Airship Training and Experimentation to designate Naval Aviators (and assign numbers). By the time this letter was issued the other training commands had already been disestablished or consolidated under the control of these three commands. In step with the previous decentralized system, the following system was established:

Chief of Naval Air Training was directed to commence a series of numbers for the foregoing designations as Naval Aviators (HTA) Number T-1, T-2, T-3, etc.

Chief of Naval Air Advanced Training is directed to commence a series of numbers for the foregoing designations of Naval Aviators (HTA) Number V-1, V-2, V-3, etc.

Chief of Naval Airship Training and Experimentation is directed to commence a similar series as Naval Aviators (LTA) using the L series, carrying on from the last number used in this series by the Commanding Officer, Naval Air Station, Lakehurst, N.J.

The Chief of Naval Air Training quit issuing Naval Aviator Numbers sometime in the 1970s.

Documentation has not been located that gives the date or provides reasons why the assignment of Naval Aviator numbers was discontinued. To date, no complete listing of all Naval Aviator numbers, including the letter-number designations, has been found. Moreover, it is highly unlikely a complete list exists because of the decentralization of the system during World War II. Bits and pieces of the listing for Naval Aviator numbers is held by the Naval Aviation History Office. However, the World War II and post-war period list is not organized in any alphabetical or chronological order, consequently, it is extremely difficult to find any individual's number.

Background on the Evolution of Naval Aviation Pilots

The evolution of the Naval Aviation Pilot designation for enlisted men is more complicated, because of the lack of a clear Navy policy regarding enlisted pilots during Naval Aviation's first decade and the misconceptions surrounding the terminology regarding designations used for enlisted pilots. By setting the standards for qualification and certification of officers as Naval Aviators in the early phase of Naval Aviation, a stable policy was put into effect. The failure to establish a clear-cut policy regarding programs for training enlisted pilots caused considerable confusion that affected the enlisted pilot program during its entire existence.

The confusion begins with terminology and how it was applied to those people "involved in actual flight." Enlisted men had been undergoing aeronautic training from the time the aeronautic station was established at Pensacola, Fla., in January 1914. Training for enlisted men can even be traced back to the first aeronautic station at Greenbury Point, Md. However, more publicity for enlisted aeronautic training and its resultant positions developed in March 1915, when a law was passed by Congress that extended increased pay and allowances to enlisted men and student aviators, as well as qualified pilots, while on duty involving flight. Prior to the passage of this law, Congress had authorized special pay only for officers detailed to duty as flyers. The allure of flight, more pay and the continued development of the small aviation section of the Navy brought about a greater interest by enlisted personnel in the naval aeronautic field. It was only natural that some enlisted men, aside from their regular duties of maintaining the craft and flying as crew members, developed an interest in piloting aircraft.

There is some confusion surrounding the first training of enlisted men as pilots. References are made to the beginning of pilot training at NAS Pensacola, Fla., for the first group of enlisted men on 6 January 1916.

In a letter to Lieutenant Commander Henry C. Mustin, Commandant, NAS Pensacola, Fla., dated 4 January 1916, Captain Mark L. Bristol, Director of Naval Aeronautics, states, "In an order issued the other day, we organized a class of men for training as aviators, specifying men of the seamen's branch. It may happen that the machinists at the present time are best fitted for this training, but we can not establish such a precedent. It would lead to all kinds of future complications, so start square on this subject." In a letter, dated 10 January 1916, written in response to Bristol's earlier one, Mustin stated, "As regards the distinction between Naval Aviator and Navy Air Pilot, I think that the term Naval Aviator, in view of the term Military Aviator used in the Army, is not altogether suitable for our enlisted men; also in view of the present wording of the law there may be some complications. However, I think we have the sense of what you desire in this line of work regardless of titles and that is a matter that can be straightened out later. In the meantime, we are going ahead with the first class of enlisted men and they are taking hold of the flying part of it very well." From these two letters we can be fairly certain the first pilot training class for enlisted men began in January 1916 at NAS Pensacola, Fla. The question regarding the designation of an enlisted pilot appears to have been left up in the air. Mustin does make a reference to using the old title "Navy Air Pilot" that had been used for officers prior to March 1913. However, Bristol left his position as Director of Naval Aeronautics in March 1916 before a decision was made on the subject.

The Bureau of Navigation's January 1916 "Course of Instruction..." mentioned above, identifies enlisted categories of Student Airman, Airman, Quartermaster, aeroplane, Quartermaster, dirigible and Machinist, aeronautic. Just like the designations involving Naval Aviator, the Navy had two organizations (the Bureau of Navigation and the CNO's Director of Naval Aeronautics) that were dealing with aviation training and issuing directives that sometimes had conflicting uses for designations. The Bureau of Navigation's January 1916 "Course of Instructions and Required Qualifications of Personnel for the Air Service of the Navy" also set up a "Certificate of Qualification for Airman." Thus, in 1916, NAS Pensacola, Fla., began issuing "Certificates of Qualification as Airman" to enlisted personnel meeting the requirements set up by the Bureau of Navigation. From a handwritten logbook maintained at Pensacola, the "Certificates" were numbered, beginning with 1 and went up to 358. The Number 1 Certificate of Qualification as Airman was issued to CMM Harry E. Adams on 15 December 1916, with a course completion date of 27 November 1916. This Airman certificate should not be confused with

the enlisted qualifications for a pilot, there is no connection between the two designations. A note in the logbook indicates the issuance of a Certificate of Qualification from the Aeronautic School at Pensacola for Airman was discontinued on 1 October 1917. It is believed Pensacola discontinued the enlisted "Certificate" program because of the changes in the "Course of Instructions", the addition of other training stations and the influx of a large number of enlisted men during World War I. However, the name Airman continued to be applied to enlisted personnel in the aviation field. Needless to say, there were other qualified enlisted men in naval aeronautics who preceded the establishment of this list of designated "Airman."

The forgoing discussion about "Airman" is provided here to clarify the fact that "Airmen" were not being defined as enlisted pilots. However, some enlisted men who received "Certificates" as Airman did become qualified pilots, and this is where the confusion begins. The first official class of enlisted men to undergo pilot training in January 1916 included: P. J. Dunleavy, CBM, F. Grompe, CMAA, A. A. Bressman, CTC, L. A. Welty, CTC, A. Hayes, CTC, A. P. Bauer, GM1c, J. Makolin, 1stSgt, USMC, W. E. McCaughtry, GunSgt, USMC and A. F. Dietrich, BM2c. The last man to join this class was Walter D. Bonner, BM2c, and he shows up on the 1 March 1916 Flying School's list of Enlisted Personnel undergoing Flying Instruction. Captain Mark Bristol, Director of Naval Aeronautics, sent a memo to the Secretary of the Navy on 4 March 1916 which stated "On the 1st of January 1916, a class of 10 enlisted men was formed and placed under instruction in flying. These men were selected from the bluejackets and marines already on duty at the station or on board *North Carolina* (ACR 12). These men are making excellent progress. There will be a class of them ordered every three months hereafter." Records do not indicate any succeeding classes of enlisted pilot training groups every three months as indicated by Bristol's letter. The next reference to a class of enlisted men undergoing flight training at NAS Pensacola is 15 May 1916, in a "Semi-Monthly Report of Aviators (Enlisted Personnel)." This report lists the following personnel undergoing training as aviators: A. A. Bressman, L. A. Welty, A. Hayes, A. F. Dietrich, W. D. Bonner, J. Makolin, W. E. McCaughtry, C. L. Allen, J. Sunderman, W. Diercks, J. Salsman, A. Ward, T. H. Murphy, and G. Verini.

In the fall of 1917 several changes were implemented in the pilot training program that affected enlisted personnel. In a CNO letter to the Commandant, Pensacola Aeronautic Station, Fla., dated 8 August 1917, paragraph 2 states, "It is desired to train no more enlisted personnel as pilots. Excellent Officer material in enlisted personnel will be treated in accordance with reference (c)." Reference (c) was the Bureau of Navigation's circular letter #9879–495 of 2 August 1917. In a letter from the Commandant, NAS Pensacola, Fla., dated 30 November 1917, to the Bureau of Navigation, clarification was requested regarding aviation designations for 10 enlisted personnel who had qualified and were given orders as Quartermaster Seaplane. This designation identified these personnel as qualified enlisted pilots. The letter goes on to ask whether new orders should be issued to these men designating them as Naval Aviators. The ten men were CBM A. F. Dietrick, CQM J. T. Sunderman, CGM G. Enos, QM2c (A) John H. Bunt, QM2c (A) James A. Whitted, CTC A. Feher, CE Carlton D. Palmer, QM2c George W. Stone, CBM Robert H. Kerr, and QM2c (A) C. A. Suber. In the Bureau of Navigation's response to the letter, dated 8 December 1917, it states, "Men mentioned in this enclosure (the enclosure was a copy of NAS Pensacola's 30 November 1917 letter listing the 10 men) will have their designations changed to Naval Aviators, but no new orders are necessary." The second paragraph of this letter indicated a new policy was being issued with regard to enlisted pilots, it stated, "In separate correspondence, instructions are being issued concerning future designations as Naval Aviators for enlisted men who qualify for pilot duty, and new blanks (Navigation Form N. Nav. 442, October 1917) are being sent out on which reports should be made in the future." It appears the Bureau of Navigation, in its Aviation Circular dated 1 January 1913, set up the policy that identified the course of instruction in flight training and the passing of flight tests for officers, and later on applied it to enlisted men who could qualify for pilot duty. However, it also appears that the Bureau of Navigation did not make any modifications in its circulars to reflect the changes that occurred in pilot designations between 1913 and 1915, such as Navy Air Pilot and Naval Aviator and the appropriate references to enlisted men who became pilots. All ten enlisted men referenced in NAS Pensacola's 30 November 1917 letter were eventually commissioned. However, several of them maintained their enlisted pilot status for over a year before receiving their commission.

In the latter part of 1917, as a result of the great need to increase the number of aviation personnel, the Navy instituted a policy of taking enlisted men for pilot training and then qualifying them for a commission and designation as a Naval Aviator. Many of the regular enlisted men who could qualify for the pilot training program would be discharged from the regular Navy and enrolled in the Naval Reserve for training and commission in the Naval Reserve Flying Corps. The majority of the personnel entering Naval Aviation service during the war came from the civilian community and joined the Naval Reserve for duty with the Naval Reserve Flying Corps. Needless to say, there were exceptions to these policies during World War I. This was particularly true for enlisted personnel who received pilot training in Europe.

On 5 June 1917, the Navy's First Aeronautic Detachment, and the first U.S. military unit sent to Europe in World War I, arrived at Pauillac, France. The second section of the detachment arrived on 8 June at St. Nazaire, France. The First Aeronautic Detachment was commanded by Lieutenant Kenneth Whiting and consisted of 7 officers and 122 enlisted men. Only four of the officers were pilots, two were supply officers, and one a doctor. The majority of the enlisted personnel were students in the aviation field. After a meeting between American and French officers, the French agreed to train the personnel of the First Aeronautic Detachment. Approximately 50 enlisted men were to be trained as seaplane pilots at Tours while another 50 would be trained as "mechanicians" at St. Raphael. On 22 June 1917, preliminary flight training for the enlisted men began in Caudron aircraft under French instructors at the Ecole d'Aviation Militaire at Tours. One of the French procedures for flight training was to teach their pilots land flying first, hence, Lieutenant Whiting had to deal with the French Army, as well as with the Navy. Changes were made to the flight training plans and 14 of the enlisted men were redirected to fill the requirement for observer training. Under French training, an observer was a prototype of aircrewmen whose duties involved observing, acting as bombardier and handling such armament as existed on the plane. On 7 July 1917, Lieutenant Whiting reported that fifty persons were undergoing pilot instruction at Tours, 38 taking machinist and 14 in observer training at St. Raphael.

The French required a ratio of 10 enlisted men for each pilot under its aviation program. Consequently, the American Navy representative in France, along with Lieutenant Whiting, requested an increase in personnel for aviation training in France. The Navy Department again found itself divided on aviation training, some wanted to continue sending men to France for aviation training, while others wanted to conduct the training in the U.S. and have some final, on site training, conducted in France. By the early summer months of 1918 many of the problems of training, organization and movement of aviation personnel abroad had begun to be solved. However, all aviation training matters were not smoothed out prior to the signing of the Armistice.

The policy regarding the enlisted pilots that were trained in Europe, either in France, Britain, or Italy, generally followed the same procedures adhered to in the U.S. at the end of 1917. Many of the enlisted pilots would receive commissions once they had completed flight training and been certified as pilots. They did not always receive their commissions immediately after their qualification as pilots. Some enlisted pilots flew many patrol missions before the administrative system authorized their commissioning in the Naval Reserve Flying Corps. When the Armistice was signed, the total strength of the U.S. Naval Aviation Force, Foreign Service (those serving overseas) was 1,147 officers and 18,308 enlisted men. The majority of them were assigned to air stations in France, followed by those in England, Ireland, and Italy.

With the end of World War I, Naval Aviation, along with other elements of the Navy, underwent a major demobilization that drastically reduced its size. Some of the officers and enlisted men on active duty in the Naval Reserve were offered a chance to convert to a regular status in the Navy. In some cases, enlisted men who had received their commissions following their completion of pilot training reverted to an enlisted status. This, of course, presented a problem for the Navy since they no longer had a program for enlisted personnel with pilot designations.

Following the massive demobilization, Naval Aviation again experienced the problems of maintaining an adequate supply of qualified aviation personnel, both enlisted men and officers. In 1919, various aviation issues were discussed by the Navy's General Board, the Commander in Chief Atlantic Fleet, Admiral H. T. Mayo, and various offices of the Chief of Naval Operations and the Bureaus. On 23 June 1919, the General Board forwarded its final recommendations on Aviation Policy to the Secretary of the Navy, via the Chief of Naval Operations. One of those recommendations was "as many enlisted men as possible should be trained and used as pilots." Captain Thomas T. Craven, the Director of Naval Aviation, submitted his comments on the General Board's recommendations on 17 July 1919. He states, "It is believed that a limited number of enlisted men should be trained as pilots". On 24 July 1919, the Secretary of the Navy added his endorsement on the Board's recommendations. However, his comments on personnel were very brief, stating, "Study will be made with regard to Aviation personnel." While these developments were important, they were eventually superseded by other events that occurred in 1919 between NAS Pensacola, Fla., other Naval Aviation organizations in the fleet, the CNO and the Bureau of Navigation. These events set in motion the eventual establishment of the designation Naval Aviation Pilot (enlisted pilots).

During 1919, a lot of correspondence took place between the Commandant, NAS Pensacola, Fla., and various upper echelon commands regarding flight training and designations for aviation personnel. In a 12 February 1919 letter from the Commandant to the Supervisor Naval Reserve Flying Corps (a CNO office), a request was made to continue flight training and give Naval Aviator designations to four enlisted men. These four men, CBM(A) Edwin Nirmaier, CQM(A) George R. Groh, CMM(GE) Lamont C. Fisher, and CQM(A) Percy M. Fuller, all had had foreign duty and had either qualified as pilots on active service or were undergoing pilot training when the war ended. None of the men wanted to be discharged from the regular Navy and reenrolled with a commission in the Reserves. The Bureau of Navigation returned the request on 31 March 1919 recommending reconsideration and further recommendation for the four enlisted men.

A 17 April 1919 letter from CNO (Aviation) to a wide range of commands, reconsidered the position on training of enlisted personnel and stated, "1. It has been decided to consider the flight training, or continuance of the interrupted flight training, of enlisted ratings of the regular service who, in addition to being unquestionable officer material, can successfully meet the following requirements: (a) That had been regularly enlisted in the Navy, and obtained the rating of second class petty officer prior to April 6, 1917, or that enlisted for Aviation duty only, in accordance with Enclosure (a)." However, the letter also indicated that these men would be commissioned in the Naval Reserve Force and retained on active duty until the issue of transferring Naval Reserve officers to the regular Navy had been definitely decided. A Bureau of Navigation letter of 18 June 1919 modified BuNav's Circular Letter No. 57–19 and authorized the enlisted pilot training policy as stated in the CNO's letter of 17 April 1919. This BuNav circular letter was instrumental in setting in motion the third class of enlisted men authorized for pilot training at NAS Pensacola, Fla. A 20 August 1919 letter from the Bureau of Navigation to the Commandants of All Naval Districts, All Naval Air Stations and Aviation Detachments, set forth the requirements for training of enlisted pilots. The letter indicated that enlisted men would be designated Naval Aviators upon successfully completing the course. However, it made no references to a requirement for commissioning in the Naval Reserves. This omission resulted in a letter from the Commanding Officer of NAS Pensacola, Fla., dated 15 September 1919, requesting Naval Aviator Appointments for Warrant Officers. The letter made a reference to Bureau of Navigation's 20 August letter, stating, "1. Reference (b) specifies that enlisted men are to be trained as Naval Aviators and, without commissioning, are to be given Naval Aviator Appointments and Insignia." In the Bureau's letter of 22 September 1919, it disapproved designating Warrant Officers as Naval Aviators, instead the Warrant Officers were to be commissioned and then designated. However, this letter made no mention of commissioning enlisted pilots as officers. It did not take long for NAS Pensacola, Fla, to send another letter, dated 3 October 1919, questioning the Bureau of Navigation's policy on Naval Aviator Appointments for Warrant Officers. In a 14 October 1919 letter from the Bureau of Navigation, the policy for training of enlisted and Warrant Officer Aviation Pilots was set forth. This letter cancelled the Bureau of Navigation letter dated 20 August 1919. This letter stated, "1. In the future it will be the policy of the Bureau to select a certain number of warrant officers and enlisted men for flight training and duty as pilots of large heavier-than-air craft and directional pilots of dirigibles. (paragraph 2. is not quoted) 3. Warrant officers and men who are selected in accordance with this letter will be given the complete course of instruction for qualification as pilot. Upon successfully completing the course, they will be issued certificates of qualification as 'Naval Aviation Pilots' by the Navy Department. Such certificates will entitle the pilots to wear the aviation insignia authorized for Naval Aviators. Warrant Officers and men who hold certificates as Naval Aviation Pilots will, while detailed for duty involving actual flying be entitled to fifty percent additional pay." This is the first official reference to the designation "Naval Aviation Pilot" and it set in motion the beginning of the enlisted pilot program. Thus, the initial program for Naval Aviation Pilots was done without authorization from Congress. The Congressional program involving enlisted pilots was not developed until the mid-1920s.

In the October and November 1919 letters from the Bureau of Navigation, the bureau notified appropriate commands of its intention to detail classes of approximately 25 enlisted men to begin flight training in heavier-than-air and lighter-than-air. The *CNO Daily Aviation News Bulletin* for 10 December 1919 stated "A class of twenty-five enlisted men has been ordered to Pensacola, Fla., to take the course preliminary to appointment as Naval Aviation Pilots." An NAS Pensacola letter of 9 December 1919 to the Bureau of Navigation stated, "This Station can start the Heavier-than-Air Course of Training for a class of twenty-five (25) enlisted men on February 1st, 1920." This was the third class of enlisted men to undergo flight training at Pensacola, Fla., but the first class whereby the graduates were identified as Naval Aviation Pilots and retained their enlisted status. A 5 February 1920 NAS Pensacola memorandum listed classes undergoing instruction in aviation. Enlisted Class No. 1 (Heavier-than-Air) has the following personnel listed: CMM(A) Floyd Bennett, CMM(A) Chas P. Brenner, CMM(A) Kenneth D. Franklin, CMM(A)

Anthony Iannucci, CMM(A) Leo C. Sullivan, CMM George N. Tibbetts, CMM(A) Jacob W. Utley, CMM(A) Thomas P. Wilkinson, CMM(A) Francis C. Barb, CMM(G) John W. Green, CMM(A) Clarence I. Kessler, CMM(A) R. B. Lawrence, CMM(A) Francis E. Ormsbee, CMM(A) Eugene T. Rhoads, CMM(A) Bert Strand, CMM(A) Harry A. Rossier, CMM(A) N. Wayne L. Carleto, CCM(A) Chas. I. Elliott, CGM(A) Ralph A. Jury, CCM(A) Herbert L. Hoobler, CE(G) William B. Livingston, CQM(A) Owen J. O'Connor, CGM George N. Strode, CEL(A) Clyde O. Switzer, BTSN(A) Lamont C. Fisher, CCM(A) Cecil H. Gurley, CEL(R) Claude G. Alexander, CGM(A) Henry Brenner, CQM(A) William August Clutne, CQM Owen J. Darling, CCM(A) Garrett H. Gibson, BM2c Harvey A. Griesy, CEL(R) Arthur E. LaPorte, CGM(A) Cyrus L. Sylvester, GM1c(A) W. T. Sweeny and CBM Stephen J. Williamson. The list for students (Lighter-than-Air) included the following enlisted men: BTSN William L. Buckley, MACH William L. Coleman, Gunner Ralph T. Bundy, Gunner Willfred H. Smart, CMM(A) L. E. Crowl, CQM(D) Horace M. Finch, CBM S. R. Soulby and CQM(A) G. K. Wilkinson. A second class of enlisted men began undergoing pilot training (Heavier-than-Air) on 1 August 1920 at NAS Pensacola, Fla., and consisted of 33 enlisted men. A third class of enlisted pilot training was scheduled to begin on 1 March 1921.

Designation List of Early Naval Aviation Pilots (NAPS)

The program for Naval Aviation Pilot designation numbers produced the same type of situation and confusion that surrounded the numbering of Naval Aviators. The Navy Department, once a policy was decided upon in late 1919 to designate enlisted men as Naval Aviation Pilots, started issuing certificates of qualification as Naval Aviation Pilots to some enlisted personnel who had qualified as pilots during World War I. Hence, the precedence list for Naval Aviation Pilots includes personnel not part of the enlisted class that began training in February 1920. It appears a number of these enlisted personnel were instructors at NAS Pensacola, Fla., in late 1919 and early 1920. CQM(A) Harold H. Karr received a letter, dated 9 March 1920, from the Bureau of Navigation that certified him as a qualified pilot and designated him a Naval Aviation Pilot. Naval Aviation Pilot designation numbers were placed on a handwritten ledger maintained at NAS Pensacola, Fla. CQM(A) Karr is listed with Naval Aviation Pilot number 1 with the date of issue as 22 January 1920. It is believed the difference between the 22 January date and the 9 March 1920 date is the time difference between the reporting from

NAS Pensacola, Fla., to the Bureau of Navigation and its response to CQM(A) Karr.

The enlisted men who were part of the first two classes to receive training as aviators in 1916 may be considered the forerunners of the enlisted men who were designated Naval Aviation Pilots (NAPS). However, because the program and designation for Naval Aviation Pilots was not established at the time of their training or because most of them received commissions and designations as Naval Aviators, they are not included in this list of early Naval Aviation Pilots. Discrepancies in the sources listing Naval Aviation Pilots made it impossible to resolve all the numbering problems. For this reason, only the first 69 Naval Aviation Pilots are listed.

Naval Aviation Pilot Designations

Pilot No.	Name	Rate	Date Designated
1	Karr, Harold H.	CQM(A)	1/22/20
2	Lee, Robert E.	NM1C(A)	1/22/20
3	Niramaier, Edwin	CBM(A)	4/14/20
4	Lovejoy, Francis E.	CQM(A)	11/22/20
5	Seiler, Walter L.	CQM(A)	1/22/20
6	Woods, Clarence	CQM(A)	1/22/20
7	Alexander, Claud G.	CE(R)	10/7/20
8	Barb, Francis C.	CMM(A)	10/8/20
9	Bennett, Floyd	CMM(A)	10/7/20
10	Byrne, Patrick J.	CMM(A)	10/8/20
11	Carleton, Wayne L.	CBM(A)	10/8/20
12	Cluthe, William A.	CQM(A)	10/8/20
13	Darling, Owen M.	CQM(A)	10/8/20
14	Elliott, Charles I.	CCM(A)	10/7/20
15	Fisher, Lawrence C.	CMM(A)	10/7/20
16	Franklin, Kenneth D.	CMM(A)	10/7/20
17	Graham, Paul E.	CMM(A)	10/8/20
18	Griesy, Harvey A.	BM2C	10/8/20
19	Hoobler, Herbert L.	CCM(A)	10/8/20
20	Insley, Cecil H.	CCM(A)	10/7/20
21	Kesler, C. I.	CMM(A)	10/8/20
22	LaPorte, Arthur E.	CE(R)	10/7/20
23	Lawrence, K. B.	CMM(A)	10/7/20
24	O'Conner, Owen J.	CQM(A)	10/7/20
25	Ormsbee, Frank E.	CMM(A)	10/8/20
26	Peterson, Allen K.	Ch.Ptr.(A)	10/8/20
27	Rhoads, Eugene S.	CMM(A)	10/8/20
28	Rossier, Harry A.	CMM(A)	10/8/20
29	Stinson, John H.	CMM(A)	10/7/20
30	Sullivan, Leo C.	CMM(A)	10/7/20
31	Tibbetts, George N.	CMM(A)	10/7/20
32	Utley, Jacob W.	CMbl(A)	10/7/20
33	Wilkinson, Thomas P.	CMM(A)	10/7/20
34	Williamson, S. J.	CBM(A)	10/8/20
35	Demshock, John J.	CE(G)A	3/8/21

Pilot No.	Name	Rate	Date Designated
36	Baker, H. T.	CMM(A)	3/8/21
37	Buckley, James W.	CMM	3/8/21
38	Elmore, William L.	CGM	3/8/21
39	Griggs, Herbert B.	CE(G)	3/8/21
40	Grobe, C. H.	MM1C	3/8/21
41	Gustafson, R. F.	MM1C(A)	3/8/21
42	Hill, William F.	CMM(A)	3/8/21
43	Jackson, Willard B.	CMM(A)	3/8/21
44	Kirkeby, C. D.	MM1C(A)	3/8/21
45	Linder, Frank M.	CE	3/8/21
46	McPeak, N. B.	MM1C	3/8/21
47	Markham, E. L.	MM2C	3/8/21
48	Merritt, R. J.	GM1C	3/8/21
49	Miller, Joseph H.	CMM	3/8/21
50	McLean, M. C.	CMM	3/8/21
51	McIntosh, Enoch B.	QM1C	3/8/21
52	O'Brien, John J.	CMM	3/8/2l
53	Preeg, Felix F.	CY	3/8/21
54	Raney, Charles B.	CY	3/8/21
55	Rawlings, John E.	CMM	3/8/21
56	Stultz, W. L.	MM1C	3/8/21
57	Steelman, Charlie	CQM(D)*	3/23/21
58	Tobin, Frederick J.	CMM(A)*	3/23/21
59	Andrews, Walter J.	ACMM	8/15/21
60	Dunn, Stephen	AMM1C	8/15/21
61	Frank, Edwin George	ACMM	8/15/21
62	Flynn, Elliott J.	AMM1C	8/15/21
63	Heinz, Edward A.	AMM1C	8/15/21
64	Holdredge, Herman J.	ACMM	8/15/21
65	Krueger, Charley E.	ACMM	8/15/21
66	Muller, Leo G.	AMM1C	8/15/21
67	Smith, Sidney N.	ACMM	8/15/21
68	Sylvester, Cyrus L.	CGM	8/15/21
69	Harrigan, John J.	ACR	8/15/21

* Airship

General Background on Training

The story of Naval Aviator training is complex and involved many changes in the various programs and where they received their training. Training of Naval Aviators first began with the assignment of Lieutenant Theodore G. Ellyson to the Glenn Curtiss camp at San Diego, Calif., (North Island) in December 1910. He arrived at the camp in January 1911. Initially, the Navy followed the policy of using the facilities of private manufacturers to train its aviators. This precedent was established by the assignment of Ellyson to the Curtiss facilities for training as an aviator. The training of these aviators by private aircraft manufacturers was tied to Navy contracts that purchased aircraft for the Navy Department. The first aircraft contracts were with

Curtiss Company and the Wright Company. So the early Naval Aviators were trained at company sites such as San Diego, Calif., and Hammondsport, N.Y., used by the Curtiss Company; Dayton, Ohio, used by the Wright Company and Marblehead, Mass., used by the Burgess Company, for training in Wright Company aircraft.

With the acquisition of aircraft and the training of several Naval Aviators, the Navy was able to terminate its dependence on private manufacturers for training its aviators. In August 1911 the Navy set up an Engineering Experiment Station and aviation school at Greenbury Point, Annapolis, Md. During the winter of 1912–1913, the aviation camp at Greenbury Point, Md., moved to Guantanamo Bay, Cuba, for its first exercises with the fleet. Captain Washington I. Chambers' report to the Chief of the Bureau of Navigation in 1913 identified the following Naval Aviators:

T. G. Ellyson, J. Rodgers, J. H. Towers, V. C. Herbster, P. N. L. Bellinger, A. B. L. Smith, G. deC Chevalier, A. A. Cunningham, W. D. Billingsley, L. N. McNair, H. C. Richardson, I. F. Dortch, H. C. Mustin and J. D. Burray. The last seven in this list of Naval Aviators were Navy-trained.

In accordance with the recommendations from the Board on Naval Aeronautic Service, the aviation school/training camp at Greenbury Point, Md., was moved to Pensacola, Fla. On 20 January 1914, the aviation unit from Greenbury Point, Md., arrived at Pensacola, Fla., to set up a flying school. It consisted of nine officers, 23 men, seven aircraft, portable hangars and other equipment.

The training of Naval Aviators at Pensacola was conducted in the same informal way that had been done at Greenbury Point. They were taught how to fly, and instructed in the rudiments of the construction and maintenance of their planes. Every man was given as much time as necessary to master his ground and flight instruction. No one washed out.

A formal training syllabus was issued by the Bureau of Navigation in June 1914, BuNav Bulletin No. 532. This syllabus established a one-year course for pilots. In January 1916, the syllabus was revised. The new syllabus, "Courses of Instruction and Required Qualification of Personnel of the Air Service of the Navy" outlined courses for Naval Aviation Pilots, Naval Aviators, Student Airmen, Quartermasters (Aviation), Quartermasters (Deck), and Machinists Mates (Aviation). During the summer of 1916, a syllabus was also established for the training of lighter-than-air pilots (dirigible and balloon pilots). Needless to say, flight instruction procedures were altered by a constant stream of suggestions from the pioneers at Pensacola.

In 1916 the Naval Appropriation Act provided for the establishment of a Naval Flying Corps. It also provided for the establishment of a Naval Reserve Force of six classes, including a Naval Reserve Flying Corps. One of the first groups to organize under the Naval Reserve Flying Corps was the First Yale Group/Unit. Most of the men in this organization received their training independently of the Navy and were later qualified as Naval Aviators. Training for many of the personnel in the Naval Reserve Flying Corps fell on the shoulders of Pensacola until a training system evolved and was established during World War I.

With the U.S. entry into World War I, numerous changes occurred in the training of naval pilots. Besides the training of pilots in England, France and Italy, a group of 24 American personnel reported at the University of Toronto on 9 July 1917 to begin flight training under the Canadian Royal Flying Corps. In the United States, flight training expanded from the site at NAS Pensacola, Fla., to include preliminary flight training at Squantum, Mass., Bay Shore (Long Island), N.Y., Miami, Fla., Key West, Fla., and San Diego, Calif. By late January 1918, the following list of air stations was conducting aviation training: Chatham, Mass., Montauk, N.Y., Bay Shore, N.Y., Rockaway, N.Y., Cape May, N.J., Hampton Road, Va., Miami, Fla., Key West, Fla., Pensacola, Fla., and San Diego, Calif. There were also Naval Aviation Detachments scattered around the country that were involved in aviation training. These included MIT at Cambridge, Mass., Great Lakes Training Station, Ill., Goodyear at Akron, Ohio, Curtiss Aeroplane at Buffalo, N.Y., Aeromarine company at Keyport, Mass., the Naval Aircraft Factory at Philadelphia, Pa., Packard Motor Car Company in Detroit, Mich., Delco Ignition Laboratories in Dayton, Ohio, Lincoln Motor Company in Detroit, Mich., and Savage Arms Corporation in Utica, N.Y. With the end of World War I, most of these stations ended their aviation training programs and NAS Pensacola, Fla., again became the primary training station.

With the beginning of World War II the training of Naval Aviators again became decentralized and expanded across the country, just as it had done during World War I. Following the end of World War II, the different phases of training for Naval Aviators continued to be conducted at several different air stations. That situation continues to exist today.

Number of Naval Aviators Designated (Trained)

Obviously, the variances in the Naval Aviator training program and its decentralization make it very difficult to provide an infallible number for the output of Naval Aviators since 1911. All the variances in the programs listed in the sections above will corroborate this statement.

Personnel trained by the Navy are designated Naval Aviators, no matter whether they serve in the U.S. Navy, Marine Corps, or Coast Guard. The list below also includes foreign personnel trained by the U.S. Navy Department as Naval Aviators, as well as a few U.S. military and civilian personnel from other federal agencies. In some cases these special groups, such as the foreign or civilian personnel from other federal agencies, were included in the number count, but in other cases they were not. It is extremely difficult to identify the years in which this group was included and the years in which they were not. Hence, the following list identifying the number of Naval Aviators trained (designated Naval Aviators) is the best available. The numbers for the more recent years are by fiscal year. In 1976 the government changed its fiscal year from 1 July–30 June time frame to 1 October–30 September. Consequently, there is an additional entry for 1976 covering the 1 July to 30 September time frame.

Year	Number Trained (Designated)
1911 to 1919	2,834
1920	82
1921	72
1922	106
1923	25
1924	32
1925	35
1926	35
1927	123
1928	140
1929	66
1930	348
1931	321
1932	168
1933	138
1934	35
1935	100
1936	212
1937	527
1938	543
1939	450
1940	708
1941	3,112
1942	10,869
1943	20,842
1944	21,067
1945	8,880
1946	2,635
1947	1,646
1948	446
1949	688

Year	Number Trained (Designated)
1950	1,691
1951	1,288
1952	932
1953	1,701
1954	2,338
1955	2,851
1956	2,571
1957	2,951
1958	2,513
1959	1,785
1960	1,602
1961	1,478
1962	1,413
1963	1,701
1964	1,701
1965	1,715
1966	1,907
1967	2,046
1968	2,334
1969	2,559
1970	2,450
1971	1,809
1972	1,853
1973	1,650
1974	1,447
1975	1,337
1976	1,375
Jul-Sep 1976	314
1977	1,196
1978	934
1979	871
1980	1,471
1981	1,482
1982	1,515
1983	1,424
1984	1,366
1985	1,343
1986	1,439
1987	1,482
1988	1,454
1989	1,528
1990	1,483
1991	1,342
1992	1,216
1993	865
1994	874
1995	1,155
Total	153,037

Aviation Commands

In order of their establishment

Officer in Charge of Aviation
Director of Naval Aeronautics
Director of Naval Aviation

CAPT Washington I. Chambers	26 Sep 1910–17 Dec 1913
CAPT Mark L. Bristol	17 Dec 1913–4 Mar 1916
CAPT Noble E. Irwin	17 May 1917–May 1919
CAPT Thomas T. Craven	May 1919–7 Mar 1921
CAPT William A. Moffett	7 Mar 1921–26 Jul 1921

The person in charge of aviation affairs for the Navy was initially designated as the officer to whom all correspondence on aviation should be referred. This position was a special duty assignment as officer in charge of aviation. The position was identified by the title Director of Naval Aeronautics on 23 November 1914. It was discontinued on 4 March 1916 and reinstituted as Director of Naval Aviation on 7 March 1918. The title Director of Naval Aviation was replaced in July 1921 by the establishment of the Bureau of Aeronautics.

Officer-in-Charge, Aviation, Headquarters Marine Corps
Director of Marine Corps Aviation
Deputy Chief of Staff (Air), Marine Corps
Director Chief of Staff for Aviation, Marine Corps

MAJ Alfred A. Cunningham	17 Nov 1919–12 Dec 1920
LCOL Thomas C. Turner	13 Dec 1920–2 Mar 1925
MAJ Edward H. Brainard	3 Mar 1925–9 May 1929
COL Thomas C. Turner	10 May 1929–28 Oct 1931
MAJ Roy S. Geiger	6 Nov 1931–29 May 1935
COL Ross E. Rowell	30 May 1935–10 Mar 1939
BGEN Ralph J. Mitchell	11 Mar 1939–29 Mar 1943
MGEN Roy S. Geiger	13 May 1943–15 Oct 1943
BGEN Louis E. Woods	15 Oct 1943–17 Jul 1944
MGEN Field Harris	18 Jul 1944–24 Feb 1948
MGEN William J. Wallace	24 Feb 1948–1 Sep 1950
BGEN Clayton C. Jerome	1 Sep 1950–1 Apr 1952
LGEN William O. Brice	1 Apr 1952–31 Jul 1955
LGEN Christian F. Schilt	1 Aug 1955–31 Mar 1957
LGEN Verne J. McCaul	1 Apr 1957–2 Dec 1957
MGEN Samuel S. Jack	14 Jan 1958–20 Feb 1958
MGEN John C. Munn	21 Feb 1958–14 Dec 1959
MGEN Arthur F. Binney	15 Dec 1959–10 Sep 1961
COL Keith B. McCutcheon	11 Sep 1961–17 Feb 1962
COL Marion E. Carl	18 Feb 1962–4 Jul 1962
BGEN Norman J. Anderson	5 Jul 1962–20 Oct 1963

MGEN Louis B. Robertshaw	21 Oct 1963–15 Jun 1966
MGEN Keith B. McCutcheon	15 Jun 1966–18 Feb 1970
MGEN Homer S. Hill	19 Feb 1970–24 Aug 1972
MGEN Edward S. Fris	25 Aug 1972–27 Aug 1974
BGEN Philip D. Shutler	28 Aug 1974–Jan 1975
MGEN Victor A. Armstrong	Jan 1975–21 Aug 1975
LGEN Thomas H. Miller, Jr.	22 Aug 1975–29 Jun 1979
LGEN William J. White	1 Jul 1979–30 Jun 1982
LGEN William H. Fitch	1 Jul 1982–31 Aug 1984
LGEN Keith A. Smith	1 Sep 1984–29 Apr 1988
LGEN Charles H. Pitman	30 Apr 1988–1 Aug 1990
LGEN Duane A. Wills	17 Aug 1990–30 Jun 1993
LGEN Richard D. Hearney	1 Jul 1993–14 Jul 1994
LGEN Harold W. Blot	15 Jul 1994–

On 1 April 1936 the title of the senior aviator attached to Headquarters, Marine Corps, changed from Officer-in-Charge, Aviation, to Director of Aviation, and on 25 April 1962 became Deputy Chief of Staff (Air). On 16 September 1972 the title changed to Deputy Chief of Staff for Aviation.

Chief of the Bureau of Aeronautics

RADM William A. Moffett	26 Jul 1921–4 Apr 1933
RADM Ernest J. King	3 May 1933–12 Jun 1936
RADM Arthur B. Cook	12 Jun 1936–1 Jun 1939
RADM John H. Towers	1 Jun 1939–6 Oct 1942
RADM John S. McCain	9 Oct 1942–7 Aug 1943
RADM Dewitt C. Ramsey	7 Aug 1943–1 Jun 1945
RADM Harold B. Sallada	1 Jun 1945–1 May 1947
RADM Alfred M. Pride	1 May 1947–1 May 1951
RADM Thomas S. Combs	1 May 1951–30 Jun 1953
RADM Apollo Soucek	30 Jun 1953–4 Mar 1955
RADM James S. Russell	4 Mar 1955–15 Jul 1957
RADM Robert E. Dixon	15 Jul 1957–1 Dec 1959

Established by act of Congress, 12 July 1921, and merged 1 December 1959 with the Bureau of Ordnance to form the Bureau of Naval Weapons.

Assistant Secretary of the Navy for Aeronautics
Assistant Secretary of the Navy for Air

Edward P. Warner	10 Jul 1926–Mar 1929
David S. Ingalls	16 Mar 1929–1 Jun 1932
Artemus L. Gates	5 Sep 1941–1 Jul 1945
John L. Sullivan	1 Jul 1945–17 Jun 1946
John N. Brown	12 Nov 1946–8 Mar 1949
Dan A. Kimball	9 Mar 1949–25 May 1949
John F. Floberg	5 Dec 1949–23 Jul 1953
James H. Smith	23 Jul 1953–20 Jun 1956
Garrison R. Norton	28 Jun 1956–5 Feb 1959

Established by act of Congress 24 June 1926 with title Assistant Secretary of the Navy for Aeronautics. Office vacant 1 June 1932 to 5 September 1941. On 11 September 1941 it was retitled Assistant Secretary of the Navy for Air and abolished on 5 February 1959.

U.S. Naval Air Forces, Pacific Fleet
Commander, Air Force, Pacific Fleet
Commander, Naval Air Force Pacific Fleet

RADM Aubrey W. Fitch	1 Sep 1942–15 Sep 1942
RADM Leigh Noyes	15 Sep 1942–14 Oct 1942
VADM John H. Towers	14 Oct 1942–28 Feb 1944
RADM Charles A. Pownall	28 Feb 1944–17 Aug 1944
RADM George D. Murray	17 Aug 1944–20 Jul 1945
RADM Alfred E. Montgomery	20 Jul 1945–31 Aug 1946
VADM John D. Price	31 Aug 1946–5 Jan 1948
VADM Harold B. Sallada	5 Jan 1948–1 Oct 1949
VADM Thomas L. Sprague	1 Oct 1949–1 Apr 1952
VADM Harold M. Martin	1 Apr 1952–1 Feb 1956
VADM Alfred M. Pride	1 Feb 1956–30 Sep 1959
RADM Murr E. Arnold	30 Sep 1959–12 Oct 1959
VADM Clarence E. Ekstrom	12 Oct 1959–30 Nov 1962
VADM Paul D. Stroop	30 Nov 1962–30 Oct 1965
VADM Thomas F. Connolly	30 Oct 1965–1 Nov 1966
VADM Allen M. Shinn	1 Nov 1966–31 Mar 1970
VADM William F. Bringle	31 Mar 1970–28 May 1971
VADM Thomas J. Walker III	28 May 1971–31 May 1973
VADM Robert B. Baldwin	31 May 1973–12 Jul 1976
VADM Robert P. Coogan	12 Jul 1976–31 Jan 1980
VADM Robert F. Schoultz	31 Jan 1980–4 Aug 1985
VADM Crawford A. Easterling	4 Aug 1982–16 Aug 1985
VADM James E. Service	16 Aug 1985–21 Aug 1987
VADM John H. Fetterman, Jr.	21 Aug 1987–14 Dec 1990
VADM Edwin R. Kohn, Jr.	14 Dec 1990–17 Jun 1993
RADM Steven R. Briggs	17 Jun 1993–26 Oct 1993
VADM Robert J. Spane	26 Oct 1993–24 Jan 1996
VADM Brent M. Bennitt	24 Jan 1996–

Established 1 September 1942 as an administrative command replacing the commands Carriers, Pacific Fleet and Patrol Wings, Pacific Fleet. The title, U.S. Naval Air Forces, Pacific Fleet was changed 14 October 1942 to Air Force, Pacific Fleet and 30 July 1957 to Naval Air Force Pacific Fleet.

Commander, Air Force, Atlantic Fleet
Commander, Naval Air Force Atlantic Fleet

RADM Alva D. Bernhard	1 Jan 1943–8 Mar 1943
VADM Patrick N. L. Bellinger	20 Mar 1943–2 Feb 1946
VADM Gerald F. Bogan	Feb 1946–Dec 1948
VADM Felix B. Stump	Dec 1948–11 May 1951
VADM John J. Ballentine	11 May 1951–1 May 1954
VADM Frederick G. McMahon	1 May 1954–29 May 1956
VADM William L. Rees	29 May 1956–30 Sep 1960
VADM Frank O'Beirne	30 Sep 1960–30 Sep 1963
VADM Paul H. Ramsey	30 Sep 1963–31 Mar 1965
VADM Charles T. Booth	31 Mar 1965–28 Feb 1969
VADM Robert L. Townsend	1 Mar 1969–29 Feb 1972
VADM Fredrick H. Michaelis	29 Feb 1972–14 Feb 1975
VADM Howard E. Greer	14 Feb 1975–31 Mar 1978

VADM George E. R. Kinnear	31 Mar 1978–31 Jul 1981
VADM Thomas J. Kilcline	31 Jul 1981–8 Dec 1983
VADM Robert F. Dunn	8 Dec 1983–23 Dec 1986
VADM Richard M. Dunleavy	23 Dec 1986–25 May 1989
VADM John K. Ready	25 May 1989–6 Aug 1991
VADM Anthony A. Less	6 Aug 1991–18 Mar 1994
VADM Richard C. Allen	18 Mar 1994–

Established 1 January 1943 as an administrative command replacing the commands Carriers, Atlantic Fleet and Fleet Air Wing, Atlantic Fleet. The original title, Air Force, Atlantic Fleet, was changed 30 July 1957 to Naval Air Force Altantic Fleet.

Deputy Chief of Naval Opeations (Air)
Deputy Chief of Naval Opeations (Air Warfare)
Assistant Chief of Naval Operations (Air Warfare)
Director, Air Warfare

VADM John S. McCain	18 Aug 1943–1 Aug 1944
VADM Aubrey W. Fitch	1 Aug 1944–14 Aug 1945
VADM Marc A. Mitscher	14 Aug 1945–15 Jan 1946
VADM Arthur W. Radford	15 Jan 1946–22 Feb 1947
VADM Donald B. Duncan	6 Mar 1947–20 Jan 1948
VADM John D. Price	20 Jan 1948–6 May 1949
VADM Calvin T. Durgin	16 May 1949–25 Jan 1950
VADM John H. Cassady	25 Jan 1950–31 May 1952
VADM Matthias B. Gardner	31 May 1952–16 Mar 1953
VADM Ralph A. Ofstie	16 Mar 1953–3 Mar 1955
VADM Thomas S. Combs	11 Apr 1955–1 Aug 1956
VADM William V. Davis, Jr.	1 Aug 1956–22 May 1958
VADM Robert B. Pirie	26 May 1958–1 Nov 1962
VADM William A. Schoech	14 Nov 1962–1 Jul 1963
VADM John S. Thach	8 Jul 1963–25 Feb 1965
VADM Paul H. Ramsey	31 Mar 1965–1 Oct 1966
VADM Thomas F. Connolly	1 Nov 1966–31 Aug 1971
VADM Maurice F. Weisner	1 Sep 1971–4 Aug 1972
VADM William D. Houser	5 Aug 1972–30 Apr 1976
VADM Forrest S. Petersen	1 May 1976–5 Oct 1976
VADM Frederick C. Turner	6 Oct 1976–30 Jun 1979
VADM Wesley L. McDonald	1 Jul 1979–1 Sep 1982
VADM Robert F. Schoultz	2 Sep 1982–27 Jan 1985
VADM Edward H. Martin	25 Feb 1985–14 Jan 1987
VADM Robert F. Dunn	15 Jan 1987–25 May 1989
VADM Richard M. Dunleavy	25 May 1989–12 Jun 1992
RADM Riley D. Mixson	12 Jun 1992–22 Nov 1993
RADM Brent M. Bennitt	22 Nov 1993–15 Jan 1996
RADM Dennis V. McGinn	15 Jan 1996–

Established by the Secretary of the Navy, 18 August 1943, as Deputy Chief of Naval Operations (Air). Changed to Deputy Chief of Naval Operations (Air Warfare) on 15 July 1971. On 1 October 1987 the Chief of Naval Operations (OPNAV) was reorganized and Deputy Chief of Naval Operations (Air Warfare) was redesignated Assistant Chief of Naval Operations (Air Warfare). On 10 August 1992 the Assistant Chief of Naval Operations (Air Warfare) was changed to Director, Air Warfare Division.

Chief of the Bureau of Naval Weapons

RADM Paul D. Stroop   10 Sep 1959–29 Oct 1962
RADM Kleber S. Masterson   27 Nov 1962–24 Mar 1964
RADM Allen M. Shinn   28 May 1964–1 May 1966

Established as the Bureau of Naval Weapons on 18 August 1959, merging the Bureaus of Ordnance and Aeronautics. It was abolished on 1 May 1966 during the reorganization of the bureaus. The reorganization assigned elements of the Bureau of Naval Weapons to three new commands: Naval Air Systems Command, Naval Ordnance Systems Command and Naval Electronic Systems Command.

Commander Naval Air Systems Command

RADM Allen M. Shinn   1 May 1966–1 Sep 1966
RADM Robert L. Townsend   1 Sep 1966–20 Feb 1969
RADM Thomas J. Walker III   20 Feb 1969–1 Apr 1971
RADM Thomas R. McClellan   1 Apr 1971–31 Aug 1973
VADM Kent L. Lee   31 Aug 1973–29 Aug 1976
VADM Forrest S. Petersen   29 Aug 1976–30 Apr 1980
VADM Ernest R. Seymour   30 Apr 1980–22 Jul 1983
VADM James B. Busey IV   22 Jul 1983–23 Aug 1985
VADM Joseph B. Wilkinson   23 Aug 1985–19 Sep 1989
VADM Richard C. Gentz   19 Sep 1989–22 Jan 1991
VADM William C. Bowes   22 Mar 1991–10 Mar 1995
VADM John A. Lockard   10 Mar 1995–

Established by a reorganization of the Navy Department effective 1 May 1966.

Following the end of World War II many carriers were placed in the mothball fleet. This photo shows six Essex *class carriers in mothballs at the Naval Ship Yard, Puget Sound, USN-428458*

Lexington *(CV 2) underway with a load of aircraft beginning their launch cycle.*

Aviation Ships
Attack Carriers (CV, CVA, CVB, CVL, CVAN, CVN)

The CVB and CVL designations were established within the original CV designation on 15 July 1943. CVA replaced CV and CVB on 1 October 1952; CVL went out of use on 15 May 1959. CV and CVN replaced CVA and CVAN on 30 June 1975 to designate the multimission character of aircraft carriers after the decommissioning of the last CVS in 1974.

During the U.S. involvement in World War II (7 December 1941 to 2 September 1945) the Navy operated 110 carriers (includes those designated CV, CVE and CVL). It commissioned 102 carriers (includes those designated CV, CVE and CVL) during the above mentioned time frame. The Navy also operated two training carriers during World War II with the designation IX. They were *Wolverine* (IX 64) and *Sable* (IX 81).

Original Classes	*Langley* Class:	1 ship (CV 1)
	Lexington Class:	2 ships (CV 2 and 3)
	Ranger Class:	1 ship (CV 4)
	Yorktown Class:	2 ships (CV 5 and 6)
	Wasp Class:	1 ship (CV 7)
	Hornet Class:	1 ship (CV 8)

Essex Class
(Long-Hull *Essex* Class
or *Ticonderoga* Class)

24 ships; CV 9 through 21, 31 through 35, 37 through 40, 45, and 47.
Of these numbers, 14, 15, 19, 21, 32–34, 36–40, 45 and 47 are sometimes referred to as "Long-Hull" *Essex* class or *Ticonderoga* Class.

Independence Class	9 ships, CVL 22 through 30.
Midway Class	3 ships, CVB 41 through 43.
Saipan Class	2 ships, CVL 48 and 49.
Enterprise Class	1 ship, CVAN-65.
Forrestal Class	4 ships, CVA 59 through 62.
Kitty Hawk Class	4 ships, CVA 63, 64, 66 and 67.
Nimitz Class	9 ships, CVN 68 through 76.

Core (CVE 11) *underway during World War II with a couple of TBM Avengers on the forward flight deck.*

Nimitz *(CVN 68), one of the Navy' current super carriers, underway with a full load of planes on her flight deck, DN-SC-84-00358.*

Carrier Listing for CV, CVA, CVB, CVAN, CVN, and CVL

Hull No.	Name	Date of Commission and Decommission or loss***	New Designation or Change of Designation	Date of Designation Change	Conversion Project*	Date Conversion Completed	Comments
1	Langley	20 Mar 1922 27 Feb 1942	CV 1 AV 3	21 Apr 1937			Lost, enemy action.
2	Lexington	14 Dec 1927 8 May 1942	CV 2				Lost, enemy action.
3	Saratoga	16 Nov 1927	CV 3				Expended, Operation Crossroads, 26 Jul 1946.
4	Ranger	4 Jun 1934 18 Oct 1946	CV 4				Sold for scrap 31 Jan 1947.
5	Yorktown	30 Sep 1937 7 Jun 1942	CV 5				Lost, enemy action.
6	Enterprise	12 May 1938 17 Feb 1947	CV 6 CVA 6 CVS 6	1 Oct 1952 8 Aug 1953			Sold, 1 Jul 1958.
7	Wasp	25 Apr 1940 15 Sep 1942	CV 7				Lost, enemy action.
8	Hornet	20 Oct 1941 26 Oct 1942	CV8				Lost, enemy action.
9	Essex	31 Dec 1942 30 Jun 1969	CV 9 CVA 9 CVS 9	1 Oct 1952 8 Mar 1960	27A 125	Feb 1951 Mar 1956	Stricken 1 Jun 1973.
10	Yorktown	15 Apr 1943 27 Jun 1970	CV 10 CVA 10 CVS 10	1 Oct 1952 1 Sep 1957	27A 125	Jan 1953 Oct 1955	Stricken 1 Jun 1973. Floating museum, Charleston, S.C., 13 Nov 1975.
11	Intrepid	16 Aug 1943 15 Mar 1974	CV 11 CVA 11 CVS 11	1 Oct 1952 31 Mar 1962	27C 27C	Jun 1954 Apr 1957	Floating Museum, New York City, N.Y.
12	Hornet	29 Nov 1943 26 May 1970	CV 12 CVA 12 CVS 12	1 Oct 1952 27 Jun 1958	27A 125	Oct 1953 Aug 1956	Stricken 1989.
13	Franklin	31 Jan 1944 17 Feb 1947	CV 13 CVA 13 CVS 13	1 Oct 1952 8 Aug 1953			Stricken 10 Oct 1964.
14	Ticonderoga	8 May 1944 1 Sep 1973	CV 14 CVA 14 CVS 14	1 Oct 1952 21 Oct 1969	27C 27C	Dec 1954 Mar 1957	Stricken 16 Nov 1973.
15	Randolph	9 Oct 1944 13 Feb 1969	CV 15 CVA 15 CVS 15	1 Oct 1952 31 Mar 1959	27A 125	Jul 1953 Feb 1956	Stricken 1 Jun 1973.
16	Lexington	17 Feb 1943 8 Nov 1991	CV 16 CVA 16 CVS 16 CVT 16 AVT 16	1 Oct 1952 1 Oct 1962 1 Jan 1969 1 Jul 1978	27C	Sep 1955	Stricken 30 Nov 1991.
17	Bunker Hill	25 May 1943 9 Jul 1947	CV 17 CVA 17 CVS 17	1 Oct 1952 8 Aug 1953			Stricken 1 Nov 1966, retained as moored electronic test ship San Diego, Calif., until Nov 1972. Scrapped 1973.

Carrier Listing for CV, CVA, CVB, CVAN, CVN, and CVL—Continued

Hull No.	Name	Date of Commission and Decommission or loss***	New Designation or Change of Designation	Date of Designation Change	Conversion Project*	Date Conversion Completed	Comments
18	Wasp	24 Nov 1943 1 Jul 1972	CV 18 CVA 18 CVS 18	1 Oct 1952 1 Nov 1956	27A 125	Sep 1951 Dec 1955	Sold for scrap 21 May 1973.
19	Hancock	15 Apr 1944 30 Jan 1976	CV 19 CVA 19 CV 19	1 Oct 1952 30 Jun 1975	27C 17C	Mar 1954 Nov 1956	Stricken 31 Jan 1976.
20	Bennington	6 Aug 1944 15 Jan 1970	CV 20 CVA 20 CVS 20	1 Oct 1952 30 Jun 1959	27A 125	Nov 1952 Apr 1955	Stricken 1989.
21	Boxer	16 Apr 1945 1 Dec `1969	CV 21 CVA 21 CVS 21 LPH 4	1 Oct 1952 1 Feb 1956 30 Jan 1959			Stricken 1 Dec 1969.
22	Independence	14 Jan 1943 28 Aug 1946	CVL 22				Sunk in weapons test 29 Jun 1951.
23	Princeton	25 Feb 1943 24 Oct 1944	CVL 23				Lost, enemy action..
24	Belleau Wood	31 Mar 1943 13 Jan 1947	CVL 24				Transferred to France 1953–1960. Stricken 1 Oct 1960.
25	Cowpens	28 May 1943 13 Jan 1947	CVL 25 AVT 1	15 May 1959			Stricken 1 Nov 1959.
26	Monterey	17 Jun 1943 16 Jan 1956	CVL 26 AVT 2	15 May 1959			Stricken 1 Jun 1970.
27	Langley	31 Aug 1943 11 Feb 1947	CVL 27				Transferred to France 1951–1963. Sold 19 Feb 1964.
28	Cabot	24 Jul 1943 21 Jan 1955	CVL 28 AVT 3	15 May 1959			Transferred to Spain on 30 Aug 1967, returned to private U.S. organization in 1989.
29	Bataan	17 Nov 1943 9 Apr 1954	CVL 29 AVT 4	15 May 1959			Stricken 1 Sep 1959.
30	San Jacinto	15 Dec 1943 1 Mar 1947	CVL 30 AVT 5	15 May 1959			Stricken 1 Jun 1970.
31	Bon Homme Richard	26 Nov 1944 2 Jul 1971	CV 31 CVA 31	1 Oct 1952			Stricken 1989.
32	Leyte	11 Apr 1946 15 May 1959	CV 32 CVA 32 CVS 32 AVT 10	1 Oct 1952 8 Aug 1953 15 May 1959			Stricken 1 Jun 1969.
33	Kearsarge	2 Mar 1946 15 Jan 1970	CV 33 CVA 33 CVS 33	1 Oct 1952 1 Oct 1958	27A 125	Mar 1952 Jan 1957	Stricken 1 May 1973.
34	Oriskany	25 Sep 1950 20 Sep 1979	CV 34 CVA 34 CV 34	1 Oct 1952 30 Jun 1975	27A 125	Oct 1950 May 1959	Stricken 1989.
36	Antietam	28 Jan 1945 8 May 1963	CV 36 CVA 36 CVS 36	1 Oct 1952 1 Aug 1953	**		Stricken 1 May 1973.

Carrier Listing for CV, CVA, CVB, CVAN, CVN, and CVL—Continued

Hull No.	Name	Date of Commission and Decommission or loss***	New Designation or Change of Designation	Date of Designation Change	Conversion Project*	Date Conversion Completed	Comments
37	Princeton	18 Nov 1945 30 Jan 1970	CV37 CVA 37 CVS 37 LPH 5	 1 Oct 1952 1 Jan 1954 2 Mar 1959			Stricken 30 Jan 1970..
38	Shangri-La	15 Sep 1944 30 Jul 1971	CV 38 CVA 38 CVS 38	 1 Oct 1952 30 Jun 1969	27C	Feb 1955	Stricken 15 Jul 1982.
39	Lake Champlain	3 Jun 1945 2 May 1966	CV 39 CVA 39 CVS 39	 1 Oct 1952 1 Aug 1957	27A	Sep 1952	Stricken 1 Dec 1969.
40	Tarawa	8 Dec 1945 13 May 1960	CV 40 CVA 40 CVS 40 AVT 12	 1 Oct 1952 10 Jan 1955 17 Apr 1961	27A	Sep 1952	Stricken 1 Jun 1967.
41	Midway	10 Sep 1945 11 Apr 1992	CVB 41 CVA 41 CV 41	 1 Oct 1952 30 Jun 1975	110	Nov 1957	In reserve.
42	Franklin D. Roosevelt	27 Oct 1945 1 Oct 1977	CVB 42 CVA 42 CV 42	 1 Oct 1952 30 Jun 1975	110	Jun 1956	Stricken 30 Sep 1977.
43	Coral Sea	1 Oct 1947 26 Apr 1990	CVB 43 CVA 43 CV 43	 1 Oct 1952 30 Jun 1975	110A	Jan 1960	Sold for scrap 30 Mar 1993.
45	Valley Forge	3 Nov 1946 15 Jan 1970	CV 45 CVA 45 CVS 45 LPH 8	 1 Oct 1952 1 Jan 1954 1 Jul 1961			Stricken 15 Jan 1970.
47	Philippine Sea	11 May 1946 28 Dec 1958	CV 47 CVA 47 CVS 47 AVT 11	 1 Oct 1952 15 Nov 1955 15 May 1959			Stricken 1 Dec 1969.
48	Saipan	14 Jul 1946 14 Jan 1970	CVL 48 AVT 6 AGMR 2	 15 May 1959 8 Apr 1965			
49	Wright	9 Feb 1947 22 May 1970	CVL 49 AVT 7 CC 2	 15 May 1959. 11 May 1963			
59	Forrestal	1 Oct 1955 30 Sep 1993	CVA 59 CV 59 AVT 59	 30 Jun 1975 4 Feb 1992			Stricken 11 Sep 1993.
60	Saratoga	14 Apr 1956 20 Aug 1994	CVA 60 CV 60	 30 Jun 1972			Stricken 30 Sep 1994.
61	Ranger	10 Aug 1957 10 Jul 1993	CVA 61 CV 61	 30 Jun 1972			Inactive in Reserve.
62	Independence	10 Jan 1959	CVA 62 CV 62	 28 Feb 1973			Active.
63	Kitty Hawk	29 Apr 1961	CVA 63 CV 63	 29 Apr 1973			Active.
64	Constellation	27 Oct 1961	CVA 64 CV 64	 30 Jun 1975			Active.

*Carrier Listing for CV, CVA, CVB, CVAN, CVN, and CVL—Continued

Hull No.	Name	Date of Commission and Decommission or loss***	New Designation or Change of Designation	Date of Designation Change	Conversion Project*	Date Conversion Completed	Comments
65	Enterprise	25 Nov 1961	CVAN 65				Active.
			CVN 65	30 Jun 1975			
66	America	23 Jan 1965	CVA 66				Inactive in Reserve.
		30 Sep 1996	CV 66	30 Jun 1975			
67	John F. Kennedy	7 Sep 1968	CVA 67				Active.
			CV 67	29 Apr 1973			
68	Nimitz	3 May 1975	CVAN 68				Active.
			CVN 68	30 Jun 1975			
69	Dwight D. Eisenhower	18 Oct 1977	CVN 69				Active.
70	Carl Vinson	13 Mar 1982	CVN 70				Active.
71	Theordore Roosevelt	25 Oct 1986	CVN 71				Active.
72	Abraham Lincoln	11 Nov 1989	CVN 72				Active.
73	George Washington	4 Jul 1992	CVN 73				Active.
74	John C. Stennis	9 Dec 1995	CVN 74				Active.
75	Harry S. Truman		CVN 75				Keel laid 29 Nov 1993.
76	Ronald Reagan		CVN 76				

* Projects 27A and the first 27Cs are axial deck modernizations; all others are angled deck conversions. For more detail, see chronology entries for 4 Jun 1947, 1 Feb 1952, 2 Sep 1953 and 27 May 1954.

** Experimental angled deck installation completed Dec 1952.

*** There were a number of carriers that were decommissioned and then recommissioned for further service. Only the final decommissioning date is listed for these carriers. Several carriers were also placed out of commission during major rennovations or yard periods. In some cases the records regarding decommissioning dates were not complete. Consequently, the decommissioning date was left blank if it was unknown.

Note 1: Construction of hull numbers omitted above were either terminated or cancelled. Numbers 35, 46, and 50–55 were scheduled for *Essex* class; 44, 56 and 57 for *Midway* class. Number 58 was *United States*.

Note 2: The contracts originally let for CV 59 and 60 (*Forrestal* and *Saratoga*) did not include an angled deck in their designs. In 1953 the Navy redesigned the flight deck plans for *Forrestal* and incorporated an angled landing deck. These changes were also made to the designs for *Saratoga*. The contract for *Forrestal* was awarded in 1951 and for *Saratoga* in 1952. The contract for *Ranger* and *Independence* (CV 61 and 62) were not awarded until 1954. Therefore, the original contract designs for *Ranger* and *Independence* would have included an angled deck. Technically speaking, *Ranger* (CVA 61) was the first carrier designed and built as an angled deck carrier.

Escort Carriers (AVG, ACV and CVE)

The original escort carrier designation AVG (Aircraft Escort Vessel) was first assigned on 31 March 1941. The classification was changed to ACV (Auxiliary Aircraft Carrier) on 20 August 1942 and to CVE (Escort Carrier) on 15 July 1943. The CVE designation went out of use when the remaining escort carriers were reclassified AKV (Aircraft Ferry) on 7 May 1959.

Classes:

Long Island	1 ship, hull number 1
Charger	1 ship, hull number 30 (originally built for Royal Navy)
Bogue	11 ships, hull numbers 9, 11–13, 16, 18, 20, 21, 23, 25 and 31
Sangamon	4 ships, hull numbers 26–29
Casablanca	50 ships, hull numbers 55–104
Commencement Bay	19 ships, hull numbers 105–123

Hull numbers not listed above are accounted for as follows:
2-5 not assigned;
6, 7, 8, 10, 14, 15, 17, 19, 22, 24, 32–54 transferred to the Royal Navy;
124–139 cancelled.

A Navy/Marine Corps HRP-1, also known as the flying banana, lands aboard Saipan, 1948, USN-706643.

Carrier Listing for CVE Designations

Hull No.	Name	Date of Commission and Decommission or loss*	New Designation or Change of Designation	Date of Designation Change	Comments
1	Long Island	2 Jun 1941 20 Mar 1946			Stricken 12 Apr 1946.
9	Bogue	26 Sep 1942 30 Nov 1946	CVHE 9	12 Jun 1955	Stricken 1 Mar 1959.
11	Card	8 Nov 1942 13 May 1946 1 Jun 1959	CVHE 11 CVU 11 AKV 40	12 Jun 1955 1 Jul 1958 7 May 1959	Stricken 15 Sep 1970.
12	Copahee	15 Jun 1942 5 Jul 1946	CVHE 12	12 Jun 1955	Stricken 1 Mar 1959.
13	Core	10 Dec 1942 4 Oct 1946	CVHE 13 CVU 13 AKV 41	12 Jun 1955 1 Jul 1958 7 May 1959	Stricken 15 Sep 1970.
16	Nassau	20 Aug 1942 28 Oct 1946	CVHE 16	12 Jun 1955	Stricken 1 Mar 1959.
18	Altamaha	15 Sep 1942 27 Sep 1946	CVHE 18	12 Jun 1955	Stricken 1 Mar 1959.
20	Barnes	20 Feb 1943 29 Aug 1946	CVHE 20	12 Jun 1955	Stricken 1 Mar 1959.
21	Block Island	8 Mar 1943 29 May 1944			Lost to enemy action.
23	Breton	12 Apr 1943 30 Aug 1946	CVHE 23 CVU 23 AKV 42	12 Jun 1955 1 Jul 1958 7 May 1959	Stricken 6 Aug 1971.
25	Croatan	28 Apr 1943 20 May 1946	CVHE 25 CVU 25 AKV 43	12 Jun 1955 1 Jul 1958 7 May 1959	Stricken 15 Sep 1970.
26	Sangamon	25 Aug 1942 24 Oct 1945	AO 28 AVG 26	23 Oct 1940 14 Feb 1942	Stricken 1 Nov 1945. *Sangamon* was a fleet oiler (AO 28) before being converted to an escort carrier.
27	Suwannee	24 Sep 1942 8 Jan 1947	AO 33 AVG 27 CVHE 27	16 Jul 1941 14 Feb 1942 12 Jun 1955	Stricken 1 Mar 1959. *Suwannee* was a fleet oiler (AO 33) before being converted to an escort carrier.
28	Chenango	19 Sep 1942 14 Aug 1946	AO 31 ACV 28 CVHE 28	20 Jun 1941 19 Sep 1942 12 Jun 1955	Stricken 1 Mar 1959. *Chenango* was a fleet oiler (AO 31) before being converted to an escort carrier.
29	Santee	24 Aug 1942 21 Oct 1946	AO 29 ACV 29 CVHE 29	30 Oct 1940 24 Aug 1942 12 Jun 1955	Stricken 1 Mar 1959. *Santee* was a fleet oiler (AO 29) before being converted to an escort carrier.
30	Charger	3 Mar 1942 15 Mar 1946			Stricken 29 Mar 1946.
31	Prince William	9 Apr 1943 29 Aug 1946	CVHE 31	12 Jun 1955	Stricken 1 Mar 1959.
55	Casablanca	8 Jul 1943 10 Jun 1946			Sold 23 Apr 1947.
56	Liscome Bay	7 Aug 1943 24 Nov 1943			Lost to enemy action.
57	Anzio (ex-*Coral Sea*)	27 Aug 1943 5 Aug 1946	CVHE 57	12 Jun 1955	Stricken 1 Mar 1959.

Carrier Listing for CVE Designations—Continued

Hull No.	Name	Date of Commission and Decommission or loss*	New Designation or Change of Designation	Date of Designation Change	Comments
58	Corregidor	31 Aug 1943 4 Sep 1958	CVU 58	12 Jun 1955	Stricken 1 Oct 1958.
59	Mission Bay	13 Sep 1943 21 Feb 1947	CVU 59	12 Jun 1955	Stricken 1 Sep 1958.
60	Guadalcanal	25 Sep 1943 15 Jul 1946	CVU 60	12 Jun 1955	Stricken 27 May 1958.
61	Manila Bay	5 Oct 1943 31 Jul 1946	CVU 61	12 Jun 1955	Stricken 27 May 1958.
62	Natoma Bay	14 Oct 1943 20 May 1946	CVU 62	12 Jun 1955	Stricken 27 May 1958.
63	St. Lo (ex-Midway)	23 Oct 1943 25 Oct 1944			Commissioned on 23 Oct 1943 as *Midway* (CVE 63) and renamed *St. Lo* (CVE 63) on 10 Oct 1944. Lost to enemy action on 25 Oct 1944.
64	Tripoli	31 Oct 1943 25 Nov 1958	CVU 64	12 Jun 1955	Stricken 1 Feb 1959.
65	Wake Island	7 Nov 1943 5 Apr 1946			Stricken 17 Apr 1946.
66	White Plains	15 Nov 1943 10 Jul 1946	CVU 66	12 Jun 1955	Stricken 1 Jul 1958.
67	Solomons	21 Nov 1943 15 May 1946			Stricken 5 Jun 1946. Launched as *USS Nassuk Bay* (CVE 67) on 6 Oct 1943 and renamed *Solomons* (CVE 67) in Nov 1943.
68	Kalinin Bay	27 Nov 1943 15 May 1946			Stricken 5 Jun 1946.
69	Kasaan Bay	4 Dec 1943 6 Jul 1946	CVHE 69	12 Jun 1955	Stricken 1 Mar 1959.
70	Fanshaw Bay	9 Dec 1943 14 Aug 1946	CVHE 70	12 Jun 1955	Stricken 1 Mar 1959.
71	Kitkun Bay	15 Dec 1943 19 Apr 1946			Sold 18 Nov 1946.
72	Tulagi	21 Dec 1943 30 Apr 1946			Stricken 8 May 1946.
73	Gambier Bay	28 Dec 1943 25 Oct 1944			Lost to enemy action.
74	Nehenta Bay	*3 Jan 1944* 15 May 1946	*CVU 74* AKV 24	*12 Jun 1955* 7 May 1959	*Stricken 1 Aug 1959.*
75	Hoggatt Bay	11 Jan 1944 20 Jul 1946	CVHE 75 AKV 25	12 Jun 1955 7 May 1959	Stricken 1 Aug 1959.
76	Kadashan Bay	18 Jan 1944 14 Jun 1946	CVU 76 AKV 26	12 Jun 1955 7 May 1959	Stricken 1 Aug 1959.
77	Marcus Island	26 Jan 1944 12 Dec 1946	CVHE 77 AKV 27	12 Jun 1955 7 May 1959	Stricken 1 Aug 1959.
78	Savo Island	3 Feb 1944 12 Dec 1946	CHVE 78 AKV 28	12 Jun 1955 7 May 1959	Stricken 1 Sep 1959.
79	Ommaney Bay	11 Feb 1944 4 Jan 1945			Lost to enemy action.

Carrier Listing for CVE Designations—Continued

Hull No.	Name	Date of Commission and Decommission or loss*	New Designation or Change of Designation	Date of Designation Change	Comments
80	Petrof Bay	18 Feb 1944 30 Jul 1946	CVU 80	12 Jun 1955	Stricken 27 Jun 1958.
81	Rudyerd Bay	25 Feb 1944 11 Jun 1946	CVU 81 AKV 29	12 Jun 1955 7 May 1959	Stricken 1 Aug 1959.
82	Saginaw Bay	2 Mar 1944 19 Jun 1946	CVHE 82	12 Jun 1955	Stricken 1 Mar 1959.
83	Sargent Bay	9 Mar 1944 23 Jul 1946	CVU 83	12 Jun 1955	Stricken 27 Jun 1958.
84	Shamrock Bay	15 Mar 1944 6 Jul 1946	CVU 84	12 Jun 1955	Stricken 27 Jun 1958.
85	Shipley Bay	21 Mar 1944 28 Jun 1946	CVHE 85	12 Jun 1955	Stricken 1 Mar 1959.
86	Sitkoh Bay	28 Mar 1944 27 Jul 1954	CVU 86 AKV 30	12 Jun 1955 7 May 1959	Stricken 1 Apr 1960.
87	Steamer Bay	4 Apr 1944 8 Aug 1946	CVHE 87	12 Jun 1955	Stricken 1 Mar 1959.
88	Cape Esperance	9 Apr 1944 15 Jan 1959	CVU 88	12 Jun 1955	Stricken 1 Mar 1959.
89	Takanis Bay	15 Apr 1944 1 May 1946	CVU 89 AKV 31	12 Jun 1955 7 May 1959	Stricken 1 Aug 1959.
90	Thetis Bay	21 Apr 1944 1 Mar 1964	CVHA 1 LPH 6	1 Jul 1955 28 May 1959	Stricken 1 Mar 1964.
91	Makassar Strait	27 Apr 1944 9 Aug 1946	CVU 91	12 Jun 1955	Stricken 1 Sep 1958.
92	Windham Bay	3 May 1944 Jan 1959	CVU 92	12 Jun 1955	Stricken 1 Feb 1959.
93	Makin Island	9 May 1944 19 Apr 1946			Stricken 5 Jun 1946.
94	Lunga Point	14 May 1944 24 Oct 1946	CVU 94 AKV 32	12 Jun 1955 7 May 1959	Stricken 1 Apr 1960.
95	Bismarck Sea	20 May 1944 21 Feb 1945			Lost to enemy action.
96	Salamaua	26 May 1944 9 May 1946			Stricken 21 May 1946.
97	Hollandia	1 Jun 1944 17 Jan 1947	CVU 97 AKV 33	12 Jun 1955 7 May 1959	Stricken 1 Apr 1960.
98	Kwajalein	7 Jun 1944 16 Aug 1946	CVU 98 AKV 34	12 Jun 1955 7 May 1959	Stricken 1 Apr 1960.
99	Admiralty Islands	13 Jun 1944 24 Apr 1946			Stricken 8 May 1946.
100	Bougainville	18 Jun 1944 3 Nov 1946	CVU 100 AKV 35	12 Jun 1955 7 May 1959	Stricken 1 Apr 1960.
101	Matanikau	24 Jun 1944 11 Oct 1946	CVU 101 AKV 36	12 Jun 1955 7 May 1959	Stricken 1 Apr 1960.
102	Attu	30 Jun 1944 8 Jun 1946			Stricken 3 Jul 1946.

Carrier Listing for CVE Designations—Continued

Hull No.	Name	Date of Commission and Decommission or loss*	New Designation or Change of Designation	Date of Designation Change	Comments
103	Roi	6 Jul 1944 9 May 1946			Stricken 21 May 1946.
104	Munda	8 Jul 1944 13 Sep 1946	CVU 104	12 Jun 1955	Stricken 1 Sep 1958.
105	Commencement Bay	27 Nov 1944 30 Nov 1946	CVHE 105 AKV 37	12 Jun 1955 7 May 1959	Stricken 1 Apr 1971.
106	Block Island	30 Dec 1944 27 Aug 1954	LPH 1 CVE 106 AKV 38	22 Dec 1957 17 Feb 1959 7 May 1959	Stricken 1 Jul 1959.
107	Gilbert Islands	5 Feb 1945 15 Jan 1955	AKV 39	7 May 1959	Stricken 1 Jun 1961.
108	Kula Gulf	12 May 1945 15 Dec 1955	AKV 8	7 May 1959	Stricken 15 Sep 1970.
109	Cape Gloucester	5 Mar 1945 5 Nov 1946	CVHE 109 AKV 9	12 Jun 1955 7 May 1959	Stricken 1 Apr 1971.
110	Salerno Bay	19 May 1945 16 Feb 1954	AKV 10	7 May 1959	Stricken 1 Jun 1960.
111	Vella Gulf	9 Apr 1945 9 Aug 1946	CVHE 111 AKV 11	12 Jun 1955 7 May 1959	Stricken 1 Jun 1960.
112	Siboney	14 May 1945 31 Jul 1956	AKV 12	7 May 1959	Stricken 1 Jun 1970.
113	Puget Sound	18 Jun 1945 18 Oct 1946	CVHE 113 AKV 13	12 Jun 1955 7 May 1959	Stricken 1 Jun 1960.
114	Rendova	22 Oct 1945 30 Jun 1955	AKV 14	7 May 1959	Stricken 1 Apr 1971.
115	Bairoko	16 Jul 1945 18 Feb 1955	AKV 15	7 May 1959	Stricken 1 Apr 1960.
116	Badoeng Strait	14 Nov 1945 17 May 1957	AKV 16	7 May 1959	Stricken 1 Dec 1970.
117	Saidor	4 Sep 1945 12 Sep 1947	CVHE 117 AKV 17	12 Jun 1955 7 May 1959	Stricken 1 Dec 1970.
118	Sicily	27 Feb 1946 4 Oct 1954	AKV 18	7 May 1959	Stricken 1 Jul 1960.
119	Point Cruz	16 Oct 1945 31 Aug 1956	AKV 19	7 May 1959	Stricken 15 Sep 1970.
120	Mindoro	4 Dec 1945 4 Aug 1955	AKV 20	7 May 1959	Stricken 1 Dec 1959.
121	Rabaul		CVHE 121 AKV 21	12 Jun 1955 7 May 1959	Stricken 1 Sep 1971. Inactivated after trials on 30 Aug 1946, never commissioned.
122	Palau	15 Jan 1946 15 Jun 1954	AKV 22	7 May 1959	Stricken 1 Apr 1960.
123	Tinian		CVHE 123 AKV 23	12 Jun 1955 7 May 1959	Stricken 1 Jun 1970. The ship was accepted by the Navy on 30 Jul 1946, but never commissioned.

* There were a number of carriers that were decommissioned and then recommissioned for further service. Only the final decommissioning date is listed for these carriers. Several carriers were also placed out of commission during major rennovations or yard periods. In some cases the records regarding decommissioning dates were not complete. Consequently, the decommissioning date was left blank if it was unknown.

World War II Training Carriers

During World War II the Navy's requirements for pilots provided an increased demand on the training command for carrier flight decks for carrier qualification training. To alleviate the need to take a front line carrier out of action for carrier qualification training, the Navy acquired two vessels that had operated on the Great Lakes and converted them to training carriers with the designation IX, miscellaneous auxiliary.

Hull Number	Name	Date of Commission and Decommission	Disposition and Status
64	*Wolverine*	12 Aug 1942 7 Nov 1945	A side-wheel steamer built in 1913 and originally named Seeandbee. She was acquired by the Navy on 12 Mar 1942 and conversion to a training carrier began on 6 May 1942. Stricken 28 Nov 1945.
81	*Sable*	8 May 1943 7 Nov 1945	The ship was built in 1924 by the American Shipbuilding Company and named Greater Buffalo. She was acquired by the Navy on 7 Aug 1942, named Sable on 19 Sep 1942 and converted to a training carrier. Stricken 28 Nov 1945.

Antisubmarine Support Aircraft Carriers (CVS)

Classification and designation for CVS (Antisubmarine Support Aircraft Carrier) established 8 August 1953.

Classes: All ships used in this role were *Essex* class carriers modified to serve in the ASW role. *Enterprise* (CV 6) was designated CVS 6 but was never used as such. This listing is for quick reference, with the reclassification dates and other data found in the Carrier Listing for CV, CVA, CVB, CVAN, CVN and CVL.

Hull Number	Name	Hull Number	Name
6	*Enterprise*	20	*Bennington*
9	*Essex*	21	*Boxer*
10	*Yorktown*	32	*Leyte*
11	*Intrepid*	33	*Kearsarge*
12	*Hornet*	36	*Antietam*
13	*Franklin*	37	*Princeton*
14	*Ticonderoga*	38	*Shangri-La*
15	*Randolph*	39	*Lake Champlain*
16	*Lexington*	40	*Tarawa*
17	*Bunker Hill*	45	*Valley Forge*
18	*Wasp*	47	*Philippine Sea*

Amphibious Assault Ships (LPH)

Hull No.	Name	Date of Commission and Decommission	New Designation or Change of Designation	Date of Designation Change	Disposition and Status
1	Block Island	30 Dec 1944 27 Aug 1954	CVE 106 LPH 1* CVE 106 AKV 38	 22 Dec 1957 17 Feb 1959 7 May 1959	Stricken 1 Jul 1959.
2	Iwo Jima	26 Aug 1961 14 Jul 1993			Stricken 10 Jul 1993.
3	Okinawa	14 Apr 1962 17 Dec 1992			Stricken 17 Dec 1992.
4	Boxer	16 Apr 1945 1 Dec 1969	CV 21 CVA 21 CVS 21 LPH 4**	16 Apr 1945 1 Oct 1952 1 Feb 1956 30 Jan 1959	Stricken 1 Dec 1969.
5	Princeton	18 Nov 1945 30 Jan 1970	CV 37 CVA 37 CVS 37 LPH 5***	18 Nov 1945 1 Oct 1952 1 Jan 1954 2 Mar 1959	Stricken 30 Jan 1970.
6	Thetis Bay	21 Apr 1944 1 Mar 1964	CVHA 1 LPH 6****	1 Jul 1955 28 May 1959	Stricken 1 Mar 1964.
7	Guadalcanal	20 Jul 1963 31 Aug 1994			Stricken 31 Aug 1994.
8	Valley Forge	3 Nov 1946 15 Jan 1970	CV 45 CVA 45 CVS 45 LPH 8*****	3 Nov 1946 1 Oct 1952 1 Jan 1954 1 Jul 1961	Stricken 15 Jan 1970.
9	Guam	16 Jan 1965			Active.
10	Tripoli	6 Aug 1966 8 Sep 1995			
11	New Orleans	16 Nov 1968			Active.
12	Inchon	20 Jun 1970	MCS 12	1 Mar 1995	Active.

* Block Island was reclassified LPH 1 on 22 Dec 1957, but the conversion was cancelled and the LPH 1 designation was not reassigned. The ship never operated with the LPH 1 designation.

** Boxer operated with the designation LPH 4 from 30 Jan 1959 until her decommissioning on 1 December 1969.

*** Princeton operated with the designation LPH 5 from 2 Mar 1959 until her decommissioning on 30 Jan 1970.

**** Thesis Bay operated with the designation LPH 6 from 28 May 1959 until her decommissioning on 1 Mar 1964.

***** Valley Forge operated with the designation LPH 8 from 1 Jul 1961 until her decommission on 15 Jan 1970.

NOTE ON DECOMMISSIONING DATES: There were a number of ships that were decommissioned and then recommissioned for further service. Only the final decommissioning date is listed for these ships. Many ships were also placed out of commission during major rennovations or yard periods.

Amphibious Assault Ships (LHA)

Class: Wasp		5 ships		
Hull Number	Name	Commissioned	Disposition and Status	
1	Tarawa	29 May 1976	Active.	
2	Saipan	15 Oct 1977	Active.	
3	Belleau Wood	23 Sep 1978	Active.	
4	Nassau	28 Jul 1979	Active.	
5	Peleliu	3 May 1980	Active.	

Amphibious Assault Ships (Multi-Purpose) (LHD)

Class: Wasp		7 ships		
Hull Number	Name	Commissioned	Disposition and Status	
1	Wasp	29 Jul 1989	Active.	
2	Essex	17 Oct 1992*	Active.	
3	Kearsarge	30 Jun 1993	Active.	
4	Boxer	11 Feb 1995	Active.	
5	Bataan		Under construction.	
6	Bonhomme Richard		Under construction.	
7	(name not assigned yet)		Authorized.	

* The ship was commissioned without ceremony on 24 Aug 1992 to permit it to go to sea to avoid a hurricane that was threatening Pascagoula, Miss. The official commissioning ceremony was held on 17 Oct 1992.

Seaplane Tenders (AV)

Classes:

Five single ships	AV 1, 2, 3, 6 and 8.
Curtiss Class	2 ships, AV 4 and 5.
Currituck Class	4 ships, AV 7, 11-13.
Pocomoke Class	2 ships, AV 9 and 10.
Kenneth Whiting Class	4 ships, AV 14 to 17.

Hull Number	Name	Date of Commission and Decommission	New Designation or Change of Designation	Date of Designation Change	Disposition & Status
1	Wright* San Clemente*	16 Dec 1921 21 Jun 1946	AZ 1 AV 1 AG 79 AG 79	17 Jul 1920 1 Nov 1923 1 Oct 1944 1 Feb 1945	Stricken 1 Jul 1946.
2	Jason	23 Jun 1913 30 Jun 1932	AC 12 AV 2	21 Jan 1930	Stricken 19 May 1936.
3	Langley**	7 Apr 1913	AC 3 CV 1 AV 3	7 Apr 1913 20 Mar 1922 21 Apr 1937	Lost to enemy action 27 Feb 1942.

Seaplane Tenders (AV)—Continued

Hull Number	Name	Date of Commission and Decommission	New Designation or Change of Designation	Date of Designation Change	Disposition & Status
4	Curtiss	15 Nov 1940 24 Sep 1957			Stricken 1 Jul 1963.
5	Albemarle***	20 Dec 1940 21 Oct 1960	T-ARVH 1	11 Jan 1966	Stricken 31 Dec 1974.
6	Patoka	13 Oct 1919 1 Jul 1946	AO 9 AV 6**** AO 9 AG 125	13 Oct 1919 11 Oct 1939 19 Jun 1940 15 Aug 1945	Stricken 31 Jul 1946.
7	Currituck	26 Jun 1944 31 Oct 1967			Stricken 1 Apr 1971.
8	Tangier	8 Jul 1940			Decommissioned sometime between May 1946 and Jan 1947. Stricken 1 Jun 1961.
9	Pocomoke	18 Jul 1941 10 Jul 1946			Stricken 1 Jun 1961.
10	Chandeleur	19 Nov 1942			Placed in reserve 12 Feb 1947. Stricken 1 Apr 1971.
11	Norton Sound	8 Jan 1945 11 Dec 1986	AVM 1	8 Aug 1951	
12	Pine Island	26 Apr 1945 16 Jun 1967			Stricken 1 Feb 1971.
13	Salisbury Sound	26 Nov 1945 31 Mar 1967			Stricken 1 Feb 1971.
14	Kenneth Whiting	8 May 1944 30 Sep 1958			Stricken 1 Jul 1961.
15	Hamlin	26 Jun 1944 15 Jan 1947			Stricken 1 Jul 1963.
16	St. George	24 Jul 1944 1 Aug 1946			Stricken 1 Jul 1963.
17	Cumberland Sound	21 Aug 1944 27 May 1947			Stricken 1 Jul 1961.

* *Wright* was renamed *San Clemente* on 1 Feb 1945 to permit the use of the name *Wright* for a carrier under construction.

** *Jupiter* was commissioned as a collier on 7 Apr 1913 and decommissioned on 24 Mar 1920 for conversion to an aircraft carrier. She was renamed *Langley* on 21 Apr 1920 and recommissioned as *Langley* (CV 1) on 20 Mar 1922.

*** *Albemarle* was decommissioned on 21 Oct 1960 and stricken from the Naval Vessel Register on 1 Sep 1962 and placed in the custody of the Maritime Administration James River Fleet. However, she was transferred back to the Navy on 7 Aug 1964 for conversion to a floating aeronautical maintenance facility for helicopters. On 27 March 1965 *Albemarle* was renamed *Corpus Christi Bay* and redesignated T-ARVH 1. On 11 Jan 1966 she was transferred to the Military Sealift Command (MSC). She was eventually taken out of service by MSC and stricken.

**** *Patoka* was authorized for conversion to AV on 25 Feb 1924 and operated as such, but was not reclassified an AV until 11 Oct 1939.

NOTE ON DECOMMISSIONING DATES: There were a number of ships that were decommissioned and then recommissioned for further service. Only the final decommissioning date is listed for these ships. Many ships were also placed out of commission during major rennovations or yard periods. In some cases the records regarding decommissioning dates were not complete. Consequently, the decommissioning date was left blank if it was unknown.

Small Seaplane Tenders (AVP)

Classes:

Lapwing Class   Converted minesweepers assigned to aviation duty in the 1920s; first given aviation designation 22 Jan 1936; 9 ships, AVP 1 to 9.

Barnegat Class   32 ships, AVP 10 to 13, 21–26, 28–41 and 48–55.

Childs Class   7 ships, AVP 14 to 20.

Hull numbers omitted may be accounted for as follows: 27, 56, and 57 were commissioned as AGPs; 42–47 and 58–67 were cancelled.

Hull Number	Name	Date of Commission and Decommission	New Designation or Change of Designation	Date of Designation Change	Disposition
1	Lapwing	12 Jun 1918 29 Nov 1945	AM 1 AVP 1	22 Jan 1936	Transferred to Maritime Commission 19 Aug 1946.
2	Heron	30 Oct 1918 12 Feb 1946	AM 10 AVP 2	22 Jan 1936	Transferred to Force Logistics Command 25 Jul 1947.
3	Thrush	25 Apr 1919 13 Dec 1945	AM 18 AVP 3	17 Jul 1920 22 Jan 1936	Stricken 8 Jan 1946 Transferred to Maritime Commission 19 Aug 1946.
4	Avocet	17 Sep 1918 10 Dec 1945	AM 19 AVP 4	22 Jan 1936	Stricken 3 Jan 1946.
5	Teal	20 Aug 1918 23 Nov 1945	AM 23 AVP 5	30 Apr 1931 22 Jan 1936	Stricken 5 Dec 1945. Transferred to Maritime Commission 19 Jan 1948.
6	Pelican	10 Oct 1918 30 Nov 1945	AM 27 AVP 6	22 Jan 1936	Stricken 19 Dec 1945. Transferred to Maritime Commission 22 Nov 1946.
7	Swan	31 Jan 1919 13 Dec 1945	AM 34 AVP 7	30 Apr 1931 22 Jan 1936	Stricken 8 Jan 1946. Transferred to Maritime Commission 12 Oct 1946.
8	Gannet	10 Jul 1919	AM 41 AVP 8	22 Jan 1936	Lost to enemy action 7 Jun 1942.
9	Sandpiper	9 Oct 1919 10 Dec 1945	AM 51 AVP 9	Jul 1920 22 Jan 1936	Stricken 17 Apr 1946. Transferred to Maritime Commission 12 Oct 1946.
10	Barnegat	3 Jul 1941 17 May 1946			Stricken 23 May 1958.
11	Biscayne	3 Jul 1941 29 Jun 1946	AGC 18	10 Oct 1944	Transferred to USCG 19 Jul 1946; returned to USN as target, 9 Jul 1968.
12	Casco	27 Dec 1941 10 Apr 1947			Transferred to USCG 19 Apr 1949.
13	Mackinac	24 Jan 1942 Jan 1947			Transferred to USCG 19 Apr 1949; returned 15 Apr 1968, expended as target.
14	Childs	22 Oct 1920 10 Dec 1945	DD 241 AVP 14 AVD 1	1 Jul 1938 1 Oct 1940	Stricken 8 Jan 1946.
15	Williamson	29 Oct 1920 8 Nov 1945	DD 244 AVP 15 AVD 2 DD 244	1 Jul 1938 2 Aug 1940 1 Dec 1943	Stricken 19 Dec 1945.
16	George E. Badger	28 Jul 1920 3 Oct 1945	DD 196 AVP 16 AVD 3 APD 33 DD 196	1 Oct 1939 2 Aug 1940 19 May 1944 20 Jul 1945	Transferred to Treasury Dept. in 1930 and returned 1934. Stricken 25 Oct 1945.
17	Clemson	29 Dec 1919 12 Oct 1945	DD 186 AVP 17	15 Nov 1939	Stricken 24 Oct 1945.

Seaplane Tenders (AVP)—Continued

Hull Number	Name	Date of Commission and Decommission	New Designation or Change of Designation	Date of Designation Change	Disposition & Status
			AVD 4	6 Aug 1940	
			DD 186	1 Dec 1943	
			APD 31	7 Mar 1944	
			DD 186	17 Jul 1945	
18	Goldsborough	26 Jan 1920 11 Oct 1945	DD 188 AVP 18 AVD 3 DD 188 APD 32 DD 188	15 Nov 1939 2 Aug 1940 1 Dec 1943 7 Mar 1944 10 Jul 1945	Stricken 24 Oct 1945.
19	Hulbert	27 Oct 1920 2 Nov 1945	DD 342 AVP 6 DD 342	2 Aug 1940 1 Dec 1943	Stricken 28 Nov 1945.
20	William B. Preston	23 Aug 1920 6 Dec 1945	DD 344 AVP 20 AVD 7	18 Nov 1939 2 Aug 1940	Stricken 3 Jan 1946.
21	Humboldt	7 Oct 1941 19 Mar 1947	AG 121 AVP 21	30 Jul 1945 10 Sep 1945	Transferred to USCG 24 Jan 1949.
22	Matagorda	16 Dec 1941 20 Feb 1946	AG 122 AVP 22	30 Jul 1945 10 Sep 1945	Transferred to USCG 7 Mar 1949; returned to USN in 1968 used as target in 1969.
23	Absecon	28 Jan 1943 19 Mar 1947			Transferred to USCG 5 Jan 1949 and then to South Vietnamese Navy on 15 Jul 1972.
24	Chincoteague	12 Apr 1943 12 Dec 1946			Transferred to USCG 7 Mar 1949.
25	Coos Bay	15 May 1943 30 Apr 1946			Transferred to USCG 5 Jan 1949; returned 16 Aug 1967 expended as target.
26	Half Moon	15 Jun 1943 4 Sep 1946			Transferred to USCG 14 Sep 1948.
28	Oyster Bay	17 Nov 1943 26 Mar 1946	AVP 28 AGP 6 AVP 28	1 May 1943 16 Mar 1949	The ship never operated as an AVP for the U.S. Navy. Transferred to Italy 23 Oct 1957.
29	Rockaway	6 Jan 1943 21 Mar 1946	AG 123 AVP 29	30 Jul 1945 26 Oct 1945	Transferred to USCG 24 Dec 1948. Stricken Sep 1966.
30	San Pablo	15 Mar 1943 29 May 1969	AGS 30	25 Aug 1949	Decommissioned as AVP 30 on 13 Jan 1947. Stricken 1 Jun 1969.
31	Unimak	31 Dec 1943 26 Jul 1946			Transferred to USCG 14 Sep 1948.
32	Yakutat	31 Mar 1944 29 Jul 1946			Transferred to USCG 31 Aug 1948, returned to USN 1970. Transferred to Navy of South Vietnam on 10 Jan 1971 until its fall in 1975, then transferred to Philippine government on 5 Apr 1976.
33	Barataria	13 Aug 1944 24 Jul 1946			Transferred to USCG 17 Sep 1948.
34	Bering Strait	19 Jul 1944 21 Jun 1946			Transferred to USCG 14 Sep 1948.
35	Castle Rock	8 Oct 1944 6 Aug 1946			Transferred to USCG 16 Sep 1948.
36	Cook Inlet	5 Nov 1944 31 Mar 1946			Transferred to USCG 20 Sep 1948. Transferred to South Vietnam as HQ-05, 21 Dec 1971.

Seaplane Tenders (AVP)—Continued

Hull Number	Name	Date of Commission and Decommission	New Designation or Change of Designation	Date of Designation Change	Disposition & Status
37	Corson	3 Dec 1944 9 Mar 1956			Stricken 1 Apr 1966.
38	Duxbury Bay	31 Dec 1944 29 Apr 1966			Stricken 1 May 1966.
39	Gardiners Bay	11 Feb 1945 1 Feb 1958			Transferred to Norway under Military Assistance Program. Stricken 1 Jul 1966.
40	Floyds Bay	25 Mar 1945 26 Feb 1960			Stricken 1 Mar 1960.
41	Greenwich Bay	20 May 1945			Stricken 1 Jul 1966.
48	Onslow	22 Dec 1943 22 Apr 1960			Stricken 1 Jun 1960.
49	Orca	23 Jan 1944 Mar 1960			Transferred to Ethiopia 31 Jan 1962.
50	Rehoboth	23 Feb 1944 15 Apr 1970	AGS 50	2 Sep 1948	Decommissioned as AVP 50 on 30 Jun 1947. Stricken 15 Apr 1970.
51	San Carlos	21 Mar 1944 30 Jun 1947	AGOR 1	15 Dec 1958	Transferred to MSTS 11 Jul 1958, renamed *Josiah Willard Gibbs* on 15 Dec 1958. Transferred to Greece 15 Dec 1971.
52	Shelikof	17 Sep 1944 30 Jun 1947			Stricken 1 May 1960.
53	Suisun	13 Sep 1944 5 Aug 1955			Stricken 1 Apr 1966.
54	Timbalier	24 May 1946 15 Nov 1954			Stricken 1 May 1960.
55	Valcour	5 Jul 1946 15 Jan 1973	AGF 1	15 Dec 1965	Stricken 15 Jan 1973.

NOTE ON DECOMMISSIONING DATES: There were a number of ships that were decommissioned and then recommissioned for further service. Only the final decommissioning date is listed for these ships. Many ships were also placed out of commission during major rennovations or yard periods. In some cases the records regarding decommissioning dates were not complete. Consequently, the decommissioning date was left blank if it was unknown.

Destroyer Seaplane Tenders (AVD)

Class: *Clemson* Class DD   14 ships, ex flush deck 1190 ton DDs converted for seaplane tending duties from 1938 to 1940.

Hull Number	Name	Date of Commission and Decommission	New Designation or Change of Designation	Date of Designation Change	Disposition & Status
1	Childs	22 Oct 1920 10 Dec 1945	DD 241 AVP 14 AVD 1	 1 Jul 1938 1 Oct 1940	Stricken 8 Jan 1946.
2	Williamson	29 Oct 1920 8 Nov 1945	DD 244 AVP 15 AVD 2 DD 244	 1 Jul 1938 2 Aug 1940 1 Dec 1943	Stricken 19 Dec 1945.
3	George E. Badger	28 Jul 1920 3 Oct 1945	DD 196 AVP 16 AVD 3 APD 33 DD 196	 1 Oct 1939 2 Aug 1940 19 May 1944 20 Jul 1945	Transferred to Treasury Dept. in 1930 and returned 1934. Stricken 25 Oct 1945.

Destroyer Seaplane Tenders (AVD)—Continued

Hull Number	Name	Date of Commission and Decommission	New Designation or Change of Designation	Date of Designation Change	Disposition
4	Clemson	29 Dec 1919 12 Oct 1945	DD 186 AVP 17 AVD 4 DD 186 APD 31 DD 186	 15 Nov 1939 6 Aug 1940 1 Dec 1943 7 Mar 1944 17 Jul 1945	Stricken 24 Oct 1945.
5	Goldsborough	26 Jan 1920 11 Oct 1945	DD 188 AVP 18 AVD 3 DD 188 APD 32 DD 188	 15 Nov 1939 2 Aug 1940 1 Dec 1943 7 Mar 1944 10 Jul 1945	Stricken 24 Oct 1945.
6	Hulbert	27 Oct 1920 2 Nov 1945	DD 342 AVP 6 DD 342	 2 Aug 1940 1 Dec 1943	Stricken 28 Nov 1945.
7	William B. Preston	23 Aug 1920 6 Dec 1945	DD 344 AVP 20 AVD 7	 18 Nov 1939 2 Aug 1940	Stricken 3 Jan 1946.
8	Belknap	28 Apr 1919 4 Aug 1945	DD 251 AVD 8 DD 251 APD 38	 2 Aug 1940 14 Nov 1943 22 Jun 1944	Sold for scrap 30 Nov 1945.
9	Osmond Ingram	28 Jun 1919 8 Jan 1946	DD 255 AVD 9 DD 255 APD 35	 2 Aug 1940 4 Nov 1943 22 Jun 1944	Stricken 21 Jan 1946.
10	Ballard	5 Jun 1919 5 Dec 1945	DD 267 AVD 10	 2 Aug 1940	Stricken 3 Jan 1946.
11	Thornton	15 Jul 1919 2 May 1945	DD 270 AVD 11	 2 Aug 1940	Stricken 13 Aug 1945.
12	Gillis	3 Sep 1919 15 Oct 1945	DD 260 AVD 12	 2 Aug 1940	Stricken 1 Nov 1945.
13	Greene	9 May 1919 23 Nov 1945	DD 266 AVD 13 APD 36	 6 Apr 1941 1 Feb 1944	Stricken 5 Dec 1945.
14	McFarland	30 Sep 1920 8 Nov 1945	DD 237 AVD 14 DD 237	 2 Aug 1940 1 Dec 1943	Stricken 19 Dec 1945.

NOTE ON DECOMMISSIONING DATES: There were a number of ships that were decommissioned and then recommissioned for further service. Only the final decommissioning date is listed for these ships. Many ships were also placed out of commission during major rennovations or yard periods. In some cases the records regarding decommissioning dates were not complete. Consequently, the decommissioning date was left blank if it was unknown.

Aviation Logistic Support Ships

Various types of ships fitted out to support operations, logistics and repair activities of Naval aircraft.

Aircraft Ferry (AKV)

Hull Number	Name	Date of Commission and Decommission	New Designation or Change of Designation	Date of Designation Change	Disposition & Status
1	Kitty Hawk	26 Nov 1941 24 Jan 1946	AVP 1 AKV 1	 15 Sep 1943	Returned to owner, Seatrain Lines, 24 Jan 1946.
2	Hammondsport	11 Dec 1941 7 Mar 1946	AVP 2 AKV 2	 15 Sep 1943	Returned to Maritime Commission 7 Mar 1946.

Note: Other ships classified AKV appear on Escort Carrier List.

Transport and Aircraft Ferry (APV)

Hull Number	Name	Date of Commission and Decommission	New Designation or Change of Designation	Date of Designation Change	Disposition & Status
4	Lafayette		AP 53 APV 4	24 Dec 1941 15 Sep 1943	Caught fire and capsized during AP conversion from French liner Normandie, never repaired or commissioned. Stricken 11 Oct 1945.

Aircraft Repair Ships (ARV)

Hull Number	Name	Date of Commission and Decommission	New Designation or Change of Designation	Date of Designation Change	Disposition & Status
1	Chourre	7 Dec 1944 13 Sep 1955	ARV 1		Stricken 1 Sep 1962.
2	Webster	17 Mar 1945 28 Jun 1946	ARV 2		Stricken 1 Sep 1962.

Aircraft Repair Ships (Aircraft) (ARVA)

Hull Number	Name	Date of Commission and Decommission	New Designation or Change of Designation	Date of Designation Change	Disposition & Status
5	Fabius	7 Jun 1945 4 Apr 1952	ARVA 5		Stricken 1 Jun 1973.
6	Megara	27 Jun 1945 16 Jan 1956	ARVA 6		Place in commission status 19 Jun 1945 for ferry purposes. Stricken 1 Jun 1973.

Aircraft Repair Ships (Engines) (ARVE)

Hull Number	Name	Date of Commission and Decommission	New Designation or Change of Designation	Date of Designation Change	Disposition & Status
3	Aventinus	30 May 1945 4 Apr 1952	ARVE 3		Transferred to Chile in Aug 1963.
4	Chloris	19 Jun 1945 9 Dec 1955	ARVE 4		Scrapped 1 Jun 1973.

Advanced Aviation Base Ships (AVB)

| 1 | Alameda County | 12 Jul 1943
25 Jun 1962 | LST 32
AVB 1 | 28 Sep 1957 | Stricken 30 Jun 1962. |
| 2 | Tallahatchie County | 24 May 1949
15 Jan 1970 | LST 1154
AVB 2 | 3 Feb 1962 | Stricken 15 Jan 1970. |

Aviation Supply Ships (AVS)

1	Supply	8 Feb 1944 4 Feb 1946	IX 147 AVS 1	25 May 1945	Stricken 25 Feb 1946.
2	Fortune	19 Feb 1944 18 Oct 1945	IX 146 AVS 2	25 May 1945	Returned to War Shipping Administration 18 Oct 1945.
3	Grumium	20 Oct 1943 20 Dec 1945	AK 112 IX 174 AVS 3	20 Jun 1944 25 May 1945	Returned to Maritime Commission 28 Dec 1945.
4	Alioth	25 Oct 1943 18 May 1946	AK 109 IX 204 AVS 4	31 Dec 1944 25 May 1945	Transferred to Maritime Commission 13 May 1947.
5	Gwinnett	10 Apr 1945 11 Feb 1946	AG 92 AVS 5	25 May 1945	Returned to Maritime Commission 11 Feb 1946.
6	Nicollet	27 Apr 1945 17 Jun 1946	AG 93 AVS 6	25 May 1945	Stricken 3 Jul 1946.
7	Pontotoc	22 Mar 1945 26 Apr 1946	AG 94 AVS 7	25 May 1945	Stricken and returned to owner 26 Apr 1946.
8	Jupiter	22 Aug 1942	AK 43 AVS 8	31 Jul 1945	Stricken 1 Aug 1965.

NOTE ON DECOMMISSIONING DATES: There were a number of ships that were decommissioned and then recommissioned for further service. Only the final decommissioning date is listed for these ships. Many ships were also placed out of commission during major rennovations or yard periods. In some cases the records regarding decommissioning dates were not complete. Consequently, the decommissioning date was left blank if it was unknown.

Patrol Craft Tenders (AGP)

These ships were fitted to service PBRs and UH-1 helicopters and worked with the Navy's riverine Task Force in South Vietnam beginning in 1967.

Hull Number	Name	Date of Commission and Decommission	New Designation or Change of Designation	Date of Designation Change	Disposition & Status
786	*Garrett County*	28 Aug 1944	LST 786 AGP 786	25 Sep 1970	Transferred to South Vietnam 23 Apr 1971.
821	*Harnett County*	22 Nov 1944	LST 821 AGP 821	25 Sep 1970	Transferred to South Vietnam 12 Oct 1970.
838	*Hunterdon County*	4 Dec 1944	LST 838 AGP 838	25 Sep 1970	Transferred to Malaysia 1 Jul 1971.
846	*Jennings County*	9 Jan 1945	LST 846 *		Stricken 25 Sep 1970.

* *Jennings County* was never redesignated AGP although she served in that capacity in Vietnam.

NOTE ON DECOMMISSIONING DATES: There were a number of ships that were decommissioned and then recommissioned for further service. Only the final decommissioning date is listed for these ships. Many ships were also placed out of commission during major rennovations or yard periods. In some cases the records regarding decommissioning dates were not complete. Consequently, the decommissioning date was left blank if it was unknown. I

The transport workhorse for carrier-onboard-delivery (COD), the C-2A Greyhound, lands aboard Kitty Hawk.

Ship Designations

AC	Collier
AG	Miscellaneous Auxiliary
AGC	Amphibious Force Flagship
AGMR	Major Communications Relay Ship
AGOR	Oceanographic Research Ship
AGP	Patrol Craft Tender (Motor Torpedo Boat Tender, Old Design.)
AGS	Surveying Ship
AKV	Aircraft Ferry; later, Cargo Ship and Aircraft Ferry.
AM	Mine Sweeper
AO	Fleet Oiler
AP	Transport
APV	Transport and Aircraft Ferry
ARG	Repair Ship, Engines
ARV	Aircraft Repair Ship
ARVA	Aircraft Repair Ship (Aircraft)
ARVE	Aircraft Repair Ship (Engines)
ARVH	Aircraft Repair Ship (Helicopter)
AV	Seaplane Tender
AVB	Advanced Aviation Base Ship
AVD	Seaplane Tender (Destroyer)
AVM	Guided Missiles Ship
AVP	Seaplane Tender (Small)
AVS	Aviation Supply Ship
AVT	Auxiliary Aircraft Transport
AZ	Lighter-than-air Tender
CV	Aircraft Carrier
CVA	Attack Aircraft Carrier
CVAN	Nuclear-Powered Attack Aircraft Carrier
CVB	Aircraft Carrier, Large (Old)
CVE	Escort Aircraft Carrier
CVHA	Assault Helicopter Aircraft Carrier until 1963—later LPH
CVHE	Escort Helicopter Aircraft Carrier (Old)
CVL	Small Aircraft Carrier
CVS	Antisubmarine Warfare Support Aircraft Carrier
CVU	Utility Aircraft Carrier
DD	Destroyer
IX	Miscellaneous auxiliary
LHA	Amphibious Assault Ship (General Purpose)
LHD	Amphibious Assault Ship (Multi-Purpose)
LPH	Amphibious Assault Ship (Helicopter)
LPD	Amphibious Assault Ship
LST	Landing Ship, Tank
T-ARVH	Associated with ARVH, indicates operated by military Sealift Command, formerly Military Sea Transportation Service.

Aviation Ships in Active Status as of 1 July

YEAR	CV **	CVS	CVL	CVE	LHA/ LPH/ LHD ***	AV	AVD	AVP	AVM	ARV	AVS	AKV	AGP	AVB	CVT/ AVT
1922	1	—	-	—	—	1	—	2	—	—	—	—	—	—	—
1923	1	—	—	—	—	1	—	2	—	—	—	—	—	—	—
1924	1	—	—	—	—	1	—	3	—	—	—	—	—	—	—
1925	1	—	—	—	—	1	—	6	—	—	—	—	—	—	—
1926	1	—	—	—	—	1	—	6	—	—	—	—	—	—	—
1927	3	—	—	—	—	1	—	8	—	—	—	—	—	—	—
1928	3	—	—	—	—	1	—	10	—	—	—	—	—	—	—
1929	3	—	—	—	—	1	—	10	—	—	—	—	—	—	—
1930	3	—	—	—	—	2	—	10	—	—	—	—	—	—	—
1931	3	—	—	—	—	2	—	11	—	—	—	—	—	—	—
1932	3	—	—	—	—	2	—	10	—	—	—	—	—	—	—
1933	3	—	—	—	—	2	—	10	—	—	—	—	—	—	—
1934	4	—	—	—	—	2	—	9	—	—	—	—	—	—	—
1935	4	—	—	—	—	2	—	8	—	—	—	—	—	—	—
1936	4	—	—	—	—	1	—	9	—	—	—	—	—	—	—
1937	3	—	—	—	—	2	—	9	—	—	—	—	—	—	—
1938	5	—	—	—	—	2	—	9	—	—	—	—	—	—	—
1939	5	—	—	—	—	2	—	11	—	—	—	—	—	—	—
1940	6	—	—	—	—	2	—	16	—	—	—	—	—	—	—
1941	6	—	—	1	—	5	14	9	—	—	—	—	—	—	—
1942	5	—	—	3	—	5	14	14	—	—	—	2	—	—	—
1943	7	—	5	17	—	6	14	20	—	—	—	2	—	—	—
1944	13	—	9	63	—	10	5	27	—	—	—	2	—	—	—
1945	20	—	8	70	—	11	5	36	—	6	7	2	—	—	—
1946	14	—	1	10	—	8	—	11	—	4	1	—	—	—	—
1947	12	—	2	8	—	5	—	9	—	1	—	—	—	—	—
1948	11	—	2	7	—	5	—	7	—	1	—	—	—	—	—
1949	8	—	3	7	—	5	—	9	—	—	—	—	—	—	—
1950	7	—	4	4	—	3	—	7	—	—	—	—	—	—	—
1951	14	—	4	10	—	4	—	9	1	4	1	—	—	—	—
1952	16	—	5	12	—	5	—	11	1	3	1	—	—	—	—
1953	17	—	5	12	—	5	—	11	1	3	1	—	—	—	—
1954	16	4	3	7	—	5	—	11	1	2	1	—	—	—	—
1955	17	5	2	3	—	5	—	8	1	2	1	—	—	—	—
1956	19	7	1	3	—	5	—	7	1	—	1	—	—	—	—
1957	16	8	1	—	1	4	—	7	1	—	1	—	—	1	—
1958	15	11	—	—	1	4	—	6	1	—	1	—	—	1	—
1959	14	10	—	—	3	3	—	6	1	—	1	—	—	1	—
1960	14	10	—	—	3	3	—	3	1	—	1	—	—	1	—
1961	15	10	—	—	4	3	—	3	1	—	1	—	—	1	—
1962	16	10	—	—	6	3	—	3	1	—	1	—	—	1	—
1963	15	10	—	—	6	3	—	3	1	—	1	—	—	1	—
1964	15	10	—	—	6	3	—	3	1	—	1	—	—	1	—
1965	15	10	—	—	7	3	—	3	1	—	1	—	—	1	—
1966	17	10	—	—	8	4	—	4	1	—	1	—	4	1	—
1967	16	9	—	—	8	4	—	—	1	—	1	—	4	1	—
1968	15	9	—	—	9	3	—	—	1	—	1	—	4	1	—
1969	15	8	—	—	8	3	—	—	1	—	—	—	4	1	1
1970	15	4	—	—	7	3	—	—	1	—	—	—	4	1	1

Aviation Ships in Active Status as of 1 July—Continued

YEAR	CV **	CVS	CVL	CVE	LHA/ LPH/ LHD ***	AV	AVD	AVP	AVM	ARV	AVS	AKV	AGP	AVB	CVT/ AVT
1971	14	4	—	—	7	3	—	—	1	—	—	—	2	—	1
1972	14	2	—	—	7	—	—	—	1	—	—	—	—	—	1
1973	14	2	—	—	7	—	—	—	1	—	—	—	—	—	1
1974	14	—	—	—	7	—	—	—	1	—	—	—	—	—	1
1975	15	—	—	—	7	—	—	—	1	—	—	—	—	—	1
1976	13	—	—	—	8	—	—	—	1	—	—	—	—	—	1
1977	13	—	—	—	9	—	—	—	1	—	—	—	—	—	1
1978	13	—	—	—	9	—	—	—	1	—	—	—	—	—	1
1979	13	—	—	—	11	—	—	—	1	—	—	—	—	—	1
1980	13	—	—	—	12	—	—	—	1	—	—	—	—	—	1
1981*	12	—	—	—	12	—	—	—	1	—	—	—	—	—	1
1982*	13	—	—	—	12	—	—	—	1	—	—	—	—	—	1
1983*	13	—	—	—	12	—	—	—	1	—	—	—	—	—	1
1984*	13	—	—	—	12	—	—	—	1	—	—	—	—	—	1
1985*	13	—	—	—	12	—	—	—	1	—	—	—	—	—	1
1986*	13	—	—	—	12	—	—	—	1	—	—	—	—	—	1
1987*	14	—	—	—	12	—	—	—	—	—	—	—	—	—	1
1988*	14	—	—	—	12	—	—	—	—	—	—	—	—	—	1
1989*	14	—	—	—	12	—	—	—	—	—	—	—	—	—	1
1990*	14	—	—	—	13	—	—	—	—	—	—	—	—	—	1
1991*	14	—	—	—	13	—	—	—	—	—	—	—	—	—	1
1992*	13	—	—	—	13	—	—	—	—	—	—	—	—	—	1
1993*	13	—	—	—	12	—	—	—	—	—	—	—	—	—	1
1994*	12	—	—	—	13	—	—	—	—	—	—	—	—	—	—
1995*	12	—	—	—	13	—	—	—	—	—	—	—	—	—	—
1996*	13	—	—	—	13	—	—	—	—	—	—	—	—	—	—

Footnotes:

* During this reporting period, 1981–1996, the total carriers listed under CV does not include the carrier undergoing a major Service Life Extension Program.

** Includes all designations CV, CVA, CVB, CVAN and CVN, that have been used for the Fleet carriers; missions the same.

*** These LHA/LPH/LHDs are counted the same since mission is very similar.

Bennington (CVS 20) underway in the 1960s with antisubmarine aircraft and helicopters on the flight deck.

Aircraft on Hand

1911–1918

1 July	Total HTA inventory	Seaplanes[1]	Flying boats	Landplanes	LTA Airships
1911	1[2]	1			
1912	3	3			
1913	6	4	2		
1914	12	6	6		
1915	15	9	6		
1916	17	14	3		
6 Apr 1917	54	45	6	3	1
11 Nov 1918	2,107	695	1,170	242	15

[1] Pontoon Type, referred to as hydroaeoplanes through 1916.
[2] The Curtis Triad which made its first flight in the hands of a naval officer on 1 July; the plane was formally accepted on 9 August.

Navy and Marine Corps Combined Including those assigned to the Air Reserve and In Storage 1920–1965

		HTA TYPES[1]					LTA TYPES[3]		
1 July	HTA Inventory	Combat	Transport and Utility[4]	Obser- vation[5]	Training	Miscel- laneous[6]	Heli- copters[2]	Rigids	Blimps
1920		1,205							16
1921		1,134							16
1922	1,234	780			484				10
1924	700	530			170			1	1
1925	860	491	134		188	47		2	1
1926	888	600			282	6		1	1
1927	886	599			284	3		1	1
1928	851	605			217	29		1	2
1929	1,038	664	7		205	162		1	2

Aircraft on Hand—Continued
1920-1965

1 July	HTA TYPES[1] HTA Inventory	Combat	Transport and Utility[4]	Obser- vation[5]	Training	Miscel- laneous[6]	Heli- copters[2]	LTA TYPES[3] Rigids	Blimp
1930	1,081	734	12		303	32		1	3
1931	1,204	776	14		300	114		1	3
1932	1,234	909	17		246	62		2	4
1933	1,375	863	38		176	303		2	3
1934	1,347	950	43		157	197		2	2
1935	1,456	1,041	67		170	178		1	2
1936	1,655	1,100	90		166	319		1	4
1937	1,637	972	113		161	393		1	4
1938	2,050	1,284	125		268	373		1	5
1939	2,098	1,316	150		262	370		1	8
1940	1,741	1,194	152		363	32			6
1941	3,437	1,774	183		1,444	31			7
1942	7,058	3,191	461		3,378	28			16
1943	16,691	8,696	878		7,021	96			78
1944	34,071	22,116	1,939		9,652	364	6		146
1945	40,912	29,125	2,897		8,370	520	27		139
1946	24,232	14,637	2,864		2,725	1,006	37		93
1947	17,602	11,181	1,288	413	3,941	779	27		66
1948	15,147	9,889	1,295	299	3,109	545	51		56
1949	14,056	9,372	1,272	144	3,118	150	103		59
1950	14,036	9,422	1,193	126	3,092	203	113		58
1951	13,473	8,713	775	101	3,527	357	163		58
1952	13,787	8,742	971	136	3,567	371	376		59
1953	14,666	8,818	1,250	194	3,700	704	661		50
1954	15,485	8,829	1,276	237	3,762	1,381	724		47
1955	16,440	8,884	1,299	217	3,679	2,361	676		61
1956	15,704	7,961	1,239	233	3,519	2,752	754		51
1957	13,904	7,591	1,287	164	3,341	1,521	821		54
1958	12,531	7,408	1,307	160	3,008	648	933		42

Aircraft on Hand—Continued
1920–1965

1 July	HTA Inventory	Combat	Transport and Utility[4]	Obser- vation[5]	Training	Miscel- laneous[6]	Heli- copters[2]	Rigids	Blimp
1959	12,030	7,030	1,355	150	3,027	468	977		37
1960	11,254	6,074	1,320	135	2,925	800	999		18
1961	11,635	6,305	1,285	129	2,769	1,147	1,032		14
1962	11,791	6,420	1,600		2,561	1,210	1,250		13
1963	11,164	6,265	1,639		2,290	970	1,274		
1964	10,586	5,420	1,727		2,149	1,290	1,265		
1965	10,101	5,127	1,681	20	2,305	968	1,285		

[1] As determined by model designation.
[2] Total on hand; also counted in pertinent columns under HTA types.
[3] Includes Los Angeles under Rigids while in non-flying status 1932-39, and the metal clad ZMC-2 under blimps, 1930-38.
[4] Includes assault transport helicopters after 1961
[5] Included under combat through 1946; thereafter VO and HO.
[6] Has different meanings at different times, but generally includes experimental and obsolete aircraft, those awaiting disposition, on loan, and other categories officially considered "nonprogram" aircraft.
Note: Data not available for fiscal year 1923.

Aircraft on Hand
1966–1995

30 June	Total Aircraft Inventory†	Total Operating Inventory‡	Combat	Transport/ Utility	Observation	Training	Miscellaneous	Rotary Wing
1966	9,509	6,485	3,163	489		1,678	3,110	1,069
1967	9,399	6,591	3,160	543	14	1,679	2,884	1,119
1968	9,326	6,962	3,362	561	36	1,876	2,300	1,191
1969	9,192	6,984	2,964	614	111	2,180	2,110	1,213
1970	8,646	6,528	3,043	549	91	1,741	1,979	1,243
1971	7,974	6,059	2,793	353	80	1,465	2,007	1,276
1972	7,836	5,658	2,663	445	63	1,369	2,223	1,073
1973	7,444	5,590	2,697	416	78	1,286	1,909	1,058
1974	7,509	5,279	2,817	402	71	1,314	1,776	1,129
1975	7,526	4,915	2,747	377	52	1,204	2,012	1,134
1976	6,836	4,931	2,344	323	63	1,067	1,952	1,087

Aircraft on Hand—Continued
1966–1995

30 Sep	Total Aircraft Inventory†	Total Operating Inventory‡	Combat	Transport/ Utility	Observation	Training	Miscellaneous	Rotary Wing
1977	6,593	4,698	2,346	268	61	879	1,943	1,096
1978	6,359	4,512	2,219	249	53	907	1,895	1,036
1979	6,390	4,463	2,207	213	55	916	1,975	1,024
1980	6,300	4,436	2,164	219	74	884	1,913	1,046
1981	6,225	4,474	2,156	221	79	908	1,803	1,058
1982	6,130	4,534	2,223	199	79	908	1,645	1,076
1983	6,178	4,469	2,418	219	78	1,004	1,230	1,229
1984	6,230	4,437	2,348	214	80	1,028	1,339	1,221
1985	5,396	4,462	2,067	183	73	845	1,004	1,224
1986	5,389	4,474	2,112	137	81	849	993	1,217
1987	5,433	4,421	2,093	131	77	816	1,106	1,210
1988**	5,424	4,174	1,945	188	68	740	1,253	1,230
1989	5,972	4,572	2,588	217	72	931	774	1,390
1990	5,895	4,766	2,550	212	57	915	722	1,439
1991	4,629	4,578	2,146	204	36	866		1,377
1992	4,684	4,403	2,235	211	43	797		1,398
1993	4,704	4,134	2,276	220	36	772		1,400
1994*								
1995*								

†Figures include aircraft in the pipeline, inactive aircraft, non-program aircraft, and aircraft in storage. Figures drawn from NAVSO P-3523 generated by the Office of the Navy Comptroller, Financial & Statistical Reports Branch.

‡Total operating inventory accounts for only operational aircraft in the reporting and physical custody of the operating unit to which assigned. Figures drawn from the Naval Aviation Summary reports (OPNAV Notice C3100).

*Figures not available.

**Date for 1988 is 30 June.

Aircraft Designations and Popular Names

Background on the Evolution of Aircraft Designations

Aircraft model designation history is very complex. In order to fully understand the designations, it is important to know the factors that played a role in developing the different missions that aircraft have been called upon to perform. Technological changes affecting aircraft capabilities have resulted in corresponding changes in the operational capabilities and techniques employed by the aircraft. Prior to World War I, the Navy tried various schemes for designating aircraft.

In the early period of naval aviation a system was developed to designate an aircraft's mission. Different aircraft class designations evolved for the various types of missions performed by naval aircraft. This became known as the Aircraft Class Designation System. Numerous changes have been made to this system since the inception of naval aviation in 1911.

While reading this section various references will be made to the Aircraft Class Designation System, Designation of Aircraft, Model Designation of Naval Aircraft, Aircraft Designation System, and Model Designation of Military Aircraft. All of these references refer to the same system involved in designating aircraft classes. This system is then used to develop the specific designations assigned to each type of aircraft operated by the Navy. The F3F-4, TBF-1, AD-3, PBY-5A, A-4, A-6E, and F/A-18C are all examples of specific types of naval aircraft designations which were developed from the Aircraft Class Designation System.

Aircraft Class Designation System

Early Period of Naval Aviation up to 1920

The uncertainties during the early period of naval aviation were reflected by the problems encountered in settling on a functional system for designating naval aircraft. Prior to 1920 two different Aircraft Class Designation Systems were used. From 1911 up to 1914, naval aircraft were identified by a single letter indicating the general type and manufacturer, followed by a number to indicate the individual plane of that type-manufacturer. Under this system:

"A" was used for Curtiss hydroaeroplanes
"B" for Wright hydroaeroplanes
"C" for Curtiss flying boats
"D" for Burgess flying boats
"E" for Curtiss amphibian flying boats

This system had been established in 1911 by Captain Washington I. Chambers, Director of Naval Aviation. The following is a list of the types of aircraft and their designations in existence from 1911–1914:

Aircraft Designation System 1911–1914

A-1 Curtiss hydroaeroplane (originally an amphibian, and the Navy's first airplane)
A-2 Curtiss landplane (rebuilt as a hydroaeroplane)
A-3 Curtiss hydroaeroplane
A-4 Curtiss hydroaeroplane
B-1 Wright landplane (converted to hydroaeroplane)
B-2 Wright type hydroaeroplane
B-3 Wright type hydroaeroplane
C-1 Curtiss flying boat
C-2 Curtiss flying boat
C-3 Curtiss flying boat
C-4 Curtiss flying boat
C-5 Curtiss flying boat
D-1 Burgess Co. and Curtiss flying boat
D-2 Burgess Co. and Curtiss flying boat
E-1 OWL (over water and land) (a Curtiss hydroaeroplane rebuilt as a short-hulled flying boat for flying over water or land and fitted with wheels for use as an amphibian)

A new Aircraft Class Designation System was established by Captain Mark L. Bristol, the second Director of Naval Aviation. He assumed the Director's position from Captain Chambers in December 1913. The new system was issued on 27 March 1914 as General Order 88, "Designation of Air Craft." This system changed the original designation of the aircraft to two letters and a number, of which the first letter denoted class; the second, type within a class; and the number the order in which aircraft within the class were acquired. The four classes set up on 27 March 1914 are as follows:

Aircraft Designation System, 1914–1920

Aircraft Classes

"A" for heavier-than-air craft. Within the "A" class:

L stood for land machines

H stood for hydroaeroplanes

B stood for flying boats

X stood for combination land and water machines (amphibians)

C stood for convertibles (could be equipped as either land or water machines)

"D" for airships or dirigibles

"B" for balloons

"K" for kites

Under this new system the A-1 aircraft (the Navy's first airplane) was redesignated AH-1, with the "A" identifying the plane as a heavier-than-air craft and the "H" standing for hydroaeroplane. General Order No. 88 also provided a corresponding link between the old aircraft designations and the new system: "The aeroplanes now in the service are hereby designated as follows:

A-1 became the AH-1

A-2 became the AH-2

A-3 became the AH-3

B-1 became the AH-4

B-2 became the AH-5

B-3 became the AH-6

C-1 became the AB-1

C-2 became the AB-2

C-3 became the AB-3

C-4 became the AB-4

C-5 became the AB-5

D-1 became the AB-6

D-2 became the AB-7

E-1 became the AX-1"

Despite the phrase, "now in the service," the A-1, B-1 and B-2 and probably the D-1 had ceased to exist before the order was issued.

The Early 1920s

In General Order 541, issued in 1920, two overall types of aircraft were identified and assigned permanent letters which have remained in effect since 1920. Lighter-than-air types were identified by the letter Z and heavier-than-air types were assigned the letter V. Within these two categories, various class letters were assigned to further differentiate the aircraft's operation or construction. Class letters assigned to the Z types were R for rigid, N for nonrigid, and K for kite. By combining the type and class designation, the different airships in the Navy's inventory could be categorized. As an example:

ZR referred to rigid dirigibles (airships)

ZN stood for nonrigid airships

ZK for kite balloons

The class letters assigned to the heavier-than-air vehicles covered a wider range and generally reflected the mission responsibilities of the aircraft classes. Class letters assigned to the V types were:

F for fighting

O for observation

S for scouting

P for patrol

T for torpedo

G for fleet (utility)

By combining the V designation for heavier-than-air vehicles with the class letters, the following aircraft class definitions were assigned in 1920:

VF for fighting plane

VO for observation plane

VS for scouting plane

VP for patrol plane

VT for torpedo and bombing plane

VG for fleet plane (most likely a general utility aircraft)

This class designation system for aircraft has continued to remain a functional system and is still used today. There have been many additions, deletions, and major changes to the system over the years but the concept has remained intact. The current naval aircraft inventory still lists VF, VS, VP, VG, VO, and VT aircraft classes. Three of these, VF, VP, and VO, still have the same definitions they were assigned in 1920. The VS, VG, and VT aircraft class designations now refer to antisubmarine (VS), in-flight refueling (VG), and training aircraft (VT).

The aircraft designation system established in July 1920 by General Order 541 was modified on 29 March 1922 by Bureau of Aeronautics Technical Note 213. It added the identity of the manufacturer to the aircraft model designation. The aircraft class designations remained the same as those issued by General Order 541 (G.O. 541); however, besides the six aircraft classes listed in G.O. 541 (VF, VO, VS, VP, VT, and VG), an additional two classes were added to the aircraft class list. The two new aircraft classes were VA for Training Aircraft and VM for Marine Expeditionary Plane.

The mid to late 1920s

Between 1922 and 1933, there were only a few modifications to the Aircraft Class Designation System. The Bureau of Aeronautics was established in July 1921 and, thereafter, made changes to the Aircraft Class Designation System. In response to a Secretary of Navy letter dated 13 February 1923, the Bureau of Aeronautics issued a Technical Note on 10 March 1923 that changed the VA designation for training aircraft to VN, dropped the VG designation, and added the VJ designation for Transport Plane. This was followed by the addition, in 1925, of the VX designation for experimental aircraft. The VX designation was dropped from the Aircraft Class Designation list in January 1927. In July 1928, the VM designation was dropped and the VJ designation was changed from Transportation Plane to General Utility. Two new designations were also instituted, VB for bombing and VH for ambulance. A new aircraft class was added in July 1930 and assigned the designation VR for transport aircraft. This VR designation has remained in effect for transport aircraft since 1930.

The 1930s

Similar changes took place in the Aircraft Class Designation System during the early 1930s. By July 1933, there were ten aircraft class designations. This list of aircraft classes did not vary much from those identified in the previous ten years. The aircraft class designations identified in July 1933 were as follows:

VB for bombing
VF for fighting
VH for ambulance
VJ for general utility
VN for training
VO for observation
VP for patrol
VR for transport
VS for scouting
VT for torpedo.

A major change was instituted to the Aircraft Designation System on 2 January 1934. Prior to 1934, aircraft classes had been established according to the primary mission the aircraft was to perform. The fact that many aircraft were capable of performing more than one mission was recognized in the revised system by assigning an additional letter to the previous two-letter aircraft class designation. In the new three-letter aircraft class designation, the first letter identified the type of vehicle, such as, V for heavier-than-air (fixed wing) and Z for lighter-than-air. For heavier-

than-air, the second letter identified the primary mission of the aircraft, using the same 10 letter designations listed in the above paragraph. The **third letter indicated the secondary mission** of the aircraft class, such as:

F for fighting
O for observation
B for bombing
T for torpedo
S for scouting

By assigning these five secondary mission letters to the primary aircraft letter designations, **seven new aircraft class designations were established**:

VBF for bombing-fighting
VOS for observation-scouting
VPB for patrol-bombing
VPT for patrol-torpedo
VSB for scouting-bombing
VSO for scout-observation
VTB for torpedo-bombing

On the eve of World War II, the Model Designation of Airplanes for 1 July 1939 was very similar to what had been identified in 1934. There were eleven primary aircraft class designations and six designations that included a secondary mission letter in its class designation. The 1 July 1939 Model Designation of Airplanes included the following Aircraft Class Designations:

Bombing (VB)
Fighting (VF)
Miscellaneous (VM)
Observation (VO)
Patrol (VP)
Scouting (VS)
Torpedo (VT)
Training (VN)
Transport (multi-engine) (VR)
Transport (single engine) (VG)
Utility (VJ)
Observation-Scouting (VOS)
Patrol-Bombing (VPB)
Scouting-Bombing (VSB)
Scouting-Observation (VSO)
Torpedo-Bombing (VTB)
Utility-Transport (VJR)

World War II

The designation changes for the aircraft classes and squadron system during World War II and the immediate post war period are identified in the Model Designation of Naval Aircraft, the Aviation Circular Letters, and in the Navy Department Bulletins.

By mid-1943, many new aircraft class designations had been added to the Model Designation of Naval Aircraft. The additions included:

VA for ambulance
VBT for bombing-torpedo
VSN for scout-training
VL for gliders
VLN for training-gliders
VLR for transport-gliders
VH for helicopters
VHO for observation-helicopters
VD for drones
VTD for torpedo-drones and/or target-drones
ZN for nonrigid airships
ZNN for nonrigid-training and/or utility airships
ZNP for nonrigid patrol and/or scouting airships

As the war progressed, more changes were made to the Model Designation of Naval Aircraft. In July 1944, a major change was instituted for the Aircraft Class Designation System. Naval aircraft were divided into **three main types identified by a letter**:

V for fixed wing vehicles (airplanes, gliders and drones)
H for rotary wing vehicles (helicopters)
Z for lighter-than-air vehicles (airships)

The three main types were then each subdivided into classes. The classes under the heavier-than-air fixed-wing type (V) included:

VF fighters
VF(M) fighters (medium or 2 engine)
VSB scout bombers
VTB torpedo bombers
VO/VS observation scout
VPB(HL) patrol bombers (heavy or 4 engine landplane)
VPB(ML) patrol bombers (medium or 2 engine landplane)
VPB(HS) patrol bombers (heavy or 4 engine seaplane)
VPB(MS) patrol bombers (medium or 2 engine seaplane)
VR(HL) transport (heavy or 4 engine landplane)
VR(ML) transport (medium or 2 engine landplane)
VR(HS) transport (heavy or 4 engine seaplane)
VR(MS) transport (medium or 2 engine seaplane)
VJ(M) utility (medium or 2 engine)
VJ utility
VSN(M) training
VSN training
VN training
VK drones
VKN drones (target training)

VL gliders
VLN gliders (training)
VLR gliders (transport)

The helicopter type (H) had the following classes:

HO helicopters (observation)
HN helicopters (training)
HR helicopters (transport)

The lighter-than-air type (Z) had the following classes:

ZN nonrigid airships
ZNN nonrigid airships (training)
ZNP nonrigid airships (patrol and escort)

This July 1944 change to the Model Designation of Naval Aircraft was still in effect at the close of World War II and only a couple of additions had been made, they included:

VKC for assault drones
HJ for utility helicopters

Post World War II and the late 1940s

On 11 March 1946, a major revision was issued to the Class Designation of Naval Aircraft. Aviation Circular Letter Number 43–46 divided naval aircraft into four types and assigned a letter designation. The four types were:

V for heavier-than-air (fixed wing)
K for pilotless aircraft
H for heavier-than-air (rotary wing)
Z for lighter-than-air

Within the class designation for **V type aircraft**, the primary mission and class designation were as follows:

Primary Mission	Class Designation
Fighter (destroy enemy aircraft in the air)	VF
Attack (destroy enemy surface or ground targets)	VA
Patrol (search for enemy)	VP
Observation (observe and direct ship and shore gunfire)	VO
Transport purposes	VR
Utility purposes	VU
Training purposes	VT
Gliders	VG

Within the class designation for **H type (rotary wing)**, the primary mission and class designation were as follows:

Air-sea rescue	HH
Observation	HO

Training	HT
Transport	HR
Utility	HU

Within the class designation for **K type (pilotless aircraft)**, the primary mission and class designation were as follows:

For attack on aircraft targets	KA
For attack on ship targets	KS
For attack on ground targets	KG
For use as target aircraft	KD
For utility purposes	KU

Within the class designation for **Z type (lighter-than-air)**, the primary mission and class designation were as follows:

Patrol and escort	ZP
Air-sea rescue	ZH
Training	ZT
Utility	ZU

This order provided that "no changes...be made in the model designation of aircraft already produced or in production, except that the mission letter of all BT class aircraft shall be changed to A." Thus, the SB2C and TBF/TBM aircraft remained in use until they were removed from the inventory, while the BT2D and BTM aircraft were redesignated as AD and AM. These aircraft were assigned to the new attack squadrons established in the latter part of 1946.

In 1947 a modification was made to CNO's Aviation Circular Letter No. 43–46 of 11 March 1946 whereby a fifth class designation was added to the naval aircraft types. The new class designation was the **M type for Guided Missiles** and the primary mission and class designation were as follows:

Air-to-air	AAM
Air-to-surface	ASM
Air-to-underwater	AUM
Surface-to-air	SAM
Surface-to-surface	SSM
Surface-to-underwater	SUM
Underwater-to-air	UAM
Underwater-to-surface	USM
Test Vehicle	TV

In 1949 the class designations were:

V type (heavier-than-air, fixed wing) Classes

VF	Fighter	Air defense and escort
VA	Attack	Surface and ground attack
VP	Patrol	ASW reconnaissance and attack

VO	Observation	Gunfire and artillery spotting
VR	Transport	Air logistic support
VU	Utility	Fleet utility support
VT	Training	Basic and fleet training
VG	Glider	

H type (heavier-than-air, rotary wing) Classes

HH	Air-sea rescue
HO	Observation
HT	Training
HR	Transport
HU	Utility

K type (pilotless aircraft) Classes

KD	Aerial target

M type (Guided Missiles) Classes

AAM	Air-to-air
ASM	Air-to-surface
AUM	Air-to-underwater
SAM	Surface-to-air
SSM	Surface-to-surface
SUM	Surface-to-underwater
UAM	Underwater-to-air
USM	Underwater-to-surface
TV	Test vehicle

Z type (Lighter-than-air)

ZP	Patrol and escort
ZH	Search and rescue
ZT	Training
ZU	Utility

The 1950s, 1960s, 1970s and 1980s

During the early 1950s several changes were made to the V (heavier-than-air fixed wing) type. The VG glider class was dropped and the following classes were added:

VS	Search	Submarine search and attack (carrier)
VW	Warning	Airborne early warning

In 1953 the nine classes of the V type were further divided into sub-classes. The **V type classes and sub-classes** were as follows:

VA	Attack	Surface and ground attack
	VA (Int'd)	Interdiction
	VA (GS)	Ground Support
	VA (AW)	All Weather and ASW
	VA (W)	Air Early Warning and ASW
	VA (H)	Heavy
	VA (P)	Photographic
VF	Fighter	Air defense and escort
	VF (Int)	Interceptor

	VF (Day)	Day, jet
	VF (Day) (Prop)	Day, reciprocating
	VF (AW)	All weather, jet
	VF (AW) (Prop)	All weather, reciprocating
	VF (P)	Photographic, jet
	VF (P) (Prop)	Photographic, reciprocating
	VF (D)	Drone control
	VF (FT)	Flight Test
VO	Observation	Gunfire and artillery spotting
VP	Patrol	ASW reconnaissance, mining and weather
	VP (L)	Landplane
	VP (S)	Seaplane
	VP (MIN)	Mining
	VP (WEA)	Weather
	VP (Q)	Countermeasure
VR	Transport	Air logistic support
	VR (H)	Heavy landplane
	VR (M)	Medium landplane
	VR (S)	Heavy seaplane
	VR (C)	Carrier
VS	Antisubmarine	Submarine search and attack
	VS	Search and attack
	VS (S)	Attack
	VS (W)	Search
VT	Training	Basic, fleet and primary training
	VT (Jet)	Jet
	VT (ME)	Two-engine, reciprocating
	VT (SE)	One-engine, reciprocating
	VT (E)	Electronic
	VT (Nav)	Navigation
VU	Utility	Fleet utility support
	VU (Gen)	General
	VU (SAR)	Search and rescue
	VU (Tow)	Tow
VW	Warning	Airborne Early Warning
	VW	Air early warning

Between 1953 and 1960 there was only one change in the V class and a few modifications in the sub-classes. The VG class, for in-flight refueling, tanker, was added in 1958. In 1960 the type letter for the heavier-than-air fixed wing class was still identified as "V", however, it was omitted from the acronym for the class designation. The class designations for the heavier-than-air fixed wing type and their basic mission were as follows:

A	Attack
F	Fighter
G	In-flight refueling tanker
O	Observation
P	Patrol
R	Transport
S	Antisubmarine (for carrier based aircraft)
T	Training
U	Utility
W	Airborne Early Warning

The **H type classes** for 1953 were as follows:

HO	Observation
HR	Transport
HS	Anti-submarine
HT	Trainer
HU	Utility
HC	Cargo

In 1955 a new H type class was added and designated HW for Aircraft Early Warning. This class remained in effect for only a short time and was removed by 1961. The only other change for the H type during the 1950s was the removal of the HC Cargo Class by 1961.

The **Z type classes** for 1953 were as follows:

ZP	Patrol
ZT	Trainer

There were several changes to the Z type classes in the 1950s. In 1954 two new classes were added, ZS Search and Anti-submarine and ZW Air Early Warning. The other changes in 1954 included the dropping of the ZT Trainer designation and modifying the ZP designation to patrol and anti-subamrine. In 1955 the ZS designation was dropped after being in effect for only a year.

The **K type classes** for 1953 were as follows:

KD	Targets

This designation was modified in 1955 to K (suffix) Target Drones. Sometime in the latter part of the 1950s the K type designation was dropped and a new **D type** was listed as Remotely Controlled Tactical Airborne Vehicle. Within this type the class was identified as DS Anti-submarine.

The **M type** for 1953 was modified as follows:

M	Tactical Weapon
RV	Research Vehicle

A Bureau of Aeronautics Aviation Circular Letter Number 25–51 of 14 July 1951 removed the guided missile type from the naval aircraft types and listed only four types of naval aircraft. The four types were:

V	Heavier-than-air (fixed wing)
H	Heavier-than-air (rotary wing)
Z	Lighter-than-air
K	Target drones

The Bureau of Naval Weapons Instruction 13100.1A "Model Designation of Naval Aircraft", dated 17 May 1961, lists the type letter designations as follows:

V	Heavier-than-air (fixed wing) (the V is omitted from the aircraft designation)

H   Heavier-than-air (rotary wing)
Z   Lighter-than-air
D   Remotely controlled tactical airborne vehicle
R   Rotorcycle

The classes within each of these five aircraft type designations were:

V type Heavier-than-air (fixed wing) Classes

VA   Attack
VF   Fighter
VG   In-flight refueling tanker
VO   Observation
VP   Patrol
VR   Transport
VS   Anti-submarine
VT   Training
VU   Utility
VW   Airborne Early Warning

H type Heavier-than-air (rotary wing) Classes

HO   Observation
HR   Transport
HS   Anti-submarine
HT   Training
HU   Utility

Z type Lighter-than-air Classes

ZP   Patrol
ZW   Airborne Early Warning

D type Remotely Controlled Tactical Airborne Vehicle Classes

DS   Anti-submarine

R type Rotorcycles Classes

RO   Observation (equipment)

In 1962 a major changed occurred in the model designation for naval aircraft. The Department of Defense consolidated the aircraft designation systems of the Navy, Army, and Air Force. A new DOD (Department of Defense) Directive was established that designated, redesignated, and named military aircraft. Under the new system the V for heavier-than-air fixed wing types was dropped completely and a single letter was used to identify the basic mission of the vehicle. The basic mission and associated type symbols were as follows:

A	Attack	Aircraft designed to search out, attack and destroy enemy land or sea targets using conventional or special weapons. Also used for interdiction and close air support missions.
B	Bomber	Aircraft designed for bombing enemy targets.
C	Cargo/transport	Aircraft designed for carrying cargo and/or passengers.
E	Special Electronic	Aircraft possessing ECM capability or installation having electronic devices to permit employment as an early warning radar station.
F	Fighter	Aircraft designed to intercept and destroy other aircraft and/or missiles.
H	Helicopter	A rotary-wing aircraft designed with the capability of flight in any plane; e.g., horizontal, vertical, or diagonal.
K	Tanker	Aircraft designed for in-flight refueling of other aircraft.
O	Observation	Aircraft designed to observe (through visual/other means) and report tactical information concerning composition and disposition of enemy forces, troops, and supplies in an active combat area.
P	Patrol	Long range, all weather, multi-engine aircraft operating from land and/or water bases, designed for independent accomplishment of the following functions; antisubmarine warfare, maritime reconnaissance, and mining.
S	Antisubmarine	Aircraft designed to search out, detect, identify, attack and destroy enemy submarines.
T	Trainer	Aircraft designed for training personnel in the operation of aircraft and/or related equipment, and having provisions for instructor personnel.
U	Utility	Aircraft used for miscellaneous missions such as carrying cargo and/or passengers, towing targets, etc. These aircraft will include those having a small payload.

V	VTOL and STOL	Aircraft designed for vertical take-off or landing with no take-off or landing roll, or aircraft capable of take-off and landing in a minimum prescribed distance.
X	Research	Aircraft designed for testing configurations of a radical nature. These aircraft are not normally intended for use as tactical aircraft.
Z	Airship	A self-propelled lighter-than-air aircraft.

The only type symbol not in use by the Navy from the above listing was the B for bomber aircraft. The O for observation aircraft was in the naval inventory but was used primarily by the Marine Corps.

Between 1962 and 1990 there were only two modifications to the listing of basic mission and aircraft type symbols in DOD's Model Designation of Military Aircraft, Rockets and Guided Missiles. These changes involved the addition of the letter "R" for Reconnaissance and the deletion of the Z type for Airships. The basic mission for the R type was an aircraft designed to perform reconnaissance missions.

Even though a consolidated DOD directive was issued on aircraft designations for the Navy, Air Force, and Army in 1962, the Navy continued to publish a listing of naval aircraft classes and sub-classes that differed slightly from the DOD directive. However, the Navy did follow the new procedures for designating its aircraft, as an example, the AD-5 Skyraider aircraft designation was changed to A-1E. The December 1962 issue of the Allowances and Location of Naval Aircraft lists the following classes and sub-classes for fixed wing aircraft (note the continued use of "V" as part of the class designation and the failure to change the VG class designation for air refueler to K, as listed by the DOD instruction):

VF	Fighter	
	VF FB	Fighter-bomber
	VF P	Photo reconnaissance

VA	Attack	
	VA L	Light Attack
	VA LP	Light Attack (Prop)
	VA M	Medium Attack
	VA H	Heavy Attack
	VA P	Photo Reconnaissance (long range)
	VA Q	ECM Reconnaissance (long range)
	VA QM	Tactical ECM
	VA QMP	Tactical ECM (Prop)

VS	ASW	(Carrier based)

VP	ASW	Patrol
	VP L	ASW Patrol (shore based)
	VP S	ASW Patrol (sea based)

VW	Airborne early warning	
	VW M	AEW Medium (carrier based)
	VW H	AEW Heavy (shore based)

VR	Transport	
	VR H	Heavy transport
	VR M	Medium transport
	VR C	Carrier transport

VG	Air refueler, heavy	

VT	Trainer	
	VT AJ	Advanced jet trainer
	VT BJ	Basic jet trainer
	VT SJ	Special jet trainer
	VT AP	Advanced prop trainer
	VT BP	Basic Prop trainer
	VT PP	Primary prop trainer
	VT SP	Special Prop trainer

VK	Drone	
	VK D	Drone control

The only change to this listing occurred in 1965 with the addition of the VO class for observation. Between 1965 and 1988 there was no change to the aircraft class listing in the Allowances and Location of Naval Aircraft. However, there were numerous changes in the listing for the sub-classes. The final publication of the Allowances and Location of Naval Aircraft was March 1988.

On 2 May 1975, the Navy selected a derivative of the YF-17 as the winner of the Navy's VFAX competition for a new multimission fighter attack aircraft. The VFAX aircraft was designed to replace two aircraft in the Navy's inventory, the F-4 Phantom II and the A-7 Corsair II. This program was reinstituting an old Navy policy, whereby, multimission requirements for attack and fighter, be incorporated into a single aircraft. Fighter and light attack missions had previously been assigned to various types of aircraft, particularly in the period prior to World War II and also in the 1950s. The Navy was now reverting to an old policy and designing a plane with a dual capacity as a fighter and an attack aircraft to meet new multimission requirements.

The VFAX aircraft was initially assigned the F-18A designation. A new model designation F/A (strike fighter) was established and assigned to the aircraft in the late 1970s. The Navy accepted its first F/A-18 Hornet on 16 January 1979. The F/A designation was identified as a sub-class and listed under the VF class in the Navy's Allowances and Location of Naval Aircraft. Under the DOD model designation listing the F/A-18 designation is listed under both the A and F symbol designations as A-18 and F-18.

The 1990s

The following is a list of the Naval Aircraft Class and Sub-classes used in the 1990s:

VF	Fighter	
	VF FA	Striker Fighter
	VF FB	Fighter
	VF P	Fighter
VA	Attack	
	VA L	Attack
	VA M	Attack
	VA H	Attack
	VA P	Attack
	VA Q	Attack
	VA QM	Attack
VS	Sea Control (was Antisubmarine until 1993)	
VP	Patrol	
	VP L	Patrol
VW	Warning	
	VP M	Warning
	VP H	Warning
VR	Transport	
	VR H	Transport

	VR M	Transport
	VR C	Transport
	VR LJ	Transport
VG	In-flight Refueling	
VO	Observation	
	VO L	Observation
VU	Utility	
	VU L	Utility
	VU S	Utility
VT	Training	
	VT AJ	Training Jet
	VT SJ	Training Jet
	VT PP	Training Prop
	VT SP	Training Prop
	VT SG	Training Jet
H	Rotary Wing	
	H F	Rotary Wing
	H A	Rotary Wing
	H G	Rotary Wing
	H S	Rotary Wing
	H H	Rotary Wing
	H M	Rotary Wing
	H L	Rotary Wing
	H T	Rotary Wing
	H R	Rotary Wing
VK	Drones	
	VK D	Drones
	VK K	Drones Jet

The R4C-1 Condor was used as a transport by the Navy, AN-32600.

Aircraft Designation List

The Aircraft Designation Listings have been divided into four separate listings to help clarify the different designation systems used by the Navy. The four listings are: **1911–1922 Designation Systems** (there were three separate systems during this period), **1922–1923 Designations**, **1923–1962 Navy System** and the **DoD Designation System, 1962 to Present**. Column headings within each of these four listings vary. However, if the popular name (official name assigned by the Navy) or common name (name usually assigned by the manufacturer) was known it is included in each of the listings. The popular or common name may not always apply to all the specific aircraft model designations. The primary emphasis for the Aircraft Designation Listings is to provide a composite list of all the aircraft designations the Navy has had in its inventory. It should also be noted, some aircraft in these listings were not assigned bureau

numbers, especially in the case of experimental aircraft. Others were one of a kind models, and some were acquired through a means other than the usual ordering via aircraft production contracts, these include foreign aircraft acquired for evaluation. A separate listing, **Naval Aircraft Redesignated in 1962**, has been added to help clarify the redesignations that occurred in 1962.

1911–1922 Designation Systems

Within this time frame there were three separate designation systems. The three separate columns identify those systems. Column three (Other Designation Systems or Popular Name) covers the period 1917–1922. During this period there was no standard designation system. During World War I the Navy generally adopted whatever designations were assigned by the developer or manufacturer.

1911 Designation System	1914 Designation System	Other Designation Systems, Popular or Common Name	Manufacturer or other Source	1911 Designation System	1914 Designation System	Other Designation Systems, Popular or Common Name	Manufacturer or other Source
A-1	AH-1	Triad	Curtiss		AH-17		Curtiss
A-2/E-1	AX-1	OWL(Over-Water-Land, also called Bat Boat)	Curtiss		AH-18		Curtiss
					AH-19	Martin S	Martin
A-3	AH-3		Curtiss		AH-20	Thomas HS	Thomas Brothers
A-4	AH-2		Curtiss		AH-21	Thomas HS	Thomas Brothers
B-1	AH-4		Wright		AH-22		Martin
B-2	AH-5		Wright		AH-23		Wright
B-3	AH-6		Wright		AH-24	Sturtevant S	Sturtevant
C-1	AB-1		Curtiss		AH-25		Burgess
C-2	AB-2		Curtiss		AH-26		Burgess
C-3	AB-3		Curtiss		AH-27		Burgess
C-4	AB-4		Curtiss		AH-28		Burgess
C-5	AB-5		Curtiss		AH-29		Burgess
D-1	AB-6		Burgess & Curtis		AH-30		Curtiss
D-2	AB-7		Burgess & Curtis		AH-31		Burgess
E-1	AX-1	OWL(Over-Water-Land, also called Bat Boat)	Curtiss (1913)		AH-32		Curtiss
	DN-1	(Navy's first LTA vehicle, D stood for dirigible and N for non-rigid)	Connecticut Aircraft Company		AH-33		Curtiss
					AH-34		Curtiss
					AH-35		Curtiss
					AH-36		Curtiss
					AH-37		Curtiss
	AH-7		Burgess-Dunne		AH-38		Curtiss
	AH-8		Curtiss		AH-39		Curtiss
	AH-9		Curtiss		AH-40		Curtiss
	AH-10		Burgess-Dunne		AH-41		Curtiss
	AH-11		Curtiss		AH-42		Curtiss
	AH-12		Curtiss		AH-43		Curtiss
	AH-13		Curtiss		AH-44		Curtiss
	AH-14		Curtiss		AH-45		Curtiss
	AH-15		Curtiss		AH-46		Curtiss
	AH-16		Curtiss		AH-47		Curtiss

1911 Designation System	1914 Designation System	Other Designation Systems, Popular or Common Name	Manufacturer or other Source	1911 Designation System	1914 Designation System	Other Designation Systems, Popular or Common Name	Manufacturer or other Source
	AH-48		Curtiss			H-12,-12L	Curtiss
	AH-49		Curtiss			H-16	Curtiss, NAF
	AH-50		Curtiss			H-4-H	Standard
	AH-51		Curtiss			HA-1,-2	Curtiss
	AH-52		Curtiss			HB-2	Levy-Lepen
	AH-53		Curtiss			HD-1,-2	Hanriot
	AH-54		Curtiss			Heinkel Seaplane	Casper Werke, Germany
	AH-55		Curtiss			HPS-1	Handley Page
	AH-56		Curtiss			HS-1,-1L	Curtiss, Boeing,
	AH-57		Curtiss				Loughead, LWF,
	AH-58		Curtiss				Gallaudet, Standard
	AH-59		Curtiss			HS-2L	Curtiss, Boeing, NAF,
	AH-60		Curtiss				Gallaudet, Standard,
	AH-61	D-1	Gallaudet				Loughead, LWF
	AH-62	R-3	Curtiss			HS-3	Curtiss, NAF
	AH-63		Paul Schmitt, Paris			HT-2	Burgess
	AH-64		Curtiss			JL-6	Junkers-Larsen
	AH-65	R-3	Curtiss			JN-4	Curtiss
		18-T Kirkham Fighter	Curtiss			JN-4B	Curtiss
		AR-1	Morane-Saulnier			JN-4H	From Army
		Avorio Prassone	Italian Government			JN-4HG	From Army
		C-1	Fokker, Netherlands			JN-6H	From Army
		C-1F	Boeing			JN-6HG-I	From Army
		Camel (F-I)	Sopwith, from Army			K Boat	Austrian Government
		Caproni Ca-44	Caproni, Italy			K-4 (variant of NO-1)	J.V. Martin
		CR-1,-3	Curtiss			KF-1 (also known as	J.V. Martin
		CS-1	Curtiss			KIV)	
		CS-II	Dornier			L-2	Curtiss
		CT	Curtiss			L-3	Longren
		D-1	Gallaudet Aircraft Corp.			Le Pen Seaplane	From Abroad
		D-1	Dornier, Swiss Agent			LePere	From Army
		D-4	Gallaudet Aircraft Corp.			LS-1	Loening Aeronautical
		D-7 or D.VII	Fokker				Engineering Co.
		DH-4	Dayton-Wright, from Army			M-3 Kitten	Loening Aeronautical
							Engineering Co.
		DH-4B/4B-1	NAF and Army			M-8	Loening Aeronautical
		DH-9A	British Govt.				Engineering Co.
		DN-1	Connecticut Aircraft Co.			M-8-0 (M-80)	Loening Aeronautical
		Donne Denhaut	French Govt.				Engineering Co.
		DT-1,-2	Douglas, NAF,LWF			M-8-1 (M-81)	NAF (Loening design)
		E-1 (M Defense)	Standard, from Army			M-8-1S (M-8-1S)	Loening
		EM-1,-2	G. Elias & Brothers			M20-1	Martin
		EO-1	G. Elias & Brothers			M.5	Macchi
		F Boat	Curtiss, Alexandria (Briggs)			M.8	Macchi
		F-5/F-5L	Curtiss, Canadian Aeroplanes Ltd., and NAF			M.16	Macchi
						MB-3	Thomas Morse
		F-6	NAF			MB-7	Thomas Morse
		FT-1	Fokker, Netherlands			MBT/MT	Martin
		Gastite Kite	Goodrich			MF Boat	Curtiss and NAF
		GS-1,-2 Gnome Speed Scout	Curtiss			MO-1	Martin
						MS-1	Martin

1911 Designation System	1914 Designation System	Other Designation Systems, Popular or Common Name	Manufacturer or other Source	1911 Designation System	1914 Designation System	Other Designation Systems, Popular or Common Name	Manufacturer or other Source
		MT/MBT	Martin			Swift	Blackburn Aeroplane Co.
		Model 10	Alexandria Aircraft			Tellier Flying Boat	French Government
		Model 39-A & -B	Aeromarine Plane & Motor Co.			TF Boat	NAF
		Model 40F	Aeromarine Plane & Motor Co.			TG-1,-2,-3,-4,-5	NAF
						TS-1	NAF and Curtiss
		Model 700	Aeromarine Plane & Motor Co.			TS-2,-3	NAF
		N-1	NAF			TR-2(TS-3 A6449 re-designated, one of a kind)	NAF
		N-9, -9H	Curtiss, Burgess				
		N-10 (2 reworked N-9)	Curtiss			TR-3,-3A	NAF (Rebuilt TS-2)
		NC-1, 2, 3 ,4	Curtiss			TW-3	Wright
		NC-5 to -10	NAF			U-1	Caspar, Germany
		Nieuport 28	From Army			U-2	Burgess
		Night Bomber	Sperry			USXB-1	Dayton Wright, from Army
		NO-1	NAF				
		NW-1, -2	Wright			VE-7,-7F	Lewis & Vought and NAF
		O-SS	British				
		Panther	Parnall			VE-7G,-7GF	NAF
		Paul Schmitt Seaplane	Paul Schmitt, Paris			VE-7H	NAF
		PT-1,-2	NAF			VE-7S,-7SF,-7SH	NAF
		R-3	Curtiss			VE-9,-9H	Chance Vought
		R-6,-6L	Curtiss			Zodiac-Vedette	French Government
		R-9	Curtiss			Viking IV	Vickers
		S-4B	Thomas Morse			VNB-1	Boeing
		S-4C	Thomas Morse Scout			WA	Dayton-Wright
		S-5	Curtiss			WP-1	Wright
		S-5 (not the same aircraft as Curtiss S-5)	Thomas Morse			WS Seaplane	Dayton-Wright
						XDH-60 Moth	DeHavilland
		SA1	NAF			XS-1	Cox-Klemin
		SA2	NAF			Exp. Seaplane	NAS Pensacola
		SC-1,-2	Martin			Glider	Am. Motorless
		SE-5	From Army			Hydroaeroplane	Pensacola and Curtiss
		SH-4	Thomas-Morse			Richardson seaplane	Washington Navy Yard
		Sopwith Baby	Sopwith			Seaplane	Aeromarine
		Sopwith Camel	Sopwith			Seaplane	DWF, Germany
		Sopwith Pup	Sopwith			Seaplane	Farman
		Sopwith 1 1/2 Strutter	Sopwith			Seaplane	Loening
		SS-Z-23	British Admiralty			Seaplane	Standard
		ST-1	Stout Metal Airplane Co.			Seaplane	Wright
						Seaplane	Wright-Martin

1922–1923 Designations

Original Navy Designation	Other Designation, Popular or Common Name	Manufacturer or other Source	Original Navy Designation	Other Designation, Popular or Common Name	Manufacturer or other Source
BR		Bee Line	HO-1		Huff-Daland
HN-1,-2		Huff-Daland	NM		NAF

1923–1962 Navy System

Post-1962 DOD Designation	Original Navy Designation	Popular or Common Name, other Designation and Miscellaneous Data	Manufacturer or Source	Post-1962 DOD Designation	Original Navy Designation	Popular or Common Name, other Designation and Miscellaneous Data	Manufacturer or Source
	AE-1	(L-4)(HE-1)	Piper		thru -3		
A-1	AD-1 thru -7	Skyraider (XBT2D-1)	Douglas		F3A-1	Corsair (F4U)	Brewster
	A2D-1	Skyshark	Douglas		FB-1		Boeing
A-3	A3D-1, -2	Skywarrior	Douglas		thru -5		
A-4	A4D-1, -2, -5	Skyhawk	Douglas		F2B-1		Boeing
	AF-2, -3	Guardian (XTB3F-1)	Grumman		F3B-1		Boeing
A-6	A2F-1	Intruder	Grumman		F4B-1 thru -4		Boeing
F-4	AH	Phantom II	McDonnell		XF5B-1		Boeing
A-2	AJ-1, -2	Savage	North American		XF6B-1		Boeing
A-5	A3J-1 thru -3	Vigilante	North American		XF7B-1		Boeing
	AM-1	Mauler (XBTM-1)	Martin		XF8B-1		Boeing
	AU-1	Corsair (XF4U-6)	Vought		F2C-1	(F2C-1 a paper designation for R2C-1, never used as F2C-1)	Curtiss
		B-314	Boeing				
		Bulldog IIA	Bristol		F4C-1		Curtiss
	BD-1,-2	Havoc (A-20)	Douglas		F6C-1 thru -4	Hawk	Curtiss
	BG-1		Great Lakes		F6C-6	Hawk	Curtiss
	XB2G-1		Great Lakes		XF6C-5 thru -7		Curtiss
	BM-1,-2	(XT5M-1)	Martin		F7C-1	Seahawk	Curtiss
	BT-1		Northrop		XF8C-1	Falcon	Curtiss
	XBT-2	(SBD-1)	Northrop/Douglas		F8C-1, -3	Falcon (OC)	Curtiss
	XBTC-2		Curtiss		F8C-4, -5	Helldiver (O2C)	Curtiss
	XBY-1		Consolidated		XF8C-2, -4	Helldiver	Curtiss
	XB2Y-1		Consolidated		XF8C-7, -8	Helldiver (O2C)	Curtiss
	XBFC-1	(XF11C-1)	Curtiss		XF9C-1, -2		Curtiss
	BFC-2	Goshawk (F11C-2)	Curtiss		F9C-2	Sparrowhawk	Curtiss
	BF2C-1	(F11C-3)	Curtiss		XF11C-1	(XBFC-1)	Curtiss
	XBTC-1	Cancelled	Curtiss		XF11C-2	Goshawk (XBFC-2)	Curtiss
	XBTC-2		Curtiss		XF11C-3	(XBF2C-1)	Curtiss
	XBT2C-1		Curtiss		F11C-2	Goshawk (BFC-2)	Curtiss
	BTD	Destroyer	Douglas		XF13C-1 thru -3		Curtiss
A-1	XBT2D-1	Skyraider (AD-1)	Douglas		XF14C-2		Curtiss
	XBTK-1	(BK-1 original designation—changed before first aircraft completed)	Kaiser-Fleetwings		XF15C-1		Curtiss
					XFD-1		Douglas
	XBTM-1	Mauler (AM-1)	Martin		FD-1	Phantom (FH-1)	McDonnell
	CS-1, -2		Curtiss		XF2D-1	Banshee (F2H)	McDonnell
	SC-1, -2	(CS-1)	Martin	F-10	F3D-1,-2	Sky Knight	Douglas
	D-558-1	Skystreak	Douglas	F-6	F4D-1	Skyray	Douglas
	D-558-2	Skyrocket	Douglas		F5D-1	Skylancer	Douglas
	XDH-80	Puss Moth	Dehavilland		FF-1, -2		Grumman
QH-50D, -50C	DSN	DASH	Gyrodyne		F2F-1		Grumman
	F-5L		NAF		F3F-1 thru -3		Grumman
	XFA-1		General Aviation		XF4F-3	Wildcat	Grumman
	F2A-1	Buffalo	Brewster		thru -6, -8		

1923–1962 Navy System—Continued

Post-1962 DOD Designation	Original Navy Designation	Popular or Common Name, other Designation and Miscellaneous Data	Manufacturer or Source	Post-1962 DOD Designation	Original Navy Designation	Popular or Common Name, other Designation and Miscellaneous Data	Manufacturer or Source
	F4F-3,-3A, -4, -7	Wildcat (FM)	Grumman	F-8	F8U-1, -2	Crusader	Vought
	XF5F-1	Skyrocket	Grumman		F8U-3	Crusader III	Vought
	XF6F-3, -4, -6	Hellcat	Grumman		F2W-1		Wright
	F6F-3, -5	Hellcat	Grumman		F3W-1	Apache	Wright
	F7F-1 thru -4	Tigercat	Grumman		XFY-1	Pogo	Consolidated
	F8F-1, -2	Bearcat	Grumman	F-7	F2Y	Sea Dart (Never used in F-7 designation)	Convair
	F9F-2 thru -5	Panther	Grumman		GB-1, -2	Traveler (JB)	Beech
F-9	F9F-6 thru -8	Cougar	Grumman		GH-1 thru -3	Nightingale (NH)	Howard
	XF10F-1	Jaguar	Grumman		GK-1	Forwarder (JK)	Fairchild
F-11	F11F-1	Tiger (F9F-9)	Grumman		GQ-1	Reliant	Stinson
	XFG-1/ XF2G-1		Eberhart	C-130	GV-1	Hercules (R8V)	Lockheed
	FG-1	Corsair (F4U)	Goodyear		HE	(L-4)(AE)	Piper
	F2G-1, -2	(FG/F4U)	Goodyear		XHL-1		Loening
	XFH-1		Hall		XHJH-1		McDonnell
	FH-1	Phantom	McDonnell		XHJP-1		Piasecki
F-2	F2H-1 thru -4	Banshee (F2D)	McDonnell		XHJS-1		Sikorsky
F-3	F3H-1, -2	Demon	McDonnell		HNS-1	Hoverfly	Sikorsky
F-4	F4H-1	Phantom II	McDonnell		XHOE-1		Hiller
	FJ-1, -2	Fury	North American	H-43	HOK-1		Kaman
F-1	FJ-3, -4	Fury	North American		HOS-1		Sikorsky
	XFJ-1, -2		Berliner-Joyce		HO2S-1		Sikorsky
	XF2J-1		Berliner-Joyce		HO3S-1		Sikorsky
	XF3J-1		Berliner Joyce		XHO3S-3		Sikorsky
	XFL-1	Airabonita	Bell	H-19	HO4S-3	(HRS)	Sikorsky
	F2L-1	Airacobra (XTDL-1)	Bell		HO5S-1		Sikorsky
	FM-1, -2	Wildcat	General Motors	H-46	HRB-1		Vertol
	FO-1	(P-38)	Lockheed		XHRH-1	Order cancelled	McDonnell
	XFR-1	Fireball	Ryan		HRP-1, -2	Rescuer (Flying Banana)	Piasecki
	FR-1	Fireball	Ryan	H-19	HRS-1 thru -3	(HO4S)	Sikorsky
	XF2R-1		Ryan	H-37	HR2S-1	Mojave	Sikorsky
	XFT-2		Northrop		HSL-1	Model 61	Bell
	F2T-1	Black Widow (P-61)	Northrop	H-34	HSS-1	Sea Bat	Sikorsky
	FU-1		Vought	H-3	HSS-2	Sea King	Sikorsky
	XF2U-1		Vought		HTE-1, -2	UH-12A	Hiller
	XF3U-1	(SBU)	Vought		HTK-1		Kaman
	XF4U-1, -3 thru -5	Corsair	Vought	H-13	HTL-1 thru -7	Did not use Sioux	Bell
	F4U-1 thru -5, -7	Corsair (AU/FG/ F3A/F2G)	Vought	H-43	HUK-1	Did not use Huskie	Kaman
	XF5U-1		Vought	H-2	HU2K-1	Seasprite	Kaman
	F6U-1	Pirate	Vought	H-13	HUL-1	Did not use Sioux	Bell
	F7U-1 thru -3	Cutlass	Vought		HUM-1	MC-4A	McCulloch
				H-25	HUP-1 thru -3	Retriever	Piasecki (Vertol)
				H-34	HUS-1	Seahorse	Sikorsky
				H-52	HU2S-1		Sikorsky
					XJA-1	Super Universal	Fokker

1923–1962 Navy System—Continued

Post-1962 DOD Designation	Original Navy Designation	Popular or Common Name, other Designation and Miscellaneous Data	Manufacturer or Source	Post-1962 DOD Designation	Original Navy Designation	Popular or Common Name, other Designation and Miscellaneous Data	Manufacturer or Source
	JR-1 thru -3	(RR)	Ford			Me-262S	Messerschmitt
	JA-1	Norseman	Noorduyn		NB-1 thru -4	Model 21	Boeing
	JB-1	Traveler (GB)	Beech		XN2B-1	Model 81	Boeing
	JD-1	Invader	Douglas		N2C-1, -2	Fledgling	Curtiss
	JE-1		Bellanca	L-4	NE-1, -2	Grasshopper	Piper
	JF-1 thru -3	Duck	Grumman		NH-1	Nightingale (GH)	Howard
	J2F-1 thru -5	Duck	Grumman		NJ-1		North American
	J2F-6	Duck	Columbia		XNK-1		Keystone
	XJ3F-1	G-21	Grumman		XNL-1		Langley
	J4F-1, -2	Widgeon	Grumman		N2M-1		Martin
	JH-1		Stearman-Hammond		N2N-1		NAF
	JK-1		Fairchild		N3N-1 thru -3	Yellow Peril	NAF
	J2K-1	Coast Guard only	Fairchild		NP-1		Spartan
	XJL-1		Colombia		XNQ-1		Fairchild
	JM-1, -2	Marauder	Martin		XNR-1		Maxon
	JO-1, -2	Model 12A	Lockheed		NR-1	Recruit	Ryan
	XJO-3		Lockheed		NS-1		Stearman
	XJQ-1, -2	(XRQ/R2Q)	Fairchild		N2S-1 thru -5	Kaydet/Caydet	Stearman/Boeing
	J2Q-1	Coast Guard (R2Q)	Fairchild		NT-1		New Standard
	XJW-1	UBF	Waco		N2T-1	Tutor	Timm
	JRB-1 thru -4	Voyager/Expediter	Beech		NY-1 thru -3	(PT-1)	Consolidated
	JRC-1	Bobcat	Cessna		N2Y-1		Consolidated (Fleet Aircraft Inc.)
	JRF-1 thru -6	Goose, G-21	Grumman		XN3Y-1		Consolidated
	XJR2F-1	Albatross (UF/UH-16)	Grumman		XN4Y-1	(PT-11)	Consolidated
	JRM-1 thru -3	Mars (XPB2M)	Martin		O2B-1	DH-4B metal fuselage	Boeing
	JRS-1		Sikorsky		OC-1, -2	Falcon (F8C-1, -3)	Curtiss
	JR2S-1	VS-44A	Vought Sikorsky		XOC-3		Curtiss
	XLBE-1	Glomb	Pratt-Read (Gould)		O2C-1,-2	Helldiver (F8C-5)	Curtiss
	LBP-1	Glomb	Piper		XO3C-1	(SOC)	Curtiss
	LBT-1	None acquired (XLBE-1)	Taylorcraft		OD-1		Douglas
	LNE-1		Pratt-Read (Gould)		XO2D-1		Douglas
	XLNP-1		Piper	O-1	OE-1, -2	Bird Dog	Cessna
	XLNR-1		Aeronca		XOJ-1		Berliner-Joyce
	LNS-1	Cancelled	Schweizer		OJ-2		Berliner-Joyce
	XLNT-1		Taylorcraft		XOK-1		Keystone
	XLRA-1		Allied		OL-1 thru -9		Loening Aeronautical Engineering Company
	XLR2A-1		Allied		XO2L-1		Loening
	XLRN-1		NAF		O2N-1	None accepted (XOSN-1)	NAF
	XLRQ-1		Bristol		OO	Schreck FBA	Viking
	LRW-1		Waco		XOP-1, -2		Pitcairn
	XLR2W-1		Waco		O2U-1 thru -4		Vought
		M-130, PanAm owned	Martin				
		Me-108B	Messerschmitt				

1923–1962 Navy System—Continued

Post-1962 DOD Designation	Original Navy Designation	Popular or Common Name, other Designation and Miscellaneous Data	Manufacturer or Source	Post-1962 DOD Designation	Original Navy Designation	Popular or Common Name, other Designation and Miscellaneous Data	Manufacturer or Source
	O3U-1, -2	(O3U-2 redes. SU-1)	Vought	P-2	P2V-1	Neptune	Lockheed
	-3, -4, -6	(O3U-4 redes. SU-2/3)			thru -7		
	XO3U-5, -6		Vought	P-3	P3V-1	Orion	Lockheed
	XO4U-1, -2		Vought		XPY-1	Admiral (P3M-1, -2)	Consolidated
	XO5U-1		Vought		P2Y-1		Consolidated
	OY-1	Sentinel (L-5) Stinson V-76	Convair (Stinson, Vultee, Consolidated)		thru -3		
					XP3Y-1	(PBY)	Consolidated
					XP4Y-1	Model 31	Consolidated
	XOZ-1		Penn Acft Syndicate	QP-4B	P4Y-2	Privateer (PB4Y-2)	Consolidated
	XOSE-1, -2		Edo		XP5Y-1	(R3Y)	Convair
	XOSN-1		NAF		XPBB-1		Boeing
	OS2N-1	Kingfisher (OS2U)	NAF		PB2B-1, -2	Catalina	Boeing
	XOSS-1		Stearman		PBJ-1	Mitchell (B-25)	North American
	OS2U-1	Kingfisher	Vought		PBM-1	Mariner	Martin
	thru -3				thru -3, -5		
		(P-59)	Bell		XPB2M	Mars (JRM)	Martin
		(P-63)(L-39)	Bell		PBN-1	Nomad	NAF
	PB-1	Flying Fortress (B-17)	Boeing		PBO-1	Hudson	Lockheed
	P2B-1, -2	Super Fortress (B-29)	Boeing		XPBS-1		Sikorsky
	PD-1	(PN-12)	Douglas		PBY-1	Catalina	Consolidated
	P2D-1		Douglas		thru -6A		
	XP3D-1		Douglas		XPB2Y-1	Coronado	Consolidated
	UF-1	Albatross(XJR2F/UH-16)	Grumman		PB2Y-2	Coronado	Consolidated
	PH-1		Hall		thru -5		
	thru -3				PB4Y-1	Liberator (B-24)	Consolidated
	XP2H-1		Hall		PB4Y-2	Privateer	Consolidated
	PJ-1, -2	FLB, Coast Guard	North American		XPTBH-2		Hall
	PK-1	(PN-12)	Keystone		R2C-1, -2	(F2C-1 paper designation for R2C-1, never used)	Curtiss
	PM-1, -2	(PN-12)	Martin				
	XP2M-1		Martin				
	P3M-1, -2	(XPY-1)	Martin		R3C-1		Curtiss
	P4M-1	Mercator	Martin		thru -4		
P-5	P5M-1, -2	Marlin	Martin		RA-1	(TA)	Altantic
P-6	XP6M-1	Seamaster (never used in P-6 designation)	Martin		thru -4		
					RB-1	Connestoga	Budd
P-6	P6M-2	Seamaster (never used in P-6 designation)	Martin		RC-1	Kingbird	Curtiss
					R4C-1	Condor	Curtiss
	PN-7		NAF	C-46	R5C-1	Commando (may not have been used under C-46 designation)	Curtiss
	thru -12						
	P2N	Never used in this designation (NC boats)	NAF				
					RD-1	Dolphin	Douglas
	P3N		NAF		thru -4		
	XP4N-1,-2		NAF		R2D-1	DC-2	Douglas
	PO-1	Constellation	Lockheed		R3D-1	DC-5	Douglas
	PO-2	Warning Star (WV)	Lockheed		thru -3		
	XPS-1, -2	(XRS-2)		C-47	R4D-1	Skytrain	Douglas
	PS-3	(RS-3)	Sikorsky		thru -7		
	XP2S		Sikorsky	C-117	R4D-8	Skytrain	Douglas
	PV-1, -3	Ventura	Lockheed	C-54	R5D-1	Skymaster	Douglas
	PV-2	Harpoon	Lockheed		thru -5		

1923–1962 Navy System—Continued

Post-1962 DOD Designation	Original Navy Designation	Popular or Common Name, other Designation and Miscellaneous Data	Manufacturer or Source	Post-1962 DOD Designation	Original Navy Designation	Popular or Common Name, other Designation and Miscellaneous Data	Manufacturer or Source
C-118	R6D-1	Liftmaster, DC-6A	Douglas		XSBC-1	(XF12C-1)	Curtiss
	XRE-1 thru -3	Skyrocket	Bellanca		XSBC-2 thru -4		Curtiss
	RG-1		Romeo Fokker, Italy		SBC-3,-4	Helldiver	Curtiss
					SB2C-1 thru -5	Helldiver (SBF/SBW)	Curtiss
	XRK-1	Envoy	Kinner				
C-3	RM-1	Model 4-0-4 (VC-3A)	Martin		XSB2C-6		Curtiss
	XRO-1	Altair	Detroit/Lockheed		SBD-1 thru -6	Dauntless	Douglas
	XR2O-1	Electra	Lockheed				
	XR3O-1	Electra	Lockheed		XSB2D-1	Destroyer	Douglas
	R4O-1	Model 14	Lockheed		SBF-1, -3 and -4	Helldiver (SB2C/SBW)	Canadian Fairchild
	R5O-1 thru -6	Lodestar	Lockheed		SBN-1	(XSBA)	NAF
	XR6O-1	Constitution	Lockheed		SBU-1, -2		Chance Vought
C-121	R7O-1	Constellation	Lockheed		SB2U-1 thru -3	Vindicator	Vought-Sikorsky, Chance Vought
	R2Q-1	(J2Q) Coast Guard	Fairchild		XSB3U-1		Vought-Sikorsky
	XR3Q-1	Reliant	Stinson		SBW-1, -3 thru -5	Helldiver (SB2C/SBF)	Canadian Car & Foundry
C-119	R4Q-1, -2	Packet	Fairchild				
	RR-4, -5	(JR)	Ford		SNJ-1 thru -7	Texan	North American
	RS-1 thru -3 & -5	(PS)	Sikorsky		XSN2J-1		North American
	RT	Delta	Northrop		SNB-1, -2	Kansan	Beech
	R6V-1	Constitution	Lockheed	C-45	SNB-5	Navigator	Beech
C-121	R7V-1	Constellation	Lockheed		SNC-1	Falcon	Curtiss
	R8V-1G	Hercules	Lockheed		SNV-1, -2	Valiant	Vultee
	RY-1 thru -3		Consolidated		SOC-1 thru -4	Seagull	Curtiss
	XR2Y-1		Convair		XSO2C-1		Curtiss
	R3Y-1, -2	Tradewind	Convair		SO3C-1 thru -3	Seamew	Curtiss
C-131	R4Y-1, -2	Convair Liner	Convair		XSOE-1		Bellanca
	ROE-1		Hiller		SON-1	(SOC-3)	NAF
	RON-1	(HOG-1)	Gyrodyne		XSO2U-1		Vought
	SC-1, -2	Seahawk	Curtiss		TB-1		Boeing
	XS2C-1	Shrike	Curtiss		T2D-1		Douglas
	XS3C-1		Curtiss		XT3D-1		Douglas
	SDW-1	(DT)	Dayton-Wright		TG-1, -2		Great Lakes
	XSE-2		Bellanca		T3M-1, -2		Martin
	SF-1	(FF-1)	Grumman		T4M-1		Martin
	XSG-1		Great Lakes		XT5M-1	(BM)	Martin
	XSL-1		Loening		XT6M-1		Martin
	XS2L-1		Loening		XTN-1		NAF
	XSS-2		Sikorsky		XT2N-1		NAF
	SU-1 thru -4	Corsair (O3U)	Vought		TA-1 thru -3	(RA)	Atlantic
S-2	S2F-1 thru -3	Tracker	Grumman		XTE-1		Edo
	XS2U-1W	Cancelled (XWU-1)	Vought		TE-2		Edo
	XSBA-1	(SBN)	Brewster	C-1	TF-1	Trader	Grumman
	SB2A-1 thru -4	Buccaneer	Brewster				

1923–1962 Navy System—Continued

Post-1962 DOD Designation	Original Navy Designation	Popular or Common Name, other Designation and Miscellaneous Data	Manufacturer or Source	Post-1962 DOD Designation	Original Navy Designation	Popular or Common Name, other Designation and Miscellaneous Data	Manufacturer or Source
	XTF-1W	Tracer (WF-2)	Grumman		XTDL-1	(P-39Q) drone	Bell
T-2	XT2J-1, -2	Buckeye	North American		TDN-1	Drone	NAF
T-2	T2J-1	Buckeye	North American		TD2N	Gorgon	NAF
T-39	T3J-1		North American		TD3N	Gorgon	NAF
T-33	TO-1, -2	Shooting Star (TV)	Lockheed		TDR-1	Drone	Interstate
	TT-1	Pinto	Temco		XTD2R-1	Drone	Interstate
T-33	TV-1, -2	Shooting Star (TO)	Lockheed		XTD3R-1	Drone	Interstate
T-1	T2V-1	Sea Star	Lockheed		TS-1		Curtiss
	TBD-1	Devastator	Douglas		XUC	(XTD4C)	Culver
	XTB2D-1		Douglas	U-1	UC-1	Otter	DeHavilland
	TBF-1	Avenger (TBM)	Grumman	U-16	UF-1, -2	Albatross (XJR2F)	Grumman
	XTBF-2, -3	Avenger (TBM)	Grumman	U-11	UO-1	Aztec	Piper
	XTB3F-1	Guardian (AF)	Grumman		UO-1	(not the same as Piper UO-1)	Vought
	XTBG-1		Great Lakes				
	TBM-1 thru -4	Avenger (TBF)	General Motors	E-1	WF-2	Tracer	Grumman
	XTBU-1	Seawolf (TBY)	Vought	E-2	W2F-1	Hawkeye	Grumman
	TBY-2	Seawolf (XTBU)	Consolidated		XWU-1	Cancelled (XS2U-1W)	Vought
	TDC-1, -2	(PQ-8) drone	Culver		WV-1	Constellation	Lockheed
	TD2C-1	(PQ-14) drone	Culver	EC-121	WV-2, -3	Warning Star	Lockheed
	XTD3C	(PQ-15) drone	Culver				
	XTD4C-1	(XUC) drone	Culver				
	TDD	(OQ-2A) drone	Radioplane				
	TD2D	Katydid, drone	McDonnell				
	TD3D	(OQ-16) drone	Frankfort				
	TD4D	(OQ-17) drone	Radioplane				

Note:

1. The list does not include all X model designations.

2. Aircraft designations in parentheses are a cross reference to a similar model or a redesignation of that aircraft. Parentheses are also used to identify Army Air Corps/Air Force designations. Civilian model designations are not placed in parentheses.

3. The designations T-28B/C, T-34B and C-130BL were used by the Navy prior to the change to the DoD Designation System in 1962.

How to Read the 1923 to 1962 Aircraft Model Designations for U.S. Naval Aircraft

There have been several systems to designate U.S. naval aircraft. However, the most common system covered the period 1923 to 1962 and consisted of four major elements:

Aircraft Type/Class
Manufacturer Type Sequence
Manufacturer
Modification

In the beginning there were just two classes: heavier-than-air (fixed wing) identified by the letter V and lighter-than-air identified by the letter Z. The letter H for heavier-than-air (rotary wing) was added with the introduction of the helicopter in the 1940s. Late in 1945 the letter K was added for pilotless aircraft, making four distinct types. In March 1946 the Type/Class designation was separated into two distinct headings of Type and Class. The letter V was omitted in the model designation, but H, K, and Z were used where applicable. The letter X was added as a prefix designating an experimental model.

In designating the first model of a class produced by a given manufacturer, the first number (1) is omitted in the Manufacturer Type Sequence position, but is shown in the Modification Sequence position. Thus, in the VJ class, the first utility aircraft produced by Grumman Aircraft Corporation was the JF-1. When a major modification was instituted for the JF-1 without changing the character of the model, that modification changed the designation to JF-2. The second modification changed the designation to JF-3. The second utility aircraft built by Grumman was designated the J2F-1 and successive modifications to this aircraft became J2F-2, J2F-3, etc. It must be remembered that the aircraft Modification Sequence Number is always one digit higher than the actual modification number. The basic designation could be expanded to show additional characteristics, as demonstrated below:

Suffix letters came into a more general use during the period of rapid expansion immediately prior to U.S. entry into World War II. Unfortunately, the use of suffix letters was not strictly defined and the same letter was frequently used to denote several different characteristics causing considerable confusion. By the time the system was abandoned, it was necessary to know the aircraft in question rather than relying on the suffix letter to tell the specific characteristics being identified.

The following lists provides all of the letter designations necessary to understand the system:

Table I
Type/Class Designation

Type/Class	Meaning	Period
A	Attack	1946–1962
A	Ambulance	1943–1946
B	Bomber	1931–1946
BT	Bomber Torpedo	1942–1946
D	Target Drone	1946–1947
F	Fighter	1922–1962
G	Glider	1946–1962
G	Transport, Single Engine	1939–1946
G	In-Flight Refueling Tanker	1960–1962
H	Hospital	1929–1942
H	Air-Sea-Rescue	1946–1962
J	Utility	1931–1946
J	Transport	1928–1931
JR	Utility Transport	1935–1946
K	Drone	1945–1962
L	Glider	1941–1945
M	Marine Expeditionary	1922–1925
N	Trainer	1922–1946

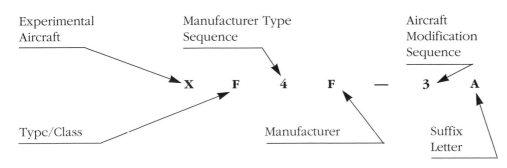

Table I—Continued
Type/Class Designation

Type/Class	Meaning	Period
O	Observation	1922–1962
OS	Observation Scout	1935–1945
P	Patrol	1922–1962
P	Pursuit	1923
PB	Patrol Bomber	1935–1946
PT	Patrol Torpedo	1922
PT	Patrol Torpedo Bomber	1937–1938
R	Transport	1931–1962
R	Racer	1923–1928
S	Scout	1922–1946
SB	Scout Bomber	1934–1946
SN	Scout Trainer	1939–1946
SO	Scout Observation	1934–1946
T	Torpedo	1922–1935
T	Transport	1927–1930
T	Training	1946–1962
TB	Torpedo Bomber	1936–1946
TD	Target Drone	1942–1946
U	Utility	1946–1962

Table II
Special Purpose Suffix

Suffix Letter	Meaning	Example
A	Target towing and photography	JRF-1A
A	Nonfolding wings and no carrier provisions	SB2C-1A
A	Armament on normally unarmed aircraft	J2F-2A
A	Arresting gear normally on noncarrier planes	SOC-3A
A	Amphibious version	PBY-5A
A	Land-based version of carrier aircraft	F4F-3A
A	Built for the Army Air Force	SBD-3A
B	Special armament version	PB4Y-2B
B	British lend lease version	JRF-6B
C	Carrier operating version of a noncarrier aircraft	SNJ-2C
C	British-American standardized version	PBM-3C
C	Equipped with two .50 cal. machine guns	TBF-1C
C	Cannon armament	F4U-1C
D	Drop tank configuration	F4U-1D
D	Special search radar	TBM-3D
E	Special electronic version	SB2C-4E
F	Converted for use as a flagship	PB2Y-3F
G	Air-sea-rescue version	TBM-5G
H	Hospital version	SNB-2H
H	Air-sea rescue version	PB2Y-5H
J	Target towing version	TBM-3J
K	Target drone version	F6F-5K
L	Search light version	P2V-5L
M	Weather reconnaissance version	PB4Y-2M
N	Night operating version (all weather)	F6F-5N
P	Photographic version	SBD-2P

Table II—Continued
Special Purpose Suffix

Suffix Letter	Meaning	Example
Q	Countermeasure version	TBM-3Q
R	Transport version	PBM-3R
S	Antisubmarine version	P5M-2S
T	Training version	R4D-5T
U	Utility version	PBM-3U
W	Special search version	PB-1W
Z	Administrative version	R4D-5Z

Table III
Manufacturer's Designation

Letter	Manufacturer	Period
A	Aeromarine Plane and Motor Co.	1922
A	Atlantic Aircraft Corp (American Fokker)	1927–1930
A	Brewster Aeronautical	1935–1943
A	General Aviation Corp (ex Atlantic)	1930–1932
A	Noorduyn Aviation, Ltd. (Canada)	1946
B	Beech Aircraft Co.	1937–1962
B	Boeing Aircraft Co.	1923–1962
B	Budd Manufacturing Co.	1942–1944
C	Cessna Aircraft Corp.	1943–1951
C	Culver Aircraft Corp.	unknown–1946
C	Curtiss Aeroplane and Motor Co.	1922–1946
C	Curtiss Wright Corp	1948–1962
C	DeHaviland Aircraft of Canada	1955–1962
D	Douglas Aircraft Co.	1922–1967
D	McDonnell Aircraft Corp.	1942–1946
D	Radioplane Co.	1943–1948
D	Frankfort Sailplane Co.	1945–1946
DH	DeHavilland Aircraft Co. Ltd. (England)	1927–1931
DW	Dayton-Wright Airplane Co.	1923
E	Bellanca Aircraft Corp.	1931–1937
E	Cessna Aircraft Co.	1951–1962
E	Edo Aircraft Corp.	1943–1962
E	G. Elias & Brothers	1922–1924
E	Gould Aeronautical Corp.	1942–1945
E	Hiller Aircraft Corp.	1948–1962
E	Piper Aircraft Corp.	1941–1945
E	Pratt-Read	1942–1945
F	Fairchild Aircraft, Ltd. (Canada)	1942–1945
F	Columbia	1943–1944
F	Grumman Aircraft Engineering Corp.	1931–1962
G	Gallaudet Aircraft Corp.	1929–1935
G	Globe Aircraft Corp	1946–1948
G	Goodyear Aircraft Corp.	1942–1962
G	Great Lakes Aircraft Corp.	1929–1935
H	Hall Aluminum	1928–1945
H	Howard Aircraft Co.	1941–1944
H	Huff, Daland & Co	1922–1927
H	McDonnell Aircraft Corp	1946–1962

Table III—*Continued*
Manufacturer's Designation

Letter	Manufacturer	Period
H	Stearman-Hammond Aircraft Corp.	1937–1939
J	Berliner/Joyce Aircraft Co.	1929–1935
J	North American Aviation	1937–1962
K	Fairchild Aircraft Corp.	1937–1942
K	Kaman Aircraft Corp	1950–1962
K	Kaiser Cargo Inc. Fleetwings Div.	1948–1962
K	Keystone	1927–1930
K	Kinner Airplane & Motor Corp.	1935–1936
L	Bell Aircraft Corp.	1939–1962
L	Columbia	1944–1946
L	Grover Loening, Inc.	1923–1933
L	Loening Aeronautical Engineering Corp.	1922–1932
M	General Motors Corp. (Eastern Aircraft Div.)	1942–1945
M	Glenn L. Martin Co.	1922–1962
N	Gyrodyne Company of America	1955–1962
N	Naval Aircraft Factory	1922–1948
N	Naval Air Development Station	1948–1962
O	Lockheed Aircraft Corp.	1931–1962
P	Pitcairn Autogyro Co.	1931–1932
P	Piasecki Helicopter Corp.	1946–1955
P	Vertol Aircraft Corp.	1955–1962
P	Spartin Aircraft Co.	1940–1941
Q	Bristol Aeronautical Corp.	1941–1943
Q	Fairchild Engine and Airplane Co.	1928–1962
Q	Stinson Aircraft Corp.	1934–1936
R	Aeronca Aircraft Corp.	1942–1946
R	Ford Motor Co.	1927–1932

Table III—*Continued*
Manufacturer's Designation

Letter	Manufacturer	Period
R	Interstate Aircraft and Engineering Corp.	1942–1962
R	Radioplanes Co.	1948–1962
R	Ryan Aeronautical Co.	1948–1962
S	Schweizer Aircraft Corp.	1941
S	Sikorsky Aviation Corp.	1928–1962
S	Sperry Gyroscope Co.	1948–1962
S	Stearman Aircraft Co.	1934–1945
T	Taylorcraft Aviation Corp.	1942–1946
T	Tempco Aircraft Corp.	1955–1962
T	New Standard Aircraft Corp.	1930–1934
T	The Northrop Corp.	1933–1937
T	Northrop Aircraft Inc.	1944–1962
T	Timm Aircraft Corp.	1941–1943
U	Lewis & Vought, Chance Vought, Vought Sikorsky	1922–1962
V	Vultee Aircraft Inc.	1943–1945
V	Lockheed Aircraft Corp.	1942–1962
W	Canadian Car and Foundry Co., Ltd.	1942–1945
W	Waco Aircraft Corp.	1934–1945
W	Willys-Overland Co.	1948–1962
W	Wright Aeronautical Corp.	1922–1926
X	Cox-Klemin Aircraft Corp.	1922–1924
Y	Consolidated Aircraft Corp.	1926–1954
Y	Convair Division (General Dynamics Corp)	1954–1962
Z	Pennsylvania Aircraft Syndicate	1933–1934

A basic company name has been used in some of the above enteries even though the company may have undergone restructuring.

Naval Aircraft Redesignated in 1962

In 1962 a standardized system for designation of U.S. aircraft went into effect. The following is a list of naval aircraft that were redesignated in 1962:

Old Designation	New Designaton	Popular Name
	Attack	
A-1		
AD-5	A-1E	Skyraider
AD-5W	EA-1E	Skyraider
AD-5Q	EA-1F	Skyraider
AD-5N	A-1G	Skyraider
AD-6	A-1H	Skyraider
AD-7	A-1J	Skyraider
A-2		
AJ-1	A-2A	Savage
A-3		
A3D-1	A-3A	Skywarrior
A3D-1Q	EA-3A	Skywarrior
A3D-2	A-3B	Skywarrior
A3D-2Q	EA-3B	Skywarrior
A3D-2P	RA-3B	Skywarrior
A3D-2T	TA-3B	Skywarrior
A-4		
A4D-1	A-4A	Skyhawk
A4D-2	A-4B	Skyhawk
A4D-2N	A-4C	Skyhawk
A4D-5	A-4E	Skyhawk
A-5		
A3J-1	A-5A	Vigilante
A3J-2	A-5B	Vigilante
A3J-3	A-5C	Vigilante
A-6		
A2F-1	A-6A	Intruder
A2F-1H	EA-6A	Intruder
	Fighters	
F-1		
FJ-3	F-1C	Fury
FJ-3D	DF-1C	Fury
FJ-3M	MF-1C	Fury
FJ-3D2	DF-1D	Fury
FJ-4	F-1E	Fury
FJ-4B	AF-1E	Fury
F-2		
F2H-3	F-2C	Banshee
F2H-4	F-2D	Banshee

Naval Aircraft Redesignated in 1962—Continued

Old Designation	New Designaton		Popular Name
F-3			
F3H-2	F-3B		Demon
F3H-2M	MF-3B		Demon
F3H-2N	F-3C		Demon
F-4			
F4H-1F	F-4A		Phantom II
F4H-1	F-4B		Phantom II
F4H-1P	RF-4B		Phantom II
F-6			
F4D-1	F-6A		Skyray
F-7			
YF2Y-1	YF-7A		Sea Dart
F-8			
F8U-1	F-8A		Crusader
F8U-1D	DF-8A		Crusader
F8U-1KD	QF-8A		Crusader
F8U-1P	RF-8A		Crusader
F8U-1T	TF-8A		Crusader
F8U-1E	F-8B		Crusader
F8U-2	F-8C		Crusader
F8U-2N	F-8D		Crusader
F8U-2NE	F-8E		Crusader
F-9			
F9F-5KD	DF-9E		Cougar
F9F-6	F-9F		Cougar
F9F-6D	DF-9F		Cougar
F9F-6K	QF-9F		Cougar
F9F-6K2	QF-9G		Cougar
F9F-7	F-9H		Cougar
F9F-8	F-9J		Cougar
F9F-8B	AF-9J		Cougar
F9F-8P	RF-9J		Cougar
F9F-8T	TF-9J		Cougar
F-10			
F3D-1	F-10A		Sky Knight
F3D-2	F-10B		Sky Knight
F3D-2M	MF-10B		Sky Knight
F3D-2Q	EF-10B		Sky Knight
F3D-2T2	TF-10B		Sky Knight
F-11			
F11F-1	F-11A		Tiger
F-111			
TFX	F-111B		

Naval Aircraft Redesignated in 1962—Continued

Old Designation	New Designaton	Popular Name
Patrol		
P-2		
P2V-4	P-2D	Neptune
P2V-5F	P-2E	Neptune
P2V-5FD	DP-2E	Neptune
P2V-5FE	EP-2E	Neptune
P2V-5FS	SP-2E	Neptune
P2V-6	P-2F	Neptune
P2V-6M	MP-2F	Neptune
P2V-6T	TP-2F	Neptune
P2V-6F	P-2G	Neptune
P2V-7	P-2H	Neptune
P2V-7S	SP-2H	Neptune
P2V-7LP	LP-2J	Neptune
P-3		
YP3V-1	YP-3A	Orion
P3V-1	P-3A	Orion
P-4		
P4Y-2K	QP-4B	Privateer
P-5		
P5M-1	P-5A	Marlin
P5M-1S	SP-5A	Marlin
P5M-1T	TP-5A	Marlin
P5M-2	P-5B	Marlin
P5M-2S	SP-5B	Marlin
Antisubmarine		
S-2		
S2F-1	S-2A	Tracker
S2F-1T	TS-2A	Tracker
S2F-1S	S-2B	Tracker
S2F-2	S-2C	Tracker
S2F-2P	RS-2C	Tracker
S2F-3	S-2D	Tracker
S2F-3S	S-2E	Tracker
Airborne Early Warning		
E-1		
WF-2	E-1B	Tracer
E-2		
W2F-1	E-2A	Hawkeye
Observation		
O-1		
OE-1	O-1B	Bird Dog
OE-2	O-1C	Bird Dog

Naval Aircraft Redesignated in 1962—Continued

Old Designation	New Designaton	Popular Name
Helicopters		
H-1		
HU-1E	UH-1E	Iroquois
H-2		
HU2K-1	UH-2A	Seasprite
HU2K-1U	UH-2B	Seasprite
H-3		
HSS-2	SH-3A	Sea King
HSS-2Z	VH-3A	Sea King
H-13		
HTL-4	TH-13L	Sioux
HTL-6	TH-13M	Sioux
HTL-7	TH-13N	Sioux
HUL-1	UH-13P	Sioux
HUL-1M	UH-13R	Sioux
H-19		
HRS-3	CH-19E	
HO4S-3	UH-19F	
H-25		
HUP-2	UH-25B	Retriever
HUP-3	UH-25C	Retriever
H-34		
HSS-1L	LH-34D	Seahorse
HSS-1	SH-34G	Seahorse
HUS-1	UH-34D	Seahorse
HUS-1Z	VH-34D	Seahorse
HUS-1A	UH-34E	Seahorse
HSS-1F	SH-34H	Seahorse
HSS-1N	SH-34J	Seahorse
H-37		
HR2S-1	CH-37C	Mojave
H-43		
HUK-1	UH-43C	
HOK-1	OH-43D	
H-46		
HRB-1	CH-46A	Sea Knight
H-50		
DSN-1	QH-50A	DASH
DSN-2	QH-50B	DASH
DSN-3	QH-50C	DASH

Naval Aircraft Redesignated in 1962—Continued

Old Designation	New Designaton	Popular Name
Bombers		
JD-1	UB-26J	Invader
JD-1D	DB-26J	Invader
Utility		
U-1		
UC-1	U-1B	Otter
U-6		
L-20A	U-6A	Beaver
U-11		
UO-1	U-11A	Aztec
U-16		
UF-1	HU-16C	Albatross
UF-1L	LU-16C	Albatross
UF-1T	TU-16C	Albatross
UF-2	HU-16D	Albatross
Cargo/Transport		
C-1		
TF-1	C-1A	Trader
TF-1Q	EC-1A	
C-45		
SNB-5P	RC-45J	
SNB-5	TC-45J	
C-47		
R4D-5	C-47H	Skytrain
R4D-5Q	EC-47H	Skytrain
R4D-5L	LC-47H	Skytrain
R4D-5S	SC-47H	Skytrain
R4D-5R	TC-47H	Skytrain
R4D-5Z	VC-47H	Skytrain
R4D-6	C-47J	Skytrain
R4D-6Q	EC-47J	Skytrain
R4D-6L	LC-47J	Skytrain
R4D-6S	SC-47J	Skytrain
R4D-6R	TC-47J	Skytrain
R4D-6Z	VC-47J	Skytrain
R4D-7	TC-47K	Skytrain
C-54		
R5D-1Z	VC-54N	Skymaster
R5D-2	C-54P	Skymaster
R5D-2Z	VC-54P	Skymaster
R5D-3	C-54Q	Skymaster
R5D-3Z	VC-54Q	Skymaster

Naval Aircraft Redesignated in 1962—Continued

Old Designation	New Designaton	Popular Name
R5D-4R	C-54R	Skymaster
R5D-5	C-54S	Skymaster
R5D-5Z	VC-54S	Skymaster
R5D-5R	C-54T	Skymaster
C-117		
R4D-8	C-117D	Skytrain
R4D-8L	LC-117D	Skytrain
R4D-8Z	VC-117D	Skytrain
R4D-8T	TC-117D	Skytrain
C-118		
R6D-1	C-118B	Liftmaster
R6D-1Z	VC-118B	Liftmaster
C-119		
R4Q-2	C-119F	Packet
C-121		
R7V-1	C-121J	Constellation
WV-2	EC-121K	Warning Star
WV-3	WC-121N	
WV-2E	EC-121L	Warning Star
WV-2Q	EC-121M	Warning Star
C-130		
GV-1U	C-130F	Hercules
GV-1	KC-130F	Hercules
C-130BL	LC-130F	Hercules
C-131		
R4Y-1	C-131F	Convair Liner
R4Y-2	C-131G	Convair Liner
C-140		
UV-1	C-140C	Jet Star
Training		
T-1		
T2V-1	T-1A	Sea Star
T-2		
T2J-1	T-2A	Buckeye
T2J-2	T-2B	Buckeye
T-28		
T-28A	T-28A	Trojan
T-28B	T-28B	Trojan
T-28BD	DT-28B	Trojan
T-28C	T-28C	Trojan

Naval Aircraft Redesignated in 1962—Continued

Old Designation	New Designaton	Popular Name
T-33		
TV-2	T-33B	Shooting Star
TV-2D	DT-33B	Shooting Star
TV-2KD	DT-33C	Shooting Star
T-34		
T-34B	T-34B	Mentor
T-39		
T3J-1	T-39D	Sabreliner
	Airship	
ZPG-2W	EZ-1B	Reliance
ZPG-2	SZ-1B	
ZPG-3W	EZ-1C	

DoD Designation System, 1962 to Present

In the following list the primary emphasis is on new aircraft model designations accepted after the Navy adopted the Department of Defense aircraft designation system in 1962. Aircraft that were in service and redesignated under the DoD Designation System will only have the primary designation (basic mission) listed. As an example, the AD-6 and AD-7 were redesignated A-1H and A-1J respectively. However, only A-1, the primary designation, will be listed instead of all the model variations. The modified mission designations will normally not be listed. Hence, designations such as RC-45J or TC-45J will not always be listed. However, the basic mission designation C-45 will be listed. Only officially designated popular names are placed in this list. A more comprehensive list of pre-1962 aircraft designations will be found in the **1923–1962 Navy System** list.

Post-1962 DOD Designation	Original Navy Designation Before 1962	Popular Name Only, other Designations and Miscellaneous Data	Manufacturer or Source
A-1	AD	Skyraider	Douglas
A-2	AJ	Savage	North American
A-3	A3D	Skywarrior	Douglas
A-4	A4D	Skyhawk	Douglas
TA-4E/F/J		Skyhawk	Douglas
A-5	A3J	Vigilante	North American
RA-5C		Vigilante	North American
A-6A/B/C/E	A2F	Intruder	Grumman
EA-6A	A2F-1Q	Intruder	Grumman
KA-6D		Intruder	Grumman
EA-6B		Prowler	Grumman
A-7A/B/C/E		Corsair II	Vought
AV-8A/TAV-8A		Harrier	Hawker-Siddeley
AV-8B/TAV-8B		Harrier II	McDonnell Douglas
F/A-18A/B/C/D/E/F		Hornet	McDonnell Douglas
EB-47E		Stratojet	Boeing
C-1	TF-1	Trader	Grumman
C-2A		Greyhound	Grumman
VC-3A	RM	Model 404	Martin
TC-4C		Academe	Grumman
UC-8A		Buffalo, DHC-5	DeHavilland
C-9B		Skytrain II, DC-9	McDonnell Douglas
UC-12B/F/M		Huron	Beech
C-20D/G		Gulfstream	Gulfstream Aerospace
EC-24A		DC-8	McDonnell Douglas
UC-27A		F-27F	Fokker (Fairchild-built)
C-28A		Model 404	Cessna
C-45H/J	SNB-5	Navigator	Beech
C-47	R4D	Skytrain	Douglas
C-54	R5D	Skymaster	Douglas
C-117	R4D-8	Skytrain	Douglas
C-118B	R6D	Liftmaster	Douglas
C-119	R4Q	Packet	Fairchild
C-121	R7V	Constellation	Lockheed
EC-121	WV	Warning Star	Lockheed
C-130	GV/R8V	Hercules	Lockheed
C-131H	R4Y	Samaritan	Convair
NKC-135A		Stratotanker	Boeing
UC-880		Convair 880	Convair
E-1	WF	Tracer	Grumman

DoD Designation System, 1962 to Present—Continued

Post-1962 DOD Designation	Original Navy Designation Before 1962	Popular Name Only, other Designations and Miscellaneous Data	Manufacturer or Source
E-2A/B/C	W2F	Hawkeye	Grumman
E-6		Hermes (redesignated Mercury)	Boeing
E-6A		Mercury	Boeing
F-1	FJ	Fury	North American
F-2	F2H	Banshee	McDonnell
F-3	F3H	Demon	McDonnell
F-4A/B/C/J/N/S	F4H	Phantom II	McDonnell
F-5E/F		Tiger II	Northrop
F-6	F4D	Skyray	Douglas
F-8	F8U	Crusader	Vought
F-9	F9F	Cougar	Grumman
F-10	F3D	Sky Knight	Douglas
F-11	F11F	Tiger	Grumman
F-14A/A+/B/D		Tomcat	Grumman
F-16N		Fighting Falcon	General Dynamics
TF-16		Fighting Falcon	General Dynamics
YF-17			Northrop
F/A-18A/B/C/D/E/F		Hornet	McDonnell Douglas
F-21A		Kfir	Israel Aircraft
F-86H		Sabre	North American
QF-86F		Sabre	North American
F-111B			Grumman/General Dynamics
AH-1G/S		Cobra	Bell
AH-1J/T/W		Sea Cobra	Bell
UH-1C/D/E/H/M/N	HU-1	Iroquois	Bell
TH-1E/F/L		Iroquois	Bell
H-2	HU2K	Seasprite	Kaman
H-3	HSS-2	Sea King	Sikorsky
OH-6A/B		Cayuse	Hughes
H-13	HTL/HUL	Sioux	Bell
H-19	HRS-3	Chickasaw	Sikorsky
H-I9	HO4S-3	Chickasaw	Sikorsky
H-25	HUP	Retriever	Piasecki (Vertol)
H-34	HSS-1	Sea Bat	Sikorsky
H-34	HUS	Seahorse	Sikorsky
H-37	HR2S	Mojave	Sikorsky
H-43	HOK	Huskie	Kaman
H-46	HRB	Sea Knight	Boeing Vertol
QH-50D,-50C	DSN	DASH	Gyrodyne
H-51		L-186, tri-service evaluation	Lockheed
H-52	HU2S	Coast Guard helo	Sikorsky
CH-53A/D		Sea Stallion	Sikorsky
CH-53E		Super Stallion	Sikorsky
MH-53E		Sea Dragon	Sikorsky
TH-57A/B/C		Sea Ranger	Bell
OH-58A		Kiowa	Bell
H-60		Sea Hawk	Sikorsky
VH-60N		White Hawk	Sikorsky

DoD Designation System, 1962 to Present—Continued

Post-1962 DOD Designation	Original Navy Designation Before 1962	Popular Name Only, other Designations and Miscellaneous Data	Manufacturer or Source
H-65		Dolphin, Coast Guard	Aerospatiale
O-1A/B/C/G	OE	L-19A	Cessna
O-2A			Cessna
P-2	P2V	Neptune	Lockheed
P-3A/B/C	P3V	Orion	Lockheed
EP-3A/B		Orion	Lockheed
RP-3D		Orion	Lockheed
QP-4B	PB4Y-2K	Privateer	Consolidated
P-5	P5M	Marlin	Martin
S-2	S2F	Tracker	Grumman
S-3A/B		Viking	Lockheed
ES-3A		Shadow	Lockheed
T-1	T2V	Sea Star	Lockheed
T-2A/B/C	T2J	Buckeye	North American
T-28A/B/C	T-28	Trojan	North American
T-29B/C		Flying Classroom	Convair
T-33	TO/TV	Shooting Star	Lockheed
T-34B/C	T-34	Mentor	Beech
T-38A/B		Talon	Northrop
T-39	T3J	Sabreliner	North American
T-41B		Mescalero	Cessna
T-42A		Cochise	Beech
T-44A		King Air 90	Beech
T-45A/B		Goshawk	McDonnell Douglas
T-47A		Cessna Citation II	Cessna
U-1	UC	Otter	DeHavilland
U-3A/B		Model 310	Cessna
U-6A		Beaver, L-20A	DeHavilland
U-8D/F/G		Seminole	Beech
U-9D		Aero Commander	Aero Design
U-11	UO	Aztec	Piper
U-16	JR2F/UF	Albatross	Grumman
U-21A		Ute	Beech
OV-1A/B/C		Mohawk	Grumman
XV-6A		Kestrels	Hawker-Siddeley
OV-10A/D		Bronco	North American
XFV-12A		Prototype of a high performance V/STOL fighter, never operational.	Rockwell International
AV-16A		Joint proposal in 1973 for an advanced version of the AV-8.	McDonnell Douglas/ Hawker-Siddeley
V-22		Osprey	Bell/Boeing
X-22A			Bell
X-25A			Bensen
X-26A			Schweizer
X-26B		QT-2PC	Lockheed/Schweizer
X-28A			Pereira
X-31A			Rockwell/DASA
YEZ-2A		Operational development - model airship.	Westinghouse Airships Inc.

How to Read the DoD Aircraft Model Designations

The Navy system had worked well for forty years, however, Congress decreed in 1962 that there should only be one system to designate military aircraft in the United States. The new system was based on the Air Force system and the aircraft manufacturer was no longer identified. While there were relatively few changes to Air Force aircraft designations, the Navy made a complete change. Aircraft models all started with the numeral 1, except for those aircraft on hand which were used by both services, in which case the existing Air Force designation applied. Thus, the FJ-3 became the F-1C, while the SNB-5P became the RC-45J. It must be emphasized that the placement of the dash is critical to distinguish aircraft under the new system from those under the previous Navy system. For example, the F4B-4 was a Boeing biplane fighter of the mid 30's, while the F-4B is an early version of the Phantom II.

The new system consisted of a Status Prefix Symbol (letter), a Basic Mission Symbol (letter), a Design Number (numeral), a Modified Mission Symbol (letter), a Series letter, and a Type Symbol (letter). A Design Number was assigned for each basic mission or type. New design numbers were assigned when an existing aircraft was redesigned to an extent that it no longer reflected the original configuration or capability. A Series Letter was assigned to each series change of a specific basic design. To avoid confusion, the letters "I" and "O" were not used as series letters. The Series letter was always in consecutive order, starting with "A".

A typical designation was as follows:

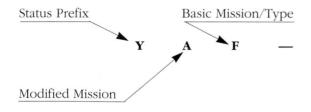
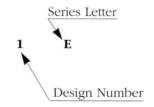

This was the Y/FJ-4B under the Navy system and the YAF-1E under the new DoD system.

Table IV
Status Prefix Symbols

Letter	Title
G	Permanently Grounded
J	Special Test, Temporary
N	Special Test, Permanent
X	Experimental
Y	Prototype
Z	Planning

Table V
Modified Mission Symbols

Letter	Title
A	Attack
C	Cargo/Transport
D	Director
E	Special Electronic Installation
H	Search/Rescue
K	Tanker
L	Cold Weather
M	Missile Carrier
Q	Drone
R	Reconnaissance
S	Antisubmarine
T	Trainer
U	Utility
V	Staff
W	Weather

Table VI
Basic Mission and Type Symbols

Letter	Title
A	Attack
B	Bomber
C	Cargo/Transport
E	Special Electronic Installation
F	Fighter
H	Helicopter
K	Tanker
O	Observation
P	Patrol
S	Antisubmarine
T	Trainer
U	Utility
V	VTOL and STOL
X	Research
Z	Airship

Alphabetical Listing of Popular Names

Aircraft Popular Names

The official assignment of names to naval aircraft began 1 October 1941 when a Navy Department press release reported that the Secretary issued orders assigning names "for popular use" to a number of in-service and developmental aircraft. This decision was first acknowledged in the April 1942 edition of the Model Designation of Naval Aircraft (SH-3AF) published by the Bureau of Aeronautics. A War Department Press Release of 4 January 1943 distributed a consolidated list of names for Navy and Army aircraft, thus beginning interservice coordination on aircraft names. This latter press release pointed out that the practice of naming aircraft had long been in effect in England, "In order that the general public may get a better idea of the character of military aircraft and more easily identify the combat planes mentioned in press dispatches from the battlefields of the world. . . ."

Prior to October 1941, manufacturers on occasion chose to use names for an aircraft model or a series of models; thus, the Curtiss Company used the name Helldiver for aircraft which they built as naval dive bombers from the late 1920's. The October 1941 action officially assigned the name Helldiver to the latest member of the family, the SB2C. Vought choose to use the name Corsair for a series of carrier-based aircraft which included the 02U and the 03U/SU; in October 1941 the Navy officially assigned the name Corsair to Vought's new fighter, the F4U.

Although assignment of aircraft names was coordinated by the Army and Navy from 1943, each service had developed its own model designation system independently. The result was that the U.S. military forces used two separate model designation systems. Moreover, when the Navy used an Army Air Forces aircraft, it assigned a designation based upon its own system; thus, the Army Air Force's B-24 became the PB4Y-l in Navy service while such trainers as the Army Air Force's AT-6 and PT-13/-17 were the Navy SNJ and N2S.

On 19 August 1952, the Joint Aircraft Committee of the Munitions Board took an initial step to eliminate multiple designations by establishing the policy that original model designations would generally be retained by the second service in the event of cross-service procurement of aircraft, thus the North American Trojan which was used as a trainer by the Air Force retained the Air Force designation T-28 when procured for naval service. Designations of aircraft already in service were not changed at that time.

On 18 September 1962, the Department of Defense issued a uniform model designation system and directed its immediate adoption. The new system, adapted from the Air Force model designation system, assigned a basic mission letter followed by a number which indicated the sequential relationship of aircraft designed for the mission. Thus, the Navy AD was redesignated A-l. To avoid compounding the confusion, the new system, insofar as was possible, correlated the new designation of naval aircraft with the older designation; thus, the F9F became the F-9 and the F8U became the F-8. By the same token, the three in-service patrol planes, the P2V, the P3V and P5M were redesignated P-2, P-3 and P-5 even though the designation P-l was not assigned.

To summarize the foregoing, the Navy developed an aircraft model designation system in the early 1920's and used it until 1962 when it was replaced by a Department of Defense unified system. The official assignment of names to naval aircraft did not begin until 1941; interservice coordination began in 1943, thus, the system for naming aircraft has changed little since the practice became official over 50 years ago.

In compiling the listing for popular names, one of the thorniest difficulties was the problem of distinguishing between what the official records said and what has long been accepted as fact. For example, few aviation historians believe that the SB2C-5 was ever assigned the name Hellcat, yet it does appear in the Bureau of Aeronautics' Model Designation of Naval Aircraft. Because this particular case is so extraordinary, there seemed ample reason to consider it an error; therefore, the SB2C-5 does not appear in this listing as a Hellcat. Others were equally questionable and were accordingly omitted. However, when sufficient doubt was present, the designation and its name were included here. As a result, some of the information in this listing will raise the eyebrows of those readers who are familiar with the popular names of naval aircraft.

Within the Alphabetical Listing of Popular Names the column headings are as follows:

Popular Names.—The popular names the Navy assigned to its aircraft are listed alphabetically. Cross-references are given when different names were assigned to different models of the same basic aircraft. In a few cases two different names were assigned to identical aircraft models. These are cross-referenced here. Also in rare instances entirely different aircraft have the same name, if so, the name is listed twice.

Original Navy Designation, pre-1962.—The original designation was the first designation under which the Navy accepted the aircraft. Basic designations are listed unless specific models were assigned different names. The Navy never officially assigned a name to

the designation in parentheses. They are listed because they were the original designations of the aircraft to which the Navy later assigned a name under a new designation.

Redesignation to the Post 1962 DOD Designation.—In 1962 the Department of Defense standardized its system of aircraft designations. Most naval aircraft, however, retained the same popular name. Basic designations are listed unless specific models were assigned different names. They are included because they are the redesignations of aircraft to which the Navy had previously assigned a name under its original designation. New aircraft acquired after 1962 and the new post 1962 aircraft designation are listed in this column.

Popular Names	Original Navy Designation, pre-1962	Redesignation to the Post 1962 DOD Designation System or New Post 1962 Designation	Popular Names	Original Navy Designation, pre-1962	Redesignation to the Post 1962 DOD Designation System or New Post 1962 Designation
Academe		TC-4C	Caydet (also Kaydet)	N2S	
Aero Commander		U-9	Cayuse		OH-6A/B
Albatross	JR2F/UF	U-16	Chickasaw	(HO4S-3)	H-19
Avenger	TBF			(HRS-3)	H-19
	TBM		Cobra		AH-1
Avenger II		A-12 (never acquired)	Cochise		T-42A
Aztec	UO	U-11	Commando	R5C	
Banshee	F2H	F-2	Connestoga	RB	
Bearcat	F8F		Constellation (see Warning Star)	PO	
Beaver		U-6		WV-1	
Bird Dog	(OE)	0-1		R70/R7V	C-121
Black Widow	F2T		Constitution	R60/R6V	
Bobcat	JRC		Convair Liner	R4Y	C-131
Bronco		OV-10	Coronado	PB2Y	
Buccaneer	SB2A		Corsair	F4U	
Buckeye	T2J	T-2		FG	
Buffalo	F2A			F3A	
Buffalo		UC-8A		AU	
				F2G	
Catalina	PBY		Corsair II		A-7
	PB2B		Cougar	F9F-6,-7,-8	F-9
	PBN		Crusader	F8U	F-8

Popular Names	Original Navy Designation, pre-1962	Redesignation to the Post 1962 DOD Designation System or New Post 1962 Designation	Popular Names	Original Navy Designation, pre-1962	Redesignation to the Post 1962 DOD Designation System or New Post 1962 Designation
Crusader III	F8U-3		Havoc	BD	
Cutlass	F7U		Hawkeye	W2F	E-2
DASH	(DSN)	QH-50	Hellcat	F6F	
Dauntless	SBD		Helldiver	SB2C SBC-3,-4 SBW SBF	
Demon	F3H	F-3			
Destroyer	(SB2D) BTD		Hercules	GV	C-130
Devastator	(XTB2D-1) TBD		Hermes (see Mercury)		E-6 (changed to Mercury)
Dolphin		H-65	Hornet		F/A-18
Duck	(JF) J2F		Hoverfly	HNS-1	
Excalibur	JR2S		Hudson	PBO	
Expediter	JRB-1 thru -4	C-45	Huron		UC-12B
Falcon	SNC		Huskie	(HOK) (HUK)	H-43
Fighting Falcon		F-16			
Fireball	FR		Intruder	A2F	A-6
Flying Classroom		T-29	Invader	JD	B-26
Flying Fortress	PB-1G, -1W		Iroquois		UH-1/TH-1
Forwarder	GK		Jaguar	F10F	
Fury	FJ	F-I	Kansan	SNB-1	
Goose	JRF		Kaydet (see Caydet)	N2S	
Goshawk		T-45	Kfir		F-21A
Grasshopper	NE		Kingfisher	OS2U OS2N	
Greyhound		C-2	Kiowa		OH-58A
Guardian	AF		Liberator	PB4Y-1/P4Y-1	
Gulfstream		C-20D	Liberator Express	RY-1	
Harpoon	PV-2		Liftmaster	R6D	C-118
Harrier		AV-8A	Lodestar	R50	
Harrier II		AV-8B	Marauder	JM	

Popular Names	Original Navy Designation, pre-1962	Redesignation to the Post 1962 DOD Designation System or New Post 1962 Designation	Popular Names	Original Navy Designation, pre-1962	Redesignation to the Post 1962 DOD Designation System or New Post 1962 Designation
Mariner	PBM		Recruit	NR	
Marlin	P5M	P-5	Reliance	ZPG-2W	EZ-1
Mars	PB2M JRM		Rescuer	HRP	
Mauler	(BTM-1), AM		Retriever	HUP	H-25
Mentor	T-34	T-34	Sabre	(F-86)	QF-86
Mercator	P4M		Sabreliner	(T3J)	T-39
Mercury (see Hermes)		E-6A	Samaritan		C-131
Mescalero		T-41B	Savage	AJ	A-2
Mitchell	PBJ		Sea Bat	(HSS-1)	H-34
Mohawk		OV-1A/B/C	Sea Cobra		AH-1J/T/W
Mojave	(HR2S)	H-37	Sea Dart	F2Y	F-7
Navigator	SNB-2C, -5	C-45	Sea Dragon		MH-53
Neptune	P2V	P-2	Seafarer	ZPG-2	SZ-1
Nightingale	GH, NH		Seagull (not official)	SOC, SO3C	
Norseman	JA		Seahawk	SC	
Orion	P3V	P-3	Sea Hawk		SH-60B
Osprey		V-22A	Seahorse	(HUS)	H-34
Otter	UC	U-1	Sea King	(HSS-2)	H-3
Packet	R4Q	C-119	Sea Knight	(HRB)	H-46
Panther	F9F-2, -4, -5	DF-9	Seamaster	P6M	
Phantom	FD, FH		Seamew	SO3C	
Phantom II	F4H	F-4	Sea Ranger	XPBB-1	
Pinto	TT-1		Sea Ranger		H-57
Pirate	F6U		Seasprite	HU2K	H-2
Privateer	PB4Y-2, P4Y-2	QP-4B	Sea Stallion		H-53 thru H-53D
Prowler		EA-6B	Sea Star	T2V	T-1
Puss Moth	XDH-80		Sea Wolf (also Seawolf)	TBY	
			Seminole		U-8

Popular Names	Original Navy Designation, pre-1962	Redesignation to the Post 1962 DOD Designation System or New Post 1962 Designation	Popular Names	Original Navy Designation, pre-1962	Redesignation to the Post 1962 DOD Designation System or New Post 1962 Designation
Sentinel	OY		Texan	SNJ	
Shadow		ES-3A	Tiger	F11F	F-11
Shooting Star	TV, TO	T-33	Tiger II		F-5
Sioux	(HTL), HUL	H-13	Tigercat	F7F	
Skyhawk	A4D	A-4	Tomcat		F-14
Sky Knight	F3D	F-10	Tracer	WF	E-1
Skylancer	F5D		Tracker	S2F	S-2
Skymaster	R5D	C-54	Trader	TF-1	C-1
Skyraider	(BT2D), AD	A-1	Tradewind	R3Y	
Skyray	F4D	F-6	Traveler	GB	
Skyrocket	D-558-2		Trojan	T-28	T-28
Skyshark	A2D		Tutor	N2T	
Skytrain	R4D-1, -5, -6, -7	C-47	Ute		U-21A
	R4D-8	C-117	Valiant	SNV	
Skytrain II		C-9	Ventura	PV-1, -3	
Skystreak	D-558-1		Vigilante	A3J	A-5
Skytrooper	R4D-2,-3,-4		Viking		S-3
Skywarrior	A3D	A-3	Vindicator	SB2U	
Stratojet		EB-47E	Volunteer	ZSG-1	
Stratotanker		NKC-135A	Warning Star (See Constellation)	WV	EC-121
Super Fortress	P2B-1		White Hawk		VH-60N
Super Stallion		CH-53E/RH-53/MH-53E	Widgeon	J4F	
Talon		T-38	Wildcat	F4F	
				FM	

The Navy and Marine Corps early helicopter, the HNS-1, demonstrates its air-sea rescue capabilities by retrieving a pilot from his ditched SBD, CG-3649.

Combat Aircraft Procured

THE FOLLOWING TABLES contain key dates relating to development, procurement and service use of combat types of airplanes obtained in quantities sufficient to equip a squadron. "Combat type" excludes trainers, transports, and utility types; however, models originally obtained for such purposes and later reported as being utilized for combat missions are included — e.g., the VE-7 and VE-9. Noncombat configurations of combat aircraft, such as TA-4E and PB2Y-3R, are also included. The term "quantities sufficient to equip a squadron" is somewhat elastic; through the 1920s (and 1930s for patrol planes) aircraft are included if as few as nine were obtained. Other than that, the table is limited to aircraft of which at least 18 were obtained.

The complete tabulation consists of five tables: attack planes, fighter planes, patrol and early warning planes, observation planes and World War I aircraft. Attack and patrol planes each include a number of specific missions identified in the heading of the table. Aircraft did not always lend themselves to the above divisions; for example, a fighter-bomber can be either a fighter or an attack plane. Arbitrary judgments, necessary to place such aircraft in one table, are reflected in designations and cross-references under alternate designations.

World War I aircraft were listed in a separate table because of the lack of data on first flight, contract date, etc., and in order to show shipments overseas.

Description of Column Headings

Designation—Basic designations and redesignations are included and are arranged alphabetically. If aircraft were procured from the Army/Air Force their designations are also listed.

First aircraft contract—This shows the date of the first contractual commitment for delivery of an airplane. If the first aircraft was ordered by amendment to a design contract, the date of the amendment is used. Letters of Intent and even telegraphic orders are treated as contracts. If a contract date could not be established, an estimate, shown as "(est)", was made from available data. The use of a year followed by a number (as 1922–2), shows that the contract was made in the quarter (in this example, the second) of the calendar year. For cross-service procurement, the date of the Navy's commitment to the Army or Air Force is shown. For World War II Army Air Force bombers, the date of the policy decision that the Navy would procure such aircraft is shown.

First flight—Refers to first flight of first aircraft, generally an "X" model. Frequently the date of first flight was estimated (shown as "(est)") usually from date of delivery for Navy flight tests. If documentation permitted, specific dates are given; otherwise the month and year are shown. No first flight date is given for aircraft which were in operation with the Army or the Air Force or commercially before they were delivered to the Navy.

Number accepted, Manufacturer, and *Models accepted*—These three columns are keyed to each other and show model designations and gross acceptances for Navy, for other services and for allies—whether lend lease, military assistance programs, or (more recently) military sales in which the Navy served as the agent of the procuring government—are shown in parentheses and included in the overall totals. For aircraft still in production, number accepted is total as of 31 December 1995.

In general, the manufacturer can be readily identified although the following may have become obscure: LWF for Lowe, Willard, and Fowler; NAF for Naval Aircraft Factory and B/J for Berliner/Joyce. No attempt was made to indicate corporate history except in the use of the family spelling "Loughead" as well as the better known "Lockheed," and in distinguishing between the Northrop subsidiary of Douglas and the Douglas Company. Thus Vought includes Lewis and Vought, the independent Chance Vought Corporation, the Vought and Vought-Sikorsky divisions of United Aircraft Corporation, the later independent Vought company and the present Vought Aeronautics Division of Ling-Temco-Vought. McDonnell and Douglas are treated as separate entities.

For aircraft redesignated while in production, both old and new designations are shown (P3V-1/P-3A), indicating that aircraft were accepted under both designations.

Squadron delivery and Last reported in squadron or inventory—These give the date when the first combat type unit received basic aircraft and similarly gives the date of the last report that such a unit had the aircraft in its custody. Thus these columns show the span of aircraft service life in combat units of the U.S. Navy and identify the first and last squadron to have custody of the aircraft. The occasional assignment of a single experimental aircraft to a combat unit is omitted; this sometimes occurred a year or more in advance of actually equipping the first squadron. For purposes of this table, combat units are defined as squadrons attached to the Atlantic or Pacific Fleet, including replacement training squadrons but excluding utility, transport, and experimental and evaluation squadrons. Thus units of the training commands and naval reserve are omitted as generally are the pre-World War II District squadrons. If squadron data is incomplete, the ships, or stations to which the unit was attached are given. Particularly, for late World War II and the early post-war years, the final squadrons with a particular aircraft could not be identified beyond the fact that they were in the Atlantic or Pacific Fleets.

A variety of sources were utilized in compiling the service history. Correspondence, individual aircraft history cards, and the monthly status report compiled by the Bureau of Aeronautics, or Deputy Chief of Naval Operations (Air). From 1926 until 1941 this report was titled, "Monthly Report, Status of Naval Aircraft," it then became "Monthly Status of Naval Aircraft"; in 1948, "Location of Naval Aircraft"; and in 1951, "Allowances and Location of Naval Aircraft." Initial assignment data is believed to be exact. The data in "last reported," is approximate; it was drawn almost entirely from the above reports, and there is uncertainty as to the currency of the data supporting any particular issue. In addition, data within the report was, at times, a month out of phase with the issue date.

Since the squadron organization did not come into being until after World War I, the table for World War I aircraft shows assignment to stations and final withdrawal from inventory.

Description—This column shows the number of wings and crew provision as a single entry, i.e., B/2 means biplane, two place. Variations in size of crew are shown in parentheses; fighters were single place, unless otherwise indicated. Other notes on equipment and structure are included to indicate basic technological advance. When mission data is shown it generally reflects a change in military requirements.

The standard engine nomenclature is used: R for radial aircooled (generally followed by a number indicating displacement); J for jet; T for turboprop; O for horizontally opposed; all others were in line or Vee-type, generally liquid cooled. Standard power terminology is used: horsepower for propeller drives and pounds thrust for jet units. The practice on turboprops has varied. Sometimes the horsepower absorbed by the propeller and the residual thrust in pounds are both given; at others, the two are combined in equivalent shaft horsepower "eshp." Identifying nomenclature for engine manufacturers was adapted from standard practice as follows:

AL, Allison; ACM, Aircooled Motors; AIR, AiResearch; AM, Aeromarine; BO, Boeing; CAM, Curtiss Aeroplane & Motor Co.; CO, Continental; FR, Franklin; GE, General Electric; LA, Lawrance; Lib, Liberty; LY, Lycoming; PKD, Packard; P&W, Pratt & Whitney Aircraft; RA, Ranger; WAC, Wright Aeronautical Corporation; WE Westinghouse; WR, Warner.

Attack Series

Includes Dive Bomber (VB), Torpedo Planes (VT), Torpedo Bombers (VTB), Scout Bomber (VSB), Carrier Scouts (VS), and Carrier ASW (VS)

Aircraft Designation	Date First Aircraft Contract	Date First Flight	Date Last Delivery	Number Accepted	Manufacturer	Models Accepted	Squadron Delivery	Last Reported in Squadron or * Inventory	Description
A-1	(Redesignation of AD)								
A-2	(Redesignation of AJ)								
A-3	9/29/49	10/22/52	1/61	282	Douglas	XA3D-1; A3D-1, -2, -2P, -2Q, -2T; A-3B; KA-3B, EKA-3B, RA-3B, EA-3B.	3/31/56 VAH-1	3/91 KA-3B	M/3 (7 in -2Q; 8 in -2T). Swept wing; 2 P&W J57, 9,500 to 10,500#.
A-4	9/13/52	6/22/54	2/27/79	2,876 (294)	Douglas	XA4D-1; A4D-1, -2, -2N, -5; A-4A, -4C, -4E, -4F, -4G, -4H, -4K, -4KU, -4M, -4N; TA-4E, -4F/J, -4H, -4J, -4K, -4KU; EA-4F	9/27/56 VA-72	3/94 A-4M	M/1 (2 in TA versions). Modified deltawing; WAC J65, 7,700# or P&W J52, 7,500 to 8500#.
A-5	8/29/56	8/31/58	11/5/70	156	North American	A3J-1; A-5A, -5B; RA-5C.	6/61 VAH-3	3/81 RA-5C	M/2. Supersonic; 2 GE J79, 17,000#.
A-6	3/26/59	4/19/60	1/31/92	890	Grumman	A2F-1; A-6A, -6E; EA-6A, -6B; KA-6D; YA-6F.	2/63 VA-42		M/2. 2 P&W J52, 8,500#.
A-7	3/19/64	9/27/65	10/86	1,491 (498)	Vought	A-7A, -7B, -7D, -7C, -7E, -7H; EA-7L.	10/13/66 VA-147	6/92 A-7E	M/1. Developed from F-8; P&W TF-30 (non-afterburning).
F/A-18	1/22/76	11/78		1196	McDonnell Douglas	F/A-18A, -18B, -18C, -18D.	1/7/83 VMFA-314		M/1 (2); 2 F404GE-400, Mach 1.8+; F/A-18D is a two seater.
AV-8	12/22/69		4/23/96	462**	Hawker Siddeley McDonnell Douglas	AV-8A, TAV-8A, AV-8B, -8C, TAV-8B	1/27/71		M/1 (2 in TA version). V/STOL Aircraft. One RR F402-RR-401, 21,500#.
AD	7/6/44	3/18/45	3/57	3,180 (20)	Douglas	XBT2D-1, -1W, -1P, -1Q, -1N; XAD-1W, -2; AD-1, -1Q, -2, -2Q, -3, -3Q, -4B, -4N, -4Q, -4W, -5, -5W, -5N, -6, -7; EA-1F.	12/6/46 VA-19A	12/31/71 EA-1F	M/1 (2 in -5; 2 to 4 in -Q, -W, -N and -S). First successful USN aircraft orginally designed as both dive bomber and torpedo plane; WAC R-3350, 2700 to 3,150 hp.
A3D	(Redesigned A-3)								
A4D	(Redesigned A-4)								
AF	2/19/45	12/46	4/53	389	Grumman	XTB3F-1, -1S, -2S; AF-2W, -2S, -3S.	10/18/50 VS-25	8/31/55 VS-37 AF-2W	M/3. ASW attack (S) and search (W); P&W R-2800, 2300 hp; also WE 19XB, 1,600 in XTB3F-1.

Attack Series—Continued

Desig.	Date	Date (est)	No.	Manufacturer	Models	Date	First Squadron	Later Squadron	Remarks
A2F	(Redesignated A-6)								
AJ	6/24/46	7/3/48	143	North American	XAJ-1; AJ-1, -2, -2P.	6/54	9/13/49 VC-5	1/31/60 VAP-62, VCP-61, AJ-2P	M/3. First heavy attack: 2 P&W R-2800, 2300 hp and J33, 4,600#.
A3J	(Redesignated A-5)								
AM	1/14/44	8/26/44	152	Martin	XBTM-1; AM-1, -1Q.	10/49	3/1/48 VA-17A	10/1/50 VC-4 AM-1Q	M/1 (2 in -1Q). P&W R-4360, 3,310 hp.
BF2C	12/16/32	5/11/33 est	28	Curtiss	XF11C-3; BF2C-1.	10/34	11/34 VB-5B	2/29/36 VB-5B BF2C-1	B/1. WAC R-1820, 700 hp.
AU	(Designated for last U.S. Navy production version of F4U)								
BFC	(Redesignation XF11C -1 & -2)								
BG	6/13/32	6/33 est	61	Great Lakes	XBG-1; BG-1	11/35	10/24/34 VT-1S	6/30/41 VMS-6, BG-1	B/2 1000# dive bomber; P&W R-1535, 700 hp.
BM	6/18/28	5/29 est	34 / 1	Martin / NAF	XT5M-1; XBM-1; BM-1, -2.	1/33	10/24/32 VT-1S	9/30/38 VCS-6, BM-2	B/2 First "heavy" 1000# dive bomber; P&W R-1690, 625 hp.
BT		10/20/38	54	Northrop	XBT-1; BT-1; XBT-2.		4/38 VB-5	1/43 PAC	M/2. 1000# dive bomber; P&W R-1535-94, 825 hp.
BTD	6/30/41	4/8/43	30	Douglas	XSB2D-1; BTD-1; XBTD-2.	10/45		(Not assigned to Fleet Squadrons)	M/1 (2 in SB2D). WAC R-3350, 2100 hp; also WE 19B Jet.
BT2D	(Initial designation for AD)								
BTM	(Initial designation for AM)								
CS	6/22 est	11/23 est	8 / 75	Curtiss / Martin	CS-1, -2. SC-1, -2.	1/26	3/1/24 VS-3	12/19/27 VT-2, SC-2	B/2, Conv't 3-in-1—torpedo, scout & bomber; steel tube fuselage & tail; WAC T-2 or T-3, 525 or 625 hp.
DT	1921	11/21 est	41 / 6 / 20 / 11	Douglas / NAF / LWF / Dayton-Wright	DT-1, -2. DT-2, -4. DT-2. DT-2.	1924-2	12/12/22	4/1/28	B/1 (2 in -2). Conv't; torpedo; welded steel tube forward fuselage and horizontal tail; fuselage skin partially aluminum; folding wings; Lib. 400 or 450 hp; WAC T-3, 650 hp in -4.

Designation	Date	Date	Date	Number	Manufacturer	Models	Service	Service	Remarks
F/A-18	(See Fighter Series)								
MBT	(Original version of Martin Bomber, see MT)								
MT	9/30/19	2/4/20	8/20	9	Martin	MT; MBT.	8/20 LANT and PAC	6/2/28 VO-8M MT	B/3. Land, folding wing on some aircraft; 2 Lib. 400 hp.
PT	1921	7/21 est	7/22	33	NAF	PT-1,-2	3/22 VT-1	7/23 VT-1, PT-2	B/2. Lib. 400 hp.
S-2	6/30/50	12/4/52	12/67	1,120 (63)	Grumman	XS2F; S2F-1, -2, -3, -2D; S2F-3S/S-2E.	2/54 VS-26	3/84 S-2E	M/4. ASW; 2 WAC F-1820, 1,525 hp.
S-3	8/69	1/21/72	9/77	187	Lockheed	S-3A, -3B.	2/20/74 VS-41		M/4. ASW Aircraft. 2 GE TF-34-GE-2, 9,000#.
SBA	(Prototype for SBN)								
SB2A	4/4/39	6/17/41	2/44	771(468)	Brewster	XSB2A-1; SB2A-1, -2, -3, -4.	1/31/43 VMF(N) -531	11/30/43 VMF(N) -532, SB2A-4	M/2. Used for training, WAC R-2600, 1700 hp.
SBC	6/30/32	6/14/34	4/41	258	Curtiss	XSBC-3, -4; SBC-3, -4.	7/17/37 VS-5	6/1/43 VMSB-151 SBC-4	B/2. P&W R-1535, 825 hp in -3; WAC R-1820, 1950 hp in -4.
SB2C	5/15/39	12/18/40	10/45	5,516(1); 834(26); 300	Curtiss; CanCar Fairchild	XSB2C-2,-5,-6; SB2C-1, -1A, -1C, -3, -4, -4E, -5. SBW-1,-1B, -3, -4, -4E, -5. SBF-1, -3, -4E.	12/15/42 VS-9	6/1/49 VA-54, SB2C-5	M/2 (XSB2C-2, sea). WAC R-2600, 1,700 to 1,900 hp; P&W R-2800, 2,100 hp in -6.
SBD	11/18/34	8/35 est	8/44	5321(338); 55	Douglas; Northrop	SBD-1, -2, -3, -3A, -4, -4A, -5, -5A, -6. XBT-1, -2; BT-1.	4/11/38 VB-5	9/30/45 PAC, SBD-6	M/2. "All metal," stressed skin; WAC R-1820, 1,000 hp in SBD-1, -2, -3; 1,200 hp in -5 & -6.
SB2D	(Redesignated to BTD)								
SBF	(SB2C manufactured by Fairchild of Canada)								
SBN	10/15/34	3/36	3/42	30; 1	NAF; Brewster	SBN-1. XSBA-1	8/41 VT-8	12/31/41 VT-8, SBN-1	M/2. Used for training; WAC R-1820, 950 hp; 725 hp in XSBA-1.
SBW	(SB2C manufactured by Canadian Car and Foundry(CanCar))								
SBU	6/30/32	6/33 est	8/37	126	Vought	XF3U-1; XSBU-1; SBU-1, -2.	11/20/35 VS-3B	4/30/41 VS-41 SBU-1	B/2. P&W R-1535, 700 hp.

Attack Series—Continued

Desig.				No.	Mfr.	Models	First Sqdn.	Last Sqdn.	Remarks
SB2U	10/11/34	1/4/36	7/41	170	Vought	XSB2U-1,- 3; SBU-1,- 2, -3.	12/20/37 VB-3	2/28/43 VB-9, SB2U-1	M/2. -3 Conv't; 1st folding winged dive bomber; P&W R-1535, 835 hp.
SC					(CS manufactured by Martin in 1920s)				
SC					(Battleship and cruiser aircraft, World War II, see Observation series)				
SF	6/9/31	8/19/32	12/34	35	Grumman	XSF-1; SF-1; XSF-2.	3/30/34 VF-2B	1/31/36 VS-3B, SF-1	B/2. Retractable landing gear; same basic airframe as FF; WAC R-1820, 700 hp.
S2F					(Redesignated S-2)				
SU					(O3U converted to carrier scout, see Oberservation series)				
TBD	6/30/34	4/15/35	11/39	130	Douglas	XTBD-1; TBD-1	10/5/37 VT-3	8/31/42 VT-4, TBD-1	M/3. P&W R-1830, 850 hp.
TBF	4/8/40	8/7/41	9/45	2,290(458)	Grumman	XTBF-1, -2, -3; TBF-1, -1B, -1C.	3/25/42 VT-8	10/31/54 VS-27, TBM-3E	M/3. WAC R-2600, 1,700 hp; 1,800 hp in -3.
				7,546(526)	Eastern	XTBM-3, -4; TBM-1,-1C, -3, -3E.			
TB3F					(Prototype for AF)				
TBM					(TBF manufactured by Eastern Aircraft Division, General Motors Corp.)				
TBU					(Produced as TBY)				
TBY	4/22/40	12/22/41	9/45	180	Consolidated	TBY-2	4/45 VT-97	3/31/45 PAC, TBY-2	M/3. P&W R-2800, 2,100 hp; 1850 hp in XTBU-1.
				1	Vought	XTBU-1			
T2D					(Initial designation for P2D, see Patrol series)				
TG					(T4M as manufactured by Great Lakes Aircraft Corp.)				
T3M	1925	7/26 est	1927	124	Martin	T3M-1, -2.	9/7/26 VT-1	7/30/32 VP-3S, T3M-2	B/3. Conv't; WAC T-3, 575 hp; PKD 3A-2500, 770 hp in -2.
T4M	6/30/27	5/27 est	12/31	103 50	Martin Great Lakes	XT4M-1; T4M-1. TG-1, -2.	8/9/28 VT-2B	3/31/38 VT-6,TG-2	B/3. Conv't; generally carrier based; P&W R-1690, 525 hp; WAC R-1820, 575 hp in -2.
T5M					(Initial prototype for BM)				
T2N					(Similar to T5M, included with BM)				

* Dates in this column through 1969 refer to squadrons. After 1969 these dates refer to the inventory.
** Includes 18 remanufactured from AV-8A to AV-8B.

Fighter Series

Aircraft Designation	Date First Aircraft Contract	Date First Flight	Date Last Delivery	Number Accepted	Manufacturer	Models Accepted	Squadron Delivery	Last Reported in Squadron or * Inventory	Description
F-1	(Redesignation of FJ-3 and -4)								
F-2	(Redesignation of F2H-3 and -4)								
F-3	(Redesignation of F3H-3)								
F-4	10/18/54	5/27/58	12/29/71	4,261 (3,057)	McDonnell	F4H-1; F-4A, -4B, -4C, -4D, -4E, -4G, -4J, -4K, -4M, -4N, -4S; RF-4B, -4C; YF-4K, -4M.	12/60 VF-121	12/89 F-4S	M/2. Mach 2 plus; all missile; 2 GE J79, 17,000#.
F-5				44	Northtop	F-5E, -5F	9/77 NFWS	12/14/89	M/2. Mach 1.5; AIM-9, M39 20mm gun. 2 GE J85-GE-21, 5,000# each.
F-6	(Redesignation of F4D)								
F-8	6/29/53	3/25/55	1/65	1264(42)	Vought	XF8U-1; F8U-1, -1P, -2, -2N, -3 -2NE/F-8E (FN); F-8J.	3/57 VF-32, VC-3	8/82 F-8J	M. Variable incidence wing; supersonic; P&W J57, 15,000# to 18,000#.
F-9	(Redesignation of F9F-5 through 8)								
F-10	(Redesignation of F3D)								
F-11	(Redesignation of F11F)								
F-14	2/3/69	12/21/70	7/10/92	679(78)	Grumman	F-14, -14B, -14A+, -14D.	1/14/73		M/2. Mach 2 plus. 2 P&W TF-30-P-44, up to 20,000#.
F-16N		9/87		22	General Dynamics	F-16N	4/87 NFWS	5/88	M/1. Mach 2 plus; 2 P&W F110, 20,000#.
F/A-18	5/75	11/18/78		1098	McDonnell	F/A-18A, -18B, -18C, -18D.	1/7/83 VMFA-314		M/1. Mach 2 plus. 2 GE F404-GE-400, 16,000#; F/A-18D a two seater.
F2A	6/22/36	12/37	4/42	503(340)	Brewster	XF2A-1; F2A-1, -2, -3.	12/8/39 VF-3	9/30/42 VMF-112, F2A-2; VMF-211, F2A-3	M/1. Midwing, cantilever monoplane; WAC R-1820, 950 to 1,200 hp.

Fighter Series—Continued

Desig.				No.	Model(s)	Mfr.			Remarks
F-21A				37	F-21A	Israel	3/85 VF-43	8/26/87	M1. Mach 2 plus. GE J79-GE-J1E, 30mm cannon, missile, bombs, rockets.
F3A					(F4U Manufactured by Brewster)				
FB	1925	11/25 est	1/27	43	FB-1, -2, -3, -5	Boeing	12/25/25 VF-2	6/30/30 VF-6M, FB-5	B. Carrier, -2 & -5; conv't, -3; radio, -5; CAM D-12, 410 hp in -1 and -2. PKD 1A-1500, 525 hp in -3 and -5.
F2B	1926	12/26 est	2/28	33	F2B-1	Boeing	12/2/27 VF-1B	5/31/35 VN-5D8, F2B-1	B. Conv't; P&W R-1340, 410 hp.
F3B	6/30/27	6/27 est	1/29	74	F3B-1	Boeing	10/17/27 VF-1B	4/28/33 VF-2B, F3B-1	B. P&W R-1340, 410 hp.
F4B	11/28/28	6/28 est	1/33	188*	F4B-1, -2, -3, -4.	Boeing	8/8/29 VB-1B	10/10/42 VJ-5 F4B-4	B. P&W R-1340, 450 hp in -1; 500 hp in -2 to -4.
F6C	1925	7/25 est	6/27	75	F6C-1, -3, -4	Curtiss	9/30/25 VF-2	10/31/32 VF-10M F6C-4	B. Conv't carrier, -2 to -4; CAM D-12, 400 hp in -1 to -3; P&W R-1340, 410 hp in -4.
F7C	6/30/27	6/27 est	1/29	18	XF7C-1; F7C-1	Curtiss	12/28/28 VF-5M	3/31/33 VF-9M, F7C-1	B. P&W R-1340, 450 hp.
F8C					(For F8C-1 -3 see OC in Observation series; F8C-3 became OC-2)				
F8C-2	3/15/28	11/28	11/31	124	XF8C-2, -4, -7 F8C-4, -5; 02C-1, -2.	Curtiss	8/30 VF-1B	7/31/38 VMJ-1 02C-1	B/2. 500# dive bomber; P&W R-1340B, 450 hp; WAC R-1820, 575 hp in 02C-2.
F9C	6/30/30	2/12/31	9/32	8	XF9C-1, -2; F9C-2.	Curtiss	9/32 Akron Unit	1/31/35 Macon Unit, F9C-2	B. Skyhook; droppable under-carriage; metal monocoque fuselage; WACR-975, 400 hp.
F11C	4/16/32	3/20/32	5/33	29	XF11C-1, -2; F11C-2 redesignated BFC-2.	Curtiss	3/22/33 VF-1B	5/31/38 VB-6, BFC-2	B. WAC R-1820, 600 hp.

Desig.	Date	Date	Date	Number	Mfr.	Models	First	Last	Description
F12C						(XF12C-1 monoplane successively modified to XS4C-1 and XSBC-1 and then crashed; it was replaced by XSBC-2 biplane which became XSBC-3)			
FD						(Original designation for FH)			
F3D	4/3/46	3/23/48	10/53	268	Douglas	XF3D-1; F3D-1, -2, -2M.	2/51 VC-3	5/31/70 EF-10B	M/2. Jet night-fighter; 2 WE J34, 3,250#; 3400# in -2.
F4D	12/16/48	1/25/51	12/58	421	Douglas	XF4D-1; F4D-1, F-6.	4/16/56 VC-3	2/29/64 VMF-115, F4D-1, F-6	M. Modified delta wing; tailless; WE J40, 13,700# in XF4D-1; P&W J57, 16,000#.
FG						(F4U manufactured by Goodyear)			
FF	4/2/31	12/21/31	11/33	28	Grumman	XFF-1; FF-1, -2.	6/21/33 VF-5B	3/31/36 VF-5B FF-1	B/2. Metal monocoque fuselage; retractable landing gear; WAC R-1820, 600 hp.
F2F	11/2/32	10/9/33	8/35	56	Grumman	XF2F-1; F2F-1.	2/19/35 VF-2B	9/30/40 VF-2, F2F-1	B. P&W R-1535, 650 hp.
F3F	10/15/34	3/20/35	5/39	164	Grumman	XF3F-1, -2, -3; F3F-1, -2, -3.	4/3/36 VF-5B	10/31/41 VMF-111, VMF-211, F3F-2	B. P&W R-1535, 700 hp in -1; WAC R-1820, 950 hp in -2 and -3.
F4F	7/28/36	9/2/37	5/45	1,978 (431)	Grumman	XF4F-2, -3; -4, -5, -6, -8; F4F-3, -3A -4, -7;	12/5/40 VF-4	11/30/45 PAC, FM-2	M. Folding wings on F4F-4/FM-1. P&W R-1830, 1,050 to 1,200 hp; WAC R-1820,1350 hp in -5 and -8/FM-1 -2.
				5,927 (651)	Eastern	FM-1, -2			
F6F	6/30/41	6/26/42	11/45	12,275 (1,182)	Grumman	XF6F-1/-3, -4, -6; F6F-3, -3E, -3N, -5, -5N.	1/16/43 VF-9	8/31/53 VC-4, F6F-5N	M. P&W R-2800, 2,000 hp to 2,325 hp.
F7F	6/30/41	11/3/43	11/46	364	Grumman	XF7F-1, -2; F7F-1, -1N, -2N, -3, -3N, -4N.	1/44 VMF-911, VMF(N)-531	3/31/54 VJ-62, F7F-3N/-4N	M. (2-place in -2N, -3N). Tricycle landing gear; 2 P&W R-2800, 2,400 hp; 2,100 hp in -4.
F8F	11/27/43	8/31/44	5/49	1,263	Grumman	XF8F-1, -1N, -2; F8F-1, -1B, -1N, -2, -2N, -2P.	5/21/45 VF-19	1/31/53 VF-921, VF-859, F8F-2	M. Medium altitude interceptor; P&W R-2800, 2,750 hp; 2,500 hp in -2.

Fighter Series—Continued

Model				Manufacturer	Models	Number			Remarks
F9F-2/-5	12/16/46	11/21/47	12/52	Grumman	XF9F-2, -3; F9F-2,- 3, -4, -5, -5P.	1,388	5/8/49 VF-51	10/31/58 VAH-7, F9F-5	M. Straight wing; P&W J42, 5,750# in -2; J48, 7,000# in -5; AL J33, 5,400# in -3; 6,500# in -4.
F9F-6/-8	3/2/51	9/20/51	12/59	Grumman	F9F-6, -6P, -7, -8, - 8P, -8T.	1,985	11/52 VF-32	2/29/60 VFP-62, F9F-8P	M. (2 place in -8T). Swept wing; P&W J48, 7,250# in -6, - 8; AL J33, 6,250# in -7.
F11F	4/27/53	7/30/54	12/58	Grumman	F9F-9; F11F-1, -1F.	201	3/8/57 VA-156	4/30/61 VF-33, VF-111, F11F-1	M. Supersonic; WAC J65, 10,500#; GE J79, 14,350# in -1F.
FH	1/7/43	1/26/45	5/48	McDonnell	XFD-1; FD-1/FH-1.	61	7/23/47 VF-17A	7/1/50 VMF-122, FH-1	M. First USN all jet; tricycle landing gear; 2 WE J30, 1,560#.
F2H	3/2/45	1/11/47	8/53	McDonnell	XF2H-1; F2H-1, -2, -2N, -2P, -3, -4.	894	3/49 VF-171	9/30/59 VAW-11, F2H-3/-4	M. Pressurized cabin; ejection seat; 2 WE J34, 3,150# in -3 and -4.
F3H	9/30/49	8/7/51	11/59	McDonnell	XF3H-1; F3H-1, -1N, -2, -2N, -2M, F-3B, -3C; MF-3B.	519	3/7/56 VF-14	8/31/64 VF-161, F-3B	M. Sparrow Missle; 1 in -2M, 3 in -2; WE J40, 13,700 and 10,900# in -1 and -1N; AL J71, 14,400#.
F4H	(Redesignated F-4)								
FJ	1/1/45	9/11/46	4/48	North American	XFJ-1; FJ-1.	33	11/18/57 VF-5A	10/1/49 VF-51, FJ-1	M. Stright wing; power boost control; GE TG-180 in XFJ-1; AL J35 (TG-180), 4,000# in FJ-1.
FJ-2/-4	2/10/51	12/27/51	5/58	North American	XFJ-2, -2B; FJ-2, -3, -3M, -4, -4B, F-1C, -1E.	1,115	1/54 VMF-122	9/30/62 VA-216, F-1E	M. Swept wing; GE J47, 6,000# in -2; WAC J65, 7,800#.
FFR	2/11/43	6/25/44	11/45	Ryan	XFR-1, FR-1	69	3/45 VF-66	6/30/47 VF-1E, FR-1	M. Combination jet-propeller; tricycle gear; WAC R-1820, 1,400 hp; plus GE I-16, 1,610#.

Desig.	Date	Date	Mfr.	Models	No.	First sq.	Last sq.	Remarks
FU				(Single seat fighter-trainer version of UO, 20 aircraft converted from UO-3, delivered January–July 1927)				
F3U				(Original XF3U-1 was replaced by XSBU-1 after original acceptance; it was later reaccepted under different serial number.)				
F4U	6/30/38	5/29/40	Vought	XF4U-1, -3, -4, -5; F4U-1, -1C, -1D, -2, -4, -4B, -4C, -4P, -5, -5N, -5NL, -5P, -7; AU-1.	7,829 (1,067)	10/3/42 VF-12	12/31/55 VC-4, F4U-5N	M. Inverted gull wing; 20mm cannon in -1C, -4B, 4C, -5 and subsequent; -2, night fighter; P&W R-2800, 2,000 hp to 2,700 hp.
			Brewster Goodyear	F3A-1 FG-1, -1D.	735(430) 4,006 (989)			
F6U	12/29/44	2/50	Vought	XF6U-1; F6U-1	33	VX-3	3/52	M. Skin of dural-balsa sandwich; afterburning, WE J34, 4,100#.
F7U	6/25/46	12/55	Vought	XF7U-1; F7U-1, -3, -3M, -3P	305	4/54 VF-81	11/30/57 VA-66 F7U-3	M. Sweptwing; tailless; 2 WE J34, 4,900# in -1; J46, 5,800# in -3.
F8U				(Redesignated F-8)				
MB-3	1921	1/22	Th. Morse	MB-3	11	Quantico 3/22	Quantico 11/23	B. WAC H, 300 hp. Land.
TS	1921	4/22 est	Curtiss NAF	TS-1 TS-1, -2, -3.	34 9	12/22 Langley	5/31/27 VF-1, TS-1	B. Conv't; LA J-1, 200 hp in -1; AM U-8-D, 210 hp in -2; WAC E-2, 180 hp in -3.
VE-7	1920	5/20 est	Vought NAF	VE-7, -7SF, VE-7, -7G, -7GF, -7H, -7SF.	60 69	7/20 GITMO	5/1/28 VT-6D-14, VE-7	B/2. (SF, single place). Land; -7H, Sea; WAC E-2, 180 hp. See Observation series.

* Dates in this column through 1969 refer to squadrons. After 1969, these dates refer to the inventory.
** Omits 23 F4B-4A obtained from Army 12/39 and 1 F4B-4 built from spares 6/34.

Patrol and Early Warning Series

Aircraft Designation	Date First Aircraft Contract	Date First Flight	Date Last Delivery	Number Accepted	Manufacturer	Models Accepted	Squadron Delivery	Last Reported in Squadron or * Inventory	Description
A-29	(See PBO)								
B-24	(See PB4Y-1)								
B-25	(See PBJ)								
B-34	(See PV)								
EC-121	(See WV)								
E-1	6/15/56	12/17/56	12/61	88	Grumman	WF-2	11/59 VAW-12	3/31/78 E-1B	M/4. Carrier parasol radome; 2 WAC R-1820, 1,525 hp.
E-2	3/12/59	10/21/60	4/1/94	215(14)	Grumman	W2F-1; E-2A, -2B, -2C.	1/64 VAW-11		M/5. Carrier; 2 position parasol rotodome; 4 vertical tails; 2 AL T56, 4,050 eshp.
E-6			5/28/92	21	Boeing	E-6A	13/4/90 VQ-3		M/18. 4 GE/SNECMA CFM-56, 24,000# each.
EC-130				25	Lockheed	EC-130G, -130Q		3/3/84	See C-130 specifications.
P-2	2/19/43	5/17/45	9/62	1,036 (193)	Lockheed	XP2V-1, -2, P2V-2, -3, -3W, -4, -5, -6, -6B, -7, -7U, -7S; SP-2H.	3/47 VP-ML-2	4/82 SP-2H	M/7-9. Land; 2 WAC R-3350, 3,090 to 3,700 hp; also in -7, 2 WE J34, 3,400#.
P-3	2/2/59		11/30/90	610(36)	Lockheed	YP3V-1; P3V-1/P-3A, -3B, -3C, -3F; YP-3C; RP-3A, -3D; WP-3D.	8/22/62 VP-8		M/12. Land; 4 AL T56, 4,500 to 4,900 eshp.
P-4	(Redesignation of P4Y-2)								
P-5	6/26/46	4/30/48	12/60	239(21)	Martin	XP5M-1; P5M-1, -2.	4/23/52 VP-44	10/31/67 VP-40, SP-5B	M/7. Boat; long hull; faired step; 2 WAC R-3350, 3,250 hp.
PB2B	(PBY-5 manufactured by Boeing of Canada, Vancouver, B.C.)								
PBJ	7/7/42		6/45	706	North American	PBJ-1, -1C, -1D, -1G, -1H, -1J.	2/43 VMB-413	1/31/46 PAC, PBJ-1J	M/4-5. Land; 2 WAC R-2600, 1,700 hp.

PBM	6/30/37	2/18/39	Martin	XPBM-1 -2, -3, 3C, -3D, -3R, -3S, -5, -5A; PBM-1, -3C, -3D, -3R, -3S, -5, -5A, -5E, -5G.	1,366	9/1/40 VP-55	7/31/56 VP-50, PBM-5S2	M/7-9. Boat; (-5A, amphibian); WAC R-2600, 1,600 to 1,900 hp; 2 P&W R-2800, 2,100 hp in -5.
PBN			(PBY manufactured by Naval Aircraft Factory; longer bow)					
PBO	9/41	10/41	Lockheed	PBO-1	20	10/29/41 VP-82	10/31/42 VP-82, PBO-1	M/5. 1st USN land type patrol; 2 WAC R-1820, 1,000 hp.
PBY	10/28/33	3/35	Consolidated	XP3Y-1; XPBY-5A; PBY-1, -2, -3, -4, -5, -6A; 0A-10, -5B, -6A.	2,387 (636)	10/5/36 VP-11F	6/1/49 VP-32, PBY-6A	M/5-8. Boat (-5A & -6A, 0A-10 & -10B, amphibian); 2 P&W R-1830, 900 to 1,200 hp.
			Boeing NAF Vickers	PB2B-1, -2 PBN-1 PBV-1A, 0A-10B.	290(270) 155(137) 230(230)			
PB2Y	7/23/36	12/17/37	Consolidated Rohr	XPB2Y-1, -3; PB2Y-2, -3, -3B. PB2Y-3R	176(33) 41	12/31/40 VP-13	11/30/45 PAC, PB2Y-3/-5	M/9-10. Boat; 4 P&W R-1830, 1,200 hp.
PB4Y-1	7/7/42	1/45	Consolidated	PB4Y-1, P4Y-1	977**	10/42 VP-51	5/31/56 VJ-62, P4Y-1P	M/6-11. Land; twin tail; 4 P&W R-1830, 1,200 hp.
PB4Y-2	5/3/43	10/45	Consolidated	PB4Y-2, P4Y-2	739***	8/44 VB-200	6/30/54 VW-3, P4Y-2S	M/11. Land; single tail; 4 P&W R-1830, 1,200 hp.
PD	12/29/27	5/29 est	Douglas	PD-1	25	7/10/29 VP-7B	10/31/36 VP-6F, PD-1	B/4. Boat; aluminum alloy with fabric covered wings; 2 WAC R-1750, 525 hp.
P2D	7/25	1/27/27	Douglas	T2D-I; P2D-I	30	5/25/27 VT-2	2/28/37 VP-3F, P2D-1	B/3. Twin float; duralumin and fabric; 2 WAC R-1820, 575 hp.
PH	12/29/27	11/29 est	Hall	XPH-1; PH-1	10	6/24/32 VP-8S	5/19/37 VP-8F, PH-1	B/5. Boat; lightweight metal structure with fabric covered wings; 2 WAC R-1820, 575 hp.
PK	11/30/29	3/31 est	Keystone	PK-1	18	9/23/31 VP-1B	7/30/38 VP-1, PK-1	B/5. Boat; twin tail; 2 WAC R-1820, 575 hp.

Patrol Series—Continued

Designation	Date 1	Date 2	Number	Manufacturer	Models	Squadron	Status	Characteristics
PM	5/31/29	7/30 est	55	Martin	PM-1, -2	8/21/30 VP-8S	4/30/38 VP-16, PM-1	B/5. Boat; 2 WAC R-1820, 575 hp.
P3M	2/28/28	12/28 est	9 / 1	Martin / Consolidated	P3M-1, XPY-1	4/29/31 VP-10S	5/31/38 VP-15, P3M-2	M/4-5.(1st monoplane patrol); 2 or 3 P&W R-1340, 450 hp.
P4M	7/6/44	9/20/46	21	Martin	XP4M-1; P4M-1	6/28/50 VP-21	5/31/60 VQ-1, P4M-1	M/9. Land; 2 P&W R-4360, 3,250 hp and 2 AL J33, 4,600#.
P5M	(Redesignated P-5)							
P0-1W	(Initial designation for WV, the Airborne Early Warning version of the Lockheed Constellation)							
PV	7/7/42		2,162	Lockheed	PV-1 -2, -2C, -2D, -3.	10/42 VP-82	12/45 VP-ML-3, PV-2	M/4. Land; 2 P&W R-2800, 2,000 hp.
P2V	(Redesignated P-2)							
P3V	(Redesignated P-3)							
PY	(Prototype for P3M)							
P2Y	5/26/31	3/26/32	47	Consolidated	XP2Y-1, P2Y-1, -2, -3.	2/1/33 VP-10S	3/31/41 VP-43, P2Y-3	Sesquiplane/5. Enclosed cabins (2 or 3 in XP2Y-1) WAC R-1820, 575 to 700 hp.
P3Y	(Initial designation of PBY)							
P4Y	(Redesignation of PB4Y-1 and -2)							
PT	(Torpedo plane manufactured by Naval Aircraft Factory, see Attack series)							
WF	(Redesignated E-1)							
W2F	(Redesignated E-2)							
WV	9/28/48	7/52	152	Lockheed	P0-1W; WV-2, -3	9/58	3/31/79 EC-121K	M/26-31. Land; vertical fin and belly radomes; 4 WAC R-3350, 2,500-3,250 hp.

* Dates in this column through 1969 refer to squadrons. After 1969, these dates refer to inventory.

** Transport versions of PB4Y-1, 3 RY-1 and 5 RY-2, not included in totals.

*** Transport versions of PB4Y-2, 33 RY-3, of which three were for U.K., not included in totals.

Observation Series

Aircraft Designation	Date First Aircraft Contract	Date First Flight	Number Accepted	Date Last Delivery	Manufacturer	Models Accepted	Squadron Delivery	Last Reported in Squadron or * Inventory	Description
M-8	1919	8/19 est	17 36	3/21	Loening NAF	M-8, M-80, M-81-S, M-81.	8/20** LANT	7/21 PAC, M-81	1st USN production monoplane; M-8 and M-80, land; M-81, conv't; M-80, 2-place reconnaissance; M-81, 1-place fighter or 2-place; Hispano Suiza, 300 hp.
MO	1922	12/22 est	36	1/24	Martin	MO-1	2/21/23 VO-2	Prior to 1/26	M/3. Conv't; aluminum frame; CAM D-12, 300 hp.
O2B	1924	3/25 est	30	1925	Boeing	O2B-1	4/25 Quantico	2/28/29 VO-9M, O2B-1	B/2. Land; DH-4B with steel tube fuselage; Lib., 400 hp.
O-1	(Redesignation of OE)								
OC	6/30/27	12/27 est	27	1928	Curtiss	F8C-1, -3; OC-1, -2.	1/21/28 VO-7M	9/35 VJ-7M, OC-2	B/2. Land; Marine obs. and attack; P&W R-1340, 410 hp.
O2C	(Redesignation for F8C-5, see Fighter Series)								
OE	6/51 est		97(4)	8/1/67	Cessna	OE-1, -2; O-1G	11/51 VMO-1, VMO-6	3/31/70 O-1C, O-1G	M/2. Land; CO O-470, 265 hp.
OJ	6/28/29	5/31 est	40	12/34	B/J	XOJ-1; OJ-2	3/33 VS-6B	2/29/36 VS-5B, OJ-2	B/2. Conv't; P&W R-985, 400 hp.
OL	1924	5/25 est	84 26	3/32	Loening Keystone	OL-1, -2, -3, -6, -8. OL-9	2/26 Quantico	7/38 NRAB Oakland	B/2-3. Amph; PKD 1500, 400 to 525 hp; Lib., 400 hp in -2; P&W R-1340, 450 hp in -8 and -9.
OS2N	(OS2U manufactured at NAF)								
OS2U	3/22/37	5/38 est	1,218 (154) 300	11/42	Vought NAF	XOS2U-1; OS2U-1, -2, -3. OS2N-1	8/16/40 VO-4	5/31/46 PAC, OS2U-3	M/2. Conv't; P&W R-985, 450 hp.
O2U	1926	11/26 est	291	2/30	Vought	O2U-1, -2, -3, -4.	12/17/27 VO-7M	4/30/36 VB-2B, O2U-2	B/2. Conv't; P&W R-1340, 450 hp.

Observation Series—Continued

Desig.	Date	Date		Qty	Mfr.	Models	Service	Service	Remarks
03U	1/18/30	6/30 est		330	Vought	03U-1, -2, -3, -6; X04U-2; X03U-6; SU-1, -2, -3, -4.	7/15/30 VO-3B	3/42 VJ-3	B/2. Conv't; amph. or land; P&W R-1340, 450 hp.
OV-10	10/15/64	7/16/65	1977	356 (239)	North American	OV-10A, -10B, -10D.	2/23/68 HML-267	4/94 VMO-4, OV-10D	M/2. Light Armed Reconnaissance Aircraft (LARA) for Counter-insurgency (COIN) missions; 2 Air T76, 715 shp.
OY	11/1/43	8/45		306	Consolidated	OY-1, -2	1/44 VMO-1, -2, -3, -4	11/30/54 VMO-1, OY-2	M/2. Land; LY O-435, 185 hp.
SC						(CS design, manufactured by Martin in 1920's, see Attack Series)			
SC	3/31/43	2/16/44		577	Curtiss	XSC-1, -1A, -2; SC-1, -2.	10/12/44 Alaska (CB 1)	10/1/49 HU-2, SC-1	M/1. Sea; WAC R-1820, 1,300 hp.
SOC	6/19/33	4/34 est		259	Curtiss	X03C-1; XSOC-1, SOC-1, -2, -3.	11/12/35 VS-5B	11/30/46 LANT, SOC-1	B/2. Sea; P&W R-1340, 550 hp.
				44	NAF	SON-1			
SO3C	5/9/38	10/6/39		794(250)	Curtiss	XSO3C-1; SO3C-1, -2, -2C, -3.	7/42 VCS-12	3/31/44 VS-46, SO3C-3	M/2. Conv't; RA V-770, 520 hp.
SON						(SOC-3 manufactured by the Naval Aircraft Factory)			
SU						(03U converted to carrier-based scout)			
UO	1922	19/22 est		163(2)	Vought	UO-1, -4, FU-1	6/14/24 Tennessee (BB 43)	12/31/29 VS-8A, VO-6M, UO-1.	B/2. Conv't; LA/WAC R-790 (J-1 to J-5) 200 to 220 hp.
VE-7						(See Fighter Series. Of the 129 total, 70 were VE-7SF fighters; 39 were VE-7 and VE-7H trainers; 20 were VE-7G observation planes)			
VE-9	1922	6/22 est		21	Vought	VE-9, VE-9H	6/22 Nevada (BB 36)	10/30/30 Navy Mission Rio de Janeiro, Brazil, VE-9	B/2. Land; -9H, Sea; WAC E-3 180 hp.

* Dates in this column through 1969 refer to squadrons. After 1969 these dates refer to the inventory.

** Estimated date.

World War I Aircraft

Designation	First Order (fiscal year)	Delivery (D) or First Flight (F)	Number Accepted	Manufacturer	Models Accepted*	Service History							Description
						Delivery Continental		For Overseas Shipment		Withdrawal from Inventory			
						Date	Destination	Date	Destination	Date	Location	Model	
DH-4	1918	5/24/18 (D)	333	Dayton-Wright	DH-4, -4B	6/4/18	Miami	5/24/18		10/31/26	Dahlgren	DH-4B-2	B/2. Land; bomber & fighter; British design; USN obtained from U.S. Army; two syn. Marlin guns, 2 flex. Lewis guns; Lib., 360 hp.
F-5	-918	7/15/18 (F)	30	Canadian Aeroplanes	F-5L	10/4/18	Hampton Roads	10/12/18	Pauillac	1/31	Hampton Roads	F-5L	B/4. Boat; ASW; British F-5 adapted to American manufacture; 5 Lewis guns, 4-230# bombs; 2 Lib., 360 hp.
			60	Curtiss	F-5L								
			137	NAF	F-5L								
H-12	1917	3/17 (D)	20	Curtiss	H-12	1/17/18	Hampton Roads		United States Only	7/17/20		H-12	B/2 to 4. Boat; training or ASW; 2-160# (Mk IV) bombs, Lewis gun, radio; 2 CAM V2-3, 200 hp or 2 Lib., 300 hp.
H-16	1918	2/1/18 (D)	124	Curtiss	H-16	2/18	Hampton Roads	3/18	England	5/30	NAF	H-16	B/4. Boat; ASW; was 1st aircraft built at NAF; radio; 5 Lewis guns, 4-230# bombs; 2 Lib., 360 hp.
			150	NAF	H-16		Pensacola						
HS	1918	10/21/17 (F) (with Lib. engine).	678	Curtiss	HS-1, -2L, -3L	1/14/18	Hampton Roads	3/25/18	Pauillac	9/28	Hampton Roads	HS-2L	B/3. Boat; pusher; ASW; some aircraft delivered as HS-1, and converted to HS-2 with 25% greater wing area; Lewis gun, 2-230# (180# in HS-1) bombs; Davis gun or radio in some machines; Lib., 360 hp.
			250	LWF	HS-2L								
			80	Standard	HS-2L								
			60	Gallaudet	HS-2L	HS-2L							
				25	Boeing								

World War I Aircraft—Continued

Designation	First Order (fiscal year)	Delivery (D) or First Flight (F)	Number Accepted	Manufacturer	Models Accepted*	Service History							Description
						Delivery		For Overseas Shipment		Withdrawal from Inventory		
						Continental						
						Date	Destination	Date	Destination	Date	Location	Model	
NC	1918	10/4/18 (F)	2 4	Loughead Curtiss	HS-2L NC-1 thru -4	5/2/19	Rockaway			5/20/24		NC-10	B/5. ASW; boat; 3 Lib., 360 or 400 hp; NC-TA (Trans-Atlantic Type) had 3 tractor and 1 pusher, Lib. 400 hp.
			6	NAF	NC-5 thru -10								
R	1916	11/16 est. (D)	200	Curtiss	R-3, -5, -6, -6L, -9.	6/20/17	Pensacola	1/18	Azores	9/26	Pearl Harbor	R-6L	B/2. Twin Float; Curtiss, 200 hp; trainer, but used for ASW; R-9 fitted for Lewis gun and small bombs; R-6L with Lib., 360 hp, used as torpedo plane.

* Excludes aircraft erected from spares at the Naval Aircraft Factory and various air stations, even when Bureau Numbers were assigned.

Transport and Training Aircraft

In basic organization and concept this table generally follows the table on combat aircraft (Appendix 6); the major difference is that these tables include only the major/primary transport and training aircraft used by the Navy since the beginning of World War II. Service history data is somewhat broader because of aircraft assignment to shore stations in some cases rather than squadrons. The descriptive data is generally self-explanatory. For explanation of engine nomenclature, see discussion of combat aircraft.

An early Navy transport, the RS-3.

Transport and Training Aircraft Data

Transport Aircraft

Aircraft Designation	Date First Aircraft Contract	Date First Flight	Date Last Delivery	Number Accepted	Manufacturer	Models Accepted	Base or Squadron Delivery	Last Reported in Squadron or * Inventory	Description
Boeing-314	(Acquired Feb 1942 from Pan AM)			5	Boeing	Boeing 314		End of WW-II	M. Flyingboat, four WAC R-2600, 1,600 hp each.
GV/C-130	6/30/59	6/13/61	3/11/95	146	Lockheed	C-130F, C-130T, C-130G; LC-130F; LC-130B; LC-130R; KC-130; EC-130Q; EC-130E; DC-130A; HC-130R; KC-130R, KC-130T.	VMGR-352		M/7 crew. In-flight refueling and transport. Four AL T56-A-16, 4,910 eshp each.
JRB/C-45	6/12/40	10/27/40	10/10/44	209	Beech	JRB-1, JRB-2, JRB-3, JRB-4.	NAS Anacostia	9/69	M/2 crew. Six passengers, two P&W R-985, 450 hp each.
JRC	4/21/43	5/24/45	12/20/43	67	Cessna	JRC-1		5/47	M/2 crew. Four or five passenger, two Jacobs R-775, 450 hp each.
JRF	4/24/39	11/29/39	12/18/45	256	Grumman	XJ3F-1; JRF-1, JRF-3, JRF-4, JRF-5, JRF-6B.	VJ-1	12/58	M/2 or 3 crew. Four to seven passengers, amphibian two P&W R-985, 450 hp each.
JRM	6/27/44	11/1/45	4/4/47	5	Martin	JRM-1	VR-2	1/57	M. Flyingboat, four WAC R-3350-8, 2,300 hp each.
J4F	6/10/42	2/28/44		131	Grumman	J4F-1, J4F-2	NAS New York	8/48	M/2 crew. Three passenger amphibian, two RA L-440, 200 hp each.
RY	3/14/44	10/12/45		47	Convair	RY-1, -2, -3	MarFair West	3/49	M/3 crew. Forty-four passengers, four P&W R-1830-94, 1,350 hp each.
R3Y	9/26/50	7/26/56	12/28/45	11	Convair	XP5Y-1; R3Y-1, R3Y-2.	VR-2	1/72	M. Nose loading door for vehicles, flyingboat, four AL XT40-A-4, 5,500 eshp each.
R4D/ C-47	9/16/40	2/9/42	5/31/45	609	Douglas	R4D-1 thru R4D-7.	BAD-1 (Marine Corps)	11/83	M/3 crew. Twenty seven passengers, two P&W R-1830-92, 1,200 hp each.
R4D-8/ C-117				100	Douglas	R4D-8	NAS Norfolk, 12/51	China Lake, 1982	M/3. Thirty passengers, Two WAC R-1820-20, 1,475 hp each, converted from earlier R4D versions.

Designation	Date	Date	No.	Manufacturer	Model	Unit	Date	Remarks
R4Q/ C-119	4/22/48	5/25/53	99	Fairchild	R4Q-1, R4Q-2.	VMR-252	5/75	M/5 crew. Forty four passenger, two WAC R-3350-36WA, 3,400 hp each.
R4Y/ C-131	9/1/50	12/30/57	39	Convair	R4Y-1; R4Y-1Z, C-131H.	Hq Marine Corps Flt. Sect.	3/88	M/4 crew. Forty four passengers, two P&W R-2800-52W, 2,500 hp each.
R5C	8/31/55	7/6/45	130	Curtiss	R5C-1	VMJ-3	8/56	M/4 crew. Fifty troops, two P&W R-2800-51, 2,000 hp each.
R5D/C-54	6/1/48	5/31/45	194	Douglas	R5D-1, R5D-2, R5D-3, R5D-4.	VR-1	7/73	M/4 crew. Thirty passengers, four P&W R-2000-7, 1,350 hp each.
R50	7/31/42	10/5/43	95	Lockheed	XR50-1; R50-1 R50-2, R50-3, R50-4, R50-5. R50-6	NAS Jacksonville	6/50	M/2 crew. Four to seven passengers, two WAC R-1820-40, 1,200 hp each.
R6D/ C-118	11/13/39	5/27/53	65	Douglas	R6D-1, R6D-1Z.	VR-3	10/83	M/4 crew. Four P&W R-2800-52W, 2,500 hp each.
R70/ R7V	8/18/50	5/28/54	55	Lockheed	R7V-1, R7V-1P, R7V-2	VR-7	9/74	M. Accomodates 72 troops, four WAC R-3350-91, 3,250 hp each.
C-1	9/26/50		87	Grumman	C-1A (TF-1)	VR-22	4/85	M/2. Accomodates 9 passengers. Designed as COD aircraft. Two WR-1820-82, 1,525 hp each.
C-2	2/6/90		39	Grumman	C-2A	VRC-50		M/3. Accomodates 39 passengers. Designed as COD aircraft. Two AL T56-A-8B, 4,050 shp each.
C-9			16	McDonnell Douglas	C-9, C-9B (DC-9)	VR-30 NAS Alameda		M. Accomodates 107 passengers. P&W JT8-D-9, 14,500#.
C-20	12/13/94		7	Gulfstream	C-20	NAF Washington		M/5. Accomodates 14 passengers, two RR Spay Mk 511-8, 11,400# each.
C-45 (See JRB)								
C-47 (See JRB)								
C-117 (See JRB)								
C-118 (See JRB)								
C-119 (See JRB)								
C-130 (See JRB)								

C-131 (See JRB)

Training Aircraft

Aircraft Designation	Date First Aircraft Contract	Date First Flight	Date Last Delivery	Number Accepted	Manufacturer	Models Accepted	Squadron Delivery	Last Reported in Squadron or * Inventory	Description
JN-4		5/10/17	4/11/23	216	Curtiss	JN-4A, -4B, -4H, -6H, -4HG.	Marine Advance Base Force, Philadelphia	4/27	B/2. Land; flight and gunnery trainer; 1 Wright-Hispano, 150 hp.
N-9		11/16/15	10/28/18	531	Curtiss	N-9H	Miami	8/28	B/2. Water, single float; primary trainer; CAM OXX -6, 100 hp; -9H Hispano-Suiza A, 150 hp.
NB		1/21/25	12/7/23	93	Boeing	NB-1, -2, -3, -4	Langley (CV 1)	12/31	B/2. Land, convert't; primary and gunnery trainer; 1 .30 machine gun on scarf ring; Law J-1, 200 hp; Wright-Hispano E-4, 180 hp.
NE		3/16/42	8/9/45	250	Piper	NE-1, -2	NRAB Anacostia	12/47	M/2. Land; primary trainer; CO O-170, 65 hp.
NH		1/15/43	3/7/44	205	Howard	NH-1	NAS Atlanta	11/47	M/4. Instrument trainer; P&W R-985, 400 hp.
NJ		11/16/37	8/28/38	40	North American	NJ-1	NAS Pensacola	8/44	M/2. Basic trainer; fixed under carrage, P&W R-1340-6, 500 hp.
NR		8/4/41	10/8/41	100	Ryan	NR-1	NAS Jacksonville	9/43	M/2. Primary trainer; all metal; Kinner R-440-3, 125 hp.
NY		5/18/26	2/21/30	292	Consolidated	NY-1, -2, -2A, -3.	Pensacola	12/37	B/2. Land, convert't; primary trainer; steel tube fuselage, wooden wings; WAC R-790-8, 220 hp.
NS				61	Stearman	NS-1		11/44	B/2. Land; primary trainer WAC R-790-8, 200 hp.
N2C		7/10/29	12/20/30	54	Curtiss	N2C-1, -2	NRAB Squantum	5/38	B/2. Land; used mainly in reserve training; 1 WAC R-790-8, 200 hp; R-760-94, 240 hp.
N2S		9/30/40	3/4/44	3700	Stearman	N2S-1, -2, -3, -5.	NAS Anacostia	6/50	B/2. Land trainer; the most prevelent trainer in WW-II;

Designation	Date	Date	Number	Manufacturer	Models	Location	Date	Remarks
N2T	4/16/42	10/11/42	262	Timm	N2T-1	NAS Pensacola	8/44	M/2. Land, primary trainer, plastic bonded plywood construction; CO R-670-4, 229 hp.
N3N	10/26/36	1/23/42	998	NAF	N3N-1, -2, -3	NAS Pensacola	10/59	B/2. Land, conver't; primary trainer; all fabric covered; WAC R-760-2, 235 hp.
SNC			305	Curtiss	SNC-1		10/44	M/2. Land; primary trainer; WAC R-974, 420 hp, all metal retractable landing gear.
SNJ	11/8/39	8/27/45	4024	North American	SNJ-1 thru -6	NAS Pensacola	6/68	M/2. Land; basic trainer; first trainer with retractable landing gear and covered cockpits; 1 P&W R-1340, 550 hp.
SNV	8/5/41	2/28/44	2000	Vultee	SNV-1, -2	NAS Corpus Christi	4/46	M/2. Land; basic trainer; retractable landing gear; P&W R-985, 450 hp.
T-28	1/28/54	10/29/57	1175	North American	T-28B, T-28C	NATC Patuxent River	4/82	M/2. Land; the first of the standardized trainers for USAF and Navy. WAC R-1820-86, 1425 hp.
T-34	6/28/56	6/18/84	423	Beech	T-34A, T-34B, T-34C.	NAS Pensacola	10/93	M/2. Land; primary trainer, CON 0-470-13, 225 hp.
T-45	4/80		100	McDonnell Douglas				M/2. Land; jet trainer; RR Mk 851 turbofan.
TO/TV	10/16/48	9/29/48	50	Lockheed	TO-1/TV-1	Undetermined	10/57	M/1. Land; advanced jet trainer; AL J33-A-20, 5,200#.
TO/TV/T-33	11/22/49	6/28/47	698	Lockheed	TO-2/TV-2/T-33	Muroc	7/74	M/2. Land.
TT		7/14/58	14	Tempco	TT-1	NAAS Saufley Field	10/60	M/2. Land; primary jet trainer; CON J69, 920#.
T2J/T-2	2/25/59	12/18/74	519	North American	T2J-1; T-2A, T-2B, T-2C.	NATC Patuxent River	6/94	M/2. Land; all-purpose jet trainer; 2 GE 085-GE-4, 2,950# each.
T2V/T-1	12/26/57	2/14/58	150	Lockheed	T2V-1/T-1A	NAS Pensacola	7/72	M/2. Land; deck-landing, advanced jet trainer; AL J33-A-24, 6,100#.

* The dates in th s column refer to either a squadron or the Navy's aircraft inventory. If only a date is listed then it refers to the inventory.

H-2 stands plane guard during flight operations K31638

HUS-1 Utility, observation and rescue helicopter 105087

Marine CH-53A, Sea Stallion, lifts large Truck NH 69965

Naval Helicopters

In basic organization and concept this table generally follows the table on combat aircraft (Appendix 6); the major difference is that these tables include practically all helicopters with which the Navy has operated. Because of the helicopter's capability for tethered flight and low altitude free flight, first flight data was not always available and was sometimes of uncertain meaning. Because of this, first acceptance was used as being somewhat analogous to first flight of a fixed wing aircraft. Service history data is somewhat broader than for fixed wing aircraft. To accommodate the broader scope of models covered, assignment to experimental squadrons (VX) is reported for models that were not later assigned to operational units. Marine Helicopter Experimental Squadron (HMX) is considered to be an operational squadron. The descriptive data is generally self-explanatory. For explanation of engine nomenclature, see discussion of combat aircraft.

A jeep is loaded aboard an HR2S-1 (H-37) for transportation ashore from the carrier, USN-1046883.

Naval Helicopter Data

Aircraft Designation	Date First Aircraft Contract	Date First Acceptance	Date Final Acceptance	Number Accepted	Manufacturer	Models Accepted	Squadron Delivery	Last Reported in Squadron or * Inventory	Description
DSN	(Redesignated QH-50, see H-50)								
H-1	6/14/62	2/64		1299	Bell	AH-1G, -1J, -1S, -1T; -1W; HH-1K; TH-1E, -1L; UH-1D, -1E, -1L, -1N.	3/64 VMO-1		Rotor 44'D & tail rotor; observation; one crew; 4 pass., LY T43, 1,150 hp.
H-2	(See HU2K for data)								
H-3	(See HSS-2 for data)								
H-12	(See HTE for data)								
H-13	(See HTL for data)								
H-19	(See HRS-3 and HO4S-3 for data)								
H-23	(See HTE for data)								
H-25	(See HUP-2 for data)								
H-34	(See HUS and HSS-1 for data)								
H-37	(See HR2S for data)								
H-43	(See HUK and HOK for data)								
H-46	9/29/61	5/62	01/31/77	677	Boeing	HRB-1/CH-46A, -46D, -46F; UH-46A, -46D.	6/64 HMM-265		Tandem rotors, 50'D; assault transport; 3 crew; 17 passenger; 2 GE T58, 1,250 hp.
H-50	12/31/58	3/60	10/20/69	633 (1)	Gyrodyne	DSN-1, -3; QH-50C, -50D.	1/23/63 Buck (DD 761)	1/31/71 QH-50C/D	Coaxil rotors, 20'D; ASW drone; BO T50, 300 hp in QH-50C.
H-53	2/7/63	5/64		733	Sikorsky	CH-53A, -53D, -53E; HH-53B, -53C; RH-53D; MH-53E.	11/2/66 HMH-463		Rotor 72'D and tail rotor; assault transport; 38 passenger or 4 ton; 2 GE T64, 2,850 hp.
H-57	1968	10/10/68		140	Bell	TH-57A, -57B, -57C.	11/10/68 HT-8		Trainer; 5 place; rotor 33'4" D and tail rotor 5'5"; -57C powered by 1 Allison 250-C-20J gas turbine, 317 shp.
H-60	2/78	3/31/80		1010	Sikorsky	SH-60B, -60F; HH-60A, -60S, -60J, -60H; UH-60A; VH-60A.	9/28/83 HSL-41		LAMPS MK III, ASW. Rotor 53' 7" D and tail rotor. 3 crew. 2 GE-401T700, 1,284 hp each.

HJP   (XHJP-1 was prototype for HUP-1)

Designation				No.	Mfr.	Models			Remarks
HNS	2/20/43	10/43	12/44	68	Sikorsky	HNS-1	11/43 NAS New York	12/31/47 VX-3, HNS-1	Rotor 38'D plus tail rotor; 1st USN helo. WR R-550, 200 hp.
HOK (H-43**)	6/26/50	4/53	12/57	83	Kaman	HOK-1	4/12/56 VMO-1	5/31/65 VMO-2, OH-43D	Side by side rotors, 47'D; utility, 2 place; CO R-975, 525 hp.
HOS	3/20/43	9/44	1/46	3	Sikorsky	XHOS-1	10/44 NAS New York	1/31/48 VX-3, HOS-1	Rotor 38'D and tail rotor; utility, 2-place; FR 0-435, 235 hp.
				102	Nash-Kel	HOS-1			
HO2S	6/22/43	12/45	12/45	44	Sikorsky	HO2S-1	2/46 NAS New York	5/31/46 CGAS Eliz. City, HO2S-1	Rotor 48'D and tail rotor; utility and rescue; 2 crew, 2 passenger; P&W R-985, 450 hp.
HO3S	9/27/46	11/46	1/50	92	Sikorsky	HO3S-1	12/47 VU-7	11/30/54 HU-1, HO4S-3	Rotor 48'D and tail rotor; utility, 4-place; P&W R-985, 450 hp.
HO4S-3 (H-19**)	4/23/50	8/50	1/58	129	Sikorsky	HO4S-1, -2, -3, -3G.	12/27/50 HU-2	12/31/60 HU-4, HO4S-3	Rotor 53'D and tail rotor; ASW, observation and rescue; crew 2 or 3. P&W R-1340, 600 hp; WAC R-1300, 800 hp in -3.
HO5S	6/30/50	2/52	2/53	79	Sikorsky	HO5S-1	7/1/52 VMO-1	6/30/57 VMO-1, HO5S-1	Rotor 33'D and tail rotor; observation, liaison and utility; 5 place; ACM 0-425, 245 hp.
HRB	(Initial designation for H-46)								
HRP	2/1/44	6/47	12/50	82	Piasecki	XHRP-1; HRP-1, -2.	4/48 HU-2	2/28/53 HS-3, HRP-1	Tandem rotors 41'D; 1st tandem conf; 2 crew, 8 passenger, P&W R-1340, 600 hp.
HRS-3 (H-19**)	8/2/50	3/51	11/57	271	Sikorsky	HRS-1, -2, -3	4/7/51 HMR-161	2/28/69 HC-5, CH-19E	Rotor 53'D and tail rotor; assault transport; 2 crew, 10 passenger; P&W R-1340, 600 to 800 hp.
HR2S (H-37**)	5/9/51	10/53	2/59	59	Sikorsky	HR2S-1, -1W	3/20/57 HMR(M)-461	3/31/66 HMH-462 CH-37C	Rotor 72'D and tail rotors; assault transport; 2 crew, 20 passenger, 2 P&W R-2800, 2,100 hp.
HSL	6/28/50	10/53	10/56	51	Bell	XHSL-1; HSL-1.		9/59	Tandem rotors, 51'6"D; ASW search or attack; 2 or 3 crew; P&W R-2800, 1,900 hp.

Designation	Date	Date	Date*	Number	Manufacturer	Models	Date	Date	Characteristics
HSS-1 (H-34**)	6/30/52	2/54	4/66	385	Sikorsky	XHSS-1, HSS-1, SH-34J.	8/55 HS-3	3/31/74 UH-34D	Rotor 56'D and tail rotor; ASW; 2 to 4 crew; WAC R-1820, 1,525 hp.
HSS-2 (H-3**)	12/24/57	3/59	11/26/75	396	Sikorsky	HSS-2/SH-3A, SH-3D, HSS-2Z/VH-3A; CH-3B, -3E.	6/61	5/96	Rotor 59'D and tail rotor; all weather ASW; "sea-worthy hull"; 4 crew, 2 GE T58, 1,050 hp.
HTE (H-12/ H-23**)	4/17/50	5/50	8/63	108	Hiller	UH-12A; HTE-1, -2.	1/19/51 HTU-1	10/31/52 HTU-1, HTE-2	Rotor 35'D and tail rotor; training and utility, 3 place; FR 0-335, 200 hp in HTE-2.
HTK	9/5/50	11/51	10/53	29	Kaman	HTK-1	1/28/53 HU-2	11/31/55 HU-2, HTK	Side by side rotors, 40'D; trainer and general utility, 3 place; LY 0-435, 255 hp.
HTL (H-13**)	6/20/46	2/47	7/59	187	Bell	HTL-1, -2, -3, -4, -5, -6, -7.	4/48 HU-2	6/30/73 UH-13P	Rotor 35'D and tail rotor; trainer and general utility, 2 or 3 place; ACM 0-325, 178-200 hp, LY 0-435, 240 hp in -7.
HU	(Redesignated H-1)								
HUK (H-43**)	12/27/56	5/58	12/58	24	Kaman	HUK-1	8/1/58 HU-2	4/30/65 VMO-2, UH-43C	Side by side rotors, 50'D; cargo and rescue; 2 crew, 3 passenger; P&W R-1340, 600 hp.
HU2K (H-2**)	11/29/57	4/59	4/28/93	256	Kaman	HU2K-1/UH-2A, -2B; SH-2F, -2B.	12/18/62 HU-2	6/94	Rotor 44'D and tail rotor; 2 crew, 4 passenger; GE T58, 1,050 hp; tandem engines prototyped in a -2B.
HUL (H-13**)	4/2/55	11/55	3/59	30	Bell	HUL-1, -1G	1/7/57 HU-2	6/30/73 UH-13P	Rotor 37'D and tail rotor; transport and utility; 1 crew, 3 passenger; LY 0-435, 240 hp.
HUP-2 (H-25**)	2/8/46	1/49	6/54	476	Piasecki	XHJP-1; HUP-1, -2, -2S; H-25A.	1/11/51 HU-2	8/31/64 VU-1, HU-1, UH-25B	Tandem rotors, 35'D; ASW and utility; 3 crew, 4 passenger, CO R-975, 550 hp.
HUS (H-34**)	10/15/54	1/57	12/30/68	549	Sikorsky	HUS-1/UH-34D; HUS-1A, -1G, -1Z; CH-34A, -34C.	2/5/57 HMR(L)-363	3/31/74 UH-34D	Rotor 56'D and tail rotor; cargo transport; 2 crew, 12 passenger or 2 ton of cargo; WAC R-1820, 1,525 hp.
K-225	9/26/49	3/50	6/50	3	Kaman	K-225 (K-5)	6/20/50 NAS Patuxent River	5/55	Side by side rotors 40'D; LY 0-435, 225 hp. K-5 was first turbine powered helo; BO-502 turbine, 175 hp.

R-4 (HNS-1 obtained from Army, YR-4 and YR-4B; Sikorsky model VS-316A)
R-5 (HO2S obtained from Army)
R-6 (HOS-1 obtained from Army, R-7A and B)
* Dates in this column through 1969 refer to squadrons. After 1969, these dates refer to inventory.
** This is the new designation assigned the helicopter in 1962.

Bureau (Serial) Numbers of Naval Aircraft

Serial number and bureau number are synonymous terms for the identifying number assigned to individual naval aircraft. The earliest system was a letter–number combination which segregated the aircraft by manufacturer (or designer) and general type. As this scheme developed, the letter "A" was used with Curtiss hydroaeroplanes, "B" for Wright type hydroaeroplanes, "C" for Curtiss flying boats, "D" for Burgess flying boats, and "E" for Curtiss amphibian flying boats. Sequential numbers beginning with one, were assigned to each set of aircraft. That scheme was replaced by AH numbers which were assigned aircraft in service. A system of construction numbers was then initiated to identify aircraft on order. The two coexisted for some 15 months when the service numbers were abandoned (See 27 Mar 1914, 10 Feb 1916, and 19 May 1917, chronology entries).

Construction numbers began with A-51 and, as serial numbers or bureau numbers, ran through A-9206 after which the letter "A" was dropped although sequential numbering continued through 9999. A second series of four digit numbers began with 0001 and ran through 7303. The last number in this series was assigned in December 1940. Beginning in 1941 a series of five digit numbers, beginning with 00001 was adopted and numbers were assigned through 99999, with 99991-100000 cancelled. A sixth digit numbering system was then added beginning with 100001 and is still in use. To summarize, the five major numbering systems are as follows:

    A-51 to A-9206
    9207 to 9999 (the A prefix was dropped)
    0001 to 7303
    00001 to 100000 (99991-100000 were cancelled)
    100001 to present (still in use but with many
        modifications)

There are several major exceptions to the assignment of numbers in the six digit numbering system. In the 1960s a block of six digit numbers, beginning with 00, were assigned to the DASH vehicle (Drone Antisubmarine Helicopter). The original designation for the unmanned helicopter was DSN. Production models of the DSN were designated QH-50C and QH-50D. All of these helos had six digit bureau numbers

that began with 00. The double zeros were part of the bureau number. These numbers obviously do not fit into the regular six digit numbering system that began with 100001. Documentation has not been found that explains why the normal six digit numbering system was not employed for these aircraft.

The other major exception to the normal sequential assignment of bureau numbers in the six digit system involves numbers beginning with 198003 and ranging up to 999794. This group of six digit numbers is not sequentially assigned. Almost all of the aircraft in this group of numbers were acquired by the Navy from the Army, Air Force, or other organizations, not directly from the manufacturer. There appears to be no logical sequence or reasoning for the assignment of these six digit numbers. It is believed that some of the numbers may have been dervied by modifying the Air Force aircraft numbering system. However, this is only conjecture since there is no documentation to verify this explanation.

Aside from the very sizable overlap stemming from the numbering schemes, the same number was never used on more than one aircraft. During the planning and contracting processes, however, numbers were often assigned to aircraft that were never obtained. Sometimes, but by no means always, these cancelled numbers were reassigned to other aircraft.

The basic sources used in compiling the following list include a master "Serial List of Designating Numbers for Naval Aircraft" prepared by the aircraft records office in the Bureau of Aeronautices. It was typed on twelve 17½ inch by 21½ inch pages and numbered consecutively 0 through 11. It was probably put in that form in 1935 when the first significant handwritten emendations appeared. Page 0 covered the pre-1916 schemes and pages 1 through 11 began with A-51 and ran through all four digit serials. For later aircraft, primarily those in the six digit system, the bureau number listing was compiled by using the "List of Serial Numbers Assigned Navy Aircraft" developed by the Aviation Statistics Office of DCNO (Air) and by reviewing the Aircraft History Card microfilm collection.

The compilations have been cross-checked against the compilation in William T. Larkins, U.S. Navy

A plate with the Bureau Number of the aircraft is shown in the upper left hand section of the F9F-5P instrument panel. 480229

Aircraft 1921–41; a compilation made by William H. Plant, Librarian, Naval Air Systems Command; and a more comprehensive listing compiled by Jack Collins, a historian and specialist in bureau numbers. Monthly and quarterly reports on the status of aircraft production, Aircraft History Cards, and the Aircraft Strike Listing were used in reconciling discrepancies.

One problem is that interpretations do not show in the final list. In addition, the compiler makes no claim to infallibility in transcribing long lists of numbers and, as a result, may have unwittingly introduced errors not in the original compilations.

The Early Designation Systems are as followings:

The First System from 1911–1914

A-1 Curtiss hydroaeroplane (originally an amphibian)
A-2 Curtiss landplane, rebuilt as hydroaeroplane. It was again rebuilt as a short-hulled flying boat variously described as OWL for over-water-land or as a Bat boat, and was fitted with wheels for use as an amphibian. This was recorded in the aircraft log for November 25, 1913: "title by order of Captain Chambers [was] changed [to] E-1."

A-3	Curtiss hydroaeroplane, received summer of 1912.
A-4	Curtiss (or Curtiss type) hydroaeroplane
B-1	Wright landplane, converted to hydroaeroplane
B-2	Wright type hydroaeroplane, built from spares, October 1912
B-3	Wright type hydroaeroplane, built from spares, October 1913
C-1	Curtiss flying boat
C-2	Curtiss flying boat
C-3	Curtiss flying boat
C-4	Curtiss flying boat
C-5	Curtiss flying boat
D-1	Burgess Co. & Curtis flying boat
D-2	Burgess Co. & Curtis flying boat
E-1	OWL or short hulled amphibious flying boat (see A-2)

The Second Designation System, 1914–1916 AH designations

General Order No. 88 of 27 March 1914 listed the corresponding designations between the above designations and the new system: "The aeroplanes now in the service are hereby designated as follows:

New Designation	Old Designation
AH-1	A-1
AH-2	A-2
AH-3	A-3
AH-4	B-1
AH-5	B-2
AH-6	B-3
AB-1	C-1
AB-2	C-2
AB-3	C-3
AB-4	C-4
AB-5	C-5
AB-6	D-1
AB-7	D-2
AX-1	E-1"

Despite the phrase, "now in the Service," the A-1, B-1, B-2 and probably the D-1 had ceased to exist before the order was issued. Other records show AH-2 as redesignation for A-4.

The designation of follow-on aircraft was as follows:

AH-7	Burgess-Dunne hydroaeroplane
AH-8	Curtiss hydroaeroplane
AH-9	Curtiss hydroaeroplane
AH-10	Burgess-Dunne hydroaeroplane
AH-11	Curtiss hydroaeroplanc
AH-12	Curtiss hydroaeroplane
AH-13	Curtiss hydroaeroplane
AH-14	Curtiss hydroaeroplane
AH-15	Curtiss hydroaeroplane
AH-16	Curtiss hydroaeroplane
AH-17	Curtiss hydroaeroplane
AH-18	Curtiss hydroaeroplane

The following listings are the five major post 1916 aircraft numbering systems:

Bureau Number	Aircraft Type	Manufacturer	Notes
A-51	Seaplane	Wright	
A-52	Seaplane	Paul Schmitt	Paris
A-53	Seaplane	DWF, German	
A-54-56	Hydro-pusher	Burgess Co.	
A-57-58	Seaplane	Thomas Bros.	AH-20 and 21
A-59	Seaplane	Gallaudet	D-1 (AH-61)
A-60-65	Hydroaeroplane	Curtiss	
A-66-67	R-3	Curtiss	AH-65 & AH-62
A-68-69	Seaplane	Martin	AH-19 and 22
A-70-75	Tractor Seaplane	Burgess	AH-25 to 31
A-76-81	Seaplane	Sturtevant	A-76 was AH-24
A-82	Richardson	Wash. Navy Yard	Seaplane
A-83-84	Hydroaeroplane	Pensacola	Curtiss type from spares
A-85-90	Seaplane	Curtiss	
A-91	Seaplane	Standard	
A-92	Seaplane	Standard	Twin engine, cx
A-93	JN Twin Tractor	Curtiss	Seaplane
A-94-95	BC-2 and 3	Goodyear	Kite Balloon
A-96-125	N-9	Curtiss	
A-126-127	Seaplane	Farman	A-127 cx
A-128-133	Seaplane	Sturtevant	
A-134-136	SH-4	Thomas-Morse	Seaplane
A-137-139	H-4-H	Standard	
A-140-141	Seaplane	Thomas Bros.	Twin tractor, cx
A-142-144	Seaplane	Aeromarine	
A-145-146	Flying Boat	Curtiss	Cx
A-147-148	Seaplane	Pacific Aero.	Boeing
A-149-150	Speed Scout	Curtiss	Seaplane
A-151	BC-4	Goodyear	Kite Balloon
A-152	H-12	Curtiss	Flying Boat
A-153-154	Seaplane, experimental	NAS Pensacola	A-154 cx
A-155-156	HT-2 Seaplane	Burgess	Speed Scout
A-157-159	JN-4B	Curtiss	
A-160-161	Kite Balloon	Goodyear	
A-162-197	R-6	Curtiss	
A-198	JN, Twin Engine	Curtiss	
A-199-200	Speed Scout	Burgess	Cx
A-201-234	N-9	Curtiss	
A-235-243	B Class Airship	Goodyear	
A-244-248	B Class Airship	Goodrich	
A-249-250	B Class Airship	Connecticut A/c	
A-251	Free Balloon	Connecticut A/c	
A-276-287	Kite Balloon	Goodyear	
A-288-290	Seaplane	Wright-Martin	
A-291-293	L-2, Triplane	Curtiss	
A-294-295	Unknown	Unknown	Cx
A-296-297	Seaplane	General/Verville	Cx
A-298-299	Unknown	Unknown	Cx
A-300-301	Seaplane	Gallaudet	Cx
A-302-341	R-6	Curtiss	

Bureau Number	Aircraft Type	Manufacturer	Notes
A-342-371	N-9	Curtiss	
A-372-373	Kite Balloon	Goodyear	
A-374-379	HT-2	Burgess	Speed Scout
A-380-385	U-2 Seaplane	Burgess	
A-386-387	F-Boat	Curtiss	
A-388-389	JN-4	Curtiss	
A-390-393	F-Boat	Curtiss	
A-394	Sopwith	British	Seaplane
A-395-406	SH-4 Seaplane	Thomas-Morse	
A-407	Sopwith	British Adm.	Seaplane
A-408	F-Boat	Curtiss	
A-409-438	N-9	Burgess	
A-439-441	Seaplane	Aeromarine	
A-442-444	Seaplane	Loening	Lawrance two cylinder engine
A-445-449	GS-2 Gnome	Curtiss	Gnome Speed Scout
A-450-649	39 A and B	Aeromarine	Seaplanes
A-650-699	Type C	Boeing	Seaplane
A-700	Kite Balloon	Goodyear	
A-701	Kite Balloon	Goodrich	
A-702-726	Kite Balloon	Goodyear	
A-727-751	Kite Balloon	Goodrich	
A-752-756	F Boat	L. S. Thompson	
A-757-762	S-5	Thomas-Morse	
A-763-764	Caquot M	British Gov't	Kite Balloon
A-765-783	H-12	Curtiss	
A-784-799	H-16	Curtiss	
A-800-815	HS-1	Curtiss	A-815 cx
A-816-817	Caquot P	French Gov't	Kite Balloon
A-818-867	H-16	Curtiss	
A-868	GS-1, Gnome	Curtiss	Speed Scout
A-869-872	Sopwith Baby	British Gov't	Seaplane
A-873-891	R-9	Curtiss	
A-892-893	R-6	Curtiss	
A-894	R-9	Curtiss	
A-895	R-6	Curtiss	
A-896-909	R-9	Curtiss	
A-910	R-6	Curtiss	
A-911-918	R-9	Curtiss	
A-919-920	R-6	Curtiss	
A-921-924	R-9	Curtiss	
A-925	R-6	Curtiss	
A-926-955	R-9	Curtiss	
A-956	R-6	Curtiss	
A-957	R-9	Curtiss	
A-958-959	R-6	Curtiss	
A-960-962	R-9	Curtiss	
A-963-966	R-6	Curtiss	
A-967-969	R-9	Curtiss	
A-970	R-6	Curtiss	
A-971-975	R-9	Curtiss	
A-976	R-6	Curtiss	

Bureau Number	Aircraft Type	Manufacturer	Notes
A-977-990	R-9	Curtiss	
A-991	R-6	Curtiss	
A-992-993	R-9	Curtiss	
A-994	R-6	Curtiss	
A-995-997	JN-4	Curtiss	
A-998	Kite Balloon	Goodrich	
A-999-1028	N-9	Burgess	
A-1029-1030	O-SS Dirigible	British	
A-1031-1048	H-16	Curtiss	
A-1049-1098	H-16	NAF	
A-1099-1398	HS-1, -1L, -2L	LWF	50 cx
A-1399-1548	HS-1 and -2L	Standard	last 70 cx
A-1549-2207	HS-1, -1L, -2L	Curtiss	
A-2208-2214	Free Balloon	Goodyear	
A-2215-2216	Free Balloon	Connecticut A/c	
A-2217-2276	HS-2L	Gallaudet	
A-2277	Flying Boat	Curtiss	
A-2278	Dunkirk Fighter	Curtiss	
A-2279-2280	F Boat	Wrigley	
A-2281	F Boat	Mitchell	
A-2282-2283	Davis Gun Carrier, N-1	NAF	A-2279 to 2284 were originally Burgess school seaplanes, probably U-2, cx
A-2284	Unknown	Unknown	Cx
A-2285-2290	N-9	Curtiss	
A-2291-2294	NC-1 to NC-4	Curtiss	
A-2295-2344	F Boat	Curtiss	
A-2345-2350	MF Boat	Curtiss	
A-2351-2650	N-9	Burgess	
A-2651-2652	F Boat	Alexandria A/c	Briggs
A-2653-2654	D-4	Gallaudet	Light bomber
A-2665-2929	Type R and M	Goodyear	Caquot Kite Balloons, 180 R and 10 M, 2845-2929 cx
A-2930-3204	Type R and M	Goodrich	Caquot Kite Balloons, 81 R and 10 M, 3021-3204 cx
A-3205-3234	JN-4H		From Army
A-3235-3244	Gnome, Speed Scouts	Thomas-Morse	From Army
A-3245-3324	DH-4	Dayton-Wright	From Army
A-3325-3326	Kirkham Fighter	Curtiss	
A-3327	F Boat	Alexandria/Briggs	
A-3328-3332	F Boat	Am. Trans-Oceanic Co. Curtiss	
A-3333-3382	F-5	Canadian Aeroplanes Ltd.	3363-3382 cx
A-3383	Balloon	Goodrich	Gastite Kite
A-3384-3458	DH-4	From Army	Dayton-Wright
A-3459-3558	H-16	NAF	
A-3559-4035	F-5	NAF	137 accepted; 343 cx: 3616-3658, 3684-3782, 3801-3858, 3881, 3883-3935, 3941-4008, 4014-4035.

Bureau Number	Aircraft Type	Manufacturer	Notes
A-4036-4037	F-6	NAF	
A-4039-4078	H-16	Curtiss	
A-4079-4108	F Boat	Curtiss	
A-4109	E-1 Dirigible	Goodyear	
A-4110-4111	Dunkirk Fighter	Curtiss	(HA)
A-4112-4117	JN-4B	Curtiss Exhibition Co.	
A-4118	C Class	Goodyear	Dirigible
A-4119	C Class	Goodrich	Dirigible
A-4120	C Class	Goodyear	Dirigible
A-4121	C Class	Goodrich	Dirigible
A-4122-4123	C Class	Goodyear	Dirigible
A-4124-4125	C Class	Goodrich	Dirigible
A-4126-4127	C Class	Goodyear	Dirigible
A-4128-4217	JN-4HG	From Army	Hispano-Suiza engine
A-4218-4227	E-1 (M Defense)	Standard	From Army
A-4228-4229	HS-2	Loughead	
A-4230	Tellier	French Gov't	Flying Boat
A-4231-4255	HS-2L	Boeing	
A-4256-4280	Unknown	Boeing	Cx
A-4281-4340	F-5	Curtiss	
A-4341-4342	N-1	NAF	
A-4343	F Boat	Carolina A/c Co.	Experimental, rejected
A-4344-4346	Unknown	Carolina A/c Co.	Cx
A-4347	C-1F	Boeing	
A-4348	F-1 Dirigible	Goodyear	
A-4349-4402	F Boat	Curtiss	
A-4403-4449	MF Boat	Curtiss	
A-4450	D-1 Airship	Goodyear	
A-4451	D-2 Airship	Goodrich	
A-4452-4453	D-3 and D-4 Airship	Goodyear	
A-4454	D-5 Airship	Goodrich	
A-4455-4469	D Class Airship	Goodrich	5 Cx
		Goodyear	10 Cx
A-4470-4819	F-5L	Curtiss	Cx
A-4820-5019	N-9	Burgess	Cx
A-5020-5021	R type, reduced	Goodyear	Caquot Kite Balloon
A-5022-5023	R type, reduced	Goodrich	Caquot Kite Balloon
A-5024	F Boat	Alexandria	
A-5025-5028	P type	Goodyear	Caquot Kite Balloon
A-5029	Kite Balloon	Goodyear	Experimental
A-5030-5039	N-1	NAF	Cx
A-5040-5089	Model 40 F Boat	Aeromarine	
A-5090-5239	Unknown	Aeromarine	Cx
A-5240	M type	British Adm.	Caquot Kite Balloon
A-5241-5242	Avorio Prassone	Italian Gov't	Kite Balloon
A-5243	Night Bomber	Sperry	
A-5244-5246	Unknown	Sperry	Cx
A-5247-5256	Model 10 F Boat	Alexandria A/c	
A-5257	B-20 Airship	Goodyear	
A-5258	F Boat	Curtiss	
A-5259-5458	F-5L	NAF	Cx
A-5459-5462	HS-3	Curtiss	

Bureau Number	Aircraft Type	Manufacturer	Notes
A-5463	Kite Balloon	Goodyear	
A-5464-5465	B-17 and B-18	Goodyear	Airship cars rebuilt
A-5466	Airship Car	Goodyear	
A-5467	B-19 Airship Car	Goodyear	
A-5468	Airship	Goodyear	
A-5469	M-3 Cat	Loening	Seaplane
A-5470-5471	JN-6HG-I	From Army	
A-5472	Astra-Torres	French Gov't	Airship
A-5473-5482	Kite Balloon	British Gov't	
A-5483-5562	MF Boat	NAF	
A-5563	SS-Z-23	British Adm.	Airship, former O-SS A-1030
A-5564-5569	HS-2	NAS Miami	from spares
A-5570-5571	SA-1	NAF	for "Ship's Airplanes"
A-5572-5573	SA-2	NAF	
A-5574-5575	Macchi	Italian Gov't	
A-5576-5579	TF Boat	NAF	Tandem engine fighting patrol plane
A-5580	NS-1	British Gov't	North Sea Dirigible
A-5581-5586	JN-6HG-I	From Army	
A-5587	O-1 Dirigible	Italian Gov't	
A-5588-5589	SE-5	From Army	
A-5590-5591	HS-3	NAF	
A-5592-5593	Vedette-Zodiac	French Gov't	Dirigible
A-5594-5605	Free Balloon	Connecticut A/c	
A-5606	LS Seaplane	Loening	
A-5607-5608	LS Seaplane	Loening	Cx
A-5609-5611	LB Flying Boat	Loening	
A-5612-5614	AS Seaplane	Aeromarine	
A-5615-5619	HS-2	NAS Hampton Rds.	from spares, one cx, apparently 5619
A-5620-5629	Hanriot	French Gov't	
A-5630	HS-2L	LWF	Formerly A-1171 rebuilt
A-5631	M-8 Airplane	Loening	
A-5632-5635	NC-5 to -8	NAF	
A-5636	Seaplane	Paul Schmitt	Paris
A-5637-5646	M-80 Airplane	Loening	
A-5647-5649	Tellier	From Abroad	5649 cx
A-5650-5651	Le Pen Seaplane	From Abroad	
A-5652-5653	Donne Denhaut	From Abroad	
A-5654	Caproni	From Abroad	
A-5655-5656	Pup	From Abroad	Sopwith
A-5657	Le Pen Seaplane	From Abroad	
A-5658-5659	Camel (F-1)	From Abroad	Sopwith
A-5660	1 1/2 Strutter	From Abroad	1A2 Sopwith
A-5661-5680	VE-7	Lewis & Vought	
A-5681-5700	VE-7G and -7GF	NAF	
A-5701-5710	M-81	NAF	Loening design
A-5711-5712	MBT	Martin	
A-5713-5720	MT	Martin	
A-5721-5724	Camel (F-1)	From Army	Sopwith

Bureau Number	Aircraft Type	Manufacturer	Notes
A-5725-5728	1 1/2 Strutter	From Army	1A2 Sopwith
A-5729-5730	Camel	From Army	Sopwith
A-5731-5733	Unknown	Unknown	Cx
A-5734-5750	1 1/2 Strutter	From Army	Sopwith
A-5751-5752	Panther	G. Parnall & Son	England
A-5753-5755	AP Type	Connecticut A/c	Kite Balloon
A-5756-5757	D-11 Seaplane	Gallaudet	Cx
A-5758-5760	D-9 Seaplane	Gallaudet	Cx
A-5761-5786	M-81 Airplane	NAF	
A-5787	HS-2L	NAS Key West	from spares
A-5788-5793	M-81-S	Loening	
A-5794-5805	Nieuport-28	From Army	
A-5806-5807	K Type Boat	Austrian Gov't	
A-5808	HS-2L	NAS Anacostia	from spares
A-5809-5814	DH-4B	From Army	
A-5815-5829	Caproni	Caproni	Cx
A-5830-5833	JN-6H	From Army	
A-5834-5839	DH-4B	From Army	
A-5840-5842	K-4	J.V. Martin	Gallaudet, subcontractor
A-5843-5854	D-7	Fokker	5849-5854 cx
A-5855-5858	S-4C Scout	Thomas Morse	From Army
A-5860-5866	Free Balloon	Goodyear	
A-5867-5869	JL-6	Junkers-Larsen	
A-5870-5884	DH-4B	From Army	
A-5885-5886	NC-9,-10	NAF	
A-5887-5889	C-1	Fokker	Netherlands
A-5890-5898	CT Seaplane	Curtiss	5891-5898 cx
A-5899-5901	ST Airplane	Stout	rejected
A-5902-5904	ST Airplane	Stout	Cx
A-5905-5911	EM-2 Seaplane	G. Elias & Bros.	
A-5912-5941	VE-7SF	Lewis & Vought	
A-5942-5955	VE-7SF	NAF	
A-5956-5971	VE-7	NAF	
A-5972	D-6 Airship	Goodyear	
A-5973	H-1 Airship	Goodyear	Towing Airship (T-1)
A-5974-5975	USXB-1	Dayton Wright	From Army
A-5976-5981	Morane Saulnier	Morane Saulnier	
A-5982-6001	DH-4B	From Army	
A-6002-6004	Exp. Ship plane	Curtiss	Cx
A-6005-6007	Macchi M-16	S.A.N.M., Italy	
A-6008-6010	Fokker FT	Netherlands A/c Co.	
A-6011-6020	VE-7SF	NAF	
A-6021-6030	VE-7SF	Lewis & Vought	
A-6031-6033	DT Seaplanes	Davis Douglas	
A-6034-6048	PT	NAF	
A-6049-6054	Seaplane	Austrian Gov't	
A-6055	Dornier CS-2	Van Berkel	
A-6056-6057	Swift	Blackburn Aeroplane Co.	
A-6058	Dornier D-1	Swiss Agent	
A-6059	Giant Boat	NAF	Cx
A-6060-6070	MB-3	Thomas Morse	From Army
A-6071	MB-7	Thomas Morse	From Army

Bureau Number	Aircraft Type	Manufacturer	Notes
A-6072	SV Airplane	Stout	
A-6073	Viking IV	Vickers	Amphibian Boat
A-6074-6076	Free Balloon	Connecticut A/c	
A-6077-6079	Unassigned		
A-6080-6081	CR Racer	Curtiss	
A-6082	WA Amphibian	Dayton-Wright	
A-6083	WS Seaplane	Dayton-Wright	
A-6084	WD Seaplane	Dayton-Wright	Cx
A-6085-6095	DT-2	Dayton-Wright	Reassigned from WA-WS-WD
A-6096-6102	WA-WS-WD		Cx
A-6103-6110	F Type	Goodyear	Kite Balloon
A-6111-6112	J Class Airship	Goodyear	
A-6113-6192	DH-4B	From Army	
A-6193-6246	JN-4H	From Army	
A-6247	JN-4H	Parris Island Marine Base	from spares
A-6248-6270	TS Airplane	Curtiss	
A-6271-6288	JN-4H	From Army	
A-6289-6290	BS-1 Boat	NAF	Cx
A-6291-6292	BS-2 Boat	NAF	Cx
A-6293-6294	BS-3 Boat	NAF	Cx
A-6295-6299	BS	NAF	Cx
A-6300-6304	TS-1	NAF	
A-6305-6315	TS-1	Curtiss	
A-6316-6325	JN-4	NAF	Cx
A-6326-6343	PT-2	NAF	
A-6344-6346	TG-1	NAF	
A-6347-6348	TG-2	NAF	
A-6349-6351	HN-1	Huff Daland	
A-6352-6401	DH-4	From Army	
A-6402-6404	HPS-1	Handley Page	Cx
A-6405-6422	DT-2	Davis Douglas	
A-6423-6428	DT-2	NAF	
A-6429-6430	BR-1	Bee Line A/c Co.	
A-6431-6433	NO-1	NAF	
A-6434-6435	Henkel seaplane submarine type	Casper Werke	Germany
A-6436-6444	VE-7H	NAF	
A-6445	Racing Balloon	NAF	
A-6446-6447	TS-2	NAF	
A-6448-6449	TS-3	NAF	
A-6450-6451	NM-1	NAF	6451 cx
A-6452-6454	M2O-1	Martin	
A-6455-6460	MO-1	Martin	
A-6461-6464	VE-9H	Vought	
A-6465-6481	VE-9	Vought	
A-6482-6499	UO-1	Vought	
A-6500-6505	CS-1	Curtiss	
A-6506	HS-2L	NAS Coco Solo	from spares
A-6507-6513	HS-2L	NAF	from spares
A-6514	DH-4B	NAF	from spares
A-6515-6520	XS-1	Cox-Klemin	
A-6521-6526	MS-1	Martin	

Bureau Number	Aircraft Type	Manufacturer	Notes
A-6527	Free Balloon	NAF	
A-6528-6542	N-9	NAS Pensacola	from spares
A-6543-6544	NW-1,-2	Wright	
A-6545	JN-4H	Port-au-Prince	from spares
A-6546-6551	UO-1	Vought	
A-6552	Libelle	Dornier	Cx
A-6553-6556	HS-2L	NAS San Diego	from spares
A-6557-6559	F-5L	NAS Hampton Rds.	from spares
A-6560-6562	HO-1	Huff-Daland	
A-6563-6582	DT-2	Douglas	
A-6583-6602	DT-2	LWF	
A-6603-6615	UO-1	Vought	
A-6616-6617	PN-7	NAF	
A-6618-6632	N-9	NAS Pensacola	from spares
A-6633-6662	MO-1	Martin	
A-6663-6688	NO-1	LWF	6684-6688 cx
A-6689-6690	F4C-1	Curtiss	
A-6691-6692	R2C-1	Curtiss	
A-6693-6695	N2N-1	NAF	
A-6696	JL-6 Junkers	Larson	
A-6697	F-5L	NAS San Diego	from spares
A-6698-6700	Free Balloon	Goodyear	
A-6701-6703	HN-2	Huff Daland	
A-6704-6705	VE-9W	Vought	Cx
A-6706-6729	UO-1	Vought	
A-6730	TW-3	Wright	
A-6731-6732	CS-2	Curtiss	
A-6733-6742	N-9	NAS Pensacola	from spares
A-6743-6744	F2W-1	Wright	
A-6745-6747	L-3	Longren	
A-6748	WP-1	Wright	
A-6749-6798	NB-1 and NB-2	Boeing	
A-6799	PN-8	NAF	
A-6800	N2M-1	Martin	
A-6801-6835	SC-1	Martin	
A-6836-6857	NB-1	Boeing	
A-6858-6877	UO-1	Vought	
A-6878	PN-8	NAF	
A-6879-6880	OL-1	Loening	
A-6881	PB-1	Boeing	
A-6882-6883	OB-1	Boeing	Cx
A-6884-6897	FB-1, -2, -3	Boeing	From Army
A-6898-6927	O2B-1	Boeing	From Army
A-6928-6967	SC-2	Martin	
A-6968-6976	F6C-1	Curtiss	
A-6977	LePere	From Army	
A-6978-6979	R3C-1	Curtiss	
A-6980-6983	OL-2	Loening	
A-6984-7023	UO-1	Vought	
A-7024-7026	TB-1	Boeing	
A-7027	TN-1	NAF	
A-7028-7029	PN-10	NAF	

Bureau Number	Aircraft Type	Manufacturer	Notes
A-7030	OL-2	Loening	
A-7031-7050	UO-1	Vought	
A-7051-7053	T2D-1	Douglas	
A-7054	R3C-1	Curtiss	
A-7055-7058	OL-3	Loening	
A-7059-7064	OL-4	Loening	
A-7065-7088	T3M-1	Martin	
A-7089-7090	FB-3	Boeing	
A-7091-7100	N-9	NAS Pensacola	reconstructed
A-7101-7127	FB-5	Boeing	
A-7128-7162	F6C-3	Curtiss	
A-7163-7202	NY-1	Consolidated	
A-7203-7204	OD-1	From Army	
A-7205-7220	NY-1	Consolidated	
A-7221-7222	O2U-1	Vought	
A-7223	F3W-1	Wright	
A-7224-7323	T3M-2	Martin	
A-7324-7350	OL-6	Loening	
A-7351-7360	NY-1	Consolidated	
A-7361-7380	FU-1	Vought	
A-7381	R Type	From Army	Kite Balloon
A-7382	J-3 Airship	Goodyear	TC Type, from Army
A-7383	PN-10	NAF	
A-7384	PN-12	NAF	
A-7385	F2B-1	Boeing	
A-7386-7389	Free Balloon	Goodyear	
A-7390-7392	Kite Balloon	Goodyear	
A-7393-7423	F6C-4	Curtiss	
A-7424-7455	F2B-1	Boeing	
A-7456-7525	NY-2	Consolidated	
A-7526	XJR-1	Ford	
A-7527	PN-11	NAF	
A-7528-7560	O2U-1	Vought	
A-7561-7563	TA-1	Atlantic Fokker	
A-7564	DH-60 Moth	DeHavilland	
A-7565	RO-1	Italian Gov't	Romeo Fokker
A-7566	XT4M-1	Martin	
A-7567-7586	O2U-1	Vought	
A-7587-7595	T2D-1	Douglas	
A-7596-7649	T4M-1	Martin	
A-7650-7652	XN2C-1	Curtiss	
A-7653	XF7C-1	Curtiss	
A-7654-7670	F7C-1	Curtiss	
A-7671-7672	F8C-1	Curtiss	
A-7673	XF8C-2	Curtiss	
A-7674-7691	F3B-1	Boeing	
A-7692	XF2U-1	Vought	
A-7693-7707	NY-2	Consolidated	
A-7708-7763	F3B-1	Boeing	
A-7764-7795	NY-2	Consolidated	
A-7796-7831	O2U-1	Vought	
A-7832-7851	OL-8	Loening	

Bureau Number	Aircraft Type	Manufacturer	Notes
A-7852-7899	T4M-1	Martin	
A-7900-7940	O2U-1	Vought	
A-7941-7943	XNK-1	Keystone	
A-7944	XFG-1	Eberhart	
A-7945-7948	F8C-1	Curtiss	
A-7949-7962	F8C-3	Curtiss	
A-7963-7969	OC-2	Curtiss	
A-7970-7977	NY-2	Consolidated	
A-7978	XJQ-1	Fairchild	
A-7979-8003	PD-1	Douglas	
A-8004	XPH-1	Hall	
A-8005	XPS-1	Sikorsky	
A-8006	PN-11	NAF	
A-8007-8008	TA-2	Atlantic	
A-8009	XFH-1	Hall	
A-8010	XN2B-1	Boeing	
A-8011	XPY-1	Consolidated	
A-8012	XJA-1	Atlantic	Cx
A-8013-8017	NY-2	Consolidated	
A-8018	TA-2	Atlantic	
A-8019	XN2Y-1	Consolidated	
A-8020-8050	N2C-1	Curtiss	
A-8051	XT5M-1	Martin	
A-8052	XT2N-1	NAF	
A-8053-8068	NK-1	Keystone	
A-8069-8088	OL-8	Loening	
A-8089-8090	XPS-2	Sikorsky	
A-8091-8127	O2U-2	Vought	
A-8128-8156	F4B-1	Boeing	
A-8157	TA-2	Atlantic	Cx
A-8158-8172	NY-2	Consolidated	
A-8173-8182	NY-1	Consolidated	
A-8183-8192	NY-2	Consolidated	
A-8193-8272	O2U-3	Vought	
A-8273-8274	JR-2	Ford	
A-8275-8276	XHL-1	Loening	
A-8277-8281	Free Balloon	Meadowcraft	
A-8282	ZMC-2 Airship	A/c Dev. Corp.	
A-8283	XN3Y-1	Consolidated	
A-8284-8287	PS-3	Sikorsky	
A-8288	XFJ-1	Berliner-Joyce	
A-8289-8313	PM-1	Martin	
A-8314	XF8C-4	Curtiss	
A-8315-8356	O2U-4	Vought	
A-8357	XOK-1		Cx
A-8358	XP2M-1	Martin	
A-8359	XOJ-1	Berliner-Joyce	
A-8360-8400	NY-1	Consolidated	
A-8401-8410	NY-2	Consolidated	
A-8411	XT6M-1	Martin	
A-8412-8420	P3M-1	Martin	
A-8421-8447	F8C-4	Curtiss	

Bureau Number	Aircraft Type	Manufacturer	Notes
A-8448-8450	F8C-5	Curtiss	
A-8451-8456	O2C-1	Curtiss	
A-8457	JR-3	Ford	
A-8458-8475	TG-1	Great Lakes	
A-8476	Free Balloon	Goodyear	
A-8477-8481	PM-1	Martin	
A-8482	XP4N-1	NAF	
A-8483-8484	XP4N-2	NAF	
A-8485	Bulldog	Bristol	
A-8486	XJQ-2	Fairchild	
A-8487-8506	NY-3	Consolidated	
A-8507-8524	PK-1	Keystone	
A-8525	XO2L-1	Loening	
A-8526-8545	N2C-2	Curtiss	
A-8546	Glider	Am. Motorless Av. Co.	
A-8547-8582	O3U-1	Vought	
A-8583-8588	NT-1	New Standard	
A-8589-8597	O2C-1	Curtiss	
A-8598-8599	JR-3	Ford	
A-8600-8605	N2Y-1	Fleet A/c Corp.	
A-8606	XO2L-1	Loening	
A-8607	Bulldog	Bristol	
A-8608-8609	C-3	Goodyear	Kite Balloon
A-8610-8612	Free Balloon	Goodyear	
A-8613-8639	F4B-2	Boeing	
A-8640	XF5B-1	Boeing	
A-8641	XO4U-1	Vought	
A-8642	XP2S-1	Sikorsky	
A-8643	XBN-1	NAF	Cx
A-8644-8661	P2D-1	Douglas	
A-8662-8686	PM-2	Martin	
A-8687-8695	PH-1	Hall	
A-8696	XSL-1	Loening	
A-8697-8728	TG-2	Detroit/Great Lakes	
A-8729	XP2H-1	Hall	
A-8730	XT3D-1	Douglas	
A-8731	XF9C-1	Curtiss	
A-8732	XFA-1	Fokker	
A-8733-8747	OL-9	Keystone	
A-8748-8790	F8C-5/O2C-1	Curtiss	Redesignated O2C-1
A-8791-8809	F4B-2	Boeing	
A-8810-8839	O3U-1	Vought	
A-8840	RR-4	Ford	
A-8841	RA-4	Fokker	Cx
A-8842-8844	RS-1	Sikorsky	
A-8845	XF8C-7	Curtiss	
A-8846	RC-1	Curtiss	
A-8847-8849	O2C-2	Curtiss	
A-8850	XOP-1	Pitcairn	Autogiro
A-8851-8871	O3U-1	Vought	
A-8872-8875	O3U-2/SU-1	Vought	Redesignated SU-1

Bureau Number	Aircraft Type	Manufacturer	Notes
A-8876	XRD-1	Douglas	
A-8877	DH-80	DeHavilland	called Puss Moth
A-8878	XFF-1	Grumman	
A-8879-8890	BM-1	Martin	
A-8891-8911	F4B-3	Boeing	
A-8912-8920	F4B-4	Boeing	
A-8921	XBY-1	Consolidated	
A-8922-8923	RS-3	Sikorsky	
A-8924-8927	Free Balloon	Goodyear	
A-8928-8937	O3U-2	Vought	
A-8938	XRE-1	Bellanca	
A-8939	XP2Y-1	Consolidated	
A-8940	XSF-1	Grumman	
A-8941-8970	O2C-1	Curtiss	
A-8971	XS2L-1	Loening	
A-8972	XSS-2	Sikorsky	
A-8973	XF2J-1	Berliner-Joyce	
A-8974	XSG-1	Great Lakes	
A-8975	XF6B-1	Boeing	
A-8976-8977	XOP-1	Pitcairn	Autogiro
A-8978	XFN-1	NAF	Cx
A-8979-8985	OL-9	Keystone	
A-8986-9007	P2Y-1	Consolidated	
A-9008	XP2Y-2	Consolidated	
A-9009-9053	F4B-4	Boeing	
A-9054	XRO-1	Detroit/Lockheed	
A-9055	RS-3	Sikorsky	
A-9056-9061	F9C-2	Curtiss	
A-9062-9076	O3U-2/SU-1	Vought	Redesignated SU-1
A-9077-9121	SU-2	Vought	
A-9122-9141	SU-3	Vought	
A-9142-9169	O3U-3	Vought	
A-9170-9185	BM-2	Martin	
A-9186	XSE-2	Bellanca	Cx
A-9187-9204	OJ-2	Berliner-Joyce	
A-9205-9206	RR-5	Ford	

A-prefix dropped

Bureau Number	Aircraft Type	Manufacturer	Notes
9207	XRE-2	Bellanca	
9208-9211	OL-9	Keystone	
9212	XBM-1	Martin	
9213	XF11C-2	Curtiss	
9214-9217	BM-1	Martin	
9218	XJF-1	Grumman	
9219	XF11C-1	Curtiss	
9220	XBG-1	Great Lakes	
9221	XB2Y-1	Consolidated	
9222	XF3U-1/XSBU-1	Vought	
9223	XFD-1	Douglas	
9224	XF3J-1	Berliner-Joyce	

Bureau Number	Aircraft Type	Manufacturer	Notes
9225	XSBC-3	Curtiss	See Note 1
9226-9263	F4B-4	Boeing	
9264	XF9C-2	Curtiss	
9265-9268	F11C-2	Curtiss	
9269	XF11C-3	Curtiss	
9270-9282	F11C-2	Curtiss	
9283-9329	O3U-3	Vought	
9330	XO3U-6	Vought	
9331-9340	F11C-2	Curtiss	
9341	RE-3	Bellanca	
9342	XF2F-1	Grumman	
9343	XF13C-1	Curtiss	
9344-9345	Kite Balloon	Air Cruisers, Inc.	
9346	XFL-1	Grover Loening Inc.	Cx
9347-9349	RD-2	Douglas	
9350-9376	FF-1	Grumman	
9377	XS2C-1	Curtiss	
9378	XF7B-1	Boeing	
9379-9398	SU-4	Vought	Cx
9399	XO5U-1	Vought	
9400	XFT-2	Northrop	
9401-9402	Glider	Franklin	
9403-9411	OJ-2	Berliner-Joyce	
9412	XO2D-1	Douglas	
9413	XO3C-1	Curtiss	
9414-9433	SU-4	Vought	
9434-9455	JF-1	Grumman	
9456-9458	XN4Y-1	Consolidated	From Army
9459	XP3Y-1	Consolidated	
9460-9492	SF-1	Grumman	
9493	XSF-2	Grumman	
9494-9520	BG-1	Great Lakes	
9521-9522	XJW-1	Waco	
9523-9527	JF-1	Grumman	
9528-9533	RD-3	Douglas	
9534-9550	BG-1	Great Lakes	
9551-9571	P2Y-3	Consolidated	
9572-9583	OJ-2	Berliner-Joyce	
9584-9585	R4C-1	Curtiss	
9586-9612	BF2C-1	Curtiss	
9613	XP3D-1	Douglas	
9614-9617	PS-2	Franklin	Glider
9618-9619	P2Y-3	Consolidated	
9620-9622	R2D-1	Douglas	
9623-9676	F2F-1	Grumman	
9677-9717	NS-1	Stearman	
9718	XR3Q-1	Stinson	
9719	F4B-4	Quantico	from spares
9720	XTBD-1	Douglas	
9721	XPTBH-2	Hall	
9722	XB2G-1	Great Lakes	
9723	XTBG-1	Great Lakes	

Bureau Number	Aircraft Type	Manufacturer	Notes
9724	XSOK-1	Kreider-Reisner	
9725	XSB2U-1	Vought	
9726	XSBA-1	Brewster	
9727	XF3F-1	Grumman	
9728	XSOE-1	Bellanca	
9729-9744	O3U-6	Vought	
9745	XBT-1	Northrop	
9746	XF3U-1	Vought	See Note 2
9747-9749	XRK-3	Kinner	
9750-9833	SBU-1	Vought	
9834	XSB3U-1	Vought	
9835-9839	JF-3	Grumman	
9840-9855	BG-1	Great Lakes	
9856-9990	SOC-1	Curtiss	
9991	XN3N-1	NAF	
9992	Free Balloon	Air Cruisers	
9993-9994	R2D-1	Douglas	
9995	XPBS-1	Sikorsky	
9996	XSBF-1	Grumman	
9997	F2F-1	Grumman	
9998	XR2K-1	Fairchild	for NACA
9999	G-1 Airship	Goodyear	

The beginning of the second series of four digit numbers

Bureau Number	Aircraft Type	Manufacturer	Notes
0001-0016	O3U-6	Vought	
0017-0101	N3N-1	NAF	
0102-0161	PBY-1	Consolidated	
0162-0190	J2F-1	Grumman	
0191-0210	NS-1	Stearman	
0211-0264	F3F-1	Grumman	
0265	XN3N-2	NAF	
0266	JF-2	Grumman	From Coast Guard
0267	XR2O-1	Lockheed	
0268-0381	TBD-1	Douglas	
0382	PM-2	NAS Norfolk	from spares
0383	XF4F-3	Grumman	
0384	PM-2	FAB Coco Solo	from spares and hull of 8480
0385	XOSN-1	NAF	
0386-0425	SOC-2	Curtiss	
0426-0450	N3N-1	NAF	Cx
0451	XF2A-1	Brewster	
0452	XF3F-2	Grumman	
0453	XPB2Y-1	Consolidated	
0454-0503	PBY-2	Consolidated	
0504-0506	JRS-1	Sikorsky	
0507-0589	SBC-3	Curtiss	0582 modified to XSBC-4
0590-0626	BT-1	Northrop	
0627	XBT-2	Northrop	
0628-0643	BT-1	Northrop	
0644-0723	N3N-1	NAF	

Bureau Number	Aircraft Type	Manufacturer	Notes
0724	ME-108b	Bayerische Flugzeugwerke	
0725	C-620 Le Simoun	Caudron	
0726-0778	SB2U-1	Vought	
0779	XSB2U-3	Vought	
0780-0794	J2F-2	Grumman	
0795	JE-1	Bellanca	
0796	XPBM-1	Martin	
0797-0799	Free Balloons	Air Cruisers	
0800	JK-1	Fairchild	
0801	JB-1	Beech	
0802-0841	SBU-2	Vought	
0842-0907	PBY-3	Consolidated	
0908-0909	JH-1	Stearman-Hammond	
0910-0949	NJ-1	North American	From Army
0950	XSO2C-1	Curtiss	
0951	XOS2U-1	Vought	
0952-0966	N3N-1	NAF	
0967-1047	F3F-2	Grumman	
1048-1051	JO-2	Lockheed	
1052	XOSS-1	Stearman	
1053	JO-1	Lockheed	
1054-1063	JRS-1	Sikorsky	
1064-1146	SOC-3	Curtiss	
1147-1190	SON-1	NAF	
1191-1194	JRS-1	Sikorsky	
1195-1209	J2F-2	Grumman	
1210	L-1 Airship	Goodyear	
1211	K-2 Airship	Goodyear	
1212	S-2	S.A.I., Italy	
1213-1244	PBY-4	Consolidated	
1245	XPBY-5A	Consolidated	
1246	PBM-1	Martin	
1247	XPBM-2	Martin	
1248-1266	PBM-1	Martin	
1267	XJO-3	Lockheed	
1268-1325	SBC-4	Curtiss	
1326-1383	SB2U-2	Vought	
1384	XJ3F-1	Grumman	
1385	XSO3C-1	Curtiss	
1386-1396	F2A-1	Brewster	
1397-1439	F2A-2	Brewster	
1440	XSO2U-1	Vought	
1441	XR4O-1	Lockheed	
1442	XF5F-1	Grumman	
1443	XF4U-1	Vought	
1444-1470	F3F-3	Grumman	
1471-1473	Free Balloon	Goodyear	
1474-1504	SBC-4	Curtiss	
1505-1519	TBD-1	Douglas	
1520	XPB2M-1R	Martin	
1521	XN5N-1	NAF	
1522-1551	SBN-1	NAF	

Bureau Number	Aircraft Type	Manufacturer	Notes
1552-1567	SNJ-1	North American	
1568-1587	J2F-3	Grumman	
1588	XFL-1	Bell	
1589-1595	GB-1	Beech	From Army
1596-1631	SBD-1	Douglas	
1632	XSB2A-1	Brewster	
1633-1637	PB2Y-2	Consolidated	
1638	XPB2Y-3	Consolidated	
1639-1670	J2F-4	Grumman	
1671-1673	JRF-1A	Grumman	
1674-1677	JRF-1	Grumman	
1678-1679	JRF-1A	Grumman	
1680	JRF-1	Grumman	
1681-1734	OS2U-1	Vought	
1735-1755	SBD-1	Douglas	
1756-1757	XNR-1	Maxson	radio controlled
1758	XSB2C-1	Curtiss	
1759-1808	N3N-3	NAF	
1809-1843	SBC-4	Curtiss	
1844-1845	F4F-3	Grumman	
1846-1847	XF4F-5	Grumman	
1848-1896	F4F-3	Grumman	
1897	XF4F-4	Grumman	
1898-1900	GB-1	Beech	
1901-1903	R3D-1	Douglas	1901 cx
1904-1907	R3D-2	Douglas	
1908-2007	N3N-3	NAF	
2008-2043	SNJ-2	North American	
2044-2100	SB2U-3	Vought	
2101	XR5O-1	Lockheed	
2102-2188	SBD-2	Douglas	
2189-2288	OS2U-2	Vought	
2289-2455	PBY-5	Consolidated	
2456-2488	PBY-5A	Consolidated	
2489-2511	F4B-4A	Boeing	From Army
2512-2538	F4F-3	Grumman	
2539-2540	XTBF-1	Grumman	2539 crashed prior to acceptance
2541	JO-2	Lockheed	
2542	XTBU-1	Vought	
2543-2547	JRB-1	Beech	
2548-2572	SNJ-2	North American	
2573-3072	N3N-3	NAF	
3073-3130	OS2U-2	Vought	
3131-3143	R4D-1	Douglas	From Army
3144	XPBB-1	Boeing	
3145-3394	N2S-1	Stearman	
3395-3519	N2S-3	Stearman	
3520-3644	N2S-2	Stearman	
3645-3845	NP-1	Spartan	
3846-3855	JRF-4	Grumman	
3856-3874	F4F-3	Grumman	

Bureau Number	Aircraft Type	Manufacturer	Notes
3875-3969	F4F-3A	Grumman	3875-3904 cx
3970-4057	F4F-3	Grumman	
4058-4098	F4F-4	Grumman	
4099-4198	NR-1	Ryan	From Army
4199-4248	SBC-4	Curtiss	
4249-4250	R50-1	Lockheed	
4251	BD-1	Douglas	From Army
4252-4351	N2S-3	Stearman	
4352-4517	N3N-3	NAF	
4518-4691	SBD-3	Douglas	
4692-4706	R4D-1	Douglas	From Army
4707-4708	R4D-2	Douglas	From Army
4709-4710	JRB-1	Beech	From Army
4711-4725	JRB-2	Beech	From Army
4726-4729	JRB-1	Beech	From Army
4730-4879	SO3C-1	Curtiss	
4880-5029	SO3C-2	Curtiss	
5030-5262	F4F-3	Grumman	
5263-5283	F4F-7	Grumman	
5284-5289	OS2U-3	Vought	
5990-6289	OS2U-3	Vought	Cx
6290-6439	SNC-1	Curtiss	
6440-6454	JRF-5	Grumman	
6455-6754	PBM-3	Martin	See Note 3
6755-7024	SNJ-3	North American	From Army
7025-7028	K Type Airship	Goodyear	
7029-7030	L Type Airship	Goodyear	
7031	XF4F-6	Grumman	
7032-7034	GK-1	Fairchild	
7035-7042	BD-2	Douglas	
7043-7242	PB2Y-3,-3R	Consolidated	
7243-7302	PBY-5A	Consolidated	
7303	R50-2	Lockheed	
7304-9999	Unassigned		

The beginning of the five digit series

Bureau Number	Aircraft Type	Manufacturer	Notes
00001-00004	SB2C-1	Curtiss	
00005	XSB2C-2	Curtiss	
00006-00200	SB2C-1	Curtiss	
00201-00370	SB2C-1C	Curtiss	
00371-00372	JF-2	Grumman	
00373-00392	TBF-1	Grumman	
00393	XTBF-2	Grumman	
00394-00658	TBF-1	Grumman	
00659-00802	J2F-5	Grumman	
00803-00882	SB2A-2	Brewster	
00883-01004	SB2A-3	Brewster	00943-01004 Cx
01005	XSB2A-1	Brewster	
01006-01007	R50-3	Lockheed	
01008-01215	SB2C-1C	Curtiss	01209-01215 Cx
01209-01212	XFO-1	Lockheed	P-38

Bureau Number	Aircraft Type	Manufacturer	Notes
01213-01215	XF15C-1	Curtiss	
01216-01515	OS2N-1	NAF	
01516-01623	F2A-3	Brewster	
01624-01646	GB-2	Beech	
01647	JF-2	Grumman	
01648-01649	R4D-1	Douglas	
01650-01673	PBM-3C	Martin	
01674-01728	PBM-3S	Martin	
01729-01730	ZNP-K-7, -8	Goodyear	K Class Airship
01731-01770	TBF-1	Grumman	
01771-01976	SNJ-3	North American	
01977-01990	R4D-1	Douglas	
01991-02152	F4F-4	Grumman	
02153-02156	F4U-1	Vought	
02157	XF4U-3	Vought	
02158-02736	F4U-1	Vought	
02737-02746	PB2Y-3R	Consolidated	
02747-02790	OY-1	Consolidated	02789-02790 Cx
02789-02790	XP4M-1	Martin	
02791-02946	PBN-1	NAF	02802 Cx
02947	R3O-2	Lockheed	
02948-02977	PBY-5A	Consolidated	
02978	V-173	Vought	
02979-02980	LNS-1	Schweizer	
02981	XF6F-4	Grumman	
02982	XF6F-3	Grumman	
02983-03182	SNV-1	Vultee	
03183	XF14C-2	Curtiss	
03184	XF14C-1	Curtiss	Cx
03185-03384	SBD-3	Douglas	
03385-03544	F4F-4	Grumman	
03545-03548	Free Balloon	Lakehurst	
03549-03550	XF7F-1	Grumman	
03551-03552	XSB2D-1	Douglas	
03553-03742	SNB-2	Beech	03563-03742 Cx
03563-03742	PBM-4E	Martin	Cx
03563-03712	PBV-1A	Vickers	Cx
03713-03742	JRF-5	Grumman	Cx
03743-03744	XSB3C-1	Curtiss	Cx
03745-03801	PBB-1	Boeing	Cx
03802-03841	F4U-1	Vought	
03842-03861	PBO-1	Lockheed	
03862-04148	SB2C-2	Curtiss	Cx
03862-04025	OY-1	Consolidated	04021-04025 Cx
04149-04198	SO3C-2	Curtiss	
04199-04348	SO3C-3	Curtiss	04290-04348 Cx
04349-04358	JRF-5	Grumman	
04359-04379	ZNPK	Goodyear	
04380-04389	LNS-1	Schweizer	
04390-04395	GH-1	Howard	
04396-04398	JR2S-1	Sikorsky	Cx
04399-04420	PBY-5A	Consolidated	

Bureau Number	Aircraft Type	Manufacturer	Notes
04421-04424	Free Balloon	Lakehurst	
04425-04514	PBY-5	Consolidated	
04515-04774	F3A-1	Brewster	
04775-04958	F6F-3	Grumman	
04959-04961	BTD-1	Douglas	
04962	XBTD-2	Douglas	
04963	BTD-1	Douglas	
04964	XBTD-2	Douglas	
04965-04971	BTD-1	Douglas	
04972-05045	PBY-5A	Consolidated	
05046-05050	R5O-4	Lockheed	
05051-05072	R4D-1	Douglas	
05073-05084	R4D-3	Douglas	
05085-05234	SNC-1	Curtiss	
05235-05434	N2S-3	Stearman	Boeing
05435-05526	SNJ-3	North American	
05527-05674	SNJ-4	North American	
05673-05874	SNV-1	Vultee	
05875-05876	N2T-1	Timm	
05877-06491	TBF-1	Grumman	
06492-06701	SBD-3	Douglas	
06702-06991	SBD-4	Douglas	
06992-06999	R4D-3	Douglas	
07000-07003	R4D-4	Douglas	
07004	JRF-1	Grumman	
07005-08004	N2S-3	Stearman	Boeing
08005	R3D-3	Douglas	
08006-08028	GH-1	Howard	
08029	GH-2	Howard	
08030-08123	PBY-5A	Consolidated	
08124-08549	PBY-5	Consolidated	
08550-08797	F3A-1	Brewster	
08798-09047	F6F-3	Grumman	
09048-09392	BTD-1	Douglas	09063-09392 Cx
09063	SNJ-4	North American	
09064	P-51H	North American	From USAAF
09085-09095	XBT2D-1	Douglas	XAD-1
09096	XBT2D-1P	Douglas	
09097	XBT2D-1	Douglas	
09098-09099	XBT2D-1N	Douglas	
09100-09106	XBT2D-1	Douglas	
09107	XBT2D-1W	Douglas	XAD-1W
09108	XAD-2	Douglas	
09109	XBT2D-1Q	Douglas	
09110-09351	AD-1	Douglas	
09352-09392	AD-1Q	Douglas	09387-09392 Cx
09393-09692	OS2U-3	Vought	
09693-09752	SBD-5A	Douglas	
09753-09764	Free Balloon	Lakehurst	
09765	GB-2	Beech	Misc. acquisition
09766	GB-1	Beech	Misc. acquisition
09767	JRF-4	Grumman	Misc. acquisition

Bureau Number	Aircraft Type	Manufacturer	Notes
09768	GB-1	Beech	Misc. acquisition
09769-09770	GH-1	Howard	Misc. acquisition
09771	JRB-2	Beech	Misc. acquisition
09772	GB-1	Beech	Misc. acquisition
09773-09774	GB-2	Beech	Misc. acquisition
09775	GH-1	Howard	Misc. acquisition
09776-09778	GB-1	Beech	Misc. acquisition
09779	GH-1	Howard	Misc. acquisition
09780	GB-1	Beech	Misc. acquisition
09781	GH-1	Howard	Misc. acquisition
09782	JRF-1	Grumman	Misc. acquisition
09783	YKS-6	Waco	Misc. acquisition
09784	YKS-7	Waco	Misc. acquisition
09785	CH400	Bellanca	Misc. acquisition
09786	Stinson	Stinson	Misc. acquisition
09787-09788	GK-1	Fairchild	Misc. acquisition
09789	J4F-2	Grumman	Misc. acquisition
09790-09797	GK-1	Fairchild	Misc. acquisition
09798-09799	GQ-1	Stinson	Misc. acquisition
09800	GB-1	Beech	Misc. acquisition
09801-09802	ZNN-L	Goodyear	L Class Airships
09803	R2Y-1	Consolidated	
09804	A-30	Martin	From England
09805-09816	J4F-2	Grumman	
09817-10316	SNJ-4	North American	
10317-10806	SBD-4	Douglas	
10807-11066	SBD-5	Douglas	
11067-11646	F3A-1	Brewster	11294-11646 Cx
11294-11646	AT-19	Stinson	Reverse Lend Lease
11647-11648	XLRA-1	Allied Aviation	
11649-11650	XLRH-1	Snead	Cx
11651-11654	XLRQ-1	Bristol	11653-11654 Cx
11655-12227	F4F-4	Grumman	
12228-12229	XF4F-8	Grumman	
12230-12329	F4F-3	Grumman	
12330-12353	GB-2	Beech	
12354-12389	SNB-2	Beech	
12390-12392	JR2S-2	Sikorsky	
12393-12404	R4D-1	Douglas	
12405-12446	R4D-5	Douglas	
12447-12453	R5O-4	Lockheed	
12454-12491	R5O-5	Lockheed	
12492-12991	SNV-1	Vultee	
12992	XF2G-1	Goodyear	
12993-13470	FG-1D	Goodyear	
13471-13472	XF2G-1	Goodyear	
13473-14690	FG-1D	Goodyear	
14691-14695	XF2G-1	Goodyear	
14696-14991	FG-1D	Goodyear	
14992-15951	FM-1	Eastern	
15952-16791	FM-2	Eastern	
16792-17091	TBM-1C	Eastern	

Bureau Number	Aircraft Type	Manufacturer	Notes
17092-17248	R4D-5	Douglas	
17249-17291	R4D-6	Douglas	
17292-17391	TDN-1	NAF	
17392-17455	F4U-1	Vought	
17456-17515	F4U-1	Vought	
17516	XF4U-3	Vought	
17517-18191	F4U-1	Vought	
18192-18307	SB2C-1C	Curtiss	
18308	XSB2C-5	Curtiss	
18309-18598	SB2C-1C	Curtiss	
18599-18619	SB2C-3, -3E	Curtiss	
18620-18621	XSB2C-6	Curtiss	
18622-19710	SB2C-3	Curtiss	
19711-21191	SB2C-4, -4E	Curtiss	
21192-21231	SBW-1	C.C.& F.	
21232	SBW-5	C.C.& F.	Cx
21232	PBY-5A	Consolidated	
21233-21645	SBW-3	C.C.& F.	
21646-21741	SBW-4E	C.C.& F.	
21742-22006	BT2D-1, -1Q	Douglas	Cx
22007-22856	SO3C-3, -4	Curtiss	22057-22856 Cx
22257-22295	AM-1	Martin	
22296	AM-1Q	Martin	
22297-22345	AM-1	Martin	
22346-22355	AM-1Q	Martin	
22356-22856	AM-1	Martin	Cx
22453-22458	HTL-1	Bell	There was no 22455
22857-23656	TBM-3, -3E	Eastern	
23657-23756	GB-2	Beech	
23757-23856	SNB-2C	Beech	
23857-24140	TBF-1	Grumman	
24141	XTBF-3	Grumman	
24142-24340	TBF-1	Grumman	
24341	XTBF-3	Grumman	
24342-24520	TBF-1	Grumman	
24521-25070	TBM-1	Eastern	
25071-25174	TBM-1C	Eastern	
25175	XTBM-3	Eastern	
25176-25520	TBM-1C	Eastern	
25521	XTBM-3	Eastern	
25522-25699	TBM-1C	Eastern	
25700	XTBM-3	Eastern	
25701-25720	TBM-1C	Eastern	
25721-26195	F6F-3,- 3N	Grumman	
26196-26425	NE-1	Piper	
26426	LNS-1	Schweizer	Cx
26427-27851	SNJ-4	North American	
27852	XP4Y-1	Consolidated	
27853-27856	XTDN-1	NAF	
27857-27858	XTDR-1	Interstate	
27859-27958	TDR-1	Interstate	

Bureau Number	Aircraft Type	Manufacturer	Notes
27959	R50-3	Lockheed	
27960-28058	N2S-4	Stearman	
28059-28829	SBD-5	Douglas	
28830	XSBD-6	Douglas	
28831-29213	SBD-5	Douglas	
29214-29375	SB2A-4	Brewster	
29376-29550	NH-1	Howard	
29551-29668	SNB-2C	Beech	29665-29668 Cx
29665-29666	XTD3C-1	Culver	
29667-29668	P-80A	Lockheed	From Army
29669-29698	NE-2	Piper	29689-29698 Cx
29689	P-80A	Lockheed	From Army
29690	P-80B	Lockheed	From Army
29691-29722	Unknown	Unknown	Cx
29723-29922	PV-1	Lockheed	
29923-30146	N2S-4	Stearman	Boeing
30147	R4D-1	Douglas	
30148-30150	R50-5	Lockheed	
30151	J4F-2	Grumman	
30152-30196	ZNP-K	Goodyear	K Class Airship, K-30 to K-74
30197-30296	AE-1	Piper	HE-1
30297-30298	XF14C-3	Curtiss	Cx
30299-31398	TBY-2	Consolidated	30368-30370 Cx 30481-31398 Cx
30368	XHJS-1	Sikorsky	
30369	TBY-2	Consolidated	
30370	XHJS-1	Sikorsky	
30481-30542	AT-19	Stinson	From UK
30543-31398	Unknown	Unknown	
31399	XBTC-1	Curtiss	Cx
31400	XBTC-2	Curtiss	Cx
31399-31400	XJL-1	Columbia	
31401-31402	XBTC-2	Curtiss	
31403-31502	LRA-1	Allied	Cx
31503-31504	XLR2A-1	Allied	
31505-31506	XLNE-1	Pratt, Read & Co.	
31507-31585	LNE-1	Pratt, Read & Co.	
31586-31635	LRH-1	Snead	Cx
31636-31685	SBF-1	Fairchild	
31686-31835	SBF-3	Fairchild	
31836-31935	SBF-4E	Fairchild	
31936-32085	PB4Y-1	Consolidated	
32086	XPB4Y-2	Consolidated	
32087-32094	PB4Y-1	Consolidated	
32095-32096	XPB4Y-2	Consolidated	
32097-32335	PB4Y-1	Consolidated	
32336-32385	GH-2	Howard	
32386	XPB3Y-1	Consolidated	Cx
32386	XTDC-2	Culver	
32387-32636	N2T-1	Timm	
32637-32786	J2F-6	Columbia	Grumman design

Bureau Number	Aircraft Type	Manufacturer	Notes
32787-32936	GH-2	Howard	32867-32936 Cx
32867-32936	GB-2	Beech	32916-32936 Cx, from UK
32937-32986	J4F-2	Grumman	
32987-32991	SNC-1	Curtiss	
32992-33066	GB-2	Beech	
33067-33466	PV-1	Lockheed	From Army
33467-33514	ZNP-K	Goodyear	Cx
33515-33614	TDR-1	Interstate	33532-33614 Cx
33532-33534	XF6U-1	Vought	
33535-33614	J2F-6	Columbia	Grumman design
33615-33714	AM-1, -1Q	Martin	Cx
33615-33621	R4D-4R	Douglas	
33622-33714	TDR-1	Interstate	
33715-33814	LRQ-1	Bristol	Cx
33815-33820	R4D-4	Douglas	
33821-33870	AM-1, -1Q	Martin	Cx
33821-33870	TO-1	Lockheed	TV-1/P-80C
33871-33920	TD3R-1	Interstate	33881-33920 Cx
33921	XTD3R-1	Interstate	
33922	XTD2R-1	Interstate	
33923-33924	XTD3R-1	Interstate	
33925-33951	PV-3	Lockheed	
33952-33957	J4F-2	Grumman	
33958-33959	XF5U-1	Vought	33959 Cx
33960-34059	PBY-5A	Consolidated	
34060-34094	JRF-5	Grumman	
34095-34096	XSC-1	Curtiss	
34097-34101	N2S-4	Stearman	Boeing
34102-34105	TBM-1C	Eastern	
34106	PB-1W	Boeing	From Army, B-17G
34107-34111	N2S-4	Stearman	Boeing
34112-34113	JK-1	Fairchild	
34114	PB-1W	Boeing	From Army, B-17G
34115-34134	LNE-1	Pratt, Read & Co.	
34135-34584	SNV-1	Vultee	
34585	J4F-2	Grumman	Misc. acquisition
34586-34997	PV-1	Lockheed	
34998-35047	PBJ-1C	North American	
35048-35096	PBJ-1D	North American	
35097	PBJ-1G	North American	
35098-35193	PBJ-1D	North American	
35194-35195	PBJ-1J	North American	
35196-35202	PBJ-1D	North American	
35203-35249	PBJ-1J	North American	
35250-35297	PBJ-1H	North American	
35298-35300	XSC-1	Curtiss	
35301	SC-1	Curtiss	
35302	XSC-1A	Curtiss	
35303-35797	SC-1	Curtiss	
35798-35921	PBN-1	NAF	Cx
35798-35920	PBJ-1J	North American	
35921	JRF-4	Grumman	

Bureau Number	Aircraft Type	Manufacturer	Notes
35922-35949	SBD-5	Douglas	
35950	SBD-6	Douglas	
35951-36421	SBD-5	Douglas	
36422-36424	XLNR-1	Aeronca	
36425-36427	XLNP-1	Piper	
36428-36430	XLNT-1	Taylorcraft	
36431-36432	XLRN-1	NAF	Cx
36433-36932	SBD-5	Douglas	
36933-36934	XTB2D-1	Douglas	
36935-37034	J2F-6	Columbia	Grumman design
37035-37064	PV-2C	Lockheed	
37065-37534	PV-2	Lockheed	
37535-37623	PV-2D	Lockheed	37551-37623 Cx
37551	HRP-1	Piasecki	
37624-37634	PV-2D	Lockheed	
37635-37636	XTDR-1	Interstate	Cx
37637-37638	AT-19	Stinson	Cx
37639-37648	LRW-1	Waco	
37649	VKS-7	Stinson	
37650-37659	Unknown	Unknown	Cx
37660-37710	R4D-1	Douglas	37681-37710 Cx
37711-37770	J4F-2	Grumman	
37771-37831	JRF-5	Grumman	
37832-37851	Unknown	Unknown	Cx
37852-37853	RS-5	Sikorsky	From Pan Am
37854-37855	RS-4	Sikorsky	From Pan Am
37856-37967	N2S-4	Stearman	Boeing
37968-37969	XHRP-1	Piasecki	37968 Cx
37970-37972	D-558-I	Douglas	
37973-37975	D-558-II	Douglas	
37976-37977	XHJP-1	Piasecki	
37978-37987	N2S-4	Stearman	Boeing
37988-38437	N2S-3	Stearman	Boeing
38438-38732	N2S-5	Stearman	38611-38732 Cx Boeing
38733-38979	PB4Y-1	Consolidated	
38980-39012	PBJ-1J	North American	
39013-39032	RY-2	Consolidated	39018-39032 Cx
39033-39055	HNS-1	Sikorsky	39053-39055 Cx, from Army
39053-39055	XFJ-1	North American	
39056	XNL-1	Langley Aviation	
39057-39095	R4D-5	Douglas	
39096-39098	R4D-6	Douglas	
39099	R4D-7	Douglas	
39100	R4D-6	Douglas	
39101-39108	R4D-7	Douglas	
39109	R4D-6	Douglas	
39110-39136	R4D-5	Douglas	39112-39136 Cx
39112-39128	R5D-4	Douglas	
39137-39181	R5D-1	Douglas	
39182-39191	N2T-1	Timm	
39192-39291	SNB-2	Beech	

Bureau Number	Aircraft Type	Manufacturer	Notes
39292-39491	RB-1	Budd	39309-39491 Cx
39318-39468	P2V-2	Lockheed	39369-39468 Cx
39469-39491	Unknown	Unknown	Most likely not used
39492-39611	R5C-1	Curtiss	
39612-39646	R5O-6	Lockheed	
39647-39712	FR-1	Ryan	
39713-39714	XF2R-2	Ryan	Cx
39715-39746	FR-1	Ryan	Cx
39747-39748	JRF-5	Grumman	
39749-39998	SNB-1	Beech	
39999-43137	F6F-3, -3N, -3E	Grumman	
43138-43637	N2S-5	Stearman	Boeing
43638-44037	SNJ-5	North American	
44038-44187	SNV-2	Vultee	
44188-44227	PB2B-1	Boeing Canada	
44228-44312	PB2B-2R	Boeing Canada	44295-44312 Cx
44313-44314	XBTK-1	Kaiser	
44315	JRB-4	Beech	
44316-44317	XOSE-1	Edo	
44318	XHJD-1	McDonnell	
44319	LRW-1	Waco	From Army
44320-44354	LBT-1	Taylorcraft	Cx
44355-44554	TDC-2	Culver	
44555-44704	JRB-4	Beech	44685-44704 Cx
44705-44904	P4Y-1	Consolidated	Cx
44905-44920	NH-1	Howard	
44921-44922	GH-3	Howard	
44923-44934	NH-1	Howard	
44935-44937	GH-3	Howard	
44938	NH-1	Howard	
44939	GH-3	Howard	
44940	NH-1	Howard	
44941-45204	GH-3	Howard	45050-45204 Cx
45205-45274	PBM-3D	Martin	
45275-45276	XPBM-5	Martin	
45277-45404	PBM-3D	Martin	
45405-45444	PBM-5	Martin	
45445-45644	TBM-1C	Eastern	
45645	XTBM-3	Eastern	
45646-46444	TBM-1C	Eastern	
46445	HNS-1	Sikorsky	
46446-46448	XHOS-1	Sikorsky	
46449	TDC-1	Culver	
46450-46638	PBY-5A	Consolidated	
46639-46698	PBY-6A	Consolidated	
46699-46723	HNS-1	Sikorsky	46701-46723 Cx
46724	PBY-6A	Consolidated	
46725-46737	PB4Y-1	Consolidated	
46738-46837	FM-1	Eastern	
46838-47437	FM-2	Eastern	
47438-47637	TBF-1	Grumman	
47638-48123	TBF-1C	Grumman	

Bureau Number	Aircraft Type	Manufacturer	Notes
48124	PBM-3D	Martin	
48125-48163	PBM-3S	Martin	
48164-48223	PBM-3D	Martin	
48224-48228	B-314	Boeing	From Pan Am
48229	JRF-5	Grumman	
48230-48231	M-130	Martin	From Pan Am
48232-48234	XFR-1	Ryan	
48235-48236	XFD-1	McDonnell	
48237-48238	XP2V-1	Lockheed	
48239-48242	ZNP-M	Goodyear	M Class Airship, M-1 to M-4
48243-48245	SOC-3A	Curtiss	
48246-48251	JRB-4	Beech	
48252-48451	PBY-5A	Consolidated	
48452-48651	Unknown	Unknown	Cx
48452-48453	Free Balloon	Lakehurst	
48652-48939	PV-1	Lockheed	
48940-49359	F3A-1	Brewster	Cx
49360-49659	PV-1	Lockheed	
49660-49762	F4U-1	Vought	
49763	XF4U-4	Vought	
49764-50300	F4U-1	Vought	
50301	XF4U-4	Vought	
50302-50359	F4U-1	Vought	
50360-50659	F4U-1D	Vought	
50660-50689	JRF-5	Grumman	Cx
50690-50739	R5C-1	Curtiss	50730-50739 Cx
50740-50839	R4D-6	Douglas	
50840-50849	R5D-1	Douglas	
50850-50868	R5D-2	Douglas	
50869-50888	R5D-3	Douglas	50879-50888 Cx
50879-50888	XBT2C-1	Curtiss	50888 Cx
50889	R5D-2	Douglas	Cx
50889-51022	J4F-2	Grumman	Cx
51023-51094	SNB-1	Beech	
51095-51199	SNB-2C	Beech	
51200-51293	SNB-2	Beech	
51294-51349	SNB-2C	Beech	
51350-51676	SNJ-4	North American	
51677-52049	SNJ-5	North American	
52050-52549	SNV-2	Vultee	
52550-53049	N2S-5	Stearman	52627-53049 Cx Boeing
52750-52761	F2T-1N	Northrop	P-61B from Army
53050-53949	TBM-3E	Eastern	
53950-54049	JRB-4	Beech	Cx
54050-54599	SBD-5	Douglas	
54600-55049	SBD-6	Douglas	
55050-55649	FM-2	Eastern	
55650-55771	N2S-4	Stearman	Boeing
55772-55783	JRC-1	Cessna	
55784-56483	F4U-1	Vought	
56484-56683	NH-1	Howard	Cx
56484-56663	R5D-3	Douglas	56550-56663 Cx

Bureau Number	Aircraft Type	Manufacturer	Notes
56684-57083	FM-2	Eastern	
57084-57656	F4U-1D	Vought	
57657-57659	F4U-1C	Vought	
57660-57776	F4U-1D	Vought	
57777-57791	F4U-1C	Vought	
57792-57965	F4U-1D	Vought	
57966-57983	F4U-1C	Vought	
57984-57986	XF8B-1	Boeing	
57987-57999	Unknown	Unknown	Cx
57987	P-51	North American	From Army
57988-57989	R5D-1	Douglas	
57990-57991	JD-1	Douglas	
57992-57994	JA-1	Noorduyn	From Army
57995-57998	HO3S-1	Sikorsky	
57999	JA-1	Noorduyn	
58000-58999	F6F-5, -5N	Grumman	
59000-59348	PBM-5, -5E	Martin	
59349	XPBM-5A	Martin	
59350-59924	PB4Y-2	Consolidated	59554 Cx
59925	PB4Y-2B	Consolidated	
59926	PB4Y-2	Consolidated	
59927	PB4Y-2S	Consolidated	
59928	PB4Y-2M	Consolidated	
59929-59937	PB4Y-2	Consolidated	
59938	PB4Y-2M	Consolidated	
59939-59944	PB4Y-2	Consolidated	
59945	PB4Y-2M	Consolidated	
59946-59948	PB4Y-2	Consolidated	
59949	PB4Y-2M	Consolidated	
59950-59954	PB4Y-2	Consolidated	
59955-59969	PB4Y-2M	Consolidated	
59970-60009	PB4Y-2	Consolidated	
60010-60035	SBW-1B	C.C.& F.	
60036-60209	SBW-4E	C.C.& F.	
60210-60459	SBW-5	C.C.& F.	60210 Cx 60296-60459 Cx
60460-60507	OY-1	Consolidated	
60508-60581	Unknown	Unknown	Cx
60582-62314	N2S-5	Stearman	60582-61036 Cx 61905-62314 Cx
62315-62914	Unknown	Unknown	Cx
62915-62929	F4U-4B	Vought	
62930	F4U-4P	Vought	
62931-62949	F4U-4B	Vought	
62950	F4U-4P	Vought	
62951-62969	F4U-4B	Vought	
62970	F4U-4P	Vought	
62971-62989	F4U-4B	Vought	
62990	F4U-4P	Vought	
62991-63009	F4U-4B	Vought	
63010	F4U-4P	Vought	
63011-63029	F4U-4B	Vought	

Bureau Number	Aircraft Type	Manufacturer	Notes
63030	F4U-4P	Vought	
63031-63049	F4U-4B	Vought	
63050	F4U-4P	Vought	
63051-63069	F4U-4B	Vought	
63070	F4U-4P	Vought	
63071-63914	F4U-4B/P	Vought	63072-63914 Cx
63915-63991	PB4Y-1	Consolidated	63960-63991 Cx
63960-63961	YP-59A	Bell	From Army
63992	PBY-5	Consolidated	
63993-64441	PBY-6A	Consolidated	64100, 64108-64441 Cx
64100	P-59B	Bell	From Army
64108-64109	P-59B	Bell	From Army
64442-64496	JRC-1	Cessna	
64497-65396	TDR-1	Interstate	64569-65396 Cx
64569-64576	XOSE-1	Edo	Cx
64577-64896	SB2C-5	Curtiss	Cx
64943-64992	PBJ-1J	North American	
64993-65285	SB2C-4, -4E	Curtiss	
65286	XSB2C-5	Curtiss	
65287-65396	SB2C-4	Curtiss	Cx
65287-65396	PB4Y-1	Consolidated	
65397-65732	SB2C-5	Curtiss	Cx
65733-65889	Unknown	Unknown	Cx
65890-66244	F6F-3	Grumman	
66245-66394	PB4Y-2	Consolidated	66325-66394 Cx
66325-66361	JRF-6B	Grumman	
66395-66594	JRB-4	Beech	66472-66594 Cx
66595-66794	JM-1	Martin	
66795-67054	PB4Y-2	Consolidated	Cx
67055-67254	FG-1D	Goodyear	67100-67254 Cx
67255-67754	FG-4	Goodyear	Cx
67100-67383	SNB-2	Beech	67130-67154 Cx
67755-67796	Unknown	Unknown	Cx
67797-67799	RY-1	Consolidated	
67800-67806	XLNT-1	Taylorcraft	
67807-67831	J4F-2	Grumman	Cx
67832-68061	PBV-1A	Vickers	Canso A, PBY-5A type
68062-69538	TBM-3	Eastern	
69539-69739	TD2C-1	Culver	
69740-69989	F7F-3	Grumman	Cx
69990-69991	LRW-1	Waco	
69992-70187	F6F-5	Grumman	
70188	XF6F-6	Grumman	
70189-70912	F6F-5,- 5N, -5P	Grumman	
70913	XF6F-6	Grumman	
70914-72991	F6F-5, -5N, -5P	Grumman	
72992-73116	PB2B-1	Boeing	
73117-73498	TBM-1C	Eastern	
73499-75158	FM-2	Eastern	
75159-75182	OY-1	Consolidated	
75183-75207	JM-1	Martin	
75208-75209	XOSE-2	Edo	Cx

Bureau Number	Aircraft Type	Manufacturer	Notes
75210-75213	XOSE-1	Edo	
75214-75215	XOSE-2	Edo	
75216-75217	XTE-1	Edo	
75218-75588	SB2C-1A	Curtiss	
75589-75688	HOS-1	Sikorsky	75625-75688 Cx
75625-75628	OSE-2	Edo	
75629-75632	TE-2	Edo	
75689-75724	HO2S-1	Sikorsky	75691-75724 Cx
75725-75726	XNQ-1	Fairchild	
75727-75728	HNS-1	Sikorsky	
75729-75730	HOS-1	Sikorsky	
75731-75738	HO2S-1	Sikorsky	Cx
75739-76138	TD2C-1	Culver	
76139-76148	FG-1	Goodyear	
76149-76449	FG-1D	Goodyear	
76450	FG-3	Goodyear	
76451-76739	FG-1	Goodyear	
76740-76759	JRB-3	Beech	
76760-76779	JRB-4	Beech	
76780-76818	SB2C-1A	Curtiss	
76819-76823	JRM-1	Martin	
76824	JRM-2	Martin	
76825-76838	JRM-1	Martin	Cx
76839-77138	PB4Y-2	Consolidated	Cx
77137-77138	PB-1W	Boeing	From Army
77139-77224	JD-1	Douglas	
77225-77244	PB-1W	Boeing	From Army
77245-77257	PB-1G	Boeing	From Army
77258	PB-1W	Boeing	From Army
77259-80258	F6F-5, -5N, -5P	Grumman	
80259-80260	F7F-1N	Grumman	
80261	XF7F-2N	Grumman	
80262-80293	F7F-1N	Grumman	
80294-80358	F7F-2N	Grumman	
80359-80547	F7F-3	Grumman	
80548	F7F-4N	Grumman	
80549-80608	F7F-3N	Grumman	
80609-80620	F7F-4N	Grumman	
80621-80758	F7F	Grumman	Cx
80621-80622	JD-1	Douglas	From UK
80759-80763	XF4U-4	Vought	
80764-82177	F4U-4	Vought	
82178-82189	F4U-1C	Vought	
82190-82259	F4U-1D	Vought	
82260-82289	F4U-1C	Vought	
82290-82369	F4U-1D	Vought	
82370-82394	F4U-1C	Vought	
82395-82434	F4U-1D	Vought	
82435-82459	F4U-1C	Vought	
82460-82539	F4U-1D	Vought	
82540-82582	F4U-1C	Vought	
82583-82632	F4U-1D	Vought	

Bureau Number	Aircraft Type	Manufacturer	Notes
82633-82639	F4U-1C	Vought	
82640-82739	F4U-1D	Vought	
82740-82761	F4U-1C	Vought	
82762-82854	F4U-1D	Vought	82853-82854 Cx
82853-82854	XJR2F-1	Grumman	
82855-82857	XF2M-1	Goodyear	Cx
82855-82857	PB-1G	Boeing	From Army
82858-83126	SB2C-4, -4E	Curtiss	
83127	XSB2C-5	Curtiss	
83128-83751	SB2C-5	Curtiss	
83752-83991	TD2C-1	Culver	
83992-84054	Unknown	Unknown	Cx
83992-84027	PB-1W	Boeing	83999-84027 Cx From Army
84028-84029	P2B-1S	Boeing	B-29 from Army
84030-84031	P2B-2S	Boeing	B-29 from Army
84032	JRB-3	Beech	
84055-84056	XTSF-1/XTB2F-1	Grumman	Cx
84057-84589	PV-2D	Lockheed	84065-84589 Cx
84590-84789	PBM-5	Martin	
84790-84818	JRF-5	Grumman	
84819-85093	SNJ-5	North American	
85094-85095	XLR2W-1	Waco	
85096-85135	JRB-4	Beech	
85136-85160	PBM-5	Martin	
85161-85162	XBTM-1	Martin	
85163-85164	XR6O-1	Lockheed	
85165-85264	LBP-1	Piper	Cx
85265-85289	LBT-1	Taylorcraft	
85290-85292	XLBE-1	Pratt, Read & Co.	
85293-85389	LBE-1	Pratt, Read & Co.	Cx
85390	XHRP-1	Piasecki	Cx
85391-85458	GB-2	Beech	Cx
85459-86296	TBM-3E	Eastern	86293-86296 Cx
86293	JRB-4	Beech	
86294	JRB-3	Beech	
86295-86296	JRB-4	Beech	
86297-87719	FM-2, -2P	Eastern	86974-87719 Cx
87720-87762	JRF-5	Grumman	87752-87762 Cx
87752	JRB-3	Beech	
87753	JRB-4	Beech	
87754-87759	R5D-3	Douglas	
87763-87787	LNT-1	Taylorcraft	
87788-88453	FG-1D	Goodyear	
88454-88458	F2G-1	Goodyear	
88459-88871	F2G-2	Goodyear	88464-88871 Cx
88872-89071	PBJ-1H	North American	
89072-89081	JD-1	Douglas	
89082-89085	P2V-1	Lockheed	
89086	XP2V-2	Lockheed	
89087-89096	P2V-1	Lockheed	
89097-89119	XTB2D-1	Douglas	Cx

Bureau Number	Aircraft Type	Manufacturer	Notes
89120-90019	SB2C-5	Curtiss	89466-90019 Cx
89466-89492	JRB-5	Beech	
89493	JRB-1	Beech	
89494	JRB-5	Beech	
90020-90131	RY-3	Consolidated	90060-90131 Cx
90060-90061	XF2L-1	Bell	P-63, Cx
90132-90384	R2Y-1	Consolidated	Cx
90132-90271	PB4Y-1	Consolidated	
90385-90395	R5D-2	Douglas	
90396-90415	R5D-4	Douglas	
90416-90436	Unknown	Unknown	Cx
90437-90459	F8F-1	Grumman	
90460-90461	XF8F-1	Grumman	
90462-90483	PB4Y-1	Consolidated	
90484-90503	XBTK-1	Kaiser	90487-90503 Cx
90504-90506	XTB3F-1	Grumman	
90507-90531	JM-2	Martin	90522-90531 Cx
90522-90523	JRB-2	Beech	
90532-90581	JRB-4	Beech	
90582-91106	SNJ-5	North American	91102-91106 Cx
91102-91103	F2L-1K	Bell	
91104	R4D-1	Douglas	
91105	R5D-1	Douglas	
91106	Mosquito	DeHavilland	From UK
91107-92006	TBM-3E	Eastern	91753-92006 Cx
91962-91993	JM-2	Martin	
91994-92006	R5D-3	Douglas	92004-92006 Cx
92007-93301	FG-1D	Goodyear	92702-93301 Cx
93302-93651	SC-1	Curtiss	93368-93651 Cx
93652-94751	F6F-5	Grumman	94522-94751 Cx
94752-95048	F8F-1	Grumman	
95049	XF8F-2	Grumman	
95050-95329	F8F-1	Grumman	
95330	XF8F-2	Grumman	
95331-96751	F8F-1	Grumman	95499-96751 Cx
96752-97295	F4U-4	Vought	
97296	XF4U-5	Vought	
97297-97363	F4U-4	Vought	
97364	XF4U-5	Vought	
97365-97414	F4U-4	Vought	
97415	XF4U-5	Vought	
97416-97531	F4U-4	Vought	
97532-97672	TBM-3	Eastern	Cx
97673-97675	XTBM-4	Eastern	
97676-98601	TBM-4	Eastern	Cx
98602-98605	PBM-5E	Martin	
98606	PBM-5N	Martin	
98607-98615	PBM-5E	Martin	
98616	XP5M-1	Martin	
98617-99073	PBM-5	Martin	Cx
99074-99077	J4F-2	Grumman	Misc. acquisition
99078	JRF-4/G-21A	Grumman	Misc. acquisition

Bureau Number	Aircraft Type	Manufacturer	Notes
99079	GK-1	Fairchild	Misc. acquisition
99080	PBY-4	Consolidated	American Export
99081-99084	B-314	Boeing	From Pan Am.
99085-99088	AT-19	Stinson	From Pan Am.
99089	Waco	Waco	From Pan Am.
99090-99092	Electra	Lockheed	From Pan Am.
99093-99095	Lodestar	Lockheed	From Pan Am.
99096-99097	Speedster	Rerwin	From Pan Am.
99098	Pilgrim	Pilgrim	From Pan Am.
99099	DC-3A	Douglas	From Pan Am.
99100-99823	Unknown	Unknown	Cx
99824-99857	R4D-7	Douglas	
99858-99860	XF2H-1	McDonnell	
99861-99990	R4D-6	Douglas	Cx
99991-100000	Unknown	Unknown	Cx

The beginning of the six digit series

Bureau Number	Aircraft Type	Manufacturer	Notes
000001	A-1	Navy & IAS	Replica-Navy's 1st a/c
001009-001023	DSN-3/QH-50C	Gyrodyne	DSN-3 redesig. QH-50C
001024-001027	QH-50C	Gyrodyne	
001029-001041	QH-50C	Gyrodyne	
001043-001049	QH-50C	Gyrodyne	
001051	QH-50C	Gyrodyne	
001053-001192	QH-50C	Gyrodyne	
001193-001196	QH-50D	Gyrodyne	
001197-001293	QH-50C	Gyrodyne	
001295-001307	QH-50C	Gyrodyne	
001309-001314	QH-50C	Gyrodyne	
001316-001327	QH-50C	Gyrodyne	
001329-001340	QH-50C	Gyrodyne	
001342-001347	QH-50C	Gyrodyne	
001349-001358	QH-50C	Gyrodyne	
001360-001362	QH-50C	Gyrodyne	
001365	QH-50C	Gyrodyne	
001367-001375	QH-50C	Gyrodyne	
001377-001381	QH-50C	Gyrodyne	
001382	QH-50D	Gyrodyne	
001383-001385	QH-50C	Gyrodyne	
001386-001493	QH-50D	Gyrodyne	
001495-001571	QH-50D	Gyrodyne	
001572	QH-50C	Gyrodyne	
001573-001613	QH-50D	Gyrodyne	
001615-001758	QH-50D	Gyrodyne	
002743-002744	X-25A	Bensen	
100001-102000	F8F-1	Grumman	Cx
102001-102275	PV-2D	Lockheed	Cx
102276-102575	PBM-5	Martin	Cx
102576-104575	TBM-4	Martin	Cx
104576-105175	FR-2	Ryan	Cx
105176-106875	F4U-4	Vought	Cx

Bureau Number	Aircraft Type	Manufacturer	Notes
106876-107875	FG-4	Goodyear	Cx
107876-108225	SB2C-5	Curtiss	Cx
108226-109272	F6F-5N	Grumman	Cx
109273-111148	F3M-1	Eastern	Cx
111149-111348	PBY-6A	Consolidated	Cx
111349-111748	F6F-5	Grumman	Cx
111749-111848	FD-1	McDonnell	111809-111848 Cx
111809-111828	HRP-1	Piasecki	
111829-111833	HRP-2	Piasecki	
111834-111848	HRP-1	Piasecki	Cx
111849-111948	SC-1	Curtiss	Cx
111949-112528	SNJ-6	North American	112360-112528 Cx
112529-114528	F8F-1	Grumman	Cx
114529-115728	F4U-4	Vought	Cx
115729-116728	FG-4	Vought	Cx
116729-117728	F7F-3	Grumman	Cx
117729-118928	TBM-4	Eastern	Cx
118929-119528	TBY-3, -4	Consolidated	Cx
119529-119778	SC-2	Curtiss	119539-119778 Cx
119779-119978	PBY-6A	Consolidated	Cx
119979-120338	TD2C-1	Culver	
120339-120341	XFJ-1	North American	Cx
120339-120340	XTD4C-1/XUC-1K	Culver	
120342-120441	FJ-1	North American	120372-120441 Cx
120442-120474	OY-1	Consolidated	
120475-121414	PBY-6A	Consolidated	Cx
121415-121438	OY-1	Consolidated	Cx
121439-121440	Unknown	Unknown	Cx
121441-121444	ME-262	Messerschmitt	
121445-121446	AR-234	Arado	
121447	DO-335	Dornier	
121448	ME-262S	Messerschmitt	
121449-121450	XSN2J-1	North American	
121451-121454	P4M-1	Martin	
121455-121456	XP5Y-1	Consolidated	
121457-121459	XF3D-1	Douglas	
121460-121462	XAJ-1	North American	
121463-121522	F8F-1	Grumman	
121523-121792	F8F-2	Grumman	
121793-121803	F4U-5	Vought	
121804	F4U-5P	Vought	
121805-121815	F4U-5	Vought	
121816	F4U-5N	Vought	
121817-121831	F4U-5	Vought	
121832-121833	F4U-5N	Vought	
121834-121851	F4U-5	Vought	
121852-121853	F4U-5N	Vought	
121854-121871	F4U-5	Vought	
121872-121874	F4U-5N	Vought	
121875-121890	F4U-5	Vought	
121891-121893	F4U-5N	Vought	
121894-121911	F4U-5	Vought	

Bureau Number	Aircraft Type	Manufacturer	Notes
121912-121915	F4U-5N	Vought	
121916-121931	F4U-5	Vought	
121932-121935	F4U-5N	Vought	
121936	F4U-5P	Vought	
121937-121951	F4U-5	Vought	
121952-121955	F4U-5N	Vought	
121956-121957	F4U-5P	Vought	
121958-121972	F4U-5	Vought	
121973-121976	F4U-5N	Vought	
121977-121978	F4U-5P	Vought	
121979-121994	F4U-5	Vought	
121995-121998	F4U-5N	Vought	
121999-122002	F4U-5P	Vought	
122003-122014	F4U-5	Vought	
122015-122018	F4U-5N	Vought	
122019-122022	F4U-5P	Vought	
122023-122036	F4U-5	Vought	
122037-122040	F4U-5N	Vought	
122041-122044	F4U-5	Vought	
122045-122048	F4U-5P	Vought	
122049-122057	F4U-5	Vought	
122058-122061	F4U-5N	Vought	
122062-122065	F4U-5P	Vought	
122066	F4U-5	Vought	
122067-122086	PBM-5A	Martin	
122087-122152	F8F-1B	Grumman	
122153-122166	F4U-5	Vought	
122167-122206	F4U-5P	Vought	
122207-122209	P4M-1	Martin	
122210-122365	AD-2	Douglas	
122366-122372	AD-2Q	Douglas	
122373	AD-2QU	Douglas	
122374-122387	AD-2Q	Douglas	
122388-122393	AM-1Q	Martin	
122394-122437	AM-1	Martin	
122438-122467	P2V-2	Lockheed	
122447-122451	F2L-1	Bell	Cx
122452-122461	HTL-1	Bell	Reassig. 22453-22458
122468-122471	PBM-5A	Martin	
122472-122474	XF7U-1	Vought	
122475	XF9F-2	Grumman	
122476	XF9F-3	Grumman	
122477	XF9F-2	Grumman	
122478-122507	F6U-1	Vought	
122508-122529	HO3S-1	Sikorsky	
122530-122559	F2H-1	McDonnell	
122560-122589	F9F-2	Grumman	
122590-122601	AJ-1	North American	
122602-122613	PBM-5A	Martin	
122614-122708	F8F-2	Grumman	
122709-122728	HO3S-1	Sikorsky	
122729-122852	AD-3	Douglas	

Bureau Number	Aircraft Type	Manufacturer	Notes
122853	AD-4	Douglas	
122854-122876	AD-3Q	Douglas	
122877-122905	AD-3W	Douglas	
122906-122907	AD-3E	Douglas	
122908-122909	AD-3N	Douglas	
122910-122911	AD-3S	Douglas	
122912-122922	AD-3N	Douglas	
122923-122951	P2V-3	Lockheed	
122952-122963	HTL-2	Bell	
122964-122987	P2V-3	Lockheed	
122988-122989	XA2D-1	Douglas	
122990-123015	F2H-1	McDonnell	
123016-123083	F9F-3	Grumman	
123084	XF9F-4	Grumman	
123085	XF9F-5	Grumman	
123086-123087	F9F-3	Grumman	123087 Cx
123088-123116	AF-2S	Grumman	Even BuNo's
123089-123117	AF-2W	Grumman	Odd BuNo's
123118-123143	HO3S-1	Sikorsky	
123144-123203	F4U-5N, -5NL	Vought	
123204-123299	F2H-2	McDonnell	
123300-123313	F2H-2N	McDonnell	
123314-123396	F2H-2	McDonnell	123383-123396 Cx
123397-123740	F9F-2	Grumman	123714-123740 Cx
123741-123770	F3D-1	Douglas	123769-123770 Cx
123771-124005	AD-4	Douglas	
124006	XAD-5	Douglas	
124007-124036	AD-4	Douglas	Cx
124037-124075	AD-4Q	Douglas	
124076-124127	AD-4W	Douglas	
124128-124156	AD-4N	Douglas	
124157-124186	AJ-1	North American	124185-124186 Cx
124187-124209	AF-2W	Grumman	Odd BuNo's
124188-124210	AF-2S	Grumman	Even BuNo's
124211-124267	P2V-4	Lockheed	
124268-124291	P2V-3W	Lockheed	
124292-124323	PF-1	Grumman	Cx
124324-124333	R4Q-1	Fairchild	124332-124333 Cx
124334-124353	HO3S-1	Sikorsky	
124354-124361	P2V-3W	Lockheed	124360-124361 Cx
124362-124373	P4M-1	Martin	
124374-124379	UF-1	Grumman	
124380-124414	F6U-1	Vought	Cx
124415-124434	F7U-1	Vought	124429-124434 Cx
124435-124436	XF10F-1	Grumman	
124437-124438	PO-1W	Lockheed	
124439-124440	XA2J-1	North American	
124441-124503	F4U-5N	Vought	
124504-124522	F4U-5NL	Vought	
124523	F4U-5N	Vought	
124524-124560	F4U-5NL	Vought	
124561-124569	HTL-3	Bell	

Bureau Number	Aircraft Type	Manufacturer	Notes
124570-124585	TO-2	Lockheed	
124586-124587	XF4D-1	Douglas	
124588-124594	HUP-1	Piasecki	
124595-124664	F3D-2	Douglas	
124665	XAU-1	Vought	
124666-124709	F4U-5NL	Vought	
124710-124724	F4U-5N	Vought	
124725-124760	AD-4NL	Douglas	
124761-124777	AD-4W	Douglas	
124778-124848	AF-2S	Grumman	Even BuNo's
124779-124849	AF-2W	Grumman	Odd BuNo's
124850-124864	AJ-1	North American	
124865-124909	P2V-4	Lockheed	
124910-124914	P5M-1	Martin	
124915-124929	HUP-1	Piasecki	
124930-124939	TO-2	Lockheed	
124940-125071	F2H-2	McDonnell	
125072-125079	F2H-2P	McDonnell	
125080-125152	F9F-5	Grumman	
125153-125225	F9F-4	Grumman	
125226-125313	F9F-5	Grumman	
125314-125321	F9F-5P	Grumman	
125322-125409	F7U-2	Vought	Cx
125410-125411	F7U-3	Vought	Cx
125412-125413	XA3D-1	Douglas	
125414-125443	F9F-5	Grumman	
125444-125445	XF3H-1	McDonnell	
125446	K-225	Kaman	
125447-125476	F9F-5	Grumman	Cx
125477-125478	K-225	Kaman	
125479-125488	A2D-1	Douglas	125485-125488 Cx
125489-125499	F9F-5	Grumman	
125500-125505	F2H-2	McDonnell	
125506-125515	HO4S-1	Sikorsky	
125516-125527	HO5S-1	Sikorsky	
125528-125531	HOK-1	Kaman	
125532	UH-12/HTE-1	Hiller	
125533-125648	F9F-5	Grumman	
125649-125679	F2H-2	McDonnell	
125680-125706	F2H-2P	McDonnell	
125707-125741	AD-4N	Douglas	
125742-125764	AD-4NA	Douglas	
125765-125782	AD-4W	Douglas	
125783-125882	F3D-2	Douglas	
125883-125892	F3D-3	Douglas	Cx
125893-126256	F9F-5	Grumman	
126257-126264	F9F-6	Grumman	
126265-126290	F9F-5P	Grumman	
126291-126350	F2H-3	McDonnell	16 to Canada
126351-126353	F2H-4	McDonnell	
126354-126489	F2H-3	McDonnell	24 to Canada
126490-126511	P5M-1	Martin	

Bureau Number	Aircraft Type	Manufacturer	Notes
126512-126513	WV-2	Lockheed	
126514-126573	P2V-6	Lockheed	126548-126573 Cx
126574-126582	R4Q-1	Fairchild	
126583-126626	TV-2/TO-2	Lockheed	
126627-126669	F9F-5	Grumman	
126670-126672	XF9F-6	Grumman	
126673-126695	F2H-2P	McDonnell	
126696-126705	HO5S-1	Sikorsky	
126706-126715	HUP-1	Piasecki	
126716-126719	ZP2N-1	Goodyear	126717-126719 Cx
126720-126737	AF-2S	Grumman	
126738-126755	AF-2W	Grumman	
126756-126821	AF-2S	Grumman	
126822-126835	AF-2W	Grumman	
126836-126875	AD-4W	Douglas	
126876-126902	AD-4N	Douglas	
126903-126925	AD-4NA	Douglas	
126926-126946	AD-4N	Douglas	
126947-126969	AD-4NA	Douglas	
126970-126987	AD-4N	Douglas	
126988-127010	AD-4NA	Douglas	
127011-127018	AD-4N	Douglas	
127019-127085	F3D-2	Douglas	
127086-127215	F9F-2	Grumman	
127216-127470	F9F-6	Grumman	
127471-127472	F9F-5P	Grumman	
127473-127492	F9F-6P	Grumman	
127493-127546	F2H-3	McDonnell	
127547-127693	F2H-4	McDonnell	
127694-127695	F2H-3P	McDonnell	Cx
127696-127719	P5M-1	Martin	
127720-127782	P2V-5	Lockheed	
127783-127843	HRS-1	Sikorsky	127843 Cx
127844-127853	AD-4	Douglas	
127854-127860	AD-4B	Douglas	
127861-127865	AD-4	Douglas	
127866-127872	AD-4B	Douglas	
127873-127879	AD-4	Douglas	
127880-127920	AD-4N	Douglas	
127921-127961	AD-4W	Douglas	
127962-128042	A2D-1	Douglas	Cx
128043-128054	AJ-2P	North American	
128055-128294	F9F-6	Grumman	
128295-128310	F9F-6P	Grumman	
128311-128322	F10F-1	Grumman	128312-128322 Cx
128323-128326	WV-2	Lockheed	
128327-128422	P2V-5	Lockheed	
128423-128432	R6D-1	Douglas	
128433	R6D-1Z	Douglas	
128434-128444	R7V-1	Lockheed	
128445-128449	R3Y-1	Consolidated	
128450	R3Y-2	Consolidated	

Bureau Number	Aircraft Type	Manufacturer	Notes
128451-128478	F7U-3	Vought	
128479-128600	HUP-2	Piasecki	
128601-128620	HO5S-1	Sikorsky	
128621-128636	HTL-4	Bell	
128637-128652	HTE-1	Hiller	
128653-128660	HTK-1	Kaman	
128661-128722	TV-2/TO-2	Lockheed	
128723-128744	R4Q-1	Fairchild	
128745-128856	F2H-3	McDonnell	Cx
128857-128886	F2H-2	McDonnell	
128887-128916	HTL-4	Bell	
128917-128936	AD-4	Douglas	
128937-128943	AD-4B	Douglas	
128944-128970	AD-4	Douglas	
128971-128978	AD-4B	Douglas	
128979-129016	AD-4	Douglas	
129017-129049	HRS-2	Sikorsky	
129050-129132	F2H-3, -3P	McDonnell	Cx
129133-129136	XHSL-1	Bell	
129137-129138	XS2F-1	Grumman	
129139-129153	YS2F-1	Grumman	
129154-129168	HSL-1	Bell	
129169-129184	HTE-1	Hiller	
129185-129195	AJ-2P	North American	
129196-129242	AF-2S	Grumman	
129243-129257	AF-3S	Grumman	
129258-129299	AF-2W	Grumman	
129300-129317	HTK-1	Kaman	
129318-129417	AU-1	Vought	
129418-129544	FJ-2	North American	Cx
129418-129522	HUP-2	Piasecki	Numbers reused, then Cx
129545-129676	F7U-3	Vought	
129677	F7U-3M	Vought	
129678-129697	F7U-3	Vought	
129698-129744	F7U-3M	Vought	
129745-129756	F7U-3P	Vought	
129757-129791	HTE-2	Hiller	
129792-129799	Unknown	Unknown	Cx
129800-129842	HOK-1	Kaman	
129843-129941	HSL-1	Bell	129878-129941 Cx
129942-129977	HTL-5	Bell	
129978-130100	HUP-2	Piasecki	130086-130100 Cx
130101-130137	HO5S-1	Sikorsky	
130138-130205	HRS-2	Sikorsky	
130206-130264	HRS-3	Sikorsky	
130265-130351	P5M-1	Martin	
130352	YA3D-1	Douglas	
130353-130363	A3D-1	Douglas	
130364-130388	AF-3S	Grumman	
130389-130404	AF-2W	Grumman	
130405-130421	AJ-2	North American	
130422-130425	AJ-2P	North American	

Bureau Number	Aircraft Type	Manufacturer	Notes
130426-130462	F3D-2	Douglas	Cx
130463-130739	F3D-3	Douglas	Cx
130740-130751	F4D-1	Douglas	
130752-130919	F9F-7	Grumman	
130920-131062	F9F-6	Grumman	
131063-131251	F9F-8	Grumman	
131252-131255	F9F-6P	Grumman	
131256-131378	F10F-1	Grumman	Cx
131379-131386	F10F-1P	Grumman	Cx
131387-131389	WV-2	Lockheed	
131390-131392	WV-2Q	Lockheed	
131393-131399	WV-2	Lockheed	Cx
131400-131543	P2V-5	Lockheed	
131544-131550	P2V-6	Lockheed	
131551-131566	P2V-6M	Lockheed	
131567-131620	R6D-1/C-118B	Douglas	From Air Force
131621-131629	R7V-1	Lockheed	
131630-131631	R7V-2	Lockheed	
131632-131659	R7V-1	Lockheed	
131660-131661	R7V-2	Lockheed	
131662-131719	R4Q-2	Fairchild	
131720-131724	R3Y-2	Consolidated	
131725-131888	TV-2/TO-2	Lockheed	131878 From Air Force
131889-131918	UF-1, -1T	Grumman	
131919-131926	ZP4K-1	Goodyear	
131927-132226	FJ-2	North American	132127-132226 Cx
132227-132391	AD-4B	Douglas	
132392-132476	AD-5	Douglas	
132477	AD-5N	Douglas	
132478	AD-5	Douglas	
132479	AD-5S	Douglas	
132480-132636	AD-5N	Douglas	
132637-132728	AD-5	Douglas	132687-132728 Cx
132729-132792	AD-5W	Douglas	132731-132792 Cx
132793-133042	A2D-1	Douglas	Cx
133043-133328	S2F-1	Grumman	133043-133044 Cx
133043-133044	WF-1	Grumman	Numbers reused, then Cx
133329-133388	S2F-2	Grumman	
133389-133488	F3H-1	McDonnell	Cx
133489-133544	F3H-1N	McDonnell	
133545-133568	F3H-2N	McDonnell	
133569	F3H-2M	McDonnell	
133570-133622	F3H-2N	McDonnell	
133623-133638	F3H-2M	McDonnell	
133639	XZP4K	Goodyear	
133640-133651	P2V-5	Lockheed	Australia
133652-133731	F4U-7	Vought	France
133732-133735	XHR2S-1	Sikorsky	
133736-133738	XHRH-1	McDonnell	Cx
133739-133753	HO4S-3	Sikorsky	UK
133754-133755	XFJ-2	North American	
133756	XFJ-2B	North American	

Bureau Number	Aircraft Type	Manufacturer	Notes
133757-133776	AD-5W	Douglas	
133777-133779	HO4S-3	Sikorsky	Netherlands
133780-133781	XS2U-1W/XWU-1	Vought	Cx
133782-133816	OE-1	Cessna	L-19A, from Air Force
133817-133818	HUM-1	McCulloch	MC-4
133819-133832	F4U-7	Vought	France
133833-133843	AU-1	Vought	
133844-133853	HO4S-3	Sikorsky	Cx
133854-134004	AD-5	Douglas	133930-134004 Cx
134004	JRB-4	Beech	
134005-134018	AD-4B	Douglas	Cx
134019-134034	ZSG-4	Goodyear	134025-134034 Cx
134035-134072	AJ-2	North American	
134073-134075	AJ-2P	North American	
134076-134233	AD-5	Douglas	Cx
134234-134244	F9F-8	Grumman	
134245-134433	F9F-6	Grumman	Cx
134434-134437	HUP-2	Piasecki	
134438-134445	A2D-1	Douglas	Cx
134446-134465	F9F-6P	Grumman	
134466-134637	AD-6	Douglas	
134638-134663	P2V-6	Lockheed	France
134664-134676	P2V-5	Lockheed	134664-134670 Cx Netherlands
134668-134670	XHSS-1	Sikorsky	
134677-134691	HUP-2	Piasecki	Cx
134692-134717	SNB-5	Beech	Netherlands/France
134718-134723	P2V-5	Lockheed	Netherlands
134724-134743	HTE-2	Hiller	UK
134744-134973	F4D-1	Douglas	
134974-135053	AD-5N	Douglas	
135054	AD-5Q	Douglas	
135055-135138	AD-5N	Douglas	Cx
135139-135222	AD-5W	Douglas	
135223-135406	AD-6	Douglas	
135407-135444	A3D-1	Douglas	
135445-135448	ZP2N-1	Goodyear	
135449-135476	P5M-1	Martin	135449-135451 Cx
135477-135543	P5M-2	Martin	
135544-135621	P2V-7	Lockheed	25 to Canada
135622-135717	HSL-1	Bell	Cx
135718-135745	HUP-2	Piasecki	Cx
135746-135761	WV-2	Lockheed	
135762-135773	YF2Y-1	Consolidated	135766-135773 Cx
135774-136162	FJ-3	North American	
136163-136392	F4D-1	Douglas	Cx
136393-136747	S2F-1	Grumman	
136748-136782	TF-1	Grumman	
136783	TF-1Q	Grumman	
136784	TF-1	Grumman	
136785	TF-1Q	Grumman	
136786	TF-1	Grumman	

Bureau Number	Aircraft Type	Manufacturer	Notes
136787-136788	TF-1Q	Grumman	
136789-136792	TF-1	Grumman	
136793-136886	TV-2	Lockheed	
136887-136911	OE-1	Cessna	
136912-136963	F7U-3	Vought	Cx
136964-136965	F7U-3P	Vought	Cx
136966-137032	F3H-2N	McDonnell	
137033-137095	F3H-2M	McDonnell	
137096-137131	F3H-1	McDonnell	Cx
137132-137155	F3H-2P	McDonnell	Cx
137156-137215	F3H-1	McDonnell	
137216-137245	F10F-1	Grumman	Cx
137246-137485	SNJ-8	North American	Cx
137486-137491	ZS2G-1	Goodyear	
137492-137632	AD-6	Douglas	
137633	Not assigned	Not assigned	
137634-137635	XF2Y-1	Consolidated	137635 Cx
137636-137637	T-28A	North American	
137638-137810	T-28B	North American	
137811	XZS2G-1	Goodyear	
137812	XA4D-1	Douglas	
137813-137831	A4D-1	Douglas	
137832	ZPG-2W	Goodyear	
137833-137835	HTK-1	Kaman	
137836-137845	HRS-3	Sikorsky	
137846-137848	P5M-2	Martin	
137849-137858	HSS-1	Sikorsky	
137859-137886	F3H-1	McDonnell	Cx
137887-137890	WV-2	Lockheed	
137891-137898	WV-3	Lockheed	
137899-137933	UF-1	Grumman	
137934-138097	TV-2	Lockheed	
138098-138102	HOK-1	Kaman	
138103-138367	T-28B	North American	
138368-138417	A2U-1	Vought	Cx
138418-138431	HR2S-1	Sikorsky	138425-138431 Cx
138432-138459	HO4S-3	Sikorsky	Cx
138460-138493	HSS-1	Sikorsky	
138494-138529	HO4S-3	Sikorsky	
138530-138534	F2Y-1	Consolidated	Cx
138535-138568	AD-5W	Douglas	Cx
138569-138576	HSL-1	Bell	Cx
138577-138601	HO4S-3	Sikorsky	
138602	HTK-1K	Kaman	
138603-138645	F11F-1	Grumman	
138646-138647	F11F-1F	Grumman	
138648-138650	XFY-1	Consolidated	
138651-138653	HOE-1	Hiller	
138654-138656	XHCH-1	McDonnell	Cx
138657-138658	XFV-1	Lockheed	
138659	XR4D-8	Douglas	
138660-138819	F3H-1	McDonnell	Cx

Bureau Number	Aircraft Type	Manufacturer	Notes
138820	R4D-8	Douglas	
138821-138822	XP6M-1	Martin	
138823-138898	F9F-8	Grumman	
138899-138901	XF8U-1	Vought	138901 Cx
138902-138976	A3D-2	Douglas	
138977-139016	TV-2	Lockheed	
139017-139029	HSS-1	Sikorsky	
139030-139207	F4D-1	Douglas	
139208-139209	F5D-1	Douglas	
139210-139278	FJ-3	North American	
139279-139280	XFJ-4	North American	
139281-139323	FJ-4	North American	
139324-139423	FJ-3	North American	Cx
139424-139530	FJ-4	North American	
139531-139555	FJ-4B	North American	
139556-139605	AD-5W	Douglas	
139606-139821	AD-6	Douglas	
139822-139867	A2U-1	Vought	Cx
139868-139917	F7U-3M	Vought	
139918	ZPG-2W	Goodyear	
139919-139970	A4D-1	Douglas	
139971-140001	HOK-1	Kaman	
140002-140052	T-28B	North American	
140053-140077	T-28C	North American	
140078-140102	OE-2	Cessna	
140103-140120	S2F-2	Grumman	140103 Cx
140121-140139	HSS-1	Sikorsky	
140140-140150	P5M-2	Martin	
140151-140160	P2V-7	Lockheed	
140161-140310	A2U-1	Vought	Cx
140311-140313	R7V-1	Lockheed	
140314-140325	HR2S-1	Sikorsky	
140326-140377	JD-1	Douglas	From Air Force
140378	R4Y-1Z	Consolidated	
140379-140413	F11F-1P/F9F-9P	Grumman	Cx
140414-140429	HSL-1	Bell	Cx
140430-140443	P2V-7	Lockheed	
140444-140446	F8U-1	Vought	
140447-140448	XF8U-2	Vought	
140449-140666	T-28C	North American	
140667-140956	T-34B	Beech	
140957	KH-15	Kellett	For ONR, test veh.
140958-140961	HRS-3	Sikorsky	Spain
140962-140986	P2V-7	Lockheed	6 to Japan
140987-140992	SNB-5	Beech	From Army
140993-141028	R4Y-1	Consolidated	
141029	HRS-3	Sikorsky	
141030-141229	F9F-8	Grumman	
141230	HRS-3	Sikorsky	
141231-141251	P2V-7	Lockheed	2 to Japan
141252-141260	P5M-2	Martin	141259-141260 Cx
141261-141288	UF-1	Grumman	

Bureau Number	Aircraft Type	Manufacturer	Notes
141289-141333	WV-2	Lockheed	
141334-141335	ZPG-2W	Goodyear	
141336-141362	F8U-1	Vought	
141363	F8U-1P	Vought	
141364-141443	FJ-3M	North American	
141444-141489	FJ-4B	North American	
141490-141558	TV-2	Lockheed	
141559-141563	ZPG-2	Goodyear	
141564-141570	ZS2G-1	Goodyear	
141571-141602	HSS-1	Sikorsky	
141603-141645	HR2S-1	Sikorsky	141618-141645 Cx
141646-141647	HR2S-1W	Sikorsky	
141648-141666	F9F-8	Grumman	
141667	YF9F-8T	Grumman	
141668-141727	F9F-8P	Grumman	
141728-141980	F11F-1	Grumman	141885-141980 Cx
141981-142009	F11F-1P	Grumman	Cx
142010	XAD-7	Douglas	
142011-142081	AD-7	Douglas	
142082-142141	A4D-2	Douglas	
142142-142235	A4D-1	Douglas	
142236-142255	A3D-2	Douglas	
142256	YA3D-2P	Douglas	
142257	A3D-2Q	Douglas	
142258	A3D-2W	Douglas	Cx
142259-142260	F4H-1	McDonnell	
142261-142268	T2V-1	Lockheed	
142269-142348	F-84 (drone)	Republic	From Air Force
142349-142357	F5D-1	Douglas	142351-142357 Cx
142358-142363	UF-1	Grumman	142363 Cx
142364-142372	HUL-1	Bell	
142373-142396	HTL-6	Bell	
142397-142399	T2V-1	Lockheed	
142400-142407	A3D-2	Douglas	
142408-142415	F8U-1	Vought	
142416-142423	A4D-2	Douglas	
142424-142427	UC-1	DeHavilland	
142428	UF-1L	Grumman	
142429	UF-1G	Grumman	
142430-142436	HRS-3	Sikorsky	Spain
142437-142532	F9F-8T	Grumman	
142533-142541	T2V-1	Lockheed	
142542-142545	P2V-7	Lockheed	
142546-142629	AD-7	Douglas	Cx
142630-142665	A3D-2	Douglas	
142666-142669	A3D-2P	Douglas	
142670-142673	A3D-2Q	Douglas	
142674-142953	A4D-2	Douglas	
142954-143013	F9F-8T	Grumman	
143014-143049	TV-2	Lockheed	
143050-143133	AD-7	Douglas	Cx
143134-143147	HUL-1	Bell	

Bureau Number	Aircraft Type	Manufacturer	Notes
143148-143171	HTL-6	Bell	
143172-143183	P2V-7	Lockheed	
143184-143230	WV-2	Lockheed	
143231	Not issued	Not issued	
143232-143366	F11F-1	Grumman	Cx
143367-143387	F11F-1P	Grumman	Cx
143388-143392	F4H-1F	McDonnell	
143393-143400	F5D-1	Douglas	Cx
143401-143402	XF12F-1	Grumman	Cx
143403-143492	F3H-2	McDonnell	
143493-143676	FJ-4B	North American	143644-143676 Cx
143677-143821	F8U-1	Vought	
143822-143827	P6M-1	Martin	
143828-143863	HR2S-1	Sikorsky	Cx
143864-143960	HSS-1	Sikorsky	
143961-143983	HUS-1	Sikorsky	
143984-144116	T-34B	Beech	
144117-144216	T2V-1	Lockheed	
144217-144218	XT2J-1	North American	
144219-144222	T2J-1	North American	
144223-144236	TT-1	Temco	
144237-144238	ZPG-2	Goodyear	Cx
144239-144241	ZS2G-1	Goodyear	
144242-144243	ZPG-3W	Goodyear	
144244-144258	HRS-3	Sikorsky	
144259-144261	UC-1	DeHavilland	
144262-144267	P2V-7	Lockheed	Cx
144268-144270	HRS-3	Sikorsky	Spain
144271-144376	F9F-8	Grumman	
144377-144426	F9F-8P	Grumman	
144427-144606	F8U-1	Vought	144462-144606 Cx
144607-144625	F8U-1P	Vought	
144626-144629	A3D-2	Douglas	
144630-144654	HUS-1	Sikorsky	
144655-144662	HUS-1A	Sikorsky	
144663-144665	OE-1	Cessna	144665 Cx
144666-144668	HRS-3	Sikorsky	Spain
144669-144674	UC-1	DeHavilland	
144675-144692	P2V-7	Lockheed	8 to France and 6 to Japan
144693-144695	HTL-3	Bell	
144696-144731	S2F-1	Grumman	
144732-144734	P2V-7	Lockheed	144733-144734 Cx
144735-144824	T2V-1	Lockheed	144765-144824 Cx
144825-144847	A3D-2P	Douglas	
144848-144855	A3D-2Q	Douglas	
144856-144867	A3D-2T	Douglas	
144868-145061	A4D-2	Douglas	
145062-145146	A4D-2N	Douglas	
145147-145156	A4D-3	Douglas	Cx
145157-145158	YA3J-1	North American	
145159-145201	F5D-1	Douglas	Cx
145202-145306	F3H-2	McDonnell	

Bureau Number	Aircraft Type	Manufacturer	Notes
145307-145317	F4H-1F	McDonnell	
145318-145415	F8U-1	Vought	
145416-145545	F8U-1E	Vought	
145546-145603	F8U-2	Vought	
145604-145647	F8U-1P	Vought	
145648-145659	F8U-1T	Vought	Cx
145660-145669	HSS-1	Sikorsky	
145670-145712	HSS-1N	Sikorsky	
145713-145836	HUS-1	Sikorsky	145813-145836 Cx
145837-145854	HTL-7	Bell	
145855-145875	HR2S-1	Sikorsky	
145876-145899	P6M-2	Martin	145880-145899 Cx
145900-145923	P2V-7	Lockheed	
145924-145956	WV-2	Lockheed	145942-145956 Cx
145957-145961	WF-2	Grumman	
145962-145963	R4Y-2	Consolidated	
145964-145976	R4Y-2, -2T	Consolidated	Cx
145977-145990	R4Y-2S	Consolidated	Cx
145991-145995	R4Y-2Q	Consolidated	Cx
145996	T2J-1	North American	
145997	XT2J-2	North American	
145998-146015	T2J-1	North American	
146016-146057	TF-1	Grumman	
146058-146237	T2V-1	Lockheed	Cx
146238-146293	T-28C	North American	
146294-146295	ZS2G-1	Goodyear	
146296-146297	ZPG-3W	Goodyear	
146298-146302	HRS-3	Sikorsky	
146303	WF-2	Grumman	
146304-146327	HUK-1	Kaman	
146328-146339	F3H-2	McDonnell	
146340-146341	F8U-3	Vought	
146342-146425	F9F-8T	Grumman	
146426-146430	UF-2	Grumman	Germany
146431-146438	P2V-7	Lockheed	Japan/France
146439	HRS-3	Sikorsky	Spain
146440-146445	P5M-2	Martin	France
146446-146447	A3D-2P	Douglas	
146448-146459	A3D-2Q	Douglas	
146460-146693	A4D-2N	Douglas	Cx
146694-146708	A3J-1	North American	146703-146708 Cx
146709-146816	F3H-2	McDonnell	146741-146816 Cx
146817-146821	F4H-1F	McDonnell	
146822-146905	F8U-1P	Vought	146902-146905 Cx
146906-147034	F8U-2	Vought	
147035-147077	F8U-2N	Vought	147073-147077 Cx
147078-147084	F8U-1P	Vought	Cx
147085-147100	F8U-3	Vought	147088-147100 Cx
147101-147136	HR2S-1	Sikorsky	Cx
147137-147146	HSS-2	Sikorsky	
147147-147201	HUS-1	Sikorsky	
147202-147205	HU2K-1	Kaman	

Bureau Number	Aircraft Type	Manufacturer	Notes
147206-147207	XP6Y-1	Consolidated	Cx
147208-147262	WF-2	Grumman	147242-147262 Cx
147263-147265	W2F-1	Grumman	
147266-147269	OF-1	Grumman	Cx
147270-147429	F9F-8T	Grumman	
147430-147530	T2J-1	North American	
147531-147538	S2F-3	Grumman	147538 Cx
147539-147542	P5M-2	Martin	France
147543-147547	T-34B	Beech	For MAP
147548	E-18S	Beech	For MAP
147549-147561	S2F-1	Grumman	
147562-147571	P2V-7	Lockheed	France
147572-147573	GV-1	Lockheed	
147574	UC-1	DeHavilland	FG-126, UK
147575-147576	P5M-2	Martin	
147577	S2F-1	Grumman	
147578-147581	HUL-1	Bell	
147582-147630	HUP-3	Vertol	For MAP
147631-147635	HSS-1N	Sikorsky	
147636-147647	S2F-1	Grumman	147646-147647 Cx
147648-147668	A3D-2	Douglas	
147669-147849	A4D-2N	Douglas	
147850-147863	A3J-1	North American	
147864-147867	A2F-1	Grumman	
147868-147895	S2F-3	Grumman	
147896-147925	F8U-2N	Vought	
147926-147945	P5M-2	Martin	147938-147945 Cx
147946-147971	P2V-7	Lockheed	
147972-147983	HU2K-1	Kaman	
147984-148032	HSS-1N	Sikorsky	
148033-148052	HSS-2	Sikorsky	
148053-148122	HUS-1	Sikorsky	
148123-148146	WF-2	Grumman	
148147-148149	W2F-1	Grumman	
148150-148239	T2J-1	North American	
148240-148245	UF-2	Grumman	
148246-148249	GV-1	Lockheed	
148250-148251	OE-1	Cessna	L-19E, for MAP
148252-148275	F4H-1F	McDonnell	
148276	YP3V-1	Lockheed	
148277	HUL-1	Bell	47G-2, for MAP
148278-148303	S2F-1	Grumman	
148304-148317	A4D-2N	Douglas	
148318-148321	UV-1L/C-130BL	Lockheed	
148322-148323	L-20	DeHavilland	Philippines
148324-148329	UF-2	Grumman	Japan
148330-148336	P2V-7	Lockheed	
148337-148362	P2V-7S	Lockheed	
148363-148434	F4H-1	McDonnell	
148435-148614	A4D-2N	Douglas	148613-148614 Cx
148615-148626	A2F-1	Grumman	148619-148626 Cx
148627-148710	F8U-2N	Vought	

Bureau Number	Aircraft Type	Manufacturer	Notes
148711-148716	W2F-1	Grumman	
148717-148752	S2F-3	Grumman	
148753-148802	HUS-1	Sikorsky	
148803-148805	HUS-1Z	Sikorsky	
148806-148822	HUS-1	Sikorsky	
148823-148882	T2J-1	North American	Cx
148883-148889	P3V-1	Lockheed	
148890-148899	GV-1	Lockheed	
148900-148923	WF-2	Grumman	
148924-148933	A3J-1	North American	
148934-148963	HSS-1N	Sikorsky	
148964-149012	HSS-2	Sikorsky	
149013-149036	HU2K-1	Kaman	
149037-149049	S2F-1	Grumman	FMS
149050-149069	UO-1	Piper	
149070-149081	P2V-7	Lockheed	Australia
149082-149087	HSS-1N	Sikorsky	Italy
149088	HUP-3	Piasecki	
149089-149130	P2V-7	Kawasaki/Lockheed	Japan
149131-149133	HSS-1N	Sikorsky	Netherlands
149134-149227	F8U-2NE	Vought	
149228-149256	S2F-3	Grumman	
149257-149275	S2F-3S	Grumman	
149276-149299	A3J-1	North American	
149300-149305	A3J-2	North American	
149306-143317	A3J-3P	North American	
149318-149402	HUS-1	Sikorsky	
149403-149474	F4H-1	McDonnell	
149475-149486	A2F-1	Grumman	
149487-149646	A4D-2N	Douglas	
149647-149666	A4D-5	Douglas	
149667-149678	P3V-1	Lockheed	
149679-149738	HSS-2	Sikorsky	
149739-149786	HU2K-1	Kaman	
149787	GV-1U	Lockheed	
149788-149789	GV-1	Lockheed	
149790	GV-1U	Lockheed	
149791-149792	GV-1	Lockheed	
149793-149794	GV-1U	Lockheed	
149795-149796	GV-1	Lockheed	
149797	GV-1U	Lockheed	
149798-149800	GV-1	Lockheed	
149801	GV-1U	Lockheed	
149802-149804	GV-1	Lockheed	
149805	GV-1U	Lockheed	
149806-149816	GV-1	Lockheed	
149817-149819	W2F-1	Grumman	
149820-149821	UV-1	Lockheed	Cx
149822-149824	UF-1	Grumman	FMS
149825-149835	P5M-2	Martin	
149836-149837	UF-1	Grumman	
149838-149839	HUL-1M	Bell	

Bureau Number	Aircraft Type	Manufacturer	Notes
149840	HSS-1N	Sikorsky	Chile
149841-149842	HSS-1N	Sikorsky	Netherlands
149843-149844	S2F-1	Grumman	
149845-149892	S2F-3	Grumman	
149893-149934	HSS-2	Sikorsky	
149935-149958	A2F-1	Grumman	
149959-150138	A4D-5	Douglas	
150139-150186	HU2K-1	Kaman	
150187-150190	R4D-6	Douglas	
150191-150192	L-20A	DeHavilland	
150193-150194	HO4S-3	Sikorsky	
150195-150264	HUS-1	Sikorsky	
150265-150278	HRB-1	Vertol	
150279-150283	P2V-7S	Lockheed	
150284-150355	F8U-2NE	Vought	
150356-150405	T-28A	North American	
150406-150493	F4H-1	McDonnell	
150494-150529	P3V-1	Lockheed	
150530-150541	W2F-1	Grumman	
150542-150551	T3J-1	North American	
150552-150580	HUS-1	Sikorsky	
150581-150600	A4D-2N	Douglas	
150601-150603	S2F-3	Grumman	
150604-150609	P3V-1	Lockheed	
150610-150617	HSS-2Z	Sikorsky	
150618-150620	HSS-2	Sikorsky	
150621-150623	HU2K-1U	Kaman	
150624-150653	F4H-1	McDonnell	
150654-150683	F8U-2NE	Vought	
150684-150690	GV-1	Lockheed	
150691	HUS-1Z	Sikorsky	Indonesia
150692-150716	T-28A	North American	S. Vietnam
150717-150729	HUS-1	Sikorsky	
150730-150732	HSS-1N	Sikorsky	Chile
150733-150807	CH-34	Sikorsky	Germany
150808-150819	HSS-1N	Sikorsky	Germany
150820	HUS-1	Sikorsky	Cx
150821-150822	HSS-1N	Sikorsky	
150823-150842	A3J-3P	North American	
150843-150932	F8U-2NE	Vought	
150933-150968	HRB-1	Vertol	
150969-150992	T3J-1	North American	
150993-151021	F4H-1	McDonnell	
151022-151261	A4D-5	Douglas	151198-151261 Cx
151262-151263	XH-51A	Lockheed	
151264-151265	UF-2	Grumman	SA-16B, Thailand
151266-151299	UH-1E	Bell	
151300-151335	HU2K-1U	Kaman	
151336-151347	T3J-1	North American	151344-151347 Cx
151348	L-20A	DeHavilland	
151349-151396	P3V-1	Lockheed	
151397-151519	F4H-1	McDonnell	

Bureau Number	Aircraft Type	Manufacturer	Notes
151520-151521	X-22A	Bell	
151522-151557	HSS-2	Sikorsky	
151558-151594	A2F-1	Grumman	
151595-151612	A2F-1Q	Grumman	151601-151612 Cx
151613-151614	CH-53A	Sikorsky	
151615-151634	RA-5C	North American	
151635-151637	SH-3A	Sikorsky	Cx
151638-151685	S-2E	Grumman	
151686-151701	CH-53A	Sikorsky	
151702-151725	E-2A	Grumman	
151726-151728	RA-5C	North American	
151729-151731	SH-34J	Sikorsky	Germany
151732-151775	F-8E(FN)	Vought	151774-151775 Cx France
151776-151779	O-1C	Cessna	L-19E, S. Korea
151780-151827	A-6A	Grumman	
151828-151839	EA-6A	Grumman	Cx
151840-151887	UH-1E	Bell	
151888-151891	C-130G	Lockheed	
151892-151901	T-41A	Grumman	TC-4B, Cx
151902-151905	UH-46A	Vertol	
151906-151961	CH-46A	Vertol	
151962-151969	RA-5C	North American	Cx
151970-151974	F-111B	Grumman	
151975-151983	RF-4B	McDonnell	
151984-152100	A-4E	Douglas	
152101	A-4F	Douglas	
152102-152103	TA-4E	Douglas	
152104-152138	SH-3A	Sikorsky	
152139	YSH-3D	Sikorsky	
152140-152187	P-3A	Lockheed	
152188	SH-34G	Sikorsky	Germany
152189-152206	UH-2B	Kaman	
152207-152331	F-4B	McDonnell	
152332-152379	S-2E	Grumman	
152380-152381	SH-34J	Sikorsky	Germany
152382-152391	T-2B	North American	
152392-152415	CH-53A	Sikorsky	
152416-152439	UH-1E	Bell	
152440-152475	T-2B	North American	
152476-152489	E-2A	Grumman	
152490-152495	UH-46A	Vertol	
152496-152553	CH-46A	Vertol	
152554-152579	CH-46D	Vertol	
152580-152582	YA-7A	Vought	
152583-152646	A-6A	Grumman	
152647-152685	A-7A	Vought	
152686	UH-34D	Sikorsky	FMS
152687-152689	C-118B	Douglas	
152690-152713	SH-3D	Sikorsky	
152714-152717	F-111B	Grumman	
152718-152765	P-3B	Lockheed	
152766-152785	E-2A	Grumman	Cx

Bureau Number	Aircraft Type	Manufacturer	Notes
152786-152797	C-2A	Grumman	
152798-152845	S-2E	Grumman	
152846-152878	TA-4F	Douglas	
152879-152885	YOV-10A	North American	
152886-152890	P-3B	Lockheed	New Zealand
152891-152964	A-6A	Grumman	152955-152964 Cx
152965-153070	F-4B	McDonnell	
153071-153088	F-4J	McDonnell	
153089-153115	RF-4B	McDonnell	
153116-153133	UH-34D	Sikorsky	
153134-153273	A-7A	Vought	
153274-153313	CH-53A	Sikorsky	
153314-153403	CH-46D	Vertol	
153404-153413	UH-46D	Vertol	
153414-153442	P-3B	Lockheed	
153443	YP-3C	Lockheed	
153444-153458	P-3B	Lockheed	
153459-153531	TA-4F	Douglas	
153532-153537	SH-3D	Sikorsky	Spain
153538-153555	T-2B	North American	
153556-153558	UH-34D	Sikorsky	
153559-153608	S-2E	Grumman	Australia, 153583-153594 Cx
153609-153610	H-23G	Hiller	
153611-153616	P-2H	Kawasaki/Lockheed	Japan
153617-153622	SH-34J	Sikorsky	Italy
153623-153642	F-111B	Grumman	Cx
153643-153659	T-28B	North American	
153660-153690	TA-4F	Douglas	
153691-153694	C-118B	Douglas	
153695-153704	UH-34D	Sikorsky	FMS
153705-153739	CH-53A	Sikorsky	
153740-153767	UH-1E	Bell	
153768-153911	F-4J	McDonnell	
153912-153950	F-4B	McDonnell	153916-153950 Cx
153951-154044	CH-46D	Vertol	
154045	UH-34D	Sikorsky	FMS
154046-154099	A-6B	Grumman	Cx
154100-154123	SH-3D	Sikorsky	
154124-154171	A-6A	Grumman	
154172-154286	A-4F	Douglas	154218-154286 Cx
154287-154343	TA-4F	Douglas	
154344-154360	A-7A	Vought	
154361-154573	A-7B	Vought	154557-154573 Cx
154574-154613	P-3B	Lockheed	154606-154613 Cx
154614-154657	TA-4F	Douglas	
154658-154729	T-28C	North American	
154730-154749	TH-1E	Bell	
154750-154780	UH-1E	Bell	
154781-154788	F-4J	McDonnell	
154789-154844	CH-46D	Vertol	
154845-154862	CH-46F	Vertol	

Bureau Number	Aircraft Type	Manufacturer	Notes
154863-154884	CH-53A	Sikorsky	
154885-154886	CH-53G	Sikorsky	
154887-154888	CH-53A	Sikorsky	
154889-154902	UH-34D	Sikorsky	FMS
154903-154910	A-4G	Douglas	Australia
154911-154912	TA-4G	Douglas	Australia
154913-154929	A-7A	Vought	Cx
154930-154942	EA-6B	Grumman	Cx
154943-154969	UH-1E	Bell	
154970-155069	A-4F	Douglas	
155070-155119	TA-4J	Douglas	
155120-155136	C-2A	Grumman	155125-155136 Cx
155137-155190	A-6A	Grumman	Cx
155191-155238	T-2B	North American	155191-155205 Cx
155239-155241	T-2C	North American	
155242-155289	A-4H	Douglas	Israel
155290	H-34G	Sikorsky	FMS
155291-155300	P-3B	Lockheed	Australia
155301-155336	CH-46F	Vertol	155319-155336 Cx
155337-155367	UH-1E	Bell	
155368-155389	CH-53A	Sikorsky	Cx
155390-155503	OV-10A	North American	
155504-155580	F-4J	McDonnell	
155581-155721	A-6A	Grumman	
155722-155730	TC-4C	Grumman	
155731-155916	F-4J	McDonnell	155904-155916 Cx
155917	LC-130R	Lockheed	
155918-156169	QT-33A	Lockheed	From Air Force
156170-156177	EC-130Q	Lockheed	
156178-156417	A-7B	Vought	Cx
156418-156477	CH-46F	Vertol	
156478-156482	EA-6B	Grumman	
156483-156506	SH-3D	Sikorsky	
156507-156546	P-3C	Lockheed	156531-156546 Cx
156547-156591	Unknown	Unknown	Cx
156592-156598	UH-34D	Sikorsky	FMS
156599-156603	P-3B	Lockheed	Norway
156604-156607	EA-6B	Grumman	Cx
156608-156653	RA-5C	North American	
156654-156677	CH-53D	Sikorsky	
156678-156685	O-1G	Cessna	FMS
156686-156733	T-2C	North American	
156734-156800	A-7C	Vought	
156801-156890	A-7E	Vought	
156891-156950	TA-4J	Douglas	
156951-156970	CH-53D	Sikorsky	
156971-156978	F-111B	Grumman	Cx
156979-156993	EA-6A	Grumman	
156994-157029	A-6A	Grumman	
157030-157101	T-2C	North American	157066-157101 Cx
157102-157126	OV-12A	Fairchild-Hiller	Cx
157127-157176	CH-53D	Sikorsky	

Bureau Number	Aircraft Type	Manufacturer	Notes
157177-157203	HH-1K	Bell	
157204-157241	AH-1G	Bell	
157242-157309	F-4J	McDonnell	
157310-157341	P-3C	Lockheed	157333-157341 Cx
157342-157351	RF-4B	McDonnell	
157352-157354	CT-39E	North American	
157355-157394	TH-57A	Bell	
157395-157428	A-4H	Douglas	Israel
157429-157434	TA-4H	Douglas	Israel
157435-157648	A-7E	Vought	157595-157648 Cx
157649-157726	CH-46F	Vertol	
157727-157756	CH-53D	Sikorsky	
157757-157805	AH-1J	Bell	
157806-157850	TH-1L	Bell	
157851-157858	UH-1L	Bell	
157859-157903	TH-1L	Bell	Cx
157904-157913	A-4K	Douglas	New Zealand
157914-157917	TA-4K	Douglas	New Zealand
157918-157925	A-4H	Douglas	Israel
157926-157929	TA-4H	Douglas	Israel
157930-157931	CH-53D	Sikorsky	
157932-157933	X-26A	Schweizer	
157934	P-3C	Lockheed	Cx
157935-157976	UH-1E	Bell	Cx
157977-157979	EA-6B	Grumman	Cx
157980-157985	F-14A	Grumman	
157986	F-14B	Grumman	
157987-157991	F-14A	Grumman	
157992-157999	S-3A	Lockheed	
158000-158001	C-130	Lockheed	Cx
158002-158028	A-7E	Vought	
158029-158040	EA-6B	Grumman	
158041-158052	A-6E	Grumman	
158053-158072	KA-6D	Grumman	Cx
158073-158147	TA-4J	Douglas	
158148-158196	A-4M	Douglas	
158197-158201	T-38A	Northrop	
158202-158203	VC-3A	Martin	
158204-158226	P-3C	Lockheed	
158227	RP-3D	Lockheed	
158228-158229	DC-130A	Lockheed	From Air Force
158230-158291	UH-1N	Bell	
158292-158309	OV-10B	North American	Germany
158310-158333	T-2C	North American	
158334-158345	CH-46F	Vertol	
158346-158379	F-4J	McDonnell	
158380-158383	CT-39G	North American	
158384-158395	AV-8A	Hawker-Siddeley	
158396-158411	OV-10C	North American	Thailand
158412-158435	A-4M	Douglas	
158436-158437	F-86H	North American	
158438-158452	UH-1N	Bell	Cx

Bureau Number	Aircraft Type	Manufacturer	Notes
158453-158527	TA-4J	Douglas	
158528-158539	A-6E	Grumman	
158540-158547	EA-6B	Grumman	
158548-158550	UH-1N	Bell	
158551-158554	VH-1N	Bell	
158555	UH-1N	Bell	
158556-158557	VH-1N	Bell	
158558-158562	UH-1N	Bell	
158563-158574	P-3C	Lockheed	
158575-158610	T-2C	North American	
158611	X-25A	Bensen	
158612-158637	F-14A	Grumman	
158638-158648	E-2C	Grumman	
158649-158651	EA-6B	Grumman	
158652-158681	A-7E	Vought	
158682-158693	RH-53D	Sikorsky	
158694-158711	AV-8A	Hawker-Siddeley	
158712-158723	TA-4J	Douglas	
158724-158725	SH-3D	Sikorsky	Spain
158726-158743	A-4N	Douglas	Israel
158744-158761	RH-53D	Sikorsky	
158762-158785	UH-1N	Bell	
158786	X-28A	Osprey	
158787-158798	A-6E	Grumman	
158799-158817	EA-6B	Grumman	
158818	X-26A	Schweizer	
158819-158842	A-7E	Vought	
158843-158844	CT-39G	North American	
158845-158846	E-2C	Grumman	
158847-158858	HH-3F	Sikorsky	USCG
158859-158873	S-3A	Lockheed	158859-158860 Cx
158874-158875	SH-3D	Sikorsky	Spain
158876-158911	T-2C	North American	
158912-158947	P-3C	Lockheed	158936-158947 Cx
158948-158977	AV-8A	Hawker-Siddeley	
158978-159025	F-14A	Grumman	
159026-159029	SH-3D	Sikorsky	
159030-159034	C-9B	Douglas	Cx
159035-159052	A-4N	Douglas	Israel
159053-159056	SH-3D	Sikorsky	
159057-159072	OV-10E	North American	Venezuela
159073-159074	U-3A	Cessna	
159075-159098	A-4N	Douglas	Israel
159099-159104	TA-4J	Douglas	
159105-159112	E-2C	Grumman	
159113-159120	C-9B	Douglas	
159121-159122	YCH-53E	Sikorsky	
159123-159128	VH-53F	Sikorsky	Cx
159129-159133	LC-130R	Lockheed	159132-159133 Cx
159134-159149	OV-10C	North American	Thailand
159150-159173	T-2C	North American	
159174-159185	A-6E	Grumman	

Bureau Number	Aircraft Type	Manufacturer	Notes
159186-159209	UH-1N	Bell	
159210-159229	AH-1J	Bell	
159230-159259	AV-8A	Hawker-Siddeley	
159260	X-26A	Schweizer	
159261-159308	A-7E	Vought	
159309-159317	A-6E	Grumman	
159318-159329	P-3C	Lockheed	
159330-159341	T-2D	North American	Venezuela
159342-159347	P-3F	Lockheed	Iran
159348	EC-130Q	Lockheed	
159349	Unassigned	Unassigned	
159350-159360	VH-3A	Sikorsky	
159361-159365	CT-39G	North American	
159366-159377	AV-8A	Hawker-Siddeley	
159378-159385	TAV-8A	Hawker-Siddeley	
159386-159420	S-3A	Lockheed	
159421-159468	F-14A	Grumman	
159469	EC-130Q	Lockheed	
159470-159493	A-4M	Douglas	
159494-159502	E-2C	Grumman	
159503-159514	P-3C	Lockheed	
159515-159545	A-4N	Douglas	Israel
159546-159556	TA-4J	Douglas	
159557-159562	AV-8A	Hawker-Siddeley	Spain
159563-159564	TAV-8A	Hawker-Siddeley	Spain
159565	UH-1N	Bell	
159566	Unassigned	Unassigned	
159567-159581	A-6E	Grumman	
159582-159587	EA-6B	Grumman	
159588-159637	F-14A	Grumman	
159638-159661	A-7E	Vought	
159662-159667	A-7H	Vought	Greece
159668-159679	A-7E	Vought	
159680-159703	UH-1N	Bell	
159704-159727	T-2C	North American	
159728-159772	S-3A	Lockheed	
159773	WP-3D	Lockheed	
159774-159777	UH-1N	Bell	
159778-159794	A-4M	Douglas	
159795-159798	TA-4J	Douglas	
159799-159824	A-4N	Douglas	Israel
159825-159874	F-14A	Grumman	
159875	WP-3D	Lockheed	
159876-159877	CH-53E	Sikorsky	
159878-159882	F-5E	Northrop	
159883-159894	P-3C	Lockheed	
159895-159906	A-6E	Grumman	
159907-159912	EA-6B	Grumman	
159913-159966	A-7H	Vought	Greece
159967-160006	A-7E	Vought	
160007-160012	E-2C	Grumman	
160013-160021	KC-130R	Lockheed	

Bureau Number	Aircraft Type	Manufacturer	Notes
160022-160045	A-4M	Douglas	
160046-160052	C-9B	Douglas	160052 Cx
160053-160058	CT-39G	North American	
160059-160098	T-2E	North American	Greece
160099-160104	RH-53D	Sikorsky	
160105-160119	AH-1J	Bell	
160120-160164	S-3A	Lockheed	
160165-160179	UH-1N	Bell	
160180-160209	A-4KU	Douglas	Kuwait
160210-160215	TA-4KU	Douglas	Kuwait
160216-160227	OV-10F	North American	Indonesia
160228-160239	T-2D	North American	Morocco
160240	KC-130R	Lockheed	
160241-160264	A-4M	Douglas	
160265-160282	T-34C	Beech	
160283-160294	P-3C	Lockheed	
160295-160298	OV-10F	North American	Indonesia
160299-160378	F-14A	Grumman	Iran
160379-160414	F-14A	Grumman	
160415-160420	E-2C	Grumman	
160421-160431	A-6E	Grumman	
160432-160437	EA-6B	Grumman	
160438-160461	UH-1N	Bell	
160462-160536	T-34C	Beech	
160537-160566	A-7E	Vought	
160567-160607	S-3A	Lockheed	
160608	EC-130Q	Lockheed	
160609	EA-6B	Grumman	
160610-160612	P-3C	Lockheed	
160613-160618	A-7E	Vought	
160619-160624	UH-1N	Bell	
160625-160628	KC-130R	Lockheed	
160629-160651	T-34C	Beech	
160652-160696	F-14A	Grumman	
160697-160703	E-2C	Grumman	
160704-160709	EA-6B	Grumman	
160710-160739	A-7E	Vought	
160740-160741	LC-130R	Lockheed	
160742-160748	AH-1T	Bell	
160749-160750	C-9K	Douglas	Kuwait
160751-160770	P-3C	Lockheed	160751-160770 Australia
160771-160774	E-2C	Grumman	Israel
160775-160785	F/A-18A	McDonnell Douglas	
160786-160791	EA-6B	Grumman	
160792-160796	F-5E	Northrop	From Air Force
160797-160826	AH-1T	Bell	
160827-160838	UH-1N	Bell	
160839-160856	T-44A	Beech	
160857-160886	A-7E	Vought	160881-160886 Cx
160887-160930	F-14A	Grumman	
160931-160963	T-34C	Beech	
160964-160966	F-5F	Northrop	

Bureau Number	Aircraft Type	Manufacturer	Notes
160967-160986	T-44A	Beech	
160987-160992	E-2C	Grumman	
160993-160998	A-6E	Grumman	
160999-161014	P-3C	Lockheed	
161015-161022	AH-1T	Bell	
161023-161056	T-34C	Beech	
161057-161079	T-44A	Beech	
161080-161081	XFV-12A	Rockwell	
161082-161093	A-6E	Grumman	
161094-161099	E-2C	Grumman	
161100-161114	A-6E	Grumman	161112-161114 Cx
161115-161120	EA-6B	Grumman	
161121-161132	P-3C	Lockheed	
161133-161168	F-14A	Grumman	
161169-161173	YSH-60B	Sikorsky	
161174-161178	EAV-8A	Hawker-Siddeley	Spain
161179-161184	CH-53E	Sikorsky	
161185-161206	UC-12B	Beech	
161207-161212	SH-3D	Sikorsky	Spain
161213-161217	F/A-18A	McDonnell Douglas	
161218-161222	TA-7H	Vought	Greece
161223	EC-130Q	Lockheed	
161224-161229	E-2C	Grumman	
161230-161241	A-6E	Grumman	161236-161241 Cx
161242-161247	EA-6B	Grumman	
161248-161251	F/A-18A	McDonnell Douglas	
161252-161265	CH-53E	Sikorsky	
161266	C-9B	McDonnell Douglas	
161267-161269	P-3C	Lockheed	Japan
161270-161305	F-14A	Grumman	161300-161305 Cx
161306-161327	UC-12B	Beech	
161328	EC-130Q	Lockheed	Cx
161329-161340	P-3C	Lockheed	
161341-161346	E-2C	Grumman	
161347-161352	EA-6B	Grumman	
161353-161367	F/A-18A	McDonnell Douglas	
161368-161380	P-3C	Lockheed	161368-161380 Netherlands
161381-161395	CH-53E	Sikorsky	
161396-161399	AV-8B	McDonnell Douglas	
161400-161403	E-2C	Grumman	
161404-161415	P-3C	Lockheed	
161416-161445	F-14A	Grumman	
161446-161493	F/A-18A	McDonnell Douglas	Cx
161494-161496	EC-130Q	Lockheed	
161497-161518	UC-12B	Beech	
161519-161528	F/A-18A	McDonnell Douglas	161526-162528 Cx
161529-161530	C-9	McDonnell Douglas	DC-9
161531	EC-130Q	Lockheed	
161532-161545	CH-53E	Sikorsky	161544-161545 Cx
161546	UC-8A	DeHavilland	DHC-5
161547-161552	E-2C	Grumman	
161553-161570	SH-60B	Sikorsky	

Bureau Number	Aircraft Type	Manufacturer	Notes
161571	X-26A	Schweizer	
161572	UC-880	Convair	
161573-161584	AV-8B	McDonnell Douglas	
161585-161596	P-3C	Lockheed	
161597-161626	F-14A	Grumman	
161627	U-8F	Beech	
161628	UC-27A	Fairchild	
161629-161640	F/A-18A	McDonnell Douglas	Cx
161641-161652	SH-2F	Kaman	
161653	YSH-2G	Kaman	
161654-161658	SH-2F	Kaman	
161659-161694	A-6E	Grumman	161691-161694 Cx
161695-161701	TH-57B	Bell	
161702-161761	F/A-18A/B	McDonnell Douglas	
161762-161773	P-3C	Lockheed	161768-161773 Cx
161774-161779	EA-6B	Grumman	
161780-161785	E-2C	Grumman	
161786-161789	E-2C	Grumman	Japan
161790-161849	T-34C	Beech	
161850-161864	F-14A	Grumman	
161865	F-14D	Grumman	
161866	F-14A	Grumman	
161867	F-14D	Grumman	
161868-161879	F-14A	Grumman	161874-161879 Cx
161880-161885	EA-6B	Grumman	
161886-161897	A-6E	Grumman	Cx
161898-161915	SH-2F	Kaman	
161916-161923	HXM		Cx
161924-161987	F/A-18A	McDonnell Douglas	
161988-162012	CH-53E	Sikorsky	
162013-162067	TH-57C	Bell	
162068-162091	AV-8B	McDonnell Douglas	162089-162091 Cx
162092-162139	SH-60B	Sikorsky	
162140-162178	C-2A	Grumman	
162179-162182	A-6E	Grumman	
162183-162187	YA-6F	Grumman	
162188-162222	A-6E	Grumman	162213-162222 Cx
162223-162246	EA-6B	Grumman	162231-162246 Cx
162247-162306	T-34C	Beech	
162307	F-5E	Northrop	
162308-162311	KC-130T	Lockheed	
162312-162313	EC-130Q	Lockheed	
162314-162325	P-3C	Lockheed	162319-162325 Cx
162326-162389	SH-60B	Sikorsky	162350-162389 Cx
162390-162393	C-9B	McDonnell Douglas	DC-9
162394-162477	F/A-18A/B	McDonnell Douglas	
162478-162498	CH-53E	Sikorsky	
162499-162526	MH-53E	Sikorsky	
162527-162531	CH-53E	Sikorsky	Cx
162532-162575	AH-1W	Bell	
162576-162587	SH-2F	Kaman	
162588-162594	F-14A	Grumman	

Bureau Number	Aircraft Type	Manufacturer	Notes
162595	F-14D	Grumman	
162596-162611	F-14A	Grumman	
162612-162613	YT-45A	McDonnell Douglas	
162614-162619	E-2C	Grumman	
162620-162649	T-34C	Beech	
162650-162655	SH-2F	Kaman	
162656-162665	P-3	For AFC TD Change	Australia
162666-162686	TH-57C	Bell	
162687	CH-53E	Sikorsky	Cx
162688-162717	F-14A	Grumman	162712-162717 Cx
162718-162720	CH-53E	Sikorsky	
162721-162746	AV-8B	McDonnell Douglas	
162747	TAV-8B	McDonnell Douglas	
162748-162752	AV-8B	McDonnell Douglas	Cx
162753-162754	C-9	McDonnell Douglas	DC-9
162755	U-8F	Beech	Cx
162755-162769	T-47A	Cessna	Civilian registration numbers
162770-162781	P-3C	Lockheed	162779-162781 Cx
162782-162784	E-6A	Boeing	
162785-162786	KC-130T	Lockheed	
162787-162790	T-45A	McDonnell Douglas	162789-162790 Cx
162791-162792	E-2C	Grumman	Egypt
162793-162796	E-2C	Grumman	Singapore
162797-162802	E-2C	Grumman	
162803-162810	TH-57B	Bell	
162811-162823	TH-57C	Bell	
162824-162825	E-2C	Grumman	
162826-162909	F/A-18A/B	McDonnell Douglas	
162910-162933	F-14A+	Grumman	162928-162933 Cx
162934-162941	EA-6B	Grumman	162940-162941 Cx
162942-162973	AV-8B	McDonnell Douglas	
162974-162997	SH-60B	Sikorsky	162992-162997 Cx
162998-163009	P-3C	Lockheed	163007-163009 Cx
163010-163021	EAV-8B	McDonnell Douglas	Spain
163022-163023	KC-130T	Lockheed	
163024-163029	E-2C	Grumman	
163030-163035	EA-6B	Grumman	
163036-163037	C-9B	McDonnell Douglas	DC-9
163038-163043	SH-60B	Sikorsky	
163044-163049	EA-6B	Grumman	
163050	EC-24A	Douglas	DC-8
163051-163089	CH-53E	Sikorsky	
163090-163091	XKB-2	Unknown	Cx
163092-163175	F/A-18A/B	McDonnell Douglas	
163176-163207	AV-8B	McDonnell Douglas	
163208	C-9B	McDonnell Douglas	DC-9
163209-163214	SH-2F	Kaman	
163215-163232	F-14A+	Grumman	163226-163232 Cx
163233-163256	SH-60B	Sikorsky	
163257-163258	UH-60A	Sikorsky	
163259-163267	VH-60A	Sikorsky	
163268-163277	F-16N	General Dynamics	

Bureau Number	Aircraft Type	Manufacturer	Notes
163278-163281	TF-16N	General Dynamics	
163282-163288	SH-60F	Sikorsky	
163289-163297	P-3C	Lockheed	163296-163297 Cx
163298-163309	F-21A	IAI	Cx
163310-163311	KC-130T	Lockheed	
163312-163347	TH-57B	Bell	
163348-163394	AV-8B	McDonnell Douglas	Cx
163395-163406	EA-6B	Grumman	
163407-163411	F-14A+	Grumman	
163412-163418	F-14D	Grumman	
163419-163426	AV-8B	McDonnell Douglas	
163427-163510	F/A-18C/D	McDonnell Douglas	
163511-163513	C-9	McDonnell Douglas	DC-9
163514-163519	AV-8B	McDonnell Douglas	
163520-163531	EA-6B	Grumman	
163532-163534	E-6A	Boeing	
163535-163540	E-2C	Grumman	
163541-163546	SH-2G	Kaman	
163547-163552	SH-2F	Kaman	Cx
163553-163564	UC-12F	Beech	
163565	E-2C	Grumman	
163566-163577	F-16N	General Dynamics	
163578-163590	P-3C	Lockheed	
163591-163592	KC-130T	Lockheed	
163593-163598	SH-60B	Sikorsky	
163599-163658	T-45A	McDonnell Douglas	
163659-163690	AV-8B	McDonnell Douglas	
163691-163692	C-20D	Gulfstream	
163693-163698	E-2C	Grumman	
163699-163782	F/A-18C/D	McDonnell Douglas	
163783-163800	HH-60H	Sikorsky	
163801-163835	HH-60J	Sikorsky	USCG 163833-163835 Cx
163836-163847	UC-12M	Beech	
163848-163851	E-2C	Grumman	
163852-163855	AV-8B	McDonnell Douglas	
163856-163861	TAV-8B	McDonnell Douglas	
163862-163883	AV-8B	McDonnell Douglas	
163884-163892	EA-6B	Grumman	
163893-163904	F-14D	Grumman	
163905-163910	SH-60B	Sikorsky	
163911-163916	YV-22A	Bell	
163917	C-28A	Cessna	
163918-163920	E-6A	Boeing	
163921-163954	AH-1W	Bell	Turkey
163955-163984	A-6F	Grumman	Cx
163985-164068	F/A-18C/D	McDonnell Douglas	
164069-164104	SH-60F	Sikorsky	
164105-164106	KC-130T	Lockheed	
164107-164112	E-2C	Grumman	
164113-164114	TAV-8B	McDonnell Douglas	
164115-164121	AV-8B	McDonnell Douglas	
164122	TAV-8B	McDonnell Douglas	

Bureau Number	Aircraft Type	Manufacturer	Notes
164123-164154	AV-8B	McDonnell Douglas	
164155-164173	T-34C	Beech	
164174-164179	SH-60B	Sikorsky	
164180-164181	KC-130T	Lockheed	
164182-164193	EA-6B	Grumman	
164194-164195	KC-130T	Lockheed	Cx
164196-164339	F/A-18C/D	McDonnell Douglas	164280-164339 Cx
164340-164351	F-14D	Grumman	
164352-164357	E-2C	Grumman	
164358-164367	CH-53E	Sikorsky	
164368-164375	MH-53E	Sikorsky	164372-164375 Cx
164376-164385	A-6E	Grumman	
164386-164388	E-6A	Boeing	
164389-164400	V-22	Bell	Cx
164401-164403	EA-6B	Grumman	
164404-164410	E-6A	Boeing	
164411-164422	F/A-18C/D	McDonnell Douglas	
164423-164440	SH-60F	Sikorsky	
164441-164442	KC-130T	Lockheed	
164443-164460	SH-60F	Sikorsky	
164461-164466	SH-60B	Sikorsky	
164467-164469	P-3C	Lockheed	Pakistan
164470-164482	CH-53E	Sikorsky	
164483-164518	E-2C	Grumman	164504-164518 Cx
164519-164523	A-12	McDonnell Douglas & General Dynamics	Cx
164524-164525	U-6A	DeHavilland	L-20A, from USDA
164526-164535	A-12	McDonnell Douglas & General Dynamics	Cx
164536-164539	CH-53E	Sikorsky	
164540-164542	TAV-8B	McDonnell Douglas	
164543-164571	AV-8B	McDonnell Douglas	
164572-164578	AH-1W	Bell	
164579-164583	T-44B	Beech	
164584-164585	X-31A	Grumman	
164586-164596	AH-1W	Bell	
164597-164598	KC-130T	Lockheed	
164599-164604	F-14D	Grumman	Cx
164605-164608	C-9	McDonnell Douglas	DC-9
164609-164620	SH-60F	Sikorsky	
164621-164626	E-2C	Grumman	
164627-164672	F/A-18C	McDonnell Douglas	
164673-164692	F/A-18D	McDonnell Douglas	
164693-164746	F/A-18C	McDonnell Douglas	
164747-164758	F/A-18D	McDonnell Douglas	
164759-164760	KC-130T	Lockheed	Cx
164761	C-28A	Cessna	
164762-164763	C-130T	Lockheed	
164764-164775	MH-53E	Sikorsky	
164776-164791	CH-53E	Sikorsky	
164792-164795	MH-53E	Sikorsky	
164796-164807	SH-60F	Sikorsky	

Bureau Number	Aircraft Type	Manufacturer	Notes
164808-164819	SH-60B	Sikorsky	
164820-164830	HH-60J	Sikorsky	
164831-164846	HH-60H	Sikorsky	
164847-164858	SH-60B	Sikorsky	
164859-164860	CH-53E	Sikorsky	
164861-164864	MH-53E	Sikorsky	
164865-164912	F/A-18C/D	McDonnell Douglas	164901-164912 Cx
164913-164938	AH-1W	Bell	Taiwan
164939-164944	V-22	Bell-Boeing	
164945-164992	F/A-18C/D	McDonnell Douglas	164981-164992 Cx
164993-164998	C-130T	Lockheed	
164999-165000	KC-130T	Lockheed	
165001-165006	AV-8B	McDonnell Douglas	
165007-165027	AV-8B	McDonnell Douglas	Italy
165028-165035	AV-8B	McDonnell Douglas	Spain
165036	TAV-8B	McDonnell Douglas	Spain
165037-165056	AH-1W	Bell	
165057-165092	T-45A	McDonnell Douglas	
165093-165094	C-20G	Gulfstream	
165095	SH-60B	Sikorsky	
165096	HH-60J	Sikorsky	USCG
165097	AH-1W	Bell	
165098-165105	P-3C	Lockheed	Korea
165106-165112	SH-60B	Sikorsky	
165113-165119	SH-60F	Sikorsky	
165120-165123	HH-60H	Sikorsky	
165124-165127	HH-60J	Sikorsky	USCG
165128-165134	SH-60B	Sikorsky	
154135-165141	SH-60F	Sikorsky	
165142-165145	HH-60H	Sikorsky	
165146-165150	HH-60J	Sikorsky	USCG
165151-165153	C-20G	Gulfstream	
165154-165157	SH-60F	Sikorsky	
165158-165161	C-130T	Lockheed	
165162-165163	KC-130T	Lockheed	
165164-165168	F/A-18E	McDonnell Douglas	
165169-165170	F/A-18F	McDonnell Douglas	
165171-165202	F/A-18C	McDonnell Douglas	
165203-165206	F/A-18D	McDonnell Douglas	
165207-165238	F/A-18C	McDonnell Douglas	
165239-165242	F/A-18D	McDonnell Douglas	
165243-165254	CH-53E	Sikorsky	
165255-165267	HH-60H	Sikorsky	
165268-165270	SH-60F	Sikorsky	
165271-165292	AH-1W	Bell	
165293-165304	E-2C	Grumman	
165305-165312	AV-8B	McDonnell Douglas	
165313-165314	C-130T	Lockheed	
165315-165316	KC-130T	Lockheed	
165317-165341	AH-1W	Bell	
165342-165343	TC-18F	Boeing	E-6A
165344-165347	CH-53E	Sikorsky	

Bureau Number	Aircraft Type	Manufacturer	Notes
165348-165351	C-130T	Lockheed	
165352-165353	KC-130T	Lockheed	
165354-165357	AV-8B	McDonnell Douglas	Remanufactured
165358-165377	AH-1W	Bell	
165378-165379	C-130T	Lockheed	
165380-165391	AV-8B	McDonnell Douglas	Remanufactured
165392-165396	AH-1W	Bell	
165397-165398	AV-8B	McDonnell Douglas	Remanufactured
165399-165416	F/A-18C/D	McDonnell Douglas	
168034	UH-1N	Bell	
198003	QF-86F	North American	
201569-201570	YF-17	Northrop	From Air Force
201970	UH-1B	Bell	From Army
210904	C-45H	Beech	
212515	UH-1B	Bell	From Army
212518	UH-1B	Bell	From Army
212522	UH-1B	Bell	From Army
212541-212543	UH-1B	Bell	From Army
212546	UH-1B	Bell	From Army
212549	UH-1B	Bell	From Army
212574-212575	CH-3B/SH-3H	Sikorsky	From Air Force
221252-221253	OH-58A	Bell	
302801	U-6A/L-20A	DeHavilland	
312908	UH-1B	Bell	From Army
312922-312923	UH-1B	Bell	From Army
312929-312931	UH-1B	Bell	From Army
312944	UH-1B	Bell	From Army
313119	OV-1A	Grumman	From Army
313128	OV-1A	Grumman	From Army
313134	OV-1A	Grumman	From Army
313988	UH-1B	Bell	From Army
349218	JC-47D	Douglas	From Army
364651	US-2E	Grumman	
413540	UH-1H	Bell	From Army
413584	UH-1D	Bell	From Army
413632	UH-1D	Bell	From Army
413646	UH-1D	Bell	From Army
413675	UH-1D	Bell	From Army
413691	UH-1H	Bell	From Army
413758	UH-1H	Bell	From Army
413765	UH-1D	Bell	From Army
413827	UH-1D	Bell	From Army
413869	UH-1D	Bell	From Army
413872	UH-1D	Bell	From Army
413901	UH-1H	Bell	
413903	UH-1B	Bell	From Army
413911	UH-1B	Bell	From Army
413919	UH-1B	Bell	From Army
413924	UH-1B	Bell	From Army
413939	UH-1B	Bell	From Army
413940	UH-1B	Bell	From Army

Bureau Number	Aircraft Type	Manufacturer	Notes
413942	UH-1B	Bell	From Army
413943	UH-1B	Bell	From Army
413948-413949	UH-1B	Bell	From Army
413952	UH-1B	Bell	From Army
413956	UH-1B	Bell	From Army
413958	UH-1B	Bell	From Army
413969	UH-1B	Bell	From Army
413975	UH-1B	Bell	From Army
413980	UH-1B	Bell	From Army
413982	UH-1B	Bell	From Army
413985	UH-1B	Bell	From Army
413989-413990	UH-1B	Bell	From Army
414001	UH-1B	Bell	From Army
414003	UH-1B	Bell	From Army
414007	UH-1B	Bell	From Army
414013	UH-1B	Bell	From Army
414020	UH-1B	Bell	From Army
414022	UH-1B	Bell	From Army
414031	UH-1B	Bell	From Army
414033	UH-1B	Bell	From Army
414036	UH-1B	Bell	From Army
414040	UH-1B	Bell	From Army
414070	UH-1B	Bell	From Army
414076	UH-1B	Bell	From Army
414081	UH-1B	Bell	From Army
414083-414084	UH-1B	Bell	From Army
414087	UH-1B	Bell	From Army
414090-414091	UH-1B	Bell	From Army
414117	UH-1M	Bell	From Army
414145	UH-1C	Bell	From Army
414235	CH-3E	Sikorsky	From Army
414243	OV-1B	Grumman	From Army
414262	OV-1B	Grumman	From Army
459186	NUH-57A	Bell	
510052	UH-1H	Bell	From Army
510054	UH-1D	Bell	From Army
510072	UH-1D	Bell	From Army
510077	UH-1D	Bell	From Army
510085	UH-1D	Bell	From Army
510104	UH-1H	Bell	From Army
510129	UH-1H	Bell	From Army
510327	T-38A	Northrop	From Army
511230	O-1A	Cessna	From Army
511696	O-1A	Cessna	From Army
512686	T-42A	Beech	
512694	T-42A	Beech	
512776	UH-1D	Bell	From Army
512868	UH-1D	Bell	From Army
512873	UH-1H	Bell	From Army
512876	UH-1D	Bell	From Army
512887	UH-1D	Bell	From Army
513278	QF-86F	North American	

Bureau Number	Aircraft Type	Manufacturer	Notes
513786	YAT-28E	North American	From Army
513788	YAT-28E	North American	From Army
513802	T-29B	Convair	From Army
514651	O-1A	Cessna	Not accepted
515117	T-29B	Convair	From Army
515124	T-29B	Convair	From Army
515129	T-29B	Convair	From Army
515145	T-29B	Convair	From Army
515165-515166	T-29B	Convair	From Army
517895	T-29B	Convair	From Army
517906	T-29B	Convair	From Army
517908	T-29B	Convair	From Army
521118-521119	T-29C	Convair	From Air Force
521160	T-29C	Convair	From Air Force
521162	T-29C	Convair	From Air Force
521167	T-29C	Convair	From Air Force
521175	T-29C	Convair	From Air Force
522090-522091	F-86H/QF-86H	North American	
522094	QF-86H	North American	
522097-522099	F-86H/QF-86H	North American	From Air Force
522116	QF-86H	North American	
522122	QF-86H	North American	
523732	F-86H	North American	
523744	F-86H	North Amreican	
524100	EB-47E	Boeing	
524120	EB-47E	Boeing	
524450	QF-86F	North American	
524647	QF-86F	North American	
525123	U-6A/L-20A	DeHavelland	
525732	QF-86H	North American	
525736	QF-86H	North American	
525744	QF-86H	North American	
525746	QF-86H	North American	
525747	F-86H	North American	From Air Force
526123	U-6A/L-20K	DeHavelland	
528176	U-3A	Cessna	
531279	F-86H	North American	
531294	QF-86H	North American	From Air Force
531314	QF-86H	North American	From Air Force
531322	F-86H	North American	From Air Force
531328	QF-86H/F-86H	North American	
531331	F-86H	North American	
531335	QF-86H	North American	
531351	QQF-86H	North American	
531373	F-86H	North American	From Air Force
531381	QF-86H	North American	
531383	QF-86H	North American	
531402	F-86H	North American	
531403	QF-86H	North American	
531406	F-86H	North American	
531408-531409	QF-86H	North American	
531413	QF-86H	North American	

Bureau Number	Aircraft Type	Manufacturer	Notes
531514	QF-86H	North American	
531521	QF-86H	North American	
531527	F-86H	North American	
532104	NB-47E	Boeing	From Air Force
532104	YOV-1	Grumman	Dup. no., from A.F.
533227-533228	C-118B	Douglas	
533257	C-118B	Douglas	
533279	C-118B	Douglas	
533291	C-118B	Douglas	
533461	T-29C	Convair	From Air Force
533477	T-29C	Convair	From Air Force
540172	U-6A/L-20A	DeHavilland	From Army
541720	U-6A/L-20A	DeHavilland	
542815	C-131H	Convair	From Air Force
542817	C-131H	Convair	From Air Force
550229	C-131H	Convair	From Air Force
552112	QF-86F	North American	
552792	QF-86F	North American	
553134	NKC-135A	Boeing	
553465	U-8G	Beech	From Army
553822-553823	QF-86F	North American	
553829	QF-86F	North American	
553838	QF-86F	North American	
553846	QF-86F	North American	From Air Force
553863-553865	QF-86F	North American	
553868	QF-86F	North American	
553875	QF-86F	North American	
553878	QF-86F	North American	
553881-553883	QF-86F	North American	
553895	QF-86F	North American	
553898	QF-86F	North American	
553900	QF-86F	North American	
553902-553903	QF-86F	North American	
553905-553906	QF-86F	North American	
553912-553913	QF-86F	North American	
553915	QF-86F	North American	
553919	QF-86F	North American	
553926	QF-86F	North American	
553932	QF-86F	North American	
553935-553936	QF-86F	North American	
553939	QF-86F	North American	From Air Force
553942	QF-86F	North American	
553945	QF-86F	North American	
553948	QF-86F	North American	
555017	QF-86F	North American	
555048	QF-86F	North American	
555052-555053	QF-86F	North American	
555057	QF-86F	North American	
555069	QF-86F	North American	
555072-555073	QF-86F	North American	
555078	QF-86F	North American	
555082	QF-86F	North American	

Bureau Number	Aircraft Type	Manufacturer	Notes
555087	QF-86F	North American	
555091	QF-86F	North American	
555095	QF-86F	North American	
555097-555099	QF-86F	North American	
555101-555102	QF-86F	North American	
555105	QF-86F	North American	
555110	QF-86F	North American	
555111-555112	QF-86F	North American	From Air Force
555114	QF-86F	North Amreican	
555890	QF-86F	North American	
556412	QF-86F	North American	
559118	C-9B	McDonnell Douglas	
560514	DC-130A	Lockheed	
560527	DC-130A	Lockheed	
562782-562784	QF-86F	North American	
562786-562787	QF-86F	North American	
562795	QF-86F	North American	
562797	QF-86F	North American	
562801	QF-86F	North American	
562804	QF-86F	North American	
562807	QF-86F	North American	
562811	QF-86F	North American	
562813-562815	QF-86F	North American	
562818-562819	QF-86F	North American	
562823	QF-86F	North American	
562825-562827	QF-86F	North American	
562829-562831	QF-86F	North American	
562836-562838	QF-86F	North American	562836 from Air Force
562840	QF-86F	North American	
562842	QF-86F	North American	
562845-562846	QF-86F	North American	
562848-562849	QF-86F	North American	
562852	QF-86F	North American	
562855	QF-86F	North American	
562858	QF-86F	North American	
562865	QF-86F	North American	
562874-562875	QF-86F	North American	
562884	QF-86F	North American	
562896	QF-86F	North American	
563596	NKC-135A	Boeing	
564039	U-8G	Beech	From Army
564044	U-8G	Beech	From Army
565103	QF-86F	North American	
566781	QF-86F	North American	
570461	DC-130A	Lockheed	
570496-570497	DC-130A	Lockheed	
570564	QT-33A	Lockheed	
570738	T-33	Lockheed	Cx
570758	T-33	Lockheed	Cx
573092	U-8G	Beech	From Army
575736	F-86H	North American	
575849	U-3A	Cessna	From Army

Bureau Number	Aircraft Type	Manufacturer	Notes
575891	U-3A	Cessna	From Air Force
575916	U-3A	Cessna	
576085	U-8G	Beech	From Army
576089	U-8G	Beech	From Army
576183-576184	U-9D	Aero Commander	From Army
576346	QF-86F	North American	
576352	QF-86F	North American	From Army
576363	QF-86F	North American	
576384	QF-86F	North American	
576388	QF-86F	North American	
576404	QF-86F	North American	
576414	QF-86F	North American	
576420	QF-86F	North American	
576422	QF-86F	North American	
576424-576425	QF-86F	North American	
576435-576436	QF-86F	North American	
576438	QF-86F	North American	
576440	QF-86F	North American	
576442	QF-86F	North American	
576444-576445	QF-86F	North American	
576447	QF-86F	North American	
576449-576450	QF-86F	North American	
576459	QF-86F	North American	
576538	OV-1A	Grumman	From Army
576539	YOV-1A	Grumman	From Army
577380	QT-33A	Lockheed	From Air Force
577580	QT-33A	Lockheed	From Air Force
580659	T-33	Lockheed	Cx
581194-581195	QT-38A	Lockheed	From Air Force
581339	U-8G	Beech	
581357	U-8G	Beech	From Army
581360	U-8G	Beech	From Army
581363	U-8G	Beech	From Army
582111	U-3A	Cessna	From Air Force
582123	U-3A	Cessna	From Air Force
582131	U-3A	Cessna	From Army
582176	U-3A	Cessna	From Air Force
583055	U-8G	Beech	From Army
583057	U-8G	Beech	From Army
583062	U-8G	Beech	From Army
583091	U-8D	Beech	From Army
586580	QT-33A	Lockheed	From Air Force
586750	QT-33A	Lockheed	From Air Force
591594-591597	QT-38A	Lockheed	
591598	QF-86F	North American	
591600	QT-38A	Lockheed	
591603-591604	T-38A	Lockheed	
592536-592538	U-8G	Beech	From Army
592625	OV-1B	Grumman	
592637	OV-1B	Grumman	
594971	NOH-13K	Bell	From Army
594990	U-8G	Beech	From Army

Bureau Number	Aircraft Type	Manufacturer	Notes
600540	UH-1C	Bell	From Army
600546	UH-1M	Bell	From Army
600582	T-38A	Lockheed	From Air Force
600610	UH-1C	Bell	From Army
603560	UH-1B	Bell	From Army
603594	UH-1B	Bell	From Army
603741	OV-1A	Grumman	From Army
603747	OV-1C	Grumman	From Army
606047	U-3B	Cessna	From Army
606068	U-3B	Cessna	From Army
610541	CT-39A	N.A. Rockwell	
610654	CT-39A	N.A. Rockwell	From Air Force
610760	UH-1B	Bell	From Army
610851	T-38A	Lockheed	From Air Force
610855	T-38A	Lockheed	From Air Force
610882	T-38A	Lockheed	From Air Force
610889	T-38A	Lockheed	
610904	T-38B	Lockheed	
610913	T-38A	Lockheed	From Air Force
610918	T-38A	Lockheed	From Air Force
610929	T-38A	Lockheed	From Air Force
613291	CH-3E	Sikorsky	From Air Force
613296	CH-3E	Sikorsky	From Air Force
613552	OV-10A	North American	From Army
615017	UH-1M	Bell	From Army
615076-615077	UH-1M	Bell	From Army
615111	UH-1M	Bell	From Army
615200	UH-1M	Bell	From Army
615217	UH-1M	Bell	From Army
615236	UH-1M	Bell	From Army
616912	UH-1H	Bell	
621881-621882	UH-1B	Bell	From Army
621912	UH-1B	Bell	From Army
621918	UH-1B	Bell	From Army
621935-621936	UH-1B	Bell	From Army
621957	UH-1B	Bell	From Army
621970	UH-1B	Bell	From Army
621984-621985	UH-1B	Bell	From Army
622007	UH-1B	Bell	From Army
622025	UH-1B	Bell	From Army
622029	UH-1B	Bell	From Army
622031	UH-1B	Bell	From Army
622034	UH-1B	Bell	From Army
622038	UH-1B	Bell	From Army
622040	UH-1B	Bell	From Army
622043	UH-1B	Bell	From Army
622048	UH-1B	Bell	From Army
622057-622058	UH-1B	Bell	From Army
622060	UH-1B	Bell	From Army
622075	UH-1B	Bell	From Army
622590	UH-1B	Bell	From Army
622602	UH-1B	Bell	From Army

Bureau Number	Aircraft Type	Manufacturer	Notes
624216	YOH-6A	Hughes	From Army
624567	UH-1B	Bell	From Army
624571-624572	UH-1B	Bell	From Army
624578-624579	UH-1B	Bell	From Army
624581-624584	UH-1B	Bell	From Army
624590	UH-1B	Bell	From Army
624594	UH-1B	Bell	From Army
624597	UH-1B	Bell	From Army
624602	UH-1B	Bell	From Army
624604	UH-1B	Bell	From Army
624897	UH-1B	Bell	From Army
625866	OV-1B	Grumman	From Air Force
625896	OV-1B	Grumman	
627469-627470	QF-86F	North American	From Air Force
627479	QF-86F	North American	
628712	UH-1B	Bell	From Army
628738	UH-1B	Bell	From Army
631034	UH-1B	Bell	From Army
638200	T-38A	Lockheed	
638501	UH-1B	Bell	From Army
638507	UH-1B	Bell	From Army
638521	UH-1B	Bell	From Army
638524	UH-1B	Bell	From Army
638540	UH-1B	Bell	From Army
638544-638545	UH-1B	Bell	From Army
638547	UH-1B	Bell	From Army
638553-638554	UH-1B	Bell	From Army
638561-638562	UH-1B	Bell	From Army
638568	UH-1B	Bell	From Army
638572	UH-1B	Bell	From Army
638587	UH-1B	Bell	From Army
638589	UN-1B	Bell	From Army
638602-638603	UH-1B	Bell	From Army
638607	UH-1B	Bell	From Army
638610	UH-1B	Bell	From Army
638614	UH-1B	Bell	From Army
638643	UH-1B	Bell	From Army
638646	UH-1B	Bell	From Army
638650	UH-1B	Bell	From Army
638664	UH-1B	Bell	From Army
638666	UH-1B	Bell	From Army
638672	UH-1B	Bell	From Army
638678-638680	UH-1B	Bell	From Army
638682-638683	UH-1B	Bell	From Army
638685	UH-1B	Bell	From Army
638687	UH-1B	Bell	From Army
638694	UH-1B	Bell	From Army
638711	UH-1B	Bell	From Army
638715	UH-1B	Bell	From Army
638727	UH-1B	Bell	From Army
638738	UH-1B	Bell	From Army
643816	UH-1D	Bell	From Army
650644	F-4D	McDonnell Douglas	From Army

Bureau Number	Aircraft Type	Manufacturer	Notes
652000	HH-65A	Aerospatiale	
652500	HH-65A	Aerospatiale	
652707	T-42A	Beech	
652728	T-42A	Beech	
652800	HH-65A	Aerospatiale	
652967	OH-6B	Hughes	
653300	HH-65A	Aerospatiale	
654500	HH-65A	Aerospatiale	
655698	CH-3E	Sikorsky	
659423	UH-1M	Bell	From Army
659476	UH-1C	Bell	From Army
659548	UH-1M	Bell	From Army
659572	UH-1D	Bell	
659598	UH-1D	Bell	From Army
659609	UH-1H	Bell	
659613-659614	UH-1D	Bell	From Army
659621	UH-1D	Bell	From Army
659632	UH-1D	Bell	From Army
659644	UH-1D	Bell	From Army
659646	UH-1H	Bell	
659662	UH-1D	Bell	From Army
659671	UH-1D	Bell	From Army
659685	UH-1D	Bell	From Army
659715	UH-1D	Bell	From Army
659735-659736	UH-1D	Bell	From Army
659739-659740	UH-1D	Bell	From Army
659777	UH-1D	Bell	From Army
659820	UH-1D	Bell	From Army
659823	UH-1D	Bell	From Army
659834	UH-1D	Bell	From Army
659853	UH-1D	Bell	From Army
659856	UH-1D	Bell	From Army
659859	UH-1D	Bell	From Army
659902	UH-1H	Bell	From Army
659945	UH-1D	Bell	From Army
659947	UH-1D	Bell	From Army
659977	UH-1D	Bell	From Army
660000	U-21A	Beech	
661012	UH-1D	Bell	From Army
661250	TH-1F	Bell	From Air Force
661534	AH-1S	Bell	From Army
664307	T-42A	Beech	
666535	UH-1M	Bell	From Army
666599	UH-1M	Bell	From Army
666655	UH-1M	Bell	From Army
666691	UH-1M	Bell	
668004	U-21A	Beech	
674623	OV-10A	North American	
674626	OV-10A	North American	
674652	OV-10A	North American	
676427	OH-6A	Hughes	
676649	OH-6A	Hughes	

Bureau Number	Aircraft Type	Manufacturer	Notes
678096	U-21A	Beech	
683796	OV-10A	North American	
683799	OV-10A	North American	
683809	OV-10A	North American	
687333	OH-6B	Hughes	
691643	AH-1S	Bell	From Army
696040-696041	OH-6B	Hughes	From Army
696044	OH-6B	Hughes	
696061	OH-6B	Hughes	From Army
701523	OH-58A	Bell	From Army
701553	OH-58A	Bell	From Army
710388	OH-58A	Bell	
710554	OH-58A	Bell	
710799	OH-58A	Bell	
712098	AH-1S	Bell	From Army
712103	AH-1S	Bell	From Army
714584	YA-7D	LTV	From Air Force
714704	CH-3E	Sikorsky	
714707	CH-3E	Sikorsky	
715106	T-41B	Grumman	From Army
715123	T-41B	Grumman	From Army
715132	T-41B	Grumman	From Army
715184	T-41B	Grumman	From Army
715218-715219	T-41B	Grumman	
715225	T-41B	Grumman	From Army
715345-715346	X-26B	Schweizer	Modified by Lockheed, from Army
715850	AH-1G	Bell	From Army
721193	OH-58A	Bell	
721300	O-2A	Cessna	From Air Force
721310	O-2A	Cessna	
721318	O-2A	Cessna	From Air Force
721349	O-2A	Cessna	From Air Force
721365	O-2A	Cessna	From Air Force
721387	F-5E	Northrop	
721404	O-2A	Cessna	From Air Force
721414	O-2A	Cessna	From Air Force
722716	UH-60A	Sikorsky	
722725	UH-60A	Sikorsky	
722791-722792	AH-1S	Bell	From Army
727709	QF-86F	North American	
727711	QF-86F	North American	
730855	F-5E	Northrop	
730865	F-5E	Northrop	
730879	F-5E	Northrop	
730881	F-5E	Northrop	
730885	F-5E	Northrop	
731635	F-5E	Northrop	
741519	F-5E	Northrop	
741528-741531	F-5E	Northrop	
741536-741537	F-5E	Northrop	
741539-741541	F-5E	Northrop	

Bureau Number	Aircraft Type	Manufacturer	Notes
741544-741545	F-5E	Northrop	
741547	F-5E	Northrop	
741554	F-5E	Northrop	
741556	F-5E	Northrop	
741558	F-5E	Northrop	
741563-741564	F-5E	Northrop	
741568	F-5E	Northrop	
741570	F-5E	Northrop	
741572	F-5E	Northrop	
741635	F-5E	Northrop	
760086	X-26A	Schweizer	
815037-815039	AH-1G	Bell	From Army
815045-815046	AH-1G	Bell	From Army
815072-815073	AH-1G	Bell	From Army
815074-815078	AH-1G	Bell	Not accepted
815079-815080	AH-1G	Bell	From Army
815081-815084	AH-1G	Bell	Not accepted
815085	AH-1G	Bell	From Army
815086-815103	AH-1G	Bell	Not accepted
815104-815105	AH-1G	Bell	From Army
815106-815111	AH-1G	Bell	Not accepted
815112-815113	AH-1G	Bell	From Army
815134	AH-1G	Bell	From Army
815140	AH-1G	Bell	From Army
815165	AH-1G	Bell	From Army
815170	AH-1G	Bell	From Army
815176	AH-1G	Bell	From Army
815190	AH-1G	Bell	From Army
815194	AH-1G	Bell	From Army
815198	AH-1G	Bell	From Army
815213	AH-1G	Bell	From Army
816695	OH-58A	Bell	From Army
816797	OH-58A	Bell	From Army
817023	AH-1G	Bell	From Army
817027	AH-1G	Bell	From Army
817041	AH-1G	Bell	From Army
817045	AH-1G	Bell	From Army
817049	AH-1G	Bell	From Army
817062	AH-1G	Bell	From Army
817066	AH-1G	Bell	From Army
817070	AH-1G	Bell	From Army
817082	AH-1G	Bell	From Army
817086	AH-1G	Bell	From Army
817090	AH-1G	Bell	From Army
817101	AH-1G	Bell	From Army
817105	AH-1G	Bell	From Army
817108	AH-1G	Bell	From Army
823507	UH-60A	Sikorsky	From Army
827806	QF-86F	North American	
827837	QF-86F	North American	From Air Force
827852	QF-86F	North American	
823507	UH-60A	Sikorsky	

Bureau Number	Aircraft Type	Manufacturer	Notes
827806	QF-86F	North American	
827837	QF-86F	North American	
827852	QF-86F	North American	
840456	F-5F	Northrop	
891038	TH-57C	Bell	
999703	F-21A	IAI	From Israel
999705	F-21A	IAI	From Israel
999708-999710	F-21A	IAI	From Israel
999716	F-21A	IAI	From Israel
999724-999728	F-21A	IAI	From Israel
999731-999732	F-21A	IAI	From Israel
999734-999735	F-21A	IAI	From Israel
999739	F-21A	IAI	From Israel
999742	F-21A	IAI	From Israel
999747	F-21A	IAI	From Israel
999749-999750	F-21A	IAI	From Israel
999764	F-21A	IAI	From Israel
999786-999787	F-21A	IAI	From Israel
999791	F-21A	IAI	From Israel
999794	F-21A	IAI	From Israel

Note 1: Originally XF12C-1, was redesignated XS4C-1 and then XSBC-1. XSBC-1 crashed during contractor's trials and was replaced by XSBC-2 which was converted to XSBC-3.

Note 2: Serial 9222 was replaced by new air frame as XSBU-1, 9222. Old 9222 was acquired as 9746.

Note 3: Variously modified to PBM-3C, -3R and -3S; 6456 reported as XPBM-3 or PBM-3R; 6656 as PBM-3D modified from PBM-3C; and 6693 as experimental PBM-3S although designated PBM-3C.

The Bureau Number for this P-3 Orion is in big numbers, 154604, on the tail and small numbers on the rear of the fuselage. The photo also shows the squadron's insignia and its tail code, YB.

*Photographs show the tail codes and insignia used by Patrol Squadron
P-3 Orion aircraft.*

Aviation Personnel on Active Duty

	Navy					Marine Corps				
	Officers			**Enlisted men**		**Officers**			**Enlisted men**	
1 July	**Pilots**	**NFO**	**Other**	**Pilots**	**Aviation Rates**	**Pilots**	**NFO**	**Other**	**Pilots**	**Aviation Rates**
1920	630		243		4,404					
1921	370		108		3,494					
1922	314		220		2,209					
1923	326		241		1,612					
1924	328		161		1,788					
1925	382		137		1,711					
1926	426		173		1,722					
1927	472		177	108	1,984					
1928	466		196	141	2,644					
1929	520		207	173	2,894					
1930	614		221	244	2,651	82		17	24	1,112
1931	737		427	330	2,806	98		15	33	999
1932	803		396	355	2,958	101		17	32	917
1933	826		450	337	11,949	103		15	30	913
1934	834		496	306	11,667	104		16	34	938
1935	867		559	280	12,129	110		15	28	985
1937	963		502	297	13,055	113		20	29	978
1938	1,059		580	447	19,463	171		23	46	1,082
1939	1,068		609	533	19,907	180		16	47	1,091
1940	2,203		145	349	5,924	304		17	45	1,677
1941	3,483		963	629	10,640	453		27	52	3,051
1942	9,059		5,716	732	27,286	1,284		345	85	12,583
1943	20,847		20,958	774	105,445	4,898		2,419	132	50,485
1944	37,367		26,596	475	183,886	10,416		4,406	41	91,246
1945	49,380		27,946	439	241,364	10,229		5,080	47	96,354
1946										
1947	10,052		3,054	537	44,201					
1948	10,232		2,475	629	56,767	1,955		213	352	11,629
1949	11,509		2,343	622	73,631	1,975		221	269	14,631
1950	9,481		1,906	920	63,505	1,922		214	255	12,017
1951	14,079		3,936	775	114,038	3,127		785	237	25,025
1952	15,774		4,633	715	129,412	4,169		1,472	210	38,359
1953	17,612		4,403	684	137,218	4,484		1,475	131	49,742
1954	16,722		4,078	631	125,102	3,848		1,647	123	39,748
1955	16,448		3,823	622	115,011	4,208		1,976	120	38,173
1956	17,193		4,209	264	135,600	4,399		1,778	109	36,232
1957	17,993		4,662	243	140,283	4,348		1,780	101	39,433
1958	18,236		4,683	210	134,212	4,225		1,697	102	37,027
1959	17,813		4,572	179	127,811	3,937		1,281	105	32,900
1960	17,090		4,977	124	121,985	3,958		1,329	96	30,326
1961	17,354		4,475	87	123,134	4,031		1,349	66	34,253

Aviation Personnel on Active Duty—Continued

| | Navy | | | | | Marine Corps | | | | |
| | Officers | | | Enlisted men | | Officers | | | Enlisted men | |
1 July	Pilots	NFO	Other	Pilots	Aviation Rates	Pilots	NFO	Other	Pilots	Aviation Rates
1962	18,301		6,436	70	135,453	4,087		1,437	51	41,476
1963	17,613		6,567	59	132,538	4,131		1,594	27	41,834
1964	17,074		7,069	51	130,742	4,234		2,132	23	41,791
1965†	16,570		7,932	43	126,988	4,372		2,346	17	41,563
1966	16,469		8,649	37	133,359	4,541		2,963	13	36,232
30 June										
1967	15,973		8,985	35	139,742	4,401		3,987	12	60,192
1968	15,767		9,633	30	141,713	4,440		3,887	9	63,361
1969	15,274		10,220	27	147,679	4,648		3,973	5	62,858
1970	14,594		8,433	22	135,945	4,892		4,241	4	62,032
1971	14,890		8,215	13	120,301	4,917		3,569	4	54,672
1972	14,245		7,978	5	114,136	4,787		2,124	3	53,605
1973	13,665		7,701	3	111,329	4,384		3,126		48,110
1974	13,236		7,690	1	108,203	4,042		2,927		32,527
1975*	13,056		7,643	1	105,619	3,921		2,671		32,454
1976‡	12,560	4,128	2,302	1	101,058	3,712		2,744		30,338
1977**	11,608	3,970	2,343	1	102,445	3,644		2,679		30,499
30 Sep										
1978	10,632	4,268	2,271	1	108,180	3,429		2,850		28,176
1979	9,707	4,327	2,123	1	107,669	3,219		2,856		29,369
1980	9,487	4,377	2,012	1	107,996	3,286		2,275		31,241
1981	9,828	4,666	1,954		109,915					34,002
1982	10,203	4,819	1,891		112,209	3,172	668			34,880
1983	10,483	5,160	2,223		114,722	3,427	640			36,808
1984	10,479	5,280	2,425		115,325	3,549	639			40,572
1985	10,559	5,566	2,685		114,866	3,666	652			41,609
1986	10,516	5,734	2,796		117,886	3,673	630			40,304
1987	10,748	5,966	2,749		122,563	3,654	605			38,531
1988	10,835	6,111	2,723		123,428	3,810	629			37,326
1989	11,022	6,241	2,641		123,651	3,712	631			36,937
1990	11,018	6,340	2,534		118,611	3,626	628			36,918
1991	10,491	6,109	2,487		114,056	3,526	635			38,400
1992	10,338	6,060	2,443		113,943	3,552	608			38,062
1993	9,162	5,222	1,116		72,182^	3,589	581			35,698
1994	8,287	4,537	977		69,725^	3,585	551			33,723
1995	7,751	4,079	939		63,309^	3,570	500			28,784

*Navy figures are for 31 Mar 1975. USMC figures are for 30 Jun 1975.
**Navy figures are for 30 Jun 1977. USMC figures are for 30 Sep 1977.
†Naval Aviation Observers (NAO) redesignated Naval Flight Officers (NFO) by BuPers Instruction 1210.4C of 8 Feb 1965, effective 1 May 1965.
‡NFO designation separated from other non-pilots.
^Annual Report, Bureau of Naval Personnel Statistics (Report 15658), discontinued in mid FY 1993. Figures for enlisted personnel in aviation rates for FY 1993–95 provided directly from BuPers, PERS 221D.

Note—Does not include men in training. Aviation rates under Navy for years 1933–39 include general service ratings assigned to aviation duty. Enlisted pilots for 1920–26 are included under aviation rates. All Navy figures for World War II period, 1940–45, include Coast Guard. Figures not available for Marine Corps, 1920–29.

Navy and Marine Corps Air Stations and Fields Named for Naval Aviators and Others

Including Temporary Advanced Air Bases and Fields

ADMIRAL A. W. RADFORD FIELD

At NAS Cubi Point, Phillipines. Dedicated 21 December 1972, in honor of former Chairman of the Joint Chiefs of Staff Admiral Arthur W. Radford (no longer active).

ALVIN CALLENDER FIELD

At NAS New Orleans, La. Dedicated 26 Apr 1958, in honor of Captain Alvin A. Callender, RFC, native of New Orleans, killed in aerial combat during World War I while flying with the Royal Flying Corps of Canada (not a U.S. Naval Aviator).

ARCHIBALD FIELD

At Managua, Nicaragua. A Marine Corps field named in late 1928 or early 1929 for Captain Robert J. Archibald, USMC, who directed the location of airfield sites in Nicaragua and was killed in line of duty in November 1928 (no longer active).

ARMITAGE FIELD

At China Lake, Calif. Name apparently assigned locally; dedicated 30 May 1945, in honor of Lieutenant John M. Armitage, USNR, killed 21 August 1944, while conducting air firing tests of a Tiny Tim rocket.

AULT FIELD

At NAS Whidbey Island, Wash. Named in honor of Commodore William B. Ault, USN, who lost his life in the Battle of Coral Sea. Designated by the Secretary of the Navy on 25 February 1943.

BARIN FIELD

At Foley, Ala. Name assigned 2 July 1942, prior to establishing as an NAAS, in honor of Lieutenant Louis T. Barin, Naval Aviator No. 56, test pilot extraordinarie and co-pilot of NC-1 on trans-Atlantic attempt, 1919. The former NAAS now an ALF to NAS Saufley Field.

BAUER FIELD

On Vila, New Hebrides Islands. Named in June 1943, for Lieutenant Colonel Harold W. Bauer, USMC, Commanding Officer of VMF-212; awarded Medal of Honor posthumously for action in South Pacific, 28 September-3 October 1942 (no longer active).

BORDELON FIELD

At NAS Hilo, Hawaii. Named for Sergeant William J. Bordelon, USMC, killed in the invasion of Tarawa; Medal of Honor (not an aviator; field no longer active).

BOURNE FIELD

At MCAS St. Thomas, V.I. Named in late 1930s for Major Louis T. Bourne, USMC, first to fly nonstop from the United States to Nicaragua (no longer active).

BREWER FIELD

At NAS Agana, Guam, in honor of Commander Charles W. Brewer, Jr. Dedicated 15 February 1973.

BRISTOL FIELD

At NAS Argentia, Newfoundland. Named, 1 June 1943 for Rear Admiral Arthur L. Bistol, who as Commander Support Force, Atlantic, contributed much toward planning and building the station (no longer active).

BRONSON FIELD

An NAAS at Pensacola, Fla. Name assigned 2 July 1942, prior to establishing of the station, in honor of Lieutenant (Junior Grade) Clarence K. Bronson, Naval Aviator No. 15, killed by premature explosion of bomb during early bomb dropping tests, 8 November 1916 (no longer active).

BROWN FIELD

An NAAS at Chula Vista, Calif. Named in honor of Commander Melville S. Brown, killed in an airplane crash in 1936. Assigned 1 June 1943, to the field at NAAS Otay Mesa and became the station name 11 June 1943 (no longer active).

BROWN FIELD

At MCAF Quantico, Va. Name assigned in 1922 in honor of Second Lieutenant Walter V. Brown, USMC, killed at Quantico in an operational crash (no longer active, present site of the Marine Corps Aviation Museum).

BYRD FIELD

A Marine Corps field at Puerto Pabezao, Nicaragua, named in the late 1920s for Captain William C. Byrd, USMC, killed in airplane crash (no longer active).

CABANISS FIELD

At NAS Corpus Christi, Tex. Dedicated 9 July 1941, in honor of Commander Robert W Cabaniss, Naval Aviator No. 36, killed in a plane crash in 1927 (the former NAAS now an OLF to NAS Corpus Christi).

CARNEY FIELD

On Guadalcanal. Named in the fall of 1942 for Captain James V. Carney, killed early in World War II (no longer active).

CECIL FIELD

An NAS near Jacksonville, Fla. Station established 20 February 1943; named in honor of Commander Henry B. Cecil, Naval Aviator No. 42, lost in the crash of the rigid dirigible Akron (ZRS-4) 4 April 1933.

CHAMBERS FIELD

At NAS Norfolk, Va. Named 1 June 1938, in honor of Captain Washington I. Chambers, first officer-in-charge of aviation and director of early efforts to find a place for aviation in the fleet (not an aviator).

CHASE FIELD

An NAS at Beeville, Tex. Named 27 April 1943, in honor of Lieutenant Commander Nathan B. Chase, Naval Aviator No. 37, killed in 1925 in an air collision while exercising his squadron in fighter tactics (no longer active).

CHEVALIER FIELD

At NAS Pensacola, Fla. Name assigned 30 December 1936, to old Station Field, in honor of Lieutenant Commander Godfrey deC. Chevalier, Naval Aviator No. 7 (no longer active).

CORRY FIELD

An NAAS at Pensacola, Fla. Name initially assigned 1 November 1922, to a temporary field and reassigned to the new station 8 December 1934, in honor of Lieutenant Commander William M. Corry, Naval Aviator No. 23; Medal of Honor awarded posthumously (no longer active).

CUDDIHY FIELD

An NAAS at Corpus Christi, Tex. Station established 3 September 1941; named in honor of Lieutenant George T. Cuddihy, test pilot and speed record holder, killed in a crash in 1929 (no longer active).

CUNNINGHAM FIELD

At MCAF Cherry Point, N.C. Dedicated 4 September 1941, in honor of Lieutenant Colonel Alfred A. Cunningham, USMC, Naval Aviator No. 5 and first Marine Corps aviator.

DOWDELL FIELD

A Marine Corps field at Apali, Nicaragua, named in the late 1920s for Sergeant Frank E. Dowdell, USMC, missing in action after a forced landing with Lieutenant Earl A. Thomas on Sapotilla Ridge, Nicaragua (not an aviator; field no longer active).

DYESS FIELD

On Roi Island, Kwajalein Atoll. Named 16 April 1944, for Lieutenant Colonel Aquilla J. Dyess, USMCR, killed leading the assault on Roi Namur; Medal of Honor awarded posthumously (not an aviator; field no longer active).

ELLYSON FIELD

An NAS at Pensacola, Fla. Station established 20 January 1943; named in honor of Commander Theodore G. Ellyson, first Naval Aviator (no longer active).

FINUCANE FIELD

On Efate, New Hebrides. Named for Lieutenant Arthur E. Finucane, USMC (no longer active).

FLATLEY FIELD

At NAS Olathe, Kans. Dedicated 20 May 1962, in honor of Vice Admiral James H. Flatley, fighter pilot, carrier commander, Director of Air Warfare Division and former commanding officer of the station (no longer active).

FLEMING FIELD

An auxiliary field to NAS Minneapolis, Minn. Named 20 July 1943, in honor of Captain Richard E. Fleming, USMC, killed leading an attack on an enemy cruiser in the Battle of Midway; Medal of Honor awarded posthumously (no longer active).

FLOYD BENNETT FIELD

At NAS New York, N.Y. Originally assigned to New York Municipal Airport, dedicated 23 May 1931, and retained as station name upon its establishing 2 June 1941. For Floyd Bennett, Naval Aviation Pilot No. 9, who with Rear Admiral Richard E. Byrd was first to fly over the North Pole (no longer an active Navy field).

FORREST SHERMAN FIELD

At NAS Pensacola, Fla., formerly Fort Barrancas Airfield. Dedicated 2 November 1951, in honor of Admiral Forrest P. Sherman, Chief of Naval Operations, 1949-1951.

FREDERICK C. SHERMAN FIELD

At San Clemente Island, Calif. Dedicated 11 January 1961, in honor of Vice Admiral Frederick C. Sherman, three-time winner of the Navy Cross and renowned leader of carrier task groups during World War II (the former NAAS now an NALF).

FREDERICK M. TRAPNELL FIELD

At NAS Patuxent River, Md. Dedicated 1 April 1976 in honor of Vice Admiral Frederick M. Trapnell.

FRANKFORTER FIELD

A Marine Corps field at Esteli, Nicaragua. Named in late 1920's for Private Rudolph A. Frankforter, USMC, killed with Captain William C. Byrd, USMC, in airplane crash (not an aviator; no longer active).

HALSEY FIELD

At NAS North Island, Calif. Dedicated 20 August 1961, in honor of Fleet Admiral William F. Halsey, Commander Third Fleet in the advance across the Pacific during World War II. Offically named Admiral Halsey Field.

HARING FIELD

On Efate, New Hebrides. Named for Second Lieutenant Richard Z. Haring, USMCR (no longer active).

HARVEY FIELD

At NAF Inyokern, Calif. Name assigned to field formerly known as Inyokern Airfield, 10 May 1944, in honor of Lieutenant Commander Warren W. Harvey, for his contributions to the development of aviation ordnance and fighter tactics (no longer active).

HAWKINS FIELD

On Betio Island, Tarawa. Named for Lieutenant William D. Hawkins, USMCR, killed while landing his platoon during assault on Tarawa; Medal of Honor awarded posthumously (not an aviator; field no longer active).

HENDERSON FIELD

At NS Midway Island. Named 19 August 1942, in honor of Major Loften R. Henderson, USMC, lost in action during the Battle of Midway. Field on Guadalcanal, also named in honor of Major Henderson in August 1942 (no longer active).

HENSLEY FIELD

At NAS Dallas, Tex. Named for Colonel William N. Hensely Jr., USMC, prominent in the Reserve program during the 1920's (not an aviator) (no longer active).

ISLEY FIELD

An NAS on Saipan, Marianas Island. Named 30 June 1944, prior to its designation as NAS, for Commander Robert H. Isely, who lost his life leading his squadron in an attack on the then enemy installation known as Aslito Airfield. (Incorrect spelling of station name became official through usage. Field no longer active.)

JOHN RODGERS FIELD

At NAS Barbers Point, Hawaii. Dedicated on 10 September 1974 in honor of Commander John Rodgers for his exploits in early Naval Aviation.

LEE FIELD

At NAS Green Cove Springs, Fla. Named in September 1940 in honor of Ensign Benjamin Lee, who lost his life in a crash at Killingholme, England, during World War I. Originally assigned as the station name, but reassigned to the landing field when station name changed to Green Cove Springs, 8 August 1943 (no longer active).

MAXFIELD FIELD

At NAS Lakehurst, N.J. Named 6 January 1944, in honor of Commander Louis H. Maxfield, Naval Aviator No. 17, who lost his life in the crash of the dirigible R-38, 24 August 1921 (no longer active).

MAX KIEL AIRFIELD

At Little America, Antarctica. Named in early 1956 in honor of Max Kiel, who lost his life while bridging a crevasse in Marie Byrd Land (not an aviator; no longer active).

McCAIN FIELD

At NAS Meridian, Miss. Dedicated with the establishing of the station 14 July 1961, in honor of Admiral John S. McCain, carrier task force commander, Chief of BuAer and Deputy Chief Naval Operations (Air).

McCALLA FIELD

At NAS Guantanamo, Cuba. Named for Captain Bowman H. McCalla, skipper of Marblehead (C 11) participating in the capture of Guantanamo Bay, and commander of a base established there, during the Spanish American war (not an aviator).

McCUTCHEON FIELD

At MCAS New River, N.C. Named in honor of General Kieth B. McCutcheon, USMC, a pioneer in Marine Corps helicopter assault tactics. Dedicated 1972.

MERRITT FIELD

At MCAS Beaufort, S.C., in honor of Major General Lewis G. Merritt, USMC. Dedicated on 19 September 1975.

MITCHELL FIELD

At NAF Adak, Alaska. Named 2 February 1944, in honor of Ensign Albert E. Mitchell, who lost his life in the Aleutians earlier in the war. Offically named Albert Mitchell Field.

MITSCHER FIELD

At NAS Miramar, Calif. Named 14 June 1955, in honor of Admiral Marc A. Mitscher, Naval Aviator No.

33, leader of Fast Carrier Task Forces in World War II and Deputy Chief of Naval Operations (Air).

MOFFETT FIELD

At NAS at Sunnyvale, Calif. Named in honor of Rear Admiral William A. Moffett, Naval Aviation Observer, first Chief of BuAer and leader of Naval Aviation through the 1920's who lost his life in the crash of the rigid dirigible Akron (ZRS-4) 4 April 1933. Name first assigned 17 May 1933, to the landing field at NAS Sunnyvale, Calif., and remained in use after the station was transferred to the U.S. Army in 1935 and after station was returned to the Navy and established as an NAS, 16 April 1942; became station name 20 April 1942 (no longer active).

MORET FIELD

On Zamboanga, Philippines. Named for Lieutenant Colonel Paul Moret, USMC, killed in a crash in 1943 (no longer active).

MULLINNIX FIELD

On Buota Island, Tarawa. Named in December 1943 in honor of Rear Admiral Henry M. Mullinnix, Carrier Division Commander, lost in sinking of Liscome Bay, during the Gilbert Islands campaign, 24 November 1943 (no longer active).

MUNN FIELD

At MCAS Camp Pendelton, Calif. The airfield was designated Munn Field on 12 January 1987 in honor of Lieutenant General John C. Munn, USMC. The general had been Assistant Commandant of the Marine Corps and the first Marine Aviator to command Camp Pendleton.

MUSTIN FIEID

An NAF at Philadelphia, Pa. Dedicated 17 September 1926, in honor of Captain Henry C. Mustin, Naval Aviator No. 11 and early exponent of aviation as the striking arm of the fleet (no longer active).

NIMITZ FIELD

At NAS Alameda, Calif. Dedicated 26 January 1967, in honor of Fleet Admiral Chester W. Nimitz, Commander-in-Chief of the Pacific during World War II and Chief of Naval Operations (not an aviator)(no longer active).

OFSTIE FIELD

At NS Roosevelt Roads, P.R. Dedicated 21 May 1959, in honor of Vice Admiral Ralph A. Ofstie, test pilot, Fleet Commander and Deputy Chief of Naval Operations (Air).

O'HARE FIELD

On Abemama, Gilbert Islands. Named in December 1943 in honor of Lieutenant Commander Edward H. O'Hare, Air Group commander, pioneer in night carrier operations and Medal of Honor winner, lost in action during the Gilberts Campaign, 26 November 1943 (no longer active).

PAGE FIELD

At MCAS Parris Island, S.C. Named 19 Sepember 1938, prior to station establishing, in honor of Captain Arthur H. Page, Jr., USMC, pioneer in instrument flying and racing pilot, who crashed to his death while leading in the Thompson Trophy Race, 1930 (no longer active).

RAMEY FIELD

At NAS Sanford, Fla. Dedicated 6 February 1959, in honor of Lieutenant Commander Robert W. Ramey, who lost his life by electing to guide his crippled plane away from a residential area (no longer active).

REAM FIELD

At NAS Imperial Beach, Calif. Named in 1943 for Major William R. Ream, MC, USA, who was a medical officer at Rockwell Field on North Island in the World War I period. Initially the station name when the station was retitled Imperial Beach, 1 January 1968 (not an aviator)(no longer active).

REEVES FIELD

At NAS Lemoore, Calif. Dedicated 20 November 1961, in honor of Rear Admiral Joseph M. Reeves, Naval Aviation Observer and farseeing pioneer in the tactical employment of aircraft carriers. Officially, Joseph Mason Reeves Field. Field at NAB San Pedro (later NAS Terminal Island), Calif., also named in honor of Admiral Reeves in the 1930's (NAS Terminal Island field no longer active).

RODD FIELD

An NAAS at Corpus Christi, Tex. Station established-ed 7 June 1941; named in honor of Lieutenant Herbert C. Rodd, Radio Officer in NC-4 on the trans-Atlantic flight 1919 (no longer active).

SAILER FIELD

On Guadalcanal. Named for Major Joseph Sailer, USMC, who lost his life leading his squadron in an attack on enemy destroyers (no longer active).

SAUFLEY FIELD

An NAS at Pensacola, Fla. Named prior to station establishing 22 August 1940, in honor of Lieutenant(jg) Richard C. Saufley, Naval Aviator No. 14, killed in a crash while on a record endurance flight.

SHEA FIELD

At NAS South Weymouth, Mass. In honor of Lieutenant Commander John J. Shea, killed in action while serving aboard Wasp in 1942. Name assigned first to the field at NAS Squantum, Mass., 15 March 1946, and upon closing of that station in 1954 was transferred to the field at South Weymouth (no longer active).

SMARTT FIELD

An outlying field to NAS St. Louis, Mo. Named in June 1943 in honor of Ensign Joseph G. Smartt, who lost his life 7 December 1941, while serving with VP-11 at Kaneohe, Hawaii (no longer active).

SOUCEK FIELD

At NAS Oceana, Va. Dedicated 4 June 1957, in honor of Vice Admiral Apollo Soucek, world altitude record holder, test pilot, task force commander and Chief of BuAer. Officially named Apollo Soucek Field.

STICKELL FIELD

On Eniwetok, Marshall Islands. Named early in 1944 in honor of Lieutenant John H. Stickell, Naval Aviator and former RAF pilot, who died from wounds received in action during a low-level attack on Jaluit in the Marshalls (no longer active).

TAYLOR FIELD

On Efate, New Hebrides. Named for Lieutenant Lawrence C. Taylor, USMCR, killed while intercepting an air attack on Guadalcanal (no longer active).

THOMAS FIELD

A Marine Corps field at Ocotal, Nicaragua. Named in the late 1920s for Lieutenant Earl A. Thomas, USMC, missing in action after a forced landing on Sapotilla Ridge, Nicaragua (no longer active).

TITCOMB FIELD

On Mindanao, Philippines. Named in February 1945 in honor of Captain John A. Titcomb, USMCR, killed while directing a close air support mission in northern Luzon (not an aviator; field no longer active).

TOWERS FIELD

At NAS Jacksonville, Fla. Dedicated 14 October 1960, in honor of Admiral John H. Towers, Naval Aviator No. 3, and an outstanding leader in Naval Aviation from 1911 to his retirement in 1947. Officially named John Towers Field.

TURNER FIELD

At MCAF Quantico, Va. Named in honor of Colonel Thomas C. Turner, USMC, Naval Aviator and Director of Marine Aviation. Name was first assigned 1 July 1936, to the field at Marine Barracks, Quantico.

VAN VOORHIS FIELD

At NAS Fallon, Nev. Dedicated 1 November 1959, in honor of Commander Bruce A. Van Voorhis, who lost his life on a low-level bombing attack on enemy positions during the Battle of the Solomon Islands; Medal of Honor, awarded posthumously.

WALDRON FIELD

At NAS Corpus Christi, Tex. Named 5 March 1943, prior to establishing of station, in honor of Lieutenant Commander John C. Waldron, killed in action leading the attack of Torpedo Squadron 8 in the Battle of Midway; 4 June 1942 (The former NAAS now an OLF to NAS Corpus Christi).

WEBSTER FIELD

A flight test field at Priest Point, Md., auxiliary to NAS Patuxent River. Named 1 June 1943 for Captain Walter W. Webster, one-time head of Naval Aircraft Factory and long associated with test and development work.

WHITING FIELD

An NAS at Milton, Fla. Named 1 June 1943, prior to establishing of station, in honor of Captain Kenneth Whiting; Naval Aviator No. 16, first to command Naval Aviation units overseas in World War I, first acting commander of the Navy's first carrier and leader in the development of carriers.

WIGLEY FIELD

On Engebi Island, Eniwetok Atoll. Named in March 1944 for Lieutenant Colonel Roy C. Wigley, USAAF, Army Air Force pilot killed in an attack on Jaluit, Marshall Islands (no longer active).

WILLIAMS FIELD

At McMurdo Sound, Antarctica. Named 16 February 1956, for Richard Williams, killed when his vehicle broke through the bay ice (not an aviator)(no longer active).

Ships Named for Naval Aviators

Ship	Named for	Commissioning Date
Abercrombie (DE 343)	ENS William W. Abercrombie, USN	1 May 1944
Adams (DM 27—ex-DD 739)*	LT Samuel Adams, USN	10 Oct 1944
Allen, Edward H. (DE 531)	LT Edward H. Allen, USN	16 Dec 1943
Antrim (FFG 20)	RADM Richard N. Antrim, USN	26 Sep 1981
Ault (DD 698)	CDR William B. Ault, USN	31 May 1944
Baker (DE 190)	ENS John D. Baker, USNR	23 Dec 1943
Baker, Paul G. (DE 642)	LT (jg) Paul G. Baker, USN	25 May 1944
Barnes, Doyle C. (DE 353)	ENS Doyle C. Barnes, USN	13 Jul 1944
Bass, Brinkley (DD 887)	LCDR Harry B. Bass, USN	1 Oct 1945
Bass, Horace A. (APD 124—ex-DE 691)*	ENS Horace A. Bass, USNR	21 Dec 1944
Bassett (APD 73—ex-DE 672)*	ENS Edgar R. Bassett, USNR	23 Feb 1945
Bauer (DE 1025)	LCOL Harold W. Bauer, USMC	21 Nov 1957
Bebas (DE 10)	ENS Gus G. Bebas, USNR	15 May 1943
Berry, Fred T. (DD 858)	CDR Fred T. Berry, USN	12 May 1945
Billingsley (DD 293)	ENS William D. Billingsley, USN	1 Mar 1920
Blakely (DE 1072)	CAPT Johnston Blakely, USN and Great Grandnephew VADM Adam Blakely, USN (aviator)	18 Jul 1970
Blessman (APD 49—ex-DE 69)**	LT Edward M. Blessman, USN	19 Sep 1943
Bowers (APD 40—ex-DE 367)**	ENS Robert K. Bowers, USNR	27 Jan 1944
Brackett (DE 41)	LT Bruce G. Brackett, USNR	18 Oct 1943
Brannon, Charles E. (DE 446)	ENS Charles E. Brannon, USNR	1 Nov 1944
Bridget (DE 1024)	CAPT Francis J. Bridget, USN	24 Oct 1957
Bristol, Arthur L. (APD 97—ex-DE 281)*	VADM Arthur L. Bristol, USN	25 Jun 1945
Brock (APD 93—ex-DE 234)*	ENS John W. Brock, USN	9 Feb 1945
Bronson, Clarence K. (DD 668)	LT (jg) Clarence K. Bronson, USN	11 Jun 1943
Brough (DE 148)	LT (jg) David A. Brough, USNR	18 Sep 1943
Brown, Jesse L. (DE 1089)	ENS Jesse L. Brown, USN	17 Feb 1973
Bull (APD 78—ex-DE 693)**	LT (jg) Richard Bull, USNR	12 Aug 1943
Bull, Richard S. (DE 402)	LT Richard S. Bull, USN	26 Feb 1944
Butler, John C. (DE 339)	ENS John C. Butler, USNR	31 Mar 1944
Byrd, Richard E. (DDG 23)	RADM Richard E. Byrd, Jr., USN	7 Mar 1964
Camp (DE 251)	ENS Jack H. Camp, USNR	16 Sep 1943
Campbell, Joseph E. (APD 49—ex-DE 70)**	ENS Joseph E. Campbell, USNR	23 Sep 1943
Campbell, Kendall C. (DE 443)	ENS Kendall C. Campbell, USNR	31 Jul 1944

Ships Named for Naval Aviators—Continued

Ship	Named for	Commissioning Date
Carpenter (DDK 825—ex-DD 825)**	LCDR Donald M. Carpenter, USN	15 Dec 1949
Chaffee (DE 230)	ENS Davis E. Chaffee, USNR	9 May 1944
Chevalier (DD 451)	LCDR Godfrey deC. Chevalier, USN	20 Jul 1942
(DD 805)		9 Jan 1945
Chourre (ARV 1—ex-ARG 14)#	LCDR Emile Chourre, USN	7 Dec 1944
Clark (FFG 11)	ADM Joseph J. Clark, USN	9 May 1980
Clark, Howard F. (DE 533)	LT (jg) Howard F. Clark, USN	25 May 1944
Collett (DD 730)	LCDR John A. Collett, USN	16 May 1944
Cook (DE 1083)	LCDR Wilmer P. Cook, USN	18 Dec 1971
Coolbaugh (DE 217)	LT (jg) Walter W. Coolbaugh, USNR	15 Oct 1943
Cooner (DE 172)	ENS Bunyan R. Cooner, USNR	21 Aug 1943
Cooper (DD 695)	LT Elmer G. Cooper, USN	27 Mar 1944
Corl, Harry L. (APD 108—ex-DE 598)**	ENS Harry L. Corl, USN	5 Jun 1945
Corry (DD 334)	LCDR William M. Corry, USN	25 May 1921
(DD 463)		18 Dec 1941
(DD 817)		27 Feb 1946
Craig, James E. (DE 201)	LCDR James E. Craig, USN	1 Nov 1943
Crommelin (FFG 37)	CDR Charles L. Crommelin, USN	
	LCDR Richard G. Crommelin, USN	
	VADM Henry Crommelin, USN	18 Jun 1983
Cross (DE 448)	LT (jg) Frederick C. Cross, USNR	8 Jan 1945
Cunningham, Alfred A. (DD 752)	LCOL Alfred A. Cunningham, USMC	23 Nov 1944
Davis, Frederick C. (DE 136)	ENS Frederick C. Davis, USNR	14 Jul 1943
Deede (DE 263)	LT (jg) Leroy C. Deede, USNR	29 Jul 1943
Dickson, Harlan R. (DD 708)	LCDR Harlan R. Dickson, USN	17 Feb 1945
Dobler (DE 48—ex-BDE 48)***	LT Joseph J. Dobler, USNR	17 May 1943
Doherty (DE 14—ex-BDE 14)***	ENS John J. Doherty, USNR	6 Feb 1943
Donnell (DE 56)	ENS Earl R. Donnell, USNR	26 Jun 1943
Doyle, Cecil J. (DE 368)	2nd LT Cecil J. Doyle, USMC	16 Oct 1944
Duffy (DE 27—ex-BDE 27)***	ENS Charles J. Duffy, USNR	5 Aug 1943
Dufilho (DE 423)	LT Marion W. Dufilho, USN	21 Jul 1944
Duncan (FFG 10)	ADM Donald B. Duncan, USN	15 May 1980
Edson (DD 946)	MGEN Merritt A. Edson, USMC	7 Nov 1958
Eichenberger (DE 202)	ENS Charles E. Eichenberger, USNR	17 Nov 1943
Eldridge (DE 173)	LCDR John Eldridge, Jr., USN	27 Aug 1943
Ellison, Harold J. (DD 864)	ENS Harold J. Ellison, USNR	23 Jun 1945
Ellyson (DMS 19—ex-DD 454) **	CDR Theodore G. Ellyson, USN	28 Nov 1941
Elrod (FFG 55)	MAJ Henry T. Elrod, USMC	18 May 1985
Estocin (FFG 15)	CAPT Michael J. Estocin, USN	10 Jan 1981
Eversole (DE 404)	LT (jg) John T. Eversole, USN	21 Mar 1944
(DD 789)		10 May 1946

Ships Named for Naval Aviators—Continued

Ship	Named for	Commissioning Date
Fechteler (DE 157)	LT Frank C. Fechteler, USN	1 Jul 1943
(DD 870)		2 Mar 1946
Fieberling (DE 640)	LT Langdon K. Fieberling, USN	11 Apr 1944
Fitch, Aubrey (FFG 34)	ADM Aubrey W. Fitch, USN	9 Oct 1982
Flatley (FFG 21)	VADM James H. Flatley, Jr., USN	20 Jun 1981
Fleming (DE 32)	CAPT Richard E. Fleming, USMC	18 Sep 1943
Fletcher (DD 445)	ADM Frank J. Fletcher, USN	30 Jun 1942
(DD 992)		12 Jul 1980
Fogg (DE 57)	LT (jg) Carleton T. Fogg, USN	7 Jul 1943
Forrestal (CVA 59)-(CV 59)	James Vincent Forrestal	1 Oct 1955
Fox, Lee (APD 45—ex-DE 65)**	ENS Lee Fox, Jr., USNR	30 Aug 1943
Gallery (FFG 26)	RADM Daniel V. Gallery, USN	
	RADM Philip Daly Gallery, USN	
	RADM William G. Gallery, USN	5 Dec 1981
Geiger (AP 197)	GEN Roy Stanley Geiger, USMC	13 Sep 1952
Gentry (DE 349)	2nd LT Wayne R. Gentry, USMC	14 Jun 1944
Gillette (DE 270)	LT (jg) Douglas W. Gillette, USNR	8 Sep 1943
(DE 681)		27 Oct 1943
Gray, John P. (APD 74—ex-DE 673)*	LT (jg) John P. Gray, USNR	15 Mar 1944
Greene, Eugene A. (DD 711)	ENS Eugene A. Greene, USNR	8 Jun 1945
Griswold (DE 7)	ENS Don T. Griswold, USNR	28 Apr 1943
Groves, Stephen W. (FFG 29)	ENS Stephen W. Groves, USNR	17 Apr 1982
Hale, Roy O. (DE 336)	LT (jg) Roy O. Hale, Jr., USN	3 Feb 1944
Halsey (DLG 23)	FADM William F. Halsey, Jr., USN	20 Jul 1963
Hammann (DD 412)	ENS Charles H. Hammann, USNR	11 Aug 1939
(DE 131)		17 May 1943
Hancock, Lewis (DD 675)	LCDR Lewis Hancock, Jr., USN	29 Sep 1943
Hanson (DD 832)	1st LT Robert M. Hanson, USMC	11 May 1945
Hart (DD 594)	LT Patrick H. Hart, USN	4 Nov 1944
Harwood (DD 861)	CDR Bruce L. Harwood, USN	28 Sep 1945
Hastings, Burden R. (DE 19—ex-BDE 19)***	LT Burden R. Hastings, USN	1 May 1943
Henderson (DD 785)	MAJ Lofton R. Henderson, USMC	4 Aug 1945
Hissem (DE 400)	ENS Joseph M. Hissem, USNR	13 Jan 1944
Hodges (DE 231)	ENS Flourenoy G. Hodges, USNR	27 May 1944
Holder (DE 401)	LT (jg) Randolph M. Holder, USNR	18 Jan 1944
(DD 819)		18 May 1946
Holt (DE 706)	LT (jg) William M. Holt, USNR	9 Jun 1944
Hopping (APD 51—ex-DE 155)**	LCDR Halsted L. Hopping, USN	21 May 1943
Hurst (DE 250)	LT Edwin W. Hurst, USN	30 Aug 1943
Hutchins (DD 476)	LT Carleton B. Hutchins, USN	17 Nov 1942
Irwin (DD 794)	RADM Noble E. Irwin, USN	14 Feb 1944
Isbell, Arnold J. (DD 869)	CAPT Arnold J. Isbell, USN	5 Jan 1946

Ships Named for Naval Aviators—Continued

Ship	Named for	Commissioning Date
Jaccard (DE 355)	ENS Richard A. Jaccard, USNR	26 Jul 1944
Johnson, Earl V. (DE 702)	LT (jg) Earl V. Johnson, USN	18 Mar 1944
Keller, Robert F. (DE 419)	ENS Robert F. Keller, USNR	17 Jun 1944
Kennedy, Jr., Joseph P. (DD 850)	LT Joseph P. Kennedy, Jr., USNR	15 Dec 1945
Kenyon, Henry R. (DE 683)	ENS Henry R. Kenyon, USNR	30 Nov 1943
King (DLG 10)	FADM Ernest J. King, USN	17 Nov 1960
Kinzer (APD 91—ex-DE 232)*	ENS Edward B. Kinzer, USNR	1 Nov 1944
Koelsch (DE 1049)	LT (jg) John K. Koelsch, USN	10 Jun 1967
Knox, Leslie L.B. (DE 580)	LT (jg) Leslie L. B. Knox, USNR	22 Mar 1944
Lansdowne (DD 486)	LCDR Zachary Lansdowne, USN	29 Apr 1942
Lewis (DE 535)	ENS Victor A. Lewis, USNR	5 Sep 1944
Lindsey (DM 32—ex-DD 771) *	LT Eugene E. Lindsey, USN	20 Aug 1944
Lough (DE 586)	ENS John C. Lough, USNR	2 May 1944
Lovelace (DE 198)	LCDR Donald A. Lovelace, USN	7 Nov 1943
Macleish (DD 220)	LT Kenneth MacLeish, USNR	2 Aug 1920
Mason (DE 529)	ENS Newton H. Mason, USNR	20 Mar 1944
Massey (DD 778)	LCDR Lance E. Massey, USN	24 Nov 1944
McCain, John S. (DL 3—ex-DD 928)*	ADM John S. McCain, USN	12 Oct 1953
(DDG 56)		2 Jul 1994
McClusky (FFG 41)	RADM Clarence W. McClusky, Jr., USN	10 Dec 1983
McCord (DD 534)	CDR Frank C. McCord, USN	19 Aug 1943
McDonnell, Edward O. (DE 1043)	VADM Edward O. McDonnell, USNR	15 Feb 1965
McCormick (DD 223)	LT (jg) Alexander A. McCormick, USNR	30 Aug 1920
Menges (DE 320)	ENS Herbert H. Menges, USNR	26 Oct 1943
Mills (DE 383)	ENS Lloyd J. Mills, USNR	2 Oct 1943
Mitchell (DE 43—ex-BDE 43)***	ENS Albert E. Mitchell, USNR	17 Nov 1943
Mitchell, Oliver (DE 417)	2nd LT Oliver Mitchell, USMCR	14 Jun 1944
Mitscher (DL 2—ex-DD 927)*	ADM Marc A. Mitscher, USN	15 May 1953
(DDG 57)		10 Dec 1994
Moore, Ulvert M. (DE 442)	ENS Ulvert M. Moore, USNR	18 Jul 1944
Mosley (DE 321)	ENS Walter H. Mosley, USNR	30 Oct 1943
Mullinnix (DD 944)	RADM Henry M. Mullinnix, USN	7 Mar 1958
Mustin (DD 413)	CAPT Henry C. Mustin, USN	15 Sep 1939
Nawman, Melvin R. (DE 416)	2nd LT Melvin R. Nawman, USMCR	16 May 1944
O'Flaherty (DE 340)	ENS Frank W. O'Flaherty, USNR	8 Apr 1944
O'Hare (DD 889)	LCDR Edward H. O'Hare, USN	29 Nov 1945
Osberg (DE 538)	ENS Carl A. Osberg, USNR	10 Dec 1945
Osmus (DE 701)	ENS Wesley F. Osmus, USNR	23 Feb 1945
Owens, James C. (DD 776)	LT James C. Owens, USN	17 Feb 1945

Ships Named for Naval Aviators—Continued

Ship	Named for	Commissioning Date
Parks, Floyd B. (DD 884)	MAJ Floyd B. Parks, USMC	31 Jul 1945
Peiffer (DD 588)	ENS Carl D. Peiffer, USN	15 Jun 1944
Pennewill (DE 175)	LCDR William E. Pennewill, USN	15 Sep 1943
Peterson, Dale W. (DE 337)	ENS Dale W. Peterson, USN	17 Feb 1944
Potter, Stephen (DD 538)	ENS Stehpen Potter, USN	21 Oct 1943
Powers, John J. (DE 528)	LT John J. Powers, USN	29 Feb 1944
Raby (DE 698)	RADM James J. Raby, USN	7 Dec 1943
Radford, Arthur W. (DD 968)	ADM Arthur W. Radford, USN	16 Apr 1977
Ramsey (DEG 2)	ADM Dewitt C. Ramsey, USN	3 Jun 1967
Raven, Julius A. (APD 110—ex-DE 600)*	LT Julius A. Raven, USNR	28 Jun 1945
Reid, Beverly W. (APD 119—ex-DE 722)*	ENS Beverly W. Reid, USN	25 Jun 1945
Rich (DE 695)	LT (jg) Ralph M. Rich, USN	10 Oct 1943
(DD 820)		3 Jul 1946
Richey (DE 385)	ENS Joseph L. Richey, USNR	30 Oct 1943
Riddle (DE 185)	ENS Joseph Riddle, USNR	17 Nov 1943
Riley (DE 579)	LT Paul J. Riley, USN	13 Mar 1944
Rinehart (DE 196)	LT (jg) Clark F. Rinehart, USN	12 Feb 1944
Roark (DE 1053)	LT William M. Roark, USN	22 Nov 1969
Roberts, John Q. (APD 94—ex-DE 235)*	ENS John Q. Roberts, USNR	8 Mar 1945
Roche (DE 197)	ENS David J. Roche, USNR	21 Feb 1944
Rodgers, John (DD 574)	COMMODORE John Rodgers	9 Feb 1943
	RADM John Rodgers	
(DD 983)	CDR John Rodgers (naval aviator)	14 Jul 1979
Rombach (DE 364)	LT (jg) Severin L. Rombach, USNR	20 Sep 1944
Rowell, Richard M. (DE 403)	ENS Richard M. Rowell, USNR	9 Mar 1944
Sample (DE 1048)	RADM William D. Sample, USN	23 Mar 1968
Saufley (DD 465)	LT (jg) Richard C. Saufley, USN	29 Aug 1942
Seaman (DD 791)##	LCDR Allen L. Seaman, USNR	
Seid (DE 256)	ENS Daniel Seid, USNR	11 Jun 1943
Sellstrom (DER 255)	ENS Edward R. Sellstrom, USNR	12 Oct 1943
Shea (DM 30—ex-DD 750)*	CDR John J. Shea, USN	30 Sep 1944
Shelton (DE 407)	ENS James A. Shelton, USNR	4 Apr 1944
(DD 790)		21 Jun 1946
Sherman, Forrest P. (DD 931)	ADM Forrest P. Sherman, USN	9 Nov 1955
Smartt (DE 257)	ENS Josesph G. Smartt, USNR	18 Jun 1943
Snyder (DE 745)	ENS Russell Snyder, USNR	5 May 1944
Sprague, Clifton (FFG 16)	VADM Clifton A.F. Sprague, USN	21 Mar 1981
Stickell (DD 888)	LT John H. Stickell, USNR	31 Oct 1945
Strickland (DE 333)	ENS Everett C. Strickland, USNR	10 Jan 1944
Stump (DD 978)	ADM Felix B. Stump, USN	19 Aug 1978
Sturtevant (DD 240)	ENS Albert D. Sturtevant, USNR	21 Sep 1920
Suesens, Richard W. (DE 342)	LT (jg) Richard W. Suesens, USN	29 Apr 1944

Ships Named for Naval Aviators—Continued

Ship	Named for	Commissioning Date
Tabberer (DE 418)	LT (jg) Charles A. Tabberer, USNR	23 May 1944
Talbot, Ralph (DD 390)	2nd LT Ralph Talbot, USMC	14 Oct 1937
Taylor, Jesse Junior (FFG 50)	CDR Jesse J. Taylor, USN	1 Dec 1984
Taylor, Lawrence C. (DE 415)	2nd LT Lawrence C. Taylor, USMC	13 May 1944
Thach (FFG 43)	ADM John S. Thach, USN	17 Mar 1984
Thomas, Leland E. (DE 420)	2nd LT Leland E. Thomas, USMCR	19 Jun 1944
Thomas, Lloyd (DE 764)	LT (jg) Lloyd Thomas, USN	21 Mar 1947
Thomason, John W. (DD 760)	COL John W. Thomason, USMC	11 Oct 1945
Thornhill (DE 195)	LT (jg) Leonard W. Thornhill	1 Feb 1944
Tills (DE 748)	ENS Robert G. Tills, USN	8 Aug 1944
Towers (DDG 9)	ADM John H. Towers, USN	6 Jun 1961
Trumpeter (DE 180)	LT (jg) George N. Trumpeter, USNR	16 Oct 1943
Tweedy (DE 532)	2nd LT Albert W. Tweedy, Jr., USMC	12 Feb 1944
Turner, Richmond K. (DLG 20)	ADM Richmond K. Turner, USN	13 Jun 1964
Underhill (DE 682)	ENS Samuel J. Underhill, USNR	15 Nov 1943
Vammen (DE 644)	ENS Charles E. Vammen, Jr. USNR	27 Jul 1944
Vandivier (DER 540)	LT (jg) Norman F. Vandivier, USNR	11 Oct 1955
Van Voorhis (DE 1028)	LCDR Bruce A. Van Voorhis, USN	22 Apr 1957
Varian (DE 798)	ENS Bertram S. Varian, Jr., USNR	29 Feb 1944
Waldron (DD 699)	LCDR John C. Waldron, USN	7 Jun 1944
Ware, Charles R. (DD 865)	LT Charles R. Ware, USN	21 Jul 1945
Weber (APD 75—ex-DE 675)**	LT (jg) Frederick T. Weber, USNR	30 Jun 1943
Whiting, Kenneth (AV 14)	CAPT Kenneth Whiting, USN	8 May 1944
Wileman (DE 22—ex-BDE 22)***	ENS William W. Wileman, USNR	11 Jun 1943
Wilhoite (DE 397)	ENS Thomas M. Wilhoite, USNR	16 Dec 1943
Wilke, Jack W. (DE 800)	ENS Jack W. Wilke, USNR	7 Mar 1944
Willis (DE 395)	ENS Walter M. Willis, USNR	10 Dec 1943
Wiltsie (DD 716)	CAPT Irving D. Wiltsie, USN	21 Jan 1946
Wingfield (DE 194)	ENS John D. Wingfield, USNR	28 Jan 1944
Wiseman (DE 667)	LT (jg) Osborne B. Wiseman, USN	4 Apr 1944
Woodson (DE 359)	LT (jg) Jeff D. Woodson, USN	24 Aug 1944

*Redesignated before commissioning.
**Redesignated after commissioning.
***Launched under different names and renamed before being commissioned.
#Redesignated and renamed from ship already in service.
##Never commissioned.

Medal of Honor Awards in Naval Aviation

To Naval Aviators and Naval Aviation Pilots in Connection with Aviation

Name	Rank/Service	N.A. Number	Occasion for Award
BAUER, Harold W.*	LCOL, USMC	4189	Action in air combat, South Pacific area; 28 Sep—3 Oct 1942
BENNETT, Floyd	CWO, USN	NAP-9	Piloted plane on first flight over North Pole; 9 May 1926
BOYINGTON, Gregory	MAJ, USMC	5160	Action in air combat, Central Solomons area; 12 Sep 1943—3 Jan 1944
BYRD, Richard E.	LCDR, USN	608	Commanded plane on first flight over North Pole; 9 May 1926
CORRY, William M.*	LCDR, USN	23	Attempted rescue of pilot from burning aircraft; 2 Oct 1920
DeBLANC, Jefferson J.	CAPT, USMC	12504	Action as leader of a fighter mission in air combat off Kolombangara Island, South Pacific; 31 Jan 1943
ELROD, Henry T.*	CAPT, USMC	4093	Action in air and ground combat in defense of Wake Island; 8–23 Dec 1941
ESTOCIN, Michael J.*	LCDR, USN		Action as leader of air attack against enemy targets in North Vietnam; 20 and 26 Apr 1967
FLEMING, Richard E.*	CAPT, USMC	6889	Action as leader of dive bombing attack, Battle of Midway; 4–6 Jun 1942
FOSS, Joseph J.	CAPT, USMC	7290	Action in air combat in defense of Guadalcanal; 9 Oct—19 Nov 1942
GALER, Robert E.	MAJ, USMC	5197	Action in air combat, South Pacific area; Aug–Sep 1942
GORDON, Nathan G.	LT, USN	11421	Rescue of 15 officers and men under fire in Kavieng Harbor; 15 Feb 1944
HALL, William E.	LT (jg), USN	6072	Determined attacks on enemy carrier, Battle of Coral Sea; 7–8 May 1942

Medal of Honor Awards in Naval Aviation—Continued

Name	Rank/Service	N.A. Number	Occasion for Award
HAMMANN, Charles H.	ENS, USNRF	1494	Rescue of fellow pilot under fire during raid on Pula, Austria; 21 Aug 1918
HANSON, Robert M.*	1st LT, USMC	5218	Action in air combat at Bougainville; 1 Nov 1943, and New Britain; 24 Jun 1944
HUDNER, Thomas J., Jr.	LT (jg), USN		Attempted rescue of squadron mate downed behind enemy lines in Korea; 4 Dec 1950
HUTCHINS, Carlton B.	LT, USN	3435	Remained at controls of his aircraft after a mid-air collision to allow his crew to escape; 2 Feb 1938
KOELSCH, John K.*	LT (jg), USN		Attempted rescue by helicopter during heavy overcast and under fire, Korea; 3 Jul 1951
LASSEN, Clyde E.	LT (jg), USN		Night helicopter rescue under enemy fire of two downed aviators in North Vietnam; 19 Jun 1968
McCAMPBELL, David	CDR, USN	5612	Action in air combat during Battle of Philippine Sea and Leyte Gulf; June and Oct 1944
O'HARE, Edward H.	LT, USN	6405	Action in air combat in defense of carrier off Rabaul; 20 Feb 1942
PLESS, Stephen W.	CAPT, USMC		Helicopter rescue under enemy fire of four American soldiers beset by a large group of Viet Cong; 19 Aug 1967
POWERS, John J.*	LT, USN	6880	Determined attacks on enemy ships during Battle of Coral Sea; 4–8 May 1942
SCHILT, Christian F.	1st LT, USMC	2741	Air evacuation of wounded under fire, Qualili, Nicaragua; 6–8 Jan 1928
SMITH, John L.	MAJ, USMC	5978	Action in air combat in defense of Guadalcanal; 21 Aug—15 Sep 1942
SWETT, James E.	1st LT, USMC	11893	Action in air combat, Solomon Islands area; 7 Apr 1943
TALBOT, Ralph	2nd LT, USMC	802	Action in air combat, Europe; 8 and 14 Oct 1918
VAN VOORHIS, Bruce*	LCDR, USN	3859	Determined low level heavy bomber attack, Battle of the Solomon Islands; 6 Jul 1943
WALSH, Kenneth A.	1st LT, USMC		Action in air combat at Vella Lavella; 15 and 30 Aug 1943

Medal of Honor Awards in Naval Aviation—Continued

Name	Rank/Service	N.A. Number	Occasion for Award
To Naval Aviators for Action not Associated with Aviation			
ANTRIM, Richard N.	LT, USN	6750	Action on behalf of fellow prisoners while POW; April 1942
EDSON, Merritt A.	COL, USMC	3026	Leading ground action in defense of the airfield at Guadalcanal; 13–14 Sep 1942
STOCKDALE, James B.	CAPT, USN		Action on behalf of fellow prisoners while POW; 4 Sep 1969
To Officers and Men later Designated Naval Aviator, NAP, and Naval Aviation Observer			
COMMISKEY, Henry A.	2nd LT, USMC		Leading ground attack on strong enemy position near Yongdungpo, Korea; 20 Sep 1950
McDONNELL, Edward	ENS, USN	18	Establishing signal station ashore and maintaining communications while under fire at Veracruz; 21–22 Apr 1914
MOFFETT, William A.	CDR, USN	NAO-1	Action in command of a ship at Veracruz; 21–22 Apr 1914
ORMSBEE, Francis, Jr.	CMM(A), USN	NAP-25	Rescuing enlisted men and attempted rescue of pilots downed in seaplane crash in Pensacola Bay; 25 Sep 1918
To Non-Aviators for Action Associated with Aviation			
CLAUSEN, Raymond M.	PFC, USMC		Repeated rescues by helicopter of men trapped by enemy fire and minefield, South Vietnam; 30 Jan 1970
FINN, John W.	Chief**, USN		Action under fire during the attack NAS Kaneohe; 7 Dec 1941
GARY, Donald A.	LT (jg), USN		Repeated rescues of trapped men on board Franklin (CV 13), severely damaged by enemy attack; 19 Mar 1945
McGUNIGAL, Patrick	Ship's Fitter 1st Class, USN		Rescue of a kite balloon pilot entangled underwater in the balloon rigging, Huntington (ACR 5); 17 Sep 1917
O'CALLAHAN, Joseph T.	LCDR, USN (CHC)		Inspiration, leadership, and repeated rescues on board Franklin (CV 13) damaged by air attack; 19 Mar 1945
RICKETTS, Milton E.*	LT, USN		Leading damage control party on board Yorktown (CV 5) damaged during Battle of Coral Sea; 8 May 1942
ROBINSON, Robert G.	GSGT, USMC		Action during air combat as gunner to LT Ralph Talbot, USMC; 8 and 14 Oct 1918

Medal of Honor Awards in Naval Aviation—Continued

To Aviators for participating in the Space Program

The Congressional Space Medal of Honor, first awarded to six former astronauts by President Jimmy Carter on 1 October 1978, was authorized by Congress on 29 September 1969 to recognize "any astronaut who in the performance of his duties has distinguished himself by exceptionally meritorious efforts and contributions to the welfare of the Nation and mankind."

Name	Rank/Service	Occasion for Award
ARMSTRONG, Neil A.		Participated in the Gemini 8 and Apollo 11 space flight missions. On Apollo 11, he became the first person to walk on the moon; 1 Oct 1978
CONRAD, Charles, Jr.	CAPT, USN	Participated in four space flight missions: Gemini 5, Gemini 11, Apollo 12, and Skylab 2. Commanded the crew of the first manned Skylab mission that conducted repairs on the orbital workshop; 1 Oct 1978
GLENN, John H., Jr.	COL, USMC	One of the original Mercury Astronauts and the first American to orbit the Earth; 1 Oct 1978
LOVELL, James A., Jr.	CAPT, USN	Participated in four space flight missions: Gemini 7, Gemini 12, Apollo 8, and Apollo 13. Commanded the crew of Apollo 13; 26 July 1995
SHEPARD, Alan B., Jr.	RADM, USN	One of the original Mercury Astronauts and the first American into space. Commanded the Apollo 14 mission; 1 Oct 1978
YOUNG, John W.	CAPT, USN	Participated in five space flight missions: Gemini 3, Gemini 10, Apollo 10, and Apollo 16, and STS-1 (Space Shuttle *Columbia*) benefitting human progress in space; 19 May 1981

* Received award posthumously
** Aviation Ordnance Chief (AOC); later promoted to commissioned status

The Medal of Honor is presented to Major Stephen W. Pless, USMC, by President Lyndon B. Johnson. A417495

Aviation Ratings

Enlisted men have served in Naval Aviation since its inception. The first men reported for duty with Lieutenant Theodore G. Ellyson and Lieutenant John Rodgers when they began flight training in 1911. Their numbers increased as the number of aviators and aircraft on hand increased. Despite the specialties involved in aviation it was a number of years before these men were required to meet special qualifications beyond those of their basic rating. Such special courses as enlisted men received in the 1916–17 period gave them a certificate to prove satisfactory completion and made them better qualified to carry out aviation duty. However, it had no effect on their basic ratings, the qualifications for which were still based on the requirements of the regular naval service.

Greater emphasis on aviation requirements accompanied the expansion for World War I and with it the basic requirements of the pre-war period were somewhat relaxed but not completely forgotten. One indication of change was a parenthetical addition to the rating to indicate aviation duty, as for example, Machinist's Mate (Aviation) or MM (A). But it was not until 1921 that aviation ratings received recognition as a special branch and the first strictly aviation ratings were established. Since then adjustments to the rating structure have been frequent. These produced a number of changes and additions to the original basic ratings as well as a great variety of subdivisions within them, some representing a mere change in title, others reflecting changing technology.

The following list covers only the basic ratings, shown in alphabetical order.

AEROGRAPHER

Rating (Aerog) established effective 1 Jul 1924 by CL 99–23 of Dec 1923; distinguishing mark approved by CL 62–26 of 29 Oct 1926*; see Aerographer's Mate.

AEROGRAPHER'S MATE

Aerographer rating (Aerog) redesignated Aerographer's Mate (AerM) by CL 113–42 of 8 Aug 1942, abbreviation changed to (AG) by CL 106–48 of 9 Jun 1948.

AIR CONTROLMAN

Rating (SP) established effective 2 Apr 1948 by CL 40–47 of 21 Feb 1947; abbreviation changed to (AC) by CL 106–48 of 9 Jun 1948; see Air Traffic Controller

AIRCRAFT MAINTENANCEMAN

A Master Chief's rating (AF) establishment approved by SecNav, 5 Nov 1963.

AIRCREW SURVIVAL EQUIPMENTMAN

Parachute Rigger rating (PR) redesignated Aircrew Survival Equipmentman effective 7 Dec 1965 by BuPers Note 1440 of 2 Feb 1966, without change of abbreviation.

AIRSHIP RIGGER

Rating (AR) established by CL 205–43 of 12 Oct 1943; distinguishing mark approved by CL 58–44 of 29 Feb 1944*; abolished effective 2 Apr 1948 by CL 246–47 of 15 Dec 1947.

AIR TRAFFIC CONTROLLER

Air Controlman rating (AC) redesignated Air Traffic Controller by BuPers Note 1220 of 10 December 1977, without change in abbreviation.

AVIATION ANTISUBMARINE WARFARE TECHNICIAN

Rating (AX) established effective 1 Dec 1962 by BuPers Note 1440 of 29 Jun 1962; see Aviation Electronics Technician

AVIATION ANTISUBMARINE WARFARE OPERATOR

Rating (AW) established effective 1 Sep 1968 by BuPers Note 1440 of 29 Feb 1968; see Aviation Warfare Systems Operator

AVIATION BOATSWAIN'S MATE

Rating (ABM) established by CL 268–44 of 14 Sep 1944; distinguishing mark approved CL 363–44 of 30 Nov 1944*; abbreviation changed to (AB) by CL 106–48 of 9 Jun 1948.

AVIATION BOMBSIGHT MECHANIC

Rating (AOMB) established as a subrating of Aviation Ordnanceman by CL 205–43 of 12 Oct 1943; see Aviation Bombsight and Fire Control Mechanic.

AVIATION BOMBSIGHT AND FIRE CONTROL MECHANIC

Aviation Bombsight Mechanic rating (AOMB) renamed Aviation Bombsight and Fire Control Mechanic by CL 355–44 of 27 Nov 1944, without change in abbreviation; see Aviation Fire Controlman

AVIATION CARPENTER'S MATE

Rating (ACM) established effective 1 Jul 1921 by CL 9–21 of 24 Mar 1921; distinguishing mark approved by CL 62–26 of 29 Oct 1926*; abolished effective 30 Jun 1940 by CL 36–40 of 21 May 1940; see Aviation Metalsmith

AVIATION ELECTRICIAN'S MATE

Rating (AEM) established by CL 129–42 of 4 Sep 1942; abbreviation changed to (AE) by CL 106–48 of 9 Jun 1948.

AVIATION ELECTRONICSMAN

Aviation Radioman rating (ARM) redesignated Aviation Electronicsman effective 2 Apr 1948 by CL 40–47 of 21 Feb 1947, without change in abbreviation; abbreviation changed to (AL) by CL 106–48 of 9 Jun 1948; abolished by BuPers Instruction 1440.10B of 18 Dec 1959.

AVIATION ELECTRONICS TECHNICIAN

Aviation Electronics Technician's Mate rating (AETM) redesignated Aviation Electronics Technician (AET) effective 2 Apr 1948 by CL 40–47 of 21 Feb 1947; abbreviation changed to (AT) by CL 106–48 of 9 Jun 1948; Ratings AQ, AX, and AV to be merged and redesignated (AT) by NAVOP 075/89 of 27 Jun 1989; (AV) rating removed so only ratings (AQ) and (AX) were absorbed into already existing rate of (AT) by amendments to NAVOP 075/89 of 23 Aug 1990, effective 1 Jan 1991.

AVIATION ELECTRONICS TECHNICIAN'S MATE

Aviation Radio Technician rating (ART) redesignated Aviation Electronics Technician's Mate (AETM) by CL 325–45 of 31 Oct 1945; see Aviation Electronics Technician.

AVIATION FIRE CONTROLMAN

Aviation Bombsight and Fire Control Mechanic (AOMB) redesignated Aviation Fire Controlman (AFC) to become basic rate by CL 39–45 of 15 Feb 1945; abolished effective 2 Apr 1948 by CL 40–47 of 21 Feb 1947; see Aviation Fire Control Technician.

AVIATION FIRE CONTROL TECHNICIAN

Rating (AQ) established in 1954 from subratings of the former Aviation Fire Controlman and in a sense a revival of that rating; see Aviation Electronics Technician

AVIATION GUIDED MISSILEMAN

Rating (GF) establishment approved by SecNav on 23 Jan 1953; abolished by BuPers Instruction 1440.25 of 10 Jun 1960.

AVIATION MACHINIST'S MATE

Rating (AMM) established effective 1 July 1921 by CL 9–21 of 24 Mar 1921; distinguishing mark approved by CL 17–41 of 11 Feb 1941*; abbreviation changed to (AD) by CL 106–48 of 9 Jun 1948.

AVIATION MAINTENANCE ADMINISTRATIONMAN

Rating (AZ) established effective 1 Jan 1964 by BuPers Note 1440 of 22 Jan 1963.

AVIATION METALSMITH

Rating (AM) established effective 1 Jul 1921 by CL 921 of 24 Mar 1921; Aviation Carpenter's Mate rating (ACM) abolished and redesignated Aviation Metalsmith (AM) by CL 36–40 of 21 May 1940; see Aviation Structural Mechanic.

AVIATION ORDNANCEMAN

Rating (AOM) established by CL 14–26 of 2 Mar 1926; abbreviation changed to (AO) by CL 106–48 of 9 Jun 1948.

AVIATION PHOTOGRAPHER'S MATES

See Photographer's Mate.

AVIATION PILOT

Rating (AP) established by CL 18–24 of 13 Mar 1924, changed to Chief Aviation Pilot and Aviation Pilot First Class by CL 66–27 of 21 Sep 1927, and abolished by a change from a rating to a designation by CL 10–33 of 28 Mar 1933; distinguishing mark approved by CL 24–33 of 30 June 1933*; reestablished as a rating by CL 43–42 of 17 Mar 1942, and again abolished by a change to a designation, effective 2 Apr 1948 by CL 40–47 of 21 Feb 1947.

AVIATION QUARTERMASTER

Rating (AR) established by BuNav Ltr N5H of 21 Mar 1917; see Aviation Rigger

AVIATION RADIOMAN

Rating (ARM) established by CL 5–42 of 13 Jan 1942; see Aviation Electronicsman.

AVIATION RADIO TECHNICIAN

Rating (ART) established by CL 169–42 of 11 Dec 1942; see Aviation Electronics Technician's Mate.

AVIATION RIGGER

Aviation Quartermaster rating (AR) redesignated Aviation Rigger effective 1 Jul 1921 by CL 9–21 of 24 Mar 1921, without a change in abbreviation; abolished effective 30 Jun 1927 by CL 13–26 of 25 Feb 1926.

AVIATION STOREKEEPER

Rating (SKV) establishment approved by SecNav on 28 Sep 1943; distinguishing mark approved by CL 65–45 of 15 Mar 1945*; abbreviation changed to (AK) by CL 106–48 of 9 Jun 1948.

AVIATION STRUCTURAL MECHANIC

Aviation Metalsmith rating (AM) redesignated Aviation Structural Mechanic effective 2 Apr 1948 by CL 40–47 of 21 Feb 1947, without change in abbreviation.

AVIATION SUPPORT EQUIPMENT TECHNICIAN

Rating (AS) established effective 1 Sep 1966 by BuPers Note 1440 of 24 Feb 1966.

AVIATION WARFARE SYSTEMS OPERATOR

Aviation Antisubmarine Warfare Operator rating (AW) redesignated Aviation Warfare Systems Operator by BuPers Note 1440 of 16 Nov 1993, without change of abbreviation.

AVIONICS TECHNICIAN

A Master Chief's rating (AV) establishment approved by SecNav, 5 Nov 1963; see Aviation Electronics Technician.

PARACHUTE RIGGER

Rating (PR) established by CL 33–42 of 24 Feb 1942; see Aircrew Survival Equipmentman.

PHOTOGRAPHER

Rating (P) established in the Aviation Branch effective 1 Jul 1921 by CL 9–21 of 24 Mar 1921, apparently later transferred to Special Branch, but returned to the Aviation Branch by CL 14–26 of 2 Mar 1926; see Photographer's Mate.

PHOTOGRAPHER'S MATE

Photographer's rating (P) redesignated Photographer's Mate (PhoM) by CL 113–42 of 8 Aug 1942 and again removed from the Aviation Branch; rating split into Photographer's Mate and Aviation Photographer's Mate (both PhoM) effective 2 Apr 1948 by CL 40–47 of 21 Feb 1947; abbreviation changed to (AF) by CL 106–48 of 9 Jun 1948; ratings combined to become Photographer's Mate (PH) of the Aviation Group by CL 116–50 of 31 Jul 1950.

PHOTOGRAPHIC INTELLIGENCEMAN

Rating (PT) established by BuPers Note 1223 of 2 Oct 1957. Merged with YN NEC 2005 to form Intelligence Specialist (IS) (not an aviation rating) by BuPers Note 1440 of 6 Dec 1974.

TRADEVMAN (Training Devices Repairman and Instructor)

Rating (TD) established by CL 106–48 of 9 Jun 1948; rate slated for disestablishment by BuPers Note 1440 of 22 Jul 1982 beginning in Fiscal Year (FY) 1984 with all conversions of personnel in this rate to be completed by the end of FY 1988.

*Distinguishing marks are for non-rated qualified as striker in a particular aviation rating (e.g. Aviation Machinist's Mate). The mark is worn mid-way between the wrist and elbow of the left sleeve. Distinguishing marks were superseded by the introduction of group rates used with striker marks by non-rated men in 1948.

The F3H Demon being refueled in the foreground has double 00s on the nose of the aircraft. Aircraft with double 00s indicates they are assigned to an Air Group Commander (CAG). The other F3H Demons in the formation are from one of the fighter squadrons assigned to the Carrier Air Group. The refueling aircraft is an AJ tanker from VAH-15. NAH 000211

Evolution of Carrier Air Groups and Wings

The term Air Group, modified by the name of a carrier, as Saratoga Air Group, came into use during the early days of carrier aviation as a collective title for the squadrons operating on board a particular carrier. It remained a mere title until 1 July 1938, when authorization for Air Group Commander billets became effective. With this action, the squadrons on board acquired the unity of a formal command and the carrier air group as such first took form.

Numerical designation of air groups began in 1942, the first being Carrier Air Group NINE (CVG-9), established 1 March 1942. The carrier air group was sometimes referred to as CAG. However, the official designation was CVG. Existing air groups continued to be known by their carrier names until they were reformed or disbanded, only two of the early groups escaping the latter fate.

On 29 June 1944, new letter designations were set up to bring them in line with standardized complements of different carrier types. The new designations, some of which had been in use for over a year, showed carrier type affiliation as follows: CVBG for large carrier air group, CVG for medium carrier air group, CVLG for light carrier air group, and CVEG for escort carrier air group. The CVEG designation was assigned to carriers of the Sangamon Class. The other CVE carrier classes were assigned Composite Squadrons (VC) and listed as air groups. They remained in that category throughout the war period. The CVBG designation was for assignment to the Midway Class carriers, sometimes referred to as the large carriers. On 15 November 1946, to correct the results of demobilization which had left squadron numbers all out of sequence and a system of no apparent order, sweeping changes were made in air

unit designations. Carrier Air Groups of four types were designated according to their assigned ship, as CVBG for Battle Carrier, CVG for Attack Carrier, CVLG for Light Carrier and CVEG for Escort Carrier. Two years later, on 1 September 1948, all carrier air groups became CVG regardless of their carrier affiliation.

Carrier Air Groups were retitled Wings on 20 December 1963, and CVG became CVW. Replacement Air Groups, which were set up in 1958, became Combat Readiness Air Groups on 1 April 1963. Popularly known by the short titles RAG and CRAG in the respective periods, their designation throughout was RCVG. When Groups became Wings, CRAG became CRAW and RCVG became RCVW.

Antisubmarine Carrier Air Groups, CVSG, were established on 1 April 1960. They were slowly phased out during the 1960s, and the last were disestablished on 30 June 1973.

On 1 July 1968, the Naval Air Reserve was reorganized into wings and squadrons similar to the active fleet air organizations to ensure a more rapid and efficient transition to combat status in the event of mobilization. Two Reserve Carrier Air Wings were established and all carrier-type squadrons in the reserves were placed in these two wings. CVWR was the acronym assigned for the Reserve Carrier Air Wings. A similar organization was established for the Reserve Antisubmarine Carrier Air Groups and assigned the acronym CVSGR. The implementation of these two reserve wings and groups did not take place until 1970.

Tabulations below have two deviations from the above: use of CVG instead of the original CAG for the period to 20 June 1944, and use of the unofficial CVAG in the period 1946–48 to identify the Attack Carrier Air Groups.

Carrier Air Wings-CVW

CVW-1	Ranger Air Group Formed	1 Jul 1938
	Reformed as CVG-4	3 Aug 1943
	Became CVAG-1	15 Nov 1946
	Became CVG-1	1 Sep 1948
	Became CVW-1	20 Dec 1963
CVW-2	CVBG-74 Established	1 May 1945
	Became CVBG-1	15 Nov 1946
	Became CVG-2	1 Sep 1948
	Became CVW-2	20 Dec 1963
CVW-3	Saratoga Air Group Formed	1 Jul 1938
	Reformed as CVG-3	25 Sep 1943
	Became CVAG-3	15 Nov 1946
	Became CVG-3	1 Sep 1948
	Became CVW-3	20 Dec 1963
CVW-4	CVG-4 Established	1 Sep 1950
	Became RCVG-4	Apr 1958
	Became RCVW-4	20 Dec 1963
	Disestablished	1 Jul 1970
CVW-5	CVG-5 Established	15 Feb 1943
	Became CVAG-5	15 Nov 1946
	Became CVG-5	1 Sep 1948
	Became CVW-5	20 Dec 1963
CVW-6	CVG-17 Established	1 Jan 1943
	Became CVBG-17	22 Jan 1946
	Became CVBG-5	15 Nov 1946
	Became CVG-6	27 Jul 1948
	Became CVW-6	20 Dec 1963
	Disestablished	1 Apr 1992
CVW-7	CVG-18 Established	20 Jul 1943
	Became CVAG-7	15 Nov 1946
	Became CVG-7	1 Sep 1948
	Became CVW-7	20 Dec 1963
CVW-8	CVG-8 Established	9 Apr 1951
	Became CVW-8	20 Dec 1963
CVW-9	CVG-9 Established	26 Mar 1952
	Became CVW-9	20 Dec 1963
CVW-10	A CVG-10 Established	1 May 1952
	Became CVW-10	20 Dec 1963
	Disestablished	20 Nov 1969
	B Established	1 Nov 1986
	Disestablished	1 Jun 1988

CVW-11	CVG-11 Established	10 Oct 1942
	Became CVAG-11	15 Nov 1946
	Became CVG-11	1 Sep 1948
	Became CVW-11	20 Dec 1963
CVW-12	CVG-102 Established for reserve squadrons 1 Aug 1950 called to active duty for Korea	
	Became CVG-12	4 Feb 1953
	Became RCVG-12	Apr 1958
	Became RCVW-12	20 Dec 1963
	Disestablished	1 Jun 1970
CVW-13	Established	1 Mar 1984
	Disestablished	1 Jan 1991
CVW-14	CVG-101 Established for reserve squadrons called to active duty for Korea	1 Aug 1950
	Became CVG-14	4 Feb 1953
	Became CVW-14	20 Dec 1963
CVW-15	CVG-15 Established	5 Apr 1951
	Became CVW-15	20 Dec 1963
	Disestablished	31 Mar 1995
CVW-16	CVG-16 Established	1 Sep 1960
	Became CVW-16	20 Dec 1963
	Disestablished	30 Jun 1971
CVW-17	Established	1 Nov 1966
CVW-19	CVG-19 Established	15 Aug 1943
	Became CVAG-19	15 Nov 1946
	Became CVG-19	1 Sep 1948
	Became CVW-19	20 Dec 1963
	Disestablished	30 Jun 1977
CVW-21	CVG-21 Established	1 Jul 1955
	Became CVW-21	20 Dec 1963
	Disestablished	12 Dec 1975

Reserve Carrier Air Wings—CVWR

CVWR-20	Established	1 Apr 1970
CVWR-30	Established	1 Apr 1970
	Disestablished	31 Dec 1994

Carrier Air Groups—CVG

CVG-1	A Established	1 May 1943
	Disestablished	25 Oct 1945
	B See CVW-1	

CVG-2	A	Established	1 Jun 1943
		Disestablished	9 Nov 1945
	B	See CVW-2	
CVG-3		See CVW-3	
CVG-4	A	CVBG-75	1 Jun 1945
		Became CVBG-3	15 Nov 1946
		Became CVG-4	1 Sep 1948
		Disestablished	8 Jun 1950
	B	See CVW-1	
	C	See CVW-4	
CVG-5		See CVW-5	
CVG-6	A	Established	15 Mar 1943
		Disestablished	29 Oct 1945
	B	See CVW-6	
CVG-7	A	Established	3 Jan 1944
		Disestablished	8 Jul 1946
	B	See CVW-7	
CVG-8	A	Established	1 Jun 1943
		Disestablished	23 Nov 1945
	B	Established	15 Sep 1948
		Disestablished	29 Nov 1949
	C	See CVW-8	
CVG-9	A	Established	1 Mar 1942
		Disestablished	15 Oct 1945
	B	CVG-20	15 Oct 1943
		Became CVAG-9	15 Nov 1946
		Became CVG-9	1 Sep 1948
		Disestablished	1 Dec 1949
	C	See CVW-9	
CVG-10	A	Established	16 Apr 1942
		Disestablished	16 Nov 1945
	B	See CVW-10	
CVG-11		See CVW-11	
CVG-12	A	Established	9 Jan 1943
		Disestablished	17 Sep 1945
	B	See CVW-12	

CVG-13	A	Established	2 Nov 1942
		Disestablished	20 Oct 1945
	B	CVG-81 Established	1 Mar 1944
		Became CVAG-13	15 Nov 1946
		Became CVG-13	1 Sep 1948
		Disestablished	30 Nov 1949
	C	Established	21 Aug 1961
		Disestablished	1 Oct 1962
CVG-14	A	Established	1 Sep 1943
		Disestablished	14 Jun 1946
	B	See CVW-14	
CVG-15	A	Established	1 Sep 1943
		Disestablished	30 Oct 1945
	B	CVG-153 Established	26 Mar 1945
		Became CVAG-15	15 Nov 1946
		Became CVG-15	1 Sep 1948
		Disestablished	1 Dec 1949
	C	See CVW-15	
CVG-16	A	Established	16 Nov 1943
		Disestablished	6 Nov 1945
	B	See CVW-16	
CVG-17	A	CVG-82 Established	1 Apr 1944
		Became CVAG-17	15 Nov 1946
		Became CVG-17	1 Sep 1948
		Disestablished	15 Sep 1958
	B	See CVW-6	
CVG-18		See CVW-7	
CVG-19		See CVW-19	
CVG-20		See CVG-9	
CVG-21	A	Established	15 Sep 1948
		Disestablished	15 Mar 1949
	B	CVG-98 Established	28 Aug 1944
		Became CVAG-21	15 Nov 1946
		Disestablished	5 Aug 1947
	C	See CVW-21	
CVG-74		See CVW-2	
CVG-75		See CVG-4	

CVG-80	Established	1 Feb 1944
	Disestablished	16 Sep 1946
CVG-81	See CVG-13	
CVG-82	See CVG-17	
CVG-83	Established	1 May 1944
	Disestablished	24 Sep 1945
CVG-84	Established	1 May 1944
	Disestablished	8 Oct 1945
CVG-85	Established	15 May 1944
	Disestablished	27 Sep 1945
CVG-86	Established	15 Jun 1944
	Disestablished	21 Nov 1945
CVG-87	Established	1 Jul 1944
	Disestablished	2 Nov 1945
CVG-88	Established	18 Aug 1944
	Disestablished	29 Oct 1945
CVG-89	Established	2 Oct 1944
	Disestablished	7 Apr 1946
CVG-92	Established	2 Dec 1944
	Disestablished	18 Dec 1945
CVG-93	Established	21 Dec 1944
	Disestablished	30 Apr 1946
CVG-94	Established	15 Nov 1944
	Disestablished	7 Nov 1945
CVG-95	Established	2 Jan 1945
	Disestablished	31 Oct 1945
CVG-97	Established	1 Nov 1944
	Disestablished	31 Mar 1946
CVG-98	See CVG-21	
CVG-99	Established	15 Jul 1944
	Disestablished	6 Sep 1945
CVG-100	Established	1 Apr 1944
	Disestablished	20 Feb 1946
CVG-101	See CVW-14	
CVG-102	See CVW-12	

CVG-150	Established	22 Jan 1945
	Disestablished	2 Nov 1945
CVG-151	Established	12 Feb 1945
	Disestablished	6 Oct 1945
CVG-152	Established	5 Mar 1945
	Disestablished	21 Sep 1945
CVG-153	See CVG-15	

Attack Carrier Air Groups—CVAG

CVAG 1	See CVW-1
CVAG 3	See CVW-3
CVAG 5	See CVW-5
CVAG 7	See CVW-7
CVAG 9	See CVG-9
CVAG 11	See CVW-11
CVAG 13	See CVW-13
CVAG 15	See CVG-15
CVAG 17	See CVG-17
CVAG 19	See CVW-19
CVAG 21	See CVG-21

Battle Carrier Air Groups—CVBG

CVBG 1	See CVW-2
CVBG 3	See CVG-4
CVBG 5	See CVW-6
CVBG 17	See CVW-6
CVBG 74	See CVW-2
CVBG 75	See CVG-4

Light Carrier Air Groups—CVLG

CVLG-1	CVLG-58 Established	15 Mar 1946
	Redesignated CVLG-1	14 Nov 1946
	Disestablished	20 Nov 1948
CVLG-21	Established	16 May 1943
	Disestablished	5 Nov 1945
CVLG-22	Established	30 Sep 1942
	Disestablished	19 Sep 1945
CVLG-23	Established	16 Nov 1942
	Disestablished	19 Sep 1945
CVLG-24	See CVEG-24	
CVLG-25	See CVEG-25	
CVLG-27	Established	1 Mar 1943
	Disestablished	26 Oct 1945

CVLG-28	CVEG-28 Established	6 May 1942
	Became CVLG-28	20 Jan 1944
	Disestablished	6 Nov 1945
CVLG-29	CVEG-29 Established	18 Jul 1942
	Became CVLG-29	1 Mar 1944
	Disestablished	10 Sep 1945
CVLG-30	Established	1 Apr 1943
	Disestablished	12 Sep 1945
CVLG-31	Established	1 May 1943
	Disestablished	28 Oct 1945
CVLG-32	Established	1 Jun 1943
	Disestablished	13 Nov 1945
CVLG-34	Established	1 Apr 1945
	Disestablished	5 Dec 1945
CVLG-38	See CVEG-38	
CVLG-39	CVEG-39 Established	15 Mar 1945
	Became CVLG-39	27 Jul 1945
	Disestablished	10 Sep 1945
CVLG-40	See CVEG-40	
CVLG-43	Established	1 Aug 1943
	Disestablished	8 Nov 1943
CVLG-44	Established	1 Feb 1944
	Disestablished	18 Sep 1945
CVLG-45	Established	1 Apr 1944
	Disestablished	10 Sep 1945
CVLG-46	Established	15 Apr 1944
	Disestablished	14 Sep 1945
CVLG-47	Established	15 May 1944
	Disestablished	21 Sep 1945
CVLG-48	Established	15 Jun 1944
	Disestablished	2 Jan 1945
CVLG-49	CVEG-49 Established	10 Aug 1944
	Became CVLG-49	2 Jan 1945
	Disestablished	27 Nov 1945
CVLG-50	See CVEG-50	
CVLG-51	Established	22 Sep 1943
	Disestablished	13 Nov 1945

CVLG-52	Established	1 Sep 1943
	Disestablished	8 Nov 1943
CVLG-58	See CVLG-1	

Escort Carrier Air Groups-CVEG

CVEG-1	CVEG-41 Established	26 Mar 1945
	Became CVEG-1	15 Nov 1946
	Became VC-21	1 Sep 1948
	Became VS-21	23 Apr 1950
CVEG-2	CVEG-42 Established	19 Jul 1945
	Became CVEG-2	15 Nov 1946
	Disestablished	1 Sep 1948
CVEG-3	Established	21 Apr 1947
	Disestablished	1 Sep 1948
CVEG-24	CVLG-24 Established	31 Dec 1942
	Became CVEG-24	15 Aug 1944
	Disestablished	25 Sep 1945
CVEG-25	CVLG-25 Established	15 Feb 1943
	Became CVEG-25	28 Aug 1944
	Disestablished	20 Sep 1945
CVEG-26	Established	4 May 1942
	Disestablished	13 Nov 1945
CVEG-28	See CVLG-28	
CVEG-29	See CVLG-29	
CVEG-33	Established	15 May 1944
	Disestablished	19 Nov 1945
CVEG-35	Established	15 Jul 1943
	Disestablished	19 Nov 1945
CVEG-36	Established	15 May 1944
	Disestablished	28 Jan 1946
CVEG-37	Established	15 Jul 1943
	Disestablished	20 Dec 1945
CVEG-38	CVLG-38 Established	16 Jun 1943
	Became CVEG-38	15 Aug 1944
	Disestablished	31 Jan 1946
CVEG-39	See CVLG-39	
CVEG-40	CVLG-40 Established	15 Jun 1943
	Became CVEG-40	15 Aug 1944
	Disestablished	19 Nov 1945

CVEG-41	See CVEG-1	
CVEG-42	See CVEG-2	
CVEG-43	Established	9 Aug 1945
	Disestablished	17 Jun 1946
CVEG-49	See CVLG-49	
CVEG-50	CVLG-50 Established	10 Aug 1943
	Became CVEG-50	1 Oct 1944
	Disestablished	29 Oct 1945
CVEG-60	Established	15 Jul 1943
	Disestablished	19 Nov 1945
CVEG-66	Established	1 Jan 1945
	Disestablished	6 Jun 1945

Night Carrier Air Groups—CVG(N)

CVG(N)-52	CVLG(N)-52 Established	20 Oct 1944
	Became CVG(N)-52	6 Jan 1945
	Disestablished	15 Dec 1945
CVG(N)-53	Established	2 Jan 1945
	Disestablished	11 Jun 1946
CVG(N)-55	Established	1 Mar 1945
	Disestablished	11 Dec 1945
CVG(N)-90	Established	25 Aug 1944
	Disestablished	21 Jun 1946
CVG(N)-91	Established	5 Oct 1944
	Disestablished	21 Jun 1946

CVLG(N)

CVLG(N)-41	Established	28 Aug 1944
	Disestablished	25 Feb 1945
CVLG(N)-42	Established	25 Aug 1944
	Disestablished	2 Jan 1945
CVLG(N)-43	Established	24 Aug 1944
	Disestablished	2 Jan 1945
CVLG(N)-52	See CVG(N)-52	

CVEG(N)

CVEG(N)-63	Established	20 Jun 1945
	Disestablished	11 Dec 1945

Ship-Named Air Groups

ENTERPRISE AIR GROUP

	Ship commissioned	12 May 1938
	Ship squadrons established	1 Jun 1937
	Air group organized	1 Jul 1938
	Disbanded	Sep 1942

HORNET AIR GROUP

	Ship commissioned	20 Oct 1941
	Air group established	6 Oct 1941
	Disbanded after ship was sunk	26 Oct 1942

LANGLEY AIR GROUP

	Ship commissioned	20 Mar 1922
	Squadrons first assigned	1925
	Air group had not formally organized when ship was reclassified AV	15 Sep 1936

LEXINGTON AIR GROUP

	Ship commissioned	14 Dec 1927
	Ships squadrons established individually	
	Air group organized	1 Jul 1938
	Disbanded after ship was sunk	8 May 1942

RANGER AIR GROUP

	Ship commissioned	4 Jun 1934
	Ship squadrons established individually	
	Air group organized	1 Jul 1938
	Reformed as CVG-4	3 Aug 1943
	See: CVW-1	

SARATOGA AIR GROUP

	Ship commissioned	16 Nov 1927
	Ship squadrons established individually	
	Air group organized	1 Jul 1938
	Reformed as CVG-3	25 Sep 1943
	See: CVW-3	

WASP AIR GROUP

	Ship commissioned	25 Apr 1940
	Air group established	1 Jul 1939
	Disbanded after ship was sunk	15 Sep 1942

YORKTOWN AIR GROUP

	Ship commissioned	30 Sep 1937
	Ship squadrons established	1 Apr 1937
	Air group organized	1 Jul 1938
	Disbanded after ship was sunk	7 Jun 1942

Antisubmarine Carrier Air Groups—CVSG

CVSG-50	Established as RCVSG	30 Jun 1960
	Disestablished	17 Feb 1971

CVSG-51	Established as RCVSG	30 Jun 1960
	Disestablished	30 Jun 1970
CVSG-52	Established	1 Jun 1960
	Disestablished	15 Dec 1969
CVSG-53	Established	1 Apr 1960
	Disestablished	1 Jun 1973
CVSG-54	Established	18 May 1960
	Disestablished	1 Jul 1972
CVSG-55	Established	1 Sep 1960
	Disestablished	27 Sep 1968
CVSG-56	Established	25 May 1960
	Disestablished	30 Jun 1973
CVSG-57	Established	3 Jan 1961
	Disestablished	30 Sep 1969
CVSG-58	Established	6 Jun 1960
	Disestablished	31 May 1966
CVSG-59	Established	1 Apr 1960
	Disestablished	30 Jun 1973
CVSG-60	Established	2 May 1960
	Disestablished	1 Oct 1968
CVSG-62	Established	25 Sep 1961
	Disestablished	1 Oct 1962

Reserve Antisubmarine Carrier Air Groups—CVSGR

CVSGR-70	Established	1 Apr 1970
	Disestablished	30 Jun 1976
CVSGR-80	Established	1 Apr 1970
	Redesignated COMHELWINGRES	1 Jan 1976

Composite Squadrons—VC

VC-1	A	VS-201 Established	5 Apr 1941
		Became VGS-1	1 Apr 1942
		Became VC-1	1 Mar 1943
		Disestablished	1 Apr 1944
	B	VOF-1 Established	15 Dec 1943
		Became VOC-1	18 Dec 1944
		Became VC-1	1 Aug 1945
		Disestablished	17 Sep 1945

VC-2	A	See VC-25	
	B	VOF-2 Established	1 Mar 1944
		Became VOC-2	13 Dec 1944
		Became VC-2	20 Aug 1945
		Disestablished	13 Sep 1945
VC-3		Established	26 Aug 1943
		Disestablished	28 Oct 1945
VC-4		Established	2 Sep 1943
		Disestablished	16 Oct 1945
VC-5		Established	16 Sep 1943
		Disestablished	1 Oct 1945
VC-6		VGS-25 Established	1 jan 1943
		Became VC-25	1 Mar 1943
		Became VC-6	1 Sep 1943
		Disestablished	5 Oct 1945
VC-7		VGS-31 Established	24 Feb 1943
		Became VC-31	1 Mar 1943
		Became VC-7	1 Sep 1943
		Disestablished	1 Oct 1945
VC-8		Established	9 Sep 1943
		Disestablished	9 Oct 1945
VC-9		VGS-9 Established	6 Aug 1942
		Became VC-9	1 Mar 1943
		Disestablished	19 Sep 1945
VC-10		Established	23 Sep 1943
		Disestablished	25 Oct 1945
VC-11	A	VGS-11 Established	5 Aug 1942
		Became VC-11	1 Mar 1943
		Became VF-21	16 May 1943
		Disestablished	5 Nov 1945
	B	Established	30 Sep 1943
		Disestablished	10 Oct 1945
VC-12	A	VGS-12 Established	28 May 1942
		Became VC-12	1 Mar 1943
		Became VT-21	16 May 1943
		Disestablished	7 Aug 1945
	B	Established	6 Oct 1943
		Disestablished	7 Jun 1945
VC-13		VGS-13 Established	5 Aug 1942
		Became VC-13	1 Mar 1943
		Disestablished	24 Sep 1945
VC-14		Established	12 Oct 1943
		Disestablished	1 Oct 1945

| VC-15 | Established | 18 Oct 1943 |
| | Disestablished | 14 Jun 1945 |

VC-16	VGS-16 Established	8 Aug 1942
	Became VC-16	1 Mar 1943
	Became VF-33	15 Nov 1945
	Disestablished	19 Nov 1945

| VC-17 | See VC-31 | |

VC-18	VGS-18 Established	15 Oct 1942
	Became VC-18	1 Mar 1943
	Became VF-36	15 Aug 1943
	Became VF-18	5 Mar 1944
	Became VF-7A	15 Nov 1946
	Became VF-71	28 Jul 1948
	Disestablished	31 Mar 1959

VC-19	VGS-23 Established	1 Jan 1943
	Became VC-19	1 Mar 1943
	Disestablished	14 Jun 1945

VC-20	A VGS-20 Established	6 Aug 1942
	Became VC-20	1 Mar 1943
	Disestablished	15 Jun 1943
	B Established	24 Oct 1943
	Disestablished	1 Oct 1945

VC-21	A VGS-21 Established	15 Oct 1942
	Became VC-21	1 Mar 1943
	Disestablished	16 Jun 1943
	B Established	30 Oct 1943
	Disestablished	15 Sep 1945

VC-22	VS-22 Established	16 Nov 1942
	Became VC-22	1 Mar 1943
	Became VT-22	15 Dec 1943
	Disestablished	22 Aug 1945

VC-23	VS-23 Established	16 Nov 1942
	Became VC-23	1 Mar 1943
	Became VT-23	15 Nov 1943
	Disestablished	19 Sep 1945

VC-24	VS-24 Established	31 Dec 1942
	Became VC-24	1 Mar 1943
	Became VB-98	15 Dec 1943
	Disestablished	25 Jun 1944

VC-25	A VS-25 Established	15 Feb 1943
	Became VC-2	1 Mar 1943
	Became VC-25	15 Sep 1943
	Became VT-25	15 Dec 1943
	Disestablished	20 Sep 1945
	B See VC-6	

VC-26	VGS-26 Established	5 May 1942
	Became VC-26	1 Mar 1943
	Became VT-26	15 Nov 1943
	Disestablished	13 Nov 1945

| VC-27 | Established | 5 Nov 1943 |
| | Disestablished | 11 Sep 1945 |

VC-28	VGS-28 Established	4 May 1942
	Became VC-28	1 Mar 1943
	Became VT-28	20 Jan 1944
	Disestablished	8 Aug 1945

VC-29	VGS-29 Established	20 Jul 1942
	Became VC-29	1 Mar 1943
	Became VT-29	15 Dec 1943
	Disestablished	1 Aug 1945

VC-30	Established	1 Apr 1943
	Became VT-30	15 Dec 1943
	Disestablished	18 Aug 1945

VC-31	A See VC-7	
	B VC-17 Established	1 May 1943
	Became VC-31	15 Sep 1943
	Became VT-31	1 Nov 1943
	Disestablished	20 Oct 1945

VC-32	Established	1 Jun 1943
	Became VT-32	1 Nov 1943
	Disestablished	20 Aug 1945

VC-33	VGS-33 Established	22 Jan 1943
	Became VC-33	1 Mar 1943
	Disestablished	16 Nov 1945

VC-34	VGS-34 Established	24 Feb 1943
	Became VC-34	1 Mar 1943
	Became VF-34	15 Aug 1943
	Disestablished	8 Jul 1944

VC-35	VGS-35 Established	28 Jan 1943
	Became VC-35	1 Mar 1943
	Became VT-35	10 Mar 1944
	Disestablished	19 Nov 1945

VC-36	VGS-36 Established	21 Feb 1943
	Became VC-36	1 Mar 1943
	Disestablished	30 Jul 1945

VC-37	VGS-37 Established	22 Jan 1943
	Became VC-37	1 Mar 1943
	Became VT-37	10 Mar 1944
	Disestablished	20 Dec 1945

VC-38	Established	16 Jun 1943
	Became VT-38	11 May 1944
	Disestablished	31 Jan 1946
VC-39	Established	1 Apr 1943
	Disestablished	15 Dec 1943
VC-40	Established	15 Jun 1943
	Became VT-40	1 Jun 1944
	Disestablished	19 Nov 1945
VC-41	Established	5 May 1943
	Disestablished	16 Nov 1945
VC-42	Established	15 Apr 1943
	Disestablished	5 Jul 1945
VC-43	Established	1 Aug 1943
	Disestablished	8 Nov 1943
VC-50	Established	10 Aug 1943
	Became VT-50	8 Nov 1943
	Disestablished	29 Oct 1945
VC-51	Established	22 Sep 1943
	Became VT-51	8 Nov 1943
	Disestablished	7 Aug 1945
VC-52	Established	1 Sep 1943
	Disestablished	8 Nov 1943
VC-55	VGS-55 Established	16 Jan 1943
	Became VC-55	1 Mar 1943
	Disestablished	21 Jun 1945
VC-58	VGS-58 Established	24 Feb 1943
	Became VC-58	1 Mar 1943
	Disestablished	8 Jun 1945
VC-60	VGS-60 Established	24 Feb 1943
	Became VC-60	1 Mar 1943
	Became VT-60	10 Mar 1944
	Disestablished	19 Nov 1945
VC-63	Established	20 May 1943
	Disestablished	23 Oct 1945
VC-64	Established	1 Jun 1943
	Became VF-39	15 Aug 1943
	Disestablished	15 Mar 1944
VC-65	Established	10 Jun 1943
	Disestablished	8 Oct 1945
VC-66	Established	21 Jun 1943
	Disestablished	12 Oct 1945
VC-68	Established	1 Jul 1943
	Disestablished	1 Oct 1945
VC-69	Established	1 Jul 1943
	Disestablished	22 Jun 1945
VC-70	Established	5 Aug 1944
	Disestablished	6 Oct 1945
VC-71	Established	20 Aug 1944
	Disestablished	6 Oct 1945
VC-72	Established	1 Sep 1944
	Disestablished	1 Oct 1945
VC-75	Established	11 Nov 1943
	Disestablished	21 Sep 1945
VC-76	Established	17 Nov 1943
	Disestablished	11 Sep 1945
VC-77	Established	23 Nov 1943
	Disestablished	17 Sep 1945
VC-78	Established	29 Nov 1943
	Disestablished	21 Sep 1945
VC-79	Established	6 Dec 1943
	Disestablished	11 Sep 1945
VC-80	Established	16 Dec 1943
	Disestablished	11 Sep 1945
VC-81	Established	22 Dec 1943
	Disestablished	20 Sep 1945
VC-82	Established	28 Dec 1943
	Disestablished	18 Sep 1945
VC-83	Established	3 Jan 1944
	Disestablished	17 Sep 1945
VC-84	Established	6 Jan 1944
	Disestablished	17 Sep 1945
VC-85	Established	12 Jan 1944
	Disestablished	15 Sep 1945
VC-86	Established	18 Jan 1944
	Disestablished	7 Jun 1945

VC-87	Established	24 Jan 1944
	Disestablished	12 Jun 1945
VC-88	Established	29 Jan 1944
	Disestablished	3 Jul 1945
VC-89	Established	3 Jan 1944
	Disestablished	1 Apr 1944
VC-90	Established	3 Feb 1944
	Disestablished	19 Sep 1945
VC-91	Established	11 Feb 1944
	Disestablished	22 Sep 1945
VC-92	Established	17 Feb 1944
	Disestablished	18 Sep 1945

VC-93	Established	23 Feb 1944
	Disestablished	11 Aug 1945
VC-94	Established	29 Feb 1944
	Disestablished	27 Jul 1945
VC-95	Established	1 Feb 1944
	Disestablished	28 Jun 1945
VC-96	Established	1 Mar 1944
	Disestablished	28 Jul 1945
VC-97	Established	8 Mar 1944
	Disestablished	24 Jul 1945
VC-98	Established	15 Mar 1944
	Disestablished	11 Oct 1945
VC-99	Established	22 Mar 1944
	Disestablished	30 Oct 1945

U.S. Navy and Marine Corps Squadron Designations and Abbreviations

The system of squadron designations was established to help define part of Naval Aviation's organizational structure and help identify the operational and administrative functions of aviation within the fleet. Just as the designations for ships, such as DD, CA, BB, etc., were used to define the duties of the specific units and their alignment within the fleet organization, so also were the squadron designations established to formulate the responsibilities and alignment within Naval Aviation and the fleet structure.

During Naval Aviation's early years, due to the limited capabilities of the aircraft there were big question marks concerning Naval Aviation's ability to succeed as a functional component of the fleet and whether it even would survive. In official publications and references, such as the Daily Aviation News Bulletin of 1 October 1919, casual terms were used to describe or identify various aircraft squadrons and units. The casual terms were used because no specific fleet aviation organizational structure for squadrons had been officially established. Prior to 1919, naval aircraft, excluding Marine Corps planes, were assigned primarily to shore stations. Therefore, in order to integrate aviation into the fleet, it was necessary to develop a fleet organization that included aviation units.

On 17 July 1920, the Secretary of the Navy prescribed a standard nomenclature for types and classes of naval vessels, including aircraft, in which lighter-than-air craft were identified by the type "Z" and heavier-than-air craft by the letter "V". Class letters assigned within the Z type were R, N and K for rigid dirigibles, non-rigid dirigibles and kite balloons respectively, while F, O, S, P, T and G were established for fighter, observation, scouting, patrol, torpedo and bombing, and Fleet planes as classes within the V type. The use of the "V" designation with fix-wing heavier-than-air squadron designations has been a question of debate since the 1920s. However, no conclusive evidence has been found to identify why the letter "V" was chosen. It is generally believed the "V" was in reference to the French word *volplane*. As a verb, the word means to glide or soar. As a noun, it described an aeronautical device sustained in the air by lifting surfaces (wings), as opposed to the bag of gas that the airships (denoted by "Z") used. The same case may be made regarding the use of "Z". It is generally believed the "Z" was used in deference to Count Ferdinand von Zeppelin, the German general and developer of the airship in 1900. However, documentation has not been located to verify this assumption.

In general terms, the Navy's system for designating naval aircraft squadrons has usually conformed to the following loose classification structure:

(1) Squadron designations were based on specific letters used for indicating the missions for each particular type of squadron and its assigned aircraft. As an example, a World War II squadron operating the F4U Corsair aircraft would have been designated a fighting squadron (VF). The letter F, for fighting or fighter, was the key in identifying the type of squadron and was also used in the aircraft's designation.

(2) Identification numbers were assigned to each squadron, such as VF-1. The number 1 separates Fighter Squadron 1 (VF-1) from Fighter Squadron 10 (VF-10).

There have been many variations to this basic system throughout Naval Aviation's history. Changes were also made to the designation system when new plane types were developed and new squadrons were formed to carry out those new missions. There is no logical sequence for the numerical designation assigned the various squadrons throughout most of Naval Aviation's history. The Marine Corps did establish a logical sequence for their squadron designations, however, there are variations to this system, too.

As Navy squadrons were established, disestablished, or redesignated, many of the same letters and numbers were reused and assigned at a later date for newly-established or redesignated units, hence, the lineage of a squadron cannot always be traced or linked by using the same designation. As an example, VF-1 from World War II has no direct relationship to VF-1 established in the 1970s. The rich tradition and heritage of the various squadrons in the Navy has not always been carried over because of the break in continuity between units. Once a squadron is disestablished that ends its history. If a new squadron is established using the same designation of a previous squadron, it does not have any direct relationship with that unit. The reuse of many of the same letters and numerical designations adds considerable confusion to the squadron designation system. A new squadron may carry on the traditions of a previous squadron, just as a ship that has been assigned the name used by a previous ship, carries on the traditions of the past ships with the same name. However, a squadron, just like a ship, cannot claim a heritage or historical link to the old unit with the same designation.

Consistency has been the major ingredient lacking in the Navy's squadron designation system. As an example, the use of "Plane" in squadron designations was not consistent during the 1920s. Sometimes the full designation would be written differently, depending on the squadron's assignment to the Battle Fleet, Scouting Fleet, or Asiatic Fleet. A designation such as Scouting Squadron and Scouting Plane Squadron, which used the same abbreviation, VS, was listed in the *Navy Directory* as Scouting Squadron under the Battle Fleet and Scouting Plane Squadron under the Scouting Fleet. The use of "Plane" in squadron designations was most likely designed to identify the squadron as an aviation unit, vice a destroyer squadron. This seems to be especially true during the 1920s when aviation was first being integrated into the fleet organization and operations. The *Navy Directory, Monthly Report, Status of Naval Aircraft,* and the *Bureau of Aeronautics, Weekly Newsletter* all list squadron designations using "Plane." The Chief of Naval Operations' "Naval Aeronautical Organization", published for each Fiscal Year, lists the squadron designations without using "Plane" in the designation. It is obvious there is no difference between the squadrons with or without the use of "Plane" in the squadron designation. The acronym remained the same, with or without the use of "Plane" in the full squadron designation. In the 1930s the squadron designations listed in all four sources identified above usually refer to the squadron using its abbreviated designation, such as VF Squadron 1 (VF-1) instead of Fighting Plane Squadron 1. In the 1940s the use of "Plane" in the full squadron designation was dropped.

In the late 1940s and early 1950s the VC squadron designation was used to identify a group of squadrons with several different missions but all assigned the VC designation. Missions for specific Composite Squadrons (VC) included all-weather night, attack and defense; air early warning; anti-submarine warfare; and photographic. The only identifying factor to separate the different types of Composite Squadrons was the numerical designation. In the late 1940s the single digit numbers were for the Composite Night or Attack and Defense units, those numbers in the teens were for Composite Air

Warning squadrons, numbers in the 20s and 30s were for Composite Anti-Submarine units, and the numbers in the 60s were for Composite Photographic squadrons.

Besides the composite squadrons (VC), several patrol squadrons (VP) had specific mission requirements that were different from its normal patrol and reconnaissance duties. However, these squadrons still maintained the normal VP designation. In the late 1940s there were two VP squadrons with a primary mission of photographic and one with an air early warning mission. VP-61 and VP-62 were the photographic squadrons and VP-51 was the air early warning squadron.

The special VC and VP designated units, were on the cutting edge of technology, which eventually lead to the development of specialized squadron designations in the 1950s and 1960s. Squadrons such as VAW (Carrier Airborne Early Warning), VAQ (Tactical Electronic Warfare), and VQ (Electronic Counter-measures or Air Reconnaissance) were the result of technical developments in the late 1940s and early 1950s.

The use of an abbreviated squadron designation with different missions occurred in the early 1950s when the VJ designation was used for both photographic squadrons and weather squadrons. VJ-1 and 2 were designated Weather Squadrons or Weather Reconnaissance Squadrons. VJ-61 and 62 were designated Photographic Squadrons. The missions were totally different for these two types of squadrons but they used a common abbreviated squadron designation.

There are four factors that play a role in developing or changing squadron designations. They have been around since the introduction of aviation in the Navy and will continue to be the primary factors effecting squadron designations. The factors are:

1. the duties or mission of a squadron
2. technical advances in aircraft or equipment
3. changes in tactics or development of new tactics
4. changes in Naval Aviation or fleet organization

The following is a list of various squadron designations used by the Navy since the early 1920s. The list is in alphabetical order rather than in the chronological order of squadron development. The general time frame for when the designation was in use is listed with most of the squadron designations. Further elaboration on the assignment of squadrons to other organizations and their designations such as: a battle group, carrier air wing, cruiser group, fleet air force, Scouting Fleet, Asiatic Fleet, naval district, reserves, etc . . . , has not been included in this list to prevent it from becoming to confusing or extensive. The only exception to this is for the reserves. Reserve squadron designations, beginning in 1970, are included in this list. In 1970 the naval air reserve was reorganized and the squadron structure and arrangement was aligned to mirror the squadron designation system in existence for active fleet units.

U.S. NAVY SQUADRON DESIGNATIONS/ABBREVIATIONS

Acronym	Full Squadron Designation	General time-frame in use
BLIMPHEDRON	LTA Headquarters Squadron	1943–1946
BLIMPRON	LTA Squadron	1942–1961
BLPHEDRON	Blimp Headquarters Squadron	1943–1946
BLPRON	Blimp Squadron	1942–1961
FASRON	Fleet Aircraft Service Squadron	1946–1960
HAL or HA(L)	Helicopter Attack Squadron Light	1967–1972
		1976–1988
HC	Helicopter Combat Support Squadron	1965–present
HCS	Helicopter Combat Support Special Squadron	1988–present
HCT	Helicopter Combat Support Training Squadron	1974–1977
HM	Helicopter Mine Countermeasures Squadron	1971–present
HS	Helicopter Antisubmarine Squadron	1951–present
HSL	Helicopter Antisubmarine Squadron (Light)	1972–present
HT	Helicopter Training Squadron	1960–present
HTU	Helicopter Training Unit	1950–1957
HU	Helicopter Utility Squadron	1948–1965
RVAH	Reconnaissance Attack Squadron	1964–1979
RVAW	Carrier Airborne Early Warning Training Squadron	1967–1983
STAGRON	Special Air Task Force Squadron (VK)	1943–1944
TACRON	Tactical Squadron or Tactical Air Control Squadron or Tactical Control Squadron	1946–present
VA	Attack Squadron	1946–present
VA(AW)	All-Weather Attack Squadron	1956–1959
VAH or VA(H)	Heavy Attack Squadron	1955–1971
VA(HM)	Attack Mining Squadron	1956–1959
VAK	Tactical Aerial Refueling Squadron	1979–1989
VAL or VA(L)	Light Attack Squadron	1969–1972
VAP or VA(P)	Heavy Photographic Reconnaissance Squadron or Photographic Reconnaissance Squadron (Heavy) or Heavy Photographic Squadron	1956–1971
VAQ	Carrier Tactical Electronics Warfare Squadron or Tactical Electronics Warfare Squadron	1968–present
VAW	Carrier Airborne Early Warning Squadron	1948
		1956–present
VAW	Carrier Tactical Electronics Warfare Squadron	1968
VB	Bombing Squadron or Light Bombing Plane Squadron	1928–1946
VBF	Bombing Fighting Squadron	1945–1946
VC	Composite Squadron	1943–1945
		1948–1956
VC	Fleet Composite Squadron	1965–present
VCN	Night Composite Squadron	1946–1948
VCP	Photographic Composite Squadron	1959–1961
VCS	Cruiser Scouting Squadron	1937–1945
VD	Photographic Squadron	1943–1946
VE	Evacuation Squadron	1944–1945
VF	Combat Squadron	1922
VF	Fighting Plane Squadron or Fighting Squadron	1922–1948
VF	Fighter Squadron	1948–present
VFA	Fighter Attack Squadron	1980–1983

U.S. NAVY SQUADRON DESIGNATIONS/ABBREVIATIONS—Continued

Acronym	Full Squadron Designation	General time-frame in use
VFA	Strike Fighter Squadron	1983–present
VF(AW)	All-Weather Fighter Squadron or Fighter (All-Weather) Squadron	1956–1963
VFC	Fighter Squadron Composite	1988–present
VFN or VF(N)	Night Fighting Squadron	1944–1946
VFP or VF(P)	Light Photographic Reconnaissance Squadron or Photographic Reconnaissance Squadron or Photographic Reconnaissance Squadron (Light) or Light Photographic Squadron	1956–1987
VGF	Escort-Fighter Squadron	1942–1943
VGS	Escort-Scouting Squadron	1942–1943
VH	Rescue Squadron	1944–1946
VJ	Utility Squadron or General Utility Squadron	1925–1946
VJ	Weather Squadron or Weather Reconnaissance Squadron	1952–1953
VJ	Photographic Squadron	1952–1956
VK	Special Air Task Force Squadron (STAGRON)	1943–1944
VN	Training Squadron	1927–1947
VO	Spotting Squadron	1922
VO	Observation Plane Squadron or Observation Squadron	1923–1945 1947–1949 1967–1968
VOC	Composite Spotting Squadron	1944–1945
VOF	Observation Fighter Squadron	1942–1945
VOS	Air Spotting Squadron or Observation Spotter Squadron	1944
VP	Seaplane Patrol Squadron	1922
VP	Patrol Squadron	1924–1944 1946 1948–present
VP-AM	Amphibian Patrol Squadron	1946–1948
VPB	Patrol Bombing Squadron	1944–1946
VP-HL	Heavy Patrol Squadron (landplane)	1946–1948
VP-HS	Heavy Seaplane Patrol Squadron	1946–1948
VPM	Meteorological Squadron	1946–1947
VP–ML	Medium Patrol Squadron (landplane)	1946–1948
VP-MS	Medium Patrol Squadron (seaplane)	1946–1948
VPP or VP(P)	Photographic Squadron or Patrol Squadron (photographic)	1946–1948
VPU	Patrol Squadron Special Unit	1982–present
VPW	Weather Reconnaissance Squadron	1945–1948
VPW	Air Early Warning Squadron	1948
VQ	Electronic Countermeasures Squadron	1955–1960
VQ	Fleet Air Reconnaissance Squadron	1961–present
VR	Transport Squadron or Air Transport Squadron or Fleet Logistic Air Squadron	1942–1958
VR	Fleet Tactical Support Squadron	1958–1976
VR	Fleet Logistics Support Squadron	1976–present
VRC or VR(C)	Fleet Tactical Support Squadron	1960–1976
VRC	Fleet Logistics Support Squadron	1976–present
VRE	Air Transport Evacuation Squadron	1945

U.S. NAVY SQUADRON DESIGNATIONS/ABBREVIATIONS—Continued

Acronym	Full Squadron Designation	General time-frame in use
VRF	Transport Ferry and Service Squadron	1943–1946
VRF	Air Ferry Transport Squadron or Air Ferry Squadron	1943–1948
VRF or VR(F)	Aircraft Ferry Squadron	1957–1986
VRJ	Utility Transport Squadron	1945–1946
VRS	Air Ferry Service Squadron or Ferry Command Service Squadron	1943–1946
VRU	Transport Utility Squadron	1946–1948
VS	Scouting Plane Squadron or Scouting Squadron	1922–1946
VS	Antisubmarine Squadron or Air Antisubmarine Squadron or Carrier Air Antisubmarine Squadron	1950–1993
VS	Sea Control Squadron	1993–present
VSF	Antisubmarine Fighter Squadron	1965–1973
VT	Torpedo & Bombing Plane Squadron or Torpedo & Bombing Squadron	1922–1930
VT	Torpedo Plane Squadron	1921
VT	Torpedo Squadron	1930–1946
VT	Training Squadron	1960–present
VTN	Night Torpedo Squadron	1944–1946
VU	Utility Squadron	1946–1965
VW	Air Early Warning Squadron or Airborne Early Warning Squadron or Fleet Early Warning Squadron	1952–1971
VW	Weather Reconnaissance Squadron or Fleet Weather Reconnaissance Squadron	1967–1975
VX	Experimental Squadron	1927–circa 1943
VX	Experimental and Development Squadron or Operational Development Squadron or Air Operational Development Squadron or Air Development Squadron	1946–1968
VX	Air Test and Evaluation Squadron	1969–present
VXE	Antarctic Development Squadron	1969–present
VXN	Oceanographic Development Squadron	1969–1993
XVF	Experimental Development Squadron	1945–1946
XVJ	Experimental Utility Squadron	1945–1946
ZJ	Blimp Utility Squadron	1944–1945
ZK	Kite Balloon Squadron	1922–1924
ZKN	Kite Balloon Training Squadron	*
ZKO	Kite Balloon Observation Squadron	*
ZNN	Non-rigid Airship Training Squadron	*
ZNO	Non-rigid Airship Observation Squadron	*
ZNP	Non-rigid Airship Patrol Squadron	*
ZNS	Non-rigid Airship Scouting Squadron	*
ZP	Airship Patrol Squadron	1942–1961
ZP	Blimp Squadron	1942–1961
ZP	Airship Patrol Squadron (All-Weather Antisubmarine) or Airship Squadron or LTA Patrol Squadron	1942–1961
ZRN	Rigid Airship Training Squadron	*
ZRP	Rigid Airship Patrol Squadron	*

U.S. NAVY SQUADRON DESIGNATIONS/ABBREVIATIONS—Continued

Acronym	Full Squadron Designation	General time-frame in use
ZRS	Rigid Airship Scouting Squadron	*
ZS	Airship Antisubmarine Squadron	*
ZW	Airship Early Warning Squadron	1956–1961
ZX	Airship Operational Development Squadron or Airship Development Squadron	1950–1957

* These squadron designations were developed, however, the Navy never established any squadrons using the designations.

MARINE CORPS SQUADRON DESIGNATIONS/ABBREVIATIONS

In 1924 the letter "M" was adopted to differentiate Marine Corps squadrons from Navy squadrons. The following is a list of Marine Corps squadron designations:

Acronym	Full Squadron Designation	General time-frame in use
AES	Marine Aircraft Engineering Squadron	1941–circa 1980
AWS	Marine Air Warning Squadron	1943–1954
H&HS	Marine Headquarters & Headquarters Squadron	1971–present
HMA	Marine Helicopter Attack	1971–1983
HMH	Marine Heavy Helicopter Squadron	1962–present
HMHT	Marine Heavy Helicopter Training Squadron	1968–1972
HML	Marine Light Helicopter Squadron	1968–1986
HMLA	Marine Light Attack Helicopter Squadron	1986–present
HMM	Marine Medium Helicopter Squadron	1962–present
HMMT	Marine Medium Helicopter Training Squadron	1966–1972
HMR	Marine Helicopter Transport Squadron	1951–1956
HMR(C)	Marine Helicopter Reconnaissance Squadron	1958–1960
HMR(L)	Marine Helicopter Transport Squadron (light)	1956–1962
HMR(M)	Marine Helicopter Transport Squadron (medium)	1957–1962
H&MS	Marine Headquarters & Maintenance Squadron	1954–1988
HMT	Marine Helicopter Training Squadron	1972–present
HMX	Marine Helicopter Squadron	1947–present
MALS	Marine Aviation Logistics Squadron	1988–present
MOTS	Marine Operational Training Squadron	1943–1944
SOMS	Station Operation and Maintenance Squadron (Marine)	1982–present
VMA	Marine Attack Squadron	1951–present
VMA(AW)	Marine All-Weather Attack Squadron	1965–present
VMAQ	Marine Tactical Electronics Warfare Squadron	1975–present
VMAT	Marine Attack Training Squadron	1951–1958
VMAT(AW)	Marine All-Weather Attack Training Squadron	1968–1986
VMB	Marine Bomber Squadron	1937–1946
VMBF	Marine Fighter/Bomber Squadron	1944–1946
VMCJ	Marine Composite Reconnaissance Squadron	1955–1975
VMD	Marine Photographic Squadron	1942–1946
VMF	Marine Fighter Squadron	1937–circa 1975
VMFA	Marine Fighter Attack Squadron	1963–present
VMFAT	Marine Fighter Attack Training Squadron	1968–present
VMF(AW)	Marine All-Weather Fighter Squadron	1948–present

MARINE CORPS SQUADRON DESIGNATIONS/ABBREVIATIONS—Continued

Acronym	Full Squadron Designation	General time-frame in use
VMF(N)	Marine Night Fighter Squadron	1942–1958
VMFP	Marine Tactical Reconnaissance Squadron	1975–1990
VMFT	Marine Fighter Training Squadron	1951–present
VMFT(AW)	Marine All-Weather Fighter Training Squadron	1955–1958
VMFT(N)	Marine Night Fighter Training Squadron	1951–1958
VMGR	Marine Aerial Refueler Transport Squadron	1962–present
VMGRT	Marine Aerial Refueling Transport Training Squadron	1986–present
VMIT	Marine Instrument Training Squadron	1951–1958
VMJ	Marine Utility Squadron	1945–1952
VMJ	Marine Photographic Squadron	1952–1955
VML	Marine Glider Squadron	1942–1943
VMO	Marine Observation Squadron	1941–1993
VMP	Marine Photographic Squadron	1946–1949
VMR	Marine Transport Squadron	1944–1962
VMS	Marine Scouting Squadron	1937–1944
VMSB	Marine Scout Bombing Squadron	1941–1946
VMT	Marine Training Squadron	1947–present
VMTB	Marine Torpedo Bomber Squadron	1943–1946

Photograph shows the tail code and insignia used by Patrol Squadron P-3 Orion aircraft.

Photographs show the tail codes and insignia used by Patrol Squadron P-3 Orion aircraft.

APPENDIX 17

The Navy in Space

Sailors have long studied the sky and have used the movements of celestial bodies to guide them across the trackless seas. Realizing the need to observe the movements of the stars and planets, the U.S. Navy established the Depot of Charts and Instruments on 6 December 1830. This is the Navy's oldest scientific institution. The Depot later became the U.S. Naval Observatory. Today it continues to provide the astronomical data necessary for navigation at sea, on land as well as in space.

In 1923 the Naval Research Laboratory (NRL) began operation. The idea for a U.S. Government-supported research laboratory was suggested by the American inventor Thomas Alva Edison during World War I. Secretary of the Navy Josephus Daniels seized the opportunity and invited Edison to become head of the Naval Consulting Board. The Board made plans to create a modern scientific research facility, which became the Naval Research Laboratory. Robert Morris Page who was at NRL from the late 1920s to the mid-1960s invented the technology for pulse radar. During World War II his invention assisted the Allies in detecting enemy planes and ships. Without radar, today's space program would be impossible.

In 1911 the Navy bought its first aircraft—the A-1 Triad. Advances were made in aviation; and aircraft were flying higher and higher. On 8 May 1929 Lieutenant Apollo Soucek set the world altitude record for landplanes by flying a Wright Apache to the height of 39,140 feet. On 4 June 1929, the same Lieutenant Souceck set the altitude record for seaplanes, also in an Apache, reaching the height of 38,560.

Altitude records were now approaching the 40,000-foot range. At these heights, the thin air and decreased pressure made it difficult for human beings to function and survive. The airplane was a poor vehicle in which to study the upper reaches of the atmosphere. The balloon proved to be more suitable.

On 4 August 1933 Lieutenant Commander Thomas "Tex" Settle ascended aloft in the sealed life-support gondola of a balloon, but the attempt failed. A similar attempt in a balloon by Soviet aeronauts the following September, achieved the height of 62,230 feet. The space race between the United States and the Soviet Union had begun.

On 20 November 1933, Lieutenant Commander Thomas "Tex" Settle and Major Chester L. Fordney, USMC, flying a 600,000 cubic-foot free balloon, set the world's altitude record of 61,237 feet. It was an official world's record, but 1,000 feet shy of the actual Soviet achievement.

In December 1941, the United States entered World War II with no rocket weapons. Germany was putting a great deal of its effort into the development of rockets, basing much of its technology on the research of the American scientist Robert H. Goddard.

At the end of the war, the U.S. rocket budget was 1.3 million. Research in the use of rockets in jet-assisted take off (JATO) had been carried out by U.S. rocket pioneer Robert Goddard, assisted by the Navy's Robert Truax. In May 1943 a JATO-equipped Catalina (PBY) made its first successful flight. JATO could reduce the takeoff run by 33 to 60 percent, or permit greater payloads. The JATO program laid the groundwork for the use of rocket power in Navy guided missiles.

After World War II, U.S. interest in high altitude research experiments resumed. The Office of Naval Research (ONR) made plans for a manned balloon flight into the upper atmosphere. Project Helios called for the construction of plastic balloons with a gondola equipped with scientific observation instruments. This ambitious plan was replaced in 1947 by Project Skyhook, which used polyethylene balloons to carry instrument packages to extreme altitudes. Thousands of these balloons were sent into the stratosphere for basic research.

In 1952 a new technique was developed in which Deacon rockets were lifted above 70,000 feet by Skyhook balloons and then fired into space. The Skyhook experiments proved to be so successful that in 1954 plans were made to entrust the lives of men to the Skyhook balloons.

Project Stratolab, a laboratory in the stratosphere, began in 1955. On 8 November 1956, Stratolab I, manned by Lieutenant Commanders Malcolm D. Ross and Morton Lee Lewis reached a record altitude of 76,000 feet. It would not, however, be with the balloon that man would reach space. It would be with the rocket.

Naval Research Laboratory scientists had been conducting experiments on the Aerobee and Viking sounding rockets during the early 1950s. An NRL study in 1954 indicated the feasibility of successfully placing a satellite in orbit, using a vehicle based on the Viking as a first stage and the Aerobee as the second.

In 1955 President Eisenhower announced that the United States would launch "small, unmanned, earth-circling satellites" as a part of the U.S. contributions to the International Geophysical Year 1957–58. The Naval Research Laboratory proposed that the Vanguard rocket, based on Viking technology, be used to launch the satellite. The NRL proposal was accepted. Project Vanguard was to have three missions: place at least one satellite in orbit during 1957–58; accomplish a scientific experiment in space; and track the flight to demonstrate that the satellite had actually attained orbit.

Before Vanguard could launch a satellite into space, however, the Soviets announced that they had put *Sputnik* into orbit on 4 October 1957. *Sputnik*, the Russian word for travelling companion, was the earth's first artificial satellite. The perception by the United States that it was the leader in space technology was shattered, and the capability of Soviet rockets to fire weapons from space became apparent.

On 31 January 1958 the Army's Jupiter-C rocket, a further development of the Redstone rocket, put the first U.S. satellite, Explorer I into orbit. On 31 March 1958, a Vanguard rocket fired from Cape Canaveral, Fla., put a second earth satellite into orbit.

In response to the Soviet challenge in space, the United States established the National Aeronautics and Space Administration (NASA) in July 1958. Project Mercury would put a man into space. On 15 May 1961, President John F. Kennedy went even further and stated in an address to Congress that the United States would commit itself to landing a man on the moon by the end of the decade. This goal was named Project Apollo.

NASA lobbed a chimpanzee into space on 31 January 1961. After this experiment proved successful, it was then believed that it was possible to put a man into a similar sub-orbital trip. Commander Alan B. Shepard, Jr., USN, was chosen to be the first American sent into space.

On 5 May 1961, Commander Shepard left earth's atmosphere in the Freedom 7 space capsule. It was a ballistic "cannon shot" with an Army Redstone rocket. The space capsule was recovered at sea by an HUS-1 helicopter from Marine Corps Squadron HMR(L)-262, which transported the capsule and Commander Shepard to the carrier *Lake Champlain*.

Subsequent Mercury missions put other men in space. On 20 February 1962, Lieutenant Colonel John H. Glenn, Jr., USMC, and his spacecraft Friendship 7 made three orbits around the earth. Other men were sent singly into space. Then, during 1965 and 1966, Project Gemini sent up two men at a time. Many were Naval Aviators.

After having succeeded in putting men into space, NASA concentrated on putting a man on the moon. In December 1968 Lieutenant Commander James A. Lovell, Jr., USN, was on the Apollo 8 flight that flew to the moon and circled around it, viewing the side that is never seen from earth. On 20 July 1969 Neil A. Armstrong, a naval aviator, became the first man to walk on the moon during the Apollo 11 flight.

The next U.S space goal was to explore space in Skylab, a space laboratory in which the astronauts could live a fairly normal life, work on scientific experiments, eat, sleep, and have regular periods of recreation. Three separate crews of Skylab astronauts were launched into space in 1973. Two of the three were all-Navy crews.

Meanwhile the Apollo space trips continued. The last Apollo mission was launched on 15 July 1975. Vance D. Brand, a former Navy pilot, was the command module pilot. On this space trip, Apollo docked with the Soviet Soyuz spacecraft. This was the first meeting between American astronauts and Soviet cosmonauts in space. The two crews then conducted scientific experiments in space. Apollo splashed down in the Pacific near Hawaii and was recovered by *New Orleans*. This was the last splash-down recovery by a Navy amphibious ship. The Space Shuttle would make splash-down recoveries unnecessary.

The Space Shuttle was launched by a rocket, but could land like an airplane, thus it could make multiple trips into space. *Columbia* was the first Space Shuttle and was launched on 12 April 1981 with an all Navy-aviator crew. Space Shuttle *Columbia* was followed by Space Shuttles *Challenger, Discovery, Atlantis,* and *Endeavour.* Subsequent Space Shuttle flights were able to take more and more astronauts on a single flight into space and stay in space for longer periods of time and continue to conduct scientific experiments. Limited cooperation with the Russian Republic, part of the former Soviet Union also continued. In 1995 Space Shuttle *Atlantis* transported two Russian cosmonauts to the Russian space station Mir where American astronaut Norman Thagard, a former naval aviator, had been living for three months. *Atlantis* docked with Mir and brought Norman Thagard back to earth.

Naval Aviation continues to play an important role in space. The following three sections provide statistical data on Naval Aviation's contributions or involvement in the manned space program.

Naval Aviation Personnel Who Have Become Astronauts

(Names with an asterisk (*) are Naval Aviators or Naval Aviation personnel but were no longer on active duty when involved in the space program)

Andrew M. Allen
Scott Altman
Neil A. Armstrong*
Jeffery Ashby
Michael A. Baker
Alan L. Bean
Charles F. Bolden, Jr.
Kenneth D. Bowersox
Vance D. Brand*
Daniel C. Brandenstein
James F. Buchli
John S. Bull
Daniel W. Bursch
Robert D. Cabana
Kenneth D. Cameron
Malcolm Scott Carpenter
Gerald P. Carr
Manley L. Carter, Jr.
Eugene A. Cernan
Roger B. Chaffee
Michael L. Coats
Kenneth Cockrell
Charles Conrad, Jr.
John O. Creighton
Robert L. Crippen
Frank L. Culbertson
R. Walter Cunningham*
Robert Curbeam
Joe F. Edwards
Ronald E. Evans
Dale A. Gardner
Jake E. Garn*
Robert L. Gibson
John H. Glenn, Jr.
Richard F. Gordon, Jr.
Dominic L. Gorie
S. David Griggs
Fred W. Haise, Jr.*
Frederick H. Hauck
Kathryn Hire
David C. Hilmers

Brent W. Jett
Joseph P. Kerwin
Wendy B. Lawrence
David C. Leestma
Don L. Lind
Michael E. Lopez-Alegria
John M. Lounge*
John R. Lousma
James A. Lovell, Jr.
Jon A. McBride
Bruce McCandless II
Michael J. McCulley
Thomas K. Mattingly II
Edgar D. Mitchell
Franklin Story Musgrave*
Carlos Noriega
Bryan D. O'Connor
Stephen S. Oswald
Robert F. Overmyer
William F. Readdy
Kenneth S. Reightler, Jr.
Richard N. Richards
Kent V. Rominger
Walter M. Schirra, Jr.
Winston E. Scott
Elliot M. See
Alan B. Shepard, Jr.
Michael John Smith
Robert C. Springer
Susan L. Still
Frederick W. Stuckow
Norman E. Thagard
Stephen D. Thorne
Pierre J. Thuot
Richard H. Truly
James D. van Hoften
David M. Walker
Paul J. Weitz
James D. Wetherbee
Clifton C. Williams
Donald E. Williams
John W. Young

Naval Aviation Personnel Who Have Made Trips Into Space and the Number of Flights Made By Each as of 31 December 1995

(Names with an asterisk (*) are former Navy)

One Flight

Malcolm Scott Carpenter
Gerald P. Carr
Manley L. Carter, Jr.
R. Walter Cunningham*
Ronald E. Evans
Jake E. Garn*
John H. Glenn, Jr.
S. David Griggs
Fred W. Haise, Jr.*
Joseph P. Kerwin
Wendy B. Lawrence
Don L. Lind
Michael E. Lopez-Alegria
Jon A. McBride
Michael J. McCulley
Edgar D. Mitchell
Kent V. Rominger
Michael John Smith

Two Flights

Andrew M. Allen
Neil A. Armstrong*
Alan L. Bean
Daniel W. Bursch
Kenneth Cockrell
Frank L. Culbertson
Dale A. Gardner
Richard F. Gordon, Jr.
Bruce McCandless II
John R. Lousma
Bryan D. O'Connor
Robert F. Overmyer
William F. Readdy
Kenneth S. Reightler, Jr.
Alan B. Shepard, Jr.
Robert C. Springer
Richard H. Truly
James D. van Hoften

Paul J. Weitz
Donald E. Williams

Three Flights

Michael A. Baker
Kenneth D. Bowersox
Robert D. Cabana
Kenneth D. Cameron
Eugene A. Cernan
Michael L. Coats
John O. Creighton
Frederick H. Hauck
David C. Leestma
John M. Lounge*
Thomas K. Mattingly II
Stephen S. Oswald
Walter M. Schirra, Jr.
Pierre J. Thuot
James D. Wetherbee

Four Flights

Charles F. Bolden, Jr.
Vance D. Brand*
Daniel C. Brandenstein
James F. Buchli
Charles Conrad, Jr.
Robert L. Crippen
David C. Hilmers
James A. Lovell, Jr.
Richard N. Richards
David M. Walker

Five Flights

Robert L. Gibson
Franklin Story Musgrave*
Norman E. Thagard

Six Flights

John W. Young

List of U.S. Space Flights with Navy/Marine Corps Pilots/Astronauts Aboard

(As of 31 Dec 1995)

Order	Date	Designation	Crew (see notes)	Duration
1	5 May 61	Mercury Redstone 3 (Freedom 7) (1st U.S. man into space, sub-orbital)	Alan B. Shepard, Jr.	15 min 22 sec
3	20 Feb 62	Mercury Atlas 6 (Friendship 7) (1st American to orbit the earth)	John H. Glenn, Jr., USMC	4 hrs 55 min 23 sec
4	24 May 62	Mercury Atlas 7 (Aurora 7)	Malcolm Scott Carpenter	4 hr 56 min 5 sec
5	3 Oct 62	Mercury Atlas 8 (Sigma 7)	Walter M. Schirra, Jr.	9 hrs 13 min 11 sec
7	23 Mar 65	Gemini 3	Virgil I. Grissom, USAF John W. Young	4 hrs 53 min
9	21–29 Aug 65	Gemini 5	Leroy G. Cooper, Jr., USAF Charles Conrad, Jr.	190 hrs 56 min 1 sec
10	4–18 Dec 65	Gemini 7	Frank Borman, USAF James A. Lovell, Jr.	330 hrs 35 min 13 sec
11	15–16 Dec 65	Gemini 6	Walter M. Schirra, Jr. Thomas P. Stafford, USAF	25 hrs 51 min 24 sec
12	16 Mar 66	Gemini 8	Neil A. Armstrong* David R. Scott, USAF	10 hrs 42 min 6 sec
13	3–6 Jun 66	Gemini 9	Thomas P. Stafford, USAF Eugene A. Cernan	72 hrs 20 min 56 sec
14	18–21 Jul 66	Gemini 10	John W. Young Michael Collins, USAF	70 hrs 46 min 45 sec
15	12–15 Sep 66	Gemini 11	Richard F. Gordon, Jr. Charles Conrad, Jr.	71 hrs 17 min 8 sec
16	11–15 Nov 66	Gemini 12	James A. Lovell, Jr. Edwin E. Aldrin, Jr., USAF	94 hrs 34 min 31 sec

List of U.S. Space Flights with Navy/Marine Corps Pilots/Astronauts Aboard—Continued

Order	Date	Designation	Crew (see notes)	Duration
17	11–22 Oct 68	Apollo 7	Walter M. Schirra, Jr. Donn F. Eisele, USAF R. Walter Cunningham*	206 hrs 9 min
18	21–27 Dec 68	Apollo 8 (1st flight to the moon)	Frank Borman, USAF James A. Lovell, Jr. William A. Anders, USAF	147 hrs 0 min 42 sec
20	18–26 May 69	Apollo 10	Thomas P. Stafford, USAF John W. Young Eugene A. Cernan	192 hrs 3 min 23 sec
21	16–24 Jul 69	Apollo 11 (first moon walk)	Neil A. Armstrong* Michael Collins, USAF Edwin E. Aldrin, Jr., USAF	195 hrs 18 min 35 sec
22	14–24 Nov 69	Apollo 12 (all Navy crew)	Charles Conrad, Jr. Richard F. Gordon, Jr. Alan L. Bean	244 hrs 36 min 25 sec
23	11–17 Apr 70	Apollo 13	James A. Lovell, Jr. John L. Swigert, Jr.(civ) Fred W. Haise, Jr.*	142 hrs 54 min 41 sec
24	31 Jan–9 Feb 71	Apollo 14	Alan B. Shepard, Jr. Stuart A. Roosa, USAF Edgar D. Mitchell	216 hrs 1 min 57 sec
26	16–27 Apr 72	Apollo 16	John W. Young Thomas K. Mattingly II Charles M. Duke, Jr., USAF	265 hrs 1 min 5 sec
27	7–19 Dec 72	Apollo 17	Eugene A. Cernan Ronald E. Evans Harrison H. Schmitt (civ)	301 hrs 51 min 59 sec
28	25 May–22 Jun 73	Skylab 2 (1st U.S. manned orbiting space station; all-Navy crew)	Charles Conrad, Jr. Joseph P. Kerwin Paul J. Weitz	672 hrs 49 min 49 sec
29	28 Jul–25 Sep 73	Skylab 3	Alan L. Bean Owen K. Garriott** John R. Lousma, USMC	1427 hrs 9 min 4 sec
30	16 Nov 73–8 Feb 74	Skylab 4	Gerald P. Carr, USMC Edward G. Gibson (civ) William R. Pogue, USAF	2017 hrs 15 min 32 sec
31	15–24 Jul 75	Apollo-Soyuz test project	Thomas P. Stafford, USAF Vance D. Brand* Donald K. Slayton, USAF	217 hrs 28 min 24 sec

List of U.S. Space Flights with Navy/Marine Corps Pilots/Astronauts Aboard—Continued

Shuttle Flights	Date	Designation	Crew (see notes)
STS-1	12–14 Apr 81	Space Shuttle *Columbia* (1st mission into space, all-Navy crew)	John W. Young* Robert L. Crippen
STS-2	12–14 Nov 81	Space Shuttle *Columbia*	Richard H. Truly Joseph H. Engle, USAF
STS-3	22–30 Mar 82	Space Shuttle *Columbia*	John R. Lousma, USMC Charles G. Fullerton, USAF
STS-4	27 Jun–4 Jul 82	Space Shuttle *Columbia*	Thomas K. Mattingly II Henry W. Hartsfield, USAF
STS-5	11–16 Nov 82	Space Shuttle *Columbia*	Vance D. Brand* Robert F. Overmyer, USMC William B. Lenoir (civ) Joseph P. Allan (civ)
STS-6	4–9 Apr 83	Space Shuttle *Challenger*	Paul J. Weitz* Karol J. Bobko, USAF Donald H. Peterson, USAF Franklin Story Musgrave*
STS-7	18–24 Jun 83	Space Shuttle *Challenger*	Robert L. Crippen Frederick H. Hauck John M. Fabian, USAF Sally K. Ride (civ) Norman E. Thagard*
STS-8	30 Aug–5 Sep 83	Space Shuttle *Challenger*	Richard H. Truly Daniel C. Brandenstein Dale A. Gardner Guion S. Bluford, Jr.,USAF William E. Thornton (civ)
STS-9	28 Nov–8 Dec 83	Space Shuttle *Columbia*	John W. Young* Brewster H. Shaw, Jr.,USAF Owen K. Garriott** Robert A. R. Parker (civ) Ulf Merbold (civ)+ Byron K. Lichtenberg(civ)+
STS-41-B	3–11 Feb 84	Space Shuttle *Challenger* (1st untethered walk in space)	Vance D. Brand* Bruce McCandless II Robert L. Gibson Robert L. Steward, USA Ronald E. McNair (civ)

List of U.S. Space Flights with Navy/Marine Corps Pilots/Astronauts Aboard—Continued

Shuttle Flights	Date	Designation	Crew (see notes)
STS-41-C	6–13 Apr 84	Space Shuttle *Challenger*	Robert L. Crippen Francis R. Scobee, USAF George D. Nelson (civ) Terry J. Hart, USAF James D. van Hoften
STS-41-D	30 Aug–5 Sep 84	Space Shuttle *Discovery*	Henry W. Hartsfield, USAF Michael L. Coats Judith A. Resnick (civ) Steven A. Hawley (civ) Richard M. Mullane, USAF Charles D. Walker (civ)+
STS-41-G	5–13 Oct 84	Space Shuttle *Challenger*	Robert L. Crippen Jon A. McBride Kathryn D. Sullivan (civ) Sally K. Ride (civ) David C. Leestma Marc Garneau (civ)+ Paul D. Scully-Power(civ)+
STS-51-A	8–15 Nov 84	Space Shuttle *Discovery*	Frederick H. Hauck David M. Walker Anna L. Fisher (civ) Joseph P. Allen (civ) Dale A. Gardner
STS-51-C	24–27 Jan 85	Space Shuttle *Discovery*	Thomas K. Mattingly II Loren J. Shriver, USAF Ellison S. Onizuka, USAF James F. Buchli, USMC Gary E. Payton, USAF+
STS-51-D	12–19 Apr 85	Space Shuttle *Discovery*	Karol J. Bobko, USAF Donald E. Williams Margaret Rhea Seddon (civ) Jeffrey A. Hoffman (civ) S. David Griggs Charles D. Walker (civ)+ Jake E. Garn*++
STS-51-B	29 Apr–6 May 85	Space Shuttle *Challenger*	Robert F. Overmyer, USMC Frederick D. Gregory, USAF Don L. Lind Norman E. Thagard* William E. Thornton (civ) Lodewijk van den Berg(civ)+ Taylor G. Wang (civ)+

List of U.S. Space Flights with Navy/Marine Corps Pilots/Astronauts Aboard—Continued

Shuttle Flights	Date	Designation	Crew (see notes)
STS-51-G	17–24 Jun 85	Space Shuttle *Discovery*	Daniel C. Brandenstein John O. Creighton Shannon W. Lucid (civ) John M. Fabian, USAF Steven R. Nagel, USAF Patrick Baudry (civ)+ Sultan Salman al-Saud (civ)++
STS-52-F	29 Jul–6 Aug 85	Space Shuttle *Challenger*	Anthony W. England (civ) Roy D. Bridges, USAF Franklin Story Musgrave* Karl G. Henize (civ) John David Bartoe (civ) Loren W. Acton (civ) Charles G. Fullerton, USAF
STS-51-I	27 Aug–3 Sep 85	Space Shuttle *Discovery*	John M. Lounge* Richard O. Covey, USAF William F. Fisher (civ) Joseph H. Engle, USAF James D. van Hoften
STS-51-J	3-7 Oct 85	Space Shuttle *Atlantis*	Karol J. Bobko, USAF Ronald J. Grabe, USAF Robert L. Steward, USA David C. Hilmers, USMC William A. Pailes, USAF+
STS-61-A	30 Oct–6 Nov 85	Space Shuttle *Challenger*	Henry W. Hartsfield, USAF Steven R. Nagel, USAF James F. Buchli, USMC Bonnie J. Dunbar (civ) Guion S. Bluford, Jr., USAF Reinhard Furrer (civ)+ Ernst Messerschmid (civ)+ Wubbo Ockels (civ)+
STS-61-B	26 Nov–3 Dec 85	Space Shuttle *Atlantis*	Brewster H. Shaw, Jr., USAF Bryan D. O'Connor, USMC Mary L. Cleave (civ) Sherwood C. Spring, USA Jerry L. Ross, USAF Rodolfo Neri Vela (civ)+ Charles D. Walker (civ)+
STS-61-C	12–18 Jan 86	Space Shuttle *Columbia*	Robert L. Gibson Charles F. Bolden,Jr., USMC Franklin R. Chang-Diaz(civ) Steven A. Hawley(civ) George D. Nelson (civ) Robert Cenker (civ)+ Bill Nelson (civ)++

List of U.S. Space Flights with Navy/Marine Corps Pilots/Astronauts Aboard—Continued

Shuttle Flights	Date	Designation	Crew (see notes)
STS-51-L	28 Jan 86	Space Shuttle *Challenger*	Francis R. Scobee, USAF Michael John Smith Judith A. Resnik (civ) Ellison S. Onizuka, USAF Ronald E. McNair (civ) Gregory B. Jarvis (civ)+ S. Christa McAuliffe(civ)++
STS-26	29 Sep–3 Oct 88	Space Shuttle *Discovery*	Frederick H. Hauck Richard O. Covey, USAF John M. Lounge* George D. Nelson (civ) David C. Hilmers, USMC
STS-27	2–6 Dec 88	Space Shuttle *Atlantis*	Robert L. Gibson Guy S. Gardner, USAF Richard M. Mullane, USAF Jerry L. Ross, USAF William M. Sheperd**
STS-29	13–18 Mar 89	Space Shuttle *Discovery*	Michael L. Coats John E. Blaha, USAF James P. Bagian (civ) James Buchli Robert Springer
STS-30	4–8 May 89	Space Shuttle *Atlantis*	David M. Walker Ronald J. Grabe, USAF Norman E. Thagard* Mary L. Cleave (civ) Mark C. Lee, USAF
STS-28	8–13 Aug 89	Space Shuttle *Columbia*	Brewster H. Shaw, USAF Richard N. Richards David C. Leestma James C. Adamson, USA Mark N. Brown, USAF
STS-34	18–23 Oct 89	Space Shuttle *Atlantis*	Donald E. Williams Michael J. McCulley Shannon W. Lucid (civ) Ellen S. Baker (civ) Franklin R. Chang-Diaz(civ)
STS-33	22–27 Nov 89	Space Shuttle *Discovery*	Frederick D. Gregory, USAF John E. Blaha, USAF Franklin Story Musgrave* Kathryn C. Thornton (civ) Manley L. Carter, Jr.

List of U.S. Space Flights with Navy/Marine Corps Pilots/Astronauts Aboard—Continued

Shuttle Flights	Date	Designation	Crew (see notes)
STS-32	9–20 Jan 90	Space Shuttle *Columbia*	Daniel C. Brandenstein James D. Wetherbee Marsha S. Ivins (civ) Bonnie J. Dunbar (civ) G. David Low (civ)
STS-36	28 Feb–4 Mar 90	Space Shuttle *Atlantis*	John O. Creighton John H. Casper, USAF David C. Hilmers, USMC Richard M. Mullane, USAF Pierre J. Thuot
STS-31	24–29 Apr 90	Space Shuttle *Discovery*	Loren J. Shriver, USAF Charles F. Bolden,Jr., USMC Bruce McCandless II Kathryn D. Sullivan Steven A. Hawley (civ)
STS-41	6–10 Oct 90	Space Shuttle *Discovery*	Richard N. Richards Robert D. Cabana, USMC William M. Sheperd** Bruce E. Melnick, USCG Thomas D. Akers, USAF
STS-38	15–20 Nov 90	Space Shuttle *Atlantis*	Richard O. Covey, USAF Frank L. Culbertson Carl J. Meade, USAF Robert C. Springer, USMC Charles D. Gemar, USA
STS-35	2–6 Dec 90	Space Shuttle *Columbia*	Vance D. Brand* Guy S. Gardner, USAF John M. Lounge* Robert A. R. Parker (civ) Jeffrey A. Hoffman (civ) Ronald A. Parise (civ)+ Samuel T. Durrance (civ)+
STS-37	5–11 Apr 91	Space Shuttle *Atlantis*	Jerry L. Ross, USAF Steven R. Nagel, USAF Kenneth D. Cameron, USMC Jay Apt (civ) Linda M. Goodwin (civ)
STS-39	28 Apr–6 May 91	Space Shuttle *Discovery*	Richard J. Hieb (civ) Guion S. Bluford, Jr., USAF Michael L. Coats Charles L. Veach, USAF Donald R. McMonagle, USAF L. Blaine Hammond,Jr., USAF Gregory J. Harbaugh (civ)

List of U.S. Space Flights with Navy/Marine Corps Pilots/Astronauts Aboard—Continued

Shuttle Flights	Date	Designation	Crew (see notes)
STS-40	5–14 Jun 91	Space Shuttle *Columbia*	Francis A. Gaffney (civ)+ Millie Hughes-Fulford(civ)+ Tamara E. Jernigan (civ) Sidney M. Gutierrez, USAF James P. Bagian (civ) Bryan D. O'Connor, USMC Margaret Rhea Seddon (civ)
STS-43	2–11 Aug 91	Space Shuttle *Atlantis*	John E. Blaha, USAF Michael A. Baker Shannon W. Lucid (civ) James C. Adamson, USA G. David Low (civ)
STS-48	12–18 Sep 91	Space Shuttle *Discovery*	James F. Buchli, USMC John O. Creighton Charles D. Gemar, USA Mark N. Brown, USAF Kenneth S. Reightler, Jr.
STS-44	24 Nov–1 Dec 91	Space Shuttle *Atlantis*	Frederick D. Gregory, USAF Terence Hendricks, USAF Franklin Story Musgrave* Thomas Hennen, USA Mario Runco, Jr. James Voss, USA
STS-42	22–30 Jan 92	Space Shuttle *Discovery*	Stephen S. Oswald William F. Readdy Roberta L. Bondar (civ)+ Ronald J. Grabe, USAF David C. Hilmers, USMC Ulf Merbold (civ)+ Norman E. Thagard*
STS-45	24 Mar–2 Apr 92	Space Shuttle *Atlantis*	Dirk D. Frimount (civ)+ Kathryn D. Sullivan Michael Foale (civ) Charles F. Bolden,Jr., USMC David C. Leestma Brian Duffy, USAF Byron K. Lichtenberg (civ)+
STS-49	7–16 May 92	Space Shuttle *Endeavour*	Kathryn C. Thornton (civ) Thomas D. Akers, USAF Kevin P. Chilton, USAF Richard J. Hieb (civ) Daniel C. Brandenstein Bruce E. Melnick, USCG Pierre J. Thuot

List of U.S. Space Flights with Navy/Marine Corps Pilots/Astronauts Aboard—Continued

Shuttle Flights	Date	Designation	Crew (see notes)
STS-50	25 Jun–9 Jul 92	Space Shuttle *Columbia*	Richard N. Richards Ellen S. Baker (civ) Bonnie J. Dunbar (civ)+ Lawrence J. DeLucas (civ) Kenneth D. Bowersox Eugene H. Trinh (civ)+ Carl J. Meade, USAF
STS-46	31 Jul–8 Aug 92	Space Shuttle *Atlantis*	Franco Malerba (civ)+ Loren J. Shriver, USAF Claude Nicollier (civ) Jeffrey A. Hoffman (civ) Andrew M. Allen, USMC Marsha S. Ivins (civ) Franklin R. Chang-Diaz(civ)
STS-47	12–20 Sep 92	Space Shuttle *Endeavour*	Robert Gibson Curtis L. Brown, USAF Mark C. Lee, USAF Jan N. Davis (civ) Mae C. Jemison (civ) Jay Apt (civ) Mamoru Mohri (civ)+
STS-52	22 Oct–1 Nov 92	Space Shuttle *Columbia*	James D. Wetherbee Michael A. Baker Charles L. Veach, USAF William M. Sheperd** Tamara E. Jernigan (civ) Steven MacLean (civ)+
STS-53	2–9 Dec 92	Space Shuttle *Discovery*	David M. Walker Robert D. Cabana, USMC Guion S. Bluford,Jr., USAF+ James Voss, USA Michael Clifford, USA
STS-54	13–19 Jan 93	Space Shuttle *Endeavour*	John H. Casper,USAF R. McMonagle, USAF Gregory J. Harbaugh (civ) Susan J. Helms, USAF Mario Runco, Jr.
STS-56	8–17 Apr 93	Space Shuttle *Discovery*	Kenneth D. Cameron, USMC Stephen S. Oswald Kenneth Cockrell Michael Foale (civ) Ellen Ochoa (civ)

List of U.S. Space Flights with Navy/Marine Corps Pilots/Astronauts Aboard—Continued

Shuttle Flights	Date	Designation	Crew (see notes)
STS-51	12–22 Sep 93	Space Shuttle *Discovery*	Frank L. Culbertson William F. Readdy Daniel W. Bursch James Newman (civ) Carl E. Waltz, USAF
STS-61	2–13 Dec 93	Space Shuttle *Endeavour*	Richard O. Covey, USAF Kenneth D. Bowersox Thomas D. Akers, USAF Jeffrey A. Hoffman (civ) Franklin Story Musgrave* Claude Nicollier (civ) Kathryn C. Thornton (civ)
STS-60	3–11 Feb 94	Space Shuttle *Discovery*	Charles F. Bolden, Jr., USMC Kenneth S. Reightler, Jr. Franklin R. Chang-Diaz(civ) Jan N. Davis (civ) Ronald M. Sega (civ) Sergey K. Krikalev (Russian)
STS-62	4–18 Mar 94	Space Shuttle *Columbia*	John H. Casper, USAF Andrew M. Allen, USMC Pierre J. Thuot Charles D. Gemar, USAF Marsha S. Ivins (civ)
STS-65	8–23 Jul 94	Space Shuttle *Columbia*	Robert D. Cabana, USMC James D. Halsell, Jr., USAF Carl E. Waltz, USAF Leroy Chiao (civ) Richard J. Hieb (civ) Donald A. Thomas (civ) Chiaki Maito-Mukai (civ)+
STS-64	9–20 Sep 94	Space Shuttle *Discovery*	Richard N. Richards L. Blaine Hammond, Jr., USAF Carl J. Meade, USAF Mark C. Lee, USAF Susan J. Helms, USAF Jerry M. Linenger**
STS-68	30 Sep–11 Oct 94	Space Shuttle *Endeavour*	Michael A. Baker Terrence W. Willcutt, USMC Thomas D. Jones (civ) Steven L. Smith (civ) Peter J. K. Wisoff (civ) Daniel W. Bursch

List of U.S. Space Flights with Navy/Marine Corps Pilots/Astronauts Aboard—Continued

Shuttle Flights	Date	Designation	Crew (see notes)
STS-63	2–11 Feb 95	Space Shuttle *Discovery*	James Weatherbee Eileen Collins, USAF Bernard A. Harris,Jr., USAF Michael Foale (civ) Vladimir Titov (Russian) Janice Voss (civ)
STS-67	2–18 Mar 95	Space Shuttle *Endeavour*	Stephen S. Oswald William G. Gregory, USAF Wendy B. Lawrence John M. Grunsfield (civ) Tamara E. Jernigan (civ) Samuel T. Durrance (civ)+ Ronald A. Parise (civ)+
STS-71	27 Jun–7 Jul 95	Space Shuttle *Atlantis*	Robert L. Gibson Charles Precourt, USAF Ellen S. Baker (civ) Bonnie J. Dunbar (civ)+ Gregory J. Harbaugh (civ) Anatoly Solovyev (Russian) Nikolay Budarin (Russian)
STS-69	7–18 Sep 95	Space Shuttle *Endeavour*	David M. Walker Kenneth Cockrell James Voss, USA James H. Newman (civ) Michael L. Gernhardt (civ)
STS-73	20 Oct–5 Nov 95	Space Shuttle *Columbia*	Kenneth D. Bowersox Kent V. Rominger Kathryn C. Thornton (civ) Catherine G. Coleman, USAF Michael E. Lopez-Alegria Fred Leslie (civ)+ Albert Sacco, Jr. (civ)
STS-74	12–20 Nov 95	Space Shuttle *Atlantis*	Kenneth D. Cameron, USMC James D. Halsell, USAF Jerry L. Ross, USAF William S. McArthur,Jr.,USA Chris Hadfield (civ)

Notes: All personnel in this flight list are Navy or former Naval personnel unless otherwise indicated. The following marks used along side an individual's name provides more amplifying information on that person:

* Naval Aviators, retired or separated from Navy or Marine Corps, assigned to the crew as civilians on space flights.

+ Payload Specialist

++ Passenger

** Navy but not connected with Naval Aviation.

STS-42 lifts off on 22 January 1992, from the Kennedy Space Center, NASA-KSC-92PC-189.

Honorary Naval Aviator Designations

The official Honorary Naval Aviator Program was initiated in 1949 to honor individuals for certain extraordinary contributions and/or outstanding performance for service to Naval Aviation. In recognition of their service, an Honorary Naval Aviator designation is bestowed on the individual with the right to wear the "Wings of Gold".

The program is managed by the Chief of Naval Operations, Director Air Warfare (previously designated Deputy Chief of Naval Operations, Air Warfare and Assistant Chief of Naval Operations, Air Warfare). Final approval of the nomination is made by the Chief of Naval Operations.

The honor designating an individual an Honorary Naval Aviator has not been bestowed lightly. The following is a list of those individuals who have received the honor:

Number and Name	Presented by	Date Received	Reason
1 CAPT Richard (Dick) Schram, (Stunt Pilot)	Chief, Naval Air Reserve	Oct 1949	"Flying Professor." Outstanding contribution to aviation since the early 1930s.
2 SGT Clifford Iknokinok (Alaskan National Guard)	James H. Smith, Jr. Asst. Secy. Navy	21 Nov 1955	Rescued 11 Navy men, shot down by Soviet MiGs over International waters, Bering Strait, Alaska.
3 SGT Willis Walunga (Alaskan National Guard)	James H. Smith, Jr. Asst. Secy. Navy	21 Nov 1955	Same as above.
4 Dr. Herman J. Schaefer	VADM Robert Goldwaite (Flight Surgeon Wings)	Jun 1960	As a scientist, made outstanding contributions to aerospace research while at the Naval School of Aviation Medicine.
5 Dr. Dietrich E. Beischer	VADM Robert Goldwaite	Jun 1960	Same as above.
6 Mr. F. Trubee Davison (Asst. Secy. of War for Air)	VADM Paul H. Ramsey DCNO (Air)	Jul 1966	Organized the 1st Yale Unit in 1916. Served as Asst. Secy. of War for Air for for 6 years, from late 1920s to 1930s.
7 Mr. Jackie Cooper (Navy Reserve Commander)	VADM Bernard M. Stean Chief, Naval Air Training	10 Jul 1970	Active in Navy's PAO program, recruiting and promoting since World War II.
8 VADM Hyman C. Rickover	VADM Thomas F. Connolly DCNO (Air Warfare)	21 Jul 1970	Vigorously supported Naval Aviation and achieved great advancements in nuclear propulsion for aircraft carriers.
9A LTC Barry R. Butler, USAF	VADM Bernard M. Strean Chief, Naval Air Training	19 Aug 1970	Made significant contributions as Advanced Training Officer, Naval Air Training Command. He flew several hundred hours in Navy aircraft and made six landings aboard Lexington (CVT 16).

Number and Name	Presented by	Date Received	Reason
10 Mr. John Warner (Secretary of the Navy)	VADM William D. Houser DCNO (Air Warfare)	14 Oct 1972	Vigorously supported Naval Aviation. Presented at establishment of VF-I and VF-2 (first F-14 squadrons) at NAS Miramar.
11 Mr. Robert G. Smith	VADM William D. Houser DCNO (Air Warfare)	8 May 1973	Artist, McDonnell Douglas Corp. National recognition as an outstanding aviation artist.
12 Mr. George Spangeberg (NAVAIRSYSCOM)	VADM William D. Houser DCNO (Air Warfare)	Sep 1975	Recognized for his many years of service as a Navy aircraft designer.
13 Mr. Jay R. Beasley	VADM E. C. Waller III Director of Weapons Sys. Eva. Grp. for VADM Houser	25 Jul 1977	Presented in recognition of 23 years of exceptionally dedicated and valuable service to Naval Aviation as production test pilot with Lockheed & P-2/P-3 instructor.
14 Mr. Robert Osborne DCNO (Air Warfare)	VADM Frederick C. Turner	21 Jan 1977	Presented for contributions to Naval Aviation safety; created Dilbert, Spoiler and Grampaw Pettibone illustrations.
15 CAPT Virgil J. Lemmon	VADM Wesley L. McDonald DCNO (Air Warfare)	23 Feb 1981	"Mr. Naval Aviation Maintenance." Awarded for 40 years of distinguished service to Naval Aviation and the Naval Aviation Maintenance establishment.
16 ADM Arleigh A. Burke	VADM Wesley L. McDonald DCNO (Air Warfare)	13 Oct 1981	Outspoken supporter of Naval Aviation; made decisions that shaped the Navy's air arm as it is known today.
17 GEN James H. Doolittle	ADM Thomas B. Hayward CNO	11 Dec 1981	In recognition of many years of support of military aviation.
18 Mr. Paul E. Garber	VADM Edward H. Martin DCNO (Air Warfare)	26 Mar 1985	Made significant contributions to Naval Aviation spanning the age of manned powered flight. Including service in World Wars I and II and impressive contributions in maintaining the history of Naval Aviation as the Ramsey Fellow and Historian Emeritus of the National Air and Space Museum.
19 Mr. Bob Hope	VADM Edward H. Martin DCNO (Air Warfare) and the Secretary of the Navy, Mr. John Lehman	8 May 1986	Presented in recognition of 45 years of selfless dedication to the well-being of those serving their nation in the Navy, Marine Corps, and Coast Guard and for making remarkable contributions to the morale of those in Naval Aviation.

Number and Name	Presented by	Date Received	Reason
20 Mr. Edward H. Heinemann	VADM Edward H. Martin DCNO (Air Warfare)	18 Oct 1986	Contributed to major achievements in the technical development of naval aircraft and as one of aviation's most highly regarded aircraft designers. The majority of the aircraft he designed served in Naval Aviation and he has become known as "Mr. Attack Aviation." A man whose professional life has been dedicated largely to designing a superb series of carrier-based aircraft.
21 CAPT Robert E. Mitchell, MC, USN	RADM E. D. Conner Deputy, CNET	25 Jun 1990	Recognized for 43 years of contributions in the field of aerospace medicine. Conducted extensive research in the Thousand Aviator Program; worked with the Navy and Marine Corps Vietnam Prisoners of War (Repatriated); wrote and published numerous medical papers; and his operational work as a Naval Flight Surgeon has helped shape the course of Naval Aviation.
22 Mr. Harold (Hal) Andrews	VADM Richard M. Dunleavy ACNO (Air Warfare)	29 Apr 1991	Outstanding contributions to Naval Aviation as a civilian engineer with 30 years of service to the Navy; provided technical advice and support for the 50th and 75th Naval Aviation anniversary celebrations; volunteered support to Naval Aviation News magazine as Technical Advisor since the 1950s and his vast knowledge of Naval Aviation events, both technical and operational, have contributed to the advancement of Naval Aviation since his association with it beginning in World War II.

Bob Hope is made an Honorary Naval Aviator during 75th Anniversary celebrations at NAS Pensacola, Fla. Mrs. Dolores Hope is pinning on his wings. Vice Admiral Edward H. Martin, DCNO (Air Warfare), is on the left and Secretary of the Navy John F. Lehman is on the right.

The Naval Aviation Hall of Honor at the National Museum of Naval Aviation.

Squadron insignia, past and present, showing squadron designation in the lower scroll.

APPENDIX **19**

Naval Aviation Hall of Honor

T he Naval Aviation Hall of Honor was established in 1980 to recognize those individuals who by their actions or achievements made outstanding contributions to Naval Aviation. A bronze plaque of the individual and their contributions is cast and placed in Naval Aviation Hall of Honor located in the National Museum of Naval Aviation at Pensacola, Fla. The first group to be inducted was in 1981. After 1984, enshrinement in the Naval Aviation Hall of Honor was placed on a two year cycle with no more than a maximum of eight inductees. The selection committee, consisting of seven to eleven members appointed by the Chief of Naval Operations, Director Air Warfare, is responsible for making the final nominatee recom-

mendations. Final approval is done by the Chief of Naval Operations.

Personnel eligible for nomination to the Naval Aviation Hall of Honor include civilian or uniformed individuals no longer employed by the Federal Government or on active duty. Criteria for nomination include:

—Sustained superior performance in or for Naval Aviation.

—Superior contributions in the technical or tactical development of Naval Aviation.

—Unique and superior flight achievement in combat or non-combat flight operations.

The following is a list of personnel enshrined in the Naval Aviation Hall of Honor:

Enshrinee	Year Enshrined
VADM Patrick N. L. Bellinger, USN	1981
CWO Floyd Bennett, USN	1981
RADM Richard E. Byrd, Jr., USN	1981
LCDR Godfrey deC. Chevalier, USN	1981
LCOL Alfred A. Cunningham, USMC	1981
Mr. Glenn H. Curtiss, Civilian	1981
CDR Theodore G. Ellyson, USN	1981
Mr. Eugene Ely, Civilian	1981
RADM William A. Moffett, USN	1981
RADM Albert C. Read, USN	1981
CAPT Holden C. Richardson, USN	1981
ADM John H. Towers, USN	1981
GEN Roy S. Geiger, USMC	1983
Mr. Glenn Martin, Civilian	1983
ADM Marc A. Mitscher, USN	1983
ADM Arthur W. Radford, USN	1983
VADM Charles E. Rosendahl, USN	1983
CDR Elmer F. Stone, USCG	1983
VADM James H. Flatley, Jr., USN	1984
Mr. Leroy R. Grumman, Civilian	1984
ADM John S. Thach, USN	1984
CAPT Kenneth Whiting, USN	1984
MGEN Marion E. Carl, USMC	1986
FADM William F. Halsey, USN	1986

Enshrinee	*Year Enshrined*
Mr. Edward H. Heinemann, Civilian	1986
RADM David S. Ingalls, USNR	1986
CAPT Donald Bantram MacDiarmid, USCG (Ret)	1986
VADM Robert B. Pirie, USN (Ret)	1986
GSGT Robert G. Robinson, USMCR	1986
VADM Frederick M. Trapnell, USN (Ret)	1986
CAPT Washington I. Chambers, USN	1988
Dr. Jerome C. Hunsaker, Civilian	1988
CAPT David McCampbell, USN (Ret)	1988
GEN Keith B. McCutcheon, USMC (Ret)	1988
ADM Thomas H. Moorer, USN (Ret)	1988
ADM Alfred M. Pride, USN	1988
CAPT Frank A. Erickson, USCG	1990
CAPT Henry C. Mustin, USN	1990
ADM James S. Russell, USN (Ret)	1990
RADM Alan B. Shepard, Jr., USN (Ret)	1990
Mr. Igor I. Sikorsky, Civilian	1990
Mr. George A. Spangenberg, Civilian	1990
VADM Gerald F. Bogan, USN	1992
ADM Austin Kelvin Doyle, USN (Ret)	1992
LT Edward H. O'Hare, USN	1992
VADM William A. Schoech, USN (Ret)	1992
Mr. Lawrence Sperry, Civilian	1992
COL Gregory "Pappy" Boyington, USMC	1994
BGEN Joseph Jacob Foss, ANG (Ret)	1994
CAPT Ashton Graybiel, Medical Corp, USN (Ret)	1994
ADM Frederick H. Michaelis, USN	1994
VADM Apollo Soucek, USN (Ret)	1994
RADM Joseph C. Clifton, USN	1996
Mr. Charles H. Kaman, Civilian	1996
GEN Christian F. Schilt, USMC	1996
ADM Forrest P. Sherman, USN	1996
VADM James B. Stockdale, USN (Ret)	1996
ADM Maurice F. Weisner, USN (Ret)	1996

Evolution of Naval Wings
(Breast Insignia)

Naval Aviator Wings

The origin of a distinctive device for Naval Aviators is somewhat obscure, but the idea was undoubtedly influenced by outside forces. It appears that the need for a distinguishing mark was voiced by the aviators themselves, particularly after Army aviators began wearing "badges" in 1913. Other influence outside the naval service also appears to have provided some of the initial impetus.

A review of the records indicates a lack of coordination within the Navy during the process to develop a Naval Aviation device. The dated correspondence of the Bureau of Navigation (BuNav) and the Chief of Naval Operations (CNO) Aviation Section relating to the "wings" does not coincide with the dated changes to the Uniform Regulations. The change to the Uniform Regulations that first identified the new "wings" was issued before the CNO's Aviation Section and BuNav had agreed upon a final design. Several separate evolutions occurred in 1917.

A 29 June 1917 letter from the G. F. Hemsley Co., stating that the sender "takes the liberty" of forwarding a design for an aviation cap and collar ornament, may well have started official action. The first official correspondence on the subject appears to have been a CNO letter to BuNav dated 19 July 1917. This letter, which forwarded a suggestion from the G. F. Hemsley Co. for aviator cap and collar ornaments, rejected the ornaments but went on to say that since foreign countries and the U.S. Army had adopted an aviation device, Naval Aviators also should be given "some form of mark or badge to indicate their qualification, in order that they have standing with other aviation services." The letter, prepared in the Aviation Section of CNO, enclosed a representative design for wings. From that date, the subject was kept alive by the exchange of correspondence concerning the design and production of the insignia by interested firms.

Lieutenant Commander John H. Towers, assigned to the aviation desk under CNO, requested the assistance of Lieutenant Henry Reuterdahl in designing the Naval Aviator wings. Reuterdahl played an important part in the design development. He was later assigned as an artist to record the first transatlantic flight in May 1919, which was originally planned to be made by four NC aircraft. (Only one, the NC-4, completed the crossing—arriving in Plymouth, England, on 31 May.) In a 28 September 1917 letter to Bailey, Banks, and Biddle Company, he recommended simplifying the wings by bolder chasing (engraving) and a reduction in the number of feathers, noting that "most naval ornaments are too fine and not broad enough in character." He also recommended changes in the anchor and rope and the introduction of a slight curve to conform to the shape of the body. He summarized his remarks by saying, "My idea has been to reduce all corners so that there will be no points which might catch in the clothing."

Several different designs were proposed and submitted for approval. The sample pins passed through a number of changes. Bronze, the first metal proposed, was quickly rejected in favor of a gold and silver combination. This, in turn, was changed to all silver and finally, in October 1917, all gold was selected. The size changed from over three inches to the final of 2¾ inches. The "U.S." was dropped from the design and stars on the shield were proposed and rejected as violating the laws of heraldry.

By October 1917 the Bailey, Banks, and Biddle Company took the lead over its competitors and on 24 October submitted its first sample pin. In early November it submitted other samples and was ready to make "prompt delivery of such number of devices as you may desire." It is believed these various sample pins added to the confusion regarding the existence of official Naval Aviator wings. On the final decision to place an order, the record is obscure but it may have been a BuNav letter to the Supply Officer at NAS Pensacola, Fla., dated 21 November 1917, selecting "the higher priced pin" ($1.15 each). The company was not named, but it seems fairly certain that it was Bailey, Banks and Biddle. Its letter to BuNav dated 19 December 1917 confirms a telegram stating: "balance aviator insignia shipped tomorrow."

The first Wings, made by Bailey, Banks, and Biddle of Philadelphia, Pa., were received by the Navy in

December 1917 and issued early in the following year. The fact that the first pins were delivered in this month is also confirmed in a 26 December letter from BuNav to NAS Pensacola reporting that the new pins had been received and "will be sent out as soon as they can be engraved to show the Aviator's number, his name and branch of service." The Bureau asked the jeweler not to sell the wings to individuals.

The requirement to engrave the aviator's number posed a problem concerning the precedence list of trained naval aviators. This was solved by the preparation of an aviators' precedence list, covering numbers 1 through 282, by the CNO Aviation Section. Thus, the development of wings was responsible for the first precedence list and, in addition, was a factor in the later assignment of fractional numbers to many aviators omitted from this first compilation.

When forwarded to BuNav on 19 January 1918, distribution of the first wings could begin. After almost eight years of Naval Aviation and nine months of war, Naval Aviators had wings—a badge of qualification that would set them apart. It seems likely that Commander Towers, senior Naval Aviator in Washington at the time, was an early—if not the earliest—recipient. The engraving of the individual's name, Naval Aviator number, and branch of service was discontinued sometime during World War I.

The official approval for Naval Aviator wings was announced before a final design had been agreed upon. On 7 September 1917, the Secretary of the Navy approved Change 12 to the 1913 Uniform Regulations. The pertinent portion read: "A Naval Aviator's device, a winged foul anchor with the letters 'U.S.', is hereby adopted to be worn by qualified Naval Aviators. This device will be issued by the Bureau of Navigation (BuNav) to officers and men of the Navy and Marine Corps who qualify as Naval Aviators, and will be worn on the left breast."

However, before any such wings were issued, the design was modified by Change 14, approved 12 October 1917 and issued in BuNav Circular Letter 40-17 of 20 November 1917: "The device for Naval Aviators will be a winged foul anchor, but the letters 'U.S.' given in Change in Uniform Regulations No. 12, have been omitted." Several other changes to the 1913 Uniform Regulations occurred regarding the Naval

Aviator wings before the design was finalized. Uniform Regulations, Change Number 18 of 1 April 1918, states "Naval Aviator's Device-Device for naval aviators will be a winged foul anchor, to be worn by qualified naval aviators. This device will be issued . . . and worn on the left breast." Change number 20 (undated) has the following pertinent information: "Chapter 10 and changes 11, 12, 14, 16, and 18 of Uniform Regulations, 1913, are annulled and in lieu thereof this chapter is substituted: NAVAL AVIATOR'S DEVICE-Device for naval aviators will be a winged foul anchor, to be worn by qualified naval aviators. This device will be issued by the Bureau of Navigation to officers and men of the Navy and Marine Corps who qualify as naval aviators, and will be worn on the left breast." Another modification to the 1913 Uniform Regulation was made by Change 29, dated 13 May 1920. In Article 262, under "Naval Aviator's Device" the title of the paragraph was changed to read "Naval Aviation Insignia" and the first sentence read: "Insignia to be worn by qualified naval aviators and by warrant officers and enlisted men holding certificate of qualification as naval aviation pilots, is a winged foul anchor."

The 1922 Uniform Regulations, approved on 20 September 1922, described the Naval Aviator wing design in more detail: "A gold embroidered or bronze gold-plated metal pin, winged, foul anchor surcharged with a shield ½ inch in height, 2¾ inches from tip to tip of wings; length of foul anchor 1 inch." Except for a reduction in the length of the foul anchor from 1 to ⅞ inch, made by Change 1 to the above Regulations, and an elaboration of the description in 1951 which added dimensions for the shield (⁷⁄₁₆ inch high and at its widest point) and for the width of the anchor (¹¹⁄₁₆ inch at the flukes and ⁷⁄₁₆ at the stock), the original design has changed very little since 1922.

The design pictured below was published by the *Air Service Journal* on 27 September 1917. A short article in the Journal identified it as a Naval Aviator's Device of gold and silver metal as described by a Change in Uniform Regulations No. 10. It is believed the article may have been referring to Change 12 in the Uniform Regulations which was issued on 7 September 1917. This published design, most likely an artist rendition, also failed to take into account the shield.

This design, published in the Air Service Journal, was never issued as the Naval Aviator wing insignia.

The following artist rendition is most likely the design referenced in Change 12 of Uniform Regulations, 1913, and issued on 7 September 1917.

This contemporary artist rendition was never issued as the Naval Aviator wing insignia.

The photograph below is of the original design authorized by Change 14 of the 1913 Uniform Regulations, approved 12 October 1917, and quoted in BuNav Circular Letter 40-17 of 20 November 1917. This is the officially approved design made by Bailey, Banks and Biddle and issued to Naval Aviators in early 1918.

Original wings issued to Naval Aviators.

The following photographs trace the evolution of the Naval Aviator wings during the 1920s, 1930s and early 1940s:

This photograph shows the highly detailed design used during the 1920s and 1930s.

This photograph shows a curved shield design used in the 1930s and 1940s.

During World War II Naval Aviator wings began showing a series of dots, or circles in the upper-part of the design where the wings break. The original design shows these as small feathers, not dots or circles.

This photograph shows the dots or circles in the upper-part of wing.

On most of the Naval Aviator wings there is a small dot or circle on one of the anchor flues. That design is part of the normal structure of an anchor and is called a becket. A becket is an eye with a line attached used for securing the anchor to the side of the ship to keep it from moving when the ship is underway.

This photograph shows the wing design, in gold or a gold finish, that has been the standard design since the 1950s.

Aircrew (Air Crew)/Combat Aircrew Wing Insignia

During World War II a new aviation breast insignia was designed in response to numerous recommendations from the Fleet to recognize the job done by enlisted aircrew personnel flying in combat. In a Navy Department press release of 18 May 1943, the new Air Crew Insignia was described as follows: "The Air Crew insignia consists of silver wings with a center disk surcharged with fouled anchor. Below the disk is a scroll with the legend 'Air Crew,' and above it is a bar on which gold stars can be placed."

The Bureau of Naval Personnel (BuPers) Circular Letter Number 90-43 of 29 May 1943 announced the approval of an Air Crew Insignia, recognizing the air-fighting ability of flight crews. The insignia was intended primarily for enlisted ratings in the flight crews of naval aircraft. However, any commissioned or warrant officer, other than pilots or designated naval aviation observers, who met the qualification requirements, were eligible to wear the insignia. The initial requirements for insignia were:

a. Having served, subsequent to 7 December 1941, for a total of three months as a regularly assigned member of the Air Crew of a combatant craft.

(1) "Combat aircraft" shall be considered as all operating aircraft of the Fleet or Frontier Forces, and excepts utility aircraft which are neither designed nor fitted out for offensive (or defensive) operations.

(2) The term "regularly assigned member of the Air Crew" shall be interpreted literally, and shall be substantiated by the battle station bill of the unit, under such instructions that may be approved and promulgated by the Bureau of Naval Personnel.

b. Having suffered injuries or other physical impairment, while engaged in combatant operations since 7 December 1941, as a regularly assigned member of a combatant aircraft, which precludes the possibility of fulfillment of the time requirements, stated in subparagraph (a) above, and is recommended by the Commanding Officer of the Unit in which injury or physical impairment was received.

c. Individual combat stars will be authorized by Unit Commanders, in conformance with instructions issued by Commander-in-Chief, United States Fleet, to those members of Air Crews who:

(1) Engage enemy aircraft, singly or in formation.

(2) Engage armed enemy combatant vessels with bombs, torpedoes, or machine guns.

(3) Engage in bombing offensive operations against enemy fortified positions.

(4) A maximum of three combat stars shall be awarded for display on the Air Crew Insignia; combat actions reports in excess of three will be credited only in the record of the individual concerned.

d. Personnel qualified by provisions of subparagraphs (a) and (b) above may wear the Air Crew Insignia permanently.

The above set of requirements for qualification to wear the Air Crew Insignia were modified several times. BuPers Circular Letter Numbers 173-43 of 8 September 1943, 22-44 of 29 January 1944 and 174-44 of 16 June 1944 all make modifications to the qualifications but do not give a detailed description of the insignia.

BuPers Circular Letter Number 395-44, dated 30 December 1944, provided a comprehensive description of the Aircrew Insignia: "The Aircrew Insignia is a silver-plated or silver-color, winged, metal, pin, with gold-color circular shield with surcharged foul anchor, superimposed on wing roots, with words "AIRCREW" below circular shield; a silver-color bar over the circu-

lar shield with three threaded holes to receive three gold-color combat stars when officially awarded. The insignia will measure two inches from tip to tip of the wings: circle on shield ⁵⁄₁₆″; total depth of the shield from the top of the circle to the bottom of the shield ⁹⁄₁₆″. The Uniform Regulations of 2 May 1947 provided the following description of the Aircrew wings: "A silver-plated or silver color, winged, metal pin, with gold circular shield surcharged with foul anchor, superimposed on wing roots, with word 'AIRCREW' in raised letters on a silver-color background below the circular shield; above the shield there shall be a silver-color scroll; the insignia to measure 2″ from tip to tip of the wings; circle on shield ⁵⁄₁₆″ in diameter; total height of the shield and silver background beneath the shield ⁹⁄₁₆″. The scroll shall be ⅛″ wide and ¾″ long and shall be centered over the wings. Gold stars to a total of three, as merited, shall be mounted on the scroll, necessary holes being pierced to receive them. A silver star may be worn in lieu of three gold stars."

This line drawing depicts an early Aircrew Insignia that was published in the Naval Aviation News *magazine in April 1943. It shows the breast insignia without the stars.*

In 1958 there was a major change in the Aircrew Insignia. On 10 April 1958 Change 5 to the 1951 Uniform Regulations was issued. The name Aircrew or Air Crew Insignia was redesignated Combat Aircrew Insignia. Besides the redesignation, there were a few minor changes to the breast insignia. The new description of the Combat Aircrew Insignia read: "A silver color, metal pin; winged, with gold color circular shield surcharged with a foul anchor, superimposed on wing roots; with word 'AIRCREW' in raised letters on a silver background below the shield. Above the shield there shall be a silver color scroll. The insignia shall measure 2″ from tip to tip of wings; the circular shield shall be ⅜″ in diameter; height of anchor ¼″ with other dimensions proportionate; total height of shield and silver background beneath ⁹⁄₁₆″; the scroll shall be ¾″ long and ¼″ wide; centered over the shield, each end to rest on top of wings. Gold stars of a size to be inscribed in a circle ⅛″ in diameter, to a total of three, as merited, shall be mounted on the scroll, necessary holes being pierced to receive them.

A silver star may be worn in lieu of three gold stars." Following the 1958 redesignation of the Air Crew insignia to Combat Aircrew Insignia, the Navy continued to allow the wearing of the redesignated Combat Aircrew Insignia for those Navy individuals who had previously been authorized to wear the device.

The Combat Aircrew Insignia as depicted in the post-1958 time frame.

With the establishment of a separate Aircrew Wing insignia the Navy no longer awarded or issued the Combat Aircrew Wing Insignia. The 1978 U.S. Navy Uniform Regulations removed the Combat Aircrew insignia from the authorized list of aviation breast insignia. However, the Marine Corps continued to use the Combat Aircrew Insignia and awarded the wings to personnel who met the qualification requirements.

A Bureau of Naval Personnel Memorandum, approved by Chief of Naval Operations on 7 November 1994, authorized Navy personnel, who flew as aircrew with Marine Corps units in combat, to wear the Combat Aircrew wings. However, the Combat Aircrew wings are not authorized for Navy personnel flying in combat aboard Navy aircraft. They are only authorized to wear the Aircrew wings. The appropriate change was made to the Navy Uniform Regulations.

Aircrew Insignia Wings

Change 5 to the 1951 Uniform Regulations, dated 10 April 1958, redesignated the Aircrew Insignia to Combat Aircrew Insignia and also established a new Aircrew Insignia. The new Aircrew Insignia was patterned along the basic lines of the Naval Aviation Observer insignia. Description for the new Aircrew insignia was: "Shall be a gold color metal pin; winged, with a circular center design and anchor upon which the block letters AC are superimposed. Width between tips of wings shall be 2¾"; circle diameter shall be ¾"; height of anchor shall be ½" with other dimension proportionate."

On 11 August 1965, BuPers Notice 1020 authorized the wearing of the Aircrew Breast Insignia on a permanent basis. From the establishment of the Aircrew

The Aircrew Insignia approved in 1958.

Insignia in 1958 and until 1965, the insignia could only be worn by qualified personnel serving in an aircrew position. If an individual was assigned to a shore billet and not involved in aircrew duties, then they were not authorized to wear the insignia. Under the new guidance, a person who qualified to wear the Aircrew Insignia could continue to wear the breast device at anytime during their military service or unless the person was disqualified for aircrew duty.

Naval Aviation Experimental Psychologists and Naval Aviation Physiologists Wings

On 12 April 1967, the Under Secretary of the Navy approved a change to the Navy Uniform Regulations that authorized a new wing insignia for Aviation Experimental Psychologists and Aviation Physiologists. In February 1966, Aviation Experimental Psychologists and Aviation Physiologists were designated as crew members and ordered to duty involving flying. These individuals were assigned to duties such as in-flight analysis of human performance in fleet and training operations covering a myriad of weapons systems and tactics, providing extensive training for all aircrew personnel in airborne protective equipment and egress systems, and test and evaluation of new and improved aircraft systems.

The gold wings of the Naval Aviation Experimental Psychologists and Naval Aviation Physiologists are similar to those worn by Flight Surgeons, except the gold oak leaf does not have the acorn. The photo below shows the wings of the Naval Aviation Experimental Psychologists and Naval Aviation Physiologists.

Photograph of Naval Aviation Experimental Psychologists and Physiologists Wings.

Naval Aviation Supply Wings

Plans began in 1982 for the establishment of a Naval Aviation Supply Officer Program and the authorization for a breast insignia for qualifying Supply Corps officers. On 8 May 1984, during the 73rd annual Aviation Ball, the first Naval Aviation Supply wings were presented by Vice Admiral Robert F. Schoultz, Deputy Chief of Naval Operations (Air Warfare), to Vice Admiral Eugene A. Grinstead, Jr., SC, USN; Rear Admiral Andrew A. Giordano, SC, USN (Ret); and Commodore John H. Ruehlin, SC, USN, Commanding Officer, Aviation Supply Office, Philadelphia, Pa.

Officers qualified to wear the Naval Aviation Supply wings must complete a demanding qualification program which required approximately 350 hours of study and practical experience. They must also pass an oral examination administered by supply and aviation maintenance officers at their operating sites.

The Naval Aviation Supply wings consist of the traditional Naval Aviator wing style with an oak leaf cluster in the center. The photograph below is a line drawing depicting the wings.

A line drawing of the Naval Aviation Supply Wings.

Enlisted Aviation Warfare Specialist Wings

In order to recognize enlisted personnel serving in Naval Aviation who were not aircrew members, a new program and set of wings was established. The Operational Navy Instruction (OPNAVINST) 1412.5 of 19 March 1980 established the Enlisted Aviation Warfare Qualification Program and the new wing insignia. The Enlisted Aviation Warfare Specialist wings are issued to enlisted personnel who acquired the specific professional skills, knowledge, and military experience that resulted in unique qualification for service in the aviation activities of the Navy.

The 1981 Uniform Regulations described the Aviation Warfare wings as follows: "A silver embroidered or silver color metal pin (for enlisted); winged, with a central device consisting of a shield with an anchor superimposed thereon and a scroll at the bottom of the insignia."

Photograph of Naval Enlisted Aviation Warfare Specialist Wings.

Balloon Pilot Wing Insignia

The exact date the Balloon Pilot wing device was approved is not clear. However, the description of the wing first appeared in the 1922 Uniform Regulations of 20 September 1922. In this Uniform Regulation the following statement appears: "Enlisted men holding certificates of qualification as balloon pilots shall wear the same insignia as in paragraph (a) but with the right wing removed." Paragraph (a) was a description of the Naval Aviator wings. There were no changes between 1922 and 1947. In the 1947 Uniform Regulations of 2 May 1947, the words "Enlisted men" are replaced by "Persons" in the above statement. The 1978 U.S. Navy Uniform Regulations removed the Balloon Pilot insignia from the authorized list of aviation breast insignia.

This photograph shows the Balloon Pilot Wings used between 1922 and 1978.

Flight Nurse Wing Insignia

A BuPers Circular Letter Number 86-45 of 30 March 1945 announced the Secretary of the Navy had approved an insignia for naval flight nurses on 15 March 1945. The change to the 1941 Uniform Regulations read as follows: "Aviation Insignia, Naval Flight Nurses—Nurses who have been designated as Naval Flight Nurses shall wear the following insignia: Gold-plated metal pin, wings, with slightly convex oval crest with appropriate embossed rounded edge and scroll. The central device shall be surcharged with gold anchor, gold spread oak leaf and silver acorn, symbol of the Nurse Corps insignia. The insignia shall measure 2″ from tip to tip of the wings; oval crest ⁹⁄₁₆″ in vertical dimension and ⁷⁄₁₆″ in width; oak leaf ¹³⁄₃₂″ in length, ⁷⁄₃₂″ in width, to be diagonally mounted surcharged on the anchor; silver acorn ⅛″ in length surmounted on oak leaf." The insignia described above was to be worn until the designation "Flight Nurse" was revoked.

On 11 August 1952, the Secretary of the Navy ap-

This photograph shows the Flight Nurse Wings as approved in 1945.

proved a revision to the Flight Nurse Insignia. The BuPers Change Memo 1-2 of 6 February 1953 described the new Flight Nurse Insignia as: "The insignia shall consist of a gold color metal pin of the same design as that prescribed for Flight Surgeons...except that the acorn shall be omitted, and the width between wing tips shall be 2″; oval width ¹⁵⁄₃₂″ vertical and ⁵⁄₁₆″ horizontal axis; thickness at leaf center, ⅛.″

This line drawing depicts the Flight Nurse Wing Insignia that was approved in 1952.

Flight Surgeon Wing Insignia

On 18 May 1942, the Chief of Naval Personnel approved an insignia for Naval Flight Surgeons. A BuPers Circular Letter Number 107-42 of 29 July 1942 announced changes to the 1941 Uniform Regulations. These changes, as approved by the Secretary of the Navy, included the establishment of the new Flight Surgeon wings. The change to the Uniform Regulations read as follows: "Officers of the Medical Corps who have qualified as Naval Flight Surgeons shall wear the following insignia on the left breast: A gold plated metal pin, winged, with slightly convex oval crest, with appropriate embossed rounded edge and scroll. The central device to be surcharged with gold oak leaf and silver acorn,

symbol of Medical Corps insignia. The metal pin shall be of dull finish. Dimensions: 2¾ inches between wing tips, central device 1 inch in vertical dimension to lower edge of fringe. Lateral width of oval crest, ¾ inch. Oak leaf ⅞ inch in length, ⁹⁄₁₆ inch in width, to be vertically mounted surcharged on oval. Silver acorn ⅜ inch in length surmounted on oak leaf." A Navy Press Release issued a few days earlier, on 27 July 1942, gave the following description: "It will consist of wings which are a modification of the Perian Feroher with a central design consisting of convex oval crest with appropriate scroll and rounded edge. The central device is to be surcharged with the gold leaf and silver acorn that serves as the Medical Corps symbol."

This line drawing depicts the Flight Surgeon Wings approved in 1942.

On 11 August 1952, the Secretary of the Navy approved a major revision to the Flight Surgeon wings. The new design superimposed the Medical Corps device (gold oak leaf and silver acorn) on the style of wings used for the Naval Aviator wing insignia. BuPers Memo 1-2 of 6 February 1953 and the change to the 1951 Uniform Regulations describes the new design for Flight Surgeon wings as follows: "A gold embroidered or gold color metal pin; winged; with an oval center design upon which the Medical Corps device (a gold oak leaf and silver acorn) is superimposed. Width between tips of wings shall be 2¾″; oval with ⅝″ vertical and ¹³⁄₃₂″ horizontal axis; thickness with acorn ³⁄₁₆″; acorn and cup ⁷⁄₃₂″ long; acorn width ⅛″; cup depth 1¹⁄₁₆″; cup width ¹¹⁄₆₄″."

This photograph shows the Flight Surgeon Wings that were approved in 1952.

Naval Astronaut (Naval Flight Officer) Wings

The 1984 Uniform Regulations, issued on 6 February 1984, authorized the wearing of the new Naval Astronaut (Naval Flight Officer) wings. The regulations described the wings as follows: *"Naval Astronaut (NFO) Insignia. A gold embroidered or solid gold metal pin; winged and containing a shooting star with an elliptical ring surrounding the trailing shafts; superimposed diagonally from bottom right to top left, on the shield of the traditional Naval Flight Officer's Wings."*

A Naval Flight Officer or an active duty officer qualified as a Naval Astronaut (Specialist), who is not a Navy pilot or NFO, may wear the Naval Astronaut (NFO) Wings if they are designated by the CNO or Commandant of the Marine Corps after meeting the following qualifications:

a. Currently on flying status as a Naval Flight Officer or a payload specialist as a shuttle astronaut (but not qualified as a Navy Pilot or NFO) in either the Navy, Marine Corps, or their Reserve components.

b. Trained, qualified, and certified to fly as a mission or payload specialist in powered vehicles designed for flight above 50 miles from the earth's surface.

c. Have completed a minimum of one flight as a mission or payload specialist aboard an extraterrestrial vehicle in a flight above 50 miles from the earth's surface.

The line drawing shows the Naval Astronaut (NFO) Wings.

Naval Astronaut (Pilot) Wings

The Navy's first Naval Astronaut (Pilot) wings were presented to Commander Alan B. Shepard, Jr., on 6 December 1961 by the Chief of Naval Operations Admiral George W. Anderson. On 18 December 1962, the Secretary of the Navy officially approved the Uniform Board's recommendation to include a description and photograph of the Naval Astronaut wing insignia in the 1959 Uniform Regulations. The Naval Astronaut (Pilot) wings are identical to the Navy Pilot wings with the addition of a shooting star superimposed over the shield. The shooting star symbolized the astronaut's spatial environment.

The Naval Military Personnel Manual states the criteria for designation as a Naval Astronaut (Pilot). A Naval Pilot may wear the Naval Astronaut (Pilot) wings upon designation by the CNO or Commandant of the Marine Corps after meeting the following qualifications:

a. Currently on flying status as a Naval Pilot in either the Navy, Marine Corps, or their Reserve components.

b. Trained, qualified, and certified to fly a powered vehicle designed for flight above 50 miles from the earth's surface.

c. Completed a minimum of one flight as a pilot or mission specialist aboard an extraterrestrial vehicle in a flight above 50 miles from the earth's surface.

The photograph shows the Naval Astronaut (Pilot) Wings that were first presented in 1961.

Naval Aviation Observer Wings

The Naval Aviation Observer (NAO) designation had its origin in an act of Congress on 12 July 1921, which created the Bureau of Aeronautics and provided that its chief qualify within one year of his appointment as an "aircraft pilot or observer." The functions and qualifications for an observer were first defined on 27 March 1922; on 17 June of the same year, Rear Admiral William A. Moffett became the first to qualify for the designation as a Naval Aviation Observer.

The 1922 Uniform Regulations, approved 20 September, provided that officers designated as Naval Aviation Observer wear the same insignia as that worn by Naval Aviators, except with the right wing and shield removed and an "O" superimposed on the foul anchor.

The line drawing is the first Naval Aviation Observer Wing Insignia. It was used by the Navy from 1922 to January 1927.

A 26 January 1927 change to the 1922 Uniform Regulations (Change Number 3) modified the Naval Aviation Observer design and changed it to the same insignia worn by Naval Aviators except that it was to be in silver.

Between January 1927 and October 1929 the design of Naval Aviation Observer Wings was the same as Naval Aviator Wings except the observer wings were silver, not gold like the Naval Aviator.

Bureau of Navigation Circular Letter 71-29 of 19 October 1929 (Change Number 7 to the 1922 Uniform Regulations) directed another change to the Naval Aviation Observer wings. This letter described the new design as: "...an insignia the same as for naval aviators as to gold wings, but that the central device shall be an 'O' circumscribing an erect plain anchor, both in silver. The 'O' and anchor to be in bold relief, the center of the 'O' being filled in gold." The 1941 Uniform Regulations, of 31 May 1941, repeated the previous description and added dimensions as follows: "...outer diameter of 'O' shall be ¾ inch, inner diameter ⁹⁄₁₆ inch. Height of anchor shall be ½ inch."

This photograph of Naval Aviation Observer Wings is the type that has been used by the Navy between 1929 to 1968.

The Naval Aviation Observer wings made the same transition that occurred to the Naval Aviator wings during World War II. A change to the 1951 Uniform Regulations, issued on 6 February 1953 as BuPers Change Memorandum 1-2, directed the wing style used by the Naval Aviator breast insignia be adopted for the Naval Aviation Observer insignia. Hence, the series of dots, or circles were incorporated into the upper-part of the design where the wings break.

The following is a detailed description of the Naval Aviation Observer wings from the Uniform Regulations of 6 April 1959: "A gold embroidered or gold color metal pin, winged, with a central device consisting of

The Naval Aviation Observer Wings showing the dots in the upper-part of the wing.

an O circumscribing an erect, plain anchor, both in silver; the O and the anchor to be in bold relief, the center of the O being filled with gold. The insignia shall measure 2¾″ between wing tips; outer diameter of O shall be ¾″; inner diameter of O shall be ⁹⁄₁₆″; height of anchor shall be ½″ with other dimensions proportionate."

In the 1950s and 1960s, the Naval Aviation Observer wings were worn by officers who were Radar Intercept Operators (RIOs), Bombardier/Navigators (BNs), and Airborne Electronic Countermeasures Operators (AECMs). They were also worn by enlisted personnel who were qualified Navigators, Airborne Electronic Countermeasures Operators, Airborne Radio Operators, VG Jet Aircraft Flight Engineers and qualified Observers.

On 18 July 1968, the CNO approved a new qualification breast insignia for Navy and Marine Corps personnel designated as Naval Flight Officers (NFOs). BuPers Notice 1020 of 24 August 1968 issued the change to the Uniform Regulations (NavPers 15665) for the new Naval Flight Officer wings: "This new insignia will replace the Naval Aviation Observer insignia currently worn by Naval Flight Officers and will be authorized for wear upon source availability. The Naval Aviation Observer insignia will become obsolete after 31 December 1968." This ended the old Naval Aviation Observer wings for a short period of time. However, they were destined for continued use by Naval Aviation.

Naval Aviation Observer and Flight Meteorologist Wings

On 21 May 1969, the CNO approved the use of the Naval Aviation Observer wings for wear by Flight Meteorologists and for those officers formerly entitled but not selected as Naval Flight Officers. This change was incorporated into the 1959 Uniform Regulations by Bureau of Personnel Notice 1020 of 16 June 1969.

The 1969 Uniform Regulations, issued on 17 October 1969, did not mention the Flight Meteorologist insignia. However, the 1975 Uniform Regulations, which replaced the 1969 edition, listed the Naval Aviation Observers and Flight Meteorologist wings. The 1975 regulations states: "Naval Aviation Observer and Flight Meteorologist Insignia. A gold embroidered or gold color metal pin; winged, with a central device consisting of an O circumscribing an erect, plan anchor, both in silver; the O and the anchor to be in bold relief, the center of the O being filled with gold. The embroidered device shall be on a background to match the color of the uniform on which worn."

Qualifications to wear the Naval Aviation Observer wings, the second oldest wings in the Navy, are outlined in the Naval Military Personnel Manual. Although not aeronautically designated, the following types of officers are authorized to wear NAO wings upon initial qualification: Flight Meteorology and Oceanography Officer; Special Evaluator (officers and warrant officers from the cryptologic community); Aviation Operations Limited Duty Officer (632X); Aviation Operations Technicain Warrant Officer (732X); and other officers assigned by the Chief of Naval Personnel to duty involving flying as technical observers and airborne command post crew members.

The Marine Corps authorized the use of the old Naval Aviation Observer wings for personnel completing the Naval Aviation Observer School at Marine Corps Air Station New River. Qualified aerial observers were to provide commanders with information of intelligence value not readily available from normal ground sources regarding enemy forces; procure information concerning terrain, and to supplement operational information of friendly forces; direct supporting fires for ground forces to include artillery, naval gunfire, and close air support; to perform utility and liaison missions as directed from an observation aircraft and to advise commanders of ground units on matters pertaining to aerial observation.

See the section on Naval Aviation Observer Wings for a photograph of the device.

Naval Aviation Observer (Navigation) Wings

BuPers Circular Letter 88-45 of 31 March 1945 announced the Secretary of the Navy had approved an insignia for Naval Aviation Observers (Navigation) on 30 March 1945. It revised the 1941 Uniform Regulations by adding the following: "Officers designated as Naval Aviation Observers (Navigation) by the Chief of Naval Personnel shall wear the following insignia: A gold-embroidered or bronze gold-plated metal pin, winged, with silver center device superimposed upon crossed gold-color foul anchors. The centerpiece shall have superimposed upon it, in bold relief and in gold color, one gold disc with eight intercardinal points of the compass; superimposed upon this gold disc will be a second disc, in bold relief and in gold color, with four cardinal points and four intercardinal points of the compass. The insignia shall measure 2¾" from tip to tip of wings; silver center device shall be approximately ¹⁵⁄₃₂" in diameter; crossed foul anchors shall be of a size to be inscribed in a circle ¾" in diameter; the inner gold disc shall be approximately ⅛" in diameter, and the outer gold disc shall be approximately ¼" in diameter. Naval Aviators and Naval Aviation Observers will not wear the Naval Aviation Observer (Navigation) insignia."

A Bureau of Naval Personnel letter dated 18 March 1947 abolished the Naval Aviation Observer (Navigation) insignia and authorized all officers designated as Naval Aviation Observer (Navigation) to wear the same insignia as that worn by Naval Aviation Observers.

The photo shows the Naval Aviation Observer (Navigation) Wing insignia used by the Navy for the period 1945–1947.

Naval Aviation Observers (Radar) Wings

The Secretary of the Navy approved the Naval Aviation Observer (Radar) insignia on 29 August 1945. BuPers Circular Letter Number 313-45 of 17 October 1945 announced the insignia and a subsequent change was made to the 1941 Uniform Regulations. The letter described the wings as follows: "Naval Aviation Observers (Radar) shall wear a gold embroidered or bronze gold-platted metal pin, winged, with silver center device superimposed upon crossed gold-color foul anchors. The center piece shall have superimposed upon it, in bold relief and in gold color, a symbolic radar manifestation. The insignia shall measure 2¾" from tip to tip of wings; silver center device shall be approximately ¹⁵⁄₃₂" in diameter; crossed foul anchors shall be of a size to be inscribed in a circle ¾" in diameter. Naval Aviation Observers (Radar) shall not wear any other aviation breast insignia."

A Bureau of Naval Personnel letter dated 18 March 1947 abolished the Naval Aviation Observers (Radar) insignia, and authorized all officers designated as Naval Aviation Observers (Radar) to wear the same insignia prescribed for Naval Aviation Observers.

The photograph shows the Naval Aviation Observers (Radar) Wing insignia used by the Navy for the period 1945–1947.

Naval Aviation Observers (Tactical) Wing

On 19 January 1946, the Secretary of the Navy approved the Naval Aviation Observers (Tactical) wings for Navy and Marine Corps officers performing duty as gunfire and artillery spotters and general liaison operations. A BuPers Circular Letter Number 28-46 of 5 February 1946 changed the 1941 Uniform Regulations to reflect that Naval Aviation Observers (Tactical) would wear a device similar to the Naval Aviation Observer (Navigation) insignia except "the centerpiece shall have two crossed guns superimposed upon it, in bold relief and in gold color." The PuPers letter provided the following description: "Naval Aviation Observers (Tactical) shall wear a gold embroidered or bronze gold-plated metal pin, winged, with silver center device superimposed upon crossed gold-color foul anchors. The center piece shall have two crossed guns superimposed upon it, in bold relief and in gold color. The insignia shall measure 2¾″ from tip to tip of wings; silver center device shall be approximately ¹⁵/₃₂″ in diameter; crossed foul anchors shall be of a size to be inscribed in a circle ¾″ in diameter and the crossed guns shall be of a size to be inscribed in a circle ¹³/₃₂″ in diameter."

A Bureau of Naval Personnel letter dated 18 March 1947 abolished the Naval Aviation Observers (Tactical) insignia and authorized all officers designated as Naval Aviation Observers (Tactical) to wear the same insignia prescribed for Naval Aviation Observers.

The photograph shows the Naval Aviation Observers (Tactical) Wing insignia used by the Navy for the period 1946–1947.

Naval Aviation Observer (Aerology)

BuPers Circular Letter Number 87-47 of 15 May 1947 established the designation Naval Aviation Observer (Aerology). Besides establishing the qualifications necessary to be designated a Naval Aviation Observer (Aerology), the circular letter also stated the following: "Officers designated naval aviation observers (aerology) by the Chief of Naval Personnel will be authorized to wear the insignia already established for naval aviation observers . . ." BuPers letter (Pers-329-MEB A2-3) of 24 February 1948 issued Change 1 to the 1947 Uniform Regulations and states: "*Naval Aviation Observer Insignia.* Officers who have been designated as naval aviation observers, Naval Aviation Observers (Aerology), Naval Aviation Observers (Navigation), Naval Aviation Observers (Radar), or Naval Aviation Observers (Tactical) by the Chief of Naval Personnel shall wear the following insignia: A gold embroidered or bronze gold-plated metal pin, winged, with a central device consisting of an "O" circumscribing an erect, plan anchor, both in silver; the "O" and the anchor to be in bold relief, the center of the "O" being filled with gold. The insignia shall measure 2¾″ between wing tips; the outer diameter of the "O" shall be ¾″, the inner diameter ⁹/₁₆″; height of anchor shall be ½″. The embroidered device shall be on a background to match the color of the uniform." See the Naval Aviation Observer Wing section for a photograph of the Naval Aviation Observer Wing.

Naval Flight Officer Wings

On 8 February 1965, a change to Bureau of Personnel Instruction 1210.4C authorized a new designator and name, Naval Flight Officer (NFO). The new designator was appropriate for "an unrestricted line officer, a member of the aeronautical organization . . . who may fill any billet not requiring actual control knowledge of an aircraft." Eight subspecialties were available at the time: bombardier, controller, electronic countermeasures evaluator, navigator, interceptor, photographer-navigator, tactical coordinator and reconnaissance navigator. The new NFOs continued wearing the Naval Aviation Observer wings.

On 18 July 1968, the CNO approved a new qualification breast insignia for Navy and Marine Corps personnel designated as Naval Flight Officers (NFOs). BuPers Notice 1020 of 24 August 1968 changed the Uniform Regulations (NAVPers 15665). The notice stated: "This new insignia will replace the Naval Aviation Observer insignia currently worn by Naval Flight Officers and will be authorized for wear upon source availability. The Naval Aviation Observer insignia will become obsolete after 31 December 1968." In this change to the Uniform Regulations (NAVPERS

15665) all references to Naval Aviation Observers were changed to Naval Flight Officer. Article 0157.2d. of the Uniform Regulations read: *"Naval Flight Officer Insignia.* A gold embroidered or gold color metal pin; winged, with a central device consisting of a shield superimposed on a set of small, crossed, fouled anchors. The embroidered device shall be on a background to match the color of the uniform on which worn."

The Naval Flight Officer wings were approved to

The photograph shows the Naval Flight Officer wings approved in 1968.

keep pace with the changes to the designators and new titles for personnel that had been designated Naval Aviation Observers. Flight officers are more closely aligned with pilots as opposed to meteorologists and other scientists. Also, the flying officer/crewmen were line officers who were allowed to compete for and earn any command assignment for which they qualify by demonstrated performance and ability, with the exception of a billet that required actual control knowledge of an aircraft. Hence, Naval Flight Officers were line officers who could qualify for command of a ship or carrier or commanding officer of a squadron just like Naval Aviators.

Navy and Marine Corps Parachutist Wing Insignia

BuPers Notice 1020 of 12 July 1963 issued information on a change to the 1959 Uniform Regulations concerning the adoption of a new wing insignia for Navy and Marine Corps Parachutists. This notice stated: "The old parachutist insignia . . . shall be renamed the 'Basic Parachutist Insignia' in conformance with the Army and Air Force nomenclature. The subject insignia shall be referred to as the 'Navy and Marine Corps Parachutist Insignia'." The description of the insignia was as follows: "A gold embroidered (Navy only) or gold-colored metal pin, same as that provided for Naval Aviator's insignia, except that a gold-colored open parachute shall be centered on the wings vice the shield and foul anchor; width of the wings from tip to tip shall be 2¾″; width of the parachute ½″ at the widest part; length of the parachute from top to bottom ¹³⁄₁₆″."

General qualifications for wearing the Navy and Marine Corps Parachutist Wings were:

(1) Have previously qualified for the Basic Parachutist insignia by completing formal parachutist training at an Armed Services installation.

(2) Have completed a minimum of five additional parachute jumps, under competent orders, with a Navy or Marine Corps organization whose mission includes parachute jumping.

Once a person qualified for the Navy and Marine Corps Parachutist insignia it will be worn in lieu of the Basic Parachutist insignia.

The photograph shows the Navy and Marine Corps Parachutist insignia approved in 1963.

Basic Parachutist Wing Insignia

The first mention of a parachutist designation and qualification badge is found in a change to the 1941 Uniform Regulations issued by a BuNav Circular Letter Number 51-42 of 31 March 1942. The circular letter stated: "The following Parachute Regulations, having been approved by the Secretary of the Navy on 6 February 1942, are published herewith for the information of all concerned:

1. (2) *DESIGNATION:* The designation (ratings) of 'Parachutist' and 'Student Parachutist' are hereby established for officers, warrant officers, and enlisted men of the Navy and Marine Corps of the United States, which designations (ratings) shall be in addition to such military or Naval ratings or ranks as are now or may hereafter be authorized by law.

(5) *RETENTION OF DESIGNATION AS PARACHUTIST OR STUDENT PARACHUTIST:* An officer, warrant officer or enlisted man of the Navy . . . who has attained a designation (rating) as a parachutist or student parachutis . . . provided, that officers, warrant officers, and enlisted men . . . who have been designated as parachutists pursuant to these regulations are authorized to retain permanently and to wear such qualification badge as parachutists as may be prescribed by competent authority."

However, the Secretary of the Navy did not authorize the parachutist badge, even though the above change to the 1941 Uniform Regulation references the wearing of such a qualification badge. There is no description of a parachutist insignia until January 1947. A BuPers letter (Pers-329-MEB A2-3) of 17 January 1947 issued changes to the 1941 Uniform Regulations as approved by the Secretary of the Navy. This letter states: "(j) A parachutist insignia, enclosure (B), has been authorized for enlisted personnel who have been designated as parachutists in accordance with the Bureau of Naval Personnel Manual. This insignia is the same as the parachutist insignia authorized by the Marine Corps and the Army. 2. The wearing of the parachutist insignia, enclosure (B), by officers and warrant officers who have been designated as parachutists in accordance with the Bureau of Naval Personnel Manual has also been authorized. Pending a revision of Chapters II and III, U.S. Navy Uniform Regulations, 1941, officers and warrant officers who are eligible to wear the parachutist insignia may do so under similar regulations contained in Art. 8-8 of enclosure (A)." A 14 February 1947 letter from BuPers issued the new Chapter II to the 1941 Uniform Regulations and included the parachutist insignia.

The 1951 Uniform Regulations described the Parachutist insignia as follows: "An open parachute, in silver, flanked on each side by wings, curved upward; the device to be 1½″ wide and ¾″ high." A BuPers Notice 1020 of 12 July 1963 issued information on a change to the 1959 Uniform Regulations concerning the adoption of a new wing insignia for Navy and Marine Corps Parachutists. This notice stated: "The old

parachutist insignia . . . shall be renamed the 'Basic Parachutist Insignia' in conformance with the Army and Air Force nomenclature."

Photograph of Basic Parachutist insignia.

Marine Aerial Navigator Wing

In June 1976, the Marine Corps approved the use of the old World War II Naval Aviation Observer (Navigation) wings for use by Marine Corps personnel who qualified as Marine Aerial Navigators. See the section on Naval Aviation Observer (Navigation) wings for a description and photograph of the wings.

Marine Aerial Observer Wing

See the section on Naval Aviation Observer and Flight Meteorologist Wings. These are the wings worn by Marine Aerial Observers.

A Bat missile on the wing of a Navy Privateer, USN-701606.

A Loon missile being launched from Carbonero (SS 337), USN-402800.

APPENDIX 21

List of Naval Aviation Drones and Missiles

Pilotless Aircraft/Drones/Targets/Remotely Piloted Vehicles

New and Old Model Designation	Manufacturer	Popular Name	Description
————	Bristol Siddeley Corp/LTV	Jindivik	Guided missile target drone
————	————	Glimps	ASW pilotless plane, released from blimps, never used
AQM-34B/KDA-1	Ryan	Firebee	Subsonic target drone
AQM-34C/KDA-4	Ryan	Firebee	Subsonic target drone
AQM-37A/KD2B-1	Beech	Challenger	Air-launched supersonic target missile
AQM-37C	Beech	Jayhawk	Supersonic missile target
AQM-38B/RP-78	Northrop Ventura	————	Army contract, missile target
AQM-127	LTV Corp.	SLAT	Supersonic low-altitude target
AQM-81B	Teledyne Ryan	Firebolt	A Navy modified AQM-81A target missile
BQM-6C/KDU-1	Chance Vought	————	BuAer managed, target drone version of Regulus I
BQM-34E/KDA series	Ryan	Firebee II	Navy version of BQM-34A, supersonic target drone
BQM-34S	Ryan	Firebee II	Upgraded BQM-34E with integrated target control
BQM-34T	Ryan	Firebee II	BQM-34E modified with transponder set and autopilot
BQM-74C	Northrop	Chukar III	Recoverable, remotely controlled, gunnery target
BQM-74E	Northrop	————	Subscale, subsonic aerial target drone
BQM-126A	Beech	————	Variable speed target missile
BQM-145A	Teledyne Ryan	Peregrine	Reconnaissance drone
BQM-147A	RPV Industries	————	Remotely/automatically piloted vehicle
CQM-10A	NAVAIR	BOMARC	Converted Air Force weapon system to missile target
DSN/QH-50C	Gyrodyne	DASH	Remotely controlled ASW helicopter
F.B./N-9	————	Flying Bomb	N-9 configured as a Flying Bomb
F.B.	Sperry-Curtiss	Flying Bomb	
F.B.	Witteman-Lewis	Flying Bomb	
KAQ	Fairchild Engine & A/c Co.	————	Pilotless aircraft
KAY	Consolidated Vultee A/c Co.	————	Ship-to-air pilotless aircraft
KDA-1(BQM-34 series)	Ryan	Firebee I	Target aircraft
KDB (see MQM-39A)	Beech	————	
KDC-1	Curtiss-Wright Corp.	————	Mid-wing monoplane target, not procured
KDD-1 (see KDH-1)	McDonnell	Katydid	
KDG-1	Globe	Snipe	Mid-wing monoplane for gunnery practice
KDG-2	Globe	Snipe	Similar to KDG-1 except for 24 volt system
KDH-1/TD2D-1/KDD-1	McDonnell	Katydid	Remotely controlled aerial target
KDM-1	Martin	Plover	High wing air launched, development of PTV-N-2
KDR-1/TD4D-1	Radioplane	Quail	Similar to TD3D-1, Army model OQ-17
KDR-2	Radioplane	Quail	Similar to KDR-1 except structural changes
KDT-1	Temco	————	Solid propellant rocket-powered drone
KDU-1	————	————	Target drone for guided missile evaluation firings
KD2C-1	Curtiss-Wright Corp.	Skeet	Pilotless aircraft target drone
KD2G-1	Globe	Firefly	Mid-wing, all metal, twin tail, monoplane target
KD2G-2	Globe	Firefly	Similar to KD2G-1
KD2N-1	NAMU	————	High mid-wing monoplane, canard design
KD2R-1	Radioplane	Quail	Wooden wings, metal monocoque fuselage target drone

Pilotless Aircraft/Drones/Targets/Remotely Piloted Vehicles—Continued

New and Old Model Designation	Manufacturer	Popular Name	Description
KD2R-2	Radioplane	Quail	Similar to KD2R-1 except 28 volt radio & stabilized
KD2R-2E	Radioplane	Quail	KD2R-2 modified system for test at NAMTC
KD2R-3	Radioplane	Quail	Similar XKD2R-4 except engine & C-2A stabilization
KD2U	Chance Vought Corp.	——	Conversion Regulus II to supersonic drones
KD3G-1	Globe	Snipe	Same as KDG-1 except for engine
KD3G-2	Globe	Snipe	Same as KD3G-1 with radio control receiver 28 volt
KD4G-1	Globe	Quail	High all metal wing gunnery trainer
KD4G-2	Globe	Quail	Similar to KD4G-1 except engine and higher speed
KD4R-1	Radioplane	——	Rocket propelled target drone
KD5G-1	Globe	——	High wing and twin tail aircraft target
KGN/KUN	NAMU	——	High wing monoplane, canard design target drone
KGW/KUW	——	——	Pilotless aircraft
KSD/KUD	——	——	Pilotless aircraft
KU2N-1/KA2N-1	NAMU	——	High midwing monoplane, canard design, liquid rocket
KU3N-1/KA3N-1	NAMU	——	High midwing monoplane, conventional, liquid rocket
KU3N-2/KA3N-2	NAMU	——	Similar to KU3N-1
KUD-1/LBD-1/KSD-1/BQM-6C	McDonnell	Regulus I	BuAer managed, target drone version of Regulus I
KUM	Glenn Martin Company	——	Pilotless aircraft for testing ram jet power plant
KUN-1/KGN-1	NAMU	——	High wing monoplane, canard design target drone
LBE-1	Gould/Pratt-Read & Co.	Glomb	Expendable bomb-carrying guided assult glider
LBP	Pratt-Read & Co.	Glomb	Was scheduled for development.
LBT-1	Taylorcraft	Glomb	Expendable bomb-carrying guided glider
LNS-1	Schweizer	Glomb	Glider test vehicle for Glomb
LNT-1	Naval Aircraft Factory	Glomb	Assault glider television controlled
LRN-1	Naval Aircraft Factory	Glomb	Large explosive carrying glider
LRW-1	——	Glomb	Test vehicle for Glomb
MQM-8	Bendix Aerospace	Vandal/Vandel ER	Reconfigured Talos for simulating cruise missile
MQM-15A/KD2U-1	Chance Vought	Regulus II	BuAer program, conversion Regulus II to target drone
MQM-36A/KD2R-5	Northrop Ventura	——	Small propeller driver target drone
MQM-39A/KDB-1	Beech	——	
MQM-61A	Beech	——	
MQM-74C	Northrop	Chukar II	Turbojet, remotely controlled drone, target training
RP-78	Northrop Ventura	——	Army contract, missile target
RPV	AAI Corp.	Pioneer	Remotely Piloted Vehicle with television camera
TD2C-1	Culver	Turkey	Target drone for aircraft and anti-gunnery training
TD2D-1/XTD2D-1	McDonnell	——	Remotely controlled aerial target, RESO-JET powered
TD2N-2/TD3N-1	NAF/NAMU	——	Target aircraft
TD2R	Interstate	——	Assault drone, program dropped
TD3C-1	Culver	——	Target drone for aircraft and anti-aircraft training
TD3D-1	Frankfort Sailplane Co.	——	Target drone, similar to TDD-3, Army model OQ-16
TD3N-1	NAF	——	Target aircraft
TD3R-1	Interstate	——	Torpedo carrying remote-controlled assault drone
TD4D-1	Radioplane	——	Target drone, Army model OQ-17
TDC-2	Culver Air	——	Target drone
TDD-1/2/3	Radioplane/Globe	Denny	Remotely controlled aerial target, gunnery practice
TDD-4	Radioplane/Globe	Denny	Same as TDD-3 except for engine
TDN	Naval Aircraft Factory	——	World War II assault drone
TDR	Interstate	——	World War II assault drone
XBDR-1	Interstate	——	WW-II jet powered, television directed assault drone
XBQ-3	Fairchild Corp.	——	Assault Drone, Army Air Corps controllable bomb
XKD3C-1	Curtiss	——	Similar to KD2C-2 with engine change, no rudder
XKD6G-1	Globe	——	Similar to KD2G-2, except for engine, new fuselage

Pilotless Aircraft/Drones/Targets/Remotely Piloted Vehicles—Continued

New and Old Model Designation	Manufacturer	Popular Name	Description
XKD6G-2	Globe	——	Similar to KD6G-1, except for engine
XQM-40A/KD6G-2	Globe Corp.		
XUC-1K	Culver	——	XUC-1 aircraft converted to target drone
YAQM-128A	TBD	——	Air launched, supersonic subscale aerial target
YBQM-126A	TBD/Beechcraft	——	Supersonic subscale target
ZBQM-90A	TBD	——	High altitude, supersonic aerial target

Note: The above list does not include aircraft modified for use as drones or towed targets.

Aircraft Configured as Drones/Flying Bombs, Early Period to 1945

Aircraft Designation	Comments
BG-1	Pre-WW-II aircraft configured as radio controlled drone
F4B	Configured as a drone.
F4U	Configured as a drone.
F6F	Configured as a drone.
JH-1	Modified aircraft, Stearman Hammond
N-9 F.B.	Experiments to make a flying bomb out of an N-9 training plane, 1917.
N2C	1937, first successful pilotless aircraft flight
NT	Modified training plane, New Standard Aircraft Corp.
O2U	Configured as a drone.
O3U	Configured as a drone.
PB4Y	Project Anvil, radio & television controlled PB4Y loaded with torpex, flown out of England against a German target, one attack flown with limited success.
PBJ	Configured as a drone.
SB2C	Configured as a drone.
SBD	Configured as a drone.
SBU	Configured as a drone.
SF-1	Configured as a drone.
SNB	Configured as a drone.
SNV	Configured as a drone.
SO3C	Matson Navigation Company converted the SO3C planes into target drones.
Sperry-Curtiss F.B.	Flying Bomb developed from a Curtiss Company Speed Scout plane, WW-I.
TBM	Configured as a drone.
TG-2	NAF converted a TG-2 plane into a radio controlled plane capable of carrying a torpedo and conducted experiments by VU-3.
VE-7H	1924 experiment with radio controlled VE-7
Witteman-Lewis F.B.	BuOrd contract with company to design a flying bomb more successful than Sperry-Curtiss F.B., airframe similar to Speed Scout, tests conducted 1919-1921.

Air-to-Ground/Air-to-Surface Missiles

New and Old Model Designation	Manufacturer	Popular Name	Description
30.5 inch Rocket	NOTS/NWC China Lake	BOAR	Bombardment Aircraft Rocket, a stand-off weapon
5 inch Rocket	——	HVAR/Holy Moses	Five inch aircraft rocket, developed during WW-II, numerous Mks and Mods for this series.
2.75 inch Rocket	NOTS/NWC China Lake	Mighty Mouse/FFAR	2.75 inch folding-fin aircraft rocket, numerous Mks and Mods for this series.
——	BuOrd/BuAer/Zenith/G.E.	Pelican/Dryden Bomb	Glide bomb, terminated late 1944
XSUM-N-2	Bureau of Standards	Grebe/Kingfisher E	Member of the Kingfisher missile projects
AGM-109C	General Dynamics	MRASM	A medium range missile, never completed development
AGM-109L	General Dynamics	Tomahawk	Medium-range, air-launched, land/sea attack missile
AGM-114B	Rockwell	Hellfire	Missile for helicopters, with various capabilities
AGM-114E	USAMICOM	Hellfire	AGM-114B modified with digital autopilot
AGM-119B	NORSK/FORSVARSTEKNOLOG	Penguin Mk-2	AGM-119A, with modified warhead, fuze, rocket motor
AGM-122	NWC China Lake/Motorola	Sidearm	Sidewinder anti-radiation missile, built from AIM-9C and designed to attack radar directed air defense system, variations of AGM-122 developed.
AGM-123A	Naval Weapons Center	Skipper	Modified laser guided bomb, with Shrike rocket motor
AGM-12A/ASM-N-7	Martin/Maxson	Bullpup	Tactical air-to-surface short range radio controlled
AGM-12B/ASM-N-7A	Martin/Maxson	Bullpup	Upgraded AGM-12A, radio-link command guidance
AGM-12C/ASM-N-7B	Martin	Bullpup	Upgraded AGM-12B
AGM-136A	Northrop Corp.	Tacit Rainbow ARM	Anti-radiation missile, long range, terminated.
AGM-45A/ASM-N-10	Texas Instruments/Sperry-Farragut	Shrike	Tactical missile used to destroy radar targets, developed by NOTS
AGM-45B	Texas Instruments/Sperry-Farragut	Shrike	Upgraded AGM-45A
AGM-53A/ASM-N-11	North American/Rockwell/NWC	Condor	Long range, electro-optical guided missile, cancelled.
AGM-53B	North American/Rockwell/NWC	Condor	Upgraded AGM-53A with EMI capability, not completed.
AGM-65E/F/G	Hughes	Maverick	Navy version of AGM-65, TV-guided, laser guided or IR guidance, tactical missile.
AGM-78A/B/C/D	General Dynamics	Standard ARM	Tactical, anti-radiation missile, upgrades listed.
AGM-83A	NWC	Bulldog	Used parts of AGM-12A, laser guided
AGM-84E SLAM	McDonnell Douglas	Harpoon/SLAM	A standoff land attack missile variant of Harpoon
AGM-84A/C/D	McDonnell Douglas	Harpoon	Air-to-surface missile designed to destroy ships, upgrades listed.
AGM-86B	——	ALCM	Air launched cruise missile, see AGM-109L Tomahawk
AGM-87A	Naval Wpns Ctr/G.E.	FOCUS I/FOCUS II	Sidewinder AIM-9B modified for air-to-surface use.
AGM-88A/B/C	Naval Weapons Center/Texas Instruments/Ford Aero	HARM	Anti-radiation missile used against surface radar, upgrades listed.
AQM-41A/AUM-N-2	Fairchild	Petrel/Kingfisher C	Air-to-underwater/surface tactical guided missile
ASM-2/ASM-N-2	Nat'l Bureau of Standards	Bat-0	Glider operational missile
ASM-N-2A	Nat'l Bureau of Standards	Bat-1	Similar to ASM-N-2
XASM-N-4/XASM-4	Eastman/BuOrd	Dove	Stand-off delivery missile, never operational
XASM-N-5	NADC	Gorgon V	Glide offensive missile
XASM-N-8/XASM-8/XM-17	Temco Aircraft Corp.	Corvus	Air to surface attack missile, never operational
XAUM-2	Bureau of Standards	Petrel/Kingfisher C	
XAUM-N-4/XAUM-4	Bureau of Standards	Diver/Kingfisher D	
XAUM-N-6/XAUM-6	Bureau of Standards	Puffin/Kingfisher F	
YAGM-114B	Rockwell	Hellfire	Navy version of AGM-114A, anti-armor missile

Note: The above list does not include training missiles, i.e. ATMs, CATMs, or DATMs.

Surface-to-Surface/Surface-to-Ship Missiles and Special Category Rockets

New and Old Model Designation	Manufacturer	Popular Name	Description
——	——	Albatross	Ship-to-ship missile
——	Consolidated-Vultee	Old Rippy	Automatic FM homing, pulse-jet, ship-to-ship
——	BuAer/BuOrd/NBS/NAOTS	Regal	Experimental program, air launched Regulus
——	Aerojet-General Corp.	Aerobee-Hi	Similar to Aerobee, a vertical sounding rocket
——	Applied Physics Lab	Triton	Program cancelled in 1957
RGM-15A/SSM-N-9	Chance Vought/LTV Aerospace	Regulus II	Surface-to-surface missile developed by BuAer
RGM-6A/SSM-8/SSM-N-8	Chance Vought	Regulus I	BuAer managed program
RGM-6B/SSM-N-8A	Chance Vought	Regulus I	BuAer managed program
RIM-7	BuWps/Raytheon	Seaspar/Sea Sparrow	Sparrow III used in a surface-to-surface or SAM mode
RTV-N-15	NADC	Pollux	Also known as Gorgon IIC, see CTV-N-2, test vehicle
RTV-N-8/RTV-8/XASR-1	BuOrd/Douglas Aircraft Co.	Aerobee	A liquid fueled rocket for upper atomosphere research
XSSM-N-6/XSSM-6/PA-VII	Grumman	Rigel	Missile fired from surface ship against land targets
XSSM-N-9	Applied Physics Lab	Lacrosse	

Note: Surface-to-surface missiles designed primarily for ship-based operations, such as the Taurus, Talos, Tartar, Terrier, and Standard Missile have not been included in the above list.

Surface-to-Air and Special Launch Test Missiles or Rockets

New and Old Model Designation	Manufacturer	Popular Name	Description
——	——	Arrow Shell	See Zeus (XSAM-N-8)
——	NAMU	Gorgon IIIB	Conventional airframe with turbo jet, eliminated.
——	NADS	Gorgon IIB	High mid-wing monoplane, canard design, turbo jet
CTV-8/RTV-6/XPM	Navy/Applied Physics Lab	Bumblebee	Program led to development of Tartar, Terrier, Talos and Typhon. The Typhon was cancelled.
CTV-N-10/KAY-1/XSAM-4	Consoliated Vultee Aircraft	Lark	Ship-to-air, variable incidence wings (test vehicle)
CTV-2/CTV-N-2/KGN-1/KUN-1	NADC	Gorgon IIC	Monoplane canard design, pulse jet, ship-to-shore
CTV-4/CTV-N-4/KA2N-1	NADC	Gorgon IIA	Monoplane, canard design with rocket, also KU2N-1
CTV-N-6/KA3N-1/KU3N-1	NADC	Gorgon IIIA	High mid-wing monoplane, conventional design, rocket
CTV-N-9/KAQ-1/XSAM-2	Fairchild	Lark	Ship-to-air guided missile, used wing flaps
CTV-N-9a/b/c	Fairchild	Lark	Ship-to-air guided missile, test vehicle
CTV-N-10	Convair	Lark	Test vehicle
KAN-1	NAMU	Little Joe	Ship-launched, use against aircraft suicidal attacks
KAN-2	NAMU	Little Joe	Similar to KAN-1, never operational.
KUD-1/RTV-2 (see RTV-N-2)	——	Gargoyle	
KUW-1 (see NTV-N-2)	USAF procurement	Loon	Test vehicle
LTV-N-2/LTV-2/KGW-1	Willys-Overland/AAF	Loon	Similar to German V-1, Launching Test Vehicle
PTV-N-2/PTV-2/KUM-1	Martin	Gorgon IV	Vehicle for testing subsonic ram jet engine
RTV-N-2/LBD-1/KSD-1	McDonnell	Gargoyle	Low wing monoplane V-tail, aerial bomb
RTV-N-4/KA3N-2/KU3N-2	NADC	Gorgon III-C	Similar to CTV-6, dual rockets, conventional design
TD2N/KDN-1	NAMU	Gorgon	Monoplane, conventional design, turbo jet
TD3N-1/KD2N-1	NADS	Gorgon	Canard, resojet power plant, similar to Gorgon IIC
XSAM-6 (see XSAM-N-6)	——	Bumblebee	
XSAM-N-6	Navy/Applied Physics Lab	Triton/Bumblebee II	Program cancelled
XSAM-N-8	NOL	Zeus	

Air-to-Air Missiles

New and Old Model Designation	Manufacturer	Popular Name	Description
——	NELC/Hughes Aircraft	Brazo/Pave ARM	Anti-radiation missile
——	——	Lady Bug	Short range, adaption of German X-4
AAM-N-3	Douglas	Sparrow II	Production version of YAAM-N-3
ADM-141A	Brunswick Defense Corp.		Air launched decoy to create a false radar image
ADM-141B	Brunswick Defense Corp.		Air launched decoy which despenses chaff
AEM-54A	Hughes	Phoenix	AIM-54A with telemetry evaluation kit
AEM-54B	Hughes	Phoenix	AIM-54A, telemetry equipment, missile flight evals
AIM-120A	Hughes	AMRAAM	Advanced medium-range, beyond visual range combat
AIM-54A/AAM-N-11/AIM-54C	Hughes	Phoenix	Long-range, tactical, air-to-air missile,upgrades listed
AIM-7A/AAM-N-2/KAS-1	Sperry	Sparrow I	Short range beam-rider missile
AIM-7B/AAM-N-3	Douglas	Sparrow II	Cancelled.
AIM-7C/AAM-N-6	Raytheon	Sparrow III	Semi-active radar homing, CW seeker radar homing, mid range
AIM-7D/E/F/M/AAM-N-6A/B	Raytheon	Sea Sparrow/Sparrow III	Supersonic launch version, upgrades listed
XAIM-95A	NWC China Lake	Agile	Short-range, for aerial combat, cancelled
AIM-9A/AAM-N-7	Philco	Sidewinder I	
AIM-9B/AAM-N-7	Philco/General Electric	Sidewinder 1A	IA Supersonic, homing weapon, passive infrared
AIM-9C/AAM-N-7	Motorola	Sidewinder 1C-SARAH	Semi-active radar guided
AIM-9D/AAM-N-7	Philco/Raytheon	Sidewinder 1C-IRAH	IR upgraded AIM-9B, infrared homing radar guiding
AIM-9G	Raytheon	Sidewinder	Upgraded AIM-9D
AIM-9H	Raytheon (GCG only)	Sidewinder	Upgraded AIM-9G with solid state guidance control
AIM-9J	Philco	Sidewinder	Upgraded AIM-9E
AIM-9L/M/N/P/S	Raytheon	Sidewinder	Upgrades listed
AIM-9R	NWC	Sidewinder	Cancelled

Note: The above list does not include training versions or electronic monitoring designations, i.e. ATMs, CAEMs, and DATMs.

Experimental or Proto-type Air-to-Air Missiles

RAAM-N-2A	Sperry	Sparrow I	Converted AAM-N-2 Sparrow I, R&D Test Missile
RAAM-N-2B	Sperry	Sparrow IA	Converted AAM-N-2, R&D Test Missile
XAAM-N-10	Bendix Aviation Corp.	Eagle/Missileer	Long range air-to-air high performance missile
XAAM-N-4/RV-N-16	Martin	Oriole	Long range antiaircraft, active radar seeker
XAAM-N-5	MIT/BuOrd	Meteor	
XAIM-54C	Hughes	Phoenix	Experimental AIM-54C with digital technology
YAAM-N-3	Douglas	Sparrow II	Preproduction version of XAAM-N-3
YAIM-120A	Hughes		Prototype AIM-120A
YAIM-54C	Hughes	Phoenix	Prototype AIM-54C
YAIM-7F	Raytheon	Sparrow	Improved version of AIM-7E
YAIM-7G	Raytheon	Sparrow	Similar to YAIM-7F, with modifications
ZAIM-9K	Raytheon	Sidewinder	Upgraded AIM-9H

Guided Weapons, Air-to-Ground

2 inch FFAR	NOTS	Gimlet	Air launched rocket development
5 inch FFAR	NOTS China Lake	Zuni	5 inch aircraft rocket, replaced the HVAR/Holy Moses
AGM-62A	NWC/Martin Marietta	Walleye I Mk 1	An electro-optical glide weapon, passive homing
——	NWC/Martin Marietta	Walleye II Mk 5/Fat Albert	Similar to Walleye I, with larger warhead
——	NWC/Martin Marietta	Walleye I Mk 22	Similar to Walleye I, with RF data link
——	NWC/Martin Marietta	Walleye II Mk 13	Similar to Walleye II, with RF data link
——	NWC	Paveway II	Laser guided bomb

HOW TO READ MISSILE DESIGNATIONS

Missile Designations (Pre-1962)
Alphabetical Symbols Used in Missile Designations

Pilotless Aircraft/Target Drones (Type K)	*Test Vehicles (Type TV)*		*Tactical Weapons—Guided Missiles (Type M)*	
KD	CTV	Control	AAM	Air-to-Air
	LTV	Launch	ASM	Air-to-Surface
	PTV	Propulsion	AVM	Air-to-Underwater
	RTV	Research	SAM	Surface-to-Air
			SSM	Surface-to-Surface

Test Vehicles

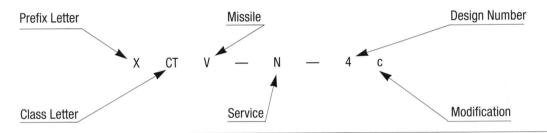

Tactical Weapon—Guided Missile

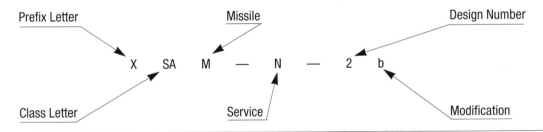

Pilotless Aircraft/Target Drone Designation

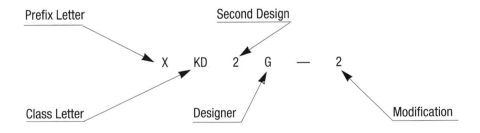

Note: Prior to 1962, normal man carrying aircraft configured as a drone used the original aircraft designation with a K at the end of the designation; i.e. F6F-5K.

Missile Designations (Post-1962)
Alphabetical Symbols Used in Missile Designations

Status Prefix		Launch Environment		Mission		Vehicle Type	
C	Captive	A	Air	C	Transport	B	Booster
D	Dummy	B	Multiple	D	Decoy	M	Guided Missile/Drone
J	Special Test (Temporary)	C	Coffin	E	Electronic/Communications	N	Probe
M	Maintenance	F	Individual	G	Surface Attack	R	Rocket
N	Special Test (Permanent)	G	Runway	I	Aerial /Space Intercept	S	Satellite
X	Experimental	H	Silo Stored	L	Launch Detection/Surveillance	K	Pilotless Aircraft
Y	Prototype	L	Silo Launched	M	Scientific/Calibration	V	Drone
Z	Planning	M	Mobile	N	Navigation		
R	Research	P	Soft Pad	Q	Drone		
		R	Ship	S	Space Support		
		S	Space	T	Training		
		U	Underwater	U	Underwater Attack		
				W	Weather		

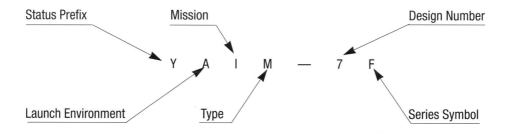

Note: After 1962, normal man carrying aircraft configured as a drone would use the original design preceded by the letter Q, i.e. QF-86D.

U.S. Navy and Marine Corps Aces

The Navy Department has never officially compiled or issued a list of "Aces". During World War II, the period with the largest number of aerial shoot downs for naval flyers, the Navy did not keep an overall record of individual scores in aerial combat, hence, there is no official list of confirmed shoot-downs.

The most comprehensive work done on Navy and Marine Corps World War II Aces was written and published by Mr. Frank Olynyk. His two books are *USN Credits for the Destruction of Enemy Aircraft in Air-to-*

Air Combat World War II, Victory List No. 2, published in 1982, and *USMC Credits for the Destruction of Enemy Aircraft in Air-to-Air Combat World War II,* published in 1981. In 1986 the *Naval Aviation News* magazine published a list of U.S. Navy and Marine Corps Aces that had been compiled by Mr. Olynyk. The following list of Aces, as published by the magazine in 1986, includes Mr. Olynyk's World War II list and also those from World War I, Korea, and Vietnam:

	Name	Service	Time Frame ****		Name	Service	Time Frame ****
*	Aldrich, Donald N.	USMC			Blackburn, John T.	USN	
	Alley, Stuart C., Jr.	USMC		**	Blair, Foster J.	USN	
	Amsden, Benjamin C.	USN			Blair, William K.	USN	
	Anderson, Alexander L.	USN			Blaydes, Richard B.	USN	
	Anderson, Robert H.	USN			Blyth, Robert L.	USN	
***	Andre, John W.	USMC			Bolduc, Alfred G.	USN	
	Axtell, George C.	USMC			Bolt, John F., Jr.	USMC	
	Bailey, Oscar C.	USN			Bolt, John F., Jr.	USMC	Korea
	Baird, Robert	USMC			Bonneau, William J.	USN	
*	Baker, Douglas	USN			Bordelon, Guy P.	USN	Korea
	Baker, Robert M.	USMC			Borley, Clarence A.	USN	
	Bakutis, Fred E.	USN		*	Boyington, Gregory	USMC	
	Balch, Donald L.	USMC			Boyle, Gerald F.	USN	
	Baldwin, Frank B.	USMC			Brassfield, Arthur J.	USN	
	Balsiger, Henry W.	USN			Braun, Richard L.	USMC	
	Banks, John L.	USN			Brewer, Charles W.	USN	
	Barackman, Bruce M.	USN			Bridges, Johnnie J.	USNR	
	Bardshar, Frederic A.	USN			Bright, Mark K.	USN	
	Bare, James D.	USN			Brocato, Samuel J.	USN	
	Barnard, Lloyd G.	USN			Brown, Carl A., Jr.	USN	
	Barnes, James M.	USN			Brown, William P., Jr.	USMC	
	Bartol, John W.	USN			Bruneau, Paul J.	USN	
**	Bassett, Edgar R.	USN			Brunmier, Carland E.	USN	
	Bate, Oscar M., Jr.	USMC			Bryce, James A.	USN	
	Batten, Hugh N.	USN			Buchanan, Robert L.	USN	
	Bauer, Harold W.	USMC			Buie, Paul D.	USN	
	Beatley, Redman C.	USN			Burckhalter, William E.	USN	
	Beaudry, Paul H. N.	USN			Burley, Franklin N.	USN	
	Beebe, Marshall U.	USN			Burnett, Roy O., Jr.	USN	
	Berkheimer, Jack S.	USN			Burriss, Howard M.	USN	
	Berree, Norman R.	USN		**	Bushner, Frances X.	USN	
	Bertelson, Richard L.	USN		*	Byrnes, Matthew S., Jr.	USN	
**	Billo, James D.	USN			Cain, James B.	USN	
	Bishop, Walter D.	USN			Carey, Henry A., Jr.	USN	

	Name	Service	Time Frame ****		Name	Service	Time Frame ****
	Carl, Marion E.	USMC			Dewing, Lawrence A.	USN	
	Carlson, Robert B.	USN			Dibb, Robert A. M.	USN	
	Carlton, William A	USMC			Dillard, Joseph V.	USMC	
	Carmichael, Daniel A., Jr.	USN			Dillow, Eugene	USMC	
	Carr, George R.	USN			Dobbin, John F.	USMC	
	Carroll, Charles H.	USN			Donahue, Archie G.	USMC	
	Case, William N.	USMC			Doner, Landis E.	USN	
	Caswell, Dean	USMC			Dorroh, Jefferson D.	USMC	
	Chambers, Cyrus J.	USN			Doyle, Cecil J.	USMC	
	Champion, Henry K.	USN			Drake, Charles W.	USMC	
	Chandler, Creighton	USMC			Driscoll, Daniel B. J.	USN	
	Check, Leonard J.	USN			Driscoll, William P. (NFO)	USN	Vietnam
	Chenoweth, Oscar I., Jr.	USN			Drury, Frank C.	USMC	
	Clark, Lawrence A.	USN			Drury, Paul E.	USN	
	Clark, Robert A.	USN			Duffy, James E.	USN	
	Clarke, Walter E.	USN			Duncan, George C.	USN	
	Clements, Robert E.	USN			Duncan, Robert W.	USN	
	Clements, Donald C.	USN			Dungan, Fred L.	USN	
	Coats, Robert C.	USN			Dunn, Bernard	USN	
	Coleman, Thaddeus T., Jr,	USN			Durnford, Dewey F.	USMC	
	Coleman, William M.	USN			Eastmond, Richard T.	USN	
	Collins, William M., Jr.	USN			Eberts, Byron A.	USN	
	Conant, Arthur R.	USMC		**	Eccles, William G	USN	
	Conant, Edwin S.	USN			Eckard, Bert	USN	
	Conger, Jack E.	USMC			Eder, William E.	USN	
	Conroy, Thomas J.	USN			Edwards, William C., Jr.	USN	
	Copeland, William E.	USN			Elliott, Ralph E., Jr.	USN	
	Cordray, Paul	USN			Elwood, Hugh M.	USMC	
	Cormier, Richard L.	USN			Enman, Anthony J.	USN	
**	Cornell, Leland B.	USN			Erickson, Lyle A.	USN	
	Cowger, Richard D.	USN			Evenson, Eric A.	USN	
	Cozzens, Melvin	USN			Everton, Loren D.	USMC	
	Craig, Clement M.	USN			Fair, John W.	USN	
	Cronin, Donald F.	USN			Farmer, Charles D.	USN	
	Crosby, John T.	USN			Farnsworth, Robert A., Jr.	USN	
	Crowe, William E.	USMC			Farrell, William	USMC	
	Cunningham, Daniel G.	USN			Fash, Robert P.	USN	
	Cunningham, Randall H.	USN	Vietnam		Fecke, Alfred J.	USN	
	Cupp, James N.	USMC			Feightner, Edward L.	USN	
	Dahms, Kenneth J.	USN			Ferko, Leo M.	USN	
	Davenport, Merl W.	USN			Finn, Howard J.	USMC	
	Davidson, George H.	USN			Fisher, Don H.	USMC	
	Davies, Clarence E.	USN		**	Flatley, James H., Jr.	USN	
	Davis, Leonard K.	USMC			Fleming, Francis M.	USN	
	Davis, Robert H.	USN			Fleming, Patrick D.	USN	
	Dean, William A., Jr.	USN			Flinn, Kenneth A.	USN	
	Dear, John W., Jr.	USN			Foltz, Frank E.	USN	
	De Blanc, Jefferson J.	USMC			Foltz, Ralph E.	USN	
	De Cew, Leslie	USN			Fontana, Paul J.	USMC	
***	Delong, Philip C.	USMC			Ford, Kenneth M.	USMC	
	Denman, Anthony J.	USN			Formanek, George, Jr.	USN	
	Denoff, Reuben H.	USN			Forrer, Samuel W.	USN	
	Devine, Richard O.	USN		*	Foss, Joseph J.	USMC	

Name	Service	Time Frame ****		Name	Service	Time Frame ****
Foster, Carl C.	USN			Heinzen, Lloyd P.	USN	
Fowler, Richard E., Jr.	USN			Henderson, Paul M., Jr.	USN	
Franger, Marvin J.	USN			Henry, William E.	USN	
Franks, John M.	USN			Hernan, Edwin J., Jr.	USMC	
Fraser, Robert B.	USMC			Hibbard, Samuel B.	USN	
Frazier, Kenneth D.	USMC			Hildbrandt, Carlos K.	USN	
Freeman, Doris C.	USN			Hill, Harry E.	USN	
Freeman, William B.	USMC			Hills, Hollis H.	USN	
French, James B.	USN			Hippe, Kenneth G.	USN	
Frendberg, Alfred L.	USN			Hoag, John B.	USN	
Funk, Harold N.	USN			Hoel, Ronald W.	USN	
Gabriel, Franklin T.	USN			Hollowell, George L.	USMC	
Galer, Robert E.	USMC			Hood, William L., Jr.	USMC	
Galt, Dwight B., Jr.	USN			Houck, Herbert N.	USN	
Galvin, John R.	USN			Hudson, Howard R.	USN	
Gayler, Noel A. M.	USN			Huffman, Charles W., Jr.	USN	
Gildea, John T.	USN			Humphrey, Robert J.	USN	
Gile, Clement D.	USN			Hundley, John C.	USMC	
Gillespie, Roy F.	USN			Hurst, Robert	USN	
Godson, Lindley W.	USN			Ingalls, David S.	USN	WW-I
Gordon, Donald	USN			Ireland, Julius W.	USMC	
Graham, Vernon E.	USN			Jaques, Bruce D.	USN	
Gray, James S., Jr.	USN			Jennings, Robert H., Jr.	USN	
Gray, John F.	USN			Jensen, Hayden M.	USN	
Gray, Lester E., Jr.	USN			Jensen, Alvin J.	USMC	
Gregory, Hayden A.	USN			Johannsen, Delmar K.	USN	
Griffin, Richard J.	USN			Johnson, Byron M.	USN	
Gustafson, Hadan I.	USN			Johnson, Wallace R.	USN	
Gutt, Fred E.	USMC			Johnston, John M.	USN	
Haas, Walter A.	USN			Jones, Charles D.	USMC	
Haberman, Roger A.	USMC			Jones, James M.	USN	
Hacking, Albert E., Jr,	USMC			Kaelin, Joseph	USN	
Hadden, Mayo A., Jr.	USN			Kane, William R.	USN	
Hall, Sheldon O.	USMC			Keith, Leroy W. J.	USN	
Hamblin, Lewis R.	USN			Kendrick, Charles	USMC	
Hamilton, Henly B.	USMC		*	Kepford, Ira C.	USN	
Hamilton, Robert M.	USN			Kerr, Leslie H., Jr.	USN	
Hanks, Eugene R.	USN			Kidwell, Robert J.	USN	
Hansen, Herman, Jr.	USMC			Kincaid, Robert A.	USN	
* Hanson, Robert M.	USMC			Kingston, William J., Jr.	USN	
Hardy, Willis E.	USN			Kinsella, James J.	USN	
Hargreaves, Everett C.	USN			Kirk, George N.	USN	
Harman, Walter R.	USN			Kirkpatrick, Floyd C.	USMC	
* Harris, Cecil E.	USN			Kirkwood, Philip L.	USN	
Harris, Leroy E.	USN			Knight, William M.	USN	
Harris, Thomas S.	USN			Kostik, William J.	USN	
Harris, William H., Jr.	USN			Kunz, Charles M.	USMC	
Haverland, Charles H., Jr.	USN			Laird, Dean S.	USN	
Hawkins, Arthur R.	USN			Laird, Wayne W.	USMC	
Hayde, Frank R.	USN			Lake, Kenneth B.	USN	
Hearrell, Frank C., Jr.	USN		***	Lamb, William E.	USN	
Heath, Horace W.	USN			Lamoreaux, William E.	USN	
Hedrick, Roger R.	USN			Laney, Willis G.	USN	

	Name	Service	Time Frame ****		Name	Service	Time Frame ****
	Langdon, Ned W.	USN			Mollenhauer, Arthur P.	USN	
	Leonard, William N.	USN			Montarpert, John R.	USN	
	Leppla, John A.	USN			Moranville, Horace B.	USN	
	Lerch, Alfred	USN			Morgan, John L., Jr.	USMC	
	Lillie, Hugh D.	USN			Morris, Bert D., Jr.	USN	
	Lindsay, Elvin L.	USN			Moseley, William C.	USN	
	Loesch, Gregory K.	USMC			Mulcahy, Douglas W.	USN	
	Long, Herbert H.	USMC			Mullen, Paul A.	USMC	
	Lundin, Walter A.	USN			Munsen, Arthur H.	USN	
	Lynch, Joseph P.	USMC			Murray, Robert E.	USN	
	Maas, John B.	USMC			Narr, Joseph L.	USMC	
	Mabarry, Lewin A.	USN			Nelson, Robert J.	USN	
	Magee, Christopher L.	USMC			Nelson, Robert K.	USN	
	Mahe, Thomas R., Jr.	USMC			Noble, Myrvin E.	USN	
	Mallory, Charles M.	USN		*	Nooy, Cornelius N.	USN	
	Mankin, Lee P., Jr.	USN			Novak, Marvin R.	USN	
	Mann, Thomas H., Jr.	USMC			Null, Cleveland L.	USN	
	Manson, Armand G.	USN			O'Hare, Edward H.	USN	
	March, Harry A., Jr.	USN			O'Keefe, Jeremiah J.	USMC	
	Marontate, William P.	USMC			O'Mara, Paul, Jr.	USN	
	Martin, Albert E., Jr.	USN			Olander, Edwin L.	USMC	
	Masoner, William J., Jr.	USN			Olsen, Austin L.	USN	
	Maxwell, William R.	USN			Orth, John	USN	
	May, Richard H.	USN			Ostrom, Charles H.	USN	
	May, Earl, Jr.	USN			Outlaw, Edward C.	USN	
	Mazzocco, Michele A.	USN			Overend, Edmund F.	USMC	
*	McCampbell, David	USN			Overton, Edward W., Jr.	USN	
	McCartney, Henry A.	USMC			Owen, Donald C.	USMC	
	McClelland, Thomas G.	USN			Owen, Edward M.	USN	
	McClure, Edgar B.	USN			Owens, Robert G., Jr.	USMC	
	McClurg, Robert W.	USMC			Parrish, Elbert W.	USN	
	McCormick, William A.	USN			Paskoski, Joseph J.	USN	
	McCuddin, Leo B.	USN			Payne, Frederick R., Jr.	USMC	
	McCuskey, Elbert S.	USN			Pearce, James L.	USN	
	McGinty, Selva E.	USMC			Percy, James G.	USMC	
	McGowan, Edward C.	USN			Philips, David P., III	USN	
	McGraw, Joseph D.	USN			Phillips, Edward A.	USN	
	McKinley, Donald J.	USN			Phillips, Hyde	USMC	
	McLachlin, William W.	USN			Picken, Harvey P.	USN	
	McManus, John	USMC			Pierce, Francis E., Jr.	USMC	
	McPherson, Donald M.	USN			Pigman, George W., Jr.	USN	
	McWhorter, Hamilton, III	USN			Pittman, Jack, Jr.	USMC	
	Mehle, Roger W.	USN			Plant, Claude W., Jr.	USN	
	Menard, Louis A., Jr.	USN			Pond, Zenneth A.	USMC	
	Mencin, Adolph	USN			Pool, Tilman E.	USN	
**	Merritt, Robert S.	USN			Pope, Albert J.	USN	
	Michaelis, Frederick H.	USN			Porter, Robert B.	USMC	
	Miller, Johnnie G.	USN			Poske, George H.	USMC	
	Milton, Charles B.	USN			Post, Nathan T., Jr.	USMC	
	Mims, Robert	USN			Pound, Ralston M., Jr.	USN	
	Mitchell, Harris E.	USN			Powell, Ernest A.	USMC	
	Mitchell, Henry E., Jr.	USN			Prater, Luther D., Jr.	USN	
	Mollard, Norman W., Jr.	USN			Presley, Frank H.	USMC	

	Name	Service	Time Frame ****		Name	Service	Time Frame ****
	Prichard, Melvin M.	USN			Slack, Albert C.	USN	
	Quiel, Norwald R,	USN			Smith, Armistead B., Jr.	USN	
**	Ramlo, Orvin H.	USMC			Smith, Carl E.	USN	
	Reber, James V., Jr.	USN			Smith, Clinton L.	USN	
	Redmond, Eugene D.	USN			Smith, Daniel F., Jr.	USN	
	Register, Francis R.	USN		*	Smith, John L.	USMC	
	Rehm, Dan R., Jr.	USN			Smith, John M.	USN	
	Reidy, Thomas H.	USN			Smith, Kenneth D.	USN	
	Reinburg, Joseph H.	USMC			Smith, Nicholas J., III	USN	
	Reiserer, Russell L.	USN			Snider, William N.	USMC	
	Rennemo, Thomas J.	USN			Sonner, Irl V., Jr.	USN	
	Reulet, Joseph E.	USN			Southerland, James J., III	USN	
	Revel, Glenn M.	USN		*	Spears, Harold L.	USMC	
	Rhodes, Thomas W.	USN			Spitler, Clyde P.	USN	
	Rieger, Vincent A.	USN			Stanbook, Richard E.	USN	
	Rigg, James F.	USN			Stanley, Gordon A.	USN	
	Roach, Thomas D.	USN			Starkes, Carlton B.	USN	
	Robbins, Joe D.	USN			Stebbins, Edgar E.	USN	
	Robinson, Leroy W.	USN			Stewart, James S.	USN	
	Robinson, Ross F.	USN		*	Stimpson, Charles R.	USN	
	Rosen, Ralph J.	USN			Stokes, John D.	USN	
	Ross, Robert P.	USN			Stone, Carl V.	USN	
	Rossi, Herman J., Jr.	USN			Stout, Robert F.	USMC	
	Ruhsam, John W.	USMC			Strane, John R.	USN	
	Runyon, Donald E.	USN			Strange, Johnnie C.	USN	
	Rushing, Roy W.	USN			Streig, Frederick J.	USN	
	Sapp, Donald H.	USMC			Sturdevant, Harvey W.	USN	
	Sargent, John J., Jr.	USN			Sutherland, John F.	USN	
	Savage, Jimmie E.	USN		*	Swett, James E.	USMC	
	Scales, Harrell H.	USN			Swinburne, Harry W., Jr.	USN	
	Scarborough, Hartwell V., Jr.	USMC			Swope, James S.	USN	
	Schecter, Gordon E.	USN			Symmes, John C. C.	USN	
	Schell, John L.	USN			Synar, Stanley T.	USMC	
	Scherer, Raymond F.	USMC			Taylor, Ray A., Jr.	USN	
	Schiller, James E.	USN			Taylor, Will W.	USN	
	Schneider, Frank E.	USN			Terrill, Francis A.	USMC	
	Seckel, Albert, Jr.	USN			Thach, John S.	USN	
	See, Robert B.	USMC			Thelen, Robert H.	USN	
	Segal, Harold E.	USMC			Thomas, Franklin C., Jr.	USMC	
	Self, Larry R.	USN			Thomas, Robert F.	USN	
	Shackford, Robert W.	USN		*	Thomas, Wilbur J.	USMC	
	Shands, Courtney	USN			Toaspern, Edward W.	USN	
	Shaw, Edward O.	USMC			Topliff, John W.	USN	
	Sherrill, Hugh V.	USN			Torkelson, Ross E.	USN	
	Shields, Charles A.	USN			Townsend, Eugene P.	USN	
	Shirley, James A.	USN			Tracey, Fredrick W.	USN	
	Shuman, Perry L.	USMC			Troup, Franklin W.	USN	
	Sigler, Wallace E.	USMC			Trowbridge, Eugene A.	USMC	
	Silber, Sam L.	USN			Traux, Myron M.	USN	
	Singer, Arthur, Jr.	USN			Turner, Charles H.	USN	
	Sipes, Lester H.	USN			Turner, Edward B.	USN	
	Sistrunk, Frank	USN			Twelves, Wendell V.	USN	
	Skon, Warren A.	USN			Ude, Vernon R.	USN	

Name	Service	Time Frame ****	Name	Service	Time Frame ****
Umphfres, Donald E.	USN		White, Henry S.	USN	
* Valencia, Eugene A.	USN		Williams, Bruce W.	USN	
Valentine, Herbert J.	USMC		Williams, Gerard M. H.	USMC	
Van Der Linden, Peter J., Jr.	USN		Wilson, Robert C.	USN	
Van Dyke, Rudolph D., Jr.	USN		Winfield, Murray	USN	
Van Haren, Arthur, Jr.	USN		Winston, Robert A.	USN	
Vedder, Milton N.	USMC		Winters, Theodore H., Jr.	USN	
Vejtasa, Stanley W.	USN		Wirth, John L.	USN	
Vineyard, Merriwell W.	USN		Wolf, John T.	USN	
Vita, Harold E.	USN		Wood, Walter A.	USN	
Voris, Roy M.	USN		Wooley, Millard J.	USN	
Vorse, Albert O., Jr.	USN		Woolverton, Robert C.	USN	
* Vraciu, Alexander	USN		Wordell, Malcolm T.	USN	
Wade, Robert	USMC		Wrenn, George L.	USN	
* Walsh, Kenneth A.	USMC		Yeremain, Harold	USN	
Ward, Lyttleton T.	USN		Yost, Donald K.	USMC	
Warner, Arthur T.	USMC		Yunck, Michael R.	USMC	
Watson, Jack O.	USN		Zaeske, Earling W.	USN	
Watts, Charles E.	USN		Zink, John A.	USN	
Webb, Wilbur B.	USN				
Weissenberger, Gregory J.	USMC				
Wells, Albert P.	USMC				
Wesolowski, John M.	USN				
West, Robert G.	USN				

* Aces with 15 kills or more.
** Unconfirmed as aces in World War II.
*** Ace status acquired from combined kills of World War II and Korea.
**** Timeframe is World War II unless indicated otherwise.

Visual Identification System for Naval Aircraft (Tail Codes)

The rapid and accurate identification of aircraft has always been of prime importance within Naval Aviation. The explosive expansion of Naval Aviation during World War II compounded this problem.

A three-part identification system had been in use in the fleet from 1923 until World War II. Under this system, the aircraft identification number 5-F-1, which was placed on the fuselage of the plane, meant this was the first airplane in Fighting Squadron 5. After July 1937, the squadron number for carrier based squadrons was the same as the hull number of the carrier. Thus Yorktown (CV 5) would have had VB-5, VS-5 and VF-5 assigned as part of her complement of squadrons. This system was modified by Commander Carriers, Pacific Fleet, on 29 April 1942. To help conceal the identity of carriers engaged in operations in enemy waters, the squadron number was eliminated, leaving just the letter designating the type of squadron and the aircraft number within the squadron. Thus, the marking on the fuselage of the plane would have been F-1 to identify it as the first plane in a fighting squadron without identifying the squadron's number. This was further modified on 22 December 1943, by the deletion of the squadron type letter. All identification as to a specific unit was now removed which allowed aircraft to be drawn from a pool as necessary without the requirement of painting identification information on them.

During World War II, with the increase in the number of fleet aircraft operating in the same area as training planes, the necessity grew even more acute to quickly differentiate the large number of training planes from the operational fleet aircraft. To alleviate this problem, Naval Air Operational Training Command, on 12 January 1943, directed that all aircraft within the command be identified by an alpha/numeric system consisting of three groups of characters. The first letter(s) designated the base assignment for the aircraft. The second letter identified the aircraft mission, while the third group was the number of the aircraft within the squadron. For an example, V-T-29 would indicate the aircraft was from Vero Beach, Fla., it was a torpedo plane, and the 29th aircraft in that Vero Beach, Fla., training unit.

During the last two years of the war, many of the aircraft assigned to the carriers in the Pacific carried symbols denoting the ship or air group to which they were assigned. No directive specifying these markings are known to exist, if there ever were any. From a review of photos of the period, it appears that the symbols were assigned to the CV designated aircraft carriers. While the Escort Carriers, designated CVE, had the symbol assigned to the squadrons that operated aboard the CVEs. Squadrons operating aboard the CVs only had that specific symbol while assigned to that particular carrier. While this was a step in the right direction, the lack of a uniform system was soon apparent when a large number of aircraft were trying to rendezvous after takeoff, before landing or over target areas.

The United States Navy Air Force, Pacific Fleet, issued a standard set of twenty-eight geometrical designs for the CV and CVL class carriers which constituted Task Force 58. These designs were assigned to the vessel and were applied to all aircraft of the attached air group as long as it was aboard. They were applied to both sides of the fin and rudder. While the drawings in the directive only showed the design on the top surface of the right wing, subsequent directives indicate that it was also to be applied on the under surface of the left wing tip.

The Commander, Air Force, Pacific Fleet, on 11 February 1945, issued an instruction for the aircraft in the Hawaiian Sea Frontier. All carrier and training type aircraft were to be identified with a letter followed by the individual aircraft number running from 1 to 99. These markings were not for the purpose of security, but rather to identify U.S. Navy aircraft after numerous reports of violations of air discipline involving flying too close to transport aircraft and ground installations.

Air Force, Pacific Fleet, on 2 June 1945, prescribed a series of recognition symbols for CVEs. These markings were to be painted on both sides of the vertical tail surfaces, as well as the upper right and lower left wing tips. All CVEGs, MCVGs and VCs assigned to ships of the Escort Carrier Force, Pacific, were to carry these designs. Each Carrier Division was assigned a basic design. The position of the individual vessel within the Division was indicated by a series of narrow stripes.

The system of geometrical symbols carried by Task Force 58 aircraft was difficult to describe over the radio and was not always readily identifiable in the air. To eliminate this problem, Commander Task Force 38, in July 1945, specified a system of 24-inch block capital letters to be used to identify the aircraft of the CVs and CVBs. These letters were to be applied to both sides of the fin and rudder as well as the top right and lower left wing tips. In its original form some ships used a single letter, while others were assigned double letters. This was the beginning of the two-letter Visual Identification System in use today.

Naval Air Stations in Hawaii were assigned letter designations on 10 September 1945, by the Commander, Air Force, Pacific Fleet. These letters were to be followed by a number from 1 to 99 inclusive. In the event all available numbers in the 1 to 99 series were used, and no additional letters were available, the use of numbers over 100 was authorized.

On 8 January 1946, Air Force, Pacific Fleet, issued instructions for the application of markings on the fast carrier aircraft. This directive also assigned new alphabetical designations for the CVs and CVBs and CVLs in place of those specified by Commander Task Force 38. This assignment of the same letter to a different carrier than previously designated, may well have caused the erroneous identification of some photographs as to what ship the aircraft were actually assigned.

All of the previous directives or instructions were a search for an easy system to rapidly identify aircraft. Finally, on 7 November 1946, the Chief of Naval Operations (CNO) established the Visual Identification System for all Navy and Marine Corps aircraft. To be effective, such a system had to be simple, readable and possess enough different combinations to cover the number of aircraft carriers and all types of squadrons to which naval aviation might expand in case of war. A system using letters satisfies these requirements as long as distinctive characters are used. The elimination of the ambiguous letters G, J, N, O, Q and Y left ample combinations to cover such expansion. Since each letter has a phonetic equivalent in communication procedures, the problem of describing geometric markings was replaced by the simple process of enunciating the names of the letters of the alphabet. Under this system each aircraft carrier had either a single or double letter symbol, some of which were a hold over from the previous system. On 12 December 1946, the Visual Identification System of Naval Aircraft was modified by CNO. Under this change the tail codes assigned to the carriers were now reassigned to individual air groups. This permit-

ted greater flexibility since an air group was not permanently assigned to a specific carrier.

Under the CNO system, non-carrier based squadrons, such as VP, VPP, VPW, VPM, VU, VRU, VX and VCN squadrons also used a letter system. In these squadrons the first of the two letters designated the wing or class while the second letter designated the squadron within the wing. Marine Corps carrier-based squadrons used the letters assigned to the parent carrier. While shore-based Marine squadrons used the first letter to designate the Wing or other command, and the second letter identified the squadron within the Wing or Command. The letters in all cases were underscored to denote Marine. It was possible under this system to have the same code letters assigned to a Navy squadron and a Marine Corps squadron concurrently. This requirement to underscore the letters on Marine Corps aircraft was rescinded on 4 August 1948.

The Training Command continued to use the letter number designation system in which the first of one or two letters designated the base or station, while the second letter identified the squadron and/or class designation. The aircraft within the squadron were identified by a one, two or three digit number. The Chief, Naval Air Training, controlled the assignment of the letter symbols within the Training Command.

Naval Air Reserve aircraft were also identified by two letters. The first letter denoted the Air Station to which the aircraft was assigned, while the second letter identified the type of squadron. From this it can be seen that it was possible to have a fleet squadron and a reserve squadron identified with the same two letters. This was resolved by the use of the orange belly band around the fuselage to denote a Reserve aircraft. Reorganization of the Naval Air Reserve in 1970 arranged the reserve squadron system along the same lines as the active fleet structure. The tail code assignments for these squadrons was redone to following the procedures used for the fleet squadrons.

Naval Air Advanced Training Command on 6 January 1947 issued a directive for identifying aircraft within the command. This alpha/numeric system used a letter to identify the Naval Air Station, followed by a second letter designating the squadron at that activity and then a three digit aircraft number. On 31 August 1950, the Chief Naval Air Basic Training issued a direcitve that involved single letters to denote aircraft assigned to the various bases. This was modified on 27 September 1950 to a two-letter system whereby the first letter designated the base and the second letter the squadron. These letters were followed by a three-digit number to denote the individual aircraft within the squadron. On 6 September 1956, Chief of Naval Air Training established a new tail code identification system for the training commands. This system included two character alpha/numberic codes whereby the number 2 designated Chief Naval Air Basic Training Command aircraft, 3 designated Chief Naval Air Advanced Training Command and 4 designated Chief Naval Technical Training Command aircraft.

One major change to occur was the move from a single letter to two letters to idenify an air group's tail code. The effective date for this change was most likely the beginning of Fiscal Year 1958 (1 July 1957). Specific documenation has not been discovered to ver-ify this date. However, the tail code (Visidual Identification System) listing in the Naval Aeronautical Organization for 1957 shows the changes for the air group tail codes to two letters.

Even though numerous changes have been made since 7 November 1946 to the Visual Identification System, the basic tenet of the system has remained intact. The following is a listing of Tail Codes (Visual Identification System for Naval Aircraft) for Naval Aviation as of the end of 1995:

Command	Tail Code
Blue Angels	BA

Carrier Air Wings (former designation Carrier Air Groups)

Command	Tail Code
CVW-1	AB
CVW-2	NE
CVW-3	AC
CVW-5	NF
CVW-7	AG
CVW-8	AJ
CVW-9	NG
CVW-11	NH
CVW-14	NR
CVW-17	AA
RCVW-4*	AD
RCVW-12**	NJ
CVWR-20	AF

Carrier AEW

Command	Tail Code
CAEWW-12	GE

ASW Air Groups

Command	Tail Code
CVSG-50***	AR
CVSG-51****	RA
HELWINGRES	NW

Fleet Composite

Command	Tail Code
VC-6	JG
VC-8	GF

Fleet Logistic Support

Command	Tail Code
VRC-30	RW
VRC-40	JK

Fleet Logistics Support Reserve

Command	Tail Code
VR-46	JS

Command	Tail Code
VR-48	JR
VR-52	JT
VR-53	WV
VR-54	CW
VR-55	RU
VR-56	JU
VR-57	RX
VR-58	JV
VR-59	RY
VR-61	RS
VR-62	JW

Helicopter Antisubmarine Light

Command	Tail Code
HSL-37	TH
HSL-40	HK
HSL-41	TS
HSL-42	HN
HSL-43	TT
HSL-44	HP
HSL-45	TZ
HSL-46	HQ
HSL-47	TY
HSL-48	HR
HSL-49	TX
HSL-51	TA
HSL-84	NW
HSL-94	NW

Naval Air Systems Command

Command	Tail Code
Test Pilot School	TPS

MARTD'S/Marine Support

Command	Tail Code
HQMC	5A
MCAS Beaufort	5B
MCAS Cherry Point	5C
MCAS El Toro	5T
MCAS Futenma	5F

Command	Tail Code	Command	Tail Code
MCAS Iwakuni	5G	HC-11	VR
MCAS New River	5D	HC-85	NW
MCAS YUMA	5Y		

Naval Air Stations (NAS)		**Patrol**	
		VP-1	YB
Alameda	7J	VP-4	YD
Brunswick	7F	VP-5	LA
Cecil Field	7U	VP-8	LC
Fallon	7H	VP-9	PD
Jacksonville	7E	VP-10	LD
Key West	7Q	VP-11	LE
Lemoore	7S	VP-16	LF
Memphis	7K	VP-26	LK
Norfolk	7C	VP-30	LL
North Island	7M	VP-40	QE
Oceana	7R	VP-45	LN
Patuxent River	7A	VP-46	RC
Point Mugu	7L	VP-47	RD
Whidbey Island	7G	VPU-1	OB
		VPU-2	SP

Naval Air Warfare Center Weapons Division			
China Lake	7P	**Patrol Reserve**	
		VP-62	LT
		VP-64	LU
Naval Air Warfarfe Center Naval Aircraft Division		VP-65	PG
Patuxent River	SD	VP-66	LV
		VP-68	LW
		VP-69	PJ
Navy Support		VP-91	PM
		VP-92	LY
NAF Atsugi	8A	VP-94	PZ
NAF El Centro	8N		
NAVSTA Guam	8J		
NAVSTA Guantanamo	8F	**Air Test and Evaluation**	
NAVSTA Mayport	8U	VX-1	JA
NAF Mildenhall	8G	VX-9	XE
NAF Misawa	8M		
COMFLTACT Okinawa	8H		
NAVSTA Roosevelt Roads	8E	**Antarctic Development**	
NAVSTA Rota	8D	VXE-6	XD
NAS Sigonella	8C		
HQ CMEF (Bahrain)	8K		
		Helicopter Mine Countermeasure Squadron	
Helicopter Combat Support		HM-14	BJ
		HM-15	TB
HC-2	HU		
HC-3	SA		
HC-4	HC	**Fleet Tactical Readiness Group**	
HC-5	RB		
HC-6	HW	COMFEWSG	GD
HC-8	BR		

Command	Tail Code	Command	Tail Code
Fleet Air Reconnaissance		VMFA-235	DB
		VMFA-251	DW
VQ-1	PR	VMFA-312	DR
VQ-2	JQ	VMFA-314	VW
VQ-3	TC	VMFA-323	WS
VQ-4	HL	VMFA-451	VM
VQ-5	SS		
VQ-6	ET	**Tactical Electronic Warfare**	
		VMAQ-1	CB
Fleet Marine and Marine Support Units		VMAQ-2	CY
Headquarters		VMAQ-3	MD
		VMAQ-4	RM
MWHS-1	SZ		
MALS-10	SE	**Aerial Refueler/Transport**	
MALS-11	TM		
MALS-12	WA	VMGR-152	QD
MALS-13	YU	VMGR-252	BH
MALS-14	CN	VMGR-352	QB
HAMS-16	WW		
MALS-24	EW	**Observation**	
MALS-26	EL		
HQSQDN-17	CZ	VMO-1	ER
MALS-31	EX	VMO-2	UU
MALS-36	WK		
HQSSDN-37	QF	**Fleet Training**	
		VMAT-203	KD
Attack		VMFAT-101	SH
		VMFT-401	WB
VMA-211	CF		
VMA-214	WE	**Fleet Readiness**	
VMA-223	WP		
VMA-231	CG	VMGRT-253	GR
VMA-331	VL		
VMA-513	WF	**Helicopter Heavy**	
VMA-542	CR	HMH-361	YN
		HMH-362	YL
All-weather Attack		HMH-363	YZ
		HMH-366	HH
VMA(AW)-332	EA	HMH-461	CJ
		HMH-462	YF
All-weather Fighter Attack		HMH-463	YH
		HMH-464	EN
VMFA(AW)-121	VK	HMH-465	YJ
VMFA(AW)-224	WK	HMH-466	YK
VMFA(AW)-242	DT		
VMFA(AW)-225	CE	**Helicopter Medium**	
VMFA(AW)-533	ED		
		HMM-161	YR
Fighter Attack		HMM-162	YS
VMFA-115	VE		
VMFA-122	DC		
VMFA-212	WD		

Command	Tail Code	Command	Tail Code
HMM-163	YP		VT-21 B
HMM-164	YT		VT-22 B
HMM-165	YW		VT-23 B
HMM-166	YX		JTTU B
HMM-261	TV		
HMM-262	ET	TRAWING FOUR	
HMM-263	EG		
HMM-264	EH	Corpus Christi	G
HMM-265	EP		VT-27 G
HMM-266	ES		VT-28 G
HMM-268	YQ		VT-31 G
HMM-364	PF		
HMM-365	YM		
		TRAWING FIVE	

Helicopter Light

Command	Tail Code
HMLA-167	TV
HMLA-169	SN
HMLA-267	UV
HMLA-269	HF
HMLA-367	VT
HMLA-369	SM

Helicopter Training

Command	Tail Code
HMT-204	GX
HMT-301	SU
HMT-303	QT

Helicopter

Command	Tail Code
HMX-1	MK

Unmanned Aerial Vehical Operations

Command	Tail Code
1st UAV	FZ
2d UAV	FF
FAST	FS
C Company	FH
VC-6 Det	FR
DUTCH	FD

Chief of Naval Air Training

TRAWING ONE

Command	Tail Code
Meridian	A
	VT-19 A

TRAWING TWO

Command	Tail Code
Kingsville	B

TRAWING FIVE

Command	Tail Code
Whiting Field	E
	VT-2 E
	VT-3 E
	VT-6 E
	HT-8 E
	HT-18 E

TRAWING SIX

Command	Tail Code
Pensacola	F
	VT-4 F
	VT-10 F
	VT-86 F

Chief of Naval Technical Training

Command	Tail Code
NATTC Lakehurst	4L
NAS Memphis	4M

Chief Naval Reserve

Command	Tail Code
Atlanta	7B
Dallas	7D
Selfridge	7Y
Glenview	7V
New Orleans	7X
South Weymouth	7Z
Washington, DC	7N
Willow Grove	7W

Naval Air Reserve

Command	Tail Code
Jacksonville	6F
Alameda	6G
Memphis	6M
Norfolk	6S

Command	Tail Code	Command	Tail Code
Fourth Marine Aircraft Wing		HMM-764	ML
HQ 4TH MAW	EZ	HML-767	MM
H&MS-41	MY	VMA-131	QG
VFMA-112	MA	VMGR-234	QH
VMA-142	MB	HML-771	QK
HMA-773	MP	HML-776	QL
HMM-774	MO	HMH-777	QM
H&MS-49	QZ	VMA-124	QP
HMH-769	MS	VMGR-452	NY
HMH-772	MT		
VMO-4	MU		
H&MS-42	MW		
HMA-775	WR		
VMA-134	MF		
VMFA-321	MG		
H&MS-46	QY		

* Disestablished on 1 June 1970. RCVW-4 tail letters retained by the following squadrons: VF-101 and VAW-120.

** Disestablished on 1 June 1970. RCVW-12 tail letters retained by the following squadrons: VAQ-129 and VS-41.

*** Disestablished on 17 February 1971. CVSG-50 tail letters retained by the following squadrons: VS-30 and HS-1.

**** Disestablished on 30 June 1971. CVSG-51 tail letters retained by the following squadron: HS-10

Squadron insignia, past and present, showing squadron designation in the lower scroll.

Squadron insignia, past and present, showing squadron designation in the lower scroll.

Current Squadron Lineage List

How to Trace Squadron Lineage

The lineage and history of U.S. Naval Aviation squadrons has been a source of confusion since the birth of Naval Aviation in 1911. Much of this confusion arose from the terminology used by the Navy, the lack of a consistent policy in selecting the alpha-numeric designations for squadrons, constantly reusing the same letter and numeric designations, and the many establishments, redesignations and disestablishments of aviation squadrons.

When dealing with a squadron's lineage, the only correct terms to use are establishment, disestablishment and redesignation. The terms commissioning and establishment have been used interchangeably for years and that is incorrect. Only ships are commissioned, decommissioned and receive commissioning pennants. Squadrons have establishment and disestablishment ceremonies.

A unit's history and lineage begins when it is established and ends at the time it is disestablished. Determining a squadron's "family tree" may seem cut and dried, but that is not the case. A squadron may undergo numerous redesignations during the period between its establishment and disestablishment. A newly established squadron bearing the same designation of a unit that had previously existed may carry on the traditions of the old organization but it cannot claim the history or lineage of the previous unit. The same is true of U. S. Navy ships and, thus, the rationale for such a policy becomes apparent. For example, *Ranger* (CV 61) is the seventh ship to bear the name Ranger and may carry on the traditions of the previous six ships. *Ranger* (CV 61) is obviously not the same Continental Navy Ship *Ranger* commanded by Captain John Paul Jones during the War of Independence. The history of *Ranger* (CV 61) begins with its commissioning date, not with the commissioning date of the first *Ranger*

The most recent squadron with the designation Fighter Squadron One (VF-1) was established 1 October 1972 and disestablished 1 October 1993. It was the seventh squadron in the Navy to be designated VF-1. This squadron is not the same VF-1 that used the designation for the first time in 1922. Designations,

like ship's names, are reused again and again. If there is a break in the active status of a unit designation as a result of a disestablishment, then there is no connection between the units bearing the same designation.

Another common problem area involved squadron insignia. The lineage or history of a squadron cannot be traced using only its insignia, because the same insignia may have been adopted and approved for official use by more than one squadron during different time frames. The insignia of a disestablished squadron may be officially approved for use by another squadron, but this does not confer upon the new squadron the right to the previous unit's history and lineage. The following outline of the Jolly Roger insignia is an example of the confusion that results if one attempts to trace the lineage and history of a squadron insignia without considering other factors.

VF-17 was established on 1 January 1943, and during World War II it produced an outstanding record as a fighter squadron. The Jolly Roger insignia for VF-17 was adopted during World War II. On 15 November 1946, all Navy squadrons were redesignated and VF-17 became VF-5B. Subsequently, it was redesignated VF-61 on 28 April 1948, and then disestablished on 15 April 1959. Commander Hoppe was the Commanding Officer of VF-61 when it was disestablished. The Jolly Roger insignia had been used by VF-17/VF-5B/VF-61 from 1943 until 15 April 1959.

On 2 July 1955, VA-86 was established and on the same day was redesignated VF-84. This squadron was equipped with the FJ Fury and adopted the nickname Vagabonds. An insignia consisting of a lightning bolt striking the world in the area of Norfolk, Va., with a sword behind the bolt, was approved on 27 September 1955. The squadron operated under this name and insignia until it replaced the FJs with F8U Crusaders in 1959. Commander Hoppe assumed command of VF-84 two days after the disestablishment of VF-61, the Jolly Roger squadron. He initiated the request to have VF-84 adopt the old Jolly Roger insignia, which had been used by VF-61 and was no longer active. This request was approved by CNO on 1 April 1960. There is no direct connection between the former Jolly Roger squadron (VF-17/VF-5B/VF-61) and VF-84, which adopted the Jolly Roger insignia. To further complicate a review of the records, there have been other squadrons with the designation VF-84. During World War II, a VF-84 was established on 1 May 1944, and disestablished 8 October 1945. Naval Air Reserve squadron VF-921 was called to active duty 1 February 1951, and was redesignated VF-84 on 4 February 1954. This squadron then became VA-86 on 2 July 1955. This occurred on the same day, the current Jolly Roger squadron was established as VA-86 and immediately redesignated VF-84. Neither of these two VF-84 squadrons had any connection with the original Jolly Rogers. Thus, the present VF-84 operating with the insignia and title of Jolly Roger can lay claim to the traditions of VF-17, VF-5B and VF-61, if it wishes to do so, but can only claim a history which commenced on 2 July 1955, and it is not a direct descendant of the original Jolly Roger squadron.

A squadron's history and lineage covers only the period during which a unit is officially declared active (established by CNO), has personnel assigned to it, and is listed in the Naval Aeronautical Organization. When a squadron is disestablished, its history and lineage ends. If a squadron is redesignated while it is active, the lineage and history of the unit is carried on by the newly redesignated squadron. The following is an example of what occurs when a squadron is redes-

ignated and its lineage and history remain unbroken.

The current VFA-25 was originally established as Torpedo Squadron 17 (VT-17) on 1 January 1943. On 15 November 1946, VT-17 was redesignated VA-6B and carried this designation until 27 April 1948, when it was redesignated VA-65. On 1 July 1959, VA-65 was redesignated VA-25 and the unit remained VA-25 until it was redesignated VFA-25 on 1 July 1983. The history and lineage of the present VFA-25 may be traced to 1 January 1943, because there was no break in active duty status of the squadron, even though its designation changed four times.

The current VFA-106 provides an example of what happens when a squadron is disestablished and then, years later, the same number is used again. This squadron was established at NAS Cecil Field on 27 April 1984. VFA-106 adopted the old insignia of VA-106 and had it officially approved. The squadron may carry on the traditions of the old VA-106, but it cannot trace its lineage and history back to VA-106. The list of commanding officers for VA-106 is not part of the list of commanding officers for VFA-106. The history of VA-106 came to an end on 7 November 1969, when it was disestablished and its personnel were transferred to other duty stations. At this time, VA-106 was removed from the active list in the Naval Aeronautical Organization.

The following is a list of the current Navy squadrons as of 31 December 1995:

Squadron Designation	Changes in Squadron Designations	Date of Change	Squadron Designation	Changes in Squadron Designations	Date of Change
Helicopter Combat Support Squadron			**Helicopter Mine Countermeasures Squadron**		
HC-2*	HC-2 Established	1 Apr 1987	HM-14	HM-14 Established	12 May 1978
HC-3	HC-3 Established	1 Sep 1967	HM-15	HM-15 Established	2 Jan 1987
HC-4*	HC-4 Established	6 May 1983	**Helicopter Anti-Submarine Squadron**		
HC-5*	HC-5 Established	3 Feb 1984	HS-1	HS-1 Established	3 Oct 1951
HC-6	HC-6 Established	1 Sep 1967	HS-2	HS-2 Established	7 Mar 1952
HC-8	HC-8 Established	3 Dec 1984	HS-3	HS-3 Established	18 Jun 1952
HC-11	HC-11 Established	1 Oct 1977	HS-4	HS-4 Established	30 Jun 1952
HC-85	HS-85 Established	1 Jul 1970	HS-5	HS-5 Established	3 Jan 1956
	HS-85 Redesignated HC-85	1 Oct 1994	HS-6	HS-6 Established	1 Jun 1956
Helicopter Combat Support Special Squadron			HS-7*	HS-7 Established	15 Dec 1969
HCS-4	HAL-4 Established	1 Jul 1976	HS-8*	HS-8 Established	1 Nov 1969
	HAL-4 Redesignated HCS-4	1 Oct 1989	HS-10	HS-10 Established	1 Jul 1960
HCS-5	HCS-5 Established	1 Oct 1988			

Squadron Designation	Changes in Squadron Designations	Date of Change
HS-11	HS-11 Established	27 Jun 1957
HS-14	HS-14 Established	10 Jul 1984
HS-15	HS-15 Established	29 Oct 1971
HS-75	HS-75 Established	1 Jun 1970

Helicopter Anti-Submarine Squadron Light

Squadron Designation	Changes in Squadron Designations	Date of Change
HSL-37	HSL-37 Established	3 Jul 1975
HSL-40	HSL-40 Established	4 Oct 1985
HSL-41	HSL-41 Established	21 Jan 1983
HSL-42	HSL-42 Established	5 Oct 1984
HSL-43	HSL-43 Established	5 Oct 1984
HSL-44	HSL-44 Established	21 Aug 1986
HSL-45	HSL-45 Established	3 Oct 1986
HSL-46	HSL-46 Established	7 Apr 1988
HSL-47	HSL-47 Established	25 Sep 1987
HSL-48	HSL-48 Established	7 Sep 1989
HSL-49	HSL-49 Established	23 Mar 1990
HSL-51	HSL-51 Established	1 Oct 1991
HSL-84	HS-84 Established	1 Jul 1970
	HS-84 Redesignated HSL-84	1 Mar 1984
HSL-94	HSL-94 Established	1 Oct 1985

Helicopter Training Squadron

Squadron Designation	Changes in Squadron Designations	Date of Change
HT-8	HTU-1 Established	3 Dec 1950
	HTU-1 Redesignated HTG-1	Mar 1957
	HTG-1 Redesignated HT-8	1 Jul 1960
HT-18	HT-18 Established	1 Mar 1972

Attack Squadron

Squadron Designation	Changes in Squadron Designations	Date of Change
VA-34*	VA-34 Established	1 Jan 1970
VA-75*	VB-18 Established	20 Jul 1943
	VB-18 Redesignated VA-7A	15 Nov 1946

Squadron Designation	Changes in Squadron Designations	Date of Change
	VA-7A Redesignated VA-74	27 Jul 1948
	VA-74 Redesignated VA-75	15 Feb 1950
VA-115	VT-11 Established	10 Oct 1942
	VT-11 Redesignated VA-12A	15 Nov 1946
	VA-12A Redesignated VA-115	15 Jul 1948
	VA-115 was in an inactive status from Aug 1967 to 1 Jan 1970. It was not disestablished during this time frame and had a very limited number of personnel assigned to the squadron which was located at NAS Lemoore during the inactive period.	
	VA-115 Reactivated	1 Jan 1970
VA-165	VA-165 Established	1 Sep 1960
VA-196	VF-153 Established	15 Jul 1948
	VF-153 Redesignated VF-194	15 Jul 1950
	VF-194 Redesignated VA-196	4 May 1955

Tactical Electronic Warfare Squadron

Squadron Designation	Changes in Squadron Designations	Date of Change
VAQ-129	VAH-10 Established	1 May 1961
	VAH-10 Redesignated VAQ-129	1 Sep 1970
VAQ-130	VW-13 Established	1 Sep 1959
	VW-13 Redesignated VAQ-130	1 Oct 1968
VAQ-131	VP-931 Reserve squadron to active duty	2 Sep 1950
	VP-931 Redesignated VP-57	4 Feb 1953
	VP-57 Redesignated VAH-4	3 Jul 1956
	VAH-4 Redesignated VAQ-131	1 Nov 1968
VAQ-132	VAH-2 Established	1 Nov 1955
	VAH-2 Redesignated VAQ-132	1 Nov 1968
VAQ-134	VAQ-134 Established	17 Jun 1969
VAQ-135	VAQ-135 Established	15 May 1969
VAQ-136	VAQ-136 Established	6 Apr 1973
VAQ-138	VAQ-138 Established	27 Feb 1976
VAQ-139	VAQ-139 Established	1 Jul 1983
VAQ-140	VAQ-140 Established	1 Oct 1985
VAQ-141	VAQ-141 Established	1 Jul 1987
VAQ-209	VAQ-209 Established	1 Oct 1977

Squadron Designation	Changes in Squadron Designations	Date of Change
	Carrier Airborne Early Warning Squadron	
VAW-77	VAW-77 Established	1 Oct 1995
VAW-78	VAW-78 Established	1 Jul 1970
VAW-112	VAW-112 Established	20 Apr 1967
VAW-113	VAW-113 Established	20 Apr 1967
VAW-115	VAW-115 Established	20 Apr 1967
VAW-116	VAW-116 Established	20 Apr 1967
VAW-117	VAW-117 Established	1 Jul 1974
VAW-120	RVAW-120 Established	1 Jul 1967
	RVAW-120 Redesignated VAW-120	1 May 1983
VAW-121	VAW-121 Established	1 Apr 1967
VAW-122	VAW-122 Established	1 Apr 1967
VAW-123	VAW-123 Established	1 Apr 1967
VAW-124	VAW-124 Established	1 Sep 1967
VAW-125	VAW-125 Established	1 Oct 1968
VAW-126	VAW-126 Established	1 Apr 1969
	Composite Squadron	
VC-6*	VU-6 Established	1 Mar 1952
	VU-6 Redesignated VC-6	1 Jul 1965
VC-8	GMSRON-2 Established (Guided Missile Service Squadron 2)	1 Jul 1958
	GMSRON-2 Redesignated VU-8	1 Jul 1960
	VU-8 Redesignated VC-8	1 Jul 1965
	Fighter Squadron	
VF-2*	VF-2 Established	14 Oct 1972
VF-11*	VF-43 Established	1 Sep 1950
	VF-43 Redesignated VF-11	16 Feb 1959
	VF-11 adopted the insignia used by the previous VF-11 which had been disestablished on 15 Feb 1959. The newly designated VF-11 (16 Feb 1959) carried on the	

Squadron Designation	Changes in Squadron Designations	Date of Change
	insignia and traditions of the Red Ripper squadron dating back to 1 Feb 1927, but not the lineage.	
VF-14*	Air Detachment, Pacific Fleet Established	Sep 1919
	Became VT-5, an element of AirDet, PacFlt	15 Jun 1920
	VT-5 Redesignated VP-4-1	7 Sep 1921
	VP-4-1 Redesignated VF-4	23 Sep 1921
	VF-4 Redesignated VF-1	1 Jul 1922
	VF-1 Redesignated VF-IB	1 Jul 1927
	VF-IB Redesignated VB-2B	1 Jul 1934
	VB-2B Redesignated VB-3	1 Jul 1937
	VB-3 Redesignated VB-4	1 Jul 1939
	VB-4 Redesignated VS-41	15 Mar 1941
	VS-41 Redesignated VB-41	1 Mar 1943
	VB-41 Redesignated VB-4	4 Aug 1943
	VB-4 Redesignated VA-1A	15 Nov 1946
	VA-1A Redesignated VA-14	2 Aug 1948
	VA-14 Redesignated VF-14	15 Dec 1949
VF-21*	VF-81 Established	2 Mar 1944
	VF-81 Redesignated VF-13A	15 Nov 1946
	VF-13A Redesignated VF-131	2 Aug 1948
	VF-131 Redesignated VF-64	15 Feb 1950
	VF-64 Redesignated VF-21	1 Jul 1959
VF-24*	VF-211 Established	Jun 1955
	VF-211 Redesignated VF-24	9 Mar 1959
VF-31*	VF-1B Established	1 Jul 1935
	VF-1B Redesignated VF-6	1 Jul 1937
	VF-6 Redesignated VF-3	15 Jul 1943
	VF-3 Redesignated VF-3A	15 Nov 1946
	VF-3A Redesignated VF-31	7 Aug 1948
VF-32*	VBF-3 Established	1 Feb 1945
	VBF-3 Redesignated VF-4A	15 Nov 1946
	VF-4A Redesignated VF-32	7 Aug 1948
VF-41*	VF-41 Established	1 Sep 1950
VF-45*	VA-45 Established	15 Feb 1963
	VA-45 Redesignated VF-45	7 Feb 1985
VF-101	VF-101 Established	1 May 1952
VF-102*	VA-36 Established	1 Jul 1955
	VA-36 Redesignated VF-102 (It should be noted that on the same day; 1 Jul 1955, the old	1 Jul 1955

Squadron Designation	Changes in Squadron Designations	Date of Change	Squadron Designation	Changes in Squadron Designations	Date of Change
	VF-102 was redesignated VA-36. This unit is separate from the VA-36 that was established on 1 Jul 1955 and then immediately redesignated VF-102.)			VF-81 Redesignated VA-81	1 Jul 1959
				VA-81 Redesignated VFA-81	4 Feb 1988
			VFA-82	VA-82 Established	1 May 1967
				VA-82 Redesignated VFA-82	15 Jul 1987
VF-103*	VF-103 Established	1 May 1952	VFA-83	VF-916 Reserve squadron called to active duty	1 Feb 1951
VF-143*	VF-871 Reserve squadron called to active duty	20 Jul 1950		VF-916 Redesignated VF-83	4 Feb 1953
	VF-871 Redesignated VF-123	4 Feb 1953		VF-83 Redesignated VA-83	1 Jul 1955
	VF-123 Redesignated VF-53	12 Apr 1958		VA-83 Redesignated VFA-83	1 Mar 1988
	VF-53 Redesignated VF-143	20 Jun 1962	VFA-86*	VF-921 Reserve squadron called to active duty	1 Feb 1951
VF-154	VF-837 Reserve squadron called to active duty	1 Feb 1951		VF-921 Redesignated VF-84	4 Feb 1953
	VF-837 Redesignated VF-154	4 Feb 1953		VF-84 Redesignated VA-86	1 Jul 1955
				VA-86 Redesignated VFA-86	15 Jul 1987
VF-201	VF-201 Established	25 Jul 1970	VFA-87	VA-87 Established	1 Feb 1968
				VA-87 Redesignated VFA-87	1 May 1986
VF-211*	VB-74 Established	1 May 1945	VFA-94*	VF-94 Established	26 Mar 1952
	VB-74 Redesignated VA-1B	15 Nov 1946		VF-94 Redesignated VA-94	1 Aug 1958
	VA-1B Redesignated VA-24	1 Sep 1948		VA-94 Redesignated VFA-94	24 Jan 1991
	VA-24 Redesignated VF-24	1 Dec 1949	VFA-97	VA-97 Established	1 Jun 1967
	VF-24 Redesignated VF-211	9 Mar 1959		VA-97 Redesignated VFA-97	24 Jan 1991
VF-213	VF-213 Established	22 Jun 1955	VFA-105*	VA-105 Established	4 Mar 1968
				VA-105 Redesignated VFA-105	17 Dec 1990
	Strike-Fighter Squadron		VFA-106	VFA-106 Established	27 Apr 1984
VFA-15	VA-67 Established	1 Aug 1968	VFA-113	VF-113 Established	15 Jul 1948
	VA-67 Redesignated VA-15	2 Jun 1969		VF-113 Redesignated VA-113	Mar 1956
	VA-15 Redesignated VFA-15	1 Oct 1968		VA-113 Redesignated VFA-113	25 Mar 1983
VFA-22	VF-63 Established	28 Jul 1948	VFA-125	VFA-125 Established	13 Nov 1980
	VF-63 Redesignated VA-63	Mar 1956	VFA-127	VA-127 Established	15 Jun 1962
	VA-63 Redesignated VA-22	1 Jul 1959		VA-127 Redesignated VFA-127	1 Mar 1987
	VA-22 Redesignated VFA-22	4 May 1990	VFA-131	VFA-131 Established	3 Oct 1983
VFA-25	VT-17 Established	1 Jan 1943	VFA 136	VFA-136 Established	1 Jul 1985
	VT-17 Redesignated VA-6B	15 Nov 1946	VFA-137	VFA-137 Established	1 Jul 1985
	VA-6B Redesignated VA-65	27 Jul 1948	VFA-146	VA-146 Established	1 Feb 1956
	VA-65 Redesignated VA-25	1 Jul 1959		VA-146 Redesignated VFA-146	21 Jul 1989
	VA-25 Redesignated VFA-25	1 Jul 1983	VFA-147	VA-147 Established	1 Feb 1967
VFA-27	VA-27 Established	1 Sep 1967		VA-147 Redesignated VFA-147	20 Jul 1989
	VA-27 Redesignated VFA-27	24 Jan 1991	VFA-151	VF-23 Established	6 Aug 1948
VFA-37	VA-37 Established	1 Jul 1967			
	VA-37 Redesignated VFA-37	28 Nov 1990			
VFA-81	VA-66 Established	1 Jul 1955			
	VA-66 Redesignated VF-81 on same day	1 Jul 1955			

Squadron Designation	Changes in Squadron Designations	Date of Change	Squadron Designation	Changes in Squadron Designations	Date of Change
	VF-23 Redesignated VF-151	23 Feb 1959		VPB-201 Redesignated VP-201	15 May 1946
	VF-151 Redesignated VFA-151	1 Jun 1986		VP-201 Redesignated VP-MS-1	15 Nov 1946
				VP-MS-1 Redesignated VP-ML-8	5 Jun 1947
VFA-192	VF-153 Established	26 Mar 1945		VP-ML-8 Redesignated VP-8	1 Sep 1948
	VF-153 Redesignated VF-15A	15 Nov 1946			
	VF-15A Redesignated VF-151	15 Jul 1948	VP-9*	VP-9 Established	15 Mar 1951
	VF-151 Redesignated VF-192	15 Feb 1950			
	VF-192 Redesignated VA-192	15 Mar 1956	VP-10*	VP-10 Established	19 Mar 1951
	VA-192 Redesignated VFA-192	10 Jan 1985			
			VP-11*	VP-11 Established	15 May 1952
VFA-195	VT-19 Established	15 Aug 1943			
	VT-19 Redesignated VA-20A	15 Nov 1946	VP-16*	VP-741 Reserve squadron called to active duty	1 May 1951
	VA-20A Redesignated VA-195	24 Aug 1948		VP-741 Redesignated VP-16	4 Feb 1953
	VA-195 Redesignated VFA-195	1 Apr 1985			
			VP-26*	VB-114 Established	26 Aug 1943
VFA-203	VA-203 Established	1 Jul 1970		VB-114 Redesignated VPB-114	1 Oct 1944
	VA-203 Redesignated VFA-203	1 Oct 1989		VPB-114 Redesignated VP-114	15 May 1946
				VP-114 Redesignated VP-HL-6	15 Nov 1946
VFA-204	VA-204 Established	1 Jul 1970		VP-HL-6 Redesignated VP-26	1 Sep 1948
	VA-204 Redesignated VFA-204	1 May 1991			
			VP-30	VP-30 Established	30 Jun 1960
	Fighter Squadron Composite				
VFC-12*	VC-12 Established	1 Sep 1973	VP 40*	VP-40 Established	20 Jan 1951
	VC-12 Redesignated VFC-12	22 Apr 1988			
			VP-45*	VP-205 Established	1 Nov 1942
VFC-13*	VC-13 Established	1 Sep 1973		VP-205 Redesignated VPB-205	1 Oct 1944
	VC-13 Redesignated VFC-13	22 Apr 1988		VPB-205 Redesignated VP-205	15 May 1946
				VP-205 Redesignated VP-MS-5	15 Nov 1946
				VP-MS-5 Redesignated VP-45	1 Sep 1948
	Patrol Squadron				
VP-1*	VB-128 Established	15 Feb 1943	VP-46	VP-5S Established	1 Sep 1931
	VB-128 Redesignated VPB-128	1 Oct 1944		VP-5S Redesignated VP-5F	1 Apr 1933
	VPB-128 Redesignated VP-128	15 May 1946		VP-5F Redesignated VP-5	1937
	VP-128 Redesignated VP-ML-1	15 Nov 1946		VP-5 Redesignated VP-33	1 Jul 1939
	VP-ML-1 Redesignated VP-1	1 Sep 1948		VP-33 Redesignated VP-32	1 Jul 1941
				VP-32 Redesignated VPB-32	1 Oct 1944
VP-4*	VB-144 Established	1 Jul 1943		VPB-32 Redesignated VP-32	15 May 1946
	VB-144 Redesignated VPB-144	1 Oct 1944		VP-32 Redesignated VP-MS-6	15 Nov 1946
	VPB-144 Redesignated VP-144	15 May 1946		VP-MS-6 Redesignated VP-46	1 Sep 1948
	VP-144 Redesignated VP-ML-4	15 Nov 1946			
	VP-ML-4 Redesignated VP-4	1 Sep 1948	VP-47	VP-27 Established	1 Jun 1944
				VP-27 Redesignated VPB-27	1 Oct 1944
VP-5*	VP-17F (VP-17) Established	2 Jan 1937		VPB-27 Redesignated VP-27	15 May 1946
	VP-17 Redesignated VP-42	1 Jul 1939		VP-27 Redesignated VP-MS-7	15 Nov 1946
	VP-42 Redesignated VB-135	15 Feb 1943		VP-MS-7 Redesignated VP-47	1 Sep 1948
	VB-135 Redesignated VPB-135	1 Oct 1944			
	VPB-135 Redesignated VP-135	15 May 1946	VP-62	VP-62 Established	1 Nov 1970
	VP-135 Redesignated VP-ML-5	15 Nov 1946			
	VP-ML-5 Redesignated VP-5	1 Sep 1948	VP-64	VP-64 Established	1 Nov 1970
VP-8*	VP-201 Established	1 Sep 1942	VP-65	VP-65 Established	16 Nov 1970
	VP-201 Redesignated VPB-201	1 Oct 1944			

Squadron Designation	Changes in Squadron Designations	Date of Change
VP-66	VP-66 Established	1 Nov 1970
VP-68	VP-68 Established	1 Nov 1970
VP-69	VP-69 Established	1 Nov 1970
VP-91*	VP-91 Established	1 Nov 1970
VP-92*	VP-92 Established	1 Nov 1970
VP-94*	VP-94 Established	1 Nov 1970

Patrol Squadron Special Unit

VPU-1	VPU-1 Established	1 Jul 1982
VPU-2	VPU-2 Established	1 Jul 1982

Fleet Air Reconnaissance Squadron

VQ-1	VQ-1 Established	1 Jun 1955
VQ-2	VQ-2 Established	1 Sep 1955
VQ-3	VQ-3 Established	1 Jul 1968
VQ-4	VQ-4 Established	1 Jul 1968
VQ-5	VQ-5 Established	15 Apr 1991
VQ-6	VQ-6 Established	5 Aug 1991

Fleet Logistic Support Squadron

VR-46	VR-46 Established	1 Mar 1981
VR-48	VR-48 Established	1 Oct 1980
VR-52*	VR-52 Established	24 Jun 1972
VR-53	VR-53 Established	1 Oct 1992
VR-54	VR-54 Established	1 Jun 1991
VR-55	VR-55 Established	1 Apr 1976
VR-56	VR-56 Established	1 Jul 1976
VR-57	VR-57 Established	1 Nov 1977
VR-58	VR-58 Established	1 Nov 1977
VR-59	VR-59 Established	1 Oct 1982

Squadron Designation	Changes in Squadron Designations	Date of Change
VR-61	VR-61 Established	1 Oct 1982
VR-62	VR-62 Established	1 Jul 1985

Fleet Tactical Support Squadron

VRC-30	VR-30 Established	1 Oct 1966
	VR-30 Redesignated VRC-30	1 Oct 1978
VRC-40	VRC-40 Established	1 Jul 1960

Air Anti-Submarine Squadron

VS-21*	CVEG-41 Established	26 Mar 1945
	CVEG-41 Redesignated CVEG-1	15 Nov 1946
	CVEG-1 Redesignated VC-21	1 Sep 1948
	VC-21 Redesignated VS-21	23 Apr 1950
VS-22*	VS-22 Established	18 May 1960
VS-24*	VS-24 Established	25 May 1960
VS-29	VS-29 Established	1 Apr 1960
VS-30*	VS-801 Reserve squadron called to active duty	9 Apr 1951
	VS-801 Redesignated VS-30	4 Feb 1953
VS-31*	VC-31 Established	28 Sep 1948
	VC-31 Redesignated VS-31	20 Apr 1950
VS-32	VC-32 Established	31 May 1949
	VC-32 Redesignated VS-32	20 Apr 1950
VS-35*	VS-35 Established	4 Apr 1991
VS-38*	VC-892 Reserve sqdn. Activated	20 Jul 1950
	VC-892 Redesignated VS-892	4 Aug 1950
	VS-892 Reserve squadron called to active duty	4 Aug 1950
	VS-892 Redesignated VS-38	4 Feb 1953
VS-41*	VS-41 Established	30 Jun 1960

Training Squadron

VT-2	BTG-2 Redesignated VT-2 (Basic Training Group-2)	1 May 1960
VT-3	BTG-3 Redesignated VT-3	1 May 1960
VT-4	BTG-9 Redesignated VT-4	1 May 1960

Squadron Designation	Changes in Squadron Designations	Date of Change	Squadron Designation	Changes in Squadron Designations	Date of Change
VT-6	Multi-Engine Training Group, Whiting Field Redesignated VT-6	1 May 1960	VT-27	ATU-402 Redesignated VT-27	1 Jul 1960
			VT-28	ATU-611 Redesignated VT-28	1 May 1960
VT-7	BTG-7 Activated BTG-7 Redesignated VT-7	1 Jun 1958 1 Jul 1960	VT-31	ATU-601 Redesignated VT-31	1 May 1960
			VT-86	VT-86 Established	5 Jun 1972
VT-10	BNAO School Redesignated VT-10 Basic Naval Aviation Officers School was established within the training department of NAS Pensacola in June 1960. BNAO School became a separate command under the Chief of Naval Air Training 15 Jan 1968.	15 Jan 1968		*Air Test and Evaluation Squadron (VX)* *Antartic Development Squadron (VXE)*	
			VX-1	Established as Aircraft Antisubmarine Development Detachment, Atlantic Fleet Aircraft Antisubmarine Development Detachment became part of a new unit called Antisubmarine Development Det, Atlantic Fleet Antisubmarine Development Det, Atlantic Fleet redesignated VX-1	1 Apr 1943 17 Sep 1943 15 Mar 1946
VT-19	VT-19 Established	2 Aug 1971			
VT-21	ATU-202 Redesignated VT-21 (Advanced Training Unit-202)	1 May 1960			
VT-22	ATU-212 Redesignated VT-22	1 May 1960	VXE-6	VX-6 Established VX-6 Redesignated VXE-6	17 Jan 1955 1 Jan 1969
VT-23	ATU-222 Established ATU-222 Redesignated VT-23	Nov 1958 1 May 1960	VX-9	VX-9 Established	30 Apr 1994

* Previous squadrons have been assigned this designation.

Carrier, Carrier Based Squadrons and Non-Carrier Based Squadron Deployments During the Korean War

Carrier, Air Group and Carrier Based Squadron Deployments

Essex (CV 9) with CVG-5 (26 Jun 1951—25 Mar 1952)

Squadron	Aircraft	Tail Code
VF-51	F9F-2	S
VF-172	F2H-2	R
VF-53	F4U-4/B	S
VF-54	AD-2/4/L/Q	S
VC-3 Det B	F4U-5NL	NP
VC-11 Det B	AD-4W	ND
VC-35 Det B	AD-4NL	NR
VC-61 Det B	F9F-2P	PP
HU-1 Det	HO3S-1	UP

Essex (CVA 9) with ATG-2 (16 Jun 1952—6 Feb 1953)

Squadron	Aircraft	Tail Code
VF-23	F9F-2	M
VF-821	F9F-2	A
VF-871	F4U-4	D
VA-55	AD-4	S
VC-3 Det I	F4U-5N	NP
VC-11 Det I	AD-4W	ND
VC-35 Det I	AD-4N	NR
VC-61 Det I	F2H-2P	PP
HU-1 Det	HO3S-1	UP

Boxer (CV 21) with CVG-2 (24 Aug 1950—11 Nov 1950)

Squadron	Aircraft	Tail Code
VF-23	F4U-4	M
VF-63	F4U-4	M
VF-64	F4U-4	M
VF-24	F4U-4	M
VA-65	AD-2	M
VC-3 Det	F4U-5N	NP
VC-11 Det A	AD-3W	ND
VC-33 Det	AD-4N	SS
VC-61 Det	F4U-4P	PP
HU-1 Det	HO3S-1	UP

Boxer (CV 21) with CVG-101 (2 Mar 1951—24 Oct 1951)

Squadron	Aircraft	Tail Code
VF-721	F9F-2B	A
VF-791	F4U-4	A
VF-884	F4U-4	A
VA-702	AD-2/4Q	A
VC-3 Det F	F4U-5NL	NP
VC-11 Det F	AD-4W	ND
VC-35 Det F	AD-4N	NR
VC-61 Det F	F9F-2P	PP
HU-1 Det	HO3S-1	UP

Boxer (CVA 21) with CVG-2 (8 Feb 1952—26 Sep 1952)

Squadron	Aircraft	Tail Code
VF-64	F4U-4	M
VF-63	F4U-4	M
VF-24	F9F-2	M
VA-65	AD-4	M
VC-3 Det A	F4U-5N	NP
VC-11 Det A	AD-4W	ND
VC-35 Det A	AD-3N/4N/2Q	NR
VC-61 Det A	F9F-2P	PP
HU-1 Det	HO3S-1	UP
GMU-90	AD-2Q/F6F-5K	V

Boxer (CVA 21) with ATG-1 (30 Mar 1953—28 Nov 1953)

Squadron	Aircraft	Tail Code
VF-111*	F9F-5	V
VF-52	F9F-2	S
VF-151	F9F-2	H
VF-44*	F4U-4	F
VF-194	AD-4NA/Q	B
VC-3 Det H	F4U-5N	NP
VC-11 Det H	AD-4W	ND
VC-35 Det H	AD-4N	NR
VC-61	F2H-2P	PP
HU-1 Det	HO3S-1	UP

*VF-111 crossdecked (transferred) from CVA 21 to CVA 39 on 30 June 1953 and returned to the U.S. in October 1953. VF-44 corssdecked from CVA 39 to CVA 21 on 30 June 1953.

Bon Homme Richard (CV 31) with CVG-102 (10 May 1951—17 Dec 1951)

Squadron	Aircraft	Tail Code
VF-781	F9F-2B	D
VF-783	F4U-4	D
VF-874	F4U-4	D
VA-923	AD-3/4Q	D
VC-3 Det G	F4U-5NL	NP
VC-11 Det G	AD-4W	ND
VC-35 Det G	AD-4N	NR
VC-61 Det G	F9F-2P	PP
HU-1 Det	HO3S-1	UP

Bon Homme Richard (CVA 31) with CVG-7 (20 May 1952—8 Jan 1953)

Squadron	Aircraft	Tail Code
VF-71	F9F-2	L
VF-72	F9F-2	L
VF-74	F4U-4	L
VA-75	AD-4	L
VC-4 Det 41	F4U-5N	NA
VC-33 Det 41	AD-4NL	SS
VC-12 Det 41	AD-4W	NE
VC-61 Det N	F2H-2P/F9F-2P	PP
HU-1 Det	HO3S-1	UP

Leyte (CV 32) with CVG-3 (6 Sep 1950—3 Feb 1951)

Squadron	Aircraft	Tail Code
VF-31	F9F-2	K
VF-32	F4U-4	K
VF-33	F4U-4	K
VA-35	AD-3	K
VC-4 Det 3	F4U-5N	NA
VC-33 Det 3	AD-4N	SS
VC-12 Det 3	AD-3W	NE
VC-62 Det 3	F4U-5P	PL
HU-2 Det 3	HO3S-1	UR

Kearsarge (CVA 33) with CVG-101* (11 Aug 1952—17 Mar 1953)

Squadron	Aircraft	Tail Code
VF-11	F2H-2	T
VF-721*	F9F-2	A
VF-884*	F4U-4	A
VA-702*	AD-4/L	A
VC-3 Det F	F4U-5N	NP
VC-11 Det F	AD-4W	ND
VC-35 Det F	AD-4N	NR
VC-61 Det F	F2H-2P	PP
HU-1 Det 15	HO3-1	UP

*CVG-101 redesignated CVG-14 on 4 February 1953.
VF-721, VF-884 and VA-702 became VF-141, VF-144 and VA-145.

Oriskany (CVA 34) with CVG-102* (15 Sep 1952—18 May 1953)

Squadron	Aircraft	Tail Code
VF-781	F9F-5	D
VF-783	F9F-5	D
VF-874	F4U-4	D
VA-923	AD-3	D
VC-3 Det G	F4U-5N	NP
VC-11 Det G	AD-3W	ND
VC-35 Det G	AD-4N	NR
VC-61 Det G	F2H-2P	PP
HU-1 Det	HO3S-1	UP

*CVG-102 redesignated CVG-12 on 4 February 1953.
VF-781, VF-783, VF-874 and VA-923 became VF-121, VF-122, VF-124 and VA-125.

Antietam (CV 36) with CVG-15 (8 Sep 1951—2 May 1952)

Squadron	Aircraft	Tail Code
VF-713	F4U-4	H
VF-831	F9F-2B	H
VF-837	F9F-2B	H
VA-728	AD-4/L/Q	H
VC-3 Det D	F4U-5N	NP
VC-11 Det D	AD-4W	ND
VC-35 Det D	AD-4NL	NR
VC-61 Det D	F9F-2P	PP
HU-1 Det	HO3S-1	UP

Princeton (CV 37) with CVG-19 (9 Nov 1950—29 May 1951*)

Squadron	Aircraft	Tail Code
VF-191	F9F-2	B
VF-192	F4U-4	B
VF-193	F4U-4	B
VA-195	AD-4	B
VC-3 Det F	F4U-5N	NP
VC-11 Det	AD-4W	ND
VC-35 Det 3	AD-4N	NR
VC-61 Det	F9F-2P	PP
HU-1 Det	HO3S-1	UP

*Air Group transferred at Yokosuka, Japan, CV 37 remained in WestPac.

Princeton (CV 37) with CVG-19X (31 May 1951—29 Aug 1951)

Squadron	Aircraft	Tail Code
VF-23	F9F-2	B
VF-821	F4U-4	B
VF-871	F4U-4	B
VA-55	AD-4	B
VC-3 Det	F4U-5N	NP
VC-11 Det	AD-4W	ND
VC-35 Det 7	AD-4N	NR
VC-61 Det	F9F-2P	PP
HU-1 Det	HO3S-1	UP

Princeton (CVA 37) with CVG-19 (21 Mar 1952—3 Nov 1952)

Squadron	Aircraft	Tail Code
VF-191	F9F-2	B
VF-192	F4U-4	B
VF-193	F4U-4	B
VA-195	AD-4	B
VC-3 Det E	F4U-5N	NP
VC-11 Det E	AD-4W	ND
VC-35 Det E	AD-4NL	NR
VC-61 Det E	F9F-2P	PP
HU-1 Det	HO3S-1	UP

Princeton (CVA 37) with CVG-15 (24 Jan 1953—21 Sep 1953)

Squadron	Aircraft	Tail Code
VF-152	F4U-4	H
VF-153	F9F-5	H
VF-154	F9F-5	H
VA-155	AD-4	H
VC-3 Det D	F4U-5N	NP
VC-11 Det D	AD-4W	ND
VC-35 Det D	AD-4N	NR
VC-61 Det D	F9F-5P	PP
HU-1 Det	HO3S-1	UP

Lake Champlain (CVA 39) with CVG-4 (26 Apr 1953—4 Dec 1953)

Squadron	Aircraft	Tail Code
VF-22	F2H-2	F
VF-62	F2H-2	F
VF-44	F4U-4	F (to 30 Jun)
VF-111	F9F-5	V (from 30 Jun)
VA-45	AD-4B	F
VC-4 Det 44	F2H-2B/F3D-2	NA
VC-12 Det 44	AD-4W	NE
VC-33 Det 44	AD-4N	SS
VC-62 Det 44	F2H-2P	PL
HU-2 Det	HO3S-1	UR

Valley Forge (CV 45) with CVG-5 (1 May 1950—1 Dec 1950)

Squadron	Aircraft	Tail Code
VF-51	F9F-3	S
VF-52	F9F-3	S
VF-53	F4U-4B	S
VF-54	F4U-4B	S
VA-55	AD-4/Q	S
VC-3 Det C	F4U-5N/AD-3N	NP
VC-11 Det	AD-3W	ND
HedRon 1 Det	F4U-5P	AZ
HU-1 Det	HO3S-1	UP

Valley Forge (CV 45) with CVG-2 (6 Dec 1950—7 Apr 1951*)

Squadron	Aircraft	Tail Code
VF-64	F4U-4	M
VF-63	F4U-4	M
VF-24	F4U-4	M
VA-65	F4U-4	M
VC-3 Det	F4U-5N	NP
VC-11 Det	AD-4W	ND
VC-35 Det 4	AD-4N	NR
VC-61 Det F	F4U-4P	PP
HU-1 Det	HO3S-1	UP

*CVG-2 crossdecked with CVG-11 from CV 47 on 28 March 1951 and CV 45 returned to San Diego, Calif., 7 April with CVG-11.

Valley Forge (CV 45) with ATG-1 (15 Oct 1951—3 Jul 1952)

Squadron	Aircraft	Tail Code
VF-111	F9F-2/B	V
VF-52	F9F-2/B	S
VF-653	F4U-4/B	H
VF-194	F4U-4/B	B
VC-3 Det H	F4U-5N/NL	NP
VC-11 Det H(7)	AD-4W/2Q	ND
VC-35 Det H(10)	AD-4NL	NR
VC-61 Det H	F9F-2P/F2H-2P	PP
HU-1 Det 20	HO3S-1	UP

Valley Forge (CVA 45) with CVG-5 (20 Nov 1952—25 Jun 1953)

Squadron	Aircraft	Tail Code
VF-51	F9F-5	S
VF-92	F4U-4	N
VF-53	F9F-5	S
VF-54	AD-4	S
VC-3 Det B	F4U-5N	NP
VC-11 Det B	AD-4W	ND
VC-35 Det B	AD-4N	NR
VC-61 Det B	F9F-5P	PP
HU-1 Det 6	HO3S-1	UP

Philippine Sea (CV 47) with CVG-11 (5 Jul 1950—26 Mar 1951*)

Squadron	Aircraft	Tail Code
VF-111	F9F-2	V
VF-112	F9F-2	V
VF-113	F4U-4B	V
VF-114	F4U-4B	V
VA-115	AD-4/Q	V
VC-3 Det 3	F4U-5N/AD-4N	NP
VC-11 Det	AD-4W	ND
VC-61 Det 3	F4U-4P	PP
HU-1 Det 3	HO3S-1	UP

*CVG-11 crossdecked with CVG-2 from CV 45; CV 47 returned to San Diego, Calif., 26 March with CVG-2.

Philippine Sea (CV 47) with CVG-2 (28 Mar 1951—9 Jun 1951)

Squadron	Aircraft	Tail Code
VF-64	F4U-4	M
VF-63	F4U-4	M

VF-24	F4U-4	M
VA-65	AD-2/Q	M
VC-3 Det	F4U-5N	NP
VC-11 Det	AD-4W	ND
VC-35 Det 4	AD-4N	NR
VC-61 Det	F4U-4P	PP
HU-1 Det	HO3S-1	UP

Philippine Sea (CV 47) with CVG-11 (31 Dec 1951—8 Aug 1952)

Squadron	Aircraft	Tail Code
VF-112	F9F-2	V
VF-113	F4U-4	V
VF-114	F4U-4	V
VA-115	AD-4	V
VC-3 Unit C	F4U-5N/NL	NP
VC-11 Unit C	AD-4W	ND
VC-35 Unit C	AD-4NL/Q/-2Q	NR
VC-61 Unit C	F2H-2P/F9F-2P	PP
HU-1 Unit	HO3S-1	UP

Philippine Sea (CVA 47) with CVG-9 (15 Dec 1952—14 Aug 1953)

Squadron	Aircraft	Tail Code
VF-91	F9F-2	N
VF-93	F9F-2	N
VF-94	F4U-4	N
VA-95	AD-4/NA/NL	N
VC-3 Det M	F4U-5N	NP
VC-11 Det M	AD-4W	ND
VC-35 Det M	AD-4N	NR
VC-61 Det M	F9F-5P	PP
HU-1 Det	HO3S-1	UP

Bataan (CVL 29) (16 Nov 1950—25 Jun 1951)

Squadron	Aircraft	Tail Code
VMF-212	F4U-4	LD (aboard 11 Dec-5 Mar)
VMF-312	F4U-4	WR (aboard 5 Mar-6 Jun)
HU-1 Det 8	HO3S-1	UP

Bataan (CVL 29) (27 Jan 1952—26 Aug 1952)

Squadron	Aircraft	Tail Code
VMA-312	F4U-4/B	WR (aboard 21 Apr-21 Jul)
VS-25	AF-2S/W	SK
HU-1 Det	HO3S-1	UP

Bataan (CVL 29) (28 Oct 1952—26 May 1953)

Squadron	Aircraft	Tail Code
VMA-312	F4U-4/B	WR (aboard 9 Feb-8 May)
VS-871	TBM-3S/W	SU

VS-21	AF-2S/W	BS
HU-1 Det	HO3S-1	UP

Rendova (CVE 114) (8 Jul 1951—22 Dec 1951)

Squadron	Aircraft	Tail Code
VMF-212	F4U-4	LD (aboard 22 Sep-6 Dec)
VS-892	TBM-3S/W	ST (aboard 16 Jul-19 Sep, 11-22 Dec)
HU-1 Det	HO3S-1	UP

Bairoko (CVE 115) (14 Nov 1950—15 Aug 1951)

Squadron	Aircraft	Tail Code
VS-21	TBM-3S/W	BS (aboard 3 Dec-16 Feb)
VS-23	TBM-3E/S/W	MI (aboard 17 Feb-15 Aug)
HU-1 Det	HO3S-1	UP

Bairoko (CVE 115) (1 Dec 1951—9 Jun 1952)

Squadron	Aircraft	Tail Code
VS-25	AF-2S/W	SK (aboard to 21 Jan, returned in May)
HU-1 Det	HO3S-1	UP

Bairoko (CVE 115) (12 Jan 1953—24 Aug 1953)

Squadron	Aircraft	Tail Code
VMA-312	F4U-4/B	WR (aboard 9 May-8 Jun)
VS-21	AF-2S/W	BS (aboard 3 Feb-8 May)
VS-23	TBM-3S/W	MI (ashore at Agana, Guam, Feb-Apr)
HU-1 Det	HO3S-1	UP

Badoeng Strait (CVE 116) (14 Jul 1950—7 Feb 1951)

Squadron	Aircraft	Tail Code
VMF-323	F4U-4B	WS
HU-1 Det	HO3S-1	UP

Badoeng Strait (CVE 116) (15 Sep 1951—1 Mar 1952)

Squadron	Aircraft	Tail Code
VMF-212	F4U-4	LD
VS-892	TBM-3S/W	ST (aboard 5 Oct-8 Dec)
HU-1 Det 18	HO3S-1	UP

Badoeng Strait (CVE 116) (19 Jul 1952—27 Feb 1953)

Squadron	Aircraft	Tail Code
VMA-312	F4U-4/B	WR (aboard 19 Oct-9 Feb)
VS-931	AF-2S/W	SV (aboard 10 Aug-19 Oct)
HU-1 Det	HO3S-1	UP

Sicily (CVE 118) (4 Jul 1950—5 Feb 1951)

Squadron	Aircraft	Tail Code
VMF-214	F4U-4B	WE (aboard 1 Aug-13 Nov)
VS-21	TBM-3E/S	BS (aboard to 3 Dec)
HU-1 Det	HO3S-1	UP

Sicily (CVE 118) (12 May 1951—12 Oct 1951)

Squadron	Aircraft	Tail Code
VMF-323	F4U-4	WS (aboard c. 5 Jun-20 Sep)
VS-892	TBM-3S/W	ST (aboard to 13 Jul)
HU-1 Det	HO3S-1	UP

Sicily (CVE 118) (8 May 1952—4 Dec 1952)

Squadron	Aircraft	Tail Code
VMA-312	F4U-4B	WR (aboard 4 Sep-19 Oct)
VS-931	AF-2S/W	SV (aboard to 9 Aug and 19 Oct-4 Dec)
HU-1 Det	HO3S-1	UP

Point Cruz (CVE 119) (11 Apr 1953—18 Dec 1953)

Squadron	Aircraft	Tail Code
VMA-332	F4U-4B	MR
VS-38	TBM-3S/W	ST (put shore at Agana, Guam, 28 Apr)
VS-23	TBM-3S/W	MI (aboard 28 Apr-Japan)
HS-2	HRS-2	HV
HU-1 Det	HO3S-1	UP

Shore Based Marine Corps Squadrons Operating in Korea

Squadron Designation	Date Departed U.S	Date Departed Korean Area	Tail Code	Aircraft Operated
VMC-1	15 May 1952		RM	AD-4N, 4NL, AD-3N, AD-2Q, AD-4Q, AD-4W
VMJ-1	23 Mar 1952		MW	F2H-2P, F9F-2P, F7F-3P, F4U-5P
VMO-6	14 Jul 1950		WB	OY-2, HO3S-1, HTL-4, TBM-3E, OE-1, HO5S-1
VMF-115	17 Feb 1952		AE	F9F-2, F9F-4, F9F-5
VMA-121	2 Oct 1951		AK	AD-2, AD-3, AD-4
HMR-161	16 Aug 1951		HR	HRS-1, HRS-2, HO5S-1
VMF/VMA-212	15 Sep 1950		LD	F4U-4, F4U-5, F4U-5N, F4U-4B, AU-1
VMF-214	14 Jun 1950	15 Nov 1951	WE	F4U-4B
VMA-251	9 Jun 1953		AL	AD-3, AD-4, AD-4B
VMF-311	14 Nov 1950		WL	F9F-2, F4U-4B, F9F-2B, F9F-5
VMF/VMA-312	24 Aug 1950	16 Jun 1953	WR	F4U-4, F4U-4B
VMF/VMA-323	14 Jul 1950		WS	F4U-4B, AU-1
VMA-332	15 May 1953		MR	F4U-4, F4U-4B
VMF(N)-513	14 Jul 1950		WF	F4U-5N, F4U-5NL, F7F-3N, F3D-2
VMF(N)-542	27 Aug 1950	9 Mar 1951	WH	F7F-3N

NOTE: Many of the Marine Corps Squadrons remained permanently assigned in the Korean operating area during the Korean War.

Navy Patrol Squadrons Deployed to Korean Area

Squadron Designation	Date Arrived in Korean Area	Date Departed Korean Area	Tail Code	Aircraft Operated
VP-1	7 Aug 1950	27 Jul 1953	CD	P2V-3/5
VP-2	1 Sep 1951	1 Dec 1951	SB	P2V-4
VP-6	28 Jun 1950	15 Jan 1952	BE	P2V-3
VP-7	30 Jun 1953	Jan 1954	HE	P2V-5
VP-9	29 Jun 1952	16 Nov 1952	CB	P4Y-2/2S
VP-22	14 Nov 1950	30 May 1953	CE	P2V-3/4/5
VP-28	14 Jul 1950	30 Nov 1952	CF	P4Y-2/2S
VP-29	27 Sep 1952	5 Apr 1953	BF	P2V-5/6
VP-40	1 Jun 1951	24 Feb 1953	CA	PBM-5/5S
VP-42	21 Aug 1950	2 Jun 1952	SA	PBM-5/5S2
VP-46	15 Jul 1950	15 Mar 1952	BD	PBM-5
VP-47	25 Jun 1950	1 Jun 1953	BA	PBM-5
VP-48	29 May 1952	15 Mar 1953	SF	PBM-5/5S2
VP-50	5 Jul 1953	27 Jul 1953	SE	PBM-5
VP-57	29 Mar 1953	27 Jul 1953	BI	P2V-5
VP-722	1 Jan 1951	1 Aug 1951		P4Y-2/2S
VP-731	29 May 1952	8 Dec 1952		PBM-5
VP-871 Det A	Oct 1951	Mar 1952	CH	P4Y-2/2S
VP-892	23 Nov 1950	1 Sep 1953		PBM-5

Note: Tail codes not available for three Reserve Patrol Squadrons, VP-722, VP-731 and VP-892. PB4Y-2 aircraft designations were changed to P4Y-2 in 1951.

APPENDIX 26

Carrier, Carrier Based Squadrons and Non-Carrier Based Squadron Deployments to Vietnam

Deployment for Carriers and Carrier Based Squadrons in the Western Pacific (WestPac) and Vietnam (1964–1975)

See the Notes Section at the end of this listing for clarification on specific entries and Tail Code List.

1964 WestPac/Vietnam Deployments

Kitty Hawk (CVA 63) with CVW-11 (17 Oct 1963—20 Jul 1964)

VA-112	A-4C
VA-113	A-4C
VA-115	A-1H
VF-114	F-4B
VF-111	F-8D
VAH-13	A-3B
VFP-63 Det C	RF-8A
VAW-11 Det C	E-1B
HU-1 D1 Unit C	UH-2A
*VQ-1Det	EA-3B
*VAP-61 Det	RA-3B

**Oriskany (CVA 34) with CVW-16 (1 Aug 1963—10 Mar 1964)

VF-161	F-3B
VF-162	F-8A
VA-163	A-4B
VA-164	A-4B
VA-165	A-1H & A-1J
VAH-4 Det G	A-3B
VFP-63 Det G	RF-8A
VAW-11 Det G	E-1B
HU-1 D1 Unit G	UH-2A
*VQ-1 Det	EA-3B

Bon Homme Richard (CVA 31) with CVW-19 (28 Jan 1964—21 Nov 1964)

VF-191	F-8E
VF-194	F-8C
VA-192	A-4C
VA-195	A-4C
VA-196	A-1J & A-1H

VAH-4 Det E	A-3B
VAW-11 Det E	E-1B
VFP-63 Det E	RF-8A
HU-1 D1 Unit E	UH-2A
*VQ-1Det	EA-3B
*VAP-61 Det	RA-3B

Ticonderoga (CVA 14) with CVW-5 (14 Apr 1964—15 Dec 1964)

*VF-51	F-8E
VF-53	F-8E
VA-52	A-1J & A-1H
VA-55	A-4E
VA-56	A-4E
VFP-63 Det B	RF-8A
VAW-11 Det B	E-1B
HU-1 D1 Unit B	UH-2A
*VAW-13 Det	(most likely used EA-1F)
*VQ-1 Det	EA-3B
*VAP-61 Det	RA-3B & KA-3B
*VAH-10 Det	A-3B
*VMCJ-1 Det	RF-8A
VAH-4 Det B	A-3B

Constellation (CVA 64) with CVW-14 (5 May 1964—1 Feb 1965)

VF-142	F-4B
VF-143	F-4B
VA-144	A-4C
VA-145	A-1J & A-1H
VA-146	A-4C
VAH-10	A-3B
VFP-63 Det F	RF-8A
VAW-11 Det F	E-1B
HU-1 D1 Unit F	UH-2A
*VAP-61 Det	RA-3B
*VQ-1 Det	EA-3B
*VF-51	F-8E
*VMCJ-1 Det	RF-8A

Ranger (CVA 61) with CVW-9 (5 Aug 1964—6 May 1965)

VF-92	F-4B
VF-96	F-4B
VA-93	A-4C
VA-95	A-1J & A-1H
VA-94	A-4C
RVAH-5	RA-5C
VFP-63 Det M	RF-8A
VAW-11 Det M	E-1B
VAH-2 Det M	A-3B
HU-1 D1 Unit M	UH-2A
*VAP-61 Det	RA-3B
*VQ-1 Det	EA-3B

Hancock (CVA 19) with CVW-21 (21 Oct 1964—29 May 1965)

VA-212	A-4E
VA-215	A-1J & A-1H
VA-216	A-4C
VF-24	F-8C
VF-211	F-8E
VAW-11 Det L	E-1B
VFP-63 Det L	RF-8A
VAH-4 Det L	A-3B
HU-1 Det L	UH-2A
*VAP-61 Det	RA-3B
*VQ-1 Det	EA-3B

Yorktown (CVS 10) with CVSG-55 (23 Oct 1964—16 May 1965)

VS-23	S-2E
VS-25	S-2E
HS-4	SH-3A
VAW-11 Det T	EA-1E
VMA-223 Det T	A-4C

Coral Sea (CVA 43) with CVW-15 (7 Dec 1964-1 Nov 1965)

VA-153	A-4C
VA-155	A-4E
VA-165	A-1H & A-1J
VAH-2	A-3B
VF-151	F-4B
VF-154	F-8D
VFP-63 Det D	RF-8A
VAW-11 Det D	E-1B
HU-1 D1 Unit D	UH-2A
(redesignated HC-1 Det D on 1 Jul 1965)	
*VAP 61 Det	RA-3B
*VQ-1 Det	EA-3B
*VAW-13 Det	EA-1F
*VMCJ-1 Det	RF-8A

Bennington (CVS 20) with CVSG-59 (20 Feb 1964—11 Aug 1964)

HS-8	SH-3A
VS-33	S-2E
VS-38	S-2E
VAW-11 Det Q	EA-1E
VA-93 Det Q	A-4B

Kearsarge (CVS 33) with CVSG-53 (19 Jun 1964—16 Dec 1964)

HS-6	SH-3A
VS-21	S-2F
VS-29	S-2F
VAW-11 Det R	EA-1E
VA-153 Det R	A-4B

1965 WestPac/Vietnam Deployments

Midway (CVA 41) with CVW-2 (6 Mar 1965—23 Nov 1965)

VF-111	F-8D
VA-22	A-4C
VA-23	A-4E
VA-25	A-1H & A-1J
VF-21	F-4B
VAH-8	A-3B
VFP-63 Det A	RF-8A
VAW-11 Det A	E-1B
HU-1 Det A	UH-2A
(redesignated HC-1 Det A on 1 Jul 1965)	
*VAW-13 Det	EA-1F
*VAP-61 Det	RA-3B
*VQ-1 Det	EA-3B

Oriskany (CVA 34) with CVW-16 (5 Apr 1965-16 Dec 1965)

VF-162	F-8E
VA-152	A-1J & A-1H
VA-163	A-4E
VA-164	A-4E
VMF(AW)-212	F-8D
VFP-63 Det G	RF-8A
VAW-11 Det G	E-1B
HU-1 Det G	UH-2B & UH-2A
(redesignated HC-1 Det G on 1 Jul 1965)	
*VMCJ-1 Det	(most likely used EF-10B)
*VAW-13 Det	EA-1F
*VQ-1 Det	EA-3B

***Independence* (CVA 62) with CVW-7 (10 May 1965—13 Dec 1965)**

VF-41	F-4B
VF-84	F-4B
VA-72	A-4E
VA-75	A-6A
VA-86	A-4E
RVAH-1	RA-5C
VAW-12 Det 62	E-1B
HU-2 Det 62	UH-2A
(redesignated HC-1 Det 62	
on 1 July 1965)	
VAH-4 Det 62	A-3B
*VAW-13 Det	EA-1F
*VQ-1 Det	EA-3B
*VAP-61 Det	RA-3B

***Bon Homme Richard* (CVA 31) with CVW-19 (21 Apr 1965—13 Jan 1966)**

VF-191	F-8E
VF-194	F-8E
VA-192	A-4C
VA-195	A-4C
VA-196	A-1H & A-1J
VFP-63 Det E	RF-8A
VAW-11 Det E	E-1B
HU-1 D1 Unit E	UH-2A & UH-2B
(redesignated HC-1 D1	
Unit E on 1 Jul 1965)	
*VQ-1 Det	EA-3B
*VAW-13 Det	EA-1F

***Hornet* (CVS 12) with CVSG-57 (12 Aug 1965—23 Mar 1966)**

HS-2	SH-3A
VS-35	S-2D
VS-37	S-2D
VAW-11 Det N	E-1B
H&MS-15 Det N	A-4C

***Ticonderoga* (CVA 14) with CVW-5 (28 Sep 1965—13 May 1966)**

VF-51	F-8E
VF-53	F-8E
VA-52	A-1H & A-1J
VA-56	A-4E
VA-144	A-4C
VAH-4 Det B	A-3B
VAW-11 Det B	E-1B
VFP-63 Det B	RF-8A
HC-1 D1 Unit B	UH-2A & UH-2B
*VQ-1 Det	EA-3B

***Enterprise* (CVAN 65) with CVW-9 (26 Oct 1965-21 Jun 1966)**

VA-36	A-4C
VA-76	A-4C
VA-93	A-4C
VA-94	A-4C
VAH-4 Det M	A-3B
RVAH-7	RA-5C
VAW-11 Det M	E-1B
VF-92	F-4B
VF-96	F-4B
HC-1 Det M	UH-2A & UH-2B
*VQ-1 Det	EA-3B
*VAP-61 Det	RA-3B

***Hancock* (CVA 19) with CVW-21 (10 Nov 1965—1 Aug 1966)**

VA-212	A-4E
VA-215	A-1J & A-1H
VA-216	A-4C
VAW-11 Det L	E-1B
VFP-63 Det 1	RF-8A
VF-211	F-8E
VF-24	F-8C
HC-1 D1 Unit L	UH-2A & UH-2B
*VQ-1 Det	EA-3B
*VAP-61 Det	RA-3B

***Kitty Hawk* (CVA 63) with CVW-11 (19 Oct 1965—13 Jun 1966)**

VA-85	A-6A
VA-113	A-4C
VA-115	A-1H & A-1J
VAH-4 Det C	A-3B
VAW-11 Det C	E-2A
VF-114	F-4B
VF-213	F-4B & F-4G
RVAH-13	RA-5C
HC-1 D1 Unit C	UH-2B & UH-2A
*VAP-61 Det	RA-3B
*VQ-1 Det	EA-3B

***Ranger* (CVA 61) with CVW-14 (10 Dec 1965—25 Aug 1966)**

VF-142	F-4B
VF-143	F-4B
VA-145	A-1H & A-1J
VA-146	A-4C
VA-55	A-4E
RVAH-9	RA-5C
VAH-2 Det F	A-3B
VAW-11 Det F	E-2A
HC-1 D1 Unit F	UH-2A & UH-2B
*VQ-1 Det	EA-3B
*VAP-61 Det	RA-3B

Bennington (CVS 20) with CVSG-59 (22 Mar 1965—7 Oct 1965)

VS-38	S-2E
VS-33	S-2E
HS-8	SH-3A
VAW-11 Det Q	E-1B
VA-113 Det Q	A-4B

1966 WestPac/Vietnam Deployments
(See note 1)

Yorktown (CVS 10) with CVSG-55 (6 Jan 1966—27 Jul 1966)

VS-23	S-2E
VS-25	S-2E
HS-4	SH-3A
VAW-11 Det T	E-1B

Intrepid (CVS 11) with CVW-10 (4 Apr 1966-21 Nov 1966)

VA-95	A-4B
VA-165	A-1H
VA-15	A-4B
VA-176	A-1H
HC-2 Det 11	UH-2A & UH-2B

Constellation (CVA 64) with CVW-15 (12 May 1966—3 Dec 1966)

VF-151	F-4B
VF-161	F-4B
VA-153	A-4C
VA-155	A-4E
VA-65	A-6A
RVAH-6	RA-5C
VAH-8	A-3B
VAW-11 Det D	E-2A
HC-1 D1 Unit D	UH-2A & UH-2B
*VQ-1 Det	EA-3B
*VAP-61 Det	RA-3B
*VAW-13 Det	EA-1F
*HS-6 Det	SH-3A

Oriskany (CVA 34) with CVW-16 (26 May 1966—16 Nov 1966)

VF-111	F-8E
VF-162	F-8E
VA-163	A-4E
VA-164	A-4E
VA-152	A-1H
VAH-4 Det G	A-3B
VAW-11 Det G	E-1B
VFP-63 Det G	RF-8G
HC-1 D1 Unit G	UH-2A & UH-2B
*VAP-61 Det	RA-3B

Franklin D. Roosevelt (CVA 42) with CVW-1 (21 Jun 1966—21 Feb 1967)

VF-14	F-4B
VF-32	F-4B
VA-12	A-4E
VA-72	A-4E
VA-172	A-4C
VAH-10 Det 42	A-3B
VAW-12 Det 42	E-1B
VFP-62 Det 42	RF-8G
HC-2 Det 42	UH-2A & UH-2B
*VQ-1 Det 42	EA-3B
*VAW-13 Det 42	EA-1F

Coral Sea (CVA 43) with CVW-2 (29 Jul 1966—23 Feb 1967)

VF-21	F-4B
VF-154	F-4B
VA-22	A-4C
VA-23	A-4E
VA-25	A-1H
VAW-11 Det A	E-2A
VAH-2 Det A	A-3B
VFP-63 Det A	RF-8G
HC-1 D1 Unit A	UH-2A & UH-2B
*VQ-1 Det	EA-3B
*VAP-61 Det	RA-3B

Ticonderoga (CVA 14) with CVW-19 (15 Oct 1966—29 May 1967)

VF-191	F-8E
VF-194	F-8E
VA-192	A-4E
VA-195	A-4C
VA-52	A-1H & A-1J
VFP-63 Det E	RF-8G
VAH-4 Det E	A-3B
VAW-11 Det E	E-1B
HC-1 D1 Unit E	UH-2B & UH-2A
*VQ-1 Det	EA-3B
*VAP-61 Det	RA-3B

Kitty Hawk (CVA 63) with CVW-11 (5 Nov 1966—19 Jun 1967)

VF-213	F-4B
VF-114	F-4B
VA-112	A-4C
VA-144	A-4C
VA-85	A-6A
RVAH-13	RA-5C
VAW-114 (previously a detachment of VAW-11)	E-2A
VAH-4 Det C	KA-3B
HC-1 D1 Unit C	UH-2A & UH-2B
*VQ-1 Det	EA-3B
*VAP-61 Det	RA-3B

Enterprise (CVAN 65) with CVW-9 (19 Nov 1966—6 Jul 1967)

VA-56	A-4C
VA-113	A-4C
VA-35	A-6A
VF-92	F-4B
VF-96	F-4B
VAH-2 Det M	A-3B
RVAH-7	RA-5C
VAW-11 Det M	E-2A
HC-1 Det M	UH-2A
*VQ-1 Det	EA-3B
*VAP-61 Det	RA-3B

Kearsarge (CVS 33) with CVSG-53 (9 Jun 1966—20 Dec 1966)

HS-6	SH-3A
VS-29	S-2E
VS-21	S-2E
VAW-11 Det R	E-1B

Bennington (CVS 20) with CVSG-59 (4 Nov 1966—23 May 1967)

VS-38	S-2E
VS-33	S-2E
HS-8	SH-3A
°VAW-11 Det Q	E-1B

1967 WestPac/Vietnam Deployments
(See notes 2 and 3)

Hancock (CVA 19) with CVW-5 (5 Jan 1967—22 Jul 1967)

VF-51	F-8E
VF-53	F-8E
VA-93	A-4E
VA-94	A-4C
VA-115	A-1H
VAH-4 Det B	A-3B
VFP-63 Det B	RF-8G
HC-1 Det B	UH-2A & UH-2B
°VAW-11 Det 31	E-1B

Bon Homme Richard (CVA 31) with CVW-21 (26 Jan 1967—25 Aug 1967)

VF-211	F-8E
VF-24	F-8C
VA-212	A-4E
VA-76	A-4C
VA-215	A-1H
VAH-4 Det 31	A-3B
°VAW-11 Det L	E-1B
VFP-63 Det 31	RF-8G
HC-1 D1 Unit L	UH-2B & UH-2A
*VAW-13 Det 31	EA-1F

Hornet (CVS 12) with CVSG-57 (27 Mar 1967—28 Oct 1967)

VS-35	S-2E
VS-37	S-2E
HS-2	SH-3A
°VAW-11 Det N	E-1B

Constellation (CVA 64) with CVW-14 (29 Apr 1967—4 Dec 1967)

VF-142	F-4B
VF-143	F-4B
VA-55	A-4C
VA-146	A-4C
VA-196	A-6A
RVAH-12	RA-5C
VAW-113	E-2A
VAH-8	KA-3B
HC-1 D1 Unit F/64	UH-2A & UH-2B
*VAP-61 Det	RA-3B
*VQ-1 Det	EA-3B
*VAW-13 Det	EA-1F
*VA-65	A-6A

Intrepid (CVS 11) with CVW-10 (11 May 1967—30 Dec 1967)

VSF-3	A-4B
VA-15	A-4C
VA-34	A-4C
VA-145	A-1H
VAW-33 Det 11	EA-1F
VAW-121 Det 11	E-1B
VFP-63 Det 11	RF-8G
VF-111 Det 11	F-8C
HC-2 Det 11	UH-2A & UH-2B

Forrestal (CVA 59) with CVW-17 (6 Jun 1967—15 Sep 1967)

VF-11	F-4B
VF-74	F-4B
VA-46	A-4E
VA-65	A-6A
VA-106	A-4E
RVAH-11	RA-5C
VAW-123	E-2A
VAH-10 Det 59	KA-3B
HC-2 Det 59	UH-2A
*VAP-61 Det	RA-3B

Oriskany (CVA 34) with CVW-16 (16 Jun 1967—31 Jan 1968)

VF-111	F-8C
VF-162	F-8E
VA-152	A-1H & A-1J
VA-163	A-4E

VA-164	A-4E
VFP-63 Det G/34	RF-8G
VAH-4 Det G/34	KA-3B
VAW-111 Det G/34	E-1B
*VAW-13 Det	EA-1F
HC-1 Det 34	UH-2A & UH-2B
*VAP-61 Det	RA-3B

Coral Sea (CVA 43) with CVW-15 (26 Jul 1967—6 Apr 1968)

VF-151	F-4B
VF-161	F-4B
VA-153	A-4E
VA-155	A-4E
VA-25	A-1H & A-1J
VFP-63 Det 43	RF-8G
VAH-2 Det 43	KA-3B
VAW-116	E-2A
HC-1 Det 43	UH-2A
*VAW-13 Det	EA-1F
*VAP-61 Det	RA-3B

Ranger (CVA 61) with CVW-2 (4 Nov 1967—25 May 1968)

VF-154	F-4B
VF-21	F-4B
VA-22	A-4C
VA-165	A-6A
VA-147	A-7A
RVAH-6	RA-5C
VAW-115	E-2A
VAH-2 Det 61	KA-3B
HC-1 Det 61	UH-2A & UH-2C
VAW-13 Det 61	EKA-3B
*VAP-61 Det	RA-3B

Kitty Hawk (CVA 63) with CVW-11 (18 Nov 1967—28 Jun 1968)

VF-213	F-4B
VF-114	F-4B
VA-75	A-6A & A-6B
VA-112	A-4C
VA-144	A-4E
RVAH-11	RA-5C
VAW-114	E-2A
VAH-4 Det 63	KA-3B
VAW-13 Det 63	EA-1F
HC-1 Det 63	UH-2C

Ticonderoga (CVA 14) with CVW-19 (28 Dec 1967—17 Aug 1968)

VF-191	F-8E
VF-194	F-8E
VA-23	A-4F
VA-192	A-4F

VA-195	A-4C
VAH-4 Det 14	KA-3B
VAW-111 Det 14	E-1B
VFP-63 Det 14	RF-8G
VAQ-33 Det 14	EA-1F
HC-1 Det 14	UH-2A & UH-2B

Kearsarge (CVS 33) with CVSG-53 (17 Aug 1967—6 Apr 1968)

HS-6	SH-3A
VS-29	S-2E
VS-21	S-2E
VAW-111 Det 33	E-1B
*HC-7 Det 110	SH-3A

Yorktown (CVS 10) with CVSG-55 (28 Dec 1967—5 Jul 1968)

VS-23	S-2E
VS-25	S-2E
HS-4	SH-3D
VAW-111 Det 10	E-1B
*HC-7 Det 111	SH-3A

1968 WestPac/Vietnam Deployments
(See notes 4, 5 and 6)

Enterprise (CVAN 65) with CVW-9 (3 Jan 1968—18 Jul 1968)

VF-92	F-4B
VF-96	F-4B
VA-35	A-6A & A-6B
VA-56	A-4E
VA-113	A-4F
RVAH-1	RA-5C
VAW-112	E-2A
VAH-2 Det 65	KA-3B
HC-1 Det 65	UH-2C
+VAW-13 Det 65	EKA-3B
*HC-7 Det 111	SH-3A

Bon Homme Richard (CVA 31) with CVW-5 (27 Jan 1968—10 Oct 1968)

VF-51	F-8H
VF-53	F-8E
VA-93	A-4F
VA-94	A-4E
VA-212	A-4F
VFP-63 Det 31	RF-8G
+VAW-13 Det 31	EKA-3B
VAW-111 Det 31	E-1B
HC-1 Det 31	UH-2C

America (CVA 66) with CVW-6 (10 Apr 1968—16 Dec 1968)

VF-33	F-4J
VF-102	F-4J
VA-82	A-7A
VA-86	A-7A
VA-85	A-6A & A-6B
VAW-122	E-2A
RVAH-13	RA-5C
VAH-10 Det 66	KA-3B
+VAW-13 Det 66	EKA-3B
HC-2 Det 66	UH-2A & UH-2B

Constellation (CVA 64) with CVW-14 (29 May 1968—31 Jan 1969)

VF-142	F-4B
VF-143	F-4B
VA-27	A-7A
VA-97	A-7A
VA-196	A-6A & A-6B
RVAH-5	RA-5C
VAW-113	E-2A
VAH-2 Det 64 (in Sep 1968, when VAH-2 was disest., VAH-2 Det 64 became a det. of VAH-10 and operated as VAH-10 Det 64)	KA-3B
+VAW-13 Det 64	EKA-3B
HC-1 Det 64	UH-2C

Intrepid (CVS 11) with CVW-10 (4 Jun 1968—8 Feb 1969)

VA-36	A-4C
VA-66	A-4C
VA-106	A-4E
VF-111 Det 11	F-8C
VFP-63 Det 11	RF-8G
VAW-121 Det 11	E-1B
VAQ-33 Det 11	EA-1F
HC-2 Det 11	UH-2B & UH-2A

Hancock (CVA 19) with CVW-21 (18 Jul 1968—3 Mar 1969)

VA-55	A-4F
VA-163	A-4E
VA-164	A-4E
VF-24	F-8H
VF-211	F-8H
VFP-63 Det 19	RF-8G
VAW-111 Det 19	E-1B
HC-1 Det 19	UH-2C
+VAW-13 Det 19	EKA-3B

Coral Sea (CVA 43) with CVW-15 (7 Sep 1968—18 Apr 1969)

VF-151	F-4B
VF-161	F-4B
VA-52	A-6A
VA-153	A-4F
VA-216	A-4C
VAH-10 Det 43	KA-3B
+VAW-13 Det 43	EKA-3B
VAW-116	E-2A
VFP-63 Det 43	RF-8G
HC-1 Det 43	UH-2C

Hornet (CVS 12) with CVSG-57 (30 Sep 1968—13 May 1969)

VS-35	S-2E
VS-37	S-2E
HS-2	SH-3A
VAW-111 Det 12	E-1B
*HC-7 Det 110	SH-3A

Ranger (CVA 61) with CVW-2 (26 Oct 1968—17 May 1969)

VA-165	A-6A
VF-21	F-4J
VAW-115	E-2A
VA-147	A-7A
VA-155	A-4F
VF-154	F-4J
RVAH-9	RA-5C
VAH-10 Det 61	KA-3B
VAQ-130 Det 61	EKA-3B
HC-1 Det 61	UH-2C
*HS-2	SH-3A
*HC-7 Det 110	SH-3A

Kitty Hawk (CVA 63) with CVW-11 (30 Dec 1968—4 Sep 1969)

VF-114	F-4B
VF-213	F-4B
VA-37	A-7A
VA-65	A-6A & A-6B
VA-105	A-7A
RVAH-11	RA-5C
VAQ-131	KA-3B & EKA-3B
VAW-114	E-2A
HC-1 Det 63	UH-2C
*HC-7 Det 110	SH-3A

Bennington (CVS 20) with CVSG-59 (1 May 1968—9 Nov 1968)

VS-33	S-2E
VS-38	S-2E
HS-8	SH-3A
VAW-111 Det 20	E-1B

1969 WestPac/Vietnam Deployments

(See note 7)

Enterprise (CVAN 65) with CVW-9 (6 Jan 1969—2 Jul 1969)

VF-92	F-4J
VF-96	F-4J
VA-145	A-6A & A-6B
VA-146	A-7B
VA-215	A-7B
VAQ-132	EKA-3B & KA-3B
VAW-112	E-2A
RVAH-6	RA-5C
HC-1 Det 65	UH-2C

Ticonderoga (CVA 14) with CVW-16 (1 Feb 1969—18 Sep 1969)

VA-87	A-7B
VF-111	F-8H
VF-162	F-8J
VA-25	A-7B
VA-112	A-4C
VFP-63 Det 14	RF-8G
VAQ-130 Det 14	EKA-3B
VAW-111 Det 14	E-1B
HC-1 Det 14	UH-2C
*HC-7 Det 110	SH-3A

Bon Homme Richard (CVA 31) with CVW-5 (18 Mar 1969—29 Oct 1969)

VF-51	F-8J
VF-53	F-8J
VA-22	A-4F
VA-94	A-4E
VA-144	A-4E
VFP-63 Det 31	RF-8G
VAQ-130 Det 31	EKA-3B
VAW-111 Det 31	E-1B
HC-1 Det 31	UH-2C
*HC-7 Det 110	SH-3A

Kearsarge (CVS 33) with CVSG-53 (29 Mar 1969—4 Sep 1969)

VS-21	S-2E
VS-29	S-2E
HS-6	SH-3A
VAW-111 Det 33	E-1B
*HC-7 Det 111	SH-3A
*HC-7 Det 110	SH-3A

Oriskany (CVA 34) with CVW-19 (14 Apr 1969—17 Nov 1969)

VF-191	F-8J
VF-194	F-8J
VA-23	A-4F

VA-192	A-4F
VA-195	A-4E
VAW-111 Det 34	E-1B
VFP-63 Det 34	RF-8G
VAQ-130 Det 34	EKA-3B
HC-1 Det 34	UH-2C

Hancock (CVA 19) with CVW-21 (2 Aug 1969—15 Apr 1970)

VF-24	F-8H
VF-211	F-8J
VA-55	A-4F
VA-164	A-4F
VA-212	A-4F
VAH-10 Det 19	KA-3B
VAW-111 Det 19	E-1B
VFP-63 Det 19	RF-8G
HC-1 Det 19	SH-3A

Constellation (CVA 64) with CVW-14 (11 Aug 1969—8 May 1970)

VF-142	F-4J
VF-143	F-4J
VA-27	A-7A
VA-85	A-6A & A-6B
VA-97	A-7A
RVAH-7	RA-5C
VAW-113	E-2A
VAQ-133	EKA-3B & KA-3B
HC-1 Det 5	SH-3A
*HC-7 Det 110	SH-3A

Coral Sea (CVA 43) with CVW-15 (23 Sep 1969—1 Jul 1970)

VF-151	F-4B
VF-161	F-4B
VA-82	A-7A
VA-86	A-7A
VA-35	A-6A
VAW-116	E-2A
VAQ-135	KA-3B & EKA-3B
VFP-63 Det 43	RF-8G
HC-1 Det 9	UH-2C

Ranger (CVA 61) with CVW-2 (14 Oct 1969—1 Jun 1970)

VF-21	F-4J
VF-154	F-4J
VA-56	A-7B
VA-93	A-7B
VA-196	A-6A
RVAH-5	RA-5C
VAQ-134	EKA-3B & KA-3B
VAW-115	E-2A
HC-1 Det 8	SH-3A
VC-3 Det	147SK Fire drones

1970 WestPac/Vietnam Deployments

Shangri-la (CVS 38) with CVW-8 (5 Mar 1970—17 Dec 1970)

VA-12	A-4C
VA-152	A-4E
VA-172	A-4C
VF-111	F-8H
VF-162	F-8H
**VAH-10 Det 38	KA-3D
VFP-63 Det 38	RF-8G
VAW-121 Det 38	E-1B
HC-2 Det 38	UH-2C

Bon Homme Richard (CVA 31) with CVW-5 (2 Apr 1970—12 Nov 1970)

VF-51	F-8J
VF-53	F-8J
VA-22	A-4F
VA-94	A-4E
VA-144	A-4F
VFP-63 Det 31	RF-8G
VAQ-130 Det 31	EKA-3B
VAW-111 Det 14	E-1B
HC-1 Det 3	UH-2C

America (CVA 66) with CVW-9 (10 Apr 1970—21 Dec 1970)

VF-92	F-4J
VF-96	F-4J
VA-146	A-7E
VA-147	A-7E
VA-165	A-6A, A-6B & A-6C
RVAH-12	RA-5C
VAW-124	E-2A
VAQ-132	EKA-3B & KA-3B
HC-2 Det 66	UH-2C
*HC-7 Det 110	SH-3A

Oriskany (CVA 34) with CVW-19 (14 May 1970—10 Dec 1970)

VF-191	F-8J
VF-194	F-8J
VA-153	A-7A
VA-155	A-7B
VAQ-130 Det 1	EKA-3B
VAW-111 Det 34	E-1B
VFP-63 Det 34	RF-8G
HC-1 Det 6	UH-2C

Hancock (CVA 19) with CVW-21 (22 Oct 1970—3 Jun 1971)

VF-24	F-8J
VF-211	F-8J
VA-55	A-4F
VA-164	A-4F
VAQ-129 Det 62	EKA-3B
VAW-111 Det 19	E-1B
VFP-63 Det 19	RF-8G
VA-212	A-4F
HC-1 Det 7	UH-2C
*HC-5 Det 103	UH-2C

Ranger (CVA 61) with CVW-2 (27 Oct 1970—17 Jun 1971)

VF-21	F-4J
VF-154	F-4J
VA-25	A-7E
VA-113	A-7E
VA-145	A-6A & A-6C
RVAH-1	RA-5C
VAQ-134	KA-3B & EKA-3B
VAW-111 Det 7	E-1B
HC-1 Det 1	SH-3G
*HC-7 Det 110	SH-3A

Kitty Hawk (CVA 63) with CVW-11 (6 Nov 1970—17 Jul 1971)

VF-114	F-4J
VF-213	F-4J
VA-192	A-7E
VA-195	A-7E
VA-52	A-6B
RVAH-6	RA-5C
VAQ-133	EKA-3B & KA-3B
VAW-114	E-2B
HC-1 Det 2	UH-2C
*HC-7 Det 110	SH-3A

1971 WestPac/Vietnam Deployments

Midway (CVA 41) with CVW-5 (16 Apr 1971—6 Nov 1971)

VF-151	F-4B
VF-161	F-4B
VA-56	A-7B
VA-93	A-7B
VA-115	A-6A & KA-6D
VAQ-130 Det 2	EKA-3B
VFP-63 Det 3	RF-8G
VAW-115	E-2B
HC-1 Det 8	SH-3G
*HC-7 Det 110	HH-3A

Oriskany (CVA 34) with CVW-19 (14 May 1971—18 Dec 1971)

VF-191	F-8J
VF-194	F-8J
VA-153	A-7A
VA-155	A-7B
VA-215	A-7B
VAQ-130 Det 3	EKA-3B
VFP-63 Det 34	RF-8G
VAW-111 Det 1	E-1B
HC-1 Det 5	UH-2C
*HC-7 Det 110	SH-3A & SH-3G

Enterprise (CVAN 65) with CVW-14 (11 Jun 1971—12 Feb 1972)

VF-143	F-4J
VF-142	F-4J
VA-97	A-7E
VA-27	A-7E
VA-196	A-6A, A-6B & KA-6D
RVAH-5	RA-5C
VAW-113	E-2B
VAQ-130 Det 4	EKA-3B
HC-1 Det 4	SH-3G

Constellation (CVA 64) with CVW-9 (1 Oct 1971—30 Jun 1972)

VF-92	F-4J
VF-96	F-4J
VA-146	A-7E
VA-147	A-7E
VA-165	A-6A & KA-6D
RVAH-11	RA-5C
VAQ-130 Det 1	EKA-3B
VAW-116	E-2B
HC-1 Det 3	SH-3G

Coral Sea (CVA 43) with CVW-15 (12 Nov 1971—17 Jul 1972)

VF-51	F-4B
VF-111	F-4B
VA-22	A-7E
VA-94	A-7E
VMA(AW)-224	A-6A & KA-6D
VFP-63 Det 5	RF-8G
VAW-111 Det 4	E-1B
VAQ-135 Det 3	EKA-3B
HC-1 Det 6	SH-3G
*HC-7 Det 110	HH-3A

Ticonderoga (CVS 14) with CVSG-59 (11 Mar 1971—6 Jul 1971)

VS-33	S-2E
VS-37	S-2E
VS-38	S-2E
HS-4	SH-3D
HS-8	SH-3D
VAW-111 Det 3	E-1B

1972 WestPac/Vietnam Deployments

Hancock (CVA 19) with CVW-21 (7 Jan 1972—3 Oct 1972)

VA-55	A-4F
VA-164	A-4F/TA-4F
VA-212	A-4F
VF-24	F-8J
VF-211	F-8J
VFP-63 Det 1	RF-8G
VAQ-135 Det 5	EKA-3B
VAW-111 Det 2	E-1B
HC-1 Det 7	SH-3G

Kitty Hawk (CVA 63) with CVW-11 (17 Feb 1972—28 Nov 1972)

VA-195	A-7E
VA-192	A-7E
VA-52	A-6A, A-6B & KA-6D
VF-114	F-4J
VF-213	F-4J
RVAH-7	RA-5C
VAW-114	E-2B
VAQ-135 Det 1	EKA-3B
HC-1 Det 1	SH-3G
*HC-7 Det	HH-3A

Midway (CVA 41) with CVW-5 (10 Apr 1972—3 Mar 1973)

VF-151	F-4B
VF-161	F-4B
VA-56	A-7B
VA-93	A-7B
VA-115	A-6A & KA-6D
VAQ-130 Det 2	EKA-3B
VFP-63 Det 3	RF-8G
VAW-115	E-2B
HC-1 Det 2	SH-3G
*HC-7 Det 110	HH-3A

Saratoga (CV 60) with CVW-3 (11 Apr 1972—13 Feb 1973)

VF-31	F-4J
VF-103	F-4J
VA-75	A-6A, A-6B &
	KA-6D
VA-37	A-7A
VA-105	A-7A
RVAH-1	RA-5C
VAW-123	E-2B
HS-7	SH-3D
*HC-7 Det 110	HH-3A
*VMCJ-2 Det	EA-6A

Ticonderoga (CVS 14) with CVSG-53 (17 May 1972—29 Jul 1972)

VS-21	S-2E
VS-29	S-2E
VS-35	S-2E
VS-38	S-2E
VAW-111 Det 3	E-1B
HS-4	SH-3D
HS-8	SH-3D

America (CVA 66) with CVW-8 (5 Jun 1972—24 Mar 1973)

VF-74	F-4J
VA-35	A-6A, A-6C &
	KA-6D
VA-82	A-7C
VA-86	A-7C
RVAH-6	RA-5C
VAW-124	E-2B
VMFA-333	F-4J
VAQ-132	EA-6B
HC-2 Det 66	SH-3G
*HC-7 Det 110	HH-3A

Oriskany (CVA 34) with CVW-19 (5 Jun 1972—30 Mar 1973)

VF-191	F-8J
VF-194	F-8J
VA-153	A-7A
VA-155	A-7B
VA-215	A-7B
VFP-63 Det 4	RF-8G
VAQ-130 Det 3	EKA-3B
VAW-111 Det 6	E-1B
HC-1 Det 5	SH-3G

Enterprise (CVAN 65) with CVW-14 (12 Sep 1972—12 Jun 1973)

VF-143	F-4J
VF-142	F-4J

VA-27	A-7E
VA-97	A-7E
VA-196	A-6E, A-6B &
	KA-6D
VAW-113	E-2B
VAQ-131	EA-6B
RVAH-13	RA-5C
HS-2 Det 1	SH-3G

Ranger (CVA 61) with CVW-2 (16 Nov 1972—23 Jun 1973)

VF-21	F-4J
VF-154	F-4J
VA-25	A-7E
VA-113	A-7E
VA-145	A-6A, A-6B & KA-6D
RVAH-5	RA-5C
VAW-111 Det 1	E-1B
VAQ-130 Det 4	EKA-3B
HC-1 Det 1	SH-3G
*HC-7 Det 110	HH-3A
*VQ-1 Det	EA-3B

1973 WestPac/Vietnam Deployments

Constellation (CVA 64) with CVW-9 (5 Jan 1973—11 Oct 1973)

VF-92	F-4J
VF-96	F-4J
VA-146	A-7E
VA-147	A-7E
VA-165	A-6A & KA-6D
HS-6 Det 1	SH-3G
VAQ-134	EA-6B
VAW-116	E-2B
RVAH-12	RA-5C
*VQ-1 Det	EA-3B

Hancock (CVA 19) with CVW-21 (8 May 1973—8 Jan 1974)

VF-24	F-8J
VF-211	F-8J
VA-55	A-4F
VA-164	A-4F & TA-4F
VA-212	A-4F
VFP-63 Det 1	RF-8G
***VAQ-135 Det 5	EKA-3B
VAW-111 Det 2	E-1B
HC-1 Det 3	SH-3G
*HC-7 Det 110	HH-3A

Coral Sea (CVA 43) with CVW-15 (9 Mar 1973—8 Nov 1973)

VF-51	F-4B
VF-111	F-4B
VA-22	A-7E
VA-94	A-7E
VA-95	A-6A, A-6B &
	KA-6D
***VAQ-135 Det 3	EKA-3B
VAW-111 Det 4	E-1B
VFP-63 Det 5	RF-8G
HC-1 Det 6	SH-3G
*HC-7 Det 110	HH-3A

Midway (CVA 41) with CVW-5 (11 Sep 1973—31 Dec 1973)
(*Midway* permanently home ported in WESTPAC)

VF-151	F-4N
VF-161	F-4N
VA-56	A-7A
VA-93	A-7A
VA-115	A-6A, A-6B &
	KA-6D
VFP-63 Det 3	RF-8G
VAW-115	E-2B
HC-1 Det 2	SH-3G
VMCJ-1 Det 101	EA-6A

Oriskany (CVA 34) with CVW-19 (18 Oct 1973—5 Jun 1974)

VF-191	F-8J
VF-194	F-8J
VA-153	A-7B
VA-155	A-7B
VA-215	A-7B
VFP-63 Det 4	RF-8G
****VAW-111 Det 6	E-1B
VAQ-130 Det 3	EKA-3B
HC-1 Det 1	SH-3G

Kitty Hawk (CV 63) with CVW-11 (23 Nov 1973—9 Jul 1974)

VF-114	F-4J
VF-213	F-4J
VA-192	A-7E
VA-195	A-7E
VA-52	A-6A & KA-6D
VAQ-136	EA-6B
RVAH-7	RA-5C
VAW-114	E-2B
VS-37	S-2G
VS-38	S-2G
HS-4	SH-3D
*VQ-1 Det 63	EA-3B

1974 WestPac/Vietnam Deployments

Midway (CVA 41) with CVW-5 (1 Jan-31 Dec 1974)
(*Midway* permanently home ported in WESTPAC)

VF-161	F-4N
VF-151	F-4N
VA-93	A-7A
VA-56	A-7A
VA-115	A-6A, A-6B &
	KA-6D
VAW-115	E-2B
HC-1 Det 2	SH-3G
VMCJ-1 Det 101	EA-6A & RF-4B
*VQ-1 Det	EA-3B

Ranger (CVA 61) with CVW-2 (7 May 1974—18 Oct 1974)

VA-25	A-7E
VA-113	A-7E
VA-145	A-6A & KA-6D
VF-21	F-4J
VF-154	F-4J
RVAH-13	RA-5C
VAW-112	E-2B
HC-1 Det 4	SH-3G
*VQ-1 Det 61	EA-3B

Constellation (CVA 64) with CVW-9 (21 Jun 1974—22 Dec 1974)

VF-92	F-4J
VF-96	F-4J
VA-146	A-7E
VA-147	A-7E
VA-165	A-6A & KA-6D
RVAH-5	RA-5C
VAW-116	E-2B
VAQ-131	EA-6B
HS-6	SH-3A
*VQ-1 Det 64	EA-3B

Enterprise (CVAN 65) with CVW-14 (17 Sep 1974—20 May 1975)

VF-1	F-14A
VF-2	F-14A
VA-27	A-7E
VA-97	A-7E
VA-196	A-6A & KA-6D
VAQ-137	EA-6B
HS-2	SH-3D
VAW-113	E-2B
RVAH-12	RA-5C
*VQ-1 Det 65	EA-3B

Coral Sea (CVA 43) with CVW-15 (5 Dec 1974—2 Jul 1975)

VF-51	F-4N
VF-111	F-4N
VFP-63 Det 5	RF-8G
VA-22	A-7E
VA-94	A-7E
VA-95	A-6A & KA-6D
RVAW-110 Det 3	E-1B
HC-1 Det 2	SH-3G

1975 WestPac/Vietnam Deployments

(See note 8)

Midway (CV 41) with CVW-5 (1 Jan-31 Dec 1975)
(Midway permanently home ported in WESTPAC)

VF-161	F-4N
VF-151	F-4N
VA-93	A-7A
VA-56	A-7A
VA-115	A-6A, A-6B & KA-6D
VAW-115	E-2B
HC-1 Det 2	SH-3G
*VMFP-3 Det	RF-4B
*VMAQ-2 Det	EA-6B
*VMCJ-1 Det 101	EA-6A & RF-4B

Hancock (CV 19) with CVW-21 (18 Mar 1975—20 Oct 1975)

VA-55	A-4F
VA-164	A-4F & TA-4F
VA-212	A-4F
VF-24	F-8J
VF-211	F-8J
RVAW-110 Det 6	E-1B
HC-1 Det 1	SH-3G
VFP-63 Det 1	RF-8G

°°*Kitty Hawk (CV 63) with CVW-11 (21 May 1975—15 Dec 1975)*

VF-213	F-4J
VF-114	F-4J
VA-52	A-6E & KA-6D
VA-192	A-7E
VA-195	A-7E
VS-37	S-2G
VS-38	S-2G
VAQ-136	EA-6B
RVAH-6	RA-5C
HS-8	SH-3G
VAW-114	E-2B
*VQ-1 Det 63	EA-3

Oriskany (CV 34) with CVW-19 (16 Sep 1975—3 Mar 1976)

VF-191	F-8J
VF-194	F-8J
VA-153	A-7B
VA-155	A-7B
VA-215	A-7B
VFP-63 Det 4	RF-8G
RVAW-110 Det 4	E-1B
HC-1 Det 4	SH-3G

Notes and explanations-specific entries:

* These squadron detachments were not aboard the carrier for the entire deployment.

** This carrier returned from deploymnant prior to the beginning of combat operations in Vietnam during 1964.

*** VAQ-135 Detachments 3 and 5 were transferred on 25 August 1973 to VAQ-130. VAQ-135 Det 3 became VAQ-130 Det 2 and VAQ-135 Det 5 became VAQ-130 Det 5.

**** VAW-111 Det 6 was transferred in March 1974 to RVAW-110 and became RVAW-110 Det 6.

° On 20 April 1967 VAW-111 was established and VAW-11 detachments became part of VAW-111. VAW-11 Det Q became VAW-111 Det 20.

°° This deployment involved an experiment with the composition of the carrier air wing in a multimission role. Several of the squadrons were shore-based in the Philippines during different periods of this deployment.

°°° VAH-10 was redesignated VAQ-129 on 1 September 1970.

+ On 1 October 1968 VAQ-13 and its detachments were redesignated VAQ-130.

Numbered Notes

1. VAW-13's records for 1966 do not specify the carriers they operated aboard. However, the records indicate VAW-13 Det 1 (located at Cubi Point, P.I.) provided detachments in support of fleet strikes from the carriers on Yankee Station.

2. VAW-13 did not submit a Command History Report for 1967, consequently, it is not possible to verify all the squadron's detachments operating aboard carriers on Yankee Station in 1967.

3. VQ-1's Command History Report for 1967 did not identify the detachments or carriers they operated from in support of combat operations against Vietnam.

4. VAP-61's Command History Report for 1968 indicated continued support of 7th Fleet carriers on Yankee Station. However, the squadron's report does not identify the detachments deployed aboard carriers in WESTPAC during 1968.

5. HC-7 was established on 1 September 1967. In 1968 an HC-7 detachment was formed and given the mission of maintaining year-round combat configured helicopters aboard carriers and other ships operating on Yankee Station for combat search and rescue missions. The 1968 Command History Report for HC-7 does not identify all the specific ships that detachment 110 operated aboard.

6. VQ-1 detachments continued to support carrier operations in Vietnam. However, the 1968 Command History Report for VQ-1 does not mention any detachments that were aboard carriers operating on Yankee Station.

7. VQ-1 and VAP-61 detachments provided support from DaNang Air Base, Republic of South Vietnam, for Fleet carriers operating on Yankee Station in 1969.

8. On 30 June 1975, all carriers with the designation CVA or CVAN were changed to CV or CVN to reflect the multimission capability of the carrier.

9. Tail codes for Carrier Air Wings (CVW) from 1964 to 1975 were as follows:

CVW-1	AB
CVW-2	NE
CVW-3	AC
CVW-5	NF
CVW-6	AE
CVW-7	AG
CVW-8	AJ
CVW-9	NG
CVW-10	AK
CVW-11	NH
CVW-14	NK
CVW-15	NL

CVW-16	AH
CVW-17	AA
CVW-19	NM
CVW-21	NP
RCVW-4	AD
RCVW-12	NJ
CVSG-50/RCVSG-50	AR
CVSG-51/RCVSG-51	RA
CVSG-52	AS
CVSG-53	NS
CVSG-54	AT
CVSG-55	NU
CVSG-56	AU
CVSG-57	NV
CVSG-58	AV
CVSG-59	NT
CVSG-60	AW

10. Tail codes for various squadrons not part of the normal air wing composition but deployed on carriers from 1964 to 1975 were as follows:

VAP-62	GB
VAP-61	SS
VFP-63	PP
VFP-62	GA
VAW-11/VAW-111	RR
VAW-12	GE
VAW-13	VR

VAW-33	GD
VAH-1/RVAH-1	GH
VAH-3/RVAH-3	GJ
VAH-4	ZB
VAH-5/RVAH-5	GK
RVAH-6	GS
VAH-7/RVAH-7	GL
VAH-9/RVAH-9	GM
VAH-11	GN
RVAH-12	GP
RVAH-13	GR
RVAH-14	GQ
VAH-21	SL
VR-30	RW
VRC-40	CD
VRC-50	RG
VQ-1	PR
VQ-2	JQ
VSF-1	NA
VAQ-130	VR
HM-12	DH

11. Some of the squadrons, such as VAQ, VAW and RVAH, lose their individually assigned tail codes in the late 1960s or early 1970s and are authorized to use the tail codes of their permanently assigned Carrier Air Wing.

12. Tail codes for Marine Corps squadrons that deployed aboard carriers were not included in the list.

Deployments for Patrol Squadrons and other Non-carrier Based Squadrons in Vietnam (1964–1972)

See the Notes Section at the end of this listing for any clarification on the entries and for the Tail Code List.

1964 Deployments

VP-48

Deployed to:	NS Sangley Point
Aircraft:	SP-5B
Date In:	May 1964

Date Out: 22 Sep 1964

VAP-61

Deployed to:	(see detachments)
Aircraft:	RA-3B
Date In:	17 May 1964

Date Out: See Note 3

Detachment Location:	NAS Cubi Point
	RTAB Don Muang
	FASU Da Nang
	RTNB U-Tapao
Detachment Date In:	17 May 1964

Date Out: 1 Jul 1971

VW-1

Deployed to:	(see detachments)
Aircraft:	EC-121K, C-121J and WC-121N
Date In:	1 Oct 1964

Date Out: See Note 3

Detachment Location:	NS Sangley Point
	NSAD Chu Lai
Detachment Date In:	1 Oct 1964

Date Out: 1 Jul 1971

VQ-1

Deployed to:	(see detachments)
Aircraft:	EC-121M, C-121J, ERA-3B and EP-3B
Date In:	1 Oct 1964

Date Out: See Note 3

Detachment Location:	RTAB Don Muang
	NAS Cubi Point
	NAF Da Nang
Detachment Date In:	1 Oct 1964

Date Out: 17 Feb 1973

VP-17

Deployed to:	NAF Naha
Aircraft:	SP-2H
Date In:	27 Apr 1964

Date Out: 30 Sep 1964

Detachment Location:	None

VP-28

Deployed to:	MCAS Iwakuni		
Aircraft:	SP-2H		
Date In:	16 May 1964	Date Out:	18 Oct 1964

Detachment Location:	NS Sangley Point		
Detachment Date In:	5 Aug 1964	Date Out:	30 Sep 1964

VP-42

Deployed to:	MCAS Iwakuni		
Aircraft:	SP-2E		
Date In:	11 Jul 1964	Date Out:	16 Nov 1964

Detachment Location:	NS Sangley Point		
Detachment Date In:	3 Sep 1964	Date Out:	18 Sep 1964
Detachment Location:	NAF Tan Son Nhut		
Detachment Date In:	18 Sep 1964	Date Out:	19 Sep 1964
Detachment Location:	NAS Cubi Point		
Detachment Date In:	6 Oct 1964	Date Out:	24 Oct 1964
Special Det Deployment:	NAF Tan Son Nhut		
Detachment Date In:	Oct 1964	Date Out:	late Feb 1965

VP-6

Deployed to:	NAF Naha and MCAS Iwakuni		
Aircraft:	SP-2E		
Date In:	12 Aug 1964	Date Out:	25 Jan 1965

Detachment Location:	NAS Cubi Point		
Detachment Date In:	1 Sep 1964	Date Out:	28 Sep 1964

VP-47

Deployed to:	NS Sangley Point		
Aircraft:	SP-5B		
Date In:	17 Aug 1964	Date Out:	28 Feb 1965

Detachment Location:	AV-13		
Detachment Date In:	various	Date Out:	various

VP-1

Deployed to:	MCAS Iwakuni		
Aircraft:	SP-2H		
Date In:	7 Oct 1964	Date Out:	1 Apr 1965

Detachment Location:	NAF Tan Son Nhut
	`Da Nang

VP-9

Deployed to:	NAF Naha		
Aircraft:	P-3A		
Date In:	12 Nov 1964	Date Out:	8 Jul 1965

Detachment Location:	None

1965 Deployments

VQ-2

Deployed to:	(see detachments)
Aircraft:	EA-3B
Date In:	1 Dec 1965

Date Out: See Note 3

Detachment Location:	NAS Cubi Point
	FASU Da Nang
Detachment Date In:	1 Dec 1965

Date Out: 30 Sep 1969

VP-2

Deployed to:	MCAS Iwakuni
Aircraft:	SP-2H
Date In:	24 Jan 1965

Date Out: 16 Jul 1965

Detachment Location:	NAF Tan Son Nhut
Detachment Date In:	15 Mar 1965
Detachment Location:	various places (Naha, Sangley Point, Iwo Jima, Bangkok, Tainan, Da Nang)

Date Out: 1 May 1965

VP-40

Deployed to:	NS Sangley Point
Aircraft:	SP-5B
Date In:	27 Feb 1965

Date Out: 3 Sep 1965

Detachment Location:	AV-13
Detachment Date In:	14 May 1965
Detachment Location:	AV-7
Detachment Date In:	29 May 1965

Date Out: 20 May 1965
Date Out: 3 Aug 1965

VP-4

Deployed to:	MCAS Iwakuni
Aircraft:	SP-2H
Date In:	26 Mar 1965

Date Out: 28 Sep 1965

Detachment Location:	NAF Tan Son Nhut
Detachment Date In:	19 Apr 1965
Detachment Location:	NS Sangley Point
Detachment Date In:	26 Mar 1965
Detachment Location:	NAS Cubi Point
Detachment Date In:	20 Apr 1965

Date Out: 19 Apr 1965
Date Out: 20 Apr 1965
Date Out: 26 Apr 1965

VP-22

Deployed to:	NS Sangley Point
Aircraft:	P-3A
Date In:	23 Apr 1965

Date Out: 13 Dec 1965

Detachment Location:	None

VP-46

Deployed to:	NAF Naha
Aircraft:	P-3A
Date In:	7 Jun 1965

Date Out: 8 Jan 1966

Detachment Location:	NS Sangley Point
Detachment Date In:	7 Jun 1965

Date Out: 8 Jan 1966

VP-17

Deployed to:	MCAS Iwakuni
Aircraft:	SP-2H
Date In:	9 Jul 1965

Date Out: 6 Feb 1966

Detachment Location:	NAF Tan Son Nhut

VP-50

Deployed to:	NS Sangley Point
Aircraft:	SP-5B
Date In:	1 Sep 1965

Date Out: 14 Mar 1966

Detachment Location:	NAF Camh Ranh Bay
Detachment Location:	AV-12
Detachment Date In:	various

Date Out: various

VP-42

Deployed to:	MCAS Iwakuni
Aircraft:	SP-2H
Date In:	26 Sep 1965

Date Out: 5 Apr 1966

Detachment Location:	NAF Tan Son Nhut
Detachment Date In:	8 Oct 1965

Date Out: 13 Feb 1966

VP-48

Deployed to:	(see detachment)
Aircraft:	SP-5B

Detachment Location:	NS Sangley Point
Detachment Date In:	Aug 1965

Date Out: 4 Sep 1966

VP-28

Deployed to:	NS Sangley Point
Aircraft:	P-3A
Date In:	2 Nov 1965

Date Out: 2 Jun 1966

Detachment Location:	None

1966 Deployments

VXN-8

Deployed to:　　(see detachment)
Aircraft:　　NC-121J

Detachment Location:	NAF Tan Son Nhut		
Detachment Date In:	Oct 1965	Date Out:	Dec 1965
Detachment Location:	NAF Tan Son Nhut		
Detachment Date In:	3 Jan 1966	Date Out:	1 Dec 1970

HC-1

Deployed to:　　(see detachment)
Aircraft:　　UH-1B

Detachment Location:	Various places in Mekong Delta		
Detachment Date In:	1 Jul 1966	Date Out:	1 Apr 1967

VRC-50

Deployed to:　　(see detachments)
Aircraft:　　C-1A, C-2A and CT-39E
Date In:　　1 Oct 1966　　　　　　Date Out:　　See Note 3

Detachment Location:	NAS Cubi Point		
Detachment Date In:	See Note 3	Date Out:	See Note 3
Detachment Location:	Da Nang		
Detachment Date In:	1 Feb 1970	Date Out	2 Jan 1971
	15 Dec 1971		19 Feb 1973

VAP-62

Deployed to:　　(see detachments)
Aircraft:　　RA-3B
Date In:　　31 Oct 1966　　　　　　Date Out:　　See Note 3

Detachment Location:	NAS Cubi Point		
	FASU Da Nang		
Detachment Date In:	31 Oct 1966	Date Out:	1 Feb 1969

VP-47

Deployed to:　　NAF Naha
Aircraft:　　P-3B
Date In:　　4 Jan 1966　　　　　　Date Out:　　30 Jun 1966

Detachment Location:　　NS Sangley Point (augmented occasionally)

VP-1

Deployed to:　　MCAS Iwakuni
Aircraft:　　SP-2H
Date In:　　3 Feb 1966　　　　　　Date Out:　　1 Aug 1966

Detachment Location:	NAF Tan Son Nhut		
Detachment Date In:	13 Feb 1966	Date Out:	27 May 1966

VP-40

Deployed to:	NS Sangley Point
Aircraft:	SP-5B
Date In:	15 Mar 1966

Date Out: 3 Sep 1966

Detachment Location:	AV-13		
Detachment Date In:	10 Mar 1966	Date Out:	26 Mar 1966
Detachment Date In:	3 Apr 1966	Date Out:	10 Apr 1966
Detachment Date In:	14 May 1966	Date Out:	3 Jun 1966
Detachment Date In:	10 Jul 1966	Date Out:	9 Aug 1966
Detachment Date In:	15 Jul 1966	Date Out:	21 Jul 1966

VP-2

Deployed to:	MCAS Iwakuni
Aircraft:	SP-2H
Date In:	1 Apr 1966

Date Out: 1 Oct 1966

Detachment Location:	NAF Tan Son Nhut
Detachment Date In:	25 May 1966

Date Out: 30 Sep 1966

VP-8

Deployed to:	NS Sangley Point
Aircraft:	P-3A
Date In:	1 Jul 1966

Date Out: 2 Dec 1966

Detachment Location: None

VP-9

Deployed to:	NAF Naha
Aircraft:	P-3B
Date In:	25 Jul 1966

Date Out: 10 Jan 1967

Detachment Location:	NAF Sangley Point
Detachment Date In:	25 Jun 1966

Date Out: 12 Dec 1966

VP-19

Deployed to:	MCAS Iwakuni
Aircraft:	P-3A
Date In:	1 Aug 1966

Date Out: 31 Jan 1967

Detachment Location: Unknown

VP-50

Deployed to:	Cam Ranh Bay, AV-7
Aircraft:	SP-5B
Date In:	19 Aug 1966

Date Out: 6 Feb 1967

Detachment Location: None

VP-17

Deployed to:	MCAS Iwakuni and NS Sangley Point		
Aircraft:	SP-2H		
Date In:	1 Oct 1966	Date Out:	30 Mar 1967
Detachment Location:	NAF Tan Son Nhut		
Detachment Date In:	1 Oct 1966	Date Out:	30 Mar 1967

VP-16

Deployed to:	NS Sangley Point		
Aircraft:	P-3A		
Date In:	2 Dec 1966	Date Out:	2 Jun 1967
Detachment Location:	NAF U-Tapao		
Detachment Date In:	18 Jan 1967	Date Out:	18 Feb 1967

1967 Deployments

VO-67

Deployed to:	RTAB Nakhon Phanom		
Aircraft:	OP-2E		
Date In:	15 Nov 1967	Date Out:	1 Jul 1968
Detachment Location:	None		

HAL-3

Aircraft:	UH-1B/1C/1L/1M and HH-1K		
Deployed to:	Vung Tau		
Date In:	1 Apr 1967	Date Out:	1 May 1969
Deployed to:	Binh Thuy		
Date In:	2 May 1969	Date Out:	16 Mar 1972
Detachment Location:	various		

VR-1

Deployed to:	(see detachment)		
Aircraft:	C-130F		
Date In:	14 Jun 1967	Date Out:	See Note 3
Detachment Location:	NAS Cubi Point		
Detachment Date In:	14 Jun 1967	Date Out:	23 Jun 1967

VP-46

Deployed to:	NAF Naha		
Aircraft:	P-3B		
Date In:	14 Jan 1967	Date Out:	30 Jun 1967
Detachment Location:	NS Sangley Point		
Detachment Date In:	5 Feb 1967	Date Out:	18 Feb 1967
Detachment Location:	RTNB U-Tapao		
Detachment Date In:	18 Feb 1967	Date Out:	30 Jun 1967

VP-4

Deployed to:	MCAS Iwakuni		
Aircraft:	P-3A		
Date In:	31 Jan 1967	Date Out:	31 Jul 1967

Detachment Location:	NS Sangley Point		
Detachment Date In:	See Note 3	Date Out:	See Note 3
Detachment Location:	NAF Naha		
Detachment Date In:	15 Jul 1967	Date Out:	20 Jul 1967

VP-40

Deployed to:	NS Sangley Point		
Aircraft:	SP-5B		
Date In:	24 Feb 1967	Date Out:	10 May 1967

Detachment Location:	AV-7		
Detachment Date In:	1 Mar 1967	Date Out:	30 Apr 1967

VP-42

Deployed to:	NS Sangley Point		
Aircraft:	SP-2H		
Date In:	31 Mar 1967	Date Out:	30 Sep 1967

Detachment Location:	NAF Cam Ranh Bay		
Detachment Date In:	2 Apr 1967	Date Out:	18 May 1967
Detachment Location:	NAF Tan Son Nhut		
Detachment Date In:	31 Mar 1967	Date Out:	30 Sep 1967

VP-1

Deployed to:	NS Sangley Point		
Aircraft:	SP-2H		
Date In:	6 May 1967	Date Out:	12 Nov 1967

Detachment Location:	NAF Cam Rahn Bay		
Detachment Date In:	15 May 1967	Date Out:	12 Nov 1967

VP-5

Deployed to:	NS Sangley Point		
Aircraft:	P-3A		
Date In:	1 Jun 1967	Date Out:	3 Dec 1967

Detachment Location:	None

VP-47

Deployed to:	NAF Naha		
Aircraft:	P-3B		
Date In:	1 Jul 1967	Date Out:	4 Jan 1968

Detachment Location:	RTNB U-Tapao		
Detachment Date In:	1 Jul 1967	Date Out:	4 Jan 1968
Detachment Location:	NS Sangley Point (dates unknown)		

VP-48

Deployed to:	MCAS Iwakuni		
Aircraft:	P-3A		
Date In:	31 Jul 1967	Date Out:	31 Jan 1968

Detachment Location:	NS Sangley Point		
Detachment Date In:	28 Dec 1967	Date Out:	8 Jan 1968

VP-2

Deployed to:	NS Sangley Point		
Aircraft:	SP-2H		
Date In:	1 Oct 1967	Date Out:	1 Apr 1968

Detachment Location:	NAF Tan Son Nhut		
Detachment Date In:	1 Oct 1967	Date Out:	Unknown
Detachment Location:	NAF Cam Ranh Bay		
Detachment Date In:	1 Feb 1968	Date Out:	30 Mar 1968

VP-17

Deployed to:	NS Sangley Point		
Aircraft:	SP-2H		
Date In:	9 Nov 1967	Date Out:	29 Apr 1968

Detachment Location:	NAF Cam Ranh Bay		
Detachment Date In:	9 Nov 1967	Date Out:	29 Apr 1968

VP-26

Deployed to:	NS Sangley Point		
Aircraft:	P-3B		
Date In:	27 Nov 1967	Date Out:	7 Jun 1968

Detachment Location:	RTNB U-Tapao		
Detachment Date In:	16 Dec 1967	Date Out:	2 Jun 1968

1968 Deployments

VAH-21

Deployed to:	(see detachment)		
Aircraft:	AP-2H		
Date In:	1 Sep 1968	Date Out:	See Note 3

Detachment Location:	NAF Cam Ranh Bay		
Detachment Date In:	1 Sep 1968	Date Out:	16 Jul 1969

VP-6

Deployed to:	NAF Naha		
Aircraft:	P-3A		
Date In:	1 Jan 1968	Date Out:	1 Jul 1968

Detachment Location:	NS Sangley Point

Detachment Date In:	21 Jan 1968	Date Out:	24 Jan 1968
Detachment Location:	NAF Cam Ranh Bay		
Detachment Date In:	13 May 1968	Date Out:	7 Jun 1968

VP-19

Deployed to:	MCAS Iwakuni		
Aircraft:	P-3B		
Date In:	1 Feb 1968	Date Out:	31 Jul 1968
Detachment Location:	NS Sangley Point		
Detachment Date In:	1 Apr 1968	Date Out:	14 Apr 1968
Detachment Location:	RTNB U-Tapao		
Detachment Date In:	1 Apr 1968	Date Out:	14 Apr 1968
Detachment Location:	NAF Cam Ranh Bay		
Detachment Date In:	15 Jun 1968	Date Out:	15 Jul 1968

VP-42

Deployed to:	NS Sangley Point		
Aircraft:	SP-2H		
Date In:	10 Mar 1968	Date Out:	3 Sep 1968
Detachment Location:	NAF Cam Ranh Bay (dates unknown)		

VP-50

Deployed to:	NS Sangley Point		
Aircraft:	P-3A		
Date In:	1 May 1968	Date Out:	1 Nov 1968
Detachment Location:	NAF Cam Ranh Bay		
Detachment Date In:	1 May 1968	Date Out:	1 Nov 1968

VP-49

Deployed to:	NS Sangley Point		
Aircraft:	P-3A		
Date In:	1 Jun 1968	Date Out:	16 Dec 1968
Detachment Location:	RTNB U-Tapao		
Detachment Date In:	1 Jun 1968	Date Out:	16 Dec 1968

VP-22

Deployed to:	NAF Naha		
Aircraft:	P-3A		
Date In:	30 Jun 1968	Date Out:	11 Jan 1969
Detachment Location:	NAF Cam Ranh Bay		
Detachment Date In:	16 Jul 1968	Date Out:	15 Aug 1968
Detachment Date In:	20 Sep 1968	Date Out:	30 Sep 1968
Detachment Date In:	1 Oct 1968	Date Out:	15 Oct 1968
Detachment Date In:	15 Nov 1968	Date Out:	10 Dec 1968

VP-4

Deployed to:	MCAS Iwakuni
Aircraft:	P-3A
Date In:	1 Aug 1968

Date Out: 29 Jan 1969

Detachment Location:	NAF Cam Ranh Bay		
Detachment Date In:	15 Aug 1968	Date Out:	15 Sep 1968
Detachment Date In:	15 Oct 1968	Date Out:	10 Nov 1968
Detachment Date In:	16 Dec 1968	Date Out:	10 Jan 1969

VP-1

Deployed to:	NS Sangley Point
Aircraft:	SP-2H
Date In:	15 Aug 1968

Date Out: 25 Feb 1969

Detachment Location:	NAF Cam Ranh Bay		
Detachment Date In:	15 Aug 1968	Date Out:	25 Feb 1969

VP-47

Deployed to:	NS Sangley Point
Aircraft:	P-3B
Date In:	1 Nov 1968

Date Out: 31 Mar 1969

Detachment Location:	NAF Cam Ranh Bay		
Detachment Date In:	1 Nov 1968	Date Out:	31 Mar 1969

VP-45

Deployed to:	NS Sangley Point
Aircraft:	P-3A
Date In:	16 Dec 1968

Date Out: 1 Jun 1969

Detachment Location:	RTNB U-Tapao		
Detachment Date In:	16 Dec 1968	Date Out:	30 May 1969
Detachment Location:	NAF Cam Ranh Bay		
Detachment Date In:	18 Apr 1969	Date Out:	28 Apr 1969

1969 Deployments

VAL-4

Deployed to:	Binh Thuy and Vung Tau
Aircraft:	OV-10A and YOV-10D
Date In:	9 Apr 1969

Date Out: 31 Mar 1972

Detachment Location:	None

VC-5

Deployed to:	(see detachment)
Aircraft:	C-1A and US-2C
Date In:	2 Oct 1969

Date Out: See Note 3

Detachment Location:	FASU Da Nang		
Detachment Date In:	2 Oct 1969	Date Out:	31 Dec 1969

VRC-30

Deployed to:	(see detactment)
Aircraft:	C-1A
Date In:	11 Oct 1969

Date Out: See Note 3

Detachment Location:	FASU Da Nang
Detachment Date In:	11 Jan 1969

Date Out: 1 Feb 1973

VP-28

Deployed to:	NAF Naha
Aircraft:	P-3A
Date In:	15 Jan 1969

Date Out: 15 Jul 1969

Detachment Location:	NAF Cam Ranh Bay
Detachment Date In:	17 Jan 1969
Detachment Date In:	29 Apr 1969
Detachment Date In:	13 Jun 1969

Date Out: 11 Feb 1969
Date Out: 15 May 1969
Date Out: 18 Jul 1969

VP-40

Deployed to:	MCAS Iwakuni
Aircraft:	P-3B
Date In:	1 Feb 1969

Date Out: 1 Aug 1969

Detachment Location:	NAF Cam Ranh Bay (dates unknown)

VP-2

Deployed to:	NS Sangley Point
Aircraft:	SP-2H
Date In:	17 Feb 1969

Date Out: 17 Aug 1969

VP-9

Deployed to:	NS Sangley Point
Aircraft:	P-3B
Date In:	1 Apr 1969

Date Out: 1 Oct 1969

Detachment Location:	NAF Cam Ranh Bay
Detachment Date In:	1 Apr 1969

Date Out: 1 Oct 1969

VP-6

Deployed to:	NS Sangley Point
Aircraft:	P-3A
Date In:	1 Jun 1969

Date Out: 15 Nov 1969

Detachment Location:	RTNB U-Tapao
Detachment Date In:	27 May 1969

Date Out: 15 Nov 1969

VP-50

Deployed to:	NAF Naha
Aircraft:	P-3A
Date In:	15 Jul 1969

Date Out: 15 Jan 1970

Detachment Location:	NAF Cam Ranh Bay
Detachment Date In:	1 Aug 1969

Date Out: 15 Jan 1970

VP-17

Deployed to:	MCAS Iwakuni
Aircraft:	P-3A
Date In:	1 Aug 1969

Date Out: 1 Feb 1970

Detachment Location:	NAF Cam Ranh Bay		
Detachment Date In:	9 Aug 1969	Date Out:	11 Sep 1969
Detachment Date In:	3 Nov 1969	Dale Oul:	15 Nov 1969
Detachment Date In:	15 Dec 1969	Date Out:	22 Dec 1969

VP-46

Deployed to:	NS Sangley Point
Aircraft:	P-3B
Date In:	1 Oct 1969

Date Out: 31 Mar 1970

Detachment Location:	NAF Cam Ranh Bay		
Detachment Date In:	2 Oct 1969	Date Out:	31 Mar 1970

VP-22

Deployed to:	NS Sangley Point
Aircraft:	P-3A
Date In:	15 Nov 1969

Date Out: 1 May 1970

Detachment Location:	RTNB U-Tapao		
Detachment Date In:	30 Nov 1969	Date Out:	29 Apr 1970

1970 Deployments

HC-3

Deployed to:	(see detachment)
Aircraft:	CH-46D
Date In:	15 May 1970

Date Out: See Note 3

Detachment Location:	NAF Tan Son Nhut		
Detachment Date In:	15 May 1970	Date Out:	1 Dec 1970

VP-47

Deployed to:	NAF Naha
Aircraft:	P-3B
Date In:	16 Jan 1970

Date Out: 13 Jul 1970

Detachment Location:	RTNB U-Tapao		
Detachment Date In:	9 May 1970	Date Out:	13 Jul 1970
Detachment Location:	NAF Cam Ranh Bay (dates unknown)		

VP-1

Deployed to:	MCAS Iwakuni
Aircraft:	P-3B
Date In:	1 Feb 1970

Date Out: 31 Jul 1970

Detachment Location:	RTNB U-Tapao		
Detachment Date In:	1 Feb 1970	Date Out:	15 Apr 1970
Detachment Location:	NAF Tan Son Nhut		
Detachment Date In:	1 May 1970	Date Out:	27 Jul 1970
Detachment Location:	NAF Cam Ranh Bay (dates Unknown)		

VP-48

Deployed to:	NS Sangley Point		
Aircraft:	P-3B		
Date In:	1 Apr 1970	Date Out:	30 Sep 1970
Detachment Location:	NAF Cam Ranh Bay		
Detachment Date In:	1 Apr 1970	Date Out:	30 Sep 1970

VP-40

Deployed to:	NS Sangley Point		
Aircraft:	P-3B		
Date In:	1 May 1970	Date Out:	30 Oct 1970
Detachment Location:	RTNB U-Tapao		
Detachment Date In:	29 Apr 1970	Date Out:	30 Oct 1970

VP-6

Deployed to:	NAF Naha		
Aircraft:	P-3A		
Date In:	14 Jul 1970	Date Out:	15 Jan 1971
Detachment Location:	None		

VP-19

Deployed to:	MCAS Iwakuni		
Aircraft:	P-3B		
Date In:	31 Jul 1970	Date Out:	30 Jan 1971
Detachment Location:	NAF Cam Ranh Bay		
Detachment Date In:	10 Oct 1970	Date Out:	24 Oct 1970
Detachment Location:	NS Sangley Point (dates unknown)		
Detachment Location:	RTNB U-Tapao (dates unknown)		

VP-50

Deployed to:	NS Sangley Point		
Aircraft:	P-3A		
Date In:	30 Sep 1970	Date Out:	31 Mar 1971
Detachment Location:	NAF Cam Ranh Bay		
Detachment Date In:	30 Sep 1970	Date Out:	31 Mar 1971

VP-17

Deployed to:	NS Sangley Point
Aircraft:	P-3A
Date In:	29 Oct 1970

Date Out: 29 Apr 1971

Detachment Location:	RTNB U-Tapao
Detachment Date In:	29 Oct 1970

Date Out: 29 Apr 1971

1971 Deployments

VP-22

Deployed to:	NAF Naha
Aircraft:	P-3A
Date In:	14 Jan 1971

Date Out: 14 Jul 1971

Detachment Location:	NAF Cam Ranh Bay
Detachment Date In:	25 Jan 1971

Date Out: 2 Feb 1971

Detachment Location:	RTNB U-Tapao
Detachment Date In:	27 Mar 1971

Date Out: 3 Apr 1971

VP-4

Deployed to:	MCAS Iwakuni
Aircraft:	P-3B
Date In:	1 Feb 1971

Date Out: 31 Jul 1971

Detachment Location: NAF Cam Ranh Bay (dates Unknown)

VP-1

Deployed to:	NS Sangley Point (1 Apr-1 Jul 1971)
	NAS Cubi Point (1 Jul-1 Oct 1971)
Aircraft:	P-3B
Date In:	1 Apr 1971

Date Out: 1 Oct 1971

Detachment Location:	NAF Cam Ranh Bay
Detachment Date In:	1 Apr 1971

Date Out: 1 Oct 1971

VP-48

Deployed to:	NS Sangley Point (1 May-1 Jul 1971)
	NAS Cubi Point (1 Jul-30 Sep 1971)
Aircraft:	P-3B
Date In:	1 May 1971

Date Out: 30 Sep 1971

Detachment Location:	RTNB U-Tapao
Detachment Date In:	1 May 1971

Date Out: 30 Sep 1971

VP-40

Deployed to:	NAF Naha
Aircraft:	P-3B
Date In:	14 Jul 1971

Date Out: 13 Jan 1972

Detachment Location: NAS Guam (dates unknown)

VP-9

Deployed to:	MCAS Iwakuni
Aircraft:	P-3B
Date In:	29 Jul 1971

Date Out: 11 Feb 1972

Detachment Locations: unknown

VP-6

Deployed to:	NAS Cubi Point
Aircraft:	P-3A
Date In:	21 Sep 1971

Date Out: 12 Jan 1972

Detachment Location:	NAF Cam Ranh Bay	
Detachment Date In:	21 Sep 1971	Date Out: 2 Dec 1971
Detachment Location:	NAS Cubi Point	
Detachment Date In:	12 Jan 1972	Date Out: 10 May 1972

VP-19

Deployed to:	NAS Cubi Point
Aircraft:	P-3B
Date In:	1 Nov 1971

Date Out: 29 Apr 1972

Detachment Location:	RTNB U-Tapao	
Detachment Date In:	1 Nov 1971	Date Out: 29 Apr 1972

1972 Deployments

VP-17

Deployed to:	NAF Naha
Aircraft:	P-3A
Date In:	13 Jan 1972

Date Out: 1 Aug 1972

Detachment Location:	NAS Cubi Point	
Detachment Date In:	9 Apr 1972	Date Out: 23 Apr 1972

VP-46

Deployed to:	MCAS Iwakuni
Aircraft:	P-3B
Date In:	1 Feb 1972

Date Out: 14 Aug 1972

Detachment Location:	NAS Cubi Point	
Detachment Date In:	23 Feb 1972	Date Out: 1 Mar 1972
Deatchment Date In:	16 Mar 1972	Date Out: 1 Apr 1972

VP-4

Deployed to:	NAS Cubi Point
Aircraft:	P-3A
Date In:	26 Mar 1972

Date Out: 1 Nov 1972

Detachment Location:	RTNB U-Tapao	
Detachment Date In:	1 May 1972	Date Out: 1 Nov 1972

VP-22

Deployed to:	NAF Naha		
Aircraft:	P-3A		
Date In:	21 Apr 1972	Date Out:	30 Nov 1972

Detachment Location:	NAS Cubi Point		
Detachment Date In:	29 Apr 1972	Date Out:	16 May 1972

VP-9

Deployed to:	(see detachment)		
Aircraft:	P-3B		
Date In:	5 May 1972	Date Out:	24 Jul 1972

Detachment Location:	NAS Cubi Point		
Detachment Date In:	5 May 1972	Date Out:	24 Jul 1972

VP-11

Deployed to:	NAS Cubi Point		
Aircraft:	P-3B		
Date In:	23 Jul 1972	Date Out:	10 Nov 1972

Detachment Location:	RTNB U-Tapao (dates unknown)

VP-40

Deployed to:	MCAS Iwakuni		
Aircraft:	P-3B		
Date In:	1 Aug 1972	Date Out:	14 Jan 1973

Detachment Location:	RTNB U-Tapao		
Detachment Date In:	16 Nov 1972	Date Out:	20 Dec 1972

VP-1

Deployed to:	NAS Cubi Point		
Aircraft:	P-3B		
Date In:	1 Nov 1972	Date Out:	30 Apr 1973

Detachment Location:	RTNB U-Tapao		
Detachment Date In:	1 Nov 1972	Date Out:	30 Apr 1973

VP-6

Deployed to:	NAF Naha		
Aircraft:	P-3A		
Date In:	30 Nov 1972	Date Out:	28 May 1973

Detachment Location:	RTNB U-Tapao		
Detachment Date In:	20 Dec 1972	Date Out:	1 Feb 1973

Notes for VP and Non-Carrier Based Squadron Deployments to Vietnam (1964-1972) and Tail Codes:

1. Date In and Date Out are normally the dates the squadron arrived and departed from the air station or base it operated from during its deployment.

2. Squadron detachment numbers or letters are not listed. There were numerous changes and rotation of patrol squadron aircraft and crews from the squadron's main base of operation during its deployment. A squadron's detachment was usually identified by using the name of the base the detachment was operating from. Some of the squadrons that deployed to Vietnam did not have or use detachments.

3. In some cases specific dates for the squadron or its detachments were not known or could not be determined from official sources.

4. The following is a list of tail codes for the VP and other non-carrier based squadrons deploying to Vietnam:

HAL-3	(no assigned tailcode)
HC-1	UP
HC-3	SA
VAH-21	SL
VAL-4	UM
VAP-61	SS
VAP-62	GB
VC-5	UE
VO-67	MR
VP-1	YB
VP-2	YC
VP-4	YD
VP-5	LA
VP-6	PC
VP-8	LC
VP-9	PD
VP-11	LE
VP-16	LF
VP-17	ZE
VP-19	PE
VP-22	QA
VP-28	QC
VP-40	QE
VP-42	RB
VP-45	LN
VP-46	RC
VP-47	RD
VP-48	SF
VP-49	LP
VP-50	SG
VQ-1	PR
VQ-2	JQ
VR-1	JK
VRC-30	RW
VRC-50	RG
VW-1	TE
VXN-8	JB

Grenada Combat Operations

25 October–2 November 1983

OPERATION URGENT FURY

The mission of Operation Urgent Fury, as stated by Admiral Wesley L. McDonald, while testifying before the Senate Committee on Armed Services on 3 November 1983, was to "protect and/or evacuate American citizens, to provide stability for the area, and at the invitation of the Organization of Eastern Caribbean States, to help establish a government which would be more democratic in nature than the existing government which had taken over rather rigorously and had placed the country into complete isolation for a period of four days." Admiral McDonald was Commander in Chief, U.S. Atlantic Command, during the Grenada operations.

The following is a list of Naval Aviation forces (does not include all Marine Corps aviation) participating in the Grenada operations:

Carriers

Independence (CV 62) with CVW-6 (Tail Code AE)

Squadron	Aircraft
VA-87	A-7E
VA-15	A-7E
VA-176	A-6E and KA-6D
VF-32	F-14A
VF-14	F-14A
VAW-122	E-2C
VAQ-131	EA-6B
VS-28	S-3A
HS-15	SH-3H

Guam (LPH 9) (Tail Code for HMM-261 was EM)

HMM-261	AH-1T and CH-53D

Saipan (LHA 2) (1-7 November 1983)

Saipan provided seaborn security, surveillance operations, communications and medical support during the operation. It did not have a deployed Marine Corps squadron aboard.

Non-Carrier Based Squadrons

Squadron	Aircraft	Tail Code
VP-10	P-3C	LD
VP-16	P-3C	LF
VP-23	P-3C	LJ
HSL-34 Dets	SH-2F	HX
HSL-32 Dets	SH-2F	HV

HSL-32 Detachments provided support for the Grenada operations between 30 October to 8 December, but were not involved in flying combat missions.

VR-56	C-9B	JU
VR-58	C-9B	JV
VR-59	C-9B	RY
VRC-40	C-1A	JK

Transport squadrons were used to provide support for units operating in Grenada, but were not involved in flying combat missions.

Operations by CVW-6 Aircraft

CVW-6 aircraft embarked on *Independence* flew SAR (Search and Rescue), MEDEVAC (Medical Evacuation), CAP (Combat Air Patrol), reconnaissance, close air support and SSSC (Surface, Sub-surface Search Coordination) missions.

Attack squadrons conducted daily surgical bombing missions (close air support) to quell enemy resistance, as well as reconnaissance missions. The following is a list of their activities:

VA-15 flew 143 combat sorties during Operation Urgent Fury.

VA-176 flew 350 combat flight hours during Operational Urgent Fury (the number of combat sorties is not listed).

VA-87 flew close air support combat missions during Operation Urgent Fury. The specific number of combat sorties was not identified.

HS-15 flew Combat SAR missions under enemy fire and were also used to drop leaflets over the central portion of the island. The squadron flew 97 sorties during Operation Urgent Fury.

Fighter squadrons flew CAP (Combat Air Patrol), reconnaissance and photographic missions over the island using the TARPS (Tactical Air Reconnaissance Pod System). VF-32 aircraft participated in the TARPS evolution. Fighter squadron activities were as follows: 256 combat sorties flown by VF-32 in 1983 (includes sorties in Grenada and Lebanon, with no break down on how many for each operation) and 82 combat sorties flown during Operation Urgent Fury by VF-14.

VAQ-131 flew electronic surveillance missions in support of Operation Urgent Fury, specific number of combat sorties not identified.

VS-28: Combat sorties unknown.

VAW-122: Combat sorties unknown.

The Navy did not loose any aircraft or aviation personnel to combat action during Operation Urgent Fury. However, several Marine Corps and Army helicopters were shot down by anitaircraft batteries and personnel lost to combat action.

Carrier Squadrons and Non-Carrier Based Squadrons Involved in 1986 Libyan Operations

(24 March–15 April 1986)

The time frames for squadron involvement in Operation Prairie Fire during March and Operation Eldorado Canyon during April 1986 are not listed. Some of the squadrons involved in the March operations were not present during the April operations, and vice versa.

Carrier Based Squadrons

America (CV 66) with CVW-1 (Tail Code AB)

VA-34	A-6E and KA-6D
VA-46	A-7E
VA-72	A-7E
VF-33	F-14A
VF-102	F-14A
VS-32	S-3A
VAW-123	E-2C
HS-11	SH-3H
VMAQ-2 Det	EA-6B
VQ-2 Det	EA-3B

Coral Sea (CV 43) with CVW-13 (Tail Code AK)

VFA-131	F/A-18A
VFA-132	F/A-18A
VA-55	A-6E and KA-6D
VAW-127	E-2C
VAQ-135	EA-6B
VQ-2 Det	EA-3B
VMFA-314	F/A-18A
VMFA-323	F/A-18A
HS-17	SH-3H

Saratoga (CV 60) with CVW-17 (Tail Code AA)

VA-81	A-7E
VA-83	A-7E
VF-74	F-14A
VF-103	F-14A
VA-85	A-6E and KA-6D
VAQ-137	EA-6B
VAW-125	E-2C
VS-30	S-3A
HS-3	SH-3H
VQ-2 Det	EA-3B

Guadalcanal (LPH 7) (Tail Code EG for HMM-263)

HMM-263	AH-1T, CH-53E and CH-46E

Note: Dets (Detachments) aboard the carriers did not use the same Tail Code assigned to the air wing (CVW).

Non-Carrier Based Squadrons

Squadron	Tail Code	Aircraft
HSL-32 Dets	HV	SH-2F
HSL-34 Dets	HX	SH-2F
HSL-36 Dets	HY	SH-2F
HSL-42 Dets	HN	SH-60B
VP-23	LJ	P-3C
VP-56	LQ	P-3C
HC-4	HC	CH-53E
HC-6 Det	HW	UH-46D and CH-46D
VR-22	JL	C-130F
VAQ-138 Det	*	EA-6B
VR-24	JM	C-2A
HC-8 Dets	BR	UH-46A and CH-46D
HS-1 Det	AR	SH-3
HC-9 Det	NW	HH-3A
VQ-2	JQ	EP-3A

See the chronology section for March and April 1986 for a more detailed account of these operations.

---

* VAQ-138 was under the control of Commander Medium Attack Tactical Electronic Warfare Wing, U.S. Pacific Fleet and did not have a permanently assigned tail code until it became part of CVW-8 in June 1986.

GBU-10E/B Paveway II laser-guided bombs are prepared for war on the deck of John F. Kennedy *the day before Desert Storm began.*

Saratoga *operating in the Red Sea during Desert Storm and the flight deck of* John F. Kennedy *is in the foreground with F-14 Tomcats on deck.*

Naval Aviation Units Involved in the Persian Gulf War

(16 January–27 February 1991)

Carrier and Carrier Based Squadrons

Saratoga (CV 60) with CVW-17 (Tail Code AA), 7 Aug 1990-28 Mar 1991

Squadron	Aircraft
VF-74	F-14A+
VF-103	F-14A+
VFA-83	F/A-18C
VFA-81	F/A-18C
VA-35	A-6E, KA-6D
VAW-125	E-2C
VAQ-132	EA-6B
HS-3	SH-3H
VS-30	S-3B

John F. Kennedy (CV 67) with CVW-3 (Tail Code AC), 15 Aug 1990-28 Mar 1991

Squadron	Aircraft
VF-14	F-14A
VF-32	F-14A
VA-46	A-7E
VA-72	A-7E
VA-75	A-6E, KA-6D
VAW-126	E-2C
HS-7	SH-3H
VAQ-130	EA-6B
VS-22	S-3B

Midway (CV 41) with CVW-5 (Tail Code NF), 2 Oct 1990-17 Apr 1991

Squadron	Aircraft
VFA-195	F/A-18A
VFA-151	F/A-18A
VFA-192	F/A-18A
VA-185	A-6E, KA-6D
VA-115	A-6E, KA-6D
VAW-115	E-2C
VAQ-136	EA-6B
HS-12	SH-3H
VRC-50 Det	C-2A

Ranger (CV 61) with CVW-2 (Tail Code NE), 8 Dec 1990-8 Jun 1991

Squadron	Aircraft
VF-1	F-14A
VF-2	F-14A
VA-155	A-6E
VA-145	A-6E
VAW-116	E-2C
VAQ-131	EA-6B
HS-14	SH-3H
VS-38	S-3A
VRC-30 Det	C-2A

America (CV 66) with CVW-1 (Tail Code AB), 28 Dec 1990-18 Apr 1991

Squadron	Aircraft
VF-102	F-14A
VF-33	F-14A
VFA-82	F/A-18C
VFA-86	F/A-18C
VA-85	A-6E, KA-6D
VAW-123	E-2C
HS-11	SH-3H
VAQ-137	EA-6B
VS-32	S-3B

Theodore Roosevelt (CVN 71) with CVW-8 (Tail Code AJ), 28 Dec 1990-28 Jun 1991

Squadron	Aircraft
VF-41	F-14A
VF-84	F-14A
VFA-15	F/A-18A
VFA-87	F/A-18A
VA-65	A-6E
VA-36	A-6E
VAW-124	E-2C
HS-9	SH-3H
VAQ-141	EA-6B
VS-24	S-3B
VRC-40 Det	C-2A

Non-carrier Based Navy Squadrons that Participated in Operation Desert Shield and Desert Storm

Squadron	Tail Code	Aircraft
HC-1	UP	SH-3G, SH-3H, and CH-53E
HC-2	SA	SH-3G and CH-53E
HC-4	HC	CH-53E
HC-5	RB	HH-46D
HC-6	HW	CH-46D, HH-46D, and UH-46D
HC-8	BR	CH-46D, HH-46D, and UH-46D
HC-11	VR	CH-46D, HH-46D, and UH-46D
HCS-4*	NW	HH-60H
HCS-5*	NW	HH-60H
HM-14	BJ	MH-53E
HM-15	TB	MH-53E
HS-75*	NW	SH-3H
HSL-32	HV	SH-2F
HSL-33	TF	SH-2F
HSL-34	HX	SH-2F
HSL-35	TG	SH-2F
HSL-36	HY	SH-2F
HSL-37	TH	SH-2F
HSL-42	HN	SH-60B
HSL-43	TT	SH-60B
HSL-44	HP	SH-60B
HSL-45	TZ	SH-60B
HSL-46	HQ	SH-60B
HSL-47	TY	SH-60B
HSL-48	HR	SH-60B
HSL-49	TX	SH-60B
VC-6	JG	Pioneer RPVs
VP-1	YB	P-3C
VP-4	YD	P-3C
VP-5	LA	P-3C
VP-8	LC	P-3C
VP-11	LE	P-3C
VP-19	PE	P-3C
VP-23	LJ	P-3C
VP-40	QE	P-3C
VP-45	LN	P-3C
VP-46	RC	P-3C
VP-91*	PM	P-3C
VP-MAU*	LB	P-3C
VPU-1	OB	P-3
VPU-2	SP	P-3
VQ-1	PR	EP-3E, UP-3A, and P-3B
VQ-2	JQ	EP-3E, EA-3B, and UP-3A
VQ-4	HL	TC-130Q
VR-22	JL	C-130F and KC-130F
VR-24	JM	C-2A and CT-39G
VR-51*	RV	C-9B
VR-52*	JT	DC-9
VR-55*	RU	C-9B
VR-56*	JU	C-9B
VR-57*	RX	C-9B
VR-58*	JV	C-9B
VR-59*	RY	C-9B
VR-60*	RT	DC-9
VR-61*	RS	DC-9
VR-62*	JW	DC-9
VRC-30	RW	C-2A
VRC-40	JK	C-2A
VRC-50	RG	C-2A, US-3A, and C-130F

* Naval Air Reserve unit.

Marine Corps Squadrons that Participated in Operation Desert Shield and Desert Storm

Squadron	Tail Code	Aircraft
HMA-773*	MP	AH-1J
HMA-775*	WR	AH-1J
HMH-362	YL	CH-53D
HMH-461	CJ	CH-53E
HMH-462	YF	CH-53E
HMH-465	YJ	CH-53E
HMH-466	YK	CH-53E
HMH-772	MT	RH-53D
Det A*		
HML-767*	MM	UH-1N
HMLA-169	TV	UH-1N and AH-1W
HMLA-269	HF	UH-1N, AH-1W, and AH-1T
HMLA-367	VT	UH-1N and AH-1W
HMLA-369	SM	UH-1N and AH-1W
HMM-161	YR	CH-46E
HMM-164(C)	YT	CH-46E, CH-53E, UH-1N, and AH-1W
HMM-165	YW	CH-46E
HMM-261	TV	CH-46E
HMM-263	EG	CH-46E
HMM-265	EP	CH-46E
HMM-266	ES	CH-46E
HMM-268(C)	YQ	CH-46E, CH-53E, UH-1N, and AH-1W
HMM-365	YM	CH-46E
HMM-774*	MQ	CH-46E
VMA-231	CG	AV-8B
VMA-311	WL	AV-8B
VMA-331	VL	AV-8B
VMA-513	WF	AV-8B
Det B		
VMA-542	CR	AV-8B
VMA(AW)-224	WK	A-6E
VMA(AW)-533	ED	A-6E
VMFA-212	WD	F/A-18C
VMFA-232	WT	F/A-18C
VMFA-235	DB	F/A-18C
VMFA-314	VW	F/A-18A
VMFA-451	VM	F/A-18A
VMFA(AW)-121	VK	F/A-18D
VMGR-252	BH	KC-130F and KC-130R
VMGR-352	QB	KC-130R
VMGR-452*	NY	KC-130T
VMO-1	ER	OV-10A and OV-10D+
VMO-2	UU	OV-10A, OV-10D, and OV-10D+

* Marine Corps Reserve Unit

List of Early Naval Jet Pilots

The first flight in a turbojet aircraft in the United States was made at Muroc, Calif., on 1 October 1942, by Robert M. Stanley, chief test pilot of the Bell Aircraft Corporation. The next day Colonel Lawrence C. Craigie of the U.S. Army Air Forces, took up the same plane for its first flight by a military pilot. The first jet flight by a Naval Aviator was made in the same plane at the same location on 21 April 1943 by Captain Frederick M. Trapnell of Flight Test, NAS Anacostia, D.C. In each instance, the plane was a Bell XP-59A powered by two General Electric 1A turbojet engines. It was the first jet aircraft built in the United States and a prototype of the first jet aircraft acquired by the United States Navy.

Before the end of the war, the Navy had acquired three of the Bell Airacomets and in the first year after the war acquired two more. All were obtained from the Army Air Forces; all were assigned to NAS Patuxent River, Md. They served two main purposes by providing a means of testing the adaptability of jet aircraft to naval requirements and a means of training pilots to fly a new aircraft type. They were used for these purposes through 1947.

Even before their acquisition, the Navy's interest in jet propulsion had been made evident. It not only monitored the progress of jet programs in the Army Air Forces and took part in certain joint studies, but also initiated a study contract which led to the development of the first Westinghouse jet engines. As early as 1943, two carrier fighter designs employing jet engines were initiated. The first with Ryan Aeronautical Company had the immediate objective of developing a fighter capable of operating from escort carriers as a replacement for the FM Wildcat. It resulted in the XFR-1 Fireball which was powered by a Wright Cyclone engine in the nose and a General Electric I-16 in the after section of the fuselage. Its development and production were handled on a crash basis and the first model flew in June 1944. Within a year it was assigned to a fleet squadron. Limited operations from escort carriers for short periods in the immediate post-war period uncovered numerous bugs and by July 1947 the decision to withdraw them from service had been made and carried out. A similar concept of composite power, carried out in the XF15C

was abandoned after experimental models had been evaluated at Patuxent, Md.

The second contract of 1943 authorized the McDonnell Aircraft Corporation to design a twin-jet carrier fighter. To avoid disrupting wartime production and to meet the not so urgent objective of using the plane to explore the feasibility of jet operations on carriers, progress was intentionally slow. Even so, the airplane took to the air for the first time on 26 January 1945. It was the XFD-1 Phantom, powered by two Westinghouse 19B jets. After another year and a half of flight testing, a production FD-1 was taken on board *Franklin D. Roosevelt* and on 21 July 1946 the first jet operations from a U.S. carrier were conducted. A year later, the Phantom became the first jet aircraft assigned to a fleet squadron when two FDs were delivered to VF-17A at NAS Quonset Point, R.I.

In the meantime, studies and contracts had been let for other jet aircraft which were to become operational. One of these, made in January 1945 with North American Aviation, produced the FJ-1 Fury equipped with a single Allison/GE jet. Claimed by some to be the hottest, straight-wing jet ever built, this airplane made its first flight in September 1946 and, in November of the next year, was delivered to VF-5A at NAS San Diego, Calif. On 10 March 1948, the squadron Commanding Officer and Executive Officer took the Fury on board *Boxer* for carrier suitability tests, conducting a number of takeoffs and landings. Shortly after, VF-17A completed carrier qualifications in the Phantom, by then redesignated FH, on board *Saipan*. The Navy's transition to jet aircraft had definitely begun.

By 1948, the number of Naval Aviators qualified to fly jets had assumed fairly generous proportions. Because it appeared desirable to have a list of the men who pioneered the Navy's effort in this field in the historical record, a project to obtain their names was initiated in October 1961 by Mr. Adrian O. Van Weyn, head of the Naval Aviation History Office.

It soon became apparent that there was no ready-made list and, further, that no official records had been kept from which one could be compiled. Even the flight logs from Patuxent, where the first jet aircraft has been assigned, seemed to have disappeared. It was then that a general appeal for help was made through a letter in *Naval Aviation News*. It appeared in the March 1962 issue.

Help came from many sources. Twenty men in all answered this call giving not only the particulars of their first flights but also the names of others who had flown in the early period. One pilot sent a list of 73 men awarded Phantom Jockey Certificates by McDonnell Aircraft Corporation commemorating their flights in the Phantom jet. Perhaps the most unexpected, but no less useful, was a report from an officer assigned to the Aviation Safety Center listing all men involved in accidents in jet aircraft through 1948. From these replies and from other sources, a list was made up of another 80 men who had probably qualified in the period 1943-48. Each was sent a letter asking for the particulars of his qualification as well as for the names of others who should be questioned. The project developed quickly into a letter writing campaign as almost every third answer added more names which in turn spawned yet other possibilities.

When these leads had been exhausted, the project seemed about complete and preparations were made to put the list in order for publication. It was then that the earlier search for the Patuxent Flight Logs produced results. They were found at the Federal Records Center in Alexandria. With some interest but only a little expectancy of finding any more than confirmation of what was already known, a few were called over for leisurely perusal. The first one dispelled all dreams of the project being finished.

About two months and 31 logs later, another 200 names had been added to the probables list. But what names! Almost without fail, the log entries identified the pilot by last name only, giving no initials, no rank and no indication of service affiliation. This should have presented no difficulty with the more unusual names but experience proved quickly that no names are unusual. Reference to unit rosters and Navy Registers helped some, and the Bureau of Personnel contributed its share, but when all available sources had been used, there were still about 100 names lacking identity.

Some of these were cleared up by a day spent at NATC Patuxent, Md., and the follow-up assistance of Rear Admiral Paul H. Ramsey's staff. Some remain only names, some of those identified could not be found, many were not heard from. Several were no longer living. Others were separated from their logs by vacation or change of duty and could not give exact information. Still others reported their logs as lost or destroyed by fire and had no means of confirming their recollections. In spite of these difficulties, the list was compiled and because publication might resolve some still unanswered questions, it was printed in the March 1963 issue of *Naval Aviation News* as a tentative list.

Tabulation of the replies revealed interesting elements of history. The early date at which many qualified was perhaps most surprising, but under the circumstances should not have been surprising at all. All aspects of early jet aircraft were highly classified. During the war years, the interests of security dictated that early jet engines be called superchargers. Even the XP-59A designation for the first jet airplane had a security angle. The original XP-59 was a conventional experimental fighter, and it was thought that use of the same designation with a suffix letter would hide the true identity of the new model. Its early operations at Muroc were also conducted under the veil of secrecy—if jet flight can be kept a secret. Admiral Frederick M. Trapnell wrote: "When flown, this aircraft was towed well out onto the lake bed, with tarpaulins covering most of the fuselage and with a fake wooden propeller on the nose. This, of course, was removed prior to run-up."

This airplane, relatively unknown even today as the Navy's first jet, was for obvious reason the one in which most Navy pilots made their first jet flights. In the period of its use through 1947, by which time 262 flights are listed, 196 were in the P-59. Because Patuxent was the center of flight testing and the first station to which jet aircraft were assigned, it topped all other locations as the scene of first flights through 1948. A number of pilots received their first indoctrination from the Army Air Forces and made their first flights at AAF bases in the southwest. Others attended RAF schools at Hullavington and Cranfield, England, and made their first flights there. When delivery of the FD Phantoms and FJ Furies began in 1947, the location of first flights extended to St. Louis, Mo., Quonset Point, R.I., Cherry Point, N.C., and San Diego, Calif.

The first Navy pilot to qualify in jets was also the first Navy pilot to fly seven post-war jets which he listed as the XFJ, XF2H, XF9F, XF3D, XF6U, XF-86, and the XF7U. Only five men with Flag rank qualified and, prior to 1948, only three qualified while holding the rank of Ensign. The majority qualified as Lieutenant Commanders (Major for the Marines) and Lieutenants (Captain for the Marines), with the former leading the pack. The pilots of VF-5A and VF-17A, on board at the time the squadrons were being equipped with jets, are all members of this early group although some that were not heard from do not appear on the list.

The replies included many interesting comments supplementing the basic information. The somewhat naive attitude of the historian was rudely jolted very early in the project. Under the assumption that some training was necessary to fly a radically different airplane, he provided a place on the questionnaire to report the extent of training received. The answers, when they were given at all, were unanimously in the vein of one report which stated: "In contrast to present practice, training consisted of looking at handbook, cockpit checkout, then go." Its elaboration by another qualifier was: "Your request for information on training is amusing. Training was very informal, to put it politely. It consisted of: 'This is the low pressure fuel cock; this is the high pressure fuel cock; it flies real easy.'" Even in the later period when the first squadrons were being equipped with jets, the training does not appear to have been extensive. One pilot reported, "VF-17A trained itself. Checkout consisted of reading the handbook and watching a movie on compressibility."

One pilot told of winning third place in the 1948 Bendix Trophy Race from Long Beach, Calif., to Cleveland, Ohio, in which he "landed at Cleveland dead stick, out of fuel the last 50 miles." Another reported ferrying an FH-1 from Patuxent, Md., to Pensacola, Fla., in 1948 with the comment: "I daresay the only jet ever to use Station Field." In similar vein, one told of his work with another pilot on chase flights out of Point Mugu, Calif., in which they, "operated P-80s off a 5,000-foot Marston mat with full ammo and fuel, for two years without incident. The P-80 was not supposed to be landed in this configuration (we later found out)."

The men who qualified in Flag rank had some toppers. The first of these, Admiral Alfred M. Pride, gave us the following account of events leading to his qualification: "I had been ordered to relieve Sallada as Chief and to report a month before the turnover date of 1 May. That gave me considerable time to look around. It then dawned on me that I would be up to my neck in jet procurement and that I had better find out a little about them at first hand. Furthermore, since no flag officer seemed to have soloed the things, it seemed appropriate that the Chief of the Bureau set the pace. So I went down and asked for a McDonnell but the Patuxent boys were not taking any chances with their new pet, I guess, and were 'so sorry, but it was out of commission.' I looked around and saw the P-59 sitting there and asked how about that one. They admitted it was 'up' and so I said that I would take it. It worked fair enough except that one engine gave out after I got out over the Bay and I had to yell for a clear runway and come on home. Never did find out what the trouble really was."

Admiral Daniel V. Gallery reported: "Rear Admirals Apollo Soucek, Edgar A. "Bat" Cruise and I checked out in Phantoms and flew a section formation at the opening of Idlewild and also at the Cleveland Air Races. Called ourselves the Gray Angels." To that somewhat noncommittal statement, Admiral Edgar A. Cruise provided a footnote quoted here in full. He wrote: "For your information Admirals Soucek and Gallery flew with me, with Gallery leading, as the Gray Angels in both the Idlewild, N.Y., dedication and later at the National Air Races in Cleveland, Ohio, in September 1948. In Idlewild on one flight I ran out of fuel on one tank resulting in a flame-out. Inasmuch as our formation was only at 2600 feet and directly over the field, I elected to land dead stick on Idlewild. I never made a more precise approach and landing in my whole life.

At Cleveland the Gray Angels caused some consternation by passing the reviewing stand simultaneously with, but in the opposite direction from, a 90-plane Air Group. The Air Group leader was flying low (about 4-500 feet) which forced us down to 75–100 feet. Needless to say flying wing, I was somewhat perturbed."

Admiral Cruise, who was Head of the Air Warfare Division in DCNO (Air) when he was making the above flights, also reported that his forced landing at Idlewild was directly involved in the subsequent installation of a positive cross connection which would prevent future flame-outs from the same cause.

As might be expected, this list of early jet pilots includes several men who later achieved other prominence in flight. Turner Caldwell set a world speed record in the D-558-I in August 1947, the first held by the Navy since Al Williams' record in 1923. Marion Carl broke that record one week later in the same plane and later soared to a new altitude record for research aircraft in the D-558-II. Carl and Caldwell were also the first of their respective services to fly faster than sound in level flight. Larry Flint took the Phantom II to a new world altitude record in 1959 and F. Taylor Brown set a time to climb record to 20,000 meters in 1962, also in the Phantom II. Thomas H. Miller set a new speed record for 500 kilometers in the Phantom II in September 1960. The first U.S. Navy jet operations on a carrier were flown by James J. Davidson; Marion Carl flew tests of the P-80 on the same ship later in the year. Najeeb Halaby, former head of the FAA, was the first to fly a jet on continuous flight across the United States from Muroc, Calif., to Patuxent, Md., which he did in a P-80A on 28 June 1945. On the other side of the ledger, the list also includes the first pilot to bail out of a jet and the first to crash-land a jet in the water, both of whom shall be nameless.

In regard to the following list itself, words of explanation and caution are necessary. In explanation of the order, flights made on the same day are in the order of time of day when known, and alphabetical when not known. When only the month and year could be given for date, the flight appears after all others made during the month. Rank is that held at the time of first flight, and all are Naval Aviators on active duty at the time. Designations for the McDonnell Phantom appear as FD initially and as FH after the change made 21 August 1947.

The cautions are particularly important. First, qualification as a jet pilot was defined loosely. For this purpose, it was considered simply as the first flight on which complete command of the aircraft was held. Whether the first flight was also the last made in a jet by a particular pilot or the beginning of a whole career of jet flying, it was accepted as meeting the requirement. Second, only flights in pure jet aircraft were considered. The question of what to do about the Ryan Fireball, FR-1 came up early in the project. Several facts of its early existence give weight to its importance in the Navy's transition to jet aircraft. Yet the fact, that it was equipped with a reciprocating engine for use in normal operations and with a turbo-jet engine for use as a booster during takeoff and maximum performance flights, removes it from the jet aircraft class. For this reason, justified or not, flights in the FR were not included.

Thirdly, only those men with whom we could make contact or about whom we could gain specific knowledge appear in the list. Those found in log books or otherwise reported as having flown jets in the early period who could neither be identified, nor located, had to be omitted. Those who died after their first jet flight (indicated by *) could be included only if the necessary information was available from another source. Their flight dates are generally the earliest found in Patuxent Flight Logs and may not be the actual first flight. Others deceased, reported as having flown in the period but for whom no specific information was found, had to be omitted from the order of precedence. They are: John E. Darden, Jr., Ralph Fuoss, Bud B. Gear, John Magda, Alfred E. Nauman, Jr., Albert D. Pollock, Jr., Horatio G. Sickel, Warren P. Smith and Conrad J. Wigge.

For the above reasons, the list is the best that could be updated and compiled. On the basis of evidence available, it is concluded that the completeness and accuracy of the list is best at the beginning and decreases as the precedence numbers increase.

The following is a list of the Early Jet Pilots in Order of First Jet Flight:

No.	Name	Rank	Date	Plane	Place
1	Trapnell, Frederick M.	CAPT	21 Apr 43	XP-59A	Muroc
2	Pearson, John B., Jr.	CDR	27 May 43	XP-59	Muroc
3	Ramsey, Paul H.	CDR	29 Jul 43	XP-59A	Muroc
4	Gayler, Noel A. M.	LCDR	13 Jan 44	YP-59A	Patuxent
5	Booth, Charles T.	CDR	14 Jan 44	YP-59A	Patuxent
6	Halaby, Najeeb E.	LTJG	21 Jan 44	YP-59A	Patuxent
7	Ferguson, John A.	LT	14 Feb 44	YP-59A	Patuxent
8	Drewelow, Robert W.	LT	21 Apr 44	YP-59A	Patuxent
9	Owen, Edward M.	LCDR	15 May 44	YP-59A	Patuxent
10	Brown, Ira W., Jr.	LCDR	28 Jun 44	YP-59A	Patuxent
11	Burroughs, Sherman E.	CAPT	11 Jul 44	XP-59	Muroc
12	Hayward, John T.	CDR	11 Jul 44	XP-59	Palmdale
13	Storrs, Aaron P.	CAPT	17 Jul 44	YP-59A	Patuxent
14	Canavan, Desmond E.	LCOL	18 Jul 44	YP-59A	Patuxent
15	Rozamus, Michael J.	LCDR	20 Jul 44	YP-59A	Patuxent
16	Davenport, M. W.	LT	21 Jul 44	XP-59A	Patuxent
17	Runyon, Donald E.	LT	21 Jul 44	YP-59A	Patuxent
18	Gerberding, Jas. H.*	LCDR	30 Aug 44	YP-59A	Patuxent
19	Elder, Robert M.	LT	28 Sep 44	XP-80	Dayton
20	Milner, Robert M.	LCDR	24 Oct 44	YP-59A	Patuxent
21	Soule, Ernest D.	LT	24 Oct 44	YP-59A	Patuxent
22	Kelly, William W.	LT	30 Oct 44	YP-59A	Patuxent
23	Flint, Lawrence E.	LT	30 Oct 44	YP-59A	Patuxent
24	Guerrieri, Mario A.	LCDR	31 Oct 44	YP-59A	Patuxent
25	Harrington, Daniel J.	LCDR	01 Nov 44	YP-59A	Patuxent
26	Davidson, James J.	LT	02 Nov 44	YP-59A	Patuxent
27	Christofferson, F. E.	LT	02 Nov 44	YP-59A	Patuxent
28	Caffey, Kenneth W.	LCDR	07 Nov 44	YP-59A	Patuxent
29	Miller, Kenneth W., Jr.	LT	08 Nov 44	YP-59A	Patuxent

No.	Name	Rank	Date	Plane	Place
30	McNeely, Henry E.	LCDR	08 Nov 44	YP-59A	Patuxent
31	Wood, Charles R., Jr.	LCDR	08 Nov 44	YP-59A	Patuxent
32	Tuttle, Magruder H.	CDR	08 Nov 44	YP-59A	Patuxent
33	Palmer, Fitzhugh L., Jr.	CDR	09 Nov 44	YP-59A	Patuxent
34	Andrews, Clyde C.	LT	09 Nov 44	YP-59A	Patuxent
35	Gough, William V., Jr.	LCDR	09 Nov 44	YP-59A	Patuxent
36	Hollar, Frank E.	MAJ	09 Nov 44	YP-59A	Patuxent
37	Bauer, Louis H.	CDR	11 Nov 44	YP-59A	Patuxent
38	Sutherland, John F.	LCDR	24 Nov 44	XP-80	Palmdale
39	Carl, Marion E.	MAJ	14 Feb 45	YP-59A	Patuxent
40	Wheatley, John P.	LT	15 Feb 45	YP-59A	Patuxent
41	Kenna, William E.	CDR	15 Feb 45	YP-59A	Patuxent
42	Connolly, Thomas F.	CDR	24 Feb 45	YP-59A	Patuxent
43	Neefus, James L.	LCOL	10 Mar 45	YP-59A	Patuxent
44	Sallenger, Asbury H.	LT	14 Mar 45	YP-59A	Patuxent
45	Cleland, Cook	LT	Mar 45	YP-59A	Patuxent
46	Schickel, Norbert H.	LT	25 Apr 45	YP-59A	Patuxent
47	Brown, Robert M.	LT	05 May 45	YP-59A	Patuxent
48	Schrefer, John F.	LCDR	09 May 45	YP-59A	Patuxent
49	Ellenburg, George W.	LCDR	23 May 45	YP-59A	Patuxent
50	Bakutis, Fred E.	CDR	11 Jun 45	YP-59A	Patuxent
51	Schroeder, F. J.	LCDR	12 Jun 45	YP-59A	Patuxent
52	Larsen, Leif W.*	LT	12 Jun 45	YP-59A	Patuxent
53	McClelland, T. G.*	LT	27 Jun 45	YP-59A	Patuxent
54	Schiller, James E.	LT	27 Jun 45	YP-59A	Patuxent
55	Beveridge, Richard A.	LCDR	18 Jul 45	YP-59A	Patuxent
56	Thomas, John M.	LT	19 Jul 45	YP-59A	Patuxent
57	Hannegan, Edward A.	CAPT	21 Jul 45	YP-59A	Patuxent
58	Billett, Dudley S., Jr.	LCDR	23 Jul 45	YP-59A	Patuxent
59	Thawley, Charles B.	LTJG	08 Aug 45	YP-59A	Patuxent
60	May, Richard H.	LT	20 Aug 45	YP-59A	Patuxent
60	Houck, Herbert N.	CDR	27 Oct 45	P-59B	Patuxent
61	Rees, Joseph R.	LT	27 Oct 45	P-59B	Patuxent
62	Tavernetti, Thomas F.	LCDR	29 Oct 45	P-59B	Patuxent
63	Mooty, Alfred F.	LT	30 Oct 45	P-59B	Patuxent
64	Franks, John M.	LT	30 Oct 45	P-59B	Patuxent
65	Earnest, Albert K.	LCDR	31 Oct 45	P-59B	Patuxent
67	Standring, Frank E.	LT	Oct 45	Meteor	England
68	MacGregor, Robert A.	LCDR	03 Nov 45	P-59B	Patuxent
69	Hackett, Hugh J.	LT	29 Nov 45	P-59B	Patuxent
70	Callan, Allie W., Jr.	LT	02 Jan 46	P-59B	Patuxent
71	Myers, Raymond F.	LCDR	05 Jan 46	P-59B	Patuxent
72	Friesz, Robert P.*	LCDR	11 Jan 46	P-59B	Patuxent
73	Leonard, William N.	CDR	23 Jan 46	P-59B	Patuxent
74	Martin, William I.	CDR	28 Jan 46	P-59B	Patuxent
75	Bolt, William H., Jr.	LCDR	07 Feb 46	P-59B	Patuxent
76	Morrison, Jack W.	MAJ	08 Feb 46	P-59B	Patuxent
77	Umphfres, Donald E.*	LT	09 Feb 46	P-59B	Patuxent
78	Holley, Edward B.	LCDR	11 Feb 46	P-59B	Patuxent
79	Quilter, Charles J.	LCOL	13 Feb 46	P-59B	Patuxent
80	Davis, Leslie D.	LCDR	19 Feb 46	P-59B	Patuxent
81	Jorgensen, John B.	LCDR	19 Feb 46	P-59B	Patuxent
82	Reedy, James R.	CDR	20 Feb 46	P-59B	Patuxent

No.	Name	Rank	Date	Plane	Place
83	Sim, Vincent M.*	LCDR	21 Feb 46	P-59B	Patuxent
84	Sollenberger, Robert L.	LCDR	21 Feb 46	P-59B	Patuxent
85	Burnett, Robert G.	LCDR	26 Feb 46	P-59B	Patuxent
86	Somerville, Henry B.	LCDR	27 Feb 46	P-59B	Patuxent
87	Pugh, Paul E.	LCDR	01 Mar 46	P-59B	Patuxent
88	Smith, James W.	LCDR	01 Mar 46	Meteor	England
89	Fleming, Francis M.	LT	09 Mar 46	P-59B	Patuxent
90	Hey, Richard J.	CAPT	20 Mar 46	P-59B	Patuxent
91	Clarke, Robert A.	LT	21 Mar 46	YP-59A	Patuxent
92	Murray, Thomas O.	CDR	22 Mar 46	YP-59A	Patuxent
93	Hanks, E. Ralph	LT	23 Mar 46	YP-59A	Patuxent
94	Smith, Francis A.	LT	26 Mar 46	YP-59A	Patuxent
95	Jackson, Mercer L.	LTJG	27 Mar 46	YP-59A	Patuxent
96	Guillory, Troy T.	LCDR	27 Mar 46	YP-59A	Patuxent
97	Kunz, Melvin M.	LT	27 Mar 46	P-59B	Patuxent
98	Kanze, Robert F.	LT	27 Mar 46	YP-59A	Patuxent
99	Mehle, Roger W.	LCDR	27 Mar 46	YP-59A	Patuxent
100	Tracy, Lloyd W.	LT	28 Mar 46	P-59B	Patuxent
101	Rodenburg, Eugene E.	LT	28 Mar 46	P-59B	Patuxent
102	Thoms, Joseph I.	LTJG	28 Mar 46	P-59B	Patuxent
103	Weaver, Victor H.	LT	01 Apr 46	P-59B	Patuxent
104	McHenry, Robert E.	LCDR	01 Apr 46	P-59B	Patuxent
105	Hoerner, Helmuth E.	LCDR	01 Apr 46	P-59B	Patuxent
106	Alford, William L.*	LT	02 Apr 46	P-59B	Patuxent
107	Hine, Thomas L.	LT	03 Apr 46	P-59B	Patuxent
108	Cain, Mahlon E.	LCDR	03 Apr 46	P-59B	Patuxent
109	Deitchman, Richard P.	LTJG	05 Apr 46	YP-59A	Patuxent
110	Ness, Dwight O.	LCDR	05 Apr 46	YP-59A	Patuxent
111	Colvin, Louis E.	LTJG	09 Apr 46	P-59B	Patuxent
112	Westover, Roland W.	LT	09 Apr 46	P-59B	Patuxent
113	Daniel, Walter E.	1stLT	09 Apr 46	YP-59A	Patuxent
114	Fitzgerald, Joseph W.	LTJG	09 Apr 46	YP-59A	Patuxent
115	Valencia, Eugene A.	LT	19 Apr 46	P-59B	Patuxent
116	Adair, Robert F.	LT	23 Apr 46	P-59B	Patuxent
117	Alley, C. John	LCDR	23 Apr 46	P-59B	Patuxent
118	David, Edmonds	LCDR	23 Apr 46	P-59B	Patuxent
119	Junk, Winfield H.	LCDR	24 Apr 46	P-80A	March Fld
120	Blackburn, John T.	CDR	13 May 46	YP-59A	Patuxent
121	Miller, Thomas H.	CAPT	17 May 46	YP-59A	Patuxent
122	Foley, Walter A.	LTJG	17 May 46	YP-59A	Patuxent
123	Candler, William R.	LT	17 May 46	YP-59A	Patuxent
124	Mechling, Wallace B.	CAPT	21 May 46	P-59B	Patuxent
125	Sanders, Roger M.	1stLT	21 May 46	P-59	Patuxent
126	Matthews, Herbert S.	LTJG	22 May 46	YP-59A	Patuxent
127	Johnson, D. H.	CAPT	22 May 46	YP-59A	Patuxent
128	Aurand, Evan P.	CDR	07 Jun 46	P-59B	Patuxent
129	Empey, Robert E.	LT	12 Jun 46	P-59B	Patuxent
130	Shryock, William A.	LCDR	13 Jun 46	P-59B	Patuxent
131	Giblin, Robert B.	LT	20 Jun 46	Meteor	England
132	Giese, Carl E.	CAPT	28 Jun 46	P-59B	Patuxent
133	Metsger, Alfred B.	CDR	10 Jul 46	P-59B	Patuxent
134	Griffin, Edwin C.	LT	11 Jul 46	P-80A	Inyokern
135	Hyland, John J.	CDR	15 Aug 46	P-59B	Patuxent

No.	Name	Rank	Date	Plane	Place
136	Pearce, James L.	LT	15 Aug 46	P-59B	Patuxent
137	Cram, Jack E.	LCOL	19 Aug 46	P-59B	Patuxent
138	Ruefle, William J.	LCDR	Aug 46	YP-59	Patuxent
139	Rembert, John P., Jr.	CAPT	04 Sep 46	P-59B	Patuxent
140	Larson, Vernon H.	LCDR	25 Sep 46	P-59B	Patuxent
141	Vatcher, Walter W.	1stLT	26 Sep 46	YP-59A	Patuxent
142	Rand, Herbert C.	LCDR	27 Sep 46	P-59B	Patuxent
143	Harris, Floyd L.	LT	03 Oct 46	P-59B	Patuxent
144	Byng, John W.	CDR	07 Oct 46	P-59B	Patuxent
145	Arnold, James T.	LT	22 Oct 46	P-59B	Patuxent
146	Deasy, Charles J.	LTJG	22 Oct 46	YP-59A	Patuxent
147	Puckett, Ronald G.	LT	19 Nov 46	P-59B	Patuxent
148	Lee, Earl C.	LTJG	21 Nov 46	P-59B	Patuxent
149	Chapman, Melvin L.	LT	29 Jan 47	FD-1	St. Louis
150	Garton, Norman F.	CAPT	29 Jan 47	FD-1	St. Louis
151	Kneeland, Kenneth P.	LTJG	31 Jan 47	FD-1	St. Louis
152	Turner, Frank	CAPT	06 Feb 47	P-59B	Patuxent
153	Caldwell, Turner F.	CDR	15 Feb 47	P-80	Muroc
154	Weems, George T.*	LCDR	04 Mar 47	P-59B	Patuxent
155	Mulvihill, Francis*	LCDR	17 Mar 47	P-59B	Patuxent
156	Pahl, Herschel A.	LT	21 Mar 47	P-80A	Chandler
157	Baumall, John F.	LT	27 Mar 47	P-59B	Patuxent
158	Nelson, Robert J.	LT	29 Mar 47	P-59B	Patuxent
159	Doerflinger, Carl	CDR	31 Mar 47	P-59B	Patuxent
160	Crocker, John A.	LT	31 Mar 47	P-59B	Patuxent
161	Provost, Thomas C.*	LCDR	31 Mar 47	P-59B	Patuxent
162	Danbury, William T.	LCDR	01 Apr 47	FD-1	St. Louis
163	O'Connor, Harry N.	LTJG	01 Apr 47	P-59B	Patuxent
164	Thompson, Harley F.	LCDR	03 Apr 47	P-59A	Patuxent
165	Whillans, Jack E.*	LT	04 Apr 47	P-59A	Patuxent
166	Wood, Robert B.	LCDR	07 Apr 47	P-59A	Patuxent
167	Krantz, William F.	LCDR	10 Apr 47	Vampire	England
168	Reeves, Roy S.	LCDR	10 Apr 47	P-59B	Patuxent
169	McKinley, Charles E.	LT	l0 Apr 47	P-59B	Patuxent
170	Coats, Robert C.	LCDR	15 Apr 47	P-59B	Patuxent
171	Hamilton, Chas. B., Jr.	LTJG	17 Apr 47	P-59B	Patuxent
172	Pride, Alfred M.	RADM	24 Apr 47	YP-59A	Patuxent
173	Clifton, Joseph C.	CAPT	01 May 47	P-59B	Patuxent
174	Ballinger, Richard R.	CAPT	01 May 47	P-59A	Patuxent
175	Bott, Alan R.	LTJG	08 May 47	P-59B	Patuxent
176	Franger, Marvin J.	LCDR	09 May 47	FD-1	Patuxent
177	McGinty, William G.	LT	19 May 47	P-80	Williams AFB
178	Cousins, Ralph W.	CDR	20 May 47	P-59B	Patuxent
179	Simpler, Leroy C.	CAPT	21 May 47	FD-1	St. Louis
180	Billo, James D.	LCDR	04 Jun 47	P-59	Patuxent
181	Timmes, Francis X.	LCDR	12 Jun 47	P-59B	Patuxent
182	Neddo, Donald N.	LCDR	13 Jun 47	P-59B	Patuxent
183	Stapler, Charles R.*	LCDR	16 Jun 47	YP-59A	Patuxent
184	Bates, Richard S.	LT	18 Jun 47	YP-59A	Patuxent
185	Smith, Joseph G.	LCDR	24 Jun 47	YP-59B	Patuxent
186	Weatherup, Robert A.	LCDR	25 Jun 47	P-59	Patuxent
187	Nester, Robert G.	LCDR	30 Jun 47	YP-59A	Patuxent
188	Dibble, Edgar J.	LT	30 Jun 47	YP-59A	Patuxent

No.	Name	Rank	Date	Plane	Place
189	Minter, Chas. S., Jr.	CDR	02 Jul 47	YP-59B	Patuxent
190	Campbell, Robert K.	LCDR	03 Jul 47	YP-59A	Patuxent
191	Gates, Clark H.	LCDR	09 Jul 47	P-59B	Patuxent
192	Weymouth, Ralph	LCDR	11 Jul 47	P-59B	Patuxent
193	Collins, Francis L.	LTJG	12 Jul 47	FD-1	St. Louis
194	Russell, Hawley	CDR	15 Jul 47	FD-1	Patuxent
195	Brehm, William W.	LCDR	17 Jul 47	FD-1	Patuxent
196	Miller, Charles G.*	LT	17 Jul 47	P-59B	Patuxent
197	Dace, Carl C.	LTJG	17 Jul 47	P-59B	Patuxent
198	Perry, Adrian H.	CDR	18 Jul 47	FD-1	Patuxent
199	Phillips, Thomas A.	CAPT	23 Jul 47	P-59	Patuxent
200	Clasen, William E.	MAJ	25 Jul 47	P-59B	Patuxent
201	Glover, John W.	LTJG	26 Jul 47	FD-1	Patuxent
202	Greenslade, John F.	CAPT	05 Aug 47	P-59B	Patuxent
203	Raposa, William C.	LTJG	06 Aug 47	FD-1	St. Louis
204	Mryo, Robert A.	LCDR	07 Aug 47	FD-1	Patuxent
205	Bicknell, John R.	LTJG	07 Aug 47	P-59B	Patuxent
206	Payne, Paul E.	LT	07 Aug 47	FD-1	Patuxent
207	Buxton, Elliott A.*	LT	08 Aug 47	FD-1	Patuxent
208	Sullivan, John*	LT	08 Aug 47	FD-1	Patuxent
209	Long, John O., Jr.*	ENS	08 Aug 47	FD-1	Patuxent
210	Cauble, Lawrence M.	LT	08 Aug 47	P-59B	Patuxent
211	Biggers, William D.*	LCDR	09 Aug 47	FD-1	Patuxent
212	Davis, William V.	CAPT	10 Aug 47	P-59B	Patuxent
213	Taylor, Donald C.	LT	12 Aug 47	P-59B	Patuxent
214	Genta, John L.*	LCDR	12 Aug 47	P-59B	Patuxent
215	McGowan, Edward C.	LT	12 Aug 47	XFD-1	NAS Mustin
216	Jensen, Alvin J.	CAPT	19 Aug 47	P-59B	Patuxent
217	Heath, Thomas W.	LCDR	23 Aug 47	FH-1	Patuxent
218	Ellis, Paul B.	LCDR	23 Aug 47	FH-1	Patuxent
219	Kimak, Charles	MAJ	26 Aug 47	P-59B	Patuxent
220	Newell, James H.	CDR	29 Aug 47	FH-1	Patuxent
221	Fox, Frank A.	LT	10 Sep 47	FH-1	Quonset
222	Laird, Dean S.	LT	10 Sep 47	FH-1	Quonset
223	Wiktorski, Peter A.	CAPT	16 Sep 47	FH-1	Patuxent
224	Turner, Frederick G.	LTJG	18 Sep 47	FH-1	Quonset
225	Roberts, Carson A.	COL	01 Oct 47	P-59B	Patuxent
226	McElroy, Richard S.	LCDR	02 Oct 47	P-59B	Patuxent
227	Werner, Ralph L.	LCDR	10 Oct 47	P-59B	Patuxent
228	James, George S., Jr.	CDR	14 Oct 47	FH-1	St. Louis
229	Torry, John A., Jr.	LCDR	14 Oct 47	P-59B	Patuxent
230	Parker, Chester A.	LT	16 Oct 47	FH-1	Quonset
231	Helms, Jonee L.	1stLT	16 Oct 47	P-80	Williams AFB
232	Blackmun, Arvid W.	MAJ	23 Oct 47	P-59B	Patuxent
233	Barnett, Marvin E.	LCDR	04 Nov 47	FH-1	Quonset
234	Sedaker, Thomas S.	LT	04 Nov 47	FH-1	Quonset
235	Sells, Warren H.	ENS	04 Nov 47	FH-1	Quonset
236	Couch, Eugene	ENS	07 Nov 47	FH-1	Quonset
237	Oelrich, Martin E. W.	MAJ	12 Nov 47	FH-1	Cherry Point
238	Domina, Walter E.	1stLT	17 Nov 47	FH-1	Cherry Point
239	Panchision, Walter	1stLT	17 Nov 47	FH-1	Cherry Point
240	Connelly, Frederick G.	1stLT	18 Nov 47	FH-1	Cherry Point
241	Jeter, Manning T., Jr.	1stLT	18 Nov 47	FH-1	Cherry Point

No.	Name	Rank	Date	Plane	Place
242	Conner, Andrew B.	LCDR	19 Nov 47	P-59B	Patuxent
243	Gordon, Donald	LCDR	19 Nov 47	P-59B	Patuxent
244	Lindley, Johnny D.	CAPT	25 Nov 47	FH-1	Cherry Point
245	Green, Robert D.	1stLT	26 Nov 47	FH-1	Cherry Point
246	Iglehart, Louis T., Jr.	1stLT	26 Nov 47	FH-1	Cherry Point
247	Mars, William G., Jr.	1stLT	26 Nov 47	FH-1	Cherry Point
248	Seaman, Milford V.	1stLT	28 Nov 47	FH-1	Cherry Point
249	Blass, Lytton F.	MSGT	05 Dec 47	FH-1	Cherry Point
250	Tate, Hugh J.	LTJG	07 Dec 47	P-59B	Patuxent
251	Schilt, C. Frank	BGEN	09 Dec 47	FH-1	St. Louis
252	Kinser, Dick R.	1stLT	09 Dec 47	FH-1	Cherry Point
253	Ramsay, Thomas W.*	LCDR	16 Dec 47	FH-1	Patuxent
254	Ives, Donald A.	MSGT	18 Dec 47	FH-1	Cherry Point
255	Bortz, William H.	1stLT	19 Dec 47	FH-1	Cherry Point
256	Roark, Walter N., Jr.	1stLT	19 Dec 47	FH-1	Cherry Point
257	McDaniel, James	1stLT	23 Dec 47	FH-1	Cherry Point
258	Bosee, Roland A.	CDR	29 Dec 47	FH-1	Patuxent
259	Kibbe, Richard L.	CDR	29 Dec 47	FH-1	Patuxent
260	Rockwell, John H.*	LCDR	29 Dec 47	FH-1	Patuxent
261	Speirs, Carl L.	LCDR	30 Dec 47	FH-1	Patuxent
262	Morton, Wilbur Y.	LCDR	31 Dec 47	FH-1	Patuxent
263	Armstrong, Alan J.	MAJ	08 Jan 48	FH-1	Patuxent
264	Morton, Wilbur Y.	MAJ	08 Jan 48	FH-1	Patuxent
265	Stefan, Karl H.	LCDR	11 Jan 48	FH-1	Patuxent
266	Beatle, Ralph H.	LT	15 Jan 48	P-59B	Patuxent
267	Vail, Malcolm E.	ENS	15 Jan 48	P-80A	Williams AFB
268	Brown, Nelson E.	1stLt	15 Jan 48	FH-1	
269	Jones, Charles D.	CAPT	15 Jan 48	FH-1	
270	Brown, F. Taylor	ENS	16 Jan 48	P-80A	Williams AFB
271	Hansen, Dale W.	1stLT	16 Jan 48	FH-1	
272	Pierozzi, C. Nello	ENS	18 Jan 48	P-80A	Williams AFB
273	Davis, Donald C.	LT	19 Jan 48	P-80A	Williams AFB
274	Pickett, Phillip G.	1stLT	22 Jan 48	FH-1	
275	Mooney, Thomas G.	MSGT	26 Jan 48	FH-1	
276	McLean, Carl T.	CAPT	26 Jan 48	FH-1	
277	Schoch, Edwin F.*	LCDR	29 Jan 48	FJ-1	Patuxent
278	Firebaugh, Gordon E.	LCDR	30 Jan 48	FH-1	Patuxent
279	Nifong, James M.	LT	31 Jan 48	FH-1	Patuxent
280	Bayers, Edward H.	LCDR	02 Feb 48	FH-1	Patuxent
281	Cotariu, Alan R.	ENS	02 Feb 48	FH-1	Patuxent
282	Stetson, Thomas H.	LCDR	02 Feb 48	FH-1	Patuxent
283	Folsom, Samuel B.	CAPT	03 Feb 48	FH-1	Patuxent
284	Kelly, Vincent F.	LT	04 Feb 48	FJ-1	San Diego
285	Thompson, Lewis E.	LT	06 Feb 48	FJ-1	N. Island
286	Roach, Walter, Jr.	LT	09 Feb 48	FH-1	Patuxent
287	Capriotti, Anthony	LT	11 Feb 48	FJ-1	San Diego
288	Ritchie, James	LT	11 Feb 48	FJ-1	San Diego
289	Davidson, Paul D.	LTJG	12 Feb 48	FJ-1	N. Island
290	Smith, Robert R.	MSGT	16 Feb 48	FH-1	Cherry Point
291	Wehmeyer, Wilbur J.	CDR	17 Feb 48	FH-1	Patuxent
292	Stacy, James M.	LT	19 Feb 48	FH-1	
293	Nemoff, Alfred J.	ENS	20 Feb 48	FJ-1	San Diego
294	Oeschlin, Robert E.	ENS	24 Feb 48	FJ-1	San Diego

No.	Name	Rank	Date	Plane	Place
295	Pettiet, Rudolph L.	LCDR	24 Feb 48	FH-1	Patuxent
296	Coppola, Earnest J.	LTJG	25 Feb 48	FH-1	Patuxent
297	Bell, William R.*	LCDR	06 Mar 48	FH-1	Patuxent
298	Meyersburg, R. B.	MAJ	10 Mar 48	Meteor	
299	Yunck, Michael R.	MAJ	11 Mar 48	P-80	Williams AFB
300	Jackson, Dewey H.	1stLT	12 Mar 48	P-80A	Williams AFB
301	Martin, Benjamin G.	1stLT	12 Mar 48	P-80A	Williams AFB
302	Ellis, James W.*	LT	13 Mar 48	FH-1	Patuxent
303	Poulson, George W.	1stLT	13 Mar 48	P-80A	Williams AFB
304	Condon, John P.	LCOL	16 Mar 48	P-80A	Williams AFB
305	Galer, Robert	COL	16 Mar 48	FH-1	
306	Starkes, C. B.	LCDR	22 Mar 48	FH-1	
307	Pankurst, Paul L.	CAPT	23 Mar 48	FH-1	
308	Whitaker, James L.	CAPT	30 Mar 48	FH-1	
309	Gibson, Charles E.	CDR	05 Apr 48	FH-1	Quonset
310	Durand, Paul H.	LCDR	06 Apr 48	FH-1	Patuxent
311	Ruehlow, Standley E.	CDR	07 Apr 48	FH-1	
312	Severson, Martin A.	LCOL	09 Apr 48	FH-1	
313	Houser, William D.	LCDR	15 Apr 48	FH-1	Patuxent
314	Spiess, Morris K.	LTJG	16 Apr 48	FH-1	Patuxent
315	McNeil, Wilfred J.*	LT	26 Apr 48	FH-1	Patuxent
316	Gray, James S., Jr.	CDR	11 May 48	P-80B	Okinawa
317	Dawson, Marion L.	COL	12 May 48	FH-1	
318	Manchester, B. B. III	LCOL	26 May 48	FH-1	
319	Roush, Martin B.	CAPT	29 May 48	FH-1	
320	Soucek, Apollo*	RADM	01 Jun 48	FH-1	Patuxent
321	Millington, W. A.	LCOL	03 Jun 48	FH-1	
322	Gallery, Daniel V.	RADM	09 Jun 48	FH-1	Patuxent
323	Peterson, Harry W.	LT	18 Jun 48	FJ-1	San Diego
324	McManus, John	1stLT	23 Jun 48	FH-1	
325	Cruise, Edgar A.	RADM	02 Jul 48	FH-1	Patuxent
326	Pawka, E. J.	CDR	02 Jul 48	TO-1	San Diego
327	Weissenberger, G. J.	LCOL	07 Jul 48	FH-1	
328	Johnson, Robert J.	LCOL	07 Jul 48	FH-1	
329	Beebe, Marshall U.	CDR	12 Jul 48	FH-1	Patuxent
330	Harris, Thomas S.	LT	15 Jul 48	FH-1	Quonset
331	Mueller, Richard C.	LCDR	22 Jul 48	FH-1	Patuxent
332	Spears, Paul H. A.	LT	Jul 48	TO-1	Burbank
333	Billings, Thomas C.	1stLT	27 Jul 48	TO-1	
334	Fiegener, Kenneth G.	1stLT	03 Aug 48	TO-1	El Toro
335	Rafferty, Edgar L.	1stLT	04 Aug 48	TO-1	
336	Harrison, Patrick	CAPT	04 Aug 48	TO-1	
337	Case, William N.	CAPT	04 Aug 48	TO-1	
338	Perry, Jack E.	1stLT	04 Aug 48	TO-1	
339	Smith, Stanley E.	LTJG	05 Aug 48	FH-1	Quonset
340	Guss, William F.	1stLT	05 Aug 48	TO-1	
341	Klingman, Robert R.	1stLT	05 Aug 48	TO-1	
342	Abbott, Edwin W. II	LTJG	05 Aug 48	FH-1	
343	Gourley, Norman W.	1stLT	05 Aug 48	TO-1	
344	Mitchell, Weldon R.	1stLT	06 Aug 48	TO-1	
345	Jarrett, Clyde R.	1stLT	06 Aug 48	TO-1	
346	Wolfe, Ted E., Jr.	LCDR	09 Aug 48	FH-1	Atl City
347	Brown, John B.	CAPT	09 Aug 48	FH-1	

No.	Name	Rank	Date	Plane	Place
348	Wilder, James H.	ENS	09 Aug 48	FH-1	
349	Ganschow, Edward F.	CAPT	11 Aug 48	FH-1	Cherry Point
350	Parker, Elwin A.	LCDR	12 Aug 48	FH-1	Patuxent
351	Moro, Albert J.	LTJG	16 Aug 48	FH-1	Quonset
352	Furney, Maynard M.	LCDR	17 Aug 48	FH-1	Patuxent
353	Prahar, T. F.	LT	17 Aug 48	FH-1	Patuxent
354	Macomber, Brainard	LCDR	18 Aug 48	FH-1	Patuxent
355	Widhelm, William J.*	CDR	19 Aug 48	FH-1	Patuxent
356	Cloud, Guy M.	1stLT	30 Aug 48	TO-1	
357	Carter, Frank B.	ENS	17 Sep 48	FH-1	Quonset
358	Nye, Robert D.	LCDR	17 Sep 48	FH-1	Quonset
359	Pugh, Edward L.	COL	17 Sep 48	FH-1	
360	Ingalls, Chas. E., Jr.	CDR	22 Sep 48	FH-1	Patuxent
361	Everton, Loren D.	MAJ	29 Sep 48	FH-1	
362	Brtek, F. C.	LTJG	06 Oct 48	FH-1	Quonset
363	Trammel, Thomas B.	CAPT	14 Oct 48	TO-1	El Toro
364	Stuckey, Harry B.	1stLT	14 Oct 48	TO-1	
365	Haley, Harold L.	1stLT	14 Oct 48	TO-1	
366	Robinson, Robert B.	1stLT	14 Oct 48	TO-1	
367	Austin, Marshall S.	1stLT	14 Oct 48	TO-1	
368	Pottinger, William K.	LCOL	14 Oct 48	TO-1	
369	Grey, Jack R.	1stLT	14 Oct 48	TO-1	
370	Read, Robert R.	MAJ	14 Oct 48	TO-1	El Toro
371	Sharp, James II	1stLT	14 Oct 48	TO-1	
372	Houser, Fred C.	CAPT	14 Oct 48	TO-1	
373	Connell, Herschell G.	1stLT	14 Oct 48	TO-1	
374	Johnson, Danny W.	1stLT	14 Oct 48	TO-1	
375	Schroeder, Charles	1stLT	14 Oct 48	TO-1	
376	Rutledge, Rockwell M.	1stLT	14 Oct 48	TO-1	
377	Frankovic, Boris J.	1stLT	14 Oct 48	TO-1	
378	Hemstad, Robert S.	1stLT	14 Oct 48	TO-1	
379	Davis, Leonard K.	LCOL	14 Oct 48	FH-1	
380	Bright, Cruger L.	MAJ	15 Oct 48	FH-1	
381	Jernigan, Curtis	1stLT	22 Oct 48	FH-1	
382	McCullough, William F.	LTJG	26 Oct 48	F-80	
383	Stapp, Donald H.	MAJ	26 Oct 48	TO-1	El Toro
384	Holloway, Harding H.	1stLT	28 Oct 48	FH-1	
385	Russell, Allard G.	LCDR	04 Nov 48	TO-1	San Diego
386	Conger, Jack E.	MAJ	04 Nov 48	FH-1	
387	Jackson, Billy	LTJG	04 Nov 48	TO-1	San Diego
388	Plog, Leonard H.	LTJG	04 Nov 48	TO-1	San Diego
389	Lizotte, Wesley E.	LTJG	04 Nov 48	TO-1	San Diego
390	Freeman, Dewitt L.	LTJG	04 Nov 48	TO-1	San Diego
391	Lloyd, Marshall O.	LT	04 Nov 48	TO-1	
392	Sears, Harry E.	CDR	05 Nov 48	FH-1	Patuxent
393	Johnson, James	1stLT	14 Nov 48	FH-1	
394	Jensen, Harvey	1stLT	15 Nov 48	TO-1	El Toro
395	King, George J.	1stLT	15 Nov 48	TO-1	
397	Oster, Eugene M.	1stLT	15 Nov 48	TO-1	
398	Meyer, Eugene W.	1stLT	15 Nov 48	TO-1	
399	Turcotte, Edward	1stLT	15 Nov 48	TO-1	
400	Toups, Thaddeus J.	1stLT	15 Nov 48	TO-1	
401	Harper, Edwin A.	CAPT	15 Nov 48	TO-1	

No.	Name	Rank	Date	Plane	Place
402	Hamilton, John	1stLT	15 Nov 48	TO-1	
403	Thornbury, Donald S.	CAPT	15 Nov 48	TO-1	
404	Croyle, Fred K.	1stLT	16 Nov 48	TO-1	
405	Keller, Harold F.	1stLT	19 Nov 48	TO-1	
406	Logan, Thomas B.	LT	01 Dec 48	TO-1	Patuxent
407	Wattenburger, Robert	LTJG	06 Dec 48	TO-1	Patuxent
408	Adams, Allan M., Jr.	LTJG	06 Dec 48	TO-1	Patuxent
409	Bunger, Samuel J.	ENS	06 Dec 48	TO-1	
410	Smith, Mercer R.	1stLT	10 Dec 48	FH-1	Cherry Point
411	Regan, Robert F.	LT	13 Dec 48	FH-1	Quonset
412	Gilman, George L.	2ndLT	14 Dec 48	FH-1	
413	Campbell, Donald L.	LTJG	15 Dec 48	FH-1	Quonset
414	Davis, Judson C.	LT	15 Dec 48	FH-1	Quonset
415	Quilty, Joseph F.	MAJ	21 Dec 48	TO-1	
416	Funk, Harold N.	CDR	22 Dec 48	FH-1	Patuxent
417	Hill, John S.	LCDR	23 Dec 48	FH-1	Patuxent
418	Penne, Harold B.	MAJ	28 Dec 48	FH-1	
419	Wenzell, R. M.	LT	28 Dec 48	FH-1	

List of Early Helicopter Pilots

The Bureau of Aeronautics issued a Planning Directive on 24 July 1942 calling for procurement of four Sikorsky helicopters for study and development by Navy and Coast Guard aviation forces. However, this was not the Navy's first interest in helicopters. That interest may be traced back to 5 December 1917 when the policy regarding helicopter development was established by the Secretaries of the Navy and War Departments on the basis of recommendations made by the Joint Technical Board on Aircraft. At that time, it was stated there was a need for improvements in powerplants and propellers if a successful helicopter was to be obtained. Actual support of development efforts was to be limited to moral encouragement until a vendor had demonstrated a helicopter of military value.

The Navy's first rotary wing vehicle was the XOP-1 autogiro ordered on 25 February 1931 from Pitcairn Aircraft. This machine was not a true helicopter since it had fixed wings and could not rise verticallly. On 12 March 1935, the Navy issued a contract to Pitcairn Autogiro Company to remove the fixed wings from the XOP-1, thereby converting it to the XOP-2 which thus became the Navy's first heavier-than-air aircraft without wings. Tests were conducted with the XOP-1, including landings on *Langley* in September 1931. However, conclusions from the tests, which compared the autogiros with fixed wing aircraft, indicated the advantages were not great enough to override the disadvantages of payload, range, and the difficulties of flying. Personnel involved in the testing of the XOP-1 included future greats in Naval Aviation such as Alfred Pride, Ralph A. Ofstie, Robert B. Pirie and Frederick M. Trapnell. Other attempts between 1932 to 1937 were made to improve rotary wing capabilities but they were not successful. The Marine Corps used the OP-1 autogiro in Nicaragua in 1932 with the comment that its chief value in expeditionary duty was in inspecting small fields recommended by ground troops as landing areas, evacuating medical "sitting" cases, and ferrying of important personnel. In 1937 the Navy also experimented with the XOZ-1, a modified N2Y-1 with a cyclic controlled rotor, but the tests were not successful.

In the early 1940s, a class desk was established in the Bureau of Aeronautics for the Navy's helicopter program and staffed by a small group of individuals who saw the potential for rotary wing development. They included Captain Clayton C. Marcy, Commander James W. Klopp and Commander Raymond Doll. The impetus for more Navy involvement in helicopters was spearheaded by the Coast Guard who were very interested in its ASW and rescue capabilities. Their vision for the use of the helicopter, whose development responsibility had been assigned to the Army Air Corps, resulted in a 15 February 1943 directive from the Commander in Chief, U.S. Fleet that assigned responsibility for sea-going development of helicopters and their operation in convoys to the Coast Guard. Tests were to be carried out to determine if helicopters operating from merchant ships would be of value in combating submarines. On 4 May 1943, to expedite the evaluation of the helicopter in antisubmarine operations, the Commander in Chief, U.S. Fleet, directed that a "joint board" be formed with representatives from the Commander in Chief, U.S. Fleet; the Bureau of Aeronautics, the Coast Guard, the British Admiralty and the Royal Air forces. The resulting Combined Board for the Evaluation of the Ship-Based Helicopter in Antisubmarine Warfare was later expanded to include representatives of the Army Air Forces (AAF), the War Shipping Administration and the National Advisory Committee for Aeronautics. A few days later, on 7 May 1943, Navy representatives witnessed landing trials of the XR-4 helicopter aboard the merchant tanker SS *Bunker Hill* in a demonstration sponsored by the Maritime Commission and conducted in Long Island Sound. The pilot, Colonel R. F. Gregory, AAF, made about 15 flights, some of which he landed on the water before returning to the platform on the deck of the ship. On 10 June 1943, Lieutenant Commander Frank A. Erickson, USCG, proposed that helicopters be developed for antisubmarine warfare, "not as a killer craft but as the eyes and ears of the convoy escorts." To this end he recommended that helicopters be equipped with radar and dunking sonar. With the foregoing proposals and developments, the Navy ordered and received its first helicopter on 16 October 1943. The helicopter was a Sikorsky YR-4B, Navy designation HNS-1. It was accepted at Bridgeport, Conn., following a 60 minute acceptance test flight by Lieutenant Commander Erickson. Commander Charles T. Booth, USN, delivered this helicopter to NAS Patuxent River, Md., on 22 October 1943. As stated by a memo from Commander Booth, he had arrived at Bridgeport "to continue instructions and to deliver to NAS Patuxent the first Navy helicopter. . . . Six hours additional flight time was obtained by Commander Booth prior to his return to NAS Patuxent, Md., on 22 October."

On the basis of his belief that tests indicated the practicability of ship-based helicopter, the Chief of Naval Operations, on 18 December 1943, separated the pilot training from test and development functions in the helicopter program. He directed that, effective 1 January 1944, a helicopter pilot training program be conducted by the U.S. Coast Guard at Floyd Bennett Field, N.Y., under the direction of the Deputy Chief of Naval Operations (Air). This planning directive of 18 December 1943, also named Rockaway, N.Y., as an outlying field for training and stated that three Coast Guard and two Navy officers had qualified as helicopter pilots to date. The directive also indicated "It has been determined that after 25 hours of dual and solo flight time, a fixed wing pilot is qualified as a helicopter pilot." Thus, during World War II, the Coast Guard, at Floyd Bennett Field, N.Y., was responsible for pilot and enlisted mechanic training in helicopter aviation for the Navy. Helicopter pilots trained by the Coast Guard unit also included personnel from the Army Air Force, the CAA, and NACA.

Following the end of World War II, the Navy established VX-3 on 1 July 1946 at NAS New York (Floyd Bennett Field). This squadron took over the helicopter pilot training duties that had been done by the Coast Guard unit at Floyd Bennett Field, N.Y. VX-3 moved to NAS Lakehurst, N.J., on 10 September 1946 and continued training helicopter pilots until they were disestablished on 1 April 1948.

Helicopter Utility Squadron 2 (HU-2) was established on 1 April 1948 and took over the responsibility for training helicopter pilots. The squadron was located at NAS Lakehurst, N.J. Many of the personnel from VX-3 helped form HU-2 when it was established. On 11 June 1948, the Chief of Naval Operations issued standards for training aviators as helicopter pilots and provided that helicopter pilots previously trained by the Coast Guard or VX-3 would retain their qualification. However, not all personnel received their qualification as a helicopter pilot from VX-3 or HU-2, even though they had been assigned the mission of training helicopter pilots. HU-2 would issue helicopter pilot qualifications to an individual that may have received training at NATC Patuxent River, Md., from HU-1, or from Connally Air Force Base in Texas.

HU-2 was not only responsible for training helicopter pilots but was also involved in providing helicopter detachments for utility services and search and rescue missions. Due to an increased demand for these services, as well as a need for more helicopter pilots, the Chief of Naval Operations decided to transfer the helicopter pilot training mission to the Naval Air Training Command at Ellyson Field, Pensacola, Fla. Helicopter Training Unit 1 (HTU-1) was established on 3 December 1950 at Pensacola, Fla. HU-2 shifted its responsibility for training helicopter pilots to HTU-1 in January 1951. HTU-1 was redesignated HTG-1 in March 1957. The HTG-1 designation was changed to HT-8 on 1 July 1960. HT-8 is still training helicopter pilots in the Pensacola area.

When a new program is established, especially one that entails listing personnel who are designated or qualified for a particular job code, the records for the evolution of that new program can be very sketchy. That is precisely what happened in the training program for helicopter pilots. The early helicopter pilots did not have a formal Navy training program to follow or the correct procedures in place to record and preserve their heliclpter pilot qualifications. In fact, in 1943 the first group to qualify were sent to East Hartford, Conn., and trained by the Sikorsky Aircraft Company. They included Lieutenant Commander Frank Erickson, USCG; Lieutenant A. N. Fisher, USCG; Lieutenant Stewart R. Graham, USCG; and Commander Charles T. Booth, USN. None of these individuals were placed on the list of early helicopter pilots. In fact, the list, which appears to originate from VX-3 and HU-2 records, does not list any Coast Guard officers. The following list is the best that could be compiled from the available records on helicopter pilot qualification and training. It does not include the Coast Guard aviators.

Helicopter Pilot Number	Name	Rank	Service	Date of Qualification Designation
1	Knapp, William G.	LT	USNR	15 Apr 1944
2	Doll, Raymond E.	CDR	USN	26 Sep 1944
3	Wood, Charles R.	CDR	USNR	26 Sep 1944
4	Brown, Percy	LT	USNR	6 Feb 1945
5	Kembro, Marcrie D.	CAPT	USN	9 Aug 1945
6	Long, Richard J.	LT	USN(T)	9 Aug 1945
7	Marcy, Clayton C.	CAPT	USN	10 Oct 1945
8	Runyon, Joseph W.	CDR	USN	31 Oct 1945
9	Houston, Charles E.	CDR	USN	18 Dec 1945
10	Hoover, George	LT	USN	27 Dec 1945
11	Lawrence, M.	LT	USNR	28 Dec 1945
12	Wilcox, Donald E.	CAPT	USN	3 Jun 1946
13	Kosciusko, Henry M.	LCDR	USN	17 Jul 1946
14	Kubicki, Edward	LT	USN	26 Jul 1946
15	Schaufler, William G.	LTJG	USN	26 Jul 1946
16	Delalio, Armand H.	MAJ	USMC	8 Aug 1946
17	Rullo, Guiseppe J.	LT	USN	28 Aug 1946
18	Reeves, George J.	LT	USN	28 Aug 1946
19	Lammi, James W.	LT	USN	27 Sep 1946
20	Junghans, Robert L.	LCDR	USN	1 Nov 1946
21	Sessums, Walter M.	LCDR	USN	5 Nov 1946
22	Tanner, Charles S.	LCDR	USN	9 Nov 1946
23	Fink, Christian	LCDR	USN	18 Dec 1946
24	Bott, Alan	LT	USN	18 Dec 1946
25	Tracy, Lloyd W.	LT	USN	23 Jun 1947
26	Glenzer, Hubert	LTJG	USN	14 Oct 1947
27	Anderson, Roy L.	1stLT	USMC	20 Nov 1947
28	Strieby, Robert A.	CAPT	USMC	20 Nov 1947
29	Garber, C. O.	CAPT	USMC	20 Nov 1947
30	Riley, Russell R.	MAJ	USMC	20 Nov 1947
31	Peters, Maurice A.	CDR	USN	21 Nov 1947
32	Shawcross, William H.	LT	USN	24 Nov 1947
33	Bagshaw, James R.	LTJG	USN	24 Nov 1947
34	Montgomery, Marvin D.	LTJG	USN	24 Nov 1947
35	Morrison, Gene W.	1stLT	USMC	1 Dec 1947
36	Carleton, R. D.	LTJG	USN	20 Dec 1947
37	Arnold, E. A.	LCDR	USN	21 Dec 1947
38	Moseley, R. H.	ENS	USN	22 Dec 1947
39	Higbee, J.	CAPT	USN	22 Dec 1947
40	Billett, Dudley S.	LCDR	USN	15 Jan 1948
41	Camp, R. W.	ADC(NAP)	USN	21 Feb 1948
42	McVicars, A. L.	1stLT	USMC	11 Mar 1948
43	Meshier, C. W.	LT	USN	12 Mar 1948
44	Blatt, W. D.	CAPT	USMC	17 Mar 1948
45	Polen, R. A.	1stLT	USMC	17 Mar 1948
46	Ward, C. E.	1stLT	USMC	19 Mar 1948
47	Pope, E. J.	1stLT	USMC	22 Mar 1948
48	Sebach, H. U.	LCDR	USN	31 Mar 1948
49	Fisher, A. G.	MSGT	USMC	1 Apr 1948
50	Schmucker, S.	ENS	USN	7 Apr 1948
51	Mathewson, F. F.	LT	USN	16 Apr 1948
52	Hanies, G. D.	LT	USN	16 Apr 1948

Helicopter Pilot Number	Name	Rank	Service	Date of Qualification Designation
53	Matthews, J. H.	CAPT	USN	20 Apr 1948
54	Mounts, L. J.	MSGT	USMC	26 Apr 1948
55	Fox, J. E.	LT	USN	29 Apr 1948
56	Leary, W.	LTJG	USN	29 Apr 1948
57	Grassi, J.	ENS	USN	29 Apr 1948
58	Longstaff, R.	1stLT	USMC	12 May 1948
59	Hamilton, D. E.	ADC(AP)	USN	12 May 1948
60	Mitchell, G. D.	ADC(NAP)	USN	18 May 1948
61	Finn, L. A.	ADC(NAP)	USN	19 May 1948
62	Collins, V. W.	LT	USN	21 May 1948
63	Nebergall, M.	1stLT	USMC	19 Jun 1948
64	Griffin, M. C.	LTJG	USN	7 Jul 1948
65	Brender, B. W.	LTJG	USN	8 Jul 1948
66	Hutto, C. H.	AC1(NAP)	USN	8 Jul 1948
67	Lynch, R. E.	ENS	USN	9 Jul 1948
68	Milner, F. D.	LT	USN	13 Jul 1948
69	Matthews, W. R.	ENS	USN	22 Jul 1948
70	Torry, J. A. H.	LCDR	USN	6 Aug 1948
71	Nickerson, R. L.	MAJ	USMC	6 Aug 1948
72	Dyer, E. C.	COL	USMC	6 Aug 1948
73	Ellis, W. Y..	LCDR	USNR	6 Aug 1948
74	Leonard, W. R.	LCDR	USN	16 Aug 1948
75	Cunha, G. D. M.	CDR	USN	19 Aug 1948
76	Cox, W. J.	ENS	USN	24 Aug 1948
77	Fridley, D. C.	ENS	USN	24 Aug 1948
78	Dixon, W. C.	LT	USN	24 Aug 1948
79	Granger, R. P.	ADC(NAP)	USN	26 Aug 1948
80	Crofoot, A. E.	LTJG	USN	27 Aug 1948
81	Johnson, F. E.	ENS	USN	2 Sep 1948
82	Carey, J. F.	LCOL	USMC	2 Sep 1948
83	Kilcore, W. H.	LCDR	USN	3 Sep 1948
84	Miller, R. A.	LTJG	USN	8 Sep 1948
85	Wrenn, E.	LTJG	USN	13 Sep 1948
86	Wheat, N. L.	ENS	USN	14 Sep 1948
87	Garrison, R. G.	ENS	USN	24 Sep 1948
88	Wiskirchen, R. L.	LT	USN	24 Sep 1948
89	Cabell, J. B.	LT	USN	24 Sep 1948
90	Zoecklein, W. O.	LCDR	USN	19 Oct 1948
91	Connolly, T. F.	CDR	USN	15 Sep 1948
92	Sherby, S. S.	CDR	USN	15 Sep 1948
93	Hyland, J. J.	CDR	USN	15 Sep 1948
94	Rand, N. C.	LCDR	USN	15 Sep 1948
95	Davis, W. V., Jr.	CAPT	USN	15 Sep 1948
96	Timmins, (init. unk.)	LCDR	USNR	8 Oct 1948
97	Reilly, J. L.	LTJG	USN	20 Oct 1948
98	Denk, H. J,	ENS	USN	20 Oct 1948
99	Little, J. C.	LT	USN	9 Nov 1948
100	Nash, D. E.	LTJG	USN	9 Nov 1948
101	Blades, J. L.	LTJG	USN	12 Nov 1948
102	Gauthier, A. C.	LT	USNR	12 Nov 1948
103	McMullen, B. E.	LTJG	USN	12 Nov 1948
104	Peterson, M. C.	ADC(NAP)	USN	12 Nov 1948

Helicopter Pilot Number	Name	Rank	Service	Date of Qualification Designation
105	Rust, D. T.	LTJG	USN	19 Nov 1948
106	Hamilton, R. C.	ENS	USNR	23 Nov 1948
107	McCarthy, J. R.		CAA	1 Dec 1948
108	Fisher, F. J.	ENS	USNR	24 Nov 1948
109	Johnson, C. R.	LT	USN	6 Dec 1948
110	Berree, N. R.	LT	USN	7 Dec 1948
111	Schmeltzer, L. B.	LTJG	USN	7 Dec 1948
112	Moore, B., Jr.	CDR	USN	10 Dec 1948
113	Lieske, J. M.	ALC(NAP)	USN	13 Dec 1948
114	Staples, C.		CAA	14 Jan 1949
115	Olmsted, P. S.	ENS	USNR	20 Jan 1949
116	Miller, H. M.	LTJG	USNR	21 Jan 1949
117	Hilton, J. J., Jr.	CDR	USN	1 Feb 1949
118	Montgomery, W. G.	LT	USN	9 Feb 1949
119	Brown, H. F.	LT	USN	10 Feb 1949
120	Armstrong, J. G.	LT	USN	23 Feb 1949
121	Starr, M. R.	ENS	USN	24 Feb 1949
122	Reed, M. (n)	LT	USN	24 Feb 1949
123	Case, R. C.	1stLT	USMC	9 Mar 1949
124	Blackwood, R. R.	ENS	USNR	11 Mar 1949
125	Cole, J. S.	LT	USN	14 Mar 1949
126	Mitchell, W. P.	MAJ	USMC	17 Mar 1949
127	Gill, R. J.	LTJG	USNR	15 Mar 1949
128	Pledger, W. G.	LTJG	USN	30 Mar 1949
129	Lueddeke, G. F.	LTJG	USN	5 Apr 1949
130	Marshall, A. R.	LT	USN	13 Apr 1949
131	Farwell, J. M.	LTJG	USN	13 Apr 1949
132	Tucci, F. A.	LT	USN	20 Apr 1949
133	Logan, I. C.	LTJG	USNR	21 Apr 1949
134	McClanan, F. H.	LCDR	USN	21 Apr 1949
135	Mayfield, A. (n)	LTJG	USN	21 Apr 1949
136	Raddatz, R. W.	LT	USN	29 Apr 1949
137	Braun, J. F.	LTJG	USN	29 Apr 1949
138	Wrigley, G. R.	LTJG	USN	29 Apr 1949
139	Kaylor, J. O.	1stLT	USMC	29 Apr 1949
140	Sullivan, R. J.	1stLT	USMC	4 May 1949
141	Bolt, G. W.	LCDR	USN	6 May 1949
142	Duffey, H. J.		CAA	9 May 1949
143	Kelley, F. E., Jr.	ENS	USN	9 May 1949
144	Rohrich, W. H.	LTJG	USN	9 May 1949
145	Griffin, (init. unk.)		CAA	15 Mar 1949
146	Titterud, S. V.	CAPT	USMC	11 May 1949
147	Lammi, W. S.	LT	USN	19 May 1949
148	Holmgren, A. F.	ENS	USN	15 Apr 1944
149	Crowe, G. T.	AD1(AP)	USN	19 May 1949
150	Taylor, C. B.	ADC(AP)	USN	20 May 1949
151	Mullen, J., Jr.	LTJG	USN	23 May 1949
152	Larkin, H. J.	LT	USN	26 May 1949
153	Close, R. A.	LTJG	USN	31 May 1949
154	Drinkwater, H. T.	LTJG	USN	31 May 1949
155	Williams, D. L.	ENS	USNR	31 May 1949
156	Mundy, E. M.	LCDR	USNR	10 Jun 1949

Helicopter Pilot Number	Name	Rank	Service	Date of Qualification Designation
157	Pennington, B. D.	LTJG	USN	15 Jun 1949
158	Highsmith, F. L.	ENS	USNR	15 Jun 1949
159	Crowell, L. T.	ENS	USNR	15 Jun 1949
160	Buerckholtz, H. M.	ENS	USNR	15 Jun 1949
161	Banks, W. F.	LTJG	USN(T)	15 Jun 1949
162	Price, W. J.	LTJG	USNR	23 Jun 1949
163	Marchand, J. L.	LCDR	USNR	23 Jun 1949
164	Heibr, W. D.	CAPT	USMC	1 Jul 1949
165	Bancroft, A. R.	1stLT	USMC	8 Jul 1949
166	Moran, F. P.	1stLT	USMC	8 Jul 1949
167	Ford, A., (n)	LT	USN	28 Jun 1949
168	Deitrich, V. S.	CDR	USN	14 Jul 1949
169	Neuman, A. E.	LT	USNR	15 Jul 1949
170	Bromka, A. C.	LTJG	USNR	19 Jul 1949
171	Leedom, H. E.	LCDR	USN	20 Jul 1949
172	Seay, G. W.	LTJG	USN	20 Jul 1949
173	Chagnon, W. G.	PRC(AP)	USN	26 Jul 1949
174	Butler, W. C.	LT	USN	26 Jul 1949
175	Dally, F. E.	CDR	USN	4 Aug 1949
176	Clabaugh, C. L.	LCDR	USNR	4 Aug 1949
177	Farish, G. B.	1stLT	USMC	8 Aug 1949
178	Armstrong, V. A.	CAPT	USMC	9 Aug 1949
179	Noble, E. V.	CDR	USN	25 Aug 1949
180	Horn, F. H.	1stLT	USMC	7 Sep 1949
181	Vest, J. P. W.	CAPT	USN	16 Sep 1949
182	Tuffanelle, G. T.	LTJG	USN	17 Sep 1949
183	Marr, R.	AO1(AP)	USN	23 Sep 1949
184	Woolley, S. R.	MSGT	USMC	26 Sep 1949
185	Barnes, R. O.	LTJG	USN	27 Sep 1949
186	Anderson, W. A.	AD1(AP)	USN	27 Sep 1949
187	Dennison, G. E.	LTJG	USN	30 Sep 1949
188	Fisher, C. E.	LTJG	USN	5 Oct 1949
189	Treon, H. J.	LT	USN	6 Oct 1949
190	Foley, F. D.	CDR	USN	7 Oct 1949
191	Asbury, D. A.	LT	USN	14 Oct 1949
192	Percy, G. (n)	MAJ	USMC	17 Oct 1949
193	Rozier, W. R.	CAPT	USMC	17 Oct 1949
194	Cozine, M. E.	ADC(AP)	USN	20 Oct 1949
195	Holman, E. D.	ADC(AP)	USN	25 Oct 1949
196	Connant, E. S.	LCDR	USN	30 Sep 1949
197	Hudson, W. N.	CDR	USNR	2 Oct 1949
198	Moody, J. T.	AO1(AP)	USN	2 Nov 1949
199	Voss, C. M.	LTJG	USNRV	4 Nov 1949
200	Scott, E. A.	LTJG	USN(T)	4 Nov 1949
201	Stokes, W. E.	ENS	USN	8 Nov 1949
202	Russell, J. B.	LT	USN	9 Nov 1949
203	Milburn, K. F.	AD1(AP)	USN	19 Nov 1949
204	Romer, R. D.	LTJG	USN	14 Nov 1949
205	Collup, W. D.	CAPT	USMC	30 Nov 1949
206	Koelsch, J. H.	LTJG	USN	9 Dec 1949
207	Proper, W. F.	LTJG	USN	14 Oct 1949
208	Harrigan, D. W.	CAPT	USN	10 Dec 1949

Helicopter Pilot Number	Name	Rank	Service	Date of Qualification Designation
209	Jenks, R. F.	AMC(AP)	USN	14 Oct 1949
210	Hamilton, C. B.	LTJG	USN	20 Jan 1950
211	Brown, S. H.	LCDR	USN	23 Nov 1949
212	Bayers, E. H.	LCDR	USN	23 Nov 1949
213	Bach, H. A.	LCDR	USN	23 Nov 1949
214	Kurtz, L. A.	LT	USN	23 Nov 1949
215	Brownfield, R. H.	ADC(AP)	USN	16 Jan 1950
216	Thorin, D. W.	AMC(AP)	USN	16 Jan 1950
217	Scroggs, F. W., Jr.	TSGT	USMC	8 Feb 1950
218	Mullkoff, E. (n)	LT	USNR	8 Feb 1950
219	Herring, G. W.	LCOL	USMC	10 Feb 1950
220	Davis, R. O.	LTJG	USN	17 Feb 1950
221	Swinburne, H. W.	LT	USN	20 Mar 1950
222	Sundberg, H. J.	LT	USN	20 Mar 1950
223	Young, R. E.	LTJG	USN	20 Mar 1950
224	Cardoza, H (n)	AD1(AP)	USN	9 Mar 1950
225	Marsh, E. D.	AD1(AP)	USN	9 Mar 1950
226	Harbour, C. C.	LT	USN	31 Mar 1950
227	Omara, P.(n)	LTJG	USN	31 Mar 1950
228	Huggins, J. C.	LT	USN	20 Apr 1950
229	Jones, C. C.	LTJG	USN	21 Apr 1950
230	Boegel, W. T.	AOC(AP)	USN	21 Apr 1950
231	Larson, C. S.	LTJG	USNR	24 Apr 1950
232	Kakol, J. F.	ADC(AP)	USN	25 Apr 1950
233	Smolen, F. E.	LT	USN	24 Apr 1950
234	Maghan, R. I.	LT	USN	28 Apr 1950
235	Richards, F. D.	LT	USN	4 May 1950
236	Felten, R. E.	LT	USN	4 May 1950
237	Jansen, T. E.	LT	USNR	4 May 1950
238	Bowen, J. B.	CAPT	USN	27 Apr 1950
239	Brock, M. A.	LT	USN	16 May 1950
240	Falabella, J. J.	LT	USNR	17 May 1950
241	Widmar, J. R.	LT	USNR	22 May 1950
242	Jensen, E. O.	LT	USNR	25 May 1950
243	Stearns, W. G.	LT	USN	2 Jun 1950
244	Hudson, F. W.	ACCA(AP)	USN	9 Jun 1950
245	McFarlane, H.	CAPT	USAF	9 Jun 1950
246	Erwin, W. L.	LTJG	USN	13 Jun 1950
247	Englehardt, L. J.	1stLT	USMC	13 Jun 1950
248	Scott, J. L.	1stLT	USMC	13 Jun 1950
249	Waring, E. S.	CDR	USN	27 Jun 1950
250	Albert, W. H.	LTJG	USNR	1 Jul 1950

Notes:
NAP and AP: Naval Aviation Pilot, an enlisted pilot.
CAA: Civil Aeroanutics Authority
init. unk.: Initials unknown

Early Helo Pilot, Commander Henry M. Kosciusko, standing along side a VX-3 HOS-1.

Gray Eagle Award

The Gray Eagle Trophy made its first appearance in 1961 during the celebration of the Fiftieth Anniversary of Naval Aviation.

In 1959, while serving as Commander in Chief, Allied Forces, Southern Europe, Admiral Charles R. Brown, USN, wrote to the Deputy Chief of Naval Operations (Air), Vice Admiral Robert B. Pirie, USN, telling of certain discussions he had with Vice Admiral George W. Anderson, then serving as Commander, Sixth Fleet. "We suggest that it be determined from official records who, at all times, is the senior aviator in point of service in flying; that a baton or similar token be awarded him, and that, with due ceremony, this symbol be handed on down to the next man with the passing years."

Admiral Pirie took the matter from there. For a time the title "Bull Naval Aviator" was a leading contender for the choice of names for the senior aviator's title. Various cups, statuettes, plaques and medals were proposed. Finally, a competition was conducted between aircraft companies desiring to sponsor the award. The Chance Vought Aircraft Company's (later LTV Corporation, Ling Temco Vought) design was selected and the Gray Eagle Award was brought into reality.

On 5 January 1961, at Naval Aviation's Fiftieth Anniversary Ball, Sheraton Park Hotel, Washington, D.C., Admiral Charles R. Brown received the Gray Eagle Trophy from Admiral James S. Russell, then serving as Vice Chief of Naval Operations.

While Admiral Brown was the first "active" aviator to receive the Trophy, replicas of the award were presented to all previous holders of the distinction, or their representative, during the ceremony. The recipients included Mrs. T. G. Ellyson, widow of Naval Aviator Number One, Commander Theodore G. Ellyson. Commander Ellyson would have held the Gray Eagle title from 1911 to 1928, if the award had been in existence.

The Trophy, donated by Chance Vought Aircraft (now Ling Temco Vought) depicts a silver eagle landing into the arresting gear of the Navy's first aircraft carrier, *Langley*. The inscription reads: "The Venerable Order of the Gray Eagle. The Most Ancient Naval Aviator on Active Duty. In recognition of a clear eye, a stout heart, a steady hand, and a daring defiance of gravity and the law of averages." Names of those who have held the title, either actively or prior to the 1961 ceremony, are inscribed on the trophy's plaque.

Eligibility for the Gray Eagle Award is determined by the official active duty precedence list for Naval Aviators, on continuous service, not recalled, who has held that designation for the longest period of time. The date of designation as a Naval Aviator is the governing factor for determining who will receive the award from the list of active duty officers. In the event that two or more aviators on active duty have been designated on the same date, the senior one qualified as the Gray Eagle. The award is passed down from the previous holder of the award on his or her retirement, or in case of death. A miniature replica is presented to each incumbent as a personal memento. The Gray Eagle Trophy may be kept in possession of and displayed by the command to which the Gray Eagle is assigned. Otherwise, it may be placed in the custody of the National Museum of Naval Aviation on a temporary basis until required for presentation to the successor. It should be noted that the ceremony date for the presentation of the Gray Eagle Award and the retirement date are not always the same.

List of Gray Eagle Award Recipients

Name	Rank Upon Retirement or Death	Naval Aviator Number	Date Designated Naval Aviator	Dates as Gray Eagle
Theodore G. Ellyson	CDR	1	2 Jun 1911*	2 Jun 1911–27 Feb 1928
John H. Towers	ADM	3	14 Sep 1911*	27 Feb 1928–1 Dec 1947
George D. Murray	VADM	22	20 Sep 1915	1 Dec 1947–1 Aug 1951
DeWitt C. Ramsey	ADM	45	31 May 1917	1 Dec 1947–1 May 1949
Henry T. Stanley	CAPT	186	17 Dec 1917	1 May 1949–1 Sep 1950
William W. Townsley	CAPT	320	13 Feb 1918	1 Aug 195l–1 Jul 1955
Alvin O. Preil	CAPT	538	11 Mar 1918	1 Jul 1955–1 Jan 1959
Irving M. McQuiston	RADM	905	12 Jun 1918	1 Jan 1959–1 Jul 1959
Alfred M. Pride	VADM	1119	17 Sep 1918	1 Jul 1959–1 Oct 1959
Thomas S. Combs	VADM	3064	21 Dec 1922	1 Oct 1959–1 Apr 1960

The above list of Naval Aviators were designated retroactively following the eastablishment of the award in 1961.

Name	Rank Upon Retirement or Death	Naval Aviator Number	Date Designated Naval Aviator	Dates as Gray Eagle
Charles R. Brown	ADM	3159	15 Aug 1924	1 Apr 1960–2 Jan 1962
Frank Akers	RADM	3228	11 Sep 1925	2 Jan 1962–1 Apr 1963
Wallace M. Beakley	RADM	3312	24 Nov 1926	1 Apr 1963–31 Dec 1963
Robert Goldthwaite	RADM	3364	20 May 1927	31 Dec 1963–1 Oct 1965
Richard C. Mangrum	LGEN(MC)	4447	20 May 1929	1 Oct 1965–30 Jun 1967
Fitzhugh Lee	VADM	3512	16 Sep 1929	30 Jun 1967–31 July 1967
Chalres D. Griffin	ADM	3647	6 Jun 1930	31 Jul 1967–1 Feb 1968
Alexander S. Heyward, Jr.	VADM	3867	23 Nov 1931	1 Feb 1968–1 Aug 1968
Robert J. Stroh	RADM	3888	25 Jan 1932	1 Aug 1968–28 Nov 1969
George P. Koch	RADM	4085	2 Jan 1935	28 Nov 1969–31 Jul 1971
Alfred R. Matter	RADM	4164	30 Oct 1935	31 Jul 1971–29 Feb 1972
Francis D. Foley	RADM	4178	1 Feb 1936	29 Feb 1972–29 Jun 1972
Thomas H. Moorer	ADM	4255	12 Jun 1936	29 Jun 1972–30 Jun 1974

Name	Rank Upon Retirement or Death	Naval Aviator Number	Date Designated Naval Aviator	Dates as Gray Eagle
Leroy V. Swanson	RADM	5921	9 Dec 1938	30 Jun 1974–29 Aug 1975
Noel A. M. Gayler	ADM	6879	14 Nov 1940	29 Aug 1975–31 Aug 1976
Martin D. Carmody	RADM	10911	22 Jan 1942	31 Aug 1976–27 May 1977
George L. Cassel	RADM	11262	3 Feb 1942	27 May 1977–31 Aug 1977
Henry Wildfang	CWO4(MC)	12766	16 Apr 1942	31 Aug 1977–31 May 1978
Frank C. Lang	MGEN(MC)		12 Mar 1943	31 May 1978–30 Jun 1978
Thomas H. Miller, Jr.	LGEN(MC)		24 Apr 1943	30 Jun 1978–28 Jun 1979
Maurice F. Weisner	ADM		May 1943	28 Jun 1979–31 Oct 1979
Andrew W. O'Donnell	LGEN(MC)		8 Jul 1944	31 Oct 1979–26 Jun 1981
Robert F. Schoultz	VADM			26 Jun 1981–17 Feb 1987
Cecil J. Kempf	VADM			25 Feb 1987–6 June 1987
James E. Service	VADM			6 Jun 1987–21 Aug 1987
Frank E. Peterson, Jr.	LGEN(MC)			21 Aug 1987–15 Jun 1988
Ronald J. Hays	ADM			15 Jun 1988–15 Sep 1988
Robert F. Dunn	VADM			15 Sep 1988–25 May 1989
Huntington Hardisty	ADM			25 May 1989–1 Mar 1991
Jerome L. Johnson	ADM			1 Mar 1991–26 Jul 1992
Edwin R. Kohn	VADM		Jun 1956	26 Jul 1992–1 Jul 1993
Jerry O. Tuttle	VADM			1 Jul 1993–19 Nov 1993
Stanley R. Arthur	ADM			19 Nov 1993–21 Mar 1995
David R. Morris	RADM			21 Mar 1995–

*Dates qualified for Pilot Certificate under Aero Club of America; Navy Air Pilot numbers were first assigned in January 1915 and Naval Aviator numbers were assigned in January 1918.

Pilots involved in an encounter with four enemy MiGs while on a mission over North Vietnam in October 1966. Left to right: LCDR C. L. Cook, LTJG W. T. Patton, LT P. F. Russell, LTJG J. W. Wiley and the commanding officer of VA-176, CDR A. R. Ashworth. LTJG Patton was credited with the shoot down of a MiG-17 in his A-1H Skyraider.

List of Navy and Marine Corps Shoot Downs Since 1950

T he following list of enemy aircraft shot down since 1950 covers only those shoot downs that are confirmed. There are a number of cases in which adequate information or verification was not available or could not be substantiated for a shoot down. These shoot downs, usually identified as "probables", are not placed on this list. The Navy Department does not have a written policy regarding the requirements for the verification of a shoot down. It is generally accepted or believed that when an aerial engagement occurs, the pilot, NFO (RIO), or other witness must actually see the enemy aircraft crash, explode or the pilot ejecting from the enemy aircraft. The Navy has used gun camera footage since World War II. However, during the 1980s the Navy began using modern equipment more extensively, such as heads-up displays and gun camera footage, to document and verify shoot downs.

AIRCRAFT SHOT DOWN DURING THE KOREAN WAR BY USN/USMC PILOTS

Date	Enemy Aircraft	Squardon	Aircraft	Weapon	Carrier	Rank	Service	Pilot	RIO/NFO
03 Jul 1950	YAK-9	VF-51	F9F-3	Guns	CV 45	LTJG	USN	Leonard H. Plog	
03 Jul 1950	YAK-9	VF-51	F9F-3	Guns	CV 45	ENS	USN	Eldon W. Brown	
04 Sep 1950	IL-4	VF-53	F4U-4B	Guns	CV 45	ENS	USN	Edward V. Laney, Jr.	
09 Nov 1950	MiG-15	VF-111	F9F-2B	Guns	CV 47	LCDR	USN	William T. Amen	
18 Nov 1950	MiG-15***	VF-52	F9F-3	Guns	CV 45	LCDR	USN	William E. Lamb	(shared with LT Parker)
18 Nov 1950	MiG-15***	VF-52	F9F-3	Guns	CV 45	LT	USN	Robert E. Parker	(shared with LCDR Lamb)
18 Nov 1950	MiG-15	VF-31	F9F-2	Guns	CV 32	ENS	USN	Frederick C. Weber	
22 Dec 1950	MiG-15	5th A.F.	F-86	Guns	*	LCDR	USN	Paul E. Pugh	
21 Apr 1951	YAK-9	VMF-312	F4U-4	Guns	CVL 29	LT	USMC	Harold D. Daigh	
21 Apr 1951	2 YAKs	VMF-312	F4U-4	Guns	CVL 29	CAPT	USMC	Phillip C. DeLong	
01 Jun 1951	MiG-15	5th A.F.	F-86D	Guns	*	LT	USN	Simpson Evans, Jr.	
01 Jul 1951	PO-2	VMF(N)-513	F7F-3N	Guns	*	CAPT	USMC	Edwin B. Long	WO Robert C. Buckingham
12 Jul 1951	PO-2	VMF(N)-513	F4U-5NL	Guns	*	CAPT	USMC	Donald L. Fenton	
23 Sep 1951	PO-2	VMF(N)-513	F7F-3N	Guns	*	MAJ	USMC	Eugene A. Van Gundy	MSgt Thomas H. Ullom
23 Oct 1951	MiG	5th A.F.	F-84E	Guns	*	LT	USN	Walter Schirra	
04 Nov 1951	MiG-15	5th A.F.	F-86	Guns	*	MAJ	USMC	William F. Guss	

AIRCRAFT SHOT DOWN DURING THE KOREAN WAR BY USN/USMC PILOTS—Continued

Date	Enemy Aircraft	Squadron	Aircraft	Weapon	Carrier	Rank	Service	Pilot	RIO/NFO
05 Mar 1952	MiG-15	5th A.F.	F-86	Guns	*	CAPT	USMC	Vincent J. Marzello	
16 Mar 1952	MiG-15	5th A.F.	F-86	Guns	*	LCOL	USMC	John S. Payne	
07 Jun 1952	YAK-9	VMF(N)-513	F4U-5NL	Guns	*	LT	USMC	John W. Andre	
10 Sep 1952	MiG	VMA-312	F4U-4B	Guns	CVE 118	CAPT	USMC	Jesse G. Folmar	
15 Sep 1952	MiG-15	5th A.F.	F-86	Guns	*	MAJ	USMC	Alexander J. Gillis	
28 Sep 1952	2 MiG-15s	5th A.F.	F-86	Guns	*	MAJ	USMC	Alexander J. Gillis	
03 Nov 1952	YAK-15	VMF(N)-513	F3D-2	Guns	*	MAJ	USMC	William T. Stratton, Jr.	MSgt Hans C. Hoglind
08 Nov 1952	MiG	VMF(N)-513	F3D-2	Guns	*	CAPT	USMC	Oliver R. Davis	WO Dramus F. Fessler
18 Nov 1952	MiG-15	VF-781	F9F-5	Guns	CVA 34	LT	USN	Elmer Royce Williams	
18 Nov 1952	MiG-15	VF-781	F9F-5	Guns	CVA 34	LTJG	USN	John D. Middleton	
10 Dec 1952	PO-2	VMF(N)-513	F3D-2	Guns	*	LT	USMC	Joseph A. Corvi	MSgt Don R. George
12 Jan 1953	MiG	VMF(N)-513	F3D-2	Guns	*	MAJ	USMC	Elswin P. Dunn	MSgt Lawrence J. Fortin
20 Jan 1953	MiG-15	5th A.F.	F-86	Guns	*	CAPT	USMC	Robert Wade	
28 Jan 1953	MiG	VMF(N)-513	F3D-2	Guns	*	CAPT	USMC	James R. Weaver	MSgt Robert P. Becker
31 Jan 1953	MiG	VMF(N)-513	F3D-2	Guns	*	LCOL	USMC	Robert F. Conley	MSgt James N. Scott
07 Apr 1953	MiG-15	5th A.F.	F-86	Guns	*	MAJ	USMC	Roy L. Reed	
12 Apr 1953	MiG-15	5th A.F.	F-86	Guns	*	MAJ	USMC	Roy L. Reed	
16 May 1953	MiG-15	5th A.F.	F-86F	Guns	*	MAJ	USMC	John F. Bolt	
17 May 1953	MiG-15***	5th A.F.	F-86	Guns	*	CAPT	USMC	Dewey F. Durnford (credit for half kill)	
18 May 1953	MiG-15	5th A.F.	F-86	Guns	*	CAPT	USMC	Harvey L. Jensen	
16 Jun 1953	PO-2	VMC-1	AD-4	Guns	*	MAJ	USMC	George H. Linnemeier	CWO Vernon S. Kramer
22 Jun 1953	MiG-15	5th A.F.	F-86F	Guns	*	MAJ	USMC	John F. Bolt	
24 Jun 1953	MiG-15	5th A.F.	F-86F	Guns	*	MAJ	USMC	John F. Bolt	
30 Jun 1953	MiG-15	5th A.F.	F-86F	Guns	*	MAJ	USMC	John F. Bolt	
30 Jun 1953	2 YAK-18s	VC-3DetD**	F4U-5N	Guns	CV 37**	LT	USN	Guy P. Bordelon, Jr.	
05 Jul 1953	2 PO-2s	VC-3DetD**	F4U-5N	Guns	CV 37**	LT	USN	Guy P. Bordelon, Jr.	
11 Jul 1953	2 MiG-15s	5th A.F.	F-86F	Guns	*	MAJ	USMC	John F. Bolt	
12 Jul 1953	MiG-15	5th A.F.	F-86H	Guns	*	MAJ	USMC	John H. Glenn	
16 Jul 1953	PO-2	VC-3DetD**	F4U-5N	Guns	CV 37**	LT	USN	Guy P. Bordelon, Jr.	
19 Jul 1953	MiG-15	5th A.F.	F-86H	Guns	*	MAJ	USMC	John H. Glenn	

Date									
20 Jul 1953	2 MiG-15s	5th A.F.	F-86	Guns		Thomas M. Sellers	MAJ	USMC	*
22 Jul 1953	MiG-15	5th A.F.	F-86H	Guns		John H. Glenn	MAJ	USMC	*

* Shore based or exchange duty with the 5th Air Force in Korea.
** Temporary additional duty (TAD) from Princeton to U.S. 5th Air Force in Korea (Navy and Marine Corps pilots had exchange duty with the 5th Air Force).
*** The credit for the shoot down of this aircraft is shared with another pilot so the person is credited for only a half a shoot down.

AIRCRAFT SHOT DOWN DURING THE VIETNAM WAR BY USN/USMC PILOTS

Date	Enemy Aircraft	Squadron	Aircraft	Weapon	Carrier	Rank	Service	Pilot	RANK AND NAME OF RIO/NFO
17 Jun 1965	MiG-17	VF-21	F-4B	AIM-7	CVA 41	USN	CDR	Louis Page	LT John C. Smith, Jr.
17 Jun 1965	MiG-17	VF-21	F-4B	AIM-7	CVA 41	USN	LT	Jack E. D. Batson, Jr.	LCDR Robert B. Doremus
20 Jun 1965	MiG-17	VA-25	A-1H	Guns	CVA 41	USN	LT	Clinton B. Johnson*	
20 Jun 1965	MiG-17	VA-25	A-1H	Guns	CVA 41	USN	LTJG	Charles W. Hartman III*	
12 Jun 1966	MiG-17	VF-211	F-8E	AIM-9D	CVA 19	USN	CDR	Harold L. Marr	
21 Jun 1966	MiG-17	VF-211	F-8E	Guns	CVA 19	USN	LT	Eugene J. Chancy	
21 Jun 1966	MiG-17	VF-211	F-8E	AIM-9D	CVA 19	USN	LTJG	Phillip V. Vampatella	
13 Jul 1966	MiG-17	VF-161	F-4B	AIM-9D	CVA 64	USN	LT	William M. McGuigan	LTJG Robert M. Fowler
09 Oct 1966	MiG-21	VF-162	F-8E	AIM-9	CVA 34	USN	CDR	Richard M. Bellinger	
09 Oct 1966	MiG-17	VA-176	A-1H	Guns	CVS 11	USN	LTJG	William T. Patton	
20 Dec 1966	An-2	VF-114	F-4B	AIM-7E	CVA 63	USN	LT	Hugh D. Wisely	LTJG David L. Jordan
20 Dec 1966	An-2	VF-213	F-4B	AIM-7E	CVA 63	USN	LT	David A. McRae	ENS David N. Nichols
24 Apr 1967	MiG-17	VF-114	F-4B	AIM-9D	CVA 63	USN	LT	Hugh D. Wisely	LTJG Gareth L. Anderson
24 Apr 1967	MiG-17	VF-114	F-4B	AIM-9B	CVA 63	USN	LCDR	Charles E. Southwick	ENS James W. Laing
01 May 1967	MiG-17	VF-211	F-8E	AIM-9D	CVA 31	USN	LCDR	Marshall O. Wright	
01 May 1967	MiG-17	VA-76	A-4C	Zuni	CVA 31	USN	LCDR	Theodore R. Swartz	
19 May 1967	MiG-17	VF-211	F-8E	AIM-9D	CVA 31	USN	CDR	Paul H. Speer	
19 May 1967	MiG-17	VF-211	F-8E	AIM-9D	CVA 31	USN	LTJG	Joseph M. Shea	
19 May 1967	MiG-17	VF-24	F-8C	AIM-9D	CVA 31	USN	LCDR	Bobby C. Lee	
19 May 1967	MiG-17	VF-24	F-8C	AIM-9D	CVA 31	USN	LT	Phillip R. Wood	
21 Jul 1967	MiG-17	VF-24	F-8C	AIM-9D	CVA 31	USN	CDR	Marion H. Isaacks	
21 Jul 1967	MiG-17	VF-24	F-8C	**	CVA 31	USN	LCDR	Robert L. Kirkwood	
21 Jul 1967	MiG-17	VF-211	F-8E	***	CVA 31	USN	LCDR	Ray G. Hubbard, Jr.	
10 Aug 1967	MiG-21	VF-142	F-4B	AIM-9	CVA 64	USN	LTJG	Guy H. Freeborn	ENS Robert J. Elliot

AIRCRAFT SHOT DOWN DURING THE VIETNAM WAR BY USN/USMC PILOTS—Continued

Date	Enemy Aircraft	Squardon	Aircraft	Weapon	Carrier	Rank	Service	Pilot	RANK AND NAME OF RIO/NFO
10 Aug 1967	MiG-21	VF-142	F-4B	AIM-9	CVA 64	USN	LCDR	Robert C. Davis	LCDR Gayle O. Elie
26 Oct 1967	MiG-21	VF-143	F-4B	AIM-7	CVA 64	USN	LTJG	Robert P. Hickey, Jr.	LTJG Jeremy G. Morris
30 Oct 1967	MiG-17	VF-142	F-4B	AIM-7E	CVA 64	USN	LCDR	Eugene P. Lund	LTJG James R. Borst
14 Dec 1967	MiG-17	VF-162	F-8E	AIM-9D	CVA 34	USN	LT	Richard E. Wyman	
17 Dec 1967	MiG-17	13 TFS	F-4D	AIM-4	432 TRW	USAF	1LT	John D. Ryan, Jr.	CAPT Doyle D. Baker USMC
26 Jun 1968	MiG-21	VF-51	F-8H	AIM-9	CVA 31	USN	CDR	Lowell R. Myers	
09 Jul 1968	MiG-17	VF-191	F-8E	**	CVA 14	USN	LCDR	John B. Nichols III	
10 Jul 1968	MiG-21	VF-33	F-4J	AIM-9	CVA 66	USN	LT	Roy Cash, Jr.	LT Joseph E. Kain, Jr.
29 Jul 1968	MiG-17	VF-53	F-8E	AIM-9	CVA 31	USN	CDR	Guy Cane	
01 Aug 1968	MiG-21	VF-51	F-8H	AIM-9	CVA 31	USN	LT	Norman K. McCoy	
19 Sep 1968	MiG-21	VF-111	F-8C	AIM-9	CVS 11	USN	LT	Anthony J. Nargi	
28 Mar 1970	MiG-21	VF-142	F-4J	AIM-9	CVA 64	USN	LT	Jereome E. Beaulier	LT Steven J. Barkley
19 Jan 1972	MiG-21	VF-96	F-4J	AIM-9	CVA 64	USN	LT	Randall H. Cunningham	LTJG William P. Driscoll
06 Mar 1972	MiG-17	VF-111	F-4B	AIM-9	CVA 43	USN	LT	Gary L. Weigand	LTJG William Freckleton
06 May 1972	MiG-17	VF-51	F-4B	AIM-9	CVA 43	USN	LCDR	Jerry B. Houston	LT Kevin T. Moore
06 May 1972	MiG-21	VF-114	F-4J	AIM-9	CVA 63	USN	LT	Rorbert G. Hughes	LTJG Adolph J. Cruz
06 May 1972	MiG-21	VF-114	F-4J	AIM-9	CVA 63	USN	LCDR	Kenneth W. Pettigrew	LTJG Michael J. McCabe
08 May 1972	MiG-17	VF-96	F-4J	AIM-9	CVA 64	USN	LT	Randall H. Cunningham	LTJG William P. Driscoll
10 May 1972	MiG-21	VF-92	F-4J	AIM-9	CVA 64	USN	LT	Curt Dose	LCDR James McDevitt
10 May 1972	2 MiG-17s	VF-96	F-4J	AIM-9	CVA 64	USN	LT	Matthew J.Connelly III	LT Thomas J. J. Blonski
10 May 1972	MiG-17	VF-51	F-4B	AIM-9	CVA 43	USN	LT	Kenneth L. Cannon	LT Roy A. Morris, Jr.
10 May 1972	3 MiG-17s	VF-96	F-4J	AIM-9	CVA 64	USN	LT	Randall H. Cunningham	LTJG William P. Driscoll
10 May 1972	MiG-17	VF-96	F-4J	AIM-9	CVA 64	USN	LT	Steven C. Shoemaker	LTJG Keith V. Crenshaw
18 May 1972	MiG-19	VF-161	F-4B	AIM-9	CVA 41	USN	LT	Henry A. Bartholomay	LT Oran R. Brown
18 May 1972	MiG-19	VF-161	F-4B	AIM-9	CVA 41	USN	LT	Patrick E. Arwood	LT James M. Bell
23 May 1972	2 MiG-17s	VF-161	F-4B	AIM-9	CVA 41	USN	LCDR	Ronald E. McKeown	LT John C. Ensch
11 Jun 1972	MiG-17	VF-51	F-4B	AIM-9	CVA 43	USN	CDR	Foster S. Teague	LT Ralph M. Howell
11 Jun 1972	MiG-17	VF-51	F-4B	AIM-9	CVA 43	USN	LT	Winston W. Copeland	LT Donald R. Bouchoux
21 Jun 1972	MiG-21	VF-31	F-4J	AIM-9	CVA 60	USN	CDR	Samuel C. Flynn, Jr.	LT William H. John
10 Aug 1972	MiG-21	VF-103	F-4J	AIM-7E	CVA 60	USN	LCDR	Robert E. Tucker, Jr.	LTJG Stanley B. Edens
12 Aug 1972	MiG-21	58 TFS	F-4E	AIM-7	432 TRW	USMC	CAPT	Lawrence G. Richard	LCDR Michael J.Ettel USN

Date	Enemy Aircraft	Squadron	Aircraft	Weapon	Carrier	Service	Rank	Pilot	Rank and Name of RIO/NFO
11 Sep 1972	MiG-21	VMFA-333	F-4J	AIM-9	CVA 66	USMC	MAJ	Lee T. Lassiter	CAPT John D. Cummings
28 Dec 1972	MiG-21	VF-142	F-4J	AIM-9	CVAN 65	USN	LTJG	Scott H. Davis	LTJG Goeffrey H. Ulrich
12 Jan 1973	MiG-17	VF-161	F-4B	AIM-9	CVA 41	USN	LT	Victor T. Kovaleski	LT James A. Wise

* These two pilots shared the credit for the shoot down of the MiG-17 and each were credited for only a half a shoot down.
** Shoot down involved use of missile (AIM-9) and guns.
*** Shoot down involved use of guns and Zuni rockets.

AIRCRAFT SHOT DOWN DURING THE LIBYAN INCIDENTS OF THE 1980s

Date	Enemy Aircraft	Squadron	Aircraft	Weapon	Carrier	Service	Rank	Pilot	Rank and Name of RIO/NFO
19 Aug 1981	Su-22	VF-41	F-14A	AIM-9L	CVN 68	USN	CDR	Hank Kleeman	LT Dave Venlet
19 Aug 1981	Su-22	VF-41	F-14A	AIM-9L	CVN 68	USN	LT	Larry Muczynski	LT Jim Anderson
04 Jan 1989	MiG-23	VF-32	F-14A	AIM-7	CV 67	USN	LT	Herman C. Cook III	LCDR Steven P. Collins
04 Jan 1989	MiG-23	VF-32	F-14A	AIM-9	CV 67	USN	CDR	Joseph B. Connelly	CDR Leo F. Enwright, Jr.

AIRCRAFT SHOT DOWN DURING THE PERSIAN GULF WAR

Date	Enemy Aircraft	Squadron	Aircraft	Weapon	Carrier	Service	Rank	Pilot	Rank and Name of RIO/NFO
17 Jan 1991	MiG-21	VFA-81	F/A-18C	AIM-9M	CV 60	USN	LCDR	Mark Fox	
17 Jan 1991	MiG-21	VFA-81	F/A-18C	AIM-9M	CV 60	USN	LT	Nick Mongillo	
06 Feb 1991	Hi-8	VF-1	F-14A	AIM-9M	CV 61	USN	LT	Stuart Broce	CDR Ron McElraft

AIRCRAFT CARRIER NAMES AND DESIGNATIONS

Intrepid (CVS 11)
Ticonderoga (CVA 14)
Hancock (CVA 19)
Bataan (CVL 29)
Bon Homme Richard (CVA 31)

Leyte (CV 32)
Oriskany (CVA 34)
Princeton (CV 37)
Midway (CVA 41)
Coral Sea (CVA 43)

Valley Forge (CV 45)
Phillipine Sea (CV 47)
Saratoga (CVA 60)
Ranger (CV 61)
Kitty Hawk (CVA 63)

Constellation (CVA 64)
Enterprise (CVAN 65)
America (CVA 66)
John F. Kennedy (CV 67)
Nimitz (CVN 68)

Sicily (CVE 118)

Acronyms:
TRW—Tactical Reconnaissance Wing
TFS—Tactical Fighter Squadron
NFO—Naval Flight Officer
RIO—Radar Intercept Officer

A VQ-1 EC-121M aircraft similar to the one shot down by the Koreans on 15 April 1969.

Cold War Incidents Involving U.S. Navy Aircraft

From 1945 to 1969, U.S. Navy aircraft were involved in a number of aerial incidents with forces of the Soviet Union, People's Republic of China, North Korea, and Czechoslovakia. These incidents resulted in the loss of eight Navy aircraft and one Coast Guard aircraft, eighty-one Navy, Marine Corps, and Coast Guard aviators and crewman, and several aircraft damaged and crewmen wounded and injured. The list below, compiled from official and unofficial sources, does not include aircraft lost in direct action in the Korean and Vietnam wars, nor aircraft shot down by Chinese forces in the vicinity of Vietnam in connection with that war.

Date	Aircraft	Squadron	Remarks
15 Nov 1945	PBM-5		While on a routine patrol mission, this aircraft was attacked by a Soviet fighter 25 miles south of Dairen (Port Arthur), Manchuria while investigating six Soviet transport ships and a beached seaplane in the Gulf of Chihli in the Yellow Sea. No damage inflicted.
20 Feb 1946	PBM-5	VP-26	Based from Tsingtao, China, during a training flight this aircraft made an unauthorized flight over Dairen (Port Arthur), Manchuria. As a result, it was fired upon by Soviet fighters firing warning bursts for twenty minutes. No damage inflicted.
8 Apr 1950	PB4Y-2	VP-26, Det A	Based from Port Lyautey, French Morocco, while on a patrol mission launched from Wiesbaden, West Germany, this aircraft (BuNo 59645) was lost when attacked by Soviet aircraft over the Baltic Sea off the coast of Lepija, Latvia. Wreckage was recovered, but unconfirmed reports stated that the missing ten crewmembers were taken prisoner.
6 Nov 1951	P2V-3W	VP-6	While conducting a weather reconnaissance mission under United Nations Command, this aircraft (BuNo 124284) was shot down by Soviet aircraft over the Sea of Japan off Vladisvostok, Siberia. Ten crewmembers reported as missing.
31 Jul 1952	PBM-5S2	VP-731	While conducting a patrol mission, this PBM-5S2 based from Iwakuni, Japan, was attacked by two Chinese MiG-15s over the Yellow Sea, resulting in two crewmembers killed and two more seriously wounded. The PBM suffered extensive damage, but was able to make it safely to Paengyong-do, Korea.
20 Sep 1952	P4Y-2S	VP-28	Aircraft attacked by two Chinese MiG-15s off the coast of China, but able to return safely to Naha, Okinawa.

Date	Aircraft	Squadron	Remarks
20 Sep 1952	P4Y-2S	VP-28	Aircraft attacked by two Chinese MiG-15s off the coast of China, but able to return safely to Naha, Okinawa.
23 Nov 1952	P4Y-2S	VP-28	Attacked without result by a Chinese MiG-15 off Shanghai, China.
18 Jan 1953	P2V-5	VP-22	P2V-5 (BuNo 127744) was shot down by Chinese anti-aircraft fire near Swatow, and ditched in the Formosa Strait. Eleven of thirteen crewmen were rescued by a Coast Guard PBM-5 under fire from shore batteries on Nan Ao Tao island. Attempting to takeoff in eight-twelve foot swells, the PBM crashed. Ten survivors out of nineteen total (including five from the P2V) were rescued by *Halsey Powell* (DD 686). During the search effort a PBM-5 from VP-40 received fire from a small-caliber machine gun, and *Gregory* (DD 802) received fire from shore batteries.
19–28 Jun 1953	PBM-5S2 P2V-5 (2)	VP-46 VP-1	Fired upon, in separate incidents, by surface ships in the Formosa Strait. No damage inflicted.
8 Jul 1953	P2V-5	VP-1	Fired upon by Chinese antiaircraft artillery (AAA) near Nantien, China. No damage inflicted.
21 Jul 1953	P2V-5	VP-1	Fired upon by Chinese antiaircraft artillery (AAA) near Amoy Island in the Formosa Strait. No damage inflicted.
2 Oct 1953	PBM-5		Damaged during attack by two Chinese MiGs over the Yellow Sea.
12 Mar 1954	AD-4 AD-4N	VA-145 VC-35, Det F	Two ADs launched from Randolph (CVA 15), on a simulated strike mission against a West German airfield, were attacked over or near the Czech border by a Czech MiG-15. The AD from VA-145 sustained damage to its tail.
26 Jul 1954	AD-4	VF-54	While searching for survivors from a Cathay Pacific airliner shot down by Chinese fighters on 22 July, two AD-4s launched from *Philippine Sea* (CVA 47) were attacked by two Chinese LA-7 fighters. During the engagement, the two LA-7s were downed by seven ADs and one F4U-5N that came to assist. The ADs encountered fire from a Chinese gunboat. No damage sustained in either situation.
4 Sep 1954	P2V-5	VP-19	Operating from NAS Atsugi, Japan, this aircraft ditched in the Sea of Japan, 40 miles off the coast of Siberia after an attack by two Soviet MiG-15s. One crewmen was lost, and the other nine were rescued by a USAF SA-16 amphibian.
Feb 1955	P2V		Aircraft sustained slight wing damage after it was fired on by Chinese antiaircraft artillery (AAA) while over the Formosa Strait.

Date	Aircraft	Squadron	Remarks
9 Feb 1955	AD-5W	VC-11, Det H	While flying an antisubmarine (ASW) patrol mission from *Wasp* (CVA 18) covering the evacuation of Chinese Nationalists from the Tachen Islands, this aircraft ditched after sustaining damage from antiaircraft fire when it overflew Chinese territory. The three-man crew was rescued by Nationalist Chinese patrol boats.
22 Jun 1955	P2V-5	VP-9	While flying a patrol mission from Kodiak, Alaska, this aircraft (BuNo 131515) crash-landed on St. Lawrence Island in the Bering Sea after an engine was set afire during an attack by two Soviet MiG-15s. Of the eleven crewmen, four sustained injuries due to gunfire and six were injured during the landing. (This was the only incident in which the Soviet Union admitted any responsibility.)
22 Aug 1956	P4M-1Q	VQ-1	While on a patrol mission from Iwakuni, Japan, this aircraft (BuNo 124362) disappeared at night after reporting an attack by hostile aircraft 32 miles off the coast of China (near Wenchow) and 180 miles north of Formosa. There were no survivors of the 16-man crew. Wreckage and one body were recovered by *Dennis J. Buckley* (DDR 808).
12 Jun 1957	AD-6	VA-145	Four AD-6s launched from *Hornet* (CVA 12) overflew the coast of China and encountered fire from Chinese anti-aircraft artillery (AAA). One AD-6 sustained slight damage.
16 Jun 1959	P4M-1Q	VQ-1	While flying a patrol mission over the Sea of Japan, this aircraft (BuNo 122209) was attacked 50 miles east of the Korean DMZ by two North Korean MiGs. During the attack, the aircraft sustained serious damage to the starboard engines and the tailgunner was seriously wounded. The P4M made it safely to Miho AFB, Japan.
15 Apr 1969	EC-121M	VQ-1	While flying a patrol mission over the Sea of Japan, this aircraft (BuNo 135749) was attacked 90 miles off the coast of Korea by North Korean fighters. All 31 crewmen were lost during the attack. Two bodies and some wreckage were recovered by search vessels.

Index

ISBN 0-16-049124-X